Texas, Our Texas

ANNOTATED TEACHER'S EDITION

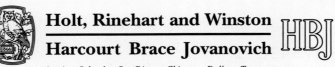

Holt, Rinehart and Winston
Harcourt Brace Jovanovich HBJ

Austin • Orlando • San Diego • Chicago • Dallas • Toronto

Printed in the United States of America   2 3 4 5 6 7   048   99 98 97 96 95 94 93

ISBN   0-03-075432-1

CONTENTS

INTRODUCTION

TEXAS, OUR TEXAS is a comprehensive program of study for Texas history and geography. It provides in-depth content as well as essential instruction and practice in a variety of skills. The content of *TEXAS, OUR TEXAS* explores the land, people, politics, economics, and government of Texas. Emphasis is placed on providing a better understanding of the forces—and their interaction—that have shaped today's Texas. An extensive review, re-teaching, and evaluation program is included as an integral part of student learning.

 ## The Goals of the Program

TEXAS, OUR TEXAS has been designed with several goals in mind. First, it provides complete coverage of the Texas Essential Elements for Texas history and geography. Second, the program challenges students while at the same time motivating them to continue the study of their state in the years to come. Third, *TEXAS, OUR TEXAS* places the story of the Lone Star State within the perspective of its relationship to the United States, Mexico, and the rest of the world. This wide perspective reveals for students the unique history of Texas as well as the important influences of regional, national, and international forces. Finally, *TEXAS, OUR TEXAS* provides beneficial instruction and practice in important study skills, critical thinking skills, writing skills, and general social studies skills.

Texas in the Twentieth Century

TEXAS, OUR TEXAS provides balanced coverage of all historical periods, from settlement by Native Americans to the most recent developments of the 1990s. Substantial content is devoted to the post-1900 years in recognition of the importance of events in the twentieth century. Fully one third of the content explores modern Texas in its geographic, historical, and governmental aspects.

Using Multicultural Perspective and Historical Imagination

Texas history has always been the history of many different cultures and ethnic groups. Special care has been taken to provide students with opportunities to experience events and is-sues from the point of view of all participants. This multicultural perspective has been interwoven throughout the content, review strategies, and teacher materials of *TEXAS, OUR TEXAS.*

The program also devotes considerable attention to the development of historical imagination. Historical imagination develops in students an empathy with the past—the ability to know or to speculate about what it was actually like to live in different periods of history and in different circumstances. Students are often asked to use their historical imaginations to place themselves in the roles of the many people they are studying. By doing so, students can more fully appreciate the motives of the people and the forces that have shaped the state of Texas and the nation.

ORGANIZATION OF THE PUPIL'S TEXT

TEXAS, OUR TEXAS is organized into twelve units of 31 chapters. The twelfth unit is a special supplement called "Handbook of Texas Government and Citizenship." Each chapter is divided into brief, titled sections. At every step, students are assisted in determining main ideas and are given opportunities to self-test their understanding of the material.

 ## Units

With the exception of the final unit, each unit of *TEXAS, OUR TEXAS* opens with a two-page spread. In the unit opener, a large, full-color illustration sparks student interest in the unit. Introductory text provides helpful background information and gives a preview of major topics, and a detailed time line highlights major events occurring in Texas and the world. Units 1–11 close with a two-page Unit Review, organized as follows:

Connecting Main Ideas: Provides reading comprehension questions designed to help students synthesize various concepts presented in the unit.

Practicing Critical Thinking Skills: Contains several questions that require students to practice critical thinking skills such as seeing cause and effect and synthesizing information.

TAAS Practice: These valuable practice items are modeled after the Reading and Writing Measurement Specifications for Texas Assessment of Academic Skills (TAAS). The activities serve to acquaint students with the format of TAAS. Teachers can use the exercises as a diagnostic tool to determine skill areas in which students need additional instruction.

Exploring Local History: Provides suggested activities for learning about local history.

Using Historical Imagination: Provides suggestions for individual and cooperative learning projects and gives students practice in using historical imagination.

For Extending Your Knowledge: Features an annotated bibliography.

Skill Lesson: Provides a full-page social studies skill presentation, which includes a **Practicing the Skill** activity.

 ## Chapters

Each chapter of *TEXAS, OUR TEXAS* begins with an introductory paragraph, along with a series of questions for students to consider as they study the material. These questions alert students to important topics

and areas of emphasis. Each chapter closes with a two-page Chapter Review, organized as follows:

Understanding Main Ideas: Includes reading comprehension questions designed to test students' understanding of key concepts of the chapter.

Thinking Critically: Provides questions that call for students to develop critical thinking skills.

Linking History and Geography: Encourages students to recognize the vital relationship between history and geography.

TAAS Practice: Provides additional practice exercises modeled after the Reading and Writing Measurement Specifications for Texas Assessment of Academic Skills (TAAS).

Practicing Skills: Gives students the opportunity to practice social studies skills such as interpreting maps and sequencing events.

Enriching Your Study of History: Provides at least one individual and one cooperative learning project.

 ## Sections

Each chapter of *TEXAS, OUR TEXAS* is organized into three to six sections. Each section concludes with a **Section Review,** which asks students to define boldfaced terms; identify key people, places, and events; relate factual information; and utilize critical thinking skills.

 ## The Vocabulary Program

TEXAS, OUR TEXAS features a strong vocabulary program. Central to the program is the development of new vocabulary in history, geography, and other fields of social studies. Key terms are introduced in **boldface** type and are explained in context. All boldfaced terms are included in the Section Review found at the end of each section of every chapter. All boldfaced terms are listed in the textbook Glossary. In the Glossary, pronunciations are given for all words, and a page reference is provided for each entry.

As a supplement to the vocabulary program, teachers will find in each **Chapter Interleaf** a helpful list of additional terms, with page references, that they may wish to preteach.

 ## The Illustration Program

TEXAS, OUR TEXAS is lavishly illustrated with photographs, drawings, maps, charts, and graphs.

Each of the illustrations found in the Pupil's Edition has been carefully selected to complement, strengthen, and extend the text material. Captions accompanying the illustrations provide explanations and sometimes questions to guide student thinking. Answers to questions are conveniently located in the **Teachertext** of the **ANNOTATED TEACHER'S EDITION**. Many of the teaching strategies in the **Teachertext** suggest additional ways in which to use various illustrations of *TEXAS, OUR TEXAS*.

TEXAS, OUR TEXAS' expanded map program includes a full-color, up-to-date world map (featuring the *latest* developments in the former Soviet Union) and a map of the United States.

 ## Special Features

Designed to increase students' enjoyment and interest in Texas history, more than 60 special feature pages in four categories complement the text. Each feature is logically placed in the unit to which the material relates. The special features include:

Lone Star Legacy: Examines events, places, and other topics that have contributed to the unique culture and heritage of Texas.

Cities of Texas: Includes geographic, historical, economic, and cultural information on various cities of Texas.

Spirit of Texas: Features colorful biographies of notable Texans.

Texas Voices: These primary-source quotations from Texans from all walks of life offer students insight into specific time periods of Texas history.

 ## Reference Section

At the back of the textbook are valuable reference materials designed to enrich and enliven the study of Texas history. An extensive Glossary lists all of the boldfaced terms found in the text, along with handy page references and pronunciations for all terms. A thorough Index is designed to be useful to students. Additional reference tools found in the Appendix include: the text of Texas' *Declaration of Independence;* a comprehensive list of Texas presidents and governors and their terms; the text and music of the state song; and illustrations of the state seal, state bird, state flower, and the six flags that have flown over Texas.

ORGANIZATION OF THE ANNOTATED TEACHER'S EDITION

The *ANNOTATED TEACHER'S EDITION (ATE)* of *TEXAS, OUR TEXAS* includes all of the Pupil's Edition pages, slightly reduced in size to create top and side margins. The *ANNOTATED TEACHER'S EDITION* is organized into three parts—**Chapter Interleaf, Teachertext,** and **Annotations**. The two-page **Chapter Interleaf** begins each chapter and offers information to help the teacher develop effective lesson plans. (See pages 1A–1B.) The **Teachertext** is printed in the side margins and top margins of the *ANNOTATED TEACHER'S EDITION*, next to and above the corresponding material in the Pupil's Edition. (See pages 2–3.) This point-of-use location will help the teacher develop effective presentation of chapter information. The **Annotations** appear in the side margins and provide a wealth of supplementary information.

 ## Chapter Interleaf

The **Chapter Interleaf** provides the teacher with several important teaching resources.

Teacher's Time Line: Lists the number and pages of each section in the chapter for each day of instruction. An additional day is suggested for Review and Assessment. Teachers may wish to adjust time allocation to fit their curriculum and the needs of their students.

Teacher Materials: Lists the available supplementary worksheets and tests that correspond to the chapter. These materials are found in the *TEXAS, OUR TEXAS* **TEACHER'S RESOURCE BINDER.**

Objectives: Outlines student objectives for the study of the chapter and provides for the teacher a handy reference around which to plan instruction.

Resources: Provides a comprehensive list of **Books for Teachers,** including many primary sources, and a list of **Multimedia Materials** complete with addresses of publishers. (In addition to the books listed in each chapter, *The Handbook of Texas* in two volumes and *The Handbook of Texas: A Supplement,* published by the Texas State Historical Association, serve as a basic reference for Texas history.)

General Strategies: Provides helpful instructional activities and suggestions designed for teaching students with special needs, including limited English proficient students, students having difficulty with the chapter, auditory learners, visual learners, tactile/kinesthetic learners, and gifted students. These strategies are designed to be used throughout the entire chapter. The **Teachertext** of the *ANNOTATED TEACHER'S EDITION* provides additional strategies designed for use during the study of specific sections of the textbook.

Included in the **Chapter Interleaf** under General Strategies is a list of vocabulary terms from the chapter that the teacher may wish to preteach. These terms are in addition to the boldfaced vocabulary terms found in the chapter. These additional terms are listed by section and include page references.

The **Chapter Interleaf** also directs the teacher to several teaching tools that can be used to introduce and/or review the chapter. These include the Chapter Time Line, Graphic Organizer, and Enrichment Worksheet, each of which is located in the *TEXAS, OUR TEXAS TEACHER'S RESOURCE BINDER.*

 Teachertext

The **Teachertext** of *TEXAS, OUR TEXAS* provides the teacher with point-of-use teaching resources. The following material can be found on the opening pages of each unit.

Unit Overview: Gives a brief overview stressing key concepts.

Unit Objectives: State the major objectives that students should have mastered upon completion of the unit.

Introducing the Unit: Connecting with Past Learning: Provides a motivational activity designed to introduce the unit to students, while expanding on previously learned material.

Motivator: Provides a motivational activity that sparks students' interest in the specific topic about to be studied.

Texas and the World: Provides a cooperative learning activity that allows students to use a time line to examine the relationship between events in Texas and the world.

The **Teachertext** of each chapter opener includes a **Chapter Overview,** which provides the teacher with a brief overview of the chapter's key concepts.

The **Teachertext** for each section of the chapter is designed around a uniform three-step **lesson cycle** that includes the following elements:

 Focus

The Focus step contains a motivational activity to spark students' interest in the section topic. Each Focus activity follows one of three formats. Students may be asked to relate past learning to what they will study in the chapter. They may be encouraged to relate their own experiences to what they will be learning. Or, they may be asked to use their current knowledge to speculate and make predictions about the course of Texas history.

 Instruction

Contains several instructional strategies, including:

Vocabulary: Provides a list of the section's boldfaced vocabulary terms and their page numbers to assist in preteaching.

Guided Practice: Provides a suggested strategy suitable to use with the entire class.

Independent Practice: Provides a suggested strategy that allows students to work independently or sometimes with a partner.

Extension: Provides a suggested strategy that requires students to reach beyond the textbook to gather information.

Reteaching: Provides a suggested activity for helping students who are having difficulty mastering the content. These strategies are part of *TEXAS, OUR TEXAS'* emphasis on helping the teacher reach students with different learning styles and abilities.

Closure: Provides a suggested strategy for bringing the lesson to a close.

Within the **Instruction** strategies of the lesson cycle, the teacher will find a wide variety of other teaching suggestions where appropriate to chapter content. These include but are not limited to activities labeled:

Geography	Brainstorming
Economics	Analysis
Cooperative Learning	Writing
Multicultural Perspective	Art and History
Historical Imagination	Illustrating

 Assessment

Assessment offers the teacher the opportunity to assess the students' understanding of key concepts. At the close of each section, **Assessment** directs the teacher to assign the Section Review. At the close of each chapter, the teacher is directed to assign the Chapter Review and other evaluation materials. At the close of each unit, the teacher is directed to assign the Unit Review and other evaluation materials.

The **Teachertext** includes model, or suggested, answers to the Section Reviews, Chapter Reviews, and Unit Reviews.

At the end of Unit 6 and the Handbook, the teacher is directed to assign the Midterm and Final tests with their corresponding worksheets, available in the **TEACHER'S RESOURCE BINDER.**

 ## Ability Guidelines

The teacher will find it helpful that the activities in the **Teachertext** are labeled **I**, **II**, or **III** according to ability guidelines. **Level I** (Basic) activities are designed for full class participation and should be within the ability range of all students. **Level II** (Average/Group) activities require group participation, selective assignments, and teacher direction. They may require the use of supplementary sources and the application of a variety of study and thinking skills. **Level III** (Challenging) activities are applicable to students who work well independently. The successful completion of Level III tasks requires the use of sources beyond the textbook and the integration of higher-level critical thinking skills.

 ## Annotations

The **Teachertext** includes **Annotations** printed in the side margins. These provide valuable background information for the teacher, suggested caption responses, and the corresponding Texas Essential Elements.

HELPING STUDENTS WITH SPECIAL NEEDS

Most classrooms include students from a variety of cultural backgrounds who have different learning styles. The *TEXAS, OUR TEXAS* program is designed to meet the needs of all types of students, including:

 ## Limited English Proficient Students (LEP)

Instructional strategies in *TEXAS, OUR TEXAS* are designed to limit the stress and anxiety of students who face difficulty in understanding instructions or communicating in the classroom. Activities found in the **Chapter Interleaf** and the **Teachertext** that will especially benefit limited English proficient students are labeled **LEP**.

Many of the teaching strategies included in *TEXAS, OUR TEXAS* provide the following opportunities to help the teacher meet the needs of limited English proficient students:

Provide intensive exposure to English. Use intensive language activities that incorporate a variety of methods and materials. Devote a high percentage of time to direct teacher instruction.

Vary the context of language learning. Have students practice using their English skills in a variety of situations.

Offer small group activities. Plan small group activities that include students who are proficient in English with those who have limited English proficiency.

Build a positive self-concept in students. Reduce stress and anxiety by accepting simple responses. Give students opportunities to achieve their goals.

Make learning comprehensible. Use exaggerated facial expressions, as well as visuals, props, and demonstrations to convey meaning.

 ## Students Having Difficulty with the Chapter

Instructional activities are included to help less prepared students who are having difficulty learning at an average rate. Teaching strategies that may help meet the needs of students having difficulty include:

Plan lessons around the interests and experiences of students having difficulty. This raises the students' interest level and increases their attention span.

Make frequent use of audio and visual materials. Often, less prepared students are auditory or visual learners. This strategy adapts the learning situation to accommodate students' learning strengths.

Provide reteaching and review activities. Students will benefit from reinforcement, reteaching, and review activities at the end of a lesson and before a quiz or test.

Strategies for Teaching Students with Varying Learning Styles

It is likely that the teacher will have auditory, visual, and tactile/kinesthetic learners in the classroom. All of the *TEXAS, OUR TEXAS* components provide ample opportunities to meet the varying needs of these students.

Auditory Learners: Auditory learners benefit from class discussions and oral activities. Activities found in the **Chapter Interleaf** and the **Teachertext** that will especially benefit auditory learners are labeled **A.**

Visual Learners: Visual learners benefit from activities such as examining pictures, analyzing charts, and interpreting other visuals. Activities found in the **Chapter Interleaf** and the **Teachertext** that will especially benefit visual learners are labeled **V.**

Tactile/Kinesthetic Learners: Tactile/kinesthetic learners benefit from hands-on activities or activities that require movement and action. Activities found in the **Chapter Interleaf** and the **Teachertext** that will especially benefit tactile/kinesthetic learners are labeled **TK.**

 ## Strategies for Gifted Students

Teaching gifted students can be a rewarding—though challenging—experience. *TEXAS, OUR TEXAS* encourages the teacher to address the individual learning styles of gifted students, while motivating and directing the students to develop their natural abilities. Activities found in the **Chapter Interleaf** and the **Teachertext** that will especially benefit gifted students are labeled **G.** Strategies to help meet the learning needs of gifted students include:

Allow gifted students to research topics of special interest. These activities tend to keep students motivated and promote independent thinking.

Utilize group activities. Activities that incorporate panel discussions, debates, and interviews encourage the exchange of ideas.

Employ activities that address real problems requiring real solutions. Having gifted students research problems facing Texas today and propose possible solutions helps broaden their perspective and increase their ability to meet challenges.

 ## Cooperative Learning Strategies

Many of the strategies in the *TEXAS, OUR TEXAS* program involve cooperative learning. In cooperative learning, small groups of students of various ability levels work together to solve problems and complete tasks. The purpose of cooperative learning is to create an environment in which students work toward a common goal. For cooperative learning to succeed, the following aspects should be incorporated:

Positive Interdependence. Students must feel that the completion of the assignment depends on the cooperation of every member of the group. For example, tell students that answers must reflect ideas from *every* member.

Individual Accountability. Stress to students that they are responsible for learning and for contributing to their group's success. For example, give each member a specific task, such as acting as reader or recorder.

Face-to-Face Interaction. Maximize learning by making sure that all students in each group exchange ideas, information, and explanations orally.

Cooperative Skill Teaching. Encourage students to take responsibility for group interaction by insisting on standards of group behavior. Behavioral standards might include: *Everyone contribute, listen carefully, ask others to explain, praise good ideas,* and *disagree with ideas, not people.*

Processing Group Effectiveness. Groups will succeed only if students evaluate their group's progress and formulate a plan for improvement. At the completion of every cooperative learning assignment, have group members list what they are doing well and how they can improve.

The **TEACHER'S RESOURCE BINDER** that accompanies *TEXAS, OUR TEXAS* contains the following items:

 ## Geography and Graph Skills

Thirty-one skill lessons provide students with an opportunity to practice geography and graph skills throughout their entire course of study. In addition, there are fourteen blackline masters from which teachers may make overhead transparencies. A separate Geography and Graph Skills Answer Key also is included.

 ## Unit Booklets

There are twelve blackline master booklets, one for each unit, organized by chapter. These booklets provide a comprehensive program for enrichment, review, and assessment. Each unit booklet contains Graphic Organizers, Enrichment Worksheets, Review Worksheets, Form A and Form B Tests, Reteaching Worksheets, and Answer Keys. In addition, Units 2 through 11 contain Time Lines and Making Global Connections Worksheets. The **ANNOTATED TEACHER'S EDITION** makes suggestions concerning when to assign these items.

 ## Informal Evaluation Forms

The Informal Evaluation Forms are designed to provide teacher, group, and self assessment on an informal basis. These materials include portfolio assessment and performance assessment items.

 ## Oral History Handbook and Teacher's Notes

The Oral History Handbook and Teacher's Notes provides a unique opportunity for students and teachers to explore aspects of Texas history on their own. The use of this teaching tool is appropriate at any time during the course of study.

 ## Map and Chart Transparencies and Teacher's Notes

This package includes 25 overhead transparencies of maps and charts taken from the student textbook. In addition, the Teacher's Notes provides comprehension and critical thinking questions for each of the 25 overhead transparencies.

 ## Test Generator

A Test Generator is available for the Apple MacIntosh, Apple II Series, and the IBM PC Series. These test generators provide teachers with an ample number of test questions with which to assess student performance. Tests may be viewed on the screen and changed, if necessary, before printing. Questions may be edited, and new questions may be written.

A Content Correlation to Rule 75.48 (e)

Key correlations of the content of ***Texas, Our Texas*** are included throughout this Annotated Teacher's Edition. Correlations with content are listed next to each section review, special feature, chapter review, and unit review/skill lesson (for example, see page 2). For the Essential Element to which each notation refers, see the Texas Essential Elements chart on pages Txii–Txvi.

Page references without a prefix denote pages in the Pupil's Edition. Page references with the ATE prefix are found in the Annotated Teacher's Edition. Page references with an asterisk (*) provide support for a skill by outlining related content and background information necessary for understanding the skill.

---

(1) Exploration and colonization of Texas. The student shall be provided opportunities to:

1a. describe the location, history, and cultures of the early inhabitants of Texas

74–75, 76–86, 87–88, 89, 90–107, 108–109, 110, 113, 124, 132, 150, 151–152, 168–169, 170, 174–176, 183

*16, 18, 20, 42–43, 63, 72, 145–146, 147, 577–578

ATE: 74, 75, 79, 81, 83, 84, 85, 92, 96, 97, 98, 100, 102, 103, 105, 112, 147

*ATE: 82, 91, 99

1b. analyze the reasons for, locations of, and results of European exploration and colonization

18, 22, 24, 26–27, 33–38, 43, 48, 57, 63–64, 70–71, 72, 86, 91, 95, 96, 97, 98, 103, 106, 110, 112–113, 114–127, 128, 129–130, 131–144, 145–149, 150, 151–152, 153–167, 168–169, 170, 173, 209

*427, 578

ATE: 9, 57, 112, 114B, 114–115, 116, 128, 147, 173

*ATE: 16, 457

1c. explain the roles of and contributions of notable individuals and groups representative of various

racial, ethnic, religious, and cultural backgrounds in the exploration, colonization, and development of Texas

16–17, 18–19, 20–21, 24, 40–41, 42–43, 48, 82, 83, 85–86, 90–95, 97–107, 114–123, 124, 125–127, 128, 129–130, 131–132, 133–145, 150, 154–156, 157, 158–167, 168–169, 170, 173, 176–191, 192–193, 194–203, 206, 231, 270

ATE: 81, 83, 112, 128, 144, 184

(2) Achievement of Texas independence and statehood. The student shall be provided opportunities to:

2a. analyze reasons for and effects of Anglo American settlement of Texas

18–19, 24, 43–44, 48, 173, 174–175, 176–191, 192, 194–210, 232, 304–306, 317–322, 346

*270

ATE: 164, 172, 174, 177, 178, 181, 184, 185, 188, 194, 208, 214, 304

*ATE: 93, 300, 302, 304

2b. analyze reasons for conflict with Mexico

24, 173, 174, 189, 205, 213–217, 218–222, 227–230, 288, 324

*481

ATE: 112, 161, 164, 172, 213, 214, 223, 227, 228, 230, 242, 243, 250

*ATE: 194, 203, 210, 218, 222, 223, 225, 226

2c. describe major events of the Texas Revolution (including the significance of the Texas Declaration of Independence, the Alamo, and the Battle of San Jacinto)

227–230, 236–237, 238–258, 259, 260–261, 270, 288

*16, 173, 218–222, 481

ATE: 238, 241, 244, 245, 246, 250, 251, 253

2d. analyze the problems and successes of the Republic of Texas

237, 262–287, 288, 294

*270

ATE: 236, 251, 262, 264, 266, 270, 277, 278, 280

*ATE: 292, 300

2e. describe the developments and events leading to annexation and statehood

291, 292–293, 294, 295–302, 307, 309–310, 324

ATE: 290, 291, 292, 295, 309

*ATE: 293, 294, 296, 300

2f. analyze the causes and results of the Mexican War

309–310, 312–317, 319, 325, 346, 347

ATE: 290, 309, 310, 311, 312–313, 314, 316, 317, 321

*ATE: 280

2g. analyze reasons for and the involvement of Texas and Texans in the Civil War

349, 350–364, 365, 366, 367, 368–382, 384

ATE: 348, 362, 363, 364, 368, 379

*ATE: 356, 357

2h. explain the roles of notable individuals of various ethnic, racial, and cultural backgrounds in Texas independence, statehood, and the Civil War

224–226, 227–230, 231, 234, 235, 237, 238–258, 259, 260–261, 262–287, 288, 289, 292–293, 294, 295–300, 302, 303, 304–306, 308, 311, 313, 315, 317–322, 325, 328–329, 333, 341, 350–356, 357–364, 365, 366, 369, 370–371, 373, 374, 378, 380, 381, 382, 383, 384, 389, 390, 391, 393–394, 396, 404, 411, 416, 420, 422, 423, 424, 428, 439, 460, 464

*16, 188, 189, 210, 219–222, 427, 453, 459

ATE: 172, 174, 175, 176, 182, 184, 189, 191, 208, 209, 210, 219, 224, 241, 245, 248, 294, 296, 300, 303, 304, 311, 342, 362, 368

*ATE: 190, 237, 293, 306, 310, 356, 363

(3) Political, economic, geographic/environmental, and social developments in Texas, post-Civil War to the 20th century. The student shall be provided opportunities to:

3a. analyze the political, economic, and social effects of the Civil War and Reconstruction on Texas

349, 378–382, 383, 384, 386–400, 401, 402, 403, 404, 405, 408–411, 480–482

ATE: 348, 382, 383, 386, 387, 391, 392, 395, 396, 397, 400, 406, 407, 468, 469

*ATE: 381

3b. analyze the effects of the Constitution of 1876 on political developments

398–400, 403

*594–606

*ATE: 394

3c. describe ethnic, racial, and cultural groups and individuals who settled in Texas (including reasons for immigration, patterns of settlement, and way of life)

401, 407, 408–416, 431–438, 439, 459, 484

*18–19, 20, 24, 33, 42–44, 48–49, 326–333

ATE: 309, 468

*ATE: 208, 209, 293, 301, 306, 355

3d. analyze the role of natural resources and major industries (e.g., agriculture, railroads, cattle) in the economic development of Texas

401, 416, 417–422, 425–433, 444, 452–455, 456–460, 461, 462, 463, 464, 483, 484, 506

*17, 20–21, 24–25, 30–33, 40–41, 42–45, 48–49, 52, 55–59, 60–62, 63–66, 70–71, 205, 333–337, 344, 345, 446–451

ATE: 326, 330, 335, 406, 407, 425, 431, 446, 448, 449, 450, 454, 456, 457, 466, 478, 495

*ATE: 34, 43, 85, 327, 333, 359, 406, 422, 435

3e. explain the extension of the frontier and its impact on settlers and Native Americans

407, 408–422, 423, 424, 430, 440–442, 464

*22, 24, 58, 70–71, 189, 208, 317–322, 325

ATE: 267, 270, 309, 320, 321, 322, 406, 407, 408, 409, 410, 412, 417, 420, 421, 422

*ATE: 184, 243, 317, 319, 320, 406

3f. identify the major political, economic, and social issues and leaders of the period

356, 386–400, 402, 403, 404, 405, 408–420, 424, 427, 430–438, 439, 441–442, 444, 447–448, 451, 453, 461, 462, 464, 480, 481, 482

*32–33, 48–49

ATE: 309, 386, 387, 388, 390, 391, 392, 394, 395, 399, 438, 446, 447, 453, 454, 466, 468, 469, 470–471, 473, 474, 476, 478, 479, 480

(4) Economic, political, and social development of Texas in the 20th century. The student shall be provided opportunities to:

4a. analyze the changes in the Texas economy and

its relationship to the United States and the world

45, 486–489, 491–493, 495–497, 504, 505, 506, 509, 514–518, 521–522, 523, 525–527, 528, 529–531, 532–535, 540, 541, 542, 545, 546, 548, 549–550, 555, 565–566, 568–569, 572–573, 575, 576, 591

*346

ATE: 437, 454, 466, 470–471, 472–473, 490, 508, 517, 521, 522, 525, 526, 527, 529, 531, 538, 546, 547, 550, 561, 564, 566, 569, 570, 572

*ATE: 24, 34, 43, 194

4b. analyze the reasons for and the effects of urbanization of the state

19, 61, 274, 323, 443, 486–489, 490, 491–493, 495–496, 497, 497–500, 504, 505, 515, 516, 517, 524, 539, 545, 546–550, 551, 559, 563–565, 567, 572, 575, 578, 584, 592

*20, 33, 64–66, 72

ATE: 466, 546, 547, 549, 561, 563, 572

*ATE: 446, 472–473, 492, 493, 519

4c. describe the involvement of Texans in foreign conflicts

501–503, 506, 509, 510–512, 535–538, 540–541, 542, 545, 550, 556, 558

ATE: 284, 466, 501, 502, 503, 513, 535, 536, 537, 538

*ATE: 24, 280, 281, 291

4d. analyze the problems and progress in the state's educational system

211, 492, 494, 496–497, 513, 519, 548–549, 550, 554, 558, 574, 576, 604–605

*203, 344–345, 481, 490

ATE: 204, 481, 508, 550, 553, 561, 572, 604, 605

*ATE: 24, 205

4e. analyze the development and the economic, political, and social impact of a changing multicultural population

486–489, 497, 498, 503, 504, 505, 512, 518–521, 524, 550, 552, 556, 558, 559, 561–563, 565, 569, 577–578, 579, 586, 591, 608

*18–19, 346

ATE: 399, 471, 496, 501, 508, 526, 544, 546, 550, 551, 552, 555, 558, 577, 578, 581, 586, 612

*ATE: 208, 316, 320, 491, 569

4f. describe changes in the structures and functions of government at the municipal, county, and state levels

489, 491, 496–497, 517, 519–520, 530–531, 534, 542, 569–570, 571–572, 591, 594–605

ATE: 398, 470–471, 472, 475, 518, 544, 551, 570, 572, 578, 594, 603, 604, 605, 609

*ATE: 519, 565, 600

4g. describe changes in the composition of political parties in Texas and their relationships to the national political scene

497–499, 500, 510–514, 518–521, 554–556, 558, 559, 569–572, 612–613

*617

ATE: 480, 498, 508, 510, 513, 518, 519, 520, 544, 546, 550, 551, 552, 569, 570, 571, 612

*ATE: 298

4h. describe developments in culturally related fields (e.g., art, music, drama, literature, etc.)

124, 274, 323, 493, 504–505, 516, 517–518, 524, 548, 551, 567, 579–586, 589, 590

*346

ATE: 303, 495, 550, 577, 578, 579, 580, 581, 583, 585, 586

*ATE: 326, 584

4i. explain the roles of and contributions by notable individuals and groups representative of the various ethnic, social, and cultural backgrounds in state, national, and international settings

58, 274, 486–489, 492–493, 494, 497, 500, 502, 503, 505, 513, 518, 521, 523, 531, 533–535, 536, 538, 550, 552–556, 557, 558, 561–562, 565, 569–572, 574, 579–586, 587, 588, 589

*18, 21

ATE: 46, 237, 298, 399, 466, 471, 473, 475, 497, 498, 499, 501, 512, 518, 519, 530, 532, 533, 535, 537, 544, 552, 553, 554, 555, 556, 557, 558, 562, 569, 570, 571, 579, 581, 582, 583, 585, 586, 587, 598, 599

*ATE: 190, 520

(5) Geographic influences on the development of Texas. The student shall be provided opportunities to:

5a. describe the major physical and cultural features of the regions of the state

2–7, 16–17, 20–21, 22–25, 26, 28–33, 34, 38, 39, 40, 50–59, 60–62, 63–66, 67–68, 69, 70–71, 72, 89, 90–97, 129, 151, 177, 207, 211, 260, 344, 521, 529

*167

ATE: 39, 50, 53, 57, 61, 63, 64, 120, 143, 177

*ATE: 28, 89, 95, 374, 584

5b. locate and explain the importance of selected places

4–7, 15, 16, 22–25, 26–27, 28–33, 38, 39, 40, 45, 47, 53, 57, 62, 64, 70–71, 72, 88, 110, 117, 133, 139, 152, 157, 159, 167, 170, 186, 187, 190, 192, 207, 211, 227, 232, 233, 234, 253, 268, 274, 278, 288, 301, 307, 323, 324, 325, 345, 353, 359, 367, 372, 375, 385, 392, 402, 418, 429, 443, 445, 449, 483, 529, 539, 551, 559, 567, 590

ATE: 2–3, 4, 5, 10, 19, 22, 24, 30, 31, 35, 51, 52, 55, 60, 61, 66, 67, 79, 84, 95, 105, 117, 120, 132, 137, 142, 154, 162, 165, 177, 186, 190, 194, 207, 239, 253, 255, 257, 272, 275, 281, 304, 310, 315, 319, 323, 335, 363, 373, 374, 409, 418, 421, 422, 432, 439, 443, 448, 457, 501, 515, 516, 519, 526, 536, 539, 547, 548, 563

5c. analyze the interrelationships of physical features and distribution of natural resources on

population movements, economic development, and patterns of settlement

2–4, 7, 11, 16–21, 22–25, 26–27, 33, 36, 37, 41, 42–43, 48, 62, 64–66, 68, 69, 72, 85, 110, 124, 125, 131–133, 134, 168, 177, 184, 211, 278, 285, 286, 300–302, 304, 307, 327, 336, 350–357, 367, 422, 425–428, 443, 449, 455, 456–460, 483, 484, 486–489, 491–493, 495–497, 504, 516, 521–522, 523, 539

ATE: 34, 43, 54, 60, 64, 67, 79, 120, 138, 139, 178, 179, 183, 197, 198, 201, 206, 207, 304, 305, 327, 328, 330, 515, 555, 584

*ATE: 351

5d. analyze impact of human activities on the natural environment of the state

20–21, 25, 31, 32–33, 39, 42–45, 46, 48–49, 52, 57, 62, 66, 69, 72, 174, 211, 307, 346, 416, 528, 530, 542, 559

ATE: 19, 530, 561, 573, 588

*ATE: 3, 7, 16, 17, 18, 23, 43, 330

(6) Respect for self and others. The student shall be provided opportunities to:

6a. be aware of and respect differing values and beliefs among individuals and groups

46, 97, 98, 104, 106, 109, 110, 127, 204–205, 234, 265, 346, 354, 356, 357–360, 365, 424, 589

ATE: 89, 131, 292, 357, 360, 363, 365, 369, 380, 401, 412, 414, 473, 511, 516, 553, 557

6b. recognize how societal values affect individual beliefs and values

97, 107, 110, 203, 204–205, 234, 270, 337–343, 346, 347, 350–356, 357–360, 365, 411, 424, 510–512

ATE: 292, 293, 357, 360, 365, 401, 408, 414, 511, 514, 516, 526, 537, 553, 557

(7) Democratic beliefs and personal responsibility. The student shall be provided opportunities to:

7a. accept the consequences of one's decisions and actions

234, 245–250, 254, 365

ATE: 245, 253, 283, 355, 473, 614

*ATE: 241, 511, 611

7b. understand the underlying principles of the Texas Declaration of Independence and Constitution, including the Bill of Rights

213–214, 223, 224–226, 251–252, 300, 337, 594–605, 608–611

ATE: 250, 251, 270, 271, 296, 297, 339, 350, 355, 361, 393, 394, 498, 511, 593, 594, 595, 596, 599, 612

*ATE: 301, 602, 608

7c. identify personal responsibility in the use and preservation of the natural environment

39, 46, 48, 49, 58, 66, 69, 72, 96, 174, 528, 530, 542, 559, 571, 573, 575, 576, 587, 588

*20–21, 346, 416

ATE: 19, 43, 454, 530, 561, 573, 588

*ATE: 7, 16, 17, 18, 23

7d. value open-mindedness, tolerance of different opinions, civic participation, and compromise as important aspects of the political process

46, 191, 234, 288, 347, 360–364, 510–512, 609–616, 617, 618

ATE: 214, 219, 224, 226, 239, 244, 251, 267, 272, 279, 350, 355, 356, 357, 360, 387, 395, 473, 497, 498, 499, 500, 511, 552, 555, 557, 602, 612, 613, 614

*ATE: 222, 315

7e. respect and support the laws of one's society and work responsibly to change laws one considers to be unjust

224–226, 354–355, 361–362, 365, 367, 480–482, 485, 496, 497–500, 506, 609–611, 613–615, 618

ATE: 203, 223, 393, 466, 479, 497, 498, 499, 500, 511, 552, 555, 601, 614, 615

*ATE: 214

7f. support the democratic processes of the republican form of government

300, 360–364, 365, 480–481, 510–512, 595, 596–597, 598–599, 600, 608–616, 617

ATE: 250, 251, 270, 271, 297, 350, 361, 387, 479, 497, 498, 557, 593, 594, 596, 598, 601, 603, 604, 611, 613, 615, 616

*ATE: 296, 612

7g. support the basic values of American society (e.g., justice, responsibility, political and religious freedom, private property, voluntary exchange, and respect for the law)

191, 213–214, 223, 367, 510–512, 608–616

ATE: 251, 297, 350, 355, 361, 387, 393, 394, 470–471, 479, 497, 498, 511, 552, 553, 557, 593, 594, 600, 601, 603, 604, 608, 610, 611, 613, 614, 615

(8) Support for the American economic system. The student shall be provided opportunities to:

8a. recognize the role of profit and competition in the American economic system

33, 41, 59, 177–178, 179, 182, 205–208, 232, 326–333, 351–352, 357, 367, 378, 425–428, 430, 439, 446–451, 452, 453, 454–455, 480, 484, 517, 521–522, 529, 531, 540, 549

ATE: 306, 327, 330, 331, 351, 425, 438, 449, 470–471, 472–473, 478, 508–509, 510, 517, 521, 566

*ATE: 301

8b. acknowledge the role of government in regulating competition of both consumers and producers

178, 182, 194–195, 378, 446–449, 452–455, 461, 512, 530–531, 532–535, 606

ATE: 273, 306, 470–471, 472, 475, 478, 479, 532, 533, 534

*ATE: 299, 331

8c. acknowledge the right of individuals to acquire, responsibly use, and dispose of property

178, 179, 194–198, 206, 232, 270, 271, 326–333, 344, 345, 353, 367, 427–428, 439, 448, 522, 550

ATE: 330, 446, 470–471, 472–473, 508–509, 510, 516, 519, 566

*ATE: 351, 355, 425, 426, 427, 455

8d. recognize that citizens, through legal political activities, can influence economic decisions made by government

337–343, 596–597

ATE: 273, 355, 466, 478, 479, 532, 533

*ATE: 472

(9) Application of social studies skills. The student shall be provided opportunities to:

9a. analyze, synthesize, and evaluate information

21, 26, 27, 33, 41, 45, 48, 49, 52, 66, 70–71, 72, 73, 86, 87, 90, 101, 104, 108–109, 110–111, 119, 127, 128, 129, 133, 139, 145, 151, 152, 156, 158, 163, 168, 169, 170–171, 176, 184, 189, 191, 192, 196, 203, 205, 210, 211, 212, 217, 232, 234, 235, 242, 244, 250, 252, 258, 260, 261, 265, 285, 286, 287, 288, 296, 300, 306, 307, 311, 314, 317, 322, 324, 333, 343, 344, 346, 347, 359, 360, 362, 364, 366, 367, 373, 382, 384, 385, 391, 402, 403, 404, 411, 420, 422, 423, 424, 428, 433, 438, 442, 444, 445, 451, 455, 461, 462, 463, 464, 465, 484, 485, 497, 500, 503, 504, 506, 507, 514, 521, 523, 535, 538, 540, 541, 542, 543, 550, 554, 559, 560, 569, 574, 575, 576, 579, 583, 589, 590, 596, 602, 604, 605, 606, 607, 609, 611, 613, 615, 616, 617

ATE: 1, 17, 18, 23, 29, 31, 36, 37, 40, 52, 58, 65, 69, 76, 77, 78, 105, 113, 115, 116, 132, 135, 136, 156, 157, 160, 178, 179, 180, 181, 183, 187, 188, 190, 195, 197, 198, 200, 207, 210, 220, 224, 229, 231, 240, 244, 248, 249, 256, 257, 263, 269, 274, 275, 277, 279, 293, 294, 295, 297, 299, 300, 304, 305, 310, 311, 313, 314, 316, 321, 331, 332, 334, 335, 336, 337, 341, 342, 343, 354, 355, 356–357, 358, 359, 360, 361, 363, 365, 370, 371, 372, 373, 374, 375, 376, 378, 380, 381, 382, 388, 389, 390, 395, 397, 398, 399, 400, 406, 409, 410, 414, 418, 419, 427, 428, 430, 431, 434, 435, 436, 437, 440, 441, 449, 450, 452, 453, 454, 455, 458, 471, 473, 476, 478, 480, 481, 482, 483, 486, 491, 493, 494, 495, 496, 497, 498, 499, 500, 502, 503, 510, 512, 513, 517, 518, 519, 520, 522, 526, 529, 530, 533, 534, 536, 537, 544, 548, 549, 550, 551, 552, 553, 555, 556, 557, 558, 561, 562, 564, 565, 566, 568, 570, 571, 573, 574, 578, 581, 584, 585, 587, 594, 595, 598, 599, 601, 603, 609, 614

9b. interpret visual materials (e.g., charts, graphs, pictures, maps)

8–15, 27, 29, 32, 35, 45, 47, 48, 49, 51, 53, 54, 57, 60, 62, 64, 71, 77, 78, 88, 90, 95, 102, 109, 110, 117, 126, 128, 129, 130, 135, 139, 143, 149, 152, 156, 157, 159, 167, 169, 170, 186, 187, 190, 192–193, 195, 207, 211, 212, 227, 232, 233, 234, 246, 250, 253, 255, 257, 260–261, 268, 278, 282, 285, 286, 287, 302, 307, 308,

312, 316, 320, 324, 325, 328, 345, 351, 353, 359, 367, 372, 375, 385, 392, 402, 403, 418, 424, 429, 445, 449, 451, 462, 463, 465, 484, 485, 487, 505, 506, 524, 529, 539, 541, 543, 560, 563, 567, 576, 589, 590, 595, 596, 601, 604, 607, 614, 615, 618

ATE: 2–3, 4, 5, 8, 9, 10, 11, 14, 18, 19, 24, 29, 30, 31, 35, 36, 41, 44, 50, 51, 52, 56, 61, 65, 77, 78, 80, 83, 86, 92, 95, 96, 99, 103, 117, 120, 133, 146, 147, 157, 162, 165, 175, 178, 183, 188, 190, 194, 195, 197, 198, 203, 206, 207, 209, 216, 220, 221, 229, 230, 239, 240, 246, 249, 250, 251, 253, 263, 268, 275, 279, 281, 283, 284, 304, 306, 310, 313, 315, 319, 323, 329, 335, 336, 353, 358, 359, 363, 364, 369, 370, 372, 373, 375, 376, 377, 380, 388, 398, 406, 409, 410, 413, 414, 416, 418, 419, 421, 422, 426, 428, 429, 431, 432, 434, 436, 438, 439, 441, 443, 448, 449, 453, 454, 457, 458, 460, 469, 473, 477, 479, 482, 486, 489, 492, 493, 500, 502, 510, 511, 512, 513, 515, 516, 517, 519, 520, 522, 526, 533, 534, 536, 538, 539, 547, 548, 549, 553, 563, 566, 567, 570, 573, 574, 578, 582, 585, 597, 599, 601, 603, 605, 611, 616

9c. distinguish fact from opinion

26, 73, 111, 344, 442, 543

*347

ATE: 236

*ATE: 431

9d. sequence historical data

27, 49, 71, 87, 88, 130, 169, 193, 233, 261, 287, 308, 325, 345, 385, 403, 416, 424, 461, 480, 507, 509, 560

ATE: 1B, 29B, 50B, 75, 75B, 87, 88B, 114B, 119, 121, 131B, 134, 153B, 155, 161, 173, 173B, 176, 193B, 212B, 220, 226, 237, 237B, 249, 258, 261B, 291, 291B, 306, 308B, 325B, 349, 349B, 361, 367B, 375, 385B, 407, 407B, 424B, 445B, 458, 461, 467, 467B, 485B, 509, 509B, 520, 524B, 537, 545, 545B, 569B, 576B

*ATE: 82

9e. perceive cause/effect relationships

7, 21, 38, 44, 45, 72, 83, 84, 86, 107, 108, 110–111, 117, 136, 139, 143, 145, 149, 151, 152, 168, 170, 189, 211, 234, 271, 280, 288, 289, 296, 306, 343, 391, 402, 415, 416, 423, 442, 458, 460, 462, 463, 482, 538, 540, 572

*383

ATE: 83, 118, 175, 215, 216, 221, 254, 269, 284, 295, 311, 322, 362, 394, 415, 420, 422, 427, 442, 451, 455, 460–461, 503, 522, 530, 538, 549

*ATE: 417, 421, 440, 442

9f. use problem-solving skills

15, 38, 66, 79, 83, 84, 182, 208, 222, 280, 337, 344, 384, 531, 540, 592, 600

ATE: 77, 90, 177, 195, 206, 214, 247, 290, 338, 340, 369, 387, 413, 415, 440, 447, 454, 459, 526, 572, 573, 599

9g. apply decision-making skills

97, 101, 108, 117, 198, 211, 230, 306, 373, 460, 482, 504, 542, 572, 605, 606, 616

ATE: 197, 245, 358

Texas, Our Texas

LARRY WILLOUGHBY

Holt, Rinehart and Winston
Harcourt Brace Jovanovich HBJ

Austin • Orlando • San Diego • Chicago • Dallas • Toronto

Texas, Our Texas

LARRY WILLOUGHBY

Larry Willoughby teaches history at Austin Community College.
His books include *Austin: A Historical Portrait* and *Texas Rhythm, Texas Rhyme.*

Janice C. May, author of the Handbook of Texas Government and Citizenship, is
Associate Professor of Government at the University of Texas at Austin.

CRITICAL READERS AND CONSULTANTS

Hispanic history:
Félix D. Almaráz, Jr., PhD
University of Texas at San Antonio

Twentieth-century history:
David DeBoe, PhD
Texas State Historical Association
Austin

Geography:
Robin Doughty, PhD
University of Texas
Austin

Women's history:
Ramona L. Ford, PhD
Southwest Texas State University
San Marcos

Texas Colonial and Republic history:
Paula Marks, PhD
St. Edward's University
Austin

History of the West:
David Murrah, PhD
Director of Southwest Collection
Texas Tech University, Lubbock

African American history:
Cary D. Wintz, PhD
Texas Southern University
Houston

Printed in the United States of America

ISBN 0-03-075431-3

1 2 3 4 5 6 7 043 99 98 97 96 95 94 93 92

ACKNOWLEDGMENTS

Front Cover photographs: Background photo by Jim Bones; inset photos, clockwise from center, Park Street; Herbert K. Barnett; Reagan Bradshaw; Texas Department of Transportation; Institute of Texan Cultures; Blagg-Huey Library, Texas Woman's University.

Credits for unit-opening pages: Unit 1, *Sunrise* (Big Bend) by William Hoey, courtesy of the artist; Unit 2, mural in Pioneer Hall by Harold D. Bugbee, Panhandle-Plains Historical Museum; Unit 3, The Granger Collection; Unit 4, *Farm Life in Central Texas* by Richard Petri, Texas Memorial Museum; Unit 5, *Dawn of the Alamo* by Henry A. McArdle, Archives Division, Texas State Library; Unit 6, *Enchanted Rock* (Scene near Fredericksburg), 1864, by Herman Lungkwitz (detail), San Antonio Museum Association; Unit 7, The Granger Collection; Unit 8, Clara McDonald Williamson, *The Old Chisholm Trail* (detail). The Roland P. Murdock Collection. Wichita Art Museum. Wichita, Kansas, photo by Henry Nelson; Unit 9, *Boomtown* (detail), 1927–28, by Thomas Hart Benton, Memorial Art Gallery of the University of Rochester, Marion Stratton Gould Fund; Unit 10, *Dust Bowl* (detail) by Alexandre Hogue, National Museum of American Art, Washington, D.C./Art Resource, New York; Unit 11, *Exit Ramp* by James B. Janknegt, courtesy of the artist.

Title page photograph: Williamson / Edwards Concepts / /The Image Bank.

Back cover photograph: Herbert K. Barnett. *Drawing on page 85 by Jack Jackson.*

For permission to reprint copyrighted material, grateful acknowledgment is made to the following sources:

Austin History Center, Austin Public Library: From letters of Jane McCallum and Minnie Fisher Cunningham, 1919 (The Jane McCallum Papers).

Barker Texas History Center: From interview with E. M. Friend from "Pioneers in Texas Oil," Mody C. Boatright and Louise Kelly, interviewers. Copyright 1953 by Barker Texas History Center. From "True Life Story of Ella Bird-Dumont, Earliest Settler in the East Part of Panhandle, Texas." Copyright by Tommy J. Boley.

A. H. Belo Corporation: From *Sunset in the East* by Ted Dealey. Copyright © 1945 by A. H. Belo Corporation.

Kathleen Benson: From *Scott Joplin* by James Haskins with Kathleen Benson. Copyright © 1978 by James Haskins and Kathleen Benson.

Chandler Historical Society on behalf of Jack Yarborough Hardee: From quote by Charles R. Yarborough from *The Chandler Area: Its History and People, 1880–1980.* Copyright © 1981 by the Chandler Historical Society.

Corona Publishing Company: From *Cisneros: Portrait of a New American* by Kemper Diehl and Jan Jarboe. Copyright © 1984 by Kemper W. Diehl and Jan Jarboe.

Editorial Herrero: From "La Guerra con los Estados Unidos" from *Un Viaje al Pasado de México,* 2a. Parte, by G.E. Gonzalez Blackaller and Luis Guevara Ramirez; translated into English by Holt, Rinehart and Winston, Inc. Copyright 1951 by Editorial Herrero.

The Encino Press: From quotes by William M. Adams and Felix Haywood from *The Slave Narratives of Texas,* edited by Ronnie C. Tyler and Lawrence R. Murphy. Copyright © 1974 by The Encino Press.

Grove Press, Inc.: From *Bullwhip Days: The Slaves Remember,* edited by James Mellon. Copyright © 1988 by James Mellon.

Gulf Publishing Company, Houston, TX: Quote by Monroe Brannon from *The Loblolly Book II* by Thad Sitton and Lincoln King, Editors. Copyright © 1986 by Gulf Publishing Company. All Rights Reserved.

Woody Guthrie Publications, Inc.: From interview with Woody Guthrie as recorded by Alan Lomax from "Woody Guthrie, Library of Congress Recordings." Copyright © 1964 by Woody Guthrie Publications, Inc. All Rights Reserved.

Hereford Brand: From editorial from *Hereford Brand,* October 12, 1935. Copyright 1935 by Hereford Brand.

The Houston Post Company: Excerpt from *The Houston Post,* 1958. Copyright © 1958 by the Houston Post Company.

Mike Kelley: From "I'm Just Not Gonna Take 'Ite' Anymore" from *My Name's Kelley and . . . That's My Opinion* by Mike Kelley. Copyright © 1977, 1978, 1979, 1981, 1982, 1983, 1984 by the *Austin American-Statesman.* Copyright © 1984 by Mike Kelley.

Alfred A. Knopf, Inc.: From *The Years of Lyndon Johnson: The Path to Power* by Robert A. Caro. Copyright © 1982 by Robert A. Caro. From *Comanches: The Destruction of a People* by T. R. Fehrenbach. Copyright © 1974 by T. R. Fehrenbach.

N. Scott Momaday: From *The Way to Rainy Mountain* by N. Scott Momaday. Copyright © 1976 by N. Scott Momaday.

William Morrow and Company, Inc.: From *Lay Bare the Heart: An Autobiography of the Civil Rights Movement* by James Farmer. Copyright © 1985 by James Farmer.

New Mexico Historical Review: From "The Rodríguez Expedition to New Mexico, 1581–1582" by George Hammond and Agapito Rey from *New Mexico Historical Review,* vol. 2: 239–269, July 1927. Copyright 1927 by New Mexico Historical Review.

Norwegian-American Historical Association: From *The Lady With the Pen: Elise Waerenskjold in Texas,* edited by C. A. Clausen. Copyright © 1961 by the Norwegian-American Historical Association.

Paramount Publishing Company: From quotes by Pauline Durrett Robertson from *Panhandle Pilgrimage.* Copyright © 1978 by Paramount Publishing Company.

Prentice Hall, a Division of Simon & Schuster, Englewood Cliffs, NJ: From *Dorothy's World: Childhood in Sabine Bottom 1902–1910* by Dorothy Howard. Copyright © 1977 by Dorothy Howard.

CONTENTS

Kevin Vandivier

Nawrocki Stock Photo

Texas Department of Transportation

Barker Texas History Center

Painting by William Huddle,
Archives Division, Texas State Library

Contents **ix**

Library of Congress

Midland County Historical Museum

Western History Collections, University of Oklahoma Library

Mural by Alexander Levin, courtesy Jasper Post Office

Roberto Valladares / The Image Bank

Gallery of the Republic

Tom Lankes /
Austin American-Statesman

Barker Texas History Center

SKILL LESSONS

LIST OF MAPS

Cartographic Collection of Mrs. Jenkins Garrett, Fort Worth

AMERICAE SIVE NOVI ORBIS, NOVA DESCRIPTIO

LIST OF GRAPHS, CHARTS, AND DIAGRAMS

USING *TEXAS, OUR TEXAS*

Texas, Our Texas is designed to provide you with an effective tool for learning about our state's geography and history. It has the standard features found in all good books. It also has some special features to make your learning more enjoyable. The following pages explain the various parts of *Texas, Our Texas.*

Finding Your Way

*T*he **Table of Contents** of *Texas, Our Texas* is found on pages vii through xvi. This table lists the titles of all units and chapters, in the same order in which they appear in the book. To the right of each unit and chapter title is the page on which each begins. Notice, for example, that Chapter 1 is titled "Texas and the World." It begins on page 2.

The Table of Contents lists page numbers for other parts of your textbook as well. It has separate listings of all special features, maps, graphs, and charts. It tells you where you can find the **Appendix.** An appendix is a section of a book that provides additional information about the book's subject. The Appendix in *Texas, Our Texas* includes information such as a list of Texas presidents and governors, the words to the state song ("Texas, Our Texas"), the pledge to the state flag, and the Texas Declaration of Independence.

The Table of Contents also tells you where you can find the **Glossary.** The glossary to *Texas, Our Texas* lists all the vocabulary words, which appear in bold black type throughout the book. Definitions and pronunciations are given for each word, and the words are listed in alphabetical order as in a dictionary.

Another important page reference in the Table of Contents tells you where to find the **Index.** An index lists the many different topics discussed in the book and the pages on which you can find them. For example, the index in *Texas, Our Texas* tells you each page on which Sam Houston is discussed. The index is also helpful to find page references for battles, the cattle industry, the environment, and many other topics of importance for Texas history and geography. The entries are listed in the Index in alphabetical order. Key words appear first. For example, the entry for Sam Houston is listed under **H** as Houston, Sam.

Organization of *Texas, Our Texas*

*T*exas, Our Texas is organized into twelve units. Each unit focuses on a particular topic or period. Unit 1 is about the geography of Texas, and the last unit is a useful handbook about Texas government and citizenship. Each of the other ten units tells the story of Texas history. The history chapters are written chronologically, or in order by time period.

Each unit in *Texas, Our Texas* is divided into two or more chapters. There are 31 chapters in all. To help you read and understand the material in the book, each chapter is divided into sections. There are pictures, maps, graphs, questions, and activities to reinforce your reading. Examples from your book are shown in reduced size on the following pages to illustrate how *Texas, Our Texas* is organized. Read over this section before you begin your study of Texas geography and history.

Unit Opening Pages

*T*he units of *Texas, Our Texas* begin with two pages that look like the ones shown here. A large picture is included in each two-page spread.

What can you guess about the topics or events of the unit from looking at the illustration? The unit title and number are a part of each unit opener. Several paragraphs explain what you will read about in the chapters that follow. Read these carefully and keep them in mind as you progress through the unit. Each unit of Texas history (Units 2 through 11) opens with a time line. Major events of Texas history are shown on the top half of the time line. Major events in the United States, Mexico, and the world that affected Texas are shown on the bottom half of the time line. You may want to refer to the time line as you read through the chapters in each unit for help in keeping the events of Texas history in order.

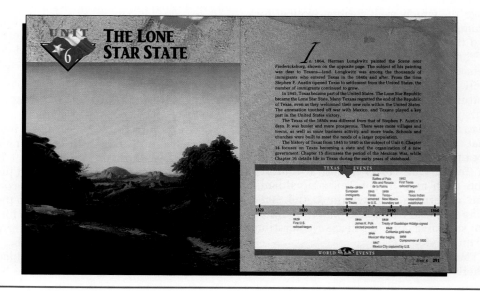

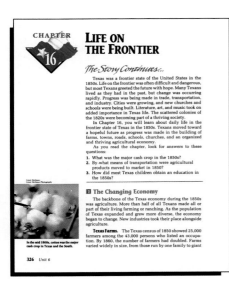

CHAPTER 16

LIFE ON THE FRONTIER

The Story Continues...

Texas was a frontier state of the United States in the 1850s. Life on the frontier was often difficult and dangerous, but most Texans greeted the future with hope. Many Texans lived as they had in the past, but change was occurring rapidly. Progress was being made in trade, transportation, and industry. Cities were growing, and new churches and schools were being built. Literature, art, and music took on added importance in Texas life. The scattered colonies of the 1820s were becoming part of a thriving society.

In Chapter 16, you will learn about daily life in the frontier state of Texas in the 1850s. Texans moved toward a hopeful future as progress was made in the building of farms, towns, roads, schools, churches, and an organized and thriving agricultural economy.

As you read the chapter, look for answers to these questions:

1. What was the major cash crop in the 1850s?
2. By what means of transportation were agricultural products moved to market in 1850?
3. How did most Texas children obtain an education in the 1850s?

1 The Changing Economy

The backbone of the Texas economy during the 1850s was agriculture. More than half of all Texans made all or part of their living farming or ranching. As the population of Texas expanded and grew more diverse, the economy began to change. New industries took their place alongside agriculture.

Texas Farms. The Texas census of 1850 showed 25,000 farmers among the 43,000 persons who listed an occupation. By 1860, the number of farmers had doubled. Farms varied widely in size, from those run by one family to giant

In the mid 1800s, cotton was the major cash crop in Texas and the South.

326 Unit 6

Chapter Pages

*E*ach chapter of *Texas, Our Texas* begins with a page that looks like the one shown above. The chapter begins with an introduction to lead you into the material that follows. Chapter introductions serve the same purpose as the introductory paragraphs on the unit opening pages. To guide your reading, each chapter introduction ends with a list of questions. Look for their answers as you read the chapter.

Just as units are divided into chapters, the chapters are divided into sections. Each section is numbered and begins with a heading in large red type. Subheadings in bold-black type break the sections into even smaller divisions.

At the end of each section, there is a Section Review. Its questions are to help

you review and understand what you just read. These Section Reviews are numbered and headed in blue type. Remember that important vocabulary words appear in bold-black type within the sentences of the chapters. If you need help understanding the meaning of any of these words, look in your Glossary.

Chapter pages in *Texas, Our Texas* are filled with photographs and art. Many pages also contain maps, graphs, and charts. Each of these illustrations has a caption that provides information about its subject. Many picture captions—and all map captions—contain questions to guide your reading. The maps, graphs, and charts are an essential part of your learning. Study them carefully because they will make the information you read clearer, and many provide additional information that you will find useful.

Texas refused to go to the reservations. Second, there was not enough land set aside for them. Nomadic tribes wanted to continue to hunt over vast areas as they had for hundreds of years. Third, most reservation land was not good farmland. East Texas Indians found it difficult to grow enough food to feed their families. Reservation Indians had to depend on government agents to supply them with food and other necessities. Sometimes these agents stole the supplies and sold them for profit.

Settlers eventually moved closer to the reservations, and this created problems. The Texans claimed that reservation Indians often raided their settlements and stole their livestock. In response to these charges, the United States government decided to move the Texas Indian reservations. In the summer of 1859, the Indians from both reservations were transferred to Indian Territory, which is today the state of Oklahoma.

The Alabama-Coushatta reservation is one of the only three Indian reservations in Texas. This photo shows a boy performing in traditional dress.

SECTION ★ REVIEW

Define: infantry, reservations
Identify: Fort Worth, Fort Duncan, Robert S. Neighbors

1. What was the United States policy toward the Indians after annexation of Texas?
2. Who was sent to guard the frontier when the United States troops went to fight in Mexico?
3. What are the only three Indian reservations in Texas?

Writing Persuasively: Imagine that you are a member of an East Texas Indian group in 1854. Write a letter to Sam Houston, asking for his help and explaining why your reservation is not meeting your needs.

Analyzing Information: What special factors caused the Texas government to create a reservation for the Alabama-Coushatta and allow them to stay in Texas?

322 Unit 6

Reservations for Texas Indians. After the reservations were moved to Indian Territory, the state of Texas recognized the right of one Indian group to remain in Texas. This group was made up of the Alabama and Coushatta tribes. They were primarily farmers and had settled along the Trinity River in East Texas in 1825. Many had fought in the Texas Revolution with the Texans.

In 1854, Texas granted the Alabama-Coushatta people 1,280 acres of land in Polk County, near present-day Livingston. Senator Sam Houston played an important role in the recognition of Alabama-Coushatta rights. In 1928, more land was added to the small Alabama-Coushatta reservation. Today the Alabama-Coushatta, the Tigua reservation near El Paso, and the Kickapoo reservation near Eagle Pass are the only Indian reservations in Texas.

The Wars Continue. The governments of Texas and the United States made efforts to end the Indian wars, but without success. People such as Sam Houston argued that the Indians should be allowed to live peacefully in Texas. Honest and hard-working Indian agents such as Robert S. Neighbors did their best to make life on reservations acceptable. Nevertheless, the basic problem went unsolved. Many Indians were naturally unwilling to give up their ways of life, and many settlers were unwilling to recognize the right of Indians to the land. Texas settlers continued to push westward, and the wars continued. ☐

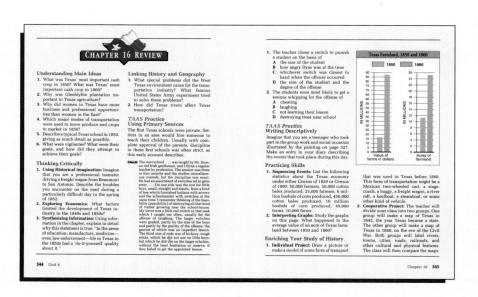

Review Pages

*E*ach chapter in *Texas, Our Texas* is followed by two pages of review material. They are printed on a cream-colored background like the pages shown here. The chapter review pages contain questions about the main ideas of the chapter, critical thinking questions about selected material in the chapter, and a variety of skill practices. These skills include using primary sources; writing persuasively or descriptively; linking history and geography (or economics); and interpreting maps, graphs, charts, pictures, or graphics, at least one of which appears in each chapter review. There also are enrichment activities for individuals and for cooperative pairs or teams.

Understanding Main Ideas is a brief review of the main points of the chapter, as covered in the chapter introduction questions. Questions under **Thinking Critically** ask you to recall information as well as to think about it in different ways. **TAAS Practice: Using Primary Sources** presents a brief primary source reading that relates to the chapter, followed by two multiple-choice questions about that reading. **TAAS Practice: Writing Descriptively** (or **Writing Persuasively**) asks you to use your historical imagination, place yourself in a given situation, and—using information you have learned from the chapter—write from a given point of view. As their name shows, TAAS Practice exercises are to help prepare you for TAAS tests. **Practicing Skills** provides practice and instruction in classifying information, making judgments, sequencing events, interpreting graphics, and other essential skills. The last section of each Chapter Review is called **Enriching Your Study of History** (or **Geography**). These sections suggest projects to be completed by individuals and by groups or pairs working cooperatively.

Besides the chapter reviews, there are one-page unit reviews at the end of each unit. They too are printed on a cream-color background. Questions and activities in the unit reviews provide opportunities for connecting main ideas of the unit, for practicing critical thinking skills, for writing practice, for exploring local history, and for individual and group learning.

Skill Lessons and Special Features

You will find several kinds of special pages in *Texas, Our Texas*. Each unit ends with a one-page **Skill Lesson** printed on a cream background. These pages offer instruction and practice in a variety of reading and writing skills. These skills will prove useful to you not only in the study of history, but also in other subject areas.

Throughout the book you will find special features to enrich your studies about Texas. Each of these special features is set off from the text by a border and its own distinctive title treatment. **Texas Voices** are primary source quotations from real people who lived Texas history. Some of these people are famous Texans. Most of them were not famous in their time, but they have important things to tell us about what life was like in our state. **Cities of**

Texas features give at-a-glance profiles of a variety of cities—large and small—in all parts of the state. Each city feature includes information on geography, economics, and history. **Lone Star Legacy** features give you insight into people and events that have made Texas what it is today, while **Spirit of Texas** features are brief biographies of notable Texans from throughout Texas history. All these features combined add even more color and life to the study of *Texas, Our Texas*. Take some time to look over these and other pages in your text.

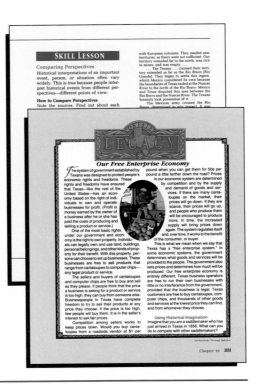

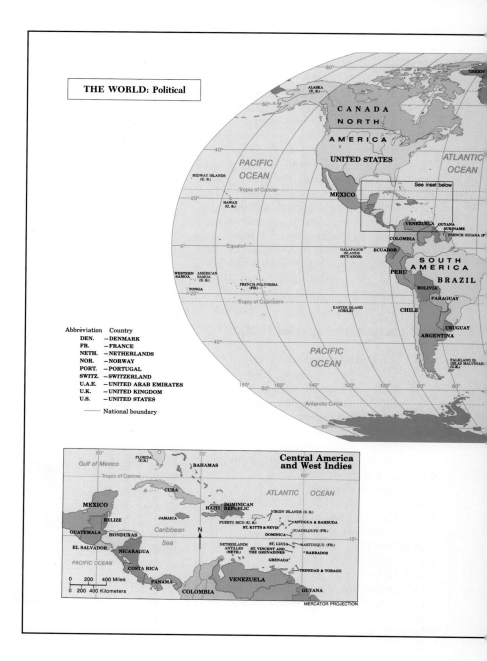

THE WORLD: Political

Abbreviation	Country
DEN.	– DENMARK
FR.	– FRANCE
NETH.	– NETHERLANDS
NOR.	– NORWAY
PORT.	– PORTUGAL
SWITZ.	– SWITZERLAND
U.A.E.	– UNITED ARAB EMIRATES
U.K.	– UNITED KINGDOM
U.S.	– UNITED STATES

—— National boundary

Central America and West Indies

MERCATOR PROJECTION

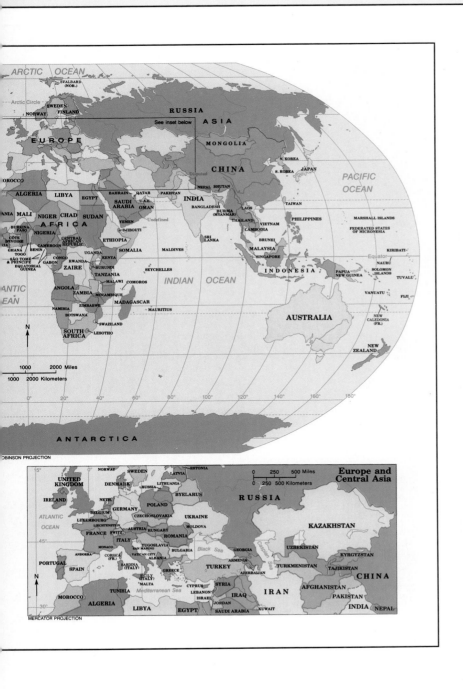

ARCTIC OCEAN

SVALBARD
(NOR.)

Arctic Circle

NORWAY SWEDEN FINLAND

EUROPE

RUSSIA

ASIA

MONGOLIA

See inset below

CHINA

Disputed

N. KOREA JAPAN
S. KOREA

PACIFIC
OCEAN

MOROCCO

ALGERIA LIBYA EGYPT

BAHRAIN QATAR PAKISTAN
SAUDI U.A.E.
ARABIA OMAN

NEPAL BHUTAN

INDIA

TAIWAN

ANIA MALI NIGER CHAD SUDAN
AFRICA
BURKINA
FASO NIGERIA
DIA CÔTE CENTRAL
D'IVOIRE AFRICAN
GHANA REPUBLIC
BENIN ETHIOPIA
TOGO CAMEROON
SÃO TOME CONGO RWANDA
& PRINCIPE GABON BURUNDI
EQUATORIAL UGANDA KENYA
GUINEA ZAIRE
TANZANIA

YEMEN

DJIBOUTI

SOMALIA

BANGLADESH LAOS
BURMA
(MYANMAR)
THAILAND VIETNAM
CAMBODIA

SRI
LANKA

MALDIVES

Undefined

PHILIPPINES

MALAYSIA
SINGAPORE

BRUNEI

MARSHALL ISLANDS

FEDERATED STATES
OF MICRONESIA

KIRIBATI

Equator

SEYCHELLES

INDIAN OCEAN

INDONESIA

PAPUA
NEW GUINEA

NAURU
SOLOMON
ISLANDS

TUVALU

ANTIC
EAN

ANGOLA ZAMBIA
MALAWI COMOROS
NAMIBIA MOZAMBIQUE
ZIMBABWE MADAGASCAR
BOTSWANA
MAURITIUS

VANUATU FIJI

SOUTH
AFRICA SWAZILAND
LESOTHO

AUSTRALIA

NEW
CALEDONIA
(FR.)

N

NEW
ZEALAND

1000 2000 Miles

1000 2000 Kilometers

0° 20° 40° 60° 80° 100° 120° 140° 160° 180°

ANTARCTICA

ROBINSON PROJECTION

**Europe and
Central Asia**

15° 0° NORWAY SWEDEN LATVIA ESTONIA

0 250 500 Miles

0 250 500 Kilometers

UNITED
KINGDOM DENMARK RUSSIA LITHUANIA

IRELAND NETH. BYELARUS RUSSIA

ATLANTIC
OCEAN

BELGIUM GERMANY POLAND
LUXEMBOURG CZECHOSLOVAKIA UKRAINE
LIECHTENSTEIN
FRANCE SWITZ. AUSTRIA HUNGARY MOLDOVA
ITALY ROMANIA

KAZAKHSTAN

45°

ANDORRA MONACO SAN MARINO
CORSICA VATICAN CITY YUGOSLAVIA
(FR.) BULGARIA
PORTUGAL SPAIN SARDINIA ALBANIA
(ITALY) GREECE TURKEY

Black Sea GEORGIA UZBEKISTAN KYRGYZSTAN

ARMENIA TURKMENISTAN TAJIKISTAN

Caspian Sea

AZERBAIJAN

CHINA

MALTA CYPRUS SYRIA
ITALY LEBANON
Mediterranean Sea ISRAEL

AFGHANISTAN

N MOROCCO TUNISIA
30° ALGERIA LIBYA EGYPT

JORDAN IRAQ IRAN
SAUDI ARABIA KUWAIT

PAKISTAN
INDIA NEPAL

MERCATOR PROJECTION

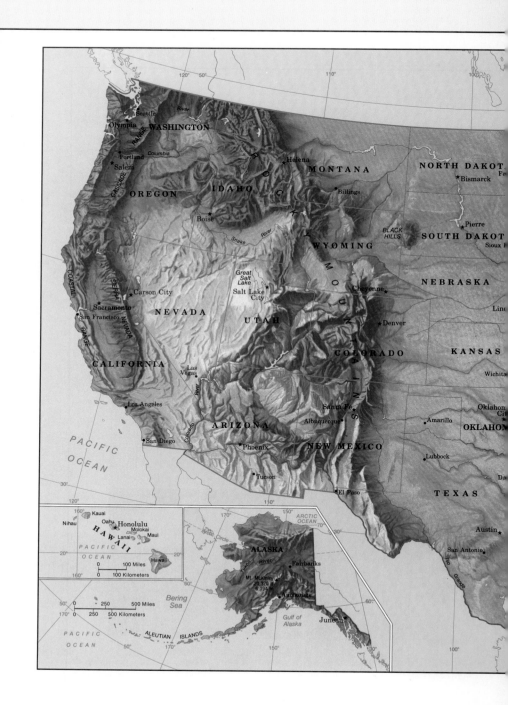

THE UNITED STATES

- ⊛ National capital
- ★ State capital
- • Other city
- —— National boundary
- —— State boundary

ALBERS EQUAL AREA PROJECTION

INTRODUCING THE UNIT

Connecting with Past Learning

Ask students the names of Texas cities where they have lived or traveled, and list the cities on the chalkboard. Ask the students to recall characteristics of the land, climate, and natural resources of these areas. Conclude with a discussion of the geographic diversity of the state.

MOTIVATOR

Ask students to tell where Texas is "located" as you record their responses on the chalkboard or overhead transparency. Encourage students to think of Texas in relation to other places in the world. Explain to students that in order to fully understand a particular place—its people, landforms, climate, economy, and so on—we must understand the significance of its location in the world.

UNIT 1 OVERVIEW

Unit 1 focuses on geography and introduces students to important terms necessary in understanding the cultural and physical geography of Texas. Chapter 1 discusses Texas' position in the world while introducing students to the tools of geographic study.

Chapter 2 provides further study of Texas' physical geography. The interaction of land and climate and effects of natural resources, settlement, and economy on a location are discussed.

Chapter 3 identifies the regions of Texas, or how the state is organized into "parts." Discussion focuses on land, climate, vegetation, resources, economic activity, and cities.

Materials Available at the Unit Level:
Oral History Handbook
Informal Evaluation Forms

UNIT 1

THE GEOGRAPHY OF TEXAS

TEXAS AND THE WORLD

Guadalupe Peak towers above the Texas landscape along the border with New Mexico. The peak is the highest point in the state and serves as a dramatic example of the geography of the vast land of Texas. The land has supported Texans throughout history, even as it has challenged those who settled it. Land was the lure that brought people from all over the world to Texas. The lives of all Texans have been influenced by the land.

History is the story of people, and the people of Texas have an exciting and, in many ways, unique story. For centuries, Texans have worked their land and sometimes fought over it. To understand the history of Texas, we must first study its geography.

The three chapters of Unit 1 describe the geography of Texas. The first chapter provides an introduction to geography and its relationship to history. It also describes the Five Themes of Geography, tools to help you understand the geography and history of Texas. Chapter 2 presents an overall view of the land. It looks at Texas as a whole, considering the shape of the land, its rivers and bodies of water, and the effects of climate. Chapter 3 takes a more detailed look at the regions of Texas. It considers each separately, giving details of where people live and how they make a living. Unit 1 sets the stage for the study of Texas history that follows.

UNIT 1 OBJECTIVES

1. Discuss the geographical diversity of Texas.
2. Describe the location of Texas in relation to the rest of the world.
3. Identify major geographic terms.
4. Identify the purpose of maps, and list the elements of a map.
5. Understand the concept of land use and how the people of Texas have shaped the land and utilized its resources.
6. Discuss the impact of Texas' diverse environments on the state's history, citing specific examples from the textbook.
7. Identify the Five Themes of Geography, and give examples from the textbook to relate these themes to the geography of Texas.
8. Identify Texas' major regions and subregions, and list the major characteristics of each.

Geography
Using a wall map of Texas, point out to students that the "Cutaway View of Texas" traces a diagonal line across the state from El Paso to Port Arthur.

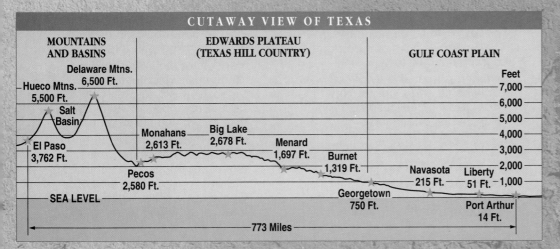

CUTAWAY VIEW OF TEXAS

MOUNTAINS AND BASINS — EDWARDS PLATEAU (TEXAS HILL COUNTRY) — GULF COAST PLAIN

Delaware Mtns. 6,500 Ft.
Hueco Mtns. 5,500 Ft.
Salt Basin
El Paso 3,762 Ft.
Pecos 2,580 Ft.
Monahans 2,613 Ft.
Big Lake 2,678 Ft.
Menard 1,697 Ft.
Burnet 1,319 Ft.
Georgetown 750 Ft.
Navasota 215 Ft.
Liberty 51 Ft.
Port Arthur 14 Ft.
SEA LEVEL
773 Miles

Feet
7,000
6,000
5,000
4,000
3,000
2,000
1,000

CHAPTER 1

TEXAS AND THE WORLD

TEACHER'S TIME LINE

Section 1 Pp. 2–7 1 Day	Section 2 Pp. 8–15 1 Day	Section 3 Pp. 16–21 1 Day	Section 4 Pp. 22–25 1 Day	Review and Assessment 1 Day

⬡ TEACHER MATERIALS

Core: Graphic Organizer 1; Enrichment Worksheet 1; Review Worksheet 1; Reteaching Worksheet 1; Chapter 1 Tests, Forms A & B

Additional: Geography and Graph Skills 1; Map and Chart Transparencies 1, 2, 3, 4, 5; Informal Evaluation Forms; Test Generator

⬡ OBJECTIVES

1. Describe the location of Texas in relation to the rest of the world, using major geographic terms.
2. Identify the purpose of a map, the features of a map, and the different kinds of maps geographers use.
3. Discuss the relationship between geography and history.
4. Identify the Five Themes of Geography, and provide examples of each.
5. Explain the relationship of people and resources and the role of resources in the economic development of Texas.

⬡ RESOURCES

BOOKS FOR TEACHERS

Arbingast, Stanley A., et al. *Atlas of Texas.* Austin: University of Texas Bureau of Business Research, 1976. Tracks economic condition and geology of Texas.

Dobie, J. Frank. *Coronado's Children.* Dallas: Southwest Press, 1930 (and later editions). Stories about lost mines and treasures of the Southwest.

Greitzer, Samuel L. *Elementary Topography and Map Reading.* New York: McGraw-Hill, 1944. Teaches map-reading skills.

Jordan, Terry G., et al. *Texas: A Geography.* Boulder: Westview Press, 1984. Overview of the land of Texas.

Martin, James C. *Maps of Texas and the Southwest, 1513–1900.* Albuquerque: University of New Mexico Press, 1984. Printed maps of Texas.

Pool, William C. *A Historical Atlas of Texas.* Austin: Encino Press, 1975. Shows links between geography and history.

Wegener, Alfred. *The Origin of Continents and Oceans.* New York: Dover Publications, 1966. Continental drift theory.

MULTIMEDIA MATERIALS

Acid Rainbows. (video, 30 min.) PBS Video, 1320 Braddock Place, Alexandria, Virginia, 22314-1698. Industry and acid rain.

Community of Living Things: Module two—Diversity. (video, 75 min.) PBS Video, 1320 Braddock Place, Alexandria, Virginia, 22314-1698. Topics in geography, beginning with forests.

Continents of the World. (video, 15 min.) Coronet Film and Video, 108 Wilmot Rd., Deerfield, Illinois, 60015. Animated visit to a space station sheds light on climate and geography.

The Language of Maps Series. (software) Focus Media Inc., 839 Stewart Avenue, P.O. Box 865, Garden City, New York, 11530. Interactive help in map reading.

⬟ GENERAL STRATEGIES

STUDENTS WITH SPECIAL NEEDS

Limited English Proficient Students (LEP)

Take students on a picture tour of the section they are about to study. Point out photographs, maps, and illustrations that provide examples of key terms and issues they will encounter. Encourage students to note specific topics and terms they are eager to learn more about. See other activities labeled **LEP**.

Students Having Difficulty with the Chapter

Organize the class into groups, and provide each group with a globe and a map. Ask students to study the globe and map and list information from each that they would like to learn more about. After a few minutes of group discussion, invite students to share their questions, and discuss the answers with the class as a whole. **LEP**

Auditory Learners

Have auditory learners prepare oral presentations on selected information discussed in Chapter 1. See other activities labeled **A**.

Visual Learners

Place a large map of Texas in the center of a bulletin board. Through-out the study of Chapter 1, ask students to bring in news articles about various places in Texas. Students should place the articles beside the map, with yarn leading from the articles to the appropriate places on the map. See other activities labeled **V**.

Tactile/Kinesthetic Learners

Have tactile/kinesthetic learners create a map of their neighborhood. Maps should include all of the elements of mapping presented in Chapter 1. Ask students to indicate on the map all of the directions that they travel on their way to school. See other activities labeled **TK**.

Gifted Students

Have students investigate the history of the development of the latitude and longitude system. Ask them also to research the types of grid systems that are used in various professions or fields of study. See other activities labeled **G**.

VOCABULARY

In addition to the boldfaced terms in each section, some students might benefit from discussing the meanings of these terms.

Section 1: *upland* (p. 4); *bottomland* (p. 4); *crossroads* (p. 4); *survey lines* (p. 7).

Section 2: *affiliations* (p. 8); *grid* (p. 8).

Section 3: *strategy* (p. 16); *technology* (p. 17); *obstacles* (p. 17); *proportion* (p. 19).

Section 4: *immigration* (p. 24); *province* (p. 25).

GRAPHIC ORGANIZER

Have students skim the chapter and then complete the Chapter 1 Graphic Organizer. *(You might wish to use this activity to review rather than to introduce the chapter.)*

ENRICHMENT

Have students complete the Chapter 1 Enrichment Worksheet.

SECTION 1

FOCUS

Past Learning (I) Ask students if they can define the word *hemisphere (half a ball)*. Using a globe, point out the Northern, Southern, Eastern, and Western hemispheres. Ask: In what hemispheres is Texas located? Encourage students to speculate on how the location of a place can influence its geography. Tell students to keep this idea in mind as they read Section 1.

INSTRUCTION

Vocabulary (I) You may wish to preteach the following boldfaced terms: *environment* (p. 3); *Northern Hemisphere* (p. 4); *equator* (p. 5); *globe* (p. 5); *maps* (p. 5); *continents* (p. 6); *countries* (p. 6); *states* (p. 7); *physical geography* (p. 7); *cultural geography* (p. 7). **LEP**

CHAPTER 1 OVERVIEW

To understand and appreciate the physical and cultural diversity of Texas, it is necessary to explore its geographic location and size. First, students must be familiar with the geographic terms and concepts used in the study of any place.

Essential Elements
5A, 5B, 5C, 5D, 7C, 9B, 9E

CHAPTER 1

TEXAS AND THE WORLD

Geography Focus

Chapter 1 begins your study of Texas geography with a look at the state's position in the world. It discusses the size and the geographical diversity of Texas. It describes the special tools and concepts that geographers use to organize information about Texas, and the way they study the close relationship between Texas geography and Texas history.

As you read the chapter, look for the answers to these questions:

1. How is the geography of Texas different from that of most other states in the United States?
2. What is the purpose of a map, and how do the features of a map help us use it effectively?
3. How can geography influence history, and how can history influence geography?
4. What are the Five Themes of Geography, and what is the meaning of each?

■ Texas in the World

Most things are understood best in comparison to something else. The same is true of Texas. In order to understand its size and location, we must compare Texas to other places.

Texas Is Big. One image of Texas has remained throughout its history. The mention of the word *Texas* brings this image to mind for people all over the world: Texas is big!

The state of Texas covers 266,807 square miles of surface area. Among the 50 states of the United States, only Alaska is larger. Texas takes in seven percent of the total land and water area of the United States. It is almost twice the size of Japan and five times the size of England. Texas is as large as New York, Pennsylvania, Ohio, Illinois, and

Larry Gatz / The Image Bank

"Big Tex" greets thousands of visitors to the Texas state fair in Dallas each year in October.

all the New England states combined. Not only is Texas bigger than 120 or more of the nations of the world, but it was once an independent nation itself. You will read about the colorful ten-year history of the Texas Republic (1836–1845) in Unit 5 of this book.

Even within Texas, distances are very great. A person can travel more than 800 miles in a straight line from the northwest corner of the Panhandle to the southern tip of Texas. El Paso in far West Texas is so far from Orange in East Texas that it is actually closer to Los Angeles, California. And Texarkana, on the border with Arkansas, is almost as close to the Atlantic Ocean as it is to El Paso.

Texas Is Diverse. "What is Texas like?" Have any of your friends from other states or countries ever asked you that question? Your answer depends on the **environment**, or natural surroundings, outside your schoolroom window. If you live in Alpine, your answer will be very different from that of a student who lives in Galveston.

Texas is so big that it stretches across four major physical areas of North America. Consequently, the Texas environment is extremely diverse, or varied. Within the borders of Texas are golden prairies and majestic mountains. There also are deserts, rolling hills, towering pine forests, cypress swamps, and sandy beaches. The vastness of the land and the variety of landscapes have long attracted people to Texas.

Texas Department of Transportation

The diversity of Texas' landscapes ranges from the subtropical Rio Grande valley, above, to the rolling hills of Central Texas, below.

Paul Montgomery

Endangered whooping cranes spend the winter at the Aransas National Wildlife Refuge near Corpus Christi.

Philip Boyer / Photo Researchers

Texas Parks and Wildlife Department

The armadillo has become a symbol of Texas throughout the nation.

The Texas you see through the window can be a land of extremes. For example, the West Texas plains might be in the middle of a drought while rivers overflow their banks in the hills of Central Texas. Texas has tropical flowers, which grow in warm moist climates, and desert cacti, which grow in dry heat. There are tall pines and twisted mesquite, river moss and tumbleweeds. The alligator, prairie dog, armadillo, and coyote all make their home in Texas.

Texas is a big land of diverse geography, plants, and animals. In some cases, this diverse geography comes together in a small area. The Big Thicket National Preserve northwest of Beaumont is a mix of upland pine forests, bottomland hardwood forests, meadows, sandhills, and swamps. In this place, "the biological crossroads of North America," plants and animals found in the Appalachian highlands, eastern forests, central plains, and southwestern deserts live side by side. Bogs covered with swamp plants sit near sandhills that support thick growths of cactus and yucca. Eastern bluebirds nest near southwestern roadrunners.

Locating Texas. But exactly where on earth is Texas? Texas is in the **Northern Hemisphere**—the northern half of the planet earth. Imagine yourself aboard a space shuttle passing in orbit directly over the North Pole. The North Pole would be at the very center of the circle of earth that

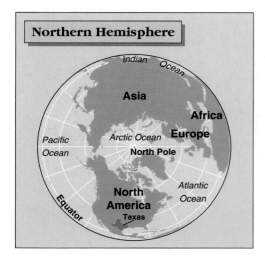

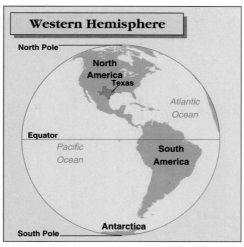

In which two hemispheres is Texas located?

you would see, and the circle's rim would be the **equator**. The equator is an imaginary line that circles the earth halfway between the North and South poles. It marks the boundary between the Northern and the Southern hemispheres. Texas is also in the Western Hemisphere.

Most of us will never be launched into orbit around the earth, but we can see Texas from the same point of view if we look at a **globe**. A globe is a model of the way the earth looks from space. Most often, we look at all or part of the earth's surface on **maps**, which are drawings on a flat surface. The map of the Northern Hemisphere above shows Texas as it looks from above the North Pole.

Already you can see some important things about the geography of Texas. It is located in the southern half of the North American continent. It borders a large body of water called the Gulf of Mexico, and it is much closer to the equator than to the North Pole. The equator (the edge of the circle) receives the most direct of the sun's rays. It is therefore one of the hottest places on the earth. And because the North Pole (the circle's center) receives the sun's rays least directly, it is one of the earth's coldest places. It is not surprising, then, that Texas' summers are much hotter than its winters are cold, and that warmth-loving armadillos far outnumber polar bears (which are found only in air-conditioned zoos)!

Robert C. Henderson

Water birds such as this lone sandpiper are frequent sights on Texas coastal beaches.

CLOSURE
Refer students to the Section 1 Focus discussion. Ask students to tell whether, after reading Section 1, they can add to their ideas about how location can influence geography.

ASSESSMENT
Have students complete the Section 1 Review on page 7.

Caption Response
Canada, the United States, and Mexico

Transparency 1
An overhead transparency of this map can be found in the Teacher's Resource Binder.

Answers to Section 1 Review
Define: *environment*—natural surroundings; *Northern Hemisphere*—the northern half of the planet earth; *equator*—imaginary line that circles the earth halfway between the North and South poles; *globe*—model of the earth; *maps*—drawings on a flat surface of all or part of the earth; *continents*—major landmasses of the earth; *countries*—areas of the world that are controlled by separate governments; *states*—major political divisions of a nation; *physical geography*—the study of the earth's surface and natural features; *cultural geography*—the study of how the land affects the way people live and how people affect the land

(Continued on page 7)

What are the three large countries in North America?

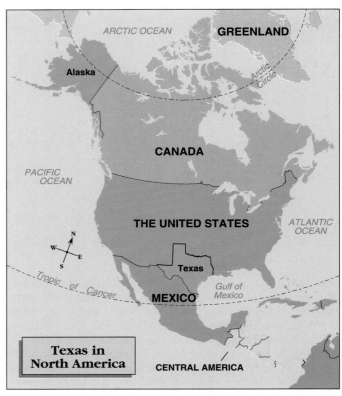

Texas in North America

Paul M. Montgomery

Alligators live in the marshes and swamps of southeastern Texas.

Continents, Countries, and States. North America, in which Texas is located, is only one of the earth's seven major landmasses, or **continents**. Besides North America, these continents are South America, Europe, Asia, Africa, Australia, and Antarctica.

Most of the world's continents are shared by a number of different **countries**, or nations. These are areas of the world controlled by separate governments. Besides the small nations of the southernmost part of North America, called Central America, the North American continent is divided into three large countries. They are Mexico, the United States, and Canada. (In the decade before 1845, Texas was an independent country in North America.)

Study the maps on these two pages. Take a close look at Texas' political neighbors. Texas is located in the south

Texas and Its Bordering States

Santa Fe
Dalhart OKLAHOMA
Amarillo Oklahoma City
ARKANSAS
NEW MEXICO UNITED STATES
Little Rock
Lubbock Wichita Falls Texarkana
Ft. Worth Dallas
Midland Abilene Shreveport
El Paso LOUISIANA
Odessa
San Angelo
TEXAS Austin Beaumont Baton Rouge
Orange
San Antonio Houston
Chihuahua Gulf of Mexico
CHIHUAHUA Corpus Christi
COAHUILA Laredo
MEXICO
NUEVO Brownsville
LEÓN
Saltillo Matamoros
Monterrey
TAMAULIPAS

• Cities
✪ Capitals

N
W—E
S

0 100 200
Scale of Miles
0 100 200
Scale of Kilometers

central United States. It is about halfway between the Atlantic and Pacific oceans. Texas is one of 50 **states**, or major political divisions of a nation. It is bordered on the west by the state of New Mexico, on the north by the state of Oklahoma, and on the northeast and east by the states of Arkansas and Louisiana. To the southwest, Texas shares an international border with the Republic of Mexico. Beginning at the Gulf of Mexico and moving west, the four Mexican states bordering Texas are Tamaulipas, Nuevo León, Coahuila, and Chihuahua.

Three of the borders of Texas are marked by rivers. Texas and Mexico are separated by the Rio Grande (called Rio Bravo in Mexico). A long stretch of the border with Oklahoma follows the Red River. The Sabine River marks a large part of the eastern border with Louisiana. The remaining boundaries are straight survey lines.

Continents are part of **physical geography**, the study of the earth's surface and natural features. Another major field of geography is **cultural geography**. Cultural geographers study how the land affects the way people live and how people affect the land. Political divisions of the land, like the country of the United States and the 50 states that make it up, are a part of cultural geography. ✪

SECTION 1 REVIEW

Define: environment, Northern Hemisphere, equator, globe, maps, continents, countries, states, physical geography, cultural geography

1. How is Texas' geography different from that of other states in the United States?
2. In which hemispheres, continent, and country is Texas located?
3. What is the difference between cultural geography and physical geography?

Writing Informatively: Imagine that you have a pen pal in Australia. Write a letter describing the physical environment of your community.

Exploring Geography: How does being near the equator affect Texas' climate?

1. Texas is bigger and more diverse, or varied.
2. Northern and Western hemispheres, North America, United States of America
3. Cultural geography is a field of study that focuses on how land affects how people live and how people affect the land they live on. Physical geography is a study of the earth's surface and natural features.

Writing Informatively:
Letters will vary, but students should discuss the landforms, vegetation, climate, and natural resources of their area.

Exploring Geography: Texas is closer to the equator than any other state except Florida and Hawaii. As a result, Texas' climate is generally mild in winter and hot in summer.

FOCUS

Past Learning (I) Refer students to several maps in their textbook. Ask them to find at least five similarities among the maps. Challenge them to identify more as you write the similarities on the chalkboard. *(The list should include a scale, directions, legends, colors, symbols, and so on.)* Then encourage students to tell what parts of maps they do not understand. *(Some students probably will respond that they do not fully understand the grid system.)* Tell students that understanding maps and their use is an important step in learning about the geography of a place.

INSTRUCTION

Vocabulary (I) You may wish to preteach the following boldfaced terms: *latitude* (p. 9); *longitude* (p. 9); *prime meridian* (p. 10); *direction indicator* (p. 12); *scale indicator* (p. 13); *map legend* (p. 14). **LEP**

Essential Elements
1B, 5B, 5C, 9B, 9F

Geography
The earth is continuously being circled by Landsat satellites. These satellites' remote sensors can detect a wide range of information that is of interest to geographers, including changes in vegetation, damage caused by natural disasters, and levels of some pollutants.

Ralph Barrera/TexaStock
Knowing how to read globes and maps helps us understand and interpret our world.

HRW Photo by Eric Beggs

Geographers and cartographers, or mapmakers, deal with maps on a daily basis.

2 Mapping Texas

Whether they are dealing with physical or cultural geography, geographers rely on maps. Maps are their most important tools. Geographers gather information on the Texas landscape from books in libraries, surveys on the ground, and photographs taken from airplanes or space satellites. Then they use this information to create maps—careful drawings of some part of the earth's surface.

Maps show the distribution—or the placement on the landscape—of whatever interests the geographer. This may be some part of physical geography, such as soil types, heights above sea level, or kinds of vegetation. Or, it may be a part of cultural geography: population distribution, agricultural products, religious affiliations, birth rates, death rates, or any one of a thousand other subjects relating to people.

Maps and Grid Systems. Geographers have developed their own special language for mapping. You should review some of this language before you go on to study the many maps of Texas in this book. To begin with, you will recall that while the earth is round, maps are flat. There is always some stretching or shrinking of the reality when a curved surface is shown on a flattened one. Geographers have developed many different kinds of mapping techniques to try to solve this problem.

Maps can show a huge variety of information, but we most commonly use them to find places. How do you tell someone where to find something on a map? How do they tell you where something is located? One common method used by geographers is the grid system. You see an example of the grid system on the map of Texas on page 9.

Notice that letters of the alphabet are placed at regular intervals across the top of the map. (They sometimes are placed across the bottom as well.) Numbers run along one or both sides. To find a town at map location B-4, you simply go down the map to "4" and then trace across to the area below the letter "B." The town should be where these two lines meet. You will see the grid system used on many Texas maps, including city maps, county maps, and Texas highway maps.

Latitude and Longitude. For some purposes, simple grid systems are not accurate enough. What is needed is

8 Unit 1

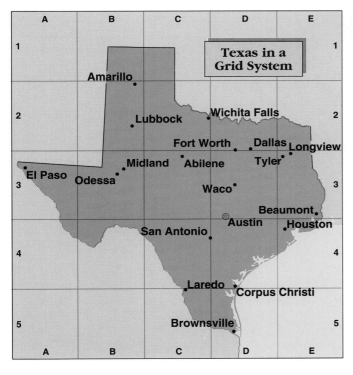

Texas in a Grid System

In what block of the grid system is Austin located? In what block is El Paso located?

some way to locate precisely any spot on earth, on globes as well as on maps. The complex grid system of **latitude** and **longitude** does exactly that job.

Study the two hemispheres divided by lines of latitude and longitude on page 10. Notice that the earth is circled by lines of latitude and longitude measured in degrees. A complete circle has 360 degrees, so each ten degrees represents 1/36 of the distance around the earth.

Lines of latitude run east and west around the earth and thus measure distances north and south of the equator. The equator is located at zero degrees (usually written 0°). Besides the equator, four of these lines of latitude have special names. Moving from the North Pole to the South Pole, these are the Arctic Circle (66½° north), the Tropic of Cancer (23½° north), the Tropic of Capricorn (23½° south), and the Antarctic Circle (66½° south).

James Newberry

Your study of Texas geography will help prepare you for your study of Texas history.

Guided Practice (I) Refer students to the General Reference Map of Texas on page 12. Ask students to practice using a map legend to identify cities, interstate highways, the state capital, rivers, and elevations. **V, TK, LEP**

EXTENSION

Community Involvement (I) Invite a city official to visit the class and speak about how maps are used by the various departments of the city in their daily work. **A, V, LEP**

Transparency 3
An overhead transparency of this map can be found in the Teacher's Resource Binder.

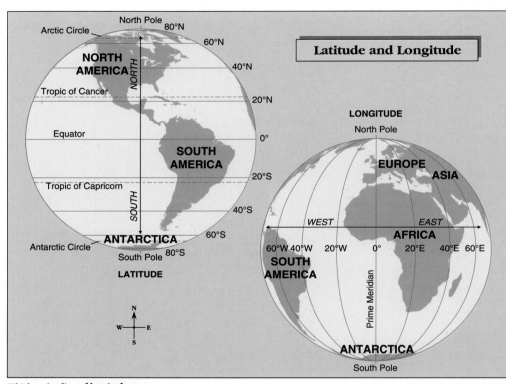

Which major line of longitude passes approximately through the center of Africa?

Caption Response
The equator

Lines of longitude, which are called meridians, are counted east and west to 180° from a line of 0° longitude. This line passes through Greenwich, England, and is called the **prime meridian**. Lines of longitude circle the earth from North Pole to South Pole and are used to measure distances east and west of the prime meridian.

The general location of a place can be given as a combination of latitude and longitude. One degree of latitude covers 69 miles. For greater precision, the distances between degrees of latitude and longitude are subdivided into minutes. There are 60 minutes within each degree, so each minute equals 1/60th of a degree. Then minutes are further subdivided into seconds, a distance equal to 1/60th of a minute. By dividing degrees into minutes and seconds, geographers can locate places precisely.

Independent Practice (II) Have each student select a topic and conduct research to create a special-feature map of Texas. The map should include the key elements of a map discussed in Section 2, including a direction indicator, scale indicator, and legend. **V, TK, G**

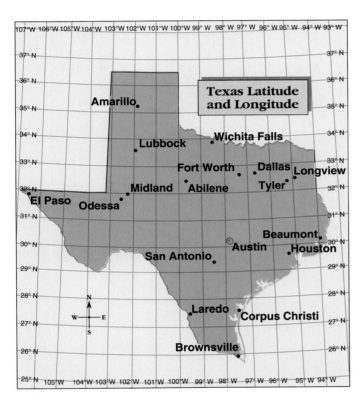

Texas Latitude and Longitude

What is the approximate location, in latitude and longitude, of Wichita Falls?

Transparency 4
An overhead transparency of this map can be found in the Teacher's Resource Binder.

Caption Response
33°54′N; 98°39′W

Geographers have developed a shorthand notation system for writing precise longitudes and latitudes. For example, the latitude of San Antonio—29 degrees, 25 minutes, 30 seconds—is written as 29°25′30″N. The "N" means that this is north latitude—north of the equator. Because Texas is very big, it should not surprise you that it covers a number of degrees of latitude and longitude. From north to south, Texas stretches from latitude 36°30′N to 25°50′N. From east to west, it reaches from longitude 93°31′W to 106°31′W. The "W" refers to west longitude: Texas begins about 93° west of the prime meridian.

Take a close look at the map on this page. What is the approximate location of your school expressed in latitude and longitude? What Texas city is located at almost exactly 32°N 102°W?

Text Question Response
Midland

Transparency 5
An overhead transparency of this map can be found in the Teacher's Resource Binder.

Caption Response
Abilene—1,000–2,000 feet;
Corpus Christi—0–500 feet;
Amarillo—2,000–5,000 feet

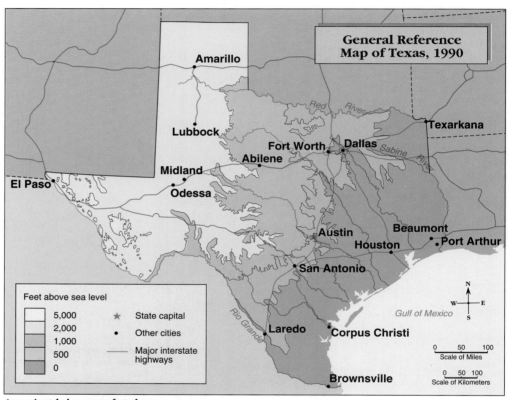

Approximately how many feet above sea level is Abilene? Corpus Christi? Amarillo?

Parts of a Map. If you study the map of Texas above, you will see that the map contains a great deal of information. To begin with, it has a title, which in this case is "General Reference Map of Texas, 1990." As is often the case, the title includes a date. The date lets us know the year or the time period to which the map refers. If the date of this map were 1950, the physical elevations would be the same, but none of the interstate highways of today would be there!

Another important part of a map is the **direction indicator**, which is used to tell the map user which way is north, south, east, west, and directions in between. Direction is usually indicated by a compass rose, which you can see on this map.

Notice the **scale indicator**, which also is found on nearly every map. A scale indicator is a numbered line that tells you how much distance on the map represents a certain distance on the earth. The scale indicator on the general reference map shows the distances that correspond to 100 miles in the real world. Using this scale, can you estimate approximately how far it is down the western border of the Texas Panhandle?

Maps can be drawn to almost any scale—the amount of area covered by each map. The scale depends on its intended use. A map the size of your textbook page could show the layout of your school building, your home town or city, your county, the state of Texas (as the map does here), or all of North America. For that matter, it could even show the Milky Way galaxy, of which our solar system is a tiny part! It all depends on the map's intended use.

People traveling Texas highways can benefit from a map's direction and scale indicators, particularly when covering unfamiliar territory.

Geography
Spend a short time allowing students to practice with the direction indicator. Ask students questions such as: Is Beaumont east or west of Austin *(east)*? Is Texarkana north or south of Beaumont *(north)*? Introduce students to the intermediary directions of northeast, southeast, southwest, and northwest. Ask students: Why is Texas considered to be part of the region of the United States that geographers call the Southwest?

Review with students the location of latitude and longitude lines on a globe or map and the significance of the equator and the prime meridian. Tell students that they will have further opportunities for practice using latitude and longitude in Section 4. Stress again the importance of location in the study of the geography and history of Texas.

ASSESSMENT
Have students complete the Section 2 Review on page 15.

Caption Response
Answers will vary depending on the county in which students live.

What is the population of the county in which you live? (Look at the map on page 47 to locate your county.)

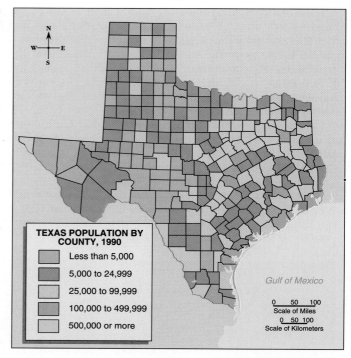

TEXAS POPULATION BY COUNTY, 1990

Less than 5,000

5,000 to 24,999

25,000 to 99,999

100,000 to 499,999

500,000 or more

Gulf of Mexico

0   50   100
Scale of Miles
0   50 100
Scale of Kilometers

**Answers to
Section 2 Review**
Define: *latitude*—imaginary lines that run east and west around the earth and are used to measure distances north and south; *longitude*—imaginary lines that run north and south around the earth and are used to measure distances east and west; *prime meridian*—the line of 0° longitude that passes through Greenwich, England; *direction indicator*—map feature that shows major directions; *scale indicator*—map feature that tells how much distance on the map represents a certain distance on the earth; *map legend*—key to map symbols

(Continued on page 15)

Often placed in a box at one edge of the map is the **map legend**, the key to using the map. It tells you what all the map symbols mean. Symbols are small drawings, numbers, or colors on the map that stand for something else. Our general reference map of Texas uses symbols both for natural and for cultural (human-made) features of the Texas landscape. These symbols make it a useful map for purposes of general reference.

The color bar in the map legend tells you the elevation (height) of land surfaces—from 0 to 5,000 feet—for every place in the state. This symbol is a physical feature of the map. The map legend also tells you that the state capital of Texas is indicated by a star. Other towns and cities are indicated by black dots. (On some maps, small towns may be indicated by small circles or other symbols.) These symbols are cultural features of the map. The map legend, then, gives you the key information for "breaking the code" and understanding the map.

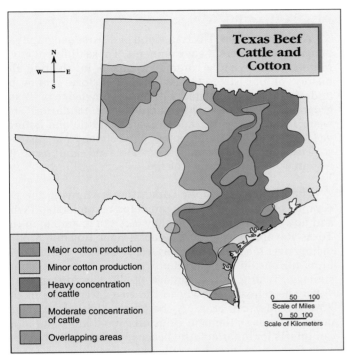

Texas Beef Cattle and Cotton

N W E S

- Major cotton production
- Minor cotton production
- Heavy concentration of cattle
- Moderate concentration of cattle
- Overlapping areas

0   50   100
Scale of Miles

0   50   100
Scale of Kilometers

Is the cotton production of far South Texas major or minor?

Kinds of Maps. We have already seen that the scale of maps may vary, from the layout of your school building to the layout of the Milky Way galaxy. The kinds of maps also vary a great deal. They are limited only by the imagination of geographers. The general reference map you have studied is a good example of a general-purpose map, which shows physical and cultural features. In this book you will find many maps that are special-feature maps. These maps focus on a single physical subject or a single cultural subject. The Texas population map on page 14 is a special-feature map. So are the physical maps in Chapter 2 that show Texas counties and rainfall distribution.

Look at the map above showing the distribution of cotton farming and cattle raising in Texas. You may find this map a little shocking if—like many people—you think that most cotton is still grown in East Texas and most cattle are still raised on the dry plains of West Texas. As the map clearly shows, the opposite is true! ✪

SECTION 2 REVIEW

Define: latitude, longitude, prime meridian, direction indicator, scale indicator, map legend

1. Name three different geographic subjects that maps may show.
2. What are the features of a map? What are their uses?
3. What are three kinds of special-feature maps?

Exploring Geography: A plane has crashed at latitude 30°N, longitude 101°W. Why might this information be inadequate for rescuers to locate the survivors quickly?

Interpreting Maps: Draw a map of your neighborhood, showing your home, major streets, and any parks or schools.

1. Students should name physical or cultural subjects such as population, rainfall, land use, and vegetation distributions.
2. Maps usually have a title, which tells the subject of the map; a date, which tells the time period to which the map refers; a direction indicator, which shows the four main directions; a scale indicator, which tells how much distance on the map represents a certain distance on the earth; and a legend, which identifies the symbols used on the map.
3. Answers may vary, but the ones mentioned in the textbook are population maps, rainfall maps, and vegetation maps.

Exploring Geography: It does not give a precise enough location to easily find the crash site. The plane could be anywhere within hundreds of square miles.

Interpreting Maps: Maps will vary but should be accurate, neat, and detailed.

SECTION ▣3

FOCUS

Student Experiences (I) Ask students if they have ever moved across town or across the country. Discuss with them the changes they encountered in the new environment and how they adapted. Next ask students how they think the problems people face when they move today compare with those faced by early Texas settlers. Explain to students that geography has always played a major role in settlement patterns.

INSTRUCTION

Vocabulary (I) You may wish to preteach the following bold-faced terms: *rural* (p. 20); *urban* (p. 20); *natural resources* (p. 20); *conservation* (p. 21); *ecology* (p. 21). **LEP**

Essential Elements
1A, 1B, 2A, 2C, 2H, 3C, 3D, 4B, 4E, 5A, 5C, 5D

Geography
Ask students how the physical landscape of their area affected the area's history.

Michael A. Murphy,
Texas Tourist Development Agency

The San Jacinto Monument in Harris County marks the site where Texans won their independence.

▣3 Texas Geography in Texas History

As we have seen, Texas is a land of diverse geography— of many very different environments. These different environments have had a dramatic impact in shaping the history of our state. In fact, Texas history cannot be understood or appreciated without a knowledge of Texas geography. This geography includes the landforms and water features, weather and climate, wildlife and natural vegetation. Just as these factors have shaped our history, so Texas peoples have shaped the land and used its resources to fit their ways of life.

The History-Geography Connection. Knowing the geography of a place in history can help you understand why and how events unfolded as they did. For example, in the Texas Revolution of 1836, General Sam Houston won a victory over the Mexican forces led by General Santa Anna. In part, Houston was victorious because of his geographic strategy. Taking full advantage of the vast distances of Texas, he retreated slowly to the east in advance of the powerful Mexican army. As he passed through the main areas of Texas settlement, Houston gained more and more volunteers for his army. And because Houston was familiar with local geography, he evaded Santa Anna's troops until just the right moment for attack. Then, as you will read in Chapter 12, he used the natural landscape of San Jacinto to take Santa Anna's army by surprise. [See the map on page 253.]

If Santa Anna had refused to pursue Houston to the east, or had not divided his troops, or had located his army in a different position on the battlefield of San Jacinto, history may well have been very different. The Texas Revolution might have been crushed. Texas might still be a part of Mexico! Seeing the geographic side of strategy allows you to judge the overall progress of any war and many of the key decisions made by both sides.

The physical landscape often influences the decisions people make. Yet in many ways, people also shape the landscape. For example, long before the first Europeans and Africans reached Texas, Native Americans altered the countryside by setting fire to wooded areas. They did so in order to drive game out into the open. In this way, the Indians could more easily kill their prey.

Kevin Vandivier

Houston is Texas' largest city. Its attractions include museums, theater, symphonies, ballet, rodeos, major-league baseball, and professional football.

Later, advances in technology enabled settlers of Texas to affect the landscape much more dramatically. By the 1890s, hundreds of miles of railroads crisscrossed the state. The railroads made it easier and faster to transport goods and people from countryside to town and from town to countryside. Along these lines of communication, new communities developed in previously unpopulated areas. Crops could quickly reach market from almost anywhere. And later, when automobiles were invented and highways were built, people were able to move goods and themselves even farther and more easily. Towns in which rail lines and highways converged became centers of trade and transport. Dallas, Fort Worth, Houston, and San Antonio grew into great cities.

Just as people overcame problems of transportation in the past, in recent times they have overcome many other obstacles created by geography. Irrigation projects now bring water to barren lands. Air-conditioning and heating systems create comfortable, human-made climates in which people live and work. Communications satellites beam messages across broad oceans and high mountains at nearly the speed of light.

TEXAS VOICES
Research (II) Ask students to prepare book reports on one of the works of J. Frank Dobie. Invite volunteers to read their reports aloud. **A, G**

EXTENSION
Research (II) Have students work in groups to create an outline, map, or chart on the natural resources of Texas. Headings should include: *Vegetation, Wildlife, Water, Minerals,* and *Soil.* Encourage students to investigate the steps being taken to conserve these resources in the state. Ask each group to share its findings with the rest of the class. **V, TK, A, G**

Reagan Bradshaw

The Alamo in San Antonio is the best-known historic shrine in Texas. It was once the chapel of the Spanish mission San Antonio de Valero.

Population Patterns. Who were the people who changed the land of Texas? Like the United States itself, Texas is a population—a society—of immigrants. First came the Native American peoples, and then—thousands of years later—immigrants from Europe and Africa. Texas was originally settled in the 1600s and 1700s by Spanish-speaking pioneers from south of the Rio Grande. Between 1820 and 1845, the first waves of North American frontiersmen and farmers came to Texas looking for cheap land and a new life. With them came thousands of African Americans, most of them enslaved.

Since statehood in 1845, settlers have come to Texas from every continent except Antarctica. In the late 1800s, tens of thousands of European immigrants poured into the farming areas and cities of the United States. Texas shared in this wave of immigration. Today, we celebrate the contributions of Indian, African, Spanish, German, Czechoslovakian, Swedish, Norwegian, Polish, French, Italian, Greek, Belgian, Swiss, Syrian, Jewish, Chinese, Japanese, Vietnamese, and Lebanese Texans, among others.

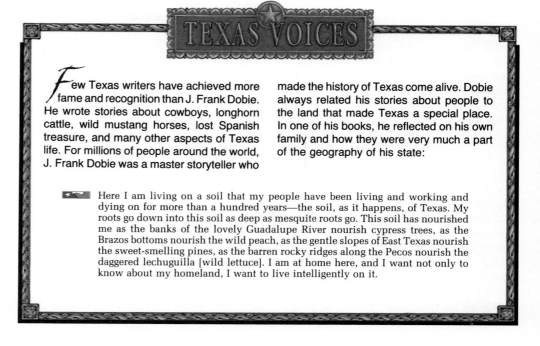

TEXAS VOICES

*F*ew Texas writers have achieved more fame and recognition than J. Frank Dobie. He wrote stories about cowboys, longhorn cattle, wild mustang horses, lost Spanish treasure, and many other aspects of Texas life. For millions of people around the world, J. Frank Dobie was a master storyteller who made the history of Texas come alive. Dobie always related his stories about people to the land that made Texas a special place. In one of his books, he reflected on his own family and how they were very much a part of the geography of his state:

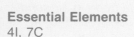 Here I am living on a soil that my people have been living and working and dying on for more than a hundred years—the soil, as it happens, of Texas. My roots go down into this soil as deep as mesquite roots go. This soil has nourished me as the banks of the lovely Guadalupe River nourish cypress trees, as the Brazos bottoms nourish the wild peach, as the gentle slopes of East Texas nourish the sweet-smelling pines, as the barren rocky ridges along the Pecos nourish the daggered lechuguilla [wild lettuce]. I am at home here, and I want not only to know about my homeland, I want to live intelligently on it.

Independent Practice (II) Organize students into pairs or small groups. Have them turn to the map on page 12. Ask each group or pair of students to select one of Texas' large urban areas along with its nearby rural area. Tell them to identify the natural resources that the urban and rural areas share and to list conflicts that might arise over the use and conservation of these resources. Ask a volunteer from each group or pair to share its conclusions with the rest of the class. **A, V, G**

RETEACHING
Ask students to skim Section 3, creating a list of terms or ideas they remain unsure about. Collect the lists, and prepare a master list on which to base a class brainstorming session to help answer questions and clarify ideas. **LEP, A**

In the first decades of the twentieth century, large numbers of African Americans hoped to gain better pay than farming offered them. They began looking for job opportunities in industry. To do so, many African Americans moved from rural communities in Texas to large cities such as Houston and Dallas. They also moved to large American cities farther north. After World War II, many Mexican immigrants also sought a better life in nearby Texas and other southwestern states.

For much of its history, the Texas population grew rapidly. Only during the Civil War of the 1860s and the Great Depression of the 1930s did the growth rate slow. Today, Texas' population continues to grow at a much faster rate than that of many older states. And although Anglos (non-Hispanic whites) still make up nearly 50 percent of the citizens of Texas, the proportion of Hispanics, African Americans, Asian Americans, and other ethnic groups in the population is increasing. Because of high birth rates and continued immigration, the two fastest-growing population groups in Texas today are the Hispanic Americans and Asian Americans.

Multicultural Perspective
Have students brainstorm about the benefits of having people from many different cultures residing in one community.

Kevin Vandivier

Dallas is one of the largest cities in the United States and the second largest city in Texas. Its economy is based on finance, industry, and fashion. Its attractions include world-class restaurants, clothing stores, the State Fair of Texas, museums, art galleries, and theaters.

CLOSURE
Have the class use the summaries presented in the Section 3 Guided Practice activity to outline Section 3 on the chalkboard.

ASSESSMENT
Have students complete the Section 3 Review on page 21.

Reagan Bradshaw

The Panhandle is one of the leading agricultural regions of the world. In the photo above, farmers harvest wheat, a major crop of the area.

As in the rest of the United States, early Texas was a **rural** society, one in which most people lived in areas outside of towns and cities. Today, Texas is an **urban**, or city-centered, society. This change came somewhat later in Texas than in many states farther east. It was not until 1950 that more Texans resided in urban areas than in the countryside. Now, however, four Texans out of five live in cities, and the trend toward urban life continues.

Land Use. Whether rural or urban, the people of Texas have used their state's many **natural resources**—vegetation, wildlife, water, minerals, and soil—to build a strong and diverse economy. In doing so, they have changed the nature of the Texas landscape.

In earliest times, Native Americans used simple tools of stone, bone, and wood in order to hunt, till the soil, and clear the land. The European settlers added metal tools such as axes, saws, plows, and firearms, and the impact on the environment was much greater. As time passed, people developed an amazing array of machines with which to harvest and use the state's resources. At first, these machines were driven by human and animal power. Later, people adapted them to use the much greater energies released by the burning of fossil fuels—coal and petroleum.

As human population and technology increased, so did their impact on the Texas environment. Certain areas of the state were completely transformed in only a few decades. Most of the original pine forests of East Texas were still in place when the first great lumber mills were

The lights of El Paso and its sister city Juárez glitter in the night of far West Texas on the border with Mexico.

Reagan Bradshaw

Robert C. Henderson

Caddo Lake is one of the main attractions of East Texas near the border with Louisiana.

built in the 1870s. If you could have flown over the landscape in a helicopter in those days, you would have seen only a few scattered clearings in what would seem to be a vast, almost unbroken forest. Fifty years later, everything had changed. The great forests had been cut and hauled to the mills on a vast network of railroads.

People such as those who cut down the East Texas forests long ago had little concern for **conservation**—planned management of resources to prevent their destruction. But during the present century, Texans have become aware that many such acts were wasteful and even dangerous. National conservationists, such as John Muir and Theodore Roosevelt, alerted the American public to threats to the country's natural beauty and resources. Scientists studying **ecology**—the interrelationships of living things and their environments—have urged people to develop sensitive areas cautiously. The federal government has set aside large areas of land as national parks and wilderness areas. Today, many Texans are concerned about conservation. This conservation has resulted in greater protection of Texas' natural gifts.

Viewed as a whole, the result of Texas conservation is impressive. Big Bend and Guadalupe Mountains national parks, Padre Island National Seashore, the Big Thicket National Preserve, National Forest Service wilderness areas, the wildlife areas administered by the Texas Parks and Wildlife Department, and more than 40 state parks now protect critical areas of the Texas landscape. ✪

SECTION 3 REVIEW

Define: rural, urban, natural resources, conservation, ecology

Identify: J. Frank Dobie

1. How can geography influence what happens in history?
2. How can history affect geography?
3. What do conservationists try to accomplish?

Exploring Geography: How do you think geography influenced the founders of your community to settle where they did?

Synthesizing Information: Of the major groups of people who migrated to Texas, which do you think had the least impact on the environment? Why?

1. The physical environment often influences the course of historic events. For example, the general who takes strategic advantage of the landscape often wins the battle.
2. By changing the environment through human activities—cutting down the trees, building cities, causing pollution, and using up natural resources
3. The preservation and careful management of natural resources

Exploring Geography: Answers will vary, but students should discuss the specific practical considerations that may have led early pioneers to choose this site. These factors may have been water resources, trade routes, and soil fertility, among others.

Synthesizing Information: The Native Americans, because their populations were smaller, and they had great respect for the natural environment

SECTION 4

FOCUS

Past Learning (I) To help students understand the geographic theme of *location*, review the grid system of latitude and longitude that was introduced in Section 2. Have students study the map of Texas on page 11, and ask them the latitude and longitude for several major cities.

INSTRUCTION

Vocabulary (I) You may wish to preteach the following bold-faced terms: *relative location* (p. 22); *absolute location* (p. 23). **LEP**

Analysis (II) Have students examine the photographs in Section 4 and identify which of the Five Themes of Geography are represented in each. **A, V, G**

Essential Elements
1B, 1C, 2A, 2B, 3E, 4A, 4D, 5A, 5B, 5C, 5D, 7C

Reagan Bradshaw

Bluebonnets bloom in the early spring in the Texas Hill Country.

The famous Paseo del Rio (River Walk) is a favorite area of San Antonio, one of Texas' oldest cities.

4 Texas and the Five Themes of Geography

Geographers organize the topics we have discussed into the *Five Themes of Geography*: location, place, relationships within places, movement, and region. Categorizing the information in this way helps geographers—and students of geography—to analyze facts and see the relationships among them.

The first theme is *location*. There are two ways of defining location: relative location and absolute location. **Relative location** is where a place is in relation to other places. Geographers describe relative location in terms of distance and direction from a certain point. For example, your home may be three miles west of your school. That is your home's relative location. If we say that Dallas is 245 miles northwest of Houston, we are describing a relative location of Dallas.

The shifting location of the Texas frontier in the nineteenth century provides another example of relative location. Texans have usually applied the term *The West* to the frontier—the farthest edge of settlement. In the first decade of Anglo and African settlement of Texas, everything west of extreme East Texas was regarded as the frontier and was referred to as West Texas. By the time of the Texas Republic (1836–1845), the line of settlement had moved farther west. San Antonio and the national capital, Austin, were then regarded as "on the frontier."

Reagan Bradshaw

Environment (I) Ask students to create a list of how people in Texas today still must adjust to the environment *(climate, types of crops that can be grown, physical features that influence economic activities)*. Conclude the discussion by asking how the environment influences the students' community. Ask: What natural disasters still occur over which you have no control, making your community little different from those of early Texas settlers? *(Possible answers include: floods, drought, tornadoes, hurricanes.)* **A, LEP**

Guided Practice (I) Organize the class into groups of five students, with each group representing one of the Five Themes of Geography. Have members of each group work together to write a paragraph summarizing how their theme relates to the study of Texas history. Summaries should be based on information presented throughout the study of Chapter 1. Ask volunteers from each group to read the summaries aloud. **A, LEP**

Richard Reynolds

Texas is home to many different varieties of plants. At left are prickly pear cacti growing in West Texas.

As you have seen, we establish **absolute location**—the exact location of any place on the earth—by the use of a grid of imaginary lines of latitude and longitude. Using this system, geographers can state a location with great precision. For example, San Antonio—and only San Antonio—is located at latitude 29°25′30″N, longitude 98°29′8″W. (You will recall that we read this as "latitude 29 degrees, 25 minutes, 30 seconds north; longitude 98 degrees, 29 minutes, 8 seconds west.")

The second of the Five Themes of Geography is that of *place*. Not only does every place on earth have its own location, but every place on earth is unique. The things that make it unique are called place characteristics. Some of these place characteristics are natural features—landforms, climate, and vegetation. Others are cultural characteristics—the roads, buildings, and farms created on the land by people. Because of the great size and diversity of Texas, Texas places are very different from each other. Texas settlers have had to adjust to places that vary widely in physical features, climate, and vegetation.

The way they adjusted to these different environments falls under the category of *relationships within places*, the third of the Five Themes of Geography. As we have seen, people adapt the environment to their needs. They clear sites for homes. They till the soil in order to grow crops. But people also adapt to their environments. To adjust to different circumstances, they change their ways of life, the

Paul Montgomery

A field of sorghum grows beside an old church near New Sweden in the Blackland Prairie region. Many European immigrants settled this region during the 1800s.

Geography
Ask students to describe some of the place characteristics of their community. Then discuss the ways in which Texas settlers had to adjust to the environment of their area.

Creating (III) Have students collect over a period of several days newspaper articles about current issues facing Texas. Have students highlight passages in the articles that serve as examples of any of the Five Themes of Geography. *(Remind students that more than one theme is likely to be illustrated in each article.)* Have students work together to create a class bulletin board displaying the articles. **V, TK, G**

Independent Practice (II) Provide students with a list of at least five major Texas cities. Ask them to use the maps in their textbook to provide the absolute location of each city. Then have the students describe each city's relative location, based on other information presented in the maps. **A, V, TK**

Multicultural Perspective

Have the class list all of the different groups of people who have settled in their area. The list should include Native American peoples as well as Mexican Americans, African Americans, Asian Americans, and European immigrants, among others.

Texas Department of Transportation

A rodeo cowboy rides a bucking bronco out of the chute. Rodeos were introduced to Texas by vaqueros, or Mexican cowboys.

Paul Montgomery

These mountain geraniums thrive in the Mountains and Basins region.

ways they earn a living, and the houses in which they live. All these are examples of relationships within places.

Another example of relationships within places is the patterns of settlement in Texas. During the centuries when Texas belonged to Spain, settlers from Mexico spread across the brush country of South Texas. This was an open or semi-open landscape similar to that of northern Mexico. It was well suited to the Hispanic system of cattle ranching. Anglo American settlers, on the other hand, preferred the timbered and well-watered lands of East Texas and the Gulf coast for their first settlements. They were farmers, and these areas were most like the places in which they had lived further east.

Then, as the Anglos and African Americans moved farther west with the moving frontier of the nineteenth century, they found that they had to adjust to different conditions of rainfall, vegetation, and landscape. They became more livestock raisers than farmers. As they did so, these new Texans found that they had much to learn from the Spanish-speaking ranchers who were there before them. To adjust to treeless conditions, they replaced their traditional log house with the adobe (mud) house in South Texas and the part-timber, part-sod house in West Texas.

The fourth of the Five Themes of Geography, *movement*, is one that you have already read about. Movement describes activities such as immigration to Texas from the United States, the movements of African Americans from rural areas to Texas cities and cities farther north, and the shift of people from rural to urban areas.

As you have read, immigrations of people play an important part in the history of Texas. Texas was settled first by Native Americans, then by the Spaniards, by Mexicans, and finally by Anglos and African Americans. In the twentieth century, many thousands of people from Mexico migrated into the state.

The theme of movement includes the movement of ideas and information as well as the movement of people. Technology has had a great influence on movement, especially in this century. Many early settlers came to the state in ox-drawn wagons, taking weeks to make the trip. Sometimes they had to camp on a river bank for days, waiting for a flooded stream to go down so they could cross. Mail took weeks—even months—for delivery.

Reagan Bradshaw

The Chisos Mountains break through morning clouds in this photograph taken at Big Bend National Park in West Texas.

These days, conditions are very different. Inventions have reduced the obstacles created by geographic barriers. Telephones, radio and television, and computers flash ideas through vast networks around the globe. Automobiles and highway systems, airplanes, and other advances in transportation speed the movement of people and goods. The movement of human ideas and information is faster and more widespread than ever before.

The fifth of the great organizing themes of geography is that of *region*. A region is a broad area of the earth that contains common characteristics. Geographers use cultural features such as language or economic activity to define cultural regions. They use physical features such as landforms and climate to define physical regions.

Geographers often identify—and historians constantly refer to—nine major physical regions of the United States. As you see in the map on page 53, these are the Atlantic Coastal Plains, the Gulf Coastal Plains, the Appalachian Highlands, the Central Plains, the Ozark Plateau, the Great Plains, the Rocky Mountains, the Plateaus and Basins, and the Pacific Coastal Ranges. The physical features of each of these regions have dominated their development. As you will learn in Chapter 3, four of these North American regions extend into Texas, making Texas the most environmentally diverse state in the nation.

These, then, are the Five Themes of Geography. As you read *Texas, Our Texas*, keep in mind these themes. They will help you understand the development of Texas from Spanish frontier province, to province of Mexico, to independent nation, to state within the United States. ✪

SECTION ✪ REVIEW

Define: relative location, absolute location

1. What are the Five Themes of Geography, and what does each theme mean?
2. The migration of different peoples to Texas is an example of which theme?
3. The adjustment of settlers from eastern states to the dry environment of West Texas is an example of which theme?

Exploring Geography: Describe four specific examples of geography influencing human activity.

Writing Descriptively: Write a brief description of your earliest childhood memories of the natural environment.

CHAPTER REVIEW RESOURCES

1. Chapter Review Worksheet 1
2. Chapter 1 Test, Form A
3. Reteaching Worksheet 1
4. Chapter 1 Test, Form B
5. **Informal Evaluation Forms:** Portfolio Assessment
6. *Texas, Our Texas* **Test Generator**

Essential Elements
1B, 5A, 5B, 5C, 9A, 9B, 9D, 9E, 9G

5. Location—relative and absolute location; place—characteristics of place; relationships within places—human/environment interactions; movement—migration and transportation; region—an area distinguished by one or more characteristics
6. Relative location is where a place is located in relation to other places. Ab-

CHAPTER 1 REVIEW ANSWERS

Understanding Main Ideas

1. Texas is a very large state with a diverse geography.
2. A globe is a round model of the earth. A map depicts the earth or some part of it on a flat surface.
3. The purpose of a map is to depict accurately some part of the earth's surface. Map features are the title (which names the map), date (which tells the period to which it refers), direction indicator (which shows the major directions), scale indicator (which tells how much distance on the map is equal to a certain distance on the earth), and legend (which identifies the map's symbols).
4. An example of geography affecting history: General Sam Houston drew the forces of Mexican general Santa Anna far to the east, into the area of densest Anglo American population, before he gave battle. As a result, Houston's army grew in size, enabling him to win the Battle of San Jacinto. An example of history affecting geography: Irrigation projects brought water to barren lands.

CHAPTER 1 REVIEW

Understanding Main Ideas

1. What are the special characteristics of Texas geography?
2. What are the differences between a globe and a map?
3. What is the purpose of a map? What are its features, and how does each feature help us use the map effectively?
4. Give one example of geography affecting history and one example of history affecting geography.
5. Name the Five Themes of Geography, and define each.
6. What is the difference between relative location and absolute location?

Thinking Critically

1. **Synthesizing Information:** Which of the Five Themes of Geography do you think is the most important to Texas history? Why?
2. **Classifying Information:** Look at the general reference map on page 12. Classify the map features according to the categories of physical geography or cultural geography.
3. **Making Decisions:** Imagine that you can live in any natural environment of Texas that you choose. Where do you prefer to live? Which environmental features determined your choice?

Linking History and Geography

1. How were the problems that faced settlers of East Texas different from those that faced settlers of West Texas?

2. In your opinion, why was the idea of conservation of resources slow to develop in Texas?

TAAS Practice
Using Primary Sources

Pioneer Noah Smithwick came to Texas in the 1820s. In his account of the early settlers, written years later, he tells how they began to farm the unfamiliar land. As you read the following excerpt, note the geographical factors that led the people to settle where they did.

[Growing corn] was no very difficult matter near the coast, where there were vast cane-brakes all along the rivers. The soil was rich and loose from the . . . crops of [wild] cane that had decayed on it. In the fall, when the cane died down, it was burned off clean. The ground was then ready for planting, which was done in a very primitive manner, a sharpened stick being all the implement necessary. With this they made holes in the moist loam and dropped in grains of corn. . . . The only water obtainable was that of the sluggish river, which crept along between low banks thickly set with tall trees, from the branches of which . . . [hung] long streamers of Spanish moss swarming with mosquitoes and . . . [swollen with] malaria.

1. Pioneers farmed the areas along the coastal rivers because
   A the dense forests there indicated a fertile soil
   B nearness to the sea encouraged a fishing industry
   C the cane along the rivers was easy to clear
   D these lands were well suited to the settlers' heavy plows

solute location is the exact location of a place in an imaginary grid of lines of latitude and longitude.

Thinking Critically

1. **Synthesizing Information:** Answers will vary, but students should provide examples to illustrate their choices.

2. **Classifying Information:** Physical—elevation, rivers; cultural—cities, state capital, highways
3. **Making Decisions:** Answers will vary, but students should offer detailed environmental reasons for their choice.

Linking History and Geography

1. Answers will vary, but students may note that East Texas pioneers faced problems of clearing the land and transportation. West Texans faced a dry climate and a scarcity of building materials.
2. Opinions will vary, but students may suggest that those resources at first seemed inexhaustible.

TAAS Practice
Using Primary Sources
1. C
2. B

TAAS Practice
Writing Descriptively
Reports will vary but should include descriptive details.

Practicing Skills
1. **Sequencing Events:** Native Americans, Spaniards, Mexicans, Anglo and African Americans
2. **Interpreting Maps:** There was a decrease. Many agricultural workers moved to towns during this period, seeking a better life. At the same time, Texas agriculture became more mechanized, with machines replacing workers.

Enriching Your Study of Geography
1. **Individual Project:** Reports will vary but should be well researched and detailed.
2. **Cooperative Project:** The maps should be detailed and accurate in scale and should include the map features suggested.

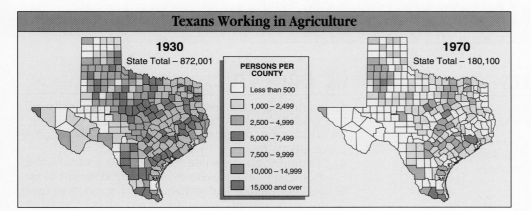

2. According to Noah Smithwick, advantages and disadvantages of settling along the rivers were
   A Spanish moss was available, but sharp sticks were difficult to use
   B water was readily available, but diseases were common
   C springs were common, but cane covered all the farmlands
   D fishing was excellent, but alligators might attack the settlers' cattle

TAAS Practice
Writing Descriptively

Imagine that you are an early Spanish explorer seeing for the first time the area in which you now live. Write a report to the king of Spain, describing how the local environment looked when it was a wilderness.

Practicing Skills

1. **Sequencing Events:** The migrations of many different peoples have made Texas what it is today. Arrange these immigrant groups in the order in which they came to Texas: Mexicans, Spaniards, Native Americans, Anglo Americans, and African Americans.
2. **Interpreting Maps:** Compare the two maps above. Was there a decrease or increase of agricultural workers in East Texas between 1930 and 1970? In your opinion, what might account for the change in numbers of farm workers during this 40-year period?

Enriching Your Study of Geography

1. **Individual Project:** Prepare a short research report on one of the following: one of the Mexican states bordering Texas, the conservation movement in Texas, the science of ecology.
2. **Cooperative Project:** With four of your classmates, prepare a map covering an area three blocks in all directions from your school. The map should include a title, a date, a direction indicator, and a scale indicator. Display your map in the classroom, and compare it to those of other groups in your class.

CHAPTER 2

A LAND CALLED TEXAS

TEACHER'S TIME LINE

Section 1	Section 2	Section 3	Section 4	Review and
Pp. 28–33	Pp. 33–38	Pp. 38–41	Pp. 42–47	Assessment
1 Day	1 Day	1 Day	1 Day	1 Day

★ TEACHER MATERIALS

Core: Graphic Organizer 2; Enrichment Worksheet 2; Review Worksheet 2; Reteaching Worksheet 2; Chapter 2 Tests, Forms A & B

Additional: Geography and Graph Skills 2; Map and Chart Transparencies 6, 7, 21; Informal Evaluation Forms; Test Generator

★ OBJECTIVES

1. Identify major landforms that shape the face of Texas.
2. List and describe Texas' water features.
3. Identify the major types of climate, and describe variations found in Texas.
4. Distinguish between natural vegetation and cultivated vegetation, and provide examples of both in Texas.
5. Discuss the different ways in which people have used the resources of Texas over time.

★ RESOURCES

BOOKS FOR TEACHERS

Bedichek, Roy. *Adventures with a Texas Naturalist.* Austin: University of Texas Press, 1961. Natural history of Texas.

Hobhouse, Henry. *Seeds of Change: Five Plants that Transformed Mankind.* New York: Perennial Library, 1987. How plants have affected culture.

Leopold, Aldo. *A Sand County Almanack, and Sketches Here and There.* New York: Oxford University Press, 1968. Natural history, geography, and wildlife preservation.

Meinig, D.W. *Imperial Texas: An Interpretive Essay in Cultural Geography.* Austin: University of Texas Press, 1969. Cultural geography of imperial Texas.

Nabhan, Gary Paul. *Enduring Seeds.* San Francisco: North Point Press, 1989. Study of Native American agriculture and conservation.

Sauer, Carl Ortwin. *Land and Life.* Berkeley: University of California Press, 1974. Tracks interface between nature and human beings, with examples from Texas.

Texas Water Commission. *Segment Identification Map for Texas River and Coastal Basins.* Austin: Texas Water Commission, 1989. Texas watersheds, rivers, estuaries, etc.

MULTIMEDIA MATERIALS

Land Use and Misuse. (film, 13 min.) Learning Corporation of America, distributed by Simon and Schuster Communications, 108 Wilmot Rd., Deerfield, Illinois, 60015. Tracks effects of accepted industrial and agricultural practice on land.

One River, One Country: The U.S.—Mexico Border. (video, 47 min.) University of California Extension Media Center, 2176 Shattuck Avenue, Berkeley, California, 94704. Importance of the Rio Grande.

Satellite Down: Rescue Adventures in Geography. (software) Focus Media Inc., 1991 catalog, 839 Stewart Avenue, P.O. Box 865, Garden City, New York, 11530. Tracks link between geography and human activity.

GENERAL STRATEGIES

STUDENTS WITH SPECIAL NEEDS

Limited English Proficient Students (LEP)

Using pictures of contrasting scenes of Texas, help students create group collages titled "Texas, Land of Contrast." Pictures should illustrate the state's varied landforms, water features, climate, and economy. Have students work together to write paragraphs describing Texas as a land of contrast. Use the collages and paragraphs as a bulletin board display. See other activities labeled **LEP.**

Students Having Difficulty with the Chapter

Organize students into small groups and assign a different area of Texas to each group. Ask students to mark on a map their assigned area. As they read the chapter, have the students list the landforms, water features, weather patterns, vegetation, and resources unique to the area. At the conclusion of the chapter, help students chart the information they have gathered. **LEP**

Auditory Learners

Have auditory learners prepare oral presentations on the information discussed in Chapter 2. See other activities labeled **A.**

Visual Learners

Have visual learners preview the chapter by studying the illustrations. Then have them complete the Chapter 2 Graphic Organizer. See other activities labeled **V.**

Tactile/Kinesthetic Learners

Have tactile/kinesthetic learners create a Texas Salt Map. Refer the students to the physical map of Texas on page 29, which shows elevations. As a class, decide on a method to convert feet above sea level to inches (height) on a map. Provide students with the following recipe to make a salt map showing Texas' elevations:

2 cups salt
1 cup flour

Add enough water to form the right consistency. Add a few drops of cooking oil.

See other activities labeled **TK.**

Gifted Students

Stress to students that the economic development of a state depends on the state's resources. Have students research how Texas' natural resources—its landforms, water features, climate, and vegetation—have affected the state's economic development. Tell students to identify Texas' major industries, supplementing their research with a map showing their location. See other activities labeled **G.**

VOCABULARY

In addition to the boldfaced terms in each section, some students might benefit from discussing the meanings of these terms.

Section 1: *plains* (p. 28); *plateaus* (p. 28); *tableland* (p. 30); *reservoirs* (p. 31).
Section 2: *torrid* (p. 34); *humidity* (p. 34).
Section 3: *native* (p. 38); *coniferous* (p. 38); *domesticated* (p. 40).
Section 4: *sulphur* (p. 42).

GRAPHIC ORGANIZER

Have students skim the chapter and complete the Chapter 2 Graphic Organizer. *(You might wish to use this activity to review rather than to introduce the chapter.)*

ENRICHMENT

Have students complete the Chapter 2 Enrichment Worksheet.

SECTION [1]

FOCUS

Student Experiences (I) Have students think about places in Texas that they have lived or visited. Ask if they can recall characteristics of the land and name any rivers or lakes of these areas. Conclude with a discussion of Texas as a land of geographic diversity.

INSTRUCTION

Vocabulary (I) You may wish to preteach the following boldfaced terms: *landforms* (p. 28); *water features* (p. 28); *ranges* (p. 28); *tributaries* (p. 30); *irrigation* (p. 31); *aquifers* (p. 31); *springs* (p. 32). **LEP**

CHAPTER 2 OVERVIEW

Texas plays host to many types of landforms. The state's valuable water features include a vast river system. While providing the state with more than its share of severe weather, Texas' several different climates support an extensive array of plant life, natural and cultivated. These natural resources are the foundation of the state's economy. While technological developments have led to greater demands on the land, people are working together to promote the wise use of natural resources.

Essential Elements
1B, 3C, 3D, 3F, 4B, 5A, 5B, 5C, 5D, 8A, 9A, 9B

CHAPTER 2

A LAND CALLED TEXAS

Geography Focus

Chapter 2 gives an overview of the major characteristics of Texas' physical geography—landforms, water features, climate, and vegetation. It then looks at the way Texans have used these natural resources over the course of Texas history.

As you read the chapter, look for the answers to these questions:

1. What are the major landforms and water features that make up the Texas landscape?
2. What are the most important characteristics of the Texas climate?
3. What two major classes of plants are found in Texas?
4. How have Texans used natural resources in the past, and how are ideas about resources changing?

■ Landforms and Water Features of Texas

The surface of the earth consists of landforms and water features—land and water. **Landforms** give the land its basic shape. They may be thought of as the face of the earth. **Water features** are formed by water draining from the land. They include rivers, lakes, and streams.

The Face of Texas. The face of Texas is shaped by landforms of many types. There are mountains, hills, plains, plateaus, canyons, valleys, and even extinct volcanoes. No two areas of the state look alike. It would be impossible to describe all of these areas here. It is possible to sketch a general picture of Texas by focusing on four major landforms: mountains, plains, plateaus, and hills.

Mountains are found in Texas west of the Pecos River. There are several different **ranges**, or groups of mountains. All are part of the Rocky Mountain system, which extends from Canada, through the United States, and into Mexico.

Reagan Bradshaw

The Texas Hill Country, with its panoramas and numerous spring-fed creeks, is admired by Texans from all areas of the state.

Illustrating (I) Provide students with the following list of landforms: mountains, plains, plateaus, hills. Ask students to draw pictures to illustrate each. Have students cut from magazines pictures of the landforms to accompany their drawings. Ask students to label the landforms. **V, TK, LEP**

Analysis (III) Ask students to study a map of Texas to note the relationship of land and water ratios to population density. Have students write a summary of their findings and present it to the rest of the class. **A, V, G**

Transparency 6
An overhead transparency of this map can be found in the Teacher's Resource Binder.

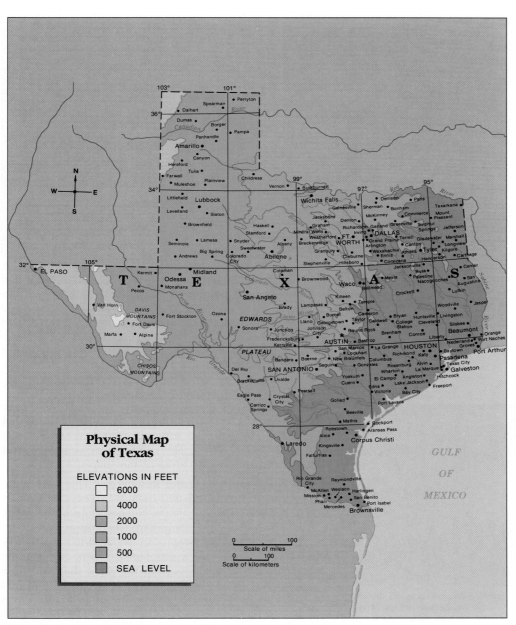

Physical Map of Texas

ELEVATIONS IN FEET

- 6000
- 4000
- 2000
- 1000
- 500
- SEA LEVEL

Scale of miles
Scale of kilometers

What is the destination of most Texas rivers? Which three Texas rivers stem from a source outside Texas?

Caption Response
The Gulf of Mexico; the Rio Grande, Pecos River, and Canadian River

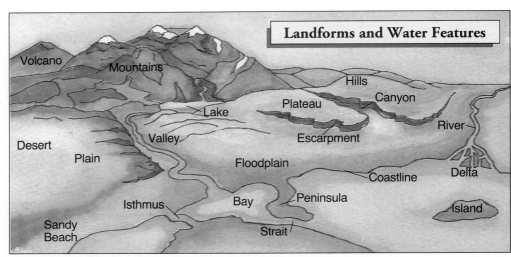

Landforms and Water Features

Volcano · Mountains · Hills · Canyon · Plateau · Lake · River · Desert · Valley · Escarpment · Plain · Floodplain · Coastline · Delta · Isthmus · Bay · Peninsula · Island · Sandy Beach · Strait

Which of these landforms and/or water features exist in the area where you live?

Texas Natural Resources Information Systems

Amistad Reservoir near Del Rio was created by the joint efforts of the United States and Mexico. Why do you think this reservoir was built?

A much larger portion of the face of Texas is formed by plains than by mountains. Plains are the major landform in several areas of the state. They cover much of West Texas, North Texas, the Gulf coast, and northwestern Texas as well.

The major plateau, or tableland, area of Texas is the Edwards Plateau in the west central part of the state. This tableland rises from land farther east.

Like plains, hills cover many parts of Texas. Much of the eastern half of Texas has gently rolling hills. Many plains areas of Texas are interrupted by hills or dotted with them. More rugged hills are found in some areas, especially Central Texas. The Hill Country west of Austin is one of the best-known areas of the state.

The Importance of Water Resources. There are more than 40 rivers and over 11,000 streams in Texas. The major rivers are the Rio Grande, Pecos, Nueces, Colorado, Brazos, Trinity, Neches, Sabine, Canadian, Guadalupe, and Red.

The Texas river system can be divided into three groups. First, there are a number of rivers and smaller streams in the northern part of the state that flow into the Mississippi River valley. These include the Red and Canadian rivers. A second group of rivers begins in Texas and flows directly into the Gulf of Mexico. The third group consists of the Rio Grande and its **tributaries**, or branches.

EXTENSION

Research (III) Ask interested students to research and report on Texas' five major aquifers. They should include in their reports the role of each aquifer as an important water source. Encourage students to supplement their reports with drawings or pictures. **A, V, TK, G**

Independent Practice (I) Provide students with blank outline maps of Texas. Ask them to draw and label on the map Texas' major rivers. **V, TK, LEP**

The most important of these is the Pecos. Eventually, water from all of the rivers and streams in Texas flows into the Gulf of Mexico.

Each of Texas' rivers has its own special character. The Rio Grande (also called Rio del Norte or Rio Bravo in Mexico) is by far the longest and most varied. It begins as a snow-fed mountain stream in Colorado and flows 1,896 miles through desert canyons and coastal lowlands to the Gulf of Mexico. For 1,200 miles of its long journey, the Rio Grande forms the international boundary between the United States and the Republic of Mexico.

At the other extreme, the Comal is the state's shortest river. Arising from big springs within the city limits of New Braunfels, the Comal River flows only 2.5 miles to its confluence (merging) with the Guadalupe River.

The Colorado River travels nearly 840 miles across Texas and drains around 40,000 square miles of Texas landscape. It is the largest river contained entirely within the state. A remarkable series of reservoirs is located along the Colorado, the largest being Lake Buchanan and Lake Travis. These artificial lakes provide water for the state capital, Austin, and other cities. They also help protect downstream areas from huge floods, which once roared down the Colorado valley.

Far to the east, the Neches River twists and turns across 416 miles of East Texas bottomlands to the Gulf of Mexico. The river takes its name from the Neche, a group of Indians who once lived nearby. For most of its length, the Neches flows through deep bottomland forests. Wilderness areas, the Big Thicket National Preserve, and two of the state's national forests are located along its banks.

There are very few natural lakes in Texas. Caddo Lake, in Northeast Texas, is the only one of any size. There are, however, hundreds of lakes built by people. Many of these serve as reservoirs to supply drinking water for towns and cities and to help control floods. They also serve as places for swimming, fishing, and boating. Reservoirs in some areas of the state are important sources for **irrigation**, or watering of crops.

An unseen source of water for Texans is underground. Much of this water lies in natural rocks, sand, or gravel formations called **aquifers**. In Texas there are seven major aquifers, which are important sources of water for farms, homes, and industry.

Laurence Parent

The Rio Grande marks the border between Texas and Mexico. In Mexico, it is also called Rio Bravo or Rio del Norte.

Laurence Parent

The human-made lake in downtown Austin, called Town Lake, is one of the city's main attractions.

Multicultural Perspective
In early times, native peoples from across the region assembled for the great annual pecan harvest. A forest of enormous trees nourished by the periodic flooding of the wild Colorado produced an abundance of delicious and healthful nuts.

RETEACHING
Create a concentration game with the Section 1 vocabulary terms and definitions listed on sets of cards. Organize the class into groups of four or five students, and provide each group with a set of cards. Group members should take turns turning over cards and matching terms to definitions.
A, V, LEP

CLOSURE
Write the following heading on the chalkboard: *Landforms and Water Features of Texas*. With the class, develop an

outline of the chapter. Example:
I. Landforms of Texas
   A. Mountains
II. Water Features
   A. Aquifers

ASSESSMENT
Have students complete the Section 1 Review on page 33.

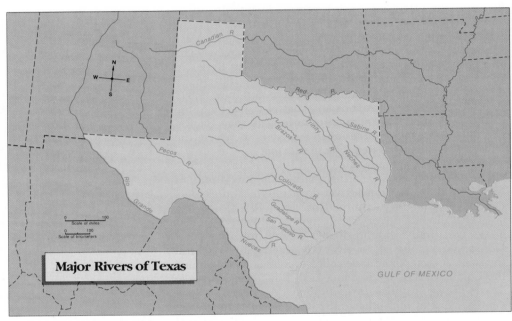

Major Rivers of Texas

Which three rivers form part of the borders of Texas?

Caption Response
Rio Grande, Red River, Sabine River

Environmental Awareness
For many years, the Ogallala Aquifer has been the only source of irrigation for the High Plains. The aquifer is being depleted so rapidly that it may cease to be an irrigation source by the year 2000.

Mike Boroff, TexaStock

Farmers in West Texas depend a great deal on irrigation from the Ogallala Aquifer to water their crops.

Water in aquifers comes from rainwater that seeps down far underground. This recharge, or refilling, of the aquifer takes place quickly in some aquifers but very slowly in others. Water in the Ogallala Aquifer, the largest groundwater source in the state, is thousands of years old and is only very slowly replenished, or replaced. The Ogallala Aquifer stretches from West Texas and New Mexico north to South Dakota. It provides water for a rich agriculture in a land of little rain. Enough water is pumped out of the Ogallala Aquifer every year to cover 7 million acres of land to a depth of one foot. This is several times more than is replenished during the year. To the south, in Central Texas, the Edwards Aquifer provides pure water for the cities of San Antonio and Austin. It gives rise to the largest **springs**—natural outpourings of water from underground—in the state.

Conservation of these underground water sources is now a major concern. The Ogallala Aquifer, West Texas' major water source, is being used up rapidly. So are the

Student Experiences (I) Ask a volunteer to read the first sentence of Section 2 on this page. Ask students if any of them can relate personal experiences that support this statement. Ask students to name the types of weather conditions they have experienced while living or traveling in Texas.

INSTRUCTION

Vocabulary (I) You may wish to preteach the following boldfaced terms: *climate* (p. 33); *precipitation* (p. 33); *northers* (p. 34); *tornadoes* (p. 36); *hurricanes* (p. 36); *blizzards* (p. 37); *drought* (p. 38). **LEP**

---

aquifers that supply the cities of Houston, Dallas, Fort Worth, and El Paso. As in the case of Austin's famous Barton Springs, which flows from the Edwards Aquifer, another problem is pollution of the aquifer caused by surface runoff.

The growth and development of Texas has always depended on water resources. Early Texas settlers established their farms and villages near springs, streams, or rivers so that they would have water for drinking, bathing, cooking, and for watering their crops and livestock. Settlers also used the rivers to transport cotton and other crops to market on rafts and steamboats.

Water resources are just as important today as they were for the first Texas settlers. Texas cities use large amounts of water. Farming would not be possible without water. The Texas fishing industry is made possible by the waters of the Gulf of Mexico, which also provide a transportation route for Texas ports, including Houston, Galveston, Port Arthur, and Corpus Christi. Hundreds of Texas industries depend on water. It is crucial to the food-processing industry, such as the canning of fruits and vegetables and to the beverage-bottling industry. Papermaking requires water, as does the manufacturing of chemicals. More than 90 electricity-generating plants in Texas use steam power, made possible by water. Other plants require water for cooling. These industries provide jobs, and they make our way of life possible. ✪

2 The Texas Climate

There is a saying in Texas, "If you don't like the weather, just wait a minute; it'll change." In many ways, the saying is accurate. The weather can change quickly and dramatically. But as in all places, the weather of Texas follows certain patterns. The term for patterns of weather over a long period of time is **climate**. Major elements of climate are wind direction, temperature, and precipitation. **Precipitation** is moisture falling as rain, snow, sleet, hail, or mist.

Wind and Weather. Because of its size, location, and closeness to the Gulf of Mexico, Texas has several climates. Yet Texas summers are always hot. Texas is located far to the south in the United States and only about 25 degrees

SECTION ★1 REVIEW

Define: landforms, water features, ranges, tributaries, irrigation, aquifers, springs

1. What four major landforms create the majority of Texas landscapes?
2. Of what major mountain system are most Texas mountain ranges a part?
3. What main sources of fresh water are found in Texas?

Classifying Information: Under the categories *Landforms* and *Water Features*, list parts of the Texas land surface discussed in this section.

Exploring Economics: Imagine that a major new reservoir is being built on the river nearest your community. What would be its positive and negative effects on the economy where you live? Why?

Reagan Bradshaw/The Image Bank

Rainfall in Texas varies greatly from region to region. This photograph shows a rainstorm over wheat fields near Amarillo.

Brainstorming (II) Organize students into groups of four or five. Ask each group to brainstorm to prepare three generalizations about the relationship between climate and economic activity in Texas. Have a spokesperson from each group present the generalizations as you write them on the chalkboard. Use the generalizations as a basis for class discussion. **A, G**

Geography
Warm, humid air can make people feel more uncomfortable than dry air at a higher temperature.

north of the equator. The line of 30° N latitude, which passes through Texas south of Austin and north of Houston, also passes through the torrid deserts of North Africa.

The eastern half of the state receives warm, moist air from the Gulf of Mexico. When this air passes over land and meets cooler air masses, it rises and often dumps rain on East Texas. Even when it does not rain, there is plenty of moisture in the air. A term for this condition is *humidity*.

Because water gains and loses heat more slowly than the land, the Gulf of Mexico acts as an air conditioner for areas all along the coast. Sea breezes keep nearby land areas cooler in summer than areas farther inland. In winter, the winds from the Gulf keep nearby land areas warmer.

In contrast to the eastern half of the state, the southwestern portion of Texas receives winds from northern Mexico. These winds usually carry warm, drier air. They bear little moisture.

Winds from the north affect the weather of the Panhandle. This area is often bombarded by air masses, or fronts, called **northers**. Temperatures can drop in a matter of

The arrival of a norther, such as the one photographed blowing into Central Texas, below, can cause temperatures to drop dramatically in only a few minutes.

Paul M. Montgomery

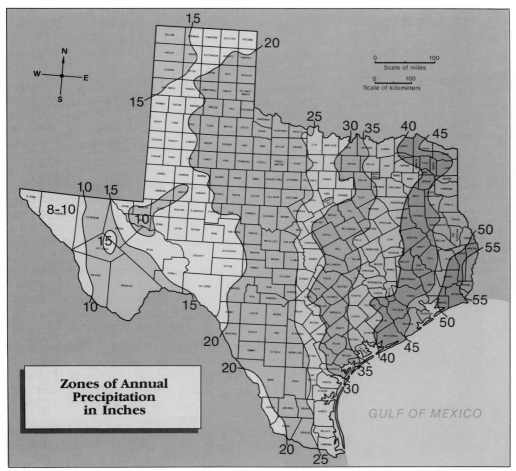

Zones of Annual Precipitation in Inches

Which part of Texas is driest? What is the average amount of precipitation in this part of Texas?

minutes when a norther hits. A norther's effects are sometimes felt as far south as Central Texas and the Gulf coast. In winter, a northern air mass can howl in with snow, ice, and freezing winds.

On an annual average, the coolest temperatures occur in the northern part of Texas. Average temperatures rise to the south. During the summer, Texas is hot. Nearly all parts of the state experience long periods of sunshine. Temperatures above 100° F are common. The highest temperatures are most often found in areas along the Rio

Caption Response
Far West Texas; 8–10 inches per year

Geography
For every 1,000 feet of altitude, the temperature drops by almost three degrees Fahrenheit.

Guided Practice (I) Have the class work together to create a large wall map of Texas illustrating the type and location of severe weather that can occur throughout the state. Encourage students to draw, or cut and paste from magazines, pictures of severe weather and place them on the map where these conditions are likely to occur. Tell students to include all of the elements of mapping that they learned about in Chapter 1. Display the finished map in the classroom. **V, TK, LEP**

EXTENSION

Research (II) Have students research a notable hurricane, tornado, blizzard, or drought in Texas history. Ask them to write and present a "news report" of the event. **A, V, G**

Texas Parks and Wildlife Department

Many areas of West Texas often face drought conditions.

Karen Dickey-Johnson,
Texas Department of Agriculture

Snowfalls are common in the Panhandle during winter, but occasionally snow falls farther south. How might snowstorms endanger livestock?

Caption Response
Livestock might freeze or starve to death.

Grande and in north central Texas. It is often cooler along the Gulf coast and in the mountains, where elevations are higher. During the winter, the coldest temperatures occur over northern Texas. The cold fronts blow down from the Rocky Mountains and Canada.

Rainfall. Extremes in rainfall throughout history reveal much about the nature of the Texas climate. For example, the West Texas town of Wink received only 1.76 inches of rain in 1956. In contrast, Clarksville in northeastern Texas had 109.38 inches of rain in 1873. On a single day in 1921, Thrall, in Central Texas, received 36.40 inches.

In spite of such extreme examples, rainfall follows a clear pattern across Texas. The amount of precipitation increases across the state from west to east. The average rainfall total in West Texas is between eight and fifteen inches per year. East Texas receives 40 to 55 inches of rain each year.

The northern area of the state gets part of its moisture from snow during the winter. The Panhandle can expect between three and five heavy snows each year. The largest snowfall on record in Texas occurred in 1956. In that year, the Amarillo area received more than 30 inches of snow.

Severe Weather. Probably because of its size, Texas seems to receive more than its share of severe weather. Severe weather includes tornadoes, hurricanes, blizzards, floods, and droughts. These weather conditions affect the Texas economy and the ways of life of Texans. At times, they are threatening to human life.

Two examples of dangerous Texas weather conditions are **tornadoes** and **hurricanes**. Tornadoes are violent circular storms that develop within severe thunderstorms. Texas is on the southern edge of "Tornado Alley." This is a region of the midwestern United States that has more tornadoes than any area in the world. The swirling winds of tornadoes can reach speeds of more than 250 miles per hour. They have claimed hundreds of lives and caused millions of dollars in damage.

Strange things happen during the passage of a tornado, as George Bomar cited in *Texas Weather*. Blades of grass and pieces of straw are driven into telephone poles and fence posts. People in automobiles are lifted off highways and smashed down in the middle of wheat fields. There

Independent Practice (I) Ask students to watch a local television weather report for one week and to take notes of the information presented. Have them write a brief summary of the week's weather conditions in their area. **V, LEP**

RETEACHING
Organize students into groups of four or five. Ask each group to select a different area of Texas and prepare a "weather report" for that area. One student from each group should play the role of the "weatherperson" and present the report to the rest of the class. **A, V, LEP**

Leon Hooten, Wichita Falls Times/Record News

Violent tornadoes often touch down in Texas. They usually occur during the spring. This photograph shows the devastating tornado that hit Wichita Falls on April 10, 1979.

are documented cases of chickens being plucked of their feathers by the strong winds—but left otherwise unhurt. In 1947, in Lipscomb County, a tornado picked a man up at his front door, carried him hundreds of feet in the air over the tops of nearby trees, then set him down uninjured. But many tornado victims have not been so lucky.

The season for tornadoes is generally over when summer begins. Toward midsummer, the season for hurricanes starts. These huge storms develop over the waters of the Atlantic Ocean, Caribbean Sea, and Gulf of Mexico. They come ashore with high winds, heavy rains, and enormous tidal surges from the Gulf. In 1900, more than 6,000 people were killed when a hurricane hit Galveston.

An even larger storm, hurricane Carla, came ashore in 1961 near Port Lavaca. With Carla came storm winds of 175 miles per hour and storm tides 18.5 feet above normal. Despite early warnings, 34 people died, and hundreds more were injured. One survivor remembers:

> "The wind would just tear at your eyeballs! That darned hurricane just laid out there and rolled over and rolled over, and the water got higher and higher and higher. The water was tremendous."

Carla also released a barrage of tornadoes as it went ashore. Four of them hit Galveston Island, killing fourteen people.

Blizzards usually hit in the Panhandle or in the north central area of Texas. High winds, snow, and ice are all part of a Texas blizzard. These storms are especially dangerous to cattle and other livestock. The Great Blizzard

Geography
Winds must blow at least 74 miles per hour before a storm is classified as a hurricane. Once formed, the storms are circular, with "eyes" of very low pressure at their centers. The air in the eye usually remains calm, but winds swirl around it at high speeds. Hurricanes typically measure 100–600 miles across. The eye of an average hurricane has a diameter of 10–25 miles.

Review with students the fact that Texas has such variations in climate because of the state's size, location, and closeness to the Gulf of Mexico.

ASSESSMENT

Have students complete the Section 2 Review on page 38.

Past Learning (I) Ask students to name some of the plants, trees, and crops that grow in their area. Ask: Of these, are any unique to the area? Review with students the importance of understanding the theme of *location* in studying the geography of Texas.

Answers to Section 2 Review

Define: *climate*—long-term weather patterns; *precipitation*—moisture falling as rain, snow, sleet, hail, or mist; *northers*—cold fronts from the north; *tornadoes*—violent circular storms that develop within severe thunderstorms; *hurricanes*—huge circular storms that come in from the Gulf; *blizzards*—storms of high winds, snow, and ice; *drought*—prolonged dry period

1. It is extremely varied, differing greatly from east to west and north to south; violent weather events are common; hot summers occur throughout the state.
2. The Gulf acts as an air conditioner to keep the coastal areas warmer in winter and cooler in summer. Moisture-bearing winds from the Gulf bring heavy precipitation and humidity to the eastern portion of the state.
3. Tornadoes—violent circular winds that can form within strong thunderstorms; hurricanes—much larger circular storms that enter Texas from the Gulf

Making Decisions: Northeast Texas is the logical choice.

Seeing Cause and Effect: Sentences will vary, but an example is: In general, the amount of yearly precipitation in Texas decreases with distance from the Gulf of Mexico.

SECTION ★ REVIEW

Define: climate, precipitation, northers, tornadoes, hurricanes, blizzards, drought

1. What are the main characteristics of the Texas climate?
2. How does the Gulf of Mexico affect Texas weather?
3. Describe the two most violent kinds of weather events that affect Texas.

Making Decisions: In which part of Texas would you choose to live if you liked plenty of rainfall but no effects of hurricanes?

Seeing Cause and Effect: Use these words in a sentence explaining a major characteristic of the state's climate: amount of precipitation, Gulf of Mexico, distance, Texas.

Paul M. Montgomery

Yucca plants abound in West Texas.

of 1886–1887 nearly destroyed the Texas cattle industry for almost a decade.

Although large areas of Texas are often dry, floods also are a threat. Early settlers were amazed at how quickly dry creek beds became raging torrents. Dams have helped control flooding in many areas of Texas. Other places remain subject to flooding following heavy downpours or long periods of rain.

Of all severe weather conditions, **drought** has been the most common problem for Texans. Long periods without much rain can kill crops and destroy livestock. In recent years, water supplies in some Texas towns and cities have fallen to very low levels during dry summer months. Reservoirs store water for many areas, but the amount of water available is limited by the Texas climate. As a result, Texans must make wise use of water resources. ⊙

3 Plant Life

Vegetation includes all the plant life of the state. Plants fall into two groups, natural and cultivated.

Natural Vegetation. Native grasses, wildflowers, trees, brush, bushes, and other forms of wild plants are natural vegetation. These are much more important than we sometimes realize. Wild plants provide food and shelter for animals. They prevent **erosion**, or soil loss, by holding the soil in place with their roots. Many wild plants help make the soil fertile. Wild plants also contribute beauty to the Texas landscape.

A great variety of wild plants is found in Texas. Landforms, climate, and soil help determine where the plants will grow. The dry lands of far West Texas support only those natural plants that can survive long periods without water. Short grasses grow in clumps, as do cacti and plants such as yucca. Stands of coniferous, or cone-bearing, trees are found in the mountains. These include piñon pines, ponderosa pines, and junipers.

The plains of South Texas are generally dry, but less dry than West Texas. Grasses cover most of the land. Mesquite trees are scattered throughout this part of Texas, with oaks found in moist places. Shrubs and cacti add to the variety of the landscape. Palm trees grow well along the Gulf coast of South Texas and in the Rio Grande valley.

Vocabulary (I) You may wish to preteach the following boldfaced term: *erosion* (p. 38). **LEP**

Cooperative Learning (II) Organize the class into four groups. Assign one of the following topics to each group: *Texas Panhandle, East Texas, West Texas, South Texas.* Have each group research and report on the plant life of its assigned area. Students should incorporate into their re-

ports the influence of climate and landforms on vegetation. Allow time for each group to present its report to the class. Suggest that students supplement their reports with drawings or pictures of various plants found in each area. **A, V, TK, G**

Padre Island and the Texas Gulf Coast

A million visitors every year enjoy the untamed beauty of Padre Island National Seashore. Padre Island is part of a chain of islands forming a barrier that protects the Texas Gulf coast from storms. The island is named for Padre (Father) Nicolás Balli, a Spanish priest who started a ranch there in about 1800.

Padre Island was created as the ocean deposited sand to form sandbars. Little by little, the sandbars were built up into what is now the longest barrier island in the world. It is 113 miles long. Its width varies from 1,000 yards to 2.5 miles. Laguna Madre, an estuary (lagoon), separates the island from the mainland.

Hurricanes are the major natural threat to the islands and to the Texas coastline. The hurricanes that strike the coast begin as tropical storms in the Atlantic Ocean, the Caribbean Sea, or the Gulf of Mexico. Hurricanes have long affected the history of the Gulf. In 1967, divers discovered a sunken Spanish treasure ship just off Padre Island. The ship had gone down during a great storm in 1553.

In the middle of Padre Island is a long row of sand dunes. The wind constantly changes the shape of these dunes because sand blows easily. Only a few plants can survive in such a sandy, windy environment, but they help hold the sand in place.

Some of the animals and plants on Padre Island and the Gulf coast are endangered. This means there are so few of them that they are in danger of disappearing

forever. Two or three Kemp's Ridley sea turtles, for example, crawl onto Padre Island each year to lay their eggs. In the entire world, there are only 380 of these turtles that can lay eggs. The endangered peregrine falcons stop on Padre Island as they migrate to South America each year.

Some seldom-seen animals also make their homes on the island. Near Padre, for example, is the only colony in North America of white pelicans that nest beside salt water. All living creatures and plants on the island and on the mainland are threatened by people. To protect them, wildlife preserves have been set aside to restrict human activity in both areas.

Using Historical Imagination
Imagine what Padre Island was like 200 years ago. How would it differ from the island today?

Reagan Bradshaw

Essential Elements
(For Lone Star Legacy)
1C, 3D, 5A, 5B, 5C, 8A, 9A

LONE STAR LEGACY
Using Historical Imagination: Answers will vary. Students might note that the shapes of the dunes were different 200 years ago. Plants and animals that are endangered today may have been plentiful 200 years ago. There would have been little human activity 200 years ago.

Essential Elements
(For Section 3)
5A, 5B, 9A, 9B

Bluebonnets climb a craggy hillside. Judging from the rocks and other plants, where do you think this photograph was taken?

Richard Reynolds

Caption Response
The Texas Hill Country

Geography
A *loblolly* is a low, swampy place. Of the three main species of Texas pine, the loblolly pine can grow in the lowest areas.

Texas Parks and Wildlife Department

Tall pines make East Texas important for growing timber.

In the Panhandle, the plains stretch for miles without trees. The soil conditions and annual rainfall support many different kinds of grasses. Unlike far West Texas, the grasses here provide a complete cover for most of the land.

In contrast to the western parts of Texas, the eastern one-third of Texas receives plenty of rain to support woody plants. The soil is very fertile. This is an area of bushes, forests, and tall grasses. Part of East Texas is known as the Piney Woods, where tall stands of shortleaf, longleaf, and loblolly pine trees grow. Other trees common to East Texas are oak, hickory, and elm.

Cultivated Plants. Cultivated, or domesticated, plants are those grown by people for food, fiber, or timber. The major cultivated crops in Texas are cotton, wheat, rice, corn, and grain sorghum. A tremendous number of trees are also raised for their fruits, nuts, or wood products.

Texas, with its wide variety of climates, can support a great number of cultivated plants. Yet irrigation is necessary in many parts of the state. In far West Texas near the Rio Grande, crops such as cotton, alfalfa, melons, and vegetables are grown on land that is irrigated. Huge crops of wheat and cotton are grown with irrigation in northwestern Texas. Irrigation is also needed in South Texas, where citrus fruits and a wide variety of vegetables are cultivated.

This part of the state has the longest growing season of any area, and two crops per season are possible for some products.

Farmers can grow an endless variety of products in East Texas, which receives ample rain. Food crops range from peanuts and watermelons to corn, tomatoes, and many other kinds of vegetables. Farmers grow rice along the wet southeastern Gulf coast. The large forest areas of East Texas provide lumber and other wood products.

Soil and weather conditions limit natural and cultivated plants, but people have managed to overcome many of these limitations. Farmers irrigate land in dry areas or during times of the year when there is little rain. They add fertilizer to poor soil to aid the growth of crops. But using irrigation and fertilizer is expensive. Their use raises the cost of farming. In some parts of Texas, it is not always practical to grow crops, because of the cost. Geography places limits on where farmers can grow crops and on what and how much they can produce. ✪

SECTION 3 REVIEW

Define: erosion

1. What are the two major classes of plant life found in Texas?
2. Which geographic factors help determine which plants will grow in a certain place?
3. What are the most important cultivated plants, or crops, grown in Texas?

Synthesizing Information: If Texas plant scientists (botanists) wanted to study cacti, palm trees, and loblolly pines, to which three parts of the state would they probably go?

Exploring Economics: Which factors might determine whether a farmer would make a profit growing a particular crop in a given year? Explain.

Grant Heilman Photography

Jesse Herrera, Texas Department of Agriculture

Rice is an important cash crop in southeastern Texas.

Cotton farming is very important to the economy of West Texas. What problems might West Texas farmers face that are geography related?

FOCUS

Past Learning (I) Write the word *Resources* on the chalkboard. Ask the class to name as many resources as they can and to identify their uses.

INSTRUCTION

Vocabulary (I) You may wish to preteach the following boldfaced terms: *economy* (p. 42); *technology* (p. 43); *solar power* (p. 44). **LEP**

Brainstorming (II) List on the chalkboard all of the resources discussed in Section 4. Then ask the class to brainstorm to classify these resources as either renewable or nonrenewable. Use the activity to prompt a discussion of the problem of resource depletion. **A, V, G**

Essential Elements
1A, 1B, 1C, 2A, 3C, 3D, 4A, 5B, 5C, 5D, 9B, 9E

Economics
Make sure that students understand the meaning of the terms *goods* and *services*. Call on students to give examples of goods and services.

Mesquite trees thrive in South Texas. Mesquite wood is popularly used to flavor smoked meats.

Texas Parks and Wildlife Department

Michael D. Sullivan, TexaStock

Produce stands in the Rio Grande valley reflect the importance of agriculture to this region.

4 People and Resources

Most people today agree that Texas is blessed with many natural resources. Among these are soil, rivers, and forests. Other resources include oil, natural gas, coal, sand, stone, gravel, and sulphur. These resources provide food, clothing, homes, and products to make our lives easier. They are the foundations of our **economy**, or system of producing and distributing goods and services.

Ideas About Resources. The first people to live in Texas arrived more than 10,000 years ago. Their ideas about the use of the land were different from those of modern Texans. Their way of life was much different. These people used nearby materials to build their homes and make their clothes. If they lived in a forest area, they built their homes of plant materials. If they lived where little wood was available, they made dwellings of animal skins or lived in caves. When food could not be found nearby, the people moved. Even after the Native American peoples of Texas

Analysis (II) Organize the class into small groups. Have students review the first paragraph of Section 4 on page 42. Ask each group to choose a resource of Texas and to use it as an example in a brief paragraph discussing the relationship between resources and the economy. Have a spokesperson from each group read the paragraph aloud. **A, V, G**

Guided Practice (I) Have students work individually or in pairs to create two lists. One list should be of Texas resources and the other of the varied uses for these re-

sources. Ask volunteers to share their lists as you create a class list on the chalkboard. **A, V, LEP**

EXTENSION

Community Involvement (I) Invite someone who works in the field of environmental protection and/or conservation to visit the class. Or, invite a member of the local water department to share information about sources of water, types of pollutants, and methods used to purify the water in your area. **A, V, LEP**

developed agriculture, their impact on the environment was still relatively slight.

Use of the land was much the same for people in Texas for thousands of years. American Indians of the 1500s—when the first European explorers arrived—lived much like earlier native peoples. Land and resources were the basic tools of their survival. Texas Indians thought of themselves as part of nature. Unlike Europeans, few of them saw resources as a way to create wealth.

The Anglo Americans, who began to settle in Texas in the 1820s, had different attitudes toward the natural environment. They saw it as a collection of resources to be used. By the mid 1800s, Texans were cutting down forests for timber, and they were mining the earth. They were building dams to store water. People were using resources to grow richer or to make their lives more comfortable. Their **technology**, or way of using resources, was becoming more complex. Texas' population increased until it was many times as large as it had been in 1500.

Ideas about resources changed along with technology. Oil provides a good example. Early residents of Texas had little use for oil. Indians used it as medicine when they found it in pools on the ground. Later, settlers sometimes used it to grease the axles of their wagon wheels. Only when people saw other uses for oil did demand for it grow.

Reagan Bradshaw

Oil has been discovered in many areas of Texas. These oil derricks rise high in the pines of East Texas.

Environmental Awareness
Ask students to consider the differences in environmental impact of people having to use only crude hand tools in contrast to the huge power machines of today.

Texas Department of Agriculture

Timber is an important resource for Texans. Lumber mills process raw timber for many uses.

Independent Practice (I) Have students draw or cut pictures from magazines and newspapers to create a collage of Texas' natural resources. Display the collages in the classroom. **V, TK, LEP**

RETEACHING
Ask students to list in note form the main ideas of Section 4. Call on volunteers to share their ideas. Have a volunteer write the students' responses on the chalkboard. **A, V, LEP**

Transparency 7
An overhead transparency of the map on page 45 can be found in the Teacher's Resource Binder.

Environmental Awareness
Explain to students the difference between renewable and nonrenewable resources. Call on volunteers to provide examples of each.

Patrick R. Dunn

Texas leads the nation in oil production. Oil pumps are a familiar sight on the West Texas plains.

When this happened, the technology developed to take oil from the ground in large amounts. Today, oil is the most important mineral resource in Texas. The state receives millions of dollars in tax money from its sale. Thousands of people depend on jobs in the oil industry.

Ideas about other resources in Texas have changed. Take sunshine, for example. Most people probably do not think of sunshine as a resource, but technology has been developed that uses sunlight to make energy. This energy can be used to heat homes and provide power for other uses. In the coming years, **solar power** could be an important natural resource.

Protecting the Environment. Because people today use many resources, great demands are placed on the land. As the population of Texas grows, demands will probably become even greater. There is a danger that valuable resources will be used up or lost. Forests may be destroyed if people do not replant trees. Soil can wash away or lose its fertility if it is not protected. Sources of water also must

David E. Kennedy, TexaStock

Homes and businesses with solar panels, or collectors, are becoming more common. Why is Texas a good state for solar power?

44 Unit 1

CLOSURE
Stress to students the importance of the wise use and conservation of Texas' natural resources.

ASSESSMENT
Have students complete the Section 4 Review on page 45.

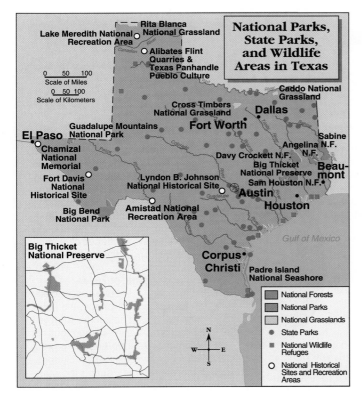

National Parks, State Parks, and Wildlife Areas in Texas

Which large areas of land owned by the federal government border on other states or another country?

be used wisely. Aquifers might dry up, reducing the amount of water available. Pollution from homes and factories can damage rivers and streams.

As you read in Chapter 1, private citizens, state government, and the national government now are working to manage and preserve the state's natural resources. This is an important task. No matter what your age, you can make a difference in your environment. You can use safe methods of waste disposal. You can organize friends to clean up public areas, plant trees, or start a recycling program.

Even with complex technology, Texans still depend on their land. If people use it properly, it will continue to serve them well. There will still be wild animals and plants to enjoy. And the land will continue to enrich the lives of all Texans. ✪

SECTION 4 REVIEW

Define: economy, technology, solar power

1. How did Native Americans' attitudes toward the environment differ from those of Anglo American pioneers?
2. Which is the most important mineral resource of Texas? Why?
3. Why is it important that the natural resources of Texas be used wisely?

Synthesizing Information: What sort of climate would be ideal for the use of solar power? Why?

Explaining Cause and Effect: Explain why Texas oil was nearly worthless in 1890 but extremely valuable in 1990.

Answers to Section 4 Review
Define: *economy*—system of producing and distributing goods and services; *technology*—ways of using resources; *solar power*—power derived from sunlight
1. Native Americans regarded themselves as part of nature and did not view the environment as a way to create wealth. Anglo Americans saw the environment as a collection of valuable resources to be used.
2. Oil, because it provides jobs and brings in tax money
3. So that they will be available for future generations of Texans
Synthesizing Information: A hot dry climate in the lower latitudes is ideal. Solar power requires direct sunlight with little interference from clouds, and a dry atmosphere and nearness to the equator are beneficial.
Explaining Cause and Effect: Oil had few uses in 1890. By 1990 modern industrial civilization had become dependent on oil and the products derived from oil.

Research (II) Ask interested students to investigate the life of Roy Bedichek, reporting on his contributions to Texas.
A, G

Essential Elements
4I, 5D, 6A, 7C, 7D

SPIRIT OF TEXAS

Roy Bedichek: Texas Naturalist

*T*oday, Texans are increasingly aware of the need to protect our natural resources and to keep the air and water pure. But more than 40 years ago, few people were. Roy Bedichek was ahead of his time then. He warned of the dangers of pollution:

> The gentle gardener poisons his soil to kill pillbugs and in so doing annihilates [wipes out] great numbers of beneficial creatures, including the lowly and lovely earthworm. An airplane spreads the deadly DDT [insecticide] over a square mile of cotton field to kill worms or weevils and in doing so kills honeybees, which fertilize the cotton, and birds, which have been attracted there to feed on these very pests.

Bedichek's words and deeds touched the lives of many Texans. To his friends and family, he was a favorite storyteller, an interesting person to talk to, and a man of warmth and sincerity. To the public, he was respected as the author of two successful books about Texas, *Adventures with a Texas Naturalist* and *Karankaway Country.* To the thousands of Texas schoolchildren he visited each year, Roy Bedichek was the Director of the Texas Interscholastic League. As head of this statewide organization, he was in charge of the organized competition among schools in sports, band, and academic skills.

Today, Roy Bedichek is best remembered as one of the first environmentalists in Texas. His love and respect for the natural beauty of his state was reflected in his writings as well as in the actions of his daily life. In *Adventures with a Texas Naturalist,* Bedichek described the vast beauty of the Texas landscape. With his words he painted vivid images of the animals and plants that lived alongside the men, women, and children of Texas.

Roy Bedichek especially loved Barton Springs, the natural swimming hole in his adopted hometown, Austin. Throughout his life, he emphasized the need to protect fragile resources such as Barton Springs. He swam there every day during the summer, even on the day before he died in 1959. On a stone ledge that came to be called Bedichek's Rock, he would sun himself between dips in the spring's cold water, and friends would stop by to join him for swimming, sunning, and conversation.

In a letter to his friend John Henry Faulk, Bedichek once expressed his joy in these daily swims:

> I go to Barton's every afternoon and have a delightful cooling off. What a poem that place is! Do you not sometimes dream of its great towering pecan trees over sparkling waters? The Apaches knew a good thing.

Roy Bedichek was a man of vision. He also was one of Texas' first ecologists.

Inset: **Roy Bedichek**

Barker Texas History Center

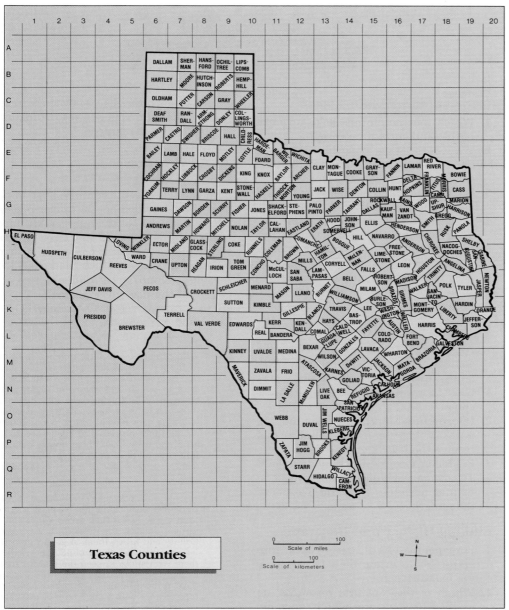

Texas Counties

0 _____ 100
Scale of miles

0 _____ 100
Scale of kilometers

N
W E
S

On the map, find the county in which you presently live. Which part of Texas has the most large counties?

CHAPTER 2 REVIEW ANSWERS

Understanding Main Ideas

1. Plains, plateaus, mountains, hills
2. Texas is located far to the south in the United States and only about 25 degrees north of the equator. The eastern half of the state receives warm moist air from the Gulf. The southwestern portion of Texas receives dry air from Mexico.
3. Natural vegetation grows wild; cultivated vegetation is planted.
4. Tornadoes are circular, often violent storms that form within thunderstorms; hurricanes are much larger circular storms that form over the ocean and come ashore, bringing high winds, high tides, and heavy rain.
5. Drought
6. Natural resources are being depleted while the population of the state is increasing rapidly.

Thinking Critically

1. **Analyzing Information:** Sources are rivers, streams, lakes, springs, and aquifers. The water comes from rainfall.
2. **Interpreting Maps:** The most—Newton and Orange counties; the least—El Paso and Hudspeth counties

48 *Unit 1*

CHAPTER 2 REVIEW

Understanding Main Ideas

1. Which four landforms make up most of the land surface in Texas?
2. Why does Texas have hot summers, and why does precipitation in the state diminish as you go farther west?
3. What is the difference between natural vegetation and cultivated plants?
4. What are the two most violent forms of Texas weather, and how do they differ?
5. What has been the most common of all severe weather conditions in Texas?
6. Why have Texas' natural resources become a source for concern in the twentieth century?

Thinking Critically

1. **Analyzing Information:** List the sources of fresh water for use by Texas cities, towns, and farms. From where does the water in all these sources come?
2. **Interpreting Maps:** Study the map on page 35. List the Texas counties that receive the least and most rainfall.
3. **Exploring Geography:** Why do today's Texans have a much greater impact on natural resources than did Texans of the mid 1800s?

Linking History and Geography

1. For what reasons did early Texas farmers prefer to locate their farms along the major rivers?
2. Which of these natural resources are easily renewable and which, once depleted, are difficult to renew: pine trees, soil, sunlight, water in reservoirs, oil, coal, water in aquifers.

TAAS Practice
Using Primary Sources

In the mid nineteenth century, huge numbers of the now-extinct passenger pigeon lived in eastern North America. Millions of these birds wintered in Texas. An observer once reported a passenger pigeon invasion of Houston that "darkened the sky like a cloud." The following two accounts of the passenger pigeon in Texas are by former governor O.M. Roberts and Charles R. Yarborough.

Wild pigeons . . . in large numbers visit us in the fall and winter, wherever they can find acorns. The wild pigeons establish a roost to which they return at night, after having gone during the day a great distance in search of food. They continue to come long after dark and crowd upon one another on the limbs of trees and bushes, so as to bend and even break them down, keeping up a noise all the time that makes the woods roar.   (Roberts)

I saw pigeons pass in the millions. . . . These passenger pigeons ate the mast, or acorns, from trees—it was their favorite food—and settlers went to their roost in Anderson County and killed them in great numbers, leaving them on the ground. They killed them with sticks to keep the pigeons from eating the acorns they wanted the hogs to have. A drove of pigeons would light on the tops of trees with a good crop of mast and would cover the entire tree.   (Yarborough)

48 *Unit 1*

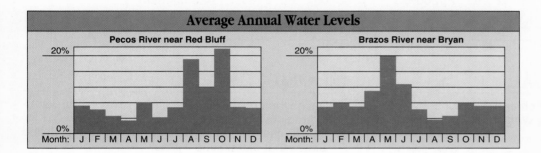

Average Annual Water Levels

Pecos River near Red Bluff

Brazos River near Bryan

1. Judging from these two accounts, the region of Texas visited by the pigeons and the time of their annual visit were
   A   the Great Plains in the spring
   B   Big Bend in the summer
   C   East Texas in the fall and winter
   D   the Rio Grande valley throughout the year
2. The reason for the passenger pigeon's extinction probably is:
   A   they died of a new pigeon disease
   B   settlers killed them because they attacked the settlers' hogs
   C   roosting pigeons were rare
   D   settlers killed them because they ate the hogs' acorns and because roosting pigeons were easy game

TAAS Practice
Writing Descriptively

Write an eyewitness description of a bird, or a flock of birds, in the community in which you live.

Practicing Skills

1. **Sequencing Events:** Arrange the following events in the history of Padre Island in chronological order: Padre Island National Seashore is created (1962); a wrecked treasure ship is discovered; Father Balli starts a cattle ranch on the island; a Spanish treasure ship sinks just offshore.
2. **Interpreting Graphs:** Compare the two graphs above. Which river is at its highest level in autumn? Which river is at its lowest level in spring?

Enriching Your Study of Geography

1. **Individual Project:** Conduct an oral history interview with a person 70 years of age or older about the natural environment he or she knew as a teenager. Ask how it was different from the present. Then report to the class about what you learned from the interview.
2. **Cooperative Project:** Your teacher will divide the class into three teams. You will conduct research and prepare a report on your county's natural resources. One team will survey water resources, another mineral resources, and another timber resources. A spokesperson from each team then will brief the rest of the class on the team's findings.

3. **Exploring Geography:** Their population is many times greater and their technology is much more developed. These factors determine the impact on the natural environment.

Linking History and Geography

1. Rivers served as sources of drinking water for people and livestock and were used for irrigation and transport.
2. Renewable—pine trees, sunlight, water in reservoirs; difficult to renew—soil, oil, coal, water in aquifers

TAAS Practice
Using Primary Sources
1. C
2. D

TAAS Practice
Writing Descriptively
Descriptions will vary but should be accurate and detailed.

Practicing Skills
1. **Sequencing Events:** From earliest to most recent—a Spanish treasure ship sinks, Father Balli starts a ranch, Padre Island National Seashore is created, a wrecked treasure ship is discovered
2. **Interpreting Graphs:** The Pecos; the Pecos

Enriching Your Study of Geography
1. **Individual Project:** Reports should be detailed and expressed clearly.
2. **Cooperative Project:** Reports should be detailed, accurate, and presented clearly.

THE REGIONS OF TEXAS

			TEACHER'S TIME LINE			
Section 1 Pp. 50–52 1 Day	**Section 2** Pp. 52–59 1 Day	**Section 3** Pp. 60–62 1 Day	**Section 4** Pp. 63–66 1 Day	**Section 5** Pp. 67–69 1 Day	**Review and Assessment** 1 Day

⊞ TEACHER MATERIALS

Core: Graphic Organizer 3; Enrichment Worksheet 3; Review Worksheet 3; Reteaching Worksheet 3; Chapter 3 Tests, Forms A & B

Additional: Geography and Graph Skills 3, Map and Chart Transparencies 8, Informal Evaluation Forms, Test Generator

⊞ OBJECTIVES

1. Define *region*, and discuss different ways of designating regions.
2. Identify the four major natural regions of the United States that extend into Texas.
3. Identify and locate the four natural regions of Texas and their subregions.
4. Discuss major characteristics of the subregions of Texas.
5. Compare land features, climate, vegetation, and resources of the subregions of Texas.

⊞ RESOURCES

BOOKS FOR TEACHERS

Cummins, William Fletcher. *Report on Geography of the Staked Plains.* Austin: State Printing Office, 1892. Report on the topography of the Staked Plains region.

Hezlep, William L. *Texas Geographic Regions.* Austin: Bureau of Business Research, University of Texas, 1976. Discusses economy and Texas regions.

Johnson, Elmer Harrison. *The Natural Regions of Texas.* Austin: University of Texas, 1931. Physical geography of Texas.

Rainwater, E.H. *Geology of the Gulf Coast and Central Texas, and Guidebook of Excursions.*

Houston: Houston Geological Society, 1962. Geology of the Gulf Coast and Central Texas regions.

Steeruwitz, W.H. Von. *Geology of Trans-Pecos Texas—Preliminary Statement.* Austin: State Printing Office, 1889. Report on the topography of the Trans-Pecos region.

Tyler, Ronnie C. *The Big Bend: A History of the Last Texas Frontier.* Washington: Office of Publications, National Park Service, 1975.

Webb, Walter Prescott. *The Great Plains.* Boston: Ginn, 1931 (and later editions). History of the Plains, West, and Mississippi Valley.

Wermund, E.G., editor; papers by L.F. Brown et al. *Approaches to Environmental Geology.* Austin: Bureau of Economic Geology, University of Texas, 1974. Discusses approaches to environmental geology and geography.

MULTIMEDIA MATERIALS

Civilization and Climate. (video, 26 min.) Southwest Media Services, Inc., P.O. Box 140, Wimberley, Texas, 78676. Shows links between climate and civilization.

Energy, Ecology, and Technology. (video) Coronet, MTI Film and Video, 108 Wilmot Rd., Deerfield, Illinois, 60015. Series covers issues relating human activity and environment.

The Geography Skills Series.(software) Focus Media Inc., 839 Stewart Avenue, P.O. Box 865, Garden City, New York, 11530. Interactive programs in map reading, geography, climate, and so on.

Only One Earth Series. (video, 1988.) University of California Extension Media Center, 2176 Shattuck Avenue, Berkeley, California, 94704. Eleven-part series examines issues of economy, geography, and environment.

Two Grasslands: Texas and Iran. (film, 22 min., LC#72-710028, 1971.) Learning Corporation of America, distributed by Simon and Schuster Communications, 108 Wilmot Rd., Deerfield, Illinois, 60015. Compares and contrasts the physical and cultural dimensions of these grasslands.

◆ GENERAL STRATEGIES

STUDENTS WITH SPECIAL NEEDS

Limited English Proficient Students (LEP)

Provide students with blank outline maps of Texas. At the conclusion of each section, instruct students to label the regions and subregions of Texas on their maps. Then have them draw arrows from each region to the margins of the maps. They should then list in the margins important facts to remember about the region and its subregions. See other activities labeled **LEP.**

Students Having Difficulty with the Chapter

At the conclusion of each section, ask students to list in note form a summary of the information presented. At the end of the chapter, help the students create on the chalkboard an outline of the chapter. **LEP**

Auditory Learners

Instruct students to work together to create a game called "Where Do I Live?" Using the information discussed in the chapter, the students will offer clues to the rest of the class. Members of the class will use the clues to name the correct region being described. See other activities labeled **A.**

Visual Learners

Have students preview the chapter by studying the illustrations. Then ask them to complete the Chapter 3 Graphic Organizer. See other activities labeled **V.**

Tactile/Kinesthetic Learners

Have tactile/kinesthetic learners cut and paste from magazines or draw pictures illustrating the regions and subregions of Texas. Have them use the pictures to create collages or posters for classroom display. See other activities labeled **TK.**

Gifted Students

Have students select for further study a famous site in Texas that is mentioned in the chapter. Direct them to use encyclopedias, atlases, almanacs, or other reference material. Then ask them to present a two-minute summary of their findings to the class. The students should supplement their reports with illustrations. See other activities labeled **G.**

VOCABULARY

In addition to the boldfaced terms in each section, some students might benefit from discussing the meanings of these terms.

Section 1: *compass* (p. 51).
Section 2: *prevalent* (p. 52); *timber* (p. 52); *lagoons* (p. 55); *sorghum* (p. 58).
Section 3: *shallow* (p. 60).
Section 4: *canyon* (p. 65).
Section 5: *preserve* (p. 67).

GRAPHIC ORGANIZER

Have students skim the chapter and complete the Chapter 3 Graphic Organizer. *(You might wish to use this activity to review rather than to introduce the chapter.)*

ENRICHMENT

Have students complete the Chapter 3 Enrichment Worksheet.

SECTION 1

FOCUS

Student Experiences (I) Ask students to identify the region of Texas in which they live. List the different responses on the chalkboard. Tell students that people often use different terms to describe the same area of a state.

INSTRUCTION

Vocabulary (I) You may wish to preteach the following boldfaced term: *region* (p. 50). **LEP**

Illustrating (II) Organize students into groups of four or five. Have each group make a list of other criteria that could be used to create geographic regions. Then ask each group to select one criterion and use it to create a map. **V, TK, G**

CHAPTER 3 OVERVIEW

Of the United States' nine natural regions, four extend into Texas. These are the Gulf Coastal Plains, the Central Plains, the Great Plains, and the Rocky Mountains. The regions of Texas are actually eleven subregions of these larger areas. Geographers divide Texas into regions on the basis of natural features. Differences within these regions affect where Texans live and the economic activities they pursue.

Essential Elements
5A, 5B, 9A, 9B

CHAPTER 3

THE REGIONS OF TEXAS

Geography Focus

Chapter 3 sketches a portrait of Texas as the regional crossroads of North America. The major geographical regions of the state—the Gulf Coastal Plains, the Central Plains, the Great Plains, and the Rocky Mountains—are described in detail.

As you read the chapter, look for the answers to these questions:

1. Which four major natural regions of North America include portions of Texas?
2. Which part of Texas is located within the Gulf Coastal Plains, and into which subregions is it divided?
3. Which part of the state is located within the Central Plains, and into which subregions is it divided?
4. Which part of the state is included within the Great Plains, and into which subregions is it divided?
5. Which part of the state is included within the Rocky Mountains, and what is its Texas subregion called?

1 Organizing the Land

There are a number of ways to organize Texas into different parts. Texans have always made up their own names for the various parts of the state. In some cases, the names they use are different from those used by geographers. Whatever terms are used, the purpose of organizing the state into regions is to understand it better.

Defining a Region. Geographers use the term **region** to mean an area that is somehow special. For example, a country might have two major sections. In one section, most of the people are farmers. In the other section, most of the people work in factories. It could be said that the country has a farming region and a factory region.

Texas Department of Transportation

Texas west of the Pecos River is sparsely populated but offers plenty of spectacular scenery.

Geography (I) Display a large wall map of the United States. Challenge students to point out the nine major natural regions of the country mentioned in Section 1. Ask them to identify the four regions that include parts of Texas. **A, V**

Guided Practice (II) Through class discussion, create a word web on the chalkboard related to the term *region*. Help students determine possible categories for regions, such as climatic, economic, agricultural, political, and so on. **A, V**

EXTENSION
Home and Community Involvement (I) Ask each student to ask five people (parents, siblings, other relatives, neighbors) the following question: "From what part of Texas are you?" If the response is a city or town, the student should ask the person to identify the region he or she is from. Ask students to share their findings with the rest of the class. **A, LEP**

A common way to organize a state or nation into regions is to look at the natural landscape. Such regions are defined by the types of plant life, landforms, climate, soil, and resources found in them.

Everyday Names. In everyday use, people sometimes make up names for the regions of a state or country. Everyday names are often based on relative locations. For example, people living in the central United States might say they are from the Midwest. People from Texas say they are from the Southwest.

Texans use many names for the various areas of their state. Some say they are from North Texas. People around Lufkin, Tyler, and Marshall say they are from East Texas. Others say they are from West Texas, South Texas, or the Panhandle. Still others claim Central Texas, the Valley, the Coastal Bend, or the Redlands as home.

Some of these names are derived from compass directions. The Coastal Bend, however, gets its name from an area where the Gulf coast "bends" near Corpus Christi. Northwest Texas is called the Panhandle because the region looks much like the handle of a pan. The Redlands is an old name for a large area of northeastern Texas that has reddish soils. And the Valley is a shortened version of the geographical term *Rio Grande valley.*

Unlike terms used by geographers, the everyday names for the regions are not always exact. Many people might

Paul M. Montgomery

The Sabine River forms much of the eastern boundary of Texas. Louisiana is visible in the distance.

Harry Seawell, Texas Tourist Development Agency

West Texas is known for its brilliant sunsets. For what do you think the windmill is used?

Caption Response
To pump water

SECTION ★1 REVIEW

Define: region

1. List four common names that Texans give to some areas of their state.
2. How do the common names for regions differ from the regional names used by geographers?
3. Texas is part of what four major natural regions?

Writing Informatively: Write a letter to an imaginary friend in New York, explaining what is special about your region of Texas. If it has a special name, explain why.

Synthesizing Information: Texas could be divided by economic activity into a manufacturing region and an agricultural region. List three other categories that could be used to divide Texas into regions.

Texas Department of Transportation

Dogwood trees bloom in early spring in the Piney Woods.

argue, for example, about the boundaries of West Texas. Still, Texans use these terms as an important means of describing their state and its divisions.

A Regional Crossroads. As part of the United States and North America, Texas shares land features with nearby states and with Mexico. Not including Alaska or Hawaii, the United States is usually divided into nine major natural regions. From east to west they are: the Atlantic Coastal Plains, the Appalachian Highlands, the Gulf Coastal Plains, the Central Plains, the Ozark Plateau, the Great Plains, the Rocky Mountains, the Plateaus and Basins, and the Pacific Coastal Ranges. Four of these regions include parts of Texas. In a sense, Texas is a crossroads of natural regions. ✪

2 The Gulf Coastal Plains

The Gulf Coastal Plains stretch from Florida to northern Mexico along the Gulf of Mexico. It is the largest region in Texas, covering more than two-fifths of the land area of the state. In places, the Gulf Coastal Plains reach inland about 300 miles. The land near the Gulf is usually low and marshy. Farther inland, the land rises, commonly becoming hilly. Dense forests of pine and hardwood trees are common in the eastern portion. In the increasingly arid west, prairies and brushlands are prevalent. This part of the state is made up of five natural **subregions**, or smaller divisions of a region. These are subregions of the Gulf Coastal Plains.

The Piney Woods. The East Texas Piney Woods is a part of a pine forest that covers the entire southern United States from the Atlantic Ocean to Texas. This forest has made the area an important source of timber and wood products for more than 100 years. Along with areas of pine, oak, gum, and hickory trees, this region is a rich farming area. The soils and climate are ideal for producing many fruits and vegetables. Cattle graze the tall grasses where the forests have been cleared to create pastures.

The land of the Piney Woods is rolling and typically hilly. Water flows into many rivers, creeks, and lakes. The Sabine, Neches, and Trinity rivers flow in a southeastward direction through this subregion. Toledo Bend Reservoir, Sam Rayburn Reservoir, and several other large reservoirs (artificial lakes) are located in this subregion.

FOCUS

Student Experiences (I) Without permitting the students to consult their textbooks, ask them to raise their hands if any of them have ever visited or traveled through the Gulf Coastal Plains region of the United States. Then refer students to the maps on this page. Ask the question again and note the different responses.

INSTRUCTION

Vocabulary (I) You may wish to preteach the following boldfaced terms: *subregions* (p. 52); *bayous* (p. 55); *prairies* (p. 58); *lignite* (p. 58). **LEP**

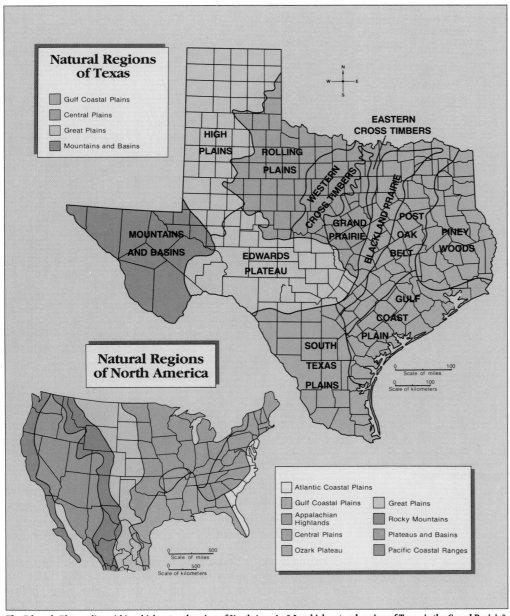

Natural Regions of Texas

- Gulf Coastal Plains
- Central Plains
- Great Plains
- Mountains and Basins

HIGH PLAINS
ROLLING PLAINS
EASTERN CROSS TIMBERS
WESTERN CROSS TIMBERS
BLACKLAND PRAIRIE
MOUNTAINS AND BASINS
GRAND PRAIRIE
POST OAK BELT
PINEY WOODS
EDWARDS PLATEAU
GULF COAST PLAIN
SOUTH TEXAS PLAINS

Scale of miles
Scale of kilometers

Natural Regions of North America

- Atlantic Coastal Plains
- Gulf Coastal Plains
- Appalachian Highlands
- Central Plains
- Ozark Plateau
- Great Plains
- Rocky Mountains
- Plateaus and Basins
- Pacific Coastal Ranges

Scale of miles
Scale of kilometers

The Edwards Plateau lies within which natural region of North America? In which natural region of Texas is the Grand Prairie?

Transparency 8
An overhead transparency of this map can be found in the Teacher's Resource Binder.

Caption Response
The Great Plains; the Central Plains

Illustrating (I) Organize the students into groups of four or five to create a Texas Economic Activity Map. Provide each group with a large sheet of poster board or butcher paper. Have the students draw a map outlining Texas and the five subregions of the Gulf Coastal Plains. Ask them to list the economic activities of each subregion. Have the students create a map key or legend with a symbol for each economic activity on their list and label each on the map. Tell students that they will add to the map throughout the study of Chapter 3. **V, TK, LEP**

Caption Response
Blackland Prairie, Post Oak Belt, Piney Woods, Gulf Coast Plain, South Texas Plains

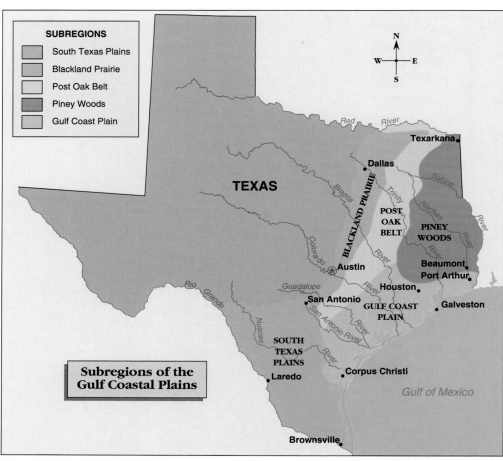

Subregions of the Gulf Coastal Plains

What subregions make up the Gulf Coastal Plains region?

Areas of the Piney Woods have been set aside as national forests to protect their valuable wood resources. Four national forests in this area are the Sam Houston National Forest, the Davy Crockett National Forest, the Sabine National Forest, and the Angelina National Forest. Cutting is controlled in these forests, and trees are carefully replanted. Several wilderness areas protect especially unspoiled parts of the national forests. The Big Thicket National Preserve also lies in this region of Texas. It was set aside because of its interesting plant and animal life.

In addition to agricultural produce, cattle, poultry, and forest products, oil is important to the Piney Woods. Large discoveries were made in the 1930s, and this industry contributes to the economy of cities such as Henderson and Kilgore.

Most of the people in the Piney Woods live in rural, or country, areas. Many small towns dot the land, serving as markets for farmers and the lumber industry. The largest cities in the Piney Woods are Longview and Texarkana. Tyler is just to the west of the Piney Woods.

The Gulf Coast Plain. West and south of the Piney Woods is a subregion called the Gulf Coast Plain. It was named for the same reasons as the larger Gulf Coastal Plains, of which it is a part. The Gulf Coast Plain extends from the eastern border of Texas near Port Arthur to Corpus Christi in the south. Lush grasslands are broken only occasionally by scattered groves of trees. Near the coast, the land is marshy and carved with shallow bays. Slow-moving, marshy bodies of water called **bayous** cross the land of the eastern Gulf Coast Plain. Most of the major Texas rivers empty into the Gulf in this region. Just off the coast is a chain of islands that runs nearly the length of the Texas coast. These islands are built up from sand and have brush and grasses growing on them. Shallow bays and lagoons separate the islands from the mainland.

People have always been attracted to the Gulf Coast Plain because of its location and resources. Resources are found on the land and under the water. The rich soil supports several important crops. Farmers grow rice in the eastern part of the Gulf Coast Plain. Maize and other grains, as well as cotton, grow in the Coastal Bend area. Cattle raising is another important activity. More cattle are raised in the Gulf Coast Plain than anywhere else in Texas.

The nearby Gulf of Mexico is the source of several important resources. Fishing (including shrimp and oysters) is a major source of income for many people in the Gulf Coast Plain. Oil rigs drill for oil just offshore.

Location is a major factor in the economy of the Gulf Coast Plain. Its largest cities are Houston, Corpus Christi, Beaumont, Galveston, and Port Arthur. They are all ports. Farm and factory products pass through these ports to other areas of the world. Materials from the rest of the world enter Texas through these same cities. The area from

Lowell Georgia

Offshore oil rigs stretch along the Texas coastline.

Guided Practice (I) Have students work together to create a Texas Subregions chart with the following column labels: *Location, Land, Vegetation, Resources, Economic Activities, Cities.* On the left side of the chart they should list Texas' five subregions of the Gulf Coastal Plains. Ask students to fill in the chart, using the information presented in Section 2. Students will add to the chart in Section 3. **V, TK, LEP**

Economics
The dramatic fluctuation of the oil business during the last two decades has caused economic ups and downs for the cities of Texas whose economies are based on oil.

Paul M. Montgomery

Chemical manufacturing provides many jobs in the coastal region.

Palm trees grow amid citrus groves in the Rio Grande valley.

Beaumont and Port Arthur to Houston is the center of the oil-refining industry in Texas. Many chemicals and petroleum products also are produced there. This part of the Gulf Coast Plain has seen the greatest industrial development in Texas since World War II. It is one of the nation's most important oil and chemical centers.

Houston is the largest city in Texas and one of the fastest-growing in the United States. The Houston metropolitan area covers a large portion of southeast Texas—more than 5,400 square miles. Houston lies about 50 miles inland from the Gulf, but because of its ship channel it is the third-largest seaport in the nation. It is also a major center for international shipping. In tonnage and value of goods shipped, Houston is surpassed only by New York City and New Orleans. Ships enter Galveston Bay from the Gulf, then follow the Houston Ship Channel and Buffalo Bayou to Houston's port facility. A world trade center, Houston is also a major manufacturing city. Its industry specializes in petroleum (oil) refining and manufacturing petrochemicals, or chemicals made from petroleum.

The South Texas Plains. West of the Gulf Coast Plain and south of San Antonio is the South Texas Plains region. Like the rest of the land along the Gulf, areas of the South Texas Plains near the coast are low and level. To the north and west, the land rises and becomes more hilly. The climate is drier than that of the regions to the east.

Greg Bryant, Texas Department of Agriculture

EXTENSION
Historical Imagination (II) Invite students to imagine them-selves as early Texas explorers traveling through the Gulf Coastal Plains subregions of Texas. Ask them to write a diary entry describing the scenes they encounter. **G**

Independent Practice (I) Ask students to list on a sheet of paper Texas' five Gulf Coastal Plains subregions. Then have them write a sentence next to each subregion, telling why the region is named as it is. **LEP**

Grasslands predominate in the coastal section, with dense brushlands further inland.

Oil and gas wells dot the landscape of the South Texas Plains. Still, farming and ranching are the most important economic activities. The major farming area is the Rio Grande valley. Temperatures there are warm for most of the year, and a freeze is unusual. The Valley has fertile soils washed down from the Rio Grande. Citrus fruits, such as grapefruits and oranges, are grown in large quantities. Texas is one of the nation's four main citrus-producing states. Sugar cane, aloe vera, and vegetable crops add to the wealth of this area. Many of the residents of this subregion work in agriculture and agriculture-related activities.

Ranches are common throughout much of the South Texas Plains. Among these is the huge King Ranch of more than 1 million acres (1,562 square miles). Rangeland for cattle first attracted Spanish and Mexican settlers to this region.

San Antonio is located on the rolling prairies of south central Texas, about 150 miles northeast of the Mexican border. Founded in 1718, the city contains many historic buildings and is thus one of Texas' major tourist attractions. Many state and national organizations hold their conventions in San Antonio. And the city is home to some of the largest military bases in the country. The bases employ many San Antonians, and military payrolls are very important to the local economy. San Antonio is a retail trade center for South Texas and a major export center for international trade with the Republic of Mexico.

San Antonio is by far the largest city in the South Texas Plains, and Laredo is a smaller city in the subregion. Brownsville, Harlingen, and McAllen are cities in the lower Valley. Outside of these urban, or city, areas, towns are widely scattered in the South Texas Plains.

The Post Oak Belt. The subregion of Texas that reaches from near San Antonio to the Red River is called the Post Oak Belt. It lies west of the Piney Woods and the Gulf Coast Plain. The Post Oak Belt has some sandy soils like the Piney Woods and some rich, black soils like the Blackland Prairie. The land of the Post Oak Belt is flat or gently rolling and was once covered by trees. These included post oaks, pin oaks, live oaks, elms, pines, and hickories.

Baylor University

Waco stretches across the Brazos River. The city is home to many industries and also Baylor University. In what region is Waco?

Mark Solomon/The Image Bank

Much of San Antonio's old architecture reflects the grandeur of the city's Spanish heritage.

Geography
The Rio Grande valley has the longest growing season in Texas—more than 300 days of the year.

Caption Response
The Gulf Coastal Plains

TEXAS VOICES
Research (II) Have interested students research and report on the plant and animal life of the Big Thicket National Preserve. Ask them to supplement their reports with pictures or drawings if possible. **A, V, TK, G**

RETEACHING
Ask students to write brief paragraphs summarizing the information presented in each subsection of Section 2. Allow them to check their textbooks to correct any misinformation. **LEP**

Essential Elements
3E, 4I, 7C

TEXAS VOICES

A frontier lifestyle survived into the twentieth century in the East Texas wilderness. During a 1969 interview, retired minister P.O. Eason gave this account of his boyhood turkey hunts in the Big Thicket to historian Campbell Loughmiller:

Of course we got pleasure out of hunting, but my greatest pleasure was being in the woods, and a lot of it was being out alone at times, next to nature. . . . There was no contamination of anything, just God's creation was out there—over me at night and around me—owls a-hollering—and I've had packs of wolves come right up and scratch within 50 yards of my camp. . . . I never had any fear of anything like that. . . .

I usually camped by myself. I loved to hunt by myself. I've stayed out when ice was on the ground with nothing but a saddle blanket. . . .

Back where we hunted, it was virgin timber. . . . But when we said "Thicket," we meant thicket! Briars and brush, possum haw, bamboo, rattan, white bay, just everything; you just had to cut your way through. . . . The best time of day to get a turkey is from four o'clock to daylight. . . . I didn't have a watch in them days, but I could tell when it was time to move out, because the owls know when the day begins to break before you do. Along about four o'clock in the morning, every owl in the woods starts just raring; they'd just jar the ground there'd be so many of 'em, just go wild! . . . You could tell it was fixing to come daylight . . . and when those owls began to kind o' die down, those old gobblers would start gobbling.

The Thicket has been my life. I've hunted just about every animal in the woods, but it wasn't just the hunting. I just enjoy being in the woods. There's hardly a time of the year you won't find flowers in bloom, and in the spring it's just a sight when the haws and the sweet bay and magnolias, and berries and jasmine and wild plum and dogwood are in bloom. My favorite is the wild honeysuckle.

Geography/Environmental Awareness
Ask students to list the ways in which people have had an impact on the natural environment of the Post Oak Belt.

Paul Montgomery

This photograph shows a view of Fayette Prairie near Ammonsville. This grassland is one of two in the Post Oak Belt.

Settlers cleared many of the trees from the Post Oak region for farming. Cotton is a major crop in this area of Texas. Other important crops are corn and sorghum. Cattle and hogs are raised in many parts of the Post Oak region.

In two parts of the Post Oak Belt there are **prairies**, or grasslands. These are called the Sandy Oak Prairie and the Fayette Prairie. They are sometimes thought of as separate subregions.

As in many other areas of Texas, oil and natural gas are important to the economy of the Post Oak Belt. Deposits of **lignite**, a type of soft coal, are mined there also.

Most people in the Post Oak Belt live in rural areas. Towns and small cities are scattered throughout the region. These include Tyler, Bryan-College Station, Paris, and Gonzales.

CLOSURE
Using a wall map of Texas, review the location of the five Gulf Coastal Plains subregions of Texas.

ASSESSMENT
Have students complete the Section 2 Review on page 59.

Larry Kolvoord / TexaStock

Austin, the capital of Texas, is one of several major cities within the Blackland Prairie.

The Blackland Prairie. Stretching alongside the Post Oak Belt is a fifth subregion of the Gulf Coastal Plains called the Blackland Prairie. This subregion of Texas has rich, black soils that are ideal for farming. Farms in the Blackland Prairie produce grains, cotton, and vegetables. Farmers in the Blackland Prairie also raise beef cattle, hogs, and chickens. Today, almost all its native vegetation has been cleared.

In addition to its soil and climate, the Blackland Prairie has other resources. Among these are oil and gas.

The Blackland Prairie and nearby areas are among the most heavily populated in Texas. The largest city is Dallas. Austin lies on the edge of the region. Smaller cities include Waco, Garland, Richardson, Plano, Grand Prairie, Mesquite, Sherman, and Temple.

Dallas is located on the rolling prairies of north central Texas, 30 miles east of Fort Worth, once a strong rival. Today, the economies of these two cities have become so interlinked that they are often referred to by a single name, the *Metroplex*. The cities share the Dallas-Fort Worth International Airport, which is located between them.

Dallas, the second largest city in Texas, is a center of the state's banking business. Many national insurance and oil companies have their corporate headquarters in Dallas. The city is also a major international cotton market. Manufacturing is important to the Dallas economy, and the city's industry is more diversified than that of Houston. Manufactured goods produced in Dallas include everything from computerized electronics and electrical equipment to missile parts and high-fashion clothing. ❂

SECTION 2 REVIEW

Define: subregions, bayous, prairies, lignite
Identify: Metroplex

1. Which area of Texas lies within the Gulf Coast Plain subregion?
2. What are the Texas subregions of the Gulf Coastal Plains?
3. What are the differences between the natural vegetation of the Piney Woods and that of the South Texas Plains?

Exploring Economics: Briefly compare the economies of Houston and Dallas.

Comparing Perspectives: Imagine that you reside in the Post Oak Belt or the Gulf Coast Plain. How would you react to proposed legislation that would raise state taxes to provide aid to major cities?

Answers to Section 2 Review

Define: *subregions*—smaller divisions of regions; *bayous*—slow-moving marshy bodies of water; *prairies*—grasslands; *lignite*—a type of soft coal
Identify: Metroplex—the combined Dallas-Fort Worth area

1. Southeast Texas bordering the Gulf of Mexico
2. The Piney Woods, Gulf Coast Plain, Blackland Prairie, South Texas Plains, Post Oak Belt
3. The Piney Woods is covered with a thick, mixed forest of pine and hardwood. The South Texas Plains is an area of brush and grasslands.

Exploring Economics: The Houston economy is dependent on oil refining and the petrochemical industry. Houston is also a major seaport. The Dallas economy is more diversified. It is based on manufacturing, banking, and insurance.

Comparing Perspectives: Answers will vary but should indicate a likely opposition to the proposed legislation from those living in the Post Oak Belt, where there are no major cities. For those living in the Gulf Coast Plain, where several large cities are located, the reverse might be true.

FOCUS

Predicting (I) Ask students to examine the map on page 60 and the photographs on pages 60–62. Ask: What do you think are the major economic activities in this region?

INSTRUCTION

Comparing and Contrasting (II) Have students write a paragraph comparing and contrasting Texas' three subre-gions of the Central Plains. Invite volunteers to read their paragraphs aloud. **A**

Illustrating (I) Ask students to use the information presented in Section 3 to add to their Texas Economic Activity maps created in Section 2. Organize students into their original groups. Tell them to add to the maps Texas' three subregions of the Central Plains, along with the economic activities of each. Students will add to the maps in Section 4. **V, TK, LEP**

Caption Response
The Grand Prairie

Essential Elements
3D, 4B, 5A, 5B, 5C, 5D, 9B

What subregion lies between the Eastern and Western Cross Timbers subregions?

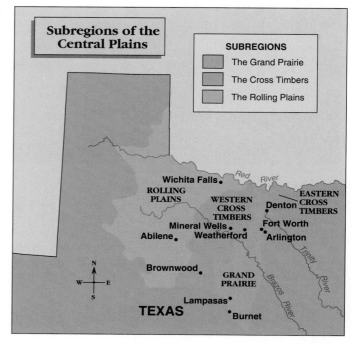

Subregions of the Central Plains

SUBREGIONS
- The Grand Prairie
- The Cross Timbers
- The Rolling Plains

Wichita Falls
ROLLING PLAINS
WESTERN CROSS TIMBERS
Red River
EASTERN CROSS TIMBERS
Denton
Mineral Wells
Fort Worth
Abilene
Weatherford
Arlington
Brownwood
GRAND PRAIRIE
Trinity River
Brazos River
Lampasas
Burnet
TEXAS

3 The Central Plains

The north central part of Texas lies within the Central Plains region of the United States. This region begins west of the Appalachian Mountains and reaches north into Canada and south and west into Texas. It is a region of gently rolling prairies, with forests growing in the river valleys. The Central Plains in Texas contains three subregions. They are the Grand Prairie, the Cross Timbers, and the Rolling Plains.

The Grand Prairie. West of the Blackland Prairie, on land several hundred feet higher in elevation, is the Grand Prairie. Some parts of this region are level while others have rolling hills. Soil is somewhat shallow, in contrast to the blacklands to the east. Grasses, shrubs, and small trees are the major types of plants. Juniper trees grow in the southern part of the Grand Prairie.

The Grand Prairie is an important region for livestock raising. Beef cattle, dairy cattle, hogs, sheep, goats, and

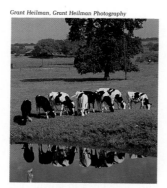

Grant Heilman, Grant Heilman Photography

Dairy farming is important to the economy of the Grand Prairie.

Paul M. Montgomery

The Grand Prairie varies in scenery. This photograph taken near Glen Rose shows the natural combination of woods and grasslands.

poultry are all important to the farm economy. Wheat, cotton, corn, and other grains are grown in the region.

Fort Worth is by far the largest city of the Grand Prairie and the largest in the Central Plains in Texas. The city and nearby towns hold more people than all other areas of the Grand Prairie combined. Fort Worth is a manufacturing, transportation, and agricultural-products center 30 miles west of Dallas. Grain milling and storage are important to the Fort Worth economy, as is the oil industry. The city also is a transport center with some of the busiest railyards in the nation. Most important, however, are Fort Worth's manufacturing industries. The city specializes in the manufacture of electronic equipment, helicopters, and airplanes. General Dynamics and other large aircraft plants are located here and employ many residents. National defense spending is therefore vitally important to the Fort Worth economy.

The Cross Timbers. Surrounding the Grand Prairie on three sides is the Cross Timbers. This subregion is made up of two narrow belts of forest land. One belt, the Western Cross Timbers, lies west of the Grand Prairie. It is located west of Fort Worth and runs south from the Red River about 200 miles. The Eastern Cross Timbers is narrower and lies between the cities of Dallas and Fort Worth.

The Cross Timbers region received its name from the presence of dense belts of hardwood trees. In the Eastern Cross Timbers, these include post oaks, hickories, and

RETEACHING

Ask students to write the following headings across the top of a sheet of paper: *The Grand Prairie, The Cross Timbers, The Rolling Plains.* Have them list under each heading the major characteristics of each subregion. **V, LEP**

CLOSURE

Using a wall map of Texas, review the location of Texas' three subregions of the Central Plains.

ASSESSMENT

Have students complete the Section 3 Review on page 62.

Caption Response
The Central Plains

Answers to
Section 3 Review

Identify: railyards—railroad transportation centers; manufacturing industries—important to Fort Worth's economy, these industries include the manufacture of electronic equipment, helicopters, and airplanes

1. The north central part of Texas
2. The Grand Prairie, Cross Timbers, and Rolling Plains
3. The natural vegetation of the Grand Prairie is grasses, shrubs, and small trees. The Cross Timbers has dense belts of hardwood trees.

Exploring Economics: Answers will vary, but students should provide reasons for their choice of subregion.

Writing Descriptively: Descriptions will vary, but students should note that the Fort Worth economy is based on defense plants (aircraft and electronics), grain milling, and rail transport.

62 *Unit 1*

Lee Angle Photography

Fort Worth is a major commercial, banking, manufacturing, and trade center for much of West Texas. The city is known for its museums, public gardens, and cultural centers. In what region is Fort Worth located?

SECTION ★3★ REVIEW

Identify: railyards, manufacturing industries

1. Which area of Texas lies within the Central Plains region?
2. What are the Texas subregions of the Central Plains?
3. What are the differences between the natural vegetation of the Grand Prairie and that of the Cross Timbers?

Exploring Economics: If you wanted to be a successful rancher in the Central Plains, which subregion would you choose for your ranch? Why?

Writing Descriptively: Describe the economy of Fort Worth, the Central Plains' largest city.

elms. Cedar, mesquite, pecan, hickory, blackjack oak, and post oak trees all grow in the Western Cross Timbers.

Because of the subregion's rich soils, farmers cut down the trees in places to allow planting of crops. Farm products range from peaches and peanuts to hay, wheat, sorghum, and oats. Ranchers also raise beef cattle, sheep, and horses there. Oil and gas are produced from wells in the Cross Timbers, but less than in the past.

In contrast to the Blackland Prairie region, the Western Cross Timbers has no large cities. Among the towns are Brownwood, Mineral Wells, and Weatherford. Arlington and Denton are cities in the Eastern Cross Timbers.

The Rolling Plains. The western part of the Central Plains consists of a subregion called the Rolling Plains. Most of this region is bounded on the north by the Red River, but some parts of it reach into the Panhandle. To the south, the Rolling Plains stretches into Central Texas.

The land of the Rolling Plains is mostly prairies, with a few high hills and mesas. There are grasslands, brush, and scattered groups of trees.

Farmers in the Rolling Plains grow wheat, cotton, and sorghum. Ranching is more important than farming, however. Large herds of cattle grow on the plains, as well as sheep and goats. These animals can survive on poorer vegetation than cattle can. Rich fields of oil are also found in the Rolling Plains.

The Rolling Plains has a population that is much smaller than those of regions to the east. Small market towns are scattered around the area. Abilene and Wichita Falls are the only sizeable cities. ✪

SECTION 4

FOCUS

Predicting (I) On a wall map, point out the Great Plains region of the United States. Then point out the High Plains subregion of Texas. Ask students to speculate about why this area of Texas is referred to as the High Plains.

INSTRUCTION
Vocabulary (I) You may wish to preteach the following boldfaced terms: *escarpments* (p. 63); *fault* (p. 66). **LEP**

4 The Great Plains

The Great Plains region is a vast area of the central United States extending from Canada to northern Mexico. It lies to the east of the Rocky Mountains and west of the Central Plains. The land of the Great Plains varies from 2,000 to 5,000 feet above sea level.

As the land of the Great Plains reaches into Texas, it is very flat. It becomes more rugged in Central and South Texas and into Mexico. In Texas, the Great Plains region consists of the High Plains and the Edwards Plateau.

The High Plains. The northwestern section of Texas is called the High Plains subregion. The name refers to its elevation above the plains farther east. Under the soil of the plains is a hard covering called the Cap Rock. Long ago, the land of the Cap Rock pushed above surrounding land. This pressure created cliffs along its eastern and western sides, which are called **escarpments**.

The High Plains has flat, open prairies. In fact, it is one of the flattest upland areas on earth. At one time this area was like an open sea of grass that supported tens of thousands of buffalo. When Spanish explorers first saw the High Plains, they named it *Llano Estacado*, or "Staked Plain." Historians disagree about the origin of the name.

The Cap Rock marks the break between the Rolling Plains and the High Plains. What are the cliffs on the sides of the Cap Rock called?

Texas Department of Transportation

Essential Elements
1A, 1B, 3D, 4B, 5A, 5B, 5C, 5D, 7C, 9A, 9B, 9F

Caption Response
Escarpments

Caption Response
The High Plains and the Edwards Plateau

What two subregions make up the Great Plains region?

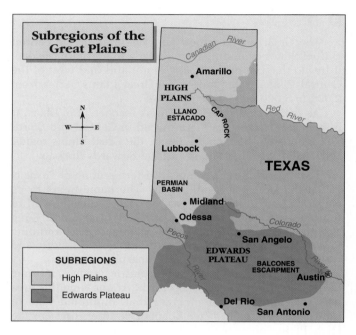

Subregions of the Great Plains

SUBREGIONS
- High Plains
- Edwards Plateau

Midland Chamber of Commerce

Midland is a center for oil, ranching, and banking. In what area of the High Plains is Midland?

Caption Response
The Permian Basin

Some think the Spaniards were referring to the plants sticking up like stakes from the flat grasslands. Others think it refers to stakes that the Spaniards used to mark their path across the treeless plateau. Most historians now believe that the explorer Coronado named it to describe the Cap Rock Escarpment—the "staked" cliffs that mark the eastern edge of the High Plains.

Indians who lived on the High Plains moved about in search of buffalo. For nearly 300 years, European explorers and settlers from the United States thought farming was not possible on the plains. Today it is part of one of the richest farming regions in the world. Ideas about the High Plains changed when Texas settlers began raising huge herds of cattle on the land. Later, irrigation with water pumped from the Ogallala Aquifer made farming possible in the rich soil. Wheat, grain sorghum, and cotton are now grown to sell to many nations of the world.

Farming, ranching, and natural gas are the backbone of the plains economy, but the land does not support large numbers of people. Lubbock, Amarillo, Odessa, and Mid-

EXTENSION
Research (III) Ask students to investigate the origins of the names *Llano Estacado, Permian Basin, Palo Duro Canyon, Edwards Plateau*, and *Balcones Escarpment*. Have them report their findings to the class. **A, G**

Independent Practice (II) Have students look through magazines and other sources to find examples of other escarpments and faults located throughout the United States. Ask them to cut and paste or draw pictures to create a poster illustrating their research. Students should write a description of each escarpment or fault, identifying the region of the country in which it is located, and place it beneath the appropriate illustration. Display the posters in the classroom. **V, TK**

Richard Reynolds, Texas Tourist Development Agency

A rancher rounds up longhorn cattle on the High Plains.

land are Plains cities. Odessa and Midland lie in an area of the High Plains called the Permian Basin.

A famous part of the region is a deep gash in the land called Palo Duro Canyon. The name means "hard wood" in Spanish. The canyon was cut into the Cap Rock over millions of years by the waters of the Prairie Dog Town Fork of the Red River. The canyon is 1,000 feet deep and more than 100 miles long. Today part of the canyon is a state park.

The Edwards Plateau. The Edwards Plateau is a high limestone tableland lying north and west of the South Texas Plains. Part of the Great Plains, it lies south of the High Plains of northwestern Texas. The land rises gently from east to west. Elevation ranges from about 850 feet at the eastern edge to about 4,000 feet at the foot of the mountains in the west. The high western part of the Edwards Plateau is level and covered with grass. Farther

Texas Department of Agriculture

Land in the Edwards Plateau region is ideal for sheep and goat ranching.

RETEACHING

Organize the class into pairs. Ask the students in each pair to take turns describing the High Plains and Edwards Plateau subregions of Texas. The students should work together to correct any misinformation. **LEP, A**

CLOSURE

Using a wall map, review the location of the Great Plains region of the United States and the High Plains and Edwards Plateau subregions of Texas.

ASSESSMENT

Have students complete the Section 4 Review on page 66.

Answers to Section 4 Review

Define: *escarpments*—cliffs along the edge of a plain; *fault*—break in the earth's crust

Identify: Llano Estacado— "Staked Plain"; Ogallala Aquifer—major aquifer lying under the High Plains

1. The Panhandle and the western part of Central Texas
2. The High Plains and Edwards Plateau
3. The High Plains is extremely level, while the Edwards Plateau rises from east to west. The eastern and southern edges of the plateau are heavily eroded, with steep hills, rugged cliffs, and deep valleys.

Exploring Economics: The High Plains is one of the most important farming areas in Texas. It has good soils, and the crops are irrigated from the Ogallala Aquifer. In contrast, the Edwards Plateau has thin, poor soils.

Solving Problems: Answers will vary, but two possible solutions are: establish an Ogallala Aquifer District to regulate the amount of water drawn from the aquifer; return to an economy based on ranching and dryland farming.

Paul M. Montgomery

Many people visit scenic Palo Duro Canyon each year.

SECTION ⍟ REVIEW

Define: escarpments, fault
Identify: Llano Estacado, Ogallala Aquifer

1. Which area of Texas lies within the Great Plains region?
2. What are the Texas subregions of the Great Plains?
3. What are the differences between the landforms of the High Plains and the Edwards Plateau?

Exploring Economics: Compare the importance of farming in the High Plains and Edwards Plateau subregions. What factors help explain this difference?

Solving Problems: Suggest two solutions to the problem of the depletion of water from the Ogallala Aquifer.

east, oak and juniper forests are common. The eastern and southern edges of the plateau are heavily eroded, with steep hills, rugged cliffs, and deep valleys.

Separating the Edwards Plateau from the Gulf Coastal Plains is the Balcones Escarpment. The Balcones Escarpment lies on a **fault**, or break in the earth's crust. The fault extends from southwestern parts of Texas through San Antonio and Austin. Large springs, such as Barton Springs in Austin, rise to the surface along the Balcones Fault. It reaches north to the Red River.

Erosion over thousands of years has left the Edwards Plateau with a thin layer of soil. For this reason, few types of farming are practical in the area. Yet, the grass, shrubs, and oak trees do provide food for sheep and goats.

Austin lies at the eastern edge of the Edwards Plateau. The largest city in this region other than Austin is San Angelo. It is a market for wool and mohair produced by nearby sheep and goat ranches. Del Rio lies between the Edwards Plateau and the South Texas Plains along the Rio Grande. Few other towns and cities are located here. ⊙

FOCUS

Past Learning (I) Using a wall map, ask students to describe the relative location of the United States' Rocky Mountain region.

Illustrating (I) Have students use the information presented in Section 5 to complete their Texas Economic Activity maps. Organize the students into their original groups. Tell them to add to the maps the Mountains and Basins subregion, along with its major economic activities. Display the maps in the classroom. **V, TK, LEP**

5 The Rocky Mountains

The land farthest west in Texas is filled with mountains, canyons, and dry plateaus. It is one of the most rugged and colorful areas of Texas. Many geographers think of this land as part of the Rocky Mountains, which rise west of the Great Plains. The Rocky Mountain region reaches from Canada, through western Texas, and into Mexico. In Texas it is called the Mountains and Basins subregion.

The Mountains and Basins. Much of the Mountains and Basins subregion lies west of the Pecos River. From the point of view of people living east of the Pecos, it is sometimes called the Trans-Pecos area (*trans* meaning "across" or "beyond"). A famous part of the subregion is the Big Bend, a vast desert wilderness located within a southward bend of the Rio Grande. It has been set aside as a national park to preserve its wilderness character. Towering peaks and deep river canyons make the area a

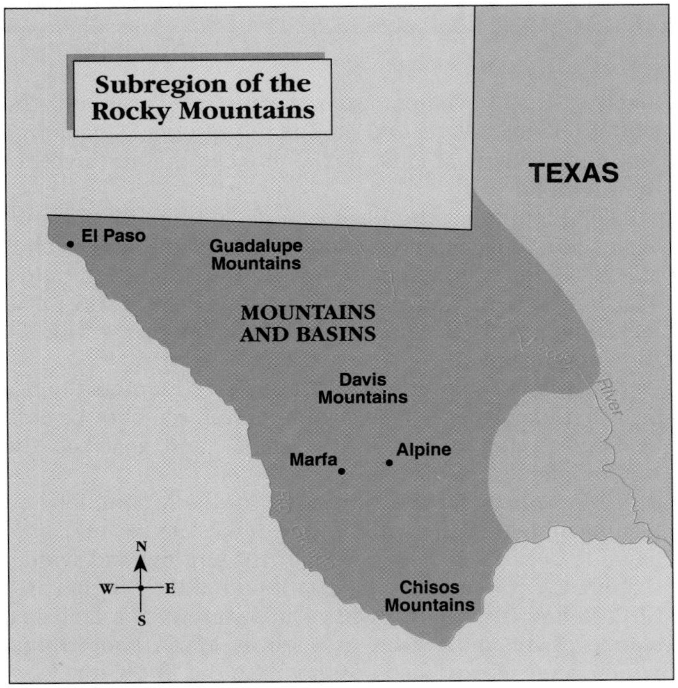

Essential Elements
5A, 5B, 5C, 9A

Subregion of the Rocky Mountains

TEXAS

El Paso

Guadalupe Mountains

MOUNTAINS AND BASINS

Davis Mountains

Marfa   Alpine

Chisos Mountains

N
W   E
S

How many subregions make up the Rocky Mountain region?

Caption Response
One

Geography (II) Provide students with blank outline maps of Texas. Ask them to use the maps in their textbooks or other sources to draw and label the mountain ranges of the Mountains and Basins subregion. Ask them to include on their maps the elevations of each. **V, TK, G**

Guided Practice (I) Refer students to the Texas Subregions chart they began in Section 2. Have them add to the chart the Mountains and Basins subregion and fill in the missing information. Display the completed chart in the classroom. **V, TK, LEP**

EXTENSION

Research (II) Ask students to write to the appropriate Chambers of Commerce or tourism offices and gather brochures and other information on the Mountains and Basins subregion. Have the class create a bulletin board display of the brochures and other information they collect. **V, TK**

Independent Practice (II) Ask students to create an advertisement or brochure promoting the physical attractions of the Mountains and Basins subregion. Tell students that their readers will be people who are unfamiliar with Texas. **V, TK, G**

Caption Response
The park offers beautiful scenery that includes towering mountains, deep valleys, and river canyons.

Richard Reynolds

Answers to Section 5 Review

Identify: Big Bend—a famous part of the Mountains and Basins subregion located within a southward bend of the Rio Grande; Chisos Mountains—a desert mountain range in the Big Bend area

1. The land farthest west
2. The Mountains and Basins
3. In the far south

Exploring Economics: These national parks are major tourist attractions.

Exploring Geography: Nearly all farming in Texas is irrigation farming. Ranches are very large in order to support cattle, sheep, and goats on the meager plant life.

Big Bend National Park is a favorite site of visitors from all over the United States. Why do you think the park attracts so many visitors?

SECTION REVIEW

Identify: Big Bend, Chisos Mountains

1. Which area of Texas lies within the Rocky Mountains region?
2. What Texas subregion is part of the Rocky Mountains?
3. Where in this subregion is Big Bend National Park?

Exploring Economics: Why are Big Bend National Park and Guadalupe Mountains National Park important to the economy of the Mountains and Basins subregion?

Exploring Geography: Explain how farming and ranching both have adapted to an extremely dry environment in Texas.

favorite site for visitors from the rest of Texas and the United States. A second national preserve, Guadalupe Mountains National Park, is 250 miles to the northwest of the Big Bend.

The Mountains and Basins subregion includes a number of different mountain ranges. Two of the higher ones are the Davis Mountains and the Guadalupe Mountains. The highest point in Texas is Guadalupe Peak, rising 8,751 feet above sea level. The Chisos Mountains rise within the Big Bend area.

Most farming in this dry part of Texas requires the use of irrigation. Ranching is very important. Ranches have to be large to support the cattle, sheep, and goats on the limited amount of plant life.

El Paso is by far the largest city in the Mountains and Basins subregion. It is one of the largest cities in Texas. Outside of El Paso, even small towns are few and widely scattered. Tourism is an important part of the economy for El Paso and the small towns. The beauty of the land is a source of income for towns such as Marfa and Alpine, which serve as entrance points to the Big Bend area. ◯

RETEACHING

Ask students to write on a sheet of paper three to five facts about the Mountains and Basins subregion. Invite volunteers to read their lists aloud. **A, LEP**

CLOSURE

Using a wall map, review the location of the Rocky Mountains region of the United States and the Mountains and Basins subregion of Texas.

ASSESSMENT

Have students complete the Section 5 Review on page 68.

Big Bend National Park

*I*n far West Texas, the Rio Grande bends in its path. North of the great bend, there lies a land that is majestic yet rugged and treacherous. It is in turn mountainous and flat, desolate and fertile. Big Bend National Park is a remote desert expanse of about 1,250 square miles. To the south lie the wild peaks of Mexico's Sierra del Carmen Mountains. Just west of the park is the 400-square-mile Big Bend Ranch State Natural Area.

Big Bend's vast beauty stretches across the desert landscape. Scattered across mountain ranges, flatlands, and hills are magnificent cacti: prickly pear, ocotillo, peyote, yucca, and other varieties. Southward across the Rio Grande, travelers can see 100 miles into Mexico. At sundown, the brilliant reds and purples of the Sierra del Carmen range appear to set the horizon on fire. On a moonlit night, the Chisos Mountains seem to shine with a ghostly glow. In fact, *chisos* means "ghost" in the Apache language.

At the feet of the Chisos, the Rio Grande rumbles through a series of deep, dark canyons that seem like another haunt of ghosts. At night in the park, coyotes howl at the moon. Mountain lions (also called cougars or pumas) stalk secluded mountainsides. A few desert bighorn sheep travel the high country. The jackrabbit, antelope, javelina, bobcat, and rattlesnake are common. Golden eagles and endangered peregrine falcons still nest on high ledges in the rocky cliffs of Big Bend.

Camping is a popular activity in the park. Many people use developed campgrounds in the Chisos Mountains and along the river. But others prefer to camp in primitive campsites deep within the walls of the Santa Elena, Mariscal, and Boquillas canyons. Many travelers reach canyon campsites by raft, kayak, or canoe. Floating down the Rio Grande towards the distant Gulf, they travel a stone's toss from Mexico on the right bank and the United States on the left. Campers in the canyons are especially careful to clean up their campsites to protect the natural beauty of this fragile environment.

Using Historical Imagination

Write a diary entry describing an imaginary camping trip in Big Bend National Park. Tell about the sights and sounds during the day and at night.

Jim Bones

Essential Elements
1C, 5A, 5C, 5D, 9A

LONE STAR LEGACY

Using Historical Imagination: Through careful reading, and by using their imaginations, students should be able to prepare colorful diary entries that include descriptive details of sights and sounds in Big Bend National Park.

cattle raising, oil; South Texas Plains—farming, ranching, oil and gas production; Post Oak Belt—agriculture, ranching, oil and gas production; Grand Prairie—livestock raising, agriculture, manufacturing; Cross Timbers—agriculture, ranching, oil and gas produc-

CHAPTER 3 REVIEW ANSWERS

Understanding Main Ideas

1. Gulf Coastal Plains, Central Plains, Great Plains, and Rocky Mountains
2. In the southeast part of the state; the Gulf Coast Plain, Piney Woods, Blackland Prairie, South Texas Plains, and Post Oak Belt
3. In the north central part of the state; the Rolling Plains, Grand Prairie, and Cross Timbers
4. In north and west central Texas; the High Plains and Edwards Plateau
5. In far West Texas; the Mountains and Basins
6. El Paso; Alpine and Marfa

Thinking Critically

1. **Evaluating Information:** The Piney Woods is a humid, hilly, tree-covered subregion within the Gulf Coastal Plains. In contrast, the Mountains and Basins subregion, in the Rocky Mountains region, is dry and mountainous, with only desert vegetation.
2. **Classifying Information:** Piney Woods—lumbering, oil production, agriculture; Gulf Coast Plain—oil refining, manufacturing, cattle raising; Blackland Prairie—farming,

CHAPTER 3 REVIEW

Understanding Main Ideas

1. Which four major natural regions of North America extend into Texas?
2. Where in Texas is the Gulf Coastal Plains? What are its subregions?
3. Where in Texas is the Central Plains? What are its subregions?
4. Where in Texas is the Great Plains? What are its subregions?
5. Where is the Rocky Mountains region, and what is its Texas subregion?
6. What is the only large city in the Mountains and Basins subregion? What two communities serve as gateways to Big Bend National Park?

Thinking Critically

1. **Evaluating Information:** Compare the natural environments of the Piney Woods subregion and the Mountains and Basins subregion.
2. **Classifying Information:** List the subregions of Texas, and list two or three important economic activities under each subregion.
3. **Synthesizing Information:** In which Texas subregions would you be most likely to find each of these: a solar energy plant, an oil refinery, a lumber mill, a sorghum farm, an irrigated cotton farm, a lignite mine?

Linking History and Geography

1. How would a Piney Woods cattle ranch likely be different from a ranch in the Mountains and Basins?

2. What do all the large cities of the Gulf Coast Plain have in common? Why?

TAAS Practice
Using Primary Sources

In his most famous book, *The Great Plains,* historian Walter Prescott Webb emphasized how Texas pioneers had to change their way of life after moving into the flat, dry country beyond longitude 98°W:

A plains environment is characterized by a plane, or level, surface, is treeless, and is sub-humid [dry]. . . . The Great Plains offered such a contrast to the region east of the ninety-eighth meridian, the regions with which American civilization had been familiar until about 1840, as to bring about a marked change in the ways of pioneering and living. For two centuries American pioneers had been working out a technique for the utilization of the humid regions east of the Mississippi River. They had found solutions for their problems and were conquering the frontier at a steadily accelerating rate. Then in the early nineteenth century they crossed the Mississippi and came out on the Great Plains, an environment with which they had had no experience. The result was a complete though temporary breakdown of the . . . ways of pioneering. . . . The ways of travel, the weapons, the method of tilling the soil, the plows and other agricultural implements, and even the laws themselves were modified.

1. According to the author, the characteristics of a plains environment are
   A peaceful Indians and herds of buffalo
   B desert conditions, flat landscapes, and irrigation farming

tion; Rolling Plains—ranching, farming, oil production; High Plains—agriculture, ranching, oil and gas production; Edwards Plateau—sheep and goat ranching, agriculture; Mountains and Basins—ranching, irrigation farming, tourism

3. **Synthesizing Information:** Solar energy plant—Mountains and Basins; oil refinery—Gulf Coast Plain; lumber mill—Piney Woods; irrigated cotton farm—High Plains; lignite mine—Post Oak Belt

Linking History and Geography

1. Because the thick grasses of the Piney Woods would sustain many more cattle on a smaller area of land, the Mountains and Basins ranch would probably be much larger. East Texas has many streams and lakes to use for watering livestock; however, water in the Mountains and Basins would probably be pumped from underground.
2. They are all located on the coast. They are important seaports.

TAAS *Practice*
Using Primary Sources

1. D
2. B

TAAS *Practice*
Writing Descriptively

Letters will vary, but students should demonstrate knowledge of the major differences in the natural environments of the Rolling Plains and Piney Woods.

Practicing Skills

1. **Sequencing Events:** Piney Woods, Edwards Plateau, Mountains and Basins
2. **Interpreting Maps:** Panhandle—winds there reach speeds of 14 miles per hour; Coastal Bend—sailboats need water, and the winds reach speeds of 12 miles per hour.

Enriching Your Study of Geography

1. **Individual Project:** Reports will vary but should be clear, accurate, and detailed, demonstrating careful research.
2. **Cooperative Project:** Reports will vary but should be clear and logical.

C fierce summer heat, cold winters, and a lack of rainfall

D a level land surface, absence of trees, dry conditions

2. The author states that pioneers reacted to the geography of the Great Plains by

A accelerating the spread of American settlement farther west

B going through a period of failure and readjustment before they successfully settled the Great Plains

C successfully applying pioneering techniques learned east of the Mississippi River

D cutting down trees, building mountain roads, and planting rice

TAAS *Practice*
Writing Descriptively

Imagine that you are a teenager in Texas during pioneer times. You and your family have recently moved from a farm in the Piney Woods to a new home on the Rolling Plains. Write a letter to your relatives in East Texas, describing your new environment. Tell them in detail what you like and dislike about your new home, and explain your reasons.

Practicing Skills

1. **Sequencing Events:** Recalling information you have learned from earlier chapters, arrange the following subregions of Texas in the order of their settlement by Anglo American and African American pioneers: Mountains and Basins, Edwards Plateau, Piney Woods.
2. **Interpreting Maps:** Study the map on this page. In which part of Texas would you expect to find the greatest soil

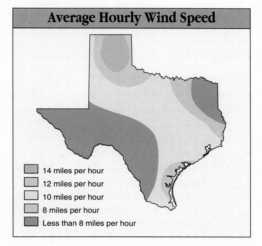

Average Hourly Wind Speed

14 miles per hour
12 miles per hour
10 miles per hour
8 miles per hour
Less than 8 miles per hour

erosion caused by wind? Why? In which part of Texas would you be likely to find sailboats? Explain your reasoning.

Enriching Your Study of Geography

1. **Individual Project:** Choose one subregion of Texas, and prepare a brief research report on one of the following of that subregion: mineral resources, wildlife, reservoirs and aquifers, agriculture, major industries, history of its largest city.
2. **Cooperative Project:** Begin a class research project to build a permanent information file on your subregion. Your teacher will assign research teams to collect information on your subregion's natural environment, agriculture, minerals, water resources, and major industries. Your research team will prepare a verbal and written report for the class.

UNIT REVIEW RESOURCES

1. Unit Review Worksheet 1
2. Unit 1 Test, Form A
3. Reteaching Worksheet 1
4. Unit 1 Test, Form B
5. **Informal Evaluation Forms:** Portfolio Assessment
6. *Texas, Our Texas* **Test Generator**

Essential Elements
1A, 1B, 4B, 5A, 5B, 5C, 5D, 7C, 9A, 9E

UNIT 1 REVIEW ANSWERS

Connecting Main Ideas

1. Relative location is the location of a place in relation to other places. Absolute location is the exact location of a place established by the use of the grid system of latitude and longitude. It could be said that the relative location of Amarillo, Texas, is the Panhandle. The absolute location of Amarillo is 35° N 102°W.
2. Plains, plateaus, mountains, hills
3. Winds carry moisture northeast from the Gulf of Mexico. The southwestern portion of Texas receives dry air from Mexico.
4. Tornadoes—violent circular winds that occasionally form within strong thunderstorms; hurricanes—huge storms of high wind and heavy rain; blizzards—blinding snowstorms that accompany strong northers
5. Gulf Coastal Plains region—Gulf Coast Plain, Piney Woods, Post Oak Belt, South Texas Plains, Blackland Prairie; Central Plains region—Grand Prairie, Cross Timbers, Rolling Plains; Great Plains region—High Plains, Edwards Plateau; Rocky Mountains region—Mountains and Basins

UNIT 1

REVIEW

Connecting Main Ideas

1. What is the difference between absolute and relative location? What is a Texas example of each?
2. What major landforms account for most features of the Texas landscape?
3. Why does rainfall in Texas diminish from east to west?
4. What are the characteristics of these three forms of violent weather: tornadoes, hurricanes, blizzards?
5. Into what geographical regions and subregions is Texas divided?

Practicing Critical Thinking Skills

1. **Synthesizing Information:** On a map of Texas, locate Nacogdoches and Alpine. How are their climates different? Why are they different?
2. **Seeing Cause and Effect:** Why is the Texas population concentrated in the eastern half of the state?
3. **Exploring Multicultural Perspectives:** Imagine that you are a Native American in Texas at the time of its early settlement by Anglo Americans and African Americans. Describe how their settlement practices are affecting the landscape, and tell what you think of their impact.

TAAS Practice
Writing Persuasively

Imagine that you are a conservationist trying to organize a community recycling program for aluminum cans, glass bottles, and plastic containers. Write a letter to a newspaper, arguing for this program.

Exploring Local Geography

1. What species of wildlife were present in the area of your community at the time of settlement? On which animals did early settlers most depend? Why?
2. Have a discussion with a parent, a guardian, or an adult friend to determine the answer to this question: What geographic factors were important in determining the original location of your community?

Using Geographical Imagination

1. **Individual Project:** Describe for an Australian pen pal what you consider to be the most beautiful environment in Texas and why.
2. **Cooperative Project:** With a partner, prepare a script for an argument between two people about whether Houston or Dallas deserves to be the new state capital of Texas. Then, with each partner taking the role of promoter of one of the two cities, read the script to the class.

For Extending Your Knowledge

Bedichek, Roy. *Adventures with a Texas Naturalist.* Garden City, NY: Doubleday, 1947. A series of essays on Texas geography and environment.

Graves, John. *Goodbye to a River.* New York: Knopf, 1960. A writer explores local environment and history during a canoe trip down the Brazos.

Practicing Critical Thinking Skills

1. **Synthesizing Information:** Nacogdoches is in the Piney Woods subregion; Alpine is in the Mountains and Basins subregion. The climate of Nacogdoches is humid, with hot summers and mild winters. The climate of Alpine is dry, with hot summers and colder winters. This difference is due to Alpine's higher elevation and because it is located much farther from the Gulf of Mexico.

2. **Seeing Cause and Effect:** Answers will vary, but students may note that the eastern half of the state has more rainfall, more natural resources, and most of the state's major industrial cities.

3. **Exploring Multicultural Perspectives:** Answers will vary, but students will probably point out that the settlers are cutting down the trees, killing and driving away the game, and harming the environment.

TAAS *Practice*
Writing Persuasively

Letters will vary, but students should point out that recycling saves valuable materials for future use and helps preserve the environment.

Exploring Local Geography

1. Answers will vary but should be valid for the student's community.
2. Answers will vary, but students should report opinions clearly.

Using Geographical Imagination

1. **Individual Project:** Descriptions will vary but should demonstrate knowledge of the chosen environment.
2. **Cooperative Project:** Scripts will vary but should be well written and presented clearly.

Skill Lesson
Practicing the Skill

1. A primary source is a firsthand record of an event. A secondary source is an account by someone who did not actually witness the event.
2. Possible answers include: newspaper articles, books, magazines, letters, diaries, official records, songs, photographs, films, paintings and drawings, political cartoons, laws, advertisements, and opinion polls.
3. Writing down, audiotaping, videotaping, filming
4. Answers will vary, but possibilities include: students' official records, written memos to teachers, teachers' handouts to students, school yearbook.

SKILL LESSON

Exploring Primary Sources

Writers of history textbooks, historians, gather accounts of events from a variety of sources, then describe the events on the basis of this evidence. Historians have observed in person few of the events they describe. For this reason, textbooks are *secondary sources* of history.

The saying "straight from the horse's mouth" describes a firsthand record of an event. Historians call such records *primary sources*. They are the primary historical evidence—the raw material—with which the historians work. Primary sources include books, newspaper articles, magazines, letters, diaries, and official records that were written by people who lived during a particular historical period. Other primary sources are recorded songs, photographs, films, paintings and drawings, political cartoons, advertisements, laws, and opinion polls.

Some primary sources are recorded as *oral histories*. Oral histories are "talking aloud" recollections of people about their past experiences. These verbal accounts may be written down or recorded onto audiotape, videotape, or film. The following oral history excerpt was recorded in 1953 by Mody C. Boatright and Louise Kelly. It is the recollection of oil ventures by E.M. Friend, a resident of Electra, near Wichita Falls. As you read, note that the words inside brackets were added to help the reader understand the subject. The ellipsis points (. . .) within the passage indicate that more was said about the topic but has been left out:

> Doc got hold of a little old spudding [digging] machine and got to drilling those shallow wells. . . . His old machine didn't amount to much. He kept it fixed up with bailing wire and anything he could get hold of. . . . And so his brother had a little money and his father had a little money. They kind of throwed in together and bought them a rotary drill. And they got some contracts and I imagine they were just about the luckiest drillers in the country. And they had the one rig, then they built it up to three or four. And when things got quiet in Electra, the East Texas field opened up and they went down there. And their luck still held good, by George.

Careful readers remember that information expressed in a primary source is not necessarily accurate or unbiased. Sometimes, these firsthand accounts include exaggeration or alteration of the facts. It is a human trait that our memory of an event or set of circumstances may grow weaker with time. It is important that we distinguish fact from opinion, whether the source is documentary or oral, whether it is primary or secondary.

Practicing the Skill

1. What is the difference between a secondary source and a primary source?
2. Name at least ten types of primary sources.
3. List four methods of recording oral history.
4. What are three primary sources from your school that could be placed in a time capsule for future historians to study?

Introducing the Unit

Connecting with Past Learning

Ask students to describe the various environments of Texas. Tell them to imagine that they are among the first inhabitants of Texas and must create a way of life for themselves and their families—food, clothing, shelter—using only the resources available to them in their environment. Have them suggest the resources on which they would come to depend and the various uses for these resources. Ask them to keep these ideas in mind as they study Unit 2.

Motivator

Before beginning the study of Unit 2, ask students to bring to class one item depicting ways of life of early Native Americans, such as pictures, artifacts, models, dolls, and so on. (As an alternative, suggest that students draw a picture depicting an aspect of Indian life.) Based on the samples, invite hypotheses about the ways of life of these first Texans. Include foods, clothing, shelter, and tools and weapons, and list them on the chalkboard. After studying the unit, evaluate with students the validity of each hypothesis.

Unit 2 Overview

Unit 2 focuses on the first Texans—the prehistoric and historic Indian peoples. Chapter 4 introduces students to the methods of studying prehistoric cultures. It describes Texas' Paleo-Indian, Archaic, and Formative eras and their major cultural characteristics.

Chapter 5 discusses the Texas Indian cultures existing at the time of European arrival. Twelve cultural groups are classified within four Indian cultural regions. Each group's way of life is detailed with discussion focusing on the Indians' adaptation to their environment.

Materials Available at the Unit Level:
Unit 2   Making Global
  Connections
Oral History Handbook
Informal Evaluation Forms

UNIT 2
THE FIRST TEXANS

TEXAS AND THE WORLD

Direct students to the map on page 78. Ask them to use the map's scale indicator to measure the distance from Asia to Texas along the migration route of early peoples. Ask students to consider how long it probably took these early peoples to reach the area now called Texas. Conclude the activity by having the students examine the time line on this page.

*H*arold D. Bugbee caught the movement, spirit, and drama of hunter, horse, and prey in his mural painting shown on the opposite page. After Texas Indians acquired horses from the Spaniards, they roamed the plains in search of buffalo herds. The Native American in the painting was a member of one of many groups who lived in Texas before it was settled by Europeans.

For thousands of years, no people lived in the land we call Texas. Later, people entered North America from Asia, and some spread into Texas. They adapted their ways of life to the land around them. Some groups found the lush forests of East Texas to their liking. Others chose the fertile lands along the Gulf coast or the prairies of Central and West Texas. As time passed, some groups disappeared while others survived. Overall, the Indians lived on the land of Texas much longer than have the descendants of Europeans and Africans.

Unit 2 is the story of the Native Americans who lived in Texas. Chapter 4 is about the ancient people who lived before any written records were kept of human activities. Chapter 5 is about the various groups of Indians living in Texas when the first Europeans arrived. Much of our knowledge of early Native Americans comes from these first European explorers.

UNIT 2 OBJECTIVES

1. Define *prehistory*, and identify sources of evidence of prehistoric people in Texas.
2. Discuss the way of life of the peoples of the Paleo-Indian Era in North America, and provide examples of Texas Paleo-Indian cultures.
3. Discuss the change from the Paleo-Indian to Archaic Era, and identify cultural differences between the two.
4. Explain the importance of agriculture in the formation of Indian civilization—the Formative Era.
5. Locate and identify the four Indian cultural regions of Texas and the twelve cultural groups that existed at the time of European exploration.
6. Compare and contrast the ways of life of the twelve Texas Indian cultural groups.

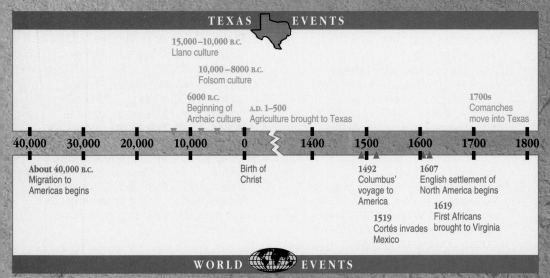

TEXAS EVENTS

15,000–10,000 B.C.
Llano culture

10,000–8000 B.C.
Folsom culture

6000 B.C.
Beginning of
Archaic culture

A.D. 1–500
Agriculture brought to Texas

1700s
Comanches
move into Texas

| 40,000 | 30,000 | 20,000 | 10,000 | 0 | 1400 | 1500 | 1600 | 1700 | 1800 |

About 40,000 B.C.
Migration to
Americas begins

Birth of
Christ

1492
Columbus'
voyage to
America

1519
Cortés invades
Mexico

1607
English settlement of
North America begins

1619
First Africans
brought to Virginia

WORLD EVENTS

PREHISTORIC CULTURES

TEACHER'S TIME LINE

Section 1	Section 2	Section 3	Section 4	Review and Assessment
Pp. 76–79	Pp. 79–83	Pp. 83–84	Pp. 84–86	
1 Day	1 Day	1 Day	1 Day	1 Day

★ TEACHER MATERIALS

Core: Chapter 4 Time Line; Graphic Organizer 4; Enrichment Worksheet 4; Review Worksheet 4; Reteaching Worksheet 4; Chapter 4 Tests, Forms A & B

Additional: Geography and Graph Skills 4, Informal Evaluation Forms, Test Generator

★ OBJECTIVES

1. Define significant terms related to the prehistoric cultures of Texas.
2. Describe methods of studying ancient cultures.
3. Distinguish among ways of life of people living during the Paleo-Indian, Archaic, and Formative eras.
4. Describe evidence of early people in Texas.
5. Discuss the impact of the development of agriculture on ways of life.
6. Identify the great civilizations of the Formative Era.

★ RESOURCES

BOOKS FOR TEACHERS

Bulletin of the Texas Archaeological Society. Austin: Texas Archaeological Society, 1953–. Articles on paleontology and archaeology concerning early Texas Indians.

Harrison, Billy R. *Lake Theo: A Stratified, Early Man Bison Butchering and Camp Site.* Canyon: Panhandle-Plains Historical museum, 1978. Fascinating account of this early Indian camp.

Newcomb, William Wilmon. *The Indians of Texas: From Prehistoric to Modern Times.* Austin: University of Texas Press, 1961. History of American Indians, including Texas.

—*The Rock Art of Texas Indians.* Austin: University of Texas Press, 1967. Rock paintings and petroglyphs.

Sauer, Carl O. *The Distribution of Aboriginal Tribes and Languages in Norwestern Mexico.* Berkeley: University of California Press, 1934.

—*Man in Nature; America Before the Days of the White Men.* New York: C. Scribner's Sons, 1939. Geography and culture in America before Columbus.

Shafer, Harry J. *Ancient Texans: Rock Art and Lifeways Along the Lower Pecos.* Austin: Texas Monthly Press, 1986. Illustrated, highly readable account of the early peoples of this region of Texas.

MULTIMEDIA MATERIALS

American Indians Before European Settlement. (video, 11 min.) Coronet Film and Video, 108 Wilmot Rd., Deerfield, Illinois, 60015. Includes Southwest groups.

The Chaco Legacy. (video, 60 min.) PBS Video, 1320 Braddock Place, Alexandria, Virginia, 22314-1698. Presents some of the wonders of this great Southwest civilization.

Maya Lords of the Jungle. (video, 60 min.) PBS Video, 1320 Braddock Place, Alexandria, Virginia, 22314-1698. Rise and fall of this magnificent culture.

Myths and Moundbuilders. (video, 60 min.) PBS Video, 1320 Braddock Place, Alexandria, Virginia, 22314-1698. Tracks the mysteries of the ancient builders.

Southwest Indians of Early America. (video, 14 min.) Coronet Film and Video, 108 Wilmot Rd., Deerfield, Illinois, 60015. Discusses early native peoples, including Hohokam and Anasazi.

GENERAL STRATEGIES

STUDENTS WITH SPECIAL NEEDS

Limited English Proficient Students (LEP)

As students study the chapter, help them create an outline showing major characteristics of the Paleo-Indian, Archaic, and Formative eras. See other activities labeled **LEP**.

Students Having Difficulty with the Chapter

Ask students to complete a four-column chart. The following labels should appear across the top of the chart: *Food Sources, Weapons and Tools, Shelter, Nomadic or Settled.* Instruct students to list on the left side of the chart the following cultures: *Paleo-Indian, Archaic, Formative.* Have students fill in the missing information as they study the chapter. **LEP**

Auditory Learners

Have auditory learners prepare oral presentations on the information presented in Chapter 4. See other activities labeled **A.**

Visual Learners

With students, select twenty to 25 words or phrases that could be used to describe life in one of the three prehistoric eras described in the chapter. Have the students design pictographs that represent the words or phrases. The students should then prepare a story that might have appeared on a prehistoric cave wall and label the era they are illustrating. Display the completed works in the classroom. See other activities labeled **V.**

Tactile/Kinesthetic Learners

Direct students to work together to create a display of a village or town of one of the early Native American cultures in Texas. Encourage the students to use sources other than their textbook. See other activities labeled **TK.**

Gifted Students

Ask gifted students to research and report on one of the four great civilizations that influenced Texas cultures—the Aztecs, Mayas, Pueblos, or Mound Builders. Reports should include the following information: location of the civilization, organization of government, economic activities, religious practices, tools and weapons, food sources, art and architecture, contributions to future ways of life. Ask students to draw a map showing the location of the civilization. See other activities labeled **G.**

VOCABULARY

In addition to the boldfaced terms in each section, some students might benefit from discussing the meanings of these terms.

Section 1: *migrations* (p. 79).
Section 2: *ancestors* (p. 80).
Section 3: *regional* (p. 83).
Section 4: *civilization* (p. 84);
cultivated (p. 84);
primitive (p. 86);
savage (p. 86);
enslaved (p. 86).

CHRONOLOGY

Have students study the Chapter 4 Time Line and identify relationships among events.

GRAPHIC ORGANIZER

Have students skim the chapter and complete the Chapter 4 Graphic Organizer. *(You might wish to use this activity to review rather than to introduce the chapter.)*

ENRICHMENT

Have students complete the Chapter 4 Enrichment Worksheet.

SECTION 1

FOCUS

Predicting (I) Ask students to brainstorm to develop a definition for the term *prehistory*. Explain that the prefix *pre* means "before." Remind students that a definition of *history* is the written or recorded knowledge of past events. Tell students that Section 1 will introduce them to the study of prehistory.

INSTRUCTION

Vocabulary (I) You may wish to preteach the following boldfaced terms: *cultures* (p. 76); *prehistory* (p. 76); *archaeologists* (p. 76); *artifacts* (p. 77); *historians* (p. 79). **LEP**

Historical Imagination (I) Ask students to write a brief paragraph answering the following questions: If you were to dig deep down into your backyard, what kinds of items would you hope to find? What might these items tell you about the people who lived there before you? **LEP**

CHAPTER 4 OVERVIEW

People have lived in the land we call Texas for thousands of years. They were among the first Americans and helped build the first civilizations in the Americas. These early peoples left many contributions that remain a part of our lives today. Their story is an important one in understanding Texas history.

Essential Elements
1A, 5B, 9B, 9F

CHAPTER 4

PREHISTORIC CULTURES

The Story Begins...

Chapter 4 tells how people migrated to North America from the continent of Asia, then gradually spread over North, Central, and South America over thousands of years. As they did so, they developed a wide variety of **cultures**, or ways of life. Each of these cultural groups was marked by distinct customs and traditions. These people were the first Americans. Their story is an important one to the understanding of Texas history. They left many contributions that are part of our society today.

As you read the chapter, look for the answers to these questions:

1. What is an archaeologist, and how do archaeologists study people who lived during the thousands of years of prehistory?
2. What were the characteristics of the Paleo-Indian cultures?
3. How were the cultures of the Archaic Era peoples different from those of the Paleo-Indians?
4. What new inventions brought about the change from the Archaic Era to the Formative Era in North America?

Paul M. Montgomery

Archaeologists discover the past.

1 Studying Prehistory

The period of time when there were no written records of human experiences is called **prehistory**. Because there are no written records, the history of the people is incomplete. But this does not mean that we know nothing about prehistoric people. There are scientists and scholars who study this ancient era. From their discoveries, they have pieced together some basic ideas of what life was like for prehistoric people.

Scientists who dig beneath the ground for evidence of past cultures are called **archaeologists**. They sift through

Art and History (I) Direct students to the painting on page 79. Point out that we can learn much about a society by studying the art that it produced. Ask: What do you think historians have learned from studying this painting and others like it? Have students speculate on how art today reflects the values of our society. **A, V, LEP**

Guided Practice (I) To illustrate how archaeologists work, display the following items for the class: a milk carton, a fork, a calculator, a ballpoint pen, a pair of earrings, and a pair of blue jeans. Then tell students that they are archaeol-

ogists in the year 2200 and that they have just discovered these artifacts. Ask them to work in groups to formulate generalizations about the society that used these items. Have the groups compare their lists. **A, V, TK, LEP**

EXTENSION

Research (II) Ask students to research Carbon-14 dating, a method used by archaeologists and scientists to determine the age of archaeological materials. Have them report their findings to the class. **A, G**

layers of earth, looking for **artifacts**—tools, weapons, and other objects that help show how people lived in the distant past. Using several scientific methods, archaeologists are able to determine the age of the artifacts. As more artifacts are discovered in an area, a pattern emerges that gives clues to the way people lived during a certain time period.

There are other sources of evidence for archaeologists. For example, prehistoric people often drew pictures on the walls of caves or on the sides of cliffs. These pictures usually describe an important activity, such as hunting or celebrating special days. In Texas, prehistoric drawings have been found in caves along the Rio Grande at Seminole Canyon, at Hot Springs in Big Bend National Park, and in Presa Canyon near the Pecos River.

These drawings sometimes give the archaeologist important clues about how people looked, the animals that they hunted, the tools that they used—even the gods

Paul M. Montgomery

Many rock paintings and prehistoric artifacts have been found at the state park at Seminole Canyon.

Historical Sidelight
A relatively new science of learning about the past is called *palynology*, the study of fossil pollen. Palynologists can learn about the paleoenvironment, determine prehistoric diet, learn the use of certain types of artifacts, and determine cultural traits by studying fossil pollen.

These Indian artifacts were all found in the Edwards Plateau region. Can you identify the uses of some of them?

Richard Pearce-Moses, L. M. Green Collection

Caption Response
Possible answers include food grinding, scraping, cutting, pounding, drilling, and killing game.

Independent Practice (II) Ask students to imagine that they are a member of an early prehistoric society in Texas. Ask them to draw a series of pictures showing how they looked, what kinds of foods they ate, their shelter, the tools they used, and so on. Have students discuss their drawings and display them in the classroom. **A, V, TK, G**

RETEACHING

Ask students to write a paragraph summarizing the information presented in Section 1. Invite volunteers to read their paragraphs aloud. **A, LEP**

CLOSURE

Remind students that archeologists search for evidence that will reveal how early peoples lived and that historians use this knowledge to write histories of early people. Tell students that they will learn about specific groups of early Texas peoples in Section 2.

ASSESSMENT

Have students complete the Section 1 Review on page 79.

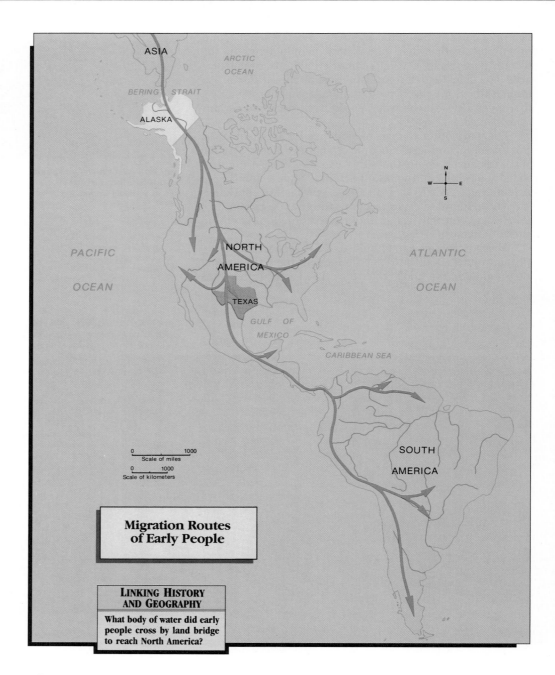

Migration Routes of Early People

LINKING HISTORY AND GEOGRAPHY

What body of water did early people cross by land bridge to reach North America?

Linking History and Geography
The Bering Strait

SECTION 2

FOCUS

Student Experiences (I) Ask students if they and their families have ever moved from one place to another. Invite them to offer reasons that people relocate to different areas. Point out that the first Americans migrated slowly from Asia to the Americas. Ask students to think about why these early peoples settled the North American continent.

INSTRUCTION

Vocabulary (I) You may wish to preteach the following boldfaced terms: *nomadic* (p. 79); *Paleo-Indians* (p. 79); *mammoths* (p. 80); *mastodons* (p. 80); *atlatl* (p. 81). **LEP**

Geography and History (I) Emphasize to students that the migration and settlement of North America took thousands of years. Refer students to the map on page 78 or to a more detailed wall map. Have them note the route from the Bering Strait to Texas. Ask them to consider geographic obstacles early peoples may have encountered. Ask: How

Watercolor by Forrest Kirkland. Texas Memorial Museum

Texas Indians represented their world through rock art. Painting natural rock surfaces is an ancient art form. This painting was found at Seminole Canyon in Val Verde County.

SECTION 1 REVIEW

Define: cultures, prehistory, archaeologists, artifacts, historians

1. What method do archaeologists usually use to study the past?
2. How is the period of prehistory different from the period that came after it?
3. On what kind of evidence is our knowledge of prehistoric peoples based?

Analyzing Information: Two artifacts are found at an archaeological site, one two feet below the surface of the earth and one five feet below. Which is likely to be the oldest? Why?

Evaluating Information: What objects are you carrying on your person that might survive as artifacts buried in the earth for 500 years? Explain.

that they worshipped. In the end, archaeologists use the evidence obtained from artifacts, cave drawings, human burials, and the traces of ancient campfires to try to piece together an accurate picture of the day-to-day activities of a prehistoric society.

Historians use the knowledge gained from the scientists and scholars to try to write a history of early people. Because of the work of historians, we can learn much about past cultures. ✪

☑ The Paleo-Indian Era

Scientists and historians believe that the first people to live in the Western Hemisphere migrated from Asia. The first of these migrations may have begun as much as 40,000 to 50,000 years ago. During the ice age, ocean levels were lower than they are today. A land bridge connected Asia and Alaska. People were able to cross this land from one continent to the other.

For thousands of years, people moved slowly into the North American continent. They were **nomadic** people, those who move periodically in search of food or following wild animals from season to season. Scientists have labeled these first settlers in North America **Paleo-Indians**. *Paleo* means "ancient," and *Indian* is the name that European

Paul M. Montgomery

This painted pebble was discovered at Seminole Canyon.

Answers to Section 1 Review

Define: *cultures*—ways of life; *prehistory*— period of time for which no written records exist; *archaeologists*—scientists who dig for evidence to learn about past cultures; *artifacts*—objects that reveal how people lived in the past; *historians*—scholars who write accounts about the past

1. Archaeologists dig artifacts from the earth to learn about past societies.
2. During prehistory there were no written records; such records do exist in the historic period that follows.
3. It is based entirely on artifacts dug from the earth at places where prehistoric people lived.

Analyzing Information: The deeper object is probably older. Artifacts accumulate over long periods of time. The general rule is that the deeper the artifact is buried, the older it is.

Evaluating Information: Answers will vary, but students should suggest objects of metal, glass, or ceramic—items that would resist rotting while buried.

Essential Elements
1A, 1C, 5B, 5C, 9B, 9E, 9F

long do you think it would take to travel this route by car? Have students compare what the first humans encountered along this route in North America to what Americans would find today. **A, V, LEP**

Synthesis and Analysis (II) Ask students to list the Five Themes of Geography that they learned about in Unit 1. *(Allow students to refer to their textbooks if necessary.)* Then ask them to write next to each theme an example from Section 2 that best represents that theme *(example:*

movement across the earth's surface—migration from Asia to North America). Collect the lists and create a master list on the chalkboard. **LEP, V**

Guided Practice (I) Have students work in groups to create posters illustrating the various animals that the Llano and Folsom cultures hunted and the weapons and methods that they used. Tell students to label their drawings, distinguishing between the two cultures. **V, TK, LEP**

Economics

Ask students to consider the population densities of Paleo-Indian societies compared to population densities today. Ask students if they think the economy of Paleo-Indians would support large populations. Have students explain their answers.

Texas Archaeological Research Labs

This rock slab and stone were used to grind food.

Richard Pearce Moses, L.M. Green Collection

This spear point probably was used to hunt buffalo.

explorers later gave to the people they met in the New World. The Paleo-Indians specialized in hunting now-extinct big-game animals that roamed North America during the last ice age. Different Paleo-Indian cultures developed over many years as these hunting peoples spread across the Americas. Evidence of several of these groups has been found in Texas.

Some Early Texans. Texas has provided evidence of some of the oldest human burials in the Americas. In 1982, archaeologists were sifting through a highway construction site near Leander. They discovered the skeleton of a Paleo-Indian woman who lived about 10,000 years ago. Named the "Leanderthal Lady" by local newspapers, this woman was five feet, three inches tall. She was found buried in charcoal, which had probably been a campfire. There was a large grinding stone beside her and spear points nearby. This is one of the oldest finds of a nearly complete human skeleton in all of North America.

In 1953, remains of a woman who lived more than 8,000 years ago were found near Midland. This Paleo-Indian woman was nicknamed "Midland Minnie."

These archaeological finds were unusual in an important way: they held the remains of human beings. Archaeological discoveries without skeletal remains are more plentiful. They tell us still more about the Paleo-Indian cultures.

The Llano Culture. When people share a common way of life, they are considered as belonging to the same culture. The very first culture known to have existed in Texas is called the Llano culture. The people of this culture lived from 10,000 to 15,000 years ago in what is now western Texas and northeastern New Mexico. These people were nomadic hunters. They chased giant **mammoths** and giant **mastodons**, both ancestors of the elephant. These animals roamed across the High Plains of Texas. The mammoths were often fourteen feet tall with tusks up to sixteen feet in length. Imagine the courage and skill needed to hunt such large animals! The Llano people hunted these thundering herds, armed only with flint-tipped spears and darts. Examples of these flint weapons have been discovered near Plainview, Denton, Lubbock, and Midland.

Research (III) Have students contact the local or state historical society or public library to find further information about the evidence of Paleo-Indian cultures in Texas. Ask students to report their findings to the class. Encourage them to supplement their reports with copies of newspaper articles about archaeological discoveries in Texas. **A, V, G**

Independent Practice (I) Have students imagine that they are some of the first settlers in Texas. Ask them to write a paragraph identifying themselves as part of either the Llano or Folsom culture, telling about their way of life. **LEP**

Ask students to list three factors that distinguish the Llano culture from the Folsom culture. Invite volunteers to read their lists aloud. **A, LEP**

Illustration by Hal M. Story, "A Paleo-American hunting scene," from W.W. Newcomb, Jr., *The Indians of Texas: From Prehistoric to Modern Times*, copyright © 1961 by the University of Texas Press. By permissions of the publisher.

Paleo-Indians of the Folsom culture hunted giant bison. These mammals were the ancestors of the buffalo that were hunted thousands of years later by Plains Indians.

The Folsom Culture. A more recent group of Paleo-Indians was the Folsom culture. Named after a town in northeastern New Mexico, the Folsom people lived between 8,000 and 10,000 years ago. They lived farther north than the Llano culture, and their weapons were improved. The Folsom people used tools made of flint, horn, and bone. Their flint points were more plentiful and elaborate. They used a spear-throwing stick called the **atlatl**, which was held in the hand and which had a hook at one end to hold the butt of the spear. The atlatl allowed ancient hunters to throw spears farther and with greater force. The Folsom culture depended on large herds of now-extinct

Richard Pearce-Moses, L. M. Green Collection

Dart points similar to these were used to tip the missiles thrown with atlatls, or spear-throwing sticks.

CLOSURE
Point out to students that the Paleo-Indian Era lasted until about 6000 B.C. Then, a new way of life gradually replaced the old.

ASSESSMENT
Have students complete the Section 2 Review on page 83.

SECTION 3

FOCUS

Past Learning (I) Ask students to examine the time line on page 75 and to recall characteristics of the Paleo-American cultures.

Essential Elements
1A, 1C

LONE STAR LEGACY
Using Historical Imagination:
Answers will vary, but students should indicate an item not available in their geographic area.

Answers to Section 2 Review

Define: *nomadic*—moving from place to place; *Paleo-Indians*—big-game hunting peoples, the first to settle North America; *mammoths* and *mastodons*—ancient ancestors of the elephant, hunted by the Llano peoples; *atlatl*—spear-throwing stick

Identify: "Leanderthal Lady"—skeleton of a Paleo-Indian woman discovered near Leander, Texas; "Midland Minnie"—remains of a Paleo-Indian woman found near Midland, Texas

(Continued on page 83)

Alibates Flint Quarries National Monument

*T*ools and weapon points found throughout North America tell us much about the first people who lived in the Texas Panhandle. The flint of which the tools and weapon points were made came from a ten-square-mile area near Amarillo. Known as Alibates Flint Quarries National Monument, it is Texas' only national monument.

The site was first reported in 1907 by Dr. Charles N. Gould, a geologist. Gould discovered a flint ledge along the Canadian River north of Amarillo. He later learned that it was part of a huge field of dolomite, a mineral usually found in crystals. Something happened many years ago to turn this dolomite into high-quality flint that is colorful and very hard. The flint was mined by Native Americans at least 12,000 years ago.

In no other place in the world has flint like this been found occurring naturally. Yet tools and weapon points made of it have been found throughout North America. At archaeological sites in New Mexico, scientists discovered Alibates weapon points embedded in the remains of ancient animals. Thus they believe that this flint was used in one of America's first mining and trading ventures. And by dating the sites where the flint has been found, geologists have determined that Alibates flint was mined continually for about 12,000 years.

Scientists also know that the early flint traders traveled on foot, because they lived before horses arrived. In animal-skin bags they kept *blanks*, chunks of flint to be made into tools. The blanks were traded for goods such as shells, red pipestone, painted pottery, turquoise, and obsidian (volcanic glass).

When Gould discovered the flint, he asked the local residents the name of a nearby creek. One of them replied, "Oh, that's where a cowboy, Allie Bates, from the LX ranch grazed a few head of his own cattle and built himself a dugout—so we call it Allie Bates Creek for him." Gould shortened the name on his maps and reports to Alibates. Consequently, scientific journals referred to the area by that name, and it has been called Alibates ever since.

Using Historical Imagination
If you were an early Texas Indian, what would you accept in trade for flint? Why?

Texas Department of Transportation

INSTRUCTION

Vocabulary (I) You may wish to preteach the following boldfaced terms: *Archaic Era* (p. 83); *extinct* (p. 83); *domesticate* (p. 84). **LEP**

Illustrating (I) Ask students to think about the ways of life of the Archaic Era and to draw pictures to illustrate what these early peoples might have drawn on caves or other surfaces. Ask: What do you think were the common subjects of these early artists? **A, V, TK, LEP**

Synthesis (I) Write the following terms on the chalkboard: *climate, extinct, environments, plant foods, domesticate.* Ask students to use the terms in a brief paragraph discussing the Archaic Era. **V, LEP**

Guided Practice (I) Have students work in pairs to develop a series of cause-and-effect statements summarizing the information in Section 3. Call on volunteers to write either a cause or an effect on the chalkboard. Have other members of the class identify the statement as a cause or an effect and complete the statement. **A, V, LEP**

giant bison, or buffalo, for their main food source. Some of these giant bison reached a height of nine feet!

Several archaeological sites in Texas give insight into the hunting skills of the Folsom people. Mounds of buffalo bones have been found at the bottom of steep cliffs. The ancient bones show cut marks made by the flint knives of the Paleo-Indians. These mounds suggest that hunters drove the buffalo over the edge of the cliffs. Then they skinned the buffalo and stripped off the meat. This method of obtaining a large supply of food was a rare achievement for the ancient Texans. Chances to ambush whole herds like this probably were uncommon. Usually they depended on the hand-held spear or the flying dart from an atlatl in order to feed their families. ✪

3 The Archaic Era

Sometime after 6000 B.C., the Paleo-Indian culture gradually changed to a new way of life. This newer period is called the **Archaic Era**. Archaeologists believe that this new age began because of changes in the climate. Larger game animals of the Paleo-Indian Era became **extinct**, or disappeared, possibly because of human hunting. This change in the available food supply forced people of the period to adapt to new conditions.

Cultural Differences. The Archaic people were similar to their Paleo-Indian ancestors in many ways, but their basic way of life was more complex and varied. Regional differences in culture were much greater than they had been in Paleo-Indian times. Archaic people still hunted on the plains, but they also spread into all the environments of the Americas. Now they chose a much wider selection of animal prey. They hunted not only buffalo but also deer, elk, bears, horses, and a variety of small game. Most important, the Archaic people used a wide variety of plant foods. They gathered berries, nuts, roots, and seeds to add to their diet.

The Archaic people used a greater variety of tools and weapons than did the Paleo-Indians. More than 30 different kinds of dart points that date from the Archaic period have been found in the Edwards Plateau region alone. The Archaic people also had knives, fishhooks, harpoons,

---

SECTION ⭐2 REVIEW

Define: nomadic, Paleo-Indians, mammoths, mastodons, atlatl

Identify: "Leanderthal Lady," "Midland Minnie"

1. What were the general characteristics of the Paleo-Indian cultures?
2. Why was it necessary for the Paleo-Indians to be nomadic?
3. What improvements of hunting techniques were made by the Folsom peoples?

Solving Problems: If you had to kill a giant mastodon with a spear, how would you go about it? Explain.

Exploring Economics: Why, in your opinion, was the Alibates flint traded so widely?

Texas Archaeological Research Labs

This ancient necklace is made of conch shells. Similar shells were traded across hundreds of miles of North America.

---

1. They were nomadic, big-game hunting cultures that spread across large areas of the Americas during the last ice age.
2. They had to follow the game that they hunted, and the game moved around.
3. They used the atlatl and more elaborate flint points. They also drove big game herds off of cliffs.

Solving Problems: Answers will vary, but students may suggest hunting in groups, driving the animals into bogs or off of cliffs, or ambushing animals from blinds.

Exploring Economics: During this period, it was the finest raw material available in North America for making stone tools.

Essential Elements
1A, 1C, 5B, 9B, 9E, 9F

Answers to Section 3 Review

Define: *Archaic Era*—period of hunting and gathering that came after the Paleo-Indian Era; *extinct*—no longer in existence; *domesticate*—to tame or control for human use

1. Smaller game was hunted, plants were now more important to the diet, and more types of tools were used.
2. Both were based on hunting game and gathering wild plant foods.
3. The domestication of plants and animals

Problem Solving: Answers will vary, but students may suggest that the food was placed on the hot stones (or that the stones were placed on the food), or that the hot stones were dropped into water-filled containers to boil the food. (The latter was most common.)

Analyzing Information: Domestication of plants, because it would require that people live close to crops they grew. Domesticated animals could accompany people as they traveled.

Essential Elements
1A, 1B, 1C, 3D, 9A, 9B, 9D, 9E

SECTION ★3★ REVIEW

Define: Archaic Era, extinct, domesticate

1. How was the culture of Archaic Era peoples different from the culture of the Paleo-Indians?
2. How were the two cultures alike?
3. What innovation at the close of the Archaic Era caused a shift to a new way of life?

Problem Solving: How could heated stones be used to cook food? Explain.

Analyzing Information: Which of these would be likely to have greater effects on a nomadic way of life: domestication of animals, domestication of plants? Why?

Texas Archaeological Research Labs

Early Texans made pottery that was both useful and decorative.

scrapers, drills, and tools for grinding seeds and nuts. They apparently used heated stones to cook some of their food.

As time passed, the Archaic people began to depend more on plants than on animals for food. As a result, they became less nomadic. The roving bands of wild game were less dependable as a food supply, and people who depended on plants for food could stay longer in one area. As they settled down, the Archaic people began to **domesticate** (tame, or control for human use) some wild animals and plants. With the domestication of plants came a shift to a whole new style of living. ○

❹ The Formative Era

Sometime around 1000 B.C., a new way of life gradually replaced that of the Archaic Era. Pottery and the bow and arrow were invented. The most important innovation was the discovery and spread of agriculture. Archaeologists call this period of great cultural change the **Formative Era** because it was a time in which Indian civilization was forming.

The Importance of Farming. The first farmers in the Americas lived in Central and South America. Sometime during the Archaic Era, people learned to grow **maize**, or corn. Growing crops increased the food supply. The development of the bow and arrow at this time also meant more food. Small villages and towns appeared as groups of people settled in one area. A more advanced society developed, partly because people had to plan farther ahead. Gradually, probably between A.D. 1 and A.D. 500, the knowledge of farming spread northward into Texas and into other areas as well.

The Formative Era people grew crops other than corn. Among them were tomatoes, pumpkins, peanuts, squash, beans, cocoa, potatoes, and sweet potatoes. They also cultivated cotton and tobacco. Many of the modern world's food crops were first developed by these early Americans. Not all of the people in Texas during this period were farmers, but those in East Texas and along the Rio Grande became excellent farmers.

As people became more productive in their farm economy, several changes took place. Population increased,

SECTION 4

FOCUS

Predicting (I) Ask the class to brainstorm to provide definitions for the word *formative*. Explain that the term relates to growth and development. Ask: Why do you think the period following the Archaic Era is called the "Formative Era"?

INSTRUCTION

Vocabulary (I) You may wish to preteach the following boldfaced terms: *Formative Era* (p. 84); *maize* (p. 84); *astronomy* (p. 86). **LEP**

Writing (I) Ask students to use the information in Section 4 to write a paragraph using the following topic sentence: "The most important innovation during the Formative Era was the discovery and spread of agriculture." Invite volunteers to read their paragraphs aloud. **A, LEP**

Drawing by Jack Jackson

Texas Indians of the Formative Era became skilled farmers in areas where the soil and climate offered favorable growing conditions.

Texas Archaeological Research Labs

and people lived longer. It took fewer people to grow more and more food. Some members of the society were free to pursue other tasks, such as art and architecture. Beautiful pieces of pottery and other brightly painted works of art have been discovered from the Formative Era. Houses became more complicated. In Central and South America, cities grew that were built around temples, palaces, and pyramids.

The Great Civilizations. No evidence has yet been found to suggest that any great cities were located in Texas at this time. Yet four of the great civilizations of the Formative Era were near Texas, and these societies influenced the Texas cultures. In Mexico and Central America, the Aztecs and Mayas developed great civilizations. The Pueblo culture in the American Southwest and the Mound Builders of the Mississippi River valley did the same.

In their own time these American civilizations were among the greatest in the world. For many years their contributions were ignored, but today, historians realize the great debt owed to these people. They built great cities, practiced complex religions, and studied mathematics.

Much time and skill was required to make pottery of this quality.

Guided Practice (I) Ask each student to make up a matching test about the Formative Era, using the information presented in Section 4. Have students exchange and complete the tests. Conclude by having pairs of students discuss and correct the answers. **LEP**

EXTENSION

Creating (II) Have students work in small groups to research and create a three-dimensional replica of one of the great cities that developed during the Formative Era. Encourage students to provide a written description of the city's organization. **V, TK, G**

Independent Practice (II) Have students work individually or in pairs to develop a three-column chart labeled: *Paleo-Indian Era, Archaic Era, Formative Era.* Tell students to complete the chart by listing major characteristics of each culture. **V, TK**

RETEACHING

Pair students who are having difficulty with the chapter with students who are performing well. Have each group skim Section 4 and list the cultural developments that took place during the Formative Era. Ask volunteers to read their lists

In Central America, the Maya civilization was highly advanced. This photograph shows ruins of a Maya city.

Superstock

SECTION ★ 4 ★ REVIEW

Define: Formative Era, maize, astronomy
Identify: Aztecs

1. What were the social effects of the development of agriculture?
2. Which crops were developed by Formative Era farmers?
3. What two civilizations developed in present-day Mexico and Central America? What two civilizations developed in North America?

Synthesizing Information: How is a domesticated plant different from a wild plant?

Seeing Cause and Effect: What is the relationship between increased food supply and the production of great works of art and architecture?

They also practiced **astronomy**, the study of the stars and planets and their movement. These early people mined and refined metals. They produced great art and music, and they organized governments. And, of course, they developed agricultural plants that remain vital to people all over the world, even today.

European Arrival. At the end of the fifteenth century, the prehistoric period in America was coming to a close. Explorers from Europe began arriving. These explorers kept written accounts of their travels. From their records, historians received the first accounts of the appearance and culture of Native Americans. This marks the start of the historic era in America.

Most Europeans looked upon the Native Americans as primitive and savage. Europeans killed or enslaved many Native Americans. But the Native Americans were people with the same human dignity as people everywhere. They placed value on the family and worked for the good of all. They and their ancestors were the first Texans. ✪

CLOSURE

Refer students to the time line on page 75. Note the end of the prehistoric period. Ask: Why did the prehistoric period come to a close with the arrival of the European explorers?

ASSESSMENT

Have students complete the Section 4 Review on page 86.

CHAPTER REVIEW RESOURCES

1. Chapter Review Worksheet 4
2. Chapter 4 Test, Form A
3. Reteaching Worksheet 4
4. Chapter 4 Test, Form B
5. **Informal Evaluation Forms:** Portfolio Assessment
6. *Texas, Our Texas* **Test Generator**

CHAPTER 4 REVIEW

Essential Elements
1A, 5B, 9A, 9B, 9D

Understanding Main Ideas

1. What are artifacts, and how do archaeologists use them to interpret the past?
2. What were the main characteristics of the Paleo-Indian way of life?
3. What was the atlatl, and by what Paleo-Indian culture was it used?
4. How were Archaic Era cultures different from Paleo-Indian Era cultures?
5. What innovations came at the beginning of the Formative Era?
6. How were Formative Era cultures different from Archaic Era cultures?

Thinking Critically

1. **Evaluating Information:** What same factors made the atlatl and dart a superior weapon to the spear, and the bow and arrow a superior weapon to the atlatl and dart?
2. **Synthesizing Information:** What characteristics of the Archaic Era way of life helped prepare the way for the development of agriculture?
3. **Classifying Information:** Write the names of the major cultural eras at the top of a sheet of paper. Then write these innovations under the appropriate era: mammoth hunting, pottery, cooking-stones, growing maize, growing cotton, growing tomatoes.

Linking History and Geography

1. How would an archaeologist use local geography to locate possible archaeological sites?

2. Why did agriculture develop far to the south in the Americas and then gradually spread north?

TAAS Practice
Using Primary Sources

As the following account from *The Smithsonian Book of North American Indians* describes, when the first Paleo-Indians reached North America, they found a fantastic variety of ice-age animals:

> Many mammals grew to extravagant size. Ground sloths reached twenty feet in length, mammoths stood fourteen feet at the shoulder and a beaver, with teeth the size of a woodsman's ax, grew as large as a black bear. There were horses and camels still about in North America and a bison with a six-foot span of horns. . . . Sustained by a flora [plant life] adapted to the cool, wet conditions of the time, these browsers and grazers [plant eaters] themselves supported a similarly impressive menagerie [animal group] of predators.
>
> The giant short-faced bear was a long-limbed predator bigger than a grizzly, but more highly adapted for running; it must have been the continent's most formidable carnivore [powerful meat eater]. Some saber-toothed cats had eight-inch canines [fangs]. An American lion was larger than any of today's lions and rivaled in size any cat that ever lived. . . . It was into this realm that the first human immigrants walked, with a well-developed arsenal of weapons and hunting skills honed by thousands of years of Old World hunting experience.

1. According to this account, the chief characteristic of most of the animal life of North America during the ice age was
A a desire to live in low, boggy areas

CHAPTER 4 REVIEW ANSWERS

Understanding Main Ideas

1. They are tools, weapons, and other objects. Archaeologists use them to study how people lived in the past.
2. Nomadism, big-game hunting, small groups
3. It was a spear-throwing stick used by the Folsom culture.
4. Archaic Era cultures had more regional diversity, hunted more kinds of animals, made greater use of plant foods, and had a greater variety of tools.
5. Domestication of plants and animals, agriculture, pottery, the bow and arrow
6. Food surpluses were larger, populations grew, cities were constructed, great works of art and architecture were created, and strong governments developed.

Thinking Critically

1. **Evaluating Information:** In each case, the flint-tipped projectile went farther and with greater accuracy.

(Continued on page 88)

2. **Synthesizing Information:**
Greater dependence on wild plant foods meant that people did not move around as much—were less nomadic—as before. This dependence on wild plant foods, along with an increased knowledge of food production, led to agriculture.

3. **Classifying Information:**
Paleo-Indian Era—mammoth hunting; Archaic Era—cooking-stones; Formative Era—pottery, maize, cotton, tomatoes

Linking History and Geography

1. Answers will vary, but students may suggest that the archaeologist would look for sites near a source of fresh water, food sources, and in sheltered locations (such as caves).

2. Answers will vary, but students may suggest that it was because of the longer growing season and the variety of wild plant foods found farther south.

TAAS Practice
Using Primary Sources

1. C
2. D

TAAS Practice
Writing Descriptively

Descriptions will vary, but students should demonstrate knowledge of the basic characteristics of Formative Era culture.

Practicing Skills

1. **Sequencing Events:** Spear, atlatl and dart, heated cooking-stones, maize, pottery
2. **Interpreting Maps:** Cultivated plants—East Texas; game—North and Central Texas; fish—along the coast; game and wild plants—far West Texas

Enriching Your Study of History

1. **Individual Project:** Answers will vary among regions in the state but should include possible game animals and edible wild plant foods from the local area.
2. **Cooperative Project:** Reports will vary but should demonstrate accurate and detailed information.

CONTINUED

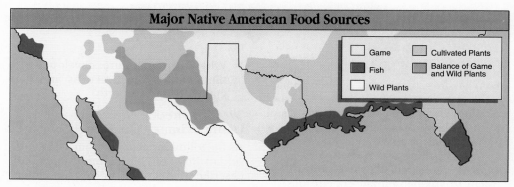

Major Native American Food Sources

Game · Cultivated Plants · Fish · Balance of Game and Wild Plants · Wild Plants

B   an ability to tolerate hot, dry environments on the Great Plains
C   the great size of many animals
D   the absence of carnivore species to prey on the plant grazers and browsers

2. The author implies that the first Paleo-Indian groups who came to North America
A   were at first unable to escape the big carnivores
B   spent several generations learning how to hunt the large animals
C   made several attempts to escape dangerous North America and return to Asia
D   had weapons and hunting skills capable of dealing with the big animals of North America

TAAS Practice
Writing Descriptively

Imagine that you are a member of an Archaic Era hunting-and-gathering group. You have just met a Formative Era group for the first time. Describe to your family your impressions of this new society.

Practicing Skills

1. **Sequencing Events:** Place the following inventions of the period of prehistory in chronological order, beginning with the oldest and ending with the most recent: pottery, atlatl and dart, spear, maize, heated cooking stones.
2. **Interpreting Maps:** Study the map on this page. It shows the dominant means of subsistence—of getting a living—of Texas Indian groups at about A.D. 1500. In what parts of the state did Indian societies get most of their livelihood from cultivated plants? from game? Where was subsistence based on fish? on a balance of game and wild plants?

Enriching Your Study of History

1. **Individual Project:** List the wild animals and plants that Archaic Era cultures in your area may have used.
2. **Cooperative Project:** With a partner, gather information from books and articles on one of these periods: Texas Paleo-Indian Era, Archaic Era, or Formative Era. Each research team will report its findings to the class.

CHAPTER 5

THE TEXAS INDIANS

TEACHER'S TIME LINE

Sections 1–2	Section 2	Section 3	Section 4	Section 5	Review and
Pp. 89–92	Pp. 92–97	Pp. 97–101	Pp. 101–104	Pp. 104–107	Assessment
1 Day	1 Day	1 Day	1 Day	1 Day	1 Day

◼ TEACHER MATERIALS

Core: Chapter 5 Time Line; Graphic Organizer 5; Enrichment Worksheet 5; Review Worksheet 5; Reteaching Worksheet 5; Chapter 5 Tests, Forms A & B

Additional: Geography and Graph Skills 5, Map and Chart Transparencies 9, Informal Evaluation Forms, Test Generator

◼ OBJECTIVES

1. Identify the four Indian cultural regions of Texas.
2. Name the twelve Indian cultural groups found within each cultural region of Texas.
3. Compare and contrast the ways of life of the Texas Indian cultural groups.
4. Cite the different ways Texas Indian cultural groups adapted to their environment.
5. Explain the origin of the name *Texas*.
6. Identify and discuss major beliefs, factors, or events that influenced the Texas Indian way of life.
7. Relate the causes for the demise of the Texas Indian cultural groups.

◼ RESOURCES

BOOKS FOR TEACHERS

Fehrenbach, T. R. *Comanches: The Destruction of a People*. New York: Knopf, 1974. History of the Comanche.

Gatschet, Albert Samuel. *The Karankawa Indians: The Coast People of Texas*. Cambridge: Peabody Museum of American Archaelogy and Ethnology, 1891. Language and culture of the Karankawa people.

Gregorz, H. F., editor. *The Southern Caddo: An Anthology*. New York: Garland Pub., 1986. Collection of anecdotes about the Caddo.

The Indian Years. Living with the Past Series No. 1. Austin: Texas Historical Commission, 1983. Discussion of the early days of Texas history involving native peoples.

Marriott, Alice Lee. *Saynday's People: The Kiowa Indians and the Stories They Told*. Lincoln: University of Nebraska Press, 1963. Tales and folklore of the Kiowa.

Newcomb, William Wilmon. *A Lipan Apache Mission: San Lorenzo de la Santa Cruz*. Austin: University of Texas, 1969. Life among the Lipan Apache at this mission.

—*The People Called Wichita*. Phoenix: Indian Tribal Series, 1976. Culture of the Wichita.

MULTIMEDIA MATERIALS

Ancient Civilizations Keyword. (software) Focus Media, Inc., 839 Stewart Avenue, P.O. Box 865, Garden City, New York, 11530. Interactive programs, aiding in comprehension of ancient civilizations, including American.

The Apache Indian. (video, 10 min.) Coronet Film and Video, 108 Wilmot Rd., Deerfield, Illinois, 60015. Culture of the Apache, including analysis of their horsemanship.

The Hopi Indian. (video, 11 min.) Coronet Film and Video, 108 Wilmot Rd., Deerfield, Illinois, 60015. Continued traditions of these Southwest Indians.

Pow-Wow. (video, 16 min.) Coronet Film and Video, 108 Wilmot Rd., Deerfield, Illinois, 60015. Display of native dances and culture.

STUDENTS WITH SPECIAL NEEDS

Limited English Proficient Students (LEP)

Ask students to write the questions from page 89 on a sheet of paper, leaving about five lines blank below each question. As students complete the study of a section, have them write an answer to the question for that section. Allow them to consult their textbooks to check and correct their answers. See other activities labeled **LEP.**

Students Having Difficulty with the Chapter

For students having difficulty with the chapter, create an identification game. Select five or six cultural groups discussed in Chapter 5. For each, write a series of identifying clues, with clues proceeding from the general to the specific. Place the series of clues in an envelope. Organize the class into small groups, and announce that the object of the game is to identify the correct cultural group using the fewest clues. Each group of students will accrue points for every clue and for incorrect guesses. The team with the fewest points is declared the winner. **LEP**

Auditory Learners

Have auditory learners select one of the cultural groups discussed in Chapter 5. Ask them to use the library to conduct additional research on the group and present their findings to the rest of the class. See other activities labeled **A.**

Visual Learners

List on the chalkboard all of the cultural groups mentioned in the chapter. Instruct students to label each group on a blank outline map of Texas. Then ask the students to select for each group one symbol that designates something distinctive or unique about the group and to create a map legend. They should then draw the symbols on the map at the appropriate locations. Display the finished maps in the classroom. See other activities labeled **V.**

Tactile/Kinesthetic Learners

Have tactile/kinesthetic learners use the Chapter 5 vocabulary terms to create an "illustrated dictionary." Ask them to select ten terms and write each at the top of a separate sheet of paper, along with its definition. Then have them draw a picture to illustrate the term. Finally, they should staple the pages to bind them into a "dictionary." See other activities labeled **TK.**

Gifted Students

Have gifted students complete the title below and use the information presented in Chapter 5 to write a three-paragraph essay in response to it.

"I Lived with the _____ Cultural Group."

See other activities labeled **G.**

VOCABULARY

In addition to the boldfaced terms in each section, some students might benefit from discussing the meanings of these terms.

Section 1: *anthropologists* (p. 89).
Section 2: *lances* (p. 90);
  council (p. 91);
  eternal (p. 91);
  intestine (p. 93);
  dominated (p. 94);
  forbade (p. 95);
  rove (p. 95).
Section 3: *descent* (p. 97);
  leagues (p. 98);
  anglicized (p. 98);
  reeds (p. 99);
  fertility (p. 99);
  turquoise (p. 100).
Section 4: *dugout* (p. 102);
  tendons (p. 102);
  mesquite (p. 104);
  agave (p. 104).
Section 5: *horticultural* (p. 105).

CHRONOLOGY

Have students study the Chapter 5 Time Line and identify relationships among the events.

GRAPHIC ORGANIZER

Have students skim the chapter and complete the Chapter 5 Graphic Organizer. *(You might wish to use this activity to review rather than to introduce the chapter.)*

ENRICHMENT

Have students complete the Chapter 5 Enrichment Worksheet.

Student Experiences (I) Ask students if their families have certain ways of doing things or follow certain rituals that they believe are unique to their family. *(Suggest holiday rituals and so on.)* Invite volunteers to share these with the rest of the class. Tell students that they will learn about four different regions of Texas and the unique ways of life of the

people who lived there. *(You might wish to review the definition of* region.*)*

Vocabulary (I) You may wish to preteach the following boldfaced term: *customs* (p. 89). **LEP**

Guided Practice (I) Ask students to write a sentence summarizing Section 1, using the following words: *customs, culture, region.* **LEP**

THE TEXAS INDIANS

CHAPTER
5

The Story Continues...

Chapter 5 describes the four cultural regions of Native Americans already living in Texas in the late 1400s, when Europeans first began exploring the Americas. It also describes the twelve different Indian cultural groups within those four regions and their various ways of life.

As you read the chapter, look for the answers to these questions:

1. What were the four Native American cultural regions of Texas in the late 1400s?
2. Which Indian cultural groups lived on the plains of West Texas? How were they similar and different?
3. Which Native American cultural groups lived in the eastern part of Texas, and how were their ways of life similar and different?
4. Which Indian cultural groups lived near the western Gulf of Mexico, and how were their cultures similar and different?
5. Which two Native American groups lived in far western and southwestern Texas, and how did their ways of life compare?

■1 Four Indian Cultural Regions

The huge area that is now Texas was home to twelve different cultural groups when Europeans first arrived. The people of each group lived in the same general location, shared the same language, and often followed the same leader or leaders. Each group had its own **customs**, or cultural ways of doing things. For example, Kiowa males sometimes took two or three different names during a lifetime. Each Indian society had its own ways of greeting people, preparing food, and raising children.

Anthropologists have grouped the twelve Texas Indian peoples into four general cultural regions, based on similarities in ways of life. These are the Plains cultural region, the Southeastern cultural region, the Western Gulf cultural region, and the Pueblo cultural region. ○

CHAPTER 5 OVERVIEW

When the Europeans arrived in America in the last part of the fifteenth century, they believed that all of the inhabitants had similar ways of life. Today we know that there were many different cultures among the Native Americans, especially in Texas.

Essential Elements
1A, 5A, 9A, 9B

Vocabulary Development
Point out to students that an anthropologist is a scientist who studies people's cultures.

Nawrocki Stock Photo

In 1832, artist George Catlin painted this portrait of Hisoosanchez (The Spaniard), a Spanish Comanche of the Plains cultural region.

CLOSURE

Review with students the names of the four Indian cultural regions of Texas. Ask: On what are these regions based *(similarities in ways of life)?*

ASSESSMENT

Have students complete the Section 1 Review on page 90.

SECTION 2

FOCUS

Student Experiences (I) Brainstorm with students all the things they think they need to survive. List their ideas on the chalkboard. Lead the class to the conclusion that basic needs can be classified according to food, shelter, and clothing. Tell students to consider as they study Section 1 how the people of the Plains cultural region met these basic needs.

Answers to Section 1 Review

Define: *customs*—cultural ways of doing things

1. The Plains cultural region, the Southeastern cultural region, the Western Gulf cultural region, the Pueblo cultural region
2. Similarities in ways of life
3. Twelve

Synthesizing Information: Answers will vary, but possible responses include: males taking two or three different names during a lifetime; a special way of greeting people, preparing food, or raising children.

Linking History and Geography

The Atakapan, the Karankawa, the Coahuiltecan; the Coahuiltecan, the Concho, the Jumano; the Caddo, the Wichita, the Kiowa, the Comanche

Transparency 9

An overhead transparency of this map can be found in the Teacher's Resource Binder.

Essential Elements

1A, 1B, 1C, 2A, 5A, 5B, 6A, 6B, 9B, 9G, 9F

Caption Response

The Comanches used the horse to chase buffalo.

90 *Unit 2*

SECTION ★ 1 REVIEW

Define: customs

1. What are the four Indian cultural regions of Texas?
2. Upon what have anthropologists based their grouping of Texas Indians into cultural regions?
3. How many Native American cultural groups lived in these four cultural regions?

Synthesizing Information: If you were a member of an Indian society, what might be a custom that would mark your group as different from others?

LINKING HISTORY AND GEOGRAPHY

Which groups lived near the Gulf Coast? the Rio Grande? the Red River?

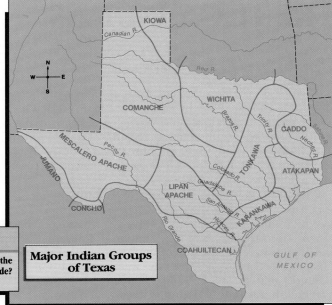

Major Indian Groups of Texas

Courtesy of the San Antonio Museum Association

Many Comanches roamed the High Plains of Texas. This painting shows a Comanche chief astride his horse. Why was the horse very important to the Comanche culture?

2 The Plains Cultural Region

Five different cultural groups lived on the plains of West Texas. These were the Comanches, the Kiowas, the Lipan Apaches, the Mescalero Apaches, and the Tonkawas. In general, these people were nomadic hunters. They depended on the roving buffalo for much of their food.

The Comanches. The Comanches rode the plains on their swift horses, chasing buffalo with lances and arrows. They lived in **tepees**, movable homes made from animal skins stretched over long poles. They often fought with other tribes for control of the land. The Comanches decorated their bodies with bright colors of paint and fancy tattoos. Over their long, braided hair, Comanche males wore headdresses made of buffalo horns. For more than 200 years, the Comanches ruled the southern plains of the present United States. When many people today think of Native Americans, they picture the Comanches.

The ancestors of the Comanches lived in the northern plains and Rocky Mountains. The Comanches moved into the plains of Texas around 1700. They came in search of

Vocabulary (I) You may wish to preteach the following boldfaced terms: *tepees* (p. 90); *bands* (p. 91); *moral code* (p. 92); *Comanchería* (p. 92); *allies* (p. 92); *pemmican* (p. 93); *rancherías* (p. 95). **LEP**

Writing (II) Tell students to imagine that they are newspaper reporters somehow transported back in time to the period of the Plains Indians in Texas. Ask students to use the information presented in Section 2 to write a newspaper story about what they see. Invite volunteers to read their stories aloud. **A**

the buffalo herds that populated most of North and West Texas. The Comanches traveled in **bands**, small groups made up of a few families. Two of the bands in Texas were the Antelopes (also known as the Quahadis) and the Honey-Eaters (the Penatekas). Other bands were the Liver-Eaters (the Tanimas), the Buffalo-Eaters (the Kotsotekas), and the Root-Eaters (the Yamparikas).

The Comanches were described as well-built, muscular people. They were the most respected and feared inhabitants of the plains. The Comanches were great warriors and expert horse breeders and riders.

The horse was a central part of the Comanche culture. The first horses were brought to the Americas by the Spaniards. Between the years 1650 and 1700, Indians on the plains of North America began to acquire horses through trade and capture. Horses gave the Comanches greater advantages in hunting buffalo. Learning to ride was as important to the Comanches as learning to walk. Boys and girls were drilled in riding skills before they were four years old. A Comanche warrior could ride full speed, pick up an injured companion, and still be ready to shoot with bow and arrows.

The Comanches had a form of government suitable to their way of life. The best rider and fighter in a Comanche band was elected its war chief, or leader in battle. In camp, the head of the band was the peace chief. The peace chief was usually an older male who had won past recognition in battle. The war chief, peace chief, and other respected men together formed a council that made important decisions for each band.

The Comanches had certain beliefs that may seem strange to us today. They believed that scalping an enemy would keep that person's soul from going to an afterlife or heaven. Scalping was also a symbol of strength and achievement to the Comanches. They believed in spirits that gave them special powers. Comanches would not eat food if a person's shadow fell on it while it was cooking. And they thought it was bad luck to boil and broil food over the same campfire.

One image of the Comanches is of warlike people who constantly raided and terrorized their enemies. But the Comanches were a religious people. They believed in a god. They also believed that a person who lived an honorable life would be rewarded with eternal life after

Thomas Gilcrease Institute of American History & Art

These Comanches were painted in war attire. The Comanches were skilled at war, but their religion enforced a strict moral code.

Texas Memorial Museum

Comanche men commonly wore head-dresses made of buffalo horns.

Historical Sidelight
Historian W.W. Newcomb suggests that Indians first learned to manage horses when they worked (or were forced to work) in the Spanish settlements of the colony of New Mexico. Indians who were able to escape left with a knowledge of how to take care of horses, and sometimes escapees were able to leave by horseback.

This photograph, taken in 1888, shows a Comanche camp near Llano.

Texas Memorial Museum

death. The Comanche religion set forth a **moral code**, or set of rules defining right and wrong. The code was strictly enforced. As a result, there was almost no crime. Their religion also stressed that people were part of nature.

The **Comanchería**, or land of the Comanches, stretched from Central Texas northward into Kansas and Colorado. The Spaniards began moving into this region after 1750. Later, other European and American settlers entered the area. Against these people, the Comanches proved to be tough fighters. Mounted on their horses, they were able to move over great distances and strike with force and power. They resisted settlement of the plains until the 1870s.

The Kiowas. Another nomadic culture that lived on the Texas plains was the Kiowas. The Kiowas were originally from the northern plains. They moved into the Texas Panhandle during the 1800s. Like the Comanches, they came in search of the gigantic herds of buffalo.

The Kiowas were among the few **allies**, or friends by treaty, of the Comanches. These two groups also had many similar customs. For example, tepees were home to nearly all the Plains Indians. Kiowa tepees consisted of 24 poles covered with buffalo hide. Both outside and inside, the buffalo hide was decorated with drawings and beautifully crafted paintings. During the summer, Kiowas rolled up the sides of the tepees to let in breezes. In winter, they built a fire in the center of the tepee, and a hole in the top acted as a vent. Kiowas made beds of blankets and buffalo hides on mattresses of willow branches.

There is no evidence that the Kiowas grew any food. They depended on their ability as hunters for survival. In addition to the buffalo, the Kiowas ate elk, antelope, deer, and bear. There are stories that Kiowas and Comanches ate their horses whenever no other source of food was available, as when they were surrounded by an enemy.

Sometimes Indians on the plains ate their meat raw, and sometimes they roasted it over a campfire. They also dried strips of meat in the sun to carry with them for a future meal. This dried meat is known today as jerky. It was probably not as tasty as fresh meat, but jerky often helped fill an empty stomach.

Another common food of the Plains Indians was called **pemmican**. Indians made pemmican by pounding dried buffalo meat into a powder and combining it with buffalo fat and juices. Then they pounded berries, nuts, fruits, or roots into a powder and mixed them in. They then stored the entire mixture in a pouch made from the intestine of a buffalo. Pemmican enabled the Plains Indians to carry food while quickly moving their camps from one location to another.

The Kiowas were known for their annual sun dance. Performance of the sun dance was thought to prevent

I. G. Holmes,
Panhandle-Plains Historical Museum

This Kiowa warrior's shield is made of painted buffalo hide, cloth, and eagle feathers.

National Anthropological Archives,
Smithsonian Institution

These Kiowa children are dressed in traditional clothing.

Institute of Texan Cultures

The buffalo was the main source of food for Plains Indian cultures. To most Indian groups, the buffalo hunt was an important event involving most of the band.

Historical Sidelight
The Kiowa Apaches joined with the Kiowas for the annual sun dance. The Kiowa Apaches were close cultural relatives of the Lipan Apaches.

sickness and disaster for the group. While dancing praises to the sun, Kiowa religious leaders asked for victory in war, many healthy children, and an unending supply of buffalo. The sun dance was held every year in mid June. It was the highlight of Kiowa life.

The Lipan Apaches. The Lipan Apaches roamed the southwestern region of Texas. Their territory extended from the western edge of the Central Texas Hill Country to areas along the Rio Grande. The Lipan Apaches dominated most of the Texas plains region until the Comanches drove them to the south in the 1700s.

The other Texas Indians feared the Lipans nearly as much as they feared the Comanches. Warfare and hunting buffalo were the primary activities of the Lipan Apaches. They were especially well known for their skills with the bow and arrow. A legend claimed that an Apache warrior could shoot twelve arrows before an enemy could fire one shot and reload a gun.

Theodore Gentilz painted this scene of a Lipan Apache camp in South Texas. Describe the events shown in this painting.

Courtesy of the San Antonio Museum Association

The Lipan Apache warrior cut his hair very short on the left side. He allowed the hair on his right side to grow long, sometimes almost to the ground. Feathers and other decorations were tied into the hair. The left ear was pierced with six to eight holes, in which earrings several inches long were worn. The men also plucked out all their beard and eyebrow hair. Women wore earrings and a few copper bracelets.

Gardening was one means for the Lipan Apaches to obtain food. This activity was not typical for Plains Indians. The Lipans grew corn, beans, and squash. Women members of the tribe worked the gardens and received a great deal of recognition from tribal leaders when they had a good harvest. After 1700, gardening became less important and hunting more important. As the Lipans acquired horses, they were better able to follow the buffalo herds. At the same time, their **rancherías**, or small farming settlements, were often raided by the Comanches.

The Lipan Apaches had a strong fear of the dead, or, as they believed, the spirits of the dead. This fear led to the quick burial of a dead person. All of the person's belongings were placed in the grave. The dead person's relatives had to move their tepees to other parts of the village. Relatives refused to visit gravesites, and they even forbade the mentioning of the dead person's name.

The Lipan Apaches faced the same fate as other Texas Indians. Their numbers were slowly reduced by attacks from Spaniards and Comanches. Others died from diseases brought by Europeans. By the 1800s, most Lipan Apaches had moved westward into the mountain regions of West Texas, New Mexico, and northern Mexico.

The Mescalero Apaches. Another band of Apaches related to the Lipans was the Mescalero Apaches. They lived to the west of the Lipans in the mountain regions of far West Texas. There were never many Mescaleros in Texas, but bands did rove in and out at various times from New Mexico and Mexico.

While Lipans were clearly Plains Indians, the Mescaleros lived much like the Pueblos, Indians of northern New Mexico. The Mescaleros depended less on the buffalo, and at times they lived in settled mountain villages.

The Tonkawas. The Tonkawas lived on the north central plains of Texas and the southeastern edge of the

Texas Memorial Museum, Courtesy of Mrs. Hunter P. Harris

This painting shows a Plains Indian woman in traditional clothing. Of what do you think her dress and ornaments are made?

Caption Response
Buffalo hide and bones

Guided Practice (I) Organize students into small groups and ask each group to design a poster illustrating a way of life of one of the five Plains cultural groups. Ask volunteers to display and explain their group's poster. **A, V, TK, LEP**

CLOSURE
Review with students the five groups of the Plains cultural region and their locations.

ASSESSMENT
Have students complete the Section 2 Review on page 97.

Essential Elements
1A, 1B, 7C

LONE STAR LEGACY
Using Historical Imagination:
Students' poems and songs will vary but should praise the natural environment and should be descriptive.

Answers to Section 2 Review
Define: *tepees*—movable homes made of animal skins stretched over long poles; *bands* —small groups made up of a few families; *moral code*—set of rules defining right and wrong; *Comanchería*—the land of the Comanches; *allies*—friends by treaty; *pemmican*—a mixture of dried, powdered buffalo meat, buffalo fat and juices, and powdered berries, nuts, fruits, or roots, stored in a pouch made from buffalo intestine; *rancherías* —small farming settlements

(Continued on page 97)

96 *Unit 2*

LONESTAR LEGACY

Gifts from the Native Americans

When Europeans arrived in the New World in the late fifteenth century, they caused many dramatic changes. Their advanced weapons gave them the power to control the economy and make decisions that affected the lives of Native Americans. But Native American peoples changed the lives of Europeans as well. They have contributed much to the development of today's culture.

A major contribution from people of the New World to people of the Old World was a vast supply of gold and silver. Some Native Americans gave these precious metals to Europeans, or they traded them. In Texas, Indians showed Spaniards where minerals were and willingly helped in mining. But in some places, Europeans enslaved Indians and forced them to work in dangerous mines.

Another major contribution of Native Americans was food. More than 60 percent of the food eaten in the world today is of American origin. Indians introduced Europeans to corn, squash, beans, potatoes, tomatoes, peppers, and cocoa beans (from which chocolate is made). Indians taught Europeans how to grow these crops and how to fertilize them. They also passed on to Europeans their special techniques of irrigation, terracing, and crop rotation.

One of the most valuable gifts of the Native American people was medical treat-ments previously unknown to Europeans. Indians taught them to use bacteria-fighting herbs, aspirin-like extracts from tree bark, and quinine for treating malaria.

Today, the Indian philosophy of respect for animals and the earth is affecting the way we live. It is present in our commitment to protect and conserve our environment. The Indian view of life reminds us of our responsibility to keep the air, land, and water clean and to preserve endangered animals. Perhaps this is the greatest of all Native American gifts: the idea that it is the duty of each person to preserve the world for future generations.

Using Historical Imagination
Imagine that you are an early Texas Indian. Write a poem or song praising the natural environment in which you live. Make your poem or song as descriptive as possible.

Inset: **Deerskin pouch**   Right: **Native American harvest**

Inset: Texas Memorial Museum   Right: Four By Five/Superstock

96 *Unit 2*

Past Learning and Predicting (I) Point out East Texas on a wall map. Ask students what they can recall from Chapter 3 about the climate, landforms, and soil conditions of this region. Tell students that the Southeastern Indian cultures that they will study in this section lived in East Texas. Ask: Based on what you have learned about this region, what do you think was the main economic activity of the people of the Southeastern cultural region *(farming)*?

INSTRUCTION

Vocabulary (I) You may wish to preteach the following boldfaced terms: *matrilineal* (p. 97); *confederacies* (p. 98); *crop rotation* (p. 99). **LEP**

Edwards Plateau. They depended on the buffalo for their food, clothing, and shelter just as the other Plains Indians did. However, they lived to the south of the largest buffalo herds, so at times the Tonkawas turned to other food sources for survival, including gardening agriculture.

Unlike their Plains Indians neighbors, the Tonkawas often ate fish. They also ate deer, birds, rabbits, and turtles. Rattlesnakes were a special treat. In the Central Texas area, there were many nuts, fruits, and berries available to the Tonkawas, which the northern Plains Indians did not have.

Like other Indians of the plains, the Tonkawas wore buffalo skins for clothing. The women wore short skirts and moccasins made of buffalo hide. Men and women both wore earrings and necklaces made of bone, shells, feathers, or stone. Tonkawa men were particularly fond of adorning their bodies. Some men tattooed themselves from head to toe. In the spring and summer, young children wore little or no clothing. On special occasions, the children wore bright ribbons or other ornaments.

The major enemies of the Tonkawas were the Comanches. The Tonkawas frequently fought the more powerful Comanches but were unable to compete successfully. There were only a few scattered bands of Tonkawas left in Texas when people from the United States entered the region. Those who did survive joined other Indians and settlers who tried to end Comanche control of the plains. ✪

SECTION 2 REVIEW

Define: tepees, bands, moral code, Comanchería, allies, pemmican, rancherías
Identify: Comanches, Kiowas, Lipan Apaches, Mescalero Apaches, Tonkawas

1. What source of food was common to all Plains Indian groups?
2. How did the Mescalero Apaches differ from the Lipan Apaches?
3. Which two Texas Plains groups were the most feared?

Writing Descriptively: Imagine that you are a Comanche in 1498. Write a poem or song praising the strengths and beliefs of your people.

Making Decisions: If you could belong to any Texas Plains Indian group, which would you choose? Why?

3 The Southeastern Cultural Region

The Southeastern Indian cultures in Texas lived in the eastern part of the state. East Texas is generally a land of forests, with good soil for farming. Hence, people of the Southeastern cultural region were primarily farmers. They also were **matrilineal**, which means they traced their descent only through their mothers' families.

The Southeastern cultural region included many Indian peoples beyond the borders of Texas. Other people of the Southeastern cultural region lived in the present states of Louisiana, Mississippi, and Alabama.

The Caddoes. Historians consider the Caddoes to have been the richest and most advanced of all Texas Indians.

Identify: Comanches—Plains cultural group of North and West Texas; Kiowas—Plains cultural group of the Panhandle; Lipan Apaches—Plains cultural group of southwestern Texas; Mescalero Apaches—Plains cultural group of far West Texas; Tonkawas—Plains cultural group that lived on the north central plains of Texas and the southeastern edge of the Edwards Plateau

1. Buffalo
2. The Mescalero Apaches depended less on the buffalo and at times lived in settled mountain villages.
3. Comanches, Lipan Apaches

Writing Descriptively: Writings will vary but should demonstrate knowledge of the Comanche culture.

Making Decisions: Answers will vary, but explanations should demonstrate knowledge of the cultural group chosen.

Essential Elements
1A, 1C, 9A, 9B, 9G

TEXAS VOICES
Role Playing (I) Have the class work together to stage an enactment of the Caddo dining customs detailed in "Texas Voices." **A, V, TK, LEP**

Cooperative Learning (I) Organize the class into groups of four or five, and have each group list the reasons that historians consider the Caddoes to have been the richest and most advanced of all Texas Indians. Have a spokesperson from each group read the lists aloud as you create a master list on the chalkboard. **A, V, LEP**

Essential Elements
1A, 1B, 6A

TEXAS VOICES

*C*addo society was highly developed. At the time of first contact with the Spaniards, their tribal groups numbered in the thousands. They were led by chiefs and other tribal officials. The Caddoes had social classes, and complicated religious rites conducted by full-time priests. The following account by Spanish friar Francisco Casañas gives us an idea of the Caddo dining customs around 1692:

> As the Indians always eat their meat boiled or roasted and without broth, they put it on very pretty little platters, which the women make of reeds. They take a long time to eat and while they are eating, they sing and talk and, from time to time, whistle. . . . Sport is made of those who eat but little, while those who eat to surfeiting [excess] are detested. It is a habit with them whenever they arrive at a house, never to ask for anything to eat. For it is customary to set whatever a host may have before a visitor as soon as he arrives. Before the meal, they take nothing until a portion of everything is first sent to the *caddi* [priest]. . . . The *caddi* takes something of everything and throws a portion into the fire, a portion upon the ground, and a portion to each side. Then he retires to a corner, and while all the others form ready to dance, he speaks—first to the corn, asking that it allow itself to be eaten. In the same way he talks to the other things they use. He tells the snakes not to bite, the deer not to be bitten. He then consecrates [devotes] the whole harvest of the house to God.

Texas Memorial Museum

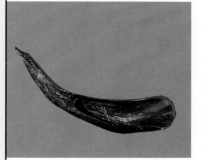

This cow horn is an artifact of early Native Americans. It was probably used as a spoon or ladle.

Their methods of farming allowed them to raise enough crops to support a large population. The Caddoes were able to trade with other people for various goods that they themselves could not produce. They built sturdy homes and produced beautiful pottery.

Caddo was the name given to three **confederacies**, or leagues, of about 25 tribal groups that lived in East Texas. A tribal group included two or more bands and had political leaders. From one of those confederacies, the Hasinai, comes the origin of the word *Texas*. The Hasinai called each other Tayshas, meaning friends or allies. Later, the Spanish referred to the Caddoes as Tayshas. The Spanish came to pronounce the word as "Tejas." The word *Tejas* was anglicized, or adapted to English, as *Texas*.

The Caddoes lived in scattered villages that stretched along the creeks and rivers of East Texas and western Louisiana. They lived in houses shaped like domes, made from tree limbs, grass, and poles. They wove colorful rugs,

Art and History (I) Organize students into small groups and ask each group to carefully plan and execute a mural depicting the way of life of each of the three Southeastern cultural groups. **V, TK, LEP**

Guided Practice (I) Refer students to the engraving on page 100. Ask them to write a detailed description of the engraving, incorporating all that they have learned about the Wichitas. Invite volunteers to read their descriptions aloud. **A, V, LEP**

baskets, wall hangings, and bedding material from reeds and tree limbs. The Caddoes were known for their useful as well as beautiful pottery.

The forests and streams of East Texas provided the Caddoes with many kinds of food—plants and animals. But the main food source of the Caddoes was corn. They were able to grow two crops of corn a year. They pounded some of the corn into flour to make bread and mixed some with other vegetables to make stew. The Caddoes wisely saved enough seed to guard against possible crop failures. Besides corn, the Caddoes grew beans, squash, sunflower seeds, and tobacco.

The Caddoes burned clearings in the forest to make more cropland. They then hoed the land. Usually, hoes were made of wood with a stone blade. Others were made from the shoulder blades of buffalo. The Caddoes used a number of modern farming methods. Among these was **crop rotation**. This means not planting the same crop in the same place two years in a row. Crop rotation helps prevent the soil from wearing out, or losing its fertility.

A practice that may have begun with the Caddoes was a method of fishing by placing bait on a series of hooks, and then stringing a line across a creek or river. The Caddoes were the first Texans to fish using this method, called a trotline.

Caddo women had the primary task of raising crops, but Caddo men helped them. (Men of most Texas Indian groups would have seen this as inappropriate.) Certain Caddo women had a strong voice in government. Their advice was sought for important decisions. They were especially respected if they were widows of important male leaders. In general, Caddo women were treated with more dignity than women were in other Indian societies.

The Caddoes had some customs that other people might regard as strange. When first meeting the Caddoes, people were usually startled by their actions. Members of the culture greeted outsiders with tears and wailing noises that sounded like crying. Their appearance also surprised strangers. In addition to binding children's heads to make them longer and narrower, the Caddo people wore many tattoos. Tattoos on faces were especially popular.

The Caddoes were a friendly people. They were also known among the Spaniards and other Indians as willing and smart traders. They traded regularly with other Indians,

Western History Collections, University of Oklahoma Library

This Indian man is dressed in clothes made of buffalo hide.

Answers to Section 3 Review

Define: *matrilineal*—descent traced through a mother's family; *confederacies*—leagues of tribal groups; *crop rotation*—alternating crops grown from year to year to avoid wearing out the soil

Identify: Caddoes—agricultural cultural group located in central East Texas; Atakapans—cultural group of mixed hunters and farmers who lived between the Caddoes and the Gulf of Mexico; Wichitas—cultural group that lived west of the Caddoes along the Red River

1. They were primarily farmers and had more complicated societies than most of the cultures immediately to their west.

(Continued on page 101)

especially those of the plains, who needed forest products. In return, the Caddoes received such things as flint and turquoise. These they used to make tools and weapons.

The Atakapans. Between the Caddoes and the Gulf of Mexico lived a people known as the Atakapans. Their homeland extended from Galveston Island to the Sabine River and into parts of Louisiana. The Atakapans had some of the same cultural links to the southeast as the Caddoes. Some Atakapans lived inland from the Gulf of Mexico on land that was suitable for farming. These people were able to grow good crops of corn. Other members of this group lived on marshy swampland. This land was subject to flooding by salt water, so farming on it was not successful. Overall, the Atakapans were not as advanced in farming as the Caddoes.

To add to their diet, the Atakapans hunted wild game and gathered nuts and berries. They also did a great deal of fishing. Often they ventured along the Gulf coast in canoes to gather shellfish. Alligators were a part of their diet. The Atakapans also took a natural fat from alligators they killed. They rubbed this on their bodies to keep off mosquitoes. Aside from their eating and hunting habits, however, little else is known about the Atakapans.

The Wichitas. Living west of the Caddoes along the Red River were the Wichitas. *Wichita* was the common name given to four different tribal groups. These four were

George Catlin was a famous American western artist of the nineteenth century. In this engraving, he shows a Wichita village along the Red River in the 1870s.

Institute of Texan Cultures

CLOSURE
Review the names of the Southeastern Indian cultures and their location. Invite volunteers to provide one or two facts about each of the three groups.

ASSESSMENT
Have students complete the Section 3 Review on page 101.

SECTION 4

FOCUS
Past Learning (I) Ask students to name the Five Themes of Geography that they learned about in Chapter 1. Tell students to keep these themes in mind as they study Section 4.

INSTRUCTION
Vocabulary (I) You may wish to preteach the following boldfaced terms: *javelinas* (p. 104); *mitotes* (p. 104). **LEP**

the Wacos, the Taovayas, the Tawakonis, and the Wichitas. Originally from Kansas and Nebraska, the Wichitas moved into north central Texas in the late 1600s. Some Wichitas lived as far south as the present city of Waco.

The Wichitas had striking features. Like most other Texas Indians, they tattooed their bodies. But the Wichitas used more tattoos and unusual designs. Women tattooed many parts of their bodies. They drew circles around their mouths, adding lines extending from the lower lip to the chin. Men had tattooed eyelids, with a short horizontal line drawn out from the corner of each eye. For this reason, they called themselves "raccoon-eyed."

In many ways, the Wichitas (another matrilineal group) lived much like others of the Southeastern culture. They lived in villages along creeks and rivers. Their homes were similar to those of the Caddoes, and they grew many of the same foods, including corn, squash, and beans.

Yet the Wichitas were different from the Southeastern cultures in two ways. Like the Plains Indians, they hunted buffalo, and they did not eat fish. For these reasons, the Wichitas were part of two different cultures.

Like some other tribes, the Wichitas were threatened by the Comanches. Eventually the Comanches ended the Wichita control of the Red River area. War and diseases brought by the Europeans also greatly reduced the population of the Wichitas. ✪

◢ The Western Gulf Cultural Region

Waters of the western Gulf of Mexico wash along the coast of Texas. Land along the water is flat or gently rolling. This land was home to two cultures of Texas Indians, the Karankawas and the Coahuiltecans.

The Karankawas. A people known as the Karankawas lived from the Galveston area south to Corpus Christi. Because they lived near the sea, they had early contacts with European explorers. The explorers left behind many accounts of the Karankawas.

The first Spanish sailors to land on the Texas coast were greeted warmly by the Karankawas. The Spaniards reported that the Karankawa women were very beautiful. They wore deerskin skirts. They also draped strands of Spanish moss about their shoulders. The Karankawa men

SECTION ★3★ REVIEW

Define: matrilineal, confederacies, crop rotation
Identify: Caddoes, Atakapans, Wichitas

1. What did the Indian cultures of the Southeastern region have in common?
2. What is the origin of the word *Texas*?
3. How did the Caddoes differ from other Indian societies in their treatment of women?
4. In what ways were the Atakapans similar to the Caddoes?
5. How were the Wichitas similar to other Texas Indians? How were they different?

Evaluating Information: Which Southeastern cultural group would you rather live among? Explain your choice.

Exploring Multicultural Perspectives: If you could have been a Texas Indian, how would you have dressed and decorated your body? Describe in detail.

Daughters of the Republic of Texas Library

Early Texas artist Theodore Gentilz captured the spirit of a proud Wichita woman in this drawing.

2. The word comes from the Caddo term *Tejas,* meaning "friends."
3. Women were treated with more respect among the Caddoes than they were in other Indian societies.
4. They were agriculturalists and had many common customs.
5. Similar—They tattooed their bodies and lived in settled agricultural villages. Different—They hunted buffalo and did not eat fish.

Evaluating Information: Answers will vary, but explanations should demonstrate knowledge of the cultural group chosen.

Exploring Multicultural Perspectives: Answers will vary, but descriptions or pictures should be detailed and based on information in the textbook.

Essential Elements
1A, 1B, 1C, 6A, 9A, 9B

Geography (II) Refer students to the Focus activity in which they named the Five Themes of Geography. Ask: That the Karankawas and the Coahuiltecans expertly adapted to their environments falls under the category of which theme *(relationships within places)*? Ask students to provide two examples of how the Karankawas and the Coahuiltecans adapted to their environments. **A**

Multicultural Perspective (I) Have the students write in note form an account of a day in their life. Tell them to include information such as the foods they eat, the people they see, the places they go, the work that they must do, and so on. Then ask them to imagine themselves as a member of either the Karankawa or Coahuiltecan culture and write an account of a day in their life. Ask students whether the lives of these Texas Indians seem harsh in comparison to their own. **A, LEP**

Guided Practice (I) Have students work in pairs to create a list of the resources that the Karankawas and the Coahuiltecans depended on for survival. Collect the lists and create a master list on the chalkboard. **LEP**

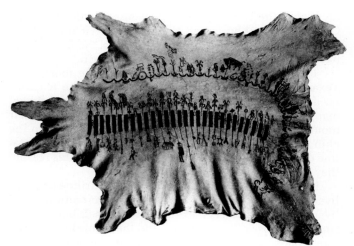

National Anthropological Archives, Smithsonian

Caption Response
Answers will vary but could include the major events in village life over a period of time.

Many buffalo hides were painted with scenes of Indian life. What do you think the artist was representing on this hide?

Texas Archeological Research Laboratory

Some Texas Indian groups, especially the Caddoes, were skilled at making pottery such as this bowl.

were reported to be tall and muscular. They brightly painted their bodies, but they wore no clothing. Some of the men pierced their lower lips and chests with short spears from stalks of sugarcane. They wore these as further decoration. All of the Karankawas rubbed alligator fat over their bodies to keep away insects.

The Karankawas wandered the bays and inlets along the coast, fishing, hunting sea turtles, and collecting shellfish. They traveled in dugout canoes, pushing them through the water with long wooden poles. Hunters carried long bows made of cedar. They made bow strings from the tendons of deer. To the Karankawas, the bow and arrow was as important for fishing as for hunting game. They also ate oysters, clams, scallops, and turtles.

The Karankawas were nomads. They traveled in small bands of no more than 30–40 people. Their homes were a clever combination of wooden hut and tepee. A frame was made of willow poles tied together as in a tepee. Animal skins and woven grass were draped over the poles. These houses could be put up or taken down quickly. To do this was important to a people always on the move.

Karankawa women were in charge of setting up and taking down the houses. They also gathered firewood, cooked meals, and carried out other jobs that were necessary to running the camps.

EXTENSION
Community Involvement (II) Have students contact the local or state historical society as well as the public library to research the Indian cultural groups who originally settled in their area. Students should present the information they gather in oral reports to the class. **A, G**

Independent Practice (I) Have students draw pictures to create collages illustrating the separate roles of women and men in the Karankawa cultural group. Display the finished collages in the classroom. **V, TK, LEP**

European reports tell of the special way Karankawas treated their children. A Spanish explorer remarked that the Karankawas "love their offspring the most of any in the world, and treat them with the greatest mildness." Small children were carried around either by mother or by father on specially made cradle boards.

Children were given two names. One name was used in public and known by everyone. The other name was a secret known only by the child's closest family members. The second name was thought to carry important magic. This magic was meant to protect children from danger while they were growing up.

Contact with European diseases greatly reduced the number of Karankawas. Warfare with settlers and other Indians eventually wiped out the remaining ones.

Thomas Gilcrease Institute of American History & Art

Lino Sánchez y Tapia painted these Karankawas fishing gracefully with a bow and arrow.

Ask students to write a paragraph comparing and contrasting the ways of life of the Karankawas and the Coahuiltecans. **LEP**

CLOSURE

Review the location of the Western Gulf cultural region and significant characteristics of the Karankawa and the Coahuiltecan cultural groups.

ASSESSMENT

Have students complete the Section 4 Review on page 104.

SECTION 5

FOCUS

Past Learning and Predicting (I) Use a wall map to point out the far western and southwestern areas of Texas. Ask students to provide adjectives to describe this region of the state. Then ask them to speculate about the way of life of the Indian groups of this area.

Answers to Section 4 Review

Define: *javelinas*—species of wild pig common to southwest Texas; *mitotes*—all-night celebrations held by the Coahuiltecans
Identify: Karankawas—nomadic hunters and gatherers who lived along the Texas coast; Coahuiltecans—hunters and gatherers who lived in the dry brush country of South Texas

1. They treated their children with great gentleness and kindness.
2. They both ate wild game. The Karankawas ate seafood and turtles. The Coahuiltecans ate cactus, mesquite beans, lizards, ant eggs, spiders, and grubworms.

Exploring Multicultural Perspectives: Letters will vary, but descriptions should be detailed and accurate.

Exploring Geography: The Karankawas lived along the coast, while the Coahuiltecans lived farther inland in the dry brush country of South Texas.

Essential Elements
1A, 1C, 5B, 6B, 9A, 9E

SECTION ★4★ REVIEW

Define: javelinas, mitotes
Identify: Karankawas, Coahuiltecans

1. How were the Karankawas special in the way they treated their children?
2. Which food did the Karankawas and Coahuiltecans have in common? Which of their foods differed?

Exploring Multicultural Perspectives: Imagine that you are a Spanish sailor landed on the western Gulf region of Texas. Write a letter to your governor, describing an Indian group that you meet.

Exploring Geography: Why did the Karankawas eat mainly fish and shellfish while the Coahuiltecans ate things such as cacti, lizards, and grubworms?

The Coahuiltecans. Living in the dry brush country of South Texas were various hunting and gathering groups, some of whom shared a common language. They are often identified as Coahuiltecans.

Today the land of South Texas supports ranching and farming. But most farming in the region is impossible without irrigation. The Coahuiltecans neither farmed nor tamed animals. By our standards today, they had a simple culture and a harsh and difficult life. But the Coahuiltecans adapted well to the land.

Wildlife was sparse on the South Texas plains. The Coahuiltecans did hunt some deer, antelope, rabbits, and **javelinas**, a type of wild pig. But they gathered most of their food from the land. The Coahuiltecans ate many foods that we might not find very appealing. They ate cacti, mesquite beans, nuts, and bulbs of the agave plant. When plant foods were scarce, they ate lizards, ant eggs, spiders, snakes, and grubworms.

Coahuiltecans sometimes held all-night celebrations called **mitotes**. These often combined feasting, dancing, and the celebrating of important events. Mitotes sometimes celebrated a special religious occasion or gave thanks for a plentiful supply of food. Celebrations were held when young women or men became adults. Often, one group of Coahuiltecans hosted another group that came to visit.

The Coahuiltecans were a strong people known for their endurance. They knew every detail of their homeland, and doing so enabled them to survive. ✪

⑤ The Pueblo Cultural Region

Two Texas Indian groups trace their culture back to the Pueblos of New Mexico and Arizona. These were the Jumanos and the Conchos. They lived in the far western and southwestern parts of Texas.

The Jumanos. Texas Indians were able to adapt to every type of environment of the vast land. The Jumanos lived in the dry and rugged area near the present city of El Paso. Jumanos lived along the Rio Grande all the way to the Big Bend region. Most Jumanos' settlements were close to the Rio Grande. Their homes were built of **adobe** bricks. These were bricks made by drying clay mud in the sun. Adobe helped to **insulate** the homes, or keep them

Paul M. Montgomery

The Jumanos lived along the Rio Grande in West Texas. They often faced difficulty surviving in this desert region with its hot, dry climate.

Geography
The Rio Grande linked the Jumanos with the Pueblo cultures of New Mexico.

cool in summer and warm in winter. The Jumano homes were one story and had flat roofs.

As was the case with other Texas Indians who lived in villages, the Jumanos farmed for most of their food. They grew corn, squash, beans, and other vegetables. Like some other horticultural tribes, they were matrilineal.

The Jumanos lived in an area where farming was often difficult. Droughts were common. There was seldom enough rain to support crops. When the Rio Grande had plenty of water, the Jumanos may have dug irrigation ditches in order to water their fields. When the Rio Grande had little or no water, the Jumanos had to find other sources of food. They ate plants that survive dry weather, such as prickly pears and mesquite beans. The Jumanos also hunted what small game they could find.

In general, the Jumanos were a peaceful people. Yet for some time they fought with Apaches who entered Jumano

Book Report (III) Ask interested students to read and present an oral report of W.W. Newcomb's *The Indians of Texas*. **A, G**

Environment (I) Display a picture of an adobe home to the class. Ask students if they can suggest other types of homes or elements of homes that are designed with the environment in mind. *(Suggestions might include log homes, homes built into the earth, skylights, solar heating, and so on.)* **A, V, LEP**

Guided Practice (I) Organize students into pairs or small groups and ask them to use the information in Section 5 to illustrate on a large sheet of paper a Jumano settlement. Illustrations should be detailed and include significant landforms and water features, homes, farms, and irrigation ditches. Display the completed drawings in the classroom. **V, TK, LEP**

Essential Elements
1A, 1B, 1C, 6A

SPIRIT OF TEXAS

W.W. Newcomb and the Jumanos

Anthropologist W.W. Newcomb, Jr. studied early Indian life for his classic book on Native Americans, *The Indians of Texas*. In his research, Newcomb often sought descriptions written by early Spanish explorers about their encounters with American Indians.

These primary source accounts are not unbiased. Like most people, the Spaniards judged strangers from their own personal and cultural viewpoints. But the accounts give anthropologists such as Newcomb the only evidence they have about the cultures of some groups.

The Jumanos of the Rio Grande valley are an example. Gradually absorbed into other groups, they had disappeared as a people by the mid eighteenth century. From reports of early explorers like the following, Newcomb and other scholars see the Jumanos as they were then.

Diego Pérez de Luxán noted in 1582:

> Upon our arrival there came to us in procession and singing more than 200 Indians, men and women, from the same Otomoacos nation. They presented us with shawls, tanned deerskins, mescal, and ornaments like bonnets with colored feathers, which they said they obtained from the direction of the sea.

In 1581, Hernán Gallegos wrote about the Jumanos in the same cultural region:

> Standing on top of their houses they showed great merriment on seeing us. These houses resemble those of the Mexicans, except that they are made of paling [vertical poles]. They build them square. They put up the bases and upon these they place timbers, the thickness of a man's thigh. Then they add the pales, and plaster them with mud.

Gallegos noted the appearance of the Jumanos as "very clean, handsome and warlike," and Diego Pérez de Luxán described them this way:

> The men have their hair cut very short, up to the middle of their heads, and from there up they leave it two fingers long and curl it with minium [red lead] paint in such a way that it resembles a small cap. They leave on the crown a large lock of hair to which they fasten feathers of white and black birds.

As Newcomb notes, "the sixteenth-century Spanish expeditions were treated with ceremony and pomp." For example, as Gallegos wrote, when his party arrived at a Jumano settlement that the Spaniards called San Bernardino:

> All the people came down within half an hour, making musical sounds with their mouths similar to those of the flute. They kissed the hand of the Father called Fray Bernardino, whom we had along. . . . They made music by beating their hands while sitting around a big fire. They sing, and in time with the singing they dance.

Illustration by Hal M. Story from W.W. Newcomb, Jr., *The Indians of Texas: From Prehistoric to Modern Times*, copyright © 1961 by the University of Texas Press. By permission of the publisher.

RETEACHING
Ask students to close their textbooks and write a brief summary of Section 5. Invite volunteers to read their summaries aloud as the class corrects any misinformation. **A, LEP**

CLOSURE
Use a wall map to review the location of the Pueblo cultural region and its two Texas Indian cultural groups.

ASSESSMENT
Have students complete the Section 5 Review on page 107.

Texas Memorial Museum, Courtesy of Mrs. Ralph A. Bickler

This painting by early Texas artist Friedrich Richard Petri shows a Plains Indian family riding a horse and a mule.

land. Eventually, the Jumanos became allies of the Apaches and later joined them as a tribal group. Many Jumano settlements had already been abandoned when the first Spanish explorers arrived. The reason may have been frequent droughts. By the nineteenth century, there was little that remained of the Jumanos.

The Conchos. A group closely linked to the Jumanos was the Conchos. Their way of life was very similar to that of their neighbors. The Conchos, however, are believed to have done more hunting than farming in order to survive. Less is known about the Conchos than about the Jumanos. By the end of the 1600s, all traces of the Conchos had disappeared. Most historians believe that they joined and became part of the Jumanos. ✪

SECTION ⑤ REVIEW

Define: adobe, insulate
Identify: Jumanos, Conchos

1. What are two ways in which the Jumanos solved the problems of surviving in a hot, dry climate?
2. What is a likely reason that the Conchos disappeared?
3. In what ways were the Conchos similar to the Jumanos? How were they different?

Using Historical Imagination: If you were an explorer and found an abandoned Jumano settlement, what conclusions might you draw about the Jumanos? What evidence would lead you to these conclusions?

Seeing Cause and Effect: Why did Indian groups who farmed for a living also usually live in villages?

Answers to Section 5 Review
Define: *adobe*—building material made from sun-dried mud; *insulate*—to protect from heat and cold
Identify: Jumanos—agricultural cultural group who lived along the Rio Grande in southwest Texas; Conchos—cultural group similar to the Jumanos but more dependent on hunting than farming
1. They practiced irrigation farming and built houses with thick walls of adobe brick.
2. They may have become part of the Jumano cultural group.
3. Like the Jumanos, the Conchos were farmers and their general way of life was similar. They differed in that hunting was more important than farming to the Conchos.

Using Historical Imagination: Answers will vary, but it is evident that the Jumanos were an advanced cultural group that built substantial houses and may have practiced irrigation farming.

Seeing Cause and Effect: Farming required people to establish permanent villages nearby so that they could tend their fields and store their agricultural produce.

CHAPTER REVIEW RESOURCES

1. Chapter Review Worksheet 5
2. Chapter 5 Test, Form A
3. Reteaching Worksheet 5
4. Chapter 5 Test, Form B
5. **Informal Evaluation Forms:** Portfolio Assessment
6. *Texas, Our Texas* **Test Generator**

Essential Elements
1A, 6A, 9A, 9B, 9E, 9G

CHAPTER 5 REVIEW ANSWERS

Understanding Main Ideas

1. Plains culture, Southeastern culture, Western Gulf culture, Pueblo culture
2. Comanches, Kiowas, Lipan Apaches, Mescalero Apaches, Tonkawas
3. Answers will vary but should demonstrate knowledge of the Indian groups of the West Texas plains.
4. They were the Caddoes, Atakapans, and Wichitas. Each group practiced agriculture to some degree. The Caddoes were more advanced in farming. All three groups were, in part, hunters and gatherers.
5. They were the Karankawas and Coahuiltecans. While both groups were hunters and gatherers, the Karankawas lived along the coast and depended on coastal species of plants and animals. The Coahuiltecans lived inland in the dry brush country of South Texas. They had to eat almost anything to survive in this harsh environment.
6. They were the Jumanos and Conchos. Their ways of life were generally similar, but hunting was much more important to the Conchos.

CHAPTER 5 REVIEW

Understanding Main Ideas

1. What were the four Indian cultural regions of Texas?
2. Which Indian cultural groups lived on the West Texas plains?
3. Compare and contrast the cultures of two or more Indian groups of the West Texas plains.
4. Which Native American cultural groups lived in the eastern part of Texas? How were their ways of life similar and different?
5. Which Indian cultural groups lived near the western Gulf of Mexico? How were their ways of life similar and different?
6. Which two Native American cultural groups lived in far western and southwestern Texas? How did their ways of life compare?

Thinking Critically

1. **Seeing Cause and Effect:** In what ways did the physical region of Texas in which an Indian group lived determine the foods that the group ate? Give two examples.
2. **Predicting Consequences:** If you were a Texas Plains Indian and all the buffalo suddenly became scarce, what do you think would happen to your people? Explain.
3. **Evaluating Information:** If you could be a member of any Texas Indian culture in the late 1400s, which would you choose? Why?

Linking History and Geography

1. Give examples of two cultural groups who adapted to different Texas environments. Explain how they did this.
2. Why do you think Texas was the home of such a large number of very different cultural groups?

TAAS *Practice*
Using Primary Sources

N. Scott Momaday is a nationally respected writer and a winner of the Pulitzer Prize. He also is a Kiowa. In the following excerpt from his book *The Way to Rainy Mountain*, he retells an old Kiowa story:

Once there was a man and his wife. They were alone at night in their tepee. By the light of the fire the man was making arrows. After a while he caught sight of something. There was a small opening in the tepee where two hides were sewn together. Someone was there on the outside, looking in. The man went on with his work, but he said to his wife, "Someone is standing outside. Do not be afraid. Let us talk easily, as of ordinary things." He took up an arrow and straightened it in his teeth; then, as it was right for him to do, he drew it to the bow and took aim, first in this direction and then in that. And all the while he was talking, as if to his wife. But this is how he spoke: "I know that you are there on the outside, for I can feel your eyes upon me. If you are a Kiowa, you will understand what I am saying, and you will speak your name." But there was no answer, and the man went on in the same way, pointing the arrow all around. At last his aim fell upon the place where his enemy stood, and he let go of the string. The arrow went straight to the enemy's heart.

Thinking Critically

1. **Seeing Cause and Effect:** The climate and environment of a region determined what plant and animal foods were available. Examples might include the following: Western tribes hunted buffalo, but rain was generally inadequate for agriculture. Eastern tribes practiced agriculture because water was available, but buffalo as a food source was not available.

2. **Predicting Consequences:** The cultural group would probably become nomadic and go in search of the buffalo herds that moved around. Permanent scarcity of buffalo would require a complete change in the group's way of life.

3. **Evaluating Information:** Answers will vary, but explanations should demonstrate knowledge of the Indian culture chosen.

Linking History and Geography

1. Answers will vary but should demonstrate knowledge of the cultural groups chosen and of the geography of the regions in which the cultural groups lived.
2. Texas is large and has many diverse environments. Cultural groups developed different ways of life in order to adapt to their environments.

TAAS Practice
Using Primary Sources

1. B
2. C

TAAS Practice
Writing Descriptively

Descriptions will vary but should demonstrate knowledge of the Comanche culture.

Practicing Skills

1. **Interpreting Pictures:** Buffalo hides, buffalo horns, wooden poles
2. **Classifying Information:** Charts will vary but should include detailed information from Chapter 5.

Enriching Your Study of History

1. **Individual Project:** Drawings will vary but should demonstrate knowledge of the cultural group chosen.
2. **Cooperative Project:** Team projects will vary but should demonstrate knowledge of the assigned cultural region.

Name of Cultural Region _____ Plains _____				
Name of Cultural Group	Major Source of Food	Type of Home	Way of Life	Region of Texas
Kiowas	buffalo, other hunting	tepee	nomadic	North Texas plains

1. Judging from the outcome of the story, the man and his wife were
   A both frightened by the outsider
   B both Kiowas
   C neither very clever
   D neither Kiowas
2. The man knew that the outsider was an enemy when
   A he shot the outsider with his newly made arrow
   B he caught sight of someone outside his tepee
   C the outsider failed to speak his name to the man
   D the man pretended to be speaking to his wife

TAAS Practice
Writing Descriptively

Imagine that you are an early Spanish explorer seeing a band of Comanches for the first time. In your diary, write a description of the Comanche group and your reaction to them.

Practicing Skills

1. **Interpreting Pictures:** Look at the photographs of the Comanche man on page 91 and the Comanche camp on page 92. Judging from what you have read in Chapter 5 about the Comanches, list the materials that were likely used to make the clothing, the tepees, and the other objects in the pictures.
2. **Classifying Information:** Make four charts like you see on this page, one for each of the four cultural regions of Texas. Fill in the blanks, using information from Chapter 5. A sample is done for you.

Enriching Your Study of History

1. **Individual Project:** Draw a picture of a person, or persons, from any of the Texas Indian cultural groups. Use a description in Chapter 5 to guide your illustration.
2. **Cooperative Project:** Your teacher will organize your class into four teams and assign each team a Texas cultural region. Your team will create an imaginary Indian group from your assigned region. Give a report to the class, telling the name of your group; their food, housing, and clothing; their special customs and beliefs; and what geographic factors most influence their culture.

UNIT REVIEW RESOURCES

1. Unit Review Worksheet 2
2. Unit 2 Test, Form A
3. Reteaching Worksheet 2
4. Unit 2 Test, Form B
5. **Informal Evaluation Forms:** Portfolio Assessment
6. *Texas, Our Texas* **Test Generator**

Essential Elements
1A, 1B, 5B, 5C, 6A, 6B, 9A, 9B, 9C, 9E

UNIT 2 REVIEW ANSWERS

Connecting Main Ideas

1. Archaeologists learn by digging up artifacts. Historians use the knowledge gained from scientists and scholars.
2. People settled in villages, people lived longer, the population increased, and architecture developed.
3. Because the landscape and climate of Texas is varied, many different cultural groups settled there.
4. Answers will vary but should demonstrate detailed knowledge of each cultural group.
5. The Europeans brought disease, killed many Indians, and forced many Indians off their land.

Practicing Critical Thinking Skills

1. **Synthesizing Information:** Answers will vary but should be supported by sound reasoning.
2. **Seeing Cause and Effect:** Answers will vary but should demonstrate detailed knowledge of the relationship between the region's physical geography and the cultures found there.
3. **Exploring Multicultural Perspectives:** Answers will vary but should demonstrate detailed knowledge of the Native American way of life.

UNIT 2

REVIEW

Connecting Main Ideas

1. How do archaeologists learn about prehistory? How do historians learn about the past?
2. What effect did the development of agriculture have on the early cultures?
3. Why is Texas a cultural crossroads?
4. Compare the ways in which Indians from two different cultural regions met their needs for food and shelter.
5. What impact did the arrival of Europeans have on Texas Indians?

Practicing Critical Thinking Skills

1. **Synthesizing Information:** Of the Native American cultural groups discussed in Unit 2, which do you find the most interesting? Why?
2. **Seeing Cause and Effect:** Choose one of the four Indian cultural regions, and explain how its geography affected the cultures of Native Americans.
3. **Exploring Multicultural Perspectives:** Imagine that you are a Native American in Texas when the first Europeans arrive. Tell how these people appear to you, and predict how you think they will affect your way of life in the future.

TAAS Practice
Writing Descriptively

Imagine that you are an archaeologist. You have just uncovered an important group of artifacts in your area. Describe several artifacts, and explain what you think they reveal about prehistoric peoples.

Exploring Local History

1. Look again at the map on page 90. What group or groups of Texas Indians once lived in your community? What evidence of Indian life exists there today (museums, historical sites)?
2. Ask parents or guardians, and adult friends: "How do the climate and landscape of the area in which you live influence your way of life (job, transportation, type of housing, type of clothing, type of food, customs)?" Write a brief report of their answers.

Using Historical Imagination

1. **Individual Project:** Research your favorite Texas Indian group and prepare an illustrated report on its customs.
2. **Cooperative Project:** With a partner, create a cave painting that shows aspects of Texas Indian life. Before you begin, discuss what you wish to show and the meaning of your illustration.

For Extending Your Knowledge

Newcomb, W.W. Jr. *The Indians of Texas: From Prehistoric to Modern Times.* Austin: University of Texas Press, 1965. The best overview of prehistoric and early Texas Indian cultures.

Turner, Ellen Sue and Thomas R. Hester. *A Field Guide to Stone Artifacts of Texas Indians.* Austin: Texas Monthly Press, 1985. A well-illustrated guide.

Wallace, Ernest and E.A. Hoebel. *The Comanches, Lords of the South Plains.* Norman, Oklahoma: University of Oklahoma Press, 1952. An excellent account of Comanche lifeways.

Writing Descriptively

Answers will vary but should demonstrate knowledge of how we can learn from artifacts.

Exploring Local History

1. Answers will vary but should demonstrate research of local history.
2. Reports will vary but should be clear and should demonstrate an understanding of the correlation between geography and way of life.

Using Historical Imagination

1. **Individual Project:** Reports will vary but should demonstrate detailed knowledge of the Indian group chosen.
2. **Cooperative Project:** Paintings will vary but should accurately illustrate an aspect of Indian life.

SKILL LESSON

Analyzing Information

To analyze information means first to break it apart into bits and pieces. These pieces can be facts and opinions, time sequences, or causes and effects. Like the pieces of a jigsaw puzzle, the pieces that result from your analyzing, or your *analysis*, must be put back together. Like a historian, you put the pieces together to reveal their relationships to each other and to the whole.

How to Analyze Information

Read the material carefully. The best way to understand what you are reading is to look for main ideas and details that support the main ideas. After a careful reading of the whole, you are ready to begin your analysis.

Ask yourself questions. Ask *who, what, when* and *where*. Ask *how*, if it is appropriate. And always ask *why*.

Separate fact from opinion. Facts can be observed and proven. They usually can be checked in one or more sources. Opinions are beliefs that may or may not be observed or proved. Certain words or phrases often precede opinions in history writing. Examples of these phrases are: *It is believed, It appears that, It seems to show.*

Search for bias. Facts can be used in such a way that they present a one-sided view. Be alert to words, phrases, or facts that support only a single viewpoint when it seems clear that more than one is possible.

Check for cause-effect relationships. Look for clue words, which indicate that part of a passage states a cause and another part states an effect. Also remember that a cause may be stated separately from its effect.

Come to a conclusion. After you assemble the bits and pieces, do something with them. Use them to draw a conclusion or form a generalization.

Practicing the Skill

Read the following excerpt from *Comanches* by historian T.R. Fehrenbach. Apply the instructions on this page. Then answer the questions that follow.

This Afro-Asian Spanish horse was a small, unlovely beast.... But no horseflesh on earth could have been better suited to the arid and semiarid mesas and grasslands of North America. Here, the mustang thrived under conditions that killed more delicately bred animals.... Because it was not impressive or beautiful in European horsemen's eyes, then and later many men discounted the Spanish mustang's performance, not understanding the breed's almost perfect symbiosis [blending] with its new environment. More than any other horse, the mustang was suited to the great bison range that ran from Canada to Texas, for the Iberian [Spanish] animal flourished in this land as well as the native buffalo.

1. What is the main idea of this paragraph?
2. What details support the main idea?
3. What cause-effect relationship is stated in the paragraph?
4. What conclusion or generalization does the author make?
5. Do you detect any bias? Explain.

Skill Lesson
Practicing the Skill

1. That the mustang is well suited to the environment of North America
2. Possible answers include: "no horseflesh on earth could have been better suited to the arid and semiarid mesas and grasslands of North America"; "the mustang thrived"; "the breed's almost perfect symbiosis with its new environment."
3. The mustang was well suited to the environment and therefore flourished.
4. Mustangs are perfectly suited to North America.
5. Answers will vary but should be supported with passages from the excerpt.

INTRODUCING THE UNIT

Connecting with Past Learning

Review with students the many Indian cultures that had developed in Texas before the arrival of the Europeans. Ask: How do you think the arrival of the Europeans would affect these cultures? How would the United States react to a similar arrival of "explorers" today? Why?

MOTIVATOR

Read the definition of *empire* to students (page 114). Ask them to imagine building an empire, and pose the following questions: Why would a country want to create an empire? What would be the benefits of establishing an empire? What would be the problems of maintaining an empire? Tell students to keep this discussion in mind as they read about the Spanish empire in the New World.

UNIT 3 OVERVIEW

Unit 3 focuses on the Spanish presence in Texas. Chapter 6 discusses Spanish exploration of the Americas and examines the reasons behind Spanish interest in Texas. It identifies significant explorers and the results of their expeditions.

Chapter 7 details Spanish plans for settling Texas and discusses the goals, problems, and achievements of the Spanish mission system. Spanish influences on Texas history are introduced.

Chapter 8 describes the changes in Spanish policy in Texas after 1760 and introduces the international events that influenced these changes. The chapter examines the challenges facing New Spain as it struggled to strengthen its control of Texas. The unit concludes with the overthrow of the Spanish government and Mexican independence.

UNIT 3
EXPLORATION AND SETTLEMENT

Materials Available at the Unit Level:
Unit 3 Making Global Connections
Oral History Handbook
Informal Evaluation Forms

TEXAS AND THE WORLD

Organize the class into small groups and direct them to the time line on this page. Ask each group to choose one world event on the time line and brainstorm about how that event might be related to events in Texas. Have a spokesperson from each group share the group's conclusions.

hristopher Columbus bids farewell to Queen Isabella and King Ferdinand of Spain in the painting opposite. After two months at sea, Rodrigo de Triana, a lookout, sighted land on October 12, 1492. Columbus, an Italian explorer sailing for Spain, went ashore on San Salvador with his crew and claimed the land in the name of the king and queen.

Columbus sailed west from Europe, hoping to find a water route to Asia. When he landed on the island he named San Salvador, he believed he had found that part of Asia called India. It was about fifteen years before Europeans realized that this land was not Asia, but the Americas. Other explorers had found America before Columbus, but it was his voyage that began an age of exploration. Less than 30 years later, European explorers were sailing along the coast of Texas.

The European exploration of Texas leading to colonization is the subject of Unit 3. Chapter 6 discusses Spanish and French exploration of Texas. Chapter 7 covers the period of Spanish settlement and control. Chapter 8 takes the story to the time when Texas, as part of Mexico, broke away from Spanish control. The chapters in Unit 3 tell an exciting tale of adventure, centered around events that helped shape the Texas of today.

UNIT 3 OBJECTIVES

1. Discuss the conquistadores and their conquest of New Spain.
2. Identify major Spanish expeditions into Texas and their results.
3. Explain the Spanish mission system and the Spaniards' reasons for establishing settlements in Texas.
4. Identify international and internal events leading to changes in Spanish policy in Texas.
5. Describe Spanish life in Texas and its impact on the history and culture of Texas.
6. Discuss major rebellions in Texas that challenged Spain's control of the region, and identify key figures.
7. Identify events leading to Mexican independence in 1821, which ended Spain's control of Mexico and Texas.

TEXAS EVENTS

1519 Piñeda explores Texas coast

1528 Cabeza de Vaca lands on Texas coast

1540 Coronado expedition

1601 Oñate expedition

1682 Ysleta mission founded

1685 La Salle lands in Texas

1718 San Antonio de Béxar founded

1767 Rubí tour of Texas

1795–1820 Filibusters invade Texas

1821 Texas becomes part of Mexico

1500   1550   1600   1650   1700   1750   1800   1850

1492 Columbus' voyage to America

1519 Cortés invades Mexico

1539 Search for Seven Cities of Cíbola

1607 English settlement of North America begins

1608 French settlement begins

1762 Louisiana given to Spain

1776 U.S. declares independence

1800 Spain returns Louisiana to France

1803 U.S. buys Louisiana

1821 Mexico declares independence

1819 Adams–Oñis Treaty signed

WORLD EVENTS

THE QUEST FOR EMPIRE

		TEACHER'S TIME LINE		
Section 1 Pp. 114–17 1 Day	**Section 2** Pp. 117–19 1 Day	**Section 3** Pp. 119–23 1 Day	**Sections 3–4** Pp. 123–28 1 Day	**Review and Assessment** 1 Day

★ TEACHER MATERIALS

Core: Chapter 6 Time Line; Graphic Organizer 6; Enrichment Worksheet 6; Review Worksheet 6; Reteaching Worksheet 6; Chapter 6 Tests, Forms A & B

Additional: Geography and Graph Skills 6, Map and Chart Transparencies 10, Informal Evaluation Forms, Test Generator

★ OBJECTIVES

1. List reasons for Spanish exploration of Texas.
2. Identify the Spanish explorers in Texas.
3. Explain the significance of various Spanish expeditions in Texas.
4. Describe the relationship between the Indians living in Texas and the Spanish explorers.
5. Discuss the results of Spanish exploration in Texas.

★ RESOURCES

BOOKS FOR TEACHERS

Cabeza de Vaca, Alvar Núñez. *Adventures in the Unknown Interior of America.* New York: Collier Books, 1961. Commentaries on his encounters in the South.

Castañeda, Pedro de. *The Journey of Coronado, 1540–1542.* Golden: Fulcrum Publishing, 1991. Account of Coronado's expeditions in the Southwest.

Columbus, Christopher. *Across the Ocean Sea: A Journal of Columbus' Voyage.* New York: Harper and Row, 1966. Primary source.

Díaz del Castillo, Bernal. *The Bernal Díaz Chronicles: The True Story of the Conquest of Mexico.* Garden City: Doubleday, 1956. Primary source.

—*The Conquest of New Spain.* Baltimore: Penguin Books, 1963. Full account of the conquest.

Las Casas, Bartolomé de. *An Account of the First Voyages and Discoveries Made by the Spaniards in America.* London: J. Darby . . . , 1964.

—*History of the Indies.* New York: Harper and Row, 1971. Focuses on the treatment of the Indians by the Spaniards.

Sauer, Carl O. *The Early Spanish Main.* Berkeley: University of California Press, 1966. Exploration of America by the Spanish.

MULTIMEDIA MATERIALS

Across the Ocean Sea. (video, 20 min.) Coronet Film and Video, 108 Wilmot Rd., Deerfield, Illinois, 60015. Tracks some of the dangers that Columbus faced when crossing the ocean.

The Ancient New World. (video, 16 min., 1964) Churchill Films, 12210 Nebraska Avenue, Los Angeles, California, 90025. Looks at some of the great civilizations in America, including the Aztecs.

For God And For Gold. (video, 19 min., 1990) Coronet Film and Video, 108 Wilmot Rd., Deerfield, Illinois, 60015. Columbus and the first Americans.

Spanish Conquest of the New World. (video, 18 min., 1988) Coronet Film and Video, 108 Wilmot Rd., Deerfield, Illinois, 60015. Broad discussion of the conquistadores, including Cortés and Coronado.

GENERAL STRATEGIES

STUDENTS WITH SPECIAL NEEDS

Limited English Proficient Students (LEP)

Provide students with a map that includes the southern United States, Mexico, and the Caribbean. Have them trace the routes of the following expeditions and identify significant sites.

Conquistadores
  Piñeda
  Cabeza de Vaca
  Coronado
  De Soto and Moscoso

Areas of Exploration
  Mexico, Gulf of Mexico,
    Rio Grande
  Galveston Island
  Mexico City, New Mexico,
    Arizona, Grand Canyon,
    Caprock Escarpment,
    Canadian River, Palo Duro
    Canyon, Oklahoma, Kansas,
    Florida, Mississippi

See other activities labeled **LEP.**

Students Having Difficulty with the Chapter

Have students use information in the chapter to complete the chart below. **LEP**

Auditory Learners

Create an identifying game for auditory learners. On separate index cards, write the following names from the chapter: Hernando Cortés, Pánfilo de Narváez, Mendoza, Cabeza de Vaca, Estéban, Fray Marcos, Coronado, El Turco, Hernando de Soto, Luis de Moscoso, Juan de Oñate. Have students work in pairs to identify the person on each card and, if applicable, his major accomplishment. See other activities labeled **A.**

Visual Learners

Have visual learners use the maps in the chapter and outside sources to create a wall map showing Spanish exploration in Texas. The explorers' routes should be labeled and dated. Maps should include a legend, a direction indicator, and a scale indicator. See other activities labeled **V.**

Tactile/Kinesthetic Learners

Have tactile/kinesthetic learners write and stage a news report about one of the Spanish expeditions into Texas. Students should create maps, pictures, or other visuals to enhance their reports. See other activities labeled **TK.**

Gifted Students

Have gifted students work together to select a Spanish expedition and identify its significant events. The students should use the events to create and present an original dramatization of the expedition. Evaluate the dramatization according to historical accuracy, creativity, special effects, and presentation. See other activities labeled **G.**

VOCABULARY

In addition to the boldfaced terms in each section, some students might benefit from discussing the meanings of these terms.

Section 1: *rival* (p. 114);
      conquests (p. 115);
      missionaries (p. 115);
      masons (p. 117).
Section 2: *treasurer* (p. 117);
      isle (p. 118);
      scalpel (p. 118).
Section 3: *stallion* (p. 122);
      muskets (p. 123);
      exaggerate (p. 126).
Section 4: *launching* (p. 128).

CHRONOLOGY

Have students study the Chapter 6 Time Line and identify relationships among the events.

GRAPHIC ORGANIZER

Have students skim the chapter and complete the Chapter 6 Graphic Organizer. *(You might wish to use this activity to review rather than to introduce the chapter.)*

ENRICHMENT

Have students complete the Chapter 6 Enrichment Worksheet.

Conquistador	Date	Route	Discoveries	Results
Piñeda				
Cabeza de Vaca				
Coronado				
De Soto and Moscoso				

SECTION 1

FOCUS

Predicting (I) Have the class brainstorm about reasons for the United States' exploration of space. Ask students what the United States hopes to gain by these explorations. Then ask them to consider the possible reasons for the Spanish exploration of Texas.

INSTRUCTION

Vocabulary (I) You may wish to preteach the following bold-faced terms: *expeditions* (p. 114); *empire* (p. 114); *conquistadores* (p. 115); *nobles* (p. 115); *friars* (p. 115); *order* (p. 115). **LEP**

CHAPTER 6 OVERVIEW

The first Europeans to enter Texas were Spanish explorers seeking riches and new lands for Spain. Their efforts resulted in Spain claiming Texas as part of its empire for many years. For the Indian culture groups already living in the region, it was the beginning of a clash of cultures.

Essential Elements
1B, 1C, 9A, 9B

Caption Response
Adventure and the search for riches

CHAPTER 6

THE QUEST FOR EMPIRE

The Story Continues...

Chapter 6 tells the story of the first Spanish explorers in Texas and the Indian cultural groups they met. It follows the Spaniards' **expeditions**, or journeys of discovery, in hopes of finding riches, winning glory for Spain, and converting the Native Americans to Christianity.

As you read the chapter, look for the answers to these questions:

1. Who were the conquistadores and what were their goals?
2. What happened to the expedition led by Pánfilo de Narváez? What then happened to Cabeza de Vaca and Estéban?
3. What was the result of the expeditions in search of Cíbola?
4. Why did Spain lose interest in further exploration of Texas?

◼ The Conquest of New Spain

After word began to spread of the voyages of Christopher Columbus, more explorers from Spain set sail westward across the Atlantic Ocean. They were seeking wealth and fame. The explorers also viewed themselves as representatives of the Spanish Crown, its people, and the Roman Catholic church. It was considered a great honor to sail under the Spanish flag.

Money for these explorations came from the Spanish government and from individuals who wanted to make personal fortunes. The rulers of Spain wanted to expand Spanish influence and the Roman Catholic religion. They hoped to create an **empire**, a rule over foreign lands, greater than that of their European rival, Portugal. The empire would supply resources for trade and gold and silver.

Drawing by José Cisneros, Barker Texas History Center

The Spanish conquistadores, dressed in armor and carrying the trappings of Spain, were impressive figures. What brought the conquistadores to the Americas?

Multicultural Perspective (I) Ask students to imagine that they are one of the following: one of Cortés' soldiers helping to capture Tenochtitlán, an Aztec captured and forced to work in the Spaniards' mines. Then have them write a letter to a friend describing Cortés' capturing of Tenochtitlán. Tell them to use the information in Section 1 to develop their letters. Invite volunteers to read their letters aloud. **A, LEP**

Guided Practice (I) Ask students to discuss the motives of the Spanish conquistadores in Mexico and Texas. Use their responses as the basis for a class discussion on the merit of these motives. **A, LEP**

EXTENSION

Research (II) Ask interested students to research and report on the history of the Franciscan order of the Roman Catholic church. Tell students to investigate its role in the church today. **A, G**

Independent Practice (II) Have students work independently or in pairs to create an advertisement that might have appeared in a Spanish newspaper for conquistadores or friars to go on an expedition to America. Display the ads on a bulletin board. **V, TK, LEP**

These would further strengthen Spain's economy and the power of the Spanish Crown. The lands in America claimed by Spain were named Nueva España, "New Spain."

The First Conquistadores. The Spaniards who led the invasion into the Americas were called **conquistadores**, meaning "conquerors." The conquistadores were military men, **nobles** (persons of high rank), and adventurers. They believed that their explorations and conquests served Spain and God. The conquistadores were warriors, and they looked the part. They wore suits of armor and steel helmets. Mounted on the finest Spanish horses, they rode in front of the soldiers they commanded. The conquistadores looked so powerful and frightening that many Indians believed they were gods.

The goal of the conquistadores was to explore and claim land for Spain. While doing this, they were to acquire as much gold, silver, and other treasures as possible. The conquistadores were also expected to bring Christianity to the Indians.

In order to spread their religion, Roman Catholic missionaries traveled with the conquistadores. Some of these missionaries were priests, others were called **friars**, meaning "brothers." Most of the missionary friars were members of the Franciscan **order**, or group, of the Roman Catholic church. The task of priests and friars alike was to build churches, schools, and missions, using them to convert the Indians to the Roman Catholic faith. Long after the conquistadores were gone, the Spanish missionaries remained, and they left a lasting influence in Texas.

One of the most famous conquistadores was a redhaired captain named Hernando Cortés. Cortés sailed from the Spanish colony of Cuba in 1519 and landed on the eastern coast of Mexico. Within two years he had conquered the great Aztec Indian empire. He captured Tenochtitlán, the capital city of the Aztecs, and imprisoned the Aztec leader, Montezuma.

The Aztecs greatly outnumbered the Spanish invaders, but Cortés and his soldiers had cannons and guns. Many Indians from other tribes joined Cortés to fight their enemies, the Aztecs. Many Aztec people were killed. Others were made slaves to work in mines and in the fields of the Spaniards. The wealth of the Aztecs—gold, silver, and jewels—was taken by ship to Spain.

The Granger Collection

Hernando Cortés conquered the great Aztec empire in Mexico.

Institute of Texan Cultures

This engraving depicts the Spaniards as they first viewed the Aztec capital of Tenochtitlán.

Historical Sidelight
Spanish conquistadores destroyed the Aztec libraries that contained picture writings, jewelry, and featherwork, greatly reducing our knowledge of Aztec civilization.

Historical Sidelight
According to Spanish chroniclers, Tenochtitlán was one of the largest and most beautiful cities in the word.

RETEACHING
Ask students to write a paragraph summarizing the information in Section 1. Instruct students to include the section's vocabulary terms in their summaries. **LEP**

CLOSURE
Review with students Spain's motives for exploration of the Americas. Invite a volunteer to write these motives on the chalkboard.

ASSESSMENT
Have students complete the Section 1 Review on page 117.

Answers to Section 1 Review

Define: *expeditions*—journeys of discovery; *empire*—rule of a country over foreign lands; *conquistadores*—conquerors; *nobles*—persons of high rank; *friars*—"brothers," or members of special religious groups; *order*—special religious group in the Roman Catholic church

Identify: Hernando Cortés—Spanish conquistador who conquered the Aztec empire in Mexico; Montezuma—leader of the Aztecs who was captured by Cortés

1. To find gold and silver, to claim new territory for Spain, and to bring Christianity to the Indians

(Continued on page 117)

Geography
The map on page 126 shows the routes of the major Spanish explorations of Texas.

The Granger Collection

When Cortés conquered Tenochtitlán, the Spaniards killed thousands of Aztecs and destroyed much of the Aztec culture.

The settlement of soldiers and priests in Tenochtitlán became the first Spanish colony on the mainland of America. The rebuilt city of Tenochtitlán was later renamed Mexico City. It became the capital of New Spain.

Piñeda and Texas. In the same year that Cortés landed in Mexico, Alonzo Alvarez de Piñeda became the first European to explore the coast of Texas. Piñeda had been told by the Spanish governor in Jamaica to sail along the coast of the Gulf of Mexico from Florida to Mexico. Piñeda's maps and charts were the first made of the Texas coast.

When Piñeda reached the mouth of the Rio Grande, he stopped and camped there for 40 days. He called the Rio Grande the Rio de las Palmas, or "River of Palms." It is not known if Piñeda or his men ventured into Texas at this time. But he wrote good reports about the land he saw and urged Spanish officials to build a permanent settlement in the Rio Grande area of Texas.

116 Unit 3

SECTION 2

FOCUS

Student Experiences (I) Ask students to share experiences of finding themselves lost. As they begin the study of Section 2, have them imagine themselves lost in a strange land thousands of miles from home.

INSTRUCTION

Vocabulary (I) You may wish to preteach the following boldfaced term: *shaman* (p. 119). **LEP**

Geography (I) Display a wall map of the world. Invite a volunteer to come to the front of the class and trace the Narváez expedition from Spain to Florida to the Texas coast. Then ask students to name all of the directions the expedition traveled on this route. Finally, ask them to describe the relative location of the crew's final destination. **A, V**

Writing (I) Ask students to imagine that they are either Cabeza de Vaca or Estéban writing his autobiography. Have them write two to three paragraphs about their experiences in Texas. **LEP**

The following year, another expedition was sent to investigate the River of Palms. Under the command of Diego de Camargo, this expedition brought along carpenters and masons to build homes and a church. Disagreements developed between the Spaniards and some Indians called the Coahuiltecans. The Coahuiltecans attacked, killing eighteen of Camargo's crew. The Spaniards withdrew, postponing plans to build in Texas. Nonetheless, Spanish interest in Texas grew stronger, and more expeditions soon headed toward the Texas shore. ○

2 Exploring Texas

The first Spaniard to enter the land of Texas did so unwillingly. His name was Alvar Núñez Cabeza de Vaca. His adventures and the stories he told about them had a great impact on the future of Spanish Texas.

The Narváez Expedition. Cabeza de Vaca was treasurer of an expedition in 1528 led by Pánfilo de Narváez. Narváez intended to follow Piñeda's route and explore the coast of the Gulf of Mexico. The Narváez expedition sailed to Florida in hope of finding treasure. While marching through the Florida swamps, Narváez and his soldiers became lost and unable to contact their ships.

Cartographic History Library, Special Collection.
The University of Texas at Arlington Libraries

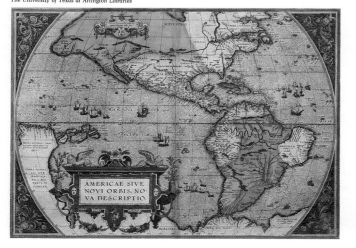

AMERICAE SIVE NOVI ORBIS, NOVA DESCRIPTIO.

This is an early Dutch map of the Americas. How does it compare with a modern map of the same area?

SECTION 1 REVIEW

Define: expeditions, empire, conquistadores, nobles, friars, order

Identify: Hernando Cortés, Montezuma

1. What were the goals of the first conquistadores?
2. What were the goals of the priests and friars who accompanied the conquistadores?
3. Who was the first European to explore the Texas coast? When did he do this?

Seeing Cause and Effect: How did the growth of Portugal's empire affect the policies of the Spanish Crown?

Writing Informatively: Imagine you are a Franciscan friar. You have just volunteered to go on a Spanish exploration of the northern frontier of Mexico. Write a letter to your parents, explaining why you did this.

2. To convert the Indians to Christianity
3. Alonzo Alvarez de Piñeda; 1519

Seeing Cause and Effect: Portugal was Spain's greatest rival as a European power. The growth of Portugal's empire caused Spain to seek an empire of its own.

Writing Informatively: Letters will vary, but the friar would probably emphasize that his decision was based on a desire to save the souls of the Indians by converting them to Christianity. He might mention the additional purpose of claiming new lands for Spain.

Essential Elements
1B, 1C, 5B, 9A, 9D, 9E

Caption Response
The shapes of North and South America are not accurate.

Guided Practice (I) Have students work in groups to create a series of story boards for a class bulletin board display titled "The Adventures of Cabeza de Vaca and Estéban." For each story board, they should draw a picture to illustrate an event in Cabeza de Vaca's and Estéban's life with the Karankawas. They should also write a brief description of the illustration for the story board. **V, TK, LEP**

EXTENSION

Role Playing (II) Organize the class into small groups, and have each group role play one of the events mentioned in Section 2. **A, V, G**

Independent Practice (II) Have students draw a cause-and-effect diagram similar to the one below, illustrating two such relationships mentioned in the section. **LEP**

Cause———Effect

RETEACHING

With the class, create on the chalkboard a time line of the events discussed in Section 2. Then have the students compare this time line with the one on page 113. **A, V, LEP**

Geography
Historians disagree about the exact route taken by Cabeza de Vaca and Estéban. Point out to students the two possible routes shown on the map on page 126.

The explorers built five small boats and decided to go west across the Gulf toward Mexico. Gulf storms destroyed three of the boats, and their crews were lost at sea. The two remaining boats, with Narváez and Cabeza de Vaca aboard, were shipwrecked on an island off the Texas coast. Cabeza de Vaca described the place where they landed as the "isle of misfortune." They probably landed on Galveston Island.

Stranded in the Texas wilderness, only fifteen of the Spaniards survived the cold winter of 1528. One of those survivors was Cabeza de Vaca. Another was a Moroccan slave named Estéban (also called Estevanico), most likely the first black person to enter and explore Texas.

The Adventures of Cabeza de Vaca and Estéban. Near starvation, Cabeza de Vaca, Estéban, and a handful of other Spaniards were captured by the Karankawas. The Indians fed the Spaniards and treated them kindly. But the Indians demanded that the Spaniards remain with them. For nearly seven years, Cabeza de Vaca, Estéban, and two other Spaniards lived with the Karankawas and other groups and traveled around southern and western Texas.

At first, the Spaniards were little more than slaves. Then one day a Karankawa warrior was struck by an enemy arrow. Cabeza de Vaca took a knife and used it as a scalpel

Cabeza de Vaca, Estéban, and their companions worked as healers among various Texas Indian tribes.

Painting by Tom Mirrat, Institute of Texan Cultures

CLOSURE

Point out that Cabeza de Vaca's unplanned exploration of Texas was very significant in encouraging further expeditions to the region.

ASSESSMENT

Have students complete the Section 2 Review on page 119.

SECTION ■3

FOCUS

Predicting (I) Review with students that Cabeza de Vaca was finally able to escape from Texas and return to Mexico. Tell students to think about the experiences of Cabeza de Vaca and Estéban in Texas. Ask: Upon his return to Mexico, what do you think Cabeza de Vaca reported to Spanish officials about his experiences?

to remove the arrow. The Indian recovered. The successful operation increased Cabeza de Vaca's reputation as a **shaman**, or healer. Estéban and the other Spaniards were also thought of as shamans. As their success in treating wounds and illnesses increased, so did their freedom.

The four Europeans soon began visiting other tribes in the South Texas area. They treated the sick and began to trade with the Indians. They wandered among various tribes, always hoping to find an escape route to lead them back to Mexico. Eventually, almost eight years after their shipwreck, Cabeza de Vaca and Estéban traveled into northwest Mexico, where they met a group of Spanish soldiers. At first, Cabeza de Vaca and his friends were mistaken for Indians. Finally the soldiers realized who they were and helped them get to Mexico City. ✪

■3 Cities of Gold

After arriving in Mexico City, Cabeza de Vaca wrote a formal report about his experiences. He described the land of Texas as rich and fertile. He told of seeing thousands of hump-backed "cows" that swept across the prairies in giant herds. They had horns and thick dark hair like wool. Cabeza de Vaca was describing the buffalo.

These stories interested Spanish officials in Mexico City, but what *excited* them was another part of Cabeza de Vaca's report. The Indians had told Cabeza de Vaca about great golden cities to the north. The streets and buildings were made of gold and silver, they said, and jewels adorned the walls and roofs. Cabeza de Vaca, Estéban, and the other survivors of the shipwreck admitted that they had not seen these cities. For that matter, they admitted that they had seen no gold at all during their stay in Texas. Still, the Indian legend was so tempting that plans were soon begun to go search for the golden cities.

Estéban and Fray Marcos. The **viceroy**, or king's representative, of New Spain in Mexico City sent out a small expedition to find the golden cities. Viceroy Antonio de Mendoza hoped that Cabeza de Vaca would lead the search, but Cabeza de Vaca wanted to go home to Spain. Mendoza ordered Estéban to go on the expedition to the north. Leading the expedition was a Franciscan friar and explorer, Fray Marcos de Niza.

SECTION ★2★ REVIEW

Define: shaman
Identify: Cabeza de Vaca, Estéban, Karankawas

1. What disaster happened to the Narváez expedition?
2. How did Cabeza de Vaca, Estéban, and others make friends with the Indians?
3. Why did Cabeza de Vaca's group travel to the southwest?

Evaluating Information: Do you think it took courage for Estéban to perform his first treatment as a shaman? Why? Why do you think he was willing to do it?

Analyzing Information: What geographic reasons can you suggest for Narváez's land forces losing their way in the Florida swamps?

Institute of Texan Cultures

The buffalo was a strange new creature to the early Spanish explorers. This drawing was first published in an early European book about the Americas.

Answers to Section 2 Review

Define: *shaman*—healer
Identify: Cabeza de Vaca—survivor of the Narváez expedition who explored much of South Texas; Estéban—Morroccan slave and probably the first black to explore Texas; Karankawas—coastal Indian group who captured Cabeza de Vaca and the other survivors of the Narváez expedition

1. The expedition got lost while exploring Florida. Only a few members of the expedition survived an ordeal that left them stranded in the Texas wilderness.
2. They acted as shamans.
3. To try to find an escape route that would lead them back to Mexico

Evaluating Information: Most students will say yes. If the first patient had died or become worse, the Indians might have killed Estéban. He was probably willing to take the chance because he was in desperate circumstances.

Analyzing Information: Possible answer: With few landmarks, the Florida swamps were difficult to navigate.

Essential Elements
1B, 1C, 5A, 5B, 5C, 9A, 9B, 9D

INSTRUCTION

Vocabulary (I) You may wish to preteach the following boldfaced term: *viceroy* (p. 119). **LEP**

Environment (I) Ask students to imagine themselves as members of Coronado's expedition. The expedition has just entered the Panhandle of Texas. Have them write a detailed account of what they see. **V, LEP**

Geography
Have students locate on the map Japan and the Tropic of Cancer. Have them compare the shape and location of Japan on this map to that of Japan on the world map on pages xxii–xxiii.

Estéban and Fray Marcos began their search for the Seven Cities of Cíbola in March of 1539. About 300 Indians from Mexico were sent along with Estéban and Marcos to protect them in case of attack. The journey began with great expectations of finding gold and planting the Spanish flag in the northern lands of New Spain.

Estéban and several others marched ahead of the main group. Estéban knew the lands, and Fray Marcos instructed him to warn the expedition if there was danger ahead. Using knowledge from his previous trip, Estéban moved northward out of Mexico into what is now Arizona. He wore bells draped over his body and tied to his wrists and ankles. He also carried rattles decorated with feathers. By dressing this way and in bright colors, Estéban was announcing to Indians he met that he was a great shaman.

After traveling for several weeks, Estéban sent back word that there were indeed seven great golden cities ahead. Marcos and the others in the expedition became

This Spanish map from the 1500s shows the location of the Seven Cities of Cíbola. The Spaniards had found great wealth in Mexico and Peru, but they found little gold in the expeditions to the northern provinces.

British Library, courtesy of American Heritage

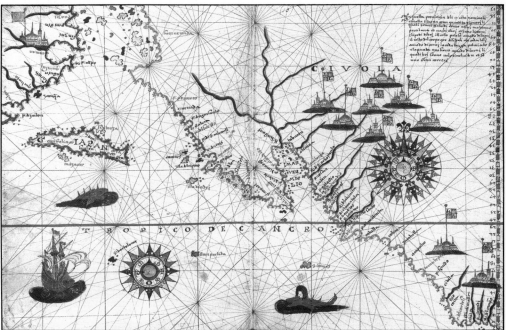

Geography (II) Tell students to select either the Coronado expedition or that of De Soto and Moscoso. First, ask them to trace on a map the route of the expedition. Then refer them to a physical map of Texas and the Southwest and ask them to describe the various landforms, water features, and other landmarks that the expedition encountered on its route. Ask: What geographic features probably created a hindrance to the expedition? **V, A**

Mural by Ben Carlton Mead, Panhandle-Plains Historical Museum, photo by I. G. Holmes

This painting shows Coronado exploring Palo Duro Canyon in 1541.

very excited, for they believed Estéban had found the riches of Cíbola. As they moved forward, tragic news reached their camp. Estéban had reached Cíbola, but the Indians there had killed him.

Despite fears that they might face the same fate as Estéban, Marcos and the rest of the expedition continued. Late one afternoon, there it was: Cíbola! From a distance, Marcos could see the seven cities sparkling in the sun. Buildings seemed to rise out of a desert landscape and shine like gold.

In reality, Cíbola was a group of Zuñi Indian villages. They were located near the present boundary of Arizona and New Mexico. The buildings were made of adobe brick. Marcos never entered the villages or got close enough to describe accurately what was there. He saw what he wanted to see: golden cities in the desert sun.

Since Estéban had been killed, Fray Marcos knew the people of Cíbola did not welcome the expedition. Instead of entering the villages, Fray Marcos decided to return to Mexico. After his arrival in Mexico City, excitement grew as Fray Marcos told the tale of the fabulous golden cities. Viceroy Mendoza made plans for a new, larger expedition to gather the treasures that Fray Marcos claimed he saw.

The Coronado Expedition. The man chosen to lead the search for fame and fortune was Francisco Vásquez de

Multicultural Perspective
The Zuñis were a peaceful group. They were mostly agricultural workers and only fought when others would not leave them alone. Their main defense against aggressive outsiders was their stone houses, which terraced into cliffs and hills and provided no entry from the floor level. The Zuñis entered and exited their houses by using ladders, which could be pulled up and in, and trap doors.

Creating (II) Divide the class into two groups. Have one group create a diorama or model of the Seven Cities of Cíbola. Have the other group create a detailed drawing of the actual Cíbola. Display the students' creations in the classroom. **V, TK, G**

Historical Sidelight
Viceroy Mendoza and Coronado invested their own money—the equivalent of almost $4 million—to finance the expedition to claim the city of Cíbola and "the kingdoms that lay beyond it."

Coronado. Coronado was 29 years old, wealthy, a noble, and greatly respected by the viceroy. The Coronado expedition was the largest one the Spaniards ever attempted into the northern provinces of New Spain. Three hundred Spanish soldiers led more than 1,000 Christian Indians into the desert Southwest. They took with them more than 1,000 horses, as well as herds of cattle and sheep. Commanding the entire army was Coronado himself. On his head was a shining steel helmet topped by bright purple feathers. He rode a majestic stallion and wore a suit of gold-plated armor.

Viceroy Mendoza sent Fray Marcos with the expedition to act as a guide. The trip began in April of 1540. A group of 100 soldiers went ahead to act as an advance guard. By early summer, Coronado would know the truth about the Seven Cities of Cíbola.

When the Coronado expedition finally reached Cíbola, the Zuñi Indians were in no mood to welcome them. The Zuñis knew that the Spaniards had come to conquer them and take what wealth and treasure they could find. A short but hard-fought battle between the Indians and the

Viceroy Mendoza planned the expedition led by Coronado to search for the Seven Cities of Cíbola.

Archives Division, Texas State Library

Spaniards took place. Making full use of their muskets and cannons, the Spaniards won. But Coronado did not feel like a conquerer when he realized there were no cities of gold.

After searching the seven little villages of the Zuñi Indians, Coronado was convinced that the entire story of the Seven Cities of Cíbola had been a lie. Members of the expedition were angry with Fray Marcos, and he was quickly sent back to Mexico City. Although greatly disappointed, Coronado refused to return to Mexico City until he had done more exploring. Thinking there might be some treasure to be found, the Coronado expedition marched on.

Coronado in Texas. Coronado divided his force into several groups. One group, led by García López de Cárdenas, traveled west and came upon the Grand Canyon in Arizona. Coronado led another group east. The main body of the Spanish expedition spent the next two years at a place in New Mexico that the Spaniards called Tiguex.

At first the Indians who lived at Tiguex were friendly toward the Spaniards and provided them with food and supplies. While staying at Tiguex, the Spaniards met an Indian whom they called El Turco (The Turk). El Turco was not one of the Tiguex Indians, but instead was from farther east. He told stories of a place called Quivira, a land of fabulous riches. With the experience of Cíbola fresh on their minds, some of the Spaniards thought the tale of Quivira was a lie. Coronado decided it was worth the risk to try to find this place. But before he could organize an expedition, trouble developed between the Indians and Spaniards. Fighting broke out, and the Spaniards killed many Indians as Coronado established control over the area around Tiguex.

In April 1541, Coronado led an expedition east toward Texas. The expedition, guided by El Turco, soon found itself on the flat lands of the Panhandle. The Spaniards had never seen a land with "no trees except at the rivers." They were amazed at the "sea of grass" that seemed to have no end. The expedition also recorded seeing the hump-backed cattle that Cabeza de Vaca had seen. Coronado and his group saw the Cap Rock Escarpment, naming the area the Llano Estacado, or "Staked Plain."

As the expedition crossed the Canadian River and moved deeper into the plains, Coronado and his soldiers became the first Europeans to see one of the most unusual sights in

Historical Picture Service, Chicago

The armor of sixteenth-century conquistadores reflected the power and wealth of Spain. When the conquistadores came to the Americas, some Indians mistook them for gods.

Paul M. Montgomery

The land and skies of the Panhandle still appear as vast and unending as they did to Coronado's expedition.

Historical Sidelight
According to Texas historian T.R. Fehrenbach, Llano Estacado was incorrectly translated by later English-speaking explorers as "staked plain." It should have been translated as "stockaded or palisaded high plain."

Other historians suggest that the name was originally El Llano Destacado. *Destacado* means "silhouetted." *Estacado* means "staked."

LONE STAR LEGACY

Using Historical Imagination:
Answers will vary, but students' diary entries should be vivid descriptions of the grandeur of the canyon.

Palo Duro Canyon

*I*n the high, flat grasslands of the Texas Panhandle, a traveler suddenly comes to the edge of a vast canyon. Palo Duro Canyon has been known to Indians, Spanish explorers, buffalo hunters, frontier cattle ranchers, and now to tourists. The canyon is 120 miles in length, several miles wide at some points, and 1,000 feet deep. Working over tens of thousands of years, the Prairie Dog Town Fork of the Red River dug this huge gash in the earth.

Native Americans camped in Palo Duro Canyon for centuries. In fact, it was Texas Indians who named the canyon. *Palo Duro* is the Spanish translation of the Indian name "hard wood." From the canyon, the Indians gathered juniper wood to make their best bows, arrows, and spears. Other trees in the canyon are cedar, cottonwood, hackberry, mesquite, mountain mahogany, salt cedar, and willow. Indians hunted deer, wild sheep, birds, and other small animals. All of these continue to live in the canyon.

Historians think that the first Europeans to see Palo Duro Canyon were Coronado and his band of Spanish explorers in 1541. After traveling for days across a flat sea of waving grass, they came upon the canyon. Like travelers today, they were surprised at its grandeur and color—surprised at its being there at all in one of the flattest places on earth.

The most scenic part of the Palo Duro Canyon, 15,103 acres, was set aside in 1933 by the state of Texas as Palo Duro Canyon State Park. Construction work at the site was done by the Civilian Conservation Corps during the New Deal of President Franklin Roosevelt. The corps constructed roads and native stone buildings.

Today, tourists enjoy camping, hiking, and musical pageants at Palo Duro's state park. During the summer, the musical drama *Texas* is presented six nights a week in the canyon's amphitheater. A large cliff is the backdrop for the production. Since 1966, the outdoor pageant has been presented to 100,000 tourists each year. Perhaps the most popular hike in Palo Duro State Park is the three-mile trail from the main road to the Lighthouse, a 300-foot rock formation that has become the hallmark of the canyon.

Using Historical Imagination

Imagine that you are Coronado in 1541. In your diary, describe the experience of seeing Palo Duro Canyon for the first time.

Texas Department of Transportation

Paul M. Montgomery

Coronado referred to Palo Duro Canyon as the "great ravine." How would you describe the geography of this area of the Panhandle?

Texas. They came upon a deep ravine cut into the plains by millions of years of erosion: Palo Duro Canyon.

Despite the beauty of Palo Duro's red soil and golden rock formations, it contained no gold. So Coronado pushed north through what is now Oklahoma and into Kansas. There he found Quivira. The story was the same as Cíbola: no gold and no riches. More angry than disappointed, Coronado had El Turco put to death.

Coronado's Report. Upon his return to Mexico City in 1542, Coronado submitted a report to Viceroy Mendoza. The report described the Llano Estacado in favorable terms. While admitting it was a harsh land, Coronado said it was similar to parts of Spain. He said he was impressed by its size and saw possible wealth in the huge herds of buffalo. Coronado also pointed out that it had no precious metals such as gold or silver. Because the Indians had no riches either, the land was of little use to the Spaniards.

Guided Practice (I) Refer students to the map on this page. Have students use the information in the map to draw a time line and place the events in the correct order. **V, TK, LEP**

Have students list in note form the major events of Section 3. Ask them to write a brief description of one of the events. **LEP**

Transparency 10
An overhead transparency of this map can be found in the Teacher's Resource Binder.

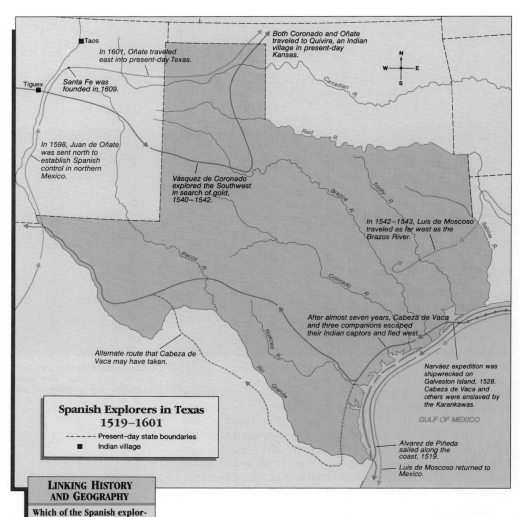

In 1601, Oñate traveled east into present-day Texas.

Both Coronado and Oñate traveled to Quivira, an Indian village in present-day Kansas.

■Taos

Tiguex■ Santa Fe was founded in 1609.

In 1598, Juan de Oñate was sent north to establish Spanish control in northern Mexico.

Vásquez de Coronado explored the Southwest in search of gold, 1540–1542.

Canadian R.

Red R.

Brazos R.

Trinity R.

Sabine R.

In 1542–1543, Luis de Moscoso traveled as far west as the Brazos River.

Pecos R.

Colorado R.

After almost seven years, Cabeza de Vaca and three companions escaped their Indian captors and fled west.

Nueces R.

Rio Grande

Alternate route that Cabeza de Vaca may have taken.

Narváez expedition was shipwrecked on Galveston Island, 1528. Cabeza de Vaca and others were enslaved by the Karankawas.

GULF OF MEXICO

Spanish Explorers in Texas 1519–1601
- - - - - Present–day state boundaries
■ Indian village

Alvarez de Piñeda sailed along the coast, 1519.

Luis de Moscoso returned to Mexico.

Linking History and Geography
Coronado (five)

LINKING HISTORY AND GEOGRAPHY
Which of the Spanish explorers crossed the most rivers on his travels through Texas?

Coronado also told the viceroy a story about El Turco. Just before his death, El Turco admitted why he had lied to Coronado about Quivira. El Turco claimed that the Indians of Tiguex had forced him to exaggerate the wealth of Quivira in order to get the Spaniards out of their lands. This is probably the reason for the Indian stories about Cíbola as well. These were part of a plan to encourage the Spanish invaders to leave the Indians in peace.

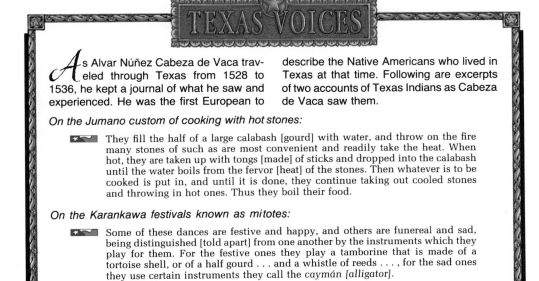

TEXAS VOICES

*A*s Alvar Núñez Cabeza de Vaca traveled through Texas from 1528 to 1536, he kept a journal of what he saw and experienced. He was the first European to describe the Native Americans who lived in Texas at that time. Following are excerpts of two accounts of Texas Indians as Cabeza de Vaca saw them.

On the Jumano custom of cooking with hot stones:

> They fill the half of a large calabash [gourd] with water, and throw on the fire many stones of such as are most convenient and readily take the heat. When hot, they are taken up with tongs [made] of sticks and dropped into the calabash until the water boils from the fervor [heat] of the stones. Then whatever is to be cooked is put in, and until it is done, they continue taking out cooled stones and throwing in hot ones. Thus they boil their food.

On the Karankawa festivals known as mitotes:

> Some of these dances are festive and happy, and others are funereal and sad, being distinguished [told apart] from one another by the instruments which they play for them. For the festive ones they play a tamborine that is made of a tortoise shell, or of a half gourd . . . and a whistle of reeds . . . , for the sad ones they use certain instruments they call the *caymán [alligator]*.

De Soto and Moscoso. While Coronado was searching for Cíbola and Quivira, Hernando de Soto was leading a Spanish expedition into Florida and the present southeastern United States. De Soto reached the Mississippi River in 1542 but died there from an illness. Command of the expedition fell to Luis de Moscoso. Moscoso led the expedition through parts of East Texas, exploring and mapping the land. The explorers intended to return to Mexico on foot, but later they changed their minds. Eventually they built several small boats and sailed along the Gulf coast to Mexico. Of De Soto's force of 600, only about 300 people survived the expedition.

In Mexico, Moscoso made a report much like Coronado's. He reported that the northern part of New Spain was a huge land of great variety but that it had no gold. Moscoso did mention one resource that would later prove to be Texas' "black gold." While in East Texas, Moscoso and his soldiers discovered a thick kind of oil seeping from the ground. ❂

SECTION ★3★ REVIEW

Define: viceroy
Identify: Viceroy Mendoza, Fray Marcos, El Turco

1. How much gold and silver did the Spaniards gain from the expeditions to Cíbola?
2. What Indian cultural group lived at Cíbola?
3. Why did Coronado say El Turco lied about Quivira?

Synthesizing Information: What did the stories about Cíbola and Quivira have in common?

Exploring Economics: In reporting to the Spanish king about his journey, Coronado said he had discovered what possible source of wealth? How do you think the king responded to this? Why?

SECTION 4

FOCUS

Student Experiences (I) Ask students: If, when trying to accomplish something, your efforts appear to be wasted, what do you do? *(Lead students to conclude that they are likely to redirect their efforts or give up the pursuit.)* Tell students that when Spain failed to find riches in Texas, it lost interest in exploring the region for nearly half a century.

INSTRUCTION

Multicultural Perspective (I) Divide the class into two groups: one representing Spaniards who saw Texas and nearby lands as theirs to claim and the other representing the Indians who saw this land as their home. Help the groups stage a debate in which representatives from each group will present their point of view. **A**

Essential Elements
1B, 1C, 9A, 9B

Answers to Section 4 Review

Identify: Juan de Oñate—Spanish explorer of the Texas Panhandle

1. No gold, silver, or other riches had been found.
2. That of Juan de Oñate; gold and silver
3. Texas had no treasures or large cities to conquer, and Texas was too far from Spanish settlements in Mexico, through land that was dry and rugged.

Evaluating Information: Spain gained much information about these northern lands, and its explorations gave the country a strong claim to this part of North America.

Interpreting Pictures: Answers will vary, but the sword could have been lost in an Indian attack or left behind when the soldier died of illness or was killed.

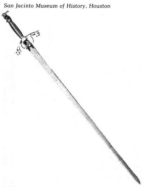

San Jacinto Museum of History, Houston

This sixteenth-century Spanish sword was found in present-day Kansas in the area explored by Coronado.

SECTION ★4★ REVIEW

Identify: Juan de Oñate

1. Why did Spain stop sending major expeditions to explore Texas?
2. What was the next expedition after Coronado's? For what was this expedition looking?
3. Besides the lack of gold and silver, why did Spanish authorities decide not to settle Texas?

Evaluating Information: In what ways were explorations of Texas useful to Spain?

Interpreting Pictures: What are two ways in which a Spanish soldier might have lost the sword shown on this page?

④ An End to Spanish Exploration

For a time after the expeditions of Coronado and De Soto, Spain showed little interest in launching any more expensive explorations of lands north of Mexico. It was almost 60 years before another expedition entered what is now Texas.

Juan de Oñate. The next Spanish exploration of Texas did not take place until 1601. In that year, a conquistador named Juan de Oñate led a group across the Texas Panhandle. Oñate had conquered the Indians of northern New Mexico in 1598 and set up a settlement at the Chama River. Oñate's trip into Texas involved more battles with Indians. Like Coronado before him, Oñate was searching for sources of gold and silver. Like Coronado, he found none. For around 75 years after Juan de Oñate's expedition, few other Spanish explorers entered the land of Texas.

Spanish Policy. Even though the Spaniards found no precious metals in Texas, their explorations had important results. One result was that Spain's claim to Texas was clear. No other European country could say it had a better right to claim Texas.

A second result of the explorations was the knowledge gained about the land. Parts of East, West, and South Texas had been seen and mapped. Several groups of explorers had traveled along the Gulf coast as well.

Despite the claim to Texas and the knowledge gained about the land, Spain decided not to settle Texas. The conquistadores had found neither treasure nor large cities to conquer. Both had been found in Mexico and Peru, so Spain was much more interested in those two areas. Besides, Texas was too far from Spanish settlements in Mexico, through land that was dry and rugged.

For some time after Oñate's trip, Texas was useful to Spain only as a barrier. It protected the lands of Mexico from Indians who were unfriendly to the Spaniards. It also protected the Spaniards from other Europeans who were exploring North America.

Throughout the southwestern United States, Spanish explorations and conquests had brought conflicts between Spaniards and Indians. Spaniards saw Texas and nearby lands as theirs to claim. The Indians saw this land as home. Clashes between the two ways of life would continue. ✪

RETEACHING
Have students write a brief paragraph summarizing Section 4. Call on volunteers to read their paragraphs aloud as you correct any misinformation. **A, LEP**

CLOSURE
Tell students that although Spain had ended its quest to find riches in Texas, it would soon renew its interest in the region north of Mexico.

ASSESSMENT
Have students complete the Section 4 Review on page 128.

CHAPTER REVIEW RESOURCES
1. Chapter Review Worksheet 6
2. Chapter 6 Test, Form A
3. Reteaching Worksheet 6
4. Chapter 6 Test, Form B
5. **Informal Evaluation Forms:** Portfolio Assessment
6. *Texas, Our Texas* **Test Generator**

CHAPTER 6 REVIEW

Essential Elements
1B, 1C, 5A, 9A, 9B, 9D

Understanding Main Ideas

1. Who were the conquistadores, and what did they want to achieve in the Americas?
2. What part did Alonzo Alvarez de Piñeda play in the exploration of Texas?
3. What disasters happened to the Narváez expedition?
4. How did Cabeza de Vaca, Estéban, and other survivors of the Narváez expedition improve their situation among the Texas coastal Indians?
5. Was the goal of the Coronado expedition accomplished? Explain.
6. Why was Juan de Oñate's expedition one of the last Spanish explorations of Texas for more than 75 years?

Thinking Critically

1. **Evaluating Information:** What was the religious task of the Spanish missionaries in Texas? In what ways did their work aid the Spanish government?
2. **Classifying Information:** Write the names Narváez, Coronado, and De Soto at the top of a sheet of paper. Then write the following under the expedition with which each is connected: Luis de Moscoso, Palo Duro Canyon, Florida, Cíbolo, Cabeza de Vaca, Quivira, shaman, El Turco.
3. **Synthesizing Information:** How were the Spaniards able to defeat American Indians, even though the Indians outnumbered them?

Linking History and Geography

1. What subregions of Texas did Cabeza de Vaca and Estéban pass through on their journey from Galveston Island?
2. Study the map on page 126 and the regions map on page 53. If Cabeza de Vaca took the northern route (of his two possible routes), which subregions of Texas did he explore?

TAAS Practice
Using Primary Sources

A Spanish missionary at Mission Guadalupe wrote about the hardships endured by the early Spanish friars and priests at the East Texas missions:

For two years, the want and hardships which the Fathers endured in the missions of Texas were keenly felt; but it seems unavoidable. From the time the missionaries entered that country, in 1716, no aid reached them, and as the supplies which they brought along were very few, they soon gave out. . . . During the years 1717 and 1718, owing to the severity of the drought, the harvest of corn and beans among the Indians was very poor. . . . The daily bread, which in that country is Indian corn, was wanting. If, perchance, after running through the rancherías, a peck of corn was gathered, there was as much ado about it as if a great train of provision had arrived. . . . When, by chance, we could get a mouthful of meat, we boiled a handful of corn and this answered the purpose of bread. Salt was entirely wanting, and thus, when we even had the good fortune to obtain beans, the lack of salt made them unpalatable [not good to eat]. . . . Meat in quantities was not to be had at all; and even if, on rare occasions, some compassionate Indian brought us a bit

CHAPTER 6 REVIEW ANSWERS

Understanding Main Ideas

1. They were Spanish adventurers, military men, and nobles whose goal was to explore and claim land for Spain. Also, they were to acquire gold, silver, and other treasures and to bring Christianity to the Indians.
2. He was the first European to explore the Texas coast.
3. They got lost in the Florida swamps, and they lost touch with their support ships. The small boats that they made to try to return to Mexico were wrecked in a storm. A few members of the expedition survived, only to land on Galveston Island and be captured by the Indians.
4. They managed to establish a reputation as shamans, thereby gaining the Indians' respect.
5. No. The fabled cities of Cíbola turned out to be Zuñi Indian villages, and there were no riches.
6. He, too, failed to find gold, silver, or any large cities to conquer.

Thinking Critically

1. **Evaluating Information:** Their task was to bring Christianity to the Indians. Doing so would create stable communities with Indian workers for the Spanish mines and ranchos. It would benefit Spain economically and politically by increasing the wealth of New Spain.
2. **Classifying Information:** Narváez—Florida, Cabeza de Vaca, shaman; Coronado—Palo Duro Canyon, Cíbola, Quivira, El Turco; De Soto—Florida, Luis de Moscoso
3. **Synthesizing Information:** The Spaniards had great superiority in weapons, which included cannons, muskets, steel swords, and steel armor, and the Indians were afraid of the Spaniards' horses. The Spaniards were fierce and disciplined fighters, and the Indians sometimes thought the Spaniards were gods.

Linking History and Geography

1. During their years with the Karankawas, they probably traveled throughout the Gulf Coast Plain and South Texas Plains subregions.
2. The Gulf Coast Plain, the South Texas Plains, the Edwards Plateau, and the Mountains and Basins

TAAS *Practice* Using Primary Sources

1. B
2. D

TAAS *Practice* Writing Descriptively

Songs will vary but should represent the Zuñis' perceptions of Coronado and their fear that he intended to conquer them and take all their wealth.

Practicing Skills

1. **Sequencing Events:** Piñeda (1519), Narváez (1528), Estéban and Fray Marcos (1539), Coronado (1540), Oñate (1601)
2. **Interpreting Maps:** France

Enriching Your Study of History

1. **Individual Project:** Reports will vary but should demonstrate research and provide detailed knowledge of the subject.
2. **Cooperative Project:** Reports will vary but should demonstrate research and provide detailed knowledge of the expeditions.

---

of venison [deer meat], the want of salt rendered it little agreeable to the taste.

Many a day dawned when there was absolutely nothing to eat at hand. . . . As we had neither bread nor vegetables, we sought to appease our hunger by means of herbs, adding nuts by way of seasoning.

1. Food was scarce at Mission Guadalupe because:
   - A the Indians refused to give the missionaries any help
   - B there was a severe drought and no fresh supplies from Mexico
   - C French agents from Louisiana burned the cornfields
   - D the missionaries refused to visit the Indian villages in search of food
2. The best statement about the Indians' support of the missionaries is:
   - A the Indians refused to give the missionaries any food
   - B the Indians gave the missionaries food even when they themselves were starving
   - C the Indians shared only their salt with the missionaries
   - D the Indians shared some food with the missionaries

TAAS *Practice* Writing Descriptively

Imagine you are a Zuñi Indian of Cíbola. Compose a song describing Coronado and his expedition.

Practicing Skills

1. **Sequencing Events:** Place these Spanish journeys of exploration in chronological order, beginning with the earliest and ending with the latest: Oñate, Coro-

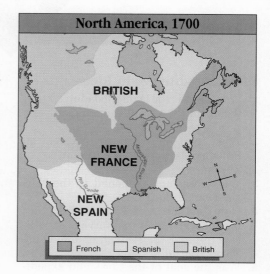

North America, 1700

French ☐ Spanish ☐ British

nado, Estéban and Fray Marcos, Piñeda, Narváez.
2. **Interpreting Maps:** Study the map on this page. What European power would Spaniards in Texas probably be most worried about in 1700?

Enriching Your Study of History

1. **Individual Project:** Prepare a short research report on one of the following: Franciscan order, Cabeza de Vaca, Estéban, De Soto, shamanism.
2. **Cooperative Project:** Your teacher will separate the class into three research teams. Each team will research the explorations of Cabeza de Vaca, Coronado, or De Soto and Moscoso. Each team will then report on interesting details of these expeditions.

CHAPTER 7

SPANISH TEXAS

TEACHER'S TIME LINE

Section 1	Section 2	Section 3	Section 4	Review and Assessment
Pp. 131–33	Pp. 133–39	Pp. 139–45	Pp. 145–49	
1 Day	1 Day	1 Day	1 Day	1 Day

TEACHER MATERIALS

Core: Chapter 7 Time Line; Graphic Organizer 7; Enrichment Worksheet 7; Review Worksheet 7; Reteaching Worksheet 7; Chapter 7 Tests, Forms A & B

Additional: Geography and Graph Skills 7, Map and Chart Transparencies 11, Informal Evaluation Forms, Test Generator

OBJECTIVES

1. Explain Spain's renewed interest in Texas in the late 1600s.
2. Describe the Spanish plan for settling Texas.
3. Identify the goals of the mission system.
4. Describe the differences between the early and later Spanish missions.
5. Locate Spanish settlements in Texas.
6. Identify lasting contributions of the Spanish in Texas.

RESOURCES

BOOKS FOR TEACHERS

Castañeda, Carlos E. *Our Catholic Heritage in Texas, 1519–1936*, 7 vols. Austin: Von Boeckmann-Jones, 1958.

La Salle, Robert Cavelier Sieur de. *Discovery of the Mississippi*. Austin: Shoal Creek Publishers, 1975. Translation of his memoirs relating discovery of the Mississippi and other subjects.

Olds, Dorris. *Texas Legacy from the Gulf*. Austin: The Texas Memorial Museum, 1976. A report on shipwreck materials recovered from the Texas tidelands.

Sauer, Carl O. *The Road to Cíbola*. Berkeley: University of California Press, 1932. Discovery and exploration of the Southwest.

—*Sixteenth Century North America: The Land and the People as Seen by the Europeans*. Berkeley: University of California Press, 1971.

Schiwetz, Edward Muegge. *Six Spanish Missions in Texas*. Austin: University of Texas Press, 1968. Paintings of missions.

Tebbel, John, and Ramon Eduardo Ruíz. *South by Southwest: The Mexican-American and His Heritage*. New York: Doubleday, 1969. Discussion of Hispanics in the Southwest, including Texas.

MULTIMEDIA MATERIALS

The French and Indian War. (video, 15 min., 1981) Coronet Film and Video, 108 Wilmot Rd., Deerfield, Illinois, 60015. Discussion of the effects of this war on Texas and American history.

French Explorations in the New World. (video, 18 min., 1988) Coronet Film and Video, 108 Wilmot Rd., Deerfield, Illinois, 60015. Tracks French explorers in America, including La Salle.

The Louisiana Purchase. (video, 15 min.) Zenger Video, 10200 Jefferson Boulevard, Room VC811, P.O. Box 802, Culver City, California, 90232. Impact of this transaction on history.

The Vocabulary of Social Studies: American History Series. (software) Focus Media, Inc., 839 Stewart Avenue, P.O. Box 865, Garden City, New York, 11530. Interactive game that includes topics such as exploration and colonization of America.

STUDENTS WITH SPECIAL NEEDS

Limited English Proficient Students (LEP)

Have students skim the chapter to find the boldfaced vocabulary terms. Ask them to write the terms on a series of index cards. They should write the term on one side of the card and the definition on the other side. Then pair students and have them use the cards as flashcards. Each pair of students should use the flashcards until both students have mastered the vocabulary. See other activities labeled **LEP**.

Students Having Difficulty with the Chapter

Have students use the Chapter 7 section and subsection headings to prepare an outline of the chapter. After they have outlined each section, ask them to write a one- or two-sentence summary of that section. **LEP**

Auditory Learners

Have auditory learners research and prepare oral reports on the origins of the names of the Spanish missions in Texas. See other activities labeled **A**.

Visual Learners

Have visual learners use a large sheet of butcher paper to complete the chart on this page as they study Chapter 7. Display the completed chart on a bulletin board. See other activities labeled **V**.

Tactile/Kinesthetic Learners

Have tactile/kinesthetic learners use the information in Chapter 7 to create a detailed illustration of a Spanish settlement. Drawings should include the following: mis-

Settlement	Year	Problems	Lasting Results
El Paso			
Ysleta			
San Francisco de los Tejas			
New East Texas Missions			
San Antonio Settlements			
La Bahía			
San Xavier			
San Sabá			

sion (chapel, kitchen, school, farm, houses, plaza, wall); presidio (barracks, officers' quarters, supply barns, headquarters building, stockade); civil settlement (farms, ranches).

Gifted Students

Refer students to the Chapter 7 subsection "The Spanish Heritage" on page 149. Have them conduct research to find examples of Spanish influence in Texas and report their findings to the class. They should supplement their reports with photographs, drawings, samples of foods, music, and so on. See other activities labeled **G**.

VOCABULARY

In addition to the boldfaced terms in each section, some students might benefit from discussing the meanings of these terms.

Section 1: *civilians* (p. 133); *merchants* (p. 133).

Section 2: *commercial* (p. 135); *contagious* (p. 139).

Section 3: *interior* (p. 139); *convert* (p. 139); *foreigners* (p. 140); *stockade* (p. 144).

Section 4: *barracks* (p. 147); *morale* (p. 148).

CHRONOLOGY

Have students study the Chapter 7 Time Line and identify relationships among the events.

GRAPHIC ORGANIZER

Have students skim the chapter and complete the Chapter 7 Graphic Organizer. *(You might wish to use this activity to review rather than to introduce the chapter.)*

ENRICHMENT

Have students complete the Chapter 7 Enrichment Worksheet.

SECTION 1

FOCUS

Student Experiences (I) Invite students to imagine that people from a faraway country have just arrived in their town. Their goal is to change the students' beliefs and way of life. Ask students how they feel about this and to keep these thoughts in mind as they read Section 1.

INSTRUCTION

Vocabulary (I) You may wish to preteach the following bold-faced terms: *missions* (p. 131); *presidios* (p. 132); *civil settlements* (p. 133). **LEP**

Cooperative Learning (I) Organize the class into cooperative learning groups of four or five students. Ask each group to imagine that it is establishing a mission in Texas during the late seventeenth century. Group members should carefully choose the location and name of the mission and outline its organization. Have each group present its plan to the class. **A, V, LEP**

SPANISH TEXAS

CHAPTER 7

The Story Continues...

Chapter 7 tells how and why the Spaniards changed their policy about settling the *despoblado*, or "unsettled land," to the north of central Mexico. Beginning in the 1680s, missions, forts, and settlements were established in the land called Texas. As was the case in other Spanish colonies, it was the Roman Catholic church that would direct the effort. A new era had begun, and Texas was to be an important part of Spain's empire in the Americas.

As you read the chapter, look for the answers to these questions:

1. What basic plan did the Spaniards choose for settling Texas and other lands of the northern frontier?
2. Why did the Spaniards choose to establish missions in East Texas first?
3. Why did the Spanish government establish new settlements in the middle of Texas after 1716?
4. What was life like in the Spanish missions, presidios, and civilian settlements of Texas?

1 Settling Texas

In the 1680s, the Spanish policies toward Texas entered a period of change. The Spaniards had long since given up the idea of finding gold in Texas. The expensive journeys of the conquistadores had been stopped. The Spaniards believed that Texas was too far from Mexico City and too dangerous to send families to settle there. But the leaders in Mexico City realized that their control over Texas had somehow to be strengthened.

The Mission System. The Spaniards decided to use a mission system to settle Texas. Catholic missionaries were to move into Texas and establish **missions**, each consisting of a church, houses, and farm buildings. Nearby Indians

Drawing by José Cisneros, Barker Texas History Center

Spanish missionaries came to Texas to convert the Indians to Christianity. Their efforts were not always welcomed by the Indians of Texas. This drawing shows one of the earliest Christian services held in Texas.

CHAPTER 7 OVERVIEW

During the 1500s and early 1600s, settlements in New Spain were concentrated in central Mexico. The Spaniards were not interested in settling Texas. In the 1680s, this policy changed and settlement slowly moved northward. Chapter 7 describes Texas' first Spanish settlements. It tells the story of the Spanish missions, Spanish policies in Texas, and the reasons behind Spanish settlement. It also examines the impact of the Spanish on Texas history and culture.

Essential Elements
1B ,1C, 5B, 5C, 6A, 9A, 9B

TEXAS VOICES

Illustrating (I) Ask students to illustrate one of the three paragraphs of Father Morfi's account. Invite students to share and discuss their drawings. **V, TK, LEP**

EXTENSION

Research (II) The Spanish established missions in California, Arizona, New Mexico, and Louisiana in addition to those in Texas. Have students research and prepare a written report on these settlements. In their reports, students

should examine how these missions differed from those of Spanish Texas. **G**

Independent Practice (II) Invite students to come to the front of the class and locate on a wall map Mexico City, El Paso, Juárez, and the Rio Grande. Then ask students to draw a map showing these sites. They should include on their maps a direction indicator and scale indicator. Tell students they will add to the maps in Section 2. **A, V, TK, LEP**

Essential Element
1C

TEXAS VOICES

*J*uan Agustín Morfi, a Spanish Franciscan chaplain of the Roman Catholic church, wrote one of the first histories of Texas. In 1777 and 1778, he traveled through Texas and described life in the Spanish missions. Much of Father Morfi's account focused on the economy of the mission system. He also described how well he thought the Indians had adapted to this new way of life. Because San Antonio was the hub of the Texas mission system, Father Morfi discussed the five missions there at great length, using mission records to aid his research. The following is an excerpt from his observations of life at the San José Mission, which still stands in San Antonio:

> The farm . . . is all fenced, the fence being in good condition. For its benefit, water is taken from the San Antonio River and distributed by means of a beautiful irrigation ditch to all parts of the field, where corn, beans, cotton, sugar cane, watermelons, melons, and sweet potatoes are raised. It also has a patch for all kinds of vegetables, and there are some fruit trees, from among which the peaches stand out, their fruit weighing at times as much as a pound.
>
> Today, the Indians here are well instructed and civilized and know how to work very well at their mechanical trades and are proficient in some of the arts. They speak Spanish perfectly, with the exception of those who are daily brought in by the missionaries. Many play the harp, the violin, and the guitar well, sing well, and dance the same dances as the Spaniards. They go about well dressed, are abundantly fed, . . . thanks to the labors and exertions of Fray Pedro Ramírez de Arellano, . . . who is in charge of this mission and is the president of all the missions in the province, and whose dedication, zeal, and religious spirit deserve all praise.
>
> In March, 1768, the mission had 350 persons, of whom 110 were capable of bearing arms; 45 of these could use guns, and the rest bows and arrows. Since that time, their number has been greatly reduced.

Historical Sidelight
The Spaniards established missions in California, Arizona, New Mexico, and Louisiana, in addition to those in Texas.

would be encouraged to live at the mission. Missionaries had done the same in Mexico years before. But now a mission system grew that was used throughout the present southwestern United States. The priests represented both the Roman Catholic church and the empire of Spain. Their job in Texas was twofold. They were to teach the Indians the Christian religion and an agricultural way of life. They also were to look after the interests of the Spanish government.

To protect the missions from Indians who opposed them, the Spaniards built **presidios**. These were small forts in which Spanish soldiers were stationed. The soldiers often had to protect several missions near a presidio.

132 *Unit 3*

RETEACHING
Have students create a three-column chart with the following headings: *Mission, Presidio, Civil Settlement.* Ask students to write under the appropriate heading three to five facts from Section 1. **V, LEP**

CLOSURE
Review with students the goals of the Spanish mission system and the location of the first Spanish missions in Texas.

ASSESSMENT
Have students complete the Section 1 Review on page 133.

SECTION 2

FOCUS
Past Learning and Predicting (I) Review with students that in 1684 French colonists landed on the Gulf coast of Texas. This event presented a threat to the Spaniards'

As the missions and presidios grew, small settlements developed nearby. These **civil settlements** eventually became small towns. They were called civil settlements because they were made up of civilians, those who were not priests or soldiers. People in civil settlements were usually farmers, ranchers, or merchants. These civilians provided products and service for the priests and soldiers.

The Founding of El Paso. Spanish settlements in northern Mexico moved closer to Texas in the middle of the 1600s. In 1659, a mission was founded where the city of Juárez, Mexico, now stands. It was named Nuestra Señora de Guadalupe de El Paso. The mission's purpose was to teach Christianity and a Spanish way of life to the Indians who lived along the Rio Grande.

In 1682, Franciscan friars established another mission along the Rio Grande. It was called Corpus Christi de la Ysleta. Located a few miles east of present-day El Paso, the Ysleta mission was the first permanent settlement in Texas by Europeans. Soon, a town called Ysleta grew up around the mission and presidio.

During the early 1680s, the Spaniards decided to begin slowly expanding their mission system. By 1684, at least two other missions and presidios had been built along the Rio Grande. One was at Socorro just to the south of El Paso. Downriver, other missions were built to serve the Jumano and Concho cultural groups. An event in 1685, however, caused the Spaniards to think about speeding up the building of missions. In that year, a group of French colonists landed on the Gulf coast of Texas. ○

2 The French Challenge

The center of the French empire in North America was Canada. But the French were involved in a struggle with the English and Spaniards for control of other areas of North America. French explorers and traders were traveling into the interior of the continent along the Ohio, Missouri, and Mississippi rivers.

La Salle and the French. The first person to be a threat to the Spaniards in Mexico was René-Robert Cavelier, Sieur de La Salle. In 1682, La Salle sailed down the Mississippi River to its mouth at the Gulf of Mexico. There he planted

Institute of Texan Cultures

Ysleta mission was the first permanent settlement made in Texas by Europeans. This photo of the mission was taken in the late 1800s.

SECTION ⭐ 1 REVIEW

Define: missions, presidios, civil settlements
Identify: Corpus Christi de la Ysleta

1. How did the Spanish government in Mexico plan to settle the lands of the north?
2. What were the two purposes of the new missions of the north?
3. Where were the first missions established in the land now known as Texas?

Synthesizing Information: After missions and presidios were successfully founded in a Texas location, what did Spanish authorities hope to see happen?

Exploring Geography: Describe the geography of Spanish settlement in Texas before 1685.

Answers to Section 1 Review
Define: *missions*—religious communities that were designed to convert nearby Indians to Christianity and teach them an agricultural way of life; *presidios*—Spanish forts; *civil settlements*—small settlements of civilians that developed near the Spanish missions and presidios
Identify: Corpus Christi de la Ysleta—first permanent settlement in Texas by Europeans, established in 1682
1. By use of the mission system
2. To teach the Indians Christianity and an agricultural way of life and to look after the interests of the Spanish government
3. Along the Rio Grande
Synthesizing Information: They hoped that civil settlements would grow up nearby.
Exploring Geography: Before 1685, Spanish settlement in Texas was concentrated along the Rio Grande.

Essential Elements
1B, 1C, 5B, 5C, 9A, 9B, 9D, 9E

control over Texas. Ask: From what you know about Texas today, how successful were the French in settling Texas?

INSTRUCTION

Vocabulary (I) You may wish to preteach the following boldfaced terms: *colonists* (p. 135); *chapel* (p. 135); *epidemic* (p. 139). **LEP**

CITIES OF TEXAS

Research (II) Ask interested students to conduct library research to chart the growth and development of El Paso from the Spaniards' arrival to the present. Have students present their findings in the form of a time line. **V, TK, G**

Essential Element
5C

CITIES OF TEXAS

El Paso

Population: 515,342

Metro area population: 591,610 (plus Juárez, Mexico, 797,679)

Size: 239.7 square miles

Relative location: On the Rio Grande in the far western tip of Texas

Region: Mountain and Basin region of West Texas

County: County seat of El Paso County

Special feature: A crossroads of two cultures: the Mexican city of Ciudad Juárez lies across the Rio Grande

Origin of name: Spaniards named the site *El Paso del Rio del Norte,* "the Pass of the River of the North."

Landmarks: The University of Texas at El Paso, Fort Bliss, William Beaumont Medical Center

Economy: El Paso's economic life is often summarized by the "Five C's": copper, cotton, cattle, clothing, and climate. The city is a center for mining operations, milling, oil refining, cotton

ginning, cement manufacturing, bottling, meatpacking, and a thriving tourist industry. More than 50 branches of the federal government also add stability to the economy of El Paso.

History: In 1659, Spaniards established a mission on the south side of the Rio Grande

where Juárez, Mexico, is now. In 1682 another mission, Corpus Christi de la Ysleta, was built on the north side of the river.

Recreation facilities: The mild, sunny climate of El Paso makes it ideal for tourism and outdoor activities. Besides the nearby Franklin Mountains, attractions include old missions, art galleries, a symphony orchestra, and diverse sports activities. And just across the river is Mexico.

Cultural activities: El Paso Museum of Art, El Paso Museum of History, historic Spanish missions, and the Tigua Pueblo reservation

Founding Dates of Early American Cities

St. Augustine, Florida — 1565
Jamestown, Virginia — 1607
Santa Fe, New Mexico — 1609
Plymouth, Massachusetts — 1620
El Paso, Texas — 1682
San Antonio, Texas — 1718
San Diego, California — 1769

the French flag and claimed all of the land drained by the Mississippi, from the Great Lakes to the Gulf of Mexico. La Salle named the land Louisiana, for his king, Louis XIV.

After exploring the Mississippi River valley, La Salle returned to France and told the king of his explorations. He asked Louis XIV for permission to return to North America to establish a settlement near the giant river's mouth. La Salle argued that the settlement would strengthen France's claim to the Mississippi River valley. It would also serve as a commercial center for the profitable fur trade.

King Louis welcomed La Salle's plans, and an expedition set sail in 1684. La Salle left France with four ships and approximately 300 people. One hundred were soldiers, and around 200 were **colonists**, or settlers. From the beginning, the expedition had problems. One ship was captured by the Spaniards, who learned of La Salle's plans from its passengers. Gulf storms separated the remaining three ships and blew them off course. Somehow, the expedition missed the mouth of the Mississippi.

The La Salle expedition finally came ashore in February 1685 at Matagorda Bay on the Texas coast. While entering the bay, one of the ships sank with valuable supplies aboard. To make matters worse, the captain of another of the ships decided to return to France with some of the colonists and many of the supplies. La Salle found himself stranded on the Texas coast with nearly 200 colonists. They had very little food and few other supplies. They were not well prepared for life in the wilderness.

Fort St. Louis. La Salle and the others quickly realized they could not live on the marshy lowlands of the coast. So they moved inland several miles and built a crude wooden fort on the banks of Garcitas Creek. They called it Fort St. Louis. Built on high ground for protection, the fort was made up of five or six houses surrounded by a wall. There was also a **chapel**, or small church. On the walls of the fort, eight cannons were mounted.

After Fort St. Louis was built, La Salle began to explore the nearby land. One journey led him westward toward the Rio Grande, perhaps in search of Spanish mines or food supplies. Meanwhile, life was not going well at Fort St. Louis. Fighting broke out with the Indians. Disease and Indian attacks lowered the number of French to only 45.

Institute of Texan Cultures

René-Robert Cavelier, Sieur de la Salle, led an expedition from France to the mouth of the Mississippi River in 1684. The expedition was blown off course and came ashore at Matagorda Bay on the Texas coast.

Institute of Texan Cultures

This engraving shows La Salle's expedition landing at Matagorda Bay. The artist had never seen the Texas coast. How can we tell this?

Geography
The Mississippi River has a series of outlets to the Gulf of Mexico. La Salle knew the latitude of the river's mouth but not the longitude, and thus he could not be sure of its location.

Caption Response
There are no mountains along the Texas coast.

Linking History and Geography
For protection

Multicultural Perspective
Hernando de Soto named the Mississippi River *Espiritu Santo.* La Salle named the river the *Colbert,* after a French minister. The Indians, however, continued to call the river *Misi Sipi,* or "Big River."

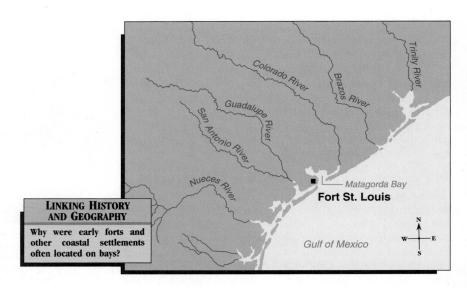

LINKING HISTORY AND GEOGRAPHY
Why were early forts and other coastal settlements often located on bays?

Crops failed, and there was little food. La Salle decided he must return to Canada for help. His first attempt to reach the Mississippi River failed. In January 1687, La Salle and seventeen men marched eastward again, looking for the Mississippi.

While on the trip through East Texas, the French argued among themselves about how poorly things had turned out. Somewhere near the present town of Navasota, La Salle was murdered by several of his own soldiers. As they wandered through the forests looking for the Mississippi, some of La Salle's murderers were later killed by Indians. A few members of the party survived and eventually made their way back to Canada.

Those who had remained at Fort St. Louis faced tragedy as well. A number of colonists died from smallpox. Then, early in 1689, Karankawas attacked the fort. They killed most of the French, and the fort was destroyed. Six of the French escaped, and two of them were later rescued by Spanish expeditions. They told the exciting and tragic tale of La Salle and Fort St. Louis.

The Spaniards Face the Challenge. There were two results of La Salle's adventure into Texas. First, it gave France at least a weak claim to Texas. Second, it presented a challenge to Spain's empire north of the Rio Grande. The

Spaniards realized that if they did not build settlements in Texas, the French might gain control of the region.

Within months after Fort St. Louis had been founded, Spaniards organized expeditions to remove the French from Texas. The Spaniards sent at least five expeditions by land and five by sea. Attempts at locating Fort St. Louis in 1686 and 1687 failed. But in 1689, a Spanish force led by the governor of the province of Coahuila, Captain Alonso de León, found two French survivors living among a group of Indians. De León took the men back to Mexico.

Viceroy Monclova ordered De León back to Texas to search for the fort. Guided by the Frenchmen, the Spanish force finally found the ruins of Fort St. Louis. Father Damián Massanet, who went along on the trip, wrote in his journal:

> There was a great lot of scattered weapons, broken by the Indians—firelocks, carbines, cutlasses—but they had not left the cannon, only one being found. We found two unburied bodies, which I interred [buried]. . . . There were many torn-up books, and many dead pigs.

Texas Department of Transportation

The interior of the chapel at La Bahía displays a fine example of Spanish religious art.

RETEACHING
Refer students to sites that they labeled in the Section 2 Independent Practice activity. Ask them to use these place names in a paragraph summarizing Section 2. Invite volunteers to read their paragraphs aloud. **A, LEP**

CLOSURE
Review with students the reasons for Spain's decision to settle the interior of Texas and why the East Texas missions failed.

ASSESSMENT
Have students complete the Section 2 Review on page 139.

Hearing of other French survivors, De León and the members of his expedition marched into East Texas. There they met a band of the Tejas confederacy of the Caddo group. The Indians were friendly and eager to listen to Father Massanet.

Spanish Missions in East Texas. De León and Father Massanet were impressed by the land and people of East Texas. After returning to Mexico, they reported to Viceroy Monclova and advised setting up missions there. They thought this was the best way to protect Spanish lands from the French. The viceroy finally gave in to Father Massanet, who was eager to bring Christianity to the Tejas. In March 1690, Captain De León and Father Massanet led several missionaries, 110 soldiers, and other Spaniards north to build a settlement in East Texas. They brought with them "twenty mules laden with wine, wax, and so on, also clothing for distribution among the Indians, and six loads of tobacco."

Arriving back in the land of the Tejas, the Spaniards claimed the land for their king and then began to build a mission. On June 1, 1690, the first Spanish mission in East Texas was dedicated. Located a few miles west of the Neches River near the present town of Weches, the mission was named San Francisco de los Tejas.

Mission San Francisco de los Tejas has been reconstructed near Weches.

Texas Department of Transportation

SECTION 3

FOCUS

Past Learning and Predicting (I) Review with students the Spaniards' failed attempt to settle East Texas in the 1690s. Have the class brainstorm reasons that the Spanish might want to return to the region.

INSTRUCTION

Analyzing (II) Ask students to consider reasons that the viceroy would not allow trade between the Spanish and the French. With the class, list the advantages and disadvantages to Spain. **A, V, G**

The mission, which was little more than a log cabin, was built in only a few days. After dedicating the mission, De León and Father Massanet returned to Mexico. Three priests were left to convert the Indians, and three soldiers were left to protect the priests. At first the Indians and priests were hopeful about the future of San Francisco de los Tejas. However, problems soon arose to upset the Spanish plan for East Texas.

Failure of the East Texas Missions. During 1691 and 1692, the San Francisco de los Tejas mission faced many problems. An **epidemic**, or contagious disease affecting large numbers of people, spread through the area, killing many Indians and one priest. Drought ruined the crops that had been planted by the Indians. Floods washed away a second mission that had been built nearby on the banks of the Neches River.

The Indians began to blame the Spanish for their troubles. They became hostile to the priests, and the Spaniards soon realized that they had to leave. On the night of October 25, 1693, the priests burned the mission to the ground, buried the mission bells, and left for Mexico. The first Spanish attempt at settling East Texas ended in failure. ⊙

3 The Spanish Return to Texas

For the next twenty years, Spain made no attempt to establish missions in the interior of Texas. Since it seemed that the French were no longer a threat, the Spaniards were satisfied with their missions and presidios along the Rio Grande. But a priest at the San Juan Bautista mission, located south of the Rio Grande near what is now Eagle Pass, wanted to rebuild the East Texas missions. Through his efforts, the Spanish returned to East Texas.

Father Hidalgo. That priest was Father Francisco Hidalgo. He wrote a letter to the French Franciscans. Somehow, it ended up in the hands of the French governor in Louisiana. It suggested that the French and Spaniards work together to establish missions for the Indians in East Texas. Governor Cadillac of Louisiana approved the plan, not so much to convert the Indians, but to trade with them and the Spaniards. Louisiana then was under control of a private company that hoped to profit from the colony. If

---

SECTION ★2★ REVIEW

Define: colonists, chapel, epidemic
Identify: Fort St. Louis, Alonso de León, Father Massanet

1. Why did the Spaniards establish their first missions in East Texas?
2. What were the two results of La Salle's expedition to colonize North America?
3. What troubles plagued the East Texas missions?

Analyzing Information: Judging from the plans of La Salle and the actions of De León and Father Massanet, how did French-Indian relations differ from Spanish-Indian relations?

Interpreting Maps: Look at the map on page 136. Why do you think it was difficult for French or Spanish ships to locate the mouth of a particular river along the Texas coast? Explain.

Answers to Section 2 Review

Define: *colonists*—settlers; *chapel*—small church; *epidemic*—contagious disease affecting large numbers of people
Identify: Fort St. Louis—crude fort built by members of La Salle's expedition; Alonso de León—governor of the province of Coahuila, who went in search of Fort St. Louis; Father Massanet—priest who accompanied De León on his search

1. To oppose the French threat and to convert the Tejas to Christianity
2. It gave France a weak claim to Texas, and it encouraged Spain to establish missions in East Texas.
3. Floods, food shortages, epidemics, lack of cooperation from the Indians

Analyzing Information: La Salle planned to promote trade with the Native Americans. In contrast, the Spanish had little to trade and wished to convert and control the Indians.

Interpreting Maps: Answers will vary, but maps of the coast were generally inaccurate. Also, there were many islands and channels located offshore at the rivers' mouths.

Essential Elements
1B, 1C, 5A, 5B, 5C, 9A, 9B, 9E

Historical Sidelight

France was more interested in making Louisiana a trading enterprise than it was in making it a colony. The French government did not encourage settlement. In 1755, the British forced more than 4,000 French farmers and fishermen out of Nova Scotia. Many of these people settled in Louisiana and came to be called *Cajuns*. (*Cajun* is a slurred form of the word *Acadian*, the French name for a Nova Scotian.)

San Jacinto Museum of History, Houston

This painting is of Father Antonio Margil de Jesus. He was with the 1716 expedition to East Texas led by Captain Domingo Ramón.

trade could be opened with the Indians and the Spaniards, perhaps Louisiana would earn money. Cadillac sent a young man named Louis de St. Denis to Texas as his agent to deal with the Spaniards and the Indians.

St. Denis began his adventure by building a trading post at Natchitoches, Louisiana, in 1713. He then crossed into the territory of the Tejas and, in 1714, headed for San Juan Bautista to find Father Hidalgo. After arriving at the presidio, St. Denis was arrested because it was against the law for foreigners to be on Spanish land. Spanish soldiers took him to Mexico City for questioning.

In his meetings with the viceroy in Mexico City, Louis de St. Denis said the French had no desire to settle East Texas. He claimed that his concern was the same as Father Hidalgo's, to expose the Indians to the Christian religion. Of course, St. Denis really wanted the Spaniards to settle in East Texas so that the French could trade with them and the Indians.

The viceroy agreed to the plan of rebuilding missions in East Texas. But he did so because he saw St. Denis as another threat. The viceroy issued a warning to St. Denis: trade between the Spanish and the French was not allowed. The viceroy made another important decision. This time, the missions in East Texas would have the support of presidios and civil settlements. In the year 1716, Spaniards returned to East Texas.

New East Texas Missions. The leader of the expedition back to East Texas was Captain Domingo Ramón. His daughter, Mañuela Sánchez, had met Louis de St. Denis when he first arrived from Louisiana. They were married as the expedition was being organized. Father Hidalgo was sent to head the new missions in the region, and St. Denis was hired by the Spaniards to act as a guide. They took with them twelve priests, 25 soldiers, and several families. They also brought gifts for the Indians, supplies from farms and the presidios, and more than 1,000 head of livestock.

The Indians welcomed the Spaniards back to their land. The bad feelings of twenty years earlier seemed to be forgotten. After an exchange of gifts, the Indians helped the Spaniards choose sites for the new missions.

Six new missions were established in the East Texas area. The first was named Nuestro Padre San Francisco de los Tejas. It was located about twelve miles east of the

Laurence Parent

Mission Concepción was originally established in East Texas. In 1731, it was relocated to San Antonio.

original Tejas mission of 1690. Father Hidalgo was placed in charge of this mission. The second mission was Nuestra Señora de la Purísima Concepción. It was about 24 miles northeast of the first mission, on the Angelina River. The third mission was Nuestra Señora de Guadalupe, located at what is now Nacogdoches. The San José de los Nazonis mission was established near present-day Cushing. Another mission was built near what is now San Augustine. A sixth mission, San Miguel de los Linares de los Adaes, was established near the French outpost at Natchitoches, Louisiana.

The Spaniards took several steps to insure the success of their East Texas missions. Captain Ramón built a presidio among the missions to offer the protection of the army. It was called Nuestra Señora de los Dolores de los Tejas. To try to guarantee the cooperation of the Indians, Ramón chose Caddo chiefs to act as representatives of the king of Spain. Ramón believed that by recognizing the authority of the tribal chiefs, the Spaniards could ultimately control the Caddoes more easily.

Chapter 7 **141**

Geography
A Spanish friar described the San Antonio area as "the best site in the world, with good and abundant irrigation water, rich lands for pasture, plentiful building stone, and excellent timber."

The San Antonio Settlements. Although the East Texas missions were firmly established by 1717, they were still over 500 miles from the nearest Spanish settlements. It was often difficult for the missions to get supplies, partly because Apaches and Comanches raided wagon trains from Mexico. The Spanish in East Texas were sometimes forced to rely on the French for supplies.

As Franciscan friar Antonio Olivares had long argued, there was a need for a Spanish outpost between the missions in East Texas and the settlements in northern Mexico. In 1718, the former governor of Coahuila, Martín de Alarcón, led an expedition to find a location for a new mission settlement.

In the spring of that year, Alarcón reached the San Pedro Springs on the San Antonio River. There he founded the presidio San Antonio de Béxar. Nearby he established the mission San Antonio de Valero, later known as the Alamo. In following years, four other missions were built in the area. As civil settlement around the missions grew, the village became known as Béxar. Today these missions lie in the heart of San Antonio.

San José mission at San Antonio is sometimes called the "Queen of the Missions" because of its fine architecture. Many people visit the museum each year.

Texas Department of Transportation

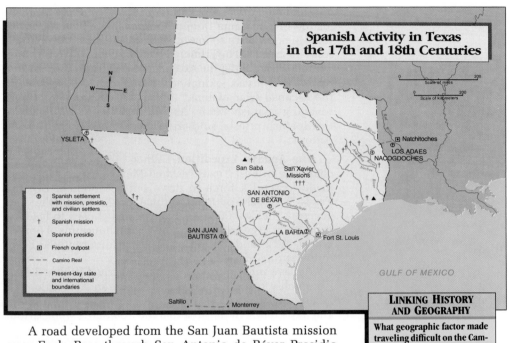

Spanish Activity in Texas in the 17th and 18th Centuries

Transparency 11
An overhead transparency of this map can be found in the Teacher's Resource Binder.

A road developed from the San Juan Bautista mission near Eagle Pass through San Antonio de Béxar Presidio and on to Nacogdoches in East Texas. It was called the Camino Real, or the "Royal Highway." The Camino Real was the major supply route from Mexico into Texas. Its importance helped make San Antonio de Béxar the largest settlement in Spanish Texas. Eventually, other such roads developed between Mexico and Texas.

Problems in East Texas. The San Antonio settlement greatly strengthened the Spanish claim to Texas, but problems continued to face the Spaniards in East Texas. French traders often had more influence with the Indians than did the Spanish missionaries. Crops failed, diseases introduced by the Spaniards sometimes broke out in the missions, and soldiers often deserted into French Louisiana. To make matters worse, France declared war against Spain in 1719.

The war in Texas had a humorous side and a serious side. A French force of seven soldiers decided to attack the mission San Miguel de Linares and demand that the Spaniards surrender. There were only two Spaniards at the

LINKING HISTORY AND GEOGRAPHY

What geographic factor made traveling difficult on the Camino Real between Mexico and Louisiana?

Linking History and Geography
Many rivers

RETEACHING

Have students list the following names on a sheet of paper: Father Hidalgo, Louis de St. Denis, Captain Domingo Ramón, Antonio Olivares, Martín de Alarcón, Marqués de Aguayo. Ask students to write a sentence next to each name, explaining that person's role in the Spanish mission system in Texas. **LEP**

CLOSURE

Ask: From what you have read in Section 3, was the Spaniards' second attempt to settle the interior of Texas a success or failure? Have students explain their answers.

ASSESSMENT

Have students complete the Section 3 Review on page 145.

mission, one of them a Franciscan friar. The only problem for the French came from a flock of squawking chickens. The chickens were so loud that they frightened the French soldiers' horses. The French commander was thrown to the ground, and, during the excitement, the friar escaped.

The event was jokingly called the "Chicken War." But the escaped friar claimed that a large French force was invading Spanish Texas. As a result of his report, most of the Spanish priests, soldiers, and settlers retreated to San Antonio.

The Aguayo Expedition. When news of the French challenge in East Texas reached Mexico City, plans were made to send a force to drive out the French. Because Texas was part of the province of Coahuila, the new governor, the Marqués de Aguayo, was chosen to lead the expedition. Aguayo was supplied with thousands of horses, mules, cattle, and sheep. He and 500 soldiers entered Texas in the spring of 1721.

Aguayo met no trouble upon his arrival in East Texas. He quickly reestablished the missions and presidio. The large number of soldiers no doubt convinced the Indians and any French in the area that the Spaniards were serious about controlling the region.

Aguayo built a new presidio near Natchitoches, Louisiana. Named Nuestra Señora del Pilar de los Adaes, the new presidio was very strong. One hundred soldiers and six cannons were stationed there. The presidio was surrounded by a stockade of pointed logs. About 28 families settled within its walls. This presidio was known as Los Adaes, and a civil settlement eventually grew up near it. The government in Mexico City made Los Adaes the capital of the province of the Tejas, or Spanish Texas.

Expansion of the Tejas Missions. The Spaniards continued to expand their mission system in other parts of Texas from the 1720s until the 1750s. One of the more important new settlements was the La Bahía mission and presidio. It was originally built near La Salle's Fort St. Louis by Marqués de Aguayo. It was later moved to a spot on the San Antonio River near the present town of Goliad.

From 1748 to 1751, the Spaniards founded three missions along the San Gabriel River near present-day Rockdale. They were called the San Xavier missions. These missions were intended to serve the Tonkawas of Central

Texas Department of Transportation

The La Bahía mission was originally established near Matagorda Bay but was eventually rebuilt along the banks of the San Antonio River near present-day Goliad.

FOCUS

Student Experiences (I) Ask students if any of them have ever visited the Spanish missions in Texas. Invite these students to describe their visits to the class. **LEP, A**

INSTRUCTION

Vocabulary (I) You may wish to preteach the following boldfaced terms: *plaza* (p. 147); *ayuntamiento* (p. 148); *alcalde* (p. 148); *fiestas* (p. 148); *vaqueros* (p. 149). **LEP**

The Beinecke Rare Book and Manuscript Library, Yale University

This sketch of Goliad and its presidio was made by Lino Sánchez y Tapia in 1829.

Texas. The missions failed because of Apache and Comanche raids, as well as an epidemic of smallpox.

Another attempt to reach the Indians of Central Texas was made in 1757. The San Sabá de la Santa Cruz mission was founded near present-day Menard. Soldiers also built San Sabá Presidio a few miles away.

Besides serving the Apaches in the area, the Spaniards hoped to mine gold and silver that was located in the region. They did mine some silver, but the San Sabá mission was soon destroyed by Comanches.

Throughout the 1700s, Spain built other missions and expanded the road system. Two missions were established on the Nueces River, and one on the Trinity. The Spaniards also tried to build a mission at Barton Springs in present-day Austin. None of these was successful, because of Indians who opposed them. The Spaniards were never able to expand the mission system into the lands of the Apaches or the Comanches.

After a century of mission activity in Texas, only a few locations proved to be successful. These were the missions and settlements in San Antonio, El Paso, Nacogdoches, Los Adaes, and Goliad. Despite years of hard work and great expense, Spanish control was limited to these areas. ✪

4 Spanish Life in Texas

To the Spanish government, the missions in Texas were a means of expanding Spanish power and influence. But to the Roman Catholic missionaries, they were a way to teach the Indians Christianity and the Spanish way of life.

SECTION ★3★ REVIEW

Identify: Father Hidalgo, St. Denis, Nuestro Padre San Francisco de los Tejas

1. How did St. Denis affect the Spanish government's Texas policies? Explain.
2. How were the Spanish settlements of 1716 in East Texas different from earlier ones?
3. What was the purpose of the Aguayo expedition of 1721?

Interpreting Information: What was the main problem with trying to start new missions in the area north and west of San Antonio? Why did the Spaniards fail to solve the problem?

Seeing Cause and Effect: What did the Spanish government try to accomplish by founding a new presidio near Natchitoches, Louisiana, in 1721?

Answers to Section 3 Review

Identify: Father Hidalgo—Spanish priest who wished to see the reestablishment of the East Texas missions; St. Denis—French trader and explorer; Nuestro Padre San Francisco de los Tejas—Spanish mission established in 1716 near the Neches River

1. His interest in East Texas renewed the Spanish government's fear of French expansion. Spain therefore decided to reestablish the East Texas missions.
2. Those of 1716 had the support of the presidios and civil settlements, and Spanish commitment was much greater.
3. To reestablish Spanish control in East Texas after the "Chicken War" incident

Interpreting Information: The main problem was hostile Indians. The Indian raiders were impossible to follow and defeat.

Seeing Cause and Effect: The Spanish government attempted to control and intimidate the French.

Essential Elements
1A, 1B, 9B, 9E

Texas Department of Transportation

Presidio San Sabá today lies in ruins near Menard.

In the places where the Indians were willing to accept these changes, the missions succeeded and towns grew. In places where Indians refused to give up their way of life, the missions usually failed. The successful mission settlements were the centers of Spanish life in Texas.

Life in the Missions. Life in the missions was busy yet routine. The day began at dawn with religious services. For at least an hour, Indians were taught the basic beliefs of the Roman Catholic faith. Then the workday began under the control and direction of the missionaries and soldiers. The Indian men worked in the fields, tending the crops of corn, beans, and cotton. The women made pottery, wove cloth, cared for the livestock, and ran the mission kitchen. Children went to classes part of the time and then trained for future jobs. The Indians were required to spend another hour in the evening learning about Roman Catholicism.

The missions in the San Antonio area were the most prosperous of all in Texas. A report in 1745 described the wealth of the San Antonio de Valero mission. It had more than 5,000 head of cattle, more than 2,000 sheep, and large herds of goats and horses. Each year, around 8,000 bushels of corn were grown, as well as large quantities of beans, melons, pumpkins, sweet potatoes, and cotton.

146 *Unit 3*

Guided Practice (I) Have students create a chart or other diagram illustrating the organization of the missions, presidios, and civil settlements. **V, TK, LEP**

EXTENSION

Home Involvement (I) With the class, plan a "Spanish Heritage" day. Invite students to bring to class samples of food and music representative of Texas' Spanish heritage. **A, V, TK, LEP**

Independent Practice (II) Ask students to imagine that they are Indians living in Texas in 1745. Have them compose a letter, a poem, or a song that describes how their lives have changed since the arrival of the Spanish missionaries. Invite volunteers to read their writings aloud. **A, TK, LEP**

Like most Texas missions, San Antonio de Valero consisted of several rows of stone houses. The houses had arched entryways, doors, and windows. Each house was furnished with high wooden beds, chests, and a supply of kitchen utensils. The houses were built around a central **plaza**, or public square. In the middle was a well surrounded by fruit and willow trees. There was, of course, a chapel near the rows of houses. The entire village was surrounded by a wall. [See drawing of the Alamo, page 246.]

The mission chapel was usually decorated with paintings, statues, tiles, and windows trimmed in gold or silver. It was a combination of Spanish and Indian artwork. Besides art, the priests and Indians shared a love of music. Much of the music that came out of the missions was religious, such as hymns and prayer chants. But the Indians often sang their tribal songs as well. Over the years, some of the Spanish and Indian music merged and came to reflect the traditions of both cultures.

Life in the Presidios. The presidios were built of timber, stone, or adobe. Inside were barracks for the soldiers. There were also quarters for the officers, storage rooms for supplies and ammunition, and a headquarters building. Surrounding these buildings was the stockade, or wall.

Manuscripts Division. New York Public Library

Converting the Indians was pictured in a 1750 manuscript by a Mexican priest. Note that the Indians are threatened by demons as they receive religious instruction (top). The demons finally disappear as the Indians are baptized (lower right).

RETEACHING

Write the following statements on the chalkboard (you may wish to add to them), and have students number a sheet of paper accordingly. Tell them to write an *M* if the statement refers to the missions, a *P* if it refers to the presidios, or a *C* if it refers to the civil settlements. **V, LEP**

1. It contained barracks for the soldiers. *(P)*
2. The day began with religious services. *(M)*
3. Horse racing was popular. *(C)*
4. The major problem was morale. *(P)*
5. Indians were taught the basic beliefs of the Roman Catholic faith. *(M)*

Barker Texas History Center

The Rose Window at San José mission is one of the finest examples in Texas of Spanish architecture from the mission era.

Geography

Display a wall map of the world, and ask a volunteer to locate the Canary Islands.

Texas Department of Transportation

The Texas longhorn resulted when wild Spanish cattle mixed with cattle brought by settlers from the United States during the 1820s and 1830s.

Several cannons were usually placed on the wall. Although there were a few soldiers stationed within the walls of each mission, most of the soldiers lived at the presidio.

The major problem at the presidios was the morale of the soldiers. They were paid a very small salary and had poor equipment. Their uniforms were often worn and tattered, and the presidios were constantly running out of supplies. The daily routine was boring, although once in a while there was the threat of an Indian attack, and fighting Indians was dangerous. The missionaries had the challenge of their work, but life for the Spanish soldiers was hard and unrewarding. Spanish reports show that soldiers often disagreed with missionaries on how to treat Indians.

Life in the Civilian Settlements. The only permanent Texas settlements that grew from the mission system were at San Antonio, Goliad, Nacogdoches, and El Paso. These were scattered over a huge area. By far the largest settlement was at San Antonio. This settlement was also the only one in which the people had a voice in their government.

San Antonio was governed by a council of landowners called the **ayuntamiento**. There was also an official called the **alcalde**, who acted as mayor, sheriff, and judge. In other settlements, the commander of the presidio ran the affairs of the government. Of course, the governor of the province had power over all of these local officials.

The settlers themselves were of several different backgrounds. Most had moved north from Mexico, hoping to find fertile land for farming or to enter the ranching business. Some of the settlers were former Spanish soldiers who married Indians. Some were free African Americans. Others were blacks brought to Texas as slaves. In San Antonio, fifteen families from the Canary Islands settled in the 1730s.

The economy of the settlements was based on farming and ranching. Men and women alike helped with the planting and harvesting of the crops. The men usually worked with the cattle and sheep. The women took charge of the goats, pigs, and chickens. Some people made their living as traders, blacksmiths, and cart drivers.

People in the civil settlements enjoyed a wide variety of social activities. Most of these activities centered around the family and the church. On most evenings, families could be seen walking around the plaza. There were parades and **fiestas**, or celebrations, that were usually

CLOSURE
Review with students Texas' Spanish legacy by asking students to give examples of Spanish influence in Texas.

ASSESSMENT
Have students complete the Section 4 Review on page 149.

Painting by Theodore Gentilz, Daughters of the Republic of Texas Library

sponsored by the church. Horse racing was popular, as were dances and musical concerts.

An important influence on the civil settlements in Texas was the growing cattle industry. Small herds of cattle had been brought to Texas by the first explorers and by every expedition that followed. By the late 1700s, there were thousands of cattle running wild. Most of these wild cattle lived in the brush country around San Antonio. The cattle adapted to the dry South Texas Plains, becoming leaner and tougher, with longer and longer horns. People in the settlements captured the wild cattle and began the Texas cattle industry. These people were the first Texas cowboys, or as the Spaniards called them, **vaqueros.**

The Spanish Heritage. Despite the mixture of successes and failures with the mission system, the Spaniards had a great impact on the history of Texas. Part of the Spanish heritage comes from the Roman Catholic church. It has given strength and guidance to millions of Texans. The first educational institutions in Texas were established here by the Franciscan missionaries.

There are other examples of Spanish influence throughout Texas history. Spanish law, art, architecture, music, language, and food are all part of Texas' heritage. The Spanish legacy is also important to the Texas economy. Spaniards brought the first horses and cattle to Texas. The cattle industry helped the city of San Antonio and many South Texas towns grow and prosper.

In the names of rivers, cities, mountains, foods, and many of our everyday words, the Spanish heritage is all around us. But the most important legacy from Spanish Texas is people. Generations of Hispanic people have called Texas their home and have helped build its future. ✪

For entertainment, dances were often held in the Spanish settlements.

Institute of Texan Cultures

Hispanic vaqueros were the earliest Texas cowboys.

SECTION ★4★ REVIEW

Define: plaza, ayuntamiento, alcalde, fiestas, vaqueros

1. What were the relationships among missions, presidios, and civil settlements in Spanish Texas?
2. What daily activities were performed by Indians at the missions?
3. How did people make a living within the civil settlements?

Interpreting Pictures: How does the picture on page 147 defend Spanish missions being in Texas? Explain.

Exploring Economics: Successful missions sometimes produced large quantities of vegetables and livestock. What do you think the missionaries did with these foodstuffs?

Essential Elements
1A, 1B, 1C

LONE STAR LEGACY

Using Historical Imagination:
Answers will vary, but students will probably describe the sounds made by combining the Indian drums and flutes with the Spanish string instruments.

LEGACY

A Sharing of Culture Through Music

*M*usic played an important role in the lives of the Texas Indians. They sang songs about harvesting their crops, hunting wild game, fighting their enemies, giving birth, becoming adults, and reaching old age with pride. Music was the foundation of Indian religious ceremonies and celebrations.

Each Native American culture had a different musical tradition. The nomadic Plains Indians (Comanches and Kiowas) sang songs with high-pitched sounds that resembled loud wails and screams. Other tribes such as the Caddoes and Tonkawas had soothing, melodic songs.

Nearly all the Texas Indians used percussion instruments. These included drums, rattles, and notched sticks. Some had flute-like instruments that resembled whistles and recorders in sound.

As the Spaniards settled Texas, they brought with them their own musical traditions. These they taught to the Texas Indians who lived in or near the Spanish missions. Over the years, there was a trading and mixing of musical styles. Music was a way of borrowing customs and sharing culture.

Father Solis, a Spanish missionary priest, observed the relationship between Spanish and Indian musical styles in 1767:

All of these Indians speak Spanish. . . . Most of them play some musical instrument, the guitar, the violin or the harp. All have good voices, and on Saturdays, the 19th of each month, and on the feasts of our Lord . . . they take out their rosaries [prayer beads] while a choir of four voices, soprano, alto, tenor, and bass, with musical accompaniment, sings so beautifully that it is a delight to hear it.

Using Historical Imagination
Write a description of what you think the music sounded like after the musical styles of Spaniards and Indians mingled.

Inset: Early stringed instrument

Inset: Robert Lightfoot, Nawrocki Stock Photo   Right: Drawing by José Cisneros. Institute of Texan Cultures

CHAPTER 7 REVIEW

Understanding Main Ideas

1. What was the purpose of the Spanish missions?
2. What were two results of La Salle's trip into Texas?
3. Why did the Spaniards return to build more missions in East Texas in 1716?
4. What three kinds of settlement were typical of Spanish colonies in northern Mexico and Texas?
5. What was the result of the "Chicken War"?
6. Why did the missions founded in Central Texas fail?
7. Give five examples of the Spanish influence in Texas.

Thinking Critically

1. **Evaluating Information:** How did a mission built in East Texas in 1716 differ from a mission built in 1690? Why did the Spaniards choose to do things differently a quarter of a century later?
2. **Synthesizing Information:** What evidence can you find in Chapter 7 that the people participating in La Salle's expedition were not in agreement about the entire trip?
3. **Classifying Information:** Write the words *French* and *Spaniards* at the top of a page. Divide the page into two columns. Then write the following names under the appropriate nationality: St. Denis, De León, La Salle, Massanet, Louis XIV, Aguayo.

Linking History and Geography

1. Why were most Spanish missions and other settlements in Texas located near rivers?
2. What basic fact of geography made it difficult to send supplies by wagon train overland from Mexico to the East Texas missions?

TAAS Practice
Using Primary Sources

When Spaniards moved north into the territories of the Apaches and Comanches, they found these Native American societies different from those they had met before. These differences were to change the course of history. In the following account, Juan Dominguez de Mendoza records his reasons for giving up a military expedition into Apache territory in 1684.

> [I am returning] because of my not being able to sustain the great war which, from the north, the common enemies, the Apache nation, have made upon us. They have attacked us three times by night and by day, and the last night they wounded a soldier, inflicting upon him three arrow wounds, besides other injuries which the Apaches have caused.
>
> From the west the bandit Indians . . . with great boldness made by night three attacks upon the . . . camp, and killed in the field two friendly Indians who had gone out to hunt. . . . And being without forces, and with only a few munitions [military supplies], I consider it best to return. . . .

1. According to Mendoza's account, he is returning to Mexico because

Essential Elements
1A, 1B, 5A, 5B, 9A, 9E

CHAPTER 7 REVIEW ANSWERS

Understanding Main Ideas

1. To convert the Indians to Christianity and to extend control of the Spanish government
2. It gave France a weak claim to Texas, and it caused the Spanish government to establish the first settlements in East Texas.
3. To prevent France from taking the area
4. Missions, presidios, and civil settlements
5. It resulted in the Aguayo expedition reestablishing the East Texas missions and founding a new settlement near Natchitoches, Louisiana.
6. Because of opposition from hostile Indians
7. Possible answers include: the influence of the Roman Catholic church; the first educational institutions; Spanish art, architecture, music, language, and food; the impact on the economy of horses and cattle, first introduced by Spaniards; place names; the Hispanic people.

Thinking Critically

1. **Evaluating Information:**
   The earlier missions were smaller. Presidios and civil settlements were added to the later missions. The presidios were added for protection. The civil settlements were added so that the missions would have a source for supplies and someone to trade with.

2. **Synthesizing Information:**
   The evidence reveals that the soldiers and colonists did not get along well. Passengers on the ship captured by the Spaniards revealed La Salle's mission in North America. One of La Salle's captains disobeyed him and refused to enter Matagorda Bay, turning back for France. Later, La Salle was murdered by his own soldiers.

3. **Classifying Information:**
   French—St. Denis, La Salle, Louis XIV; Spaniards—De León, Massanet, Aguayo

Linking History and Geography

1. For a source of water and transport
2. Too many rivers to cross

TAAS Practice
Using Primary Sources

1. C
2. A

TAAS Practice
Writing Descriptively

Diary entries will vary but should demonstrate knowledge of Spanish mission life and should include positive and negative aspects of mission life.

Practicing Skills

1. **Seeing Cause and Effect:** *Cause:* La Salle established Fort St. Louis *Effect:* East Texas missions were founded; *Cause:* the "Chicken War" took place *Effect:* East Texas missions were abandoned

2. **Interpreting Maps:** San Antonio and Nacogdoches

Enriching Your Study of History

1. **Individual Project:** Reports should be detailed, accurate, and well written.

2. **Cooperative Project:** Answers will vary but should demonstrate knowledge of the two empires.

A he has failed to find enough food and water on the deserts of the Southwest

B he has successfully completed his military assignment and is ready to go home

C the Apaches have made repeated attacks on his expedition

D his Indian guides refused to go any further because of the weather

2. The reasons Mendoza gives for the Apaches' success against him are

   A they are bold and attack at night

   B his friendly Indians refused to fight against them

   C they had newer weapons than the Spanish soldiers

   D they always took Mendoza's soldiers by surprise and refused to fight fairly

TAAS Practice
Writing Descriptively

Imagine that you are an Indian living at the San Antonio de Valero mission in the years after 1740. In your diary, describe your activities on an average workday. What do you find most satisfying and least satisfying about life in the mission?

Practicing Skills

1. **Seeing Cause and Effect:** A cause is an event that brings about another event. The second event is an effect of the first. Match the following causes with the correct effect. *Causes:* La Salle established Fort St. Louis; the "Chicken War" took place. *Effects:* East Texas missions were founded; East Texas missions were abandoned.

Spanish Last Names in Texas, 1850

● Spanish last names
1 Dot = 100 persons

(Note: El Paso census was not taken in 1850.)

2. **Interpreting Maps:** Study the map on this page. With what eighteenth-century Spanish settlements were the Central Texas grouping and the East Texas grouping connected?

Enriching Your Study of History

1. **Individual Project:** Choose a Spanish mission or presidio mentioned in this chapter and prepare a research report on its history.

2. **Cooperative Project:** Your teacher will separate the class into small groups to discuss this question: How would Texas history have been different if France, not Spain, had added Texas to its empire? Each group will agree on its answer to this question and write it on a sheet of paper. Then a speaker from each group will share the group's ideas with the entire class.

CHAPTER 8

CONFLICTS OF EMPIRE

TEACHER'S TIME LINE

Section 1 Pp. 153–56 1 Day	Section 2 Pp. 156–58 1 Day	Section 3 Pp. 158–63 1 Day	Section 4 Pp. 163–67 1 Day	Review and Assessment 1 Day

⭐ TEACHER MATERIALS

Core: Chapter 8 Time Line; Graphic Organizer 8; Enrichment Worksheet 8; Review Worksheet 8; Reteaching Worksheet 8; Chapter 8 Tests, Forms A & B

Additional: Geography and Graph Skills 8, Map and Chart Transparencies 12, Informal Evaluation Forms, Test Generator

OBJECTIVES

1. Discuss reasons that the Spaniards changed their policy toward Texas settlement.
2. Describe the relationship between the Spaniards and the Texas Indians.
3. Identify boundary changes that influenced Spanish policy in Texas.
4. Discuss the results of the Adams-Oñis Treaty.
5. Explain the goals of the filibusters.
6. Describe major rebellions against Spanish control of Texas.
7. Explain how Mexico gained its independence.

⭐ RESOURCES

BOOKS FOR TEACHERS

Bolton, Herbert Eugene. *Texas in the Middle Eighteenth Century: Studies in Spanish Colonial History and Administration*. Austin: Unversity of Texas Press, 1970. History of the Spanish colonial period.

Faulk, Odie B. *A Successful Failure, 1519–1810. The Saga of Texas Series*. Austin: Steck-Vaughn, 1965. Texas history.

Flores, Dan L., editor. *Jefferson and Southwestern Exploration*. Norman: University of Oklahoma Press, 1984. Louisiana Purchase and other important events.

Haley, J. Evetts. *The Alamo Mission Bell*. Austin: Encino Press, 1974. History of San Antonio.

McDonald, Archie P. *The Old Stone Fort*. Austin: Texas Historical Association, 1981. Story of Antonio Gil Ybarbo.

Moore, Effie Missouria Pitchford. *Alone by the Sea: The Story of Jane Wilkinson Long, Mother of Texas*. San Antonio: Naylor, 1951. Story of Jane Long's experiences in Texas.

MULTIMEDIA MATERIALS

Archive of the New World. (video, 18 min.) Southwest Media Services, Inc., P.O. Box 140, Wimberley, Texas, 78676. Important look at the people of the New World at the time of the conquest and colonial period.

Colonial America: Life in the Maturing Colonies. (video, 17 min.) Encyclopaedia Britannica Educational Corporation, 310 South Michigan Avenue, Chicago, Illinois, 60604.

The Great Knowledge Race; U.S. History Series. (software, Series No. 1) Focus Media, Inc., 839 Stewart Avenue, P.O Box 865, Garden City, New York, 11530. Program covers exploration, Indians, and colonization.

Spanish Influences in the United States. (video, 11 min., 1972) Coronet Film and Video, 108 Wilmot Road, Deerfield, Illinois, 60015.

◈ GENERAL STRATEGIES

STUDENTS WITH SPECIAL NEEDS

Limited English Proficient Students (LEP)

List the Chapter 8 vocabulary terms on the chalkboard or an overhead transparency. Ask students to pronounce and define as many of the words as possible. After all of the words have been defined, have the students use each word in a sentence within the context of Chapter 8. See other activities labeled **LEP.**

Students Having Difficulty with the Chapter

List on the chalkboard the names of all of the people mentioned in Chapter 8. Have students select ten names and write clues to the identity of each. Place the names in a seek-and-find puzzle or a crossword puzzle, and list the clues below the puzzle. Distribute copies of the puzzle to students to review the chapter. **LEP**

Auditory Learners

Have auditory learners work together to host a "talk show" based on the information presented in Chapter 8. They should select a theme for the program and four appropriate guests from the chapter. Students should select a moderator and prepare a list of two questions per guest. The group will then present a ten-minute talk show to the rest of the class. See other activities labeled **A.**

Visual Learners

Allow time for visual learners to study the illustrations in the chapter. Then ask them to choose one of the illustrations and write an essay expanding on the information offered in the illustration's caption. See other activities labeled **V.**

Tactile/Kinesthetic Learners

Have tactile/kinesthetic learners complete four maps representing four time periods. Ask them to designate the following boundaries for each time period:

1763–1800	New Spain (including Texas), Louisiana
1800–1803	New Spain (including Texas), Louisiana, United States
1806–1819	New Spain (including Texas), Louisiana Territory of the United States, Neutral Ground
1821	Texas province, Mexican territory, United States

On each map, students should use different colors to distinguish national boundaries. See other activities labeled **TK.**

Gifted Students

Have interested students conduct further research on the Seven Years' War, also called the French and Indian War. Ask them to present oral reports, supplemented with maps illustrating the results of the war's peace treaty. See other activities labeled **G.**

VOCABULARY

In addition to the boldfaced terms in each section, some students might benefit from discussing the meanings of these terms.

Section 1: *peace treaty* (p. 153); *inspection tour* (p. 154).

Section 2: *tremendous* (p. 156); *disputed* (p. 158).

Section 3: *freebooters* (p. 158); *executed* (p. 160); *lieutenant* (p. 161); *impose* (p. 161); *siege* (p. 161).

Section 4: *smugglers* (p. 164); *pirating* (p. 164); *proposals* (p. 165); *rebel* (p. 167).

CHRONOLOGY

Have students study the Chapter 8 Time Line and identify relationships among the events.

GRAPHIC ORGANIZER

Have students skim the chapter and complete the Chapter 8 Graphic Organizer. *(You might wish to use this activity to review rather than to introduce the chapter.)*

ENRICHMENT

Have students complete the Chapter 8 Enrichment Worksheet.

SECTION 1

FOCUS

Predicting (I) Direct students to the painting and caption on page 154. Ask students to consider how the events illustrated might affect the Spanish empire in Texas. Lead students to conclude that Britain now replaced France as a threat to Spanish presence in Texas.

INSTRUCTION

Vocabulary (I) You may wish to preteach the following boldfaced term: *ceded* (p. 154). **LEP**

CONFLICTS OF EMPIRE

CHAPTER 8

The Story Continues...

Chapter 8 tells how France lost its vast empire in North America. Spain then faced a new threat to its territories north of the Rio Grande. This threat came in the form of adventurers from the United States.

As you read the chapter, look for the answers to these questions:

1. How did Spain's Texas policies change after it acquired Louisiana from France?
2. What was the dispute over the Neutral Ground? How was it finally settled?
3. What were the filibusters trying to accomplish?
4. Who were Henry Perry and James Long? Who were Jane Long and Kiamatia?

◼ Changes in the Spanish Empire

The development of the Texas mission system was directly related to the Spaniards' fears of the French. The explorations of La Salle and the trading adventures of Louis de St. Denis excited the Spaniards to action, but then Texas was ignored for many years. By the 1760s, events in Europe and elsewhere began to change the Spanish empire and its policies toward Texas.

Spain Acquires Louisiana. Several major countries of Europe were involved in a world war from 1756 to 1763. Known in Europe as the Seven Years' War, it was called the French and Indian War in North America. The war in America actually began in 1754 between the British colonies and the French in Canada. Both the results of the war and the peace treaty greatly affected the future of Texas. First, the French lost nearly all of their empire in North America to the British. All the land east of the Mississippi River, as well as Canada, came to be controlled by Britain.

National Museum of American Art / Art Resource

This Iroquois chief, Not-to-way, was painted by artist George Catlin. Many Iroquois fought in the French and Indian War.

CHAPTER 8 OVERVIEW

As the French threat to the Spanish empire faded, more serious threats from other interests arose. Chapter 8 is the story of the end of Spanish control in Texas.

Essential Elements
1B, 1C, 5B, 9A, 9B, 9D

Synthesis (I) Tell students to imagine that they are settlers at the East Texas missions in 1772. Ask them to write a paragraph explaining to their families why the family must abandon its home and relocate to San Antonio. Invite volunteers to read their paragraphs aloud. **A**

Geography (I) Provide each student with a blank outline map of Texas. Ask students to label on the map the location of the East Texas missions, San Antonio, Ybarbo's settlement in present-day Madison County, and Nacogdoches.

Then have them add to the map arrows showing the settlement pattern of the East Texas settlers who relocated to San Antonio and later established Nacogdoches. Allow students to refer to maps in their textbooks. **V, TK, LEP**

Guided Practice (I) With the class, write on the chalkboard in sequence the chain of events that led to the Spanish empire's change of policies toward Texas. Have students describe the new policies. **A, V, LEP**

Geography
Refer students to the map of North America on page 159.

The Granger Collection

This painting shows the defeat of British troops by a French force during the French and Indian War in North America. Britain, however, eventually won the war with France and took possession of most of the French lands in North America.

Second, the city of New Orleans and the land west of the Mississippi River was **ceded**, or given over, to Spain by France. This huge piece of land was called Louisiana, and it remained under Spanish control from 1762 until 1800.

After 1763, the Spaniards had little to worry about from the French. But they now had to worry about the British. The Spanish government wanted to consider the condition of New Spain now that its empire had changed. For this reason, an inspection tour was sent to look over the northern areas of New Spain.

The Marqués de Rubí Report. In 1766, a tour led by a Spanish officer, the Marqués de Rubí, set out to check the northern areas of New Spain from California to Louisiana. Rubí entered Texas at Eagle Pass in 1767 and visited most of the missions in the present state. At the end of his trip, he had traveled around 7,000 miles in two years. During the trip, Rubí discovered what others had been trying to tell the Spanish government. Spain had neither the wealth nor the power to maintain all of the missions and presidios in its northern lands. This fact was especially true of the missions and presidios in Texas.

EXTENSION

Research and Map Work (II) Have interested students work together to create wall maps showing the extent of the Spanish, French, and British empires in North America in 1754 and in 1763. Students should use a different color to highlight each empire. Display the finished maps in the classroom. **V, TK, G**

Independent Practice (II) Ask students to imagine that they are the Marqués de Rubí or Athanase de Mézières. Ask them to write a description of their role in shaping Spanish policies in Texas. **LEP**

RETEACHING

Draw a time line on the chalkboard. Call on students to select an event from Chapter 8 and come to the chalkboard and write the event in the proper place on the time line. Have other students describe the event. **A, V, TK, LEP**

CLOSURE

List on the chalkboard in note form the series of events that led to changes in the Spanish empire and its policies toward Texas.

There was another consideration in the case of Texas. Spanish Louisiana now lay to the north and east of Texas, between Texas and the British colonies. Adding Louisiana to the empire meant that Texas was no longer an outer part of New Spain. For this reason, Spanish officials saw less need to have missions and settlements in Texas.

Rubí's report was issued in Madrid, Spain, in 1772. It suggested that all the missions in Texas be abandoned, except San Antonio and La Bahía. The report also stated that all the settlers from East Texas should be sent to live in San Antonio. In addition, Rubí called for a new policy toward the Indians in Texas. He wanted Spain to establish friendly relations with northern tribes such as the Comanches and Wichitas. However, Rubí claimed that a war against the Apaches was needed, in order to protect Spanish interests. This was because the Apaches had been pushed closer to Spanish settlements when the Comanches entered Texas from the north.

Rubí's recommendations were accepted by the Spanish government. The missions of East Texas were again abandoned. Most of the settlers in the area moved to San Antonio. They were homesick, however, and soon asked for the right to return to East Texas. The leader of these people was Antonio Gil Ybarbo. He was born at Los Adaes in 1729, after his parents had settled there from Spain.

In 1774, Gil Ybarbo and the others from East Texas were allowed to return east as far as the Trinity River. There they built a settlement in present-day Madison County that they called Bucareli. Still, the East Texans felt unsettled, and, without asking for permission, they moved

Institute of Texan Cultures

Gil Ybarbo and the Spanish colonists returned to East Texas after several years at Bucareli and established the town of Nacogdoches.

ASSESSMENT

Have students complete the Section 1 Review on page 156.

SECTION 2

FOCUS

Past Learning (I) Ask students to define *treaty.* Ask: What is a key factor in the development of any treaty? *(negotiation)* Tell students that in Section 2 they will learn about a

significant treaty in the history of Texas and the United States.

INSTRUCTION

Vocabulary (I) You may wish to preteach the following boldfaced terms: *neutral* (p. 158); *diplomats* (p. 158). **LEP**

CITIES OF TEXAS

Compare and Contrast (III) Ask students to compare and contrast the historical development of San Antonio with that

Answers to Section 1 Review

Define: *ceded*—given over

Identify: Marqués de Rubí—Spanish officer who reported on the northern areas of New Spain; Gil Ybarbo—leader of Spanish settlers in East Texas; Athanase de Mézières—former French soldier who directed Texas' Spanish Indian policy in the 1770s

1. Abandon all missions except those at San Antonio and La Bahía, move East Texas settlers to San Antonio area, establish friendly relations with the Comanches and other northern tribes, wage war with the Apaches. He believed that with the addition of Spanish Louisiana, the threat from France and the United States was no longer as great.
2. It was ceded to Britain and Spain; Spain obtained the land beyond the Mississippi River.
3. The goal of removing the Indians as a threat to the Spaniards in Texas was never met.

(Continued on page 157)

Essential Elements
1B, 1C, 9A

SECTION 1 REVIEW

Define: ceded

Identify: Marqués de Rubí, Gil Ybarbo, Athanase de Mézières

1. What changes in Spanish policy were suggested by Rubí? Why did he suggest them?
2. What happened to France's empire in North America in 1762?
3. What was the result of Spain's new Indian policy?

Synthesizing Information: How did the Apaches and Comanches differ from the Caddoes of East Texas?

Interpreting Pictures: Look at the watercolor painting reproduced on page 155. Which person do you think is Gil Ybarbo? Explain your answer.

The Granger Collection

Napoléon Bonaparte sold the huge area of Louisiana to the United States for $15 million.

east again. In 1779, they rebuilt the town of Nacogdoches on one of the old mission sites.

Indian Relations. To direct the new policy toward the Indians, the Spaniards turned to a former French soldier, Athanase de Mézières. Mézières had served at Natchitoches for a number of years and had traded with most of the Indian groups. While at Natchitoches, Mézières married the daughter of Louis de St. Denis, the Frenchman who had caused so much worry for Spain in the early 1700s.

Mézières lost no time in contacting the Texas Indians. During the 1770s, he held talks with Wichitas, Comanches, and others. He even persuaded a band of Comanches to join the Spaniards to fight the Apaches.

Mézières never reached his goal of removing the Indians as a threat to the Spaniards in Texas. Just after he was appointed governor of Texas in 1779, Mézières died. With his death, his Indian policy fell apart.

Spanish presidios and missions continued to be targets of raids by Comanches and Apaches. The Comanches did wage war on the Lipan Apaches, but this did not stop them from raiding the Spaniards too. It also did not put an end to raids by the Lipans. Spanish attempts to stop the raids were a failure. The Spaniards simply did not have enough soldiers to fight the Comanches and Apaches. These Indian groups were nomadic, and they were capable of covering hundreds of miles in a short period of time. The Spaniards quickly realized they could not hunt down the Indians in the vast land of Texas. ✪

2 The United States Becomes a Threat

In 1800, events in Europe once again had an effect on New Spain and Texas. The French emperor, Napoléon Bonaparte, forced Spain to return Louisiana to France. Then, in 1803, Bonaparte decided to sell Louisiana. He sold it to the United States for only $15 million, or three cents per acre, a tremendous bargain for the young country. The Louisiana Purchase doubled the size of the United States. The United States now bordered Texas. Thus Spain's interests in Texas were threatened.

The Neutral Ground. The purchase of Louisiana by the United States created a dispute with Spain over boundaries. The United States government claimed that the Sabine

of El Paso, from the years of the Spanish missions to the present. Students should present their findings in an oral report. **A, G**

Cooperative Learning (II) Organize students into two groups who will debate the terms of the Adams-Oñis Treaty. Act as moderator as one group argues in favor of the terms while the other argues that the terms are unfair to Spain. Encourage students to create maps for their presentations. **A, V, TK, G**

Guided Practice (I) Have students draw a map on which they highlight the Neutral Ground in one color and the border between Texas and United States as a result of the Adams-Oñis Treaty in another color. **V, TK**

EXTENSION

Research (III) Have students research and report on the authors of the Adams-Oñis Treaty. *(United States Secretary of State John Quincy Adams and Spanish minister Luis de Oñis)* In their reports, students should address Adams' motivation of continental expansion. **A, G**

Essential Elements
5B, 9B

Synthesizing Information: The Comanches and the Apaches were nomadic raiders who depended on the buffalo herds. The Caddoes were peaceful, settled villagers and farmers.

Interpreting Pictures: Accept all logical answers. The artists probably depicted Ybarbo as the older authority figure to the left.

CITIES OF TEXAS

San Antonio

Population: 935,933

Metro area population: 1,302,099

Size: 263 square miles

Relative location: On the San Antonio River

Region: The rolling prairies of south central Texas

County: Bexar county seat

Special features: Texas' major tourist destination and site of military bases

Origin of name: The original mission (San Antonio de Valero) and presidio (San Antonio de Béxar) on the site (*San Antonio* is Spanish for Saint Anthony)

Landmarks: The Alamo, Tower of the Americas, the Paseo del Rio, or Riverwalk

Economy: A major American center of trade with Mexico, San Antonio also is the financial and manufacturing center for the South Texas region. Ranching, farming, and oil contribute to the area economy. Tourism is a major source of income. The Alamo, the Paseo del Rio,

and Sea World, a theme park, are chief attractions. Five major military installations also contribute to the city's vibrant economy.

History: When Spanish priests established a mission in 1718, they founded the modern-day site of San Antonio. Previously a small Indian village along the San Antonio River, the mission and nearby fort grew to be

the major city in the northern Spanish frontier. When Texas became a Republic in 1836, San Antonio was the largest city in Texas.

Recreation facilities: Human-made tourist attractions as well as the warm climate and beautiful natural environment make San Antonio a city rich in recreation facilities. Parks, nearby rivers, Sea World, and the famous Riverwalk offer a variety of activities.

Cultural activities: San Antonio Missions National Historical Park, HemisFair Plaza, La Villita, McNay art museum, Institute of Texan Cultures, the Brackenridge Park and Zoo, Witte Memorial Museum, and the Spanish Governor's Palace

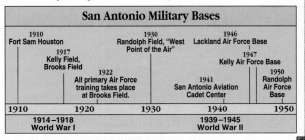

San Antonio Military Bases

1910 Fort Sam Houston		**1930** Randolph Field, "West Point of the Air"	**1946** Lackland Air Force Base	
	1917 Kelly Field, Brooks Field		**1947** Kelly Air Force Base	
		1922 All primary Air Force training takes place at Brooks Field.	**1941** San Antonio Aviation Cadet Center	**1950** Randolph Air Force Base
1910	**1920**	**1930**	**1940**	**1950**
1914–1918 World War I			**1939–1945** World War II	

Independent Practice (II) Tell students that they are travelers in the year 1810. They must get from Nacogdoches to Natchitoches but do not wish to enter the Neutral Ground. Ask them to sketch a map outlining the alternate routes available. **V, TK**

RETEACHING
Ask students to write a sentence identifying the Neutral Ground and a sentence identifying the Adams-Oñis Treaty. **LEP**

CLOSURE
Tell students that with the expansion of the United States, Spain's interests in Texas would continue to face threats.

ASSESSMENT

Have students complete the Section 2 Review on page 158.

Caption Response
The Sabine, Arroyo Hondo, and Calcasieu rivers

Answers to Section 2 Review

Define: *neutral*—not belonging to either side; *diplomats*—persons who represent a country in foreign affairs

Identify: James Wilkinson—United States general who helped settle the boundary dispute between the U.S. and Spain in 1806; Simón de Herrera—Spanish officer who assisted Wilkinson in settling the U.S. and Spain boundary dispute

1. Wilkinson and De Herrera declared the disputed territory to be neutral until diplomats could settle the issue.
2. Outlaws came to the area because no authorities could enforce their laws there.

(Continued on page 159)

Essential Elements
1B, 1C, 2B, 5B, 9A, 9B, 9D

The Neutral Ground

UNITED STATES

·Natchitoches

Nacogdoches·

NEUTRAL GROUND

TEXAS

The Neutral Ground was bordered by which rivers?

SECTION ★2★ REVIEW

Define: neutral, diplomats
Identify: James Wilkinson, Simón de Herrera

1. How did the Neutral Ground come to be?
2. What sorts of persons came to the Neutral Ground between 1806 and 1819? Why did they come there?
3. What were the terms of the Adams-Oñis Treaty?

Analyzing Information: Which country did the Adams-Oñis Treaty seem to favor? Explain.

Synthesizing Information: Why did the Spaniards see the United States as a greater threat to their North American empire than the French had been?

River was the dividing line between Texas and Louisiana. The Spanish government said that Texas was bordered by Arroyo Hondo, a small stream east of the Sabine.

The Spanish and United States governments argued over the Texas boundary line for many years. Meanwhile, the Spaniards renewed their interest in Texas. More troops were sent to the Nacogdoches area, and settlers were encouraged to move to East Texas.

No one wanted to go to war over the boundary issue. In 1806, an agreement was worked out by General James Wilkinson of the United States and Lieutenant Colonel Simón de Herrera of New Spain. These two commanders declared that the disputed territory was to be **neutral**, or not belonging to either side. The issue would have to be worked out by **diplomats**, or persons who represent a country in foreign affairs.

From 1806 until 1819, no one controlled the Neutral Ground. Because no authorities could enforce their laws in the area, outlaws moved into the region, and traveling through it became very dangerous.

The Adams-Oñis Treaty. In 1819, the United States and Spain signed a treaty that settled the dispute over the Neutral Ground. This agreement was called the Adams-Oñis Treaty. It established the Sabine River as the border separating Texas and the United States. The Neutral Ground became part of the United States. In addition to this part of the treaty, there were three other important items. Spain ceded Florida to the United States, and the United States gave up all claims to Texas. Finally, the treaty set boundaries between all areas of the United States and New Spain, extending west to the Pacific Ocean. ○

❸ Filibusters and Rebellions

The disagreement over boundaries turned out to be a minor problem in comparison to others facing Spain in the early 1800s. People called **filibusters** began entering Texas from the United States. The term comes from the Spanish *filibusteros*, meaning freebooters or adventurers. Most of these people had ideas about overthrowing the Spanish government in Texas, hoping that Texas would become a separate country or a part of the United States. Other filibusters looked for adventure or easy wealth. Also,

158 *Unit 3*

Student Experiences (I) Ask students to speculate on what it would be like if Texas were an independent nation. Explain that in the early 1800s, people fought and died trying to make independence a reality.

Vocabulary (I) You may wish to preteach the following boldfaced terms: *filibusters* (p. 158); *rebellion* (p. 161). **LEP**

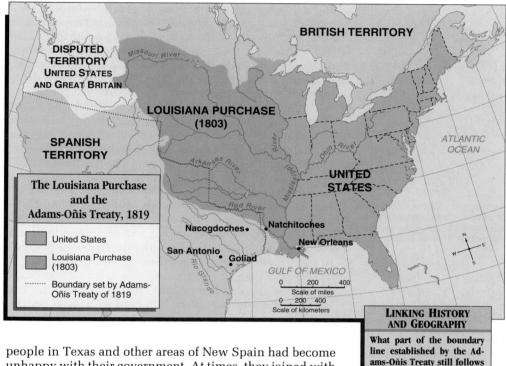

The Louisiana Purchase and the Adams-Oñis Treaty, 1819

United States

Louisiana Purchase (1803)

.... Boundary set by Adams-Oñis Treaty of 1819

LINKING HISTORY AND GEOGRAPHY

What part of the boundary line established by the Adams-Oñis Treaty still follows modern Texas boundaries?

3. It established the Sabine River as the border separating Texas and the United States, with the Neutral Ground becoming part of the United States; Spain ceded Florida to the United States; the United States gave up all claims to Texas; and boundaries were set between all areas of the United States and New Spain, extending west to the Pacific Ocean.

Analyzing Information: The United States, because it received much more territory

Synthesizing Information: The United States was much larger and more densely populated than the French empire in North America had been. In addition, the Americans were aggressively moving west in search of land.

Transparency 12
An overhead transparency of this map can be found in the Teacher's Resource Binder.

Linking History and Geography
The part along the Red River in the north, along the east of the Panhandle, and along the border between Louisiana and Texas

people in Texas and other areas of New Spain had become unhappy with their government. At times, they joined with the filibusters to fight against Spanish control in Texas.

Philip Nolan. By the early 1800s, settlers from the United States had pushed to the borders of Texas and beyond. A number of people from Arkansas crossed the Red River and settled small farms and villages. Others settled illegally in East Texas around Nacogdoches to trade with the Spaniards and Indians. For the most part, these people obeyed Spanish laws, and Spanish officials did not worry much about them. But the filibusters were a major concern.

The first, and best known, of the filibusters was Philip Nolan. Nolan was the bookkeeper and friend of General James Wilkinson, commander of the United States forces in Louisiana. Nolan had come to Texas in 1791 as a trader. He captured wild horses known as *mesteños* (from which came the word *mustangs*) that roamed Texas. The ancestors of these horses had escaped from the early explorers, who brought them from Spain. As a mustang trader, Nolan

Analysis (I) Organize the class into groups of four or five students. Have each group review the information presented on Philip Nolan on pages 159–60. Ask students in each group to discuss and vote whether Nolan was guilty or innocent of being a spy. Have a spokesperson from each group give the group's final vote as you tally the votes on the chalkboard. Spokespersons should explain why the group voted as it did. **A, LEP**

Cooperative Learning (I) Organize a "round table" discussion, with students assuming the roles of the following persons: Philip Nolan, Father Hidalgo, Bernardo Gutiérrez, William Magee, Major Samuel Kemper, General Joaquín de Arredondo. Begin the discussion by having each "guest" identify himself and his role in Texas history. Act as moderator and solicit questions from the class "audience." Questions should focus on the information presented in Section 3. **A**

The Granger Collection

General James Wilkinson worked out an agreement with Lieutenant Colonel Herrera of New Spain concerning the boundary of Texas and Louisiana.

Institute of Texan Cultures

Peter Ellis Bean was the sole survivor of Philip Nolan's ill-fated force in Texas.

Biography
Peter Ellis Bean left Mexico and arrived in New Orleans in 1814, in time to join Andrew Jackson's army in its fight against the British in the War of 1812.

entered Texas several times with the permission of Spanish officials in Louisiana and took out wild horses, which he then sold. By 1800, the Spaniards suspected that Nolan was a spy working for General Wilkinson. They believed that Nolan and Wilkinson were plotting to gain a foothold in Texas. Therefore, the Spaniards warned Nolan not to return to Spanish lands.

Nolan chose to ignore the warning, and in late 1800, he returned with a force of approximately twenty men. Nolan and his men ventured deep into Central Texas and spent the rest of the year capturing horses. During the winter months, they built a camp on the banks of the Brazos River a few miles from present-day Waco.

The Spanish commander at Nacogdoches sent over 100 soldiers to arrest Nolan. In March 1801, they found Nolan and his men. Nolan decided to fight and was killed. The other Americans soon ran out of ammunition and surrendered to the Spaniards. The survivors were marched to Mexico and thrown into prison in Chihuahua.

For six years the American survivors of the Nolan expedition remained in prison. Finally, in 1807, the king of Spain ordered that every fifth man be hanged and the rest be sentenced to ten more years in prison. There were only nine Americans still alive, so the Spaniards decided to execute only one man. The survivors threw dice to see who would be hanged. Ephraim Blackburn was the unlucky man who threw the lowest number. He was executed as an enemy of the king of Spain. The other Americans were sent to a prison where all but one later died. The survivor was Peter Ellis Bean. He was released from prison during fighting between rebels and the Spanish government.

The Philip Nolan affair is still something of a mystery. The reasons behind Nolan's trips into Texas have never been fully explained, probably because no one knew the complete truth except Nolan himself. He may have been simply a trader and adventurer. But why then did he map the territory he covered in Texas? The rumor persisted that Nolan really was an agent of General Wilkinson, planning to invade Texas and overthrow the Spanish government.

The Gutiérrez-Magee Expedition. There were other sources of unrest in Spanish Texas during the early nineteenth century. A desire for independence from Spain began to grow among the people. In 1810, the Roman Catholic

Guided Practice (I) Ask students to imagine that they are settlers in Spanish Texas. Have them write a paragraph justifying acts of rebellion against Spanish control of Texas. Invite volunteers to read their paragraphs aloud. **A, LEP**

EXTENSION
Creating (II) Ask students to create a time line incorporating significant events from Section 3 with events related to the United States winning its independence from Britain. **V, TK, G**

priest Father Miguel Hidalgo led an attempt to free New Spain from Spanish control and set up a new government. Although the Spanish army put down Father Hidalgo's **rebellion**, the movement for independence continued.

One of the followers of Father Hidalgo was Bernardo Gutiérrez de Lara. When Father Hidalgo first challenged Spanish rule, Gutiérrez was sent to the United States to raise money and look for people to help. After Father Hidalgo was defeated, Gutiérrez decided to invade Texas and continue Father Hidalgo's movement of rebellion.

In Louisiana, Gutiérrez was introduced to a young American named Augustus William Magee, a former lieutenant in the United States Army. Magee was a graduate of the United States Military Academy at West Point. When he was passed over for a promotion, he resigned from the army and joined Gutiérrez as a colonel.

Gutiérrez and Magee believed that by invading Texas they could carry on the rebellion of Father Hidalgo. They thought that Spain had no right to impose its will on the Mexican people. As an example, they pointed to the United States, which had recently won its independence from Britain. So Gutiérrez and Magee began recruiting volunteers for their Republican Army of the North.

Gutiérrez and Magee had no trouble finding volunteers for their invasion force. They moved into Texas in August 1812 with around 130 people. Their ranks included citizens from the United States, Mexicans, Indians, and French. There was also a variety of adventurers who claimed no homeland. The expedition took Nacogdoches, where the Spaniards surrendered without a fight. The expedition then moved southward toward San Antonio. When Spanish forces moved to defend San Antonio, the expedition headed for the La Bahía presidio at Goliad.

The Republican Army of the North captured La Bahía (Goliad) in November 1812. The filibusters held the fort through the winter, even though they were surrounded by about 800 Spanish soldiers. During the winter siege, Colonel Magee died. He was replaced by another American, Major Samuel Kemper. After failing to take La Bahía, the Spanish soldiers retreated to San Antonio. Major Kemper and the Republican Army followed, defeating the Spaniards in a battle near San Antonio.

After the victory, more people joined the revolutionary army. Gutiérrez and his followers drafted a document

Painting by Michael Waters, Institute of Texan Cultures

This watercolor shows Bernardo Gutiérrez and Augustus Magee during their invasion of East Texas.

Institute of Texan Cultures

Father Miguel Hidalgo led a rebellion against Spain in 1810. Spain defeated the rebellion, and Father Hidalgo was executed.

Independent Practice (II) Have students work individually or in pairs to create maps illustrating the Gutiérrez-Magee expedition. Ask students to label on their maps significant place names, dates, and outcomes. **V, TK, LEP**

RETEACHING
Refer students to the three subsections of Section 3 on pages 159–63. Ask them to write a series of cause-and-effect statements to summarize the material in each of these subsections. Have volunteers copy their statements onto the chalkboard. **V, LEP**

CLOSURE
Tell students that these rebellions were only the beginning of the challenges that the Spanish government would face in Texas.

ASSESSMENT
Have students complete the Section 3 Review on page 163.

Historical Sidelight
Disagreements also arose between those people who hoped Texas would become part of an independent Mexico and those who hoped Texas would become part of the United States.

Answers to Section 3 Review

Define: *filibusters*—adventurers; *rebellion*—attempt to overthrow an established government

Identify: Philip Nolan—filibuster and mustang trader suspected by the Spaniards of being a spy, killed by Spanish soldiers in 1801; Father Hidalgo—Roman Catholic priest who led an unsuccessful rebellion against Spain in 1810; Republican Army of the North—army led by Gutiérrez and Magee that invaded Texas in 1812 in an attempt to free Texas from Spain

(Continued on page 163)

stating that Texas was free and independent. But before the celebrations ended, trouble developed among the leaders of the army. Gutiérrez and the Americans had different views of what a free and independent Texas was to mean.

Defeat of the Rebellion. The Americans and the Mexicans could not agree on what kind of government Texas should have. The Americans wanted a form of government similar to that of the United States. They believed that the officials of the government should be elected by the citizens. The Mexicans felt that power should be held by a governor and a ruling body of appointed officials, as under Spanish rule.

A second disagreement arose between the two sides in San Antonio. A force under the command of Antonio Delgado killed thirteen Spanish prisoners as well as the governor of Texas. The Americans blamed Gutiérrez for allowing the murders. Gutiérrez was forced to give up

The La Bahía presidio was captured by the Republican Army of the North in 1812.

Texas Department of Transportation

SECTION 4

FOCUS

Student Experiences (I) Write the term *pirate* on the chalkboard. Encourage students to discuss pirates about whom they have read or heard and to give their associations for the term. Then direct them to the drawing on page 164. Ask: Does Jean Lafitte look like a pirate?

INSTRUCTION

Vocabulary (I) You may wish to preteach the following boldfaced terms: *pardon* (p. 164); *revolution* (p. 167). **LEP**

Painting by Bruce Marshall. Institute of Texan Cultures

control of the expedition, but many of the Americans still decided to return home to the United States. Included in that group was Major Kemper. With its leadership changing and many of its soldiers gone, the Republican Army of the North was left weak and confused.

Meanwhile, the Spaniards were moving troops into Texas to end this serious rebellion. General Joaquín de Arredondo and his troops defeated the 1,400-man Republican Army in August 1813 near the Medina River, about fifteen miles south of San Antonio. Called the Battle of Medina, this Spanish victory crushed the Republican Army of the North. About 300 survivors escaped back to the United States. General Arredondo's forces then swept through San Antonio, Goliad, and Nacogdoches, searching for supporters of the rebellion. Hundreds of Texans were put in prison or executed, and the rebellion was ended. ○

◢ Rebellions and Revolution

Even though Nolan, Gutiérrez, and Magee had been stopped, others continued to challenge Spanish control of Texas. Most of these new adventurers and filibusters organized in Louisiana to strike at Texas. But the Spanish government was eventually overthrown by forces in Mexico.

The Republican Army was effectively crushed in the Battle of Medina. The Republican Army is shown in the foreground of this painting with the Spanish army in the background.

SECTION 3 REVIEW

Define: filibusters, rebellion
Identify: Philip Nolan, Father Hidalgo, Republican Army of the North

1. What were the goals of the filibusters? Were they all the same? Explain.
2. Why is the Nolan affair still a historical mystery?
3. What disagreement weakened the Republican Army of the North?

Evaluating Information: Which of the filibusters' expeditions seemed to be the greatest threat to the government of New Spain? Why?

Analyzing Information: What do you think was the filibusters' attitude toward the Adams-Oñis Treaty? Why?

1. Most of the filibusters wanted to take Texas from Spain. Some of these wanted to make Texas an independent country, while others wanted to make it part of the United States.
2. It is still not known whether Nolan was, as the Spaniards suspected, a spy, or a mustang trader as he claimed.
3. The American and Mexican members disagreed on what form of government to set up after independence. They also argued over who was responsible for the killing of some prisoners.

Evaluating Information: The greatest threat was the expedition led by Gutiérrez and Magee. They had hundreds of men, won several military victories, and took several towns.

Analyzing Information: Answers will vary. The filibusters resented the treaty because it gave up all United States' claims to Texas.

Essential Elements
1B, 1C, 2A, 2B, 5B, 9B, 9C

Biography

Bernardo de Gálvez was born in Spain in 1746. As a young man, he distinguished himself as a soldier in several wars, both in Spain and in the New World. He became a colonel in 1776, and he was made governor of Louisiana in 1777, serving until 1783. During the American Revolution, Gálvez aided the Americans, recognizing the independence of the United States and capturing Florida, Jamaica, and the Bahamas from the British. For these actions, he was honored by the king of Spain and given the title of *conde* (count).

While he was governor of Louisiana, Gálvez ordered a survey of the Texas coast, and Galveston Bay was named in his honor. Because he sympathized with efforts to extend Spanish influence in North Texas, the village called San Bernardo (on the north bank of the Red River) was also named for him. In 1785, Gálvez was made viceroy to Mexico, and he died in Mexico in 1786.

Barker Texas History Center

LAFITTE.

From 1817 to 1820, Jean Laffite raided Spanish ships from his base on Galveston Island.

Pirates on the Coast. Among those who made attempts to invade Texas was Henry Perry. Perry had been a member of the Gutiérrez-Magee expedition. In 1815, he gathered a force of about 150 people and moved into Texas. This group settled near Point Bolivar, across the bay from Galveston Island.

Galveston Island, named for Bernardo de Gálvez, a former governor of Louisiana, was the home of a number of pirates and smugglers. After some time, Henry Perry was able to talk pirate-adventurer Louis Aury into helping with an invasion of Texas. A Frenchman, Aury had been raiding Spanish ships in the Gulf of Mexico and had taken part in fighting against the Spaniards in other places. He helped sail Perry and a group of Mexicans to the coast of Mexico for an attack. The attack failed, and Perry was later surrounded in Texas, where he committed suicide.

While Aury was away from Galveston Island, the area was taken over by another famous French pirate, Jean Laffite. For years, Laffite and his brother had lived as pirates and slave smugglers in Louisiana. They had fought for the United States in the Battle of New Orleans. For his help, Laffite had been given a **pardon**, or official forgiveness, for his crimes by the president of the United States. But Laffite continued pirating from Galveston Island. He claimed that he was fighting for the independence of Mexico. But he was most likely interested only in Spanish treasure.

From 1817 until 1820, Laffite raided Spanish ships and gathered a large fortune. But when he began attacking American ships, the United States Navy took action. A warship sailed to Galveston Island and drove away Laffite and other pirates.

James Long. A more serious fighter for independence was Dr. James Long. Texas was the prize he sought. Like many Americans, Long was unhappy with the Adams-Oñis Treaty of 1819, which recognized Texas as part of Spanish territory. A growing number of people in the southern United States felt that Texas should be part of their country or, at least an independent land. From his home in Natchez, Mississippi, Long organized an invading force to free Texas from Spanish control.

In the summer of 1819, Long led a force into Texas and captured the town of Nacogdoches. The invaders declared

Guided Practice (I) Have students work individually or in pairs to create a poster, sketch, or other graphic to illustrate an event discussed in Section 4. Ask students to display and explain their illustrations. **A, V, TK, LEP**

EXTENSION

Community Involvement (II) Have interested students contact the local or state historical society or visit the public library to find out about events that were occurring in their area of the state during the time period covered in Section 4. Ask students to share their findings with the rest of the class. **A, V, G**

Institute of Texan Cultures

This drawing of Galveston Harbor shows how the island may have looked during Jean Laffite's time.

Texas free and independent. Then they established a government with Long as president. One of the leaders of the Long expedition was Bernardo Gutiérrez, who had earlier invaded Texas with the Republican Army.

Following the capture of Nacogdoches, Long traveled to Galveston Island to get help from Jean Laffite. Laffite had no interest in Long's proposals, and he declined to assist. While Long and Laffite discussed the future of Texas, Spanish troops moved toward Nacogdoches. Before Long could return to his base in East Texas, Colonel Ignacio Pérez, from San Antonio, with a force of more than 500 Mexican soldiers, ran Long's supporters out of Texas. Long's brother was killed, and many of Long's men were captured.

Long crossed over into the United States, joining his wife and child. Then he went to New Orleans to recruit more men and plan another invasion of Texas. In 1820, he had a new force that sailed for the Texas coast. They landed on Point Bolivar, near the mouth of Galveston Bay, where a fort had been built in 1819.

Soon, Long and his party moved inland to La Bahía presidio at what is now Goliad. They were forced to surrender to Mexican forces from San Antonio. Long was captured and taken to Mexico City for trial. While awaiting trial, he was shot and killed by a Mexican soldier. Officials claimed that it was an accident, but Long's friends called it murder.

Geography
Display a map of Texas, and ask a volunteer to locate Galveston Harbor.

This map of New Spain was completed in 1809 by Alexander von Humboldt, a famous scientist and geographer. Some of the information on the map is incorrect, but at the time it was made, it was one of the best maps available of this area.

Barker Texas History Center

Biography

Jane Long was 23 years old during the winter of 1821.

Jane Long. Jane Long, who was soon to have a baby, had remained at the fort at Point Bolivar. With her were her young daughter Ann, a twelve-year-old black servant named Kiamatia, and a handful of soldiers. The soldiers at the fort returned to New Orleans in the fall of 1821, but Jane Long and the two girls stayed on at Point Bolivar.

They faced the winter of 1821 alone. A second daughter, Mary James, was born in December. For food, they fished,

Have each student list ten items (people, places, events) from Section 4 on a sheet of paper. Then ask students to exchange papers with a partner and write a one-sentence identification for each item. Allow students to use their textbooks to verify their identifications. **LEP**

CLOSURE
With the class, summarize on the chalkboard in note form the events leading to Mexican independence in 1824.

ASSESSMENT
Have students complete the Section 4 Review on page 167.

shot birds, and gathered oysters from the bay. When a group of Karankawas appeared on the beach, Long fired a cannon and frightened them away. The winter was harsh, and the damp cold made survival difficult for Long, Kiamatia, and the two little girls.

Help finally arrived in the summer. From friends, Jane Long learned of her husband's death. She decided to try to seek money for his services. She traveled to San Antonio but had no success. After a short trip to the United States, Long returned to Texas in 1824 as one of Stephen F. Austin's Old Three Hundred colonists.

Jane Long lived to see the dream of an independent Texas come true. She became a successful businesswoman, operating a boarding house before becoming a farmer. Her farm became one of the most prosperous in Fort Bend County. Through all of Long's adventures, Kiamatia remained a close companion. Jane Long lived until 1880.

Mexican Independence. Since the rebellion led by Father Hidalgo in 1810, many citizens of Mexico had dreamed of winning independence from Spain. Hidalgo was executed by Spanish authorities, but others carried on his fight. By 1815, however, Spanish troops had crushed almost all of the rebel armies. It looked as if the Mexican rebellion was over.

Soon, however, events in Europe weakened Spain's hold on its empire and breathed new life into the Mexican cause. In 1820, a revolt by liberals swept across Spain and weakened the power of the government. Mexican leaders saw this as their chance to gain independence. A military officer, Agustín de Iturbide, allied with rebel troops in a **revolution**, or overthrow of the government, in 1821.

Spanish forces offered little resistance. Wealthy and powerful persons, led by Iturbide, soon gained control of the revolution. Iturbide took over as emperor, but he was such a poor ruler that he was driven from power by a military revolt in 1823. Mexico completed its constitution in 1824, officially becoming a republic.

Despite the new republic, the average Mexican citizen had little political power. Still, Mexicans were proud of their new country and glad to be free of Spanish control. Their problems with the government were just beginning, however. These problems, along with events in the United States, would soon have a great effect on Texas. ✪

Fort Bend County Museum

Jane Long was one of the first Anglo women to settle in Texas and became one of the best-known women in the Republic.

SECTION ✪ 4 REVIEW

Define: pardon, revolution
Identify: Henry Perry, Jean Laffite, Jane Long, Kiamatia

1. What did James Long hope to accomplish in Texas?
2. Why were the Galveston Island pirates important to the plans of Henry Perry?
3. What event in Europe led to Mexican independence from Spain?

Comparing Perspectives: What did the filibusters think of themselves and their goals? What did the authorities in New Spain think of them?

Exploring Geography: Compare the Von Humboldt map of New Spain on page 166 with the physical map of Texas on page 29. In general, what is wrong with Von Humboldt's map?

Answers to Section 4 Review

Define: *pardon*—official forgiveness by a government; *revolution*—an attempt to overthrow an established government

Identify: Henry Perry—filibuster who attempted to invade Texas in 1815; Jean Laffite—French pirate based on Galveston Island; Jane Long—filibuster James Long's wife, who later became a member of Austin's colony; Kiamatia—servant who assisted Jane Long

1. He wanted to win Texas' independence from Spain.
2. They could offer military assistance.
3. In 1820, an internal revolt weakened the Spanish government, weakening Spanish military and political control of New Spain and breathing new life into the Mexican cause.

Comparing Perspectives: They thought that they were noble. Authorities in New Spain saw them as rebels trying to overthrow a government.

Exploring Geography: The shape of the Texas coast is wrong, and the Rocky Mountains are positioned too far to the east.

CHAPTER REVIEW RESOURCES

1. Chapter Review Worksheet 8
2. Chapter 8 Test, Form A
3. Reteaching Worksheet 8
4. Chapter 8 Test, Form B
5. **Informal Evaluation Forms:** Portfolio Assessment
6. *Texas, Our Texas* **Test Generator**

Essential Elements
1A, 1B, 1C, 5C, 9A, 9B, 9D, 9E

CHAPTER 8 REVIEW ANSWERS

Understanding Main Ideas

1. Spain acquired French Louisiana as part of the settlement at the end of the Seven Years' War, and the French threat to New Spain ended. The new Spanish-United States border, however, was now far to the east of Texas. Texas was no longer a critical border province between two empires. As a result, the East Texas missions and presidios were not as important.
2. The Apaches
3. East Texas was his home and the home of the settlers he led.
4. After the United States purchased Louisiana, the Spanish-United States boundary came into dispute. The United States claimed the Sabine River as the boundary; the Spanish government claimed that the boundary was the Arroyo Hondo, east of the Sabine. It was agreed to designate the land in between as the Neutral Ground and to settle the dispute through diplomacy. The Adams-Oñis Treaty gave this territory to the United States.
5. Adventurers seeking to win Texas' independence from Mexico
6. Both men were filibusters who led unsuccessful armed

CHAPTER 8 REVIEW

Understanding Main Ideas

1. What happened to Spain's Texas policies after 1763?
2. Who did Rubí believe to be the main Indian group opposing the Spaniards?
3. Why did Gil Ybarbo want to return to East Texas?
4. Explain the dispute over the Neutral Ground. How did it end?
5. Who were the filibusters and what were their goals?
6. Who were Henry Perry and James Long? Who were Jane Long and Kiamatia?

Thinking Critically

1. **Evaluating Information:** The government of New Spain had a different view of the filibusters than the filibusters had of themselves. Which view do you think was more correct? Why?
2. **Synthesizing Information:** How do you explain the failure of all the filibuster attempts before 1821?
3. **Analyzing Information:** Do you think Mézières' Indian policy would have solved the government's Indian problem in Texas? Explain.

Linking History and Geography

1. What was the effect of the Louisiana Purchase on the Spanish government's position in Texas?
2. Why do you think pirates such as Laffite chose Galveston Island as their base on the Texas coast?

TAAS Practice
Using Primary Sources

In her book *A History of Texas For Schools* (1895), Anna Pennybacker, a respected historian of her time, gave this description of social life in Spanish Texas:

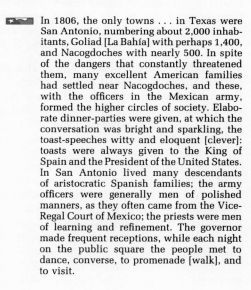

In 1806, the only towns . . . in Texas were San Antonio, numbering about 2,000 inhabitants, Goliad [La Bahía] with perhaps 1,400, and Nacogdoches with nearly 500. In spite of the dangers that constantly threatened them, many excellent American families had settled near Nacogdoches, and these, with the officers in the Mexican army, formed the higher circles of society. Elaborate dinner-parties were given, at which the conversation was bright and sparkling, the toast-speeches witty and eloquent [clever]: toasts were always given to the King of Spain and the President of the United States. In San Antonio lived many descendants of aristocratic Spanish families; the army officers were generally men of polished manners, as they often came from the Vice-Regal Court of Mexico; the priests were men of learning and refinement. The governor made frequent receptions, while each night on the public square the people met to dance, converse, to promenade [walk], and to visit.

1. According to the author, social life in Nacogdoches was characterized by
   A bad relations between Spaniards and Americans
   B little social activity of any kind
   C racial, cultural, and political disagreements
   D friendly relations between Spanish officers and American families

expeditions to establish Texas independence. Jane Long was the wife of James Long, and she later became a member of Austin's colony. Kiamatia was Jane Long's black servant.

Thinking Critically

1. **Evaluating Information:** Answers will vary but should be based on sound reasoning. Students should note that the filibusters were trying to overthrow a legal government and were viewed as outlaws.
2. **Synthesizing Information:** Filibuster armies generally were outnumbered by Spanish military forces. The filibusters often had mixed goals, and their leaders often failed to cooperate with each other. They were operating far from any bases of supply in the United States. None of the filibusters had the support of the United States government.
3. **Analyzing Information:** His plan might not have solved the problem. The Native Americans outnumbered the Spaniards and could travel great distances quickly.

Linking History and Geography

1. The Louisiana Purchase reestablished Texas as the frontier province of New Spain facing a powerful foreign power—the United States.
2. Galveston Island had a good offshore harbor and was easy to defend. Any enemies had to attack by sea.

TAAS **Practice**
Using Primary Sources
1. D   2. C

TAAS **Practice**
Writing Descriptively
Diary entries will vary but should provide a detailed and accurate account of the battle.

Practicing Skills

1. **Sequencing Events:** Philip Nolan, Gutiérrez and Magee, Henry Perry, James Long
2. **Interpreting Maps:** the Apaches. The advancing Comanches pressured the Apaches to the south and into Spanish territory.

Enriching Your Study of History

1. **Individual Project:** Reports and maps will vary but should be based on thorough research.
2. **Cooperative Project:** Reports and accompanying illustrations will vary but should demonstrate careful research.
3. **Cooperative Project:** Maps will vary but should be based on information in the textbook.

---

2. According to Anna Pennybacker's account of Spanish Texas, the leaders of social life in San Antonio were
   A Coahuiltecan and Tonkawa chiefs
   B Anglo American businessmen and traders
   C Spanish officials, army officers, and priests
   D dancers, public speakers, promenaders, and visitors

TAAS **Practice**
Writing Descriptively

Imagine that you are a young Spanish soldier commanded by General Joaquín de Arredondo at the Battle of the Medina River in 1813. Write a diary entry about what happened to you during the battle. Make your entry as descriptive as possible. Use your historical imagination.

Practicing Skills

1. **Sequencing Events:** Place the following filibusters in chronological order, beginning with the earliest and ending with the most recent: James Long, Henry Perry, Gutiérrez and Magee, Philip Nolan.
2. **Interpreting Maps:** Study the map on this page. With which Indian group would the Spaniards in Texas probably have come into the most direct conflict? Explain, in terms of geography, why you think your answer is true.

Enriching Your Study of History

1. **Individual Project:** Conduct research in the library, and prepare a written report on the impact of the Louisiana Purchase on Spanish Texas. Prepare a colorful map to illustrate your report.

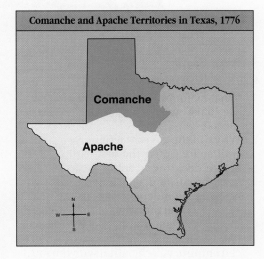
Comanche and Apache Territories in Texas, 1776
Comanche
Apache

2. **Cooperative Project:** Your teacher will divide your class into three groups to research the major towns in Spanish Texas in 1800: San Antonio, La Bahía (Goliad), and Nacogdoches. At the end of the research, each team will present a class report on the political, economic, and cultural life of its assigned town. Your group should decide how best to illustrate your report, and then together create a map, a drawing, or a three-dimensional model of your assigned town.
3. **Cooperative Project:** With a partner, create a map of Texas, poster size. On the map, show the movements and major locations of Philip Nolan, Bernardo Gutiérrez de Lara, William Augustus Magee, General Joaquín de Arredondo, Jean Laffite, Henry Perry, James Long, Jane Long and Kiamatia. A careful study of your textbook should help you decide how much territory your map must cover.

UNIT REVIEW RESOURCES

1. Unit Review Worksheet 3
2. Unit 3 Test, Form A
3. Reteaching Worksheet 3
4. Unit 3 Test, Form B
5. **Informal Evaluation Forms:** Portfolio Assessment
6. *Texas, Our Texas* **Test Generator**

Essential Elements
1A, 1B, 1C, 5B, 9A, 9B, 9E

ANSWERS TO UNIT 3 REVIEW

Connecting Main Ideas

1. Trouble with the Indians and the French, epidemics, drought, soldiers' poor morale, and a threat from the United States
2. They had no economic reason to settle Texas, and they did not feel that their interests were threatened.
3. It was begun by Father Hidalgo; Iturbide ended it.
4. Spain; France. Spain gained from France the city of New Orleans and the land west of the Mississippi.
5. Drought, epidemics, Indian raids

Practicing Critical Thinking Skills

1. **Synthesizing Information:** Coronado was seeking riches; De León and Massanet were seeking ways to protect Spanish land from the French. The Indians did not welcome Coronado as they did De León and Massanet.
2. **Seeing Cause and Effect:** 1690s—withdrawn because of drought and epidemics; 1716—reestablished to convert the Indians to Christianity and to protect against the French; 1770s—Spain did not have the financial means to maintain the missions, and Spanish authorities felt

UNIT 3

REVIEW

Connecting Main Ideas

1. What major problems did Spanish people have when they tried to settle Texas?
2. Why did the government in New Spain wait so long after the first explorations before deciding to settle Texas?
3. Who began and who ended the fight for Mexican independence from Spain? What was the outcome of the struggle?
4. In the struggle among Spain, France, and Great Britain for the North American empire, which nation won the most in 1763? Which nation lost the most? Explain your answers.
5. What troubles plagued the East Texas missions throughout their history?

Practicing Critical Thinking Skills

1. **Synthesizing Information:** Compare and contrast Coronado's expedition with that of De León and Massanet.
2. **Seeing Cause and Effect:** The Spaniards established missions in East Texas in the 1690s, withdrew them a few years later, established the missions again in 1716, and abandoned them again in the 1770s. In each case, explain the main cause for the Spanish policy decision regarding the missions.
3. **Exploring Multicultural Perspectives:** You know that some Texas Indian cultures were very different from each other. How might the Apaches describe the Spanish missionaries? How might the Caddoes describe them?

TAAS *Practice*
Writing Persuasively

Imagine that you are a Spanish priest trying to convince a band of Tonkawas to come to San Antonio and live at your mission. Write the short speech you will use to convince them to do this.

Exploring Local History

1. Study a map of the county in which you live. How many Spanish place names can you find?
2. Ask parents or guardians, and adult friends: "In what ways has the Spanish heritage influenced life in Texas?" Write a brief report of the answers.

Using Historical Imagination

1. **Individual Project:** Research a figure from the Spanish period of Texas history. Using what you learn about the person's life, write a brief autobiography as if you were that person.
2. **Cooperative Project:** Working in two- or three-student teams, research either Spanish missions or presidios. Each team will present a drawing or model and a brief report on its structure.

For Extending Your Knowledge

Bolton, H. E. *Texas in the Middle Eighteenth Century.* Austin: University of Texas Press, 1915. A standard work on Spanish Texas.

Cabeza de Vaca, Alvar Nuñez. *La Relación.* New York: Macmillan, 1988. Cabeza de Vaca's account of his adventures.

SKILL LESSON

Synthesizing Information

In studying history, it is often necessary to synthesize information that you are reading. To synthesize information, you must combine ideas or facts from more than one source. Chapter 8, which you have just read, is a synthesis. The author studied a number of historical sources and used that information to create his own story about the last century of Spanish rule in Texas. You, too, are asked to synthesize information in this course and in other courses. Each time you read two sources and then combine ideas from each in your own work, you are synthesizing information.

How to Synthesize Information

The following four steps will help you understand how to synthesize information. Study them carefully before you go on to practice the skill.

- *Select sources carefully.* Make sure that the sources you are studying cover the same information and complement, or add to, each other.
- *Read for understanding.* Identify main ideas and important supporting evidence in each source. Sometimes, you may need to read a source more than once to understand its contents completely.
- *Compare and contrast.* Note where sources agree or build on each other. More importantly, note where they differ from each other.

- *Interpret all the information.* Use what you have found to interpret the information. Interpretation is the key step in synthesizing.

Practicing the Skill

Read carefully the two sources that follow. Then, using the synthesizing tips above, combine the information in both sources to write one paragraph.

The following two paragraphs about Jean Laffite are excerpted from *The World Book Encyclopedia**:

> In 1814, the British were at war with the United States. They offered Laffite $30,000, a pardon, and a naval captaincy if he would aid them in attacking New Orleans. He refused, informed the United States government of the plans, and offered the services of the Barataria smugglers to the United States. Laffite fought for General Andrew Jackson in the Battle of New Orleans on January 8, 1815, and received a pardon from President James Madison.
>
> American forces had destroyed the community at Barataria, so Laffite moved to Galveston Island. There, he established a town called Campeachy, and returned to piracy.

The following two paragraphs are excerpted from *Texas: A Modern History* by David G. McComb:

> Jean with his brother set up smuggling operations at Barataria near New Orleans around 1808. In spite of the destruction of their base by the governor of Louisiana in 1814, Laffite and his pirates aided Andrew Jackson in the defense of New Orleans early in 1815.
>
> Although pardoned for their past because of their support in the war, the Laffite brothers went back into business as brokers to pirates on Galveston Island in 1817.

*Excerpted from The World Book Encyclopedia. © 1991 World Book, Inc. By permission of the publisher.

that there was no longer a need to populate an area that was no longer the outer edge of New Spain.

3. **Exploring Multicultural Perspectives:** Descriptions will vary but should demonstrate knowledge of the two Indian groups and their relationship with the Spanish missionaries.

TAAS *Practice*
Writing Persuasively

Speeches will vary but should present a clear and persuasive argument.

Exploring Local History

1. Answers will vary but should demonstrate an awareness of Spanish place names.
2. Reports will vary but should be clear and logical.

Using Historical Imagination

1. **Individual Project:** Autobiographies will vary but should be based on thorough research of the person's life.
2. **Cooperative Project:** Projects will vary but should demonstrate knowledge of missions and presidios.

Skill Lesson
Practicing the Skill
Paragraphs will vary but should synthesize accurately the information presented.

INTRODUCING THE UNIT

Connecting with Past Learning

Review with students the settlement of Texas and Mexico's break from Spanish control, leaving Texas now a part of Mexico. Have the class review the map on page 159. Ask students to speculate on what Mexican control might mean for the future of Texas as thousands of settlers pour into the region.

UNIT 4 OVERVIEW

Unit 4 focuses on the colonization of Texas by settlers from the United States and the events leading to the Texas Revolution. Highlighting the major role of Stephen F. Austin, Chapter 9 describes the first organized settlement of Texas by empresarios.

Chapter 10 examines daily life in colonial Texas and covers politics, religion, education, occupations, and social life.

Chapter 11 describes the road to revolution. It presents the causes of unrest in Texas and the reasons for conflict between the colonists and the Mexican government. The first battle of the Texas Revolution is described.

Materials Available at the Unit Level:
Unit 4   Making Global
         Connections
Oral History Handbook
Informal Evaluation Forms

UNIT 4
AMERICAN COLONIZATION

MOTIVATOR

Announce to students that in Unit 4 they will be studying the colonization of Texas. Ask them to imagine that they are among the first U.S. citizens chosen to settle Texas. Have students list ten items they would be certain to take with them when traveling to a new home in an unfamiliar territory. Assign the students to groups to compare their lists. Compare the lists as a class, and create one group list on the chalkboard.

TEXAS AND THE WORLD

Organize the class into small groups, and have each group study the time line on this page. Select one of the world events, and have the groups brainstorm about how that event might relate to events of that period in Texas. Continue the activity for other key events on the time line.

Spain sent few settlers to Texas during the long period of its control. Yet the population of Texas began to grow after Mexico won its independence from Spain in 1821. Thousands of settlers from the United States entered Texas to establish colonies under Mexican control. Settlers also came from other areas of Mexico and from Europe.

Richard Petri, a German Texan, painted the scene opposite of farm life in Central Texas. Thousands of people from all backgrounds came seeking land and a new life. The large majority settled on farms. A smaller number opened businesses. Soon, churches and schools were established. Small towns began to grow, and roads were developed.

Texas remained part of Mexico from 1821 to 1836. During this period, settlers from the United States came to outnumber all others in Texas. Disagreements grew between Texans and the Mexican government. Gradually these disagreements grew into conflict, and Texans sought to break away from Mexican control.

Unit 4 covers the period when Texas was part of Mexico. Chapter 9 centers around Stephen F. Austin's role in bringing settlers to Texas. Chapter 10 is about life in Texas during the 1820s and 1830s. Chapter 11 discusses the areas of disagreement that developed between Texans and the Mexican government.

UNIT 4 OBJECTIVES

1. Identify Moses Austin and Stephen F. Austin, and explain the role of the empresarios in the settlement of Texas.
2. Discuss the impact of Mexico's National Colonization Law on colonial Texas.
3. Identify and discuss the contributions of Stephen F. Austin to the history of Texas.
4. Explain reasons for the influx of settlers from the United States into Texas during the 1820s and 1830s.
5. Identify and give examples of the early Texas settlers' ways of life, and discuss the physical and economic hardships the settlers faced.
6. Discuss the role of education and religion in colonial Texas.
7. Identify causes of unrest among the colonists regarding Mexican control of Texas.
8. List and discuss events leading to the Texas Revolution.

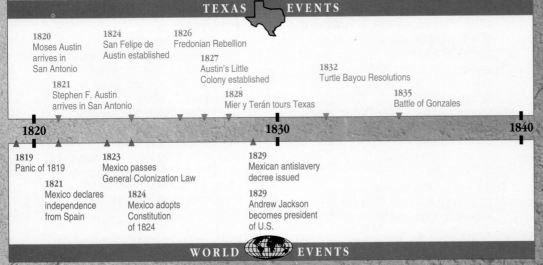

TEXAS EVENTS

1820
Moses Austin arrives in San Antonio

1821
Stephen F. Austin arrives in San Antonio

1824
San Felipe de Austin established

1826
Fredonian Rebellion

1827
Austin's Little Colony established

1828
Mier y Terán tours Texas

1832
Turtle Bayou Resolutions

1835
Battle of Gonzales

1820 — 1830 — 1840

WORLD EVENTS

1819
Panic of 1819

1821
Mexico declares independence from Spain

1823
Mexico passes General Colonization Law

1824
Mexico adopts Constitution of 1824

1829
Mexican antislavery decree issued

1829
Andrew Jackson becomes president of U.S.

STEPHEN F. AUSTIN AND THE EMPRESARIOS

TEACHER'S TIME LINE

Section 1	Section 2	Section 3	Section 4	Section 5	Review and Assessment
Pp. 174–76	Pp. 176–82	Pp. 182–84	Pp. 184–89	Pp. 189–91	
1 Day	1 Day	1 Day	1 Day	1 Day	1 Day

⬟ TEACHER MATERIALS

Core: Chapter 9 Time Line; Graphic Organizer 9; Enrichment Worksheet 9; Review Worksheet 9; Reteaching Worksheet 9; Chapter 9 Tests, Forms A & B

Additional: Geography and Graph Skills 9, Informal Evaluation Forms, Test Generator

⬟ OBJECTIVES

1. Discuss the role of Moses Austin in Texas history.
2. List reasons for choosing the location of Stephen F. Austin's original colony.
3. Explain why settlers from the United States were eager to come to Austin's colony.
4. Explain how changes in Mexico affected Austin's colony.
5. Analyze the impact of new colonization laws on Anglo settlement in Texas.
6. Identify empresarios who brought settlers to Texas.
7. Examine reasons for the recognition of Stephen F. Austin as the "Father of Texas."

⬟ RESOURCES

BOOKS FOR TEACHERS

Austin, Moses. *Austin Moses, Papers*. Austin: Barker-MS. Important papers of Moses Austin.

Barker, Eugene C. *The Life of Stephen F. Austin: Founder of Texas, 1793–1836*. Austin: University of Texas Press, 1969. Biography of Stephen F. Austin.

Binkley, William C. *Law in the Lone Star State*. Austin: State Bar of Texas, 1976. Three activities: *Law Comes to Texas, Wagons to Texas, Law in Early Texas*.

Duval, John C. *Early Times in Texas*. Austin: Steck, 1892. History of the colonial period.

Everett, Dianna. *The Texas Cherokees: A People Between Two Fires, 1819–1840*. Norman: University of Oklahoma Press, 1990. Describes the adaptation of the Cherokees to environments in Texas.

Yoakum, H. *History of Texas from Its First Settlement in 1685 to Its Annexation to the United States in 1846*. New York: Redfield, 1855. Facsimile edition, Steck-Vaughn.

MULTIMEDIA MATERIALS

The Frontier Experience. (video, 25 min.) Learning Corporation of America, Distributed by Simon and Schuster Communications, 108 Wilmot Road, Deerfield, Illinois, 60015. The westward movement from a woman's perspective.

Sacajawea. (video, 24 min.) Southwest Media Services, Inc., P.O. Box 140, Wimberley, Texas, 78676. Portrait of the American frontier, focusing on the Indian guide Sacajawea.

Wagons West. (software) Focus Media, Inc., 839 Stewart Avenue, P.O. Box 865, Garden City, New York, 11530. Interactive program covers pioneer life, Plains Indians, and so on.

STUDENTS WITH SPECIAL NEEDS

Limited English Proficient Students (LEP)

Have students draw on a sheet of paper a time line for use throughout the study of Chapter 9. As students complete each section of the chapter, ask them to fill in the time line with appropriate dates and events from that section. After they have completed the time line, instruct them to choose one event and write a brief summary. See other activities labeled **LEP**.

Students Having Difficulty with the Chapter

List all of the boldfaced terms on the chalkboard. In a second list, write the following complementary words and phrases:

edge of settlement
taking a business risk in hopes of obtaining a quick gain
settlers without titles
proof of ownership
volunteer army
seat of government
businesspeople who brought settlers to Texas
law-making body
sudden and massive withdrawals of money from banks
newcomers
request

Invite individual students to come to the board and match a term with its description. Conclude the activity by asking students to write sentences using each term in the appropriate context. **LEP**

Auditory Learners

Have auditory learners select one of the following situations. Each student should prepare a brief speech to present to the class. See other activities labeled **A**.

a. Baron de Bastrop influencing Governor Martínez to approve Moses Austin's land grant petition
b. Stephen F. Austin convincing settlers to join his expedition to Texas
c. Stephen F. Austin requesting recognition of his Texas colony from the Mexican government

Visual Learners

Provide visual learners with blank outline maps of Texas. Ask them to locate and label the colony sites of the following empresarios:

Stephen F. Austin
Green DeWitt
David Burnet, Joseph Vehlein, and Lorenzo de Zavala
Sterling Robertson
James Power and James Hewetson
John McMullen and James McGloin
Haden Edwards
Martín de León

See other activities labeled **V**.

Tactile/Kinesthetic Learners

Assign pairs of students to compose an advertisement and an application for settlers interested in moving to Texas with Stephen F. Austin. Each pair should list the criteria to be used in evaluating individual applications. Display the advertisements and applications on the bulletin board. See other activities labeled **TK**.

Gifted Students

Have students evaluate the leadership qualities of Stephen F. Austin. Ask them to list five important standards, such as intelligence, by which they would judge a leader. Have them apply their standards to Stephen F. Austin by writing a *Y* for yes or an *N* for no next to each standard in answer to the following question: Did Austin meet this standard? Finally, ask students to write a paragraph summarizing the leadership qualities of Stephen F. Austin. See other activities labeled **G**.

VOCABULARY

In addition to the boldfaced terms in each section, some students might benefit from discussing the meanings of these terms.

Section 1: *ambitious* (p. 174).
Section 2: *legislator* (p. 176); *eligible* (p. 178); *cargo* (p. 179); *prosperous* (p. 182).
Section 3: *authorized* (p. 182); *sojourn* (p. 184).
Section 4: *grant* (p. 186); *land commissioner* (p. 189).
Section 5: *isolated* (p. 189); *adviser* (p. 191).

CHRONOLOGY

Have students study the Chapter 9 Time Line and identify relationships among the events.

GRAPHIC ORGANIZER

Have students skim the chapter and complete the Chapter 9 Graphic Organizer. *(You might wish to use this activity to review rather than to introduce the chapter.)*

ENRICHMENT

Have students complete the Chapter 9 Enrichment Worksheet.

SECTION ▪1▪

FOCUS

Past Learning (I) Write the date 1821 on the chalkboard. Ask volunteers to name the significance of this date *(Mexico declares independence from Spain).* Ask students to recall that now Texas was under Mexican control.

INSTRUCTION

Vocabulary (I) You may wish to preteach the following boldfaced terms: *financial panic* (p. 175); *petition* (p. 175); *immigrants* (p. 176). **LEP**

Analysis (I) Have students write from the point of view of the Mexican government a paragraph defending or condemning Moses Austin's plan for bringing 300 families into Texas. Invite volunteers to read their paragraphs aloud. **A**

CHAPTER 9 OVERVIEW

Mexico's independence from Spain in 1821 began a new era for Texas. During the 1820s, the colonization of Texas by settlers from the United States began. The United States was expanding westward, and Texas meant cheap land and unlimited opportunity. When the Mexican government removed restrictions on settlement, thousands of people entered Texas from the United States. Chapter 9 tells the story of Moses and Stephen F. Austin, two men who were most important in the colonization of Mexican Texas.

Essential Elements
1C, 2A, 2B, 2H, 5D, 7C, 9A, 9B, 9D, 9E

CHAPTER 9

STEPHEN F. AUSTIN AND THE EMPRESARIOS

The Story Continues...

Chapter 9 tells how Texas' colonial policies changed after Mexico declared its independence from Spain in 1821. It also explains how thousands of settlers from the United States entered Texas to establish colonies under Mexican control.

As you read the chapter, look for the answers to these questions:

1. Who was Moses Austin, and what did he request of the Spanish governor in San Antonio?
2. Why were American settlers eager to come to Stephen F. Austin's colony in Texas?
3. What problems troubled the early days of Austin's colony?
4. What new colonization policies were put into effect in 1825 by the state of Coahuila y Texas?
5. What personal traits of Stephen F. Austin made him a successful empresario?

Stark Museum of Art, Orange, Texas

The famous painter John James Audubon produced this hand-colored engraving of a Texas whooping crane in 1834. Today, the whooping crane is an endangered species.

▪1▪ Moses Austin and Texas

In December 1820, Moses Austin rode his horse into the Plaza de Armas at San Antonio de Béxar hoping to meet with the Spanish governor of Texas, Antonio Martínez. Austin, a 59-year-old businessman, wanted Governor Martínez to grant him a contract to bring 300 families from the United States to settle in Texas. Bringing that many people was an ambitious plan and one that the Spaniards greeted with suspicion. Their experiences with the filibusters made them distrustful of any American. But Moses Austin had staked his future on the settlement of Texas.

Taking a Chance. Moses Austin was born in Connecticut, but at the time of his trip to Texas, he lived in Missouri. For several years he had operated a lead mine there. Austin

Economics (II) Have students write a series of cause-and-effect statements outlining the financial panic in the United States in 1819. Ask volunteers to write their statements on the chalkboard. **A, V**

Guided Practice (I) Have students work individually or in pairs to create a map or other drawing to illustrate Bastrop's idea that the Texas settlers would act as a buffer against the Indians at war with the Spaniards. **V, TK**

EXTENSION

Role Playing (II) Ask interested students to play the role of Moses Austin as he petitions Governor Martínez to bring settlers to Texas. Have other students role play Baron de Bastrop as he presents Austin's plan to Governor Martínez. **A, V**

Independent Practice (I) Have students write an inscription for a historical marker for Moses Austin. Tell students they must be brief but descriptive. **V, LEP**

Missouri Historical Society

Moses Austin lived to see his plan for settling Texas approved by Spanish officials in Mexico. Unfortunately, the long and difficult trip back to Missouri and the strain of organizing settlement plans caused his death. His dying wish was for his son Stephen to take over his leadership of the Texas colony.

invested his profits from the mine in a bank and other businesses. Then in 1819, a **financial panic** swept the United States. Banks had loaned too much money to people buying land in the West. People with money in the banks grew fearful and rushed to withdraw their savings. Many banks failed, and land values fell sharply. One of the failed banks was the Bank of St. Louis, which Moses Austin had helped found. His family fortune was lost overnight.

Moses Austin understood Spanish ways of life and policies of government. When he first went into Missouri, it was part of Louisiana and under Spanish control. He admired and respected the Spanish and had always worked well with them. Now, broke and with little hope for a future in Missouri, Moses Austin struck out for Texas.

At his first meeting in San Antonio with Governor Martínez, Austin's **petition**, or formal request, to bring settlers to Texas was refused. In low spirits, Austin left the governor's office. He walked across the plaza to meet

RETEACHING

List major events from Section 1 in random order on the chalkboard. Ask volunteers to number the events in chronological order. Then call on students to summarize each event. **LEP, A**

CLOSURE

With the class, list on the chalkboard three reasons Baron de Bastrop gave the Spaniards that convinced them to accept Moses Austin's colonization plan.

ASSESSMENT

Have students complete the Section 1 Review on page 176.

SECTION 2

FOCUS

Predicting (I) Remind students of Moses Austin's dying wish that his son Stephen carry out his dream of colonizing Texas. Ask: From what you know about Texas history, did Stephen Austin fulfill his father's dream?

Answers to Section 1 Review

Define: *financial panic*—fear of bank failures that causes people to withdraw their money, which in turn actually may cause bank failures; *petition*—formal request; *immigrants*—persons who come into a country to live

Identify: Moses Austin—Missouri businessman who began colonization of Texas; Baron de Bastrop—friend of Governor Martínez who helped Moses Austin deal with the Spanish government; Governor Martínez—Spanish governor of Texas

1. To bring families from the United States to settle Texas
2. Bastrop was a friend of Governor Martínez and had the respect of Spanish officials.
3. Pneumonia

Analyzing Information: Austin had just lost his fortune and was seeking a new start. He had lived in Spanish territory and got along well with the Spaniards. He saw Texas as a great opportunity.

Evaluating Information: Answers will vary. Students should note that Austin's plan had already been rejected by the Spanish government in San Antonio and that Austin probably would have returned home without an agreement if he had not had Bastrop's help.

SECTION ★ 1 REVIEW

Define: financial panic, petition, immigrants
Identify: Moses Austin, Baron de Bastrop, Governor Martínez

1. What did Moses Austin ask Spanish officials to allow him to do?
2. Why was the Baron de Bastrop important to Austin's success?
3. What probably caused Moses Austin's death?

Analyzing Information: What factors contributed to Moses Austin's decision to seek permission for an American colony in Texas?

Evaluating Information: How might history have been different if Moses Austin had not chanced to meet the Baron de Bastrop while in San Antonio?

Richmond, a slave and his personal servant. There, by chance, Austin met Philip Hendrik Nering Bögel, known as Baron de Bastrop.

Baron de Bastrop. Bastrop and Moses Austin may have known each other from earlier days in Spanish Louisiana. Bastrop had come from Holland, but he now lived in San Antonio and was a close friend of Governor Martínez. Austin explained his plan to bring settlers into Texas. Bastrop understood Austin's desire for a fresh start in Texas and promised to help him. The Baron had no money, but he did have the respect of the Spanish officials.

Because Bastrop was friendly with Governor Martínez, he was the perfect person to present Austin's colonization plan. Bastrop convinced the Spaniards that families from the United States would be good for Texas and would help the Spanish economy. He also pointed out that the **immigrants**, or persons who come into a country to settle, would act as a buffer, or shield, against the Indians at war with the Spaniards. Governor Martínez and General Joaquín de Arredondo back in Monterrey saw the wisdom in Bastrop's argument. Austin's plan was approved.

The Death of Moses Austin. Moses Austin, accompanied by Richmond, set out for Missouri to begin recruiting settlers. Cold, damp winds slowed their journey. Icy, flooded streams had to be crossed. Richmond became ill, and Austin had to leave him with a family on the Sabine River. When he finally reached home in Missouri, Austin had developed a case of pneumonia. Within months, he lay dying. On his deathbed, Moses Austin asked that his son, Stephen, carry out his dream of colonizing Texas. ○

❷ Stephen F. Austin

At the time of his father's death, Stephen Fuller Austin was 27 years old. He was born in Virginia on November 3, 1793. He had been successful in Missouri and Arkansas as a legislator, a businessman, and a judge. He was a patient and understanding man with a great deal of energy. Stephen was as determined as Moses, and in the summer of 1821, he set out to honor his father's wish.

Exploring the Land. Stephen F. Austin arrived in San Antonio in August 1821. He was escorted into the city by

Vocabulary (I) You may wish to preteach the following boldfaced terms: *titles* (p. 178); *militia* (p. 182). **LEP**

Geography (I) Review with students the geographic theme of *location* that they learned about in Unit 1. Ask students to name the countries and bodies of water that border the continental United States *(Canada on the north, Mexico and the Gulf of Mexico on the south, Atlantic Ocean on the east, Pacific Ocean on the west)*. Point out that the borders of the United States did not extend from coast to coast until almost the mid 1880s, and that the first moves in this direction occurred when Americans began settling in Texas and Oregon. **A, V**

Cooperative Learning (I) Organize the class into groups. Direct students to a map of Texas, and have each group choose a location in which to establish a colony. The group leader should record three reasons for the choice. Compare the students' choices with that of Stephen F. Austin. **A, V, LEP**

Archives Division, Texas State Library

Stephen F. Austin was a young man when he agreed to carry out his father's plan to settle Texas.

Essential Elements
(For Section 2)
1C, 2A, 2H, 5A, 5B, 5C, 8A, 8B, 8C, 9A, 9B, 9F

Historical Sidelight
When his father died, Stephen F. Austin was not present at his bedside. Stephen's mother wrote him a letter, passing on Moses' dying wish that Stephen continue Moses' colonization plan.

a representative of Governor Martínez, Erasmo Seguín, a local business leader and rancher. After extending a warm greeting, Governor Martínez officially transferred Moses Austin's contract to Stephen.

Stephen F. Austin spent the next few weeks exploring the area east of San Antonio for colony sites. After looking over much of the land between San Antonio and Nacogdoches, he chose an area near the Brazos and Colorado rivers. The land offered rich soil and plenty of trees for building. Rainfall was plentiful, and there were many wild game animals. Besides being near rivers, the land was close to the Gulf coast. In Austin's words, this country was "as good in every respect as man could wish for, land first rate, plenty of timber, fine water—beautifully rolling." The location was also well removed from Comanches.

Austin Recruits Colonists. Excited by the success of his journey into Texas, Stephen F. Austin returned to the United States and began promoting his colony. Word of the Austin plan had already spread from Louisiana all the way to the New England states. In southern newspapers,

Stark Museum of Art, Orange, Texas

John James Audubon was a famous artist and naturalist. He studied many animal species in their natural settings and made realistic illustrations of them, such as this painting of a Texas red wolf (1845).

Paul M. Montgomery

Prairies along the Colorado and Brazos rivers looked like promising farmland to Stephen F. Austin.

Historical Sidelight
Austin received about 100 letters in response to his advertisement.

Austin advertised his colony and the terms he was offering. Applications poured in from men and women eager for land.

Individual settlers chosen by Austin would receive 640 acres of land. A husband and wife were eligible for an additional 320 acres. For each child, settlers could obtain another 160 acres. Because most of the settlers were from the southern United States, many had African American slaves. Each slave added 80 acres to the total land grant. Austin was to receive 12.5¢ per acre from each settler to cover the costs of surveying the land and recording the **titles**, or proofs of ownership. Because land was selling for $1.25 per acre in the United States, Austin's terms were very attractive.

By the terms of his agreement with the Spaniards, Austin set up strict guidelines for granting land titles. He realized that the success or failure of the colony depended upon his ability to choose honest settlers who were willing to work. Austin felt a responsibility to the Spanish government and to the immigrants from the United States to make this new colony successful.

Austin's rules for the colony stated that "no drunkard, no gambler, no profane swearer, no idler" would be allowed. At first, he sought only farming and ranching families. Austin wanted people who would also respect the Spanish law, tradition, and religion. This meant that the settlers had to promise loyalty to the Roman Catholic church. After he was sure of their good character, Austin extended credit to settlers or agreed to accept goods as payment for land. Many times Austin took no payment if a settler faced hard times and could not pay the fee of 12.5¢ per acre.

The Colony Begins Settlement. Austin returned to New Orleans to make arrangements for his colony. In November 1821, he went into partnership there with an old friend, Joseph Hawkins, a lawyer. Hawkins loaned Austin $4,000 for necessary expenses. Austin used part of the money to buy a small ship, the *Lively*, to transport supplies to Texas. The *Lively* sailed from New Orleans in November with eighteen colonists and a cargo of tools, seed, and building materials. Austin agreed to meet this group of settlers at the mouth of the Colorado River in several weeks.

After seeing the *Lively* off, Austin traveled from Louisiana to Nacogdoches. A party of colonists awaited him there, and together they left for Austin's colony. Upon their arrival, Austin discovered that several families had already settled in scattered places along the Brazos and Colorado rivers. In that group was Josiah Bell, Austin's friend and

Stephen F. Austin issued land titles to hundreds of colonists. He more than fulfilled his father's dream of settling Texas. His personal concern with the development of the colony made the settlement successful.

Drawing by Norman Price, Barker Texas History Center

Chapter 9 **179**

Historical Sidelight
Austin spent the late summer and fall of 1821 traveling and mapping the Guadalupe, Colorado, and Brazos rivers.

former business partner. Other early settlers were the Kuykendall brothers—Abner, Joseph, and Robert—and their wives and children. The first person to enter the new colony was most likely Andrew Robinson. He began running a ferry along the Brazos River in 1830 at a spot where the town Washington-on-the-Brazos later grew up. This town later became one of the early capitals of Texas.

One of the best equipped of the early settlers was Jared Groce. With at least 50 wagons, livestock, seed, and about 90 slaves, he settled near present-day Hempstead. More typical of the first settlers were Clement and Sarah Dyer. The Dyers had come from Tennessee with only a few supplies. They were eager to own a plot of land and build a family farm.

As settlers poured in, Austin kept busy having the land surveyed and recording titles. He tried to help the new colonists adjust to life in the Texas wilderness. From the beginning, the colony was short of food, equipment to clear land, and farming supplies. A crisis came when the supply ship *Lively* was lost on its second trip. The *Lively* wrecked near the tip of Galveston Island with settlers and supply cargo on board. A number of people were killed, and tools and seed were lost. Some survivors became discouraged and returned to the United States.

Austin in Mexico. Another and much larger problem soon faced Austin. In March 1822, he filed a report with

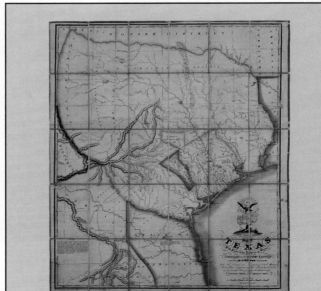

Library of Congress

Stephen F. Austin drew this map of the Texas colonies in 1822.

RETEACHING
Have students list the subheadings from Section 2 across the top of a sheet of paper: *Exploring the Land, Austin Recruits Colonists, The Colony Begins Settlement, Austin in Mexico.* Then ask them to select and list under each subheading three important ideas from that subsection. Finally, have students use the lists to write a paragraph summarizing Section 2. **LEP**

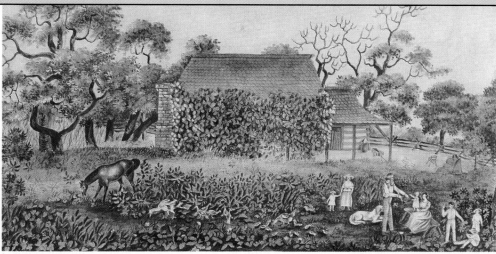

San Antonio Museum Association

Louis Hoppe painted this impression of life on an early Texas farm. What do you think life was like for the early colonists in Texas?

Caption Response
Possible answer: Life was very difficult. Colonists were starting a new life from scratch, and they had to face many hardships.

Historical Sidelight
According to one historian, the band of Comanches that robbed Austin at first thought that he and his small party were Mexicans. When the Indians discovered Austin's identity, they returned the group's belongings—except for a Spanish-English dictionary.

Governor Martínez in San Antonio on the progress of his colony. There he was told that Mexico had recently won its independence from Spain. The Mexican officials said they could not honor Austin's colonization grant. After talking over the new policy with Governor Martínez, Austin had no choice. If he hoped to save his colony, he had to go to Mexico City.

Stephen F. Austin set out immediately on his long journey to Mexico City. He hoped to return quickly, but it would be more than a year before he saw Texas again. He left his friend Josiah Bell in charge of the colony.

The road to Mexico was rugged and dangerous. Once, Austin was robbed by a band of Comanches. On the road from Monterrey to Mexico City, he dressed as a beggar to fool robbers. The disguise worked, for the hundreds of thieves along the road ignored him. He finally arrived in Mexico City in late April 1822. But events there did little to lift his spirits after his long trip.

Following the revolution that ended Spanish control, the situation in Mexico was confusing. Austin spent much of his time learning to speak Spanish and trying to understand which people held power in the government. Delay after delay extended Austin's stay in Mexico City. But he dared not leave until he knew the future of his Texas colony. Finally the Mexican congress passed a colonization law on January 3, 1823. The terms of the new law were

CLOSURE

Review with students Stephen F. Austin's success in setting up a colonization agreement with the Mexican government in 1823. Ask: What was the most important result of Austin's trip to Mexico City *(the relationship he developed with the Mexican government)*?

ASSESSMENT

Have students complete the Section 2 Review on page 182.

FOCUS

Student Experiences (I) Ask students to name qualities found in a leader and why they think it is important for a group to have a leader. Tell them to keep this discussion in mind as they read about the early problems facing Stephen Austin's colony.

Answers to Section 2 Review

Define: *titles*—legal proofs of ownership; *militia*—army made up of citizens who serve only when needed

Identify: Stephen F. Austin—Moses Austin's son who took over the colonizing of Texas; Erasmo Seguín—San Antonio business leader and rancher who befriended Stephen F. Austin; Washington-on-the-Brazos—early Texas settlement located at a ferry crossing on the Brazos River, became one of the early capitals of Texas; Jared Groce—wealthy plantation owner in Austin's colony

1. Land in Austin's colony was cheap.
2. The area offered rich soils, trees for building, plentiful rainfall, wild game, and was near rivers and close to the Gulf coast. It was also well removed from the Comanches.

(Continued on page 183)

Essential Elements
1A, 1C, 2A, 3E, 5C, 9A, 9B

SECTION 2 REVIEW

Define: titles, militia
Identify: Stephen F. Austin, Erasmo Seguín, Washington-on-the-Brazos, Jared Groce

1. Why did Stephen F. Austin have little difficulty in recruiting American settlers?
2. What were the reasons that Austin established his colony where he did?
3. What were the terms of Stephen F. Austin's agreement with the Mexican government in 1823?

Solving Problems: Imagine that you are planning to found a new colony in an unknown land. Make a list of the geographical factors that you will take into account in choosing its location.

Exploring Economics: What economic factors may have led Mexican officials to allow Austin to go ahead with his Texas colony?

Institute of Texan Cultures

This painting shows Stephen F. Austin and Baron de Bastrop issuing land titles at San Felipe de Austin.

favorable to Austin. But then another crisis in the Mexican government kept him from returning to Texas.

The emperor of Mexico, Agustín de Iturbide, was overthrown shortly after the colonization law was passed. Austin had to remain in Mexico City, trying to get a contract from the new government. Once again, Austin's patience and determination paid off. He was soon rewarded with permission to continue his Texas colony. The new agreement increased the amount of land for married settlers to a total of 4,605 acres, with 4,428 acres for ranching and 177 for farming.

Despite the length of his stay, the trip to Mexico proved to be successful for Austin. As the founder of the colony, Austin was to receive 100,000 acres of land. He was appointed judge for his colony, and he had the power to organize a **militia**. Unlike a regular army, a militia is made up of citizens who serve only when necessary. The most important result of Austin's trip was the relationship that he had developed with the Mexican government. Mexican leaders were impressed by Austin's knowledge, his honesty, and his determination. They were confident of his ability to set up a prosperous colony of people who would obey the law. This trust in Stephen F. Austin was a key to insuring the future growth of Texas. ✪

◾ The Austin Colony

Stephen F. Austin returned to his colony in August 1823. With him came his father's old friend, Baron de Bastrop. Bastrop had been authorized by the Mexican government to issue land titles for Austin's colony. When Austin and Bastrop rode into the first settlements along the Colorado River, they met a discouraged group of men and women. Austin's return had come none too soon.

Early Problems. The major problem facing the colonists was a shortage of food. A drought had destroyed the corn crop, and lack of seed kept the settlers from planting another. Most of the colonists had been living off the land, hunting wild game or gathering nuts and berries. There were a great many wild turkeys and deer in the area, but most of the ammunition had to be saved for Indian attacks. To add to their small food supply, some colonists had even killed wild mustangs.

INSTRUCTION

Vocabulary (I) You may wish to preteach the following boldfaced term: *capital* (p. 183). **LEP**

Environment (I) Ask students to skim Section 3 and find examples of how the colonists depended on their environment for survival. List students' responses on the chalkboard. **A, LEP**

Guided Practice (I) Have students work in pairs or small groups to draw a diagram illustrating San Felipe de Austin and the colonists' way of life. Ask students to display and discuss their illustrations. **A, V, TK, LEP**

EXTENSION

Research (II) Ask interested students to research and report on the fate of the Karankawa and Tonkawa culture groups in Texas after 1825. **A, G**

There were also problems with the Karankawas and Tonkawas. These Indians did not like the settlers invading their hunting grounds. Austin had some success negotiating with the Indians, but raids against the colony continued. There were also several gangs of thieves that sometimes attacked the colonists. Austin tried to solve both problems by organizing the settlers into a militia.

Some of the colonists were also fighting among themselves. Because much of the land had not yet been surveyed, there were disagreements over land titles and boundaries. Bastrop helped Austin settle these disputes.

The Old Three Hundred. Stephen F. Austin soon restored the good spirit of the colony. By the spring of 1825, 297 families were living in Austin's colony. These original Texas immigrants became known as the "Old Three Hundred" because the original grant had been for 300 families. Most of the Old Three Hundred were from the southern United States. Almost all of them were Anglo Americans, tracing their ancestors to Britain. Among them were many of the most influential and interesting citizens of early Texas.

One of the most famous of the Old Three Hundred was Jane Long. The first settlers in the colony had heard the story of her courage on Point Bolivar in the winter of 1821. Her survival against many hardships showed the spirit of these early settlers of Texas.

San Felipe de Austin. During the summer of 1823, Stephen F. Austin chose a place for the **capital**, or seat of

Institute of Texan Cultures, from Original in Texas State Capitol

Robert M. Williamson, known to the early colonists as "Three-Legged Willie," was a well-known member of the Old Three Hundred.

Barker Texas History Center

This sketch of Stephen F. Austin's residence at San Felipe de Austin shows a log cabin that was typical of the homes built by settlers from the United States.

3. Austin could continue his colony; the amount of land for married settlers was increased to a total of 4,605 acres; Austin would receive 100,000 acres of land, was appointed judge for his colony, and had the power to organize a militia. In return, the Mexican leaders expected Austin's colonists to obey Mexican law.

Solving Problems: Answers will vary, but possible responses include: soil, climate, grasslands, timber for building, water resources, access to the coast.

Exploring Economics: Answers will vary. Two centuries of Spanish and Mexican attempts to settle Texas had resulted in only a small population there. A thriving colony in Texas would bring increased trade and tax revenues to Mexico.

Historical Sidelight
A peace treaty was signed with the Karankawas, but the Indians continued to harass the colonists. The Mexican government sent troops to assist the colonists. The Mexicans and colonists won a crushing victory over the Indians. Almost half of the Karankawas were killed.

Independent Practice (II) Ask students to write a brief paragraph explaining how Stephen Austin might have been able to successfully negotiate with the Karankawas and Tonkawas concerning the settlers' invasion of the Indians' hunting grounds. Invite volunteers to read their paragraphs aloud. **A**

RETEACHING
Ask students to list what they would have liked or disliked about living in Austin's colony. Ask volunteers to read their lists aloud. **A, LEP**

CLOSURE
Point out to students that the leadership qualities of Stephen F. Austin helped to ensure his colony's success. Soon, others would seek permission to settle Texas.

ASSESSMENT
Have students complete the Section 3 Review on page 184.

Answers to Section 3 Review

Define: *capital*—seat of government

Identify: Old Three Hundred—name given to first 300 families who settled Austin's colony; San Felipe de Austin—capital of Austin's colony, located on the Brazos River; Noah Smithwick—early resident of San Felipe; Luciano García—Mexican governor of Texas who chose the name San Felipe de Austin; Gail Borden—newspaper publisher who joined the colony at San Felipe

1. Droughts, crop failures, loss of a supply ship, Indian raids, attacks by outlaws, squabbling over property lines, Austin's prolonged absence
2. Most of them were from the southern United States, and most of them were Anglo Americans.
3. Log cabins, sometimes double log cabins called "dog-run houses"

(Continued on page 185)

Essential Elements
1C, 2A, 2B, 2H, 5B, 9A, 9B, 9E

Barker Texas History Center

Gail Borden was a famous inventor and successful businessman.

SECTION ⭐3 REVIEW

Define: capital
Identify: Old Three Hundred, San Felipe de Austin, Noah Smithwick, Luciano García, Gail Borden

1. What serious problems troubled Austin's colony in its early years?
2. Describe the settlers known as the Old Three Hundred.
3. What sort of houses were built at San Felipe?

Problem Solving: Imagine that you need to found a capital for a new colony. Describe the geography of an ideal location for your new seat of government.

Analyzing Information: What evidence can you find in this section to suggest that the Old Three Hundred may have been people of education and culture, rather than rough pioneers?

government, of his colony. He established the capital near the Atascosito ferry crossing on the Brazos River in what is now Austin County. Luciano García, the Mexican governor of Texas, chose the name San Felipe de Austin to honor both Saint Philip and Stephen F. Austin.

San Felipe de Austin gained population quickly. Soon it was the center of business, social, and political life. Most of the early buildings in town were log cabins with only one or two rooms. Austin built his own home at San Felipe. Noah Smithwick, an early resident, described it as "a double log cabin with a passage through the center, a porch with dirt floor on the front with windows opening upon it, and a chimney at each end of the building." This kind of double log cabin was called a dog-run, or dogtrot, house.

Of the people of San Felipe, Smithwick wrote, "They were a social people these Old Three Hundred. . . . There were a number of weddings and other social gatherings during my sojourn in that section."

Among the well-known people of San Felipe was Robert M. Williamson, a lawyer. Williamson was known by the colonists as "Three-Legged Willie." He wore a wooden leg to support his bent and crippled right leg. Another citizen of San Felipe was a publisher, Godwin B. Cotten. Cotten owned the *Texas Gazette*, the first newspaper in the colony. In 1829, Gail Borden, another newspaper publisher, joined the colony at San Felipe. In addition to being publisher of the *Telegraph and Texas Register*, Borden was a part-time surveyor and inventor. He gained his greatest fame as the inventor of canned condensed milk. Borden later became one of the most successful businesspeople in the United States. ✪

❹ Colonization Laws and Empresarios

With the success of Stephen F. Austin's colony, other people sought to follow his lead. The Mexican government decided to develop a permanent program to deal with the growing number of applications for settlement in Texas.

New Colonization Laws. In 1824, the Mexican congress passed the National Colonization Law. This law gave each Mexican state the right to govern its own lands and set its own colonization policies. The two former Spanish provinces of Coahuila and Texas were united as one

SECTION 4

FOCUS

Predicting (I) Pose the following question to students: When the success of Austin's colony became well known, what do you suppose happened? Lead students to conclude that the idea of Texas as a land of opportunity caught on, and soon many others wanted to follow Austin's lead and bring settlers to Texas.

INSTRUCTION

Vocabulary (I) You may wish to preteach the following boldfaced terms: *legislature* (p. 185); *empresarios* (p. 185); *speculation* (p. 187); *squatters* (p. 187). **LEP**

Synthesis (II) Invite students to imagine that they are newspaper reporters for *The Texas Gazette*. Ask them to write an editorial about the Mexican congress having just passed the National Colonization Law and speculate on what impact this might have on the future of Texas. Select several editorials to read aloud. **A, G**

Mexican state. Texas was then considered to be a department within the state of Coahuila. The capital city of this new state called Coahuila y Texas was Saltillo, a beautiful city 50 miles southwest of Monterrey.

The first representative from Texas to serve in the state **legislature**, or law-making body, at Saltillo was Baron de Bastrop. In the spring of 1825, the Coahuila y Texas legislature passed a state law that would have important effects on the future settlement of Texas. Under this law, Texas was declared open to all foreign immigration. A family could receive as much as 4,428 acres with a down payment of only $30. New immigrants did not have to pay taxes to the Mexican government for ten years. The only requirements for settlement were to show evidence of good character and to honor the Roman Catholic faith.

More than five years had passed since Moses Austin received permission to settle Texas. Now the Mexican government had finally set up clear rules and regulations. No longer was Stephen F. Austin the only person allowed to bring in settlers. It was the beginning of a new era, as thousands of people in the United States looked to Texas for free land and a new beginning.

The Empresarios. Following passage of the Coahuila y Texas colonization law, about 25 new "empresario" contracts were granted by the Mexican government. The Mexicans used the term **empresarios** to describe the businesspeople who brought in settlers to occupy lands in Texas. Each empresario received 23,000 acres of land for every 100 families he brought into Texas. That is almost 36 square miles of land, an area six miles long and six miles wide! Less than a month after the new law went into effect, many families were approved for settlement in Texas.

After Stephen F. Austin, the most successful empresario was Green DeWitt, also from Missouri. DeWitt was authorized to settle 400 families between the Guadalupe and Lavaca rivers. The colony was settled on the rich soil of the Gulf Coast Plain and the Post Oak Belt. The most important town established in DeWitt's colony was Gonzales. It was named in honor of Rafael Gonzales, the governor of Coahuila y Texas at the time. Despite repeated attacks by the Comanches, the DeWitt colony slowly grew. It eventually became one of the most prosperous farming and ranching areas in colonial Texas.

Barker Texas History Center

THE TEXAS GAZETTE.

The Texas Gazette was the first newspaper published in Austin's colony.

Daughters of the Republic of Texas Library

José Antonio Navarro was a land commissioner for Green DeWitt. He was also a signer of the Texas Declaration of Independence.

Problem Solving: Answers will vary. The ideal site would be centrally located, perhaps on a river crossing or on a main road. It would be on high ground, secure from flooding, and would have good water resources.

Analyzing Information: Among them were many of the most influential citizens of early Texas. Some of the well-known people included a lawyer and two newspaper publishers, one of whom became one of the most successful businesspeople in the United States.

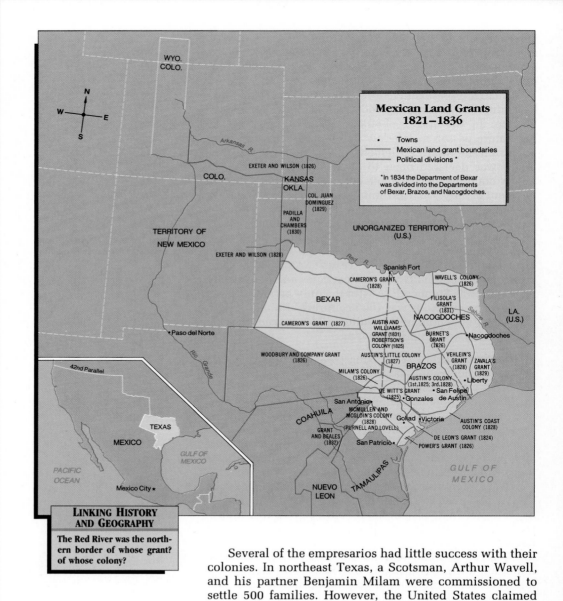

Mexican Land Grants 1821–1836

- Towns
- Mexican land grant boundaries
- Political divisions *

*In 1834 the Department of Bexar was divided into the Departments of Bexar, Brazos, and Nacogdoches.

WYO.
COLO.

N
W E
S

Arkansas R.

EXETER AND WILSON (1826)

COLO.

KANSAS
OKLA.

COL. JUAN DOMINGUEZ (1829)

PADILLA AND CHAMBERS (1830)

TERRITORY OF NEW MEXICO

UNORGANIZED TERRITORY (U.S.)

EXETER AND WILSON (1828)

Red R.

Spanish Fort

CAMERON'S GRANT (1828)

WAVELL'S COLONY (1826)

FILISOLA'S GRANT (1831)

BEXAR

NACOGDOCHES

LA. (U.S.)

• Paso del Norte

CAMERON'S GRANT (1827)

AUSTIN AND WILLIAMS' GRANT (1831) ROBERTSON'S COLONY (1825)

BURNET'S GRANT (1826)

• Nacogdoches

Sabine R.

WOODBURY AND COMPANY GRANT (1826)

AUSTIN'S LITTLE COLONY (1827)

VEHLEIN'S GRANT (1828)

ZAVALA'S GRANT (1829)

BRAZOS

• Liberty

MILAM'S COLONY (1826)

AUSTIN'S COLONY (1st,1825; 3rd,1828)

Rio Grande

DE WITT'S GRANT (1825)

• San Felipe de Austin

• Gonzales

San Antonio •

COAHUILA

MCMULLEN AND MCGLOIN'S COLONY (1828) (PURNELL AND LOVELL)

Goliad • Victoria

AUSTIN'S COAST COLONY (1828)

GRANT AND BEALES (1832)

San Patricio •

DE LEON'S GRANT (1824)

POWER'S GRANT (1826)

TAMAULIPAS

NUEVO LEON

GULF OF MEXICO

42nd Parallel

TEXAS

MEXICO

GULF OF MEXICO

PACIFIC OCEAN

Mexico City ★

LINKING HISTORY AND GEOGRAPHY

The Red River was the northern border of whose grant? of whose colony?

Several of the empresarios had little success with their colonies. In northeast Texas, a Scotsman, Arthur Wavell, and his partner Benjamin Milam were commissioned to settle 500 families. However, the United States claimed that the Wavell grant was inside its territory. This dispute created uncertainty over land titles, and for this and other reasons, the colony failed to grow.

Guided Practice (I) Have pairs of students work together to write dialogue that might have occurred in a conversation between Stephen F. Austin and a land speculator. The dialogue should present the point of view of both persons. Ask volunteers to perform their dialogue for the class. **A, V**

EXTENSION

Research (III) Have students visit the library to investigate current immigration trends in Texas. Ask them to report their findings in the form of a chart, graph, map, or other graphic. **V, TK, G**

South of the Wavell property, in East Texas, empresario contracts went to David G. Burnet, Joseph Vehlein, and Lorenzo de Zavala. Their land grants were later transferred to the Galveston Bay and Texas Land Company. Stephen F. Austin disliked land companies such as this because he felt they often used unfair sales methods. He believed that the land companies were too concerned with high profits and rarely worked for the best interest of their customers.

Another land company, the Nashville Company, represented by Sterling Robertson, had conflicts with Austin. Robertson had acquired land northwest of Austin's first colony. He then turned over areas of his land to other people to sell. This system angered Austin because it often led to too much land **speculation**. Speculators were people who bought land hoping its value would quickly rise. When it did, they sold it for a profit. The speculators had no desire to settle the land for farming or ranching.

Some colonies were established with the idea of bringing immigrants directly from Europe. James Power and James Hewetson from Ireland settled Irish families along the Gulf coast near the present city of Refugio. Another Irish colony was founded south of San Antonio by John McMullen and James McGloin.

In far East Texas, empresario Haden Edwards received the right to settle people near the Sabine River. His colony had problems over land titles from its beginning. New colonists argued with old settlers in the Nacogdoches area as well as with **squatters**, people who settled land on their own without titles. The colony eventually failed.

One of the more successful empresarios was Martín de León. De León was a native of Mexico and had been a rancher in South Texas. He brought in nearly 200 families from Mexico. His colony extended along the Guadalupe River near the Gulf coast. Martín and Patricia de León founded the city of Victoria. The colony became the center of business and trade between Mexico and Texas.

The Tejanos. Martín de León and Lorenzo de Zavala were native-born Mexicans who were empresarios. They were among 3,500 to 4,000 Tejanos, or native Mexicans living in Texas, in the 1820s.

Most of the Tejanos lived near the Rio Grande. When De León and De Zavala acquired grants in the 1820s, some Tejanos began moving northward. Like settlers from the

12 TEXAS IMMORTALS by Lajos Markos

Lorenzo de Zavala was one of the most influential citizens of Texas during the 1820s and 1830s. He was given a land grant and established a colony in East Texas. During the Revolution, he supported the Texas struggle against Mexico and later served as vice president of the Republic of Texas.

Institute of Texan Cultures

Martín de León was an important empresario. This painting by Bruce Marshall depicts De León supervising the building of Victoria, which he founded. Locate Victoria on a map.

Historical Sidelight
The main economic activity of De León's colony was trade in horses and cattle. These animals were driven from the large ranches of the colony to markets in Louisiana. At the time of De León's death in 1833, the estimated wealth of the colony was more than $1 million.

188 *Unit 4*

The Tejanos and Tejanas

The Tejanos and Tejanas were the early men and women of Mexican descent who lived in Texas. Although most of them resided in South Texas, they were the majority in towns such as San Antonio and La Bahía (present-day Goliad) and were a sizeable minority in Nacogdoches. Many Tejanos owned ranches near these towns and raised large herds of livestock. The vaqueros who worked for them were the first cowboys in Texas. They made cattle drives to Louisiana and south of the Rio Grande as early as the 1770s. Some of the rancheros, or ranchers, became wealthy and influential citizens.

The Tejanas played an important role on Texas ranches and farms. These women had jobs that contributed to the household economy as well as to the family. They often were in charge of the domestic animals, and they prepared food, made clothing, tended the family garden, and organized household chores for the children. Many Tejanas kept business records and handled the financial affairs of the ranch or farm. Gertrudis Seguín, wife of rancher Juan N. Seguín, became a respected citizen in the San Antonio area because of her many duties on the Seguín ranch. Another famous Tejana, Patricia de León, helped her husband, Martín, found the city of Victoria. After his death, she continued the operation of his empresario grant in the 1830s.

Typical of the Tejano ranchers was the Seguín family. Erasmo Seguín (Juan's father) was a successful and prosperous rancher, as were his father and grandfather before him. The Seguín ranch, La Mora (The Mulberry Tree), was on the San Antonio River near present-day Karnes City.

When Mexico gained independence from Spain, Erasmo Seguín represented Texas in the Mexican congress. He helped write the Constitution of 1824. And he was one of the Mexican citizens sent to welcome Stephen F. Austin to Texas. Seguín and Austin became close friends, and Seguín worked hard to help Austin's colonists. He also spoke for them in the congress.

Juan Seguín continued the work for an independent Texas. When Texans revolted against the Mexican government, he gathered a company of Tejano volunteers to fight for independence. They joined the army formed by Austin and took part in the capture of San Antonio. Erasmo Seguín contributed supplies to feed the rebel army.

Juan Seguín served two terms as a senator to the Congress of the Republic of Texas and was elected mayor (alcalde) of San Antonio. The present-day town of Seguin, which is located near San Antonio on Interstate Highway 10, is named for this young Tejano hero who helped Texas win its independence.

Inset: Juan Seguin

Archives Division, Texas State Library

SECTION 5

FOCUS

Past Learning (I) Ask students to provide facts they have learned about Stephen F. Austin as you list their responses on the chalkboard. Allow students to add to the list as they study Section 5.

INSTRUCTION

Vocabulary (I) You may wish to preteach the following boldfaced term: *frontier* (p. 189). **LEP**

United States, most were ranchers and farmers. The government in Mexico City hoped to send more Mexican settlers to Texas. But the idea of Texas as a land of opportunity never caught on in Mexico. By 1831, settlers from the United States outnumbered the Tejanos ten to one.

There were some conflicts between the Tejanos and settlers from the United States, as each group had different ways of life. But for the most part, there was peace and cooperation during the colonial era. One example is the relationship between the Austin and Seguín families. Moses Austin and Erasmo Seguín became close friends when Austin first arrived in San Antonio. When Stephen F. Austin came to Texas, it was Erasmo Seguín who welcomed and helped him. Later, Erasmo's son Juan and Stephen F. Austin worked closely together.

Other Tejanos were well known in Texas. José Antonio Navarro was a businessman and land commissioner for Green DeWitt. Plácido Benavides was an important member of De León's colony, holding government office in Victoria. Juan Antonio Padilla, also a land commissioner, later served in the revolution for independence from Mexico. ○

5 Stephen F. Austin's Contribution

Even with the coming of other empresarios, Stephen F. Austin continued to be the most important figure in Texas after the colonization law of 1825. He received a number of other contracts to bring in settlers, but his importance went beyond his success as an empresario.

Austin's Little Colony. The second of Austin's additional grants was awarded in 1827. It provided for 100 families to be brought into Texas. They settled east of the Colorado River and north of the Camino Real, also known as the Old San Antonio Road. This settlement became known as Austin's "Little Colony."

The town of Bastrop on the Colorado River was chosen as the capital of the Little Colony. Bastrop was farther out on the **frontier**, or edge of settlement, than any other place. It presented some new problems for Stephen F. Austin. The colony was so far west and so isolated that recruiting new settlers became difficult. Also, Bastrop was close to Comanche country. In order to attract settlers, Austin advertised the pine forests, the rolling farmland, and the

SECTION ★4★ REVIEW

Define: legislature, empresarios, speculation, squatters

Identify: Coahuila y Texas, Sterling Robertson, Green DeWitt, Lorenzo de Zavala, Tejanos

1. What new Texas colonization policies went into effect in 1825?
2. Who were the empresarios, and how did they profit by bringing in new settlers to Texas?
3. What did Austin dislike about land companies?

Synthesizing Information: Using evidence in this section (and previous sections), write a brief paragraph describing Austin's probable attitude toward other empresarios.

Seeing Cause and Effect: Explain how the National Colonization Law affected the policies of the state of Coahuila y Texas and how these policies affected Texas history.

ernment for ten years; the only requirements for settlement were to show evidence of good character and to honor the Roman Catholic faith.

2. They were businesspeople who brought in settlers to occupy lands in Texas. Each empresario received 23,000 acres of land for every 100 families he brought into Texas.

3. He thought that they used unfair sales methods, were too concerned with profits, and rarely worked for the best interests of customers.

Synthesizing Information: Paragraphs will vary. If the empresario worked in good faith and for the good of the colonists, Austin probably approved of him. Austin was distrustful of persons who seemed interested only in profit.

Seeing Cause and Effect: The National Colonization Law left matters of immigration policy up to the states. Coahuila y Texas used this freedom to set up a liberal immigration policy that brought thousands of new settlers to Texas, most of them from the United States. This set the stage for serious conflict with the government of Mexico.

Essential Elements
1C, 2A, 2H, 3E, 4I, 5B, 7D, 7G, 9A, 9B

Analyzing and Comparing (II) Ask students to think of a present-day politician or other leader whom they admire. Ask them to write an essay comparing the leadership qualities of this person with those of Stephen F. Austin. Invite volunteers to read their essays aloud. **A, G**

Guided Practice (I) Provide students with blank outline maps of Texas. Then direct them to the map on this page. Ask students to locate and draw on the outline maps the boundaries of Austin's colony. Then, using a current political map of Texas, ask them to label the cities, towns, and other landmarks found within those borders today. **V, TK, LEP**

EXTENSION

Research (II) Ask interested students to prepare an oral book report on Stephen F. Austin and his role in Texas history. **A**

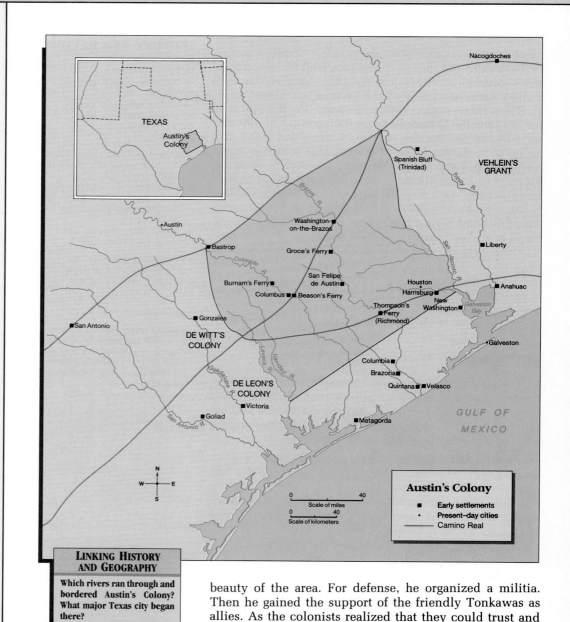

Linking History and Geography
San Jacinto, Brazos, Colorado, Navidad, Lavaca; Houston

LINKING HISTORY AND GEOGRAPHY

Which rivers ran through and bordered Austin's Colony? What major Texas city began there?

beauty of the area. For defense, he organized a militia. Then he gained the support of the friendly Tonkawas as allies. As the colonists realized that they could trust and depend on Stephen F. Austin, the colony grew. Again, Austin was successful in overcoming what others saw as impossible problems. John Holland Jenkins wrote of life near present-day Bastrop in 1830:

> Here we began life in Texas, squatting out on the raw prairie. . . . It is surprising how much can be done when bone and muscle are used with a will. The change we made upon the solitary wilderness would have seemed almost like magic to one who looked upon the scene as we came upon it, and then looked a few days later upon the huts which stood ready for us to enter.

During the late 1820s, Austin received other grants along the Gulf coast and to the north of his original colony. In fewer than ten years, Austin had helped more than 1,500 families settle in Texas. For his role in opening Texas to settlement from the United States, Stephen F. Austin is often called the "Father of Texas."

Empresario and Friend. Historians have recognized Austin as the most important colonizer in all of North America from 1821 until his death in 1836. This was not because he was the first or most powerful colonizer in Texas. It was, instead, because he saw his task as providing a future for families. Austin was more than an empresario: he was a friend and adviser to his colonists.

Known as Don Estévan Austin to his Mexican friends, Stephen was not typical of the frontier hero often seen in the American West. He was a slender, rather small man. He was quiet and soft-spoken. Austin believed in discussing rather than arguing or fighting. He was equally at ease with high government officials in Mexico and farmers on the Brazos River.

Probably the thing that contributed most to Austin's success was his ability to deal well with people of different cultures. Trusted and respected by the Mexicans and Americans alike, he eventually became the victim of his own patience and understanding. As differences between the settlers from the United States and the Mexican government grew during the 1830s, Austin was caught in the middle. This problem troubled him for the last years of his life. There was nothing he could do to prevent the coming conflict. He feared that the Texas that he and his father had worked for would be destroyed if a war came. After he spoke out about these concerns, some called Austin weak and a coward. Others said he was a traitor. Stephen F. Austin ignored these people, believing that Texas should be born in peace, not war. ✪

Archives Division, Texas State Library

Stephen F. Austin had many talents. His fairness and generosity helped the settlement of Texas.

SECTION ★ 5 REVIEW

Define: frontier
Identify: Austin's Little Colony, Old San Antonio Road, Bastrop

1. What formed the southern boundary of Austin's Little Colony?
2. What was the capital of the Little Colony, and where was it located?
3. What personal traits of Austin made him important to Texas history?

Evaluating Information: Why do you think Stephen F. Austin was a successful empresario?

Using Historical Imagination: Imagine you are an empresario about to address a Mississippi town meeting to try to convince people to come to your colony in Texas. What arguments would you use in your speech?

CHAPTER REVIEW RESOURCES

1. Chapter Review Worksheet 9
2. Chapter 9 Test, Form A
3. Reteaching Worksheet 9
4. Chapter 9 Test, Form B
5. **Informal Evaluation Forms:** Portfolio Assessment
6. *Texas, Our Texas* **Test Generator**

Essential Elements
1C, 2A, 5B, 9A, 9B, 9D

CHAPTER 9 REVIEW ANSWERS

Understanding Main Ideas

1. That he be allowed to bring settlers from the United States to Texas
2. Land was priced at 12.5 cents an acre; each husband and wife were eligible for 320 acres; additional land could be added to the grant for each child and each slave accompanying the settlers
3. Droughts, crop failures, supplies not reaching them, conflicts with Indians and outlaws, arguments over property boundaries, Stephen F. Austin's absence
4. A law passed by the Mexican legislature allowing Mexican states to pass their own immigration policies
5. He was intelligent, tactful, patient, and skilled at dealing with persons from other cultures.
6. Martín de León—along the Guadalupe River near the Gulf coast; Lorenzo de Zavala—in southeast Texas

Thinking Critically

1. **Evaluating Information:** Answers will vary, but an opponent might have argued that the law could result in the eventual loss of Mexican

---

CHAPTER 9 REVIEW

Understanding Main Ideas

1. What did Moses Austin propose to Spanish officials in San Antonio?
2. What was offered to settlers who agreed to come to Austin's colony?
3. What early troubles did the Old Three Hundred face?
4. What was the National Colonization Law of 1824?
5. What special personal traits of Stephen F. Austin contributed to his success as an empresario?
6. Who were the Tejano empresarios, and where did they establish their colonies?

Thinking Critically

1. **Evaluating Information:** When the National Colonization Law of 1824 was being debated in the Mexican legislature, what arguments might an opponent have used against it?
2. **Synthesizing Information:** In what ways do you think Stephen F. Austin was different from most of the American settlers who came to his colony?
3. **Classifying Information:** Place the following under the names of the empresarios with whom they were connected: Nashville Company, Gonzales, San Felipe, Noah Smithwick.

Linking History and Geography

1. Look at the map on page 186. Considering problems experienced by DeWitt's colony and Austin's Little Colony, why do you think the Cameron land grant and the Woodbury and Company land grant remained unsettled in 1836?
2. Which colony on this map included some of the earliest disputed American settlements in Texas?

TAAS Practice
Using Primary Sources

Although he ended up at San Felipe in Austin's colony, pioneer Noah Smithwick was originally recruited by empresario Sterling C. Robertson. In the passage below, Smithwick describes how Robertson tempted settlers to Texas:

What the discovery of gold was to California the colonization act of 1825 was to Texas. In the following year Sterling C. Robertson, who had obtained a grant for a colony . . . went up into Kentucky recruiting. The glowing terms in which he [described] the advantages to be gained by emigration, were well calculated to further his scheme. To every head of a family . . . was promised 177 acres of farming land . . . and 4,428 acres of pasture land for stock. . . . The climate was so mild that houses were not essential; neither was a superabundance of clothing or bedding. . . . Corn in any quality was to be had for the planting. . . . Of the hardships and [lack of necessities], the every increasing danger from the growing dissatisfaction of the Indians, upon whose hunting grounds the whites were steadily encroaching, and the almost certainty of an ultimate war with Mexico, he was discreetly silent. . . .

I was but a boy in my nineteenth year, and in for adventure. . . . I started out . . . with all my worldly possessions, consisting of a few dollars in money, a change of clothes, and a gun, of course, to seek my fortune in this lazy man's paradise.

territories to the United States.
2. **Synthesizing Information:** Austin seemed less interested in personal gain and more interested in promoting the general success of the Texas colony.

3. **Classifying Information:** Sterling Robertson—Nashville Company; Green DeWitt—Gonzales; Stephen F. Austin—Noah Smithwick, San Felipe

Linking History and Geography

1. This land was Comanche territory and far from the nearest Anglo settlement. The Comanches made it impossible for the empresarios to bring in settlers.
2. Wavell's colony in far northeast Texas

TAAS **Practice**
Using Primary Sources
1. B
2. D

TAAS **Practice**
Writing Persuasively
Letters will vary but should indicate that a farmer's chance of acceptance by Austin would increase if the farmer emphasized that he and his family were sober, industrious, and hard-working people, or "solid citizens," and that they were willing to formally accept the Roman Catholic faith and to obey Mexican laws.

Practicing Skills
1. **Sequencing Events:** Moses Austin, Stephen F. Austin, Green DeWitt
2. **Interpreting Maps:** Upper southerners

Enriching Your Study of History
1. **Individual Project:** Reports will vary but should demonstrate detailed knowledge of the Texas pioneer or early settlement chosen.
2. **Cooperative Project:** Team reports should demonstrate thorough research of the assigned colony and should be well organized and well presented.

---

1. Major arguments used by Robertson to convince Kentuckians to move to Texas were
   A the presence in Texas of schools, churches, and towns
   B the availability of free land, an abundance of wild game and plant foods, and a mild climate
   C the presence in Texas of friendly Indians and the right to import slaves
   D the support of Roman Catholic priests and Mexican soldiers
2. Smithwick's attitude toward Robertson's arguments is best described as
   A acceptance of Robertson's claims about Texas
   B bitter rejection of all Robertson's claims
   C agreement that Texas really was a "lazy man's paradise"
   D amusement that Robertson exaggerated the good and left out the bad about Texas

TAAS **Practice**
Writing Persuasively
Imagine that you are a farmer from Alabama, hoping to be accepted as a member of Austin's colony. Write a letter to Stephen F. Austin, telling him why your family meets all his requirements for settlement in Texas.

Practicing Skills
1. **Sequencing Events:** Place the following empresarios in chronological order, beginning with the earliest and ending with the most recent: Green DeWitt, Stephen F. Austin, Moses Austin.

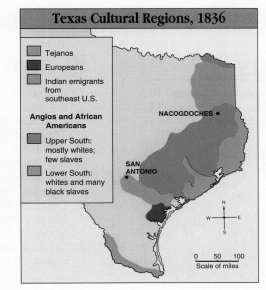

Texas Cultural Regions, 1836

Tejanos
Europeans
Indian emigrants from southeast U.S.

Anglos and African Americans

Upper South: mostly whites; few slaves
Lower South: whites and many black slaves

NACOGDOCHES
SAN ANTONIO

0   50   100
Scale of miles

2. **Interpreting Maps:** Study the map on this page. In 1836, what group or groups occupied the largest part of colonial Texas?

Enriching Your Study of History
1. **Individual Project:** Using the *Handbook of Texas* as a resource, present an oral report to the class about a Texas pioneer or an early Texas settlement mentioned in the chapter.
2. **Cooperative Project:** Your teacher will place your class into three teams. Each team will do library research to gather additional information about one of three major Texas colonies: Austin's colony, DeWitt's colony, and Martín de León's colony. Then all three teams will report their research findings to the entire class.

CHAPTER 10

COLONIAL TEXAS

TEACHER'S TIME LINE

Section 1	Section 2	Section 3	Section 4	Section 5	Section 6	Review and
Pp. 194–96	Pp. 196–98	Pp. 198–203	Pp. 203–05	Pp. 205–08	Pp. 208–10	Assessment
1 Day	1 Day	1 Day	1 Day	1 Day	1 Day	1 Day

⭐ TEACHER MATERIALS

Core: Chapter 10 Time Line; Graphic Organizer 10; Enrichment Worksheet 10; Review Worksheet 10; Reteaching Worksheet 10; Chapter 10 Tests, Forms A & B

Additional: Geography and Graph Skills 10, Informal Evaluation Forms, Test Generator

⭐ OBJECTIVES

1. Discuss the reasons for immigration to Texas during the 1820s.
2. Describe the types of food, shelter, and clothing of Texas colonists.
3. Name early forms of economic activity in Texas.
4. List the leisure activities of Texas colonists.
5. Cite different opportunities for education available in colonial Texas.
6. Describe the religious practices of Texas colonists.
7. Identify the modes of transportation for people and goods of colonial Texas.
8. Discuss the contributions of significant individuals in colonial Texas.

⭐ RESOURCES

BOOKS FOR TEACHERS

Almaráz, Félix D. Jr. *Empty Echoes in a Howling Wind.* Discussion of the Tejano community. El Paso: University of Texas at El Paso, 1986.

—*Crossroad of Empire: The Church and State on the Rio Grande Frontier of Coahuila and Texas.* San Antonio: Center for Archaeological Research, University of Texas at San Antonio, 1979. History of early Texas.

—*Tragic Cavalier: Governor Manuel Salcedo of Texas, 1808–1813.* Austin: University of Texas Press, 1971. Life of this Texas governor.

Baker, Nina Brown. *Texas Yankee: The Story of Gail Borden.* New York: Harcourt, Brace, 1955. Biography of Gail Borden.

Barker, De Witt Clinton. *A Texas Scrapbook Made Up of the History, Biography, and Miscellany of Texas and Its People.* New York: A.S. Barnes and Co., 1875. Primary sources of early Texas.

Hart, Mary Bell, editor. *Biography of José Antonio Navarro.* Austin: Hart Graphics and Office Centers, 1976. Life and times of Navarro.

Rabb, Mary Crownover. *Travels and Adventures in the 1820's:* *Being the Reminiscences of Mary Crownover Rabb, with an Introduction by Ramsey Yelvington.* Waco: W.M. Morrison, 1962. Memoirs of Mary Rabb.

Poyo, Gerald E., and Gilberto M. Hinojosa, editors. *Tejano Origins in Eighteenth-Century San Antonio.* Austin: University of Texas Press, 1991. Growth and development in San Antonio.

Weber, David J. *Troubles in Texas: A Tejano Viewpoint from San Antonio.* Dallas: Wind River Press, 1983. Personal view of Texas before 1833.

MULTIMEDIA MATERIALS

The Journals of Lewis and Clark. (video, 27 min.) Encyclopaedia Britannica Educational Corporation, 310 South Michigan Avenue, Chicago, Illinois, 60604. Lewis and Clark expedition and the wonders of the frontier.

The Romantic Horizon. (video, 52 min.) Southwest Media Services, Inc., P.O. Box 140, Wimberley, Texas, 78676. Tracks the Lewis and Clark expedition and presents a vivid image of the frontier.

Westward Movement. (video, 53 min.) Zenger Video, 10200 Jefferson Boulevard, Room VC 811, P.O. Box 802, Culver City, California, 90232. Pioneers in the Southwest in the eighteenth century.

◼ GENERAL STRATEGIES

STUDENTS WITH SPECIAL NEEDS

Limited English Proficient Students (LEP)

Use the chapter vocabulary terms, along with other unfamiliar terms from Chapter 10, as a review. Provide students with a list of terms, and ask them to classify each term as a form of food, shelter, or clothing, or as a term related to economic activity. Discuss the definitions aloud, and then ask students to write sentences using each term in context. See other activities labeled **LEP.**

Students Having Difficulty with the Chapter

Have students complete an outline of the chapter using the framework below. **LEP**
I. Reasons for coming to Texas
II. Traveling to Texas
III. Shelter
IV. Food
V. Clothing
VI. Education
VII. Religion
VIII. Leisure Activities
IX. Trade
X. Transportation
XI. Ethnic backgrounds of colonists

Auditory Learners

Provide auditory learners with a list of prominent Texas citizens discussed in the chapter. Have

students select one person to research and then present a brief oral report. See other activities labeled **A.**

Visual Learners

Ask students to review the information in Chapter 10 about trade and transportation in colonial Texas. Have them prepare a newspaper advertisement for a colonial product, a colonial business, or a colonial transportation service. Display the posters in the classroom. See other activities labeled **V.**

Tactile/Kinesthetic Learners

Instruct students to review the information in Chapter 10 about shelter and clothing in colonial Texas. Refer students to additional sources of information. Ask them to create a model or an illustration of a colonial Texas home or of colonial clothing. See other activities labeled **TK.**

Gifted Students

Have students prepare a travelogue or diary of a family or individual moving to Texas. The travelogue should include a map of the route to the final destination, a list of supplies needed for the journey, chosen methods of transportation, and a daily calendar of events in two- or three-sentence descriptions. See other activities labeled **G.**

VOCABULARY

In addition to the boldfaced terms in each section, some students might benefit from discussing the meanings of these terms.

Section 1: *merchants* (p. 195); *flatboat* (p. 196).
Section 2: *horizontally* (p. 197); *lean-tos* (p. 197).
Section 3: *excess* (p. 198); *insufficient* (p. 201); *legends* (p. 202).
Section 4: *worshipped* (p. 204).
Section 5: *entrepreneur* (p. 206); *unpredictable* (p. 208).
Section 6: *heritage* (p. 208); *dominate* (p. 209).

CHRONOLOGY

Have students study the Chapter 10 Time Line and identify relationships among the events.

GRAPHIC ORGANIZER

Have students skim the chapter and complete the Chapter 10 Graphic Organizer. *(You might wish to use this activity to review rather than to introduce the chapter.)*

ENRICHMENT

Have students complete the Chapter 10 Enrichment Worksheet.

FOCUS

Student Experiences (I) Ask students if they know anyone who has moved to Texas in recent years for economic reasons. Tell students that during the 1820s and 1830s thousands of settlers came to Texas seeking new opportunities.

Cooperative Learning (I) Organize the class into three groups. Each group will plan a move to Texas in 1830. Students should select their point of origin in the United States and their final destination in Texas. They should choose one of three methods of travel: on foot, by wagon, or using water transport. Have each group map its route, estimating the total miles it will travel and the time the journey will take. Students should list rivers and other landforms they will encounter on their route. Have each group present its plan to the class. **A, V, TK, LEP**

CHAPTER 10 OVERVIEW

Texas was part of the Republic of Mexico from 1821 until 1836. During this period, Texans followed Mexican laws and traditions. Yet, most of the colonists were from the United States. Thousands of settlers poured in, farms and ranches were begun, towns and villages appeared, and trade and business grew. Chapter 10 describes life in colonial Texas. It tells where the people came from and how they lived after they arrived. It is the story of life in Texas under Mexican rule.

Essential Elements
1C, 2A, 2B, 4A, 5B, 8B, 8C, 9A, 9B, 9F

CHAPTER
10

COLONIAL TEXAS

The Story Continues...

Chapter 10 explains how "Texas fever" swept the United States. In the 1820s and 1830s, thousands of settlers from the southern states came to Texas looking for cheap land, new homes, and a better life. The daily lives of these colonists were hard, but opportunities were everywhere.

As you read the chapter, look for the answers to these questions:

1. Why were people from the southern United States eager to come to Texas?
2. What sorts of homes did the colonists build on their new land?
3. What was daily life like in colonial Texas?
4. How did colonial Texans meet their needs for education and religious worship?
5. Why was transportation a problem in colonial Texas?
6. What were the ethnic origins of early Texas settlers?

■1 Texas Fever

Texas fever swept the United States during the 1820s and 1830s. Although a few settlers moved to Texas from Mexico and Europe, the large majority of colonists came from the southern United States. Most came from Tennessee, Kentucky, Georgia, Alabama, Mississippi, Louisiana, Missouri, and Arkansas. Most were farmers and stock raisers. Some brought with them African American slaves.

Gone to Texas. Land was opportunity. While land sold for 12.5¢ per acre, most people from the United States could afford to buy. With land came hope of a new life. The first settlers to buy land from empresarios like Stephen F. Austin and Martín de León were interested mainly in starting a family farm or ranch. As empresarios encouraged wider settlement, however, people began to arrive in Texas

Institute of Texan Cultures

Flatboating down the Mississippi to New Orleans was a first step in the journey for many settlers on their way to Texas.

Art in History (I) Point out to students that we learn much about the people of a historical period by studying the art from the period. Ask students to study the painting on page 196 and list generalizations about the way of life of Texas colonists. Discuss their generalizations as a class. **A, V**

Guided Practice (I) Invite students to imagine that they are hopeful colonists who have just arrived at Galveston Bay from New Orleans during the 1820s. Ask them to write a paragraph describing their initial reaction at seeing Texas. Then have them list five things they must do upon arrival. Ask students to compare their lists. **A, LEP**

EXTENSION

Research (I) Have students work individually or with a partner to research and report on occupations in colonial Texas. If possible, reports should include demonstrations. **A, V, TK**

Independent Practice (I) Ask students to use their historical imagination to write a detailed account of one day's events during a journey from the United States to Texas. Students should indicate whether they are traveling over land or by water and the hardships they encounter. Invite volunteers to read their accounts aloud. **A, LEP**

The Granger Collection

Many settlers came to Texas during the 1820s and 1830s in covered wagons. From what area of the United States did most Texas settlers come?

Caption Response
Most settlers came from the southern United States.

for different reasons. Some of them were carpenters or blacksmiths who could start a business. Others were merchants who hoped to buy and sell goods and to open stores in the new villages of the colony.

In the late 1820s and early 1830s, some people came to Texas because they had trouble with debts or with the laws of the United States. Stephen F. Austin had hoped to keep people with such problems out of Texas, but the growth of the colony made it difficult to do this. Word spread in the United States that Texas was filling with undesirable people. Whenever people left town owing money or under suspicion of breaking the law, it was said, "Oh, they've probably gone to Texas." Eventually it became common in the South to refer to any missing person as "Gone to Texas." Many overdue accounts were closed and marked "G.T.T." (Gone to Texas).

Getting to Texas. For most people, Texas remained a land of great appeal. Men and women scraped together whatever savings they had and headed west. Some rode in wagons pulled by oxen or mules. A few rode on horses, with their only belongings tied across the horses' backs.

RETEACHING

Ask students to list three reasons that colonists came to Texas and three methods of getting there. **LEP**

CLOSURE

Review with students the idea of Texas as a land of opportunity during the 1820s and 1830s.

ASSESSMENT

Have students complete the Section 1 Review on page 196.

SECTION 2

FOCUS

Past Learning and Predicting (I) Review with students the distinction between *needs* and *wants*. As you list their responses on the chalkboard, ask students to name the colonists' immediate needs upon their arrival in Texas. Ask students to keep this list in mind as they study the remainder of Chapter 10.

Answers to Section 1 Review

Identify: "G.T.T."—"Gone to Texas," a common reference in the South to any missing person

1. Cheap land and the hope for a better life and a new start
2. Many early settlers were chosen by empresarios such as Austin. While many of the later settlers were solid citizens, some came to Texas because of debts or legal trouble in the United States.
3. Some took flatboats down to New Orleans and then sailed to Galveston. Others came by wagon, on horseback, and on foot.

Synthesizing Information: Some people came to Texas to escape bad debts or the laws of the United States. It became known that Texas was filling with undesirables.

Analyzing Information: Possible answers include: finding their way over land that had few and poor roads, enduring weeks of hard travel, and crossing the many large rivers on their route.

Essential Elements
1C, 2A, 5C, 8C, 9A, 9B, 9G

The population of Texas grew rapidly during the colonial era. Most colonists were farmers. This painting of an early Texas farm is by Carl G. von Iwonski.

SECTION 1 REVIEW

Identify: "G.T.T."

1. What attracted early settlers to colonial Texas?
2. Why were later settlers somewhat different from earlier ones? How did they differ?
3. What were the means of transportation that settlers used to get to Texas?

Synthesizing Information: How does this section help explain the old southern saying from the 1830s "There's no law in Texas"?

Analyzing Information: Judging from this section, what do you think were the greatest problems faced by settlers coming to Texas by overland routes?

Daughters of the Republic of Texas Library

Some even walked. Many rode a flatboat down the Mississippi to New Orleans, then took a ship to Galveston.

For those people who had to walk or ride in a wagon, the journey was long and hard. They usually covered only ten or fifteen miles a day, stopping to camp just before dark. They lived off the land, always hoping to shoot a deer or wild turkey for their evening meal. Some immigrants brought cattle, pigs, oxen, or goats to stock their land in Texas. But more often than not, these animals ended up as food during the trip.

For those who could afford it, the fastest and most comfortable way to reach Texas was by water. Thousands of people made their way to New Orleans. From there, sailing ships left regularly for Galveston. It was not unusual to see several flatboats hitched to the back of a ship pulling out of the harbor at New Orleans. The ships were packed with hopeful colonists. Once they landed at Galveston Bay, the colonists moved in all directions to claim their land. All had a spirit of adventure. Tired travelers became hopeful and excited once they saw their own piece of land. ✪

2 Home Away from Home

Finding land was the first order of business for the colonists arriving in Texas. A few settlers were assigned land by an empresario, but most were able to choose their own.

INSTRUCTION

Cooperative Learning (I) Organize students into their original groups from Section 1 in which they mapped their journey to Texas from the United States. Tell students that they have finally arrived in Texas and must choose an area in which to settle. Tell them to keep in mind the part of the United States from which they came. Have a spokesperson from each group announce the group's decision and explain its reasoning. **A**

Compare and Contrast (I) Have students write a brief essay comparing and contrasting the features of a typical 1820s colonial Texas home with those of a home that might be constructed today. Suggest that students supplement their essays with drawings or diagrams. **V, LEP, TK**

Guided Practice (I) Ask students to list characteristics of colonial Texas homes. Ask: On what in their natural environment did the colonists depend most in meeting their need for shelter *(the local woods)*? **LEP**

Choosing Land. Settlers usually wanted to live in an area that looked like their old home. Many settlers passed up good, fertile land because it did not look familiar. For example, southerners from the hills of Tennessee wanted to settle in land that was hilly. They often refused to buy land on the Gulf Coast Plain because it was too flat. Some southerners from the pine forests of Alabama passed by other areas so they could settle in the East Texas pine country.

Settlement was also affected by Indians who lived in the area. It was generally accepted that it was unsafe to live north of the Camino Real. Traveling, and especially settling, in that region was dangerous. The colonists most feared the Comanches, the Apaches, and the Wichitas. South of the Camino Real, the Indians who remained were more friendly and less willing to resist settlement.

Building Houses. Once a family picked out its land, the first task was to build a house. Often, neighbors and new arrivals in an area helped each other with the construction. The typical house in colonial Texas was small and built of logs cut from the local woods. In describing the homes of the time, an observer claimed that early Texas homes were "plain, rough, strong, angular, and open."

The walls of the houses were built with rough logs laid horizontally on each other. They fit together with notches cut on the ends. The spaces between the logs were filled with a mix of clay, grass, and sticks. Settlers sometimes knocked out a space in summer to let in the breezes. Of course, bugs came in too! Long, thin wooden shingles were cut to cover gaps in the walls and to go on the roofs. The floors were usually either dirt or clay. Sometimes a wooden floor was made by splitting logs and placing their flat side up. Caroline von Hinueber, who was eleven when her family came to Texas from Germany, wrote this about her first house, which was different from American-built cabins:

> It was roofed with straw and had six sides, which were made out of moss. The roof was by no means waterproof, and we often held an umbrella over our bed when it rained at night, while the cows came and ate the moss. Of course we suffered a great deal in the winter. My father had tried to build a chimney and fireplace out of logs and clay, but we were afraid to light a fire because of our straw roof. So we had to shiver.

Most homes were one- or two-room cabins. Lean-tos were often built against one of the walls to add space. Some

Paul M. Montgomery

Some settlers chose land in the Piney Woods of East Texas. Why did settlers from southern states often choose to settle in this area of the state?

Caption Response
It most resembled the area from where they had come.

This reconstructed interior of a settler cabin shows how a typical East Texas dwelling looked during colonial days.

Mike Hawkins, Gregg County Historical Museum, Longview

SECTION ★2★ REVIEW

1. What sort of home was built by most early newcomers to Texas?
2. Why was it dangerous for settlers to live north of the Camino Real?
3. Describe a dog-run style house.

Making Decisions: Imagine that you are a settler coming to Texas from your family home in the hills of Tennessee. In what part of Texas will you probably choose to settle? Why?

Writing Descriptively: Write a paragraph describing the typical house of an early East Texas settler.

families built a two-room cabin with an open passage connecting the rooms. This was the dog-run style home that Stephen F. Austin lived in at San Felipe de Austin.

The colonists used building materials found close at hand. In East Texas, they usually used pine logs. In other locations, they used oak or cedar. Where they could find limestone or sandstone, they used it to build chimneys. They carved very simple chairs, tables, and beds of wood from nearby trees. In the 1830s and 1840s, settlers began to replace their log cabins with larger, fancier homes. But in the first years of settlement, the home provided little escape from the hard frontier life. ○

3 Colonial Styles of Life

Because most of the colonists were farmers and stock raisers, the life of early Texans was that of country people. There were few villages, and people within the same colony were sometimes spread over hundreds of miles. All the activities of a family were influenced by its environment.

Foods of the Colonists. The eventual goal of every farm family was to feed itself and then to sell or trade excess food for a profit. The early Texas farmers all started with corn. It was fairly easy to grow and harvest, and it could be used to make many kinds of dishes.

The settlers had learned from Indians many different ways to prepare corn. They roasted it or boiled it on the

SECTION 3

FOCUS

Student Experiences (I) Write the term *self-sufficient* on the chalkboard, and ask students to provide a definition. Tell them that the colonists' way of life depended on their ability to be self-sufficient.

INSTRUCTION

Vocabulary (I) You may wish to preteach the following boldfaced terms: *venison* (p. 199); *buckskin* (p. 200); *ethnic group* (p. 203). **LEP**

cob. They often grated the corn and made it into a sweet bread. They made cornmeal by drying the kernels and then grinding them with a stone or a metal grinder. The meal was mixed with milk, molasses, or butter, then baked into corn bread. If the cornmeal batter was cooked over a bed of hot coals, it was called johnnycake. If it was baked in an oven, it was called corn pone. The colonial Texans used corn as their main grain and bread source because there was plenty of it, it was cheap, and it was nutritious. They obviously liked its taste as well. But one visitor from England had a different view. He remarked that Texas corn bread was a "modification of sawdust."

There were not many other vegetables in the typical settler's diet. Some people had small gardens of sweet potatoes, cabbages, turnips, and peas. In many places, berries, grapes, and peaches grew wild. Pecan trees were abundant along the river banks. There were a few banana trees grown on Galveston Island, but vegetables and fruits were a luxury that few colonists enjoyed.

At a typical meal in the 1820s, a Texas family had fried or roasted meat, corn bread, and black coffee. Most often, they ate beef, pork, and **venison**, or deer meat, because wild cattle, hogs, and deer were present in large numbers. Occasionally a wild turkey, duck, prairie hen, or bear added variety to the standard diet. In Central Texas, buffalo were hunted. There were times when the colonists had to eat wild mustangs and other less desirable foods. Some settlers were reported eating wildcats, pigeons, and skunks.

Texas Department of Transportation

This photograph shows examples of early Texas kitchen utensils.

Texas Department of Transportation

Meals in early colonial days were usually simple and lacked variety.

As the settlers began to raise domestic hogs, cattle, and goats during the 1830s, they hunted less wild game for food.

The colonists began eating a greater variety of food as people of different backgrounds came to Texas. Anglo, Mexican, German, Swedish, French, and African American settlers all brought their own kinds of foods to the frontier.

Clothing of the Colonists. As with their food, clothing for the settlers came from local resources. Many people wore leather clothes made from deer, cattle, or buffalo in the region. Smooth, tanned deerhide, called **buckskin**, was worn by men, women, and children. It was often decorated with beads or fringe. Shoes and hats were also made of buckskin. It was strong, but it was not comfortable.

Colonists gladly switched to more comfortable clothing when it became available. Cotton replaced buckskin in the late 1820s and early 1830s. Most of the cotton was grown in Texas. It was spun by women, who dyed it with bark

Daughters of the Republic of Texas, the Alamo

Most Texans in the colonial era had few luxuries. This painting by W. G. M. Samuel shows a Texas frontiersman in buckskin clothing.

or berry juice. They then wove it into cloth. Women and girls wore full-length cotton dresses with bonnets to match. Men wore cotton shirts in the fields. For more formal occasions they wore dark brown cotton suits. To fight the cold, men and women often wore cotton blankets draped over their shoulders, with a slit in the middle for their heads to go through. Borrowed from the Mexican style, these blanket coats were called ponchos.

When Texas towns began to grow, merchants started stocking ready-to-wear clothes imported from the United States. By the 1830s, a family could go to a "dry goods" store and buy work clothes or better wear for Sundays and holidays. Stores in San Antonio, Galveston, and Nacogdoches had calico dresses, silk gowns, men's suits, vests, overcoats, and a wide variety of leather shoes and boots.

The problem facing most Texas shoppers of the day was that store-bought goods were usually too expensive because merchants had to pay shipping costs. Caroline von Hinueber wrote:

> Our shoes gave out, and we had to go barefoot in winter, for we did not know how to make moccasins. Our supply of clothes was also insufficient, and we had no spinning wheel, nor did we know how to spin and weave like the Americans. It was 20 miles to San Felipe de Austin, and besides, we had no money. When we could buy things, my first calico dress cost 50 cents per yard.

One article that every well-dressed Texan needed was a hat. Hats were in fashion on the farm as well as in town. Women made their own cotton bonnets or sun hats. But a store-bought hat from New York or New Orleans was something very special. The men wore buckskin hats or coonskin caps to keep the sun off, but they also followed the fashions of the day for dressier occasions. They wore beaver hats, Mexican sombreros, or tall "stovepipe" hats. Expensive clothing and hats were not seen often in the rural areas of Texas. But on holidays and at other special times, it seemed that everyone had at least one fashionable outfit.

Leisure Activities. There was little free time during the early years of Texas settlement. Men, women, and children had a full day of work and chores to keep them busy. But in the evenings, on Sunday afternoons, and on holidays, the Texans enjoyed themselves.

One of the most common leisure activities combined group work and visiting. This was the house-raising or

Paul M. Montgomery

Pecan trees provided early Texans with the popular pecan nut. The pecan was chosen as the state tree of Texas in 1919.

Independent Practice (II) Ask students to imagine that they are living in colonial Texas. Tell them to write a letter to a friend back home expressing what they like and dislike about colonial ways of life in Texas. Encourage them to be specific. Invite volunteers to read their letters aloud. **A**

RETEACHING

Provide students with a list of words or phrases from Section 3 that can be categorized as related to colonial Texas foods, clothing, or leisure activities. Ask students to write next to each item an *F* for foods, a *C* for clothing, or an *L* for leisure. Explain that some items might be placed into more than one category. **LEP**

CLOSURE

With the class, list on the chalkboard examples of the foods the colonists ate, the kinds of clothing they wore, and their leisure activities.

ASSESSMENT

Have students complete the Section 3 Review on page 203.

This quilt was made in Texas more than 100 years ago. Colorful quilts added a touch of comfort and beauty to the rustic existence of settlers.

Courtesy of the San Antonio Museum Association

Institute of Texan Cultures

Texas settlers were quick to lend a hand to neighbors needing help constructing homes, barns, and other structures.

barn-raising for a new settler. People gathered from miles around to help build a new log cabin or barn. While the men sawed and hammered, the women barbecued meat and prepared corn bread. The women also made quilts for the new neighbor and helped decorate the inside of the new home. The children played games of tag or learned to dance. Sometimes the house-raising lasted all day and into the night. After the work was finished, the men sometimes competed in log-rolling, rail-splitting, or shooting contests.

Much of the settlers' free time was in the evening hours. Some read books. Settlers from the United States usually read the Bible. Parents often took this time to teach their children to read and do basic arithmetic. There was a great deal of storytelling as well. Stories and legends were passed from one generation to the next as the entire family sat around the fireplace.

One of the favorite Texas pastimes was dancing. In the settlements, there were balls to celebrate every occasion. Music was provided by a fiddle band that usually played southern folk songs. People of all ages attended the dances. Mothers even brought their babies to the dances, wrapped them in blankets, left them beneath the benches in the dance hall, and then joined in the dancing. The rural areas

FOCUS

Predicting (I) Present the following scenario to students: You live in Texas but must follow the customs and traditions of Mexico even though these differ greatly from your own. Ask: How do you feel about this? Will you work to change it? Tell students to keep these thoughts in mind as they study Section 4.

INSTRUCTION

Art and History (II) Display several newspaper pages that feature editorial cartoons. Explain that the purpose of an editorial cartoon is to use a drawing to promote a point of view on an issue. Organize students into small groups, and ask each group to develop an editorial cartoon with a caption promoting one of the following points of view:

(1) that colonial Texas needs a public school system
(2) that freedom of religion is necessary in colonial Texas

Have each group display and discuss its cartoon. **A, V, TK, G**

probably had fewer dances because of the great distances that people had to travel. Their barn dances were less formal, but their enthusiasm was just as great.

Frontier music and dances were influenced by each **ethnic group**, or people of the same cultural background. The music of southern blacks influenced the style, sound, and choice of instruments in Texas. However, Anglos learned Mexican dances and musical styles. And German polkas and accordion sounds affected the dancing steps. Everyone learned something new and different from all the groups that now lived side by side.

Of all the leisure activities of the period, horse-racing was probably the favorite. In the early 1830s, many towns had a racetrack. Entire families went to the races together, picnicked, and then attended the party or dance that was held afterward. ✪

4 Education and Religion

Because the Texas colonists lived under Mexican law, their schools and churches were affected by Mexican tradition and custom. Still, the majority of colonists in Texas were from the United States, and their traditions and customs were different.

Education in Colonial Texas. There were very few schools in Texas in the 1820s and 1830s. The Mexican government claimed that it wanted to provide public schools, but it never went forward with plans in Texas. Lack of money was always a problem. The government tried only once to start a public school system. In 1829, the Coahuila y Texas state legislature passed a law that called for the establishment of primary schools. The schools were never opened. Mexican officials said they could not find capable teachers.

The colonists did open private schools all over Texas. Wealthy citizens often hired a teacher to give classes in their homes. Others sent their children to school in the United States. But most private schools were built in the community, and everyone shared the costs. As early as 1823, a school was opened in Austin's colony. Two years later, Nacogdoches had a school. There were several teachers in San Antonio who gave classes. Juan Zambrano had established a school there in 1811 and opened another in

SECTION ★3★ REVIEW

Define: venison, buckskin, ethnic group

1. What was the most common food crop grown in colonial Texas?
2. Describe a typical meal of a Texas family in the 1820s.
3. What material replaced buckskin for making clothing?

Evaluating Information: Imagine that you are a member of a family of early Texas settlers. Write a letter to a friend back east, describing your leisure activities and telling which you enjoy most.

Exploring Multicultural Perspectives: Imagine that you are an enslaved person brought to the Texas colonies from a plantation in Mississippi. What advantages and disadvantages do you see to this move to a new land?

Richard Pearce-Moses

Dancing was a favorite pastime among Texas settlers. Spanish fandangos became popular, and other such dances came out of the blending of cultures in colonial Texas.

Answers to Section 3 Review

Define: *venison*—deer meat; *buckskin*—tanned deerhide; *ethnic group*—people of the same cultural background
1. Corn
2. Fried or roasted meat, corn bread, and black coffee
3. Cotton

Evaluating Information: Letters will vary but might include activities such as reading, playing music, dancing, horse-racing, house-raising, and visiting friends.

Exploring Multicultural Perspectives: Answers will vary. While the slaveholder might go to Texas for a new start, there would not be a new start for the slave.

Essential Elements
2A, 2B, 4D, 6A, 6B, 7E, 9A, 9B

Using Historical Imagination (I) Ask students to write a poem about what life might have been like for an African American slave in colonial Texas. Invite volunteers to read their poems aloud. **A**

Guided Practice (I) The textbook explains that colonial families treated education and religious activity as a private matter that was left up to the wishes of each family. Ask students to write a brief paragraph answering the following question: If you were a parent in colonial Texas, what would be your wish for your children concerning education and religious activity? **LEP**

EXTENSION

Community Involvement (II) Ask interested students to research the development of the public school system in their community. Suggest that they find the information by writing to the local board of education. **G**

Independent Practice (I) Have students write a paragraph on one of the following topics: **LEP**
"Educational Opportunities in Colonial Texas Prior to 1834"
"Religious Opportunities in Colonial Texas"

La Bahía in 1818. Still another school was started in San Antonio in 1826. By the late 1820s, nearly every village had at least one teacher who offered basic reading, writing, and arithmetic classes. But such classes were not offered to African American slaves.

Formal schooling was usually considered important only for boys. There was, however, some interest in providing an education for girls. The first girls' school was opened in 1834 by Frances Trask Thompson at Independence.

Without government support, there were never enough schools to teach all the children. Only a small number of school-age children ever attended formal classes. Most children who could read and write learned from their parents. The demands of farm life kept many children in the fields rather than at a school desk.

The Mexican government sent an inspector to Texas in 1834. He reported that the Texans had no interest in education. He remarked, "The wealthier colonists prefer sending their children to the United States, and those who have not had the advantage of fortune care little for the education of their sons, provided they can wield an axe and cut down a tree, or kill a deer." Yet the early Texans did believe in education. When government support became available and when the demands of frontier life eased, schools appeared all over Texas.

Religion in Colonial Texas. The Roman Catholic church was the official church of the Republic of Mexico. The colonists in Texas were all expected to honor its traditions and support it. Stephen F. Austin had promised the Mexicans that his settlers would obey their rules, but he knew it would be difficult. Most Texas colonists were Protestants who were unwilling to change their beliefs. Still, the arrangement worked fairly well through the 1820s. Publicly, the Texans who were not Catholics stated support for the Roman Catholic church. But in private, they worshipped as they pleased, and the Mexican government left them alone.

Since only Roman Catholic churches were legal, there were no organized Protestant churches in Texas until 1836, when the Texans achieved their independence. There was, however, a good bit of religious activity. Camp meetings with traveling preachers from the United States were held from time to time. Protestant missionaries came to Texas regularly and passed out Bibles. The most famous was a

Archives Division, Texas State Library

Thomas J. Pilgrim moved to Texas in 1828. The following year, he started a Sunday school at San Felipe de Austin. The school was open to everyone.

RETEACHING
Ask students to write a two- or three-sentence summary of each of the Section 4 subsections. **LEP**

CLOSURE
Write the following headings on the chalkboard: *Education in Colonial Texas, Religion in Colonial Texas.* Ask students to provide facts that they have learned about each.

ASSESSMENT
Have students complete the Section 4 Review on page 205.

SECTION 5

FOCUS

Past Learning (I) Review with students the Five Themes of Geography that they learned about in Unit 1. Ask: Which geographic theme best represents colonial trade *(movement)*? Stress that the lack of an adequate transportation system was a major obstacle for colonial business and trade.

Presbyterian named Sumner Bacon. He traveled the Camino Real, giving sermons and handing out Bibles from Gonzales to Nacogdoches. Another Presbyterian, Melinda Rankin, was one of the few women who preached on the traveling circuit. One preacher, Joseph Bays, was arrested for preaching at San Felipe de Austin. But usually, the Mexican officials just turned their heads at such religious activity.

Even though no official Protestant churches were to be found, Sunday school teachers conducted classes. In 1829, Thomas J. Pilgrim, a Baptist from New York, operated a Sunday school in San Felipe de Austin. In the same year, Mary Helm opened a Sunday school nearby. These Protestant Sunday school teachers sometimes performed weddings or spoke at funerals, since the only priests were in San Antonio and Nacogdoches. There was one priest named Father Michael Muldoon. He was the only representative of the Roman Catholic church that most settlers from the United States ever saw.

Most colonists treated religious activity the way they handled education. It was a private matter that was left up to the wishes of each family. ✪

5 Trade and Transportation

As the colonists became more prosperous, they had goods to sell for profit. By the 1830s, Texas farmers and merchants had crops to **export**, or send to other areas for sale. These included cotton, corn, sugarcane, cattle, cowhides, and animal skins. But a major problem for business and trade was the lack of a transportation system.

Business and Trade. Texas products were sold to traders from the United States by way of New Orleans or to Mexican businesspeople. The increase in trade and business helped towns grow. Ports developed along the coast, and the population increased.

Despite the early signs of business growth in Texas, there was little **industry**, or activity making products or preparing them for sale. There were a few **cotton gins**, places where cotton fiber was separated from the seeds. There were also a few sawmills, but, like the cotton gins, most were small operations. Jared Groce, the wealthy landowner who lived near present-day Hempstead, had the largest cotton gin and cotton plantation.

SECTION ★ 4 REVIEW

Identify: Juan Zambrano, Frances Trask Thompson, Sumner Bacon, Melinda Rankin, Thomas J. Pilgrim

1. What was the official church of Mexico?
2. How did most children learn to read and write in colonial Texas?
3. What was the religious background of most colonists in Texas?

Exploring Multicultural Perspectives: How might a Mexican official's attitude toward his country's religious laws be different from that of an Anglo or African American colonist?

Analyzing Information: In what ways did pioneer religious life show adjustments to Mexican religious laws?

Answers to Section 4 Review
Identify: Juan Zambrano—founded the first school in San Antonio in 1811; **Frances Trask Thompson**—opened the first school for girls at Independence in 1834; **Sumner Bacon**—traveling preacher who handed out Bibles on the Camino Real; **Melinda Rankin**—Presbyterian preacher who preached on the traveling circuit; **Thomas J. Pilgrim**—Baptist from New York who ran a Sunday school in San Felipe de Austin
1. The Roman Catholic church
2. They were taught at home by their parents.
3. Most colonists were Protestants.

Exploring Multicultural Perspectives: Mexico had an official state religion, and colonists were expected to obey Mexico's religious laws. Colonists from the United States were accustomed to separation of church and state and wanted to follow their own beliefs.

Analyzing Information: The colonists would publicly support the Roman Catholic faith, but in private, worshipped as they pleased. There were camp meetings and traveling preachers but no established church organizations.

Essential Elements
2A, 3D, 3E, 5A, 5B, 5C, 8A, 9A, 9B, 9F

Vocabulary (I) You may wish to preteach the following boldfaced terms: *export* (p. 205); *industry* (p. 205); *cotton gins* (p. 205). **LEP**

SPIRIT OF TEXAS

Analysis (I) Direct students to the inscription from Gail Borden's tombstone. Ask them to find and list examples from the special feature that support this statement. **LEP**

Geography (II) Ask students to use the information in Section 4 to write a paragraph discussing how the geography of a region can influence or deter an area's economic development. Use the essays as a basis for class discussion. **A**

Cooperative Learning (I) Organize students into groups of four or five. Review with students the lack of an adequate transportation system in colonial Texas. Ask members of each group to brainstorm to devise a solution to the colonists' problem. Have each group present its plan to the class, using illustrations or other graphics if applicable. **A, V, TK**

Essential Elements
1C, 8A, 8C

SPIRIT OF TEXAS

Gail Borden: Texas Entrepreneur

I tried and failed, I tried again and again, and succeeded.
(inscription on Gail Borden's tombstone)

Throughout the world Gail Borden is best known as the inventor of canned condensed milk. During his lifetime, 1801 to 1874, he failed at many experiments. But he finally succeeded because he believed in his ideas, insisted upon quality products, and asked fair prices. The dairyman to a nation, Borden struggled financially most of his life before he found fame and fortune.

Born in upstate New York, Borden struck out for Texas at age 21. His marriage to Penelope Mercer and a career in Mississippi delayed his arrival in Galveston until Christmas Eve, 1829. In San Felipe, Borden began his contribution to the Texas Revolution by setting up a newspaper, the *Telegraph and Texas Register*. The newspaper played an important role in promoting the idea of revolution against Mexico and in unifying the Texas settlers. Mexican soldiers destroyed the office three times, but Borden did not give up. Finally his presses resumed in Houston.

By 1846, Borden had lost his wife and a son to yellow fever. He then turned to his experiments. Borden knew there was a need among sailors and westward pioneers for food that would not spoil and was neither heavy nor bulky. Through trial and error, he attempted to condense figs and turnips by removing their water. His products failed. Then, in 1849, Borden invented a meat biscuit by condensing chunks of beef, mixing them with flour, and baking the mixture. Added to boiling water, the biscuits made soup for travelers. Americans never accepted the biscuit, but Borden was given the Gold Medal Award in England.

Sailing back to America, Gail Borden witnessed the death of a baby who had drunk the spoiled milk of seasick cows. He devoted much of his time to the invention of canned condensed milk. On August 17, 1856, he was granted a patent "for condensing milk in a vacuum over low heat, with exclusive rights to manufacture and sell the same." During the Civil War, the Union army bought all the condensed milk that Borden's factory could produce, so Borden built other factories. It was not long before the general public was using Borden's new product as well.

Gail Borden and his third wife, Emeline Eunice Church, became philanthropists, people who give money for the benefit of large numbers of less wealthy people. The Bordens gave generously and organized schools for freedmen and black children. In later years, Borden lived in the Texas town named for him. He died in Borden, Texas, in 1874.

Inset: **Gail Borden**

Rosenberg Library

Guided Practice (I) Have students draw or cut and paste from magazines pictures to create posters showing the major export products of colonial Texas. Display the posters in the classroom. **V, TK, LEP**

EXTENSION
Community Involvement (II) Ask interested students to contact the local historical society or visit the public library to find out what crops or industries played a role in the growth of their community. Have them present the information in an oral report. **A, V, G**

Independent Practice (I) Display a wall map of Texas. Ask volunteers to come to the front of the class and trace the water route from New Orleans to various Texas ports and point out the place names mentioned in Section 5. **A, V, LEP**

RETEACHING
Ask each student to make a word search puzzle using terms, people, and places from Section 5. Then have students exchange and complete the puzzles with a partner. Have each pair of students work together to discuss and correct the completed puzzles. **LEP**

Painting by Harley Murray. Texas Historical Foundation

The *Yellow Stone* was a famous Texas steamer. Built in Kentucky, the *Yellow Stone* made its first trip to Texas in 1835. It carried Stephen F. Austin's body from Columbia to Peach Point for burial in December 1836. Why were Texas rivers generally unsuitable for steamboats?

Economics
The establishment of industries requires capital, available resources, means of transportation, and a market for finished products. Discuss these requirements in terms of colonial Texas.

Caption Response
They were too shallow.

Roads, Rivers, and Ports. To have a successful economy, a region must have good means of transportation. This was a major problem in colonial Texas. There were no roads between many towns, and some roads were little more than trails. In dry weather, the roads were dusty and bumpy. During the wet seasons they became nearly impassable mud swamps. Creeks and rivers also became barriers to travel when they flooded.

Most people traveled on horseback. A person who had baggage or supplies to transport used a wagon drawn by oxen or horses. The roads were so bad, however, that wagon travel was slow and sometimes impossible. Many a wagon was stuck in the mud of a Texas river bottom and

CLOSURE
Tell students that despite the transportation problems facing the colonists, business and trade increased and the population of Texas continued to grow.

ASSESSMENT
Have students complete the Section 5 Review on page 208.

SECTION 6

FOCUS

Predicting (I) Tell students that Texas' population continued to grow with people from many different ethnic backgrounds. Ask them to speculate about the changes that might have taken place in colonial Texas society because of this mixture of cultures. Remind students that Texas was still controlled by Mexico.

Answers to Section 5 Review

Define: *export*—send goods to other areas for sale; *industry*—activity of making products or preparing them for sale; *cotton gins*—places where cotton fiber was separated from the cotton seeds

Identify: Jared Groce—wealthy cotton plantation owner who lived near present-day Hempstead; Galveston Bay—harbor on the inland side of Galveston Island; Indianola—main port at Matagorda Bay; Henry Austin—owner of the *Ariel,* the first steamboat to operate in Texas

1. On horseback or by wagon
2. Cotton, corn, sugarcane, cattle, cowhides, animal skins
3. They were too shallow for much of the year and had many sandbars and logjams. They were unpredictable.

Using Historical Imagination: Answers will vary. Some students might suggest that the group wait for the river to recede or find a less swift area of the river at which to try to cross.

Exploring Economics: It limited trade and business. Shipping was expensive, and it was often too costly to ship bulk items such as agricultural produce to market.

Essential Elements
1B, 2A, 2B, 2H, 3C, 4E, 9A, 9B

SECTION  5 REVIEW

Define: export, industry, cotton gins
Identify: Jared Groce, Galveston Bay, Indianola, Henry Austin

1. How did most people travel in Texas?
2. What Texas products were exported for sale in the 1820s and 1830s?
3. Why were Texas rivers not very suitable for navigation?

Using Historical Imagination: Imagine that you are with a group of settlers coming to Texas in a wagon train from Alabama. You arrive at the east bank of the Sabine River and find it swift and nearly overflowing its banks. How will your group manage to cross to the Texas side of the river?

Exploring Economics: How did the lack of good roads affect trade and business in colonial Texas?

New York Public Library. Special Collections Office

Mary Austin Holley first visited her cousin's colony in 1831. Her letters and observations about the colony were published in a book titled *Texas.*

not recovered until months later. Horse buggies, known as "pleasure carriages," did not appear on Texas roads until the late 1830s.

The best transportation in colonial Texas was by water. Ships sailed and steamed through the Gulf of Mexico to several Texas ports. The busiest port was Galveston Bay. Settlers and merchants either stopped on Galveston Island or went into the bay at the mouth of the Trinity River near Anahuac. The main port at Matagorda Bay was the village of Indianola. Other ships landed regularly at Velasco, near the mouth of the Brazos River.

Settlers always felt that the rivers of Texas should be the solution to their transportation problems. But the history of river navigation in Texas is one of failure and frustration. Small boats and rafts could navigate the Texas rivers, but large boats constantly had trouble. The rivers were too shallow and full of snags and sandbars to be safe. During rainy seasons they overflowed and were blocked by driftwood.

The first steamboat to navigate the Texas rivers was the *Ariel.* The *Ariel* was owned by Henry Austin, a cousin of Stephen F. Austin. Austin operated his boat on the lower part of the Rio Grande and traded with Mexican merchants. Later he took the *Ariel* up the Brazos River and Buffalo Bayou, the slow-moving waterway between Galveston Bay and present-day Houston. Other steamboats tried to navigate the Texas waterways throughout the 1850s. Some of them had limited success, but most of them failed because the Texas rivers were too unpredictable. When railroads began to appear in the 1850s, the dreams of water transportation in Texas began to fade. ○

6 The People of Colonial Texas

People of many different ethnic backgrounds settled in Texas. Few places in the United States or in the rest of North America had such a mix of different people living and working together.

A Common Goal. Most of the colonists from the United States were of English, Irish, or Scottish ancestry. However, there were also Texans whose heritage was German, French, Swedish, Italian, or African. Tejanos represented a fairly large population, particularly in San Antonio and

INSTRUCTION

Writing (II) Ask students to assume the identity of a European settler who has just arrived in colonial Texas. Have them write a letter home to a friend describing their first impressions of Texas and colonial society. They should incorporate into their letters as much information from Section 6 as possible. Select several letters to read aloud. **A**

Multicultural Perspective (I) Ask students to imagine that they are an enslaved African American in colonial Texas. Have them write a paragraph explaining their role in colonial Texas and how they feel about their status. Invite volunteers to read their paragraphs aloud. **A**

Guided Practice (I) Display a world map for the class. Ask students to point out the different countries that were represented by the heritage of Texas colonists in 1835. **A, V, LEP**

EXTENSION

Research (III) Have students investigate and report on the rights of women in colonial Texas. Ask them to answer the following questions: Did single women have the same rights as married women? Could women own property? **A, G**

Institute of Texan Cultures

William Goyens was an important citizen of Nacogdoches. He was trusted by Indians, Tejanos, and Anglo Americans in East Texas. In this painting by M.A. Emanuel, Goyens is conducting business in front of his blacksmith shop.

along the Rio Grande. Nearly all these different people were looking for land on which they could build new lives.

There were more Anglo Americans in Texas than any other group, and they began to dominate political and economic affairs. Three important Anglo Texans were Stephen F. Austin, David G. Burnet, and Henry Smith. They would all play an important role in the Texas struggle for independence. The richest citizen in the colony was probably Jared Groce. Stephen F. Austin's cousin Mary Austin Holley was a respected writer of colonial Texas. Another Anglo American woman, Nancy Tevis, helped found the city of Beaumont.

Leading Tejano citizens included Erasmo and Juan Seguín, Lorenzo de Zavala, and Martín de León. Patricia de León was a key figure in the settlement of the city of Victoria. Another Tejano who served Texas throughout his lifetime was José Antonio Navarro.

A number of settlers arrived directly from Europe. The first German to come to Texas with a family was probably Frederich Ernst. He settled in Stephen F. Austin's colony in 1831. One of the first French settlers was William Alley. He, his American wife, Cynthia, and their children were members of Austin's original Old Three Hundred. New Yorker Jane McManus Cazneau was the only woman to take on the responsibilities of an empresario. She was given the right to settle German families near Matagorda Bay.

Edna Schroeder Kirschke, courtesy of Institute of Texan Cultures

Louise Ernst Stoehr was one of the first German immigrants to arrive at Austin's colony. Her husband was Frederich Ernst.

RETEACHING
Ask students to list the ethnic backgrounds found in colonial Texas by 1835. Ask: What was the dominant ethnic group *(Anglo American)*? **LEP**

TEXAS VOICES
Analysis (I) As students read the special feature, ask them to list adjectives that might be used to describe Mary Rabb's feelings. Use their lists to create a master list on the chalkboard. **LEP**

CLOSURE
Tell students that as Texas' population grew, the colonists' relationship with the government of Mexico became strained.

ASSESSMENT
Have students complete the Section 6 Review on page 210.

Essential Elements (For Texas Voices)
2H, 9A

Answers to Section 6 Review

Identify: Mary Austin Holley— Stephen F. Austin's cousin and a respected writer; Nancy Tevis—helped found the city of Beaumont; Frederick Ernst— German settler in Austin's colony; William Goyens—successful black businessman who lived in the Nacogdoches area

1. Possible answers include: Anglo American, African American, Tejano, German, French, Scottish, English, Irish, Swedish, and Italian.
2. They were enslaved people, most of whom worked on plantations or farms. Some worked at skilled trades in the settlement towns.
3. They arrived in the greatest numbers, and they had the most money and property.

Evaluating Information: A settler from Georgia would have found Texas similar to what he or she was accustomed to in Georgia. The German settler would have to cope with a strange environment, a new language, and unfamiliar ethnic groups.

Synthesizing Information: Answers will vary. Because most blacks in colonial Texas were slaves, free blacks might have had to prove that they were free and not runaway slaves. Some Anglo Americans probably feared that free blacks would encourage slaves to revolt or run away.

*M*ary Crownover Rabb was one of the original "Old Three Hundred" colonists. She and her husband, John, moved to Texas in 1823 with their children and other family members. The Rabb family had difficulty finding a good place to settle and begin their new life in Texas.

Mary Rabb left a journal describing the experiences of her family. The following is a portion written to her children:

 We got to my pa's about 4 or 5 days after we left Indian Hill. I found my father and mother well and well pleased there. We had plenty of cornbread and bear meat and venison [deer meat] and honey and milk and butter. We stayed there a few weeks. We had no neighbors nearer than eight miles, and the mosquitoes was so bad, it was almost impossible to do any work like sewing and churning unless we were in a mosquito bar [netting]. The flies was eating the cattle and horses up, and so we concluded we would leave there and go higher up the Brazos River. As the flies and mosquitoes was so bad, we knew we would have to travel pretty much altogether in the night. . . .

How many trials and troubles we passed through together here in Texas, and no opportunity of going to church, yet God was mindful of us and blessed us and gave us his spirit and made us feel that we was His.

SECTION REVIEW

Identify: Mary Austin Holley, Nancy Tevis, Frederich Ernst, William Goyens

1. List six ethnic groups in Texas during the colonial period.
2. What was the status of most African Americans in colonial Texas? Explain.
3. Why did Anglo American settlers in Texas dominate economic and political affairs?

Evaluating Information: Explain the following: A settler coming to Texas from Germany had to make more adjustments than one from Georgia. What were these adjustments?

Synthesizing Information: How might the presence of enslaved blacks in Texas have made life difficult for free blacks?

Nine out of ten black Texans were enslaved people—about fourteen percent of the population in 1836. Slaves were the one group who did not see Texas as a land of opportunity. They worked the farms and plantations and were the backbone of many rural communities. A few of the slaves lived in the towns, working as carpenters, blacksmiths, or laborers. During the 1820s, about 150 free blacks lived in Texas. Their numbers included citizens such as Samuel Hardin and Lewis Jones. Two other free black Texans, Greenberry Logan and Hendrick Arnold, later distinguished themselves as heroes in the Texas Revolution. The most famous of the free black Texans probably was William Goyens. Goyens became a successful businessman in the Nacogdoches area.

Becoming Texans. By 1835, there were more than 30,000 settlers in Texas. No matter where they came from or what their background, most began to see themselves as Texans. Many no longer felt that they were a part of Mexico. This troubled the government of Mexico City. Texans would soon find themselves fighting a revolution. ◯

CHAPTER REVIEW RESOURCES

1. Chapter Review Worksheet 10
2. Chapter 10 Test, Form A
3. Reteaching Worksheet 10
4. Chapter 10 Test, Form B
5. **Informal Evaluation Forms:** Portfolio Assessment
6. *Texas, Our Texas* **Test Generator**

Essential Elements
2H, 4D, 5A, 5B, 5C, 5D, 9A, 9B, 9E, 9G

CHAPTER 10 REVIEW

Understanding Main Ideas

1. Why were many citizens of the United States eager to move to Texas?
2. What sorts of homes were built by the early Texas colonists?
3. What foods were eaten at a typical meal in colonial Texas?
4. How did most colonial Texas children learn to read and write?
5. Why was transportation a major problem for residents of colonial Texas?
6. Name four ethnic groups that were represented in colonial Texas.

Thinking Critically

1. **Seeing Cause and Effect:** Most of the population of colonial Texas was scattered on farms. How might this fact affect the development of schools?
2. **Evaluating Information:** On the basis of information in Chapter 10, do you think people in colonial Texas were friendly and neighborly? Explain.
3. **Making Decisions:** If you were the head of a family in colonial Texas, would you have thought it more important for your children to work on the farm or go to school? Why?

Linking History and Geography

1. Why might the natural environment of a rural Texas community have a greater impact on daily life in 1830 than it did in 1930?
2. In what ways did rivers affect transport and trade in early Texas?

TAAS *Practice*
Using Primary Sources

Pioneering was a risky business and not always successful. The following story by Solomon Wright illustrates this fact. He heard this story when he was a boy in the 1800s in East Texas:

A man moving to this promised land from Missouri drove two spans of powerful, spirited Thoroughbred horses to two brand new wagons. He drove mighty proud, and when anybody would ask him where he was going, he'd boom out in the heartiest voice you can imagine, "Goin' to Texas to get rich."

After a couple of years in the alligator-swamp country, this man and his family had been shaken by so many chills and burned up by so much fever that they were as yellow as pumpkins, and just about as spirited. He'd had to dispose of his fine horses and painted wagons to buy medicine. Finally he started back to Missouri in an old shackly [rickety] wagon, each of its four wheels trying to go in a different direction, pulled by a pair of ewe-necked, rabbit-hipped prairie ponies. When anyone would ask him where he was going, he would squeak out in a weak, whiney voice, "Goin'-back-to-Missouri, Mister-please-give-me-a-chaw-of-tebaccer."

1. A serious truth lies behind this humorous story. This truth is
   A that horses and wagons often broke down in Texas
   B that disease and failure struck many hopeful settlers
   C that self-confidence and hard work always assured success on the Texas frontier
   D that prairie ponies and pumpkins sold well in Missouri markets

CHAPTER 10 REVIEW ANSWERS

Understanding Main Ideas

1. The lure of cheap land and the opportunity for a fresh start
2. Simple log cabins
3. Fried or roasted meat, corn bread, and black coffee
4. They were taught at home by their parents.
5. Travel overland meant few and poor roads, with many difficult rivers to cross. These rivers were unpredictable and difficult to navigate and did not lend themselves to water transportation.
6. Possible answers include: Anglo American, African American, Tejano, German, Irish, Swedish, English, Scottish, French, and Italian.

Thinking Critically

1. **Seeing Cause and Effect:** Because it was difficult to establish and maintain schools, most children were taught at home.
2. **Evaluating Information:** Answers will vary, but people generally were considered friendly and neighborly. They lived in isolated areas and desired social interaction, and they often depended on one another for help.
3. **Making Decisions:** Answers will vary, but children's help on farms was usually necessary for survival.

Linking History and Geography

1. The environment provided basic resources to a rural community in 1830. The community lacked good roads, adequate transportation, electricity, and so on. People depended on the natural environment in order to grow or make much of what they needed.
2. Because they were generally shallow and undependable, they limited transport and trade.

TAAS *Practice*
Using Primary Sources

1. B
2. D

TAAS *Practice*
Writing Persuasively

Entries will vary but should demonstrate knowledge of problems of river transportation in colonial Texas.

Practicing Skills

1. **Classifying Information:** *education*—Juan Zambrano, Frances Trask Thompson; *religion*—Thomas J. Pilgrim, Sumner Bacon, Melinda Rankin, Joseph Bays, Mary Helm; *settlement*—Lorenzo de Zavala, David Burnet, Nancy Tevis, Jane McManus Cazneau, William and Cynthia Alley, Patricia de León; *transportation*—Henry Austin
2. **Interpreting Charts:** 1821 to 1831; these were the years during which empresarios brought settlers to Texas from the United States, Mexico, and Europe; 1806 to 1821

Enriching Your Study of History

1. **Individual Project:** Drawings and reports will vary but should be based on knowledge of the colonial way of life in Texas.

2. **Cooperative Project:** Reports will vary but should be well organized, detailed, and demonstrate thorough research.

CONTINUED

2. This story was told as a joke by East Texans to other East Texans. It most likely makes fun of
   A people who use prairie ponies to pull rickety wagons
   B people from West Texas
   C people who drive expensive wagons but beg things from strangers
   D outsiders who were quitters or too sure of themselves

TAAS *Practice*
Writing Persuasively

Imagine that you are the captain of the steamboat *Yellow Stone*, making a trip up the Colorado River. You have just had a terrible day on the river. All the problems that beset Texas river travel seem to have beset you. Write an entry in the ship's log for May 18, 1834, reporting everything that has happened to you and your vessel during your journey.

Practicing Skills

1. **Classifying Information:** Group the following persons under the categories *education, religion, settlement,* or *transportation*—the areas of Texas colonial life to which they contributed: Henry Austin, Lorenzo de Zavala, Thomas J. Pilgrim, Nancy Tevis, Sumner Bacon, Melinda Rankin, Juan Zambrano, William and Cynthia Alley, Frances Trask Thompson, Patricia de León, Jane McManus Cazneau, Joseph Bays, Mary Helm, David Burnet.
2. **Interpreting Charts:** Study the population chart on this page. Then refer to the chart to answer the following questions: Within which ten-year

Texas Population Growth	
Year	Population
1744	1,500
1792	2,992
1806	7,000
1821	7,000
1831	20,000
1834	24,700
1836	38,470

period did the Texas population increase most dramatically? How do you explain this great increase? Within which period did the population remain the same?

Enriching Your Study of History

1. **Individual Project:** Using information in this chapter and additional library research, make a drawing of a typical pioneer home during the colonial period. Use your drawing to illustrate an oral report to your class, in which you explain the various activities that took place in the typical pioneer home.
2. **Cooperative Project:** Your teacher will divide your class into eight teams and assign each team one of the following research topics on Texas colonial history: agriculture, stock-raising, house construction, education, wild game and wild plant foods, religion, entertainment, transportation. Each team will prepare an oral report for the class, detailing its topic well beyond the factual coverage in the chapter.

THE ROAD TO REVOLUTION

TEACHER'S TIME LINE

Section 1	Section 2	Section 3	Section 4	Review and Assessment
Pp. 213–17	Pp. 218–22	Pp. 222–26	Pp. 227–30	
1 Day	1 Day	1 Day	1 Day	1 Day

▩ TEACHER MATERIALS

Core: Chapter 11 Time Line; Graphic Organizer 11; Enrichment Worksheet 11; Review Worksheet 11; Reteaching Worksheet 11; Chapter 11 Tests, Forms A & B

Additional: Geography and Graph Skills 11, Map and Chart Transparencies 13, Informal Evaluation Forms, Test Generator

▩ OBJECTIVES

1. Explain the reasons for conflict between the Mexican government and the Texas colonists.
2. Describe the impact of the recommendations of the Mier y Terán report.
3. Explain the Decree of April 6, 1830, and its impact on the Texas colonists.
4. Identify sources of conflict in incidents at Anahuac and Velasco.
5. Explain the purpose of the Conventions of 1832 and 1833.
6. Identify problems encountered by Stephen F. Austin in Mexico.
7. Discuss reasons Texans opposed Santa Anna's rule.

▩ RESOURCES

BOOKS FOR TEACHERS

Barker, Eugene Campbell. *Mexico and Texas, 1821–1835*. Dallas: P. L. Turner Co., 1928. Causes of the Texas Revolution.

Bartlett, Robert Merrill. *Those Valiant Texans*. Portsmouth: P. E. Randall, 1989. Events leading to the Texas Revolution.

Callcott, Wilfrid Hardy. *Santa Anna: The Story of an Enigma Who Once Was Mexico*. Norman: University of Oklahoma Press, 1936. Study of this man.

Henson, Margaret Swett. *Anahuac in 1832: The Cradle of the Texas Revolution*. Texas: Fort Anahuac Committee of Chambers County Historical Commission, 1982. Discusses conflicts at Anahuac in 1832.

Holley, Mary Austin. *Letters of an Early American Traveller*. Dallas: Southwest Press, 1933. First book printed in English on life in colonial Texas.

McDonald, Archie P. *Travis*. Austin: Jenkins Publishing Co., 1976. Life and times of W.B. Travis.

MULTIMEDIA MATERIALS

The Golden Land. (video, 52 min.) Southwest Media Services, Inc., P.O. Box 140, Wimberley, Texas, 78676. Saga of manifest destiny, the Texas Revolution, and pioneer spirit.

Texas. (video, 21 min.) Coronet Film and Video, 108 Wilmot Road, Deerfield, Illinois, 60015. Dramatic story leading to the Texas Revolution.

Texas and the Mexican Cession. (video, 14 min.) Encyclopaedia Britannica Educational Corporation, 310 South Michigan Avenue, Chicago, Illinois, 60604. Portraits of the men and women who fought for the Texas territory. Includes the stories of Austin, Crockett, Bowie, Travis, and Santa Anna.

⊛ GENERAL STRATEGIES

STUDENTS WITH SPECIAL NEEDS

Limited English Proficient Students (LEP)
Have students skim the chapter and list the names of important people, places, and events mentioned. Then ask them to write next to each name a related fact from the textbook. Instruct them to use the list to review the chapter. See other activities labeled **LEP**.

Students Having Difficulty with the Chapter
Organize students into several cooperative learning groups. Have each group prepare a ten-item objective test of the material covered in Chapter 11. As students are preparing the tests, check to be sure that all group members are contributing items. After the groups have completed their tests, have them administer the tests to the other groups. **LEP**

Auditory Learners
Have auditory learners work together to write a series of questions for use during a "Who Am I?" game. They should develop the game so that the entire class can play. See other activities labeled **A.**

Visual Learners
Have visual learners work together to create an illustrated time line. Have them draw a time line on a large sheet of butcher paper or newsprint. Ask them to add to the time line significant events and corresponding dates from Chapter 11. Then have them draw at each point on the time line an illustration representative of the event. Display the completed time line in the classroom. See other activities labeled **V.**

Tactile/Kinesthetic Learners
Have tactile/kinesthetic learners locate the following sites on a map titled "The Road to Revolution":

Nacogdoches
San Antonio
San Felipe de Austin
Anahuac
Velasco
Mexico City
Washington-on-the-Brazos
Gonzales
Goliad
the United States

Then have the students identify events and dates related to the map's title at each location. See other activities labeled **TK.**

Gifted Students
Have students prepare two written speeches that might have been presented at the Consultation of October 1835. One speech should represent the point of view of the peace faction, and the other the point of view of the war faction. Invite students to present the speeches to the class. See other activities labeled **G.**

VOCABULARY
In addition to the boldfaced terms in each section, some students might benefit from discussing the meanings of these terms.

Section 1: *jury* (p. 214); *alliance* (p. 215).
Section 2: *exempted* (p. 218); *suspended* (p. 218); *public works* (p. 220).
Section 3: *convention* (p. 224); *resolutions* (p. 224); *solitary confinement* (p. 226).
Section 4: *dictatorship* (p. 230).

CHRONOLOGY
Have students study the Chapter 11 Time Line and identify relationships among the events.

GRAPHIC ORGANIZER
Have students skim the chapter and complete the Chapter 11 Graphic Organizer. *(You might wish to use this activity to review rather than to introduce the chapter.)*

ENRICHMENT
Have students complete the Chapter 11 Enrichment Worksheet.

THE ROAD TO REVOLUTION

CHAPTER 11

The Story Continues...

As more and more settlers arrived in Texas, relations between the Mexican government and the settlers became strained. The settlers wanted a different kind of government. In the 1830s, the problem became more serious. Chapter 11 looks at the conflicts and how they paved "the road to revolution."

As you read the chapter, look for the answers to these questions:

1. What were the reasons for unrest between the Mexican government and settlers in Texas?
2. How did Mexico's response to Mier y Terán's report and the first conflict at Anahuac cause more problems between Mexico and the United States?
3. What demands did Texans make at the conventions of 1832 and 1833? How were their demands met?
4. Why were Texans divided in their feelings toward Mexico? How did the Battle of Gonzales unite them?

1 Causes of Unrest

Some of the differences between Mexico City and the Texas colonists were political, involving questions of government. Others involved issues of religion and economics. A lack of trust and understanding developed because of these differences.

Different Views. Mexico had just gone through a revolution. Many people wanted a **democracy**, or government elected by the people, that gave important powers to the states. Others favored less democracy and a strong central government. In the 1830s, the argument between these two groups was still going on, and there was much confusion. Although groups in Mexico were working to change the government, it remained much as it had been under Spanish rule.

Kevin Vandivier

This photograph shows Galveston Bay today. Nearby Anahuac on the bay was the site of conflict over the Mexican government's decree of April 6, 1830.

Chapter 11 **213**

Historical Imagination (I) Direct students to the discussion on pages 213–14. Ask them to list the different views that existed between the Mexican government and the colonists as you copy students' responses onto the chalkboard. Then divide the class into two groups: one representing the Mexican government and the other representing the colonists. Have the groups sit face to face and discuss these issues as you moderate the discussion. **A**

Brainstorming (II) Have the class brainstorm to develop a compromise solution between Haden Edwards and the settlers living near Nacogdoches whose property rights were threatened. **A, G**

Analysis (I) Point out that Haden Edwards eventually returned to settle in Nacogdoches. Have students consider how Edwards might have been received by the other settlers. Ask them to express their opinions in a brief paragraph. Invite volunteers to read their paragraphs aloud. **A, LEP**

Amon Carter Museum

Stephen F. Austin wanted Galveston established as a port as early as 1825. Yet settlement did not really begin until the early 1830s. In 1832, Galveston had only about 300 settlers, but the city had grown to more than 3,000 by 1838. Galveston eventually became one of the largest ports in the United States.

Constitutional Heritage
A fundamental concept of our government today is civilian control of the military. The governor of Texas is the commander of the state forces, and the president is commander-in-chief of the national military.

Settlers in Texas from the United States wanted a system like the one they had left behind. For example, they believed in a trial by a jury when a person was accused of a crime. They also thought a person should be allowed to post bail, or pay to be released from jail until a trial was held. Under Mexican law, local military officials could legally deny these rights to people who were arrested. In the United States, the military was under the control of elected government leaders. The tradition in Mexico placed the military in control of the government.

Two other subjects concerned the colonists in Texas. Although the Mexican government had never pressed the issue, many settlers from the United States disliked having to say they accepted the beliefs of the Roman Catholic church. Many settlers were also uneasy over the growing issue of slavery. They worried that the Mexican government would end slavery, and many Texas settlers believed they had a right to hold slaves.

The Fredonian Rebellion. The first conflict between the Mexican government and Texas colonists occurred in East Texas. In 1825, a United States citizen named Haden Edwards received a land grant near Nacogdoches. Mexican officials granted him the right to settle 800 families. When

Guided Practice (I) Have students develop five or more statements illustrating cause and effect in Section 1. Ask them to save these for later use. **LEP**

EXTENSION
Role Playing (II) Invite two students to stage the meeting that took place between Mier y Terán and Stephen F. Austin during the general's inspection tour of Texas. The students should present in detail each side's position. **A, V, G**

Edwards and his family reached Nacogdoches in September 1825, there were already several hundred families in the region. Edwards was required by his land contract to respect the holdings of all settlers who had proper title to their land.

Edwards promptly ordered all landowners to produce their land titles. Those who could not do so had to pay Edwards to secure one for them. Many of the settlers did not have an official land title. Among them were some families who had moved in from Louisiana and some whose Mexican ancestors had settled in East Texas years before. There were also some Cherokee families who had asked for land titles in 1820 but never received them. The Cherokees had entered Texas after being forced from their homes in Tennessee and Georgia by the white settlers.

These older settlers resented Edwards and the threat he posed to their homes. They decided to petition José Antonio Saucedo, the chief Mexican political official in the San Antonio area, for help against Edwards. Saucedo sided with the old settlers and told Haden Edwards that he could not charge them for new land titles. For the next few months, Edwards argued with the Mexican government. In 1826, he returned to the United States.

Benjamin Edwards, Haden's brother, began to organize to oppose the Mexican government. He tried unsuccessfully to make an alliance with the Cherokees through two members of their group, John Hunter and Richard Fields. Then he recruited a small band of settlers and declared war on the Mexican government. Edwards declared that a part of Texas was now the Republic of Fredonia.

On December 16, 1826, Benjamin Edwards and a small group of his supporters rode into Nacogdoches waving a red and white flag. This Republic of Fredonia banner bore the words *Independence, Liberty, and Justice*. The armed riders took over a building in Nacogdoches generally known as the Old Stone Fort. For over a month, Edwards and his supporters occupied the fort as the capital of Fredonia.

The Fredonian revolt had no support from most Texas citizens. Anglo Texans and Tejanos both refused to be part of it. The Cherokees also opposed the Fredonian Rebellion.

After learning in January 1827 that Mexican troops were coming, the Fredonians fled Nacogdoches. Several escaped across the Sabine River into the United States. Others were captured by the Mexicans. They were later

Institute of Texan Cultures

Haden Edwards, his wife Susanna, and their family settled in Nacogdoches after Edwards received a land grant in East Texas. Many settlers had been in the area for some time and were angry when Edwards threatened their property rights.

Biography
Richard Fields was born in 1780. He was the great grandson of a Scottish man and a Cherokee woman. At the age of 21, Fields began working as a diplomat among groups of Native Americans. For example, in 1812, he was the interpreter in a treaty between the Creeks and Chickasaws. He probably made his way to Texas around 1819 or 1820.

Fields was unsuccessful in his attempts to obtain land titles for the Cherokees. After the Fredonian Rebellion, in which he tried to align the Cherokees with the rebels, the Cherokee tribal council ordered that Fields and John Hunter be executed. According to tribal law and custom, Fields and Hunter had violated a law prohibiting a person from working against the best interests of the community to benefit an enemy.

Independent Practice (II) Ask students to create a journal that Mier y Terán might have written during his inspection tour of Texas. Journals should include a map showing the route of his tour. Encourage students to use their creativity and historical imagination to make the journals seem authentic. **V, TK**

RETEACHING
Refer students to the cause-and-effect statements that they wrote for the Section 1 Guided Practice activity. Ask them to organize the statements into the form of a two-column chart. **V, TK, LEP**

The painting at right shows a view of the Old Stone Fort at Nacogdoches, which served briefly as the capital of Fredonia.

The Granger Collection

President John Quincy Adams thought that Mexico might be interested in getting rid of Texas after the Fredonian Rebellion. The United States offered $1 million for Texas, but Mexico was not interested.

The Granger Collection

President Andrew Jackson was also interested in buying Texas. Mexico refused. The Mexicans were very upset with the United States' continued interest in acquiring Texas.

Painting by Rev. George L. Crockett. Barker Texas History Center

released, after Stephen F. Austin spoke in their behalf. Eventually, Haden Edwards returned to Texas and settled in Nacogdoches.

Results of the Fredonian Rebellion. The Fredonian Rebellion was a minor event, but it attracted much attention. Newspapers in the United States carried stories about the revolt. They exaggerated the support that the Edwards brothers had. Many people in the United States believed that the Mexican government had treated Benjamin Edwards unfairly and that most Texans were in favor of his rebellion.

The Mexican government was greatly concerned by the United States' interest in Texas. Mexican leaders suspected that the Fredonian Rebellion was part of a plot by the United States to acquire Texas. Because of this worry, the Mexicans sent more troops into East Texas. Two hundred soldiers were sent to Nacogdoches under the command of Colonel José de las Piedras. Piedras was instructed to watch all new settlers from the United States and report on their activities.

The government of the United States increased the fears of Mexican leaders. In 1825, President John Quincy Adams offered to pay Mexico to move the Texas border west of

CLOSURE

Tell students that the Fredonian Rebellion was the first of many conflicts on the "road to revolution." Like the Spanish before them, Mexican officials would try to strengthen their hold on Texas.

ASSESSMENT

Have students complete the Section 1 Review on page 217.

the Brazos River. This offer angered the Mexicans. In 1827, soon after the Fredonian Rebellion, the United States offered to buy all of Texas for $1 million. President Andrew Jackson later offered $5 million for Texas. Once again, the Mexicans were offended. Texas had always been part of New Spain, and they were determined to keep it as an important part of Mexico.

Because of its concern, the Mexican government decided to send a group to investigate conditions in Texas. The group was headed by General Manuel de Mier y Terán. Mier y Terán was instructed to tour Texas and then make proposals on how Texas could be kept as part of Mexico.

The Mier y Terán Report. General Mier y Terán made his inspection tour in 1828–1829, beginning in Laredo. He traveled on to San Antonio. He then met with Stephen F. Austin at San Felipe de Austin. Austin convinced Mier y Terán that the colonists were loyal to Mexico. But he explained that the Texans were unhappy in some ways. Austin described the frustrations of the Texans with the Mexican court system. He also told Mier y Terán that the Texans did not like being ruled by the military government that enforced Mexican laws.

Mier y Terán continued his tour of Texas in Nacogdoches. While in East Texas, he wrote to the president of Mexico saying that Mexican influence in Texas decreased as one moved northward. He observed that the Mexican settlers in the Nacogdoches area were outnumbered by Anglo Americans ten to one. United States influence in Texas was growing stronger every day. Mier y Terán expressed his concern over this trend.

In his letter, Mier y Terán claimed that "Texas could throw the whole nation into revolution" unless certain steps were taken. He made several recommendations for keeping Texas under Mexico's control. He proposed that a separate Department of Nacogdoches be created in East Texas. Trade between Mexico and Texas should be increased, since colonists depended too much on trade with the United States. More Mexican soldiers should be sent to show Mexican power and determination to keep Texas. He also suggested that more Mexicans be encouraged to settle in the region. Mier y Terán believed that the immigration of more Mexican settlers into East Texas was the only way Mexico could hold Texas. ✪

Institute of Texan Cultures

General Manuel de Mier y Terán was an important official in the Mexican government. His inspection tour of Texas in 1828–1829 resulted in the passage of the much-hated Decree of 1830. He thought correctly that Texas was ripe for revolution.

SECTION ① REVIEW

Define: democracy
Identify: Haden Edwards, John Hunter, Republic of Fredonia, Manuel de Mier y Terán

1. What were the differences between how Mexico governed and how settlers in Texas wanted to be governed?
2. What was the cause of the Fredonian Rebellion?
3. How did the governments of the United States and Mexico respond to the Fredonian Rebellion?
4. What recommendations did Mier y Terán make to the Mexican government?

Comparing Perspectives: Write two letters to the editor, one arguing that Mexico should govern Texas, one arguing that Texas should govern itself.

Analyzing Information: In your opinion, why was Mexico offended by the offers of payment for Texas?

Answers to Section 1 Review

Define: *democracy*—government elected by the people

Identify: Haden Edwards—U.S. citizen given a land grant by Mexico, who quarreled with the Mexican government; John Hunter—Cherokee whom Benjamin Edwards unsuccessfully tried to ally; Republic of Fredonia—part of Texas declared independent during Fredonian Rebellion; Manuel de Mier y Terán—Mexican general sent by the Mexican government to investigate conditions in Texas

1. Mexico had a military government, while the Texas settlers wanted a democratic one.
2. After his brother had difficulties with the Mexican government over a land grant, Benjamin Haden opposed Mexico by forming the independent Fredonian Republic.
3. The U.S. government tried to buy Texas, and the Mexican government sent troops.
4. That a separate Department of Nacogdoches be created; that trade with Texas be increased; that more troops be sent to Texas; that more Mexicans settle Texas

Comparing Perspectives: Letters will vary but should be rational arguments and should be based on information discussed in the textbook.

Analyzing Information: Opinions will vary but should be well thought out and presented clearly.

SECTION 2

FOCUS

Student Experiences (I) Present this scenario to students: Beginning tomorrow, the following rules will be in effect in our school as decreed by our new principal.

1. There will be no talking in the halls.
2. Lunch prices will increase by one dollar.
3. One hour of homework per subject will be assigned each day.

Ask students how they might respond to this situation and what actions they might take. Tell them to keep these ideas in mind as they read about Mexico's change in policy toward Texas.

INSTRUCTION

Vocabulary (I) You may wish to preteach the following boldfaced terms: *decree* (p. 218); *customs duties* (p. 218); *garrison* (p. 219); *constitution* (p. 221). **LEP**

Essential Elements
2B, 2C, 2H, 7D, 9A, 9B, 9D, 9E, 9F

The Granger Collection

Many Texas settlers came from southern states, where slavery was well established. Some settlers brought enslaved people with them to Texas and continued to use slave labor on their farms and plantations.

Benson Latin American Collection.
The University of Texas at Austin

President Vicente Guerrero issued a decree in 1829 abolishing slavery in Mexico.

2 Beginnings of Conflict

Before acting on Mier y Terán's proposals, the Mexican government passed a law that greatly worried the Texans. The president of Mexico, Vicente Guerrero, issued a **decree** (official order) in 1829, abolishing slavery in Mexico. The decree never went into effect. Still, slaveholders protested. They complained that the new law threatened what they thought was their right to own slaves.

The Decree of April 6, 1830. On April 6, 1830, the Mexican government made a dramatic change in policy toward Texas. In response to Mier y Terán's report, a new law was passed to end all immigration from the United States. The law also suspended any empresario contract that was in progress. Furthermore, no new slaves could be brought into Texas. Mexican and European settlers could continue coming to Texas, however. To encourage these settlers, the Mexican government offered land and money.

There were other provisions of the law. More soldiers were to be sent to Texas, and taxes were to be collected on goods coming to Texas from the United States. These taxes, or **customs duties**, would add to the cost of goods. They were intended to discourage trade between the Texans and the United States. The Mexican government hoped that Texas would trade more with Mexico instead.

Texans were very angry about the Decree of April 6, 1830. They believed that the new tax law would hurt the growing Texas economy. The Texans were also bitter because the decree meant that relatives and friends in the United States would not be able to join them in Texas. Stephen F. Austin voiced his concern and tried to negotiate with Mexican officials. But he realized that serious damage had been done to the relations between Texans and their government in Mexico City.

Conflict at Anahuac. As a result of the Decree of April 6, 1830, Mexican troops began to move into Texas. Forts at San Antonio, Goliad, and Nacogdoches were strengthened. New ones were built at the ports of Anahuac, Lavaca, and Velasco. Anahuac, located at the mouth of the Trinity River on Galveston Bay, was the site of the first conflict over the new Mexican policy.

The **garrison**, or station of troops, at Anahuac was commanded by Colonel Juan Davis Bradburn. Bradburn

The Decree of 1830 provided for additional troops of Mexican soldiers to be sent to Texas. For the most part, these troops did little to discourage revolution in Texas.

Painting by Frederic Remington. Amon Carter Museum

Guided Practice (I) Organize students into three groups. Have each group work together to create a time line, map, or chart illustrating the events discussed in Section 2. Ask each group to display and discuss its finished illustration. **V, TK, LEP, A**

EXTENSION

Research (III) Have students research to find out similarities in Mexico's Constitution of 1824 and the government established by the United States Constitution. **G**

was from Kentucky. He had probably come to Texas with the Henry Perry expedition, and he remained in Mexico. He had supported the Mexicans in their struggle for independence against Spain and was later made a colonel in the Mexican army. Most Texans disliked him because he supported Mexican policies.

Bradburn arrested a special land commissioner named Francisco Madero in February 1831. Madero had come to the area to issue land titles to settlers along the Trinity River. Bradburn claimed that Madero had no authority and threw him in jail. The Texans protested this action, threatening to rebel against Bradburn. Bradburn made matters worse by abolishing the ayuntamiento in the town of Liberty. He took supplies from the colonists without paying for them. He also used colonists' slaves for local public works projects but refused to pay their owners for the labor.

Tension increased in November 1831 over collection of taxes. George Fisher, the new collector of customs at Anahuac, was similar to Bradburn in some ways. He, too, was from the United States and had become a Mexican citizen. Fisher demanded that all ships landing at the mouth of the Brazos River pay their customs duties to him at Anahuac. To do this was very difficult because it was nearly 100 miles from Anahuac to the mouth of the Brazos.

In December 1831, two ships decided to disobey Fisher's rules. They forced their way through the mouth of the Brazos at Brazoria. Mexican soldiers at Brazoria tried to stop the ships, and in the short fight, one Mexican soldier was wounded. The affair might have become a battle if Stephen F. Austin had not been close by. He convinced both sides to lay down their guns.

Fisher resigned soon after the incident, but conditions did not improve. Bradburn was still the commander of Anahuac, with military control of the area. In the spring of 1832, Bradburn arrested several citizens who had protested his policies. Among those were William B. Travis, Patrick Jack, and Sam Allen. These men were well liked and respected by their fellow Texans, and they felt that they had committed no crimes. Their friends decided to take action against the decisions of Bradburn.

The Texans Fight Back. Many Texans were outraged by the imprisonment of the men arrested by Bradburn. In June 1832, a group organized in Brazoria to demand their

Archives Division, Texas State Library

George Fisher became the customs collector at Anahuac in 1831. He made difficult demands upon the colonists and almost created a bloody incident at Brazoria.

220 *Unit 4*

Independent Practice (II) Have students work independently or with a partner and draw a diagram showing a cause-and-effect chain reaction. They should use the Decree of April 6, 1830, as the initial cause of the resulting chain of events. Ask volunteers to discuss their diagrams and explain how each event listed in the chain helped cause the next event. **A, V, TK**

RETEACHING
With the class, use the framework below to create on the chalkboard an outline of the material presented in Section 2.
  I. Decree of April 6, 1830
  II. Conflict at Anahuac
  III. Texans Fight Back
  IV. The Turtle Bayou Resolutions
  V. The Battle of Velasco

Allow students to ask questions to clarify information about which they are unsure. **A, V, LEP**

release. Bradburn ignored the demand. A force of 160 people then marched toward Anahuac. In Anahuac, the Texans exchanged gunfire with the Mexican soldiers at the fort. Bradburn then agreed to release the prisoners if the Texans would withdraw. But he went back on his promise after the Texans withdrew, and he took the opportunity to strengthen his forces.

The Turtle Bayou Resolutions. After withdrawing, the Texans camped at Turtle Bayou, a spot between Anahuac and Liberty. They sent John Austin and William Russell to Brazoria to get two cannons. While they waited, the Texans adopted a series of statements known as the Turtle Bayou Resolutions. They declared in these resolutions that they were not rebelling against Mexico. The Texans claimed that they supported Antonio López de Santa Anna, who was then leading a democratic revolt in Mexico. There, President Bustamante had taken complete control of the government, ignoring the Constitution of 1824. This **constitution**, or plan of government, favored democracy and local self-government. Like Santa Anna, the Texans strongly supported the Constitution of 1824.

Soon after the Turtle Bayou Resolutions were drawn up, a Mexican force led by Colonel José de las Piedras

San Jacinto Museum of History, Houston

Antonio López de Santa Anna led a revolt against President Bustamante in support of the Constitution of 1824. At first, Texans supported Santa Anna, but he later became absolute ruler and led Mexican forces against the Texan revolutionaries in 1836.

Point out to students that Texans felt hopeful with news that Santa Anna would soon be in power; nevertheless, tensions between Mexico and Texas continued to mount.

ASSESSMENT

Have students complete the Section 2 Review on page 222.

FOCUS

Student Experiences (I) Ask students to define the word *compromise. (Both sides give up something they want and get something they want in return.)* Invite them to tell the class about a controversy in which they were involved and were able to compromise in order to reach an agreement.

Answers to Section 2 Review

Define: *decree*—an official order; *customs duties*—taxes collected on goods entering or leaving a country; *garrison*—station of troops; *constitution*—a plan of government

Identify: Juan Davis Bradburn—Mexican army colonel who commanded the forces at Anahuac; George Fisher—tax collector at Anahuac; Turtle Bayou Resolutions—a collection of statements made by Texans in support of Santa Anna; Antonio López de Santa Anna—leader of a revolt in Mexico in 1832

1. They thought that the decree would hurt the Texas economy and that their friends and relatives in the United States would not be able to join them.
2. He arrested Madero, abolished the ayuntamiento in Liberty, took supplies without paying for them, and used the colonists' slaves.
3. They wanted Bradburn to free the citizens he had arrested. He agreed to release the prisoners if the Texans would withdraw. They withdrew, but he went back on his promise and then strengthened his forces.

(Continued on page 223)

Essential Elements
2B, 2C, 2H, 7B, 7D, 7E, 9A, 9D

Institute of Texan Cultures

President of Mexico Anastacio Bustamante lost a power struggle with Santa Anna, partly because he ignored the Constitution of 1824.

SECTION ★2 REVIEW

Define: decree, customs duties, garrison, constitution
Identify: Juan Davis Bradburn, George Fisher, Turtle Bayou Resolutions, Antonio López de Santa Anna

1. Why did the Decree of April 6, 1830, anger many Texans?
2. What actions did Bradburn take that upset many Texans?
3. Why did 160 people march on Anahuac, and what was the outcome?
4. Why did Texans support Santa Anna against President Bustamante?
5. Who fought the Battle of Velasco, and why?
6. What did Stephen F. Austin and other Texas leaders tell Mexía?

Exploring Economics: What were the economic demands that Bradburn and Fisher made of the Texans? Why did the Texans oppose these demands?

Evaluating Information: Did Piedras take the right actions at Nacogdoches to solve the problems there? Why or why not?

---

arrived from Nacogdoches. Piedras believed that Bradburn was at fault for the uprising, and he restored peace. He released the prisoners who had been arrested by Bradburn. They were turned over to officials for trial. The Texans were paid for property that Bradburn had taken from them. Bradburn then resigned.

The Battle of Velasco. A serious battle was avoided at Anahuac, but fighting did break out at Velasco, near the mouth of the Brazos River. John Austin, William Russell, and their supporters had loaded their two cannons on a ship at Brazoria and headed for Anahuac. When the Texans reached Velasco, the Mexican commander, Colonel Domingo de Ugartechea, refused to let them pass. The fighting that followed was called the Battle of Velasco.

After three days of fighting, the Mexicans ran out of ammunition and were forced to surrender. Men were killed and wounded on both sides. The Mexican soldiers were allowed to return to Mexico. The Texans resumed their journey to Anahuac, only to find the conflict settled.

Events in Mexico. Following the incidents at Anahuac and Velasco, Mexican troops began to leave Texas. In Mexico, Santa Anna and President Bustamante were at war, and the Mexican soldiers in Texas headed south to take sides. By the end of August 1832, the only Mexican soldiers remaining in Texas were at San Antonio and Goliad. Once again, Texans were nearly free of the Mexican army. Then good news came from Mexico. Santa Anna was winning a revolution and would soon be in power.

One of Santa Anna's supporters was Colonel José Antonio Mexía, who captured the city of Matamoros. There Mexía met Stephen F. Austin, who was returning to Texas from a meeting of the Coahuila y Texas legislature. Austin sailed to Texas with Mexía and discussed conditions there. He and other Texas leaders convinced Mexía that Texas was loyal to Santa Anna. Mexía returned to Mexico with a favorable report on Texas. ○

[3] Conventions and Petitions

Texans had been unhappy with the government in Mexico since the Antislavery Law of 1829 and the Decree of April 6, 1830. Now Santa Anna was becoming head of

Ask students to consider as they read Section 3 whether Texas and Mexico ever came close to settling their differences through compromise.

INSTRUCTION

Vocabulary (I) You may wish to preteach the following boldfaced term: *delegates* (p. 224).

LONE STAR LEGACY

The Mexican Constitution of 1824

When the Texans made their stand at the Alamo [which you will read about in Chapter 12] against General Santa Anna's army, the flag they flew had a large *1824* in the middle. That flag represented the Mexican Constitution of 1824. Rights and privileges guaranteed under this document were important to the Texans. When Santa Anna ignored these rights, Texas citizens were determined to oppose him and fight him if necessary. The Texas Revolution began as people in Texas tried to defend the Mexican Constitution of 1824.

In the same year as the Colonization Law was passed, the Mexican congress wrote the Constitution of 1824. The Colonization Law contained rules for owning land and for settling the Texas territory. The Constitution of 1824 set forth the rules of government for the Republic of Mexico.

Much of the Constitution of 1824 was based on the Constitution of the United States. For example, the president and vice president held four-year terms, and the Mexican congress was made up of two houses.

The Constitution of 1824 was different from the United States Constitution in some ways. For example, the Roman Catholic religion was made the national faith, and money from the national treasury supported the church. All dealings with the Mexican government had to be conducted in Spanish.

The Constitution of 1824 established the state of Coahuila y Texas. Many Texans hoped that Texas would someday be a state separate from Coahuila. They believed that separate statehood would give Texas more power in dealing with the national government in Mexico City. Their dreams of a separate Texas were shattered when Santa Anna seized power and ignored the Constitution of 1824.

Many historians have argued that the Texans would not have revolted if the Constitution of 1824 had remained in force. That is uncertain, of course. Change was taking place rapidly as thousands of Americans poured into Texas. It is certain, however, that on March 6, 1836, more than 180 Texans were willing to stand and die for the rights they held under the Constitution of 1824.

Using Historical Imagination
Imagine that you are a Texan in 1836. If the Constitution of 1824 were brought back, would you still wish to revolt against Mexico? Why or why not?

Inset: **Coahuila y Texas flag** Right: **Texas Revolution flag**

Inset: *Institute of Texan Cultures* Right: *Gallery of the Republic*

---

4. They thought that Santa Anna, unlike Bustamante, would follow the Mexican Constitution.
5. It was fought by Texans and Mexicans. A group of Texans was trying to take cannons to Anahuac but was stopped by Mexicans at Velasco.
6. They told him that Texans supported Santa Anna.

Exploring Economics: Bradburn took supplies that the settlers needed and used slaves without paying for their labor. Fisher demanded that ships landing at the Brazos River travel to Anahuac to pay their customs duties nearly 100 miles away. These demands cost the Texans money and time.

Evaluating Information: Answers will vary but should be supported with logical reasons.

Essential Elements
2B, 7B, 7E, 7G

LONE STAR LEGACY
Using Historical Imagination: Answers may vary. Some students may say that they would not revolt if the rights promised them under the Constitution of 1824 were reinstated. Other students may suggest that there were other reasons for revolt, such as being forced to follow a national faith.

Historical Imagination (II) Select students to write and perform a play depicting the key figures in the Convention of 1832 and the Convention of 1833. Have other class members participate by playing the roles of delegates. **A, V, TK**

Categorizing (I) Pair students and provide each pair with a list of statements referring to the Convention of 1832, the Convention of 1833, or both. One student will read a statement as the other tells in what category it belongs. Have students continue the activity until all statements have been categorized correctly. **A, LEP**

Guided Practice (I) Write the following names on separate index cards: *Santa Anna, Stephen F. Austin, William H. Wharton, Rafael Manchola, Erasmo Seguín; Dr. James B. Miller, Valentín Gómez Farías.* Lay the cards face down on your desk in random order. A student will choose a card and then give the class an identifying clue from Section 3. The class must guess whose name is on the card. Continue until all names have been identified correctly. **A, TK**

the government. Texans expected that the Constitution of 1824 would again be followed. The Texans believed that this was the time to ask for reforms. Each settlement in Texas was asked to send a representative to San Felipe de Austin on October 1, 1832. The **delegates** (representatives) to this convention would discuss the concerns of Texans. They would then send their proposals to Santa Anna in Mexico City.

The Convention of 1832. When the convention met, 58 delegates from sixteen settlements were present. Delegates from Goliad arrived only after the convention was over, but they approved of what had been decided. San Antonio was the only major settlement not represented.

Stephen F. Austin was elected president of the convention, which adopted several resolutions. The most important resolution asked the Mexican government to allow immigration from the United States once again. There was also a request to exempt Texas from paying certain customs duties. The delegates asked for better protection from the Indians, for the creation of a public school system, and for the appointment of a land commissioner in East Texas. The delegates also asked to separate Texas from Coahuila so that it could have its own state government.

Two delegates, William H. Wharton and Rafael Manchola, were selected to present the resolutions to Mexican officials. But the resolutions were never presented because leaders in San Antonio did not support the convention. Stephen F. Austin decided that it was wise to wait until there was full support of the measures.

The Convention of 1833. Stephen F. Austin realized that the only hope for reforms in Texas lay in cooperation among Anglo Texans, Tejanos, and Mexican officials. He set out on a tour of San Antonio and Goliad to gain support from the Tejano communities. While Austin was meeting with leaders in San Antonio and Goliad, a group of impatient Texans called for another convention.

The second convention met at San Felipe de Austin on April 1, 1833. Only fourteen members of the Convention of 1832 were among the 55 delegates to the second convention. William H. Wharton was chosen president. He was the leader of a group that wanted to push harder and more quickly for changes in Mexican policy. Stephen F. Austin was not in favor of the convention, but he gave his support.

Thomas Gilcrease Institute of American History and Art

Jean Louis Berlandier painted this Mexican soldier in about 1830. The soldier was probably a member of a Texas garrison responsible for defending settlers against Indian raids. What caused many Mexican troops to leave Texas and return to Mexico during 1832?

Caption Response
They went to take sides in the war in Mexico.

EXTENSION
Role Playing (I) Organize the class into two groups. Have members of one group imagine that they are friends of Stephen F. Austin who have come to Mexico City in an attempt to get Austin out of jail. Have them write a plea to the Mexican authorities on Austin's behalf. They should include Austin's original intentions for coming to Mexico, and why he and other colonists feel as they do toward the Mexican government. Have members of the other group imagine that they are Mexican leaders. They should develop an argument justifying their actions against Texas settlers, as well as telling why they have jailed Austin. Have students from both sides present their pleas or arguments to the class. **A, V**

He hoped to keep the delegates from taking actions that would anger the government.

One of the new members of the convention was Sam Houston of Nacogdoches. Houston, who had only recently arrived in Texas, was already well known in the United States. He had served as governor of Tennessee and as a member of the United States Congress.

The Convention of 1833 adopted many of the same resolutions as the first convention. The members again asked that immigration from the United States be allowed. They also wrote a constitution in the hope that Texas would be made a separate state. Three delegates were chosen to take the resolutions to the Mexican government. They were Stephen F. Austin, Erasmo Seguín, and Dr. James B. Miller. Neither Seguín nor Miller could make the trip, so Austin set out for Mexico City alone.

Austin in Mexico. Austin left San Felipe de Austin in April 1833. The trip to Mexico City took nearly three months. When he finally arrived, Austin faced one problem after another. Because Santa Anna was out of the city, Austin was unable to meet with him. Austin did see the vice president, Valentín Gómez Farías. But Gómez Farías said there would be a delay in presenting Austin's plan to the congress. He explained that the Mexican government was busy with a cholera epidemic that had swept the city, killing thousands of people. Austin pressed Gómez Farías for a quick approval of the convention's proposals. Gómez Farías thought Austin was threatening him. Following the meeting, Austin was discouraged because he had made little progress.

In October 1833, Austin wrote a letter to the San Antonio ayuntamiento. He told of his frustration in dealing with the Mexican government. Austin claimed that government leaders could not, or would not, act on the convention's proposals. He encouraged Texans to begin organizing a separate state government without waiting for official permission. This letter later caused much suffering for Stephen F. Austin.

The situation improved the following month. Santa Anna returned to Mexico City and met with Austin. He agreed to nearly all of the resolutions of the Convention of 1833. Immigration from the United States was again allowed. Santa Anna promised better mail service and

Painting by J. Wood. Library of the Daughters of the Republic of Texas at the Alamo

Sam Houston is one of the most colorful figures in American history. He came to Texas in 1832. He quickly stood out as a leader and was a delegate from Nacogdoches to the Convention of 1833.

Independent Practice (II) Ask students to imagine that they are colonists at San Felipe de Austin in 1833. The news of Stephen F. Austin's arrest has just reached them. Each student should draft a letter to Mexican officials in an attempt to gain Austin's release. Encourage students to suggest to Mexico a plan for compromise. Invite students to read their letters aloud. **A**

RETEACHING

Have students create a time line illustrating the events in Section 3. Ask them to choose one of the events from the time line and write a brief description. **TK, LEP**

CLOSURE

Tell students that it was now clear that Mexico had no intention of allowing Texas to become a separate state.

ASSESSMENT

Have students complete the Section 3 Review on page 226.

Answers to Section 3 Review

Define: *delegates*—representatives to conventions

Identify: Convention of 1832—called to discuss the concerns of Texas; William H. Wharton—delegate to the Convention of 1832 and president of the Convention of 1833; Sam Houston—former governor of Tennessee, delegate to the Convention of 1833; Valentín Gómez Farías—vice president of Mexico with whom Stephen F. Austin spoke about the resolutions of the Convention of 1833

1. Allow immigration from the United States again; exempt Texas from certain customs duties; provide better protection from Indians; create a public school system; appoint a land commissioner in East Texas
2. A constitution
3. Immigration was allowed, better mail service and improvements in the court system were promised, and he set fairer tax policies on goods from the United States.
4. Austin was put in jail because of a letter he wrote suggesting that Texans organize a separate state government.

(Continued on page 227)

226 *Unit 4*

Delays and frustration were Stephen F. Austin's constant companions during his 1833 stay in Mexico City. In 1834, Austin was thrown into prison in Mexico City as a result of his letter encouraging Texans to organize a state government. This scene shows the seat of city government in Mexico City, the Municipal House.

SECTION 3 REVIEW

Define: delegates

Identify: Convention of 1832, William H. Wharton, Sam Houston, Valentín Gómez Farías

1. What resolutions were adopted at the Convention of 1832?
2. What was written at the Convention of 1833 that was not written at the Convention of 1832?
3. What resolutions were met by Santa Anna?
4. Why was Austin put in jail in Mexico?

Writing Descriptively: Imagine that you are Stephen F. Austin in solitary confinement in Mexico. Write a letter home, describing your reaction to your present situation.

Exploring Perspectives: Imagine that you are a government official in 1834. You have just read a copy of Austin's letter to the leaders in San Antonio. What is your reaction? Why?

Lithograph by C. Castro. Benson Latin American Collection. The University of Texas at Austin

improvements in the court system. He also granted the Texans' request for fairer tax policies on goods coming from the United States. He rejected, however, the idea of making Texas a separate state.

Austin Is Arrested. Austin left Mexico City on December 10, 1833. He had failed to gain permission to make Texas a state. Yet his other successes made him hopeful about the future of Texas. When he reached the city of Saltillo in northern Mexico, Austin was arrested. Mexican officials had read the letter he wrote to the leaders in San Antonio. The officials thought the letter challenged their authority. They accused Austin of being disrespectful to the Mexican government, but he was never formally charged.

Austin was returned to Mexico City under armed guard and put in prison in February 1834. For the next three months, he was held in solitary confinement. He was not allowed to see or speak to anyone. He was not given a trial. When he was finally released from solitary confinement, Austin was moved from jail to jail. After nearly a year in prison, Austin was released on Christmas Day, 1834. But he was still required to remain in Mexico City. Austin was at last permitted to return to Texas in July 1835, after two years away from home. ○

Past Learning (I) Ask students to trace the rise of tensions between Texas and Mexico from 1830 to 1835 as you list their responses on the chalkboard. Tell students that they will learn in this section how these and other events resulted finally in revolution.

Vocabulary (I) You may wish to preteach the following boldfaced term: *faction* (p. 228). **LEP**

4 The Revolution Begins

While in prison, Stephen F. Austin wrote many letters to his friends. He pleaded with them not to take any violent action. To his brother-in-law, Austin wrote:

> I have no idea when I shall be at liberty. . . . It is much in my favor that all remains quiet in Texas. I was confident that no friend of mine would try to get up an excitement but I feared that my enemies would. Such a thing would have increased my difficulty.

Austin did not have to worry about the Texans. They were concerned about his imprisonment, yet they took no strong actions. Austin soon had cause to worry about Santa Anna, however. In 1835, Santa Anna rejected the Constitution of 1824, which the Texans supported. Austin feared that Santa Anna was becoming absolute ruler, a leader with complete power. Events in 1835 supported Austin's fears. Santa Anna took complete control of the Mexican government. But the Texans refused to live under his rule.

New Conflict at Anahuac. In January of 1835, Santa Anna decided to strengthen his control over Texas. He sent

Writing Descriptively: Letters will vary but should be descriptive and written in character.

Exploring Perspectives: Answers will vary but should reflect an understanding of the point of view of the Mexican government.

Essential Elements
2B, 2C, 2H, 5B, 9A, 9B, 9G

Linking History and Geography
From Presidio on the Old San Antonio Road to San Antonio, then on another road east to Gonzales, and from there on the northeast road to Columbus

Transparency 13
An overhead transparency of this map can be found in the Teacher's Resource Binder.

LINKING HISTORY AND GEOGRAPHY

What route would you have to take if you were traveling from Presidio to Columbus?

Important Settlements in 1836
— Major roads
--- Present-day state boundary

Analysis (I) Organize the students into small groups. Write the following question on the chalkboard: *Should Texas colonists fight for independence from Mexico?* Below the question, make two columns headed by *Yes* and *No.* Each group should discuss reasons for and against going to war as you list the reasons on the board. The groups should then evaluate the reasons and make a group decision regarding the issue. Write the votes in the appropriate columns. **A, V, LEP**

Historical Imagination (I) Organize students into two groups, one representing the "peace faction" and the other representing the "war faction." Ask each group to prepare a news conference in which it presents its position. Allow members from the opposing group to ask questions. **A**

Guided Practice (I) Ask students to write an essay defending or attacking William Travis' actions at Anahuac. **LEP**

Historical Sidelight
General Cós was Santa Anna's brother-in-law.

Caption Response
"Three-Legged Willie"

Rosenberg Library

Samuel Williams was Stephen F. Austin's close friend and chief assistant. In 1835, the Mexican government made many efforts to capture him, but he managed to evade capture.

Richard Pearce-Moses

Robert M. Williamson was a highly respected member of the Texas colony. He had settled at San Felipe in 1826. Williamson was one of the first to speak out against the Mexican government. After the Revolution, he became a member of the Texas Supreme Court and also served in the Texas House of Representatives and Senate. What was Robert Williamson's nickname?

more Mexican troops and tax collectors into Texas. Once again, there was conflict between Texans and Mexican officials at Anahuac.

The commander of the customs house at Anahuac was a Mexican captain, Antonio Tenorio. Tenorio arrested a merchant, Andrew Briscoe, for refusing to pay customs duties to the Mexican government. Briscoe and other citizens at Anahuac argued that they should not have to pay the taxes. Actually, taxes had not been collected for some time. They feared that more Mexican troops would soon arrive.

A meeting was held at San Felipe de Austin to talk about the arrest at Anahuac. William B. Travis organized a group of people who wanted to take immediate action in response to the arrest. They decided to attack Tenorio's forces at Anahuac. Travis and about 25 supporters marched on the customs house, demanding the surrender of Tenorio. Tenorio agreed to lay down his arms and leave Texas. Travis and his group believed that they had won a great victory.

Most Texans, however, were disturbed by Travis' actions. They believed such actions would only make things worse. As it turned out, they were correct. The official in charge of the province of Texas, General Martín Perfecto de Cós, was angered. He refused to accept the apology of the many Texans who were embarrassed by Travis' actions. Instead, Cós demanded the arrest of the leaders of the attack on Anahuac. He also ordered more troops into Texas to restore the authority of Santa Anna.

Cós demanded that the Texans arrest William Travis, Robert Williamson, Samuel Williams, Francis W. Johnson, and Lorenzo de Zavala. Even though many Texans disagreed with the actions at Anahuac, they were not willing to turn their friends over to Cós. They knew that Cós would put the Texans on trial in a military court, and that was unacceptable to them.

The Consultation. Reports that General Cós was bringing in more troops upset the Texans even further. They decided to call another meeting to discuss matters. This convention was set to meet on October 15, 1835, in the town of Washington-on-the-Brazos. They called the convention the Consultation. It eventually met at San Felipe de Austin.

Two groups held different ideas about the coming Consultation. One **faction**, or group, argued that Texans should

228 *Unit 4*

EXTENSION
Research (III) General Santa Anna called himself "the Napoléon of the West." Ask interested students to find out why and then report back to the class. **A, G**

Independent Practice (II) Refer students to the illustration on this page, and ask them to describe what they see. Then have them write a speech that Stephen F. Austin might have given at this gathering. Invite volunteers to present their speech to the class. **A, V**

Archives Division, Texas State Library

Stephen F. Austin spent many years trying to resolve with Mexican officials the problems of settlement in Texas. He supported the Revolution after he realized that Texas' best interests would not be served by Santa Anna.

Historical Sidelight
By mid 1835, Santa Anna was flaunting his power. He nullified the Constitution of 1824, and he ordered his army to crush a rebellion in Zacatecas, a state neighboring Coahuila y Texas. Many in Texas were alarmed that Santa Anna would soon move against them.

remain calm. This "peace faction" wished to keep peaceful relations with Mexico. They believed that the Consultation was not needed and that it would only anger the Mexican government. Another group, the "war faction," argued for the Consultation. This group was led by William Wharton and William Travis. Some members of the war faction wanted Texas to declare its independence from Mexico.

While the debate over the Consultation continued, Stephen F. Austin returned from his imprisonment in Mexico. The people of Texas looked to Austin for guidance. Nearly all Tejanos, Anglos, and other groups of Texans trusted his judgment. Austin declared his support for the Consultation. He explained that the people of Texas must

RETEACHING

Direct each student to make a crossword puzzle using names, events, and terms from Section 4. Clues should be in identification or fill-in-the-blank format. Have students exchange and complete the puzzles. Then have partners work together to discuss and correct the answers. **LEP**

CLOSURE

Pose the following question to students: Which side began the war between Texas and Mexico? Allow students with differing opinions to express their views. Lead students to conclude that both sides contributed to the war.

ASSESSMENT

Have students complete the Section 4 Review on page 230.

Answers to Section 4 Review

Define: *faction*—group that is in opposition to another group

Identify: Antonio Tenorio—Mexican captain who commanded the customs house at Anahuac; Andrew Briscoe—merchant arrested by Tenorio for refusing to pay customs duties; William B. Travis—Texan who organized a group to attack Tenorio's forces at Anahuac; Martín Perfecto de Cós—Mexican general who demanded the arrest of the leaders of the attack on Anahuac

1. He angered Texans and Mexicans by taking the law into his own hands.
2. One faction wanted to make peace with Mexico, whereas the other wanted to hold the Consultation.
3. The Texans refused to give to the Mexicans the cannon that they used for protection from the Indians.

Making Decisions: Answers will vary but should be supported by sound reasoning.

Exploring Perspectives: Paragraphs will vary but should reflect an understanding of the Mexicans' point of view.

230 *Unit 4*

Texas Department of Transportation

A mosaic depicting the Battle of Gonzales, the first battle of the Texas Revolution, is displayed at the Municipal Building at Gonzales.

Define: faction

Identify: Antonio Tenorio, Andrew Briscoe, William B. Travis, Martín Perfecto de Cós

1. How did Travis' actions at Anahuac worsen relations with Mexico?
2. What were the differences between the two factions attending the Consultation?
3. Why was the Battle of Gonzales fought?

Making Decisions: Which faction would you have joined, the peace faction or the war faction? Explain.

Exploring Perspectives: Imagine that you were a Mexican fighting at the Battle of Gonzales. Write a paragraph describing your thoughts or reaction when you saw the Texans' flag.

unite. Austin said that Texans had to stand against the dictatorship of Santa Anna and prepare for the oncoming troops of General Cós.

The Battle of Gonzales. Two weeks before the Consultation was to begin, Texans and Mexican troops clashed at Gonzales. The Battle of Gonzales took place on October 2, 1835. It was the first battle of the Texas Revolution.

The battle began when the Mexican commander at San Antonio, Colonel Ugartechea, sent a force of soldiers to the town. The soldiers, led by Lieutenant Francisco Castañeda, had been ordered to bring back a brass cannon used for protection against the Indians. The Texas force of 160 people, led by Colonel John H. Moore, refused to surrender the cannon. Both sides discussed the issue, but no agreement could be reached.

In the early morning of October 2, the Texas force attacked the Mexicans. The fighting lasted only a few minutes. After one of the Mexican soldiers was killed, Castañeda's troops withdrew and returned to San Antonio. No Texans were killed. The Texans used the cannon in the battle. It was mounted on a wagon and loaded with iron balls and pieces of chain. Flying above the cannon was a white flag bearing the words *Come And Take It.*

The Texans had challenged Mexican military authority at the Battle of Gonzales. Most citizens in Texas now realized that there was no turning back. A war had begun. ○

SPIRIT OF TEXAS

Mary Austin Holley

*T*he role of women has been overlooked in many Texas history books. But historians know that the diaries, letters, and journals of early Texas women provide new understanding of the history of our state. These primary sources reveal attitudes and values that colonial women held when settlement in Texas by people from the United States was just beginning. These accounts of life in early Texas, along with the views of people in other walks of life, give us a broader and more accurate picture of our past history.

One of the widely read accounts of life in colonial Texas was written by a woman named Mary Austin Holley. Mary Holley was a well-educated and highly cultured woman from Connecticut. She traveled throughout the United States, and she kept a journal in which she described all she saw and experienced. At the urging of her cousin Stephen F. Austin, Mary Holley ventured to Texas in 1831. While there, she wrote many letters to friends back home, telling them of life in this new and exciting place.

Mary Austin Holley traveled through much of the United States by horse, stagecoach, train, steamboat—and even on foot. After all her travels, she chose to live in Texas. She saw in the rugged frontier wilderness of Texas a special place. In her own words, "One's feelings in Texas are unique and original, and very like a dream or youthful vision realized."

In 1833, a book was published containing the journal and letters of Mary Austin Holley. Titled *Texas Observations,* it was advertised as the first book published in English about Texas. The book was full of vivid descriptions of the land and people of Texas. In one passage, Mary Holley tells a friend back east what a person can expect to find if moving to Texas:

He will find, here, abundant [plentiful] exercise for all his faculties, both of body and mind, a new stimulus to his exertions [efforts], and a new current for his affections. He may be obliged to labour hard, but riches are a very certain reward for his exertions. He may be generous, without fear of ruin. He will learn to find society in nature, and repose [rest] in solitude, health in exertion, and happiness in occupation. If he have a just ambition, he will glow with generous pride, while he is marking out an untrodden path . . . and founding for himself, and his children after him, a permanent and noble independence.

Holley's book *Texas,* a history, was published in 1836. Many people in the United States read it and, as a result, decided to move to Texas. Because of her writings, Mary Austin Holley was called "first lady ambassador-at-large" for Texas.

Barker Texas History Center

CHAPTER REVIEW RESOURCES
1. Chapter Review Worksheet 11
2. Chapter 11 Test, Form A
3. Reteaching Worksheet 11
4. Chapter 11 Test, Form B
5. **Informal Evaluation Forms:** Portfolio Assessment
6. *Texas, Our Texas* **Test Generator**

Essential Elements
2A, 5B, 8A, 8C, 9A, 9B, 9D

CHAPTER 11 REVIEW ANSWERS

Understanding Main Ideas

1. The Texans wanted democratic rule, while the Mexican government wanted to maintain control of Texas without allowing self-government.
2. He traveled to Texas to find out how Texas and Mexico could maintain peace. He recommended sending more soldiers to Texas and increasing trade with Texas, and he encouraged Mexicans to settle in Texas.
3. The Decree of April 6, 1830; the conflict at Anahuac; the Turtle Bayou Resolutions; the Battle of Velasco
4. They hoped that Mexico would allow immigration from the United States, exempt Texans from some customs duties, provide better protection from the Indians, create a public school system, and appoint a land commissioner for East Texas. Their requests were met. Members of the Convention of 1833 wrote a constitution in the hope that Texas would be made a separate state. This wish was not granted.
5. They believed that his intervention made matters worse.
6. By proving that there was no turning back and that war was certain

CHAPTER 11 REVIEW

Understanding Main Ideas

1. What differences did the Texans and the Mexican government have about Texas?
2. Why did Mier y Terán travel to Texas, and what did he report when he returned to Mexico?
3. What conflicts occurred between 1830 and the fall of 1832 to worsen relations between Mexico and the United States?
4. What did Texans at the Conventions of 1832 and 1833 hope to get from Mexico? How were their hopes met?
5. Why did many Texans disagree with Travis' actions at Anahuac in 1835?
6. How did the Battle of Gonzales unify Texans against Mexico?

Thinking Critically

1. **Exploring Perspectives:** Imagine that you are a high-ranking official of the Mexican government. In your own words, write the Decree of April 6, 1830.
2. **Exploring Economics:** In what ways was trade important to the Texans and to the government of Mexico? How was trade an issue between Texans and Mexico?
3. **Analyzing Information:** What did the Texans' flag at the Battle of Gonzales show about their attitude toward the Mexicans?

Linking History and Geography

1. Study the map on page 227. Notice where most of the important settlements were located. Why do you think many Texans wanted to have a peaceful relationship with Mexico?
2. From what country did most Texans come at the time covered in this chapter? How do you think this fact affected trade between Texas and the United States?

TAAS Practice
Using Primary Sources

On February 4, 1834, the Mexican government issued this decree urging Mexicans to settle in Texas:

NATIONAL DECREE

The Vice President of the Mexican United States, exercising the Supreme Executive Power, and impressed by the necessity of aiding the multitude of persons whose fate has been, and still is, unfortunate . . . finds himself resolved to open its coffers [treasury] to remedy . . . such a pitiful condition. The territories situated next to the boundary line of our Republic . . . open to commerce . . . and extremely fertile, are offering, for robust Mexican arms, and industry, all kinds of things which are unavailable elsewhere. . . . The Republic finds itself plagued with families which, for one reason or another, have lost their fortune and their peace of mind. The Supreme Government invites all of them to better their fate in the peaceful pursuits of agriculture. They will build up their fortunes. They will cause them to forget the errors of their ways, and will convert into useful citizens a multitude of persons . . . driven away from the present towns.

1. The Mexican government says the decree was issued because

Thinking Critically

1. **Exploring Perspectives:** Writings will vary but should be based on knowledge of the decree and the Mexican government's point of view.
2. **Exploring Economics:** Texans needed goods from the United States and Mexico; Mexico earned money from taxes on goods exported to Texas, and it depended on resources from Texas. Texans did not want to pay customs duties, while Mexico needed the money from the duties.
3. **Analyzing Information:** The flag showed that the Texans were willing to challenge the Mexicans.

A   the government of Mexico needed a way to help its poor people

B   Texans wanted more settlers from Mexico

C   the government of Mexico wanted more agriculture in Texas

D   Texas needed more commerce and agriculture

2. The Mexican government hopes that new settlers in Texas

A   will be peaceful and wealthy farmers

B   will become rebels

C   will forget about Mexico

D   will become citizens of the Mexican United States

TAAS Practice
Writing Persuasively

Imagine that you are a Mexican who moved to Texas. Write a letter to Santa Anna, dated after the Battle of Gonzales. Explain to him why you want a democratic government and what you think he should do to make peace with Texas.

Practicing Skills

1. **Sequencing Events:** Make a time line of the major events leading to the Revolution. Include a brief description of each event.
2. **Understanding Point of View:** Study the newspaper advertisement on this page. Who wrote the ad, and why did they write it? What do they hope will be the result of this ad?

Enriching Your Study of History

1. **Individual Project:** Make a map of Texas and Mexico showing the location of important events leading up to the Revolution. Your teacher will display your map in the classroom.
2. **Cooperative Project:** The teacher will divide your class into two groups, the "peace faction" and the "war faction" of the Consultation. Your group will prepare your argument for peace or war. Take into consideration the Battle of Gonzales. Then your faction will hold a class debate with the other.

FREEMEN OF TEXAS

To Arms!!! To Arms!!!

"Now's the day, & now's the hour."

CAMP OF THE VOLUNTEERS,
Friday Night, 11 o'clock
October 2, 1835

Fellow Citizens:—

We have prevailed on [asked] our fellow citizen Wm. H. Wharton, Esq. to return and communicate to you the following express [urgent message], and also to urge as many as can . . . leave their homes to repair to Gonzales immediately, "armed and equipped for war even to the knife." On the receipt of this intelligence [secret information] the Volunteers immediately resolved to march to Gonzales to aid their countrymen. We are just now starting which must apologize for the brevity of this communication. We refer you to Mr. Wharton for an explanation of our wishes, opinions and intentions, and also for such political information as has come into our hands. If Texas will now act promptly; she will soon be redeemed from that worse than Egyptian bondage which now cramps her resources and retards her prosperity.

P.S. An action took place on yesterday at Gonzales, in which the Mexican Commander and several soldiers were slain—no loss on the American side

---

Linking History and Geography

1. Many settlements were near Mexico and located on important roads connecting Mexico and the United States.
2. Most came from the United States. It meant a comfortable trade relationship.

TAAS Practice
Using Primary Sources

1. A
2. D

TAAS Practice
Writing Persuasively

Letters will vary but should focus on the advantages of democratic rule.

Practicing Skills

1. **Sequencing Events:** Time lines should include the Fredonian Rebellion, the Mier y Terán visit, the Decree of April 6, 1830, the conflict at Anahuac, the Turtle Bayou Resolutions, the Battle of Velasco, the Conventions of 1832 and 1833, and the Battle of Gonzales. Descriptions should be based on information from the textbook.
2. **Understanding Point of View:** It was written by men who fought at the Battle of Gonzales. They wanted more men to join them. They hoped that more Texans would join the fight for independence.

Enriching Your Study of History

1. **Individual Project:** Maps will vary but should include the events described in the chapter.
2. **Cooperative Project:** Debates should demonstrate knowledge of issues facing Texans in 1835.

UNIT REVIEW RESOURCES

1. Unit Review Worksheet 4
2. Unit 4 Test, Form A
3. Reteaching Worksheet 4
4. Unit 4 Test, Form B
5. **Informal Evaluation Forms:** Portfolio Assessment
6. *Texas, Our Texas* **Test Generator**

Essential Elements
2H, 5B, 6A, 6B, 7A, 7D, 9A, 9B, 9E

UNIT 4 REVIEW ANSWERS

Connecting Main Ideas

1. Cheap available land
2. Hardships of frontier life, being made to follow the Roman Catholic religion, battles with Indians
3. They were businesspeople who brought settlers to establish colonies in Texas.
4. The Mexican government's demand that the colonists accept the Roman Catholic faith; the Decree of April 6, 1830; and the colonists' desire for a democratic form of government
5. The relationship was generally good. Both groups supported the Mexican Constitution of 1824 and opposed certain policies of the Mexican government.

Practicing Critical Thinking Skills

1. **Synthesizing Information:** They resented the government's collecting of customs duties and prohibiting further immigration from the United States; they preferred the legal system they had in the United States; they resented having to publicly accept the Roman Catholic faith.
2. **Seeing Cause and Effect:** His view was fairly accurate. His reforms resulted in re-

UNIT 4

REVIEW

Connecting Main Ideas

1. What did new colonists like most about Texas?
2. What things about Texas did new colonists like the least?
3. Who were the empresarios, and what was their role in the settling of Texas?
4. What were the sources of conflict with the Mexican government that eventually led Texas colonists to revolt?
5. Describe the relationship between settlers from the United States and Tejanos during the 1820s and 1830s.

Practicing Critical Thinking Skills

1. **Synthesizing Information:** Describe the attitude of Anglo colonists toward the Mexican government (including its local officials), Mexican law, and the Catholic church.
2. **Seeing Cause and Effect:** How accurate was Mier y Terán's view of the situation in Texas? What was the result of the reforms he suggested to the Mexican government?
3. **Exploring Multicultural Perspectives:** Imagine that you are a Tejano planning to attend the Consultation of 1835. Why have you decided to join the war faction that wants to gain Texas' independence from Mexico?

TAAS Practice
Writing Descriptively

Imagine that you are a new settler coming to colonial Texas from Tennessee. You come upon a typical Texas farm, recently cleared from the pine forest. Describe it in a letter to relatives back home.

Exploring Local History

1. On a county map, mark the locations of ten of the oldest buildings in your county. These might include farmsteads, houses in town, industrial buildings, forts, and such. Conduct your research at city or county libraries, or your county historical commission.
2. Ask several adults their opinions of why Texas revolted against Mexico. How much agreement do you find in their answers?

Using Historical Imagination

1. **Individual Project:** Choose some individual mentioned in this unit and research his or her life. Write a brief autobiography as that person.
2. **Cooperative Project:** With a partner, create a detailed drawing of some physical object used in daily life in colonial Texas. This could be a log house, a steamboat, a flintlock rifle, or an article of clothing, for example. Your teacher will display all the students' drawings.

For Extending Your Knowledge

Barker, Eugene C. *The Life of Stephen F. Austin, Founder of Texas, 1793–1836.* Dallas: Cokesbury Press, 1926. Classic early biography of the empresario.

Jenkins, John Holland. *Recollections of Early Texas,* ed. by John Holmes Jenkins III. Austin: University of Texas Press, 1958. Award-winning memoir.

SKILL LESSON

Evaluating Historical Information

To evaluate information means to study information carefully, compare it to other things you know, and then come to a conclusion about it. Is the information accurate or inaccurate? Is it true or false? Is it good or bad?

How to Evaluate Information

Evaluation always involves what is known in sports as a "judgment call," or a personal judgment. Because evaluation is personal, two individuals may evaluate the same information and come to different conclusions about it. Evaluating information, especially historical information, involves these steps:

Study the information carefully. Decide which parts of the information are facts and which parts are the author's own judgments of the events described.

Look for signs of the author's bias. Bias is a kind of evaluation. But it is based not on careful judgment but on prejudice and emotion. Can you detect bias in the author's judgments? Can you determine any reason for the author's being biased on the subject?

Come to your own conclusions. Make your own judgments about the information you are to evaluate. Come to conclusions and be prepared to explain these conclusions to others. Know *why* you have

evaluated the historical information as you have.

Practicing the Skill

Read the following passages from two of Stephen F. Austin's letters, then follow the instructions that follow. Austin's first letter was mailed to his brother-in-law during Austin's eighteen months of imprisonment in Mexico City. (It is also on page 227.) The second letter was sent to Austin's cousin from New Orleans soon after Austin had been released from prison and allowed to leave Mexico.

(Letter One)
I have no idea when I shall be at liberty. . . . It is much in my favor that all remains quiet in Texas. I was confident that no friend of mine would try to get up an excitement but I feared that my enemies would. Such a thing would have increased my difficulty.

(Letter Two)
A great immigration from Kentucky, Tennessee, etc., *each man with his rifle* . . . would be of great use to us—very great indeed. . . . I wish a great immigration this fall and winter from Kentucky, Tennessee, *everywhere; passports or no passports, anyhow.* For fourteen years I have had a hard time of it, but nothing shall daunt my courage or abate my exertions to complete the main object of my labors to *Americanize* Texas. This fall and winter will fix our fate—a great immigration will settle the question.

Write a paragraph explaining the difference in Austin's attitude (and what he says he hopes to see happen) between Letter One and Letter Two.

sentiment among Anglo settlers, which eventually led to the Texas Revolution.
3. **Exploring Multicultural Perspectives:** Answers will vary. A Tejano probably would join the war faction because of opposition to Santa Anna.

TAAS *Practice*
Writing Descriptively
Letters will vary but should demonstrate knowledge of a typical colonial Texas farm.

Exploring Local History
1. Maps should demonstrate careful research of local history.
2. Responses will vary but will probably emphasize the invasion of Texas by Santa Anna.

Using Historical Imagination
1. **Individual Project:** Autobiographies will vary but should demonstrate careful research.
2. **Cooperative Project:** Drawings will vary but should be accurate and detailed.

Skill Lesson
Practicing the Skill
Explanations will vary. The first letter may have been written before Austin concluded that Santa Anna was becoming an absolute ruler and that Texans had no choice but to resist him.

INTRODUCING THE UNIT

Connecting with Past Learning

Review with students the characteristics of facts and opinions. Ask them to recall what they already know about the Texas Revolution and the years of the Texas Republic. On a large sheet of paper or poster board, list their statements under the headings *Facts* and *Opinions*. Display the lists throughout the study of the unit. After completing the unit, have students assess the accuracy of their classifications.

UNIT 5 OVERVIEW

Unit 5 focuses on Texas' fight for independence, its efforts to form a new government, and its years as a new nation. Chapter 12 details the progress of the battles of the Texas Revolution and the victory at San Jacinto. The Texans' attempts to create a new government are outlined.

Chapter 13 describes the years of Texas as an independent republic. The problems facing the new nation are explored, along with the different policies of the Republic's four presidents. The nation's effort to achieve recognition from foreign countries also is discussed.

UNIT 5
THE REPUBLIC OF TEXAS

Materials Available at the Unit Level:
Unit 5   Making Global Connections
Oral History Handbook
Informal Evaluation Forms

Ask students to identify persons whom they consider to be modern heroes. Have them brainstorm the characteristics of a heroic person and list these on the chalkboard. Ask: Do all heroes have the same characteristics? Explain that Unit 5 discusses many persons who are remembered as heroes in Texas history. Tell students to think about the characteristics of heroes as they study the unit. After completing the unit, have them review their list of characteristics and make revisions if necessary.

TEXAS AND THE WORLD

Organize the class into small groups, and have the groups study the time line on this page. Select one of the world events, and ask students to brainstorm about how that event is related to events in Texas. Ask volunteers to share their group's answer. Continue the activity for other key events on the time line.

*I*n the early morning hours of March 6, 1836, Mexican soldiers under the command of General Santa Anna attacked the small Texas army in San Antonio. The ferocity of the fighting is depicted in Henry A. McArdle's painting opposite, *Dawn at the Alamo*. The battle is perhaps the most famous in Texas history, but it was only one of many in the Texas struggle for independence.

After its freedom was won, Texas became an independent country. The Republic of Texas existed from 1836 to 1845. Texans faced many challenges in the years of the Republic. Conflicts with Mexico continued. Indian wars broke out as Texans moved into new lands. A government had to be organized for the new country. Policies of government had to be set and ways found to pay the new country's debts.

Texans found solutions to their problems, and the country continued to grow. Thousands of new settlers entered the Republic to find land and seek opportunity.

Unit 5 is about one of the most exciting periods in the long history of Texas. Chapter 12 discusses not only the Battle of the Alamo but the other events of the Texas revolution against Mexico. Chapter 13 begins after Texas won independence and discusses the period when it was an independent country.

UNIT 5 OBJECTIVES

1. List and describe the opening battles of the Texas Revolution.
2. Discuss the purpose and results of the Consultation of 1835.
3. Describe the Battle of the Alamo and its legacy in Texas history.
4. Discuss the significance of the Consultation of 1835 and the Convention of 1836.
5. Describe the Battle of San Jacinto, and explain its significance in Texas history.
6. Discuss the early years of the Republic of Texas and that nation's relations with Mexico.
7. Compare and contrast the policies of the Republic's presidents, including those regarding Indian affairs.
8. Identify the Republic's successes and failures in establishing foreign relations.

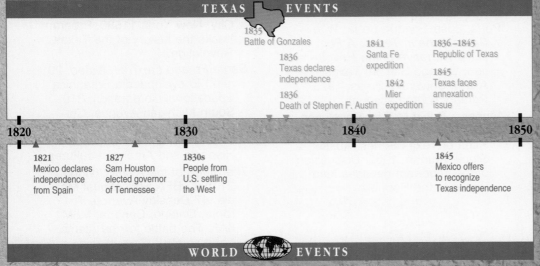

TEXAS EVENTS

1835
Battle of Gonzales

1836
Texas declares
independence

1836
Death of Stephen F. Austin

1841
Santa Fe
expedition

1842
Mier
expedition

1836–1845
Republic of Texas

1845
Texas faces
annexation
issue

1820   1830   1840   1850

1821
Mexico declares
independence
from Spain

1827
Sam Houston
elected governor
of Tennessee

1830s
People from
U.S. settling
the West

1845
Mexico offers
to recognize
Texas independence

WORLD EVENTS

CHAPTER 12

REVOLUTION AND INDEPENDENCE

TEACHER'S TIME LINE

Section 1	Section 2	Section 3	Sections 4–5	Section 6	Review and Assessment
Pp. 238–42	Pp. 242–44	Pp. 244–50	Pp. 250–55	Pp. 255–58	
1 Day	1 Day	1 Day	1 Day	1 Day	1 Day

TEACHER MATERIALS

Core: Chapter 12 Time Line; Graphic Organizer 12; Enrichment Worksheet 12; Review Worksheet 12; Reteaching Worksheet 12; Chapter 12 Tests, Forms A & B

Additional: Geography and Graph Skills 12; Map and Chart Transparencies 22, 14; Informal Evaluation Forms; Test Generator

OBJECTIVES

1. List and describe the major battles of the Texas Revolution and their outcomes.
2. Identify historical figures who played key roles in the Texas Revolution.
3. Discuss the Consultation of 1835 and the Convention of 1836.
4. Explain the function of the three branches of government created by the Texas Constitution.
5. Identify the major principles that underlie the Texas Declaration of Independence, Constitution, and Bill of Rights.

RESOURCES

BOOKS FOR TEACHERS

Adair, Anthony Garland. *Heroes of the Alamo*. New York: Exposition Press, 1957. Story of the siege at the Alamo.

Binkley, William C. *The Texas Revolution*. Austin: Texas State Historical Association, 1979. Important events shaping the Texas Revolution.

Castañeda, Carlos E. *The Mexican Side of the Texas Revolution*. Austin: Graphic Ideas, 1970. The Texas Revolution told from Mexico's point of view.

King, Richard C. *Susanna Dickinson: Messenger of the Alamo*. Austin: Shoal Creek Publishers, 1976. Story of this survivor.

Lord, Walter. *A Time to Stand: The Epic of the Alamo*. Lincoln: University of Nebraska Press, 1961. Story of the Alamo.

Pēna, José Enrique de la. *With Santa Anna in Texas: A Personal Narrative of the Revolution*. College Station: Texas A & M University Press, 1975. Primary source account.

Vigness, David M. *The Revolutionary Decades, 1810–1836*. The Saga of Texas Series. Austin: Steck-Vaughn, 1965. Discussion of the important decades leading up to the Republic.

MULTIMEDIA MATERIALS

The Fight for Texas. (software) Focus Media Inc., 839 Stewart Avenue, P.O. Box 865, Garden City, New York, 11530. Program tracks the history of the Texas Revolution.

Santa Fe and the Trail. (video, 20 min.) Encyclopaedia Britannica Educational Corporation, 310 South Michigan Avenue, Chicago, Illinois, 60604. Portrayal of cultural interface between Hispanic and American cultures.

The Siege of the Alamo. (video, 21 min.) BFA Educational Media, 47 Densley Avenue, Toronto, Ontario, Canada, M6M 5A8. The battle for the Alamo.

Limited English Proficient Students (LEP)

Pair LEP students with students who are proficient in English. Have the pairs skim the chapter to find the boldfaced vocabulary terms. Students should write the terms on one side of a series of index cards. They should write the terms' definitions on the opposite sides of the cards. Have students use the cards as flashcards until students in each pair have mastered the vocabulary. See other activities labeled **LEP.**

Students Having Difficulty with the Chapter

Have students use the information in the chapter to create a chart of the major battles of the Texas Revolution. Headings should include: *Battle, Location, Date, Mexican Leader(s), Texan Leader(s), Outcome, Significance.* **LEP**

Auditory Learners

Have auditory learners select and research one of the heroes of the Revolution and give an oral report. See other activities labeled **A.**

Visual Learners

Have students work together to prepare a large wall map showing the battles of the Texas Revolution. Ask them to indicate on the map, when possible, troop movements and to distinguish between Mexican and Texan forces. Display the map in the classroom. See other activities labeled **V.**

Tactile/Kinesthetic Learners

Have students create a booklet or a poster titled "Who's Who in the Texas Revolution." Students should prepare biographical sketches of famous persons and assemble them in book form or as a classroom poster. See other activities labeled **TK.**

Gifted Students

Have students locate copies of Texas' Declaration of Independence and Constitution and those of the United States. Ask them to prepare a report identifying the similarities and differences between the documents of the two nations. See other activities labeled **G.**

VOCABULARY

In addition to the boldfaced terms in each section, some students might benefit from discussing the meanings of these terms.

Section 1: *disband* (p. 239); *artillery* (p. 239); *mourned* (p. 241).
Section 2: *citizenship* (p. 243).
Section 3: *revenge* (p. 246); *humanity* (p. 250).
Section 4: *chaired* (p. 250); *importation* (p. 252).
Section 5: *escorted* (p. 253); *smoldering* (p. 253); *executed* (p. 254).
Section 6: *sentries* (p. 257); *subdued* (p. 258); *gesture* (p. 258); *compassion* (p. 258).

CHRONOLOGY

Have students study the Chapter 12 Time Line and identify relationships among the events.

GRAPHIC ORGANIZER

Have students skim the chapter and complete the Chapter 12 Graphic Organizer. *(You might wish to use this activity to review rather than to introduce the chapter.)*

ENRICHMENT

Have students complete the Chapter 12 Enrichment Worksheet.

SECTION 1

FOCUS

Past Learning (I) Have students recall the Battle of Gonzales. Ask students to explain the significance of the battle. *(Texans realized that there was no turning back. It was the beginning of the war.)*

INSTRUCTION

Vocabulary (I) You may wish to preteach the following boldfaced terms: *strategy* (p. 239); *reinforcements* (p. 239). **LEP**

CHAPTER 12 OVERVIEW

After the Battle of Gonzales, most Texans were ready to fight to resolve their differences with Santa Anna. General Cós made it clear that he considered the actions of the Texans at Gonzales to be a declaration of war. Chapter 12 tells how Texas began to govern itself and sets forth the battles of the Texas Revolution. The chapter relates the dramatic story of sacrifice and determination on the part of the people of Texas.

Essential Elements
2C, 2H, 5B, 7A, 7D, 9A, 9B

CHAPTER 12

REVOLUTION AND INDEPENDENCE

The Story Continues...

The Battle of Gonzales marked the beginning of the Texas Revolution. Chapter 12 tells the story of that revolution, from the occupying of Goliad by the Mexican army to the fall of the Alamo to the Texans' final victory at San Jacinto. The fight for Texas independence lasted only a few months, but it was a bitter struggle. In the end a new nation, the Republic of Texas, was born.

As you read the chapter, look for the answers to these questions:

1. What happened in the Battle of San Antonio?
2. What did the Consultation accomplish?
3. What were the results of the siege of the Alamo?
4. What was accomplished by the Convention of 1836?
5. What defeats did the Texans suffer following the fall of the Alamo?
6. What happened at the Battle of San Jacinto?

Gonzales Historical Museum

Ben Milam assisted in the attack and capture of Mexican forces at Goliad.

1 Opening Battles

The Battle of Gonzales followed the trouble between Texans and the Mexican officials in Anahuac. Because of these troubles, General Martín Perfecto de Cós decided to send more troops into Texas. These new troops landed at Copano on the Gulf coast and marched through Goliad to San Antonio.

The Capture of Goliad. General Cós left 30 soldiers to guard Goliad. On the night of October 9, 1835, a force of 50 Texans under the command of George Collinsworth, assisted by Ben Milam, attacked the Mexican garrison. A brief fight occurred, and one Mexican soldier was killed. The rest of the garrison, outnumbered and surrounded, surrendered to the Texans.

The victory at Goliad was important to the Texans in a number of ways. It gave Texans more confidence and encouraged more of them to join the army. The Texans also captured much-needed ammunition and arms at the Goliad fort. The Texas army seized 300 muskets, two cannons, and $10,000 worth of military supplies. Of equal importance was the location of Goliad. Capturing Goliad cut off the supply route between Copano and General Cós in San Antonio.

Despite the sudden success of the Texans at Gonzales and Goliad, they knew that the major contest would be at San Antonio. There, General Cós and the Mexican army were waiting. Texans began to organize at Gonzales for the coming attack.

The March on San Antonio. As volunteers poured into Gonzales, the Texans attempted to organize into army units. At first, there were disagreements in selecting commanders for the military companies. For a brief period, these disagreements over who would control the army and make decisions nearly caused the Texas forces to disband. Then Stephen F. Austin arrived in camp, and he was chosen to be commander-in-chief.

Austin was not a trained military leader, but he had the respect of most Texans. Once he had established order and organized the 600 volunteers into companies, plans were made to attack General Cós at San Antonio. The march to San Antonio began October 12, 1835. Austin and his army set up camp on the outskirts of the city in late October to talk about their **strategy**, or military plans.

One minor battle occurred on October 28. A force of 90 Texans led by James W. Fannin and James Bowie was sent ahead to find a campsite nearer to San Antonio. About a mile from Mission Concepción, they were attacked by 400 Mexican soldiers. In the battle, the Texans won a quick and clear victory.

Like the capture of Goliad, this victory boosted the Texans' confidence. When Austin and the rest of the Texans arrived at Mission Concepción, many wanted to attack General Cós in San Antonio immediately. But Austin and Bowie decided to wait for **reinforcements**, or additional troops. Because the Mexicans at San Antonio had more soldiers and artillery than the Texans, the delay proved to be a wise move.

The Grass Fight. While part of the Texas army remained at Mission Concepción, Austin and the other

Archives Division, Texas State Library

James W. Fannin moved to Texas in 1834. Along with Bowie, he commanded the victorious Texas army at the Battle of Concepción in October 1835. He was later shot, along with hundreds of other Texans, at the massacre at Goliad.

Texans moved their camp to the Old Mill. This mill was located about a half mile from the main plaza in San Antonio. Austin then left to go to the United States as a diplomatic agent to seek help. Edward Burleson took command of the Texas forces stationed at the Old Mill.

On November 26, one of Burleson's scouts, Erastus "Deaf" Smith, rode into camp with the news that Mexican soldiers were bringing horses and mules to San Antonio. Deaf Smith and the other Texans believed that the soldiers were bringing silver so that General Cós could pay his troops. About 100 Texans ambushed the Mexicans and captured their horses and mules.

When the Texans opened the bags that supposedly held silver, they were greatly disappointed. The bags contained only grass to feed the hungry horses of General Cós' army. Out of frustration, the Texans burned the grass and then returned to camp. This incident became known afterwards as the Grass Fight.

Victory at San Antonio. After the Grass Fight, the Texans became discouraged. They knew that they did not have enough soldiers or weapons to defeat General Cós,

In this painting by Henry McArdle, Ben Milam is leading the call for volunteers in the attack on the Mexican army at San Antonio. The Mexican forces under General Cós were defeated in the Battle of San Antonio and were forced to leave Texas.

Daughters of the Republic of Texas, the Alamo

RETEACHING
Have each student make up a matching review with ten to fifteen names and identifications from Section 1. Ask students to exchange and complete the reviews. Then have partners work together to correct and discuss the answers. **LEP**

CLOSURE
Review with students the outcome of the Battle of San Antonio and the reasons for the Texans' feelings of optimism.

ASSESSMENT
Have students complete the Section 1 Review on page 242.

and winter was coming on. Many of the volunteers were worried about their families at home and began to leave camp. Colonel Burleson and the Texans agreed to withdraw from San Antonio and return to Gonzales and Goliad.

On the next day, however, a captured Mexican soldier was brought into camp. The soldier reported to Colonel Burleson that the Mexican army in San Antonio was weak and disorganized. The soldiers were suffering from a lack of supplies. He claimed that the troops of General Cós could not defeat the Texans.

Upon hearing that report, Colonel Ben Milam shouted to the Texans, "Who will go with old Ben Milam into San Antonio?" Three hundred people answered Milam's call and gathered that night at the Old Mill. Ben Milam and Francis W. Johnson each took command of a group for the attack on San Antonio.

The Texans attacked on December 5, 1835. For the next four days, the battle raged for control of San Antonio. The Texans fought from house to house, slowly driving the Mexican forces into retreat.

On the third day of the attack, Milam was killed. Johnson took over the command of both groups of Texans. On December 9, the Mexican forces had been driven from the center of the town and into the abandoned San Antonio de Valero mission, also known as the Alamo. Even though General Cós had received reinforcements that same day, he decided to surrender. On December 10, the Mexican army agreed to the terms demanded by the Texans. General Cós agreed not to interfere with Texans in their fight to restore the Constitution of 1824. Cós was then allowed to lead the Mexican army out of Texas. All public property and military supplies were turned over to the Texans.

The Battle of San Antonio had been a long struggle with many heroic acts. All Texans mourned the death of Ben Milam and praised the others who had fought bravely. Colonel Burleson and Francis Johnson were recognized for their leadership. Appreciation was shown the many Tejanos who joined in the fight. Two black Texans, Hendrick Arnold and Greenberry Logan, were singled out for their heroic contributions. In the battle, Logan received a wound that left him crippled for the rest of his life.

Many Texans believed that the victory at San Antonio would end the fighting. The defeat of General Cós and his troops left Texas free of Mexican soldiers. The Texans

Painting by Thorgh, Institute of Texan Cultures, from Original in Texas State Capitol

Edward Burleson was elected colonel of a regiment organized by Stephen F. Austin. When Austin went to the United States for aid, Burleson took over command of the regiment.

Biography
Ben Milam was born in Kentucky in 1788. He was a veteran of the War of 1812, and after that war, he traded goods with the Comanches. In 1819, he was involved in the filibustering activities of James Long. After Long's death, Milam became a Mexican citizen and joined the Mexican army. During the Texas Revolution, Milam joined the Texas volunteers shortly before the attack on La Bahía.

SECTION 2

FOCUS

Predicting (I) Write the term *consultation* on the chalk-board. Ask the students to speculate about a definition. You might begin by asking them to define *consult*. Ask a volunteer to find the term's definition in a dictionary and read it aloud.

INSTRUCTION

Vocabulary (I) You may wish to preteach the following bold-faced term: *provisional* (p. 243). **LEP**

Writing (II) Have students write a persuasive argument for or against declaring independence from Mexico. Arguments should incorporate the point of view of both the war and the peace factions. Invite students to read their arguments aloud. **A**

Answers to Section 1 Review

Define: *strategy*—military plans; *reinforcements*—additional troops

Identify: Ben Milam—Texas colonel who sparked the Texas assault on San Antonio; Edward Burleson—took command of the Texas forces at San Antonio after Stephen Austin left for the United States; Deaf Smith—scout for Burleson who participated in the Grass Fight; Greenberry Logan—African American who was wounded in the fight for San Antonio

1. It boosted the Texans' confidence. They captured much-needed arms and cut off General Cós' supply route.
2. The bags on the Mexicans' horses and mules turned out to carry only grass instead of silver.
3. Cós agreed not to interfere with the Texans in their fight to restore the Constitution of 1824 and to lead the Mexican army out of Texas. All public property and military supplies were turned over to the Texans.

Analyzing Informaton: It had more soldiers and artillery than the Texas army.

Evaluating Information: They were untrained, quarreled over leadership, and were undisciplined. As volunteers, they felt free to go home at any time.

Essential Elements
2B, 2C, 2H, 3E, 7D, 9A

242 *Unit 5*

Hendrick Arnold and Greenberry Logan fought heroically at the Battle of San Antonio.

SECTION ★ 1 REVIEW

Define: strategy, reinforcements
Identify: Ben Milam, Edward Burleson, Deaf Smith, Greenberry Logan

1. Why was victory at the Battle of Goliad important for the Texas cause?
2. How did the Grass Fight get its name?
3. What terms did General Cós agree to after the capture of San Antonio by the Texans?

Analyzing Information: What were the strengths of General Cós' army in San Antonio that made Texan leaders Austin and Bowie wait before attacking it?

Evaluating Information: From your reading of this section, what do you think were the main weaknesses of the Texans as a fighting force?

Painting by Kermit Oliver. Institute of Texan Cultures

went wild in celebration. Many believed they could now become a separate state within Mexico and operate under the laws of the Constitution of 1824. But Santa Anna had different ideas. The ruler of Mexico was gathering an army south of the Rio Grande to destroy the Texas rebellion. He would personally lead the attack. ⊙

▣ The Consultation and Its Work

While the Texas army was fighting at San Antonio, the convention known as the Consultation had assembled. The first session of the Consultation opened on November 3, 1835, at San Felipe de Austin. Branch T. Archer was elected president of the Consultation. During the Consultation, 58 delegates attended one or more meetings.

Debating War and Peace. Debate at the Consultation first centered around arguments over the reasons for the Texas rebellion. The war faction delegates argued that Texas should declare its independence from Mexico. The peace faction claimed that Texas should remain a part of Mexico. They stated that the reason Texans rebelled against Santa Anna was to restore the Constitution of 1824.

When the question came to a vote, the peace faction won. It was led by Sam Houston. This decision of the

Guided Practice (I) Tell students to imagine themselves as newspaper reporters observing the Consultation of 1835. Have them write an article outlining the convention's events. Tell students that as newspaper reporters they must remain neutral. **LEP**

EXTENSION

Role Playing (III) Invite several students to role play the peace treaty negotiations that took place among Sam Houston, William Goyens, and the Cherokees of East Texas. Encourage students to conduct additional research in order to address the exact terms of the treaty, Goyens' role as an agent of Mexico, and reasons for the Cherokees agreeing to remain neutral in the conflict between Texas and Mexico. **V, G, A**

Consultation was stated in the famous Declaration of the People of Texas on November 7, 1835. In this document the delegates pledged their loyalty to Mexico and the Constitution of 1824. They explained that they had used force only to defend themselves against Santa Anna. To encourage supporters from both Mexico and the United States, the delegates offered land and citizenship to anyone who joined them in the revolt against Santa Anna.

The Provisional Government. The next order of business for the Consultation was to create a government. It was considered a **provisional**, or temporary, government because it would govern only until problems with Mexico were straightened out. The Consultation elected Henry Smith provisional governor and James Robinson provisional lieutenant governor. Both were members of the war faction. Sam Houston was selected as commander-in-chief of the army. Three commissioners were chosen to travel to the United States to recruit volunteers for the army and to raise money. They were Stephen F. Austin, William Wharton, and Branch T. Archer.

The Consultation also created a council of delegates to help the provisional government. Because the duties of the council were not clearly defined, problems arose. Disagreements between Governor Smith and the council brought the provisional government to a halt. Governor Smith questioned the loyalty of many of the Tejanos and argued for immediate independence. Many members of the council were from the peace faction. They disliked Smith's attitude.

Sam Houston faced problems also. The provisional government had appointed him commander of the army, but Houston had no army to command. Texas had no power to raise an army and no money to pay soldiers. The volunteer soldiers fighting at San Antonio were under the command of Francis Johnson. A disagreement arose over a plan to attack Matamoros in northern Mexico. Houston opposed the attack, but others went ahead with plans to carry it out.

While the council and Governor Smith argued, Sam Houston and William Goyens went to East Texas to negotiate a peace treaty with the Cherokees. Goyens, an African American businessman, was an Indian agent appointed by the Mexican government. By the terms of the treaty, the Cherokees agreed to remain neutral in the conflict between the Texans and the Mexicans.

Barker Texas History Center

TEXAS!!

Emigrants who are desirous of assisting Texas at this important crisis of her affairs may have a free passage and equipments, by applying at the **NEW-YORK and PHILADELPHIA HOTEL,** On the Old Levee, near the Blue Stores.

Now is the time to ensure a fortune in Land: To all who remain in Texas during the War will be allowed 1280 Acres.
To all who remain Six Months, 640 Acres.
To all who remain Three Months, 320 Acres.
And as Colonists, 4600 Acres for a family and 1470 Acres for a Single Man.

New Orleans, April 23d, 1836.

Appeals were posted in the United States, encouraging volunteers to come to the aid of Texas in exchange for land.

Historical Sidelight
Matamoros was the principal outlet for trade in the lower Rio Grande region. Some Texans believed that much of what is now northern Mexico might break away and join Texas against the Mexican government. Exiled Mexican leaders encouraged an invasion attempt.

Independent Practice (II) Ask students to list the problems that existed within Texas' provisional government. Then have them choose one of the problems and develop a possible solution. Invite volunteers to share their ideas with the class. **A**

RETEACHING

Have volunteers summarize in note form the results of the Consultation of 1835 on the chalkboard. Ask the class to vote whether the convention was a success and tell why or why not. **LEP, A**

CLOSURE

Tell students that the Texans were unprepared for Santa Anna's army. Have them keep the following question in mind as they begin Section 3: Would it have made a difference had they had more time to prepare?

ASSESSMENT

Have students complete the Section 2 Review on page 244.

Answers to Section 2 Review

Define: *provisional*—temporary
Identify: Branch T. Archer—elected president of the Consultation of 1835; Henry Smith—elected provisional governor by the Consultation; Sam Houston—elected commander-in-chief of the Texas army by the Consultation; William Goyens—African American businessman and Indian agent who helped Houston negotiate a treaty with the Cherokees

1. A provisional government was set up to govern until the trouble with Mexico ended. Delegates pledged their loyalty to Mexico and the Constitution of 1824.
2. At first the delegates argued over reasons for the Texas rebellion. The war faction wanted Texas to declare its independence from Mexico. The peace faction wanted Texas to stay a part of Mexico. Later, the delegates argued over whether or not to attack Matamoros in northern Mexico.

(Continued on page 245)

Essential Elements
2C, 2H, 7A, 9A, 9B, 9D, 9F, 9G

In this painting, William Goyens and Sam Houston are pictured trying to work out a peaceful settlement with the Cherokees of East Texas. Both Goyens and Houston were well trusted by the Cherokees.

SECTION ★ 2 REVIEW

Define: provisional
Identify: Branch T. Archer, Henry Smith, Sam Houston, William Goyens

1. What happened at the Consultation of 1835?
2. What did the two factions argue about during the Consultation?
3. Why did Houston and Goyens meet with the East Texas Cherokees?

Analyzing Information: Explain why the name *peace faction*, used for one group at the Consultation, might be thought of as an inappropriate term.

Using Historical Imagination: Imagine that you are a military expert from Great Britain attending the Consultation as a neutral observer. Do you think it is likely that the Texans will achieve a military victory over Mexico? Why or why not?

Painting by Kermit Oliver. Institute of Texan Cultures

From November 1835 until March 1836, there was confusion in the provisional government of Texas. Texas did not have a clear policy or capable leadership. Stephen F. Austin, the person the Texans always depended upon in times of trouble, was in the United States to rally support for the Texans' cause. While Texans were arguing among themselves, Santa Anna was on the move.

A new convention was scheduled to meet on March 1, 1836. The Texans believed they had plenty of time to prepare for war. But Santa Anna had crossed the Rio Grande in early February and was headed for San Antonio. The most dramatic event in all of Texas history was about to unfold. ○

❸ The Siege of the Alamo

Mexican forces moving north into Texas were organized into three groups. The two most important of these were commanded by Santa Anna and General José Urrea. Santa Anna was leading his forces to San Antonio while General Urrea's army marched along the Gulf coast toward Goliad and Victoria. Texas forces were scattered in small groups, some organized for an attack on Matamoros. Colonel James Neill had about 100 troops in San Antonio. More than 400 soldiers were in Goliad under the command of James

SECTION ■3

FOCUS

Student Experiences (I) Write the following names on the chalkboard: *William Travis, James Bowie, Davy Crockett.* Ask students: With what do we generally associate these names *(the Alamo)?* Invite volunteers to tell what they know about the famous battle at the Alamo.

INSTRUCTION

Vocabulary (I) You may wish to preteach the following boldfaced term: *siege* (p. 246). **LEP**

Analysis (I) Organize students into groups of four or five. Ask students to discuss and vote on the following question: Considering the outcome of the battle, should Colonel Travis have chosen to fight or surrender at the Alamo? Have a spokesperson from each group give the group's final vote and present its reasoning. **A, LEP**

Fannin. Colonel Francis Johnson and James Grant had more than 100 troops at San Patricio, but the Texans were unprepared for an advance by the Mexican army.

Before the Battle. Sam Houston knew that Santa Anna was on the march. He was alarmed that the Texans were so unprepared and disorganized. On January 17, he ordered James Bowie to go to San Antonio. Bowie was to destroy the Alamo, remove all weapons and ammunition, and withdraw Texas forces there. This action would allow the Texans time to strengthen their army.

When Bowie arrived at San Antonio, he and Colonel James Neill agreed that the Alamo was too important to leave undefended. They disobeyed Houston's orders. Bowie explained their actions to Governor Smith in a letter on February 2: "Colonel Neill and myself have come to the solemn resolution that we would rather die in these ditches than give it up to the enemy."

Meanwhile, reinforcements began to arrive in San Antonio. Colonel William Travis and 30 soldiers rode in from San Felipe de Austin. Juan Seguín and ten other Tejanos were among the defenders. James Bonham and a group from Gonzales also joined the Texas force. Bonham had come to Texas with a group of volunteers from Alabama known as the Mobile Grays.

Thirteen volunteers from Tennessee rode into San Antonio a few days after Travis arrived. They were led by David Crockett. Crockett was a famous frontiersman who was nearly a legend in the United States. Once a member of the United States Congress, Davy Crockett was well known for standing up for a just cause. He had heard about the Texas rebellion, and he believed that the Texans were right in opposing Santa Anna.

After Colonel Neill left the Alamo to care for an ill family member, Travis and Bowie were left in command. Both had strong personalities, and they quarreled over who was in charge. When Bowie became ill, command of the Alamo went to Colonel Travis.

The Mexicans Advance. The first part of Santa Anna's army arrived in San Antonio on February 23, 1836. The Texans were caught by surprise. Travis and Bowie had thought that the cold and rainy weather would delay the Mexicans for at least three more weeks. They had underestimated the anger and determination of Santa Anna.

Institute of Texan Cultures, from Original in Texas State Capitol

James Bowie came to Texas in 1828. He became a colonel in the Texas Rangers. During the siege of the Alamo, Bowie was stricken with typhoid-pneumonia and fought Santa Anna's final charge from his cot.

12 TEXAS IMMORTALS by Lajos Markos

Colonel William B. Travis was only 26 years old when he became the commander of the Texas forces at the Alamo. His appeal for aid in the letter of February 24 has been described as one of the most heroic documents in American history. He died, along with the others, defending the Alamo.

3. To negotiate a treaty in which the the Cherokees would agree to remain neutral in the conflict between Texas and Mexico

Analyzing Information: This group was willing to go to war to defend Texas from the forces of Santa Anna.

Using Historical Imagination: Answers will vary; however, students should note that the Texans were untrained and disorganized. When Sam Houston was made commander-in-chief he had no army yet, whereas Santa Anna's forces were already on their way.

Historical Sidelight

Davy Crockett refused Travis' offer of a position of authority. Calling himself a "high private," Crockett told Travis, "Assign me some place, and I and my Tennessee boys will defend it all right."

Synthesis (II) Organize the class into four groups, each representing one of the following subsections from Section 3: "Before the Battle," "The Mexicans Advance," "The Siege Begins," "The Fall of the Alamo." Tell students that they will "teach" a class about the Alamo, focusing on their assigned topic. Allow each group time to prepare its presentation. Suggest that students incorporate into their presentations wall maps, diagrams drawn on the chalkboard, illustrations from the textbook, and so on. Allow the rest of the class to ask questions of each group. **A, V, TK, G**

Caption Response
They were firing platforms.

Transparency 22
A transparency of this diagram can be found in the Teacher's Resource Binder.

Santa Anna wanted revenge for the defeat of General Cós. He pushed his troops hard to achieve it quickly and completely.

As the Mexican army marched into the city, Travis ordered all the Texans into the Alamo. Food, ammunition, and other supplies were gathered. Cannons were mounted on the walls around the old mission. The Texans expected a **siege**, with the Mexican army surrounding them to force their surrender. The area enclosed by the buildings and walls of the Alamo was more than two acres. An area that size required about 1,000 soldiers to defend it properly. The Texas soldiers in the Alamo at this time numbered little more than 150.

Santa Anna and the remainder of his force arrived just after the Texans were safely inside the walls of the Alamo. At a meeting between the two sides, Santa Anna demanded that the Texans surrender. The response of the Texans was clear. Travis ordered a cannon shot fired toward the Mexican army. The siege of the Alamo was under way.

The Siege Begins. On February 24, the fighting began. Mexican cannons bombarded the Alamo for hours at a

What was the purpose of the wooden platforms at the corners and far end of the Mission Square?

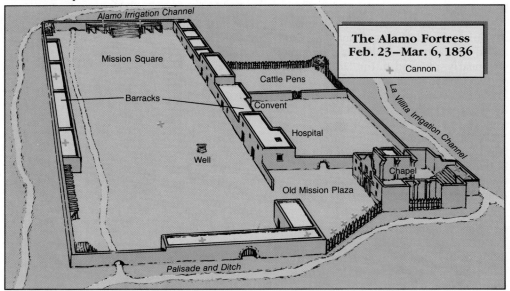

The Alamo Fortress
Feb. 23–Mar. 6, 1836
+ Cannon

Brainstorming (I) Have the class brainstorm to answer the following questions: What should Colonel Travis have done differently at the Alamo? Was there a way the Texas forces could have escaped the siege? **A, LEP**

Guided Practice (I) Tell students to imagine that they are one of the men and women spared by Santa Anna at the Alamo. Ask them to write a letter to a relative in the United States, explaining the events of the siege as they unfolded. **LEP**

time. Occasionally the Texans fired back. But they saved most of their ammunition because they expected a full attack. On the evening of February 24, Travis wrote his famous plea for help in a letter "To the People of Texas & all Americans in the world." The letter was a request for aid in the face of certain death:

> Commandancy of the Alamo—
> Bejar, Fby. 24th 1836—
>
> To the People of Texas & all Americans in the world—
>
> Fellow Citizens—& compatriots—
>
> I am besieged, by a thousand or more of the Mexicans under Santa Anna—I have sustained a continual Bombardment & cannonade for 24 hours & have not lost a man—The enemy has demanded a surrender at discretion, otherwise, the garrison are to be put to the sword, if the fort is taken—I have answered the demand with a cannon shot, & our flag still waves proudly from the walls—I shall never surrender or retreat. Then, I call on you in the name of Liberty, of patriotism & everything dear to the American character, to come to our aid, with all dispatch—The enemy is receiving reinforcements daily & will no doubt increase to three or four thousand in four or five days. If this call is neglected, I am determined to sustain myself as long as possible & die like a soldier who never forgets what is due to his own honor & that of his country—
>
> VICTORY OR DEATH
> William Barret Travis
>
> Lt. Col. comdt.
>
> P.S. The Lord is on our side—when the enemy appeared in sight we had not three bushels of corn—we have since found in deserted houses 80 or 90 bushels and got into the walls 20 or 30 heads of Beeves.
>
> Travis

Painting by C. B. Normann, Archives Division, Texas State Library

James Bonham came to Texas at his friend William Travis' request. He may have arrived at the Alamo in company with James Bowie.

Travis sent out several more requests for help. On February 25, Juan Seguín and Antonio Cruz Arocha rode through the Mexican lines in an attempt to reach Sam Houston. The next day, James Bonham escaped through Santa Anna's forces to seek help from Colonel Fannin at Goliad. He returned without Fannin. Later, Bonham passed through Mexican lines a second time to seek help and again returned safely to the Alamo.

Finally, on March 1, some help did arrive. Thirty-two volunteers from Gonzales rode into the Alamo under cover

Vocabulary

Explain to students that the "Beeves" mentioned in Travis' postscript refer to beef cattle.

EXTENSION

Research (II) Have students research to find out more about the heroes of the Alamo. Ask them to present their findings in the form of biographical sketches that can be displayed along with illustrations of the Alamo and monuments honoring those who died for Texas' independence. **V, TK**

Independent Practice (I) Tell students that they have been chosen to write the inscription for the historical marker at the Alamo. Point out that their inscriptions should be descriptive but brief. Invite volunteers to read their inscriptions aloud. **A, LEP**

of early morning darkness. They were led by Captain Albert Martin. Yet because there would be no other help, it became obvious to the Texans that they were doomed. They had between 182 and 188 soldiers. The Mexican forces numbered more than 5,000.

During most of the siege, both sides watched and waited. There were long breaks between bursts of gunfire, though the Mexican cannons pounded the thick limestone walls of the Alamo regularly. The Texans were kept busy repairing damaged walls, building cannon platforms, and sneaking out for supplies or to try to get help. At night the Texans could see the Mexican soldiers gathered around their campfires. They often heard music coming from the Mexican camp. One Mexican soldier reported that he saw Davy Crockett standing on the wall playing his fiddle. No doubt, soldiers on both sides were thinking of home and more peaceful days.

Travis made one last appeal for help on March 3 in a letter to the delegates at the convention meeting at Washington-on-the-Brazos. A famous Texas legend claims that later that day, Travis gave his troops a choice. He took his sword and drew a line on the ground. Those who wished to stay and defend the Alamo were asked to cross over the line. All but one person crossed the line to face certain death. Whether the story is true or not will never be known. Still, it is clear that the people in the Alamo were willing to die for their cause.

The Fall of the Alamo. In the early morning hours of March 6, 1836, the Texans were awakened by the sound of music from the Mexican camp. Santa Anna's army band was playing "El Degüello." The Texans knew that this music meant no prisoners were to be taken and no mercy was to be shown.

The final attack began before dawn. One column of Mexican soldiers opened fire on the Alamo as another tried to mount ladders on the walls of the fort. The Texans fought back with rifles and cannons. The Mexicans retreated. Another wave of Mexicans attacked, trying to break through the wall. Once again, the Texans forced the Mexicans back.

On its third try, the Mexican army overwhelmed the Texans. With ladders in place along the wall, the Mexicans entered the fort by the hundreds. They captured a cannon,

Harry Ransom Humanities Research Center. The University of Texas at Austin

David Crockett was a well-known Tennessee folk hero, a United States representative, and a legendary hunter. Crockett moved to Texas to take part in the Revolution. In January 1836, he wrote, "I would rather be in my present situation than to be elected to a seat in Congress for life." He died at the Alamo.

Historical Sidelight

From their positions on the walls, the defenders of the Alamo could see the flag that Santa Anna displayed from the cathedral tower in the middle of San Antonio. The flag was not the red, green, and white tricolor Mexican flag but a solid red flag. The flag (along with the song "El Degüello," meaning "the massacre") relayed the chilling message that no one would be taken alive.

TEXAS VOICES

Illustrating (I) Have students select and illustrate one of the paragraphs from Suzanna Dickenson's report. **V, TK, LEP**

RETEACHING

Have students work independently or with a partner to create a time line showing the events leading up to the fall of the Alamo. Time lines should incorporate the events and dates mentioned in Section 3 only. **V, TK, LEP**

CLOSURE

Point out that after the fall of the Alamo, the Texans' cause appeared hopeless as Santa Anna continued his march through Texas. Ask: Despite this fact, what did the Alamo symbolize for Texans *(that they must defeat Santa Anna at any cost)*?

ASSESSMENT

Have students complete the Section 3 Review on page 250.

TEXAS VOICES

Suzanna Dickenson and her daughter, Angelina, were survivors of the Alamo. Suzanna was the wife of Almaron Dickenson, who died at the Alamo. Santa Anna chose her to tell Sam Houston and other Texans of the Alamo battle. The Mexican general hoped her report would make the Texans surrender. But her description of the heroism inspired the people of Texas. Late in her life, she recalled:

> Travis called up his men, drew a line with his sword, and said: "My soldiers, I am going to meet the fate that becomes me. Those who will stand by me, let them remain. But those who desire to go, let them go, and who crosses the line that I have drawn, shall go!"
>
> Then the horde [Mexican troops] came on like a swoop, in divisions. They came in the form of a semi-circle that extended from the northeast to the southwest, but the strongest attack was from about where the Military Plaza now is. . . . Three times they were repulsed [driven back] by our cannon.
>
> The enemy gradually approached by means of earthworks [protected trenches]. . . . We looked for reinforcements, but they never came. The final struggle lasted more than two hours. Then my husband rushed into the church where I was with my child and exclaimed, "Great God, Sue! The Mexicans are inside our walls! All is lost! If they spare you, save our child!" Then with a parting kiss, [he] drew his sword and plunged into the strife that was raging in the fort. . . .

turned it inward, and opened fire. Hand-to-hand combat followed for at least half an hour. It was a bloody and tragic scene. One of Santa Anna's officers wrote of the battle grounds:

Institute of Texan Cultures

> The bodies of the Texians lay as they had fallen; and many of them were covered by those of Mexicans who had fallen upon them. The close of the struggle seemed to have been a hand to hand engagement; and the number of slain Mexicans exceeded that of the Texians. The ground was covered.

As the smoke cleared, at least 182 Texans and perhaps as many as 1,600 Mexicans lay dead. Crockett, Travis, Bowie, Fuentes, Losoya, and Bonham were just a few of the Texas names among the dead. There were some survivors. Suzanna Dickenson, whose husband had been artillery officer Almaron Dickenson, and her daughter survived the battle. Another survivor was Anna Salazar de Esparza, whose husband was fighter Gregorio Esparza. Santa Anna also spared Travis' black slave, Joe, Bowie's black slave, Sam, and several women and children.

Essential Elements
2H, 7A, 9B

Suzanna Dickenson was one of the survivors of the Alamo. Her account of the Texans' bravery there inspired further revolt.

Past Learning (I) Ask students to tell what they know about the United States Declaration of Independence. Ask: From whom was the United States declaring its independence *(Great Britain)*? Ask students if they can note any similarities between Texas' desire for independence from Mexico and the American colonists' fight for independence from Great Britain.

Vocabulary (I) You may wish to preteach the following boldfaced terms: *unanimous* (p. 250); *executive branch* (p. 251); *legislative branch* (p. 251); *judicial branch* (p. 251); *ad interim* (p. 252). **LEP**

Answers to Section 3 Review

Define: *siege*—the surrounding of an enemy fortification to force a surrender

Identify: General Urrea—Mexican commander who marched along the Gulf as Santa Anna moved on San Antonio; James Bowie—Texas colonel ordered by Houston to destroy the Alamo but who stayed to defend it; William Travis—commander of Texas forces at the Alamo; Juan Seguín—a Tejano who defended the Alamo

1. They chose to stay and defend the Alamo.
2. To get reinforcements
3. It became a symbol to Texans that they must fight Santa Anna at any cost.

Evaluating Information: The Texans were excellent fighters and riflemen and killed many attacking troops; however, the leaders of the Alamo garrison disobeyed Houston's orders and remained in an indefensible position.

Interpreting Pictures: Answers will vary. The Texans did not have enough troops to defend the walls that surrounded most of the compound.

Essential Elements
2B, 2C, 2D, 2H, 7B, 7D, 7F, 7G, 9A, 9B

SECTION ★3 REVIEW

Define: siege
Identify: General Urrea, James Bowie, William Travis, Juan Seguín

1. How did James Bowie and James Neill disobey Houston's orders?
2. What was the purpose of the various messengers sent by Travis from the Alamo?
3. How did the fall of the Alamo help the Texans' cause?

Evaluating Information: How do events at the Alamo serve to illustrate both the strengths and the weaknesses of the Texans as a fighting force?

Interpreting Pictures: Look at the drawing of the Alamo on page 246. What do you think was the Texans' basic problem in defending it? Why?

Barker Texas History Center

George C. Childress was elected a delegate to the Convention of 1836. He was selected as head of the committee to write the Texas Declaration of Independence.

The Legacy of the Alamo. Santa Anna believed that the fall of the Alamo would warn Texans that his army could not be defeated. But the Alamo became a symbol to the Texans that they must fight Santa Anna at any cost. Citizens of the United States also rallied around the Texas cause after they heard about the courageous stand at the Alamo. The battle cry "Remember the Alamo" became the inspiration for Texans during the rest of the war.

The Alamo has a special meaning in Texas and United States history both. It represents the high price that people sometimes have to pay for freedom. As 22-year-old Daniel Cloud wrote before entering the walls of the Alamo, "If we fail, death in the cause of Liberty and humanity is not a cause for shuddering." ✪

■4 The Convention of 1836

On March 1, 1836, while the Texans were defending the Alamo, a convention began at Washington-on-the-Brazos. The 59 delegates to the Convention of 1836 included many people with experience in government. Those with experience in the United States included Sam Houston, Richard Ellis, Robert Potter, Martin Parmer, and Samuel Carson. One of the delegates, Lorenzo de Zavala, had served in the Mexican congress. Two other Tejanos joined Zavala at the convention, José Antonio Navarro and José Francisco Ruíz.

The task of the convention was clear to all the delegates. They planned to declare the independence of Texas from Mexico. Then they would create a government for the new country, the Republic of Texas.

The Declaration of Independence. The first order of business for the Convention of 1836 was to write a declaration of independence. As their guide, the delegates used the United States Declaration of Independence, written in 1776 by Thomas Jefferson. George C. Childress chaired the committee in charge of writing the document. In fact, Childress himself apparently wrote most of the Texas Declaration of Independence.

The declaration was presented to the convention and adopted on March 2, 1836. March 2 is now celebrated as Texas Independence Day. The vote in favor of the declaration was **unanimous**, or agreed to by all. The declaration

Analysis (I) Ask students: Which part of Texas' Constitution of 1836 would be deleted from a constitution written today *(the right to hold slaves)*? **A**

Guided Practice (I) Have the class work together to write a constitution for your classroom. The constitution could provide the basic rules of class conduct to be followed throughout the year. **LEP**

EXTENSION

Research (II) Ask interested students to conduct research to compare and contrast the organization of Texas govern-

ment today with that set up in the Constitution of 1836. Have students create charts or diagrams to illustrate their findings. **TK, V, G**

Independent Practice (II) Ask students to write a brief paragraph answering the following question: Texas' Constitution of 1836 contained a Bill of Rights. As an African American in 1836, what are your rights? Invite volunteers to read their paragraphs aloud. **A**

---

listed the complaints of the Texans against Santa Anna's government. It stated that Mexico had denied the Texans freedom of religion, the right to trial by jury, a public school system, and the right to petition the government. It described the abuses of Santa Anna and his use of force to silence Texans. Then the document declared Texas a free and independent country.

The Constitution of 1836. After declaring Texas independent, the convention began work on a constitution, or plan of government. After two weeks of debate, the delegates finished the Constitution of 1836. The model for this document also came from the United States. The government was to have three branches. The **executive branch**, which would carry out the laws, was to be headed by a president. Laws were to be made by the **legislative branch**, called the Congress. The **judicial branch** was the court system.

Daughters of the Republic of Texas Library

The Convention of 1836 was held in a building belonging to a blacksmith at Washington-on-the-Brazos.

In the painting below by Charles and Fanny Normann, the delegates to the Convention of 1836 are shown as they listen to the reading of the Texas Declaration of Independence.

Mrs. Artie Fultz Davis, Fultz Estate, Navasota

Citizenship
Refer students to the chart on page 595 in the "Handbook of Texas Government and Citizenship," and have them compare the organization of the Texas government today to the information contained in this section.

RETEACHING
With the class, create on the chalkboard an outline showing the main ideas of Section 4. Use the section subheadings as a framework for the outline. **LEP, A, V**

CLOSURE
Review with students the results of the Convention of 1836. Ask: What is the next step for the Texans in their quest for independence *(to defeat Santa Anna)*?

ASSESSMENT
Have students complete the Section 4 Review on page 252.

SECTION 5

FOCUS
Past Learning (I) Review with students the fall of the Alamo. Point out that Sam Houston was still trying to organize an effective fighting force. Ask: Do you think Texans were optimistic or pessimistic about the course of the Revolution?

Answers to Section 4 Review

Define: *unanimous*—agreed to by all; *executive branch*—branch of government that carries out the laws; *legislative branch*—branch of government that makes the laws; *judicial branch*—the court system of a government; *ad interim*—temporary

Identify: Lorenzo de Zavala—Tejano delegate to the Convention of 1836, chosen as vice president of the ad interim government; George C. Childress—thought to have written most of the Texas Declaration of Independence; David G. Burnet—president of the ad interim government

1. To declare Texas' independence and to organize a government
2. It claimed that Mexico had denied Texans freedom of religion, the right to trial by jury, a public school system, and the right to petition the government, and that Santa Anna had used military force against Texas.
3. President—David G. Burnet; vice president—Lorenzo de Zavala

(Continued on page 253)

Essential Elements
2C, 2H, 5B, 7A, 9B, 9E

Archives Division, Texas State Library

David G. Burnet was named the first president of the Republic at the Convention of 1836.

SECTION ★ 4 REVIEW

Define: unanimous, executive branch, legislative branch, judicial branch, ad interim

Identify: Lorenzo de Zavala, George C. Childress, David G. Burnet

1. What was the purpose of the Convention of 1836?
2. How did the Texas Declaration of Independence justify the Texans' revolt against Santa Anna?
3. Who were chosen as president and vice president of the ad interim government?

Using Historical Imagination: Imagine that you are a delegate to the Convention of 1836. You supported the Mexican Constitution of 1824. Now you have changed your mind and voted for Texas independence. Why?

Analyzing Information: Why did the ad interim government do a poor job of governing Texas after March 17, 1836?

The Constitution of 1836 contained a Bill of Rights. These were statements of basic rights that the government could not take away. The Bill of Rights guaranteed freedom of speech, meaning people could speak their minds without fear of arrest. Freedom of religion gave the people the right to worship as they pleased. Freedom of the press meant newspapers could print what they believed to be true. The right to trial by jury was also included in the Bill of Rights. In addition to these rights, the Constitution of 1836 encouraged immigration, created a school system, and developed a free land policy.

Yet the Constitution did not pass laws freeing slaves or stopping their importation from the United States. In fact, the law was strengthened to guard the right to hold slaves. Free blacks had to petition Congress to stay in Texas. Among those who had to do so were Samuel McCullough, Hendrick Arnold, and Greenberry Logan, who had fought heroically for Texas during the Revolution.

The Ad Interim Government. Because Texas was still at war, the delegates created an **ad interim**, or temporary, government. Leaders were chosen by the convention until elections could be held. David G. Burnet was selected as president. Lorenzo de Zavala was chosen as vice president. Other officers were Samuel Carson, Bailey Hardeman, Thomas Rusk, Robert Potter, and David Thomas.

The officers were sworn in on March 17 at Washington-on-the-Brazos. But later that day, they fled after hearing that the Mexican army was near. The government was set up at Harrisburg but was again forced to flee under the threat of Santa Anna's troops. Constantly on the move, the ad interim government could accomplish little. The future of the Republic of Texas was now in the hands of General Sam Houston and the Texas army. ✪

5 The Fighting Continues

With the ad interim government in retreat and with the tragic news coming from the Alamo, the Texans seemed near defeat. Houston was trying to organize the army to make it more effective. But he was short on troops, guns, ammunition, supplies, and money. Meanwhile, after the fall of the Alamo, Santa Anna began his march toward the Texas army stationed at Gonzales.

INSTRUCTION

Cooperative Learning (I) Organize the class into small groups. Tell students that they are Texans charged with developing a strategy to defeat Santa Anna quickly. Allow each group time to develop its strategy and then present its plan to the class. Then have the class work together to develop a single strategy to defeat Santa Anna. **A, V**

Map Reading (I) Direct students to the map on this page. Have them number a sheet of paper from one to five and answer the following questions:

1. Which Mexican army entered Texas at Laredo? *(Santa Anna's)*
2. How many battles are shown on the map? *(Six)*
3. In which general direction from Gonzales to San Jacinto did Houston's army move—west, east, north, or south? *(East)*
4. Of the battles shown, which involved Houston's army? *(San Jacinto)*
5. Which Mexican army did not reach the Battle of San Jacinto? *(General Urrea's)*

Call on volunteers to share their answers aloud. **A, V, LEP**

The Runaway Scrape. Houston had left before the convention of Washington-on-the-Brazos ended. He reached Gonzales on March 11 and tried to find out what was happening at San Antonio. He sent his best scout, Deaf Smith, to investigate. Two days later, Smith escorted Suzanna Dickenson and a few other survivors of the Alamo into Gonzales. Houston and the Texas army then heard for the first time the details of the massacre at the Alamo.

Smith also told the Texans that Santa Anna and his force of thousands were marching toward them at Gonzales. The army and the people of Gonzales became frightened, and many panicked. Houston, realizing they were in danger, ordered a retreat. All supplies were removed from Gonzales. The people in the area packed their belongings and left. On the night of March 12, the entire town of Gonzales was burned on Houston's orders. When the Mexicans arrived at Gonzales, they found nothing but smoldering ashes.

The people of Gonzales fled eastward to escape Santa Anna. As they reached other settlements along the Colorado and Brazos rivers, word spread about the Alamo and other

Barker Texas History Center

Erastus "Deaf" Smith, a prominent scout in the Texas army during the Revolution, played an important role in the Battle of San Jacinto.

LINKING HISTORY AND GEOGRAPHY

How much distance was covered by Houston's army from Gonzales to San Jacinto?

Using Historical Imagination: Answers will vary; however, students should consider that all hope of peace was gone by the time of the Convention. Santa Anna's armies had invaded Texas and, even as the Convention met, the Alamo was under siege.

Analyzing Information: Santa Anna's invading army forced it to flee. During the remainder of the Revolution, it was always on the move.

Linking History and Geography
Almost 200 miles

Transparency 14
A transparency of this map can be found in the Teacher's Resource Binder.

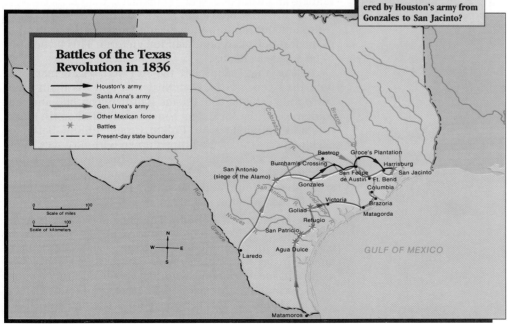

Battles of the Texas Revolution in 1836

- → Houston's army
- → Santa Anna's army
- → Gen. Urrea's army
- → Other Mexican force
- ✳ Battles
- –·–· Present-day state boundary

0   100
Scale of miles

0   100
Scale of kilometers

Bastrop · Groce's Plantation
Burnham's Crossing
San Antonio (siege of the Alamo)
San Felipe de Austin · Ft. Bend · Harrisburg · San Jacinto
Gonzales
Columbia
Victoria · Brazoria
Goliad · Matagorda
Refugio
San Patricio
Agua Dulce
Laredo
GULF OF MEXICO

Matamoros

Guided Practice (I) Ask students to assume the role of Suzanna Dickenson or Deaf Smith and write an eyewitness account of the Runaway Scrape. **LEP**

EXTENSION

Writing/Illustrating (II) Have students choose either the Texan or the Mexican point of view and write a newspaper editorial or draw an editorial cartoon about the massacre at Goliad. Invite students to read their editorials aloud or display and discuss their editorial cartoons. **V, TK, G, A**

Independent Practice (I) Have students work independently or with a partner to create a series of cause-and-effect statements, using the information in Section 5. Collect the statements to use in Section 5 Reteaching. **LEP**

RETEACHING

Using the cause-and-effect statements from the Independent Practice activity, create a matching review game for students. Separate the cause statements from the effect statements and write them on individual index cards. Challenge students to match a cause with its effect. **A, V, LEP**

Historical Sidelight

General Urrea was outraged at Santa Anna's order to execute the prisoners. Urrea had utmost respect for the "much esteemed and fearless Fannin." Urrea, however, as an army officer, was obliged to follow Santa Anna's orders.

Painting by Nola Montgomery, courtesy Texas Department of Parks and Wildlife

Outnumbered and surrounded on the open prairie, the Texas force under Colonel Fannin surrendered to General Urrea at the Battle of Coleto. The prisoners were taken to Goliad and executed seven days later.

Mexican victories. Fearing for their lives, more Texas settlers fled eastward. For over a month, Texans left their homes, towns, and farms to avoid the Mexican army. This movement of settlers was called the Runaway Scrape.

Defeat in South Texas. While the Alamo was under siege, scattered Texas forces suffered defeats in South Texas. Mexican General Urrea led 900 Mexican troops against about 40 Texans at San Patricio. All but six of the Texans were killed or captured. Urrea then won a battle on March 2, 1836, at Agua Dulce Creek. Once again, the Texans were no match for the Mexican force.

While Santa Anna was stalled at the Alamo, General Urrea continued his move north along the Gulf coast. On March 14, he won the Battle of Refugio. A number of Texans escaped, only to be captured by Urrea's troops near Victoria. Urrea's next target was Colonel James Fannin's army at Goliad.

Fannin in Retreat. Sam Houston had ordered Fannin to withdraw to Victoria on March 14. Fannin, however, did not act immediately. He had sent troops to help at Refugio and waited for word of them. On March 18, General Urrea's advance force met Fannin and his troops in a short series of fights. Fannin then decided to leave the protection of the fort at Goliad and head for Victoria. This turned out to be a bad decision.

Just as the Texans left the fort and began marching onto the open prairie, General Urrea and his main army surrounded them. The Texans had between 300 and 400 soldiers, and the Mexicans had around 450. Fannin chose to stand and fight near Coleto Creek. In the Battle of Coleto, the Texans were pinned down with no cover. After reinforcements arrived for General Urrea on the morning of March 20, Fannin decided to surrender. Following the surrender, Fannin and the other Texans were marched back to the La Bahía fort at Goliad.

The Massacre at Goliad. The prisoners were held at Goliad for a week. General Urrea wrote to Santa Anna, asking him for permission to hold the Texans as prisoners of war instead of killing them. Santa Anna's reply was swift and clear. Anyone who had taken up arms against the government of Mexico must be executed immediately.

On March 27, the prisoners were divided into three groups and marched onto the prairie near the fort. Mexican

CLOSURE
Point out that after these serious defeats, pressure was on Sam Houston to develop a sound strategy for defeating the Mexican armies.

ASSESSMENT
Have students complete the Section 5 Review on page 255.

SECTION 6

FOCUS

Past Learning (I) Direct students to the map on page 253. Ask the class to point out the general location of Houston's army at this point in the campaign. *(It has left Gonzales and is moving east toward the Brazos River.)* As students read the first several paragraphs of Section 6, have them use the map to trace Houston's movements.

Painting by Andrew J. Houston. Archives Division. Texas State Library

This painting, *The March to the Massacre*, shows Fannin's troops being led to their death near La Bahía.

Identify: San Patricio, James Fannin, Battle of Coleto, Francisca Alvarez

1. What military reverses did the Texans suffer after the fall of the Alamo?
2. What happened in the Runaway Scrape?
3. Why did Fannin not act immediately to leave Goliad?

Interpreting Maps: Judging from the map on page 253, what do you think was Santa Anna's plan to defeat the Texans?

Using Historical Imagination: How do you think Santa Anna would justify his order of execution for Fannin and his men?

firing squads then shot about 350 Texans. When the firing began, a few of the Texans ran and were thus able to escape. A number of others survived the massacre by hiding before the shooting took place. Francisca Alvarez, a nurse whose husband was a Mexican officer, hid some people who escaped. The Texans later referred to her as the "Angel of Goliad." As a result of the massacre, the Texans had another battle cry: "Remember Goliad!" ✪

6 Victory at San Jacinto

With news of the defeats, pressure began to mount on Sam Houston to attack and gain a victory. The Texas troops were angry about what had happened at the Alamo and Goliad, and they demanded action. But Houston was afraid that the Texas army was still too small and untrained. He decided to pull the main Texas force away from Santa Anna.

The Texans in Camp. Houston and the army moved eastward toward the Brazos River. Santa Anna's army was close behind. Several Texans openly rebelled against Houston, criticizing him for retreating. Even President Burnet challenged Houston to fight. He wrote to Houston, "The enemy are laughing at you in scorn."

Houston ignored the criticism. He moved the Texas army to Groce's Crossing near Hempstead. There, they camped at the plantation home of Jared Groce. For two weeks, Houston drilled the troops and taught them military strategy. He created a scouting unit led by Deaf Smith and Henry Karnes. The Texans also increased their stock of

INSTRUCTION

Art in History (I) Have students examine the painting on this page. Lead a discussion on how battle tactics have changed since the Texas Revolution. Ask: What impact has technology had on warfare? **V, A**

Geography (I) Point out that Houston's strategy in the Battle of San Jacinto depended greatly on the area's physical geography. Ask students to provide an example from the textbook to support this fact. **V, A**

Historical Imagination (I) Pose the following questions for class discussion: How do you think history might have been different if the Mexicans had won the Battle of San Jacinto? How might historians have viewed Sam Houston? **A, LEP**

Historical Sidelight

Santa Anna had hoped to catch the members of the ad interim Texas government. At Harrisburg, Mexican troops tossed Gail Borden's printing press into the Bayou.

supplies and ammunition. The citizens of Cincinnati, Ohio, sent two cannons to the soldiers. The Texans named the cannons the Twin Sisters.

The Texans left Groce's Crossing on April 14 and marched toward Harrisburg. Santa Anna's army had already crossed the Brazos at what is now Richmond. Five days later, Houston learned from his scouts the location of Santa Anna's army. It was camped near Harrisburg on the San Jacinto River. Houston made his decision. The stage was set for the final battle against Santa Anna.

The Battle of San Jacinto. The Texans moved down Buffalo Bayou and, on April 20, camped beside the San Jacinto River. They were in a grove of live oak trees, with a wide prairie in front of them. The only way the Mexicans could attack them was to cross the open prairie. On the afternoon of April 20, there was a short fight between a small number of Texans and Mexicans. The Mexican charge was stopped by the pounding of the Texas cannons, the Twin Sisters. After a few hours of fighting, Santa Anna pulled his forces back.

The next day, Houston called a meeting of the Texas officers. They argued over what to do. Some wanted to attack immediately. Others wanted to wait for Santa Anna

The Battle of San Jacinto was the deciding victory of the Texas Revolution. Santa Anna was captured, and his army suffered a devastating loss at the hands of the Texas army under General Sam Houston.

Painting by Henry McArdle, Archives Division, Texas State Library

Guided Practice (I) Organize the class into groups of three or four. Provide each group with a detailed map (such as a road map) of present-day Texas. Ask each group to examine the map and list the cities, counties, and landmarks that derive their names from the people and events of the Texas Revolution. After each group completes its list, have the students compile the information into a class list. **V, LEP**

EXTENSION

Research (III) Have interested students research and report on the leadership of Santa Anna. Reports should address the following questions: How long did Santa Anna remain in power after the Battle of San Jacinto? What were later relations with Texas and the United States like? **A, G**

Independent Practice (I) Ask students to write a brief paragraph telling whether they think Sam Houston made the correct decision in sparing Santa Anna. Invite volunteers to read their paragraphs aloud. **A, LEP**

to attack. Houston decided that the assault would begin at around three o'clock that afternoon. About 900 Texans began preparations to charge approximately 1,200 Mexican troops. Meanwhile, Houston sent Deaf Smith to destroy a bridge over Vince's Bayou, the only escape route to Harrisburg. This was the bridge that General Cós had crossed with reinforcements earlier.

When the Texans moved from the woods onto the prairie, they were still out of sight of the Mexican sentries. High ground in front of the Mexicans kept the Texans from being seen. Many of the Mexicans, exhausted from the previous day's battle, were sleeping. When a Mexican warning shot finally rang out, the Texans charged. The Mexicans were caught by complete surprise. They were

Star of the Republic Museum, Washington-on-the-Brazos

In this painting by Stephen Seymour Thomas, General Sam Houston is shown as the fearless commander of the Texas army, leading his troops into battle and final victory.

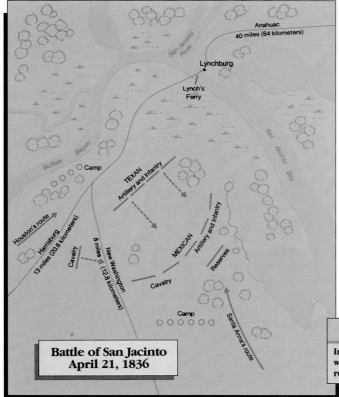

Battle of San Jacinto April 21, 1836

Anahuac
40 miles (64 kilometers)

Lynchburg

Lynch's Ferry

San Jacinto River

San Jacinto Bay

Buffalo Bayou

Camp

TEXAN Artillery and Infantry

MEXICAN Artillery and Infantry

Reserves

Cavalry

Houston's route

Harrisburg 13 miles (20.8 kilometers)

Cavalry

New Washington 8 miles (12.8 kilometers)

Camp

Santa Anna's route

LINKING HISTORY AND GEOGRAPHY

In case of the need to retreat, which army had the easiest route of escape? Why?

Linking History and Geography

The Mexican army—they had no rivers to cross.

RETEACHING
Organize students into pairs. Have each pair use the information in Section 6 to create a calendar dated April 1836. Students should draw the calendar on a large sheet of paper and then fill in the month's events leading up to the Battle of San Jacinto on April 21. **V, TK, LEP**

CLOSURE
Tell students that now Texans faced the challenge of creating their new nation independent of Mexico.

ASSESSMENT
Have students complete the Section 6 Review on page 258.

General Houston was wounded in the ankle at the Battle of San Jacinto. In this painting by William Huddle, Houston is accepting the surrender of Santa Anna.

Archives Division, Texas State Library

258 *Unit 5*

SECTION ⑥ REVIEW

Identify: Twin Sisters, "Will You Come to the Bower?"

1. Why were Texas politicians upset with Houston before the Battle of San Jacinto?
2. Why were the Texans able to win the Battle of San Jacinto?
3. Why did Houston spare the life of Santa Anna?

Analyzing Information: Why do you think Sam Houston delayed for more than a month before launching his major battle with General Santa Anna?

Evaluating Information: Many Texans wanted Santa Anna executed after the Battle of San Jacinto. Do you think they were right or wrong? Explain.

awakened by Texas bullets and battle cries of "Remember the Alamo!" and "Remember Goliad!" Musicians played a tune called "Will You Come to the Bower?"

The battle lasted only about eighteen minutes. Unprepared, many Mexican soldiers fled into the woods or tried to surrender. But the anger of the Texans could not be subdued, even by Houston. The Texans continued firing on the Mexicans and killed many unarmed soldiers. The bitter memories of the Alamo and Goliad led to a massacre. When the shooting stopped, 630 Mexicans had been killed. Only nine Texans died. Among the wounded was Sam Houston, whose ankle was shattered by a musket ball.

Santa Anna had disappeared during the fighting, but he was found the next day hiding in the woods. Many of the Texans wanted to execute Santa Anna on the spot. But Houston refused to let the soldiers kill the general. Houston explained his reason later: "My motive in sparing the life of Santa Anna was to relieve the country of all hostile enemies without further bloodshed, and to secure his acknowledgement of our independence." The war was over. Houston's gesture was meant to begin the new country on a note of compassion, not revenge. ◐

The Texas Flag

Between 1821 and 1836, the Mexican flag flew over Texas. But during this period, Texans began to fight for independence, and groups of men across the territory fought under various flags. Almost every flag was designed and sewn by a woman who supported Texas independence.

Two of the battle flags are still in existence. The flag of the New Orleans Greys was made by women in Texas. They gave the flag to the volunteers from New Orleans, Louisiana, who had come to help fight for Texas. This flag was captured at the Battle of the Alamo. Its exact whereabouts today is uncertain, but it may be in the National Museum of Anthropology in Mexico City. The flag carried by Kentucky volunteers was made by women in Kentucky. The Kentucky volunteers fought with General Sam Houston in the Battle of San Jacinto. This flag still hangs in the state capitol building in Austin.

When Texas declared independence from Mexico in March 1836, a new flag was needed. Lorenzo de Zavala, the first vice president of the Republic, is credited with the design of the first flag. It was used for two years. David G. Burnet drew up a second design. Finally, under President Mirabeau Lamar, the Lone Star flag was adopted as the national flag of the Republic of Texas. Its design was the same as today's Texas flag.

Historians have debated who should receive credit for designing the first Lone Star flag for Texas. Best known as the possible creator is Joanna Troutman, pictured here. She was a Georgian and never visited the Republic of Texas. The Georgia volunteers carried her flag into Velasco in December 1835. Her design was a blue five-pointed star on a white background. Troutman was called "the Betsy Ross of Texas," probably because the first two official flags of the new Republic in 1836 were similar to the one she designed.

The Texas flag today looks more like the one below. It was made by Sarah Dodson, who moved from Kentucky to Harrisburg, Texas, when she was a child. It was Dodson's flag that flew over the building in which the Texas Declaration of Independence was signed. She had made the flag a year earlier for her husband, Lieutenant Archaelaus Dodson, to carry into battle.

Using Historical Imagination

Imagine that you are in favor of Texas independence in 1836. Design a battle flag or a flag for the new Republic of Texas.

Inset: **Joanna Troutman**   Right: **Dodson's flag**

Inset: *Texas Department of Transportation;*   Right: *Gallery of the Republic*

CHAPTER REVIEW RESOURCES

1. Chapter Review Worksheet 12
2. Chapter 12 Test, Form A
3. Reteaching Worksheet 12
4. Chapter 12 Test, Form B
5. **Informal Evaluation Forms:** Portfolio Assessment
6. *Texas, Our Texas* **Test Generator**

Essential Elements
2C, 2H, 5A, 9A, 9B, 9D

CHAPTER 12 REVIEW ANSWERS

Understanding Main Ideas

1. The Texans won. General Cós agreed to lead his army back to Mexico and to give up all military supplies to the Texans.
2. The war faction wanted to declare independence from Mexico, whereas the peace faction wanted to affirm Texas' allegiance to the Mexican Constitution of 1824. The delegates pledged their loyalty to Mexico in the Declaration of the People of Texas and created a provisional government.
3. It left the Texas army determined to defeat Santa Anna at any cost.
4. An independent Republic of Texas
5. They were massacred by order of General Santa Anna.
6. The Mexican army was defeated, and Santa Anna was captured.

Thinking Critically

1. **Synthesizing Information:** He held Texas troops in some contempt.
2. **Evaluating Information:** Answers will vary, but students might note that the fort would have offered protection for Fannin and his men.

CHAPTER 12 REVIEW

Understanding Main Ideas

1. Who won the Battle of San Antonio? What were the terms of surrender?
2. What basic disagreement divided delegates to the Consultation? What did the Consultation accomplish?
3. What were the historical consequences of the fall of the Alamo?
4. What was created by the Convention of 1836?
5. What happened to the Texan forces at Goliad under the command of Colonel James Fannin?
6. What was the result of the Battle of San Jacinto?

Thinking Critically

1. **Synthesizing Information:** Judging from his actions described in this chapter, what was General Santa Anna's opinion of Texan troops?
2. **Evaluating Information:** Do you think Colonel Fannin could have won his battle with General Urrea if he had remained in the Goliad fort? Explain.
3. **Classifying Information:** List these battles of the Texas Revolution under the appropriate heading, *Texas Defeats* or *Texas Victories*: Coleto, Refugio, San Jacinto, San Antonio, Grass Fight.

Linking History and Geography

1. Study the map on page 253. How did Santa Anna's military strategy differ from that of General Urrea? (What did he do that Urrea did not?)

2. How did Sam Houston use the geography of the San Jacinto battlefield to increase his chances of victory over Santa Anna's army?

TAAS Practice
Using Primary Sources

General Sam Houston was commander-in-chief of the Texas forces, but at first he had few troops to command. Before leaving for Gonzales to organize his army, he issued this call to arms:

★✦ ARMY ORDERS.

Convention Hall, Washington, March 2, 1836

War is raging on the frontiers. Bejar [San Antonio] is besieged by two thousand of the enemy, under the command of general Siezma. Reinforcements are on their march, to unite with the besieging army. By the last report, our force in Bejar was only one hundred and fifty men strong. The citizens of Texas must rally to the aid of our army, or it will perish. Let the citizens of the East march to the combat. The enemy must be driven from our soil, or desolation must accompany their march upon us. *Independence is declared*, it must be maintained. Immediate action, united with valor, alone can achieve the great work. The services of all are forthwith required in the field.

SAM HOUSTON
Commander-in-Chief of the Army

P.S. It is rumored that the enemy are on their march to Gonzales, and that they have entered the colonies. The fate of Bejar is unknown. The country must and shall be defended. The patriots of Texas *are appealed to, in behalf of their bleeding country.*

S.H.

1. Houston told Texans that they should volunteer their services to the Texas army because
   A they will be ashamed of themselves in the future if they do not
   B the Alamo must be avenged
   C the enemy will destroy them if they do not defend themselves
   D the enemy has been burning cities and attacking civilians

2. Houston's call to arms is directed at
   A anyone who will volunteer to fight
   B men between 18 and 25 years of age
   C persons with military experience
   D landowning citizens of Texas who can read and write

TAAS Practice
Writing Descriptively

Imagine that you are one of the Tejano soldiers serving with Houston's army at the Battle of San Jacinto. Write a letter to your family, describing what you saw and experienced on April 21, 1836.

Practicing Skills

1. **Sequencing Events:** List the following battles of the Texas Revolution in the order that they occurred: Goliad, San Jacinto, San Antonio, the Alamo, Coleto, Gonzales.
2. **Interpreting Graphics:** The fall of the Alamo was sensational news throughout the United States. The emotional headlines (above right) began a long newspaper article about the Texas Revolution. It ran in the Columbia, Tennessee, *Observer* on April 14, 1836. How might this kind of newspaper coverage have helped the Texas cause? Explain.

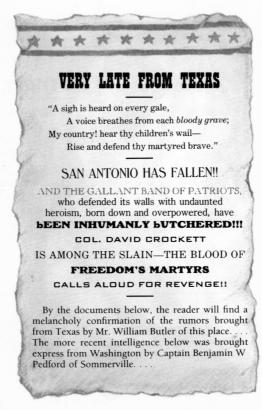

★ ★ ★ ★ ★ ★ ★ ★ ★ ★ ★

VERY LATE FROM TEXAS

"A sigh is heard on every gale,
A voice breathes from each *bloody grave*;
My country! hear thy children's wail—
Rise and defend thy martyred brave."

SAN ANTONIO HAS FALLEN!!

AND THE GALLANT BAND OF PATRIOTS, who defended its walls with undaunted heroism, born down and overpowered, have
bEEN INHUMANLY bUTCHERED!!!
COL. DAVID CROCKETT
IS AMONG THE SLAIN—THE BLOOD OF
FREEDOM'S MARTYRS
CALLS ALOUD FOR REVENGE!!

By the documents below, the reader will find a melancholy confirmation of the rumors brought from Texas by Mr. William Butler of this place. . . . The more recent intelligence below was brought express from Washington by Captain Benjamin W Pedford of Sommerville. . . .

Enriching Your Study of History

1. **Individual Project:** Collect information about a person who participated in the Texas Revolution. Then tape record a brief oral biography of the person.
2. **Cooperative Project:** Your class will conduct research and prepare a large model of the Alamo. Show the troops during the final attack. Your model should be as accurate as possible. A good resource is Walter Lord's *A Time to Stand.*

3. **Classifying Information:** *Texas Defeats*—Coleto, Refugio; *Texas Victories*—San Jacinto, San Antonio, Grass Fight

Linking History and Geography
1. Santa Anna was willing to divide his army.
2. He destroyed a bridge to cut off Mexican resupply. He then took the Mexican army by surprise, advancing across a field that hid the Texas soldiers.

TAAS Practice
Using Primary Sources
1. C
2. A

TAAS Practice
Writing Descriptively
Letters will vary but should demonstrate knowledge of the details relating to the Battle of San Jacinto.

Practicing Skills
1. **Sequencing Events:** Gonzales, Goliad, San Antonio, the Alamo, Coleto, San Jacinto
2. **Interpreting Graphics:** It probably attracted many potential soldiers.

Enriching Your Study of History
1. **Individual Project:** Reports will vary but should demonstrate careful research.
2. **Cooperative Project:** The model should be detailed as well as an accurate representation of the final battle at the Alamo.

A NEW NATION

TEACHER'S TIME LINE

Section 1	Section 2	Section 3	Section 4	Section 5	Review and Assessment
Pp. 262–65	Pp. 265–71	Pp. 271–78	Pp. 278–80	Pp. 280–85	
1 Day	1 Day	1 Day	1 Day	1 Day	1 Day

◾ TEACHER MATERIALS

Core: Chapter 13 Time Line; Graphic Organizer 13; Enrichment Worksheet 13; Review Worksheet 13; Reteaching Worksheet 13; Chapter 13 Tests, Forms A & B

Additional: Geography and Graph Skills 13, Map and Chart Transparencies 15, Informal Evaluation Forms, Test Generator

◾ OBJECTIVES

1. Identify the first elected president of the Republic of Texas.
2. Analyze the major problems faced by the new Republic of Texas.
3. Compare and contrast the policies of presidents Houston and Lamar.
4. Explain the impact of the Indian wars on the Republic of Texas.
5. Identify and discuss international policy concerns of the new Republic.

◾ RESOURCES

BOOKS FOR TEACHERS

Carter, Samuel. *Cherokee Sunset: A Nation Betrayed: A Narrative of Travail and Triumph, Persecution and Exile*. Garden City: Doubleday, 1976. The tragic story of the Cherokees.

Cash, Joseph H. *The Comanche People.* Phoenix: Indian Tribal Series, 1974. Story of the Comanches.

Flanagan, Sue. *Sam Houston's Texas*. Austin: University of Texas Press, 1964. Pictorial study.

Friend, Llerena B. *Sam Houston: The Great Designer*. Texas History Paperbacks Series. Austin: University of Texas Press, 1969. Story of Sam Houston.

Gregory, J. N. *Fort Concho: Its Why and Wherefore*. San Angelo: Newsfoto Pub. Co., 1962. History of the Comanches and Fort Concho.

Haynes, Sam W. *Soldiers of Misfortune: The Somervell and Mier Expeditions*. Austin: University of Texas Press, 1990. An examination of the "black bean episode" and its political and diplomatic contexts.

Schmitz, Joseph William. *Texas Culture in the Days of the Republic, 1836–1846*. San Antonio: Naylor, 1960. Texas during the years of the Republic.

MULTIMEDIA MATERIALS

Indians of North America. (video) Zenger Video, 10200 Jefferson Boulevard, Room VC811, P.O. Box 802, Culver City, California, 90232. Presents a portrait of the culture and life of the Indians of the Southwest.

Westward Ho! the Wagons. (video) Coronet/MTI Film and Video, 108 Wilmot Road, Deerfield, Illinois, 60015. Portrait of the pioneers on a wagon train west.

Westward Wagons. (video, 24 min.) Southwest Media Services, Inc., P.O. Box 140, Wimberley, Texas, 78676. Journey across America as seen through the eyes of a ten-year-old boy.

STUDENTS WITH SPECIAL NEEDS

Limited English Proficient Students (LEP)

Have students use the Chapter 13 vocabulary terms as a review. Ask them to list the terms on a sheet of paper, allowing space for writing under each. Point out that all but one of the terms *(emancipating)* can be related to the concept of government. Have students use their textbook glossary to write a definition for each term. Then ask them to write a complete sentence for each term within the context of Chapter 13. See other activities labeled **LEP.**

Students Having Difficulty with the Chapter

Have students skim the chapter and make a list of key people discussed. Then ask them to prepare a one-sentence "Who am I?" clue for each. *(Example: "I served the Republic as the fourth president. Who am I?")* Provide the students with graph paper, and have them hide the names in a seek-and-find puzzle. Have students exchange the papers with a partner. They should answer the questions and then find the names in the puzzle. **LEP**

Auditory Learners

Have auditory learners research and prepare an oral report on one of the four presidents of the Re-public of Texas. See other activities labeled **A.**

Visual Learners

Have visual learners preview and/ or review the chapter by studying the illustrations and their captions. Allow students to ask questions about any terms or concepts they do not fully understand. See other activities labeled **V.**

Tactile/Kinesthetic Learners

Have tactile/kinesthetic learners create a series of drawings that they think capture the most important events of Texas during the period from 1836 to 1845. Ask them to share and discuss their drawings with the class. See other activities labeled **TK.**

Gifted Students

Have gifted students conduct additional research on the military and political careers of Sam Houston. Ask them to assess Houston's role in the history of Texas from the time he was commander-in-chief of the army through his terms as president of the Repub-lic. Was he a hero? Was he a great military commander? Was he a great president? See other activities labeled **G.**

VOCABULARY

In addition to the boldfaced terms in each section, some students might benefit from discussing the meanings of these terms.

Section 1: *majority* (p. 262); *custody* (p. 262); *violated* (p. 263).

Section 2: *legend* (p. 265); *duel* (p. 267); *sympathetic* (p. 269).

Section 3: *polls* (p. 271); *charter* (p. 272); *aggressive* (p. 278); *prospect* (p. 278).

Section 4: *salaries* (p. 279); *ambush* (p. 279); *status* (p. 280); *codes* (p. 280).

Section 5: *recognition* (p. 281); *embassy* (p. 281); *documents* (p. 283); *pardoned* (p. 285).

CHRONOLOGY

Have students study the Chapter 13 Time Line and identify relationships among the events.

GRAPHIC ORGANIZER

Have students skim the chapter and complete the Chapter 13 Graphic Organizer. *(You might wish to use this activity to review rather than to introduce the chapter.)*

ENRICHMENT

Have students complete the Chapter 13 Enrichment Worksheet.

SECTION 1

FOCUS

Predicting (I) Write the following statement on the chalkboard: *The Republic of Texas: What Lies Ahead?* Ask students to reflect on the challenges the newly independent nation might face. List their responses on the chalkboard. *(Challenges might include: stabilizing the economy, insuring national security, establishing foreign policy, and providing governmental services.)*

INSTRUCTION

Vocabulary (I) You may wish to preteach the following boldfaced terms: *republic* (p. 262); *cabinet* (p. 262); *annexation* (p. 263). **LEP**

CHAPTER 13 OVERVIEW

After the Texans' victory over Santa Anna at San Jacinto, Texans needed to turn to the task of beginning a new nation. Chapter 13 details the first three administrations of the new nation's government—their problems and policies, and their relations with the Indians. The chapter ends with a discussion of the Republic's international relations and the concern about annexation.

Essential Elements
2D, 2H, 6A, 9A, 9B

CHAPTER 13

A NEW NATION

The Story Continues...

Chapter 13 tells the story of the years from 1836 to 1845 when Texas was an independent country. The young Republic of Texas faced many problems and dangers during its decade of independence, but it survived and prospered.

As you read the chapter, look for the answers to these questions:

1. Who was elected first president of the Republic?
2. What problems did Houston face during his term in office?
3. What policy changes did President Lamar make?
4. What measures did Houston take to restore peace and order during his second term?
5. What caused the continuing conflict between the Republic of Texas and the Republic of Mexico?

1 First Days of the New Nation

Under its constitution, Texas was a **republic**. A republic is a form of government in which voters elect representatives to carry out the wishes of the majority of citizens. A republic is a type of democracy because its government is run by the people. As an independent country, Texas was known as the Republic of Texas.

Any celebration in the Republic of Texas after the Battle of San Jacinto could not last long. The new country faced many challenges. The work of the ad interim government began when it met at Velasco. The first task facing President Burnet and the **cabinet**, or group of advisers, was what to do with Santa Anna.

The Treaties of Velasco. Following the Battle of San Jacinto, Santa Anna was held in custody by Sam Houston. Because Houston had been shot in the ankle during the battle, he needed to go to New Orleans for treatment. He left Santa Anna in the care of President David G. Burnet.

Tracy W. McGregor Library, University of Virginia

In this political cartoon, Sam Houston (left) is shown accepting the surrender of Santa Anna (center). The Mexican general is pictured as grateful that Houston has spared his life. Many Texans thought that Santa Anna should have been executed.

Cooperative Learning (I) Organize students into groups of four or five. Tell students in each group to imagine that they are President Burnet and his advisers, and they must decide what to do with Santa Anna. Explain that their decision should be based not on emotion but on what is best for the Republic of Texas. Have a spokesperson from each group report its group's decision. **A, LEP**

Illustrating (II) Direct students to the political cartoon on page 262. Organize students into small groups and have them work together to create a political cartoon illustrating the Mexican point of view concerning Houston's treatment of Santa Anna. **V, TK, G**

Star of the Republic Museum, Washington-on-the-Brazos

This Republic of Texas flag was carried by Texas soldiers in 1842. The Lone Star flag was adopted as the official flag of the Republic in 1839 and has remained the flag of Texas ever since. This is why Texas is often referred to as the Lone Star state.

At Velasco, Santa Anna signed two treaties with the Texans. In the first treaty, which was made public, Santa Anna agreed to end the fighting against Texas. The first treaty also provided that prisoners held by Mexico and Texas would be exchanged. Then Santa Anna promised to take Mexican forces with him when he was freed and never to return to Texas. The second treaty was a secret one. In it, Santa Anna pledged to try to get the Mexican government to recognize the independence of Texas.

The promise to release Santa Anna was not popular with many Texans. There were demands that he be executed or put in prison. Dissatisfaction with the way President Burnet handled the treaties erupted into revolt.

In June 1836, Santa Anna was put aboard the ship *Invincible* for his return to Mexico. A force of Texans led by Thomas Green kept the ship from leaving Velasco. Texans demanded that Santa Anna be put to death. President Burnet refused but instead ordered Santa Anna to prison. Even though Santa Anna was later allowed to return to Mexico, the Texans had violated part of their agreement in the first Treaty of Velasco. Relations remained unsettled between Texas and Mexico.

The Election of 1836. To meet the requirements of the Constitution of 1836, President Burnet called for an election to be held in September. Texans were to elect new leaders of the Republic and to vote on the Constitution of 1836. Texans were also to consider **annexation**, or being added,

Historical Sidelight
The *Invincible* was one of four ships of the Texas navy, which was created in 1836.

San Jacinto Museum of History, Houston

Mirabeau B. Lamar was elected vice president of the new Republic. Lamar, a hero of San Jacinto, was popular and a great speaker. He was elected the second president of the Texas Republic in 1838.

Institute of Texan Cultures, from Original in Texas State Capitol

Thomas J. Rusk was a signer of the Texas Declaration of Independence. He was elected secretary of war and took part in the Battle of San Jacinto. He was later elected chief justice of the Texas Supreme Court and became one of the first Texans elected to the United States Senate.

to the United States. More than 6,000 Texans turned out to vote in this first election.

Sam Houston was elected president of Texas by a large majority. Mirabeau B. Lamar, another hero of the Battle of San Jacinto, was elected vice president. The voters approved the Constitution of 1836 as the law of the land. They also expressed their wish to ask the United States to annex Texas.

Once in office, President Houston appointed a cabinet to assist him in running the government. He chose people he believed were best able to solve the country's problems and to unite different points of view. Stephen F. Austin was appointed secretary of state, Thomas Rusk secretary of war, and Henry Smith secretary of the treasury.

Stephen F. Austin was able to serve the Republic of Texas for only a few months. As a result of overwork and exposure to the winter cold, he caught pneumonia. Austin died on December 27, 1836, at the age of 43. Texans of every political viewpoint mourned the loss of the man who had dedicated his life to Texas. President Houston honored

Richard Pearce-Moses

The small village of Houston was selected as the new capital of the Republic in 1836. Houston remained the capital until 1839. This engraving shows the old capitol building in Houston.

Stephen F. Austin by declaring a period of 30 days for mourning. In his official statement, Houston said, "The Father of Texas is no more. The first pioneer of the wilderness has departed."

Selecting a Capital. The first elected Congress of the Republic of Texas met at Columbia on October 3, 1836. President Burnet had earlier declared Columbia the temporary capital city. Because Columbia was too small, a movement grew to find a more suitable seat of government.

One of the acts passed by the first Congress was to move the capital to Houston. Houston was little more than a village itself in 1836. Two brothers, John and Augustus Allen, had recently founded the city five miles from Harrisburg on Buffalo Bayou. Named in honor of Sam Houston, the hero of San Jacinto, the new capital city grew rapidly to meet the needs of government. ✪

◪ President Sam Houston

When Sam Houston first rode into Texas in 1832, he was already well known as an American hero and western legend. He was born in Virginia on March 2, 1793. When his father died in 1807, Sam Houston moved with his mother to a Tennessee farm.

SECTION ★ 1 REVIEW

Define: republic, cabinet, annexation

Identify: Thomas Green, Mirabeau Lamar, John and Augustus Allen

1. What were the terms of the public Treaty of Velasco?
2. What propositions were approved by Texas voters during the first national election?
3. Who won the first presidential election held by the Republic of Texas?

Evaluating Information: If you had been elected president of the Republic of Texas, what qualities would you look for when selecting your cabinet members?

Exploring Multicultural Perspectives: How might the Mexican government have justified its refusal to recognize the Treaty of Velasco?

INSTRUCTION

Vocabulary (I) You may wish to preteach the following boldfaced terms: *administration* (p. 267); *specie* (p. 267); *poll tax* (p. 267); *ratify* (p. 269). **LEP**

Analyzing (I) Have students select one of the following problems facing the new government and create a chart evaluating possible solutions:

A. What should the government do about the growing debt?

B. What should the national policy be toward the Indians? The chart should appear as follows:

PROBLEM

Solution		Solution	
Positive	Negative	Positive	Negative

V, TK

Painting by Martin Johnson Heade. Archives Division, Texas State Library

Sam Houston was the first elected president of the Republic of Texas. Although he had many political enemies, the hero of San Jacinto remained popular with most Texans and was reelected president in 1841.

Early Fame. Sam Houston received some education in frontier schools, but most of his knowledge was gained from his father's library and from the Cherokees, with whom Houston spent much of his youth living and working in Tennessee. Cherokee Chief John Jolly adopted Sam and gave him a special name, "The Raven."

At the age of 21, Houston joined the United States Army and served under General Andrew Jackson. Jackson was later elected president of the United States. Houston and Jackson became good friends and remained so for the rest of their lives. After leaving the army, Sam Houston entered politics and was elected to represent Tennessee in the United States Congress. Later he was elected governor of Tennessee.

Just before his arrival in Texas, Houston spent another three years with the Cherokees in Arkansas. He admired the Native Americans and their way of life. He sometimes dressed in Indian blankets and leather moccasins. On several occasions, the president of the United States asked Houston to try to settle disputes between Indians and the United States government. By 1832, Houston's fame had spread all over the United States.

Cooperative Learning (I) Organize students into four groups, each representing one of the following: *the Cherokees, nomadic Indians living to the west of Texas settlements, land speculators, settlers moving west.* Allow time for members of each group to discuss Houston's Indian policy and its impact on them. Then have each group select a spokesperson to present its point of view of the issue. **A**

Multicultural Perspective (I) Present the following scenario to students: You are a Cherokee living in Texas in 1836. You have just learned of the new Texas land policy. What is your reaction? Will this affect your relationship with Sam Houston? Have students develop their responses in a brief paragraph. Invite volunteers to read their paragraphs aloud. **A, LEP**

Houston's First Administration. Serious problems faced Sam Houston when his first **administration**, or term of office, began on October 22, 1836. Texas government lacked order. County governments were also unorganized. Money was scarce. There was no clear land policy, and conflicts with Mexico and the Texas Indians continued.

A major problem that troubled President Houston was control of the army. Even during the Revolution, some members of the army refused to follow orders. At the beginning of Houston's first administration, control of the army was becoming difficult to maintain. A group of new settlers in Texas tried to take over the army to invade Mexico. President Houston appointed a new commander, Albert Sidney Johnston, but Johnston was wounded in a duel with the previous commander, Felix Huston. To bring the army under control, Houston placed all but 600 troops on leave and never recalled them to duty.

The Economic Crisis. Money to pay the costs of the army and of running the government was another major problem for the Republic of Texas. The country had a debt of $1.25 million when Sam Houston took office, and it had few means of raising money. To provide a money supply, the Republic printed paper money. But the government had no **specie**, or gold and silver, to back up the paper money. In other words, people could not exchange their paper money for gold or silver. They accepted the paper money only out of confidence that it could be used to purchase goods. But as confidence in the government's ability to pay its debts fell, the Republic's money began to lose its value. By accepting it, people were running a risk that it would become worthless.

To raise money, the government began collecting customs duties. The Republic also passed a wide variety of other tax laws. Taxes were placed on various businesses, property, and land titles. There was also a **poll tax**, a tax that must be paid in order to vote. And Texas public lands were put up for sale. Still, the government continued to spend more money than it raised. Despite the efforts of the congress and President Houston, the Republic's debt grew steadily. Eventually, Texas began to look to the United States for help in solving its financial problems.

Texas Land Policy. During Sam Houston's first term, a policy was established for the distribution and sale of

Economics
Make sure that students understand that paper money has no value in itself; rather, it represents something else of value.

Archives Division, Texas State Library

Republic of Texas paper money, such as this $20 bill, could not hold its face value because it was not supported by specie.

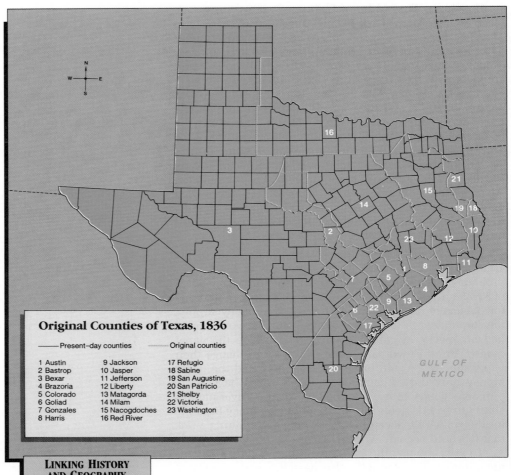

Original Counties of Texas, 1836

——— Present–day counties   ——— Original counties

1 Austin	9 Jackson	17 Refugio
2 Bastrop	10 Jasper	18 Sabine
3 Bexar	11 Jefferson	19 San Augustine
4 Brazoria	12 Liberty	20 San Patricio
5 Colorado	13 Matagorda	21 Shelby
6 Goliad	14 Milam	22 Victoria
7 Gonzales	15 Nacogdoches	23 Washington
8 Harris	16 Red River	

GULF OF MEXICO

Linking History and Geography
Bexar (3)

LINKING HISTORY AND GEOGRAPHY

Which 1836 county gave rise to the greatest number of present-day counties?

public lands. The Constitution of 1836 stated that every head of household in Texas before March 4, 1836, would receive 4,605 acres of free land. Heads of families who arrived in Texas after March 4, 1836 could get 1,280 acres. Veterans of the Texas Revolution were also eligible for free land. But African American Texans and Indians were not. By giving away land, the government hoped that the population would grow, thus strengthening the economy. This, in turn, would help the government raise funds.

EXTENSION
Research (III) Ask students to research and report on Texas' current laws regarding homestead protection. **A, G**

Independent Practice (I) Have students create a cause-and-effect diagram of the information discussed in Section 2. Invite several students to copy their diagrams onto the chalkboard. **V, TK**

The land law did not require settlers to live on the land they received from the government. Therefore, many speculators took free land and sold pieces of it, sometimes for rather high prices. After paying high prices for land, some newcomers later lost their homes when they could not pay their debts.

A law passed in January 1839 gave settlers additional land if they would live on it for three years. This law was intended to prevent people from buying land only to sell it. A family's home was also protected from sale to pay debts. The Homestead Law was based on similar laws passed by the legislature of Coahuila y Texas. These laws protected certain personal belongings from sale to pay debts.

Houston's Indian Policy. The Republic had an urgent need for a national Indian policy. As the population of Texas expanded, settlers again came into conflict with Texas Indians over land. Many members of the Texas army wanted to attack the Indians and remove them from Texas. President Houston was against such a policy for two reasons. First, the Republic had financial problems, and spending money on war would hurt the economy. Second, and more important, Houston was sympathetic to the Indians. He had lived with the Cherokees and cared about them. He knew they only wanted peace and control of their land.

Trouble was brewing in East Texas between the Republic and the Cherokees. Agents of the Mexican government hoped to encourage the Cherokees to fight the Texans. The Cherokees themselves were angry because the Texas government had not given them title to land occupied since 1820. In 1836, a treaty was signed to guarantee the Cherokees control of their land. But the Senate of the Republic of Texas refused to **ratify**, or approve, the treaty.

President Houston urged the Cherokees to be patient. He told them that he would do everything in his power as president to help. At the same time, he discouraged other Texans from settling in Cherokee territory. The Cherokees trusted Houston because they knew he was sincere. For a while, relations between the Republic and the Indians in East Texas were peaceful.

The nomadic Indians living to the west of Texas settlements presented a greater challenge for President Houston. Settlers were moving west by the hundreds, and they expected the government to protect them. Houston

Daughters of the Republic of Texas Library at the Alamo

Sam Houston often dressed in Indian clothing, a reminder of his longtime friendship with Native Americans. In this portrait he wears a Cherokee-style headdress.

National Museum of American Art, Washington, D.C. / Art Resource, New York

Artist George Catlin painted this portrait of Cherokee band chief Col-Lee.

Multicultural Perspective
Some Cherokees were in favor of cooperation with Mexico in hopes of gaining an independent land in East Texas.

SPIRIT OF TEXAS

Research (II) Ask interested students to research and report on the tragic "Trail of Tears"—the forced relocation of the Cherokees from their homelands in the southeastern United States to Oklahoma in 1838. Thousands of Cherokees died during the long march. **A, G**

RETEACHING

Have students list the problems facing Houston's first administration. Then ask them to list next to each problem the government's proposed solutions, if any. **LEP**

CLOSURE

Ask students: If the Texas Constitution had permitted a person to serve as president two times in a row, do you think Sam Houston would have been reelected? Why or why not?

Essential Elements
1C, 2A, 2C, 2D, 2H, 3E, 6B, 8C

**Answers to
Section 2 Review**

Define: *administration*—a president's term of office; *specie*—gold and silver; *poll tax*—tax paid in order to vote; *ratify*—approve

Identify: "The Raven"—name given to Sam Houston by the Cherokees; Andrew Jackson—president of the United States and friend of Sam Houston's; Albert Sidney Johnston—appointed commander of the Texas army by Houston, wounded in a duel by Felix Huston; Felix Huston—commander of the army before Johnston

1. The Texas government lacked order, money was scarce, there was no clear land policy, and conflicts with Texas Indians and the Mexican government continued.

(Continued on page 271)

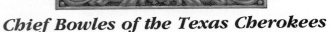

Chief Bowles of the Texas Cherokees

*I*n 1819 or 1820, a small group of Cherokees made a journey west to Texas. They were led by a man who played an important role in the history of Texas, Mexico, and the United States. He was Chief Bowles, and his Cherokee name was Diwali.

Chief Bowles' father was a Scotch-Irish trader and his mother was a Cherokee. When Diwali was growing up in Tennessee, the United States government constantly forced his people to move from their homelands. The government refused to recognize the Cherokees' right to own land.

The Cherokees were farmers, and they heard about the rich farmlands in Texas. In 1824, Chief Bowles and a group of Cherokees crossed the Sabine River and settled along the Angelina River in Northeast Texas.

For several years, life was peaceful and prosperous for the Texas Cherokees. Their farms flourished, and their settlements grew. One reason for their success was that the Mexican government in Texas recognized their right to the land. The future looked bright for Chief Bowles and his people.

In 1836, when war broke out between Mexico and Texas, the Cherokees agreed to a treaty with the Texans. This treaty would insure the Cherokees' right to stay on their land. It was signed by Chief Bowles and Sam Houston, the president of the Republic of Texas and a friend to the Cherokees. But soon after, trouble began for the Texas Cherokees. The Texas Senate failed to approve President Houston's treaty. The next president of Texas, Mirabeau B. Lamar, ignored Houston's Indian policies. Lamar allowed war to be declared on the Cherokees, and he ordered troops to attack and remove them from Texas.

Chief Bowles had hoped that his fighting days were over. Yet he knew that the pride of his people would not allow them to give up the land they had worked and loved. Chief Bowles and the Cherokees decided to fight to defend their homes.

In mid July of 1839, the Cherokees met the Texas army along the Neches River. The Cherokees were greatly outnumbered by the Texans, who killed hundreds of Cherokees. They then burned the Indian villages and farmlands. The Cherokees' years of hope and success in Texas were destroyed in just two days of fighting. Chief Bowles was killed in the last battle. When his body was found, he was holding a tin box. In it was the peace treaty made with Houston.

Cherokee lands were quickly settled by Texans. Only Sam Houston challenged the policy of the Texas government. He continued to campaign for Indian rights in memory of his respected friend Chief Bowles.

Inset: **Chief Bowles**

Inset: Courtesy Jenkins Company/Archives Division, Texas State Library

SECTION 3

FOCUS

Past Learning (I) Ask students to name the current president of the United States. Ask: How many terms in a row can a president serve *(two)*? Point out that the Texas Constitution did not allow a president to serve two times in a row; therefore, Houston could not run for reelection.

and the Texas Congress reacted with several policies. A line of forts was planned on the frontier to separate Indian territory from the rest of Texas. Law officers known as Texas Rangers were to patrol the frontier. Houston hoped to use these forts to keep Texans out of Indian lands. He also wanted to promote trade with the Indians, using the forts as centers for business activity.

Land speculators felt that Houston's policy was delaying settlement to the west and thus costing them money. Houston believed that an Indian war would be unjust and would prove to be too costly in lives and money. Every national election during the Republic years centered around this debate.

Houston attempted to make peace with each Indian group in Texas. Whenever treaties were signed, he tried to include the right of the Indians to own title to their land. In this respect, he was one of the few leaders in American history to believe that white settlers and Native Americans could live side by side in peace. ✪

3 President Mirabeau B. Lamar

In November of 1838, the people of Texas once again went to the polls to elect their leaders. The Texas Constitution did not allow anyone to serve as president two times in a row, so Houston could not run. Mirabeau B. Lamar was elected president of Texas in 1838. David G. Burnet was chosen as his vice president. Both men disagreed with Houston's policies and personally disliked him. It was clear that the government's policies would change.

A Commitment to Education. Mirabeau Lamar is perhaps best remembered for his commitment to education. At his **inaugural address**, or opening speech when he became president, in December 1838, Lamar stressed the need for the nation to set up a system of public education. He proclaimed that "a cultivated mind is the guardian genius of Democracy, and while guided and controlled by virtue, the noblest attribute to man."

Congress responded to Lamar's stirring speech with education acts passed in 1839 and 1840. To support public schools, the Republic set aside 17,712 acres of land in each county. To support the future establishment of two universities, the government set aside 221,400 acres.

SECTION 2 REVIEW

Define: administration, specie, poll tax, ratify
Identify: "The Raven," Andrew Jackson, Albert Sidney Johnston, Felix Huston

1. What major problems did President Houston face during his first two years in office?
2. How did the new republic try to raise money to pay its debts?
3. What were Houston's Indian policies? What special-interest group opposed them?

Exploring Economics: Explain how the Republic of Texas hoped to raise money by giving away public lands.

Seeing Cause and Effect: What political event of Houston's first term strongly affected the Cherokees? What consequences do you think this event might have?

---

2. By printing paper money and by establishing taxes and customs duties
3. Houston tried to establish peace treaties with the Indians and keep settlers off their lands. Land speculators opposed Houston's policies.

Exploring Economics: If land were given away, the population and prosperity of Texas would grow and tax revenues would increase, strengthening the economy.

Seeing Cause and Effect: The Texas Senate rejected the treaty that guaranteed the Cherokees the right to their lands. This action meant that the Cherokees had no legal claim to their lands.

Essential Elements
2D, 2H, 5B, 5C, 7B, 7D, 7F, 8B, 8D, 9A, 9B

Geography
Remind students that although Austin is near the center of Texas today, it was on the western edge of settlement in the early 1840s.

INSTRUCTION

Vocabulary (I) You may wish to preteach the following boldfaced term: *inaugural address* (p. 271); *capitol* (p. 273). **LEP**

Geography (I) Ask volunteers to come to the front of the class and locate on a wall map of Texas the location of the universities opened during the years of the Republic. **A, V, LEP**

Geography (I) To reinforce the geographic theme of *location,* ask students why Austin as the capital seemed too far west to many Texans. Then ask them what location they would select if Texas were to build a new capital city and why. **A, V**

Rutersville College was the first college to open in Texas. The college had both a female and male division. This early photo is of the main building, completed in 1842. The school was later moved to Georgetown and became Southwestern University.

Institute of Texan Cultures

The Texas Collection, Baylor University

This photo shows the ruins of Baylor University at Independence. The campus at Independence was abandoned when the university relocated in Waco in 1886.

Public universities were not built until after the 1860s, but several private colleges did appear during the Republic years. The first college to begin operation in Texas was Rutersville College. It opened in February 1840 in Rutersville, a small town near La Grange. Other colleges also appeared in the 1840s. Among them were Galveston University, the University of San Augustine, and Nacogdoches University. In 1845, the Republic granted a charter to Baylor University, and it began classes the next year.

A New Capital for Texas. President Lamar and many members of Congress were unhappy with the town of Houston as a capital for the Republic. They complained that Houston was too far from inland cities of Texas. Lamar had a personal dislike for the capital city because it was named for his chief rival.

In 1839, Congress created a commission to locate a permanent capital. The commissioners were instructed to find a site between the Trinity and Colorado rivers and north of the Old San Antonio Road. They chose a little village known at the time as Waterloo. Located on the Colorado River, Waterloo was about 30 miles northwest of Bastrop. The village, populated by only a few families in 1839, was renamed Austin in honor of Stephen F. Austin.

After the site for the capital was selected, Judge Edwin Waller was sent to Austin to lay out the streets and begin

Multicultural Perspective (I) Present the following to students for class discussion: You are a historian writing a biography of President Lamar. As a native Texan and a descendant of the Cherokees, will your biography be objective? Why or why not? **A**

Guided Practice (I) Ask students to write a brief paragraph summarizing the economic condition of the Republic of Texas during Lamar's presidency. Then pair students and have them brainstorm to develop a possible solution to the nation's economic problems. **A**

The Granger Collection

In 1839, President Mirabeau B. Lamar appointed a commission to select a site for a permanent capital. The village of Waterloo on the banks of the Colorado River was chosen. The small town was renamed Austin in honor of Stephen F. Austin. This lithograph shows the settlement around 1840.

constructing government buildings. A **capitol**, or building in which the legislature meets, was built. Homes appeared, and businesses sprang up along the main street, Congress Avenue. But many people were disappointed by the choice of Austin as the capital. They claimed that it was too far west and subject to constant Comanche raids. Life in frontier Austin was difficult and dangerous. But as more people moved in and peace was made with the nearby Tonkawas, most Texans became satisfied with their new capital city.

Continuing Economic Problems. The financial problems of the Republic grew during the administration of Mirabeau Lamar. The public debt increased, and the value of the Texas dollar decreased. To meet the crisis, President Lamar and the Texas Congress issued more paper money called "redbacks." The value of the redbacks also fell. In comparison to the United States dollar, the Texas dollar was worth only about two cents by 1841.

The reason for the continued decline in the value of Texas money was quite clear. The government was spending more than it collected in taxes. The extra government expense was largely a result of spending more money for

Archives Division, Texas State Library

"Redbacks" were issued during President Lamar's administration, but their value quickly fell.

Chapter 13 **273**

Chapter 13 **273**

Predicting (II) Have students use the information presented in the special feature to speculate about why people might want to live in Austin. Then have students study the chart and predict the population of Austin in the year 2000. Ask students to provide explanations for their predictions. **A, V**

Essential Elements
4B, 4H, 4I, 5B, 9A

Austin

Population: 465,622

Metro area population: 559,173

Size: 130 square miles

Relative location: On the Colorado River, 160 miles west of Houston

Region: Central Texas, edge of the Blackland Prairie

County: County seat of Travis County

Special feature: The capital of Texas

Origin of name: Named for Stephen F. Austin

Landmarks: The Texas State Capitol, the University of Texas, the Lyndon Baines Johnson Library

Economy: State, local, and federal governments employ more than one-third of Austin's work force. The University of Texas is the largest single employer, but more than 200 trade organizations and associations have their headquarters in Austin. In recent years, the city has become a center for the production of elec-

tronic equipment and for research of various kinds.

History: Settlers first arrived in the early 1800s, when the area was inhabited by Tonkawas. The settlers called their small community Waterloo. In 1839, Judge Edwin Waller, the first mayor, mapped the original plan for the city, which was chosen as the new capital of the Republic

of Texas. The original grid pattern of Waller's plan is still visible in the layout of downtown Austin.

Recreation facilities: Austin has several dams on the Colorado River, which have created artificial lakes within the city. These— along with many city parks, hike-and-bike trails, and Barton Springs—provide recreation facilities that attract many visitors.

Cultural activities: Austin has long been the home of many writers, artists, dancers, craftspeople, and musicians of regional and national renown. A wide variety of music is performed throughout the city, including jazz, blues, rock, *conjunto*, country-western, and classical.

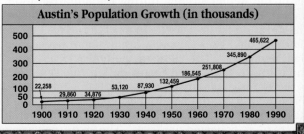

Austin's Population Growth (in thousands)

Year	Population
1900	22,258
1910	29,860
1920	34,876
1930	53,120
1940	87,930
1950	132,459
1960	186,545
1970	251,808
1980	345,890
1990	465,622

EXTENSION

Community Involvement (II) Have students prepare an oral and visual demonstration of the culture of a Native American group they have selected and researched. If there are Native American students in your class, you may wish to invite them to ask their family members for help with their project. Other students may consult the local historical society or Native Americans living in their community. Presentations should include costumes, food, or other articles belonging to the Native Americans, as well as a map showing reservations where many Native Americans still live. **A, V, TK, G**

Barker Texas History Center

The first capitol in Austin was a one-story frame building surrounded by a stockade as protection against raids by Indians.

the army. President Lamar's reversal of Houston's Indian peace policy began costing lives and money.

Lamar's Wars with Texas Indians. President Lamar disliked the Indians and wanted them removed from Texas. He disagreed with Houston's claim that the Indians had a right to their land. Albert Sidney Johnston, secretary of war, and George W. Bonnell, Houston's commissioner of Indian affairs, joined Lamar in this new policy. It was a plan that proved to be a disaster for the Indians.

The Cherokees were the first to feel the effects of Lamar's policy. In 1839, Lamar declared that they had no claim to their land and ordered them to leave Texas. When the Cherokees refused, 500 Texas soldiers led by Kelsey Douglass marched into East Texas to remove them. In July of 1839, war broke out west of the present-day city of Tyler. The Texans won this conflict, known as the Battle of the Neches, and drove the surviving Indians north of Texas into Indian Territory in present-day Oklahoma. Some other Indian groups, including the Shawnees and Caddoes, were also removed at this time.

War with the Comanches had never really stopped. The Comanches raided a number of Texas settlements in 1836. In these raids, the Comanches sometimes carried away captives. In May 1836, a band of Comanche and Kiowa warriors attacked Parker's Fort, located near present-day

Independent Practice (II) Tell students to imagine that they are Cynthia Ann Parker writing a diary entry describing the Council House Fight and the Battle of Plum Creek. Remind students that although Parker was an Anglo American, she grew up with the Comanches. Invite students to share their entries with the class. **A**

Historical Sidelight
Texas Indian historian W.W. Newcomb suggested that this particular band of Comanches only had the two captives, although other bands of Comanches probably held others.

Quanah Parker, son of Cynthia Ann Parker and Peta Nocona, became one of the last great Comanche chiefs and participated in the Indian wars in Texas. He later became well known for his efforts to establish better relations between the United States government and Indians.

Gibbs Memorial Library

Groesbeck in Limestone County. After killing most of the settlers, the Indians kidnapped two women and three children. One of the captives was Cynthia Ann Parker. Named Naduah by the Comanches, Parker grew up living a nomadic life on the plains. As a young woman, Parker married a Comanche chief named Peta Nocona. Their son, Quanah Parker, became a great Comanche chief. [You will read more about Quanah and Cynthia Ann Parker in Chapter 20.]

The raids of the 1830s angered Texans and made them wish to strike at the Comanches. President Lamar sent Colonel John Moore westward in 1839 to attack the Comanches living on the western frontier of Texas. Moore and his troops raided several villages northwest of Austin along the San Saba and Colorado rivers. Because of the raids by Moore, the Comanches met in San Antonio to talk about peace.

The Council House Fight. On March 19, 1840, about 65 Comanche men, women, and children arrived in San Antonio. They had agreed to bring their Texas captives to the meeting. When the Comanches arrived with only two captives, Matilda Lockhart and a Mexican boy, the Texans tried to take all of the Indians prisoner. A battle broke out in San Antonio's central plaza next to the Council House. Twelve Comanche chiefs, several Comanche women, and more than 20 Comanche warriors were killed. At least seven Texans died in the Council House Fight.

When other Comanches heard about the fight, they were enraged. They put their Texas captives to death. A large raiding party struck the Texas settlements of Victoria and Linnville, killing people, burning houses, and stealing livestock. The Council House Fight probably destroyed any chance that peace could be achieved between the Texans and Comanches.

The Battle of Plum Creek. Texans were in turn angered when they heard about the Comanche raids. A force of volunteers, soldiers, and Texas Rangers began searching for the band of Comanches that had raided Victoria and Linnville. Under the command of Felix Huston, Edward Burleson, and Ben McCulloch, the Texans caught up with the Comanches on August 11, 1840. In the battle that followed at Plum Creek just outside Lockhart, the Comanches lost more than 100 men.

The Texans were not satisfied, and they decided to strike farther into Comanche country. Colonel John Moore was sent northwest, again in search of Comanche camps. He found them along the Colorado River nearly 200 miles upriver from Austin. The Texans caught the Comanches by surprise and destroyed an Indian village. More than 125 Comanches were killed, and two Texans died. The Texans killed men, women, and children in the raid.

Historical Sidelight
Many citizens of Linnville escaped death only by boarding boats and rowing out into the bay.

The Battle of Plum Creek, near present-day Lockhart, was a decisive defeat for the Comanches.

Painting by Lee Herring, courtesy William Adams, Dallas

TEXAS VOICES

Analyzing (I) Ask a volunteer to read Sam Houston's poem aloud. Then, through class discussion, help students determine Houston's message in the poem. **A, LEP**

CLOSURE

Ask students: For what is President Lamar best remembered *(his commitment to education)*?

ASSESSMENT

Have students complete the Section 3 Review on page 278.

SECTION 4

FOCUS

Past Learning (I) Ask students to recall ways in which President Lamar's policies differed from Sam Houston's. Point out that after the Lamar administration, voters were ready to welcome Houston back into office.

Essential Element
2H

Answers to Section 3 Review

Define: *inaugural address*—a president's opening speech; *capitol*—building where the legislature meets

Identify: Battle of the Neches—East Texas battle that resulted in the surviving Cherokees being driven into Indian Territory; Council House Fight—San Antonio battle between Comanches and Texans; Battle of Plum Creek—battle near Lockhart in which more than 100 Comanches were killed

1. Lamar moved the capital from Houston to Austin and tried to force the Indians to leave Texas.
2. Houston supporters wanted the capital to remain in their leader's namesake town. They saw Austin as a frontier town still subject to Indian attack.
3. They killed all of their captives and launched raids on Victoria and Linnville.

Exploring Geography: Possible flooding

Interpreting Pictures: Some of the Indians appear to be wearing hats and other clothing items taken from the settlers.

Essential Elements
2D, 2F, 2H, 4C, 7D, 9A, 9B, 9E, 9F

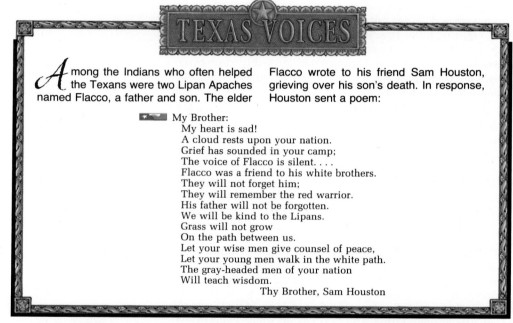

TEXAS VOICES

*A*mong the Indians who often helped the Texans were two Lipan Apaches named Flacco, a father and son. The elder Flacco wrote to his friend Sam Houston, grieving over his son's death. In response, Houston sent a poem:

 My Brother:
My heart is sad!
A cloud rests upon your nation.
Grief has sounded in your camp;
The voice of Flacco is silent. . . .
Flacco was a friend to his white brothers.
They will not forget him;
They will remember the red warrior.
His father will not be forgotten.
We will be kind to the Lipans.
Grass will not grow
On the path between us.
Let your wise men give counsel of peace,
Let your young men walk in the white path.
The gray-headed men of your nation
Will teach wisdom.
                    Thy Brother, Sam Houston

SECTION 3 REVIEW

Define: inaugural address, capitol

Identify: Battle of the Neches, Council House Fight, Battle of Plum Creek

1. How did President Lamar change policies about the state capital and the Indians?
2. Why did people object to Lamar's new state capital?
3. How did the Comanches react to the Council House Fight?

Exploring Geography: Study the early lithograph of Austin on page 273. What danger to the new capital can you see in this illustration?

Interpreting Pictures: Look at the painting on page 277. What evidence of the Comanches' raid on Victoria and Linnville can you find in the picture?

The Cost of Indian Wars. Many Texan and Indian lives were lost as a result of President Lamar's aggressive Indian policy. The Indian wars cost the Republic of Texas $2.5 million. By the end of his term, Lamar had achieved his goal of removing the Cherokees from East Texas. The Comanches had been pushed farther west, opening vast lands for settlement. Speculators and new immigrants to Texas were pleased with the prospect of more land, but others were unhappy about the growing national debt. ○

4 Houston Returns

In the fall of 1841, Texas voters returned to the polls to elect a new president. The people were unhappy over constant war with the Indians, worthless Texas redbacks, and the rising national debt. Once again, they chose Sam Houston to lead them. Houston defeated David G. Burnet, the candidate favored by Lamar, by about 4,300 votes.

Economy in Government. Houston sought to reduce the debt of the Republic during his second administration. The

INSTRUCTION

Vocabulary (I) You may wish to preteach the following boldfaced term: *emancipating* (p. 280). **LEP**

Analyzing (II) Ask students to review the Section 4 subsection "A Return to Peace." Ask: What does the author mean by "if only for a short period"? Why is Houston's peace policy destined for failure? *(Lead students to conclude that as the frontier moves farther west, these Indian lands will be sought after by settlers.)* **A**

Guided Practice (I) Have students imagine that they are an African American in Texas in 1840 writing a letter to a distant friend. Tell them to explain why they think they were better off before independence from Mexico. Invite students to read their letters aloud. **A**

Independent Practice (II) Ask students to use their historical imagination to write a speech that will be given in 1844 promoting the election of Dr. Anson Jones. Tell them to explain why it is important that Sam Houston's policies be continued. Invite several students to give their speech aloud. **A**

size of the government was reduced to save money. Workers who did not lose their jobs found their salaries cut. The Texas army and the Texas Rangers also suffered cuts in staff. In 1843, Houston convinced Congress to sell the navy. He believed the four ships were too expensive to maintain. But his wish to sell the ships was never carried out.

To help maintain the value of its paper money, the government of the Republic passed a law restricting the amount issued. This policy did not succeed, because the value of the paper money continued to fall.

A Return to Peace. In addition to other economic measures, President Houston hoped to reduce military spending. He wanted the Republic to return to the peace policy of his first administration. In September 1843, a peace treaty was signed between the Republic and the Wacos and Tawakonis at Bird's Fort, just west of present-day Dallas. In October 1844, Houston met with Chief Buffalo Hump of the Penateka band of Comanches. The two leaders agreed to the Treaty of Tehuacana Creek, a peace and trading treaty.

A key part of Houston's peace policy was to open trade between the Indians and Texas merchants. Trading houses were encouraged on the frontier to keep Indians supplied with goods so that they would not raid Texas homes or businesses. Once again, peace came to the western frontier of Texas. Houston had proved, if only for a short period, that Texans and Indians could live together peacefully.

The Regulator-Moderator War. Meanwhile, a feud between old settlers and newcomers in East Texas was becoming violent. It began over land titles in the old Neutral Ground. Gradually, more people were drawn in on each side. In the Neutral Ground, law enforcement was weak and outlaws were everywhere. Local officials were unable to stop the feud. Some were personally involved on one side or the other. Calling themselves Regulators or Moderators, each side claimed to have formed to fight crime. They attacked each other and anyone else who got in their way.

Violence began in Shelby County in 1840. It then spread to surrounding counties in Texas and Louisiana. Crops went untended, men were shot from ambush, prisoners were hung without trial, houses were burned, and people were driven from their homes. Eventually, each side numbered in the hundreds. In August 1844, President Houston

Drawing by Emil Bunjes. Rosenberg Library

The *Independence* was a schooner in the Texas navy. It was captured by Mexico in 1837.

Economics
Stress the connection between revenues and expenditures by the Republic government. Point out that all governments face the issues of spending and taxation.

RETEACHING
Ask students to write a brief summary of each of the sub-sections of Section 4. **LEP**

CLOSURE
Point out that the challenges facing the Republic of Texas included establishing relations with Mexico and the United States. Tell students that they will learn more about these issues in Section 5.

ASSESSMENT
Have students complete the Section 4 Review on page 280.

Answers to Section 4 Review

Define: *emancipating*—freeing
Identify: Chief Buffalo Hump—Penateka Comanche chief who signed the Treaty of Tehuacana Creek; the Regulator-Moderator War—East Texas feud that began between old settlers and newcomers; Dr. Anson Jones—the last president of the Texas Republic

1. By signing trade and peace treaties
2. He restricted the size of the government, cut government salaries, reduced the size of the Texas army and Texas Rangers, and tried to sell the Texas navy.
3. Sam Houston sent several hundred troops to restore order. Both sides were forced to negotiate.

Solving Problems: Answers will vary. The blacksmith might try to remain aloof from both sides; however, the only effective option was to leave the area.

Seeing Cause and Effect: It was too late for Houston to help the Cherokees. Lamar had defeated them and forced them to leave Texas.

Essential Elements
2D, 2H, 4C, 5B, 5C, 7A, 9A, 9B, 9E

SECTION 4 REVIEW

Define: emancipating
Identify: Chief Buffalo Hump, the Regulator-Moderator War, Dr. Anson Jones

1. How did Houston try to establish peace with the Indians during his second term as president?
2. What measures did Houston take to reduce government spending?
3. How was the Regulator-Moderator conflict brought to a close?

Solving Problems: Imagine that you are a blacksmith in Shelby County during the early 1840s. You do not wish to take part in the Regulator-Moderator feud. What might you do to stay out of the conflict?

Seeing Cause and Effect: Why did Houston's Indian policy after 1842 have nothing to do with his friends the Cherokees?

---

sent 600 soldiers into the region to stop the feud. The soldiers finally broke up the Regulators and Moderators.

Blacks in the Republic of Texas. The status of African American Texans changed dramatically following independence. The Texas Constitution of 1836 legalized slavery. It prohibited the Texas Congress from restricting the importation of new slaves from the United States. It also prohibited the Congress from **emancipating**, or freeing, Texas slaves. At the same time, Congress passed slave codes that defined the status of slaves in Texas society.

Because of this legal encouragement, many more slaves were brought to Texas. The number of slaves increased from about 5,000 in 1836 to about 46,000 ten years later. Free blacks also suffered. Texas law made it difficult for free blacks to reside in Texas. Most free African Americans needed an act of Congress to remain legally in the state. A few free blacks, such as Samuel McCullough, received this permission because of their military service during the Revolution. Others, such as Hendrick Arnold, a hero of the Battle of San Antonio, stayed without obtaining permission. But most free blacks left the state. By 1860 there were only about 355 free blacks in Texas, fewer than in any other southern state.

Dr. Anson Jones. The major political factions during the years of the Republic were those favoring Sam Houston's policies and those favoring Mirabeau Lamar's. In the last election under the Republic, in 1844, a president was elected who carried on most of Houston's policies. He was Dr. Anson Jones. Jones was a successful doctor from Brazoria who had served as secretary of state under Sam Houston. He was also a veteran of the Battle of San Jacinto and had served in the Texas Congress.

Jones defeated Edward Burleson by a vote of 7,037 to 5,668. His vice president was Kenneth Anderson. During the Jones administration, peace was maintained with the Indians, and the government tried to limit its spending. ○

5 Relations with Foreign Governments

Even as the Republic sought to work out its problems at home, it faced the challenge of **foreign relations**, or dealings with other countries. One of the first goals of the

SECTION 5

FOCUS

Past Learning (I) Explain to students the distinction between the terms *domestic* and *international*. Draw on the chalkboard a two-column chart with these terms as headings. Have students classify as domestic or international the Republic's problems that they have read about thus far in Chapter 13. Instruct students to copy the chart onto a sheet of paper to save for later use.

INSTRUCTION

Vocabulary (I) You may wish to preteach the following boldfaced terms: *foreign relations* (p. 280); *archives* (p. 283). **LEP**

Republic was to persuade other countries to recognize the independence of Texas. The first government to offer recognition was the United States.

Recognition from the United States did not come easily. Many Americans did not wish to anger Mexico, which still considered Texas part of its territory. Some Americans were opposed to slavery, in Texas as well as in the southern United States. Finally, the government of Andrew Jackson recognized Texas and sent Alcée La Branche as a United States diplomat to Texas. In return, Texas sent Memucan Hunt and William H. Wharton to Washington as representatives of the Republic.

Efforts to achieve recognition from the European nations began soon after United States recognition. James Pinckney Henderson was sent to Europe by President Houston in 1837. France was the first European country to recognize Texas, and Holland, England, and Belgium soon followed. The French sent a diplomat and built an embassy in Austin. The French *chargé d'affaires* to Texas, Count Alphonse de Saligny, moved to Austin in 1840.

Conflict with Mexico. Mexico refused to recognize Texas as an independent nation. It rejected the Treaty of Velasco. And numerous times during the Republic years, fighting broke out between Texas and Mexico.

President Lamar believed that he could use the navy to force Mexico to recognize Texas. The Texas fleet was expanded to include six warships. Lamar ordered the navy into Mexican waters to aid rebels fighting the Mexican government.

The Santa Fe Expedition. One specific disagreement between Texas and Mexico was the location of the western boundary of Texas. Texans argued that the boundary extended into New Mexico and included all land east of the Rio Grande. By this argument, the city of Santa Fe was in Texas. Of course, the Mexicans disagreed. President Houston made no effort to enforce this claim. But President Lamar tried to take control of the Santa Fe area.

In June of 1841, Lamar sent an expedition of about 320 people to Santa Fe. In the expedition were 270 soldiers under the leadership of Brigadier General Hugh McLeod. Their goal was to secure the Santa Fe region for Texas and to open up trade between New Mexico and Texas. From

Richard Pearce-Moses

Dr. Anson Jones was elected president in September 1844. He was the last president of the Republic and retired to his farm near Washington-on-the-Brazos after the annexation of Texas in 1845.

Richard Pearce-Moses

France was the first European nation to recognize the Republic of Texas. In 1840, Count Alphonse de Saligny came to Texas as the French *chargé d'affaires*. The French Legation still stands in Austin and is maintained by the state.

Historical Sidelight
Britain and France hoped to gain influence in Texas while limiting the influence of the United States. These two countries were rivals of the United States in other areas of North America and the world.

Writing (II) Instruct students to write a newspaper editorial titled "Should Texas Be Recognized as an Independent Nation?" for a newspaper in one of the following countries: Texas, Mexico, the United States, or France. Invite four students representing each of the four countries to read their editorials aloud. **A, G**

Geography (I) Display a wall map showing Texas and New Mexico. Invite a volunteer to come to the front of the class and use the map's scale indicator to calculate the distance that Lamar's Santa Fe expedition traveled. *(The student should measure the distance from Austin to Santa Fe.)* Have students examine the wall map and the maps in their textbooks to name the geographic features (such as mountains, rivers, plains, and so on) that the expedition encountered on its trip. **A, V, LEP**

Transparency 15
A transparency of this map can be found in the Teacher's Resource Binder.

Linking History and Geography
Santa Fe was claimed as part of Texas at the time.

Economics
President Lamar and some others hoped that Texas might gain the rich trade of New Mexico, which was being carried on from Santa Fe to Independence, Missouri. Texas ports could have offered a convenient outlet for this trade.

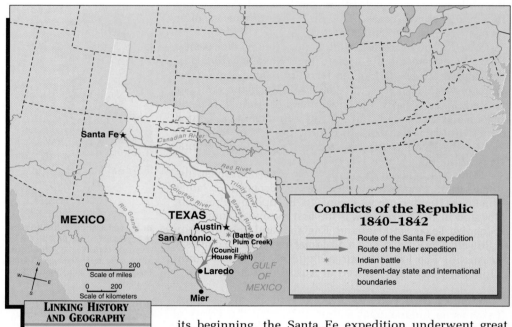

LINKING HISTORY AND GEOGRAPHY

According to the map, why did Texans think they had a right to send an expedition to Santa Fe?

its beginning, the Santa Fe expedition underwent great hardships. Crossing the High Plains proved to be difficult, just as it had been for the Spanish conquistadores. The Texans lost their way and faced unfriendly Indians. Food and water were in short supply.

When they reached Santa Fe, the Texans were exhausted. The people of Santa Fe did not welcome the expedition. A large Mexican military force easily captured the Texans. From Santa Fe the Texans were marched more than 2,000 miles to Mexico City and thrown into prison.

Lamar's Santa Fe expedition was a failure. Many Texans died, and the expedition cost a great sum of money. It so angered the Mexicans that they began similar raids into Texas.

The Mexicans Invade Texas. As a result of the Santa Fe expedition, a Mexican force entered Texas in 1842. General Rafael Vásquez and 500 soldiers invaded San Antonio, Goliad, and Refugio. While at San Antonio, General Vásquez flew the Mexican flag over the city and declared Mexican control over Texas. But he soon went back to Mexico.

Many people in Texas panicked when they heard that Mexican troops were invading. President Houston called

Historical Imagination (I) Have students imagine that they are a survivor of the Mier expedition. They must write a letter to Sam Houston criticizing or defending Colonel William Fisher's actions. Ask several students to read their letters aloud. **A**

Guided Practice (I) Refer students to the chart they created in this section's Focus activity. Ask them to add to the chart the information discussed in Section 5. **V, TK, LEP**

Austin History Center, Austin Public Library

The Archives War was touched off by fear that President Houston intended to return the capital to Houston from Austin. Angelina Eberly led a group of Austinites who fired on government officials as they removed papers from the state capitol.

up the Texas militia. He then started to withdraw the government **archives**, or records, from Austin. Some people suspected that the president wanted to return the capital to the city of Houston. Citizens in Austin were against this move. Led by Angelina Eberly, they even fired at government officials when the officials began loading documents onto wagons. This short conflict, called the Archives War, ended with the documents back in Austin.

On September 11, 1842, Mexico invaded Texas again. General Adrián Woll and 1,500 Mexican soldiers captured San Antonio. Fighting broke out as hundreds of Texas militia and Texas Rangers made their way to San Antonio. The Texans ambushed General Woll's force on Salado Creek, about six miles from San Antonio. The Mexicans suffered heavy losses and then retreated to Mexico. As General Woll marched south, he took a number of captives with him. The people of Texas were angry, and many demanded a declaration of war against Mexico.

The Mier Expedition. In November 1842, President Houston ordered General Alexander Somervell and 750 Texas soldiers to the Rio Grande in southern Texas. They

Current Events (II) Ask students to search daily newspapers or listen to news reports for one week to find accounts of current problems or issues facing our nation's government. Have them record and classify these issues in a chart labeled *Domestic* and *International*. At the end of one week, invite students to share and discuss their charts. **A, V, TK**

Museum of Fine Arts, Houston, The Hogg Brothers Collection, gift of Miss Ima Hogg

Members of the Mier expedition were forced to draw beans from a jar. Prisoners who drew black beans were immediately executed. This painting is by Frederic Remington.

Historical Sidelight

President Houston's desire for peace was unpopular with many Texans, especially after the latest invasions. The Mier expedition revealed just how unpopular Houston's policy was. In fact, the expedition increased public opinion in favor of annexation.

were to protect the border and insure that the Mexican armies had left Texas. When Somervell reached the Rio Grande, he concluded that the Mexican threat was over. He then ordered his soldiers home. Three hundred of the Texans refused to obey Somervell's orders. They were determined to invade Mexico. Under the command of Colonel William Fisher, the 300 Texans crossed the Rio Grande in December and made their way toward the little Mexican town of Mier.

The Texans knew there was a Mexican force at Mier, but they did not know that it consisted of 2,000 soldiers. For two days, a battle raged. Finally, after nearly defeating the large Mexican force, the Texans surrendered. As prisoners of war, they began the long march to Mexico City. During the march south, 193 Texans escaped. Wandering in the mountains without food and water, most of these Texans either died or were recaptured within a week.

RETEACHING
With the class, create on the chalkboard an outline of the information discussed in Section 5. **LEP, A, V**

CLOSURE
Review with students the last paragraph of Section 5. Ask: Which is the best choice for Texas?

ASSESSMENT
Have students complete the Section 5 Review on page 285.

Barker Texas History Center

This photograph shows the surviving members of the Mier expedition. The picture was taken years after the ill-fated expedition.

Santa Anna, who was once again the ruler of Mexico, ordered every tenth person shot as punishment for the escape attempt. The 176 prisoners had to draw beans from a jar to determine who would live and who would be executed. The jar was filled with 159 white beans and 17 black beans. The prisoners who drew the black beans were removed from prison, blindfolded, and shot.

Of the remaining captives, eight eventually managed to escape, a few died in prison, and some were pardoned by the Mexican government. In September of 1844, the last of the Mier prisoners were released.

Mexico Offers Recognition of Texas. Through the efforts of England and France, peace was slowly restored between Texas and Mexico. Both European countries wanted Texas to remain an independent nation. They put great diplomatic pressure on Mexico to recognize Texas in order to keep it from becoming part of the United States. Finally, in 1845, Mexico did agree to recognize the independence of Texas. But the Mexican offer required that the Texans reject annexation by the United States.

The Texans had a choice. They could accept the Mexican offer and finally have a secure relationship with their southern neighbor. Or they could reject the Mexican offer and go ahead with plans to join the United States. ✪

SECTION ⑤ REVIEW

Define: foreign relations, archives

Identify: Brigadier General Hugh McLeod, General Rafael Vásquez, General Adrián Woll, General Alexander Somervell

1. Why was the United States slow to recognize the independence of Texas?
2. Why did military conflicts with Mexico continue in the years after 1836?
3. How did Mexico retaliate for the Santa Fe expedition?

Evaluating Information: Which part of the foreign policy of the Republic of Texas do you think was the most successful? Which was the least successful? Explain.

Exploring Geography: What prevented the Republic of Texas from exercising any real control over the northwestern part of the area it claimed?

Answers to Section 5 Review

Define: *foreign relations*—dealings with other countries; *archives*—records

Identify: Brigadier General Hugh McLeod—led Lamar's Santa Fe expedition; General Rafael Vásquez—Mexican army leader who captured San Antonio in retaliation for the attack on Santa Fe; General Adrián Woll—led a later Mexican army that also captured San Antonio; General Alexander Somervell—led Texas forces to protect the southern border of Texas

1. Many Americans did not want to anger Mexico, and many were opposed to slavery.
2. Mexico rejected the Treaty of Velasco and refused to recognize an independent Texas.
3. It sent armies to capture San Antonio twice in 1842.

Evaluating Information: Answers will vary. The Republic was successful in getting formal recognition from several foreign nations, including France, Holland, England, Belgium, and the United States. It had little success in establishing better relations with Mexico because, until 1845, Mexico refused to recognize Texas' independence.

Exploring Geography: It was far from settlements, and the Comanches and other hostile Indians claimed it as theirs.

CHAPTER REVIEW RESOURCES

1. Chapter Review Worksheet 13
2. Chapter 13 Test, Form A
3. Reteaching Worksheet 13
4. Chapter 13 Test, Form B
5. **Informal Evaluation Forms:** Portfolio Assessment
6. *Texas, Our Texas* **Test Generator**

Essential Elements
2D, 2H, 5C, 9A, 9B, 9D

CHAPTER 13 REVIEW ANSWERS

Understanding Main Ideas

1. Sam Houston
2. Disorganization in government, lack of revenue, threat of Mexican attack
3. He tried to improve public education, moved the capital to Austin, launched expeditions to assert Texas' authority over Mexico, and fought to remove the Texas Indians.
4. He reduced government spending, cut back on the army and the Texas Rangers, and sought peace and trade treaties with the Indians.
5. Mexico refused to recognize Texas' independence.

Thinking Critically

1. **Using Historical Imagination:** Answers will vary. The Comanches were probably outraged at the attack, because they thought they were attending the meeting to talk about peace. They may not have understood why the Texans were angry that the Comanches had not brought all of their captives.
2. **Exploring Economics:** A lack of money, inflation, a rising national debt; none was solved

(Continued on page 287)

CHAPTER 13 REVIEW

Understanding Main Ideas

1. Who was elected the first president of the Republic of Texas?
2. What problems did the new president face in his first term?
3. What major new policies did President Lamar begin?
4. What did Houston do in his second term to change Lamar's policies?
5. Why were relations between Texas and Mexico poor during the Republic?

Thinking Critically

1. **Using Historical Imagination:** Imagine that you are a Comanche chief who survived the Council House Fight. You have just returned to tell your band members about it. What will you say about the actions of the Texans?
2. **Exploring Economics:** What economic problems troubled the Republic of Texas throughout its existence? Which, if any, of these problems were solved?
3. **Evaluating Information:** Judging from events described in this chapter, who do you think was the most successful president of the Republic of Texas?

Linking History and Geography

1. How did geography influence the success of the Santa Fe expedition?
2. Describe the argument over the choice of a capital for Texas. What were the geographic disadvantages of Houston and the geographic disadvantages of Austin?

TAAS Practice
Using Primary Sources

On July 11, 1839, officials from the Lamar administration met with Chief Bowles and other chiefs to discuss Indian removal from East Texas. About 24 Indians and two interpreters were present. Vice President Burnet addressed them with these words:

> The Mexicans are our enemies and the Cherokees are their friends. They have protected Mexican traitors. . . . The President believes that we cannot live together here in peace. Therefore the Cherokees had better go away. . . . The President desires peace but is always ready for war. The Cherokees are few whilst the Texans are like leaves on the trees, and are daily increasing from the United States. They [the Cherokees] had better go in peace to that place where they will be protected and remain at peace, [rather] than stay here where they will be destroyed.

1. Burnet says that he is ordering the Cherokees to leave Texas because
   A the Texans want their land
   B the Cherokees are weak while the Texans are strong
   C Cherokees waged war against Texan settlers
   D Cherokees aided the Mexicans
2. The message given by the Lamar government to the Indians is
   A leave the state at once or face war
   B prepare for immediate war
   C give up the Mexican traitors they are protecting
   D send a representative to Austin to explain their side

Presidents of the Republic of Texas
1. President Burnet (March 1836–October 1836)   Event(s)
2. President Houston (October 1836–December 1838)   Event(s)
3. President Lamar (December 1838–December 1841)   Event(s)
4. President Houston (December 1841–December 1844)   Event(s)
5. President Jones (December 1844–February 1846)   Event(s)

TAAS Practice
Writing Persuasively

Imagine that you are a supporter of Mirabeau B. Lamar, residing in San Antonio in 1836. Write your brother, a Sam Houston supporter, to persuade him to vote for Lamar.

Practicing Skills

1. **Sequencing Events:** Each of the following three events helped cause the invasion that came after it. Place them in the proper order, and tell whether each invasion was Texan or Mexican: Woll and Vásquez invasions of San Antonio, Mier expedition, Santa Fe expedition.
2. **Interpreting Charts:** Copy the chart on this page onto a sheet of paper. Then place the letter of the following events beside the name of the person who was president at the time: **a.** Homestead Law passed, **b.** Battle of Plum Creek, **c.** James Pinckney Henderson sent to Europe, **d.** Santa Fe expedition, **e.** Ru-

tersville College opened, **f.** Mier expedition, **g.** Treaties of Velasco, **h.** Council House Fight, **i.** Regulator-Moderator War settled, **j.** Woll invaded Texas, **k.** Mexico agreed to recognize Texas independence, **l.** Battle of the Neches, **m.** Treaty of Tehuacana Creek.

Enriching Your Study of History

1. **Individual Project:** Research and prepare a written report providing more detailed information about one person or event mentioned in this chapter. Your teacher will retain these reports as a class resource on the period of the Texas Republic.
2. **Cooperative Project:** Your teacher will assign several groups to conduct research on various historical topics in the period of the Texas Republic. Each group must choose one member to make an oral report to the class on its topic. Examples of topics are: the Texas Navy, the Santa Fe expedition, the Battle of the Neches.

3. **Evaluating Information:** Answers will vary, although most students probably will respond that Sam Houston was the most successful. He tried to keep peace with the Indians and with Mexico and tried to solve the Republic's economic problems.

Linking History and Geography

1. The expedition had to cross vast distances and was troubled by hostile Indians and a lack of food and water. As a result, the Texans were exhausted by the time they reached Santa Fe.
2. Austin was too far from the center of Texas settlement and too close to hostile Indians. Houston was too far from the inland cities of Texas.

TAAS Practice
Using Primary Sources
1. D   2. A

TAAS Practice
Writing Persuasively

Letters will vary but should demonstrate knowledge of Lamar's plans for the Republic.

Practicing Skills

1. **Sequencing Events:** Santa Fe expedition (Texan), Woll and Vásquez invasions of San Antonio (Mexican), Mier expedition (Texan)
2. **Interpreting Charts:** Sam Houston—a, c, f, i, m; Burnet—g; Lamar—b, d, e, h, j, l; Jones—k

Enriching Your Study of History

1. **Individual Project:** Reports will vary but should demonstrate accurate research.
2. **Cooperative Project:** Reports will vary but should demonstrate accurate and detailed research.

Practicing Critical Thinking Skills

1. **Synthesizing Information:** Texans wanted a democratic form of government and freedom of religion, and they feared that Mexico would extend its abolition of slavery into Texas. They also resented Mexico's law prohibiting further immigration to Texas

REVIEW

Connecting Main Ideas

1. What was the outcome of the Battle of San Antonio?
2. How did events at the Alamo both hurt and help the Texan cause?
3. What was accomplished by the Convention of 1836?
4. About which policies did Sam Houston and Mirabeau Lamar strongly disagree?
5. Why did Mexico finally offer to recognize Texas' independence in 1845?

Practicing Critical Thinking Skills

1. **Synthesizing Information:** What political conflicts with Mexico caused the Texas Revolution? Which, if any, of these conflicts remained unresolved after Texas won its independence?
2. **Seeing Cause and Effect:** How did the victory at San Jacinto prepare the way for the political conflicts between Lamar and Houston during the decade of the Republic of Texas?
3. **Exploring Multicultural Perspectives:** Imagine that you are a Mexican political leader in Mexico City. You have just been informed of the defeat at San Jacinto and the two treaties of Velasco. What is your opinion of these two treaties? Explain.

TAAS Practice
Writing Persuasively

Imagine that you are Samuel McCullough, a black hero of the Battle of San Antonio. Petition Congress to be allowed to remain in Texas.

Exploring Local History

1. Conduct research to discover what your county was like during the years of the Republic of Texas. Questions to answer include: Was the county part of a larger county at this time? What settlements were present in the period from 1836 to 1845? What were the main roads in the county during the Texas Republic?
2. Ask several adults—parents or guardians, and adult friends: Does the decade of the Texas Republic still affect how Texans think and feel about their state?

Using Historical Imagination

1. **Individual Project:** Imagine that your family emigrated to Texas during the period of the Texas Republic. Using what you can learn about Texas settlers during this period, write a brief account of your trip to Texas. Tell how you traveled and how you chose a place to settle.
2. **Cooperative Project:** Your team will research a major battle of the Texas Revolution or Texas Republic. You will gather information and prepare a large-scale, detailed battle map. Your map should show the geographical features of the field of battle, the placement of opposing troops, and so on. A designated speaker will explain to the class, using the map, what took place during the battle and why.

For Extending Your Knowledge

Lord, Walter. *A Time to Stand: The Epic of the Alamo.* Lincoln: University of Nebraska Press, 1978. A vivid, well-researched account of the Alamo.

from the United States. These conflicts were resolved by the Texas Revolution, even though Mexico refused to recognize the independence of Texas.
2. **Seeing Cause and Effect:** Both men emerged as heroes of the battle, ready to use their fame to gain political office.

3. **Exploring Multicultural Perspectives:** Answers will vary, but the political leader probably would view these treaties as invalid since they were made while General Santa Anna was being held captive by the Texans.

Writing Persuasively
Responses will vary but should point out McCullough's long residence in Texas and his courageous service to the cause of the Texas Revolution during the Battle of San Antonio.

Exploring Local History
1. Findings will vary but should demonstrate careful research.
2. Responses will vary. Many historians believe that today's Texans' feelings of pride in their state are influenced by Texas' years as a Republic.

Using Historical Imagination
1. **Individual Project:** Accounts will vary but should be based on information covered in Unit 5 as well as additional research.
2. **Cooperative Project:** Presentations will vary but should demonstrate detailed knowledge of a major battle.

Skill Lesson
Practicing the Skill
1. Sam Houston was wounded, and he was recuperating away from the Texas army.
2. Land rewards offered to those who served in battle
3. Possible answers: Santa Anna was prevented from being sent back to Vera Cruz; a group of horse marines captured a Mexican warship; there was fear that a rash act by unruly soldiers would cause fighting.
4. Diagrams should demonstrate students' understanding of cause and effect.

SKILL LESSON

Recognizing Cause and Effect

Determining cause and effect relationships is crucial for the reader of history. A cause is a condition, person, or event that makes something happen. An effect is the outcome of a cause. A cause may have many effects. An effect may itself be the cause of other effects. Visually, the relationship would look like this example from the unit:

Cause	Effect/Cause	Effect
Texas Santa Fe expedition	→ Mexican raids on San Antonio	→ Texas Mier expedition

To fully understand the reasons for an event, you must be able to recognize the cause-effect relationships.

How to Recognize Cause and Effect

Look for cause-effect clues. Certain words are immediate clues to cause and effect. Cause clues include *led to, brought about, produced, because, the source of,* and *the reason.* Some effect clues are *the outcome of, as a consequence, resulting in, gave rise to,* and *depended on.*

Remember, however, that writers do not always state the link between cause and effect. Sometimes you must read closely to see the relationship between the events.

Check for complex connections. Note that many cause-effect relationships have complex connections. A single cause may have many effects. Likewise, a single effect may have root in many causes. And remember that an effect may itself be a cause.

Practicing the Skill

Read the following paragraph from *Texas: A Modern History* by David G. McComb. Identify all the cause-effect relationships you can find, then check them by answering the questions that follow.

With Sam Houston attending to his wound in New Orleans, the Texan army became a problem. Hundreds of mercenaries [persons who fight only for payment] continued to arrive to join the Texas cause, aching for a battle in order to participate in the generous land rewards offered to those who served. A group of them under General Thomas J. Green prevented Burnet from sending Santa Anna back to Vera Cruz. They removed him from the warship *Invincible*, and Burnet had to keep the fallen dictator under guard for his own safety. Isaac Burton's horse marines, who patrolled the coast, captured a Mexican ship at Copano Bay in June, and there was talk once again of marching on Matamoros in search of plunder. Mirabeau B. Lamar, whom Burnet appointed to head the army, could not control it, and the ad interim president feared fighting would flare up again through some rash act of the unruly soldiers.

1. What two causes contributed to the effect, "the Texas army became a problem"?
2. What caused the new mercenaries to "be aching for a battle"?
3. What effects were caused by the problem with controlling the Texas army?
4. Using the arrow diagram at left as your model, draw a cause-effect diagram of the passage above. Show the two causes of "problem with the Texas army." Then draw an arrow, or arrows, from this effect/cause to its further effects.

INTRODUCING THE UNIT

Connecting with Past Learning

Present the following situation to the class, and have students brainstorm to complete the assignment: A newly discovered island has requested statehood in the United States. Your input is needed to design the government plan for this new state. Think about what you currently know about the organization of state government. What recommendations will you present? Indicate to students that in Chapter 14 of this unit they will learn how Texans organized their state government.

UNIT 6 OVERVIEW

Unit 6 focuses on the early years of Texas statehood. Chapter 14 discusses annexation to the United States and the organization of the new government. It describes the growth of Texas' population and cities.

Chapter 15 introduces the concept of manifest destiny and examines the role of Texas in the Mexican War. The chapter also discusses the Indian wars and subsequent government policies.

Chapter 16 explores Texas society during the 1850s. It is the study of a changing economy, developing cultural institutions, and the social interactions of the people.

Materials Available at the Unit Level:
Unit 6   Making Global Connections
Oral History Handbook
Informal Evaluation Forms

UNIT 6

THE LONE STAR STATE

MOTIVATOR

Organize students into groups of four or five. Write the following chart headings on the chalkboard:

Annexation of Texas

Advantages   **Disadvantages**

Allow students in each group ten minutes to fill in the chart on a sheet of paper. They should base their responses on their current knowledge. Collect their responses and combine them into a single chart on the chalkboard.

TEXAS AND THE WORLD

Organize the class into small groups, and ask each group to study the time line on this page. Select one of the world events, and have the groups brainstorm about how that event is related to events in Texas. Ask volunteers to share their group's answer. Continue the activity for other key events on the time line.

*I*n 1864, Herman Lungkwitz painted the *Scene near Fredericksburg*, shown on the opposite page. The subject of his painting was dear to Texans—land. Lungkwitz was among the thousands of immigrants who entered Texas in the 1840s and after. From the time Stephen F. Austin opened Texas to settlement from the United States, the number of immigrants continued to grow.

In 1845, Texas became part of the United States. The Lone Star Republic became the Lone Star State. Many Texans regretted the end of the Republic of Texas, even as they welcomed their new role within the United States. The annexation touched off war with Mexico, and Texans played a key part in the United States victory.

The Texas of the 1850s was different from that of Stephen F. Austin's days. It was busier and more prosperous. There were more villages and towns, as well as more business activity and more trade. Schools and churches were built to meet the needs of a larger population.

The history of Texas from 1845 to 1860 is the subject of Unit 6. Chapter 14 focuses on Texas becoming a state and the organization of a new government. Chapter 15 discusses the period of the Mexican War, while Chapter 16 details life in Texas during the early years of statehood.

UNIT 6 OBJECTIVES

1. Identify issues of debate over annexation of Texas.
2. Discuss the creation of Texas' new state government and the provisions of the Constitution of 1845.
3. Discuss the growth of Texas during the early years of statehood, and identify the state's diverse population groups.
4. Define and discuss the concept of manifest destiny within the context of Texas history.
5. Identify the causes, events, and results of the Mexican War, and discuss the Compromise of 1850.
6. Explain the Indian policies of the federal government after Texas' annexation and their impact on Texas Indians.
7. Discuss Texas as a frontier state in terms of economy, transportation, and social and cultural institutions.

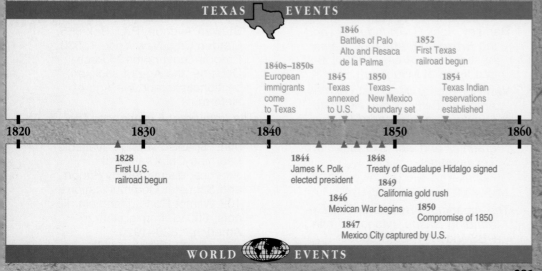

TEXAS EVENTS

1840s–1850s
European immigrants come to Texas

1845
Texas annexed to U.S.

1846
Battles of Palo Alto and Resaca de la Palma

1850
Texas–New Mexico boundary set

1852
First Texas railroad begun

1854
Texas Indian reservations established

1820   1830   1840   1850   1860

1828
First U.S. railroad begun

1844
James K. Polk elected president

1846
Mexican War begins

1847
Mexico City captured by U.S.

1848
Treaty of Guadalupe Hidalgo signed

1849
California gold rush

1850
Compromise of 1850

WORLD EVENTS

CHAPTER 14

EARLY STATEHOOD

TEACHER'S TIME LINE

Section 1	Section 2	Section 3	Review and
Pp. 292–96	Pp. 296–300	Pp. 300–06	Assessment
1 Day	1 Day	1 Day	1 Day

▣ TEACHER MATERIALS

Core: Chapter 14 Time Line; Graphic Organizer 14; Review Worksheet 14; Enrichment Worksheet 14; Reteaching Worksheet 14; Chapter 14 Tests, Forms A & B

Additional: Geography and Graph Skills 14, Map and Chart Transparencies 16, Informal Evaluation Forms, Test Generator

▣ OBJECTIVES

1. Present the issues of the debate regarding the annexation of Texas.
2. List the requirements made of Texas for statehood.
3. Describe the structure and functions of Texas' new state government.
4. Identify leaders of Texas during early statehood.
5. Discuss political issues that continued to trouble Texas after statehood.
6. Identify different groups of people who settled in Texas, and discuss reasons for migration to Texas.

▣ RESOURCES

BOOKS FOR TEACHERS

The Anti-Texass [sic] *Legion: Protest of Some Free Men, States and Presses Against the Texass* [sic] *Rebellion, Against the Laws of Nature and of Nations.* Albany: Sold at the Patriot Office, 1844. Primary source material regarding the Texas rebellion.

Biesele, Rudolph L. *The History of the German Settlements in Texas, 1831–1861.* Austin: Von Boeckmann Press, 1930. German settlements in Texas.

Eberstadt, Edward Emory. *Eberstadt Collection.* Austin: Barker Center Manuscripts. Description of early Texans, including James Pinckney Henderson.

Clarke, Mary Whatley. *Thomas J. Rusk, Soldier, Statesman, Jurist.* Austin: Jenkins Pub. Co., 1971. Biography of this Texan.

Jordan, Terry. *German Seed in Texas Soil.* Austin: University of Texas Press, 1966. German settlements in Texas.

Ramsey, Jack C. *Thunder Beyond the Brazos: Mirabeau B. Lamar.* Austin: Eakin Press, 1985. Life and times of Mirabeau Lamar.

Van Rosenberg, Marjorie. *German Artists of Early Texas: Herman Lungkwitz and Richard Petri.* Austin: Eakin Press, 1982. Biographies and works of these two Texas artists.

MULTIMEDIA MATERIALS

The American Adventure, The Expanding Nation. (video, 30 min.) PBS Video, 1320 Braddock Place, Alexandria, Virginia, 22314. Tracks the expansion of America until 1860.

The Great Knowledge Race: U.S. History Series. (software, No. 3.) Focus Media, Inc., 839 Stewart Avenue, P.O. Box 865, Garden City, New York, 11530. Program covers the Monroe Doctrine, the Age of Jackson, sectionalism, and the Age of Reform.

The Immigrant Experience: The Long, Long Journey. (video, 28 min., Spanish version available) Learning Corporation of America, distributed by Simon and Schuster Communications, 108 Wilmot Road, Deerfield, Illinois, 60015. Immigration to America, 1820–1920.

STUDENTS WITH SPECIAL NEEDS

Limited English Proficient Students (LEP)

Ask students to skim the chapter and create a time line showing major events discussed. Have them use the time line to review the chapter. You might wish to have students add to the time line in Chapters 15 and 16 to use as a unit review. See other activities labeled **LEP.**

Students Having Difficulty with the Chapter

Have students locate the following on a map of Texas:

Galveston	Fredericksburg*
San Antonio	El Paso*
Houston	Laredo*
Marshall	Brownsville*
Austin	Dallas*
Jefferson	Praha*
New Braunfels*	Brownsboro*

Have the students make a chart of immigrant groups that settled in the towns designated with asterisks. Ask them to list the town, dates of settlement given in the chapter, and the name of the immigrant group. **LEP**

Auditory Learners

Pair auditory learners, and assign each pair the topic *Texas Annexation.* In each pair, one student should prepare arguments in favor of annexation, and the other should prepare arguments against annexation. Each pair should then present a debate on the issue. See other activities labeled **A.**

Visual Learners

Have visual learners select one of Texas' early governors and research his background. Students should then prepare a campaign poster to tell voters significant facts about the candidate and his position on issues of the time. Display the posters in the classroom. See other activities labeled **V.**

Tactile/Kinesthetic Learners

Have tactile/kinesthetic learners create a three-column chart labeled *Executive Branch, Legislative Branch, Judicial Branch.* Ask them to add to the chart under the correct heading the following descriptions:

a. Headed by the governor
b. Representatives are elected for two-year terms
c. Includes the court system
d. Members meet every two years
e. Composed of the House of Representatives and the Senate
f. Representatives are elected for four-year terms
g. The supreme court was the highest court of this branch
h. James Pinckney Henderson was its first leader
i. John Hemphill was the first chief justice.

See other activities labeled **TK.**

Gifted Students

Assign gifted students to select one of the early immigrant groups of Texas. Ask them to compile a report folder including the following material.

1. A world map showing the country of origin and a map showing the location(s) of settlements in Texas
2. A written report that includes
   a. Reasons for the group's migration to the United States
   b. Key leaders of the immigrant group and their contributions
   c. Areas of settlement and the group's contributions to Texas culture
   d. The group's reasons for selecting the settlement location or a geographical description of the area
   e. The status of the settlement today

See other activities labeled **G.**

VOCABULARY

In addition to the boldfaced terms in each section, some students might benefit from discussing the meanings of these terms.

Section 1: *petitioned* (p. 292); *expansion policy* (p. 292); *resolution* (p. 295).

Section 2: *chief justice* (p. 297); *succeeded* (p. 299); *parcels* (p. 300).

Section 3: *estimates* (p. 300); *nobles* (p. 304); *prospered* (p. 304).

CHRONOLOGY

Have students study the Chapter 14 Time Line and identify relationships among the events.

GRAPHIC ORGANIZER

Have students skim the chapter and complete the Chapter 14 Graphic Organizer. *(You might wish to use this activity to review rather than to introduce the chapter.)*

ENRICHMENT

Have students complete the Chapter 14 Enrichment Worksheet.

SECTION 1

FOCUS

Student Experiences (I) Ask students: When faced with an important decision, have you ever listed the issue's pros and cons, or arguments for and against, before making a choice? Explain that during the 1840s many people wanted Texas to remain independent, while many others favored statehood. In Section 1 they will learn the arguments for and against annexation of Texas.

INSTRUCTION

Vocabulary (I) You may wish to preteach the following boldfaced term: *nominated* (p. 293). **LEP**

Cooperative Learning (I) Tell students that they are news reporters in 1844 and that they are going to interview people in Texas about their positions on the issue of annexation of Texas. Then organize the students into pairs, and have the students take turns interviewing their partners, asking and answering questions that they have prepared. **A, LEP**

CHAPTER 14 OVERVIEW

After nearly ten years as an independent country, Texas became part of the United States. On December 29, 1845, President James K. Polk signed the act that made Texas the twenty-eighth state. Once annexation was achieved, a new state constitution had to be written and a state government organized. Certain responsibilities once held by Texas were turned over to the United States. Policies had to be worked out to deal with the public debt and public land. During this same period, the population of Texas was increasing at a tremendous rate. People migrated to Texas from other parts of the United States and from other countries.

Essential Elements
2D, 2E, 2H, 3C, 6A, 6B, 9A, 9E

CHAPTER 14

EARLY STATEHOOD

The Story Continues...

Chapter 14 describes the early years of Texas statehood, when a new flag, the Stars and Stripes, flew over the state. It tells the story of Texas' annexation, the organization of its new government, and its growth of population during the 1840s and 1850s.

As you read the chapter, look for the answers to these questions:

1. Why did many people in the North oppose the annexation of Texas?
2. What major political issues from the days of the Texas Republic still troubled Texas after statehood?
3. Which region of the United States contributed the largest number of immigrants to Texas after 1845?

1 The Annexation of Texas

Texas showed interest in joining the United States as soon as it won its independence from Mexico in 1836. During his first term as president of Texas, Sam Houston petitioned his old friend, President Andrew Jackson, for annexation. Although he favored admitting Texas, Jackson was unable to gain approval of the United States Congress.

Debate over Annexation. Texas became the subject of debate during the late 1830s and early 1840s. Some members of the United States Congress did not want to annex Texas for fear of bringing on a war with Mexico. Other issues were involved in the debate, however.

Many people in the United States at this time were split over the expansion policy of the United States. Members of Congress from the North were generally against admitting states in which slavery was allowed. Members of Congress from the South were generally in favor of new slave states. North and South also disagreed over policies of government affecting trade and business. Neither section

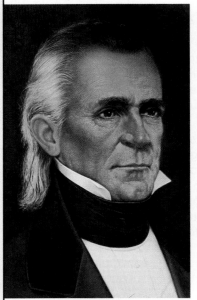

The Granger Collection

President James K. Polk strongly favored the annexation of Texas, which was a major issue in the United States presidential election of 1844.

Guided Practice (I) Ask students to summarize the presidential election of 1844 by completing the following information.

Candidates:
Parties:
Stand on Issues Related to Texas:
Election Results:
Call on volunteers to write their answers on the chalkboard.
V, LEP

Historical Imagination (I) Tell students to imagine that they are Texas voters in 1845. Have the class consider and vote on the issue of annexation. Call on voters to give their reasons for or against annexation. **A**

Texas Memorial Museum

The annexation of Texas was hotly debated in the United States during the 1830s and 1840s. The major issue was the existence of slavery in Texas. This painting, titled *Hauling Water*, is by Friedrich Richard Petri.

wanted the other to gain more power in Congress when new states were admitted.

In 1841 and again in 1844, the annexation issue arose in Texas. Many Texans wanted Texas to remain a republic and perhaps to expand westward toward California. Among this group was Mirabeau Lamar, who sent an expedition to Santa Fe in 1841 to claim all land east of the Rio Grande. But President Houston and other Texas leaders wanted to join the United States. The majority of Texans were most likely in favor of annexation.

The issue of annexation was an important one in the United States presidential election of 1844. James K. Polk of Tennessee was **nominated**, or chosen to run, for president by the Democratic party. Polk and his supporters favored the annexation of Texas, partly because they feared the interest of Britain in Texas. The United States and Britain were also involved in a dispute over control of Oregon. Polk hoped to annex Oregon as well as Texas and give the United States control of North America to the Pacific Ocean.

Polk's opponent in the election of 1844 was Whig party candidate Henry Clay of Kentucky. Clay did not want annexation, because he feared the country would split over the slavery issue. There was a powerful feeling in the United States that opposed the spread of slavery to any western region. Nevertheless, most voters wanted more land added to the United States, and Polk was elected president.

Research (II) Have students investigate and report on the United States' dispute with Britain over control of Oregon. How was the dispute resolved? What was President Polk's role in the dispute? Suggest that students supplement their findings with a map. **A, TK, V, G**

Essential Elements
2D, 2E, 2H

LONE STAR LEGACY
Using Historical Imagination
Answers will vary, but students should demonstrate knowledge of the debate over annexation.

LONE STAR LEGACY

The Great Debate: Statehood or Empire

A great debate raged in Texas and in the United States during the early 1840s. Should Texas become a state, or should it remain a separate country? Emotions were high on both sides of the issue, and the debate dominated the United States presidential election of 1844. In Texas, the argument revolved around the views of the two leading political opponents during the Republic years, Sam Houston and Mirabeau B. Lamar.

Sam Houston supported annexation to the United States. He thought that annexation would bring more security and economic stability to Texas. Houston shared the vision of many people in the United States who believed that the United States should encompass all the land from the Atlantic Ocean to the Pacific. In his writings, Houston expressed his hope that part of this massive country would be set aside as a separate Indian nation.

Houston's political opponent, Mirabeau Lamar, wanted Texas to remain a republic. As president of Texas, he sent military expeditions west to try and claim more land for Texas. Ironically, the policies of Lamar helped lead to annexation. His military adventures weakened Texas financially, and the resulting high inflation led many Texans to demand annexation by the more powerful, wealthier United States. Lamar's desire for a larger Texas empire also worried some American politicians who had their eyes on California.

When annexation to the United States finally came, some Texans still had mixed emotions. The following passage is from Noah Smithwick's *Recollections of Old Texas Days,* published in 1900:

Anson Jones, its [the Texas Republic's] last president, standing on the steps of the old capitol, lowered the old flag from the mast and reverently furling [folding] it, announced amidst breathless silence, "The Republic of Texas is no more." Many a head was bowed, many a broad chest heaved, and many a manly cheek was wet with tears when that broad field of blue in the center of which, like a signal light, glowed the lone star . . . was laid away among the relics of the dead republic. But we were most of us natives of the United States, and when the stars and stripes, the flag of our fathers, was run up and catching the breeze unrolled its heaven-born colors to the light, cheer after cheer rent [tore] the air. Methinks the star in the lower left-hand corner should have been especially dedicated to Texas.

Using Historical Imagination
If you had been a Texan in the early 1840s, which side would you have taken in the great debate? Explain in detail why you would have taken that side.

Inset: **Noah Smithwick**

Archives Division, Texas State Library

Independent Practice (I) Have students work independently or with a partner to create a series of cause-and-
effect statements using the information presented in Section
1. Ask volunteers to read their statements aloud. **A, LEP**

RETEACHING
Pair students who are having difficulty with those who are
performing well. Then have each pair review the section
and list the arguments in favor of and against annexation of
Texas. Have each pair exchange its list with another pair to
check for accuracy. **LEP, A**

The Annexation Resolution. The election of Polk was
a signal to the United States Congress that a majority of
Americans wanted Texas in the United States. On February
28, 1845, both houses of Congress passed a resolution
allowing annexation. The resolution contained certain requirements that Texas had to meet in order to become a state.

The first requirement was that citizens of Texas approve
annexation by holding a convention and an election. Texans
were also to write and adopt a new state constitution at that
convention. Texas was required to turn over some of its
public property to the United States, including the navy, all
army forts, and military supplies. Some land was to be sold
to pay off the public debt. Another part of the resolution
allowed Texas to divide into four other states if the people
so desired. All decisions regarding the boundary of Texas
were to be made by the United States government.

Texas Joins the United States. After the United States
passed the annexation resolution, representatives from
France and Britain pressed the Texans to wait before accepting it. They wanted Texas to remain independent. They
urged Mexico to recognize Texas as an independent country.

Texans were proud of being independent, but there
were good reasons for joining the United States. Most
Texans were from the United States, and many had families
still living there. There were strong business and trade ties

Barker Texas History Center

President Anson Jones declared, "The
Republic of Texas is no more," when
the flag of the Republic was lowered
and replaced by the United States flag.

Ask students how Texas history might have been different had Henry Clay won the United States presidential election of 1844. *(Clay was opposed to the annexation of Texas; therefore, it probably would not have taken place in 1845.)*

ASSESSMENT

Have students complete the Section 1 Review on page 296.

FOCUS

Student Experiences (I) Ask students if they have ever had to make rules for running a club or other organization. Then ask what kinds of problems they encountered. Explain that the first task facing the state of Texas was the creation of a new government.

Answers to Section 1 Review

Define: *nominated*—chosen to run for election

Identify: James K. Polk—Democrat and president of the United States at the time of Texas' annexation; Henry Clay—Whig party candidate who unsuccessfully opposed Polk in the 1844 presidential election

1. Some people feared war with Mexico, and others were concerned that another slave state would be added to the United States.
2. Polk, who favored annexation, was elected president, signaling that most Americans wanted annexation.
3. Its independence

Seeing Cause and Effect: The United States and Britain were competing for territory. The annexation of Oregon and Texas would give the United States control of North America.

Evaluating Information: Arguments for statehood include: a better postal service, military protection, a sound money system, and help in solving debt problems. Arguments against include: a desire to maintain independence and the privileges that come with having one's own government.

Essential Elements
2E, 2H, 4G, 4I, 7B, 7F, 7G, 8B, 9A

SECTION 1 REVIEW

Define: nominated
Identify: James K. Polk, Henry Clay

1. Why was the question of annexation of Texas a major political issue in the United States?
2. What effect did the presidential election of 1844 have on this debate?
3. What did Texas have to give up to join the United States?

Seeing Cause and Effect: How did the relations between the United States and Britain help bring about Texas statehood?

Evaluating Information: Imagine that you are a Texas voter in 1845, trying to make up your mind whether to vote for annexation. What arguments can you make for, and against, statehood?

Barker Texas History Center

James Pinckney Henderson took office as the first governor of the state of Texas on February 19, 1846, after Texas was admitted to the United States as the twenty-eighth state.

---

between Texas and the United States. And Texans looked forward to having the postal service and military protection offered by the United States. They also looked to the United States for a sound money system and for help in solving the debt problems of the Republic of Texas. For these reasons, public opinion was strongly in favor of annexation, and Texas President Anson Jones called for a convention to consider the issue.

On July 4, 1845, the delegates to the annexation convention assembled. With only one vote against, the convention approved annexation. By August 27, a new constitution had been written. On October 13, Texas voters approved annexation by a vote of 4,254 to 257, and they ratified the constitution by a vote of 4,174 to 312.

On December 29, 1845, after the United States Congress accepted the Texas Constitution, President Polk signed the act making Texas a state. On February 19, 1846, Texas President Anson Jones officially turned over the powers of government to Texas' first governor, James Pinckney Henderson. President Jones concluded the ceremonies with these memorable words: "The final act in this great drama is now performed; the Republic of Texas is no more." ✪

2 The New State Government

The creation of a state government was the first issue facing the new state of Texas. The plan for that government was the Constitution of 1845, which was a requirement for annexation. The constitution was modeled on the constitutions of the Republic of Texas and the United States as well as the newly written constitution of Louisiana. When finished, it was regarded as an excellent law of the land. The great statesman from Massachusetts, Daniel Webster, proclaimed it the best of all American state constitutions.

The Constitution of 1845. Most of the people who wrote the Texas Constitution of 1845 were experienced legislators, lawyers, and judges. Before arriving in Texas, most had lived in the southern United States. Only one member, José Antonio Navarro, was a native Texan. Thomas J. Rusk served as president of the convention that wrote the Constitution of 1845. He was assisted by many able delegates. James Pinckney Henderson had been a

INSTRUCTION

Vocabulary (I) You may wish to preteach the following boldfaced terms: *biennial* (p. 297); *corporations* (p. 298); *federal government* (p. 298); *political parties* (p. 298). **LEP**

Analysis (I) Point out to students that the textbook states that the Texas Constitution of 1845 was regarded as "an excellent law of the land." Ask students to defend or reject this statement using information from Section 2 to support their arguments. Allow time for students to present their views. **A**

Synthesis (I) Tell students to imagine that they were one of the delegates of the convention that wrote the Texas Constitution of 1845. Ask them to write a letter to a friend or relative explaining why they believe the constitution is a great document. Tell students to use the information presented in Section 2 to write their letter. Invite volunteers to read their letters aloud. **A**

cabinet member under President Sam Houston. N.H. Darnell was a former speaker of the Texas House of Representatives. Hiram Runnels once had been governor of Mississippi. Abner Lipscomb was a former chief justice of the Supreme Court of Alabama, and Isaac Van Zandt had served in the Texas Congress.

The Constitution of 1845 provided for a governor to run the executive branch of government. The governor would serve a two-year term and was not allowed to serve more than four years in any six-year period. The constitution created a legislative branch of government consisting of a senate and a house of representatives. House members were elected for terms of two years. Senators were elected for four-year terms. The state legislature was to meet once every two years, or in **biennial** sessions.

The governor and members of the legislature were to be elected by the voters of Texas. At this time, only white males 21 years of age or older were allowed to vote. This was the case in other states as well. Under this law, blacks, Indians, and white women were denied the rights to vote and to hold office. The constitution also prohibited ministers or priests from serving in the legislature.

One section of the constitution denied the right to hold office to anyone who took part in a duel. Its purpose was to put an end to dueling, which was used to settle many disputes. Felix Huston, the commander of the Texas army, challenged Albert Sidney Johnston to a duel when Johnston tried to take over command of the army. Johnston was badly wounded. At another time, President Burnet challenged Sam Houston to a duel, though Houston refused. President Lamar once challenged a person who criticized his decision to send an expedition to Santa Fe.

In addition to a governor and a legislature, the constitution provided for a judicial branch, or court system. The Supreme Court was the highest state court. District courts were also organized. At first, the governor appointed judges, but in 1850, a law was passed to allow voters to elect them.

The Constitution of 1845 continued the Homestead Law passed in 1839. Up to 200 acres of a homestead were exempted from being taken for payment of debts. Under the constitution, a married man could not sell a homestead without the consent of his wife. The constitution also protected the right of women to own property separately from their husbands.

Archives Division, Texas State Library

The Constitution of 1845, written as a requirement for admission to the United States, was ratified by a majority of Texas voters.

Archives Division, Texas State Library

Felix Huston was commander of the Texas army for a brief period after independence from Mexico was achieved. When Albert Sidney Johnston was sent to replace Huston as commander, Huston challenged Johnston to a duel and wounded him.

Constitutional Heritage
Point out to students that state constitutions must not conflict with the general principles of the United States Constitution, which is the supreme law of the land.

Cooperative Learning (I) Organize students into groups of four or five. Tell students in each group that they are forming a new political party in Texas in the late 1840s. Have each group select a name for its party and identify the issues it supports and whose views it represents. Have a spokesperson from each group tell about the new party. **A**

Guided Practice (I) Write the following headings on the chalkboard: *Democrats, Republicans, Whigs, Know Nothings.* Ask students to provide information to describe what each party represented in Texas in the 1840s and 1850s. **A, V**

EXTENSION

Community Involvement (II) Have students find out the names of Texas' senators and of the representatives from their area. Then have students choose an issue facing Texans today. Ask students to find out where each representative and senator stands on this issue by calling or writing the offices of these officials. Have students report their findings to the class. **A, G**

Archives Division. Texas State Library

John Hemphill participated in the Council House Fight at San Antonio. He became chief justice of the Texas Supreme Court in 1842. When Texas entered the United States, he became the first chief justice of the Texas state Supreme Court. He was later elected to the United States Senate.

The constitution included a number of measures reflecting the feelings of Texans about debts and money. The legislature was forbidden to go into debt more than $100,000. Banks were prohibited from operating in Texas. This was because the vast majority of Texans at that time were farmers who saw little need for banks. Most of these farmers mistrusted banks because many banks had failed during bad economic times. **Corporations**, or groups of people organized into one body to do business, needed permission from the legislature to operate. The legislature could take away a corporation's right to operate if it was found to be using unfair business methods.

The First State Election. The first election of state officials was held on December 15, 1845. James Pinckney Henderson of San Augustine won the governor's race by a large vote over James B. Miller. Albert C. Horton of Matagorda was elected lieutenant governor. The state legislature later selected Sam Houston and Thomas Rusk as the first United States senators from Texas. Today, voters elect United States senators, but in 1845 they were chosen by members of the legislature. Governor Henderson named John Hemphill the first chief justice of the Texas Supreme Court. Hemphill had served as chief justice of the Republic.

After Governor Henderson appointed other state officials and judges, the new government began its work. Its first duty was to transfer the daily operations of government from the Republic to the state. The Texas postal system was transferred to United States control. Army posts, public buildings, arms and ammunition, and certain other property were turned over to the **federal government**, or government of the United States. As Governor Henderson took charge of the state's business, Senators Houston and Rusk headed for Washington, D.C., to represent the interests of the Texas people.

Texas Politics. **Political parties**, or organized groups representing people with similar views about government, did not exist in Texas before the 1840s. Texans supported a particular person, such as Houston or Lamar, or they voted to support or reject certain issues. But there were no parties to organize voters around a group of issues.

In the late 1840s, the politics of Texas were changing. People began to join and support political parties organized in the United States. Most leaders in Texas joined the

Independent Practice (I) Have students list on a sheet of paper three ways in which Texas was able to pay its public debt. Have students share their lists as you make a master list on the chalkboard. **A, V, LEP**

RETEACHING
With students, outline the information from this section on the chalkboard. Main topics should include: *the Constitution of 1845, the first state election, political parties, early governors of Texas,* and *debts and land*. Call on volunteers to come to the chalkboard and list subtopics and details in proper outline form. **LEP, A, V**

Democratic party. One of its founders had been Thomas Jefferson, who wrote the United States Declaration of Independence in 1776. Andrew Jackson of Tennessee, a former president of the United States and a favorite of Texans, was a Democrat. In general, the Democratic party represented the views of farmers and owners of small businesses. The party had supported the annexation of Texas and was very strong throughout the southern United States.

The other major political party in the United States was the Whig party. The Whigs represented the views of merchants, owners of factories, and wealthier people. They had much less support in the South than did the Democrats. In the 1850s, the Whig party broke apart because its members disagreed over slavery. Those in the North joined with some smaller groups to form the Republican party. The Republican party believed that slavery should not be allowed to spread into any new areas of the United States. For that reason, it had almost no support in Texas and the South.

During the 1850s, a third political party appeared for a short time. The American, or Know Nothing, party wanted to keep foreign immigrants and Roman Catholics from taking part in government. It gained some support in Texas, but most Texans were not interested in its views. Many people in Texas were recent immigrants or Roman Catholics or both. Also, Texans in general did not like the fact that the Know Nothings usually held their political meetings in private. By the late 1850s, the Know Nothing party had nearly disappeared.

Early Governors of Texas. James Pinckney Henderson, Texas' first governor, served only one term. During part of that term he was away commanding Texas troops in the Mexican War of 1846. While he was away, Lieutenant Governor Albert C. Horton filled the office. Governor Henderson did not run for reelection and was succeeded by George T. Wood in 1847. Wood was a plantation owner from the Trinity River area near Liberty. Wood ran again in 1849, but he was defeated by Peter Hansborough Bell. Bell, a veteran of the Texas Revolution and the Mexican War, won reelection in 1851. One month before his term expired, Bell resigned to take a seat in the United States Congress. He gave up his office to Lieutenant Governor J. W. Henderson.

One of Texas' most popular governors was Elisha M. Pease, who was elected in 1853 and 1855. Originally from

Archives Division, Texas State Library

Governor Elisha M. Pease played an active role in Texas politics during his two terms in office. Railroad construction was pushed, public education was improved, a new capitol was constructed, and new health institutions were begun. When Pease left the governor's office, Texas was nearly free of debt.

Historical Sidelight
Governor Elisha Pease was the first governor to reside in the governor's mansion in Austin, completed in August 1856. Governor Pease held an open house for the citizens of Austin.

Have students choose one of the topics from the outline that they created in the Reteaching activity, and ask them to write a brief summary.

ASSESSMENT

Have students complete the Section 2 Review on page 300.

Past Learning (I) Ask students to recall the discussion in Unit 4 on American colonization of Texas during the 1820s and 1830s. Ask: What attracted colonists to Texas *(available land, economic opportunities)*? Tell students that Texas' population grew even more rapidly as Texas experienced its first years of statehood. Texas as a land of opportunity continued to draw settlers from all over the world.

**Answers to
Section 2 Review**

Define: *biennial*—occurring every two years; *corporations*—groups of people organized into one body to conduct business; *federal government*—the government of the United States; *political parties*—groups of people sharing similar views about government

Identify: James Pinckney Henderson—first governor of Texas; George T. Wood—second governor of Texas; Thomas J. Rusk—president of the convention that wrote the Constitution of 1845; Peter Hansborough Bell—third governor of Texas

1. James Pinckney Henderson; Sam Houston, Thomas Rusk
2. The Democratic party
3. Public debt and land policy

(Continued on page 301)

Essential Elements
2A, 2D, 2E, 2H, 3C, 5B, 5C, 7B, 8A, 8B, 9E, 9G

SECTION ★ REVIEW

Define: biennial, corporations, federal government, political parties

Identify: James Pinckney Henderson, George T. Wood, Thomas J. Rusk, Peter Hansborough Bell

1. Who was elected Texas' first governor? Who became the first United States senators from Texas?
2. To what national political party did most Texas political leaders belong?
3. What major political issues from the days of the Texas Republic continued to trouble Texas after statehood?

Analyzing Information: Texas began as a province of New Spain and then was a province of the Republic of Mexico. Is there evidence in this section that the new Texas Constitution was influenced by Mexican law and politics? Explain.

Synthesizing Information: Why do you think the Texas Constitution prohibited ministers and priests from serving in the state legislature?

Connecticut, Pease was called an "Old Texan." He came to Texas in 1835 and fought in the Battle of Gonzales. Following Pease in the governor's office was Hardin R. Runnels. Runnels won the office by defeating Sam Houston, who was a United States senator at that time. Then Houston challenged Runnels in 1859 and won. With that victory, Sam Houston had served Texas as commander of the Republic army, president of the Republic, United States senator, and governor of the state.

Debts and Land. The issues facing the early political leaders of the state were similar to those of the Republic. Two of the most important problems were the public debt and land policy.

The debt was especially troublesome. By 1846, it was nearing $12 million and rising steadily. The annexation resolution provided for the payment of the Texas debt from the sale of public lands. Texas had plenty of land to sell, but at the price of 50 cents per acre, there were few buyers. Most settlers could get some free land by homesteading. Meanwhile, the state's creditors, those people who had loaned it money, began demanding repayment. This was a problem that took nearly ten years to solve. During the late 1840s and early 1850s, the United States helped the state pay this large debt. In 1850, the federal government gave Texas money in exchange for land claimed by Texas in present-day New Mexico, Oklahoma, Wyoming, and Colorado. The United States also credited money to Texas for future land sales. With the assistance of the United States, the Texas debt was paid by 1855.

During the early days of statehood, Texas continued much of the land policy developed during the Republic years. Land was given to people if they settled on it and improved it in some way. This homesteading policy usually entitled a person to 320 acres. Additional land could be bought from the state. Other parcels of state land were set aside for public schools, colleges, universities, and public improvements such as roads, harbors, and railroads. ✪

3 Growth and Immigration

In its early years as a state, Texas experienced a tremendous growth in population. Estimates place the population of Texas in 1845 at around 100,000. This

Vocabulary (I) You may wish to preteach the following boldfaced terms: *census* (p. 301); *socialist* (p. 306); *free enterprise* (p. 306). **LEP**

Courtesy of the San Antonio Museum Association

By 1860, San Antonio had become the largest town in Texas. This engraving shows San Antonio around 1850.

number increased rapidly as people from other states and countries poured into Texas, the huge new state.

Texas Population. According to the **census**, or official count of population, the total number of Texans in 1850 was 212,592. The census revealed that Texas had around 154,000 whites and 58,000 blacks. Among the whites was a wide variety of ethnic groups. Texas was one of the faster-growing regions in the United States. Its people were as diverse as those of any other area.

The 1850 census also showed that more than 95 percent of Texans lived in rural areas. The towns and villages that did exist were small. Galveston was the largest town in the state, with 4,177 people. By 1860, San Antonio replaced Galveston as the largest town, with a population of 8,235. Other large towns included Houston, Marshall, Nacogdoches, Jefferson, and New Braunfels. But even these were little more than villages. Austin, even though it was the state capital, had fewer than 1,000 residents when Texas became a state.

When the census figures for 1860 were released, the growth of Texas was even more surprising. The population was 604,215, or three times as large as in 1850! Towns

Analyzing Information: By copying the United States' Constitution instead of Mexico's, Texas demonstrated that it identified with the United States and not Mexico. In addition, students might suggest that the prohibition of ministers and priests from serving in the legislature was a reaction against Mexican law.

Synthesizing Information: Answers will vary, but students should mention that Texas wanted to keep religion and government separate, and that it was a reaction against Mexico's law requiring that citizens accept the Roman Catholic faith.

Vocabulary Development
Explain to students that the term *immigrant* refers to a person who *comes* to a country to settle. The term *emigrant* refers to a person who *leaves* one country to settle in another. The difference is one of perspective.

became cities, and the line of settlement moved steadily westward. It was still the land that lured people to Texas, and they were coming faster than ever before.

New Arrivals. Most of the people who arrived in Texas after 1845 were from the lower South, mainly the Gulf Coastal Plain states of Alabama, Georgia, Mississippi, and Louisiana.

Some southerners brought slaves with them from the cotton plantations of the Old South. Just as the total population exploded during the 1840s and 1850s, so did the black population in Texas. The 1850 census reported that there were 58,558 blacks, and in 1860 the number rose

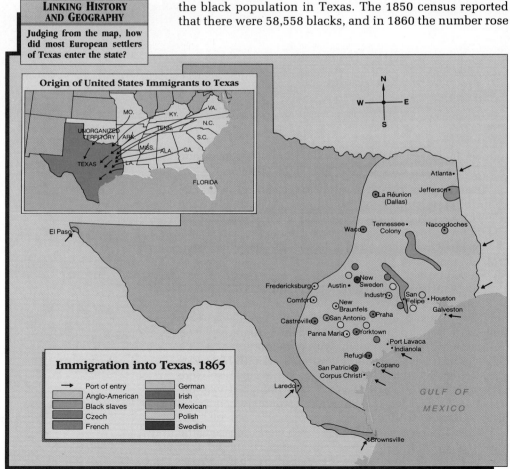

LINKING HISTORY AND GEOGRAPHY

Judging from the map, how did most European settlers of Texas enter the state?

Origin of United States Immigrants to Texas

Immigration into Texas, 1865

→ Port of entry
Anglo-American
Black slaves
Czech
French
German
Irish
Mexican
Polish
Swedish

SPIRIT OF TEXAS

Friedrich Richard Petri: Frontier Artist

Land was the lure that brought most people to Texas. But among the thousands who settled in Texas in the 1800s, one young man from Germany came looking for something besides land. Friedrich Richard Petri arrived in Texas in 1850 seeking artistic freedom—the right to draw and paint whatever he chose.

Richard Petri was born in Dresden, Germany, in 1824. At age fourteen he was recognized as a talented artist while attending the Dresden Academy of Fine Arts. But for the next few years, life became difficult for serious artists in Germany. Political groups forced them to produce only those works of art that pleased the government. Desiring the freedom to control his own work, Petri decided to move to Texas.

It was a frightening experience to leave home for an unknown land. Still, in the summer of 1850, Petri joined friends and family on the great adventure of an ocean voyage to America. Traveling with Petri was another artist and close friend, Herman Lungkwitz. Petri and Lungkwitz later became two of the most respected artists of early Texas.

When their ship arrived in the United States, their trip to Texas had just begun. The small group of German immigrants traveled by train from Hoboken, New Jersey,

to Wheeling, Virginia. They then boarded a riverboat on the Ohio River and made their way to the Mississippi River. After several days on a big paddle-wheel boat, they arrived in New Orleans. Another boat took them from New Orleans to the Texas coastal town called Indianola. The last segment of their long and difficult journey was by horse-drawn oxcart to New Braunfels, Texas.

The families of Richard Petri and Herman Lungkwitz eventually settled near Fredericksburg, beside the banks of the Pedernales River. Life in the Texas wilderness was not easy for them. But the Petri and Lungkwitz families survived and eventually prospered. Petri and Lungkwitz both became well known for their beautiful paintings of the life and landscapes of Central Texas.

Richard Petri spent much of his time with the Indians around Fredericksburg. As he gradually became more friendly with them, he began painting and drawing portraits of them. He was the first artist to create a series of paintings of Texas Indians. Petri's successful career was cut short, however, in 1857. While trying to cool a fever by swimming in the river, he drowned. The artist was only 33 years old when he died. Several of his paintings are reproduced in this textbook.

Inset: **Self-portrait by Friedrich Richard Petri**

Texas Memorial Museum

Geography (I) Direct students to a physical map of Texas. Ask the class to list the geographic factors that might have influenced Prince Carl in the selection of a settlement site in 1844. *(Lead students to discuss water resources, climate, soil, and so on.)* **V, A**

Guided Practice (I) Provide students with blank outline maps of Texas. Ask them to use the information on pages 304–06 to locate and label the sites of European settlements in Texas in the 1840s and 1850s. **V, TK, LEP**

Courtesy of the Sophienberg Museum and Archives, New Braunfels

Prince Carl of Solms-Braunfels prepared for the arrival of German immigrants in Texas.

Photography Collection. Harry Ransom Humanities Research Center. The University of Texas at Austin

John O. Meusebach settled many German families in Texas. He also studied Texas plant and animal life and opened his extensive private library to scientific researchers.

Geography

Throughout history, the German people had been unable to form an enduring union. In the mid 1800s, Germany was a patchwork of independent states with no central government. Germans came to Texas from a number of different states and kingdoms.

to 182,921. There were about 355 free blacks in Texas at this time. But laws restricting their freedom prevented the growth of the free black population.

Immigrants continued to enter Texas from Mexico during the early years of statehood. They settled primarily in the border regions of the Rio Grande and in the farming regions of South Texas. San Antonio, El Paso, Laredo, and Brownsville were centers of Mexican American population then (and continue to be so today). From 1850 to 1860, the number of Mexican American Texans increased from around 4,000 to more than 12,000.

European Immigrants. Nearly all the immigration to Texas from outside the United States and Mexico came from Europe. A few Europeans had come to Texas in the years before the Texas Revolution. But during the Republic years, agents from the United States encouraged large numbers of people to come to America. In 1850, it was estimated that more than 30,000 Texans were immigrants from Europe.

The immigrants from Europe usually came in large groups, often from the same city or region. Many were escaping revolutions that had failed to bring democracy to their countries. Others sought the opportunity to own land or to worship as they pleased. During the Republic, they bought their land in Texas from empresarios. Later, land companies and speculators sold land to immigrants. The largest ethnic group to immigrate to Texas came from German-speaking areas of Europe. Two-thirds, or 20,000, of the European immigrants who came to Texas during this period were Germans.

The Germans Arrive. In 1842, a group of German nobles formed an organization known as the Adelsverein, or Association of Noblemen. This group later became the Society for the Protection of German Immigrants in Texas. The group wanted to start a German colony in Texas, and they began the process of choosing and acquiring land. In 1844, the society sent Prince Carl of Solms-Braunfels to Texas with about 200 settlers. They acquired land along the Guadalupe River near Comal Creek. The settlement of New Braunfels was named in honor of Prince Carl's hometown. Prince Carl returned to Germany two months later, but New Braunfels grew and prospered.

TEXAS VOICES
Creating (I) Have students work in small groups to create a modern-day *Guide to Texas Emigrants.* Tell them to think about the state's climate, available housing, cities, recreation facilities, and so on. Allow time for students to display and discuss their guidebooks. **A, V, TK, LEP**

EXTENSION
Research (III) Ask interested students to research and report on the leisure activities of Texas settlers during the 1840s and 1850s. What types of leisure activities did immigrants from other countries bring with them to Texas? Did life in Texas during this period allow time for leisure? **A, G**

TEXAS VOICES

*B*efore emigrating to Texas, future Texans often consulted guidebooks to prepare them for the pioneer experience. The following passages are from David Woodman's *Guide to Texas Emigrants,* published in 1835. It offered suggestions on what the well-equipped settlers should bring with them to Texas:

> Emigrants should be well provided with necessary farming tools, a wagon, comfortable clothing (principally cotton), a good rifle, and a strong dog. Seeds of useful plants and different grains must not be forgotten. It would be best to carry articles of bedding and tents for shelter until the house is built. . . .
>
> Some household utensils should also be taken. The following would serve: two pots for boiling (one large and one small), one hook pot, one tin water-can, tinderbox and matches, three lbs. candles, one tin hand-basin, two tin pint cups, two square deep tin baking pans, one wooden bowl, three tin plates, knives, forks and spoons, and a small washtub.
>
> The light traveling wagons are hardly strong enough for Texas. A party of emigrants who plan to go inland should have a strong large wagon and buy a couple of oxen at the place of landing. These oxen will be invaluable to the settler when he starts the working of his land.

After Prince Carl left Texas, Baron Ottfried Hans Freiherr von Meusebach replaced him. In Texas, the baron changed his name to John O. Meusebach. Meusebach continued the work begun by Prince Carl and settled many German families. By 1847, the German society had sent 7,380 immigrants to Texas. They settled communities such as Fredericksburg, Boerne, Comfort, Sisterdale, and Bettina. Many Germans came into Texas at the port of Indianola, which grew into one of the largest in Texas at the time. Some Germans settled in established towns. By 1860, there were more German-born Texans in San Antonio than there were Tejanos. Wherever German immigrants went, they established prosperous farms, businesses, and communities. German settlers generally disapproved of slavery and almost never had any slaves.

German settlers were well organized, but they endured their share of hardships on the Texas frontier. One Fredericksburg woman remembered:

> People who have never gone through it can't realize how these people who started the little Texas towns and made

Barker Texas History Center

Henri Castro, a Frenchman of Portuguese ancestry, established the town of Castroville on the Medina River west of San Antonio in 1844. He was dedicated to the successful settlement of his colony. His wisdom, fairness, and generosity were comparable to that of another famous Texas empresario, Stephen F. Austin.

Biography
Baron von Meusebach knew five languages and was educated in political science, economics, law, mining, and forestry.

Analysis (I) Direct students to the boldfaced terms *socialist* and *free enterprise* on this page. Ask the class to consider the positive and negative aspects of living in a socialist society. List their responses on the chalkboard. **A**

Independent Practice (II) Have students work individually or in pairs to draw a graph showing the total population of Texas in the years 1845, 1850, and 1860. **V, TK**

RETEACHING

Have students create a time line using the information discussed in Section 3. **LEP, TK**

CLOSURE

Ask students: What do you think were the positive aspects of immigration to Texas during the 1840s and 1850s? Were there any negative aspects? Allow time for students to present their views.

ASSESSMENT

Have students complete the Section 3 Review on page 306.

Answers to Section 3 Review

Define: *census*—official count of a population; *socialist*—society in which people share all of the work and rewards equally; *free enterprise*—system in which people work for their own profit
Identify: Prince Carl of Solms-Braunfels—representative of German nobles who began a German colony in New Braunfels; John O. Meusebach—replaced Prince Carl in settling German families when Prince Carl returned to Germany; Henri Castro—brought the first group of French settlers to Texas; Victor Considérant—Frenchman who established a settlement in North Texas, which later became the city of Dallas
1. The lower South
2. It tripled.
3. To escape revolution, search for land, or gain religious freedom

Synthesizing Information: Most European immigrants did not speak English and brought with them new customs and traditions. Most were not slaveholders.

Seeing Cause and Effect: Answers will vary, but students might mention that the transition to a new location within the United States would be easier. The government, postal service, and military would remain the same. Also, it would be easier to contact relatives living in the United States.

Special Collections. The University of Texas at Arlington Libraries

This photograph shows the colony of La Réunion, the French socialist settlement established in 1855. The colony failed, but the skilled and cultured Europeans remaining in the area added to the growth and prosperity of the community of Dallas.

SECTION ★3★ REVIEW

Define: census, socialist, free enterprise
Identify: Prince Carl of Solms-Braunfels, John O. Meusebach, Henri Castro, Victor Considérant

1. After 1845, from where did the largest group of American settlers come?
2. How much did Texas' population grow between 1850 and 1860?
3. Why did the new European immigrants decide to come to Texas?

Synthesizing Information: How was European immigration to Texas different from immigration from the United States?

Seeing Cause and Effect: Imagine that you are a farmer from Georgia. You were tempted to move to Texas during the decade of the republic, but you decided to do so only after Texas became a state. How did annexation influence your decision to move?

them grow had to starve and do. . . . We did not know what it was to have shoes. All summer we went barefooted—part of the winter, too. We had to save the shoes we had. Even the grown people went barefooted.

The French Immigrants. The first group of French settlers in Texas was brought by Henri Castro. Castro and 300 French colonists founded the town of Castroville in 1844. It was located 25 miles west of San Antonio, on the Medina River. By 1847, Castro had brought in more than 2,000 colonists to settle along the Medina River. They helped establish D'Hanis, Quihi, and Vandenburg. Many of Castro's settlers spoke German because they were from the French province of Alsace, a German-speaking area.

Another Frenchman, Victor Considérant, established a settlement in 1855 in North Texas. It was located near the cabin of Margaret and John Neely Bryan on the Trinity River. This area later became the city of Dallas. This French colony of about 350 settlers was called La Réunion. The La Réunion colony was founded as a **socialist** society. In such a society, the people agree to share all work and rewards equally. The colony failed, however. Few of the people knew how to farm. Those who worked hard grew unhappy with sharing equally. They decided it was best to work for their own profit. That is, they preferred the **free enterprise** system.

Other European Immigrants. During the 1840s and 1850s, thousands of settlers from all over Europe came to Texas. Polish colonists founded Panna Maria in Karnes County in 1854. Czech immigrants settled in towns such as Praha, New Bremen, and Fayetteville. Slavic settlers known as Wends came to Central Texas. There were hundreds of Jewish settlers in various Texas towns. The first Norwegian settlement in Texas was at Normandy, near Brownsboro. Swedish settlers arrived in Central Texas in the early 1840s. Immigrants from Italy, the Netherlands, and Belgium began to arrive in large numbers during the 1850s.

Texas had become a land of immigrants in the 1820s, when the Austins opened it for settlement. After Texas became a state, the movement of people into Texas grew at its fastest rate. The newcomers were ready to share with older residents the problems as well as the promises of Texas. ✪

CHAPTER REVIEW RESOURCES

1. Chapter Review Worksheet 14
2. Chapter 14 Test, Form A
3. Reteaching Worksheet 14
4. Chapter 14 Test, Form B
5. **Informal Evaluation Forms:** Portfolio Assessment
6. *Texas, Our Texas* **Test Generator**

Essential Elements
2E, 2H, 5B, 5C, 5D, 9A, 9B, 9D

CHAPTER 14 REVIEW

Understanding Main Ideas

1. What political issue delayed the annexation of Texas?
2. What political issues from the days when Texas was a republic still remained after Texas became a state?
3. What United States region contributed the largest number of settlers to Texas after 1845?

Thinking Critically

1. **Synthesizing Information:** Why did northerners oppose the annexation of Texas? How were their fears justified in the first decade of Texas statehood?
2. **Evaluating Information:** How do you think the ever-increasing numbers of slaves brought to Texas would affect the lives of free blacks already there?
3. **Classifying Information:** Classify the following Texas settlements as German, French, Polish, Czech, or Norwegian: Normandy, Panna Maria, New Braunfels, Comfort, Fayetteville, Boerne, Sisterdale, Castroville, La Réunion.

Linking History and Geography

1. Imagine that you were able to examine satellite photographs of East Texas taken in 1845 and 1860. What environmental changes might you see?
2. Judging from the map on page 302, what Texas communities were located on the extreme western and southern boundaries of the state?

TAAS *Practice*
Using Primary Sources

Mathilda Doebbler Gruen Wagner's father came to Texas from Germany around 1850. After working for several years as a stonemason, he was granted a homestead near Fredericksburg. Soon after, he sent for his wife and children. Mathilda Wagner wrote this account of German-Indian relations on the Texas frontier:

The Indians often came to Fredericksburg to trade their beads and pecans they gathered, or whatever they had made for things the settlers had. They would sometimes trade a big sack of pecans for a handful of salt or tobacco. As the church was just next to the market square they were often around it. . . . The Indians were friendly and helpful until the settlers started driving them out as though they were cattle. Then they became mean and would steal and sometimes kill. . . . The houses in those early days were all built on the corners of the farms, where a number of farms came together. This was done so that . . . each neighbor could hear signals from the others and in this way have a little protection from the Indians. Every house had a horn made from a cow's horn, and when the other settlers heard it blow, they knew there were Indians around. My father blew the horn and the neighbors came running with their guns.

1. According to Mathilda Doebbler Gruen Wagner, trouble started with the Indians because
   A setters began to drive the Indians from the area
   B the Indians refused to trade with the German settlers

CHAPTER 14 REVIEW ANSWERS

Understanding Main Ideas
1. Slavery
2. Debt and land policy
3. The lower South

Thinking Critically
1. **Synthesizing Information:** Northerners feared that Texas would be a slave state. Ways in which their fears were justified included: many people who moved to Texas brought slaves with them, Texas' new constitution did not make slavery illegal, and the number of free blacks who could live in Texas was limited.
2. **Evaluating Information:** Answers will vary, but students should recognize that if most blacks in Texas were slaves, free blacks would probably be viewed as outcasts. Also, slaveholders might fear that the free blacks would influence the slaves to run away or revolt.
3. **Classifying Information:** German—New Braunfels, Comfort, Boerne, Sisterdale; French—Castroville, La Réunion; Polish—Panna Maria; Czech—Fayetteville; Norwegian—Normandy

Linking History and Geography
1. Possible answers include: more farms and villages and larger towns in 1860.
2. El Paso, Laredo, Brownsville

TAAS *Practice*
Using Primary Sources
1. A 2. C

TAAS *Practice*
Writing Descriptively

Letters will vary but should be based on information presented in the chapter.

Practicing Skills

1. **Sequencing Events:** Henry Clay is nominated for president, James Polk becomes president, the United States Congress passes a resolution allowing annexation, the Texas annexation convention meets, President Polk signs the act making Texas a state, Texas voters ratify the Texas Constitution

2. **Interpreting Maps:** Most chose south Central Texas. Many Germans were farmers, and this area was an ideal farming region with a mild climate and long growing season. Other Germans who were businesspeople were attracted to Central Texas cities such as San Antonio, where there was a large market for business.

Enriching Your Study of History

1. **Individual Project:** Reports should accurately characterize the account chosen.

2. **Cooperative Project:** Outlines should demonstrate thorough investigation of the assigned communities.

CONTINUED

C the Indians attacked the settlers without reason
D the Indians had nothing that the settlers wanted to take in trade

2. As a defense against the Indians, German settlers in the countryside around Fredericksburg
A organized a militia
B signed a peace treaty
C settled close to each other
D blew horns to scare them away

TAAS *Practice*
Writing Descriptively

Imagine that you are a member of a German family who has recently settled in the Fredericksburg area. Write a letter to a cousin in Germany, describing your new life and your new home on the Texas frontier. Tell what you like best about your new home, and explain why. Also describe the difficulties of your new life.

Practicing Skills

1. **Sequencing Events:** Place the following historical events in proper sequence, beginning with the earliest and ending with the latest: President Polk signs the act making Texas a state, Texas voters ratify the Texas constitution, the Texas annexation convention meets, Henry Clay is nominated for president, James Polk becomes president, the United States Congress passes a resolution allowing annexation.

2. **Interpreting Maps:** Study the map on this page. In what part of Texas did

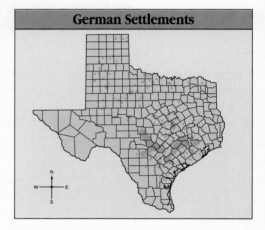

German Settlements

most German settlers choose to make their homes? Why do you think they chose to settle there?

Enriching Your Study of History

1. **Individual Project:** With the help of your teacher or librarian, locate a written account by some person who moved to Texas between 1836 and 1860. Then prepare a brief written report on the person's experiences.

2. **Cooperative Project:** Your teacher will divide your class into six teams to research Texas communities begun by European immigrants. The teams will investigate communities formed by German, French, Polish, Czechoslovakian, Swedish, and Norwegian settlers. Each team will then compose an outline of its findings about its community and report its findings to the entire class.

TEXAS AND THE UNITED STATES

TEACHER'S TIME LINE

Section 1	Section 2	Section 3	Section 4	Review and Assessment
Pp. 309–11	Pp. 312–14	Pp. 314–17	Pp. 317–23	
1 Day	1 Day	1 Day	1 Day	1 Day

TEACHER MATERIALS

Core: Chapter 15 Time Line; Graphic Organizer 15; Enrichment Worksheet 15; Review Worksheet 15; Reteaching Worksheet 15; Chapter 15 Tests, Forms A & B

Additional: Geography and Graph Skills 15, Map and Chart Transparencies 17, Informal Evaluation Forms, Test Generator

OBJECTIVES

1. Outline causes of the Mexican War.
2. Discuss the role of Texas in the Mexican War.
3. List the major provisions of the Treaty of Guadalupe Hidalgo.
4. Explain the boundary dispute between Texas and New Mexico.
5. Specify the provisions of the Compromise of 1850.
6. Discuss the treatment of the Tejanos during and after the Mexican War.
7. Analyze government policies toward Texas Indians.

RESOURCES

BOOKS FOR TEACHERS

Anderson, John B. *Corpus Christi Caller: Centennial Journey*. Corpus Christi: Caller-Times Pub. Co., 1983. History of Corpus Christi.

Benton, Thomas Hart. *Mr. Benton's Anti-compromise Speech*. Washington, 1850. Benton argues against the Compromise of 1850 before the U.S. Senate.

The Causes and Justice of the Mexican War. Concord: N.H. Patriot's office, 1846. Primary source material regarding the Mexican War.

Connor, Seymour V. *Adventures in Glory, 1836–1849*. The Saga of Texas Series. Austin: Steck-Vaughn, 1965. Story of the days

of the Texas Republic and just after.

Singletary, Otis A. *The Mexican War*. Chicago: University of Chicago Press, 1960. Discussion of the Mexican War.

Stevens, Isaac Ingalls. *Campaigns of the Rio Grande and of Mexico*. New York: D. Appleton and Co., 1851. Some campaigns of the Mexican War.

The Treaty Between the United States and Mexico. Washington: Wendell and Van Benthuysen, 1848. Treaty ending the war.

Webb, Walter Prescott. *The Texas Rangers: A Century of Frontier Defense*. Austin: University of Texas Press, 1965. History of the Texas Rangers.

MULTIMEDIA MATERIALS

Gomez, Fernando Chacon. *The Intended and Actual Effect of Article VIII of the Treaty of Guadalupe Hidalgo: Mexican Treaty Rights Under International and Domestic Law*. (film) Austin: Benson Latin American Collection.

The History of the U.S. Demo-comp Package, America Moves West, and *European Immigration to the U.S.* (software) Focus Media, Inc., 839 Stewart Avenue, P.O. Box 865, Garden City, New York, 11530. These two programs respectively trace the movement west across the early frontier and the rise of European immigration.

◆ GENERAL STRATEGIES

STUDENTS WITH SPECIAL NEEDS

Limited English Proficient Students (LEP)
Have students skim the Chapter 15 illustrations and captions. Ask them to write down terms or concepts about which they are unsure. Allow time to discuss their lists and clarify ideas. See other activities labeled **LEP.**

Students Having Difficulty with the Chapter
Ask students having difficulty to create a matching review based on the people and events discussed in Chapter 15. Have students exchange the review with a partner. Allow pairs of students to work together to check and correct their answers. **LEP**

Auditory Learners
Pair auditory learners with visual learners. Have auditory learners select one of the topics below and prepare an oral report to the class. Refer to the "Visual Learners" activity for further instructions.

The Texas Rangers
Battles of the Mexican War
The Colt Six-Shooter
Indian Reservations in Texas

See other activities labeled **A.**

Visual Learners
Have visual learners prepare drawings, maps, or other graphics to accompany the oral reports given by the auditory learners. Encourage the students in each pair to work together to conduct research. See other activities labeled **V.**

Tactile/Kinesthetic Learners
Have students draw on a large sheet of paper or poster board a map of the United States. Ask them to use different colors to designate the following: the boundaries of Texas from 1836 to 1850, the area of Texas ceded to the United States in 1850, the area disputed between Texas and Mexico, the Nueces River, the Rio Grande, the territory of the Mexican Cession, Santa Fe. Display the completed maps in the classroom. See other activities labeled **TK.**

Gifted Students
Refer gifted students to the political cartoon on page 315. Ask them to review the major topics discussed in Chapter 15 and create a cartoon based on one of these issues. Ask students to display and discuss their cartoons. See other activities labeled **G.**

VOCABULARY
In addition to the boldfaced terms in each section, some students might benefit from discussing the meanings of these terms.

Section 1: *journalist* (p. 309); *overspread* (p. 309); *destined* (p. 309); *westward expansion* (p. 309); *turmoil* (p. 311); *encamped* (p. 311).

Section 2: *protest* (p. 312); *sacrifice* (p. 313); *reckless* (p. 313).

Section 3: *restrict* (p. 316); *survey line* (p. 317); *prejudiced* (p. 317).

Section 4: *mounted* (p. 319); *clashes* (p. 320).

CHRONOLOGY
Have students study the Chapter 15 Time Line and identify relationships among the events.

GRAPHIC ORGANIZER
Have students skim the chapter and complete the Chapter 15 Graphic Organizer. *(You might wish to use this activity to review rather than to introduce the chapter.)*

ENRICHMENT
Have students complete the Chapter 15 Enrichment Worksheet.

Predicting (I) Direct students to the first two paragraphs of Section 1. You might wish to ask a student to read the second paragraph aloud. Ask students if they think that the United States was correct in believing that it had a "right" to continue to expand its territory westward. Ask: What might be the consequences of such a belief? *(Lead students to* conclude that this belief might lead to the idea that nothing and no one should stand in the way of expansion.)

INSTRUCTION

Analysis (I) Lead the class to define and discuss *manifest destiny* in the context of the 1990s by posing the following question: Does the concept of manifest destiny still exist as a driving force in the United States today? *(One example is space exploration.)* **A**

TEXAS AND THE UNITED STATES

The Story Continues...

The decade after Texas became a state was a time of western expansion for the United States. Chapter 15 explores the troubles that arose when the interests of Texas and the United States came into conflict with those of Mexico and the Indian nations.

As you read the chapter, look for the answers to these questions:

1. What was manifest destiny, and how did belief in it lead to a war with Mexico?
2. What role did Texans play in the Mexican War?
3. What were the terms of the Treaty of Guadalupe Hidalgo?
4. How did the United States government try to deal with the problem of the western Indians in the decade after the Mexican War?

1 Expansion and Conflict

While Texans were working to achieve statehood in 1845, a journalist in the United States named John L. O'Sullivan wrote an important article in his newspaper. He discussed the tremendous growth in the West, and he claimed that Texas must be allowed to become part of the United States.

Manifest Destiny. In his newspaper article, O'Sullivan stated that nothing must interfere with "the fulfillment of our manifest destiny to overspread the continent." The term *manifest destiny* was thereafter used to describe the belief that the United States was clearly destined to expand from the Atlantic Ocean to the Pacific.

O'Sullivan's words reflected the views of many United States citizens. But not all Americans supported the idea of manifest destiny. Many people worried that westward expansion would lead to war with Mexico over control of

Library of Congress

John L. O' Sullivan is credited with inventing the term *manifest destiny*.

CHAPTER 15 OVERVIEW

The annexation of Texas was part of the westward expansion of the United States in the 1840s. Texas statehood was one step in fulfilling the dream of many Americans to control all western land from the Mississippi River to the Pacific Ocean. As people migrated to Texas, others trekked across the Great Plains and through the Rocky Mountains into Oregon and California. Westward expansion, however, created problems for Texas and the United States. Boundary disputes arose, war with Mexico occurred, and conflicts with Indians increased as people rushed to settle new territory.

Essential Elements
2E, 2F, 2H, 3C, 3E, 3F, 5B, 9A, 9B, 9E

Illustrating (I) Provide each student with a blank outline map of Texas and northern Mexico (or ask them to draw a map). Have students illustrate on the map the boundary dispute between Texas and Mexico. Then ask them to illustrate on the map the information presented under the subheading "Fighting Breaks Out." You might wish to refer them to the map on page 312 as a guide. Suggest to students that they utilize symbols and a map legend. To conclude the activity, ask: Which side do you think started the Mexican War? **A, V, TK**

Guided Practice (I) Write on the chalkboard the topic *Causes of the Mexican War*. Have the class work together using the information in Section 1 to prepare an outline of the topic as you copy their responses on the board. Have students copy the outline on a sheet of paper and save it for use in Section 2. **A, V, TK, LEP**

EXTENSION

Research (III) Ask students to investigate and report on the presidency of James Polk. How is Polk viewed by historians? What do historians consider to be Polk's achievements and failures? **A, G**

The Granger Collection

Americans moved westward in large numbers during the 1840s and 1850s. Texas was the destination of many of these western settlers.

Texas, California, and other areas of the Southwest. In the Northwest, the British in Canada claimed land in what is now Washington and Oregon. Some people believed it was wrong to continue to take land from the Indians. And many other people, mainly those from the northeastern United States, warned that movement west would bring more slave states into the country.

When James Polk won the presidency in 1844, it was clear that most people in the United States favored expansion. The first step in achieving manifest destiny was the annexation of Texas. The fear that annexation might lead to war with Mexico appeared to be coming true, however. Signs of war could be seen in the gathering of troops by both sides near the Rio Grande.

Troubles with Mexico. Relations between the United States and Mexico had been unfriendly for some years. The Mexicans had resented efforts by the United States to buy Texas, and they were troubled when people in the United States supported the Texas Revolution. Most Mexicans continued to believe that the Revolution was a United States plot to steal Texas. They became even more upset when the United States annexed Texas.

President Polk sent a representative named John Slidell to Mexico to negotiate an agreement between the two nations. Many United States citizens had claims against Mexico for damage done to their property during Mexican uprisings. Slidell's task was to try to settle these claims

Independent Practice (II) Have students examine the illustration on page 310. Ask them to select one of the persons in the illustration and use their historical imagination to write a journal entry recalling the day's events. Invite students to share their entries with the class. **A, V**

RETEACHING

Refer students to the class outline from the Guided Practice activity. Ask them to write a brief summary of the topic *Causes of the Mexican War.* **LEP**

CLOSURE

Ask students to write a cause-and-effect statement incorporating the following terms: *manifest destiny, Mexican War.* Call on volunteers to read their statements aloud.

ASSESSMENT

Have students complete the Section 1 Review on page 311.

with Mexico. He was also instructed to make an offer to buy California and to negotiate the Texas boundary with Mexico. The Mexican government was in turmoil at this time, and no Mexican leader would even talk to Slidell. The Mexican representative to the United States, Juan Almonte, left Washington, D.C., in anger as soon as it was announced that Texas had been annexed.

The spark that set off a war was the disagreement over the boundary line between Texas and Mexico. Mexico claimed that the Nueces River marked the Texas boundary. The United States accepted the Texas argument that the boundary was the Rio Grande.

Fighting Breaks Out. A United States force commanded by General Zachary Taylor was encamped along the Nueces River. After Texas Governor James Pinckney Henderson took office in February 1846, Taylor moved his troops across the Nueces River. In April 1846, Taylor had Fort Brown built near the Rio Grande at what is now Brownsville. The Mexican commander in the region, General Mariano Arista, ordered Taylor and the United States troops to leave the disputed territory. When Taylor refused to withdraw, General Arista moved his army north of the Rio Grande. On May 8 and 9, battles were fought at Palo Alto and Resaca de la Palma near Fort Brown. Taylor claimed victories for the United States in both battles.

Both Mexico and the United States declared war within days after the two battles. The Mexican government claimed it was fighting against the aggressive actions of the United States. President Polk stated that "American blood has been shed on American soil." ✪

Lithograph by Carl Nebel, Amon Carter Museum, Fort Worth

The Battle of Palo Alto was a draw, but General Taylor claimed it as a victory for the United States troops.

Chicago Historical Society

General Zachary Taylor marched his army to the Rio Grande and established Fort Brown at present-day Brownsville.

SECTION 1 REVIEW

Identify: John Slidell, General Zachary Taylor, Fort Brown, General Mariano Arista

1. How did the belief in manifest destiny help cause the war with Mexico?
2. What long-term quarrels between the United States and Mexico troubled their relations in the years before the Mexican War?
3. What incident started the Mexican War?

Analyzing Information: Why did some citizens oppose both the annexation of Texas and the Mexican War?

Evaluating Information: If James Polk had been defeated in his race for the presidency in 1844, do you think the Mexican War might have been avoided? Explain.

Answers to Section 1 Review

Identify: John Slidell—sent by President Polk to Mexico to negotiate an agreement between the United States and Mexico; General Zachary Taylor—commanded the United States forces that battled Mexico near the Rio Grande, beginning the Mexican War; Fort Brown—built by Texas forces near present-day Brownsville; General Mariano Arista—commanded the Mexican forces in the first two battles of the Mexican War

1. Manifest destiny reflected the attitude of many Americans that they were destined to overspread the continent. The United States' annexation of Texas angered Mexico, and war seemed the only solution.
2. United States' efforts to buy Texas, Americans' support of the Texas Revolution, the annexation of Texas
3. General Taylor's refusal to withdraw from disputed territory along the Rio Grande

Analyzing Information: They believed that annexation would lead to war, and they did not want the United States to become involved in a war with Mexico.

Evaluating Information: Answers will vary. Some students may note that if Polk had been defeated, Texas might not have been annexed.

SECTION ▣2

FOCUS

Student Experiences (I) Ask students if they think that war is an effective solution to the disputes between nations. *(Suggest that they consider recent conflicts involving the United States.)* Ask them if they believe that war with Mexico could have been avoided.

INSTRUCTION

Vocabulary (I) You may wish to preteach the following boldfaced term: *offensive* (p. 313). **LEP**

Using Historical Imagination (II) Organize the class into two groups. Have students in the first group imagine that they are newspaper reporters from Texas covering the Mexican War. They are traveling with the United States forces in Mexico. Ask them to write newspaper articles describing

Essential Elements
2F, 2H, 9A, 9B

Linking History and Geography
Mexico

Transparency 17
A transparency of this map can be found in the Teacher's Resource Binder.

▣2 The Mexican War

Many people in the United States were opposed to the Mexican War. They believed that President Polk had deliberately angered the Mexicans, in order to force them to fight. In fact, nearly everyone in the northeastern states was against the war. Many participated in protest marches to let the president and Congress know they wanted peace.

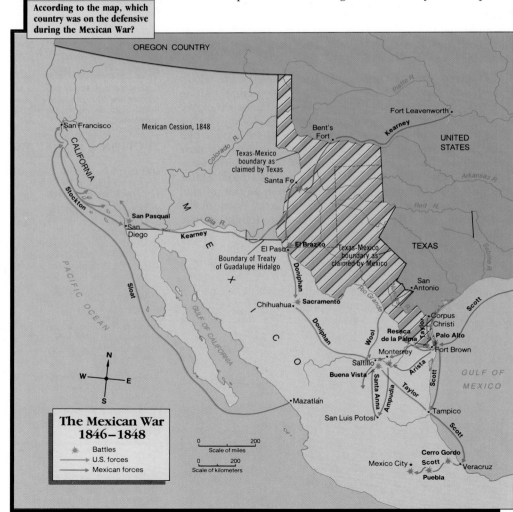

LINKING HISTORY AND GEOGRAPHY

According to the map, which country was on the defensive during the Mexican War?

The Mexican War 1846–1848
* Battles
→ U.S. forces
→ Mexican forces

The Role of Texans. Most Texans strongly supported war with Mexico. Texas and Mexico had been involved in disputes since 1835. The Texans still had bitter memories of the Alamo and Goliad. They thought the war was a chance to end the threat from Mexico. Many Texans welcomed the chance to fight the commander of the Mexican army, their old rival, General Santa Anna.

More than 8,000 Texans volunteered to fight in the Mexican War. Governor Henderson took a leave from office to serve in the army. Other Texas leaders who fought included former Texas president Mirabeau Lamar, several future governors, and the commander of the army under the Republic, Albert Sidney Johnston. Most of the Texans, however, were average young people who left homes and families to serve. It was a great sacrifice, and it created difficulties for those who stayed behind.

The Texas Rangers joined the United States forces in the war. Because they were familiar with the geography of South Texas and northern Mexico, the Rangers served as scouts for General Zachary Taylor and General Winfield Scott. Their fame as fighters spread quickly among Mexican troops as well as United States forces. Several Texas Rangers were recognized for their leadership and bravery in the war. Ben McCulloch, Jack Hays, John "Rip" Ford, Samuel Walker, and William A. A. "Bigfoot" Wallace became heroes to their troops and to many of the people of Texas.

Despite their reputation as fighters, the Texas Rangers received much criticism. Many United States Army officers felt that the Rangers were reckless and did not follow orders well. It was reported that Rangers often went their own way, attacking Mexican villages and towns as the United States forces pushed into Mexico. Many Mexicans were terrified of the Rangers. They called them the Texas Devils.

Even as many Texans served in the war, one served in making peace. Jane McManus Cazneau was sent to Mexico City by Secretary of War James Buchanan. Cazneau had brought German settlers into Texas and was well respected by leaders in the United States government. Cazneau's discussion with Mexican leaders became part of the final agreement ending the Mexican War.

The United States Victory. After battles at the mouth of the Rio Grande near Fort Brown, General Taylor began an **offensive**, or forward troop movement, into northern

Institute of Texan Cultures

Ben McCulloch, a veteran of San Jacinto, organized a company of Texas Rangers during the Mexican War.

Library of Congress

John Coffee Hays was a surveyor for the Republic of Texas and became captain of a Texas Ranger company. During the Mexican War, "Captain Jack" played an important role in the battles at Monterrey and Mexico City. He became one of the best-known Texas Rangers.

Historical Sidelight
Former Ranger Captain Bob Crowder once defined a Texas Ranger thus: "A Ranger is an officer who is able to handle any given situation without definite instructions from his commanding officer or higher authority. This ability must be proven before a man becomes a Ranger."

TEXAS VOICES

*W*hile Americans argued the pros and cons of a war with Mexico, the citizens of Mexico also debated the issues of war. To rally support for a war with the United States, General Francisco Mejia wrote a letter to his troops and the citizens of the northern states of Mexico. His words reflect the bitterness and anger that marred relations between the United States and Mexico in 1846.

FELLOW-Citizens:—The annexation of the department of Texas to the United States, projected and consummated [carried out] by the tortuous policy of the cabinet of the Union, does not yet satisfy the ambitious desires of the degenerate sons of Washington [immoral Americans]. The civilized world has already recognized in that act all the marks of injustice, iniquity [wickedness], and the most scandalous violation of the rights of nations. Indelible is the stain which will forever darken the character for virtue falsely attributed to the people of the United States; and posterity [future generations] will regard with horror their perfidious [unfaithful] conduct, and the immorality of the means employed by them to carry into effect that most degrading depredation [corrupt plundering]. . . . The United States . . . has . . . put in practice . . . the basest treachery, in order to obtain possession, in the midst of peace, of the territory of a friendly nation, which relied upon the faith of promises and the solemnity of treaties.

SECTION ★2★ REVIEW

Define: offensive
Identify: General Winfield Scott, Veracruz

1. How did Texans take part in the Mexican War?
2. What special role did the Texas Rangers play?
3. What happened at the battles of Buena Vista and Veracruz?

Using Historical Imagination: Imagine that you are Jane McManus Cazneau, sent to talk peace with Mexican leaders after the capture of Mexico City. Do you think it will be easy or difficult to make a treaty? Explain.

Evaluating Information: Do you think President Polk intentionally caused the Mexican War? Why or why not?

Mexico. The United States forces won victories at Monterrey and Buena Vista. Another United States force under the command of General Scott landed on the Mexican coast near Veracruz in March 1847. From there the United States Army moved inland to capture Mexico City. In each case, Texas Rangers led the advance into battle.

Meanwhile, United States forces took control of California and regions of New Mexico. After the capture of Mexico City, the war came to a quick end. Yet fighting continued through October of 1847. ✪

❸ Results of the Mexican War

The end of the Mexican War had far-reaching effects on the future of Texas, the United States, and Mexico. The long dispute between Texas and Mexico was over. New boundaries were set, which remain today. More than one-fourth of the present-day United States was acquired as a result of the Mexican War. Mexico lost about half its territory. The goal of manifest destiny had been achieved.

SECTION 3

FOCUS

Past Learning and Predicting (I) Direct students to the map on page 312 and ask them to recall the boundary dispute that sparked the Mexican War. Then ask a student to point out on a wall map the current boundary between Texas and Mexico *(the Rio Grande).* Ask: What do you think was one of the terms of the peace treaty ending the war? *(The Rio Grande was recognized as the border between Texas and Mexico.)*

INSTRUCTION

Vocabulary (I) You may wish to preteach the following boldfaced terms: *compromise* (p. 317); *exiled* (p. 317). **LEP**

Cooperative Learning (I) Tell students that it is 1850 and that they are going to interview ordinary people about their positions on the Compromise of 1850. Have each student prepare a list of questions to ask. Then organize students into pairs. Have them take turns interviewing their partners, asking and answering the prepared questions. **A, LEP**

Treaty of Guadalupe Hidalgo. The peace treaty formally ending the war was signed on February 2, 1848. Representatives from Mexico and the United States agreed to terms at Guadalupe Hidalgo, a village near Mexico City.

In the Treaty of Guadalupe Hidalgo, Mexico agreed to recognize Texas as a part of the United States and give up all claims to Texas territory. The Rio Grande was recognized as the border between Texas and Mexico. Mexico also ceded a vast amount of its northern land to the United States. That territory included present-day California, Nevada, Utah, and parts of Arizona, New Mexico, Colorado, and Wyoming. The United States paid Mexico $15 million for this land, often referred to as the Mexican Cession. The United States also took over $3.25 million in claims against the Mexican government by United States citizens. Mexican Americans were promised all rights of citizenship.

The Texas–New Mexico Boundary Dispute. With the southern boundary of Texas settled, attention turned to its western border. Texas had always claimed that the Rio Grande was not only its southern border, but its western border as well. According to this claim, nearly one-half of New Mexico was part of Texas, including the trading center of Santa Fe. But the people of Santa Fe rejected the Texas claim. They had been willing to fight over the issue as early as the Republic years. Now that both New Mexico

The Granger Collection

Many Americans, especially in northern states, were opposed to armed conflict with Mexico. This American cartoon, published in 1846, is critical of Americans volunteering for war against Mexico. How did most Texans feel about war with Mexico?

Santa Fe was within the borders claimed by the Republic of Texas, but most of Santa Fe's people supported Mexico. Santa Fe had long been a center of trade with Mexico. It was the capital of New Mexico Territory for more than 200 years before Texas gained independence from Mexico.

Caption Response
Most were in favor of war.

Institute of Texan Cultures

Guided Practice (I) Refer students to the class outline from the Section 1 and 2 Guided Practice activities. Write on the chalkboard the topic *Results of the Mexican War* and have the class complete the outline. **A, V, TK, LEP**

Independent Practice (II) Have students write a paragraph explaining the link between the issue of slavery and the Texas–New Mexico boundary dispute. Invite volunteers to read their paragraphs aloud. **A**

Multicultural Perspective (I) Have students imagine that they are Tejanos after the Treaty of Guadalupe Hidalgo. Many of them have lost their land to new settlers. Ask them to write an appeal to the United States government pleading the cause of the Tejanos. Invite students to read their pleas aloud. **A**

RETEACHING
Refer students to the outline that they completed in the Guided Practice activity. Ask them to write a brief summary of the topic *Results of the Mexican War*. **LEP**

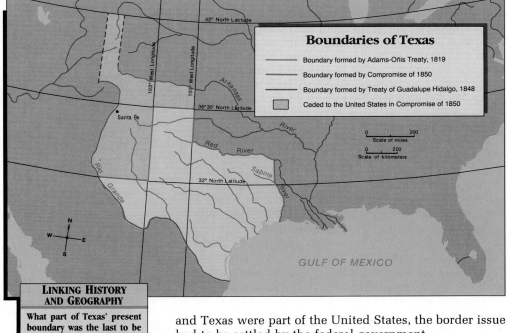

Boundaries of Texas

— Boundary formed by Adams-Oñis Treaty, 1819
— Boundary formed by Compromise of 1850
— Boundary formed by Treaty of Guadalupe Hidalgo, 1848
☐ Ceded to the United States in Compromise of 1850

Linking History and Geography
That of Northwest Texas and the Panhandle

LINKING HISTORY AND GEOGRAPHY
What part of Texas' present boundary was the last to be established?

Historical Sidelight
In August 1846, long before the end of the Mexican War, David Wilmot of Pennsylvania introduced the Wilmot Proviso in the United States House of Representatives. The proviso called for the prohibition of slavery in any territory gained by the United States as a result of the Mexican War. The proviso was not adopted but was indicative of the fight over slavery that was yet to come.

and Texas were part of the United States, the border issue had to be settled by the federal government.

The people of Santa Fe tried to convince the federal government that New Mexico should become a separate territory of the United States. Most New Mexicans spoke Spanish and had close ties to Mexico. They were still angry at the Texans for the invasions that occurred under President Lamar. Most people in Santa Fe were also against slavery, and they had no desire to be part of Texas.

The United States Congress was divided over the Texas–New Mexico boundary issue. Southern leaders wanted to recognize the Texas claim. They hoped to keep the territory acquired from Mexico open to slavery. Members of Congress from the North sided with the New Mexicans. They wanted to restrict the size of Texas in the hope of keeping slavery out of the new western territories.

While the United States Congress debated, the Texas legislature passed laws protecting the Texas claim to New Mexico. In March 1848, the state legislature declared all of New Mexico east of the Rio Grande to be Santa Fe County, Texas.

CLOSURE
Write the following headings across the chalkboard: *Treaty of Guadalupe Hidalgo, Texas–New Mexico boundary dispute, Compromise of 1850.* Have the class list key facts about each topic as you write their responses under the appropriate headings.

ASSESSMENT
Have students complete the Section 3 Review on page 317.

SECTION 4

FOCUS

Predicting (I) Ask students to consider the impact that manifest destiny might have had on the Indians living in Texas in the 1840s and 1850s. Ask: From what you have read in previous chapters, do you think that the Indians could expect to be treated fairly by the governments of the United States and Texas?

The Compromise of 1850. In 1850, the United States Congress made a decision about the Texas boundary and the issue of slavery in the West. Congress passed a set of laws known as the Compromise of 1850. A **compromise** is an agreement in which each side gives up something it wants in order to reach a settlement. Texas was paid $10 million in exchange for giving up all claims to New Mexico. Texas needed the money to pay its debts, and the people in Santa Fe did not want to be part of Texas. For these reasons, the voters in Texas accepted the agreement. A survey line was drawn between Texas and New Mexico, setting the boundary as its remains today.

Other provisions of the Compromise of 1850 dealt with the slavery issue. California became a state in which slavery was forbidden. The rest of the territories gained from Mexico would make their own decisions regarding slavery. Because these regions had small populations, they would not become states for many years. In this way, Congress postponed dealing with the problem until a later time.

Tejanos and the War. Following the Texas Revolution, Tejanos were often regarded as enemies of Texas. Most had supported and fought for Texas independence. But many new settlers from the United States were prejudiced against all people of Mexican ancestry. These new settlers were unaware of the contributions of Tejanos such as Juan Seguín, José Antonio Navarro, and Patricia de León.

When Mexican troops invaded Texas in 1842, some Texans assumed that the Tejanos supported Mexico. Tejanos were criticized and sometimes attacked. To protect themselves, Tejanos, including the De León and Benavides families, left Texas. Tejanos were hurt and angry over their treatment. They had doubts about being part of the United States if it meant that the bad treatment would continue. At the time of the Mexican War, loyal Tejano citizens such as Juan and Gertrudis Seguín, Antonio Pérez, and Manuel Flores were **exiled**, or forced to flee their country. Most returned after the Mexican War to find that they had lost their land, livestock, and other property. ✪

◢ Texas, the United States, and the Indians

After being annexed to the United States, the people of Texas expected the federal government to take care of

SECTION 3 REVIEW

Define: compromise, exiled
Identify: Treaty of Guadalupe Hidalgo, Santa Fe County, Compromise of 1850

1. What lands were added to the United States in the Treaty of Guadalupe Hidalgo?
2. What did Texas receive in exchange for giving up claims to land in New Mexico?
3. What happened to many Tejano families in the 1840s?

Analyzing Information: Explain why the results of the Mexican War had long-term effects on the slavery issue in the United States.

Evaluating Information: If you were a Texas political leader, would you have voted for the terms of the Compromise of 1850? Why or why not?

INSTRUCTION

Vocabulary (I) You may wish to preteach the following boldfaced terms: *infantry* (p. 319); *reservations* (p. 320). **LEP**

Art and History (I) Direct students to the painting on this page. Invite volunteers to describe what they see in the painting. Ask: Do the Indians in the painting look like warriors? Does the painting's caption influence your perceptions? Have students continue the activity, using other illustrations in the textbook. **A, V**

any conflicts with the Indians. A steady rise in Texas population, along with movement westward, brought hundreds of settlers into new Indian homelands. As a result, Indian wars continued for more than 30 years after annexation. In many cases, Texans came to feel the need to provide their own forces to help those of the United States in the wars.

Rangers and Indians. After annexation, the United States policy was to make treaties with the Indians while stationing troops along the frontier. The troops were supposed to guard Texas settlements as well as keep settlers from moving farther west into Indian lands. In 1846, the United States made a treaty with the Penateka band of Comanches in an effort to keep the peace. With the outbreak

Comanches controlled a large area of West Texas. This painting by Theodore Gentilz shows a Comanche raiding party in far West Texas during the 1840s.

Courtesy of the San Antonio Museum Association

of the Mexican War, United States troops were withdrawn from the Texas frontier to fight in Mexico.

When the United States troops left, five companies of Texas Rangers were sent to guard the frontier. Throughout 1847 and 1848, the Comanches and Kiowas made a series of raids. Texas leaders then sent four more companies of Texas Rangers to the frontier between San Antonio and the Rio Grande.

The Rangers saw their job as protecting Texans while punishing Indians. When a group of Indians raided an area, the Texas Rangers struck back, sometimes attacking Indians whether or not they had taken part in the raiding. The Indians feared the Texas Rangers and were less likely to sign treaties because of their actions.

In general, the Rangers were more effective in fighting the Indians than were the troops of the United States. The first United States troops sent to the Texas frontier were **infantry**, or foot soldiers. They were unable to match the fighting style of the Indians, particularly the Comanches and Kiowas. These Indians moved swiftly across the plains on their horses, and they knew the land. The Rangers, however, were mounted too. Gradually they learned the land almost as well as the Texas Indians. In the 1840s, the Rangers acquired a powerful new weapon, the Colt six-shooter. This handgun was capable of firing six shots in rapid order, unlike the old one-shot weapons. This gun gave the Rangers a great advantage in frontier warfare.

Establishment of Forts. When the Mexican War ended, the United States again sent troops to the frontier. By that time, the line of settlement in Texas had moved westward to Sherman and Dallas in North Texas and Fredericksburg in Central Texas. To protect these and other settlements, the federal government built a line of forts just to the west of them. By 1849, there were eight army posts stretching from the Red River to the Rio Grande. Among the forts was Fort Worth, built where the city now stands. In the south, Fort Duncan was built near Eagle Pass on the Rio Grande.

A new line of forts was soon built to the west of the first line. These new forts were built to protect travel routes that were being established in West Texas and along the Rio Grande. Routes were developed to connect Austin and San Antonio to El Paso. Additionally, people were traveling along the Rio Grande to El Paso on their way to California.

This early photograph is of James Buckner Barry, who served under Captain Jack Hays. With the outbreak of the Mexican War, Barry joined the Texas Rangers and was wounded at the Battle of Monterrey.

The invention of the Colt six-shooter greatly aided the Texas Rangers along the frontier. This version of the Colt six-shooter is called a Walker pistol.

Geography
From north to south, these forts were Fort Worth; Fort Graham, on the Brazos River; Fort Gates, on the Leon River; Fort Croghan, near Burnet; Fort Martin Scott, at Fredericksburg; Fort Lincoln, 55 miles west of San Antonio; Fort Inge, near Uvalde; and Fort Duncan, at Eagle Pass. Have students locate these forts on the map on page 320 and write a sentence summarizing the pattern formed by this first line of forts. *(The forts formed a vaguely diagonal line from the Rio Grande to the Red River, an attempt to block Indians from moving into Anglo settlements to the east.)*

Cooperative Learning (I) Organize the class into two groups. Have one group represent Comanches or Lipan Apaches who do not want to move onto reservations. The other group will represent government officials who want to move the Indians. Have the groups prepare their arguments and then meet to discuss their differences and try to reach a compromise. Conclude the activity by asking whether the government was justified in moving the Indians onto reservations. Ask: Can you think of an alternative to this policy? **A, LEP**

Multicultural Perspective (I) Direct students to the quotation from the Comanche chief on page 321. Invite a student to read the quote aloud. Ask students: How does the chief feel about the move? What adjectives might you use to describe the chief's emotions? How do you think you would feel if you were he? **A, LEP**

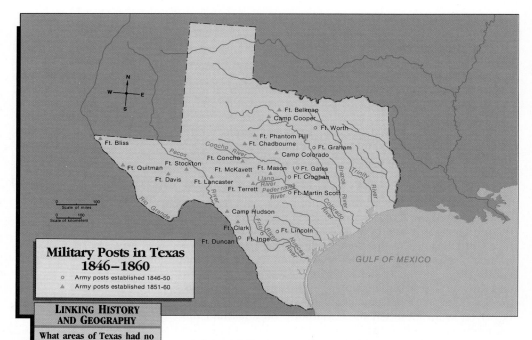

Military Posts in Texas 1846–1860
- ○ Army posts established 1846-50
- ▲ Army posts established 1851-60

LINKING HISTORY AND GEOGRAPHY

What areas of Texas had no military posts? Why do you think army posts were absent from these areas?

Linking History and Geography

The Panhandle, far East Texas, and far South Texas had no military posts. There were few settlers and no threat of attack in these areas.

Gold was discovered in California in 1849, and people from many areas of the world were rushing to get there. When the new line of forts was finished, settlers pressed westward once more. Soon they had again moved to the line of defense.

The army built a third line of posts on or near the Rio Grande. The purpose of these forts was to protect Texas from raids by Mexicans and Indians who lived south of the Rio Grande. They were also built to keep Texas Indians from raiding northern Mexico.

The Reservation Policy. The attempt to prevent clashes between Indians and settlers by building forts failed. As a result, the government decided to try to move the Texas Indians onto **reservations**. These were sections of land set aside, or reserved, for Indian use. Reservations had been established by the United States government in many places throughout the West.

In 1854, two reservations were created in Texas. The state set aside 53,140 acres of land for this purpose. One reservation was for use by Texas Indians who were mainly

Guided Practice (I) Tell students to imagine that they are members of the Texas Rangers sent to guard the frontier during the Mexican War. Ask them to list in note form their duties and responsibilities. **LEP**

Independent Practice (II) Tell students to imagine that they are members of a Texas Indian group that has been resettled on a reservation. Ask them to write a letter to a friend, describing their feelings about the move and how it will affect their way of life. Invite volunteers to read their letters aloud. **A**

EXTENSION

Community Involvement (II) Have interested students prepare a report on the Indian groups that live or lived around their community. Suggest that they contact the local historical society, along with a local museum and library. They should supplement their findings with drawings, maps, or other visuals. **A, V, TK, G**

Archives Division. Texas State Library

John Meusebach held council with a group of Comanche chiefs on March 2, 1847. The meeting produced a treaty allowing Meusebach's German settlers to enter Indian territory unharmed and settle in the San Saba River area.

farmers. It was located on the Brazos River just west of the present-day town of Graham. It was supposed to be home for Caddoes, Wacos, Tonkawas, and some other groups.

A second reservation was located about 40 miles west of the first one. It was on the Clear Fork of the Brazos River. About 500 Penateka Comanches settled on this reservation. When asked how he felt about moving, one Comanche chief replied, "Over this vast country where for centuries our ancestors roamed . . . free and happy, what have we left? . . . Give us a country we can call our own where we may bury our people in quiet."

The Lipan Apaches refused to move to a third reservation planned near Graham. Around 500 Comanches refused to settle on the reservation with the Penatekas. Instead, they moved north to join other Comanches, who continued to fight against Texas settlers.

For a brief period, the reservation system seemed to slow conflict between the Indians and Texans. But the policy eventually began to fail. First, many Indians in

RETEACHING

Have students work in pairs to write one or more cause-and-effect statements, using each subsection of Section 4. Call on volunteers to copy their statements on the chalkboard. Use the statements to review the main ideas of Section 4. **LEP, A**

CLOSURE

Ask students to recall their comments in this section's Focus activity. Ask: After studying the information in Section 4, do you think that the Texas Indians were treated fairly? Allow time for students to express their views.

ASSESSMENT

Have students complete the Section 4 Review on page 322.

Answers to Section 4 Review

Define: *infantry*—foot soldiers; *reservations*—sections of land set aside for Indian use

Identify: Fort Worth—fort built by the federal government on the western frontier where the city of Fort Worth now stands; Fort Duncan—fort located on the Rio Grande near Eagle Pass; Robert S. Neighbors—Indian agent who worked to make reservation life acceptable

1. To make treaties while stationing troops along the frontier
2. Texas Rangers
3. The Alabama-Coushatta, Tigua, and Kickapoo reservations

Writing Persuasively: Letters will vary but might mention that there is too little land, the land is unsuitable for farming, and that Indian agents often steal the supplies.

Analyzing Information: Many members of this group had fought in the Texas Revolution on the side of Texas and had settled as farmers in East Texas.

Reagan Bradshaw

The Alabama-Coushatta reservation is one of the only three Indian reservations in Texas. This photo shows a boy performing in traditional dress.

SECTION 4 REVIEW

Define: infantry, reservations
Identify: Fort Worth, Fort Duncan, Robert S. Neighbors

1. What was the United States policy toward the Indians after annexation of Texas?
2. Who was sent to guard the frontier when the United States troops went to fight in Mexico?
3. What are the only three Indian reservations in Texas?

Writing Persuasively: Imagine that you are a member of an East Texas Indian group in 1854. Write a letter to Sam Houston, asking for his help and explaining why your reservation is not meeting your needs.

Analyzing Information: What special factors caused the Texas government to create a reservation for the Alabama-Coushatta and allow them to stay in Texas?

Texas refused to go to the reservations. Second, there was not enough land set aside for them. Nomadic tribes wanted to continue to hunt over vast areas as they had for hundreds of years. Third, most reservation land was not good farmland. East Texas Indians found it difficult to grow enough food to feed their families. Reservation Indians had to depend on government agents to supply them with food and other necessities. Sometimes these agents stole the supplies and sold them for profit.

Settlers eventually moved closer to the reservations, and this created problems. The Texans claimed that reservation Indians often raided their settlements and stole their livestock. In response to these charges, the United States government decided to move the Texas Indian reservations. In the summer of 1859, the Indians from both reservations were transferred to Indian Territory, which is today the state of Oklahoma.

Reservations for Texas Indians. After the reservations were moved to Indian Territory, the state of Texas recognized the right of one Indian group to remain in Texas. This group was made up of the Alabama and Coushatta tribes. They were primarily farmers and had settled along the Trinity River in East Texas in 1825. Many had fought in the Texas Revolution with the Texans.

In 1854, Texas granted the Alabama-Coushatta people 1,280 acres of land in Polk County, near present-day Livingston. Senator Sam Houston played an important role in the recognition of Alabama-Coushatta rights. In 1928, more land was added to the small Alabama-Coushatta reservation. Today the Alabama-Coushatta, the Tigua reservation near El Paso, and the Kickapoo reservation near Eagle Pass are the only Indian reservations in Texas.

The Wars Continue. The governments of Texas and the United States made efforts to end the Indian wars, but without success. People such as Sam Houston argued that the Indians should be allowed to live peacefully in Texas. Honest and hard-working Indian agents such as Robert S. Neighbors did their best to make life on reservations acceptable. Nevertheless, the basic problem went unsolved. Many Indians were naturally unwilling to give up their ways of life, and many settlers were unwilling to recognize the right of Indians to the land. Texas settlers continued to push westward, and the wars continued. ✪

Geography (I) On a wall map of the United States, have several volunteers locate the ten port cities listed in the chart on this page. Then ask students what effect being a major port might have on a city. *(Lead students to understand that the city might have more cultural influences from other parts of the United States and other parts of the world, and that these cultural influences might be a major factor in drawing tourists. Students might mention that being a port city would have an economic impact. Many* people in the port city would work at jobs related to the shipping industry.) **V, A**

Analysis (I) Ask students if they have ever heard or read about the Mediterranean region called the Riviera. Ask a volunteer to look up the region in an atlas or geographical dictionary. Ask students: Why do you think Corpus Christi is sometimes referred to as "the Texas Riviera"? *(Its beaches and warm climate make it a major tourist destination.)* **A**

CITIES OF TEXAS

Corpus Christi

Population: 257,453

Metro area population: 349,894

Size: 395.2 square miles

Relative location: On the Gulf Coast at the mouth of the Nueces River

Region: Southern edge of the Gulf Coast Plain

County: County seat of Nueces County

Special feature: Largest city on the Coastal Bend

Origin of name: Legend claims that Alonzo de Piñeda named the nearby bay Corpus Christi because he arrived there on the festival day of Corpus Christi, the Latin name for "body of Christ."

Landmarks: Downtown Corpus Christi is located on the ocean front, with the main street winding along the water's edge.

Economy: Since enlarging and improving its channel system, Corpus Christi has become a major port city. Ocean freighters and oil supertankers serve the en-

tire South Texas area through Corpus Christi Bay. Other industries include fishing, aluminum manufacturing, and oil refining. Tourism is also vital to the city.

History: For centuries, the Corpus Christi Bay area was a center of trade among Indians and later with Spain.

In 1840, H.L. Kinney established a trading house and ranch on the site of present-day Corpus Christi. As industry and tourism increased, Corpus Christi grew to be the largest city on the Coastal Bend.

Recreation facilities: Beach and water sports abound in the Corpus Christi area. The city lies at the northern tip of 110-mile-long Padre Island.

Cultural activities: The Texas State Aquarium, the Bayfront Arts and Science Park, the Corpus Christi Museum, the Botanical Gardens, and the Museum of Oriental Cultures.

Commerce of Top Ten U.S. Ports *(by tonnage)*	
	Total
1. New Orleans, LA	175,500,858
2. New York, NY	155,061,783
3. Houston, TX	124,886,883
4. Valdez Harbor, AK	107,144,515
5. Baton Rouge, LA	78,857,473
6. Corpus Christi, TX	57,931,945
7. Tampa Harbor, FL	50,252,299
8. Norfolk Harbor, VA	46,872,002
9. Long Beach, CA	46,559,885
10. Los Angeles, CA	45,213,855

Essential Elements
4B, 4H, 5B, 9B

CHAPTER 15 REVIEW ANSWERS

Understanding Main Ideas

1. Manifest destiny was the belief that the United States was destined to expand from the Atlantic Ocean to the Pacific. The United States' desire to annex Texas angered Mexico.
2. Many Texans volunteered to fight.
3. Present-day California, Nevada, and Utah, and parts of Arizona, New Mexico, Colorado, and Wyoming
4. By making treaties with the Indians, stationing forts along the frontier to protect settlers, and setting aside reservations for the Indians

Thinking Critically

1. **Synthesizing Information:** Paragraphs will vary. During the Mexican War, the Texas Rangers became famous for their fighting abilities. They also had a reputation for being reckless and feared, however. After the war, the Texas Rangers were sent to fight the Indians, where the Rangers had the advantage because of the Colt six-shooter.
2. **Evaluating Information:** Answers will vary but should demonstrate sound reasoning.
3. **Analyzing Information:** The annexation of Texas, the Mexican War

CHAPTER 15 REVIEW

Understanding Main Ideas

1. What was manifest destiny? How did belief in it lead to the Mexican War?
2. What role did Texas play in the Mexican War?
3. What territory did the United States gain from the Treaty of Guadalupe Hidalgo?
4. How did the United States government try to solve problems with Texas Indian groups after annexation?

Thinking Critically

1. **Synthesizing Information:** Based on discussions in this chapter, write a paragraph evaluating the behavior of the Texas Rangers as a fighting force.
2. **Evaluating Information:** Do you think the United States was justified in making war on Mexico? Why or why not?
3. **Analyzing Information:** What historical events contributed to the worsening situation of the Tejanos between 1836 and 1848?

Linking History and Geography

1. Which of the following battles of the Mexican War took place in what is now the United States? Which took place in what is now Mexico? Refer to the map on page 312: Buena Vista, Santa Fe, Monterrey, Veracruz, El Brazito.
2. Look at the map on page 320. How are the military posts established between 1851 and 1860 different from those established between 1846 and 1850?

What factors do you think explain this change? Explain.

TAAS *Practice*
Using Primary Sources

In his memoirs, *My Eighty Years in Texas*, William Physick Zuber wrote about many historical events that took place during his long life. He fought in the Texas Revolution and the Civil War. But in the passage below, he explains why he did not fight in the 1846 war against Mexico:

> At that time [1845] many people of Texas were opposed to annexation. Our population was divided.... The annexationists tried by intimidation [frightening them] to convert the anti's or, failing this, to prevent them from voting....
>
> I opposed annexation for several reasons. First, I was proud of the honor we had won by founding one of the nations of the world, and wished to hold it. Second, I was indignant that the United States had rejected us in 1837, and I wished to remain independent of them. And third, I was opposed to dividing Texas into five states and especially to restraining Negro servitude in part of our present territory. Had I been aware that our financial embarrassments were so great I think I would have been an annexationist....
>
> I took no part in the Mexican War of 1845 and 1846, which resulted from annexation, because, since we had given ourselves to the United States, I believe that government ought to take war off our hands.

1. Zuber said that he opposed annexation because
   A he thought that only United States troops could save Texas from Mexico

Linking History and
Geography
1. The United States: Santa
   Fe, El Brazito; Mexico:
   Buena Vista, Monterrey,
   Veracruz
2. Those established after 1850
   were farther west than those
   established earlier. As the Indians were pushed farther
   west, more military forts were
   needed to protect settlers.

B   he was proud of the honor won by
    the Texas Republic in becoming an
    independent nation
C   he resented the political tactics of
    the people who were opposed to
    annexation
D   he was aware of the financial prob-
    lems of the Texas government
2. Zuber did not participate in the Mexi-
   can War, because
   A   he was angry about annexation and
       thought the United States govern-
       ment should do its own fighting
   B   his old war wounds from the Texas
       Revolution prevented it
   C   he was opposed to slavery and the
       expansion of territory in which
       slavery was allowed
   D   he had left Texas in disgust after
       annexation and moved to the North

TAAS Practice
Writing Persuasively
Imagine that you are a Texas politician in
1846. Write a letter to your brother in
Pennsylvania, who disagrees with the idea
of manifest destiny. Your letter should
persuasively argue that he should support
the Mexican War, as you do.

Practicing Skills
1. **Sequencing Events:** Place the following
   events in order, beginning with the
   earliest and ending with the most recent: the Treaty of Guadalupe Hidalgo
   is signed, John O'Sullivan writes about
   manifest destiny, the Battle of Palo Alto
   takes place, James K. Polk is elected
   president of the United States, the
   United States Army under General
   Winfield Scott captures Mexico City.

Herb Peck, Jr.

2. **Interpreting Photographs:** Study the
   early photograph on this page. It is of
   a United States trooper who fought in
   the Mexican War. With what weapons
   is he armed? Why do you think he
   carried two pistols?

Enriching Your Study of History
1. **Individual Project:** Prepare an illustrated research paper on one of the
   following persons or places: John
   Slidell, General Zachary Taylor, General Mariano Arista, Fort Brown, Jane
   McManus Cazneau, General Winfield
   Scott, Santa Fe County, Fort Worth,
   Fort Duncan, Robert S. Neighbors.
2. **Cooperative Project:** Your teacher will
   divide your class into debate teams to
   prepare two class debates. One pair of
   teams will debate whether or not the
   United States should go to war with
   Mexico. The other pair of teams will
   debate whether or not New Mexico
   should be part of Texas.

TAAS Practice
Using Primary Sources
1. B   2. A

TAAS Practice
Writing Persuasively
Letters will vary but should be
persuasive.

Practicing Skills
1. **Sequencing Events:** James
   K. Polk is elected president of
   the United States, John
   O'Sullivan writes about manifest destiny, the Battle of Palo
   Alto takes place, the United
   States Army under General
   Winfield Scott captures Mexico City, the Treaty of Guadalupe Hidalgo is signed.
2. **Interpreting Photographs:**
   He has two pistols or hand-
   guns and a rifle. Answers to
   the second part of the question may vary, but students
   might suggest that before
   the general availability of
   six-shooters, a trooper
   needed to be able to fire as
   often as possible before
   reloading.

Enriching Your Study of
History
1. **Individual Project:** Research papers should
   demonstrate careful and
   thorough research.
2. **Cooperative Project:**
   Debates should demonstrate
   careful preparation, and arguments should be based
   on sound reasoning.

LIFE ON THE FRONTIER

TEACHER'S TIME LINE			
Section 1 Pp. 326–33 1 Day	**Section 2** Pp. 333–37 1 Day	**Section 3** Pp. 337–43 1 Day	**Review and Assessment** 1 Day

TEACHER MATERIALS

Core: Chapter 16 Time Line; Graphic Organizer 16; Enrichment Worksheet 16; Review Worksheet 16; Reteaching Worksheet 16; Chapter 16 Tests, Forms A & B

Additional: Geography and Graph Skills 16, Informal Evaluation Forms, Test Generator

OBJECTIVES

1. Describe economic activity in Texas during the 1850s, and explain the importance of agriculture in the state.
2. Discuss the growth of industry in Texas, and identify the types of industries found in Texas in the 1850s.
3. Identify the various professions found in Texas during the 1850s, and describe the role of women in frontier life.
4. Discuss the growth of transportation in Texas in the 1850s, and identify forms of transportation available to Texans.
5. Identify important social and cultural institutions of Texas in the 1850s and their impact on Texans' quality of life.
6. Describe developments in Texas in communications, health care, and the arts.

RESOURCES

BOOKS FOR TEACHERS

Berry, Wendell. *The Unsettling of America: Culture and Agriculture.* San Francisco. Sierra Club Books, 1977. Agricultural aspects of the United States, including the South.

Crawford, Ann Fears, and Crystal Sasse Ragsdale. *Women in Texas: Their Lives, Their Experiences, Their Accomplishments.* Austin: Eakin Press, 1982. Women in Texas.

Emmett, Chris. *Texas Camel Tales.* Austin: Steck-Vaughn, 1969. Early Texas fiction.

Jenkins, John Holmes, editor. *Recollections of Early Texas, Memoirs of John Holland Jenkins.* Austin: University of Texas Press, 1991. Personal account of life in early Texas.

Michener, James A. *Texas.* Austin: University of Texas Press, 1986. Important moments in the history of Texas, with drawings by Charles Shaw.

Montejano, David. *Anglos and Mexicans in the Making of Texas, 1836–1986.* Austin: University of Texas Press, 1987. History of Mexican-Anglo rela-

tions in Texas since the nineteenth century.

Roland, Charles P. *Albert Sidney Johnston, Soldier of Three Republics.* Austin: University of Texas Press, 1964. Life and times of Johnston.

Wheeler, Kenneth W. *To Wear a City's Crown: The Beginnings of Urban Growth in Texas, 1836–1865.* Cambridge: Harvard University Press, 1968. Beginnings of urbanization in Texas.

MULTIMEDIA MATERIALS

The American Adventure: Agitation and Compromise. (video, 30 min.) PBS Video, 1320 Braddock Place, Alexandria, Virginia, 22314. Includes the events leading to the Mexican-American War.

Industrialism in America—An Economic History: The Industrial Revolution Comes to the U.S. (software) Focus Media, Inc., 839 Stewart Avenue, P.O. Box 865, Garden City, New York, 11530. Interactive program about the Industrial Revolution.

Manifest Destiny. (video, 30 min.) PBS Video, 1320 Braddock Place, Alexandria, Virginia, 22314. Includes events and effects of Mexican-American War.

GENERAL STRATEGIES

STUDENTS WITH SPECIAL NEEDS

Limited English Proficient Students (LEP)
Have LEP students work together to create a pictorial essay titled "Life on the Frontier." They should compile their drawings into booklet form. See other activities labeled **LEP.**

Students Having Difficulty with the Chapter
Ask students to review the chapter and then write a paragraph telling whether or not they would have enjoyed living in Texas in the 1850s. Tell them to explain why or why not, using specific examples from the chapter. **LEP**

Auditory Learners
Have auditory learners select any aspect of frontier life in Texas discussed in the chapter. Ask them to conduct further research and present an oral report. See other activities labeled **A.**

Visual Learners
Have visual learners review the chapter and compile a list of economic activities in Texas in the 1850s. Ask them to create advertisements featuring the types of goods and services available during this period. See other activities labeled **V.**

Tactile/Kinesthetic Learners
Have tactile/kinesthetic learners work together to produce a newspaper portraying characteristics of life in Texas in the 1850s. They should include articles on economic activity, transportation, communications, religion, education, law enforcement, and the arts. Encourage students to be creative in their approach to illustrating each aspect of Texas frontier life. See other activities labeled **TK.**

Gifted Students
Several numerical figures are given in the chapter to demonstrate changes in Texas. Have students calculate the following statistics based on data in the chapter:

a. The percentage of increase in cotton production from 58,073 bales in 1849 to 431,645 bales in 1859

b. The approximate population of Texas in 1860 based on this statement: "The 3,786,000 cattle in Texas outnumbered people six to one."

c. The percentage of increase in the Methodist Texas Conference from 1,878 members in 1840 to 30,661 members in 1860

d. The percentage of increase in the number of newspapers from twenty in 1840 to 80 in 1860

Ask students to present their calculations in the form of a diagram, chart, graph, or other visual. See other activities labeled **G.**

VOCABULARY
In addition to the boldfaced terms in each section, some students might benefit from discussing the meanings of these terms.

Section 1: *occupation* (p. 326); *cash crop* (p. 327); *enterprising* (p. 329); *slaughtered* (p. 329); *breweries* (p. 332); *ironworks* (p. 332).

Section 2: *freight companies* (p. 335); *contractors* (p. 335).

Section 3: *hewed* (p. 338); *denomination* (p. 339); *quinine* (p. 340); *memoirs* (p. 342).

CHRONOLOGY
Have students study the Chapter 16 Time Line and identify relationships among the events.

GRAPHIC ORGANIZER
Have students skim the chapter and complete the Chapter 16 Graphic Organizer. *(You might wish to use this activity to review rather than to introduce the chapter.)*

ENRICHMENT
Have students complete the Chapter 16 Enrichment Worksheet.

FOCUS

Student Experiences (I) Direct students to the painting on page 327. Ask volunteers to describe what they see. Ask students if there is any aspect of life depicted in the painting that reflects experiences in their own lives. Stress the importance of agriculture in Texas in the 1850s. Ask: Using this painting as a basis of comparison, how have our lives changed since then?

CHAPTER 16 OVERVIEW

Texas was a growing, changing society in the 1850s. Although most people made their living as farmers or ranchers, industry began to grow and new modes of transportation were introduced. As the Texas economy and population expanded, people practiced new and different kinds of professions. Social and cultural life gained importance, with churches remaining the center of Texas life. As a frontier state, Texas welcomed advances in art, literature, and music.

Essential Elements
2H, 3C, 3D, 5C, 5D, 8A, 8B, 8C, 9A, 9B

CHAPTER

LIFE ON THE FRONTIER

The Story Continues...

Texas was a frontier state of the United States in the 1850s. Life on the frontier was often difficult and dangerous, but most Texans greeted the future with hope. Many Texans lived as they had in the past, but change was occurring rapidly. Progress was being made in trade, transportation, and industry. Cities were growing, and new churches and schools were being built. Literature, art, and music took on added importance in Texas life. The scattered colonies of the 1820s were becoming part of a thriving society.

In Chapter 16, you will learn about daily life in the frontier state of Texas in the 1850s. Texans moved toward a hopeful future as progress was made in the building of farms, towns, roads, schools, churches, and an organized and thriving agricultural economy.

As you read the chapter, look for answers to these questions:

1. What was the major cash crop in the 1850s?
2. By what means of transportation were agricultural products moved to market in 1850?
3. How did most Texas children obtain an education in the 1850s?

Grant Heilman /
Grant Heilman Photography

In the mid 1800s, cotton was the major cash crop in Texas and the South.

1 The Changing Economy

The backbone of the Texas economy during the 1850s was agriculture. More than half of all Texans made all or part of their living farming or ranching. As the population of Texas expanded and grew more diverse, the economy began to change. New industries took their place alongside agriculture.

Texas Farms. The Texas census of 1850 showed 25,000 farmers among the 43,000 persons who listed an occupation. By 1860, the number of farmers had doubled. Farms varied widely in size, from those run by one family to giant

INSTRUCTION

Vocabulary (I) You may wish to preteach the following boldfaced terms: *tallow* (p. 329); *manufactured products* (p. 332); *grist mill* (p. 332); *tanneries* (p. 332); *textile* (p. 332); *architects* (p. 333). **LEP**

Dallas Museum of Art

H. O. Kelly painted this winter scene of Central Texas from memory during his old age. The painting, titled *Hog Killing Time*, is a fine image of farm life in Central Texas.

plantations covering thousands of acres. On large farms and small ones, nearly all Texas farmers worked to produce a cash crop to sell for profit.

Cotton was the major cash crop in Texas and the southern United States. It grew well in the soil, and there was a market for it in the northern states and Europe. From the Republic days, cotton production in Texas increased every year except for times when drought or insects destroyed part of the crop. Cotton production was 58,073 bales in 1849 and 431,645 bales in 1859.

Before the 1850s, cotton was grown in East Texas and along the Gulf coast. Some people doubted that it could be raised in places farther west. By the 1850s, however, some cotton was being grown in what is now Central Texas. Texas' other cash crop, sugarcane, was grown only along the Gulf coast.

As in the early years of settlement, corn remained the major food crop. It was used to make many dishes and was fed to farm animals as well. Other common food crops included sweet potatoes, wheat, and sugarcane.

Economics
The cotton grown in Texas was of a finer grade than that grown in other southern states and therefore commanded higher prices on the European market. The average cotton grower earned nine cents on a pound of cotton that cost five cents to grow.

Synthesis (I) Tell students to imagine that they are a Texas farmer who has been invited to present a speech at the state fair in Dallas in 1859. Ask them to write a speech citing the progress Texas farmers have made in the last decade. Allow time for several students to present their speeches. **A**

Linking History and Economics
Production of cotton bales

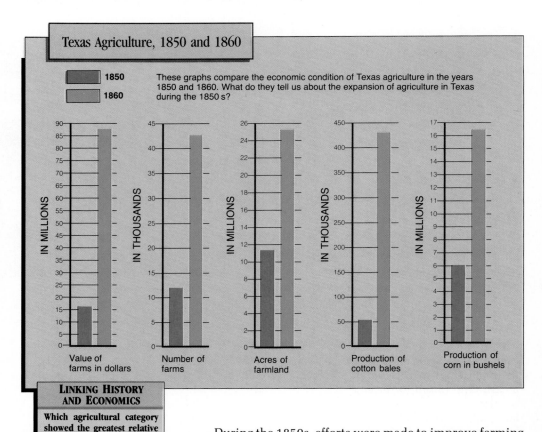

Texas Agriculture, 1850 and 1860

■ 1850
■ 1860

These graphs compare the economic condition of Texas agriculture in the years 1850 and 1860. What do they tell us about the expansion of agriculture in Texas during the 1850 s?

Value of farms in dollars (IN MILLIONS)	Number of farms (IN THOUSANDS)	Acres of farmland (IN MILLIONS)	Production of cotton bales (IN THOUSANDS)	Production of corn in bushels (IN MILLIONS)

LINKING HISTORY AND ECONOMICS

Which agricultural category showed the greatest relative increase in the decade between 1850 and 1860?

During the 1850s, efforts were made to improve farming methods. Agricultural societies were formed so that farmers and ranchers could share information. In 1852, the first farm exposition, or fair, was held at Corpus Christi. The first state fair was held at Dallas in 1859. Formally chartered in 1886, the Texas State Fair in Dallas continues to be one of the nation's largest fairs promoting agriculture.

During the 1850s, a well-known agricultural expert, Thomas Affleck, moved to Texas. Affleck, originally from Scotland, settled near Brenham with his wife, Anna Dunbar Smith. They established a famous plantation called Glenblythe. A large nursery for plant research and a beekeeping operation were developed at Glenblythe. The plantation, thriving with cotton and corn, served as a model for other farmers in Texas and in the South. Affleck wrote numerous articles and books on agriculture, and he helped develop modern farming techniques.

Texas Ranches. Texas ranching grew rapidly between 1845 and 1860. Prior to that time, most Texas farmers had raised livestock primarily for food and hides. But after the Republic years, many ranchers began raising cattle for profit, in the way cotton was grown as a cash crop. Cattle ranching began to have an important impact on the Texas economy as it increased ten times in value from 1850 to 1860. The 3,786,000 cattle in Texas in 1860 outnumbered people six to one.

Ranches in Texas dated to the 1700s. Tomás Sánchez established a huge ranch at Laredo in 1755. Other large ranches were established under Spanish rule and, later, Mexican rule in South and Southwest Texas. In the 1840s, enterprising Texans rounded up hundreds of thousands of wild cattle and established ranches. Some cattle were taken to port cities such as Indianola, Copano, and Aransas Pass. Auctions were held, where the cattle were sold to the highest bidder. Some cattle were slaughtered to provide food, hides, and **tallow**, or animal fat used in making soap and candles. Many of the cattle were shipped from the Texas ports to New Orleans or Havana, Cuba.

This nineteenth-century photograph shows a typical farm family in Central Texas. What cash crop was grown in Central Texas by the 1850s?

Caption Response
Cotton

Kilmar Studio, Fredericksburg, Texas

The Texas cattle industry grew rapidly after Texas was admitted to the United States. Many ranchers and ranch hands were Mexican Texans. This newspaper illustration of Texas ranchers was published in 1859.

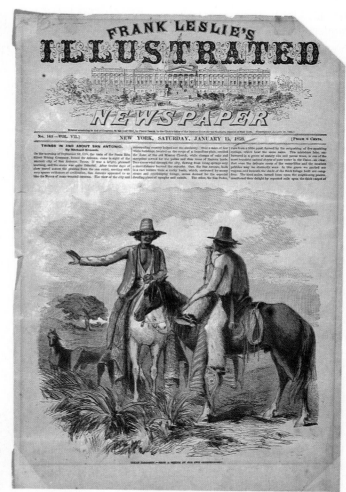

Courtesy of the San Antonio Museum Association

Richard Pearce-Moses

Richard King acquired the Santa Gertrudis grant in 1852. This tract of land eventually grew into the huge King Ranch in South Texas.

One of the most prosperous ranchers of the 1840s was James Taylor White. From his ranch near Anahuac in Chambers County, he drove cattle overland to New Orleans. H.L. Kinney expanded his trading post at Corpus Christi into a cattle business in the same period. Richard King and Mifflin Kenedy came to Texas during the Mexican War. In 1852, they bought the huge Santa Gertrudis grant of 75,000 acres and soon dominated South Texas ranching. Aaron

Cooperative Learning (I) Organize students into small groups. Have each group select one occupation or profession described in Section 1. Present the following situation: You are business owners in Texas in the 1850s. In order to meet the demands of your customers, your business must expand. In applying for a business loan, you must provide the following information:

1. What is your business?
2. Do you provide a product or a service?
3. Who are your potential customers?
4. What materials and supplies do you need to operate your business?
5. Why do you want to expand?
6. What are your business goals?
7. What problems may prevent you from achieving your goals?
8. How would your success benefit other Texans?

Have each group present its "application" to the rest of the class. **A, V, TK**

LONE STAR LEGACY

Our Free Enterprise Economy

The system of government established by Texans was designed to protect people's economic rights and freedoms. These rights and freedoms have ensured that Texas—like the rest of the United States—has an economy based on the right of individuals to own and operate businesses for profit. (Profit is money earned by the owner of a business after he or she has paid the costs of producing and selling a product or service.)

One of the most basic rights under our government and economy is the right to own property. Individuals can legally own and use land, buildings, personal belongings, and other kinds of property for their benefit. With this property, persons can choose to set up businesses. These businesses are free to sell products that range from cantaloupes to computer chips—any legal product or service.

The sellers and buyers of cantaloupes and computer chips are free to buy and sell as they please. If people think that the price a business is asking for a product or service is too high, they can buy from someone else. Businesspeople in Texas have complete freedom to try to sell their products at any price they choose. If the price is too high, few people will buy them. It is in the seller's interest to ask fair prices.

Competition among sellers works to keep prices down. Would you buy cantaloupes from a roadside vendor at $1 per pound when you can get them for 50¢ per pound a little farther down the road? Prices in our economic system are determined by competition and by the supply and demand of goods and services. If there are many cantaloupes on the market, their prices will go down. If they are scarce, their prices will go up, and people who produce them will be encouraged to produce more. In time, the increased supply will bring prices down again. The system regulates itself and, over time, it works to the benefit of the consumer, or buyer.

This is what we mean when we say that Texas has a "free enterprise system." In some economic systems, the government determines what goods and services will be provided to the people. The government also sets prices and determines how much will be produced. Our free enterprise economy is entirely different. Texas business operators are free to run their own businesses with little or no interference from the government, provided that the business is legal. Texas customers are free to buy cantaloupes, computer chips, and thousands of other goods and services at the lowest price they can find, and from whomever they choose.

Using Historical Imagination

Imagine that you are a saddlemaker who has just arrived in Texas in 1858. What can you do to compete with other saddlemakers?

Ted Kawalerski / The Image Bank West

Chapter 16 **331**

Essential Elements
8A, 8C

LONE STAR LEGACY
Using Historical Imagination: Answers will vary but might include: setting up the business where the most customers would be found, making saddles to meet the needs of the customers, and charging what the customers are able to pay. One could compete by offering better saddles at lower prices.

Chapter 16 **331**

RETEACHING

Write on the chalkboard the title of this section—"The Changing Economy." Ask students to give five statements that could be used to summarize the section. List their responses on the chalkboard. **LEP, A**

CLOSURE

Direct students to the statements from the Reteaching activity. Ask them to use the statements to create a paragraph summarizing Section 1.

ASSESSMENT

Have students complete the Section 1 Review on page 333.

Answers to Section 1 Review

Define: *tallow*—animal fat used in making soap and candles; *manufactured products*—products made by hand or machine in large numbers for sale; *grist mill*—machine for grinding grain into meal or flour; *tanneries*—places where animal hides and skins were prepared; *textile*—cloth; *architects*—building designers

Identify: Glenblythe—plantation that served as a model for other plantations; Richard King and Mifflin Kenedy—dominated the ranching industry in the 1850s; Hiram and James Wilson—freed slaves who became well known as pottery makers; Elise Waerenskjold—Texas journalist and writer

(Continued on page 333)

332 *Unit 6*

Ashworth was a free black who owned a large ranch in Jefferson County in southeastern Texas. John Chisum was one of the first ranchers in North Texas, establishing a large operation in Denton County. In 1854, Manuel Músquiz settled near Fort Davis in the Trans-Pecos region. His was the first large ranch in that area of Texas, but it failed because of raids by the Apaches.

Samuel and Mary Ann Maverick established a large ranch in the San Antonio area. Samuel Maverick, who was a businessman, served as mayor of San Antonio. Because the Mavericks kept a small herd of unbranded cattle, the term *mavericks* eventually came to mean unbranded cattle. Today the word is also used to describe someone who acts independently or free of others.

Institute of Texan Cultures

Samuel Maverick was a well-known rancher in the San Antonio area. He served as mayor of San Antonio and in the Texas legislature.

Henry F. Wilson, Institute of Texan Cultures

Hiram Wilson made excellent pottery, and his remaining works are now valuable collector's items.

The Growth of Industry. As was the case in other southern and western states, industry was but a small part of the Texas economy. Raising enough money to start a business was difficult. In an agricultural society, people grow or make at home much of what they need. In the 1850s, demand in Texas was low for **manufactured products**, those made either by hand or machine in large numbers for sale. Because of low demand, there was little encouragement to open large manufacturing plants. Industries in Texas manufactured products for local markets. But most manufactured items were shipped into Texas from the northern United States or Europe.

A number of small industries prospered in the 1850s. Nearly every town had a **grist mill**, or machine for grinding grain into meal or flour. Cotton gins were also common. In East Texas, there were a number of sawmills. By the 1850s, businesses were established to build wagons and carriages. Most were owned and operated by one person or family.

As the towns gained population, other industries became more common. They included breweries, ironworks, brickyards, and **tanneries**, where animal hides and skins were prepared. Houston had a hat factory, and there was a large **textile**, or cloth, factory in Harrison County. Two slaves, Hiram and James Wilson, became well known in Seguin as pottery makers. After they became free in the 1860s, their products were sold across the state and in other areas of the United States.

Professions in Texas. Texas had a higher percentage of professional people than any other southern state.

SECTION 2

FOCUS

Past Learning (I) Ask students to recall the transportation problems that faced settlers during colonization *(lack of roads, difficult rivers to cross)*. Point out that these problems still existed in the 1850s but that some advances were made as the state's population grew.

INSTRUCTION

Geography (I) Ask students which of the Five Themes of Geography best illustrates the role of transportation in the Texas economy *(movement)*. **A**

Lawyers were well represented among the professional people. Texas had a large supply of doctors as well. In 1860, there were 1,471 doctors, a large number for a frontier state. However, methods for granting licenses to doctors and lawyers had not yet been established. As a result, some practiced these professions without proper training or qualifications. Many doctors, for example, learned to treat illnesses simply by working with older doctors.

Other professionals in Texas included dentists, teachers, and ministers. The 1860 census listed 758 preachers but only 65 dentists. Eight people claimed to be **architects**, or building designers. Many professional people were involved in other businesses to add to their income. Many teachers, for example, taught part-time and did other jobs too.

Women in the Economy. Texas women were a central part of the economy. Many professions and jobs were closed to women by law or custom. Still, women worked as hard as men in the support of their families.

On the farm, women commonly performed tasks such as churning butter, tanning animal hides, sewing, and weaving cloth. They also prepared and cooked food and tended livestock such as chickens, pigs, and goats. Farm women often grew vegetable gardens to add to the food supply. Running the home, which was usually a dawn-to-dusk job, was the sole responsibility of women in most families.

Women in Texas had more business and professional opportunities than did women in the East. When there was a need for goods or services on the frontier, women sometimes supplied them. For example, Angelina Eberly, who had fired the cannon in the Archives War, ran hotels in Austin and Port Lavaca. She also bought and sold land in Indianola. Elise Waerenskjold was a journalist and writer. Jane McManus Cazneau was a novelist, an empresario, and a diplomat. Melinda Rankin was a missionary and teacher. Sally Scull was a rancher who caught and sold wild horses in South Texas. Two free black women, Zelia Husk and Diana Leonard, operated a laundry business. ✪

2 The Growth of Transportation

The lack of a good transportation system slowed the growth of the Texas economy. Farmers, ranchers, traders,

Mrs. O'Belle Harris, Institute of Texan Cultures

Grist mills, like this one in Norse, became more numerous in Texas during the 1850s. What function did grist mills serve?

SECTION ★ 1 REVIEW

Define: tallow, manufactured products, grist mill, tanneries, textile, architects

Identify: Glenblythe, Richard King and Mifflin Kenedy, Hiram and James Wilson, Elise Waerenskjold

1. What cash crop was the basis of the economy of Texas and the South in 1850?
2. How did the Texas cattle industry change after 1845?
3. Name four tasks normally performed by women living on farms.

Analyzing Information: What factors restricted the growth of Texas industry in the 1850s?

Evaluating Information: Why did women sometimes have more business and professional opportunities in Texas than in the older states of the East?

Caption Response
They ground grain into meal or flour.

1. Cotton
2. After 1845, the cattle were raised for profit.
3. Possible answers include: churning butter, tanning animal hides, sewing, weaving cloth, preparing food, tending livestock, and growing vegetable gardens.

Analyzing Information: The difficulty in raising money to start a business and too little demand for manufactured goods

Evaluating Information: Fewer people on the frontier meant more opportunities for women. When goods or services were needed, women sometimes supplied them.

Essential Elements
3D, 5B, 5C, 9A, 9B, 9F

and merchants sought better roads and other improved means of transportation. But Texas was a large area, and improvements in transportation required money that was not always available. Still, as the economy grew, some advances were made.

The Road System.   Roads in Texas were not much better in the 1850s than they had been during the days of Spanish control. There were more of them, but they still turned to mud during wet weather. A visitor to Texas in 1855, Frederick Law Olmsted, commented on the terrible road conditions. He described a road in Leon County as "little better than a cowtrack." He called the road from Victoria to Port Lavaca "a mere collection of straggling wagon ruts."

Stage and Freight Lines.   Many people traveled around Texas on stagecoaches. The 1850s saw an improvement in the coaches themselves as well as more stage lines. A typical stagecoach could carry as many as nine passengers on the inside and a few more outside. The stagecoaches were drawn by teams of four or six horses. Passengers were usually charged ten cents per mile. Rates were higher if conditions were bad, which was often the case. Muddy roads, flooded rivers, and severe weather made travel uncomfortable and dangerous. The possibility of Indian attacks and holdups by robbers made stagecoach travel an adventure as well. A passenger could expect to help repair a broken wheel, fight a band of roving robbers, or push the coach out of a muddy stream.

Within the state, stage lines connected most cities and towns along the major roads. The major lines ran on the Old San Antonio Road from San Antonio to Nacogdoches, the Old Military Road from Dallas to Austin, a road from Indianola to San Antonio, and a road from Dallas to Houston. In 1857, passenger and mail service was opened between San Antonio and San Diego, California. The 30-day trip cost $200. In 1858, another stage service came to Texas, the Butterfield Mail Line. The Butterfield Line entered North Texas and passed through El Paso on its route from St. Louis, Missouri, to San Francisco, California. Butterfield stages ran twice weekly and made the 2,700-mile journey in 25 days.

The stagecoach lines delivered the mail throughout the United States, including Texas. The stages were not large enough, however, to transport heavy freight such as food

Institute of Texan Cultures

Stage lines increased in Texas during the 1850s. This engraving shows a typical stagecoach from this period.

Guided Practice (I) Have students draw and label maps illustrating stage line, railroad, and river transportation routes in Texas in the 1850s. (Direct them to the discussion on pages 334–36.) Allow them to refer to maps in their textbooks. **V, TK, LEP**

EXTENSION
Research (III) Ask interested students to research and report on the role of railroads in the Texas economy today. Are railroads still an important means of transportation in the state? **A, G**

The Granger Collection

Construction of railroad lines did not begin in Texas until the early 1850s. After the Civil War, however, rail-line mileage and railroad transportation greatly increased.

products, dry goods, and farm supplies. As a result, freight companies sprang up all over Texas to handle the increasing business and trade. Freight contractors used heavy wagons with iron axles and wheels that were typically five or six feet high. These strong freight wagons, reinforced with iron bars, were drawn by teams of ten to twenty mules, horses, or oxen. Most of the freight companies were located along the Gulf coast near the ports of Galveston, Indianola, Houston, Port Lavaca, and Corpus Christi.

The Railroads Come to Texas. The first railroads were built in the United States in the 1820s and 1830s. In 1852, construction was begun on the first railroad line in Texas. It was the Buffalo Bayou, Brazos, and Colorado Railroad, commonly known as the Harrisburg Railroad. Charges on the Harrisburg Railroad were five cents per mile for passengers and one cent per mile for each 100 pounds of freight. By 1855, it ran 32 miles from Harrisburg on Buffalo Bayou to Richmond on the Brazos River. Within five years, the Harrisburg Railroad had expanded westward nearly 30 more miles to the Colorado River. More rail lines were built in the Houston area during the 1850s.

Geography
Refer students to the map "The Growth of Railroads in Texas, 1853–1920" on page 449.

Independent Practice (I) Have students work individually or in pairs to create a chart illustrating the information in Section 2, using the following headings: *Method of Transportation, Advantages, Disadvantages.* **V, TK, LEP**

RETEACHING
Refer students to the charts that they created in the Independent Practice activity. Ask them to write a brief paragraph summarizing the information in the chart. **LEP**

Captain T. K. Treadwell, Institute of Texan Cultures

The rail line spanning Buffalo Bayou was the first line constructed in Texas.

Barker Texas History Center

THE NEW-ORLEANS AND GALVESTON STEAM PACKET NEPTUNE,

Newspapers advertised steamboat transportation in Texas.

By 1861, a railroad linked Victoria with Port Lavaca. Shreveport, Louisiana, was connected with Marshall by rail in 1864. Early rail lines connected riverports and seaports with nearby towns. After the 1860s, railroads expanded to every region of Texas and became the most important means of transportation.

River Transportation. Texans continued their effort to use the Texas rivers for transportation. But they were not much more successful in the 1850s than they had been in the 1820s. It always seemed that the Texas rivers were either flooded or too low for safe navigation. Sandbars often prohibited passage of larger steamboats. On rivers like the Colorado, great masses of driftwood usually blocked travel.

During the 1850s, some river routes were dependable. Ships could travel safely up the Brazos as far as Brazoria. Boats loaded with cotton departed from Jefferson, traveled along Big Cypress Bayou to Caddo Lake, into the Red River, and then down the Mississippi River to New Orleans. When rainfall was plentiful, boats loaded with cotton could travel the Sabine, Neches, Trinity, and San Jacinto rivers. Boats crossed Buffalo Bayou to reach Houston from Galveston. Goods shipped from Houston were placed on larger ships in Galveston for the trip over the Gulf of Mexico.

Several attempts were made to reach the capital city of Austin by boat. Steamboats such as the *Kate Ward* and the *Colorado Ranger* were sometimes successful. The shallow river made the trip uncertain and even dangerous, so regular service was never established.

The Camel Experiment. During the 1850s, the United States Army chose Texas for a unique experiment in transportation. The army was seeking animals that could survive better than horses and mules in the dry climate of West Texas. Jefferson Davis, the secretary of war, had 34 camels imported into Texas through Indianola. Forty-one more camels were brought in later. On their journey to Camp Verde, northwest of San Antonio, they passed through Victoria. Pauline Shirkey was ten years old at the time. She later wrote:

> Major Wayne came over to our house and ate supper with us, and then he told us when he intended to leave with the camels, and he gave me a special invitation to come over and take a ride on one of them.
>
> While the camp was under the trees, Major Wayne presented to my mother, Mrs. Mary A. Shirkey, some of

.Ask students: Of the methods of transportation discussed in Section 2, which would you have preferred to use for travel in Texas in the 1850s? Why? Allow time for students to express varying opinions.

ASSESSMENT

Have students complete the Section 2 Review on page 337.

SECTION 3

FOCUS

Predicting (I) Locate and bring to class artifacts illustrating life in Texas during this time period. Examples might include a McGuffey Reader, advertisements, newspapers, and doctors' supplies. Use these sources to stimulate discussion of Texas frontier life.

---

the hair which he had clipped from one of the camels, and she knit a pair of socks for the President of the United States, Franklin Pierce. Mother had a great deal of trouble making those socks.

The camels were stronger than mules and horses, so they could carry more. They could also travel greater distances with less water. They were faster over long distances and needed less rest. Despite these advantages, camels were not brought into Texas in large numbers. When the army turned its attention to the Civil War in 1861, it sold most of the camels to freight companies, who used them in Arizona and California. The army never returned to its camel experiment. ✪

3 Social and Cultural Institutions

As the population of Texas expanded in the 1850s, changes occurred in institutions such as schools, churches, newspapers, health and medical care, and law enforcement. Texans desired a higher quality of life. They welcomed advances in literature, art, music, and other forms of entertainment.

Schools in Texas. Texas had a commitment to education since the Republic days. The Constitution of 1845 provided for a public school system. However, little had been done to establish schools by 1850, and people began to demand action. The state legislature acted by passing the School Law of 1854. Supported by Governor Elisha M. Pease, the law set aside $2 million for a permanent school fund. The School Law of 1854 was a start, but money was lacking to build schoolhouses and pay teachers, even with state aid. San Antonio was an exception. It had free public schools beginning in 1853. German settlements also established and supported free public schools.

To meet the demands for education, private schools opened in nearly every Texas community. Parents had to pay a fee for their children to attend these schools. Some private schools were owned by individuals, but most were operated by churches. The same held true for the few colleges in Texas. Rutersville College was established by the Methodist church in 1840. Baylor University was opened by the Baptist church in 1845, and Austin College was organized in 1849 by the Presbyterian church.

SECTION ★2★ REVIEW

Identify: Butterfield Mail Line, Jefferson Davis, Pauline Shirkey

1. What means of transport were available to get Texas farmers' cotton to market in 1850?
2. How was the mail delivered in the 1850s?
3. What problems kept people from using Texas rivers for transportation?

Exploring Economics: Why do you think a poor transportation system would be limiting to industry? Explain.

Solving Problems: If you were setting up a new freight company in Texas around 1850, where would you locate your headquarters? Explain.

Barker Texas History Center

Schul-Eroeffnung!
Miss N. E. DAVIS,
ein Zögling des J. O. O. F. Collegiate-Instituts in Rogersville, Tenn., und zuletzt eine Lehrerin in demselben, hat soeben in der Presbyterian-Kirche in San Antonio eine Schule eröffnet, und hofft durch ihre Schule Jedermann zufrieden zu stellen.
Lehr-Bedingungen:
Für die Vorbereitungs Classen
pr. Monat - - $3 00
" " höheren Classen - $4 00
☞ Keine weiteren Forderungen werden gemacht.

This advertisement announces the opening of a German-language school in San Antonio.

Answers to Section 2 Review

Identify: Butterfield Mail Line—stage service that passed through Texas on its way from St. Louis to San Francisco; Jefferson Davis—United States secretary of war in the 1850s who conducted the camel experiment in Texas; Pauline Shirkey—young girl in Victoria, Texas, who wrote about the camel experiment

1. Freight wagons, railroad, boats
2. By stagecoach
3. Often the rivers flooded or were too shallow, or driftwood and sandbars blocked passage.

Exploring Economics: A poor transportation system would limit an industry's ability to transport its goods to the people who need them.

Solving Problems: Answers will vary but should provide a reasonable explanation for the choice of location.

Essential Elements
2H, 6B, 7B, 8D, 9A, 9E, 9F

INSTRUCTION

Vocabulary (I) You may wish to preteach the following boldfaced terms: *literacy* (p. 339); *vigilante* (p. 341). **LEP**

Historical Imagination (I) Organize the class into two groups. As you provide each group with instructions, do not allow the other group to hear. Tell students in the first group that it is 1860 and that they are going to list fifteen items to be placed into a time capsule. The items should represent different aspects of life on the Texas frontier. The capsule will be opened in the year 2000. Tell members of the second group that it is the year 2000. They have just unearthed a time capsule from the year 1860. They should list the fifteen items found in the capsule. Have the class compare the items on each list. **A, LEP**

Amon Carter Museum, Fort Worth

The Methodist church was the largest Protestant denomination in Texas after independence from Mexico was won. This engraving is of an early Methodist church and parsonage in Corpus Christi.

In the rural areas, where timber was locally available, one-room log schools were common. One such school was built by Bird Slover in Parker County in the 1850s or 1860s. Slover cut trees, hewed them square with a broadax, and built a one-room schoolhouse. Inside the school, benches and desks, also hewn from logs, rested on a dirt floor. At this very early school, boys carried pistols as protection from Indians.

Early schools in Tarrant County were also made of logs. Some, built without windows, relied instead upon light from the large cracks between the logs. On dark winter days, children in these schools did their lessons by the light from torches and lanterns. Seats were typically planks set on logs sunk in the dirt floor. One such school had a crack in its door that was put to good use. The schoolmaster, who lived only a short distance away, always went home at noon to take a nap. The older students were told to watch the progress of sunlight from the crack. When it reached a certain spot the schoolmaster had marked on the floor, the students blew a cowhorn to call him back.

Country schools were very plain, but students often enjoyed attending them. They found them welcome relief from the never-ending farm work at home. One elderly woman from Bell County recalled:

> Our seats for sitting in were long, two-foot-by-twelve-foot boards placed on top of two rocks placed at each end of the twelve-foot boards. We used our knees for desks to do our writing. In spite of all our handicaps when compared with today's schools, my school days were golden to me.

River baptisms were common events in Texas.

Barker Texas History Center

School in the nineteenth century was a combination of strict discipline and a broad course of study. Even in the early grades, students in some schools were expected to learn ancient history and languages such as Latin and Greek. Newspaper advertisements described a school's course of study and its rules for behavior. One ad boasted of "a strict discipline rigidly enforced." Another ad claimed, "Course of study full, instruction thorough, and discipline strict." Although Texas lacked a public school system, state records claimed that **literacy**, or the ability to read and write, rose by ten percent from 1850 to 1860.

Churches in Texas. After Texans overthrew Mexican rule in 1836, restrictions on religion were removed. No longer was the Roman Catholic faith required of settlers. After Texas independence, Protestant churches appeared and grew rapidly. Of all the factors that affected Texas social life, none had more influence than the churches.

The Methodist church was the largest denomination in Texas at this time. The Methodist Texas Conference was organized in 1840 with 1,878 members. By 1860, that number had grown to 30,661. The Methodists not only built churches, but they also sent missionaries around the state to hold revivals and other worship services.

The Baptists were the second largest Protestant group. They formed the Texas Baptist Convention in 1848. By 1860, the Baptists had 280 church buildings, while the Methodists had 410. The next largest Protestant group was the Presbyterian church. Episcopalians were also active in Texas. The Roman Catholic church was dominant in San Antonio, Nacogdoches, Victoria, and small towns in South Texas and along the Rio Grande.

Social life in Texas usually revolved around the local church. Besides sermons and Sunday school, the churches sponsored fairs, picnics, and bazaars to raise funds for charity. Traveling preachers held outdoor revivals called camp meetings. Churches helped set the moral standards of the communities, and they improved social and cultural life by encouraging people to learn to read and write.

Newspapers in Texas. In a state as large and isolated as Texas, communication was very important. For a frontier region, Texas had a surprisingly large number of newspapers. The number grew from around twenty in 1840 to more than 80 in 1860.

Institute of Texan Cultures

The Vereins Kirche, or "Coffeemill Church," in Fredericksburg was built in 1846 to serve all religious denominations. A replica of the church was built in 1930, the original having been torn down in 1897.

Constitutional Heritage
Remind students that the United States Constitution and the Texas Constitution protect freedom of religion. They establish no official religion.

Historical Sidelight

National and world news was transmitted by telegraph. The artist and inventor Samuel Morse sent the first public telegraph on May 24, 1844. He transmitted the message "What hath God wrought?" over a 40-mile line between Washington, D.C., and Baltimore, Maryland.

Barker Texas History Center

Many medicines were sold by people with no medical training, and "quack" cures for almost any ailment were readily available.

The *Telegraph and Texas Register* had the largest circulation of any Texas newspaper. It was published in Houston. *The Daily News*, published in Galveston, was its main rival. Other notable papers were *The State Gazette* in Austin and *The Weekly Herald* in Dallas.

Most Texas newspapers were published only once or twice a week. They chiefly contained public notices and information about local events. Partly because of poor communications with other states, newspapers carried little national and world news until the 1850s, when the first telegraphs appeared. The newspapers rarely discussed social problems, nor did they include women. Editors then thought it was in poor taste to print women's names.

Health and Medicine. One of the attractions of Texas was its climate, claimed by many to be very healthful. Still, many Texans fell victim to disease and died at an early age. The average life span was around 45 years. Many more newborn babies and children died than do today. The lack of medical knowledge and hospitals, as well as the poor training of doctors, contributed to the high death rate.

Epidemics were a major threat. Cholera swept through Texas in the 1830s and again in 1849, 1850, and 1854, killing hundreds of people. Typhoid, yellow fever, and smallpox sometimes spread out of control. Other common diseases were pneumonia, measles, and hepatitis.

All kinds of cures were used to fight sickness and disease. Most were homemade medicines containing alcohol, petroleum products, castor oil, quinine, or herbs and roots. A favorite cure was to have a patient take mustard and pepper treatments. Home remedies ranged from the practical to the ridiculous. Bleeding, for example, was treated by such remedies as placing pine resin on the cut, putting a pair of scissors down the victim's shirt collar, covering the wound with spider webs, or getting the victim to hold a coin under his lip. Some home treatments actually worked, but untrained "quacks" took advantage of sick people, selling a wide variety of strange medicines.

A step was taken in the 1850s to improve medical care in Texas. The Medical Association of Texas was organized in 1853. Two of its founding members were Dr. Ashbel Smith and Dr. James W. Throckmorton. The association attempted to regulate the training and education of doctors practicing in the state.

TEXAS VOICES

Jane McManus Cazneau arrived in Texas in 1832 and played an important role in the early history of Texas. She was a journalist and a novelist who was respected throughout the United States for her writing ability. Her newspaper articles helped gain support in the United States for the annexation of Texas. Her novel *Eagle Pass* was one of the first literary descriptions of life in Texas during the 1830s and 1840s. In this excerpt from *Eagle Pass*, Cazneau's main character describes her first view of Texas:

> I landed in March, in Texas, and, as almost everybody is, was led captive by the fresh and verdant [green] beauty of the coast region. The north was still shivering in the frost and sleet of lingering winter, but already green and laughing spring was holding her revels on a carpet of flowers in the bright sunshine. A gay and radiant freedom seemed to pervade this land of fertility and promise, and with every drawback, in the shape of confused land titles, and the beginner's privations [lack of comforts], there is no country under the sun in which a sober, sensible and industrious man can more certainly realize a quick independence and a delightful home. Somewhere or other in its vast extent, everyone can find the features and productions that interest him most. . . . All these sections [of Texas] offer sure employment and independent homes on the easiest terms. If a healthy man is poor and homeless in Texas, it is because he is not manly enough to turn his hands to useful labor.

Law Enforcement. The crime rate in Texas was no higher than in other western states, but law enforcement was a concern of most citizens. Because Texas is huge, there were not enough law officers to patrol such a vast area. Nearly everyone carried a gun on the frontier, and people often solved their disputes with guns.

While the Texas Rangers had the responsibility of keeping peace statewide, local sheriffs and police officials had the job of enforcing local laws. They were sometimes outnumbered by gangs of criminals, however, and their jails were small. When crime was seen as a big problem, communities sometimes organized **vigilante** committees. Vigilantes are citizens who enforce the law as they see fit, sometimes without following legal procedures. In 1852, a vigilante committee in San Antonio hanged between twelve and fifteen people. The victims had been accused of committing crimes but were not given their right to a trial.

To aid in the fight against crime, a state penitentiary, or prison, was built in 1849. More Texas Rangers were hired in the 1850s. Crime did not disappear, but Texans continued to fight it.

Archives Division, Texas State Library

EAGLE PASS:
OR,
Life on the Border.
BY CORA MONTGOMERY.

NEW YORK:
GEORGE P. PUTNAM & CO., 10 PARK PLACE.
MDCCCLII.

Jane McManus Cazneau wrote newspaper articles that encouraged annexation of Texas. Under a pen name, she wrote the novel *Eagle Pass*.

Essential Elements
2H, 9A

Guided Practice (I) Create a "Who Am I?" game for students, using the information presented on pages 342–43. Provide students with index cards with identifying clues and have the class guess "Who am I?" **A, V, LEP, TK**

EXTENSION

Art and History (II) Have students select one of the authors or artists mentioned in Section 3. They should research and prepare a biographical profile of the person. Some students may wish to prepare a book report on a book published during this period. **A, V**

*Humanities Research Center,
The University of Texas at Austin*

Mayne Reid was a well-known novelist of the nineteenth century. Perhaps his best work is the Texas legend he recreated in *Headless Horseman*.

Friends of the Governor's Mansion

This portrait of Herman Lungkwitz was painted by his friend and fellow artist Friedrich Richard Petri.

This painting by William Huddle illustrates the musical heritage that enslaved people contributed to the culture of Texas.

Literature and Art. Books were scarce in frontier Texas. Most families had a Bible or a McGuffey Reader to teach their children to read. In the 1840s, libraries and large book collections were rare. Between 1850 and 1860, however, the number of libraries rose from twelve to 132. One of the few large book collections was owned by Svante Palm, a Swedish settler in Austin. He later donated his entire collection of books to the University of Texas.

Most books published in Texas after the Texas Revolution dealt with the history of the state. Accounts of life in early Texas settlements were written by Mary Austin Holley and later, in his memoirs, by Noah Smithwick. In 1841, an Englishman named William Kennedy published

Dallas Museum of Art

RETEACHING

With the class, create on the chalkboard an outline of the information presented in Section 3. Use the section sub-headings as outline topics. **LEP, A, V**

CLOSURE

Ask the class: Would you like to have lived during this period of Texas history? Why or why not? Encourage students to provide examples from the textbook to support their points of view.

ASSESSMENT

Have students complete the Section 3 Review on page 343.

Austin History Center, Austin Public Library

German Texans greatly enjoyed saengerfests, or statewide song festivals. This arch, constructed on Congress Avenue in 1889, welcomed participants to Austin.

The Rise, Progress, and Prospects of Texas. In 1855, Henderson Yoakum released a *History of Texas.*

Related to history books were travel accounts of Texas. The most famous travel journal about Texas was Frederick Law Olmsted's *Journey through Texas.* Matilda Houston wrote her impressions of a visit to Texas in *Texas and the Gulf of Mexico.* Many of these travel books encouraged people to move to Texas from the eastern United States and Europe.

Several Texans wrote successful fiction during this time. Jane McManus Cazneau published the novel *Eagle Pass,* which was about life on the Rio Grande. Mayne Reid wrote about Southwest Texas legends in *Headless Horseman.* Mirabeau Lamar, who had served as president of the Republic, was well regarded as a poet.

Art grew in importance along with literature. José Sánchez was a Mexican citizen who spent time in Texas creating hundreds of sketches of the land and people. Friedrich Richard Petri, Herman Lungkwitz, and Carl von Iwonski were also highly respected artists of the 1850s. Louisa Heuser Wueste was San Antonio's most popular portrait painter. Frenchwoman Eugenie Lavender was a famous painter in Europe before she settled in Texas in 1851. Another French immigrant, Theodore Gentilz, painted scenes of Texas life. ✪

SECTION ★3★ REVIEW

Define: literacy, vigilante

Identify: *Telegraph and Texas Register,* Dr. Ashbel Smith, Dr. James W. Throckmorton, Svante Palm

1. Describe a typical Texas school around 1850.
2. What were four diseases causing epidemics among Texans in the 1840s and 1850s?
3. Why did some Texans resort to vigilante action against lawbreakers?

Seeing Cause and Effect: Explain how the School Law of 1854 affected Texas education.

Analyzing Information: How was religion in Texas after the Mexican War different from the way it had been in the days of Mexican rule?

CHAPTER 16 REVIEW

Understanding Main Ideas

1. What was Texas' most important cash crop in 1850? What was Texas' most important cash crop in 1860?
2. Why was Glenblythe plantation important to Texas agriculture?
3. Why did women in Texas have more business and professional opportunities than women in the East?
4. Which major modes of transportation were used to move produce and crops to market in 1850?
5. Describe a typical Texas school in 1850, giving as much detail as possible.
6. What were vigilantes? What were their goals, and how did they attempt to achieve their goals?

Thinking Critically

1. **Using Historical Imagination:** Imagine that you are a professional teamster driving a freight wagon from Beaumont to San Antonio. Describe the troubles you encounter on the road during a particularly difficult day in the spring of 1852.
2. **Exploring Economics:** What factors limited the development of Texas industry in the 1840s and 1850s?
3. **Synthesizing Information:** Using information in the chapter, explain in detail why this statement is true: "In the areas of education, manufacture, medicine— even law enforcement—life in Texas in the 1850s had a 'do-it-yourself' quality about it."

Linking History and Geography

1. What special problems did the West Texas environment cause for the transportation industry? What famous United States Army experiment tried to solve these problems?
2. How did Texas rivers affect Texas transportation?

TAAS Practice
Using Primary Sources

The first Texas schools were private. Settlers in an area would hire someone to teach their children. Usually with complete approval of the parents, discipline in these first schools was often strict, as this early account describes:

The next school . . . was taught by Mr. Dyas, an old Irish gentleman, and I think a regular teacher by profession. The session was three or four months and the studies miscellaneous [varied], but the discipline was exact. He had an assortment of switches set in grim array. . . . On one side was the row for little boys, small, straight and elastic, from a kind of tree which furnished Indians with arrows and the schoolmaster with switches at the same time. I remember thinking of the feasibility [possibility] of destroying all that kind of timber growing near the school-house. My terror was a little red switch in that rank which I caught too often, usually for the offense of laughing. The larger switches were graded, partly by the size of the boys and partly by the gravity of the offense, the gravest of which was an imperfect lesson. The third size of rods was of hickory, tough sticks, which he did not use on little boys, but which he did use on the larger scholars, without the least hesitation or reserve, if they failed to get the appointed lesson.

1. The teacher chose a switch to punish a student on the basis of
   A the size of the student
   B how angry Dyas was at the time
   C whichever switch was closest to hand when the offense occurred
   D the size of the student and the degree of the offense
2. The students were most likely to get a serious whipping for the offense of
   A cheating
   B laughing
   C not learning their lesson
   D destroying trees near school

TAAS *Practice*
Writing Descriptively

Imagine that you are a teenager who took part in the group work and social occasion illustrated by the painting on page 327. Make an entry in your diary describing the events that took place during this day.

Practicing Skills

1. **Classifying Information:** List the following statistics about the Texas economy under either *Census of 1850* or *Census of 1860*: 50,000 farmers, 50,000 cotton bales produced, 25,000 farmers, 6 million bushels of corn produced, 450,000 cotton bales produced, 16 million bushels of corn produced, 45,000 farms, 10,000 farms.
2. **Interpreting Graphs:** Study the graphs on this page. What happened to the value of Texas farms between 1850 and 1860?

Enriching Your Study of History

1. **Individual Project:** Draw a picture or make a model of some form of transport

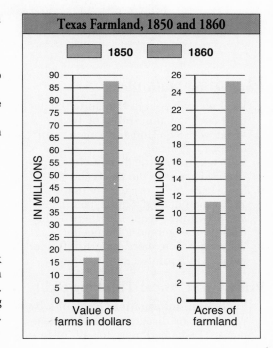

Texas Farmland, 1850 and 1860

1850 1860

Value of farms in dollars (IN MILLIONS)
Acres of farmland (IN MILLIONS)

that was used in Texas before 1860. This form of transportation might be a Mexican two-wheeled cart, a stagecoach, a buggy, a freight wagon, a river raft, a keelboat, a steamboat, or some other kind of vehicle.
2. **Cooperative Project:** The teacher will divide your class into two groups. One group will make a map of Texas in 1845, the year Texas became a state. The other group will make a map of Texas in 1860, on the eve of the Civil War. Both groups will label rivers, towns, cities, roads, railroads, and other cultural and physical features. The class will then compare the maps.

3. **Synthesizing Information:** Explanations should include that there was little state or federal aid for programs and that there was a limited number of qualified people to carry out professional tasks.

Linking History and Geography

1. Water was scarce and there were great distances between settlements. In the camel experiment, the army imported camels to Texas with the idea that they could travel long distances without water.
2. They limited transportation. Often, rivers were either flooded or too low for safe navigation.

TAAS *Practice*
Using Primary Sources
1. D
2. C

TAAS *Practice*
Writing Descriptively
Diary entries will vary but should reflect the events portrayed in the painting.

Practicing Skills
1. **Classifying Information:** *Census of 1850:* 25,000 farmers, 50,000 cotton bales produced, 6 million bushels of corn produced, 10,000 farms; *Census of 1860:* 50,000 farmers, 450,000 cotton bales produced, 16 million bushels of corn produced, 45,000 farms
2. **Interpreting Graphs:** It increased from about $15 million to about $87 million.

Enriching Your Study of History
1. **Individual Project:** Pictures and models should be accurate representations of the subject.
2. **Cooperative Project:** Students' maps should be accurately labeled.

UNIT REVIEW RESOURCES

1. Unit Review Worksheet 6
2. Unit 6 Test, Form A
3. Reteaching Worksheet 6
4. Unit 6 Test, Form B
5. **Informal Evaluation Forms:** Portfolio Assessment

6. *Texas, Our Texas* **Test Generator**
7. Midterm Review Worksheet
8. Midterm Test, Form A
9. Midterm Reteaching Worksheet
10. Midterm Test, Form B

Essential Elements
2A, 2F, 4A, 4E, 4H, 5D, 6A, 6B,
7C, 7D, 9A, 9C

UNIT 6 REVIEW ANSWERS

Connecting Main Ideas

1. They feared war with Mexico, and they disagreed about adding another slave state to the United States.
2. He served Texas as commander of the Republic's army, president of the Republic, United States senator, and governor of the state.
3. People on the frontier had little money and lived simple lives.
4. Helped to provide food, clothing, and shelter
5. Because there was a small population on the frontier, women were needed to help meet settlers' needs for goods and services.

Practicing Critical Thinking Skills

1. **Evaluating Information:** Answers will vary but should demonstrate sound reasoning and should mention Texas' proximity to Mexico.
2. **Synthesizing Information:** Answers will vary but should be supported with examples from the textbook.
3. **Exploring Multicultural Perspectives:** Descriptions will vary but should reflect the poor treatment of the Tejanos during that period.

UNIT 6

REVIEW

Connecting Main Ideas

1. Why were people in the United States split over the annexation of Texas?
2. What were Sam Houston's main contributions to Texas?
3. Why was there little demand for manufactured goods in the 1840s and 1850s?
4. Industries in Texas in the 1840s and 1850s included grist mills, cotton gins, and sawmills. What did these industries do that served local needs?
5. Why were there more opportunities for women in a frontier state? Explain.

Practicing Critical Thinking Skills

1. **Evaluating Information:** Explain why you agree or disagree with this statement: "Texas had more to gain or lose by the outcome of the Mexican War than other states."
2. **Synthesizing Information**: Do you think that life for the average Texan changed much from 1845 to 1860? Why or why not?
3. **Exploring Multicultural Perspectives:** Imagine that you are a Tejano historian writing in the late 1800s about the events of 1836-1860—events that you lived through yourself. Describe what happened to the Tejano community in Texas during these years.

TAAS Practice
Writing Descriptively

Imagine that you are a modern geographer writing about changes in the natural environment of Texas during the period from 1836 to 1860. Write a paragraph giving an overview of these changes.

Exploring Local History

1. Find out when your town, city, or county government was organized. Create a diagram to illustrate the organization of your local government.
2. Ask several adults to tell you about home remedies they know of. Write them down and compare with those collected by other students.

Using Historical Imagination

1. **Individual Project:** Read a section of a newspaper about arts or entertainment. Write a similar article as you think it might have appeared in a Texas newspaper of the 1850s.
2. **Cooperative Project:** Organize a campaign between two candidates for governor of Texas during the years covered in this unit. Decide on campaign managers, workers, and candidates. Each side in the campaign should prepare speeches and posters reflecting issues of importance discussed in the unit.

For Extending Your Knowledge

Marks, Paula Mitchell. *Turn Your Eyes Toward Texas: Pioneers Sam and Mary Maverick.* College Station: Texas A&M University Press, 1989. A couple comes to Texas to start a cattle ranch.

Olmsted, Frederick Law. *A Journey Through Texas.* Austin: University of Texas Press, 1978. A sharp-tongued easterner travels Texas in the 1850s.

SKILL LESSON

Comparing Perspectives

Historical interpretations of an important event, person, or situation often vary widely. This is true because people interpret historical events from different perspectives—different points of view.

How to Compare Perspectives

Note the sources. Find out about each author, or source.

Compare the main ideas expressed. Note the similarities and differences. Some points will be quite similar.

Conduct research. Find out as much as you can about the situation.

Use your critical thinking skills. Use your historical imagination—and your ability to analyze, synthesize, and evaluate information—to understand why people have different views. Decide which point of view you think is most reliable.

Practicing the Skill

Read the following accounts, which express very different perspectives about the origins of the Mexican War. Then apply the instructions listed above and answer the questions that follow.

The first interpretation is from a textbook used in Mexico in 1951. The second is from a popular Texas history book published in the early 1900s.

War with the United States (Mexican Perspective)

This was the greatest of all the disgraces suffered by Mexico in the last century. . . . The United States had practically filled up with European colonists. They needed new territories, as theirs were not sufficient. Our territory extended far to the north, was rich in mines, and was empty. . . .

. . . The Texans . . . claimed their territory extended as far as the Rio Bravo [Rio Grande]. They began to settle this region, which Mexico considered its own because the boundaries of Texas ended at the Nueces River to the north of the Rio Bravo. Mexico and Texas disputed this area between the Rio Bravo and the Nueces River. The Texans brazenly took possession of it. . . .

The Mexican army crossed the Rio Bravo, determined to win respect. It was then that the United States . . . cried, "Mexico has invaded my territory."

Our government tried to explain to the North Americans its reasons for crossing the Rio Bravo, but they would not listen. They wanted to fight. And there was no other recourse; war with the United States began.

Causes of War with Mexico (Texan Perspective)

When Mexico saw that in spite of all her efforts Texas was to become one of the United States, she became indignant. . . . Preparations were made for war. The Congress of the Republic of Texas in 1836 declared the Rio Grande to be its western boundary, but Mexico asserted . . . that the Nueces River formed the dividing line between the two countries. The United States government ordered General Zachary Taylor, with a strong force, to occupy the disputed territory. . . . The Mexicans tried to resist this movement, but failed. . . . So much bad feeling had been created by the boundary dispute and the question of debts that the declaration of war against Mexico by Congress was welcomed by most of the American people.

1. Where do these two histories of the origin of the war agree?
2. Using both sources (and the interpretation in Chapter 15), write your own account of why the war began.

INTRODUCING THE UNIT

Connecting with Past Learning

Write the term *civil war* on the chalkboard. Ask volunteers to provide a definition. Explain that a civil war is a war fought between groups within one nation. Using a world map, challenge students to point out locations of past civil wars *(Spain, 1930s; Pakistan, 1970; Lebanon, 1970s–1980s; Yugoslavia, 1990s)*. Mention other wars in history and explain how these differ from civil wars.

MOTIVATOR

Bring to class samples of spirituals sung by slaves in the pre-Civil War South, either as a record or as lyrics on a transparency. Have the students listen to the songs or read the lyrics and analyze the feelings being expressed. Ask students to draw conclusions about life for slaves prior to the Civil War.

UNIT 7 OVERVIEW

Unit 7 focuses on the Civil War in the history of Texas and the United States. Chapter 17 examines life in the South prior to the war and presents the debate over slavery. It concludes with a discussion of Texas secession and the creation of the Confederacy.

Chapter 18 explores events of the Civil War and examines the conflicts between the North and South. Emphasis is placed on Texas battles and reasons for Union interest in Texas. Wartime politics, economics, and ways of life also are discussed.

Chapter 19 describes the period of Reconstruction and Texas' relationship to other states. Political change and the new role in society for freedmen is examined.

Materials Available at the Unit Level:
Unit 7 Making Global Connections
Oral History Handbook
Informal Evaluation Forms

UNIT 7

CIVIL WAR AND RECONSTRUCTION

*T*he northern states and the southern states went to war in 1861. Their armies met for the first time in July 1861 between Washington, D.C., and Richmond, Virginia. Six companies of Texans reached Virginia in time to fight for the South in the First Battle of Bull Run, also known as the First Battle of Manassas. The battle, shown in the lithograph on the opposite page, was won by the South. It brought on four terrible years of fighting.

The North and South disagreed over the addition of new states to the country and over slavery. In 1861, a number of southern states withdrew from the United States and formed the Confederate States of America. Texas became one of the states in this new nation.

The split between the North and the South led to the most bitter war in the country's history. Historians have called this era the nation's most tragic period. After the war was over, the defeated southern states had to be rebuilt and brought back into the United States. This process aroused almost as much emotion and bitterness as the war itself.

The three chapters in Unit 7 describe events between the 1850s and 1876. Chapter 17 examines the issue of slavery leading to the Civil War. Chapter 18 tells the story of the war in Texas and the major role of Texans in the war. The unit concludes with Chapter 19, which examines the period after the war, when Texas again became part of the United States.

UNIT 7 OBJECTIVES

1. List arguments made for and against slavery in Texas in the 1850s.
2. Describe the lives of Texas slaves.
3. Discuss the dispute over slavery in the 1850s that split the nation politically.
4. Discuss the role of the doctrine of states' rights in secession, and identify events leading up to Texas secession.
5. Discuss the role of Texans in the Civil War, and identify key battles in Texas and the Southwest.
6. Describe the economic and political impact of the Civil War on Texas.
7. Define *Reconstruction*, and discuss its impact on Texas.
8. Outline the terms of the Constitution of 1876, and understand the document's importance in Texas today.

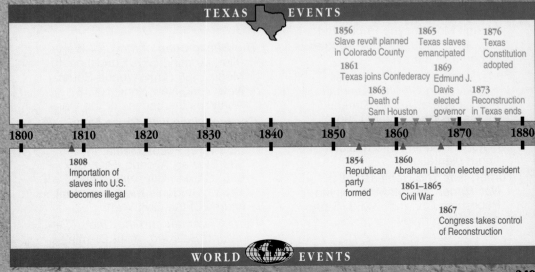

TEXAS EVENTS

1856
Slave revolt planned
in Colorado County

1865
Texas slaves
emancipated

1876
Texas
Constitution
adopted

1861
Texas joins Confederacy

1869
Edmund J.
Davis
elected
governor

1863
Death of
Sam Houston

1873
Reconstruction
in Texas ends

1800   1810   1820   1830   1840   1850   1860   1870   1880

1808
Importation of
slaves into U.S.
becomes illegal

1854
Republican
party
formed

1860
Abraham Lincoln elected president

1861–1865
Civil War

1867
Congress takes control
of Reconstruction

WORLD EVENTS

SLAVERY AND SECESSION

TEACHER'S TIME LINE

Section 1	Section 2	Section 3	Section 4	Review and
Pp. 350–57	Pp. 357–60	Pp. 360–62	Pp. 362–65	Assessment
1 Day	1 Day	1 Day	1 Day	1 Day

⯃ TEACHER MATERIALS

Core: Chapter 17 Time Line; Graphic Organizer 17; Enrichment Worksheet 17; Review Worksheet 17; Reteaching Worksheet 17; Chapter 17 Tests, Forms A & B

Additional: Geography and Graph Skills 17, Informal Evaluation Forms, Test Generator

⯃ OBJECTIVES

1. Describe the role of African Americans in the economy of the South prior to the Civil War.
2. Discuss characteristics of the plantation system.
3. Describe life for free blacks in the South during the 1850s.
4. Cite arguments used for and against slavery.
5. Explain the meaning of *states' rights* and its role in secession.
6. Discuss Sam Houston's opposition to secession.

⯃ RESOURCES

BOOKS FOR TEACHERS

Bluenger, Walter Louis. *Secession and the Union in Texas*. Austin: University of Texas Press, 1984. Discusses secession in Texas.

Braden, Josephine Clarke. *Monograph*. Austin: Barker Texas History Center, 1941. Slavery and the Republic of Texas.

Campbell, Randolf. *An Empire for Slavery: The Peculiar Institution in Texas, 1821–1865*. Baton Rouge; LSU Press, 1989. Slavery in Texas.

Coss, Carrie B. *Liendo Plantation*. (S.L.): Waller County Historical Commission, 1977. History of this plantation.

Douglass, Frederick. *The Narrative and Selective Writings*. New York: Modern Library, 1984. Life and philosophy of Douglass.

The Life, Trial and Execution of Capt. John Brown: Being a Full Account of the Attempted Insurrection at Harper's Ferry. Miami: Mnemosyne Publishing Co., Inc., 1969. Primary source account of the event.

Perry, James Franklin. *James Franklin and Stephen Samuel Perry Papers*. Austin: Barker Texas History Center, 1790–1853. Documents about Texas history, including information about plantations.

Turner, Nat. *The Confessions of Nat Turner*. Miami: Mnemosyne Publishing Co., Inc., 1969. Story of his slave revolt.

Waerenskjold, Elise. *The Lady with the Pen: Elise Waerenskjold in Texas*. New York: Arno Press, 1979. Life and writing of this Norwegian immigrant.

MULTIMEDIA MATERIALS

The Background of the Civil War. (film, 20 min.) BFA Educational Media, 468 Park Avenue South, New York, New York, 10016. Analyzes the causes of the war.

Conversations with Great Americans. Civil War and Expansion. (software) Focus Media, Inc., 839 Stewart Avenue, P.O. Box 865, Garden City, New York, 11530. Students meet important figures of the Civil War.

Harriet Tubman and the Underground Railroad. (film, 21 min.)

BFA Educational Media, 468 Park Avenue South, New York, New York, 10016. Traces one of Tubman's dangerous trips leading slaves to freedom.

The Heritage of Slavery. (film, 53 min.) BFA Educational Media, 468 Park Avenue South, New York, New York, 10016. Examination of slavery and its effects.

The South's Slave System. (video, 30 min.) PBS Video, 1320 Braddock Place, Alexandria, VA 22314. Multifaceted examination of the institution of slavery.

GENERAL STRATEGIES

STUDENTS WITH SPECIAL NEEDS

Limited English Proficient Students (LEP)
Have students preview the chapter by studying the illustrations. If necessary, assign a language-proficient student to help read and explain the captions. Ask students to write down words that might be used to describe the life of a slave in Texas, based on what they see in the illustrations. After they have studied the chapter, ask them to review their list and expand on it. Encourage them to develop the list into a written paragraph. See other activities labeled **LEP.**

Students Having Difficulty with the Chapter
Direct students to review the main ideas of the chapter by listing the topic and topic sentence of the first paragraph of each section. If there is no topic sentence, have them create one from two or more related sentences. **LEP**

Auditory Learners
Have auditory learners work together to present a "talk show" for the class, based on the information discussed in the chapter. They should select a talk-show host and several guests to represent different types of people living in Texas before the Civil War. The other auditory learners should prepare a list of questions that contrasts the ways of life of the guests. Guests may include a plantation owner, a free black, a slave, a merchant, or a farmer. See other activities labeled **A.**

Visual Learners
Have visual learners work together to conduct research and prepare a chart for classroom display showing the political parties that came into being in the 1850s. The chart should include information about the party platforms, candidates, and region of strongest support. See other activities labeled **V.**

Tactile/Kinesthetic Learners
Have students choose a person or type of person to represent a point of view in pre-Civil War Texas. Suggestions might include a family member of a plantation owner, a slave, a free black, a Unionist, a secessionist, an abolitionist, and so on. Ask them to write several journal entries to describe that person's life. See other activities labeled **TK.**

Gifted Students
Have gifted students conduct library research to find nineteenth-century political cartoons dealing with issues discussed in Chapter 17. Challenge them to locate two cartoons representing opposing points of view for each issue. Ask them to display and discuss the cartoons in class. See other activities labeled **G.**

VOCABULARY
In addition to the boldfaced terms in each section, some students might benefit from discussing the meanings of these terms.

Section 1: *enslaved* (p. 350); *institution* (p. 350); *auctions* (p. 351); *status* (p. 352); *ideals* (p. 354); *brickmasons* (p. 355).

Section 2: *quarters* (p. 358); *cotton gin* (p. 359); *catering* (p. 360); *uprooted* (p. 360); *spirituals* (p. 360).

Section 3: *traitor* (p. 361); *denouncing* (p. 361).

Section 4: *gallant* (p. 363); *postmaster general* (p. 364).

CHRONOLOGY
Have students study the Chapter 17 Time Line and identify relationships among the events.

GRAPHIC ORGANIZER
Have students skim the chapter and complete the Chapter 17 Graphic Organizer. *(You might wish to use this activity to review rather than to introduce the chapter.)*

ENRICHMENT
Have students complete the Chapter 17 Enrichment Worksheet.

SECTION 1

FOCUS

Past Learning (I) Ask students what they think the nation's founders meant when they said that "all men are created equal." Ask them if they think that the founders meant to exclude African Americans. Women? Indians? Allow time for students to express varying opinions.

INSTRUCTION

Vocabulary (I) You may wish to preteach the following boldfaced terms: *secede* (p. 350); *abolitionists* (p. 355). **LEP**

CHAPTER 17 OVERVIEW

Black slaves were brought to Texas by the first Europeans who settled the region. Many of the settlers who entered Texas from the United States brought slaves with them. The number of slaves in Texas continued to grow. During the 1850s, Texas entered the conflict brewing between the northern and southern states over slavery. In 1861, Texans elected to secede from the United States and join the Confederate States of America.

Essential Elements
2G, 3F, 5C, 6B, 7B, 7D, 7E, 7F, 7G, 8A, 8C, 8D

CHAPTER 17

SLAVERY AND SECESSION

The Story Continues...

Texas had fewer slaves than most other southern states, but in 1860, one out of four Texans was an enslaved person. In the 1860s, debate over slavery between northern and southern states split the nation. Most Anglo Texans supported the southern point of view. The disagreement became so serious that southern states began threatening to **secede**, or separate from the United States. This chapter looks at the institution of slavery in Texas, the status of free black Texans, and the events that led to the separation of Texas and the rest of the South from the United States.

As you read the chapter, look for the answers to these questions:

1. What role did blacks play in the economy of Texas?
2. What were the lives of enslaved people like, and how did they try to make their lives better?
3. How did the issues of slavery and states' rights play a part in the secession of southern states from the Union?
4. How did Sam Houston try to stop Texas from seceding, and what events led to secession?

1 Slavery in Texas

The number of enslaved people in Texas was estimated at around 5,000 at the time of independence in 1836. As agriculture expanded, the demand for slaves grew. In fact, the slave population grew faster than that of any other group in Texas. By 1860, census figures listed 182,566 black slaves in a total population of 604,215. Only about 25 percent of the white families in Texas had any slaves, but the institution of slavery was of major importance to the Texas economy.

Plantations and Slavery. Slavery developed in the South as a cheap source of labor for plantations. Plantations

The Granger Collection

Many opponents of slavery felt that slave auctions were the cruelest expression of the slave system. Family members were sometimes separated as individual slaves were sold to the highest bidder.

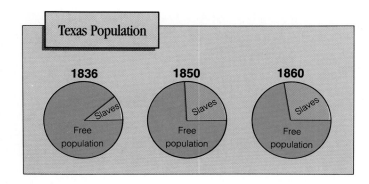

Texas Population

1836   1850   1860

Slaves

Free population

Between which years did the population of slaves increase the most?

were large farming operations producing cash crops, usually cotton or tobacco. Africans had been brought as slaves to the colony of Virginia in 1619. During the 1700s and 1800s, the plantation system spread westward from southern states along the Atlantic coast of the United States. There, cotton grew well in the warm climate and rich soil. Eventually, plantations growing cotton and sugarcane were established in the rich lands of Texas.

Cotton, the major cash crop, was grown in the South and exported to the northern United States and Europe. These areas could not grow cotton because of their colder climates. But they did have hundreds of textile mills where cotton was made into cloth. Cotton and a few other cash crops became the only items that the South could export for a good profit in return.

Slaves greatly increased the profits of the plantation owners. Growing cotton required many hours of labor by hand to plant the seeds, pick the cotton, and separate the fiber. Many workers were needed. Plantation owners did not have to pay slaves, so costs were limited mainly to food, clothing, and shelter. In the 1600s and 1700s, blacks had continually been brought from Africa to America to satisfy the demand for more slaves.

The United States Congress passed a law that made importing slaves illegal by 1808. It had little effect on Texas, because it was not a state at the time. Besides, most slaves were brought to Texas from states in the southern United States, not from overseas. The slave trade became a business in itself. In Texas, slave auctions were held in Galveston and Houston. The average price for a slave was

Texas Department of Transportation

Although most farming operations in Texas before the Civil War were small, a few large plantations did exist. The Liendo Plantation in Waller County had thousands of acres of farmland worked by about 300 slaves.

around $800, but a strong field hand could bring as much as $2,000, a large amount of money in those days. Slaves were not citizens. They were bought and sold as property.

Not all slaves worked on plantations. Many worked on small farms, or in towns or cities. On the farm, slaves helped plow fields, harvest crops, tend livestock, and prepare meals. In towns and cities, they worked as servants, wagon drivers, or laborers in industries. Some performed skilled labor as carpenters or blacksmiths. In small industries and on small farms, slaveholders worked side by side with slaves. In such situations, slaves and slaveholders sometimes developed friendships. They often shared in the care of family members. Yet slaves were not free to do as they wished and could never forget their status as slaves.

The Planters. Nearly 80 percent of the 21,878 Texas slaveholders had fewer than nine slaves. The other 20 percent of slaveholders held two-thirds of the slaves in Texas. This second group, made up of plantation owners known as planters, had at least twenty slaves each. There were not a great many plantation owners in Texas, probably around 2,000. But they controlled the state's economy and held great influence in government.

352 Unit 7

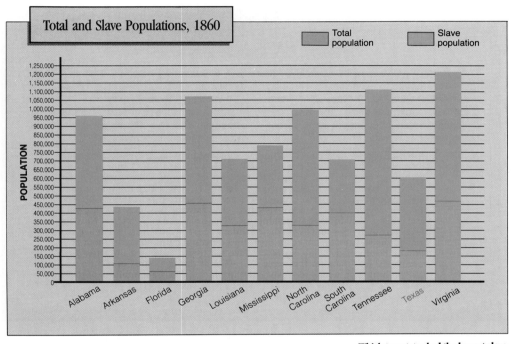

Total and Slave Populations, 1860

Which two states had the largest slave populations? Which state had the smallest slave population?

The planters were the wealthiest citizens in Texas and lived better and more comfortably than most people. The planter who had the largest number of slaves in Texas was David G. Mills. In 1860, he held more than 300 slaves. His home in Brazoria County was similar to other large plantation houses of the era. These houses were often large, two-story mansions of brick or stone. Many were built in the Greek style with huge columns in the front. The plantation homes had expensive furniture, sometimes brought from New Orleans or imported from Europe. The homes had luxuries that few Texans ever saw, such as marble-topped dressing tables and fancy bathtubs.

The plantation families had an abundant supply of food. While most Texans lived on a simple diet of beef, pork, and corn, the planters ate a variety of foods. They had slaves to tend large vegetable gardens, and they had the money to buy other foods from merchants in the cities. Fine clothing was another luxury the planters could afford. For special occasions, the plantation women had fancy

TEXAS VOICES

Analyzing (I) After students have read the special feature, pose the following questions for class discussion: What does the author mean when she says that "For great numbers of them, life will be harsher now than when they were slaves"? Is she defending slavery? **A**

Essential Elements
2H, 6A, 6B, 9A

During the Civil War, many abolitionists were forced to leave Texas. But Elise Waerenskjold stayed. A Norwegian immigrant who spoke her mind, she has been described as "an independent spirit, a tradition-breaker, a woman ahead of her time." She was a writer, teacher, artist, and community activist.

In letters written between 1851 and 1865, Waerenskjold often expressed her concerns about slavery. The following was written in 1865 to a friend in Norway:

Union men were those who did not favor secession of the southern states from the union with the North. Practically all the Norwegians were Union men. . . .

Until the war I did not really know the laws on slavery. But I know now that according to these laws, I was guilty of . . . offenses [punishable by imprisonment] more than 100 times, because the law decreed several years of [imprisonment] only for saying in private conversation that slavery was unjust. The same punishment was stipulated for helping a fugitive slave in any way. . . . Now the slaves are finally free, but as yet their freedom does not mean very much because their former owners try to scare them into remaining, and many of them have actually been killed. Some, however, have left their masters, or the latter have voluntarily sent them on their way. But what of the thousands of people who have nothing with which to make a start in life? . . . For great numbers of them, life will be harsher now than when they were slaves.

floor-length gowns. They wore silk stockings and fine shoes and hats from London or Paris. The men wore vested suits with long coats. Their high-topped boots often cost more money than an average Texas farmer earned in a year.

Opposing Slavery. Many people were opposed to the system of slavery. They pointed out that planters lived well because they had the advantage of slave labor. Some opposed it for religious reasons. They said that even if many slaveholders were kind to their slaves, it was wrong for one person to own another. Others argued against slavery for political reasons. They believed that slavery went against the American ideals of democracy and freedom.

Opponents of slavery pointed to the terrible lives of slaves. There were slaveholders who beat their slaves or overworked them. Enslaved people had no future and could take little pleasure in the present. Slave families were sometimes torn apart because members were sold to different slaveholders. Slaves lived under the threat of violence for not doing as they were told. For all of these reasons, they said slavery was an evil institution.

Analysis (II) Review with students the definition of the term *abolitionists*. Help students understand the ethical issues that abolitionists faced. Explain that people who are involved in reform movements sometimes face moral dilemmas, or choices. Point out that during this period, slavery was protected by the United States Constitution. Legally, slaves were property. People were forbidden to help slaves escape and were required by law to return runaway slaves to their owners. The abolitionists' choice—or dilemma—was to break the law or accept the institution of slavery. Pose the following questions for class discussion: Are there ever circumstances in which breaking the law is an acceptable form of protest? Why or why not? **A**

Guided Practice (I) Have students write the following headings across the top of a sheet of paper: *Planter, Abolitionist, Slave, Free Black*. Ask them to write under each heading three characteristics of each. Ask students to provide their responses as you copy them onto the chalkboard. **A, V, LEP**

People who organized to abolish, or do away with, slavery were called **abolitionists**. Most of them lived in the northern United States, where slavery had never been widespread. There were only a few abolitionists in Texas.

One of the leading opponents of slavery in Texas was a Presbyterian missionary named Melinda Rankin. A staunch Unionist, she wrote books and articles against the system but was forced to leave Texas in 1862. Another who occasionally spoke out was Elise Waerenskjold, a writer and journalist. A high percentage of Mexican Texans also opposed slavery.

Defending Slavery. Most Anglos in Texas and throughout the South defended slavery. Even those who owned no slaves felt that the system should be continued. Many small farmers envied the planters and hoped one day to have a plantation themselves. Nearly all defenders of slavery pointed out that the system supported the economy of the South. Without slavery, they argued, their cash crops could not be grown, and money could not be earned from exports. Other people defended slavery by pointing to history. They claimed that great civilizations in the past such as those in Egypt, Greece, and Rome had slave labor.

Slaveholders and their defenders responded to abolitionists who argued that slaves were treated badly. Slaves were expensive, they said. It would be foolish to hurt them so that they could no longer work. Others even argued that blacks were better off as slaves in America than they had been as free people in Africa.

Free Blacks in Texas. Not all blacks in Texas were enslaved. There was a small number of free blacks. Most free black families entered Texas during the years of Spanish and Mexican control. Others entered later from the United States. Still others were able to earn money to buy their freedom, which was occasionally possible when a slaveholder agreed to it.

Free blacks worked at the same occupations as most other Texans. Some had small farms. Others were businesspeople. William Goyens, for example, operated a farm, an inn, and a freight company. Some free blacks worked on ranches as cowboys, while others such as Aaron Ashworth owned their ranches. Other free blacks lived in towns and cities. They worked as carpenters, seamstresses, brickmasons, blacksmiths, servants, and freight haulers.

Norwegian-American Historical Association, Northfield, MN

Elise Waerenskjold was a champion of various social causes. A Norwegian, she moved to Texas in 1847. Like many immigrants from northern Europe, Waerenskjold was highly critical of slavery.

Library of Congress

Among the occupations of free blacks in Texas was that of cowboy. More African Americans became cowboys after the Civil War.

Community Involvement (I) Invite a member of the local historical society or someone else familiar with local history to discuss with the class how the issue of slavery affected your community. Find out if there were slaves in your community and, if so, the kinds of work they performed. **A, LEP**

Independent Practice (II) Tell students to imagine that they are either Melinda Rankin or Elise Waerenskjold. Ask them to write a fiery letter criticizing slavery to send to the editor of a Texas newspaper. Invite students to read their letters aloud. **A, G**

RETEACHING
Organize students into small groups. Have each group make up a quiz on the information in Section 1. Make certain that each student in each group contributes at least one question. Have each group exchange its quiz with

---

Essential Elements
2H, 3F, 6A

LONE STAR LEGACY
Using Historical Imagination: Answers will vary greatly but should be thoughtful and creative.

Answers to Section 1 Review

Define: *secede*—separate from; *abolitionists*—people who wanted to abolish, or do away with, slavery

Identify: David G. Mills— planter who owned the largest number of slaves in Texas; Elise Waerenskjold—Texas writer and journalist who spoke out against slavery; William Goyens—free black Texan who operated a farm, an inn, and a freight company; Mary Madison—free black who successfully petitioned to remain in Texas as a "free woman"

1. Plantations were large farms that produced cash crops. Slaves provided the labor on plantations.
2. People opposed slavery for religious reasons—because they felt it was wrong for one person to own another—or for political reasons—because they believed it went against the nation's ideals of democracy and freedom.

(Continued on page 357)

From Africa to America

From 1619 until 1865, slavery existed in the southern region of the United States. Most of the enslaved people were brought by force to America from the nations of western Africa. Despite the efforts of some slaveholders to "Americanize" the enslaved people, the link between southern black Americans and their previous lives in Africa was never broken completely.

One way in which African Americans stayed close to their memories of their home country was through what is called an oral tradition. This means that each generation passes along information to their children through stories, songs, and family history. Usually, the oldest member of a family tells the younger ones a daily tale of family adventures and accomplishments. This method of passing along family tradition was exceptionally strong during the years of slavery.

In addition to telling stories about Africa, black Americans succeeded in keeping alive many African customs. Their music, dances, and plays were similar to those that had existed in places such as Nigeria, Ghana, and other African nations. Marriage ceremonies were a combination of American and African traditions. The same was true for burial customs. Some of the language used by southern blacks, from Virginia to Texas, showed the influences of older African languages.

Many of the skills used in daily activities relied on African ways. The black slaves often used farming methods that their ancestors in Africa had developed. These included forms of irrigation and crop cultivation. Home designs, carpentry techniques, and decoration of the home also had an African flair. Other African connections could be found in slaves' artwork, food preparation, and homemade medicines for treating illness and injuries.

Soon after their arrival in America, most blacks practiced the Christian religion. But they often blended African religious customs into the ceremonies and traditions of the Christian church. Despite its harshness and many difficulties, slavery could not destroy the spiritual nature of African Americans.

The traditions of Africa can still be seen today throughout American society. The African influence is present almost everywhere we look. People of all colors and cultures in America are richer because of this African connection.

Using Historical Imagination
Imagine that you are an African American enslaved in the South during the early nineteenth century. Write a brief story to tell your grandchildren, one that will give them a link to their African heritage.

Inset: African dance in Texas

Columbia Artists Management Inc.

another group and answer the questions. Review the quizzes as a class and correct any misinformation. **LEP, A**

CLOSURE
Ask students what they consider to be the strongest argument against slavery. Allow time for several students to express their opinions.

ASSESSMENT
Have students complete the Section 1 Review on page 357.

SECTION 2

FOCUS

Past Learning (I) Remind students that some defenders of slavery claimed that slaves were better off in America than they had been as free people in Africa and that slaves were generally well treated. Ask students to imagine themselves in the role of an enslaved person. Ask: How would you respond to these arguments? Tell students that in Section 2 they will learn more about the lives of Texas slaves.

It was difficult for free blacks to live in Texas or any other state where slavery was legal. They were regarded by many whites as a threat to the slavery system because they were symbols of freedom to thousands of people who wished to be free.

Because free blacks were a threat to slavery, they were not treated as equals. They could not vote or hold office, and many jobs were closed to them. All free blacks, even black heroes of the Texas Revolution, had to petition the government to be allowed to stay in Texas. In 1850, Mary Madison petitioned the state to be allowed to live in Texas as "a free woman of color." Her petition was approved, but many were not. Because of their uncertain status, the number of free blacks in Texas declined. ✪

2 The Lives of Texas Slaves

Defenders of slavery in Texas argued that slaves in the state led better lives than those in other states. Records of people who witnessed slave life suggest that this may be true. Nevertheless, Texas slaves longed for the day when they could be free and live their own lives. They dreamed of a time when their labor was their own and their families would be safe and secure. Many Texas slaves were willing to risk their lives to escape.

SECTION ★ REVIEW

Define: secede, abolitionists
Identify: David G. Mills, Elise Waerenskjold, William Goyens, Mary Madison

1. What were plantations, and how were slaves important to plantation operations?
2. What were the reasons that people opposed slavery?
3. Why were many Texans in favor of slavery?
4. What were some jobs held by free blacks in Texas?

Exploring Economics: How did the economy of Texas depend on the system of slavery?

Comparing Perspectives: Write two paragraphs comparing the attitudes toward slavery of abolitionists and planters.

3. Many Texans believed that slavery was necessary to the South's economy, and many farmers hoped to own plantations someday. Some people used history as a defense of slavery by pointing to the slaveholding civilizations of the past.
4. Answers might include: farmers, cowboys, ranch owners, carpenters, seamstresses, brickmasons, blacksmiths, servants, and freight haulers.

Exploring Economics: The plantations exported cash crops for profit, and slaves provided the plantation labor. Therefore, slavery was a vital part of the economy.

Comparing Perspectives: Paragraphs will vary but should mention that abolitionists opposed slavery for religious and political reasons, while planters favored slavery primarily for economic reasons.

Essential Elements
2G, 2H, 3D, 5B, 6A, 6B, 7D, 9A, 9B, 9G

Caption Response
Most were in favor of slavery.

The Granger Collection

Many slaves worked long, hard hours in the cotton fields of Texas. Picking cotton, the major cash crop, was difficult and very tiring. What was the attitude held by most Anglos in Texas about the system of slavery?

INSTRUCTION

Historical Imagination (II) Direct students to the illustration on this page. Ask them to write a fictional account of a slave escape, using this illustration and information from Section 2. Allow time for several students to read their accounts aloud. **A, V**

Cooperative Learning (I) Have students work in groups of three or four to prepare presentations depicting the life of slaves in Texas. Each group should choose an appropriate method of presentation. For example, students might pre-sent dramatic readings using primary sources, secondary sources, or spirituals. They might illustrate some aspect of slave life with original drawings. They might display and explain reproductions of paintings or other illustrations from the time period. **A, V, TK, LEP**

Multicultural Perspective (I) Present the following scenario to students: You are a slave who is considering an escape. It will mean never seeing your family again. Will you attempt the escape? Write a paragraph explaining your difficult decision. **LEP**

Historical Sidelight

In early summer 1860, in Dallas, mounting tensions between abolitionists and slaveholders had reached a breaking point. On the afternoon of July 8, 1860, a huge fire broke out in the courthouse square. It eventually destroyed 25 buildings in the Dallas business district, including the city's newspaper, the post office, two hotels, and all its stores. Fires were also reported the same day in towns across North Texas, and more fires followed weeks later.

In the resulting panic, vigilance committees claimed that the fire was planned by northern abolitionists, acting with slaves to weaken Dallas. These committees feared that while the city was thus vulnerable, abolitionists, slaves, and Indians would begin a war. Some evidence indicates that these fires had been part of an attempted rebellion aimed at overthrowing the slaveholders and freeing the slaves. Whether there existed a "grand plot" is still a matter of speculation.

Caption Response
To Mexico, Indian Territory, or Canada

The Granger Collection

Some slaves tried to escape to freedom, but many were caught and beaten severely as a warning to other slaves. Where did runaway slaves in Texas try to go?

Slave Escapes and Rebellions. Texas newspapers and plantation records tell of an occasional escape attempt by slaves during the 1840s. By the 1850s, the number of slave escapes increased into the hundreds. A runaway slave would head for Mexico or Indian Territory or even attempt the long journey northward to Canada. Most slaves who tried to escape were caught and returned to their masters. Many were punished severely as examples to others.

The idea of a large slave rebellion frightened the white population. Concern about slave violence was particularly high in East Texas, where the majority of slaves were held. Several slaves planned an uprising in Colorado County in 1856. They acquired guns and hid them in their quarters. They intended to kill the plantation masters and then escape to Mexico. Before the slave rebellion could take place, the guns were discovered. The uprising was crushed by angry, frightened whites. They killed several of the slaves and beat another 200 as punishment.

Slaves faced a terrible decision when considering escape. Most of them would have to leave family members whom they would never see again. They also faced the possibility of being caught. For these reasons, the vast majority of Texas slaves went about life on plantations, on small farms, and in cities as their ancestors had for generations. It was a difficult existence for black Texans. But they survived the challenges of slave life with dignity and strength.

Slaves' Work. Slaves had to work at least six days a week. They usually had Sunday off, but there were many chores and family duties that had to be done on Sunday. For the plantation field hands, work began at daybreak. They ate a breakfast of bread, pork fat, and coffee in the fields. They also ate lunch near the workplace. Lunch might consist of bread and corn or potatoes, or maybe a vegetable stew. Then the slaves plowed or harvested until the sun went down. The evening meal was usually prepared by the slaves themselves. Many had gardens that provided fresh vegetables. Corn, bacon, sweet potatoes, and more bread rounded out the big meal of the day. On special occasions, beef was added to the diet.

When working in the cotton fields, slaves were expected to pick many pounds of cotton. Mary Kincheon Edwards, who lived near Austin, reported that she "picked two and three hundred pounds a day, and one day I picked 400."

Guided Practice (I) Have students work independently or in pairs to create a series of rough drawings that represent one of the following topics: *slaves' work, slaves' time off, slave rebellions.* Have students display the drawings (drawings should not be labeled) while the rest of the class guesses which of the topics is illustrated. **A, V, TK, LEP**

EXTENSION

Research (II) Choose volunteers to read and write a report on Harriet Beecher Stowe's 1852 book *Uncle Tom's Cabin.*

Ask students to investigate the book's impact on society at the time. **G**

Independent Practice (II) Have students use the discussion "Slaves' Work" and "Slaves' Time Off" on pages 358–60 to write two detailed diary entries: one that a slave in Texas might have written of a typical Saturday and the other of a typical Sunday. Invite volunteers to read their entries aloud. **A**

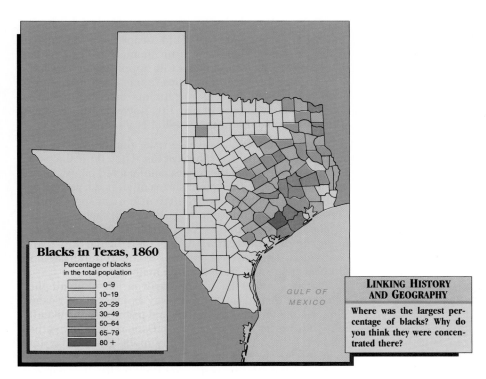

Blacks in Texas, 1860

Percentage of blacks in the total population

	0–9
	10–19
	20–29
	30–49
	50–64
	65–79
	80 +

GULF OF MEXICO

LINKING HISTORY AND GEOGRAPHY

Where was the largest percentage of blacks? Why do you think they were concentrated there?

Linking History and Geography
The largest percentage of blacks was in Southeast Texas. Most cotton plantations were located in this region.

Plantation slaves had other jobs in the cotton fields. Mariah Snyder, a slave woman in Panola County, ran a mule-powered cotton gin. Men usually did the heaviest work, such as plowing fields behind mules or teams of oxen.

Slaves in the cities worked at a variety of jobs. Some labored in factories. Others performed skilled labor such as carpentry. Slave women in the cities were housekeepers, cooks, or babysitters. Slaves helped build the roads and railroads that brought the produce from country to city. And slave labor was very important to the docks and warehouses of Houston and Galveston. Slaves helped build the business buildings whose activities enriched these cities. Before the Civil War, slaves were about 25 percent of the population of Houston and Galveston.

As a rule, slaves in the cities had more freedom and led more rewarding lives than slaves on plantations. Many of them were "hired out" by their masters to work for other businesspeople. The slaveholders liked the hiring-out

Chapter 17 **359**

RETEACHING
Have students write a one- or two-sentence summary of each of the subsections of Section 2. **LEP**

CLOSURE
Write the title of Section 2 on the chalkboard—"The Lives of Texas Slaves." Call on volunteers to provide adjectives that might be used to summarize this topic. List their responses on the chalkboard.

ASSESSMENT
Have students complete the Section 2 Review on page 360.

SECTION 3

FOCUS

Past Learning (I) Review with the class the reasons given by southerners in defense of slavery. Ask: What was the South's primary defense of slavery? What were the reasons presented in opposition to slavery? Tell students that the dispute over slavery grew, dividing the nation.

Answers to Section 2 Review

Identify: Mary Kincheon Edwards—Texas slave who reported picking 200 to 300 pounds of cotton a day; Mariah Snyder—Panola County slave who drove a mule-powered cotton gin

1. Many did not want to leave their families, and many feared being caught.
2. Slaves on plantations had less freedom than slaves in cities. Some urban slaves were able to open their own businesses.
3. Religion held the slave community together and gave slaves strength and determination.

Analyzing Information: Answers will vary. Students should mention that many slaves risked their lives trying to escape. Others planned rebellions to gain their freedom. Neither of these efforts proved very effective. Punishment for running away was severe, and participants in slave rebellions were killed or severely beaten.

Writing Descriptively: Letters will vary but should reflect the point of view of a plantation slave in Texas.

Essential Elements
2G, 2H, 6A, 6B, 7B, 7D, 7E, 7F, 7G, 9A, 9D, 9E

SECTION ⭐ 2 REVIEW

Identify: Mary Kincheon Edwards, Mariah Snyder

1. Why did many slaves not try to escape, despite the chance for freedom?
2. How did the lives of slaves on plantations and in cities differ?
3. Why was religion an important part of the lives of many slaves?

Analyzing Information: What efforts did slaves make to improve their lives? How effective do you think these efforts were? Explain.

Writing Descriptively: Imagine that you are a slave on a Texas plantation. Write a letter to your sister in Illinois, explaining why you have decided to escape.

system because they got cash for the work of their slaves. Slaves liked it because they could escape the watchful eyes of their masters, live away from them, and keep part of their wages. Urban slaves took this opportunity to start the first African American churches. Some even managed to open businesses, such as restaurants catering to slaves. Despite the advantages of city life, however, urban slaves still could be sold and uprooted at any moment.

Slaves' Time Off. Slaves on the plantations lived in small one-room or two-room cabins. They built their own homes and furnished them with hand-carved tables, chairs, and beds. Outside the cabin, slaves often had a garden or a small cotton patch. Much of their free time was spent tending these gardens and doing personal chores. If slaves sold their vegetables or cotton, they could usually keep the money. Some slaves worked extra jobs after their regular duties were completed. They used the extra income to purchase food, clothes, or special gifts for family members.

Slaves spent what little time was left after all their work was finished in the same way as most other Texans. They visited with their families and friends. In the evening they told stories or played games. Dances or family gatherings were often held on Saturday night. On Sunday they went to church, had picnics, or played music.

Music and religion were important in the slave community. While working in the fields, slaves sang songs called "field hollers" and "work chants." After work, they played instruments such as fiddles and banjos. Music was a major part of the worship service at black churches as well. Spirituals rang through every southern black church, carrying messages of hope and faith. Religion held the slave community together and gave the people the strength and determination to face their lives of enslavement. ○

❸ The Slavery Dispute

During the 1850s, the dispute over slavery, and whether it would be allowed to spread westward, dominated politics in the United States. The debate became very bitter and emotional as North and South divided over the issue. Some of the most heated arguments were heard in the United States Congress, where decisions were being made that would determine the future of the entire country.

INSTRUCTION

Vocabulary (I) You may wish to preteach the following boldfaced term: *states' rights* (p. 362). **LEP**

Historical Imagination (II) Have a student play the role of a Texas newspaper reporter writing a follow-up story on John Brown's raid on Harpers Ferry and the events that followed. Other students should portray people the reporter might interview and, in these roles, present the points of view that people might have had toward the

events. Possible roles include: an abolitionist, a northerner, a Texas planter, a member of Congress. **A, G, V**

Guided Practice (I) Have students list the major events of Section 3. Then ask them to write a brief description of one of the events. Call on volunteers to read their lists and descriptions aloud. **A, LEP**

Independent Practice (II) Have students use the events and dates in Section 3 to create a time line. Ask them to select one of the events and write a brief paragraph speculating about its impact on Texas. **TK, V**

The Debate in Congress. The United States Congress was faced with a difficult decision after the Mexican War. Congress had to decide if slavery would be allowed in the territory acquired from Mexico. In the Compromise of 1850, Congress sidestepped the issue. It declared that the people in the new territories would wait to decide about slavery until after they applied for statehood. The members of Congress realized that the regions of Arizona, Nevada, Utah, and New Mexico, which held few people, would not be ready for statehood for many years.

In 1854, the nation's eyes were on the Kansas and Nebraska territories. Congress had to determine if slaves would be allowed in these regions, which were ready to become states. A law called the Kansas-Nebraska Act passed, giving the people of Kansas and Nebraska the right to vote on the issue. If a majority voted for slavery, it would be legal to take slaves into the region. Most Texans and southerners were happy with this decision.

Texas' most famous leader in Washington, D.C., Senator Sam Houston, voted against the Kansas-Nebraska Act. He believed that allowing slavery to spread would split the North and South and eventually destroy the United States. In the North, people praised Sam Houston for his courage. People in the South, and particularly many Texans, said Houston was a traitor.

Emotions Run High. As Congress debated, people in Kansas began to fight each other over the slavery issue. Citizens in every region of the United States took sides. In the North, people made speeches denouncing the violence in Kansas and placing the blame on southern slaveholders. Southerners responded with speeches claiming that abolitionists were trying to destroy the southern way of life.

In 1854, the Republican party was formed. This new political party claimed that its major goal was to stop the spread of slavery and keep it out of the western United States. Southerners believed that the Republicans' real goal was to win control of the federal government and use this power to abolish slavery where it already existed. Citizens in the South were afraid that if a Republican was elected president, slavery would be ended and the southern economy would be ruined.

States' Rights and Secession. The debate over slavery raised an old question about the relationship between the

Massachusetts Historical Society

John Brown dreamed of freeing all slaves, but his ill-planned raid on Harpers Ferry failed. He was tried for treason and hanged, but his actions terrified many white southerners.

Have students work in pairs to create a cause-and-effect diagram of the events discussed in Section 3. Call on volunteers to copy their diagrams onto the chalkboard. **LEP**

CLOSURE
Ask students: What major events occurred in 1859 and 1860 that led to the secession of southern states *(John Brown's raid on Harpers Ferry and Lincoln's election)*? Based on what you have read, will Texas choose to secede *(yes)*?

ASSESSMENT
Have students complete the Section 3 Review on page 362.

SECTION   4

FOCUS
Past Learning (I) Review with students the status of the nation soon after Lincoln's election in 1860 *(six states had seceded from the Union)*. Ask: What decision now faced the people of Texas *(whether to secede as well)*?

Answers to Section 3 Review

Define: *states' rights*—view that each state had the right to determine whether to follow federal laws

Identify: Kansas-Nebraska Act—allowed Kansas and Nebraska to vote on the issue of slavery; John Brown—abolitionist who led an unsuccessful raid on Harpers Ferry and was later hanged; Abraham Lincoln—Republican president of the United States, elected in 1860

1. Most accused Houston of being a traitor.
2. To stop the spread of slavery to the western United States
3. Several southern states seceded from the Union.

Evaluating Information: Answers will vary but should be supported with sound reasoning.

Analyzing Information: Southerners believed that states chose to join the Union and that each state had the right to determine whether to follow federal law. According to this view, if the federal government tried to pass a law prohibiting slavery in any state, it was violating the property laws of the state. If a state chose to leave the Union, it had that right.

Essential Elements
2G, 2H, 5B, 6A, 7D, 7F, 9A, 9B

The Granger Collection

Abraham Lincoln's election as president started a chain reaction that led to secession of eleven states. Many white southerners feared that Lincoln would abolish slavery.

SECTION REVIEW

Define: states' rights
Identify: Kansas-Nebraska Act, John Brown, Abraham Lincoln

1. How did Texans react to Sam Houston's vote on the Kansas-Nebraska Act?
2. What was the main goal of the newly formed Republican party?
3. What happened as a result of Lincoln's victory in the election of 1860?

Evaluating Information: Do you think Congress made the right decision by passing the Kansas-Nebraska Act? Explain.

Analyzing Information: How did the southerners' beliefs about states' rights lead to secession?

---

federal government and the states. The southern point of view was that each state had the right to determine whether or not to follow federal laws. Most leaders in Texas and other states in the South took the view that if a state did not agree with a federal law, it could choose not to obey or enforce it. They also said that the nation had been formed when states chose freely to join the Union, or United States. If a state chose to leave the Union, it had that right.

Southern leaders applied this **states' rights** view to slavery. They said that the federal government had no right to pass laws keeping slavery out of any state or territory. If the federal government tried to do so, it would violate the state's property laws, and that state could then leave the Union.

The view of most leaders in the North was that states did not have the right to leave the Union. They also said that federal laws applied to all states in all cases.

Events soon led to southern states carrying out their threat to secede, or leave the Union. In 1859, an abolitionist named John Brown led a raid on Harpers Ferry, Virginia. He hoped to seize army supplies there to lead a slave revolt. Even though Brown's attempt failed and he was hanged, people throughout the South were seized with fear. Many white southerners believed that most people in the North supported Brown.

In the national election of 1860, Abraham Lincoln, a Republican, was elected president. To leaders in the South, Lincoln's election was unacceptable. The Republican party had no support in Texas or in the South. Southern leaders felt that Lincoln was not president of the whole country. They feared that his election meant that slavery would soon be abolished. As a result of Lincoln's victory, South Carolina became the first state to secede. Soon Mississippi, Florida, Alabama, Georgia, and Louisiana joined South Carolina in seceding. Now Texans faced the most important decision in their short history as a state. ✪

◪ The Secession Decision in Texas

John Brown's raid and the election of Abraham Lincoln alarmed a majority of Texas citizens. Some communities reacted violently against slaves, free blacks, and people suspected of being abolitionists. There were threats against many respected leaders in the state who opposed secession.

INSTRUCTION

Vocabulary (I) You may wish to preteach the following boldfaced terms: *ordinance* (p. 363); *allegiance* (p. 364). **LEP**

Illustrating (I) Provide students with blank outline maps of the United States dated March 2, 1861. Ask them to label the Confederate States of America. **V, TK**

Guided Practice (I) Conduct a mock election and ask students to vote for or against Texas secession. Collect and tally the votes on the chalkboard. Invite volunteers to express reasons for voting as they did. **A, LEP**

Independent Practice (II) Ask students to write a paragraph in response to the following question: In your opinion, what were the personal costs and benefits of Sam Houston's stand on secession? Invite volunteers to read their paragraphs aloud. **A**

The Unionists. The people who wanted to stay in the Union and try to work out differences over slavery were called Unionists. They spoke out against secession in the debate in Texas. A number of Unionists were well-known Texas leaders who had served the state for many years. Their number included Sam Houston, Elisha Pease, David Burnet, Andrew J. Hamilton, James W. Throckmorton, John Hancock, Edmund J. Davis, and George Hancock. Sam Houston was the leader of the Unionists. He ran for governor in 1857 and 1859 in order to strengthen the Unionist position and keep Texas in the United States. He won the election in 1859 and argued the Unionist cause from the governor's mansion in Austin.

Governor Houston, now nearly 70 years old, made a gallant effort to keep Texas in the United States. He claimed that secession would lead to a war in which North and South both would be losers. In one of his last speeches, Houston pleaded with the citizens of Texas:

> Some of you laugh to scorn the idea of bloodshed as the result of secession. But let me tell you what is coming. Your fathers and husbands, your sons and brothers, will be herded at the point of the bayonet. You may, after the sacrifice of countless millions of treasure and hundreds of thousands of lives, as a bare possibility, win Southern independence . . . but I doubt it. The North is determined to preserve this Union.

The Secession Convention. After South Carolina seceded, many Texas politicians called for a special meeting of the Texas legislature to consider secession. Governor Houston refused their request. Despite Houston's opposition, other leaders organized a secession convention to meet on January 28, 1861. The convention quickly adopted an **ordinance**, or order, of secession on February 1, 1861. This ordinance declared that the United States government had abused its power in order "to strike down the interest and prosperity of the people of Texas."

The secession convention scheduled an election among the people of Texas to see if they wished to leave the Union. On February 23, 1861, the people voted for secession by 44,317 to 13,020. Only in a few counties did a majority of people vote against it.

Texas Joins the Confederacy. Texas became the seventh state to secede from the United States. Representatives from the other six states met in Montgomery, Alabama, in

Painting by William Huddle.
Archives Division, Texas State Library

Governor Sam Houston was strongly opposed to secession and refused to support the Confederate government. He was removed from office in 1861 and retired to his home in Huntsville. He died in July 1863, deeply saddened about division of the nation and the horror of the Civil War. During the war he stated, "I wish no epitaph to be written to tell that I survived the ruin of this glorious Union."

RETEACHING

Ask each student to make up a matching review using names, terms, and identifications from Section 4. Have students exchange and complete the reviews. Allow partners to work together to check and correct their answers. **LEP**

CLOSURE

Ask students: Why did Texas secede from the Union?

ASSESSMENT

Have students complete the Section 4 Review on page 364.

Linking History and Geography
They depended heavily on slavery.

Answers to Section 4 Review

Define: *ordinance*—an order; *allegiance*—loyalty

Identify: Unionists—people who wanted to stay in the Union and work out differences over slavery; Confederate States of America—name of the new nation formed by the states that seceded from the Union; Jefferson Davis—president of the Confederacy; Edward Clark—replaced Sam Houston as governor of Texas in 1861

1. That it would lead to a war in which both sides would be losers
2. Voters chose to join the Confederacy.
3. He refused to take an oath of allegiance to the Confederacy.

Using Historical Imagination: Reactions will vary but might mention fear over possible war between the North and South.

Evaluating Information: Possible answer: He would not have been able to provide effective leadership if most people were against him.

364 *Unit 7*

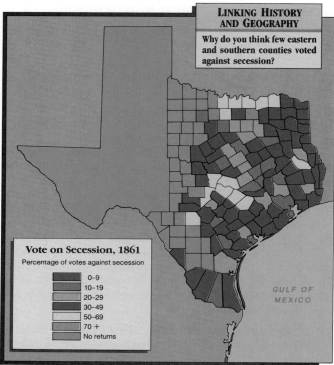

Austin History Center, Austin Public Library

Jefferson Davis was president of the Confederacy. Davis had served as one of Mississippi's senators in the United States Congress. This photograph was taken in 1865.

February of 1861 to form a new nation, the Confederate States of America. They elected a president, Jefferson Davis of Mississippi, and other officers to run the country. John H. Reagan of Texas was named postmaster general.

On March 5, 1861, the Texas Secession Convention voted officially to join the Confederacy. All state officials were required to take an oath of **allegiance**, or loyalty, to the Confederacy. Governor Sam Houston refused. Consequently, he was removed from office and replaced by Lieutenant Governor Edward Clark.

President Lincoln offered Houston the help of the federal government to remain in office if he so desired. But Houston declined the offer. He told his supporters that he would leave office peacefully because he loved Texas "too much to bring civil strife and bloodshed upon her." Sam and Margaret Houston quickly left Austin and retired to Huntsville. Sam Houston died on July 26, 1863, during the terrible war he had tried to prevent. ○

SECTION  REVIEW

Define: ordinance, allegiance
Identify: Unionists, Confederate States of America, Jefferson Davis, Edward Clark

1. What did Sam Houston predict would be the result of secession?
2. What was the result of the secession convention?
3. Why was Sam Houston forced from office as governor?

Using Historical Imagination: Imagine that you are a Texan in 1861 with relatives in the North. What is your reaction to Texas' having joined the Confederacy?

Evaluating Information: Did Sam Houston make the right decision in turning down Lincoln's offer of help? Why or why not?

LINKING HISTORY AND GEOGRAPHY

Why do you think few eastern and southern counties voted against secession?

Vote on Secession, 1861
Percentage of votes against secession

- 0–9
- 10–19
- 20–29
- 30–49
- 50–69
- 70 +
- No returns

GULF OF MEXICO

SPIRIT OF TEXAS

Texas Unionists

$\mathcal{S}$ome Texas Unionists claimed that the majority of Texans would have remained loyal to the Union if the true feelings of the people had been known. Andrew Jackson Hamilton, the United States congressman from Texas, charged that the Texas Secession Convention had been assembled illegally and that its actions were unconstitutional and revolutionary. He also said that the Secession Ordinance was approved through the use of threats and by means of indecent haste. In Travis County, where the state capital is located, the vote on the ordinance of secession was 436 for leaving the Union to 694 against. The district's judge, Alexander W. Terrell, reported that all of the counties in his judicial district voted against it. Historian Claude Elliott wrote in "Union Sentiment in Texas, 1861–1865" that only one-third of all Texans supported the war, while one-third wanted to stay in the Union and one-third remained neutral.

During the war, however, most Texans clearly resented Unionists. Perhaps the most despised Unionist in Texas was Edmund Jackson Davis, even though he was elected governor in 1869. A 1958 story about Davis in *The Houston Post* said:

> He fled to Mexico after refusing to take the oath of allegiance to the Confederacy. As a recruiter of Unionist Texans from Matamoros, he was captured once by Texans and narrowly missed hanging. He returned to Mexico but that government protested. So he spent the remainder of the war in Northern Louisiana with federal forces as a brigadier general. . . .
>
> He advocated disfranchisement [taking away the right to vote] of former Confederates and unrestricted Negro suffrage [the right to vote]. He led an almost successful movement to divide Texas into three states.

Even after the war ended, bitterness toward Texas Unionists lingered. Judge John Hancock, "a Union man," was accused in several Texas newspapers of being a traitor. But the *San Antonio Express* spoke in his defense on September 3, 1874: "Thank God, there were no 'traitors' during our late war. The American name has no such stain on either side. It was a war in which men were divided by honest convictions and sacred affections."

Inset: E. J. Davis, Right: A. J. Hamilton

Both photographs: Archives Division, Texas State Library

CHAPTER REVIEW RESOURCES

1. Chapter Review Worksheet 17
2. Chapter 17 Test, Form A
3. Reteaching Worksheet 17
4. Chapter 17 Test, Form B
5. **Informal Evaluation Forms:** Portfolio Assessment
6. *Texas, Our Texas* **Test Generator**

Essential Elements
2G, 2H, 5B, 5C, 7E, 7G, 8A, 8C, 9A, 9B

property laws of the states would be violated and these states could secede.
5. The Unionists were people who wanted to stay in the Union and try to work out differences. Houston was the Unionists' leader. He ran for governor to try to strengthen the Unionists' position and to keep Texas in the United States. As governor, he argued for the Unionists' cause.
6. John Brown's raid and the election of Abraham Lincoln alarmed many

CHAPTER 17 REVIEW ANSWERS

Understanding Main Ideas

1. Slaves provided cheap labor for the plantation owners.
2. Opposing: It was wrong for one person to own another, it was against the ideals of democracy and freedom, enslaved people had terrible lives and their families were often torn apart. In favor of: It was necessary for the economy, it had been practiced by great civilizations in history, farmers hoped to be wealthy plantation owners.
3. Slaves worked six days a week, could be sold and uprooted at any time, and were often separated from their families. Free blacks worked at the same occupations as many other Texans. Some owned farms or were businesspeople. Yet, because free blacks were regarded as a threat to slavery, whites did not treat them as equals. They could not vote or hold office, and many jobs were closed to them.
4. Southern states wished to protect their right to own slaves. They believed that each state had the right to determine whether to follow federal laws and that they had the right to leave the Union if they desired. According to this view, if the government tried to pass laws abolishing slavery in any state, the

Understanding Main Ideas

1. How were slaves necessary to the plantation system?
2. List three criticisms given by people opposing slavery and three reasons given in favor of slavery.
3. Compare the lives of slaves to the lives of free blacks.
4. Why did several states choose to secede, and how did they use the argument of states' rights?
5. Who were the Unionists, and how did Sam Houston fight for their cause?
6. What led to Texas' decision to secede?

Thinking Critically

1. **Analyzing Information:** Explain the relationship between states' rights and secession.
2. **Evaluating Information:** Did Sam Houston represent the views of most Texans on secession? Do you think he acted correctly in this case, or should government officials always represent the views of the people who elect them? Explain the reasons for your answer.
3. **Exploring Multicultural Perspectives:** How do you think the enslaved people in Texas reacted when Texas seceded? Why do you think this?

Linking History and Geography

1. Why do you think most plantations were in northern and eastern Texas?
2. Why was cotton grown in the South but not in northern states or Europe?

TAAS Practice
Using Primary Sources

The following description of a southern plantation was written by Frederick Law Olmsted, who traveled around the South in the 1850s:

They [house servants] live in brick cabins, adjoining the house and stables, and one of these, into which I have looked, is neatly and comfortably furnished.... Slaves brought up to housework dread to be employed at field labour; and those accustomed to the ... life of the negro settlement [field work], detest the close control and careful movements required of the house servants.

After a ride of several miles through the woods, in the rear of the plantations we came to his largest negro-settlement. ... Each cabin was a framed building, the walls boarded and whitewashed on the outside, lathed and plastered within, the roof shingled; forty-two feet long, twenty-one feet wide, divided into two family tenements, ... each tenement divided into three rooms. ... There was a brick fireplace in the middle of ... each living room. ... Each tenement is occupied, on an average, by five persons. ... Each cabin has a front and back door, and each room a window, closed by a wooden shutter.

1. Olmsted said slaves who worked in the fields did not want to be house servants because
   A house servants were very closely watched
   B field servants dreaded housework
   C field servants wanted to know just what was expected of them
   D field servants did not like brick cabins

Texans and caused them to consider seceding from the Union.

Thinking Critically

1. **Analyzing Information:** According to the view of states' rights, each state could determine whether to follow federal laws. If the government tried to force a law on the states, it was violating the rights of the states. Because the states had chosen to join the Union, they believed that they could leave the Union freely.

2. **Evaluating Information:** No. Answers to the second part of the question will vary but should be supported with sound reasoning.

3. **Exploring Multicultural Perspectives:** Answers will vary, but students should note that secession meant that Texans retained the right to hold slaves. Therefore, most enslaved people probably were not in favor of secession.

Linking History and Geography

1. Northern and eastern Texas had the best land and climate suitable for growing major cash crops such as cotton and sugarcane.
2. The climates of the northern states and Europe are not suitable for growing cotton. Cotton needs a warm climate in which to grow.

TAAS Practice
Using Primary Sources

1. A
2. B

TAAS Practice
Writing Descriptively

Entries will vary but should reflect information presented in the chapter.

Practicing Skills

1. **Interpreting Maps:** Counties with many slaves voted in favor of secession.
2. **Analyzing Information:** $7,000; $15.00 per slave per year. Answers to the third question will vary. Students might note that without the slave labor on the plantation, the overseer would not have a job.

Enriching Your Study of History

1. **Individual Project:** Posters will vary but should be visually appealing and should demonstrate further research.
2. **Cooperative Project:** Newspapers will vary but should demonstrate accurate information regarding secession and slavery.
3. **Cooperative Project:** Oral reports should be well organized and demonstrate careful research.

---

2. From the description of the slaves' tenements we can conclude
   - **A** that slaves were unhappy with their homes
   - **B** that the tenements were crowded
   - **C** that slaves took good care of the tenements
   - **D** that slaves did not get enough air

TAAS Practice
Writing Descriptively

Imagine that you are a slave on a plantation in East Texas. Write a diary entry at the end of a typical Sunday, describing what you did, with whom you spent time, and what your plans are for next week.

Practicing Skills

1. **Interpreting Maps:** Study the maps on pages 359 and 364. What conclusion can you draw about the relationship between counties with many slaves and the way those counties voted regarding secession?
2. **Analyzing Information:** Study the plantation budget on this page. What was the value of the cotton produced by the slaves? How much, total, was spent to feed and clothe each slave? Compare this cost to the wages of an overseer. Who do you think was more necessary to the economy of the plantation, a slave or an overseer? Why?

Enriching Your Study of History

1. **Individual Project:** Use the library to find out more about the lives either of plantation owners or of slaves. Then use the information you learned to create a poster illustrating the life of a plantation owner or a slave.

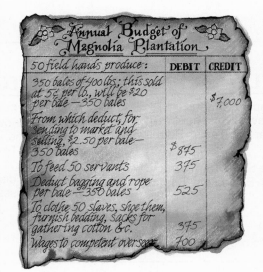

Annual Budget of Magnolia Plantation

50 field hands produce:	DEBIT	CREDIT
350 bales of 400 lbs.; this sold at 5¢ per lb., will be $20 per bale—350 bales		$7,000
From which deduct, for sending to market and selling, $2.50 per bale—350 bales	$875	
To feed 50 servants	375	
Deduct bagging and rope per bale—350 bales	525	
To clothe 50 slaves, shoe them, furnish bedding, sacks for gathering cotton &c.	375	
Wages to competent overseer	700	

2. **Cooperative Project:** The teacher will divide your class into several small groups. Work together to create the front page of a Texas newspaper on the day the Texans voted to secede. You might include articles describing the events leading up to secession, information from the map on page 364, editorials about the role of slavery in Texas, and a prediction of where secession will lead. Your teacher will display each group's newspaper page in the classroom.

3. **Cooperative Project:** With a partner, conduct research on African American spirituals to produce an oral report for your class. If you can find recordings of some of these songs, play them as part of your report. Also, make copies of the words to a spiritual, give them to your classmates, and teach them to sing the song.

TEXAS AND THE CIVIL WAR

TEACHER'S TIME LINE

Section 1	Section 2	Section 3	Review and Assessment
Pp. 368–73	Pp. 373–78	Pp. 378–83	
1 Day	1 Day	1 Day	1 Day

TEACHER MATERIALS

Core: Chapter 18 Time Line; Graphic Organizer 18; Enrichment Worksheet 18; Review Worksheet 18; Reteaching Worksheet 18; Chapter 18 Tests, Forms A & B

Additional: Geography and Graph Skills 18, Map and Chart Transparencies 18, Informal Evaluation Forms, Test Generator

OBJECTIVES

1. Discuss the Union plan to conquer the Confederacy.
2. Explain how Texans contributed to the war effort at home and in battle.
3. Identify Texans who played important roles in the Civil War.
4. List and discuss important battles fought in Texas.
5. Identify issues facing Texas at the end of the Civil War.

RESOURCES

BOOKS FOR TEACHERS

Burke, Benjamine F. *Letters of Pvt. Benjamine F. Burke: Written While in the Terry's Texas Rangers.* Austin: Barker Texas History Center, 1985. Primary source account of a Texas Ranger.

Foster, Samuel T. *One of Cleburne's Command: The Civil War Reminiscences and Diary of Capt. Samuel T. Foster, Granbury's Texas Brigade.* Austin: University of Texas Press, 1980. Primary source account of the Civil War.

Franklin, John Hope. *The Emancipation Proclamation.* Garden City: Anchor Books, 1963. Examination of the effects of this important proclamation.

Gragg, Rod. *The Illustrated Confederate Reader.* New York: Harper & Row, 1989. Collection of personal experiences, eyewitness accounts, and interesting facts by and about southern soldiers and civilians.

Seraile, William. *New York's Black Regiment During the Civil War.* New York: City University, 1977. Description of participation and bravery of black soldiers during the Civil War.

Tapert, Annette, ed. *The Brothers' War: Civil War Letters to Their Loved Ones from the Blue and Gray.* New York: Vintage Books, 1989. Primary source accounts of the Civil War.

MULTIMEDIA MATERIALS

American History Keyword Series. Civil War Keyword. (software) Focus Media, Inc., 839 Stewart Avenue, P.O. Box 865, Garden City, New York, 11530. Vocabulary builder related to important people and events of the Civil War.

Crisis of Union. (video, 30 min.) PBS Video, 1320 Braddock Place, Alexandria, Virginia, 22314. Examination of the causes leading to the Civil War.

A Frightful Conflict. (video, 30 min.) PBS Video, 1320 Braddock Place, Alexandria, Virginia, 22314. Examination of the military conflicts of the Civil War.

STUDENTS WITH SPECIAL NEEDS

Limited English Proficient Students (LEP)

Have students work independently or in pairs. Ask them to select one of the sections of Chapter 18 and create a collage to illustrate the topics discussed. Tell them to use their own drawings as well as pictures cut from magazines and newspapers. See other activities labeled **LEP.**

Students Having Difficulty with the Chapter

Pair students who are having difficulty with students who are performing well. Have students skim the chapter to find key terms, events, place names, and persons mentioned. Have them write the terms and names on one side of a series of index cards. They should write a brief definition or identification on the other side. Have each pair use the cards as flashcards until both students have mastered the definitions and identifications. **LEP**

Auditory Learners

Have auditory learners create a series of questions to use in a "Who Am I?" game. They should develop the game so that the entire class can play it when reviewing for the chapter test. See other activities labeled **A.**

Visual Learners

Have visual learners present a report to the class comparing and contrasting the images of war conveyed in various media, including paintings, photographs, television, and movies. Ask them to bring in references from the library containing photographs by Mathew Brady, considered one of the greatest photographers of the Civil War. See other activities labeled **V.**

Tactile/Kinesthetic Learners

Pair tactile/kinesthetic learners and have them draw a series of political cartoons that might have appeared in a Texas newspaper during the Civil War. Ask them to display and discuss their cartoons. See other activities labeled **TK.**

Gifted Students

Assign the following topic to gifted students: *Geography and the Civil War.* Ask them to investigate and report on how geography influenced the war strategy of the Union. Did Union strategy work? See other activities labeled **G.**

VOCABULARY

In addition to the boldfaced terms in each section, some students might benefit from discussing the meanings of these terms.

Section 1: *reunite* (p. 368); *cavalry* (p. 370); *distinction* (p. 371).

Section 2: *militia* (p. 373); *retreat* (p. 374); *mainland* (p. 375); *transports* (p. 376); *morale* (p. 377).

Section 3: *scarce* (p. 378); *parched* (p. 378); *brigadier general* (p. 380); *valor* (p. 380); *proclamation* (p. 382).

CHRONOLOGY

Have students study the Chapter 18 Time Line and identify relationships among the events.

GRAPHIC ORGANIZER

Have students skim the chapter and complete the Chapter 18 Graphic Organizer. *(You might wish to use this activity to review rather than to introduce the chapter.)*

ENRICHMENT

Have students complete the Chapter 18 Enrichment Worksheet.

Past Learning (I) Use the following brainstorming activity to assess the extent of students' knowledge of the Civil War. Write *Civil War* on the chalkboard. Ask students to name people who they think had some role in the war. Write each response on the board and give a brief identification of the person. Use the same procedure to elicit names of battles, types of weapons used, battle sites, and so on.

Vocabulary (I) You may wish to preteach the following boldfaced terms: *regiments* (p. 369); *draft* (p. 369); *blockade* (p. 372). **LEP**

CHAPTER 18 OVERVIEW

The Civil War began when South Carolina troops fired on the United States Army at Fort Sumter in Charleston Harbor. Having seceded from the Union, South Carolina considered the fort its property. President Abraham Lincoln soon called for additional troops to end what he considered a rebellion by southern states. But the southern states were determined to establish an independent country. Chapter 18 examines Texas' role in the Civil War, the battles fought on Texas soil, and the impact of the war on the state and its people.

Essential Elements
2G, 2H, 5B, 6A, 9A, 9B, 9G

CHAPTER 18

TEXAS AND THE CIVIL WAR

The Story Continues...

The Civil War began in April 1861, when South Carolina troops fired on Fort Sumter, held by the U.S. Army. President Abraham Lincoln was determined to use force if necessary to keep the Union together. For four years, soldiers from the United States and from the Confederate States of America fought one another. More than 600,000 Americans died in the war. Thousands of others at home suffered losses and sacrifices. In this chapter you will read about the role Texans played in the Civil War.

As you read the chapter, look for the answers to these questions:

1. How did Texans respond to the call to battle?
2. What important battles of the Civil War were fought in Texas?
3. What were the experiences of Texans who stayed home during the war?

Archives Division, Texas State Library

Francis R. Lubbock was elected governor in 1861. Lubbock had held a number of public offices before he defeated Edward Clark in the election for governor. He did not seek reelection, and in 1864, he became an assistant to Confederate president Jefferson Davis.

1 The War Begins

When the war began, the Confederacy faced great disadvantages that the United States did not face. The North had a population of about 22 million, compared to about 9 million in the South. Among the South's population were about 3.5 million slaves, who could not be expected to fight to keep slavery. The North had more miles of railroads and far more factories than did the South.

The major resources of the South were its leaders and the determination of its people. Many military leaders who joined the Confederate forces had been among the best officers in the United States Army. Many young men in the South, and especially in Texas, were experienced in riding horses and using firearms. Also, the South was fighting on its own land. Union troops had to invade the Confederacy in their effort to reunite the country.

Analysis (I) Pose the following questions for class discussion: Do you think it was wrong for the United States government to use force to try to preserve the Union? Was there an alternative? Allow time for students to present varying viewpoints. **A**

Illustrating (I) Point out to students that the Civil War was portrayed as glamorous and exciting in posters and advertisements. Have students work in small groups to create posters that might have been used to recruit volunteers in Texas. Have each group display and discuss its posters. **A, V, TK, LEP**

The Granger Collection

In this lithograph, Jefferson Davis is with his cabinet in the council chamber at Richmond, Virginia, the capital of the Confederacy. Davis is seated at center left, and General Robert E. Lee, the commander of Confederate forces, stands in the center.

Texans Answer the Call. When word reached Texas that the war had begun, thousands of Texans joined the Confederate army. Many people in Texas and other parts of the South believed it was wrong for the federal government to use force against states wishing to leave the United States. After Lincoln's call for troops, four additional states seceded, bringing the total in the Confederacy to eleven.

By late September 1861, ten Texas **regiments**, units of around 1,000 troops, had been organized. In the next few months, Governor Lubbock reported that fifteen more regiments of Texans were in service. At first, service in the army was voluntary. But this method failed to provide enough troops for the Confederate forces.

In April 1862, the Confederate government passed a conscription act, or a **draft**, by which people were required by law to serve in the military. The law required all healthy white males between eighteen and 35 years of age to serve

Biography

John Bell Hood was 29 years old when the Civil War started. Born in Kentucky, he resigned from the Union Army to take command of the 4th Texas Infantry, which took the name Hood's Texas Brigade. Hood believed in fighting alongside his troops. He was wounded in the arm at Gettysburg, and he lost his right leg at the Battle of Chickamauga.

In July 1864, Hood took over as commander of the Army of Tennessee. After a crushing defeat at Nashville, a Union officer said of Hood's leadership abilities, "I doubt if any soldiers in the world ever needed so much cumulative evidence to convince them they were beaten."

Lawrence Jones Collection

This photograph shows two young Texas soldiers in Confederate uniforms. The Civil War was fought by young men, many not even eighteen years old.

when called. The age limit was later broadened to include white males between seventeen and 50 years of age. There was some dissatisfaction with the draft law among Texans because it allowed exemptions, or exceptions. Persons holding public office and those considered important in industry and agriculture were exempted from the draft. Also, those drafted could hire a substitute to serve in their place. Those who could not afford substitutes commonly resented this provision of the law.

Despite any dissatisfaction with the draft laws, a very high percentage of Texans joined the fight. At some time during the war, around 60,000 Texans were members of the Confederate forces. Other states with larger populations sent more soldiers, but there were only about 92,000 white males between the ages of eighteen and 45 in the entire Texas population in 1860.

Texans usually joined units from their hometowns or local areas. The units took the names of people who organized or commanded them. Among the best-known Texas units were Terry's Texas Rangers, Hood's Texas Brigade, and Ross' Texas Brigade. These units fought in many battles outside Texas. Terry's Rangers, led by B. F. Terry, was a cavalry unit that fought in more battles than

Painting by Carl von Iwonski, San Antonio Museum Association

Terry's Texas Rangers, a well-known Confederate cavalry unit, saw a great deal of action during the war. When the unit organized, Terry's Rangers numbered about 1,000 men. At the end of the war, only about a third of them were alive.

The Granger Collection

This lithograph by Kurz and Allison commemorates the Battle of Shiloh, Tennessee, in 1862. Many Texans took part in the fighting of this major Civil War battle.

any other unit in the Confederate army. It lost two-thirds of its members during the war, including its commander.

Texas contributed many talented officers to the Confederate cause. Among them were more than 130 generals and colonels. The highest-ranking Texan in the Confederate army was Albert Sidney Johnston. The Confederate commander, Robert E. Lee, called Johnston the South's finest military leader. Johnston was the second-highest ranking officer in the Confederate army at the time he was killed at the Battle of Shiloh, Tennessee, in 1862. Other notable Texas leaders were John B. Hood, John Wharton, Thomas Green, Felix H. Robertson, and Samuel Bell Maxey.

Thousands of less well-known Texans served with distinction during the war. Texas troops gained a reputation for spirit and daring in battle. But they paid a terrible price for their courage. The exact number of Texans killed and wounded is not known, but it is estimated to have been around 20,000.

Texas in the War. After the firing on Fort Sumter, the plans of the United States to conquer the Confederate states began to unfold. Union forces intended to invade Virginia to capture Richmond, the capital of the Confederacy. At

Brown Brothers

Albert Sidney Johnston was appointed a general in the Confederate army. He was the highest-ranking Texan on the Confederate side. The South suffered a great loss when he was killed at the Battle of Shiloh.

RETEACHING
Have each student use the names, terms, and events from Section 1 to create a word puzzle. *(You may wish to show students samples of various kinds of word puzzles.)* Have students exchange the puzzles with a partner. After completing the puzzles, partners should work together to check and correct their answers. **LEP, A**

CLOSURE
Present the following scenario to students: You are a Texan who has volunteered to fight in the Confederate army. Considering the disadvantages facing the South, do you believe that the South can win? Tell students to consider all of the material in Section 1 before responding. Allow time for students to present varying opinions.

the same time, Union forces planned to take control of the Mississippi River. This would cut the Confederacy in two, separating Arkansas, Texas, and part of Louisiana from other southern states. To cripple the South's economy, the Union navy would **blockade**, or block, ports in the Confederate states so ships could not enter or leave. The blockade was to extend from Virginia to Florida on the Atlantic coast and from Florida to the southern tip of Texas.

The war was fought on land in three areas. The heaviest fighting took place in Virginia between Washington, D.C., and Richmond. A second major battleground developed in Tennessee. The third area of fighting was west of the Mississippi River, and this included Texas. While Texas was not at the center of the Civil War, the state played a major role. Its soldiers fought not only in their own state, but also in major battles in all areas. President Jefferson Davis welcomed the first Texas troops to Richmond in 1861 with the words, "Texans! The troops from other States have their reputation to gain, but the sons of the defenders of the Alamo have theirs to maintain. I am sure you will be faithful

Linking History and Geography
24

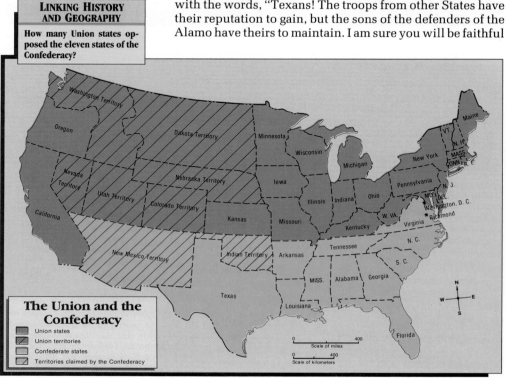

LINKING HISTORY AND GEOGRAPHY

How many Union states opposed the eleven states of the Confederacy?

The Union and the Confederacy
- Union states
- Union territories
- Confederate states
- Territories claimed by the Confederacy

ASSESSMENT
Have students complete the Section 1 Review on page 373.

SECTION 2

FOCUS

Predicting (I) On a wall map of Texas, place stars where key Civil War battles were fought. Help students brainstorm about reasons for the Union army seeking to control Texas from these points. Tell students to keep their hypotheses in mind as they read Section 2.

Painting by Bruce Marshall

This painting captures the break-through of Hood's Texas Brigade at Gaines' Mill on June 27, 1862.

to the trust." Hood's Texas Brigade became the leading unit in Robert E. Lee's Army of Northern Virginia, and it fought in some of the most important battles of the war.

At times, Texans found themselves fighting against units in which they had served before secession. At Gaines' Mill, Virginia, Hood's Texas Brigade was charged by a unit of United States cavalry in which Hood had once served. A Confederate officer later wrote:

> At the most desperate moment of the fight, Captain Whiting who had been Hood's captain on the frontier of Texas, and was now leading the charge, had his horse shot from under him, and fell stunned at the feet of Hood's men and was taken prisoner. . . . [Later, a Union captain] begged that word be carried to Hood, that his old friend and fellow-soldier in the Second Cavalry, Captain Chambliss, was lying on the battle-field desperately wounded. The word was brought to Hood and he immediately sent a messenger to tell the captain [Chambliss] he would come as soon as possible, and instructed him to give all possible aid to the wounded man. ☼

2 Battles in Texas and the Southwest

Texas moved to seize several United States military posts even before the state had officially seceded. Militia commanded by Ben McCulloch, Henry McCulloch, and John S. Ford accepted the surrender of Major General David E. Twiggs, commander of United States forces in Texas. Without firing a shot, the Texas militia took about ten

SECTION 1 REVIEW

Define: regiments, draft, blockade
Identify: B.F. Terry, Albert Sidney Johnston, Robert E. Lee, John B. Hood

1. Why did the Confederate government pass a draft law?
2. Why did the Union forces plan to take control of the Mississippi River?

Making Decisions: Would you have volunteered to fight for the Confederacy? Why or why not?

Analyzing Information: Why do you think Jefferson Davis reminded Texans of the Battle of the Alamo?

Answers to Section 1 Review

Define: *regiments*—military units of around 1,000 troops; *draft*—an act by which people are required by law to serve in the military; *blockade*—to block

Identify: B.F. Terry—leader of the Texas unit known as Terry's Texas Rangers; Albert Sidney Johnston—highest-ranking Texan in the Confederate army; Robert E. Lee—commander of the Confederate forces; John B. Hood—notable Texas leader who served in the Confederate army

1. Not enough men volunteered for the army.
2. They wanted to weaken the Confederacy by dividing it.

Making Decisions: Answers will vary. Students should give reasons for their answers.

Analyzing Information: Davis knew that by reminding them of the Alamo he could appeal to Texans to fight hard and give their all.

Essential Elements
2G, 2H, 5A, 5B, 9A, 9B, 9D

INSTRUCTION

Historical Imagination (I) Have students select one of the battles fought in Texas. Ask them to assume the role of a Confederate or Union soldier and write a letter home describing the battle. Invite volunteers to read their letters aloud. **A**

Geography (I) Organize the class into small groups. To highlight the importance of the geographic theme of *place*, assign each group a battle fought in Texas and the Southwest. Have groups research how the physical geography of the area, including its weather, might have influenced the outcome of the battle. Ask each group to create a map to illustrate its findings and then give a brief presentation to the class. **A, V, TK**

Archives Division, Texas State Library

This photograph shows the surrender of General Twiggs' Union army to a force of Texas Confederate militia at San Antonio.

percent of the United States Army and between $3 million and $6 million in military supplies.

The New Mexico Campaign. Shortly after the war started, Texas forces led by Colonel John Baylor marched into southern New Mexico. Baylor claimed the area, as well as Arizona, for the Confederacy. In January 1862, General Henry H. Sibley took three Texas regiments to secure northern New Mexico for the Confederacy. The goal of General Sibley and the Texans was to take control of the Southwest from New Mexico to California. By doing so, the Confederacy would gain the wealth of gold and silver mines there, as well as ports on the Pacific Ocean.

Marching north from Mesilla, New Mexico, Sibley's army won a battle over Union forces at Valverde. They continued north along the Rio Grande, seizing Albuquerque and Santa Fe. Gradually, however, the army was weakened by disease and by lack of food and water.

United States forces were gathering to attack Sibley's army and cut it off from Texas. Union troops from Colorado met part of Sibley's force at Glorieta Pass, and a fierce battle followed in which the Confederate supply train was destroyed. Sibley and his small army were forced to retreat to Texas, and Union forces kept control of the Southwest for the rest of the war.

Fighting at Galveston Island. During July 1861, the Union navy began to blockade Texas ports. Ports in other Confederate states had been blockaded, and some captured, by the Union. In October 1862, a Union fleet sailed into

Barker Texas History Center

General Henry H. Sibley led three Texas Confederate regiments into New Mexico in early 1862. Sibley's goal of controlling the Southwest was crushed when Union forces defeated his army at Glorieta Pass.

Illustrating (I) Have students work in small groups to create a pictorial essay of "Battles in Texas and the Southwest." Allow time for groups to display and discuss their projects. **A, V, TK, LEP**

Guided Practice (I) Have students work individually or in pairs to create a time line showing battles in Texas and the Southwest. Have them list Confederate victories above the line and Union victories below. **V, TK, LEP**

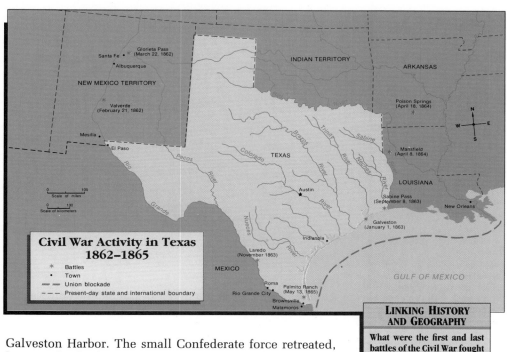

Civil War Activity in Texas 1862–1865

* Battles
• Town
— — Union blockade
- - - Present-day state and international boundary

LINKING HISTORY AND GEOGRAPHY

What were the first and last battles of the Civil War fought in Texas?

Galveston Harbor. The small Confederate force retreated, leaving the harbor in Union hands. Galveston was the most important seaport in Texas and was vital to the Confederacy. The commander of forces in Texas, General John B. Magruder, made plans to recapture it.

Two steamboats were converted to gunboats by Magruder's men. Troops led by Tom Green boarded the boats, whose sides were lined with cotton bales to protect the riflemen. The two boats, the *Neptune* and the *Bayou City*, were to attack Union ships in the harbor at the same time the forces crossed from the mainland to attack the Union forces in Galveston.

In the early morning hours of January 1, 1863, Magruder's attack began. The *Bayou City* rammed a Union ship in the harbor, sinking it. Confederate land forces overran the Union troops in Galveston and captured several hundred Union soldiers. The city of Galveston was again under Confederate control.

The Battle of Sabine Pass. In the summer of 1863, United States leaders made plans to invade Texas through

EXTENSION
Research (II) Ask interested students to research and report on (1) one of the battles of the Civil War, (2) military
uniforms of the period, or (3) weapons used by both sides
in the war. Encourage students to supplement their reports
with drawings or other illustrations. **A, V, TK, G**

Institute of Texan Cultures

**Confederate success at the Battle of
Sabine Pass was an important victory
for the South. This view of the battle
was drawn by an eyewitness.**

Biography
Lieutenant Richard W. Dowling
was a 25-year-old, redheaded
businessman from Houston. He
had come to the United States
as a child, fleeing the potato
famine in County Galway,
Ireland.

Sabine Pass. This is the outlet of the Sabine and Neches
rivers into the Gulf of Mexico. General William B. Franklin
and about 5,000 troops sailed from New Orleans, which
had been captured earlier in the war by the Union. Franklin
hoped to land his army near Sabine City and then march
overland to attack Houston and Beaumont.

Sabine Pass was guarded by Fort Sabine, also called Fort
Griffin. This small post was surrounded only by earthworks,
or trenches and protective mounds. The garrison of the fort
consisted of around 40 soldiers known as the Davis Guards.
They were led by Lieutenant Richard Dowling. Although
small, the fort had six cannons, and the soldiers had
practiced for a long time hitting targets in the pass.

On September 8, 1863, Union gunboats and several
transports attacked Sabine Pass. General Franklin planned
to have the gunboats silence Fort Griffin so that his troops
could land. The Union gunboats shelled Fort Griffin for
more than an hour. Dowling and his men held their fire
until the Union gunboats were close, then opened up with
the cannons. Two of the gunboats were hit and later
captured. The rest of the Union ships turned back. In the
short but fierce fight, the United States lost about 65
soldiers. Dowling and his forces captured more than 300,
marking a complete victory for the Confederacy.

Independent Practice (I) Have students use the information in Section 2 to create a five-column chart titled "Battles in Texas and the Southwest." Students should write the following headings across the top of the chart: *Battle, Confederate Leader, Union Leader, Goal of Battle, Results of Battle.* **V, TK, LEP**

RETEACHING
Ask students to survey the illustrations and captions in this section. Ask them to write a brief paragraph explaining how the illustrations supplement the written text. Allow time for students to discuss their responses. **LEP, V, A**

The victory at Sabine Pass excited people in Texas and the rest of the South. The Confederacy had lost two major battles during the summer. Now, the Battle of Sabine Pass helped restore morale. Lieutenant Dowling and his troops were given special medals for their actions by order of President Jefferson Davis.

The Coast and South Texas.   Despite victories at Sabine Pass and Galveston, Texas was not safe from Union forces. Two months after the Battle of Sabine Pass, the Union army and navy captured Brazos Island off the mouth of the Rio Grande. The goal of the Union forces was to capture Brownsville and stop trade between Texas and Mexico. Texans were shipping cotton and other goods to Mexico to avoid the blockade. Mexico was providing Texas with war supplies in return, then shipping the Texas goods to other countries and to the United States.

From Brazos Island, the Union troops captured weakly defended Brownsville. After taking Brownsville, they sailed northward along the coast, capturing St. Joseph and Matagorda islands and occupying Indianola.

In November 1863, Edmund J. Davis of Texas, leading forces for the Union, captured Rio Grande City and Roma along the Mexican border. But his attack on Laredo failed against Texas troops led by Santos Benavides.

When Union forces were called away from Brownsville for an attack into northeastern Texas, Colonel John S. Ford recaptured the town. Some Union troops remained on Brazos Island, but none remained on the mainland.

The Red River Campaign.   By 1864, the United States army was in control of New Orleans and other areas of Louisiana. In the spring of 1864, it planned to use its Louisiana base to attack northeastern Texas along the Red River. An army led by General Nathaniel P. Banks moved northwest up the river toward Texas, hoping to link with another Union army moving south from Arkansas.

On April 8, 1864, Confederate units from Texas, Arkansas, Louisiana, and Missouri intercepted General Banks at Mansfield, Louisiana. The Confederate victory over a large opponent forced Banks to turn back. On April 18, Confederate units, including many Texas troops, defeated the second Union army at Poison Springs, Arkansas. The Union armies were never able to join forces, and Texas was once again saved from invasion.

Point out to students that the Civil War is considered the nation's first "modern war" because of the innovations in weaponry and warfare used. *(You might wish to invite a volunteer to investigate this further and report back to the class.)*

ASSESSMENT

Have students complete the Section 2 Review on page 378.

FOCUS

Predicting (I) Ask students to imagine that they are financial advisers in Texas in 1861. Tell them that they are being asked to predict the economic consequences of the war for Texas. Copy their responses on the chalkboard. Have students check the accuracy of their predictions after completing the study of Section 3.

Answers to Section 2 Review

Identify: Colonel John Baylor—led the forces that marched into southern New Mexico, claiming that area as well as Arizona for the Confederacy; Tom Green—led the troops that recaptured Galveston; Lieutenant Richard Dowling—led Confederate forces at Sabine Pass; Santos Benavides—led the Texas troops that successfully resisted Davis' attack on Laredo

1. To gain the area's wealth of gold and silver mines and ports on the Pacific Ocean
2. Two converted battleships attacked Galveston from the harbor while troops attacked from the land, surrounding Union soldiers.
3. To stop trade between Texas and Mexico
4. Confederate troops intercepted Banks in Louisiana, forcing him to turn back. He was unable to link up with a second Union army—which Texas troops later defeated—that was moving south from Arkansas.
5. The Battle at Palmito Ranch

(Continued on page 379)

Essential Elements
2G, 2H, 3A, 6A, 8A, 8B, 9A, 9B

Caption Response
The Union blockade caused a severe shortage of most goods.

SECTION 2 REVIEW

Identify: Colonel John Baylor, Tom Green, Lieutenant Richard Dowling, Santos Benavides

1. Why did Texans want to control the area from New Mexico to California?
2. How did Texans recapture Galveston from the Union troops?
3. Why did Union forces want to capture Brownsville?
4. How were Confederate troops able to keep Texas from being invaded by General Banks and his army?
5. What was the last battle of the Civil War?

Exploring Economics: How did Texas depend on Mexico during the war?

Writing Informatively: Write the telegram that might have been sent to President Jefferson Davis after the Battle of Sabine Pass.

Taylor Johnson

Confederate money fell in value as the war continued, and the prices of almost everything soared. Why did prices inflate, or rise, so dramatically during the war?

Battle at Palmito Ranch. On May 12, 1865, units of the Union army moved inland once again to occupy Brownsville. The next day, they collided with Confederate troops led by John S. Ford at Palmito Ranch. In the victory, Ford's troops captured over 100 Union prisoners. From them Ford learned that General Robert E. Lee, commanding the main Confederate army in Virginia, had been forced to surrender more than one month earlier. The last shot of the Civil War may have been fired at the Palmito Ranch battle, but the Confederacy had already lost the war. ○

3 The War Years at Home

Texas was removed from the major battles of the Civil War and suffered little of the damage experienced by other Confederate states. Its cities were not invaded or burned, nor were its roads, railroads, and bridges destroyed as they had been in Virginia, Tennessee, North Carolina, and other states. Still, the war had great impact on the lives of Texans. They had to make sacrifices to feed and equip an army. Many families suffered because husbands, fathers, brothers, and sons had been killed in the fighting.

Wartime Economy. The Union blockade gradually became more effective as the war went on. Ships known as blockade runners sometimes slipped past the Union navy, but they were unable to carry on regular trade. Most goods once shipped into Texas from northern factories could no longer be found. Dresses, shoes, suits, and similar goods became very scarce. Because they were scarce, the price of such goods rose ever higher. Soon, few Texans could afford to buy the few goods available. Many newspapers stopped operation because of lack of paper. Salt and medicines were always in short supply. Shortages caused by the blockade became more severe because supplies had to be sent to the armies of the Confederacy within Texas, as well as to those fighting in other southern states.

Texans soon learned to adapt to the shortages. When coffee was not available or was too expensive, people used parched peanuts, sweet potatoes, rye, or okra to make drinks. The ashes of corncobs were used to make a type of soda for washing and bleaching clothes. Texans began to make more homespun clothing. According to Mrs. E. M. Loughery, "Good cloth was not to be had except in very

INSTRUCTION

Vocabulary (I) You may wish to preteach the following boldfaced terms: *martial law* (p. 381); *assassinated* (p. 382). **LEP**

Analysis (I) Ask students to use the information in Section 3 to refute or defend the following statement: "For Texas, the war created more problems than it solved." Have them write their responses in a brief paragraph. Ask volunteers to read their paragraphs aloud. **A**

Synthesis (I) Tell students to imagine the following: You are a woman whose husband or son is a Confederate soldier. Write a letter to him expressing your bitter feelings about some Texas Unionists and the newly formed Peace party. Tell him what you will do to assist in the war effort. Invite volunteers to read their letters aloud. **A**

small quantities and at fabulous prices. Calico of the best quality cost $50 per yard, Confederate money." Women made their hats from corn husks and straw.

Because Texas was not overrun by the United States army, agriculture remained quite productive during the war. To feed the army, farmers were urged to grow more corn and wheat and less cotton. Women, as well as children and men not able to serve in the army, took on added responsibilities to run farms and plantations. The number of slaves increased during the war, as slaveholders in other states sent slaves to Texas to prevent their being freed by Union forces. With all of this labor, good crops were raised every year.

Women played other roles in keeping the economy going during the war. They worked in small factories or made items at home. Women organized special groups to support the war effort. These groups made uniforms, bandages, and medical supplies. They also provided aid and support for soldiers' families. Black women also shared in the hardships of war. Not only did they work long hours spinning thread, but like Anglo women they often had to endure the absence of their loved ones. Some of these attended their masters in the battlefield. Others ran away and joined the Union forces.

Texas became an important center of trade for the Confederacy because it bordered Mexico. Because the Union navy did not blockade Mexican ports, goods were shipped across the Rio Grande to Mexico and exchanged for needed supplies. Many Texas products were sent to the Mexican port of Matamoros.

To produce war supplies, Texas established new industries when the war began. Thomas Anderson operated a mill near Austin to produce gunpowder. A factory in Tyler made cannons and ammunition. Iron foundries were opened in Jefferson and Rusk. Workers at the state penitentiary at Huntsville produced a million and a half yards of cloth per year. Smaller industries scattered about the state made wagons, saddles, uniforms, and tents. Texas' plentiful resources of cotton and cattle provided fiber, leather, and meat. But as the Mississippi River fell under Union control, it became difficult to ship items east.

Wartime Political Activity. Once the Civil War began, political party differences and activity in Texas ceased.

Exploring Economics: When Union forces blockaded ports along the Texas coast, Texans kept their economy healthy by trading with Mexico.

Writing Informatively: Telegrams will vary but should reflect the spirit of elation at the victory.

Austin History Center, Austin Public Library

Anderson Mill was built in 1863 by Thomas Anderson. The mill was used as a factory for gunpowder.

Guided Practice (I) Have students use the information in Section 3 to create a two-column chart labeled: *Economic Problems, Solutions.* **V, TK, LEP**

EXTENSION

Historical Imagination (II) Ask interested students to conduct further research on one of the issues affecting Texans at home during the war, such as shortages, the draft, or relations with slaves. Have students work together to write and present skits based on their findings. **A, V, TK, G**

Independent Practice (II) Tell students to imagine that they are abolitionists in Texas in 1863. Ask them to write a letter to a northern friend expressing their feelings about the Emancipation Proclamation and their worries about the future of freed slaves. Invite volunteers to read their letters aloud. **A**

Archives Division, Texas State Library

Pendleton Murrah was governor of Texas during the difficult closing years of the Civil War. He fled to Mexico when the Confederate armies surrendered in 1865. He died in Monterrey in July of that year.

Texas Historical Foundation

Elisha M. Pease was governor of Texas during the 1850s. He opposed the Confederacy and took little part in public life during the war.

Historical Sidelight
Many Unionists fled Texas early in the war, some to Matamoros, Mexico, where they were rescued by Union ships. Some Unionists hid in isolated places such as the Big Thicket in East Texas.

The most important issue was the war. All office holders strongly supported the Confederate cause.

In the election of 1861, Francis R. Lubbock defeated Edward Clark in the race for governor. In the same election, representatives were chosen to serve in the Confederate Congress in Richmond, Virginia. Louis T. Wigfall and Williamson Simpson Oldham served Texas as senators in the Confederate Congress.

Governor Lubbock joined the Confederate army in 1863 and did not seek reelection. Pendleton Murrah became the new governor of Texas. Like Lubbock, Murrah struggled during the war with state debts and the problems of raising troops and defending the frontier against Indian raids.

Unionists and the War. Large numbers of Texans joined the Confederate army, and office holders were strong supporters of the Confederate cause. Still there were Texans who did not agree with secession. At the time of the vote on secession, about one-third of Texans voted against leaving the United States. Once the war began, these Unionists could be divided into three groups.

The largest group opposed to secession decided to support Texas in the war. The best known among this group was James W. Throckmorton. He became a brigadier general in the Confederate army.

A smaller number of Unionists tried to remain neutral during the war. They supported neither side in the conflict. Among well-known Texans in this group were Sam Houston, David G. Burnet, Elisha M. Pease, and George Paschal. Many German Texans and Mexican Texans were counted in this group as well.

A third group of Unionists actively supported the United States. Approximately 2,000 Texans joined the Union army. Among those were about 50 black Texans. Milton Holland, an African American soldier born in Texas, won the Congressional Medal of Honor for courage and valor during the Battle of Chaffin's Farm, Virginia, in 1864. Other Texans who fought for the Union included John Haynes and Edmund J. Davis. Davis organized a regiment of cavalry and eventually became a brigadier general. He later served as governor of Texas.

Those Unionists who stayed in Texas during the war generally faced a difficult time. Well-known leaders such as Sam Houston and Elisha M. Pease were left alone, but

TEXAS VOICES

The Texas slave narratives were collected in the late 1930s by interviewers working under the Federal Writer's Project of the Works Progress Administration. These 308 original accounts of lives spent in slavery were given by elderly ex-slaves living in various places in Texas. William M. Adams from San Jacinto County told the following story about what the enslaved people called "the great freedom war."

Just before the war, a white preacher came to us slaves and said: "Do you want to keep your homes where you get all to eat, and raise your children, or do you want to be free to roam around without a home, like the wild animals? If you want to keep your homes, you'd better pray for the South to win. All that want to pray for the South to win, raise the hand." We all raised our hands because we were scared not to, but we sure didn't want the South to win.

That night all the slaves had a meeting. . . . Old Uncle Mack, he got up and said: "One time over in Virginia there were two old black men, Uncle Bob and Uncle Tom. They were mad at one another, and one day they decided to have a dinner and bury the hatchet. So they sat down, and when Uncle Bob wasn't looking, Uncle Tom put some poison in Uncle Bob's food, but he saw it, and when Uncle Tom wasn't looking, Uncle Bob turned the tray around on Uncle Tom, and he got the poison food." Uncle Mack, he said, "That what we slaves are going to do, just turn the tray around and pray for the North to win."

many Unionists were threatened and sometimes attacked. In August 1862, sixty-five German Texans tried to flee to Mexico but were caught and attacked by the Texas militia. Thirty-four of the Unionists were killed. When German communities in Central Texas organized to protest, 50 more German Texans were hanged. Confederate officials were fearful of Unionist activities, and some areas of Texas were placed under **martial law**, or rule by armed forces.

In northeastern Texas, an organization known as the Peace party was formed to oppose the draft. Confederate troops arrested 150 men in Gainesville who were suspected of belonging to the party. Forty were hanged without trial. Five other men were hanged in Wise County for opposing the war. These troubles revealed how deep the feelings about the war ran and added to the widespread sorrow.

The End of the War. The surrender of General Robert E. Lee on April 9, 1865, marked the end of the Civil War, even though some smaller Confederate forces did not stop fighting for another month. As word spread of the war's end, Texas troops began making their way home.

Painting by Bruce Marshall, Institute of Texan Cultures

Milton M. Holland was the first black Texan to win the Congressional Medal of Honor. He led his unit in a daring attack against Confederate forces at the Battle of Chaffin's Farm, Virginia.

Essential Elements
2H, 9A

Historical Sidelight
In his Second Inaugural Address, delivered only a month before his assassination, President Lincoln called for northerners to move toward the postwar period "with malice toward none, with charity for all; with firmness in the right, as God gives us to see the right."

* **This marker in Central Texas is dedicated to the memory of German Unionists who were hanged at this site during the Civil War.**

Texas Department of Transportation

SECTION **3** REVIEW

Define: martial law, assassinated

Identify: James W. Throckmorton, Milton Holland, John Wilkes Booth, Emancipation Proclamation

1. What role did women play during the Civil War?
2. How did politics in Texas change after the war had started?
3. Into what three groups did the Unionists fall?
4. What was the status of slaves at the end of the Civil War?

Using Historical Imagination: How would you have reacted, as a Texan, upon hearing the news of Robert E. Lee's surrender?

Evaluating Information: What risks did Texas Unionists take during the Civil War? Think of as many as you can. Do you think these risks were worth taking? Why or why not?

Victory was greeted with celebration in the North. The celebration turned to sorrow, however, when President Abraham Lincoln was **assassinated**, or murdered. He was shot while at Ford's Theater in Washington, D.C., by John Wilkes Booth, a Confederate supporter. Lincoln died on April 15, 1865, the day after he was shot.

The death of Lincoln only added to the uncertainty facing the United States following the war. In 1863, Lincoln had issued the Emancipation Proclamation, which said that slaves were free in those areas rebelling against the United States. As the Union army advanced into Confederate states, the slaves were freed. But at war's end, no one was certain what would become of the freed slaves. They were left without jobs, land, and money.

Texas faced the issue of free slaves, as well as other problems, following the war. The Confederate government of Texas was considered by the United States to be illegal. Unsure of what would become of them, Governor Murrah and other officials fled to Mexico. Texans in general were not sure whether Union forces would enter the state and, if they did, how they would treat Texans.

The war left the economy in shambles. The cotton trade had nearly ceased. The death of many men placed hardships on Texas farms, plantations, and businesses. The effects of the Civil War would be felt in Texas for many years to come. ✪

LONE STAR LEGACY

The Effects of Emancipation

On June 19, 1865, almost three years after President Lincoln's Emancipation Proclamation, Texas slaves were officially freed by an officer of the federal government. General Gordon Granger arrived at Galveston to announce that all slaves were emancipated. Today, Texans celebrate emancipation on June 19, or "Juneteenth," as it is called, a state holiday observed every year.

During the years after the proclamation, some of the former slaves developed new skills and trades. But many continued to live on farms and plantations, doing the only work that they had ever known.

The Freedmen's Bureau—set up by the United States government to assist "freedmen," or freed slaves—helped African Americans adjust to their new life of freedom. In Texas, the main role of the bureau was to educate the former slaves. African Americans, young and old, were eager to learn. But a lack of properly qualified and trained teachers slowed the bureau's progress.

Freedmen were offered the "three R's" (reading, 'riting, and 'rithmetic), along with instruction that prepared them for manual labor. In time, many became teachers in bureau schools after graduation from high school. Throughout the state, the rate of illiteracy among former slaves dropped from 75.4 percent in 1880 to 38.2 percent in 1900.

During the twentieth century, educational opportunities for African Americans in Texas have continued to improve. Federal laws and policies have insured the right of equal education for all citizens. State-supported colleges and universities have promoted the enrollment of all ethnic groups, and it is now illegal to require separate public schools for blacks and whites. New ideas and solutions continue in the original spirit of emancipation.

Using Historical Imagination

Imagine that you are General Granger on June 19, 1865. Write a diary entry describing how slaves reacted to your announcement. Predict how you think the new Freedmen's Bureau will affect their future.

Inset: **Abraham Lincoln**   Right: **General Granger announcing Emancipation**

Inset: *The Granger Collection*   Right: *Institute of Texan Cultures*

Essential Elements
2H, 3A, 9E

LONE STAR LEGACY
Using Historical Imagination: Answers will vary. The diary entry should reflect the slaves' elation upon hearing Granger's news. Granger would probably express hope for the future of the Freedmen's Bureau, but he may note the lack of qualified teachers.

5. Some decided to support Texas in the war, some tried to remain neutral, and others actively supported the Union.

Thinking Critically

1. Analyzing Information: Physically, Texas was barely touched—its towns and cities were never successfully invaded by Union forces. As a result of blockades, however, Texas' economy

CHAPTER 18 REVIEW ANSWERS

Understanding Main Ideas

1. Thousands joined the Confederate army; others were drafted.
2. (1) Capture Richmond, Virginia, the capital of the Confederacy; (2) take control of the Mississippi River, thereby dividing the Confederacy; (3) blockade southern ports so that ships could not enter or leave
3. Galveston Island: After Union troops captured Galveston, Confederate troops surrounded them and won it back. Sabine Pass: A small group of Confederate soldiers fought off a much larger Union force by waiting until Union gunboats were within close range and then firing heavily on them. The Red River Campaign: Texas forces fought off a Texas invasion by driving General Banks' forces back into Louisiana before Banks was able to link up with another Union army in Arkansas, which the Texas forces defeated as well. Palmito Ranch: The last battle of the war was fought here, after Lee had already surrendered.
4. Some trade was cut off, many businesses suffered, and there was a shortage of goods.

CHAPTER 18 REVIEW

Understanding Main Ideas

1. How did Texans answer the call to fight during the Civil War?
2. The Union plan to conquer the Confederacy had three parts. Describe each of these parts of the plan.
3. Briefly describe the important battles fought in Texas during the Civil War.
4. How was the economy of Texas affected by the war?
5. What different attitudes did the Texans have who sided with the Union?

Thinking Critically

1. **Analyzing Information:** Compare the effect the war had on Texas physically and economically.
2. **Comparing Perspectives:** Compare the efforts of Texans at home with those fighting the war. How did each group contribute to the war effort?
3. **Evaluating Information:** Why do you think Unionists such as James W. Throckmorton decided to fight for the Confederacy? Should all Unionists in the South have supported the Confederate cause? Why or why not?
4. **Writing Descriptively:** Imagine that you are the wife of a Confederate Texas soldier. Write your husband a letter describing your life at home and the sacrifices you are making.

Linking History and Geography

1. How was Mexico important to Texas and the rest of the Confederacy?

2. Confederate forces in Texas had to defend a coastline of more than 350 miles. What problems do you think this caused them? What problems do you think it caused for the Union blockade?

TAAS *Practice*
Using Primary Sources

Captain Samuel T. Foster was a soldier with Granbury's Texas Brigade. During the war he kept a diary. The following excerpt is from 1865, when Foster was on his way back to Texas.

May 19th

> I saw some negro children going to school this morning, for the first time in my life. In fact I never heard of such a thing before. . . . I stopped a little negro girl about 12 years old dressed neat and clean, going to school with her books. . . . I opened the Grammar about the middle of the book and asked her a few questions—which she answered very readily and correctly. . . . I never was more surprised in my life! The idea [of an educated black child] was new to me. . . .
>
> I can see that all the negro children will be educated the same as the white children are. . . . I can see that our white children will have to study hard, and apply themselves closely, else they will have to ride behind, and let the negro hold the reins—I can see that the next generation will find lawyers doctors preachers, school teachers farmers merchants . . . divided some white and some black, and the smartest man will succeed without regard to his color. . . .
>
> The color will not be so much in the future as knowledge. The smartest man will win—in every department of life. . . .
>
> And the man that is the best mechanic lawyer, doctor or teacher . . . will succeed.

suffered. Many businesses, plantations, and farms shut down or were hurt severely.

2. **Comparing Perspectives:** Around 20,000 Texans lost their lives fighting in the war. Texans at home sacrificed to feed and equip Texas forces, adapted to wartime shortages, and kept the economy going.

3. **Evaluating Information:** Answers will vary but should consider Throckmorton's loyalty to Texas.
4. **Writing Descriptively:** Letters will vary but should be based on information presented in the chapter.

Linking History and Geography

1. During the Union blockade, Texas was able to trade with Mexico for needed goods.
2. Accept answers that suggest that there were not enough Confederate troops to defend such a long coastline effectively. Such a long coastline made it easier for blockade runners to land without being detected by Union forces.

TAAS **Practice**
Using Primary Sources
1. B   2. A

TAAS **Practice**
Writing Persuasively

Letters will vary but should be persuasive and based on information presented in the chapter.

Practicing Skills

1. **Sequencing Events:** Time lines should present information found in the chapter as well as information found through research.
2. **Interpreting Maps:** Piedras Negras—Eagle Pass; Nuevo Laredo—Laredo; Guerrero—Carrizo; Matamoros—Brownsville. Houston was a railroad hub. Goods probably would be routed from Sabine through Liberty, Houston, Alleyton, and King's Ranch, and then to Brownsville, where they would cross into Matamoros, Mexico.

Enriching Your Study of History

1. **Individual Project:** Oral reports will vary but should demonstrate thorough research and should be illustrated with photographs or drawings.
2. **Cooperative Project:** Cooperative projects should demonstrate careful preparation.

---

1. Foster probably had never met an educated black person before because
   A   he had been a soldier most of his life
   B   he came from Texas, where most blacks were slaves
   C   he had never before met a black person
   D   he had never been to school
2. Foster thought that the most important way to success after the war would be
   A   knowledge
   B   race
   C   physical strength
   D   money

TAAS **Practice**
Writing Persuasively

Imagine that you are the leader of a Confederate regiment from your community during the Civil War. Write a letter to the people of your community, describing things that they can do to help win the war, and persuading them to do those things.

Practicing Skills

1. **Sequencing Events:** Create a time line that includes the major battles in Texas. Use your library to learn the major events that occurred in the Civil War nationally. Include those events on your time line.
2. **Interpreting Maps:** Study the map on this page. Through what pairs of cities would goods going between Texas and Mexico have to pass? Which Texas city was a hub for goods transported by train? Describe the route that goods would probably take from Sabine to Matamoros.

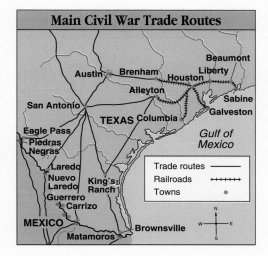

Main Civil War Trade Routes

Beaumont · Liberty · Austin · Brenham · Houston · Alleyton · San Antonio · Sabine · Galveston · TEXAS · Columbia · Eagle Pass · Piedras Negras · Gulf of Mexico · Laredo · Nuevo Laredo · King's Ranch · Guerrero · Carrizo · MEXICO · Brownsville · Matamoros

Trade routes ——
Railroads ++++
Towns ●

Enriching Your Study of History

1. **Individual Project:** Research information about a person or family who lived in your community during the Civil War, or find information about one of the Texas brigades. Prepare a brief oral report for the class. You may wish to illustrate your report with copies of photographs, or you may prefer to draw your own illustration.
2. **Cooperative Project:** Work with a partner to find a song that was sung by a Texas regiment during the Civil War. Your librarian may be able to assist you in your research. After you and your partner have selected an appropriate song, make copies of it for everyone in your class, including your teacher. Learn the song and then teach it to your entire class.

RECONSTRUCTION IN TEXAS

◈ TEACHER MATERIALS

Core: Chapter 19 Time Line; Graphic Organizer 19; Enrichment Worksheet 19; Review Worksheet 19; Reteaching Worksheet 19; Chapter 19 Tests, Forms A & B

Additional: Geography and Graph Skills 19, Informal Evaluation Forms, Test Generator

◈ OBJECTIVES

1. Explain the requirements for Texas' readmission to the Union under President Johnson's Reconstruction plan.
2. Explain what Texas had to do in order to be readmitted to the Union under the Congressional plan for Reconstruction.
3. Cite the main ideas of the Thirteenth and Fourteenth amendments.
4. Relate significant events during the administrations of Texas Reconstruction governors.
5. Specify characteristics of the Constitution of 1876.
6. Discuss results of Reconstruction in Texas.

◈ RESOURCES

BOOKS FOR TEACHERS

Adams, Larry Earl. *Economic Development in Texas During Reconstruction*. Denton: North Texas State University, 1980.

Carrier, John Pressley. *A Political History of Texas During the Reconstruction*. Vanderbilt University, 1971. History of Texas during Reconstruction.

Conner, John Coggswell. *Carpet Bag Rule*. Washington: Gibson Brothers, 1871. History of Texas during Reconstruction.

Ramsdell, Charles William. *Reconstruction in Texas*. Texas History Paperbacks Series. Austin: University of Texas Press,

1970. History of Texas during Reconstruction.

Wallace, Ernest. *Texas in Turmoil, 1849–1875*. Austin: Steck-Vaughn, 1964. Examination of these crucial years.

Woodward, C. Vann. *Origins of the New South, 1877–1913*. Rev. ed. Baton Rouge: LSU Press, 1971. The postwar period in the South.

MULTIMEDIA MATERIALS

The Background of the Reconstruction Period. (film, 21 min.) BFA Educational Media, 468 Park Avenue South, New York, New York, 10016. Rebuilding of the post-Civil War South.

The End of an Era. (video, 30 min.) PBS Video, 1320 Braddock Place, Alexandria, Virginia, 22314. The postwar period in the South.

Reconstructing the South. (video, 30 min.) PBS Video, 1320 Braddock Place, Alexandria, Virginia, 22314. Examines the period following the Civil War.

The U.S. History Series. Constitution to Civil War and *Civil War to World Power*. (software) Focus Media, Inc., 839 Stewart Avenue, P.O. Box 865, Garden City, New York, 11530. These two programs aid students in reviewing important information concerning the Civil War.

STUDENTS WITH SPECIAL NEEDS

Limited English Proficient Students (LEP)

Have students review the chapter by creating a time line of events during the period of Reconstruction. Ask students to select one event and summarize it. See other activities labeled **LEP.**

Students Having Difficulty with the Chapter

Organize students into pairs. Have each pair use the section headings and subheadings to outline the chapter. Have them write a one-sentence summary of each entry in their outline. **LEP**

Auditory Learners

Have auditory learners select one of the issues, events, or persons mentioned in the chapter to research. Ask them to present an oral report to the class. See other activities labeled **A.**

Visual Learners

Locate in the library resources and other history textbooks that contain political cartoons from the Reconstruction period. Cover the captions of the cartoons and show them to students. Explain to students that the cartoons represent editorial comment about Reconstruction issues. Ask students to select a cartoon and write a caption for it. Compare and discuss the captions. See other activities labeled **V.**

Tactile/Kinesthetic Learners

Have tactile/kinesthetic learners use the information from the chapter to create a chart classifying Texas' four Reconstruction governors. The chart should include the following headings: *Governor, Elected/Appointed, Former Unionist/Confederate, Years in Office, Significant Events of Term.* See other activities labeled **TK.**

Gifted Students

Refer gifted students to a copy of the Texas Constitution and the United States Constitution. Ask them to compare the two documents and identify similar features *(Preamble, Bill of Rights, amendments, organization of the three branches of government).* Invite a volunteer to share the information with the rest of the class. See other activities labeled **G.**

VOCABULARY

In addition to the boldfaced terms in each section, some students might benefit from discussing the meanings of these terms.

Section 1: *legalize* (p. 387); *informal* (p. 387); *testify* (p. 390).

Section 2: *override* (p. 392); *impediment* (p. 393); *fraud* (p. 395); *obnoxious* (p. 395); *bribes* (p. 396).

Section 3: *landslide* (p. 397); *margin* (p. 397); *corrupt* (p. 398).

CHRONOLOGY

Have students study the Chapter 19 Time Line and identify relationships among the events.

GRAPHIC ORGANIZER

Have students skim the chapter and complete the Chapter 19 Graphic Organizer. *(You might wish to use this activity to review rather than to introduce the chapter.)*

ENRICHMENT

Have students complete the Chapter 19 Enrichment Worksheet.

SECTION 1

FOCUS

Predicting (I) Write the term *radical* on the chalkboard. Ask students to provide a definition. Explain that a radical is someone who supports a sudden or dramatic change. Point out to students that they will learn how this term relates to Reconstruction in Section 1.

INSTRUCTION

Vocabulary (I) You may wish to preteach the following boldfaced terms: *Reconstruction* (p. 386); *freedmen* (p. 387); *amendment* (p. 390). **LEP**

CHAPTER 19 OVERVIEW

The Civil War ended in 1865. The United States then began the task of reuniting the southern states with the Union. In the plan for Reconstruction, new state governments had to be organized and representation restored to Congress. In Texas and other southern states, Reconstruction was a slow and difficult process. For eight years, Texans debated the restoration of its state government.

Essential Elements
2H, 3A, 3F, 7D, 7F, 7G, 9A, 9B, 9E, 9F

CHAPTER 19

RECONSTRUCTION IN TEXAS

The Story Continues...

When the Civil War ended in the spring of 1865, the United States faced the problem of **Reconstruction**, or bringing the former Confederate states back into the Union. In Chapter 19, you will learn about the period of Reconstruction in Texas.

As you read the chapter, look for the answers to these questions:

1. What did Texas have to do to be readmitted to the Union under President Johnson's plan for Reconstruction?
2. What new requirements for readmission were added by the Congressional Plan for Reconstruction?
3. What were the writers of the Texas Constitution of 1876 trying to accomplish?

1 Reconstruction Under President Johnson

Before the Civil War ended, President Abraham Lincoln had devised a plan to reunite the nation. Lincoln hoped to bring the southern states back into the United States as quickly as possible. He did not want to punish the South or increase feelings of bitterness. After Lincoln was assassinated, the responsibility of Reconstruction passed to the new president, Andrew Johnson.

Emancipation. The first United States troops to arrive in Texas after the Civil War landed at Galveston on June 19, 1865. Their commander, General Gordon Granger, issued a proclamation freeing the slaves of Texas in the name of the president. President Lincoln had declared all slaves in the rebelling states free in 1863. But because Union forces did not control Texas at that time, the Emancipation Proclamation had no effect in the state until Granger read his order in Galveston. Since 1865, June 19

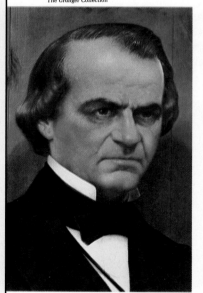

The Granger Collection

President Andrew Johnson, a southerner, favored a moderate policy of Reconstruction. He was opposed by Radical Republicans in both houses of Congress, and his policies for reuniting the Union were overturned.

Austin History Center, Austin Public Library

Juneteenth has been celebrated in Texas for more than 120 years. This photograph of a Juneteenth meeting was taken around 1900.

has been celebrated in Texas as a day of freedom. Many Texans refer to the day as "Juneteenth." It is a state holiday marked by picnics, parades, and family gatherings.

There was much confusion in Texas following emancipation. Some areas of the state had not received word that slaves were free. Many **freedmen**, as the former slaves were known, expected help in adjusting to a new way of life. They hoped to receive some land and farm animals to start their own farms. A small number of freedmen, weary from years of forced labor, collected at military posts. They hoped to receive government aid.

The first reaction slaves had to the news of emancipation was to leave the plantations. During the summer and fall of 1865, Texas roads were crowded with former slaves loaded down with their possessions. They were moving to cities, from one county to another, or out of Texas to a different state. For a few, the freedom to travel was in itself an attraction. But most former slaves had specific goals. Some hoped to find paying jobs in nearby towns where Union troops would protect them. Others traveled in search of family members from whom they had been separated. The desire to reunite families and legalize informal slave marriages sent blacks to Texas courthouses in droves. But

Guided Practice (I) List the following headings on the chalkboard: *Johnson's Plan, Congress' Reactions.* Call on volunteers to list President Johnson's actions with regard to his Reconstruction plan and the reactions of Congress. **A, V**

EXTENSION

Research (II) Ask interested students to locate information on Texas governors from the Civil War to the present. Have them record in chart form the party of each governor. **V, TK**

Barker Texas History Center

These Texans were once slaves. This photograph was taken years after emancipation. Almost no photographs were taken of blacks in Texas before the Civil War.

Biography

President Johnson was a Democrat from Tennessee. He had served in both houses of Congress and as governor of Tennessee. Johnson was one of the few pro-Union politicians who came from a Confederate state.

Throughout his career, President Johnson, a self-educated man, had been a champion of the small farmer. He favored homestead laws and laws to improve public education. He was critical of great wealth and called southern planters "traitorous aristocrats."

despite the freedmen's desire for a better life, harsh economic necessities forced many of them back to the rural areas—even to their old plantations—within a few months.

The freedmen were given no land or farm animals following emancipation. Before the end of the war, however, Congress had created the Bureau of Refugees, Freedmen, and Abandoned Lands in order to assist former slaves. This Freedmen's Bureau began work in Texas in late 1865, providing food, shelter, and medicine for freedmen. It also represented former slaves in court to work out contracts with employers.

Perhaps the most lasting contribution of the Freedmen's Bureau was in the field of education. The bureau opened the first schools for blacks in Texas. By 1870, more than 100 such schools were in operation. The bureau itself, however, ceased to operate in Texas after 1868.

Johnson's Plan. The troops sent to the southern states had the responsibility of supporting President Johnson's Reconstruction plan. The first step in that plan was the creation of provisional, or temporary, state governments. The provisional governments were required to meet several conditions. First, the Confederate states had to end slavery officially. They were also required to declare their acts of secession illegal. Because the federal government considered secession to be illegal, the states had to agree that

388 *Unit 7*

debts acquired under the Confederacy would not be paid. Adult white males had to take an oath of allegiance to the United States. Men who had been officials of the Confederate government or high-ranking army officers were required to request a pardon from the president. Upon receiving a pardon, these people could take part in government once again.

After meeting these conditions, the southern states could write new constitutions and hold elections. State governments could then resume operation. This plan was acceptable to many Texans. They felt it was fair, and they supported President Johnson in his attempts to bring about a quick and easy Reconstruction.

Governor Hamilton Takes Charge. President Johnson appointed Andrew J. Hamilton the provisional governor of Texas in June 1865. Hamilton had been a Unionist in Texas before the Civil War. When war broke out, he went north and became a general in the Union army. Although he fought for the Union, the majority of Texans welcomed him to Austin, the capital city, when he arrived there in August 1865. Because Hamilton had previously served Texas as a member of the United States Congress, he was respected and considered to be a wise choice of leader to begin the Reconstruction effort.

Governor Hamilton started by appointing officers to help run the government. Many of the people he appointed were Unionists whom he knew and had worked with before. He also appointed some former Confederate leaders. Because of these appointments, Hamilton was recognized for his fairness and for his desire to restore order and confidence in the state government.

On November 15, 1865, Governor Hamilton called an election to select delegates to a constitutional convention. The convention assembled in Austin on February 7, 1866. Two old political factions, the Unionists and the secessionists, faced each other at the convention.

The Constitutional Convention of 1866. The constitutional convention did its work in two months. The delegates met President Johnson's Reconstruction requirements to declare secession illegal, recognize the end of slavery, and cancel the Confederate war debt. Debate was heated and lengthy, however, over proposals for granting certain rights to freed slaves.

Institute of Texan Cultures

Schools for former slaves were opened all across the South after the Civil War. These schools were established to educate young and old. Before emancipation, it had been illegal in the South for slaves to receive any formal education.

Archives Division, Texas State Library

Andrew J. Hamilton was appointed provisional governor of Texas in 1865. Although Hamilton had served as a general in the Union army, many Texans held him in high regard.

Constitutional Heritage

Section 1 of the Thirteenth Amendment to the Constitution reads:

Neither slavery nor involuntary servitude, except as a punishment for crime whereof the party shall have been duly convicted, shall exist within the United States, or any place subject to their jurisdiction.

Answers to Section 1 Review

Define: *Reconstruction*—bringing the former Confederate states back into the Union; *freedmen*—former slaves; *amendment*—an addition that changes part of a constitution

Identify: Andrew Johnson—United States president after Lincoln; Freedmen's Bureau—agency set up to help freed slaves; Andrew J. Hamilton—appointed provisional governor

(Continued on page 391)

Archives Division, Texas State Library

James W. Throckmorton was elected governor in 1866. He had served in the Confederate army as a brigadier general. In 1867, the Texas state government was declared illegal, and Throckmorton was removed from office.

Even though the convention agreed to end slavery in Texas, it refused to formally ratify the Thirteenth Amendment to the United States Constitution, which prohibited slavery. An **amendment** is an addition that changes a part of the Constitution. The convention provided for basic security and protection for black Texans, but it failed to grant them equal rights. For example, blacks could own property and were given the right to trial by jury. But black Texans were not allowed to vote. They could not hold office. And they were not permitted to testify at trials in cases involving whites.

According to the demands of President Johnson's plan, the convention wrote a new constitution and presented it to Texas voters. In June 1866, the voters approved the Constitution of 1866 and elected state officials. Former Confederate James W. Throckmorton won the election over the Unionist Elisha M. Pease, probably because he opposed granting blacks the right to vote. The first Reconstruction government in Texas soon was ready to begin work.

Congress Reacts. The newly elected state legislature met for the first time on August 6, 1866. Three days later, Governor Throckmorton was sworn into office, and, on August 20, President Johnson proclaimed that the rebellion in Texas was ended. Texas, with a new government, could resume operation. The people of Texas believed that Reconstruction was over. They soon discovered, however, that it was only beginning.

From the start of President Johnson's Reconstruction plan, many members of the United States Congress were opposed to it. Congress was controlled by the Republicans, and they had major points of disagreement with the course of Reconstruction. One group of Republicans in particular wanted Congress to take over Reconstruction. Known as the Radicals, they wanted to give full rights of citizenship to former slaves.

The Radicals were angry that most southern states had elected former Confederate leaders as their representatives. For example, one newly elected Texas senator, Oran Milo Roberts, had been president of the secession convention in 1861. Governor Throckmorton had been a general in the Confederate army. And all of the Texas members of the United States House of Representatives had been loyal to the South during the war. The Radicals and many other

CLOSURE
Point out to students that President Johnson attempted to pursue a moderate policy of Reconstruction. Congress, however, opposed Johnson's plan and the course of Reconstruction.

ASSESSMENT
Have students complete the Section 1 Review on page 391.

Institute of Texan Cultures

Republicans were furious. They believed that the war had been pointless because southern states were now electing to office the very people who had led the rebellion.

The Republicans were further angered because Texas refused to ratify the Thirteenth Amendment. Nor would the Texas legislature ratify the Fourteenth Amendment, which stated that blacks were citizens of the United States and of the states in which they lived.

The Black Codes. Still another point of disagreement between the Republicans in Congress and the southern states was over a series of laws that came to be called the "black codes." Under these laws, if freedmen did not have jobs, they could be put in jail. They could not leave one job to take another without permission from their former employers. A black person could not have visitors at work, and the laws stated that blacks had to obey and respect their employers. Many cities and counties also passed vagrancy laws. These restricted the time of day when blacks could be out in public and the places they could go. Although the black codes in Texas were less severe than some in other southern states, still they were undemocratic. ✪

During Reconstruction, the Alamo was used as a supply center by the United States Army. This photograph was taken in 1868. Army wagons are storing supplies in the famous San Antonio mission.

SECTION ① REVIEW

Define: Reconstruction, freedmen, amendment

Identify: Andrew Johnson, Freedmen's Bureau, Andrew J. Hamilton, James W. Throckmorton

1. What did Texas have to do to rejoin the Union under Johnson's plan?
2. Why did Radical Republicans dislike this plan?
3. What were the black codes?

Seeing Cause and Effect: How might Reconstruction have been different if President Lincoln had lived? Explain.

Evaluating Information: In your opinion, what were the black codes meant to accomplish?

of Texas in 1865; James W. Throckmorton—elected governor of the first Reconstruction government of Texas

1. Create a provisional government that would: pass a bill officially ending slavery, declare the state's act of secession illegal, agree that debts acquired under the Confederacy would not be paid, require all adult white males to take an oath of allegiance to the United States, and require former Confederate officials and high-ranking army officers to request a pardon from the president
2. It allowed former Confederate officials and officers to assume immediate control of state government, and it did not require the states to ratify the Thirteenth and Fourteenth amendments to the Constitution which would have given freedmen full citizenship rights.
3. A series of undemocratic laws that restricted the rights of freedmen

Seeing Cause and Effect: Answers will vary, but students might suggest that if Lincoln had lived Reconstruction might not have lasted as long, and there might have been less political animosity and turmoil.

Evaluating Information: Opinions will vary, but students should note that the black codes were an attempt to keep blacks in a condition of semi-slavery.

SECTION 2

FOCUS

Past Learning (I) Ask students to list the disagreements between Congress and President Johnson over Reconstruction. List their responses on the chalkboard. Tell students that the Radical Republicans soon gained control of Congress and the course of Reconstruction.

INSTRUCTION

Vocabulary (I) You may wish to preteach the following boldfaced term: *veto* (p. 392). **LEP**

Linking History and Geography
Louisiana

Essential Elements
2H, 3A, 3B, 3F, 5B, 7B, 7D, 7E, 7G, 9A, 9B, 9E

Reconstruction Military Districts

■ Military district

LINKING HISTORY AND GEOGRAPHY
What other state was linked with Texas in the Fifth Reconstruction Military District?

2 Congressional Reconstruction

President Johnson chose to do nothing to interfere with a quick Reconstruction, even though he was not happy about the black codes. Congress, on the other hand, thought that Reconstruction was moving too swiftly. The Radicals and their supporters were determined to take control. Some Radicals cared deeply about the rights of former slaves, and most Republicans believed it was wrong for former Confederate leaders to be back in power. Republicans also realized that if blacks were given the right to vote and hold office, they would support the Republican party.

The Reconstruction Acts. When national elections were held in November 1866, the Radical Republicans won enough support in Congress to gain control of Reconstruction. They had enough votes in Congress to override President Johnson's **veto**, or cancellation of a proposed law. With their new power, the Radicals passed several Reconstruction acts, beginning in March 1867.

The new state governments in the South were declared illegal. Then the South was divided into five military

Austin History Center, Austin Public Library

This building in Austin served as the headquarters of the Fifth Reconstruction Military District in Texas.

districts, each under the control of an army officer. The southern states were then to write new constitutions that guaranteed rights for black citizens. States were also required to ratify the Fourteenth Amendment.

Texas was included in the Fifth Reconstruction Military District. Its commander was Philip H. Sheridan, a famous Union army general. Under Sheridan's command, federal forces made sure that black males were registered to vote.

In order to vote, adult white males were required to take an "ironclad oath." This was an oath that they had never voluntarily supported the Confederacy. Thousands of Texans thus were declared ineligible to vote. That suited the Radicals, who believed that former Confederates should be prevented from taking part in any new state government.

Appointment of Governor Pease. One of the first acts of General Sheridan was the removal of Governor Throckmorton from office on July 30, 1867. Sheridan claimed that Throckmorton was "an impediment to Reconstruction."

To fill the office of governor, Sheridan appointed Elisha M. Pease. Pease, a former governor, had been a Unionist and was more sympathetic to the goals of the Republicans in Congress. Pease was also well respected by most Texans. He was an excellent choice to try to keep order between the military and Texas citizens.

Many Texans, nevertheless, were angry at people such as Pease who supported the military rule of the Republicans. Texans who supported the Republican plan were

Brown Brothers

A native of Ohio, General Philip H. Sheridan became the commander of the Fifth Reconstruction Military District. Sheridan was a famous general of the Union army and strongly supported the Reconstruction policies of the Radical Republicans.

The Granger Collection

In this political cartoon, the carpetbagger, the symbol of northern domination, is represented as crushing the South.

called "scalawags." The small number of northerners who had come to Texas since the war and supported the Republicans were called "carpetbaggers." People who disliked these northerners claimed they came to the South for political gain, often carrying all they owned in bags made of carpet. More likely they came seeking employment.

Governor Pease held office for the next two years. The most important political event of his term was another constitutional convention. This convention was called to meet the requirements of Congress for Reconstruction.

The Convention of 1868. Those eligible to vote elected delegates to a new constitutional convention. The delegates met in Austin on June 1, 1868. Only six of the delegates had been members of the convention of 1866. The majority were Texas Unionists, but there were some former Confederates. Nine of the delegates were black, and several were northerners who had moved to Texas at the end of the Civil War.

The convention was divided into two factions over the new constitution. One faction wanted radical changes and hoped to put strong Union supporters, including blacks, in control of the state government. This faction was led by Edmund J. Davis and George T. Ruby. Ruby was a black delegate and a leader of the Loyal Union League in Texas. The league was an organization that worked to promote support among black Texans for the Republican party.

Painted under supervision of Dr. John Biggers, Texas Southern University

George T. Ruby of Galveston was a leader of the Loyal Union League. He was elected a delegate to the Convention of 1868. Ruby was next elected to the Texas Senate, where he introduced a number of important bills. In this painting, he is shown seated at right.

EXTENSION
Debate (II) Organize the class into two teams to debate the success or failure of Reconstruction. Have each team select three members to present its views. Arguments should be based on information from the textbook or outside references. Allow ten minutes for presentations and five minutes for rebuttals for each side. **A, G, V**

Independent Practice (II) Ask students to list three positive aspects and three negative aspects of the Davis administration. Collect their lists and compile a class list on the chalkboard. Call on volunteers to give their opinions of Governor Davis. **A, V**
RETEACHING
Using names and events from Section 2 as clues, create a crossword puzzle for students to use as a review. Allow students to work in pairs or small groups to check and correct their completed puzzles. **LEP**

The second faction was led by Andrew J. Hamilton. Hamilton was known as a moderate Republican. He and his supporters favored few changes from the past, and they wanted to restore the right of former Confederates to take part in government.

The convention, controlled largely by the Radicals, finished a new constitution for Texas in February 1869. The law gave the vote to former Confederates and to blacks. In contrast to past constitutions, the new one gave the governor the power to appoint numerous state officials and judges. The governor's term of office was lengthened from two to four years. The legislature was to meet every year, instead of once every two years.

The Constitution of 1869 made important changes in public education. Funds were to be provided from the sale of public lands, from one-fourth of state revenues, and from a poll tax of one dollar per voter. Attendance at school was made compulsory, or demanded by law.

The constitution was adopted by a wide margin. In the election for governor, Edmund J. Davis defeated Andrew J. Hamilton by a vote of 39,901 to 39,092. Many Texans charged that the army had made sure that Davis would win and that there had been fraud, or cheating, in the voting. Nevertheless, the Radicals in Congress now had a supporter in the Texas governor's office.

The Davis Administration. The four years under Governor Davis were marked by great controversy. A majority of Texans, who were Democrats and had supported the Confederacy, felt that Davis did not represent them. They opposed the governor at every opportunity. Davis and his supporters, on the other hand, felt that the government of Texas had to be run by people loyal to the Union and to the Republican party.

Davis and his supporters had a majority in the Texas legislature. They used their power to pass a series of laws labeled by Democrats the "obnoxious acts." One of the laws granted the governor the power to declare martial law. Under martial law, people accused of crimes could be tried in military courts. Governor Davis believed that martial law was necessary to maintain law and order. His opponents claimed that the governor used the power to arrest people who did not support him. He created a state police force with many black officers. The governor said it

Archives Divsion, Texas State Library

Edmund J. Davis was elected governor in 1869. His four years in office were troubled, making him unpopular with many Texans. Davis was soundly defeated in his reelection attempt in 1873. Reconstruction in Texas ended with his defeat.

Historical Sidelight
One irregularity of the election was that the returns were never made public. In fact, the returns have never been found.

Answers to Section 2 Review

Define: *veto*—cancellation of a proposed law

Identify: Philip H. Sheridan—United States general and commander of the Fifth Reconstruction Military District; Elisha M. Pease—Texas governor appointed by General Sheridan; Edmund J. Davis—Republican who was elected governor of Texas in 1869; George T. Ruby—black Republican who served as a delegate to the Convention of 1868

1. Under the Congressional plan, state governments established under Johnson's plan were declared illegal and the South was divided into five military districts. The southern states had to write new constitutions guaranteeing rights for black citizens and had to ratify the Fourteenth Amendment. To be eligible to vote, adult white males had to take an oath that they had never supported the Confederacy.

(Continued on page 397)

Essential Elements
2H, 3A, 3B, 3F, 4F, 9A, 9B

SECTION 2 REVIEW

Define: veto
Identify: Philip H. Sheridan, Elisha M. Pease, Edmund J. Davis, George T. Ruby

1. What was required of the southern states under the Congressional plan for Reconstruction?
2. What major changes were made by the Constitution of 1869?
3. What were the "obnoxious acts"?

Analyzing Information: How did the Constitution of 1869 strengthen the power of the office of governor?

Interpreting Pictures: Look at the political cartoon on page 394. How is the carpetbagger being maintained in power? What figure symbolizes the South?

For many Texans, Governor Coke's inauguration at the capitol in January 1874 was a joyous celebration. Texans were eager to put the bitterness of Reconstruction behind them and get on with the business of their fast-growing state.

was needed to protect the freedmen, fight crime, and help with frontier defense. But many Texans said the force was used against opponents of Governor Davis.

Another act gave the governor the power to appoint many state and local officials. Critics claimed that Governor Davis used the power to appoint those who supported him, while removing anyone who did not like his policies. Those opposed to the governor also charged that these officials were making money by fraud. Evidence suggests that Governor Davis was honest and did not enrich himself, but a number of officials accepted bribes or made money at the state's expense.

Many Texans were upset over the increase in spending by the state government under Governor Davis. Yet the increased spending brought about some positive changes. New roads were built, defense of the frontier was improved, and the school system was given funds to operate. To pay for these improvements, taxes were raised to bring in more money. Even with new taxes, the state debt increased. ◗

3 The End of Reconstruction

Opponents of Governor Davis organized to vote him out of office. Davis had the support of Radical Republicans and blacks in the election of 1873. His opponent, Richard Coke, was supported by Democrats and moderate Republicans. Coke, a former Confederate army officer from Waco,

Austin History Center, Austin Public Library

INSTRUCTION

Historical Imagination (I) List on the chalkboard five types of people living in Texas after the Civil War.

a. A freed black
b. A plantation owner
c. A returning Confederate general
d. An appointed governor
e. A woman who operated a farm while her husband served in the Confederate army

Organize the class into five groups, each group representing one of these persons. Ask each group to consider the information presented in this section as well as in previous sections to speculate about what life was like for that person during Reconstruction. Students should list their ideas in note form. Have a spokesperson from each group report its descriptions to the class. **A, LEP**

Austin History Center, Austin Public Library

Democrats occupied the old capitol building on January 12, 1874, by using ladders to reach the second floor. This photograph shows the Texas capitol that was built in the early 1850s. It was destroyed by fire in 1881.

won the election by a landslide. He received 85,549 to 42,663 for Davis.

Coke Takes Over. Despite losing by a huge margin, Governor Davis refused to leave office. He claimed that the election had not been fair. Davis sent word to President Ulysses S. Grant, asking for United States support to keep him in office. By 1873, however, many people in the North had lost interest in Reconstruction. Radicals in Congress had begun to lose their power. President Grant refused to back Davis.

Davis reacted by ordering the state militia to guard the capitol. Armed guards were stationed on the ground floor. In this way, Davis believed he could keep the legislature from meeting and stop the inauguration of Richard Coke.

Late on the night of January 12, 1874, Democrats placed ladders on the side of the capitol building and sneaked into the second floor. There they organized the legislature. There were threats of violence when Davis found out, but no violence occurred. On January 15, Richard Coke was sworn in as governor of Texas. Another appeal by Edmund Davis to the United States government was ignored. The period of Republican control of Texas was over. It marked the end of Reconstruction in the state.

2. The governor was given the power to appoint many state officials, the governor's term was lengthened from two to four years, the legislature was to meet every year rather than every two years, state funds were provided for public education, and school attendance was made compulsory.

3. A series of laws passed during the Davis administration, some of which gave the governor the right to declare martial law, to set up a state police force, and to appoint more state and local officials

Analyzing Information: It extended the governor's term of office from two to four years and expanded the list of state offices to which the governor could appoint officials.

Interpreting Pictures: By the military; the woman laboring under the weight of the carpetbag

Historical Sidelight
When Davis asked President Grant for United States support to keep him in office, Grant advised that it would "be prudent as well as right" to accept the decision of the voters.

Analysis (I) Ask students to identify what they consider to be the greatest accomplishment and the greatest failure of Reconstruction. Record responses on the chalkboard and attempt to reach a class consensus. **A**

Guided Practice (I) Have students work individually or in pairs to create a diagram, chart, or other graphic to illustrate one of the topics discussed in Section 3. **V, TK, LEP**

EXTENSION
Community Involvement (II) Ask a student to find out what percentage of your school district's budget is provided by the state and report back to the class. **A**

Members of the constitutional convention met in Austin in the fall of 1875 to write a new constitution. Many Democrats objected to the Constitution of 1869, which had been written by Republicans.

Archives Division, Texas State Library

Austin History Center, Austin Public Library

Richard Coke was elected governor of Texas in 1873. Coke was a veteran of the Confederate army and won a landslide victory over Governor Davis. Coke was reelected in 1876 but resigned shortly thereafter to take a seat in the United States Senate.

The Constitution of 1876. Governor Coke and the Democrats worked to reverse the changes made by the Davis administration. They removed officials they thought to be corrupt. They also removed those who disagreed with their policies. They cut government spending, and they set about writing still another constitution to replace that of 1869.

The constitutional convention met in Austin in the fall of 1875. Unlike the previous convention, this one had 75 Democrats. Of the fifteen Republicans, six delegates were African Americans. In February 1876, the constitution

398 *Unit 7*

Essential Elements
3A, 4E, 4I, 9A

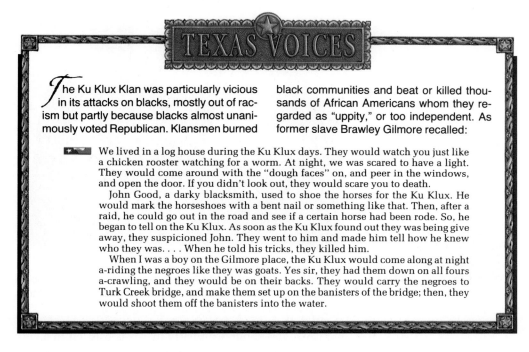

TEXAS VOICES

The Ku Klux Klan was particularly vicious in its attacks on blacks, mostly out of racism but partly because blacks almost unanimously voted Republican. Klansmen burned black communities and beat or killed thousands of African Americans whom they regarded as "uppity," or too independent. As former slave Brawley Gilmore recalled:

We lived in a log house during the Ku Klux days. They would watch you just like a chicken rooster watching for a worm. At night, we was scared to have a light. They would come around with the "dough faces" on, and peer in the windows, and open the door. If you didn't look out, they would scare you to death.

John Good, a darky blacksmith, used to shoe the horses for the Ku Klux. He would mark the horseshoes with a bent nail or something like that. Then, after a raid, he could go out in the road and see if a certain horse had been rode. So, he began to tell on the Ku Klux. As soon as the Ku Klux found out they was being give away, they suspicioned John. They went to him and made him tell how he knew who they was. . . . When he told his tricks, they killed him.

When I was a boy on the Gilmore place, the Ku Klux would come along at night a-riding the negroes like they was goats. Yes sir, they had them down on all fours a-crawling, and they would be on their backs. They would carry the negroes to Turk Creek bridge, and make them set up on the banisters of the bridge; then, they would shoot them off the banisters into the water.

written by the delegates was approved by Texas voters. It remains the basic law of the state today.

The goal of the framers of the Constitution of 1876 was to limit the power of state government. For this reason, the governor's term was once again set at two years, and the power of the governor to appoint state officials was reduced. The legislature was again scheduled to meet once every two years instead of every year. Special importance was placed on limiting the ability of the legislature to spend money. The legislature could not go into debt for more than $200,000, and many proposals for spending had to be approved by Texas voters.

The Texas constitution is very long and complex. Because of this fact, a number of attempts have been made to rewrite it. These attempts have failed, but many amendments have been added over the years.

Results of Reconstruction. The period of Reconstruction in Texas affected education, government, and the status of African Americans. When the constitution was written, state spending was reduced, greatly affecting

Historical Sidelight
The list of illustrious delegates to the Convention of 1876 included Lawrence Sullivan Ross, who later would become governor of Texas and president of Texas A&M College; John S. Ford, famous editor and Texas Ranger; Charles DeMorse, an editor and ex-Confederate colonel; John H. Reagan, who had been postmaster general of the Confederacy and recently had been elected to serve in the U.S. House of Representatives; and Thomas Nugent, who would go on to become a leader in the farmers' revolt of the 1890s.

Institute of Texan Cultures

Ku Klux Klan members used terror to keep blacks from exercising their rights after the Civil War. At times, carpetbaggers and moderate southern whites were also targets of the Klan's violence.

SECTION 3 REVIEW

Identify: Richard Coke, Ulysses S. Grant, the Ku Klux Klan

1. What national changes caused the end of Congressional Reconstruction in Texas?
2. What was the major purpose of the writers of the Constitution of 1876?
3. How did the Constitution of 1876 affect public education?

Analyzing Information: In what ways was the Constitution of 1876 a reaction against the Constitution of 1869?

Evaluating Information: Besides keeping blacks from voting, what do you think were the other purposes of the Ku Klux Klan?

education. Control of public schools was returned to local authorities. Funds often were not available to schools, and school attendance was no longer compulsory.

With the return of the Democrats to power under Governor Coke, the Republican party in Texas was left in a very weak condition. It continued to operate but lacked the power to win elections. For years after Reconstruction, the Democrats in Texas won nearly all state and local offices.

No group was affected more by Reconstruction than black Texans. Reconstruction brought emancipation but new problems as well. Because blacks supported the Republicans as the party of emancipation, blacks were resented by many white Texans who were Democrats. Some whites did not want blacks to take part in government at all. Secret organizations were sometimes formed to keep blacks from voting or registering to vote. One such organization was the Ku Klux Klan. Dressed in long robes and white hoods to hide their faces, Klan members threatened, attacked, and sometimes murdered blacks. As the Republican party declined in Texas, so too did the influence of blacks. Later, laws were passed to keep them from voting.

For black Texans, Reconstruction had been a new beginning. Steps had been taken toward gaining voting rights and other rights of citizenship. The first schools had been opened for black children. Yet many of these gains had been lost. The promise of emancipation remained to be fulfilled. ⊙

CLOSURE
Ask students to summarize the problems that blacks in Texas faced during Reconstruction. List key ideas on the chalkboard.

ASSESSMENT
Have students complete the Section 3 Review on page 400.

LONE STAR LEGACY

Freedom Colonies in Texas

Economic realities, especially the lack of land, education, and job opportunities, forced many former slaves back to their old plantations within a few months after emancipation.

Other freedmen managed to take a different course, however. In many locations across Texas, former slaves banded together to buy their own land and start African American "freedom colonies." In communities such as Jake's Colony, Peyton Colony, and St. John Colony, former slaves lived lives of independence and freedom. They were poor, but they had obtained something very precious: they owned their own land.

Peyton Colony was located on 5,000 acres in Blanco County. Soon after slaves were officially freed in Texas, black families began making their way to this colony 40 miles from Austin. There they began setting up homesteads and farms. Later, Peyton Colony attracted blacks from across the United States.

In Caldwell County, close to the Bastrop County line, is St. John Colony. In the late 1970s, the Reverend S.L. Davis, a 90-year-old Baptist minister, told a historian the following about how this community was established:

> It was just a little bit after slavery. They [freed slaves] all wanted homes, permanently. This [fellow] told them that he'd sell them all the land they wanted. And

the heads of the families, they all rode horseback from Hog Eye [Webberville] to the place now called St. John. It was nothing but forest at that time.

So, they came out then, they selected land, those heads of families. There were seventeen of them. They went back and got their families. By horse-team, mule team, oxen, and horseback is how they made it up there. They got together and organized themselves. They began to build cabins—going into the forest, cutting logs, hewing them out, notching them, and then dabbing them with red clay. One door, one window. You had to cook outdoors and sleep in that room. They did that until they got everybody in a home.

Using Historical Imagination

Imagine that you are a former slave who has just purchased your first piece of land. Record your thoughts about this event in your life.

Inset: **Austin Jones of Peyton Colony**   Right: **Hattie Mae Coffee of Peyton Colony**

Both photographs: Tom Lankes, Austin American-Statesman

Chapter 19 **401**

Essential Elements
3A, 3C, 3D, 6A, 6B

LONE STAR LEGACY
Using Historical Imagination: Answers will vary but should reflect the pride, excitement, and determination to succeed that the former slave most likely felt.

CHAPTER REVIEW RESOURCES

1. Chapter Review Worksheet 19
2. Chapter 19 Test, Form A
3. Reteaching Worksheet 19
4. Chapter 19 Test, Form B
5. **Informal Evaluation Forms:** Portfolio Assessment
6. *Texas, Our Texas* **Test Generator**

Essential Elements
3A, 3B, 3F, 5B, 9A, 9B, 9D, 9E

5. The Democratic party
6. The Constitution of 1879 reduced the powers of the governor and limited the governor's term of office to two years. The state legislature's powers to spend money were reduced.

Thinking Critically

1. **Synthesizing Information:** Both sought to control the behavior and curb the freedom of blacks. The

CHAPTER 19 REVIEW ANSWERS

Understanding Main Ideas

1. It had to create a provisional state government that would: end slavery officially, declare Texas' secession illegal, agree that debts created under the Confederacy would not be paid, require adult white males to take an oath of allegiance to the United States, and require former Confederate officials and high-ranking army officers to request a pardon from the president. After these conditions were met, Texas could write a new constitution and hold elections.

2. State governments established under Johnson's plan were declared illegal. Texas was placed in one of five military districts, and a provisional governor was appointed. To vote, adult white males were required to take an oath that they had never supported the Confederacy. A new constitutional convention was held, and the Constitution of 1869 was then established.

3. The Radical Republicans' loss of political power, and a decrease in public support for the policies of Reconstruction

4. A series of laws passed to control the freedmen

CHAPTER 19 REVIEW

Understanding Main Ideas

1. What did Texas have to do in order to be readmitted to the Union under Johnson's plan of Reconstruction?
2. What did Texas have to do in order to be readmitted under the Congressional plan?
3. What national changes brought about the end of Reconstruction?
4. What were the black codes?
5. What political party regained power in Texas in 1874?
6. How was the Texas Constitution of 1876 different from the Texas Constitution of 1869?

Thinking Critically

1. **Synthesizing Information:** Compare the aims of the black codes to the goals of the Ku Klux Klan.
2. **Exploring Economics:** How do you think Texas plantation owners would have treated their newly freed slaves? What do you think they would have wanted the freedmen to do? Explain.
3. **Analyzing Information:** What events in Texas during early Reconstruction angered Radical Republicans?

Linking History and Geography

1. Why was the Ku Klux Klan most active in Texas counties with the greatest cotton acreages?
2. Look at the map on page 392. How many Reconstruction military districts were there? Which district was the smallest? Which district was made up of the most states? Which Confederate state was not included in a military district? (See the map on page 372.)

TAAS Practice
Using Primary Sources

When Texas slaves first learned of their emancipation after June 19, 1865, most of them reacted with great joy. Former slave Felix Haywood described his first responses to freedom in this oral account recorded in the 1930s:

> Everybody went wild. We all felt like heroes, and nobody had made us that way but ourselves. We were free. Just like that, we were free. It didn't seem to make the whites mad, either. They went right on giving us food just the same. Nobody took our homes, but right off colored folks started on the move. They seemed to want to get closer to freedom, so they knew what it was like—like it was a place or a city.
>
> We knew freedom was on us, but we didn't know what was to come with it. We thought we were going to get rich like the white folks. We thought we were going to be richer than the white folks, because we were stronger and knew how to work, and the whites didn't, and we didn't have to work for them any more. But it didn't turn out that way. We soon found out that freedom could make folks proud but it didn't make them rich.

1. Haywood said that many former slaves left their homes because
   A they were seeking work
   B their old masters made them leave
   C they were trying to experience their new freedom

black codes were laws designed to restrict the rights of blacks to travel about or to change employers. The Ku Klux Klan was a secret organization whose members terrorized and intimidated blacks.

2. **Exploring Economics:** Answers will vary, but students should recognize that plantation owners still needed the labor that the former slaves could pro-

vide. They would have wanted the freedmen to continue working on the plantations.

3. **Analyzing Information:** The black codes, the state's refusal to ratify the Thirteenth and Fourteenth amendments, and the election of former Confederate officials and army officers to positions of power in state government

Linking History and Geography
1. These counties had the most plantations and the largest populations of former slaves.
2. Five; the First District; the Third District; Tennessee

TAAS ***Practice***
Using Primary Sources
1. C
2. A

TAAS ***Practice***
Writing Persuasively
Speeches will vary but should argue that the governor's policies have been important in re-establishing order, promoting public education, building roads, and protecting the rights of African Americans.

Practicing Skills
1. **Sequencing Events:** General Gordon Granger issues his proclamation of emancipation, Andrew J. Hamilton is appointed provisional governor, Edmund J. Davis is elected governor, Governor Richard Coke takes office, the Constitution of 1876 is approved
2. **Interpreting Graphs:** 1870; 1890; between 1870 and 1880

Enriching Your Study of History
1. **Individual Project:** Diary entries will vary but should be based on conclusions drawn from studying the chapter and from further research on the effects of Reconstruction.
2. **Cooperative Project:** Debate presentations should be supported with factual information regarding Governor Davis and his policies.
3. **Cooperative Project:** Illustrated time lines should include the major events of Texas Reconstruction.

D Yankee troops told them they could

2. According to this passage, the former slaves thought they were going to get rich because
   A they were strong and knew how to work
   B the Union forces would give them money
   C the wealth of the planters would be distributed among them
   D their former owners would take care of them

TAAS ***Practice***
Writing Persuasively
Imagine that you are a speechwriter for Governor Davis during the election campaign of 1873. Write a short speech for Governor Davis to use in his campaign, strongly defending his policies while he has been in office.

Practicing Skills
1. **Sequencing Events:** Place the following events of Reconstruction in Texas in chronological order, beginning with the earliest and ending with the most recent: the Constitution of 1876 is approved, Governor Richard Coke takes office, General Gordon Granger issues his proclamation of emancipation, Andrew J. Hamilton is appointed provisional governor, Edmund J. Davis is elected governor.
2. **Interpreting Graphs:** Study the graph of southern cotton production on this page. When was the low point of southern cotton production after the war? What was the high point of southern cotton production during the period? Between which years did cotton pro-

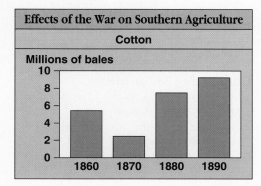

Effects of the War on Southern Agriculture

Cotton

Millions of bales

duction surpass the level of production before the war began?

Enriching Your Study of History
1. **Individual Project:** Imagine that you are traveling through Texas in 1867. Use your historical imagination to write three diary entries describing the effects of Reconstruction.
2. **Cooperative Project:** Your class will present a debate on the policies of Governor Davis. Half the class will prepare a statement defending Davis and his policies. The other half will prepare a statement criticizing him. After the two statements are presented, the entire class will vote by secret ballot for, or against, Davis. Your teacher will tally the ballots and announce the winner of the election.
3. **Cooperative Project:** Working with a partner, create a large poster-size time line of Texas Reconstruction. Include as many major events as possible. Make colorful drawings of people and symbols to illustrate your time line. Your teacher will display your poster in the classroom.

UNIT REVIEW RESOURCES

1. Unit Review Worksheet 7
2. Unit 7 Test, Form A
3. Reteaching Worksheet 7
4. Unit 7 Test, Form B
5. **Informal Evaluation Forms:** Portfolio Assessment
6. *Texas, Our Texas* **Test Generator**

Essential Elements
2H, 3A, 3F, 9A

UNIT 7

UNIT 7 REVIEW ANSWERS

Connecting Main Ideas

1. The economy of the South was based on cash crops such as cotton and sugarcane. Plantation owners depended on slave labor to grow these crops. As the cash crops expanded—especially cotton—so did the system of slavery.

2. The doctrine of states' rights claimed that states had the right to determine whether to obey federal laws and that, because they had chosen freely to join the United States, they also had the right to secede.

3. Soldiers, food crops, money from trade with Mexico

4. Hard feelings divided Texans during Reconstruction. Those who had supported the Union were important in the Reconstruction governments and were resented by ex-Confederates, who were largely excluded from government until 1874.

5. Coke was a Democrat and a former Confederate. With his election, the conservative group that had controlled Texas before the war resumed political power.

REVIEW

Connecting Main Ideas

1. Why did slavery become important to the economy of the South?
2. Explain the connection between states' rights and secession.
3. List three contributions that Texas made to the South during the Civil War.
4. How did feelings about the Civil War affect politics during Reconstruction?
5. Why did the election of Richard Coke as governor mark the end of Reconstruction in Texas?

Practicing Critical Thinking Skills

1. **Synthesizing Information:** Compare the status of blacks under slavery to their status under the black codes.
2. **Evaluating Information:** Do you think confusion in government such as occurred during Reconstruction creates opportunities for fraud? Explain.
3. **Exploring Multicultural Perspectives:** Imagine that you are a slave on a Texas plantation the day General Granger announces your emancipation. Describe the reaction of the woman who owns the plantation. Her son and husband both died in the Civil War.

TAAS Practice
Writing Descriptively

Imagine that you are a Texas reporter in January 1874. Write a newspaper article describing the events that followed the election of Richard Coke as governor.

Exploring Local History

1. Find out what military activities took place in your area of Texas during the Civil War. Were any military units organized in your community?
2. Ask several adults—parents or guardians, and adult friends—their memories of what they were taught in school about the Civil War. How do their interpretations compare with that of your textbook? Why do you think historical interpretations of past events change over time?

Using Historical Imagination

1. **Individual Project:** Write an editorial for a newspaper during Reconstruction, in which you express your views of the Ku Klux Klan.
2. **Cooperative Project:** Your class will nominate a list of five people from Unit 7 to be included in the Texas Hall of Fame. Then five groups will each prepare an acceptance speech for one of the historic figures selected.

For Extending Your Knowledge

Smyrl, Frank H. *Texas in Gray: The Civil War Years, 1861–1865.* Boston: American Press, 1983. A recent history of Texans during the Civil War.

Tyler, Ronnie C. and Lawrence R. Murphy (eds.). *The Slave Narratives of Texas.* Austin: The Encino Press, 1974. Former slaves recall what their lives were like during their enslavement.

Wintz, Cary D. *Reconstruction in Texas.* Boston: American Press, 1983. A fine account of this troubled era.

Practicing Critical Thinking Skills

1. **Synthesizing Information:** Under slavery, blacks were owned as property. After 1865, blacks were freed and could not be bought and sold. The black codes, however, were an attempt to reestablish control over the former slaves and tie them to plantation life.

2. **Evaluating Information:** Answers will vary but should be supported with examples from the textbook.

3. **Exploring Multicultural Perspectives:** Descriptions will vary. Most students will probably describe the woman as having a bitter reaction.

TAAS **Practice**
Writing Descriptively

Students' articles will vary but should note that after Coke's election, the Republicans lost control, and Reconstruction came to an end in Texas.

Exploring Local History

1. Students should consult a library as well as local and state historical societies to research this information.

2. Answers will vary. Some comparisons might reveal a more biased interpretation. Interpretations change as more information is gathered.

Using Historical Imagination

1. **Individual Project:** Views expressed in editorials should be supported with sound reasoning.

2. **Cooperative Project:** Acceptance speeches should demonstrate detailed knowledge of the persons' lives and accomplishments and of the issues of the period.

Skill Lesson
Practicing the Skill

Students' editorial letters will vary but should follow the outline for writing persuasively.

SKILL LESSON

Writing Persuasively

To write persuasively means to write in such a way as to persuade others that your opinion about an issue or controversy is the correct one. By means of your written arguments, you attempt to convert the reader to your point of view.

How to Write Persuasively

In order to write persuasively, follow these steps:

Decide what is your own opinion on the issue in question. To be able to persuade others, you must determine what you yourself believe.

Determine the specific audience that you wish to persuade. You would probably make slightly different arguments in order to persuade various groups. Decide which audience is the specific target of your persuasive essay.

Practice using your historical imagination. To determine which arguments will have the most effect on your targeted audience, put yourself in their place. Use your imagination. If you were one of them, which arguments would likely influence you the most?

Write your persuasive essay, organizing it in terms of these elements:
1. a topic sentence, stating your position on the issue in question
2. three main arguments for your position, chosen in order to best persuade your target audience

3. after *each* main argument, two or three details or examples illustrating that argument
4. a concluding sentence, in which you restate your opinion on the issue

Practicing the Skill

Imagine that you are a citizen of Texas during the period covered by Unit 7. Choose a political controversy or issue about which you have strong opinions. Then write a letter to the editor of a local newspaper to persuade its readers that your opinion about the controversy is the correct one. Follow the steps for persuasive writing outlined on this page.

To assist you in writing your letter to the editor, there is an outline in the box below. Copy the outline onto a separate sheet of paper, and fill it in with elements of your persuasive essay.

Outline of Persuasive Essay

1. Political controversy chosen:
2. Topic sentence stating your opinion on the controversy:
3. Main argument #1, followed by two or three supporting details or illustrative examples:
4. Main argument #2, followed by two or three supporting details or illustrative examples:
5. Main argument #3, followed by two or three supporting details or illustrative examples:
6. Concluding sentence, restating your opinion:

INTRODUCING THE UNIT

Connecting with Past Learning

Ask students to define the term *progress.* Ask: Are the effects of progress always positive? Allow time for students to express varying opinions. Point out that this unit describes an era of Texas history characterized by change and progress. As settlers pushed westward, advances in agriculture, industry, and technology changed the ways of life for Texans. Have students evaluate the positive and negative effects of such progress as they study the unit.

MOTIVATOR

Organize students into three groups, and assign each group one of the chapters in Unit 8. Ask students to skim their assigned chapter, focusing on the illustrations and captions. Have each group list at least four main ideas or generalizations about the chapter. Then have a spokesperson from each group share the group's list with the class, referring to any visuals that help illustrate a main idea.

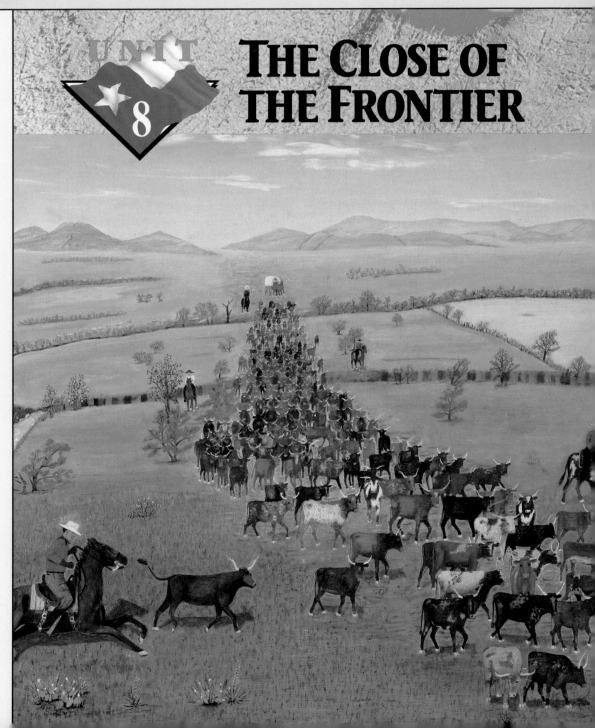

UNIT 8 OVERVIEW

Unit 8 describes the major changes that Texas experienced during the last half of the nineteenth century. Chapter 20 discusses the wars between Native Americans and government troops. These wars left Native Americans confined to reservations and brought an end to their independence.

Chapter 21 explores the "Cattle Kingdom" that developed on the grasslands of Texas. Between the 1860s and 1880s, cowhands herded thousands of cattle across Texas from the open range to northern railroad towns. By the 1880s, the era of the open range was coming to an end.

Chapter 22 describes the development of the modern Texas economy caused by the expansion of railroads and advances in agriculture, industry, and technology.

Materials Available at the Unit Level:
Unit 8 Making Global Connections
Oral History Handbook
Informal Evaluation Forms

UNIT 8

THE CLOSE OF THE FRONTIER

TEXAS AND THE WORLD

Clara Williamson lived in the town of Iredell, southwest of Fort Worth, during the days of the cattle drives. Some years after the last drive, she painted the scene on the opposite page showing cattle being driven along the Chisholm Trail.

When the Civil War ended in 1865, settlers surged westward seeking land on the Texas frontier. New wars erupted between Texans and the Plains Indians of West Texas over control of the land. As the Indians were driven from the land, settlers moved in to start ranches, farms, and towns. Huge ranches were established in South and West Texas to provide cattle for the large populations in the northern United States. In the late 1800s, the first railroad lines were built across West Texas. Soon, new businesses and industries began springing up throughout the state. These developments marked the closing of the frontier in Texas, as almost all areas of the state were settled.

Unit 8 traces the changing of Texas from a frontier state to a modern industrial state. The story of the Texas Indian wars is told in Chapter 20. Cowboys, cattle, and ranches are discussed in Chapter 21. Chapter 22 describes the changes in Texas brought by the rise of major businesses and industries in the late 1800s and early 1900s.

UNIT 8 OBJECTIVES

1. Explain the effects of government policies on Native American ways of life during the late 1800s.
2. Identify important events and leaders in the wars between Native Americans and the United States government.
3. Describe the development of the Texas cattle industry.
4. Explain reasons that the open range came to an end in the 1890s.
5. Discuss the effects of railroad expansion on Texas.
6. Describe nineteenth-century developments in agriculture and their impact on Texas.
7. Identify major industries in Texas in the late 1800s and the technological advances within them.

TEXAS EVENTS

1852 First Texas railroad built

1865 Trail drives begin

1866 First Texas oil well

1873 Buffalo hunters enter Panhandle

1874 Battle of Palo Duro Canyon

1882 T&P Railroad completed

1885 XIT ranch established

1901 Spindletop oil boom

1840 — 1850 — 1860 — 1870 — 1880 — 1890 — 1900 — 1910

1849 California gold rush

1860s Killing of buffalo on Great Plains

1867 Treaty of Medicine Lodge Creek

1867 Stockyards developed at Abilene, Kansas

1869 First railroad line built across U.S.

1873 Barbed wire invented

1890s Automobile developed

WORLD EVENTS

THE INDIAN WARS

TEACHER'S TIME LINE				
Section 1	**Section 2**	**Section 3**	**Section 4**	**Review and**
Pp. 408–12	Pp. 412–16	Pp. 417–20	Pp. 420–22	**Assessment**
1 Day	1 Day	1 Day	1 Day	1 Day

◼ TEACHER MATERIALS

Core: Chapter 20 Time Line; Graphic Organizer 20; Enrichment Worksheet 20; Review Worksheet 20; Reteaching Worksheet 20; Chapter 20 Tests, Forms A & B

Additional: Geography and Graph Skills 20, Informal Evaluation Forms, Test Generator

◼ OBJECTIVES

1. Explain the impact of westward expansion on Native Americans and reasons for their hostility.
2. Trace the sequence of events in the Texas Indian wars from 1860 to 1890.
3. Identify significant Native American and United States government leaders.
4. Describe changes in government policy and attitudes toward Native Americans.
5. Discuss problems of the reservation system.
6. Discuss the effects of the slaughter of the buffalo on the Native American way of life.

◼ RESOURCES

BOOKS FOR TEACHERS

Black Elk. *Black Elk Speaks: Being the Life Story of a Holy Man of the Ogalala Sioux as Told to John G. Neihardt (Flaming Rainbow), Illustrated by Standing Bear*. New York: W. Morrow and Company, 1932. Primary source by this great man.

Foreman, Paul. *Quanah, The Serpent Eagle*. Flagstaff: Northland Press, 1983. Life of Quanah Parker.

Gard, Wayne. *The Great Buffalo Hunt*. Lincoln: University of Nebraska Press, 1968. Descriptions of the buffalo hunt.

Leckie, William H. *The Buffalo Soldiers: A Narrative of the Ne-gro Cavalry in the West*. Norman: University of Oklahoma Press, 1968. Narrative account of these African American troops.

Mayhall, Mildred P. *Indian Wars of Texas*. Waco: Texian Press, 1965. History of the Indian wars in Texas.

—*The Kiowas*. Norman: University of Oklahoma Press, 1971. History of the Kiowas.

Wallace, Ernest. *Ranald S. Mackenzie on the Texas Frontier*. Lubbock: West Texas Museum Association, 1965. Includes Mackenzie's adventures among the Comanche and Kiowa.

MULTIMEDIA MATERIALS

Geronimo and the Apache Resistance. (video, 60 min.) PBS Video, 1320 Braddock Place, Alexandria, Virginia, 22314. Story of Geronimo.

Heroes and the Test of Time. (video, 60 min.) PBS Video, 1320 Braddock Place, Alexandria, Virginia, 22314. Includes the defeat of General Custer at the Little Bighorn.

Sitting Bull. (video, 26 min.) Learning Corporation of America, distributed by Simon and Schuster Communications, 108 Wilmot Road, Deerfield, Illinois, 60015. Life story of Sitting Bull.

GENERAL STRATEGIES

STUDENTS WITH SPECIAL NEEDS

Limited English Proficient Students (LEP)

For each section of the chapter they are about to study, have students skim the section and list the boldfaced terms and other words they do not understand. Collect the lists and prepare a master list. As the terms are encountered during the ensuing class periods, have the class brainstorm about definitions and usage. See other activities labeled **LEP.**

Students Having Difficulty with the Chapter

Ask students to copy the questions from page 408 on a sheet of paper. They should leave several blank lines beneath each question. As students study a section, have them write an answer to the question that pertains to that section. Ask volunteers to read aloud their answers. Through class discussion, clarify any misinterpretations or misinformation. **LEP**

Auditory Learners

Have auditory learners select one of the topics discussed in Chapter 20 and present an oral report. See other activities labeled **A.**

Visual Learners

Have visual learners preview the chapter by studying the illustrations and their captions. Then have them complete the Chapter 20 Graphic Organizer. See other activities labeled **V.**

Tactile/Kinesthetic Learners

Have tactile/kinesthetic learners create a diorama, stage set, or other display of a Texas Indian village. See other activities labeled **TK.**

Gifted Students

Have students research the major Native American groups in Texas and prepare a class presentation. Reports should include where the groups lived, aspects of the groups' cultures or ways of life, and how the events of the late nineteenth century affected their cultures. Encourage students to illustrate their presentations with maps and drawings. See other activities labeled **G.**

VOCABULARY

In addition to the boldfaced terms in each section, some students might benefit from discussing the meanings of these terms.

Section 1: *frontier* (p. 408); *freighting business* (p. 409); *pleas* (p. 411).

Section 2: *convicted* (p. 413).

Section 3: *casualties* (p. 417); *decisive* (p. 417); *humiliated* (p. 417); *elimination* (p. 417); *headwaters* (p. 418); *tributaries* (p. 418); *refuge* (p. 419); *descending* (p. 420); *plunder* (p. 420).

Section 4: *skirmishes* (p. 420); *cunning* (p. 421); *fates* (p. 422).

CHRONOLOGY

Have students study the Chapter 20 Time Line and identify relationships among the events.

GRAPHIC ORGANIZER

Have students skim the chapter and complete the Chapter 20 Graphic Organizer. *(You might wish to use this activity to review rather than to introduce the chapter.)*

ENRICHMENT

Have students complete the Chapter 20 Enrichment Worksheet.

SECTION 1

FOCUS

Past Learning (I) Write the term *Native American* on the chalkboard. Ask students to provide associations for the term as you list their responses on the chalkboard. Use the list to review with students the relationship between the Indians and settlers in Texas in the mid 1800s.

INSTRUCTION

Vocabulary (I) You may wish to preteach the following boldfaced terms: *ransom* (p. 409); *graft* (p. 412). **LEP**

Multicultural Perspective (I) Organize students into small groups. Have students review the discussion of the Plains Indians on pages 90–97. Ask each group to create a list of ten elements of Texas Plains Indian culture. Collect the lists and make a master list on the chalkboard. With the class, discuss which of the elements would be most affected by widespread settlement and why. **A, V**

CHAPTER 20 OVERVIEW

Relations between Native American groups and Texans steadily deteriorated in the mid 1800s, especially during and after the Civil War. Settlers continued to push westward onto Indian lands, while Indian raids against this encroachment increased. After the war, the United States government attempted to remove the Indians by treaty. When this attempt failed, federal troops battled the Indians for more than two decades. Finally, the slaughter of the buffalo and the strength of the United States Army ended Native American independence in Texas and elsewhere.

Essential Elements
2H, 3A, 3C, 3E, 3F, 5B, 6B, 9A, 9B

CHAPTER

20

THE INDIAN WARS

The Story Continues...

Imagine what it must have been like to witness the bitter struggle between Texas settlers and Native Americans, each group convinced of its right to the land. In this chapter, you will learn the story of the last Indian wars fought on Texas soil. You also will find out the federal government's policy toward the Indians and the effects that policy had in Texas. Indian leaders, United States military commanders, and Texas settlers are all part of this dramatic and tragic story.

As you read the chapter, look for the answers to these questions:

1. What events led to a crisis on the frontier, and how did the government respond to this crisis?
2. What attempts did the United States government make to end the Indian raids? How did the Indians respond?
3. What were the causes and consequences of the Red River Wars?
4. What happened to Victorio, Satanta, Quanah Parker, and the Texas Indians after the Indian wars?

Painting by Katie Oliver,
Texas Southern University Art Department

Black Seminole leader John Horse, above, joined Chief Coacoochee, also called Wild Cat, in helping his people escape to Mexico, rather than be forced onto reservations. Black Indians were often threatened by slave-hunters seeking bounty.

1 A New Government Policy

During the Civil War, most available Texas troops were sent to fight for the Confederacy, leaving few to defend the frontier against raids by Indians. Not only were settlers along the frontier stopped from advancing westward, but many were forced back to the east. As a result of Indian attacks, the frontier line moved east as much as 100 miles during the war years.

The Frontier Crisis. With the frontier stripped of troops by the Civil War, Indians of West Texas saw their opportunity to drive settlers from their lands. The Comanches were especially active, as they had always been. Many settlers' homes were attacked and destroyed while others were abandoned by fearful owners. The Comanches raided along

Geography (I) Direct students to the map "Major Indian Groups of Texas" on page 90. Have them locate the areas occupied by the Kiowa, Comanche, and Apache groups. Point out that these were the Indian groups involved in conflicts with settlers after the Civil War. Assign interested students to create a detailed map of Indian lands and settlements in 1865. **A, V, TK, LEP**

Guided Practice (I) Organize the class into small groups. Assign each group a subsection of Section 1. Ask the groups to create a news report of the main ideas of the

subsection. Encourage students to use maps and other illustrations in their news report. Have each group select a spokesperson to present the group's report. **A, TK, LEP, V**

EXTENSION

Historical Imagination (II) Have students work in pairs or small groups to create a "You Are There" type of report. Some students should act as news reporters, while others assume the roles of Native American leaders, government leaders, or Quakers. You might wish to videotape the reports to present as a news program. **TK, A, V, G**

Texas Memorial Museum

Indian raids along the frontier regions of Texas became more frequent during the Civil War. This painting by Friedrich Richard Petri shows a Plains Indian family. The warrior appears ready for battle. Why did Indian raids in Texas increase during the war?

a line from Gainesville in the north to Fredericksburg in Central Texas.

In 1864, a large group of Comanches and Kiowas raided a settlement along Elm Creek in Young County. They burned a number of homes, killed several settlers, and kidnapped other settlers. Some settlers fared better, however. Two men of the Hamby family rode to the ranch of George Bragg to warn the people there of an Indian raid. The Hambys took refuge at the Bragg home. With the women reloading the guns and the three men firing through windows, the settlers managed to fight off the attackers.

Mary and Britton Johnson, a black couple, lost one son in the same raid. The Comanches carried away Mary Johnson and two children, along with several other settlers. In early 1865, Britton Johnson rode north into Indian Territory in what is now Oklahoma. He managed to **ransom,** or pay for the return of, his wife and two children as well as several other captives. Britton Johnson later entered the freighting business around Fort Belknap. While on a trip in 1871, he was attacked and killed near the fort by a group of Kiowas.

Caption Response
There were fewer troops on the frontier during the war.

Historical Sidelight
The Indian raiders in Young County were led by an ambitious man named Little Buffalo. He was killed during the attack on the Bragg home.

Independent Practice (II) Have students create a three-column chart with the following labels: *Native American Concerns, U.S. Government Plans, Quaker Policy.* Call on volunteers to share their summaries. **A, V, TK**

RETEACHING
Organize students into pairs. Ask students to copy the following terms from the chalkboard: *frontier crisis, Treaty of Medicine Lodge Creek, Satanta, Quaker peace policy, Lawrie Tatum.* Have each pair of students brainstorm about each term and write ideas associated with it. Have students share their results. **LEP, A**

Geography
The frontier line in 1860 was in what is now the central part of Texas.

Elm Creek was only one of many sites raided by Indians. In 1866, a Waco newspaper reported that four of every five ranches in the area had been deserted in fear of attack. Seventy-eight people were killed by Indians in 1865. That number rose to 163 by the first half of 1867. During the same period, 43 people were taken as captives, a possibility that particularly frightened many frontier families. Between 1860 and 1870, more than half the population of Wise, Young, and Denton counties moved to what they considered to be safer locations.

After the end of the Civil War, Texas officials petitioned the federal government for better frontier protection. But the troops sent to Texas were there to enforce Reconstruction more than to protect the frontier settlements from Indians. Because the number of troops was small, the army was unable to patrol the entire frontier.

The Treaty of Medicine Lodge Creek. The United States government sent commissioners to negotiate a peace treaty with the Plains Indians in 1867. These commissioners met with chiefs of the Comanche, Kiowa, and Kiowa-Apache tribes at Medicine Lodge Creek in Kansas. The representatives from the government proposed that the tribes accept reservation land in Indian Territory (present-day Oklahoma). To receive the land, the Indians had to live within the boundaries of the reservation and stop making raids on settlements. At the peace meeting, the United States representatives gave out thousands of pounds of sugar, coffee, bread, and tobacco as gifts. The United States government set aside approximately 3 million acres of land in Indian Territory for the reservation. This was far smaller than the Comanchería, the old range of the Comanches.

Some of the Indian leaders at the peace meeting agreed to the terms of the treaty. But Satanta, a Kiowa chief, bitterly opposed the reservation policy. He claimed that the Texas Panhandle belonged to the Kiowas and their Comanche allies. At the meeting, Satanta made a famous speech to the commissioners:

I don't want to settle. I love to roam over the prairies. There I feel free and happy, but when we settle down we grow pale and die. . . . A long time ago this land belonged to our fathers; but when I go up to the river I see camps of soldiers on its banks. These soldiers cut down my timber; they kill my buffalo; and when I see that, my heart feels like bursting; I feel sorry.

National Anthropological Archives, Smithsonian Institution

Satanta, a famous Kiowa chief, participated in various treaty meetings. Satanta could not bear the thought of being placed on a reservation, however, and so he continued to lead raids against United States troops and frontier settlers.

CLOSURE
Point out that as settlers continued to move onto Indian lands, conflicts increased. Attempts by the United States government and a group of Quakers failed to settle the problems.

ASSESSMENT
Have students complete the Section 1 Review on page 412.

National Anthropological Archives, Smithsonian Institution

Quaker Lawrie Tatum worked hard to resolve the many difficulties associated with the Indian reservation in southwestern Oklahoma.

After the Treaty of Medicine Lodge Creek was signed, several thousand Indians who had lived on the plains moved to Indian Territory. Many others, including some bands of Kiowas and Comanches, did not move. They traveled at times to the reservation in Oklahoma for food and other supplies. But they were determined to remain free on the Texas plains.

The Quaker Peace Policy. Despite the pleas of officials in Texas, the United States did not want to wage war against the Indians. In 1869, President Ulysses S. Grant established a Board of Indian Commissioners. The board was to carry out a policy of peace toward the Plains tribes. Many Quakers, members of a church group called the Society of Friends, were appointed to act as Indian agents. Their aim was to promote peace in place of violence. The Quakers argued that it would be less costly to keep peace than to wage war. Like most Anglos of their time, however, they had little regard for the Indian way of life.

FOCUS

Student Experiences (I) Ask students to describe how they might react if people from another country came into their neighborhood and, at gunpoint, demanded that everyone abandon their homes and most of their belongings and move to another place that they will never be allowed to leave. *(Most students will respond that they would be angry; some might suggest that they would fight to avoid moving.)* Point out that this situation is what the Native Americans faced.

INSTRUCTION

Vocabulary (I) You may wish to preteach the following boldfaced terms: *parole* (p. 413); *extermination* (p. 416). **LEP**

Essential Elements
(For Section 2)
2H, 3C, 3D, 3E, 3F, 5D, 6A, 7C, 9B, 9D, 9E, 9F

Answers to Section 1 Review

Define: *ransom*—to pay for the return of something; *graft*—making profit illegally

Identify: George Bragg—held off an Indian attack on his ranch; Mary Johnson—African American kidnapped by the Comanches and later ransomed by her husband; Satanta—Kiowa chief who bitterly opposed the reservation system; Lawrie Tatum—Quaker Indian agent for the Comanches and Kiowas

1. The war left the frontier with few troops, and the Indians took the opportunity to attempt to reclaim their lands.
2. That the Indians accept the reservation land in Indian Territory, live within the reservation's boundaries, and halt raids on settlements

(Continued on page 413)

The Granger Collection

General William Tecumseh Sherman inspected conditions on the Texas frontier in the spring of 1871.

SECTION ★ REVIEW

Define: ransom, graft
Identify: George Bragg, Mary Johnson, Satanta, Lawrie Tatum

1. How did the Civil War make the conflict between Indians and settlers worse?
2. What were the terms of the Treaty of Medicine Lodge Creek?
3. What were the aims of the Quaker peace policy? What problems did the Quakers face in reaching their goals?

Comparing Perspectives: Write two imaginary accounts of an Indian raid on settlers, one from the settlers' perspective and the other from the Indians' point of view.

Evaluating Information: Why can the conflict between Indians and settlers be seen as a clash of cultures?

The Quakers hoped to teach the Indians how to farm so that they could make a living the Anglo way. Schools and churches would be built on the reservations. Lawrie Tatum was appointed Indian agent for the Comanches and Kiowas at the reservation in southwestern Oklahoma. For a while, Tatum achieved some success.

There were problems with the reservation system, however. From the time the reservations were established in present-day Oklahoma, some people argued that the land could not support farming to feed the Indians. Others said that the government did not provide all of the additional food and clothing it had promised. Those who were supposed to supply the reservations sometimes took part in **graft**, or making profit illegally. Goods bought by the government for the reservation were sometimes sold before reaching their destination. Undoubtedly, some Indians, like Satanta, were simply determined to remain free.

Those Indians who were raiding stepped up their attacks on Texas settlements. They took hundreds of cattle and horses and destroyed many farms. Many raiders returned to the reservation after the attacks to avoid army troops. Even Lawrie Tatum came to believe that the military would be needed to stop the raids. ●

2 War on the Plains

William Tecumseh Sherman, a famous Civil War general, was sent by the United States Army to investigate conditions on the Texas frontier. In 1871, Sherman and General Randolph Marcy set out for a visit to forts in West Texas. They stopped at Fort Richardson on May 18. Events the next day led to a new policy toward the Plains Indians.

The Salt Creek Raid. Early on the morning of May 19, 1871, a wounded man was brought into Fort Richardson. He told the story of a raid by the Indians at Salt Creek prairie, on the road between Fort Griffin and Fort Richardson. More than 100 Indians had attacked a wagon train, killing seven people and destroying the train.

The story told by the survivor convinced General Sherman that military action was necessary. He sent troops after the Indian raiders and then set out for Fort Sill, Oklahoma, the army post near the reservation. At the reservation, Satanta admitted to Lawrie Tatum that he had led the raid.

Cooperative Learning (I) Organize students into small groups of three or four. Tell half of the groups that they are Native Americans and the other half that they are representatives of the United States government. Have each group develop a plan to end the disputes between the Indians and settlers. Ask a spokesperson from each group to present its plan to the class. Have the class decide the best solution to end the conflicts. **A, LEP**

Geography (II) Have students create maps illustrating the Indian wars and the events mentioned in Section 1 and Section 2. **V, TK**

When Sherman was told, he ordered that Satanta and two other chiefs be arrested. The three were taken to Jacksboro to stand trial. One of the chiefs was killed on the way to Texas when he attacked the guards. Satanta and the other chief were convicted of murder and sentenced to hang.

The trial of Satanta gained attention throughout the country. It appeared very likely that the angry Kiowas and Comanches would fight again. Lawrie Tatum convinced Governor Davis that hanging Satanta would only make matters worse on the frontier. Davis shared Tatum's concern, and he placed Satanta on **parole**, or released him under condition of good behavior. In August 1873, Satanta was allowed to return to the Kiowas.

As a result of the raid on Salt Creek, General Sherman obtained permission from the United States War Department to launch a series of raids against the Indians who did not live on the reservations. The man selected to lead the attacks was a young cavalry officer named Ranald Mackenzie.

Mackenzie's Raiders. Colonel Ranald Mackenzie was the commander of the Fourth Cavalry regiment stationed at Fort Concho near San Angelo. President Grant once called Mackenzie the most talented young officer in the United States Army. During the four-year period from 1871 to 1875, Mackenzie and his troops achieved great fame fighting on the Texas frontier. The soldiers who served under Mackenzie were called Mackenzie's Raiders.

Mackenzie began his raids in the fall of 1871. He and his men traveled northwest from Camp Cooper on the Clear Fork of the Brazos River. At Blanco Canyon, Mackenzie's cavalry troops fought a group of Comanches of the Quahadi band led by Quanah Parker. The Battle of Blanco Canyon was a minor one. The Indians escaped to the northwest in a heavy snowstorm.

Following several Indian raids in the spring of 1872, Mackenzie renewed his warfare on the Comanches in Northwest Texas. He also crossed the Texas Panhandle into New Mexico, chasing cattle thieves. One of his most famous raids occurred on September 29, 1872. Mackenzie's Raiders surprised and defeated Comanches camped along McClellan Creek, a few miles southeast of the present-day town of Lefors. They killed many Indians and took others prisoner. Several hundred horses, mules, and cattle were captured by the soldiers.

Western History Collections, University of Oklahoma Library

Colonel Ranald S. Mackenzie was in command of a series of campaigns against the Indians of Texas during the 1870s. A string of victories over various Indian groups by Mackenzie and his soldiers succeeded in halting most of the Indian raids in Texas.

Library of Congress

The Comanche chief Quanah Parker led much of the fighting in Northwest Texas against the United States Army. He finally surrendered in 1875.

3. The Quakers wanted to promote peace and cooperation between Native Americans and settlers. There were problems with the reservation system: the land could not support farming to feed the Indians; promised supplies did not always reach the Indians; some Indians were determined to remain free, so they continued to raid settlements.

Comparing Perspectives: Accounts by settlers should reflect the settlers' fear of the Indians and anger at illegal raids. Accounts by Indians should include the Indians' desire to reclaim their land.

Evaluating Information: Possible answer: Each group had a different view of land ownership. The reservation system forced Indians to stay within a certain boundary, which was a new concept to them. The settlers did not understand the Indians' reluctance to stay on reservations.

Multicultural Perspective (I) Ask students which they believe was more difficult for Cynthia Ann Parker to endure—being captured as a child by the Comanches or being recaptured by Texas Rangers and forced to live out her life with her Anglo relatives. Allow time for students to express their opinions. **A, LEP**

Guided Practice (I) Have students work individually or in pairs to create a three-column chart with the following labels: *Indian Goal, U.S. Government Goal, Result.* Ask students to list at least four goals in each of the first two columns. In the third column, they should describe the results of conflicting goals. **V, TK, LEP**

Essential Elements
3E, 3F, 6A, 6B

SPIRIT OF TEXAS

Cynthia Ann and Quanah Parker

On the morning of May 19, 1836, Comanches raided Parker's Fort in present-day Limestone County. They killed five of the Parker men and took as captives two women and three children. Among the captives was nine-year-old Cynthia Ann Parker. Parker was taken to live with the Noconi (Wanderers) band of the Comanches. She was adopted by an Indian family and named Naduah.

Separated from her relatives, Naduah gradually forgot their language and way of life. She entered into Comanche life and eventually became the wife of young Peta Nocona, who was later a chief. They had two sons, Quanah and Pecos, and a daughter, Topsannah. Naduah roamed the plains with the Comanches for 24 years.

In 1860, Naduah and her two-year-old daughter were recaptured by a force of Texas Rangers. Her sons were away on a hunting trip. No one knows whether Chief Nocona was away, too, or if he was killed during the battle.

When Texas forces discovered Naduah's identity as Cynthia Ann Parker, they contacted her uncle, Isaac Parker, who took the frightened woman and child into his home in Birdville. Cynthia Ann Parker lived the last decade of her life relearning the language and skills of her relatives. She tried several times to escape and never found contentment in her new life. She grieved for Nocona and her children.

Topsannah died at age five. Pecos died before reaching adulthood. Quanah, who grew up with the Quahadis on the Llano Estacado, was the last surviving child of Cynthia Ann Parker.

Quanah Parker, who took his mother's name, became a famous leader. As chief of the Quahadi band of the Comanches, he led his people in peace as he had in war. From 1875 until his death in 1911, his influence grew in dealings between Indians and Anglos. Parker dealt with United States Indian agencies in charge of the Oklahoma Territory reservations. He rode his horse in the inaugural parade of President Theodore Roosevelt. With an Indian father and an Anglo mother, Quanah Parker became a force for peace between two cultures.

Inset: **Cynthia Ann Parker**   Right: **Chief Quanah Parker**   Inset: *The Texas Collection, Baylor University*   Right: *Amon Carter Museum, Fort Worth*

EXTENSION
Role Playing (II) Ask interested volunteers to reenact Satanta's trial. One group of students should represent the United States government and present its case against the chief. Another group should represent the defense and present Satanta's plea for the Indian way of life. **A, V, G**

Independent Practice (I) Have students work individually or in pairs to create a cause-and-effect diagram of the events discussed in Section 2. Call on volunteers to share their diagrams with the class. **V, TK, A**

Quanah Parker and his warriors attacked Mackenzie's camp the following night and stampeded the animals, recapturing many of them. Still, Mackenzie succeeded in stopping further Indian raids for awhile.

With troubles temporarily halted in Northwest Texas, Colonel Mackenzie and the Fourth Cavalry headed for the area along the Rio Grande. Stationed at Fort Duncan near Eagle Pass, Mackenzie led a campaign to stop Kickapoo and Lipan Apache raids along the Mexico border. By the end of 1873, Mackenzie had stopped most of the raids by forcing the Indians south into Mexico.

The Killing of the Buffalo. For hundreds of years, the nomadic Indians of the American plains had depended on the buffalo herds. The Indians ate buffalo meat, wore buffalo hides and fur as clothing, and used the hides for tepees. Millions of buffalo grazed on the brush and grasslands from Texas to Canada. By 1870, the survival of these giant herds of buffalo was threatened. As a result, the Indians of the plains were threatened as well.

The coming of the railroads to the Great Plains after the Civil War signaled the end of the nomadic life of Plains Indian tribes and the almost total destruction of the buffalo. Buffalo hunters went to the plains to make their fortunes by supplying buffalo hides to meet a growing demand. How did the destruction of the great buffalo herds bring an end to the way of life of the Plains Indians?

Caption Response
The Plains Indians depended on the buffalo for survival. The total destruction of the buffalo made it impossible for the Indians to continue their way of life.

The Granger Collection

RETEACHING

Organize students into groups. Have each group create a poster illustrating a main idea of Section 2. Ask volunteers to display and explain their group's poster. **A, V, TK, LEP**

CLOSURE

Point out to students that the purpose of Mackenzie's Raiders was to end Indian raids and to move the Indians onto reservations or chase them into Mexico.

ASSESSMENT

Have students complete the Section 2 Review on page 416.

Answers to Section 2 Review

Define: *parole*—to release under condition of good behavior; *extermination*—the complete destruction of something

Identify: William Tecumseh Sherman—army general who recommended that the United States take military action against the Indians; Mackenzie's Raiders—troops led by Colonel Ranald Mackenzie that carried out raids against the Indians; Quanah Parker—son of Cynthia Ann Parker and a leader of the Comanches

1. Satanta and two other chiefs were arrested and taken to Jacksboro to stand trial. One chief attacked the guards and was killed. Satanta and the other chief were convicted and sentenced to hang. Satanta was later paroled and allowed to return to the Kiowa tribe.
2. He forced the Indians into northern Mexico.
3. They knew that the Indians depended on the buffalo for survival. By killing off the buffalo, they hoped to end the Indians' independence and force them onto the reservations.

(Continued on page 417)

416 *Unit 8*

Charles M. Russell's painting *Shooting the Buffalo* illustrates the slaughter of buffalo on the Great Plains. Buffalo had no fear of humans and did not flee at the sound of gunfire, which made them easy targets for the buffalo hunters.

Amon Carter Museum, Fort Worth

SECTION ⭐ 2 REVIEW

Define: parole, extermination
Identify: William Tecumseh Sherman, Mackenzie's Raiders, Quanah Parker

1. What happened to the leaders of the Salt Creek Raid?
2. How did Mackenzie stop most raids along the Mexican border with Texas?
3. Why did some military leaders encourage the extermination of the buffalo?

Sequencing Events: Make a list of the actions of Mackenzie's Raiders between 1871 and 1873.

Seeing Cause and Effect: How did the coming of the railroad affect the Plains Indians' way of life?

After the Civil War, railroads began to stretch into the middle of the United States from east of the Mississippi River. When railroads reached towns in Kansas, buffalo hides could be transported quickly and cheaply to cities in the East. Many buffalo were killed to feed the crews building the railroad lines. About the same time, a new method of tanning buffalo hides was developed to make them into good-quality leather. Demand for the hides increased, and their price shot up. With an average buffalo hide worth three dollars on the market, buffalo hunters swarmed onto the plains to make their fortune.

The buffalo hunters first destroyed the herds in Kansas and Nebraska. By 1873, they had moved into the Texas Panhandle. The hunters were expert shots and used the latest in long-range rifles, the Sharps Big 50. These rifles were known throughout the West as buffalo guns. The buffalo hunters could kill, skin, and ship thousands of buffalo in a month. By 1880, only a handful of buffalo remained in the Texas Panhandle.

The **extermination**, or complete destruction, of buffalo herds was encouraged by some United States military leaders. Without the buffalo, the Plains Indians had no means of survival. It was believed that the Indians would have no choice but to accept life on the reservations. The Indians were well aware of this strategy. It probably explains the renewal of warfare in the spring of 1874, the final major attacks by the tribes on the Texas plains. ✪

416 *Unit 8*

SECTION 3

FOCUS

Past Learning (I) Review with students the relationship between the Native Americans and Texans in 1874. Ask: What events happened between 1870 and 1874 that directly affected Native Americans in Texas? *(Sherman recommended military action against the Indians, Mackenzie's Raiders battled the Indians throughout northwestern and* *western Texas, railroads moved across the region, and hunters began destroying the buffalo herds.)*

INSTRUCTION

Synthesis (I) Write the following heading on the chalkboard or overhead transparency: *Conflicts Between Native Americans and the U.S. Government.* Have students suggest the main issues causing conflicts as you record their responses under the heading. Ask: Which issue created the most conflict? A, V, LEP

3 The Red River Wars

In 1874 and 1875, a series of clashes occurred that ended the warfare on the Texas plains. The battles were fought in Northwest Texas along the Red River and in the upper reaches of the Texas Panhandle. The Red River Wars were the final attempt of Texas Plains Indians to continue their nomadic way of life.

Battle of Adobe Walls. In June of 1874, leaders of the remaining Indian tribes on the Texas plains met to discuss a plan to drive away the buffalo hunters. The Comanches were represented by Quanah Parker, the Kiowas by Lone Wolf, and the Cheyennes by Stone Calf. They decided to attack Adobe Walls in the Texas Panhandle. Adobe Walls was a small settlement that served as a trading center for the buffalo hunters in the area. It was located on the Canadian River about 20 miles northeast of present-day Borger.

In the early morning hours of June 27, 1874, the Indians attacked the settlement at Adobe Walls. Twenty-eight men and one woman defended the settlement against several hundred Indians. The Indians attacked repeatedly throughout the day, but the hunters at Adobe Walls caused many casualties with their long-range rifles. One of the defenders at Adobe Walls was a young man named Bat Masterson. Years later, Masterson became a respected lawman and one of the most famous figures in the American West. After his career as a western lawman and gunfighter, he went to New York and achieved recognition as a sportswriter.

The buffalo hunters scored a decisive victory at Adobe Walls. The Indians greatly outnumbered their opponents, but the power of the buffalo guns was too much for them. Yet the results of the battle proved disastrous for other hunters on the plains. Humiliated by the defeat at Adobe Walls, the Indians began a widespread war against all buffalo hunters in the region. Within the next two months, 190 settlers and hunters were killed on the plains of Kansas, New Mexico, Colorado, and Texas. Thirty of those were killed in the Texas Panhandle.

The Army Attacks. The Indians believed that the elimination of the buffalo hunters was their last hope of living on the plains. The United States Army saw the latest series of Indian raids as an opportunity to formally end the Quaker peace policy and settle the conflict by force.

Western History Collections, University of Oklahoma Library

A Kiowa woman, Noble Star, poses for a late-nineteenth-century photographer. The Kiowas were among the last Texas Indian groups to surrender to the United States Army.

Brown Brothers

Bat Masterson fought at the Battle of Adobe Walls and later became a legendary figure of American history and folklore.

Essential Elements
2H, 3D, 3E, 3F, 5B, 9A, 9B, 9E

Sequencing Events: Lists should include: the Battle of Blanco Canyon, the renewal of warfare in Northwest Texas, the McClellan Creek raid, and raids along the Mexico border.

Seeing Cause and Effect: Many buffalo were killed to feed the railroad workers. Also, the railroad made it easy and cheap to transport buffalo hides, so many buffalo hunters came to the area. The extermination of the buffalo meant that the Indians could no longer survive on the plains.

Geography (I) Direct students to the map on this page. Ask them to locate on the map the following battles: Adobe Walls, Palo Duro Canyon, Tule Canyon. Ask: In what part of Texas did these battles take place *(the Panhandle)*? Why were the confrontations in this area? *(Buffalo hunters were killing the herds, which were concentrated here.)* **V, A**

Guided Practice (I) Have students list the major events of Section 3. Ask them to select one event and write a brief description. Call on volunteers to read their descriptions aloud. **A, LEP**

Linking History and
Geography
The Panhandle

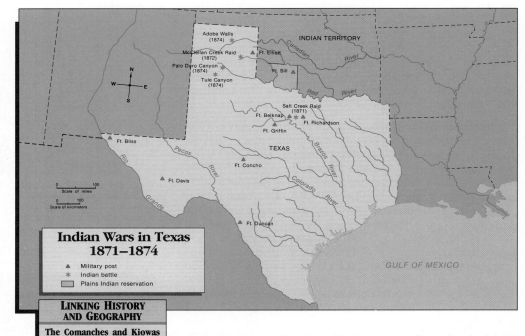

Indian Wars in Texas 1871–1874

▲ Military post
✳ Indian battle
☐ Plains Indian reservation

LINKING HISTORY AND GEOGRAPHY

The Comanches and Kiowas were finally defeated in a series of battles between 1871 and 1874. In what part of Texas were most of the battles fought?

President Grant denounced the peace policy after he heard about the start of the Red River Wars. All Indians, even those living peacefully on the reservation, were put under control of the military. A large military campaign was organized to destroy or remove the Indians remaining in the Panhandle.

In August of 1874, the army offensive began. Forty-six companies of cavalry and infantry, about 3,000 soldiers, marched into the Texas Panhandle. They came from different directions, moving toward the Indian encampments along the headwaters and tributaries of the Red River.

Colonel Nelson Miles led a force of 750 soldiers into Texas from Oklahoma. These soldiers defeated around 500 Indians and burned their village to the ground at Tule Canyon, just east of present-day Tulia. Major William Price and four companies of troops advanced from the west. They were stationed at Fort Union, New Mexico, before being called to join forces with Colonel Miles. Price defeated a band of Indians near Sweetwater Creek in the eastern Panhandle. Two other military forces also were

Analysis (II) Ask a volunteer to read aloud the excerpt from Ten Bears' speech. Have the class list the complaints that Ten Bears voices. Ask: How does his speech summarize the position of all Native Americans? *(Possible answer: Native Americans feel great bitterness and resentment that white settlers are taking over the Indians' land and forcing them onto reservations.)* **A**

Creating (I) Have students create a series of storyboards, a collage, or other visual that illustrates the way of life of the Plains Indians. **V, TK, LEP**

Independent Practice (II) Have students imagine that they are historians writing a brief history of the Red River Wars. Encourage them to illustrate their work with sketches of famous people and maps of battles. **V, TK**

patroling the region. One was commanded by Colonel John Davidson, and the other was led by Lieutenant Colonel George Buell. Both forces destroyed Indian villages and forced hundreds of the survivors onto the reservation in present-day Oklahoma.

The Battle of Palo Duro Canyon. The final blow to the Indians on the Texas plains was struck by Colonel Mackenzie. Mackenzie and the Fourth Cavalry marched northward from Fort Concho to join the other columns searching for Indians. By late September 1874, Mackenzie realized that most of the remaining Comanches, Kiowas, and Cheyennes were seeking refuge in Palo Duro Canyon.

Palo Duro Canyon had been a refuge for Indians for hundreds of years. Fresh water and wild game were abundant there, and its steep walls provided excellent cover from surprise attacks. The Indians in the canyon included the Quahadi Comanches led by Quanah Parker, the Kiowas under Lone Wolf, and a few Cheyennes. Feeling secure, the Indians were making preparations for the rugged Panhandle winter to come.

National Anthropological Archives, Smithsonian Institution

Lone Wolf led the Kiowas in the Battle of Adobe Walls.

Essential Elements
3E, 3F, 9A

TEXAS VOICES

*I*n October 1867, the United States government called together the Plains Indians for a great council meeting at Medicine Lodge Creek in what is now Barbour County, Kansas. At the meeting, Ten Bears, a chief of the Comanches, spoke of his peoples' concerns. The following is an excerpt from his speech:

My heart is filled with joy when I see you here, as the brooks fill with water when the snow melts in the spring; and I feel glad as the ponies do when the fresh grass starts in the beginning of the year. . . .

But there are things which you have said to me which I do not like. They were not sweet like sugar, but bitter like gourds. You have said that you want to put us on a reservation, to build us houses and make us medicine lodges. I do not want them. I was born under the prairie, where the wind blew free and there was nothing to break the light of the sun. . . .

If the Texans had kept out of my country, there might have been peace. But that which you now say we must live in, is too small. The Texans have taken away the places where the grass grew the thickest and the timber was best. Had we kept that, we might have done the things you ask. But it is too late. The whites have the country which we loved, and we wish only to wander on the prairie until we die.

RETEACHING

Have students work individually or in pairs to make a cause-and-effect diagram using the information in Section 3. Diagrams should include the causes and effects of the Red River Wars. Have students share their diagrams as you create one on the chalkboard. **A, V, TK, LEP**

CLOSURE

Discuss with students the final attempts by the Texas Plains Indians to continue their way of life, and the government's response.

ASSESSMENT

Have students complete the Section 3 Review on page 420.

Answers to Section 3 Review

Identify: Red River Wars—wars between Indians and U.S. government troops along the Red River and the final attempt by the Indians to continue their nomadic way of life; Battle of Adobe Walls—Indian attack on buffalo hunters in the Texas Panhandle; Bat Masterson—famous lawman present at the Battle of Adobe Walls; Nelson Miles—army colonel whose troops were victorious at Tule Canyon

1. The Indians were humiliated by their defeat and began a widespread attack on buffalo hunters in the region.
2. The government sent 3,000 troops to remove all of the remaining Indians from the Panhandle.
3. They quietly descended a narrow path to the canyon bottom, surprising the Indians there.

Analyzing Information: The Indians' supplies and horses were taken or destroyed, leaving the Indians unprepared for the winter. They had no choice but to go to the reservation.

Writing Persuasively: Speeches should indicate why the buffalo hunters and settlers were a threat to the Plains Indians' way of life.

Essential Elements
2H, 3D, 3E, 5B, 5C, 9A, 9B, 9E

420 Unit 8

SECTION ③ REVIEW

Identify: Red River Wars, Battle of Adobe Walls, Bat Masterson, Nelson Miles

1. How did the outcome of the Battle of Adobe Walls affect the region's buffalo hunters?
2. How did the federal government react to the renewed Indian raids?
3. How did Mackenzie and his men defeat the Indians at the Battle of Palo Duro Canyon?

Analyzing Information: Why was the Battle of Palo Duro Canyon a serious blow to the Plains Indians?

Writing Persuasively: Imagine that you are a Plains Indian on trial for taking part in the Red River Wars. Write a speech explaining why it was necessary to attack the buffalo hunters and settlers.

Just before dawn on September 28, 1874, Mackenzie and about 500 soldiers eased along the rim of Palo Duro Canyon. After quietly descending a narrow path to the canyon bottom, the soldiers surprised the villages of Indians. Most of the Indians escaped, many by scaling the cliffs of the canyon and fleeing onto the prairie. There were few casualties. But the victory was an important one for the army. In their haste to escape, the Indians were forced to abandon most of their supplies and possessions—including more than 1,400 horses.

Following the fighting, Mackenzie ordered his men to plunder and burn the villages. He also had most of the captured horses taken to nearby Tule Canyon and shot by a firing squad. Past experience had taught him not to give the Indians the chance to retake their horses. Only about 350 of the healthiest animals were spared for the army's use. With their homes, food supplies, and horses destroyed, the Indians faced a terrible choice. They could try to survive the coming winter unprepared, or they could return to the reservation.

Except for a few determined Indians still wandering the Panhandle, most chose to accept defeat and follow the soldiers to Oklahoma. Minor battles continued through the winter of 1874 and into the spring of 1875. But without their horses and adequate supplies, the Indians were unable to maintain enough warriors to continue the fighting. By June of 1875, even Quanah Parker and his followers had been forced into Fort Sill, hungry and exhausted by constant warfare. The army established Fort Elliott in 1875 to insure that reservation Indians would not try to return to Texas. ✪

◪ The End of an Era

The end of the Red River Wars opened the Texas Panhandle to cattle ranching, railroad building, and settlement. In the following years, one way of life replaced another. After the wars, only one area of Texas remained in which Indians had not been destroyed or successfully confined to reservations—the Rio Grande border between Texas and Mexico. From 1876 to 1880, this area was the site of numerous Indian raids and skirmishes between the Indians and the armies of the United States and Mexico.

SECTION 4

FOCUS

Past Learning (I) Review with students the causes of the Indian Wars. Ask: Why did the government begin battling the Native Americans? *(The Indians were raiding settlements and refused to move to reservations.)* What would happen to the Native American lands after the Indians moved to the reservations? *(Settlers and the United States government would claim them.)*

INSTRUCTION

Geography (I) Direct students to the map "Major Indian Groups of Texas" on page 90. Ask them to locate on the map the Pecos River and the Rio Grande. Explain that this was the last area of Texas under Indian control. Have students identify the Native American groups that lived in the region *(Mescalero Apache, Concho, Jumano)*. Point out that the Apaches presented the greatest challenge to government forces. **A, V**

Barker Texas History Center

◄ The end of the Indian wars opened West Texas to settlement and the railroads. This nineteenth-century photograph shows a train along the Sunset-Limited Route near El Paso.

Among the most successful of the Indian raiders was a group of Apaches under the leadership of the cunning Victorio.

Victorio and his followers fiercely resisted life on the reservation. Rather than lose their independence, they escaped over the border and into the mountains. From their hidden camps, they tormented their American and Mexican enemies with daring raids and ambushes.

The Buffalo Soldiers. Important to the army effort in the Red River Wars and the fight against Victorio were the black soldiers of the Ninth and Tenth Cavalry. Although white officers served with the regiments, all of the troops were African American. The Indians so respected the bravery of the black troops that they named them "buffalo soldiers," after the animal the Indians held sacred. The name caught on, and a buffalo was even added to the Tenth Cavalry's crest.

Black soldiers were stationed at Fort Davis in far West Texas, as well as in other areas. They participated in campaigns against the Apaches in the region. Henry Flipper, the first black graduate of the United States Military

Institute of Texan Cultures

Lieutenant Henry O. Flipper, the first black graduate of West Point, campaigned against Victorio while stationed at Fort Davis. Flipper later spent many years as an engineer in El Paso and several years in government service in Washington, D.C.

Brown Brothers

Victorio, leader of the Mescalero Apaches, was a chief of the last Indian group to wage war in Texas.

SECTION 4 REVIEW

Identify: Victorio, Henry Flipper

1. Who were the buffalo soldiers? How did they get their name?
2. Why was it difficult for Mackenzie's troops to end Victorio's raids?
3. How did the fates of Victorio, Satanta, and Quanah Parker differ?

Exploring Geography: How did geographic factors affect the fighting along the Rio Grande?

Synthesizing Information: Why can it be said that the Indians' old ways of life were dead by the 1880s?

Academy, took part in a campaign against the Mescalero Apache leader Victorio while stationed at Fort Davis.

Mackenzie Returns to the Rio Grande. In 1878, Ranald Mackenzie was again sent to the Rio Grande area. Mackenzie's task was to end the raids by the Apaches under Victorio. Stopping the raids was not an easy task. Victorio raided into Texas from his base in the mountains and deserts of Mexico. Towns in the Trans-Pecos region were widely scattered. There were miles and miles of lonely roads where travelers could be easily attacked. Any army troops following the Apaches had to carry their own supplies of food and water in order to survive in the dry and rugged Trans-Pecos area.

Mackenzie and other officers led forces after Victorio for two years. Troops from Fort Bliss and Fort Davis sometimes trailed the Apaches for weeks, only to find they had crossed the Rio Grande into Mexico. The raids were not stopped until the Mexican Army became active in the chase. In 1880, Mexican soldiers killed Victorio, the last Indian leader in the nineteenth century to wage war against Texas.

The Indian Legacy. Two other famous Indian leaders met fates that were different from that of Victorio. Satanta, the Kiowa leader, had been jailed again in 1876 for refusing to live on the reservation. He was returned to the prison at Huntsville. Unable to live freely and unwilling to resign himself to living on a reservation, Satanta took his own life at the prison.

The story of Quanah Parker was more positive. After surrendering in 1875, Parker took an active role in governing Oklahoma reservations. He sometimes went to Washington, D.C., to negotiate on behalf of the Indians with the United States government. He also became involved in a number of businesses in Texas and Oklahoma. Quanah Parker managed to live successfully in the cultures of Indians and whites alike. He once remarked about his white mother, "If she could learn the ways of the Indian, I can learn the ways of the white man."

Military attacks, the slaughter of the buffalo, and disease and starvation took a terrible toll on the Texas Indians. By the 1880s, their population had been greatly reduced. Their life of freedom on the Texas plains was over. ✪

ASSESSMENT
Have students complete the Section 4 Review on page 422.

Essential Elements
2H, 3E, 3F, 6A, 6B,
9A, 9B, 9D, 9E

CHAPTER REVIEW RESOURCES

1. Chapter Review Worksheet 20
2. Chapter 20 Test, Form A
3. Reteaching Worksheet 20
4. Chapter 20 Test, Form B
5. **Informal Evaluation Forms:** Portfolio Assessment
6. *Texas, Our Texas* **Test Generator**

CHAPTER 20 REVIEW

Understanding Main Ideas

1. What actions did the Indians take against the settlers during the Civil War? Why were the Indians able to take these actions?
2. How did the government first attempt to restore peace to the frontier after the Civil War? Why did these efforts fail?
3. How did the Salt Creek Raid change the government's Indian policy?
4. Why was Satanta paroled rather than hanged for his part in the Salt Creek Raid? What finally happened to him?
5. Why did the number of buffalo hunters on the Texas plains increase after the Civil War? Why were these hunters a threat to the Indian way of life?
6. What role did each of the following play in the Indian Wars: William T. Sherman? Ranald Mackenzie? Quanah Parker? Victorio?

Thinking Critically

1. **Synthesizing Information:** How did the government's policies toward the Indians change between 1867 and 1880? Why did they change?
2. **Classifying Information:** Group the raids and battles discussed in the chapter according to their main cause: **(a)** the movement of settlers onto Indian land; **(b)** the extermination of the buffalo; or **(c)** opposition to reservation life.
3. **Analyzing Information:** In the speech on page 419, what reasons does Ten Bears give for being unhappy? What

does he say the Texans did to cause the Indians to wage war?

Linking History and Geography

1. In the Panhandle the average low temperature in January is 25 degrees. Could the Indians there survive the winter after the army took or destroyed their animals and food supply? Explain.
2. What problems did the army face in defending the Rio Grande border in the Trans-Pecos region? How was this border with Mexico an advantage to the Indian raiders?

TAAS Practice
Using Primary Sources

Texas Ranger B. Frank Gholson gave the following account of an attempt to persuade Cynthia Ann Parker to dress like other white women, soon after her recapture from the Comanches. As you read the account, note how the viewpoints of Parker and her "rescuers" differ, then answer the questions that follow.

The women took her out of the tent in which she was staying and took her up to one of their tents. They found enough clothes to clothe her, prepared some hot water and washed her thoroughly, combed her hair and let her look at herself in a mirror. She submitted to all this willingly enough, apparently, until she got a good opportunity to get out the door of the place. When this opportunity occurred she made a dive for the door. . . . The next time she reappeared she had got rid of the remnants of her civilized garb and had somewhere raked up some more Comanche garments.

CHAPTER 20 REVIEW ANSWERS

Understanding Main Ideas

1. They began raiding settlements, which they could do because there were few soldiers available to protect the settlers on the frontier.
2. The government created a reservation where the Indians could live. Many Indians refused to move to the reservation.
3. The government decided that the only way to control the Indians was through military force.
4. The government believed that if it hanged Satanta, the Indians would retaliate with even greater force. Satanta took his own life in prison.
5. The railroads provided an easy method of transporting the buffalo hides. The hunters were exterminating the buffalo, on which the Indians depended for survival.
6. William T. Sherman—led an investigation into the Texas Indian raids; Ranald Mackenzie—led the fights against the Texas Indians; Quanah Parker—was a leader among the Indians during the wars and eventually became a negotiator between the Indians on the reservations and the government; Victorio—was the last Indian to wage war against the government in Texas.

Thinking Critically

1. **Synthesizing Information:** At first, the government sought to end the conflict peacefully. When the Indians refused to move to the reservations and continued to raid settlements, the government turned to military force.

2. Classifying Information:
(a) Elm Creek Raid; (b) Battle of Adobe Walls, Tule Canyon, Sweetwater Creek, Battle of Palo Duro Canyon, raids against Victorio; (c) Salt Creek Raid, Battle of Blanco Canyon, McClellan Creek

3. Analyzing Information: Ten Bears says that the Indians wish to continue their way of life on the prairie. He says that the Texans took the Indians' land from them and that the land given to them by the government is too small.

Linking History and Geography

1. The Indians probably could not have survived. Food would be difficult to find, and, without horses, they could not have traveled in search of additional food.

2. Settlements were few in the region, so troops had to carry their own supplies and water, which slowed them. Indian raiders could easily cross the border and escape into Mexico.

TAAS *Practice*
Using Primary Sources

1. C
2. A

TAAS *Practice*
Writing Persuasively

Letters will vary but should be written from the perspective of settlers, who believed that the land was rightfully theirs.

Practicing Skills

1. **Sequencing Events:** Time lines should illustrate the following sequence of events: Elm Creek Raid, 1864; Treaty of Medicine Lodge Creek, 1867; Salt Creek Raid, May 1871; Satanta's parole, August 1873; Battle of Adobe Walls, June 1874; Battle of Palo Duro Canyon,

September 1874; Quanah Parker's surrender, June 1875; Victorio's defeat, 1880.

2. **Interpreting Graphs:** As the number of farms grew, the number of buffalo fell. More farms meant less land for the Indians. The elimination of the buffalo meant the end of the Indians' means of survival.

Enriching Your Study of History

1. **Individual Project:** Reports should demonstrate research beyond information presented in the chapter.

2. **Cooperative Project:** Debates should be supported by sound reasoning and should demonstrate differing points of view.

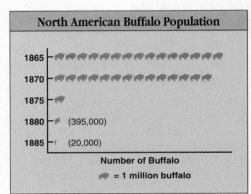

North American Buffalo Population

1865
1870
1875
1880 (395,000)
1885 (20,000)

Number of Buffalo

= 1 million buffalo

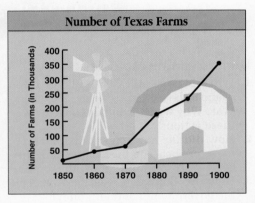

Number of Texas Farms

Number of Farms (in Thousands)
400
350
300
250
200
150
100
50

1850 1860 1870 1880 1890 1900

1. Parker probably replaced her new clothes with Comanche clothes because
   A she liked white women's clothes
   B she disliked wearing Comanche garments
   C she was more comfortable wearing Comanche garments
   D she was more comfortable wearing white women's clothes

2. Parker's reactions probably surprised her rescuers because
   A they expected her to prefer white women's clothes to Indian clothes
   B they expected her to take time to readjust to white people's ways
   C she was grateful for being rescued from the Indians
   D she made no attempt to escape from her rescuers

TAAS *Practice*
Writing Persuasively

Imagine that you are a settler who has come to Texas to start a new life. Write a letter to a relative in the East. Explain why you must be allowed to remain on the

frontier, even if it means forcing all the Indians onto reservations.

Practicing Skills

1. **Sequencing Events:** Arrange the following on a time line: Victorio's defeat, Treaty of Medicine Lodge Creek, Battle of Adobe Walls, Satanta's parole, Quanah Parker's surrender, Salt Creek Raid, Elm Creek Raid, Battle of Palo Duro Canyon.

2. **Interpreting Graphs:** Study the two graphs on this page. How might the figures depicted in the graphs be related? How might both figures have affected the Texas Indians?

Enriching Your Study of History

1. **Individual Project:** Prepare a short research report on one of the following: Quanah Parker, Satanta, Ranald Mackenzie, Lawrie Tatum, Victorio.

2. **Cooperative Project:** With your classmates, prepare a debate on the following question: Can people with different ways of life live together in peace as equals? Then hold the debate for the entire class.

CHAPTER 21

THE CATTLE KINGDOM

TEACHER'S TIME LINE

Section 1	Section 2	Section 3	Section 4	Review and Assessment
Pp. 425–28	Pp. 428–33	Pp. 433–39	Pp. 440–43	
1 Day	1 Day	1 Day	1 Day	1 Day

⬥ TEACHER MATERIALS

Core: Chapter 21 Time Line; Graphic Organizer 21; Enrichment Worksheet 21; Review Worksheet 21; Reteaching Worksheet 21; Chapter 21 Tests, Forms A & B

Additional: Geography and Graph Skills 21, Map and Chart Transparencies 19, Informal Evaluation Forms, Test Generator

⬥ OBJECTIVES

1. Describe the longhorn cattle, and discuss their adaptation to the Texas open range.
2. Identify the major cattle trails, and discuss why they were developed.
3. Describe life on a cattle drive.
4. Identify the four largest ranches in Texas history.
5. Identify significant persons in the history of the open range in Texas.
6. Explain the causes for the end of open-range ranching.

⬥ RESOURCES

BOOKS FOR TEACHERS

Adams, Andy. *The Log of a Cowboy: A Narrative of the Old Trail Days*. Boston: Houghton Mifflin, 1927. Primary source account of life on the trail.

Dale, Edward Everett. *Cow Country*. Norman: University of Oklahoma Press, 1965. Story of the cattle business.

Dick, Everett. *The Sod-House Frontier, 1854–1890*. Lincoln: Johnson, 1954. Life and times along the extending frontier.

Gard, Wayne. *The Chisholm Trail*. Norman: University of Oklahoma Press, 1954. Story of this important cattle trail.

Haley, J. Evetts. *The XIT Ranch of Texas and the Early Days of the Llano Estacado*. Norman: University of Oklahoma Press, 1953. Story of early ranching days.

Lea, Tom. *The King Ranch*. Boston: Little Brown, 1957. Story of this famous ranch.

Siringo, Charles A. *A Texas Cowboy*. New York: Sloans, 1950. Personal memoir.

MULTIMEDIA MATERIALS

The Ballad of the Iron Horse. (video, 29 min.) Learning Corporation of America, distributed by Simon and Schuster Communications, 108 Wilmot Rd., Deerfield, Illinois, 60015. History of the railroad.

Do You Mean There Are Still Real Cowboys? (video, 60 min.) PBS Video, 1320 Braddock Place, Alexandria, Virginia, 22314. The old and the new West.

On the Cowboy Trail. (video, 60 min.) PBS Video, 1320 Braddock Place, Alexandria, Virginia, 22314. Contemporary cowboys and their way of life.

STUDENTS WITH SPECIAL NEEDS

Limited English Proficient Students (LEP)

Have students skim the chapter and list all of the boldfaced terms as well as other terms related to the Texas cattle kingdom. Ask them to indicate which terms they feel they already know and the source of their knowledge. *(Some students may indicate western movies.)* Discuss the terms and their usage. Point out compound words such as *stockyards, round-up, chuckwagon,* and *longhorn.* Ask students to separate the compounds and then decide whether the individual words combine into appropriate descriptions for each term. See other activities labeled **LEP.**

Students Having Difficulty with the Chapter

Have students work in pairs to create diagrams to represent answers to the following questions:

a. What industries grew from the increased demand for Texas longhorns?

b. How were Texas longhorns useful to Texas?

c. What cowboy terms grew out of the cattle industry?

Review the diagrams with students. **LEP**

Auditory Learners

Have auditory learners read one of the works of Texas author J. Frank Dobie and present an oral book report. You might wish to ask some students to research and present a report on Dobie's life. See other activities labeled **A.**

Visual Learners

Have visual learners work together to create a series of illustrated "want ads" to be placed in an eastern newspaper during the 1800s. Students are advertising for persons necessary to conduct trail drives, including trail bosses, cooks, ramrods, pointers, flankers, and scouts. The ads should include the job duties as well as the origin and destination of the trail drives. Display the ads in the classroom. See other activities labeled **V.**

Tactile/Kinesthetic Learners

Provide the following scenario to students: It is the year 1873, and you have decided to open a cattle ranch in Texas. Using a blank map of the United States, indicate the following: the location of your ranch, labeling any physical features of the area that influenced your decision to locate there, and the trail you will follow to move your cattle to market. Ask students to display their maps and address the following questions: Why have you chosen this location? Why have you chosen this trail? See other activities labeled **TK.**

Gifted Students

Have gifted students work in small groups to practice creative problem solving. Ask them to consider the economic opportunities created by the Texas cattle industry in the 1800s. Then have them select a business to start in Texas today. They should prepare a business plan, which includes a description of the business, estimated costs, products, necessary employees, and potential customers. They should also indicate what their greatest barrier to success will be. Allow time for groups to present their business plans to the class. See other activities labeled **G.**

VOCABULARY

In addition to the boldfaced terms in each section, some students might benefit from discussing the meanings of these terms.

Section 1: *industry* (p. 425); *predators* (p. 426); *enterprising* (p. 427); *open range* (p. 427).

Section 2: *relays* (p. 431); *North Star* (p. 432).

Section 3: *emerged* (p. 434); *tribute* (p. 434); *dominant* (p. 436).

Section 4: *lease* (p. 442).

CHRONOLOGY

Have students study the Chapter 21 Time Line and identify relationships among the events.

GRAPHIC ORGANIZER

Have students skim the chapter and complete the Chapter 21 Graphic Organizer. *(You might wish to use this activity to review rather than to introduce the chapter.)*

ENRICHMENT

Have students complete the Chapter 21 Enrichment Worksheet.

SECTION 1

FOCUS

Past Learning (I) Write on the chalkboard the terms *supply* and *demand*. Ask students if they can provide a sentence describing the relationship between the two terms. *(Example: As supply decreases, demand increases.)* Tell students that in Section 1 they will learn more about the concept of supply and demand and its effect on the Texas cattle industry after the Civil War.

INSTRUCTION

Vocabulary (I) You may wish to preteach the following boldfaced term: *brand* (p. 427). **LEP**

THE CATTLE KINGDOM

CHAPTER 21

CHAPTER 21 OVERVIEW

After the Civil War, the demand for beef increased in the North. With railroads in the Midwest linked to the growing cities of the Northeast, Texans took full advantage of this economic opportunity. Cattle ranching in Texas became a huge, profitable industry. By the mid 1800s, the Texas cattle kingdom had spread to the open lands of West Texas and north into the plains states.

The Story Continues...

The Spanish conquistadores brought herds of cattle with them from Spain. Soldiers and priests at Spanish missions depended on cattle for their food. Thousands of cattle roamed free until, in the nineteenth century, enterprising Texans rounded up and began marketing the wild cattle. The Texas cattle kingdom was born.

Cattle ranches became important to the Texas economy. After the Civil War the demand for beef grew even greater. Texans drove cattle north to the railroad lines, where the cattle were then shipped east. The Texas cattle industry became a booming business. In this chapter you will read about types of cattle, cowboys, cattle trails, ranchers, and how Texas came to be king of the cattle kingdom.

As you read the chapter, look for the answers to these questions:

1. How did the cattle kingdom begin in Texas?
2. What trails did cattle ranchers follow, and what was life like on the trail?
3. What were some of the famous Texas ranches? What was the life of a cowboy like?
4. What caused the end of cattle ranching on open ranges?

■ The Open Range in Texas

The Texas cattle kingdom was different from the cattle industry in more settled regions of the United States. In the East, cattle were raised on farms. Herds were usually small, and they were kept in fenced pastures. In Texas, much of the industry grew upon a vast, open range. This rangeland was public and open to anyone who wanted to use it. Cattle in Texas could graze on nearly endless grass prairies. The Texas ranchers grazed thousands of cattle under the care of cowboys on horseback.

Michael Murphy,
Texas Tourist Development Agency

The longhorn was the primary breed of cattle during the cattle-drive days in Texas. Today, other cattle breeds are much more common in the state, but the longhorn is important to the history of the Texas cattle kingdom.

Essential Elements
1B, 2H, 3D, 3F, 5C, 8A, 8C, 9A, 9B, 9E

Illustrating (I) Have students work together to create a life-sized drawing of a Texas longhorn for classroom display. For accuracy in size and color, have them consult an encyclopedia or other reference. **V, TK, LEP**

Synthesis and Analysis (I) Read aloud the following statement from the textbook: "By the 1860s, those who had the will and the nerve found new opportunities for wealth in Texas." Ask students: What does the author mean? Ask them to find examples in the text to support this statement. **A**

Guided Practice (I) Have students create on the chalkboard a flow chart that illustrates the development of the Texas cattle kingdom. Ask them to copy the chart on a sheet of paper. Later during the study of the chapter, have students add to the chart the reasons for the closing of the open range. **A, V, TK, LEP**

Painting by Theodore Gentilz, San Antonio Museum Association

Mexican vaqueros worked the first large-scale ranches in Texas. The vaqueros passed on the methods and general know-how of ranching to later generations of cowboys.

The Texas Longhorns. The Spaniards brought a hardy, lean breed of cattle to Mexico in the sixteenth century. In Texas, these cattle mixed with heavier cattle brought by Anglo Americans. A new breed developed called the longhorn.

Just before Texas won its independence from Mexico in 1836, there were more than 100,000 longhorns in Texas. That number had jumped to more than 3 million by 1860. The longhorns were well suited for the open range of South Texas. They were strong animals who could endure hot weather as well as cold. They thrived on the native grasses and during droughts ate brush and prickly pear. Their long, pointed horns protected them from predators such as wolves and cougars. Long-legged and strong, they could travel great distances to find water in a dry, harsh land.

The Texas longhorns were, of course, most distinguished by their long, sharp horns. The average horn was

426 *Unit 8*

EXTENSION

Economics (III) Challenge students to complete the following information:

Number of longhorns in 1836: 100,000
Number of longhorns in 1860: 3 million
Percent increase:
Price of cattle in Texas: $4 per head
Price of cattle in Northeast: $40 per head
Percent increase:

Have students develop a conclusion based on the figures above. Then have them compare findings. **G, A**

Independent Practice (I) Refer students to the discussion on supply and demand in the Focus activity. Ask students to use these terms in a two- or three-sentence paragraph summarizing the subsection "The Demand for Cattle Grows." Invite volunteers to read their paragraphs aloud. **A**

RETEACHING
Have students work in pairs to create a series of cause-and-effect statements based on the information in Section 1. Call on volunteers to read their statements aloud. **A, LEP**

about six feet from tip to tip. Some were even longer. Early Texas settlers displayed these horns on their walls, and from the horns they made buttons, spoons, cups, furniture, decorations, and household utensils. Gunpowder stayed dry when stored in the end of a horn.

The Early Ranchers. The first ranchers in Texas were the Spanish missionaries and soldiers who raised cattle near their missions and forts. Numerous Mexican settlers operated ranches from Laredo to San Antonio in the early 1800s. Martín de León and Placido Benavides had a huge ranch near Victoria. The De Leóns claimed to have the oldest Texas **brand**, or design burned into the hide of cattle as proof of ownership. The De León brand was *EJ*, which stood for Espíritu de Jesús, or "Spirit of Jesus."

The Texas cattle industry expanded somewhat in the 1840s. Large-scale operations were begun by James Taylor White, who took his cattle from Liberty County to market in New Orleans. In 1846, Edward Piper took a herd of Texas cattle to Ohio. Some Texans drove cattle to California after gold was discovered there in 1849. Samuel Maverick in San Antonio sold cattle to other Texans and to the Mexican army. He sometimes shipped them to New Orleans. H.L. Kinney operated a large ranch near Corpus Christi. Perhaps the most famous of all Texas ranchers began operations in the 1850s. Richard King's ranch in South Texas was later expanded to more than 1 million acres. Unlike most Texans who started ranches later, King acquired title to the land on which his cattle grazed.

The availability of good grasslands and wild cattle made it possible for any enterprising person to enter the cattle business. The writer J. Frank Dobie noted an old saying that all it took to become a rancher in Texas was "a rope, a branding iron, and the nerve to use it." By the 1860s, those who had the will and the nerve found new opportunities for wealth in Texas.

The Demand for Cattle Grows. When the Civil War broke out, the demand for Texas beef increased. At first, attempts were made to ship Texas cattle to Confederate troops east of the Mississippi River. But as the war dragged on, it became more difficult to get beef to the battle fronts. Also, many ranchers were off fighting the war, so the Texas herds were neglected. The number of Texas cattle running wild on the open range grew.

Panhandle-Plains Historical Museum

Cattle were marked with brands that identified their owners.

CLOSURE

As you write their responses on the chalkboard, ask students to list at least three factors that contributed to the development and growth of the cattle kingdom in Texas.

ASSESSMENT

Have students complete the Section 1 Review on page 428.

SECTION 2

FOCUS

Student Experiences (I) Have students review the illustrations in this section. Ask them to relate any tales or stories they know regarding cowboys and cattle drives. Ask them if they think the stories are exaggerations. Tell them to keep these stories in mind as they read the section.

Answers to Section 1 Review

Define: *brand*—design burned into the hide of cattle as proof of ownership

Identify: Martín de León—owned a large ranch near Victoria in early 1800s; Samuel Maverick—sold cattle to Texans and the Mexican army; Richard King—rancher in South Texas, whose ranch later expanded to more than 1 million acres; J. Frank Dobie—noted Texas writer

1. They were strong, could endure hot and cold weather, lived on native grasses, ate brush and prickly pear during droughts, and could walk great distances to reach water.
2. King owned title to the land on which his cattle grazed.
3. The population in the Northeast was growing, as was the demand for beef.

Exploring Economics: Possible answers: Many of the ranchers were off fighting the war and could not supply the beef; the armies needed to feed the troops.

Synthesizing Information: Stockyards, packing houses, and beef-processing plants are mentioned in the chapter. Businesses not mentioned in the chapter might include tanners and leatherworkers.

Essential Elements
3C, 3D, 3E, 3F, 5B, 8A, 9A, 9B, 9C

SECTION 1 REVIEW

Define: brand
Identify: Martín de León, Samuel Maverick, Richard King, J. Frank Dobie

1. How were longhorns suited to the open range of South Texas?
2. How did the King ranch differ from other ranches at the time?
3. Why was a head of cattle worth more in the Northeast than in Texas?

Exploring Economics: Why do you think the demand for beef grew during the Civil War?

Synthesizing Information: What businesses were created to serve the cattle industry? Can you think of any that are not mentioned in the chapter?

When the war ended, new cattle markets opened. Railroads now connected cities in midwestern states such as Missouri with the larger cities of the Northeast. The growing population in the Northeast demanded beef, and Texans jumped at the opportunity. In Texas, cattle were selling for $3 or $4 per head. In the cities of the Northeast, the cattle were worth between $30 and $40 per head!

By 1865, stockyards and packing houses were opening in Chicago. Soon, more beef-processing plants appeared farther west in St. Louis and Kansas City. These plants were built to prepare the beef for shipment to cities in the North and East. Other markets were available as well. Army posts and Indian reservations in the Midwest and West wanted Texas beef. The major problem faced by the Texas ranchers was how to get the cattle to the nearest railroad lines. The tough longhorns provided a simple solution: they could walk. ○

② The Texas Cattle Trails

In the fall and winter of 1865–1866, ranchers in South and Central Texas rounded up thousands of cattle. When the grass began to turn green in the spring, the herds were driven north to the nearest railroad line in Sedalia, Missouri. More than 200,000 head of cattle made the journey of around 800 miles.

The Granger Collection

The cattle-drive era started after the Civil War, in response to the growing demand for Texas beef.

Vocabulary (I) You may wish to preteach the following boldfaced terms: *roundup* (p. 431); *remuda* (p. 431). **LEP**

Art and History (I) Have students examine the paintings on pages 428 and 433 and the photograph on page 432. Stimulate class discussion by asking individual students to describe what they see in the illustrations. Ask: From what you see in the paintings and photograph, do you think you would have liked to have been a cowboy? Why or why not? **A, V, LEP**

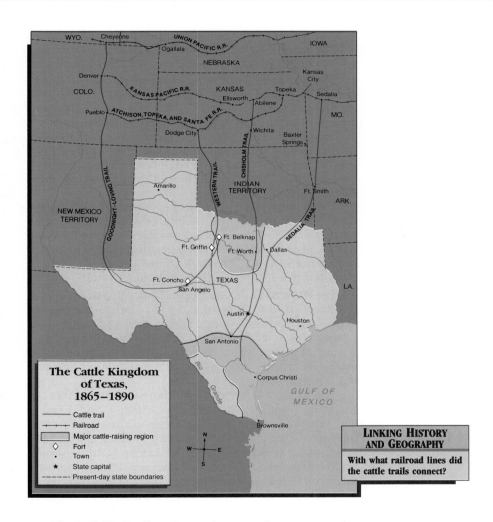

The Cattle Kingdom of Texas, 1865–1890

- ——— Cattle trail
- ╫╫╫ Railroad
- ▨ Major cattle-raising region
- ◇ Fort
- • Town
- ★ State capital
- ------ Present-day state boundaries

LINKING HISTORY AND GEOGRAPHY

With what railroad lines did the cattle trails connect?

Transparency 19
An overhead transparency of this map can be found in the Teacher's Resource Binder.

Linking History and Geography
Union Pacific Railroad; Kansas Pacific Railroad; and the Atchison, Topeka, and Santa Fe Railroad

The Sedalia Trail. The cattle were driven over what came to be called the Sedalia Trail. From South Texas, the trail reached northward through Northeast Texas and western Arkansas to the rail line in Central Missouri.

These first cattle drives encountered serious problems. The Sedalia Trail passed through farmland in Missouri. Farmers there claimed that the cattle ruined their crops. They also claimed that the Texas cattle carried a disease called Texas fever caused by ticks. This disease spread to

Historical Imagination (I) Tell students to imagine that they are magazine reporters in 1875. Have them compose an article titled "A Day on the Cattle Trail." Invite volunteers to read their articles aloud. **A**

Guided Practice (I) Pose the following questions for class discussion: It is the late 1800s. You can be a rancher or a cowboy. Which occupation will you choose? Why? Allow time for students to present varying opinions. **A, LEP**

Western History Collections,
University of Oklahoma Library

Jesse Chisholm was of Scottish and Cherokee ancestry. He was a well-known Indian trader and guide. Chisholm also served as an interpreter at various Indian treaty councils in Texas, Indian Territory, and Kansas.

Austin History Center, Austin Public Library

This photograph shows cowboys at Doan's Store at Doan's Crossing. Doan's Crossing was a stopping point at the Red River.

animals in Missouri. The Texans were sometimes attacked and their cattle scattered by angry farmers. They needed a new route to bring cattle to the railroad lines.

The Chisholm Trail. A businessman named Joseph McCoy convinced Texans to drive their cattle farther west. At Abilene, Kansas, McCoy built corrals and loading pens near the Kansas Pacific rail line. He sent messengers south to Texas ranches to encourage ranchers to drive their cattle to Abilene for shipment eastward. In 1867, only 35,000 longhorns passed through the Abilene stockyards. By 1869, however, the number of cattle sold in Abilene was more than 350,000.

Cattle were herded to Abilene from Texas on the Chisholm Trail. Jesse Chisholm was a trader who blazed part of the trail while traveling in Indian Territory (present-day Oklahoma). The new trail began near San Antonio and moved northward to Austin. It passed west of Fort Worth, went through Indian Territory, and then to Abilene.

The Western Trail. As the Indians were removed from the plains in the 1870s, the Texas population grew and expanded westward once again. Farms and settlements sprang up along the Chisholm Trail. To avoid the new settlers, Texas ranchers again sought cattle trails farther west. The favorite cattle-drive route by the mid 1870s was the Western Trail.

The Western Trail ran north from San Antonio through Kerrville, passed Brady, Coleman, Albany, and Vernon, and crossed the Red River at Doan's Crossing. The trail then went through Indian Territory to reach the railroad line in southwestern Kansas at Dodge City. Cowtowns such as Dodge City and Abilene grew from small frontier villages to boomtowns almost overnight. There the exhausted cowboys relaxed, their pockets full of money after the long cattle drive. Many of the legends and stories about the American West came from the wild and rowdy days when the Texas cowboys rode into Kansas cowtowns.

The Goodnight-Loving Trail. Not all of the Texas longhorns driven north went to markets in Kansas. In some years, more than half of the Texas cattle were driven elsewhere. They were sold to military posts and to the Cheyenne and Sioux reservations in Nebraska and the Dakota Territory. Many of the Texas longhorns were sold to ranchers in Colorado, Montana, and Wyoming. Texas cattle helped expand

EXTENSION
Relating History to Geography (II) Have students report on the impact of the railroads on life in Texas. Their reports should focus on the geographic theme of *movement*. Ask them to supplement their reports with maps, photographs, or other visuals. **A, V, TK, G**

Independent Practice (II) Ask students to write an essay titled "The Legend of the American West: Myth vs. Reality." Tell them to base their essays on information in Section 2 as well as on information they have gathered from movies, television, and books. Invite volunteers to read their essays aloud. **A**

the cattle kingdom from South Texas to Canada. Most Texas cattle were driven to markets along a trail beginning in West Texas called the Goodnight-Loving Trail.

Before the Civil War, John Chisum had established a cattle operation in Denton County in North Texas. After the war, the cattle kingdom spread in North and West Texas. In 1866, Charles Goodnight and Oliver Loving drove cattle from Fort Belknap in north central Texas, southwestward to Fort Concho, then along the Middle Concho River. When they reached the Pecos River, they shifted northward into New Mexico. They then drove the herd through Fort Sumner, New Mexico, over Raton Pass, and into eastern Colorado. On their third trip along this trail, Oliver Loving eventually died of wounds received during an Indian attack. Goodnight continued driving herds over the trail. In 1876, Charles Goodnight established the first permanent ranch in the Texas Panhandle, the JA Ranch.

Life on the Cattle Trail. A trail drive began with a **roundup**. Cowboys rode the open range, herding the longhorns to a central camp. Cowboys from different ranches usually worked together to collect the cattle. They branded calves and unmarked strays, and they separated the animals into herds.

The drive north followed one of the cattle trails. It began when the grass was green so that the cattle could eat as they moved. Some ranchers rode along and used their own cowboys, but most hired others to move the cattle. Charles Schreiner, John Lytle, and John Henry Stephens made large sums of money herding other people's cattle to market.

Herds on the trail ranged in size from several hundred cattle to as many as 3,000. The larger herds required fifteen to twenty or more cowboys. The cowboys needed 50 to 60 horses to do their work. Each cowboy used several horses in relays of two or three, so a fresh mount was always available. The group of horses on the drive was called the **remuda**, the Spanish word for "exchange." A trail boss was in charge of the entire outfit. The boss had to plan the drive, keep the business records, and handle about fifteen independent cowboys. To help with these duties, the trail boss usually had a ramrod, or assistant.

A good camp cook was also a necessity. The cook usually traveled ahead of the herd and had meals prepared

Paramount Publishing Co., Amarillo

Oliver Loving helped establish the cattle kingdom in Texas. While traveling ahead of the herd on a cattle drive in 1867, Loving was wounded during an Indian attack. Taken to Fort Sumner, New Mexico, Loving died three weeks later. His last words to his partner, Charles Goodnight, were, "Take me back to Texas. Don't leave me in foreign soil." Goodnight brought his body back to Texas and buried him at Weatherford.

The Kansas State Historical Society

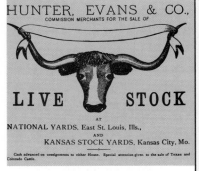

The cattle-trail era was well established at the time of this 1874 newspaper advertisement for livestock.

RETEACHING

Call on students to come to a wall map and trace the four Texas cattle trails mentioned in Section 2. Call on others to explain the reasons for the development of the trails along these routes. **LEP, A, V**

CLOSURE

Point out to students that much of what we hear and see on television and in the movies and read in books is glamorized. The actual life of the cowboy was difficult, dangerous, and lonely.

ASSESSMENT

Have students complete the Section 2 Review on page 433.

The chuckwagon served as a café, meeting point, and directional guide for the entire cattle drive.

The Southwest Collection, Texas Tech University

Answers to Section 2 Review

Define: *roundup*—process of herding cattle to a central location; *remuda*—the group of horses used on a cattle drive, Spanish word for "exchange"

(Continued on page 433)

when the outfit caught up. The cook was in charge of a chuckwagon loaded with food. Meals on the trail consisted of beans, beef, cornbread, molasses, and coffee. Every night the cook pointed the tongue of the chuckwagon toward the North Star, thus providing an accurate direction for the next day's drive. Nearly as important as the camp cook was the scout. The scout rode ahead and reported on trail conditions, water sources, or signs of trouble.

A day on the trail began before sunrise. After breakfast, the cowboys would choose their horses from the remuda. The two or three most experienced cowboys, known as pointers, rode in front of the herd to guide it in the right direction. Most of the cowboys rode along the sides, or flanks, of the herd to keep it together. The least-experienced cowboys rode in the rear, or drag position. A large herd was spread out over a half mile, and the riders in the rear "ate" dust the whole trip. On a good day, a trail-driving outfit could cover fifteen to eighteen miles.

Lack of water and the summer heat were constant problems on the trail. The cowboys always had to be alert

SECTION 3

FOCUS

Student Experiences (I) Allow students to experience the atmosphere of the West by playing music that features cowboy ballads or other western songs. Have them discuss how the lyrics related to the lives of the people.

Frederic Remington, Thomas Gilcrease Institute of American History & Art

This painting, titled *Stampeded by Lightning*, illustrates the danger of thunderstorms and lightning during a cattle drive. Many head of cattle could stampede and trample cowboys.

for rustlers, or cattle thieves, and the possibility of Indian attacks. A burst of thunder and lightning could stampede thousands of cattle in every direction, trampling everything and everyone in their path. In 1882, a thunderstorm stampeded eleven herds of cattle waiting to cross the Red River at Doan's Crossing. For ten days, more than 125 cowboys chased some 30,000 frightened cows.

Lightning storms on the Great Plains were terrifying events. As cowboy E.C. "Teddy Blue" Abbott remembered:

 Lots of cowpunchers were killed by lightning. . . . I was knocked off my horse by it twice. The first time I saw a ball of fire coming toward me and felt something strike me on the head. When I came to, I was lying under old Pete [his horse] and the rain was pouring on my face. . . . The cattle were always restless when there was a storm at night, even if it was a long way off, and that was when any little thing would start a run. Lots of times I have ridden around the herd, with lightning playing and thunder muttering in the distance, when the air was so full of electricity that I would see it flashing on the horns of the cattle, and there would be balls of it on the horse's ears and even on my mustache, little balls about the size of a pea. ○

3 Ranches, Ranchers, and Cowboys

By the early 1880s, cattle ranching was a thriving and profitable business in Texas. There were giant ranches in South Texas and all the way to the northern tip of the

SECTION ★2 REVIEW

Define: roundup, remuda

Identify: Joseph McCoy, Jesse Chisholm, Charles Goodnight, Oliver Loving

1. What problems did Texans face when driving cattle through Missouri? Why?
2. What did McCoy do in Abilene to attract cattle ranchers?
3. How did the cattle industry affect towns like Dodge City and Abilene?
4. Where besides Kansas were Texas cattle sold?

Using Historical Imagination: Imagine that you are a cowboy on a cattle drive. Write a cowboy song about your life on the trail.

Classifying Information: Make two lists of problems or dangers that ranchers and cowboys faced on the trail. Title one list *Nature* and the other list *Human*.

Identify: Joseph McCoy—businessman who developed the stockyards in Abilene, Kansas; Jesse Chisholm—blazed the Chisholm trail; Charles Goodnight—with Oliver Loving, blazed the Goodnight-Loving Trail, established the first permanent ranch in the Texas Panhandle; Oliver Loving—helped blaze the Goodnight-Loving Trail

1. Texans were sometimes attacked and their cattle scattered by angry farmers who claimed that the cattle ruined their crops and spread Texas fever.
2. He built corrals and loading pens near the Kansas Pacific rail line.
3. The cowboys passing through brought business with them, and the towns grew.
4. To military posts, to Indian reservations, and to ranchers in other states

Using Historical Imagination: Songs will vary but should be based on information presented in the chapter.

Classifying Information: *Nature*—heat, drought, storms; *Human*—cattle rustlers, Indian attacks, angry farmers

Essential Elements
3C, 3F, 4A, 8A, 9A, 9B

INSTRUCTION

Vocabulary (I) You may wish to preteach the following boldfaced term: *lariat* (p. 438). **LEP**

Writing (I) Have students use the information in Section 3 to write an obituary for Charles Goodnight. Call on volunteers to read their obituaries aloud. **A, LEP**

Comparison (I) Have students create a chart comparing the JA Ranch and the XIT Ranch. Labels on the chart should include: *Date Established, Location, Acres of Land, Number of Cattle.* Then draw the chart on the chalkboard and call on students to provide the information. **A, V, TK, LEP**

Vocabulary Development
Charles Goodnight was a trailblazer. Have students brainstorm about what might be involved in blazing a trail. Tell students that we still use the term *trailblazer* to signify someone who is a pioneer or leader.

Western History Collections,
University of Oklahoma Library

Charles Goodnight was one of the best-known Texas ranchers. Along with his partner Oliver Loving, Goodnight established the Goodnight-Loving Cattle Trail from Fort Belknap, Texas, to Cheyenne, Wyoming. This trail became one of the most widely used cattle trails.

Paramount Publishing Co., Amarillo

Mary Ann Dyer Goodnight was one of the early leading pioneers and citizens of the Panhandle.

Panhandle. Investors from other states and from Europe put money into these ranches, hoping for large profits from the sale of cattle. The famous ranchers and cowboys who emerged set the image of the West that is held to this day in many parts of the world.

Charles Goodnight. Charles Goodnight began his ranching career in Palo Pinto County in 1857. He raised cattle, drove them to market, served as a scout for the army, and rode with the Texas Rangers. During the 1850s and early 1860s, Goodnight blazed trails over which approximately 10 million cattle were moved northward from Texas. Few cattle drivers or ranchers left as much of an impact on the industry as Goodnight.

After his ranching ventures in New Mexico and Colorado, Goodnight started a ranch near Palo Duro Canyon in the Texas Panhandle in 1876. The area provided a good supply of water, plenty of grass, and a shelter from the winds that sweep across the Panhandle. Goodnight entered into a partnership with an Irish investor, John Adair. They named the Panhandle ranch the JA. By the mid 1880s, the JA Ranch covered more than 1.3 million acres of land and supported about 100,000 head of cattle. Cornelia Adair, John's widow, later bought out the Goodnights' share. She ran the JA Ranch from 1887 to 1921.

Charles and Mary Goodnight were leading figures in opening the Panhandle to settlement. In tribute to his wife, Charles Goodnight presented her with a clock inscribed:

> In Honor of Mrs. Mary Dyer Goodnight
> Pioneer of the Texas Panhandle
>
> For many months, in 1876–1877, she saw few men and no women, her nearest neighbor being seventy-five miles distant, and the nearest settlement two hundred miles. She met isolation and hardships with a cheerful heart, and danger with undaunted courage. With unfailing optimism, she took life's varied gifts, and made her home a house of joy.

The XIT Ranch and the Capitol. The largest and one of the most famous Texas ranches was the XIT Ranch. It was established in 1885 in the northwest corner of the Panhandle. The XIT covered 3,050,000 acres and extended nearly 200 miles along the Texas–New Mexico border. The ranch was almost the size of the entire state of Connecticut. At its peak, the XIT Ranch employed more than 150 cowboys to care for 150,000 head of cattle.

TEXAS VOICES

Thomas and Ella Bird were two of the first Anglo settlers to move into the Texas Panhandle. After their marriage in 1876, the couple settled in Cottle County near present-day Paducah. At first they survived by hunting buffalo, antelope, and deer. They were constantly on the move and lived in tepees, much like the Comanches and Kiowas who also roamed the plains. Tom tanned and sold hides. Ella made leather gloves and vests and sold them to cowboys. Because Ella was often paid with a newborn calf, the Birds gradually found themselves with a small herd of cattle. When their first child was born, Tom began working as a cowboy. The family lived on several different ranches during their marriage, until Tom died in 1886. In her later years, Ella recalled the changes that she had witnessed during her life on the Texas plains:

> How I would like to have laid everything aside and worked in this rock and nothing else. I wanted to be a sculptor. It bore on my mind [unceasingly], though I said nothing about it to anyone, for I felt that we were not able to devote my time to something I could not see any profit in. . . . Though I was never any hand to worry, I feel thankful I have always tried to make the best of life's possibilities; it is usually hard enough at best. . . .
>
> At times I seemed to stand and gaze on the progress of the country almost in wonderment. Only a little while ago it seemed when there were nothing but buffalo; then a space of time elapsed when there was nothing left but ourselves; yet we remained. This was a time ever to be remembered. There were months and months that I did not see the face of even one woman; next the cattle were being moved in, then the ranches, then a long space of time ere [before] the farming and building of towns, schools, etc., began, and then the present. What a change! But this was a change I had longed to see, for I wanted my children to grow up with the advantages of a civilized country.

The land for the XIT was given to a group of Chicago and British investors by the state of Texas. In return, the investors agreed to construct a new state capitol building in Austin. The old capitol had burned in 1881. The new capitol was completed in 1888, built from pink granite taken from Marble Falls in the Texas Hill Country. It is still the seat of Texas government.

The owners of the XIT Ranch said that their brand was rustler-proof. The block letters *XIT* could not be changed to another brand by cattle thieves. Others dispute this origin of the ranch's name. They claim that XIT stands for "Ten In Texas," representing the ten counties in which the ranchland is found. Others claim that the *X*, or *ten*, refers to ten investors in the ranch.

Institute of Texan Cultures

Bose Ikard was a top hand for Charles Goodnight, who called him "my detective, my banker, and everything else."

Essential Elements
3C, 3D, 3F, 9A

Historical Sidelight
A railroad was built between Austin and Marble Falls to haul the granite for the capitol.

Spindletop Museum, Lamar University, Texas Historical Foundation

This photograph shows the interior of the XIT Ranch headquarters. The XIT Ranch was established in 1885 and originally covered parts of ten Texas counties.

Economics
Emphasize that the large ranches were businesses. They existed to earn profits for the investors and owners.

Institute of Texan Cultures

Daniel Webster Wallace was one of the best-known trail hands and black ranchers in Texas. He made several trail drives to markets in Kansas and later purchased a ranch in Mitchell County.

Other Texas Ranches. Other large ranches were developed in the Panhandle with money from investors from the East or from Europe. Besides the XIT, these included the Spur, the Pitchfork, the LX, the Diamond F, and the Matador ranches.

The Matador Ranch came to be one of the largest ranching operations in North America. It was purchased in 1882 by the Matador Land and Cattle Company of Dundee, Scotland. Its headquarters was located in Motley County. The Matador began with 300,000 acres of land and 60,000 head of cattle. The manager of the Matador was a Scot named Murdo Mackenzie. Under his control, the Matador company continued to grow until it included a number of ranches from Texas to Canada.

Charles Goodnight, the XIT, and the Matador all played a part in spreading the fame of ranching in the Texas Panhandle. But the one ranch that continued as a large and dominant part of the Texas cattle industry was the King Ranch in South Texas. It originated in 1852, when Richard King and Mifflin Kenedy acquired a large grant of land southwest of Corpus Christi. King and Kenedy divided their property in 1868 and went on to increase their individual holdings. Richard King died in 1885, but his wife, Henrietta King, continued operation of the ranch. King and her son-in-law, Robert Kleberg, built the King Ranch into the largest Texas ranch of the twentieth century. King used her wealth and vast landholdings to establish

EXTENSION
Research (II) Ask students to conduct research to compare cattle ranching in Texas in the late 1800s with cattle ranching today. They should include in their reports the King Ranch and the XIT Ranch. **A, G**

Independent Practice (II) Have students write a fictional diary entry of a cowboy's typical day on the trail. Invite volunteers to read their entries aloud. **A**

the city of Kingsville. She also donated great amounts of money to build churches throughout South Texas.

A number of women operated ranches and worked cattle on trail drives. Margaret Borland ran her own ranch and led a trail drive to Kansas in 1873. Elizabeth Johnson Williams was also in the ranch business. Although she rode the Chisholm Trail with her husband, Hezekiah, Williams maintained her own separate herd and brand.

The Cowboys. The famous ranchers and giant ranches could never have produced cattle and profit without the cowboys. Most cowboys were young men, usually in their early twenties. They faced stampedes, Indian attacks, blizzards, floods, and hours of hard labor. On trail drives, it was not unusual for a cowboy to sleep in the saddle while riding 24 hours at a stretch. For all of their work and hardship, cowboys received only about $20 to $25 per month in salary.

On many Texas ranches, at least half of the cowboys were African Texans or Mexican Texans. Bose Ikard, a black cowboy, was one of Charles Goodnight's most trusted hands. Jim Perry and Matthew "Bones" Hooks were two other well-known black cowboys. Mexican Texan Ramón Alvarado was a famous boss on the King Ranch. Daniel Webster "80 John" Wallace was a respected black cowboy who eventually bought his own ranch. The ranch covered 8,000 acres of Mitchell County.

Mrs. Ron Brown, Institute of Texan Cultures

After the Civil War, Margaret Borland ran her own Texas ranch. By 1873, she owned more than 10,000 cattle. She became the first woman to drive her own cattle to market in Kansas, though she died of a fever after reaching Wichita. Her trail hands brought her body back to Texas. She was buried at Victoria.

Institute of Texan Cultures

"Bones" Hooks was a well-known and skilled cowboy. In later life, Hooks became a pioneer settler of the Panhandle. He is also credited with establishing one of the first churches for blacks in West Texas.

Vocabulary Development
Students may enjoy learning some of the following terms used by real cowboys. First, read the terms to students and ask them if they know their meanings. Then read to them the actual definitions.

Bronco Spanish word for "mean," often shortened to *bronc*. In cowboy parlance, this was a vicious unbroken horse.

Brush Popper a cowboy who works in the brush country

Cutting a Rusty doing your best

Eating Gravel being thrown from a bucking bronc or wild steer

Eyeballer anyone poking his nose into the business of others

Goosy very nervous or touchy

Moss Head a very old steer

Sweater an outsider hanging around camp in hope of obtaining a free meal

Telling a Windy telling a boastful story

To Tooth to look at the teeth of an animal to determine its age

Wide Place in the Road a very small town

Have each student use the names, terms, and identifications from Section 3 as clues to create a crossword or other word puzzle. Have students exchange and complete the puzzles. Allow pairs of students to work together to check and correct their answers. **LEP**

Remind students that the Texas ranches were operated for the purpose of making a profit from the sale of cattle. Profit is a major goal of our free enterprise system.

ASSESSMENT

Have students complete the Section 3 Review on page 438.

Answers to Section 3 Review

Define: *lariat*—long, light rope used by cowboys

Identify: Mary Dyer Goodnight—with Charles Goodnight, leading pioneer in opening the Panhandle to settlement; Elizabeth Johnson Williams—rode the Chisholm Trail, maintaining her own herd and brand; Ramón Alvarado—Mexican Texan who was a famous boss on the King Ranch; Daniel Webster "80 John" Wallace—respected black cowboy who eventually bought his own ranch

1. He blazed trails over which about 10 million cattle were moved northward from Texas.
2. It was given in exchange for construction of a new state capitol to replace the one that burned.
3. She established the city of Kingsville and donated money to build churches throughout South Texas.
4. Mexico

Writing Persuasively: Letters should demonstrate knowledge of the skills required of a cowboy.

Analyzing Information: James believed that cowboys were clever. For example, he agreed with the idea that cowboys could make the top of a steamboat from rawhide.

Austin History Center, Austin Public Library

By 1871, "Lizzie" Johnson Williams had a sizable herd of cattle and had registered her own brand. She later made cattle drives up the Chisholm Trail to Kansas with her husband.

SECTION 3 REVIEW

Define: lariat

Identify: Mary Dyer Goodnight, Elizabeth Johnson Williams, Ramón Alvarado, Daniel Webster "80 John" Wallace

1. What did Charles Goodnight contribute to the cattle kingdom?
2. Why did the state of Texas give land to establish the XIT ranch?
3. How did Henrietta King use the money she earned from ranching?
4. From where did much of the language and style of cowboys come?

Writing Persuasively: Imagine that you are a cowboy looking for work. Write a letter to Henrietta King, convincing her that she should hire you.

Analyzing Information: What do you think was Will S. James' opinion of cowboys? How can you tell?

Some of the black cowboys first learned their trade farther east. When African Americans and Anglo Americans first moved to Texas, they practiced a tradition of stock raising that was common across the American South. In this tradition, cattle and hogs were left to roam the deep woods, where they ate grass, switch cane, and acorns. Owners rounded them up from time to time and notched their ears with distinctive marks to identify them. They herded cattle and hogs by using stock dogs, and the southern stockman was more likely to carry a whip than a rope for herding in the dense woodlands. As the southern tradition of stock raising moved west, it mixed and merged with the stock-raising tradition of South Texas. In one generation, the stockman became a cowboy.

The tradition and style of the South Texas and West Texas cowboys began in Mexico. Many words used by cowboys came from the Spanish language. Among these are *remuda* as well as *ranch*, from the Spanish word *rancho*. All cowboys used a long, light rope called a **lariat**, from the Spanish word *la reata*. The lariat was also known as a *lasso*, from the Spanish word *lazo*. Contests of roping and riding took the name *rodeo*, from the Spanish word for "roundup" or "surrounding."

Some cowboys wrote books about life on the ranges and during the cattle drives. Charles Siringo wrote *A Texas Cowboy: or Fifteen Years on the Hurricane Deck of a Spanish Pony*. Later, Siringo wrote more books on his experiences along the Chisholm Trail and his years as a detective tracking down cattle rustlers. Will S. James wrote about the cowboy's equipment in *27 Years a Mavrick*:

> The bridle was hardly to be called a creation of fancy, as it was all they had, and was made from the hide of a cow, rubbed and grained until it was pliable.
>
> Some men broke the monotony by adopting the Mexican plan of making them of hair, which was a very popular article of which to make ropes. Some made their bridles of rawhide by platting [braiding], which made quite an artistic one. . . . The rope used for catching and handling horses and cattle was a platted one and was one of the best ropes for the purpose I ever used. . . . For several years after the war, long after reconstruction days in Texas, it was said—and not without some foundation—that a Texan could take a butcher knife and rawhide and make a steamboat, of course he could not have made the boiler, but when it came to the top part he would have been at home. One thing for certain, if the thing had broken to pieces, he could have tied it up. ○

Research (I) Ask students to consult a current detailed map of Texas and locate names of cities, counties, or landmarks that might have derived from important Texas ranchers mentioned in the chapter. Have them compile their findings on a blank map of Texas. **V, TK, LEP**

Essential Elements
2H, 3C, 3F, 5B, 8A, 8C, 9B

SPIRIT OF TEXAS

C.C. Slaughter: Texas Cattle King

Great fortunes were made in the Texas cattle business in the late 1800s. One of the most successful entrepreneurs on the open range was Christopher Columbus (C.C.) Slaughter, a ranching pioneer in West Texas. In 1873, a Dallas newspaper called Slaughter "the Cattle King of Texas."

C.C. Slaughter was born in 1837 near Nacogdoches. His father, a veteran of the Texas Revolution, was in the freight business and began raising cattle to add to the family income. C.C. went on his first cattle drive at the age of twelve. As a teenager, he learned about raising, driving, and selling cattle, and he realized then that ranching would be his life's work.

Before he was twenty, C.C. Slaughter recognized the potential value of the rich grasslands of the Texas Plains region. He convinced his father to move west and expand their ranching operation from hundreds of acres of land to millions of acres. Slaughter knew that it was a risk but that the rewards could be great.

The Slaughter family moved to the southern plains of West Texas, along the Brazos River near present-day Palo Pinto. They raised thousands of cattle and sold them to the United States Army and to Indians in nearby Oklahoma. It was not long before C.C. struck out on his own and began his ranching operation. He moved farther west and stead-ily built up one of the great ranching fortunes in Texas history.

C.C. Slaughter's ranching empire, known as "Slaughter Country," stretched from north of Big Spring for 200 miles to the New Mexico border west of Lubbock. By 1900, the Slaughter ranch included more than a million acres and 40,000 head of cattle.

It took courage, skill, and determination to survive and prosper in the rugged and unpredictable region of West Texas. People such as C.C. Slaughter helped open up that vast country to make it more productive and livable for millions of Texans to follow. His biographer, David Murrah, described Slaughter as a symbol and example of the early Texas cattle kings:

> C.C. Slaughter was a true entrepreneur [business owner]. He exhibited . . . flexibility by adapting from trail driving to cattle raising to improved breeding. He demonstrated a willingness to work at regional and national levels to improve the cattle industry as a whole, thereby aiding his own business. Always an optimist, he possessed the daring of a gambler as he risked cattle herds on a war-ravaged frontier, as he moved forty-two thousand dollars in an open wagon across sixty miles of dangerous roads to open a bank, and as he bought half a county of West Texas land considered to be worthless. Slaughter gambled, and his risks paid off handsomely.

Inset: **C.C. Slaughter**

Southwest Collection, Texas Tech University

FOCUS

Predicting (I) Bring in a piece of barbed wire to show students. Ask students if they can identify it. Then direct them to the title of Section 4: "The Closing of the Open Range." Ask students to speculate about how barbed wire might relate to this topic.

INSTRUCTION

Using Historical Imagination (I) Organize the class into two groups. Ask students in one group to imagine that they are cattle ranchers and students in the other group to imagine that they are sheep ranchers. They are at war because neither side can understand the other's point of view. Instruct students to review the information in the subsection "The Range Wars" and prepare an argument why their side is right. Have students choose a spokesperson to argue their side's case before the class. The rest of the class should act as arbitrator and suggest solutions. **A**

Essential Elements
3E, 3F, 9A, 9B, 9C, 9E, 9F

Economics
The large cattle companies found it profitable to sell their enormous land holdings in small parcels to ranchers and farmers.

Prairie fires could destroy valuable grazing land quickly. This mural, *Ranchers of the Panhandle*, shows cowboys using a dead steer to help put out a blaze.

Frank Mechau, Police Department Headquarters, Brownfield

4 The Closing of the Open Range

The success of the open-range cattle industry helped bring about its end. As more profits were made and as the Panhandle and other areas of West Texas were opened for settlement, the range became more crowded. The open range was soon fenced into individual ranches and farms.

Fencing the Open Range. As more people moved into West Texas, many ranchers felt the need to fence in their cattle and keep others' cattle off their land. By the 1880s, farmers were also pushing into this part of Texas, and they wanted to protect their cropland from stray cattle. The introduction of barbed wire made it possible to fence huge areas of land. Joseph F. Glidden of DeKalb, Illinois, is given credit for inventing barbed wire in 1873. He had a very simple but practical idea. Two wires were twisted together and held with small barbs about two inches apart. The sharp points of the barbs kept cattle off the fences without hurting the animals.

Uvalde Leader-News, courtesy Texas Historical Foundation

This photograph of a sheep ranch near Cotulla was taken around 1900.

Henry Sanborn, who also founded the city of Amarillo in the Panhandle, was the salesman who brought barbed wire to Texas in 1875. At first, Sanborn had trouble selling the wire in Texas because many people opposed fencing the range. But by the end of the 1880s, barbed-wire fences could be found in nearly every Texas county.

The Range Wars. Fencing the open range caused trouble. On the open range, cattle could wander freely to available water. It was important that they be able to do so in areas subject to drought. Fencing cut off sources of water, and some ranchers fought over water rights. Owners of small properties complained that they were being surrounded by the fences of giant cattle companies. Fencing to support sheep ranching angered cattle ranchers. They said that sheep ate the grass all the way to the root, making it useless for grazing cattle.

These disagreements led to fence-cutting wars in the 1880s. Gunfights sometimes broke out between guards and

The Kansas State Historical Society

The invention of barbed wire dramatically changed the open range and brought an end to the cattle-trail era.

RETEACHING

Have students work in pairs to create a cause-and-effect diagram titled "The Closing of the Open Range." Call on several students to draw their diagrams on the chalkboard. **V, TK, LEP**

CLOSURE

Ask students: With the close of the open range, what do you suppose happened to the cowboys who made their living driving cattle? Allow time for students to express varying opinions.

ASSESSMENT

Have students complete the Section 4 Review on page 442.

Answers to Section 4 Review

Identify: Joseph F. Glidden—inventor of barbed wire; Henry Sanborn—founded Amarillo and brought barbed wire to Texas; John Ireland—Texas governor who called a special meeting of the legislature to deal with the fence-cutting wars

1. Barbed wire consisted of two wires twisted together and held by small barbs about two inches apart. The sharp points of the barbs kept cattle off the fences without hurting the animals.
2. On the open range, cattle could wander freely to water. When ranchers began fencing the land, they cut off sources of water, and ranchers fought over water rights. Cattle ranchers claimed that fencing to support sheep ranches ruined the land for grazing cattle.
3. They allowed ranchers to pump water from underground.

Seeing Cause and Effect: Ranching became so successful that soon the open range developed into large fenced pastures as more farmers moved into the Panhandle and other areas of West Texas.

Evaluating Information: Responses will vary, but students should support their arguments with examples from the textbook.

The windmill greatly changed the development of West Texas. It tapped underground water supplies, so that ranchers were no longer forced to rely on the limited natural surface water of the region.

Archives Division, Texas State Library

Governor John Ireland called a special session of the Texas legislature to deal with the fence-cutting wars.

SECTION ★4★ REVIEW

Identify: Joseph F. Glidden, Henry Sanborn, John Ireland

1. How did barbed wire work?
2. Why did the fence-cutting wars begin?
3. What was the purpose of windmills in the Panhandle?

Seeing Cause and Effect: How did open-range ranching lead to its own end?

Evaluating Information: In your opinion, did ranchers effectively solve their problems caused by fencing? Why or why not?

Panhandle-Plains Historical Museum

fence cutters. One estimate of the damage resulting from this conflict in Texas was $20 million.

The Big Pasture Country. In 1883, Governor John Ireland called a special session of the legislature to meet in January of 1884 to deal with the problem of fence cutting. A law was passed making fence cutting illegal. Gates were required in fences every three miles to allow passage for roads and railroads. It was also made illegal for people to fence land they did not own or lease. To enforce the law, Texas Rangers were sent to the open-range country.

By 1890, the open range had nearly disappeared. Railroad lines were built into the Texas cattle country, ending the need for long trail drives to Kansas. Windmills were developed to bring underground water to the surface in the Panhandle. Wind blowing against the blades of a windmill supplied the power to pump water from deep underground. Windmills eased the problem created when natural water supplies were fenced. However, more farmers moved into the Panhandle and other areas of West Texas when windmills were developed. Soon the land of the open range became large fenced pastures. Ranches remained and continued to bring wealth to Texas, but the era of the cowboys and cattle drives was over. ✪

Geography (I) Have students choose one of the cities discussed in the special feature and write a paragraph describing its relative location. Have them consult outside references, such as an atlas or a gazetteer, to find its absolute location in terms of latitude and longitude. Invite volunteers to read their paragraphs aloud. **A**

Geography (I) Have students study the elevation and average temperature graphs in the special feature. Ask students to write a sentence describing the relationship between elevation and temperature. *(Example: Cities located at higher elevations generally have cooler temperatures.)* **V, LEP**

CITIES OF TEXAS

Amarillo and Lubbock

Population:
Amarillo—157,615;
Lubbock—186,206

Metro area population:
Amarillo—187,547;
Lubbock—222,636

Size: Amarillo—86.6 sq. mi.;
Lubbock—103.9 sq. mi.

Relative location: Amarillo lies in the center of the Texas Panhandle. Lubbock is 105 miles due south of Amarillo.

Region: Amarillo and Lubbock both are located in the High Plains region.

County: Amarillo—Potter and Randall counties. Lubbock—Lubbock County.

Special feature: The Texas Panhandle is one of the nation's major producers of cattle, oil, natural gas, and cotton.

Origin of name: *Amarillo*, the Spanish word for "yellow," described the banks of a nearby creek. Lubbock was named for Colonel Thomas S. Lubbock.

Landmarks: Amarillo—the World's Largest Cattle Auction; Lubbock—Texas Tech University

Economy: Amarillo is a major business and transportation center. Cattle, oil, natural gas, and helium production are the mainstays of the Amarillo economy. Lubbock is a major producer of cotton, food and dairy products, oil-field and irrigation equipment, and manufactured goods. Texas Tech University and School of Medicine add to

the stability of the Lubbock economy.

History: The first major settlement of the region was in 1887 near the site of the Fort Worth and Denver Railroad. Amarillo had been named by Mexicans who traded in the area. It quickly became the center of commerce in the Panhandle. Lubbock was founded in 1891 as a compromise between two other frontier towns competing for settlers. Its growth began when oil was found in the 1910s and 1920s.

Recreation facilities: Nearby Palo Duro Canyon and Lake Meredith provide recreation to the Amarillo area. Lubbock also has lake and park facilities, including Mackenzie State Park.

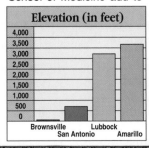

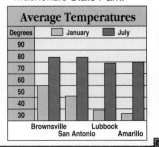

Essential Elements
4B, 5B, 5C, 9B

CHAPTER REVIEW RESOURCES

1. Chapter Review Worksheet 21
2. Chapter 21 Test, Form A
3. Reteaching Worksheet 21
4. Chapter 21 Test, Form B
5. **Informal Evaluation Forms:** Portfolio Assessment
6. *Texas, Our Texas* **Test Generator**

Essential Elements
3D, 3F, 5B, 9A, 9B

CHAPTER 21 REVIEW

CHAPTER 21 REVIEW ANSWERS

Understanding Main Ideas

1. The cattle could withstand cold, hot, and dry weather, could walk long distances, and could eat the grasses of the Texas plains.
2. After the Civil War, the population of the Northeast grew, and the demand for beef grew with it.
3. They were developed for ranchers to drive their cattle to the rail lines in the Midwest and then ship them to the East.
4. A trail boss controlled the drive. A cook was in charge of the chuckwagon, and a scout rode ahead to check trail conditions. Cowboys rode in front, on the flanks, and to the rear of the herd.
5. The government of Texas gave land to the owners of the XIT ranch in exchange for the construction of the capitol.
6. Farmers and ranchers began fencing the land.

Thinking Critically

1. **Synthesizing Information:** The longhorn originated there, and the first Texas ranches were begun there.

Understanding Main Ideas

1. How was the longhorn especially suited to open-range ranching?
2. What happened to the demand for beef when the Civil War ended?
3. Why were cattle trails developed?
4. Describe the organization of cowboys on a trail drive. Who did which jobs? How were cowboys arranged to control the herd?
5. How did the Texas capitol come to be built?
6. What caused the end of open-range ranching?

Thinking Critically

1. **Synthesizing Information:** The word *cradle* can mean a place where something begins or is born. Why might South Texas be called "the cradle of the cattle kingdom"?
2. **Evaluating Information:** Why do you think cowboys have been the subject of many books and films? Do cowboys deserve their heroic reputation? Explain your answer.
3. **Analyzing Information:** How were the open-range ranches dependent on the railroads?

Linking History and Geography

1. How did Charles Goodnight deal with the problem of high winds in the Texas Panhandle? How was wind used to solve the problem caused by fencing of water sources?

2. Describe the creation of the four trails described in the chapter. Give the reasons that each trail was created.

TAAS Practice
Using Primary Sources

E.C. "Teddy Blue" Abbott was a cowboy during the 1870s and 1880s. In 1937, he recalled his days as a cowboy in a book titled *We Pointed Them North.*

I heard a story once about a school teacher who asked one of these old Texas cow dogs to tell her all about how he punched cows on the trail. She said: "Oh, Mister So-and-So, didn't the boys used to have a lot of fun riding their ponies?"

He said: "Madam, there wasn't any boys or ponies. They was all horses and men."

Well, they had to be, to stand the life they led. Look at the chances they took and the kind of riding they done, all the time, over rough country. . . . If a storm come and the cattle started running—you'd hear that low rumbling noise along the ground and the men on herd wouldn't need to come in and tell you, you'd know—then you'd jump for your horse and get out there in the lead, trying to head them and get them into a mill before they scattered. . . . It was riding at a dead run in the dark, with cut banks and prairie dog holes all around you, not knowing if the next jump would land you in a shallow grave.

1. The teacher's attitude toward cowboys was that they
   A were tough and hardworking
   B were old and fun-loving
   C were young and fun-loving and did not work very hard
   D were young and hardworking

2. **Evaluating Information:** Answers will vary but should be supported with sound reasoning.
3. **Analyzing Information:** Ranchers depended on the railroads to transport the cattle to faraway markets.

Linking History and Geography
1. He established his ranch near Palo Duro Canyon, which provided a shelter from the winds. The winds powered the windmills that pumped water from underground.

2. Sedalia Trail: ran from South Texas to Sedalia, in Central Missouri—created to reach a railroad line; Chisholm Trail: ran from Texas to Abilene, Kansas—created to avoid angry farmers and because McCoy had built corrals and loading pens in Abilene; Western Trail: ran from San Antonio to the rail line at Dodge City, Kansas—created to avoid farms and settlements on the Chisholm Trail; Goodnight-Loving Trail: ran from Fort Belknap in north central Texas south to Fort Concho and then north through New Mexico—created to move cattle to northwestern markets

2. The author knew that cowboys had to be tough because
   A life was easy for them
   B their lives were always in danger
   C they often had to work during storms
   D they didn't have time to be afraid

TAAS *Practice*
Writing Persuasively

Imagine that you own an open-range cattle ranch. Your neighbor has built a fence around his grazing land, which includes a spring. Write him a letter asking that he take down his fence. Tell him why he should cooperate with you, and predict what might happen if other ranchers followed his example.

Practicing Skills

1. **Interpreting Pictures:** Study the picture of the chuckwagon on page 432. What can you tell about life on the trail from this picture? Explain.
2. **Interpreting Symbols:** Study the sixteen cattle brands on this page (above right). Branding cattle was especially important in the days of the open range, when cattle roamed the countryside. The brand on each cow showed who owned it. Brands made it difficult for rustlers, or cattle thieves, to steal the cattle and sell them as their own. Brands often reflected the names of the ranch to which the cattle belonged. The first symbol in the second row, for example, could be the brand of the Running W Ranch. Select five of the brands pictured, copy them onto a sheet of paper, and make up a ranch name for each one. Note that straight horizontal lines were

Cattle Brands

called "bars," and diagonal symbols often meant "lazy."

Enriching Your Study of History

1. **Individual Project:** Use the library to research the cowboys' special clothing and tools (lariat, branding iron, saddle, chaps, and so on). Create a poster showing the clothing and tools and explaining their uses.
2. **Cooperative Project:** Work with a partner to prepare an oral report about one of these topics: brands and branding of cattle, cattle rustlers, the history of barbed wire, types of Texas cattle, female "cowboys," cowboys' horses, cowboy songs.
3. **Cooperative Project:** Working with two or three partners, write and perform a ten-minute play. The setting is a Texas ranch in the 1800s. Your characters should represent typical ranch dwellers and workers. Their conversations should give your audience a clear idea of what ranch life was like in those days. Try presenting your play to the class. Wear convincing costumes.

TAAS *Practice*
Using Primary Sources
1. C
2. B

TAAS *Practice*
Writing Persuasively
Letters will vary but should predict the end of the open range.

Practicing Skills
1. **Interpreting Pictures:** Responses will vary but should incorporate information discussed in the chapter about life on the trail.
2. **Interpreting Symbols:** Students' interpretations of the brands will vary but should be logical and creative.

Enriching Your Study of History
1. **Individual Project:** Posters should be based on thorough research.
2. **Cooperative Project:** Oral reports should be well organized and based on thorough research.
3. **Cooperative Project:** Plays should be based on an understanding of ranch life during the 1800s.

THE INDUSTRIAL REVOLUTION

TEACHER'S TIME LINE

Section 1	Section 2	Section 3	Section 4	Review and Assessment
Pp. 446–51	Pp. 452–55	Pp. 456–60	Page 461	
1 Day	1 Day	1 Day	1 Day	1 Day

 ## TEACHER MATERIALS

Core: Chapter 22 Time Line; Graphic Organizer 22; Enrichment Worksheet 22; Review Worksheet 22; Reteaching Worksheet 22; Chapter 22 Tests, Forms A & B

Additional: Geography and Graph Skills 22, Map and Chart Transparencies 20, Informal Evaluation Forms, Test Generator

 ## OBJECTIVES

1. List the advantages of railroads over other available forms of transportation after the Civil War.
2. Discuss the ways in which state and local governments promoted the building of railroads in Texas.
3. Identify the major railroad lines and cities of Texas in the late 1800s.
4. Explain the effects of railroads on urban development.
5. Identify developments that had an impact on agricultural growth in Texas.
6. Explain the beginning of the oil industry in Texas, and list oil-related industries that developed in Texas in the late 1800s.
7. Discuss the effects of new inventions on the quality of life in Texas.

RESOURCES

BOOKS FOR TEACHERS

Boatright, Mody C. *Folklore of the Oil Industry*. Dallas: Southern Methodist University Press, 1963. Story of the oil industry.

Clark, Ira G. *Then Came the Railroads*. Norman: University of Oklahoma Press, 1958. Story of the coming of the railroads.

Proctor, Ben H. *Not Without Honor: The Life of John H. Reagan*. Austin: University of Texas Press, 1969. Life and times of this man.

Rister, Carl Coke. *Oil! Titan of the Southwest*. Norman: University of Oklahoma Press, 1949. Story of the discovery of oil and its impact.

Safford, H.R. *Railroads as a Factor in the Industrial Development of Texas*. Austin: Barker Texas History Center, 1930. Railroads and industrial development in Texas.

Schofield, Donald F. *Indians, Cattle, Ships, and Oil*. Austin: University of Texas Press, 1985. Economic forces shaping Texas.

Spratt, John Stricklin. *The Road to Spindletop: Economic Change in Texas, 1875–1901*. Texas History Paperbacks Series. Austin: University of Texas Press, 1985. Examines the effect of oil on Texas economics.

MULTIMEDIA MATERIALS

God Bless Standard Oil. (video, 60 min.) PBS Video, 1320 Braddock Place, Alexandria, Virginia, 22314. History of Standard Oil.

The Independents. (video, 60 min.) PBS Video, 1320 Braddock Place, Alexandria, Virginia, 22314. History of the independent oil wildcatters.

The Industrial Revolution. (video, 23 min.) Encyclopaedia Britannica Educational Corporation, 310 South Michigan Avenue, Chicago, Illinois, 60604. Examines the beginnings of the Industrial Revolution in the United States.

Oil. (video, 8 part series) PBS Video, 1320 Braddock Place, Alexandria, Virginia, 22314. Examines the global rise and influence of oil.

⬛ GENERAL STRATEGIES

STUDENTS WITH SPECIAL NEEDS

Limited English Proficient Students (LEP)

Provide students with a skeletal outline of the chapter, using the section and subsection headings as topics. As students study each section, they should complete the outline by writing in note form three to five facts about each topic. Have them use the outline to review the chapter. See other activities labeled **LEP.**

Students Having Difficulty with the Chapter

Ask students to skim the chapter, looking only at the illustrations. Point out that these portray many of the changes that took place in Texas from the mid 1800s to 1900. Select one illustration and explain the changes suggested. Ask students to find other "portraits of change" in the chapter. This activity will remind students that illustrations are important tools to use in studying history and will also establish readiness to begin the chapter. **LEP**

Auditory Learners

Have auditory learners select one of the topics discussed in the chapter and present an oral report. See other activities labeled **A.**

Visual Learners

Point out to students that in the late 1800s railroad companies encouraged settlers to move to West Texas. Have visual learners work together to develop advertising campaigns that these companies might have used. The advertisements should present the benefits of moving west and should suggest solutions to problems that settlers might face in this region. Have students present the advertising campaigns to the class, and have class members rate the effectiveness of each advertisement. See other activities labeled **V.**

Tactile/Kinesthetic Learners

Have tactile/kinesthetic learners choose one of the topics of the chapter and create a map, illustration, or model. For example, they might create a detailed map of the United States railroad system in 1900, a detailed illustration of a locomotive, or a model of an oil derrick, or they might demonstrate a nineteenth-century invention. See other activities labeled **TK.**

Gifted Students

Assign students a geographic region of Texas of which to prepare a map showing the following: major cities, forms of transportation, major rivers and bodies of water, natural resources, agricultural products. After reviewing the information on the map, students should decide on a business to establish in the region. The decision should reflect the use of the information on the map. Have students display their map and explain the reasons for their decision. See other activities labeled **G.**

VOCABULARY

In addition to the boldfaced terms in each section, some students might benefit from discussing the meanings of these terms.

Section 1: *authorized* (p. 447); *issuer* (p. 447); *interest* (p. 447); *finance* (p. 447); *prosperity* (p. 448).

Section 2: *potential* (p. 452); *erosion* (p. 453); *sorghum* (p. 453); *cultivated* (p. 454); *commercial farming* (p. 454).

Section 3: *venture* (p. 457).

Section 4: *turbines* (p. 461); *industrial revolution* (p. 461).

CHRONOLOGY

Have students study the Chapter 22 Time Line and identify the relationships among the events.

GRAPHIC ORGANIZER

Have students skim the chapter and complete the Chapter 22 Graphic Organizer. *(You might wish to use this activity to review rather than to introduce the chapter.)*

ENRICHMENT

Have students complete the Chapter 22 Enrichment Worksheet.

FOCUS

Past Learning (I) Ask students what advantages railroads might have over river transportation *(faster, dependable, able to reach areas boats cannot)*. Ask: Which of the Five Themes of Geography best represents railroad transporta-tion *(movement)*? Point out that the expansion of the rail-roads had a great impact on Texas and the rest of the United States. Railroad hubs grew into large cities, and people moved into previously unsettled areas.

CHAPTER 22 OVERVIEW

Texas experienced vast changes during the late nine-teenth century. With the coming of the railroads, the frontier all but disappeared as the popula-tion expanded westward. Rail lines brought new businesses and eased travel and trade; in-dustry and agriculture grew. New inventions changed the way people lived.

Essential Elements
3D, 3F, 4B, 5B, 5C, 8A, 8B, 8C, 9A, 9B, 9E, 9F

CHAPTER 22

THE INDUSTRIAL REVOLUTION

The Story Continues...

The growth of the railroads after the Civil War dramati-cally changed the lives of Texans. Because the railroad made travel easier and faster, more and more people moved to Texas. New businesses opened along the rail lines to serve the needs of travelers and new arrivals. Industry and agriculture also grew. Texas was feeling the effects of the national commercial and industrial revolution.

Chapter 22 focuses on the railroads, agriculture, and industries during this exciting time. You will read about the growth of the economy of modern Texas.

As you read the chapter, look for the answers to these questions:

1. How did state and local governments help promote the building of railroads in Texas? How did railroads affect Texas communities?
2. How did agriculture change in Texas during the 1870s and 1880s?
3. How did the oil industry begin in Texas?
4. What new inventions in the 1880s and 1890s affected life in Texas?

Institute of Texan Cultures, courtesy Mrs. Ford Boulware

This 1890s photograph shows a Texas and Pacific passenger train boarding at the Colorado City depot in West Texas.

1 The Expansion of the Railroads

In the years after the Civil War, new railroad lines were built in nearly every section of the United States. Railroads were the fastest means of transportation available. Towns, cities, and states in every region welcomed new rail lines to carry passengers and haul their products from farm and factory to market. In 1869, the first line connecting the Atlantic and Pacific coasts was completed. By 1860, the United States counted 30,626 miles of railroads. That figure increased to approximately 52,900 miles by 1870.

INSTRUCTION

Vocabulary (I) You may wish to preteach the following boldfaced terms: *bonds* (p. 447); *land grant* (p. 448); *junctions* (p. 450). **LEP**

Cooperative Learning (I) Organize students into small groups. Tell students in each group that they are local government officials of a Texas town in the 1860s. Have them create a plan to encourage a railroad company to pass through their city. Students should identify the town and explain how the railroad as well as the town will benefit from the plan. Have a spokesperson from each group present its plan to the class. **A, V, TK, LEP**

Amon Carter Museum, Fort Worth

The city of Fort Worth grew up around the military post established in the area in 1849. The arrival of the railroad marked the beginning of Fort Worth's growth as a major Texas city.

Demand for New Lines. The first railroad in Texas was the Buffalo Bayou, Brazos, and Colorado Railway, begun in 1852. Railroad lines built at this time all connected ports on rivers or the Gulf with nearby farm areas. For a number of years, the railroad system in Texas was slow to expand. By 1860, there were only 307 miles of track in Texas. Little progress was made in the 1860s, partly because of the Civil War and its effects. Even in 1870, Texas had only 583 miles of railroads.

Despite the lack of progress, many Texans saw the rail lines as the wave of the future. Rivers in Texas were unpredictable and unreliable for transportation. Roads turned to mudholes during wet weather. Railroads, on the other hand, promised fast, dependable, and cheap transportation. Farmers, businesspeople, and government leaders called for a rapid expansion of the Texas rail system.

Aid for the Railroads. In the 1850s, various cities and counties offered aid to railroad companies to encourage them to build new lines. Some local governments, such as San Antonio's, authorized the sale of **bonds**. These certificates were sold with the promise that the issuer would pay back the full amount, plus additional money as interest, after a certain period of time. The income from the sale of bonds was used to finance railroad construction. Other local governments offered loans or gave land to the

Midland County Historical Museum

This early photograph is of the Texas and Pacific Railroad. It was the first rail line to stretch from East Texas to West Texas.

railroad companies. The city of Fort Worth offered cash bonuses to any railroad passing through.

There was much competition for railroad service. Many people felt that railroads meant prosperity. A new line provided jobs for people building it. New businesses might open up near the line. A community that did not have a railroad might stop growing, while places near a railroad attracted businesses and prospered.

Land Grants to the Railroads. The most common form of aid to railroads was a **land grant**. In 1876, the Texas legislature passed a general land grant law for railroad companies that wished to build in the state. After completing ten continuous miles of track, a company could receive sixteen sections of land for each mile. The railroads were required to sell the land to finance surveying and construction of their lines. Texas eventually gave 32,153,878 acres of land to 41 railroad companies.

New Texas Railroad Companies. In 1880, the Texas and Pacific Railway Company began laying track west of Fort Worth. Working furiously, track gangs averaged a mile per day across the plains of West Texas. Supply camps were moved every 30 to 60 days to keep up with the construction crews. Through 1880 and 1881, the towns of Gordon, Baird, and Abilene were established along the new rail route. Eastland, Sweetwater, Colorado City, and Big Spring were also towns that grew with the railroad.

Guided Practice (I) Have students use the information in Section 1 to create a three-column chart with the following labels: *Railroad Company, Date Begun, Cities Linked.* **TK, LEP**

EXTENSION

Geography (II) Provide students with outline maps of the United States. To help students visualize the geographic extent of the railroad network, ask them to use library resources to make maps of the railroads built by the end of the nineteenth century. Use the maps as the basis for a class discussion of how the extension of railroad lines might have influenced the lives of ordinary people. **V, A, TK, G**

The track crews were in a race to reach El Paso and then build into New Mexico. Their company had been authorized by the United States to build to California. Now, however, a company called the Southern Pacific was building from California toward Texas. The company that built the most miles of track would receive the largest land grants.

On January 1, 1882, the two lines met at Sierra Blanca, about 90 miles east of El Paso. The owner of the Texas and Pacific, Jay Gould, was disappointed that his line had not reached El Paso. But for Texas it was a great day. The

Historical Sidelight
Jay Gould was among the rail owners who sought control of many different railroad companies across the United States. His goal was to establish national connections and eliminate his competition.

Linking History and Geography
Houston

LINKING HISTORY AND GEOGRAPHY

What city was the earliest major rail center in Texas?

The Growth of Railroads in Texas 1853–1920

NEW MEXICO

OKLAHOMA

ARK.

Amarillo

Lubbock

Wichita Falls

Texarkana

Fort Worth · Dallas

Longview

El Paso

TEXAS AND PACIFIC R.R.

Abilene

San Angelo

Waco

LA.

Sierra Blanca

TEXAS

SOUTHERN PACIFIC R.R.

Austin

Beaumont

Houston

San Antonio

Galveston

0   100
scale of miles
0   100
scale of kilometers

Eagle Pass

Indianola

Corpus Christi

Laredo

GULF OF MEXICO

Brownsville

Rail lines built before 1861
Rail lines built 1861–1880
Rail lines built 1881–1920

Transparency 20
An overhead transparency of this map can be found in the Teacher's Resource Binder.

Independent Practice (I) Have students create two lists: one of the Texas cities on which the railroad had a positive impact and another of those cities on which the railroad had a negative impact. Lists should be based on the information in Section 1. **LEP**

RETEACHING

Have students create an outline of Section 1, using the section subheadings as topics. After outlining each topic, they should write a one-sentence summary. Have students work together to create a class outline on the chalkboard. **LEP, TK, V**

Historical Sidelight

Most of the railroads built in Texas during the 1870s and 1880s were soon absorbed by a small number of large companies that dominated railroading throughout the Southwest. Among these large companies were the Atchison, Topeka, and Santa Fe; the Southern Pacific; the Missouri Pacific; the Texas and Pacific; and the Chicago, Burlington, and Quincy.

Answers to Section 1 Review

Define: *bonds*—certificates sold with the promise that the issuer will pay back the full amount, plus interest; *land grant*—section of land given to railroad companies to encourage construction of new lines; *junctions*—meeting points of two or more rail lines

Identify: Sierra Blanca—town 90 miles east of El Paso where the Texas and Pacific Railroad and the Southern Pacific met to complete the first rail line across Texas; T&P—Texas and Pacific Railway Company, first rail line to connect Texas from east to west

1. Railroads were fast, dependable, and cheap. Texas rivers were unpredictable and unreliable, and Texas roads became full of mudholes during wet weather.

(Continued on page 451)

San Antonio Light Collection, Institute of Texan Cultures

In the late 1800s, this frame building in San Antonio served as the railroad station for the San Antonio and Aransas Pass Railway.

Texas and Pacific Railroad and the Southern Pacific now connected Marshall in East Texas with El Paso in far West Texas. This same line provided rail service from Louisiana, through Texas, to California.

The T&P, or Texas and Pacific, was but one of the many new lines built in Texas during the 1870s and 1880s. Other lines soon linked the Gulf coast with North Texas and states beyond. The Houston and Texas Central was built from Galveston through Houston, Hearne, Dallas, and Denison. At Denison, it was met by the Missouri, Kansas, and Texas line, providing service north to St. Louis, Missouri.

In 1873, the Gulf, Colorado, and Santa Fe began building a line that connected Fort Worth with Galveston. The Southern Pacific connected El Paso with San Antonio and Houston. By building new lines and buying other ones, the company soon provided rail service through Texas to New Orleans.

Rails linked Texas to Mexico at this time as well. The International and Great Northern built a line through Longview south to Austin and San Antonio. It joined with the Mexican railways at Laredo on the border.

The Texas Panhandle was the last large region of Texas to have rail service. By 1882, the Fort Worth and Denver City Railroad was begun to connect Colorado with the Texas Gulf coast. The line extended from Denver, Colorado, into Texas at Texline. It passed through Dalhart, Amarillo, Childress, Wichita Falls, and Fort Worth. Branch lines were built to connect other major routes throughout the state.

Effects of the Rail Boom. By 1880, Texas had 3,244 miles of railroad tracks. By 1890, much of the state was crisscrossed with approximately 8,700 miles of railroads, and, by 1900, Texas led the nation with 9,866 miles of railway lines.

The new rail lines gave Texas a fast and dependable system of transportation. They also helped connect Texas with the rest of the United States. By 1890, people and goods could be transported from Texas to almost anywhere in the United States over various railroad lines.

The railroads brought great changes for most of the communities through which they passed. Cities grew rapidly at **junctions**, or meeting places, of two or more lines. Shops to repair locomotives and railroad cars were often built at junctions. New businesses were located at junctions

CLOSURE
Ask students to name one positive and one negative effect
of railroad expansion in the late 1800s. Allow time for students to discuss their responses.

ASSESSMENT
Have students complete the Section 1 Review on page 451.

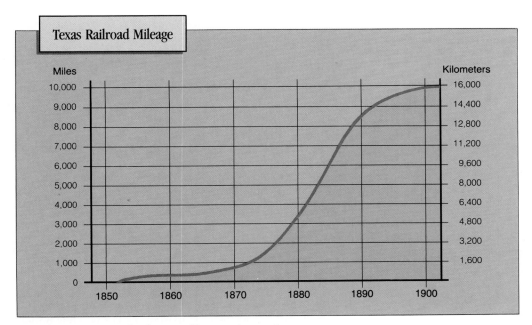

Texas Railroad Mileage

The greatest growth in railroads occurred between what years?

to take advantage of various routes available for shipping products. Dallas, Fort Worth, Houston, San Antonio, Galveston, Waco, El Paso, and Austin were among the cities that felt the benefits of railroads. Fort Worth grew as a meat-packing center because it was near the large cattle ranches of West Texas. It had a number of railroad lines to ship the beef to market. Railroad car repair shops built by the Texas and Pacific helped Marshall's economy.

The establishment of rail lines hurt some communities and helped others. Jefferson was a prosperous cotton-trading center before the Civil War. It had a water connection through Caddo Lake to the Red River, which flowed into the Mississippi and on to New Orleans. As Marshall grew and prospered from the railroad lines, however, Jefferson declined in importance. In the Panhandle, the settlement of Tascosa had developed as a trading center for sheep ranchers and cattle ranchers. When the railroad junction was built 35 miles away at Amarillo, Tascosa also declined in importance. Trade and business shifted to the cities on the rail lines. ✪

SECTION ★1★ REVIEW

Define: bonds, land grant, junctions
Identify: Sierra Blanca, T&P

1. Why would railroads be better transportation than rivers or roads?
2. How could a railroad company receive a land grant?
3. Why were some communities hurt by the railroads?

Analyzing Information: Why would a city such as Fort Worth choose to offer bonds to a railroad company?

Using Historical Information: If you lived in a town in the Panhandle, how would you react to not having railroad service when most of Texas did? Why?

Caption Response
Between 1880 and 1890

2. After completing ten continuous miles of track, a company could receive sixteen sections of land for each mile. The railroads were required to sell the land to finance construction of the lines.
3. Some communities that were once centers of trade because of their location were bypassed by the rail lines.

Analyzing Information: Cities wanted to attract railroads so that they could connect with other cities in Texas and the United States. Railroads brought new business to the cities. Cities such as Fort Worth would benefit from the railroad's ability to transport goods (in this case, cattle) to and from their markets.

Using Historical Information: Reactions will vary, but students should recognize the advantages of having railroad service.

Student Experiences (I) Bring to class food-section advertisements from newspapers. Point out selected staple items, such as bread, milk, eggs, beef, and so on. Discuss any changes that have occurred in prices and possible causes for changes. Tell students that they will discuss in Section 2 the impact that price changes have on farmers.

INSTRUCTION

Vocabulary (I) You may wish to preteach the following boldfaced terms: *mechanized* (p. 454); *tenant farmers* (p. 455); *sharecroppers* (p. 455). **LEP**

Essential Elements
3D, 3F, 4A, 5C, 7C, 8A, 8B, 8C, 9A, 9B, 9E, 9F

This photograph of the Pecos High Bridge, built by the Santa Fe Railroad, illustrates the difficulty of providing rail service to parts of West Texas.

Barker Texas History Center

Mural by Peter Hurd, photo by I. G. Holmes, Texas Tech University

This mural depicts Dora Nunn Roberts, a pioneer of West Texas. Along with her family, Roberts endured much hardship, especially during the great drought of 1886–1887. Oil was discovered on Roberts' land in 1927, making her wealthy. She donated millions to Texas colleges.

2 Growth and Change in Agriculture

In order to sell the land obtained from their grants, the railroads encouraged people to move to Texas. They hoped that farmers would buy railroad land and then raise crops or livestock to ship over the lines. New businesses would then locate along the railroads to sell goods needed by the farmers. The railroads not only influenced the growth of agriculture, but they changed the way many farmers thought about farming.

The Farmers Move West. The railroads were especially important in attracting people to settle West Texas. The companies began advertising campaigns to encourage people to settle along their routes. They printed brochures describing the rich farmland of Texas and distributed them all over the United States. Some companies ran trains that took potential land buyers to selected areas. Demonstration farms were established to show the varieties of crops that could be grown in West Texas. Cities such as Odessa were established by railroad companies. Partly as a result of these efforts, the population of West Texas jumped to 750,000 by 1900.

Farmers in West Texas quickly discovered that new techniques were needed to raise crops in the dry climate. Windmills helped in some areas to bring water for irriga-

TEXAS VOICES
Research (II) Ask interested students to research and report on the major farmer organizations that were active during the late nineteenth century. What were the farmers' grievances? Were the organizations effective? **A, G**

Art and History (I) Have students examine the mural on page 452. Ask them to write three generalizations about farm life in West Texas in the late 1800s, basing their observations on the mural. Then ask them to find examples in the textbook to support their generalizations. Call on volunteers to share their responses. **A, V**

Essential Elements
2H, 3D, 3F, 8A, 9A

TEXAS VOICES

Farmers faced rough economic times during the 1870s and 1880s. Foreign competition, high interest rates, droughts, and high transportation costs made it difficult for them to make a profit from the sale of their agricultural goods. Adding to their problems were political leaders who came from large Texas cities and who often represented the desires of industry, not those of farmers.

In the mid 1880s, Texas farmers found a voice to champion their cause. His name was Dr. Charles W. Macune. Macune, an attorney as well as a physician, became a dynamic leader of the Texas Farmers' Alliance. He was an impressive speaker and an energetic organizer. Macune encouraged farmers to join together and speak as one political voice. Through his efforts, Texas farmers became a more powerful political force. Dr. Macune emphasized cooperation among farmers to save money on purchases, to get better prices for their goods, and to raise their political power. In this excerpt from one of his speeches, he discusses the need for farmers to continue their tough political approach:

> We have been talking co-operation for twenty years. Now we have made an aggressive movement. It has thrown the whole community into the wildest confusion. . . . It saved us last year from one to five million dollars on our cotton. It saved us forty percent on our plows, thirty percent on our engines and gins, sixty percent on sewing machines, thirty percent on wagons. . . .
> The question today is: shall we endorse [support] the aggressive movement, or shall we go back home and say to the people, we stirred up the bees in the bee tree and made them make the biggest fuss you ever heard . . . but we declined the fight and have come back home to starve and let our children grow up to be slaves. In a nut-shell then, the question is: will you cease an aggressive effort that promises certain relief, simply because the opposition howl?

tion. But in the nineteenth century, this method was used on a very small scale. Most farmers turned to methods of dry farming. Terraces, or small ridges, were built to catch runoff from rainfall. They also helped stop soil erosion. The soil in the Panhandle and some other areas of West Texas was quite rich but often very hard on the surface. A special type of plowing left a layer of loose soil on top to allow crops to absorb any moisture in the air.

Farmers soon learned that certain crops grow well in West Texas. Corn, which had long been a favorite of farmers in East Texas, was not one of them. Instead, West Texas farmers turned to wheat and grain sorghum. One East Texas crop that proved to grow well in West Texas was

Library of Congress

Dugout houses sometimes served as homes on the plains of West Texas. In this photograph, taken in 1908, H.H. Campbell of the Matador Ranch stands in front of the dugout he lived in during his final years.

Austin History Center, Austin Public Library

Railroad companies encouraged commercial farming and offered quick transportation of goods to market. This 1894 photograph shows railroad cars loaded with cotton at the Grand Central Depot in Houston.

Painting by Peter Hurd,
photo by J. G. Holmes,
Texas Tech University

The circuit rider played an important role for many settlers on the Texas frontier. This mural depicts Robert Franklin Dunn, a Methodist minister whose territory in West Texas covered an area larger than Massachusetts. Dunn established the first churches at Sweetwater, Big Spring, Colorado City, and Snyder.

cotton. By 1900, cotton was grown on about half the cultivated land in Texas.

Commercial Farming in Texas. The railroads encouraged more commercial farming, or the raising of crops for sale. Railroads provided fast and reliable transportation to carry farm products to Texas cities, to other states, and to ports for shipment overseas. Farmers in Texas had always raised some cash crops, but in the late 1800s, commercial farming became even more important to the state's economy.

Other changes occurred in Texas agriculture. It became more **mechanized**, meaning farms used machinery to perform tasks. Threshers drawn by horses were used on wheat farms. Steam-powered tractors came into use. The number of large farms increased as farmers sought to work as much land as possible to produce crops for sale. Mechanization allowed farmers to increase production.

Farm income in Texas soon exceeded income from cattle ranching. Cotton farming led the way. Rice and sugarcane continued to be important in Southeast Texas. Soon the railroads helped develop fruit and vegetable farming in the Rio Grande valley.

Despite the great changes and growth in agriculture, all was not well in Texas farming. Many farmers borrowed

454 *Unit 8*

454 *Unit 8*

The Texas Collection, Baylor University

Cotton has long been the leading cash crop in Texas. This old photograph shows the entrance to the Cotton Festival in Waco. King Cotton reigns among the cotton bales at the gate leading to the Cotton Palace.

money to buy land or equipment. Prices were not good for some crops. Texas farmers were competing with farmers in other states and in foreign countries to sell wheat and cotton. With many farmers growing the same crops, prices fell because the supply was so high.

Tenant Farmers. Life was especially hard for **tenant farmers**, who rented land on which to grow crops. Nearly half the Texas farmers in the late nineteenth century were tenant farmers. The landowners received a part of a farmer's crop as payment for land rental. Sometimes the tenant farmer also promised part of the crop in return for tools, seeds, or a house. Such farmers were **sharecroppers**.

The tenant farm system developed throughout the South following the Civil War. Many plantation owners who had once held slaves were left without money to pay workers. Black and white farmers alike were without money to buy land of their own. The tenant farm system met the needs of landowners and farmworkers both.

Many tenant farmers fell deeply in debt. If insects or bad weather struck, they could not produce enough crops to cover their land rental. If crop prices were low, farmers earned too little to pay for food and clothing. Many were unable to repay loans completely and had to borrow more money each year. As long as they owed money, tenant farmers and their children could not leave the land. ✪

SECTION 2 REVIEW

Define: mechanized, tenant farmers, sharecroppers

1. What efforts did railroad companies make to attract settlers to Texas?
2. How did mechanization affect farming?
3. When did the tenant farm system develop?

Synthesizing Information: How did the railroads affect agriculture in Texas?

Exploring Geography: How did farmers in West Texas adapt to the land and climate? Which of the Five Themes of Geography does this represent?

Chapter 22 **455**

Chapter 22 **455**

SECTION 3

FOCUS

Student Experiences (I) Ask students: What is the most important industry in Texas *(oil)*? Point out that Section 3 details the growth of industry in Texas.

INSTRUCTION

Vocabulary (I) You may wish to preteach the following boldfaced term: *refinery* (p. 457). **LEP**

Essential Elements
2H, 3D, 5B, 5C, 9B, 9D, 9E, 9G

Sam Houston Regional Library

The lumber industry of East Texas was the leading industry in the state at the close of the nineteenth century. Lumber remains a vital force in the Texas economy.

3 The Growth of Industry

Although Texas has many natural resources, industry and manufacturing were still a small part of the economy in the late 1800s. Only one percent of Texans were industrial workers in 1865. Texas industries were entering a period of rapid growth, however, and new industries were being developed.

Leading Industries. Of major importance to Texas industry was the processing of farm products. Flour milling and the production of cottonseed oil were leading industries by the 1880s. Prior to 1860, cottonseeds were considered to have very little value, and most farmers threw them away. After 1870, cottonseeds became popular as a fertilizer and as a fuel. Oil extracted from cottonseeds was used to make shortenings and margarine. Meat-packing in Texas began in Victoria in the 1860s. Fort Worth eventually became the leading meat-packing center in Texas.

Coal mining developed in Palo Pinto and Erath counties. By 1890, the leading industry in Texas was lumber. The thousands of square miles of timber in East Texas had provided Texans with one of their first industries before

American Petroleum Institute

The first important oil refinery in Texas was built at Corsicana. The refinery first began operations in 1898. It was under construction when this photograph was taken.

the Civil War. After the war, sawmills sprang up throughout East Texas as railroad lines were built deep into the forests. The number of lumber mills increased from 324 in 1870 to 637 in 1900. The value of lumber products increased many times over.

The Early Oil Industry in Texas. The most important Texas industry got its start in the late 1800s. The first known oil well in Texas was drilled in 1866 by Lyne Barret in Nacogdoches County. Barret used a drill powered by a steam engine to reach oil 106 feet below the surface of the earth. The venture failed when Barret ran out of money. There was little demand for the product at the time anyway.

Other oil discoveries were made in Texas during the 1870s and 1880s, and demand for the product began to climb. In 1894, important deposits of oil were discovered near Corsicana. J.S. Cullinan built the first large refinery near the oil fields. A **refinery** is a place in which crude oil is processed into various products. The oil refined at Corsicana was used to fuel locomotives, to lubricate machinery, to make kerosene for lamps, and to cover roads to hold down dust. By 1900, wells at Corsicana had produced more than 800,000 barrels of oil.

Institute of Texan Cultures

Lyne Barret drilled the first known oil well in Texas in 1866.

Chapter 22 **457**

Chapter 22 **457**

Guided Practice (I) Have students draw an illustrated time line, detailing the growth of industry in Texas. Select several time lines to display in the classroom. **V, TK, LEP**

EXTENSION

Research (II) Ask students to conduct library research to find Texas' crude oil production for the years 1870, 1880, 1890, and 1900. Ask them to illustrate their findings in the form of a chart or graph. **V, TK, G**

Spindletop Museum, Lamar University

Spindletop. Pattillo Higgins thought there was oil near Beaumont, and he told everyone so. Higgins believed that the oil was located at Spindletop, about three miles south of Beaumont. He helped form a company to drill for oil, but it failed. In an attempt to find support for a new drilling venture, Higgins advertised in newspapers. His ad was answered by Captain Anthony F. Lucas, a mining engineer.

Lucas and Higgins both believed that there were oil deposits in the salt domes along the Gulf coast. The domes are underground formations, one of which lay under a rise of twelve to fifteen feet in the coastal plain at Spindletop. Lucas directed the drilling that began in October 1900. On January 10, 1901, the fabulous Lucas gusher came in. With it came a new era for Texas industry.

The oil of the gusher spouted high into the air, blowing out over six tons of metal pipe and drilling equipment. Historian C. C. Rister described the gusher at Spindletop:

> Without warning, a large volume of heavy mud shot out of the well with the sound of a cannon shot, followed by a sustained, deafening roar. First came a strong flow of gas, then oil by head flows. The flow increased in force so that within a short time rocks shot upwards for hundreds of feet. Then black oil in a powerful stream, increasing in volume, gushed skyward for more than twice the height of the derrick, crested, and settled back to earth in a greasy shower.

The Spindletop Boom. By 1902, Spindletop was producing one-fourth of the oil in the United States. When word spread about the discovery at Beaumont, people scrambled to drill new wells. All hoped to become rich from the oil boom. Many people did become rich from investments in oil wells, or from selling land or drilling equipment. Others lost money investing in fake land deals. Adventurers and gamblers, too, flocked to Spindletop.

Caption Response

It meant a new era for Texas industry, as oil would become the state's most important industry.

The Lucas gusher at Spindletop marked the beginning of the oil age in Texas. The gusher took nine days to cap and led to a spectacular oil boom in the area. What did the Lucas gusher mean to the future of Texas?

Sam Houston Regional Library

A forest of oil derricks is shown in this early photograph of the oil field at South Liberty near Beaumont.

458 *Unit 8*

LONE STAR LEGACY

Spindletop

Although Texas is known for its oil derricks, petroleum was not a major Texas industry until the early twentieth century. In fact, Texas was not even the first state to produce oil. The first oil well was drilled in Pennsylvania in 1859.

Soon after that, Texans in Nacogdoches County found traces of oil and gas in the water of what is now Oil Springs. In 1895, oil was discovered in Corsicana. J.S. Cullinan developed the petroleum industry there and established the first oil refinery in Texas.

By 1898, hundreds of wells had been dug in East Texas. But the boom was yet to come. Near Beaumont, Captain Anthony F. Lucas, an Austrian immigrant and mining engineer, set up a wooden derrick and drilled an exploratory well in a field called Spindletop. The field was possibly named for a group of oak trees that resembled a child's toy top.

On the morning of January 10, 1901, Spindletop exploded. Gas whistled out of the well, drill pipe flying through the air. Mud followed. Sludge fizzed up, then sand, rock, and finally brown-black oil. The greasy geyser roared into the sky. It shot up twice the height of the 56-foot derrick. The "black gold" fell gently to the ground.

That morning, only the three drillers working on the derrick knew about the gusher. But by evening, word had flashed around the world by telegraph and newspaper. The well ran full blast for nine days and produced around 800,000 barrels before workers managed to put a cap on it.

Within three months, Beaumont swelled in population from 9,000 to 50,000. The 200 acres of the Spindletop field itself sold for $900,000 per acre. During the next four years, 12,000 oil wells were dug in the area.

The last wooden derricks disappeared from Spindletop in about 1950, replaced by steel derricks. Steel derricks were gone by the early 1970s. Today Spindletop is still a working oil field with approximately 50 wells.

The success of Lucas' gusher marked the beginning of development of many productive oil fields on the Gulf Coastal Plain. More important, it signalled the beginning of Texas' prominence as an oil-producing state. Spindletop was more than a lucky discovery. It was the start of the modern petroleum industry.

Using Historical Imagination

Imagine that you could travel in a time machine back to the morning of January 10, 1901. What might you do to help the people working at Spindletop avoid wasting 800,000 barrels of oil?

Inset: Anthony F. Lucas

Texas Memorial Museum

Essential Elements
2H, 3C, 9F

LONE STAR LEGACY
Using Historical Imagination: Answers will vary, but students should help solve the problem by using modern know-how or technology not available in 1901.

RETEACHING
Have students create a collage that represents the growth of industry in Texas. Invite volunteers to display and discuss their collages. **A, V, TK, LEP**

CLOSURE
As you copy their responses on the chalkboard, have students list the changes that occurred in Texas as a result of the oil boom.

ASSESSMENT
Have students complete the Section 3 Review on page 460.

SECTION 4

FOCUS

Student Experiences (I) Ask students to name recent advances in technology that are changing the way we live *(computers, for example)*. Tell them to consider the impact

The Spindletop field at Beaumont produced 17,420,949 barrels of oil in 1902, one-fourth of the nation's total. No one had dreamed that one field could produce that much oil.

Brown Brothers

Answers to Section 3 Review
Define: *refinery*—place in which crude oil is processed into various products

Identify: Lyne Barret—drilled the first Texas oil well; J.S. Cullinan—built the first large Texas refinery; Pattillo Higgins—the first to stir interest in Spindletop, the site of Texas' first major oil boom; Anthony F. Lucas—engineer who drilled the Spindletop gusher

1. Lumber mills were able to use the newly built railroad lines to transport lumber to market.
2. 1866
3. Possible answers include: construction of refineries, storage facilities, and pipelines; oil shipping.

Seeing Cause and Effect: In the years following the Spindletop gusher, many uses for oil developed, and oil became the most important industry in Texas.

Making Decisions: Answers will vary but should be supported with sound reasoning.

SECTION 3 REVIEW

Define: refinery
Identify: Lyne Barret, J.S. Cullinan, Pattillo Higgins, Anthony F. Lucas

1. Why did the number of lumber mills increase from 1870 to 1900?
2. When was oil first drilled in Texas?
3. What are three industries that were started because of the Spindletop boom?

Seeing Cause and Effect: How did Spindletop usher in a new era for Texas industry?

Making Decisions: Would you have invested money in Pattillo Higgins' plans for oil drilling? Why or why not?

Many oil-related industries developed as a result of the Spindletop boom. Refineries were built nearby. Storage facilities were constructed to hold oil and oil products before shipment to market. Pipelines were laid to carry some of the oil, while business increased for the railroad lines in the area.

Ports near Beaumont benefited from the oil business. One of the first large shipments of oil by tanker left Port Arthur in 1901. Tankers were soon plying the waters of Sabine Pass in large numbers.

Giant companies such as Gulf and Texaco grew from the oil discovery at Spindletop and the related industries that followed. In the early 1900s, demand grew for gasoline to fuel the new horseless carriages, or automobiles. In later years, large discoveries of oil were made in other areas of Texas. New fields opened in Odessa, Borger, Ranger, Burkburnett, and Kilgore. As a result, Texas led the nation in oil production through most of the twentieth century ⊙

INSTRUCTION

Guided Practice (I) Have students create a time line of the dates and events mentioned in Section 4. Ask them to select one of the events and summarize its significance. **LEP, TK**

CLOSURE

Tell students that the advances in technology during this era contributed to transforming a rural society into the industrial society we know.

ASSESSMENT

Have students complete the Section 4 Review on page 461.

4 New Technology and Texas

Scientific knowledge and technology grew along with industry. Hundreds of new inventions came into being as a result. This new technology greatly affected the lives of all Texans.

New Inventions. New technology first affected Texans living in the cities. Rural Texans felt its effects later, but after 1900, modern conveniences were available in most areas of the state.

Telegraph lines had spread throughout Texas after the 1850s. In 1878, the first telephone line in Texas was installed in Galveston. Houston soon had telephone service, and by 1900, telephone exchanges linked most Texas cities.

Electric power plants were built in Texas beginning in the 1880s in Galveston. In these early plants, steam drove turbines to generate electricity. Water power was used in some places to provide energy for electricity generation. The larger towns and cities had electric service in the following years. The city of Austin had indoor electric service in 1887 and electric street lamps in 1888. By 1891, Austin had electric streetcars. In 1895, the city built tall "moonlight towers" to support electric lights. At night, the capital was bright with electric moonlight.

Shortly after 1900, the automobile rolled into Texas. The first automobiles were slow and uncomfortable. There were few good roads and highways, especially between cities. Yet autos soon competed with railroads as the major form of transportation for Texans.

Challenges of the New Technology. Most Texans greeted the changes of the commercial and industrial revolution with enthusiasm. The economy was expanding, and prosperity seemed possible for everyone. Home life became more comfortable. The progress brought new challenges for Texans. Some people worried that traditional values might be lost by the emphasis on progress and wealth.

The growth of business and industry presented new challenges for government. Regulations had to be worked out to encourage orderly growth. Issues of taxation arose concerning the railroads and other companies. Concerns were raised about protection for Texas workers in new industries. People had different opinions about these issues. New political movements soon formed to deal with them. ○

Texas Department of Transportation

The lack of adequate roads sometimes made travel in early autos difficult.

SECTION ★4 REVIEW

Identify: "moonlight towers"

1. When was the first telephone line installed in Texas?
2. What was the attitude of most Texans toward the commercial and industrial changes?

Sequencing Events: Make a time line that shows the inventions described in this section.

Synthesizing Information: Where in Texas would electricity be slow to arrive if water was needed in order to generate it?

Answers to Section 4 Review

Identify: "moonlight towers"—tall towers built to support electric lights in the city of Austin in 1895

1. 1878
2. They were enthusiastic. Prosperity seemed possible for everyone.

Sequencing Events: Time lines should include: 1850s—telegraph lines spread throughout Texas; 1878—Texas' first telephone line installed in Galveston; 1880s—electric power plants built in Texas; 1887—indoor electric service in Austin; 1888—electric street lamps in Austin; 1891—electric streetcars in Austin; 1895—"moonlight towers" built in Austin; early 1900s—automobile appears in Texas.

Synthesizing Information: Electricity would be slow to arrive in the Panhandle and in far West Texas, where it is very dry.

CHAPTER REVIEW RESOURCES

1. Chapter Review Worksheet 22
2. Chapter 22 Test, Form A
3. Reteaching Worksheet 22
4. Chapter 22 Test, Form B
5. **Informal Evaluation Forms:** Portfolio Assessment
6. *Texas, Our Texas* **Test Generator**

Essential Elements
3D, 3F, 9A, 9B, 9E

CHAPTER 22 REVIEW ANSWERS

Understanding Main Ideas

1. Little progress was made before 1870, in part because of the Civil War. After 1870, progress was rapid.
2. Railroads offered fast, dependable, and cheap transportation, whereas river and road transportation were unpredictable and unreliable.
3. It allowed farmers to increase production.
4. The system developed after the Civil War. Many plantation owners did not have the money to pay workers. The system allowed farmers to rent land from landowners.
5. At first, there was little demand for oil. As new developments and inventions began requiring oil or oil products, the industry boomed.
6. It brought streetcars, streetlights, and indoor electric service to the city.

Thinking Critically

1. **Classifying Information:** Charts should provide the following information. Effects on industry: allowed industries to transport goods across the state and country; effects on agriculture: farmers could transport their products cheaply and quickly; effects on communities: some communities

CHAPTER 22 REVIEW

Understanding Main Ideas

1. Compare the building of railroad lines before 1870 with progress after 1870.
2. What advantages did railroads offer over river and road transportation?
3. How did mechanization affect farming in Texas?
4. Why did the tenant farming system come into being?
5. Describe the growth of the oil industry in Texas.
6. How did electricity change the city of Austin?

Thinking Critically

1. **Classifying Information:** Make a chart showing the effects of railroads on (a) industry, (b) agriculture, and (c) Texas communities.
2. **Analyzing Information:** Explain why the late 1800s in Texas might be considered as the beginning of a communications revolution. Consider what changes occurred in communications and the effects these changes might have had on Texans.
3. **Evaluating Information:** What was the most important development affecting the Texas economy in the late 1800s? Explain your answer.

Linking History and Geography

1. How did farmers try to adapt to the dry climate of West Texas? Consider crops as well as farming methods before you decide upon your answer.

2. List three natural resources used by Texas industry in the late 1800s.

TAAS Practice
Using Primary Sources

A train engine of the Missouri, Kansas & Texas Railway first chugged into Denison, Texas, in 1872. At that time, Denison was only a few tents and small buildings. Within months, however, it grew into a bustling city. Here is a reporter's description of the new city.

> It was like magic, the building of Denison. . . . It is exceedingly remarkable [very surprising], also, that in a community one-half of which is undoubtedly made up of professional ruffians [bullies], . . . gamblers, and the offscourings [outcasts] of society, there is not more of terrorism. Every third building in the place is a drinking saloon with gambling appurtenances [equipment]. Robberies are, of course, of frequent occurrence in the gambling halls; but in the primitive hotels where passengers from the M.K.&T. Railway await transfer by stage to Sherman, they are as safe from robbery or outrage as in any first-class hotel. The businessmen of Denison are a stern, self-reliant, confident company. They have a thorough belief in Northern Texas; intend to tame its wildness, and make it one of the gardens of the world.

1. The reporter is surprised that in Denison
   A   there are not more businessmen
   B   there are not more gamblers and robbers
   C   there is not more crime
   D   there are not more travelers

prospered because the railroads brought in businesses. Other communities declined in importance if a railway was not built nearby.

2. **Analyzing Information:** Answers may vary. New forms of communication such as the telegraph and telephone were developed, and transportation improvements speeded communications. Ways in which these changes affected Texans might include: faster pace of life, jobs in communication industries, and exchange of information.

3. **Evaluating Information:** Answers will vary but should be supported with sound reasoning.

Linking History and Geography

1. Some farmers used windmills for irrigation, while others used methods of dry farming. They began growing crops such as wheat and grain sorghum that were more suited to the climate.
2. Oil, coal, and wood

TAAS Practice Using Primary Sources

1. C
2. A

TAAS Practice Writing Descriptively

Letters will vary but should mention the new technology and inventions discussed in the chapter.

Practicing Skills

1. **Writing Descriptively:** Descriptions will vary but should be written in character and based on information presented in the textbook.
2. **Interpreting a Table:** Corn; the 1880 price was higher than that of 1900; accept any reasonable generalization supported by information in the table.

Enriching Your Study of History

1. **Individual Project:** Research findings should contain information specific to the student's community.
2. **Cooperative Project:** Maps should be based on the information provided in the chapter.
3. **Cooperative Project:** Projects will vary but should be based on information provided in the chapter.

	Crop	Acres Planted	Quantity	Value ($)
1880	Wheat	373,570	2,567,737 bushels	2,441,918
	Corn	2,468,587	29,065,172 bushels	11,509,808
	Oats	238,010	4,893,359 bushels	1,761,609
	Cotton	2,178,435	805,284 bales	39,458,916
1900	Wheat	1,027,947	12,266,320 bushels	7,592,852
	Corn	5,017,690	109,970,350 bushels	39,259,415
	Oats	847,225	24,190,668 bushels	6,241,192
	Cotton	6,960,367	2,506,212 bales	107,510,010

2. The reporter feels that the businessmen are the
   A future of Denison
   B gardeners of Denison
   C wealthiest men in Denison
   D gamblers or ruffians of Denison

TAAS Practice Writing Descriptively

Imagine that you are a citizen of Austin in 1894. Write a letter to a relative in California, describing the changes that have come to Austin and how they have affected your life.

Practicing Skills

1. **Writing Descriptively:** Reread C.C. Rister's description of the gusher at Spindletop. Imagine that you are Pattillo Higgins, and write a description of your reactions as you watched that gusher come in.
2. **Interpreting a Table:** Study the table above. Which food crop had the greatest total value in 1880? You can determine the average value per bale of cotton by dividing the number of bales

into the total value. How did the price per bale in 1880 compare with that of 1900? What generalization can you make about the relative importance of the crops listed in the table?

Enriching Your Study of History

1. **Individual Project:** Use the library to find out how your community was affected by either the growth of railroads or the discovery of oil.
2. **Cooperative Project:** Work with a partner to create a map of railroad lines in Texas. Use the information in this chapter to draw the railroad lines on your map.
3. **Cooperative Project:** Working with two partners, use the information in Chapter 22 to create a poster titled "Effects of the Railroad in Texas." Your poster should feature an illustrated word web, with the word RAILROADS in the web's inner circle. If you prefer, your group can create a brief skit featuring a conversation among three Texans riding a train in the 1800s. Talk about how the new railroad has affected you.

UNIT REVIEW RESOURCES

1. Unit Review Worksheet 8
2. Unit 8 Test, Form A
3. Reteaching Worksheet 8
4. Unit 8 Test, Form B
5. **Informal Evaluation Forms:** Portfolio Assessment
6. *Texas, Our Texas* **Test Generator**

Essential Elements
2H, 3D, 3E, 3F, 9A, 9B

UNIT 8 REVIEW ANSWERS

Connecting Main Ideas

1. The Indians were angry that the settlers were moving onto their land and that the buffalo hunters were killing off the herds. The government decided that military force was the only way to stop the raids.
2. The Indians depended on buffalo, and the ranchers depended on cattle. These animals both survived on the flat grazing lands.
3. Killing off the buffalo and fencing the land
4. Possible answers include: growth in business, growth of towns, increased population, growth of the cattle kingdom.
5. Answers might include: By 1900, most of Texas had electricity, telephones, and access to the railroads.

Practicing Critical Thinking Skills

1. **Exploring Economics:** The settlers moved onto Indian lands in order to begin farms and ranches. Ranchers wanted the Indian lands for cattle grazing. Buffalo hunters killed the buffalo to make money from the sale of their hides, but the Indians depended on the buffalo for their survival.
2. **Evaluating Information:** Answers will vary but should demonstrate sound reasoning.

UNIT 8

REVIEW

Connecting Main Ideas

1. Why did the Indians raid settlers and buffalo hunters? Why was the army called in to stop these raids?
2. How did the geography of Texas suit the Indians and ranchers both?
3. What actions by settlers and ranchers closed the Texas frontier for the Native Americans?
4. Describe three changes in Texas that were brought about by the railroads.
5. Describe three ways that Texas in 1900 was different from Texas in 1850.

Practicing Critical Thinking Skills

1. **Exploring Economics:** How did economics play a role in the settlers', ranchers', and buffalo hunters' treatment of the Indians?
2. **Evaluating Information:** How do you think Texas would have been different if there had been no rail service? Explain your answer.
3. **Exploring Multicultural Perspectives:** Indians and buffalo hunters valued the buffalo for different reasons. What were the reasons? How did these differences lead to conflict?

TAAS *Practice*
Writing Descriptively

Imagine that you are an oilfield worker in the late 1800s. Write a letter to a cousin in the East, describing how the oil boom has changed Texas and how it has affected your life.

Exploring Local History

1. When was the first railroad line established in your county or local community? What forms of transportation serve your community today?
2. Ask parents or guardians and adult friends how oil is important to their lifestyle. Take notes on their answers, and give them to your teacher.

Using Historical Imagination

1. **Individual Project:** Write a poem or a song about one of these: the Indian wars, life on a cattle drive, working for the railroad, settling the frontier, striking oil.
2. **Cooperative Project:** With a partner, prepare an interview with one of these: Cynthia Ann Parker, Quanah Parker, Ranald Mackenzie, Charles Goodnight, Mary Goodnight, Anthony F. Lucas. Prepare questions and answers, then present the interview to the class.

For Extending Your Knowledge

Exley, Jo Ella Powell, ed. *Texas Tears and Texas Sunshine.* College Station: Texas A&M University Press. First-person accounts of the experiences of sixteen Texas frontier women.

Gipson, Fred. *Old Yeller.* New York: Harper. Novel about a young boy and his dog managing the farm while his father is on a cattle drive.

Haley, James L. *The Buffalo War.* Norman: University of Oklahoma Press. An illustrated history of the Red River Indian uprising.

3. **Exploring Multicultural Perspectives:** Indians depended on the buffalo for survival—they ate the meat and made use of the hides. Hunters valued the buffalo because their hides brought high prices in the North. As the hunters killed off the buffalo, the Indians' way of life was threatened.

Writing Descriptively

Letters will vary but should emphasize the wealth that the oil boom has brought to the state, the new dependence on oil, and the jobs the boom has created.

Exploring Local History

1. Answers will vary, depending on the community in which students live.
2. Responses will vary but might include: fuel for automobiles, farm equipment, and airplanes; fuel for heat; petroleum products such as paving materials, phonograph records, detergents, plastics, and so on.

Using Historical Imagination

1. **Individual Project:** Poems and songs will differ but should reflect knowledge of the topic chosen.
2. **Cooperative Project:** Interviews should demonstrate accuracy and careful preparation.

Skill Lesson
Practicing the Skill

1. Answers should provide examples that compare the general nature of the topics in the first account with the specific details provided by the second account.
2. Answers might include: "a play pritty," "bladder balloons," and "lost to a blue norther."
3. Charts will vary but should include at least five descriptive images in each category.
4. Paragraphs will vary but should include references to each of the five senses.

SKILL LESSON

Writing Descriptively

Description brings your writing to life. Making your writing lively and immediate is an important skill for you to have. The following is an account of a turn-of-the-century Texas breakfast, written with very little description:

> Breakfast consisted of meats, along with other food and drinks. Condiments [things people put on their food, such as salt and pepper, sugar, ketchup, syrup, and so forth] were available on the table. From her memory, Mother made biscuits, which were eaten last.

While that paragraph informs the reader, it does not make the breakfast seem very appealing, does it? Consider by way of contrast the next passage, which is excerpted from Dorothy Howard's book titled *Dorothy's World: Childhood in Sabine Bottom, 1902–1910*.

> Breakfast consisted of ham, bacon, sausage, or hog brains or calf brains (at hog-killing time), eggs, scrambled or fried, and biscuit—always biscuit, coffee (for adults) with cream and sugar, sweet milk (for the children), and ribbon cane syrup or sorghum molasses in the syrup pitcher sitting in the middle of the table in the cluster with the pepper sauce bottle and the spoon holder. The biscuits were made with buttermilk, soda, salt, lard, and flour by a recipe in Mama's memory and never written down. Breakfast ended with biscuit and molasses or syrup. The molasses was poured over the open biscuit, and the biscuit cut into bite-size pieces.

That paragraph also is informative, but it differs from the first one. Howard "paints pictures with words." She uses the senses to create a scene that can easily be imagined by the reader. She provides details that allow us to see, taste, and smell the breakfast. If she had described the scraping of chairs being pulled up to the table, she would have touched our sense of hearing too.

In the following descriptive account, "Bladder Balloons," Howard summons the senses of sight and touch. Notice how her original expressions also enhance the images.

> At hog-killing time, the hog bladders were washed, blown up by mouth, and given to the children for a play pritty [toy]. The children punched the bladder balloon with their fists to see how high they could make the bladder go. If caught by an upwind, it could rise and soar off into the fields, with the children racing wildly after it. It could be lost to a blue norther.

Practicing the Skill

1. Compare the general topics in the first account (meat, food, drinks, condiments, biscuits) with detailed information in Howard's account.
2. What are two original expressions that offer imagery in "Bladder Balloons"?
3. Make a chart with the five senses at the top (sight, hearing, smell, taste, touch). Below each sense, list at least five words or images that would describe a breakfast that you ate recently.
4. Using your chart, write a paragraph describing that breakfast. Try to make your readers experience all their senses while reading it. Include in your paragraph references to things you saw, heard, smelled, tasted, and touched.

INTRODUCING THE UNIT

Connecting with Past Learning

Direct students to study the painting on this page. Ask them to identify forms of technology that represent a new age of industry in the late 1800s and early 1900s *(the railroad, oil wells, telephone lines, automobiles, movie theaters)*. Ask: How does the scene in this painting differ from illustrations of life in Texas found in earlier units of the textbook? *(Lead students to conclude that the painting illustrates urban life, whereas earlier illustrations focused on a rural society.)*

MOTIVATOR

Ask students to identify groups in society today that are seeking to make social changes. *(They might include MADD, groups that trace lost children, consumer advocates, ACORN, and so on.)* Explain that these groups are seeking reforms in society. Point out that Chapter 23 introduces groups that were seeking reforms in Texas in the late 1800s and early 1900s. As students study the chapter, have them compare the goals and methods of these early groups with those of present-day groups.

UNIT 9 OVERVIEW

Unit 9 examines the political and economic changes in Texas in the late 1800s and early 1900s. Chapter 23 focuses on government and politics and examines the relationship between government and the economy. The chapter also introduces various groups seeking political reform. Their goals, methods, and accomplishments are presented.

Chapter 24 describes changes taking place in Texas between 1900 and 1920. Farm life and urban life are compared and contrasted, and the pace of industrial development is examined. The chapter concludes with the role of Texas in world affairs.

Materials Available at the Unit Level
Unit 9   Making Global
         Connections
Oral History Handbook
Informal Evaluation Forms

UNIT 9
A NEW CENTURY

TEXAS AND THE WORLD

Organize the class into small groups, and have students study the time line on this page. Select one of the world events, and ask groups to brainstorm about how that event is related to events in Texas. Ask volunteers to share their group's responses. Continue the activity for other events on the time line.

*A*new century began in 1900, and in many ways it was like the beginning of a new age for Texas. New towns and cities sprang up with the growth of business and industry. Texas had been born as a rural, farming society. The new century marked the growth of Texas into an urban, industrial state.

Farmers experienced problems even as towns and cities boomed. Agricultural problems began in the 1870s. Throughout the late 1800s, farmers in Texas and across the United States organized to bring about changes in government to aid agriculture. They sought to elect new leaders and pass new laws to meet changing conditions. After 1900, groups in the cities of Texas began to demand changes in government in response to new ways of life in urban areas.

In Unit 9 you will learn about the changes in the Texas economy, politics, and government from the late 1800s to the early 1900s. Chapter 23 examines how farmers and others were affected by changes in the economy and how they responded to those changes. Chapter 24 looks at the shift of population from farms to cities after 1900 and the impact of that shift on Texas.

UNIT 9 OBJECTIVES

1. Discuss politics in Texas during the years following Reconstruction.
2. Identify reform groups in Texas and their goals, and discuss their impact on state government.
3. Discuss successful reform measures that benefited the people of Texas.
4. Distinguish between the Populists and Progressives, and list reforms sought by each group.
5. Discuss the growth of cities in Texas and reasons for this population shift from rural to urban.
6. Contrast life in rural and urban Texas in the early 1900s.
7. Identify and discuss the dominant political issues in Texas between 1900 and 1920.
8. Provide examples of Texas' role in world affairs in the late 1800s and early 1900s.

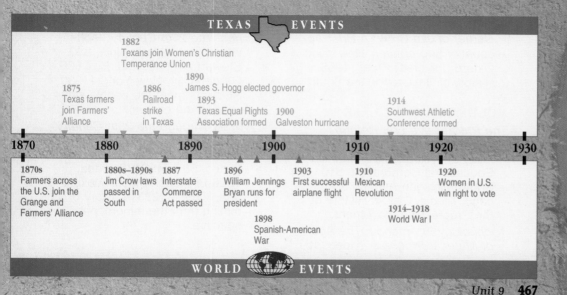

TEXAS EVENTS

1882 Texans join Women's Christian Temperance Union

1890 James S. Hogg elected governor

1875 Texas farmers join Farmers' Alliance

1886 Railroad strike in Texas

1893 Texas Equal Rights Association formed

1900 Galveston hurricane

1914 Southwest Athletic Conference formed

1870 — 1880 — 1890 — 1900 — 1910 — 1920 — 1930

1870s Farmers across the U.S. join the Grange and Farmers' Alliance

1880s–1890s Jim Crow laws passed in South

1887 Interstate Commerce Act passed

1896 William Jennings Bryan runs for president

1898 Spanish-American War

1903 First successful airplane flight

1910 Mexican Revolution

1914–1918 World War I

1920 Women in U.S. win right to vote

WORLD EVENTS

TEXAS IN THE AGE OF REFORM

TEACHER'S TIME LINE

Section 1	Section 2	Section 3	Section 4	Review and Assessment
Pp. 468–72	Pp. 472–78	Pp. 478–80	Pp. 480–83	
1 Day	1 Day	1 Day	1 Day	1 Day

⬥ TEACHER MATERIALS

Core: Chapter 23 Time Line; Graphic Organizer 23; Enrichment Worksheet 23; Review Worksheet 23; Reteaching Worksheet 23; Chapter 23 Tests, Forms A & B

Additional: Geography and Graph Skills 23, Informal Evaluation Forms, Test Generator

⬥ OBJECTIVES

1. Describe government in Texas after Reconstruction.
2. Discuss reasons that farmers wanted reform of the railroad industry in the late 1800s.
3. Name results of the efforts of the Grange and the Farmers' Alliance.
4. Outline the Populist party platform.
5. Identify the accomplishments of James Hogg.
6. Identify changes Progressives worked for in Texas.
7. Explain the new plan of city government adopted after the Galveston hurricane.

⬥ RESOURCES

BOOKS FOR TEACHERS

Cortner, Robert Crawford. *James Stephen Hogg: A Biography*. Austin: University of Texas Press, 1969. Life and times of this popular governor.

Gard, Wayne. *Sam Bass*. Lincoln: University of Nebraska Press, 1969. Biography of this notorious outlaw.

Hare, Maud Cuney. *Norris Wright Cuney: A Tribune of the Black People*. Austin: Steck-Vaughn, 1968. Important African American publication in Texas.

Martin, Roscoe C. *The People's Party in Texas*. Texas History Paperbacks Series. Austin: University of Texas Press, 1970. Study of this third party in Texas.

Weems, John E. *A Weekend In September*. College Station: Texas A & M Press, 1980. Story of the great Galveston storm of 1900.

Woodward, C. Vann. *The Strange Career of Jim Crow: A Brief Account of Segregation*. New York: Oxford University Press, 1955. History of Jim Crow in the South.

MULTIMEDIA MATERIALS

The Progressive Era: Reform Works in America. (video, 23 min.) Encyclopaedia Britannica Educational Corporation, 310 South Michigan Avenue, Chicago, Illinois, 60604. History of the Progressive movement.

Technology in America: The Age of Material Progress. (video, 18 min.) Coronet Film and Video, 108 Wilmot Road, Deerfield, Illinois, 60015. A new century in America brings technological and cultural changes.

The Time Tunnel: American Series. The 20th Century. (software) Focus Media, Inc., 839 Stewart Avenue, P.O. Box 865, Garden City, New York, 11530. Students meet the people who shaped the century.

A Walk Through the 20th Century with Bill Moyers. Out of the Depths—The Miners' Story. (video, 58 min.) PBS Video, 1320 Braddock Place, Alexandria, Virginia, 22314. Story of mining from the miners' perspective.

GENERAL STRATEGIES

STUDENTS WITH SPECIAL NEEDS

Limited English Proficient Students (LEP)

Have students work in pairs. Ask them to skim the chapter and make a list of important dates to include on a time line. After students have placed the dates on their time lines, ask them to draw pictures illustrating some of the major events. See other activities labeled **LEP.**

Students Having Difficulty with the Chapter

Have students complete the following chart as they read the chapter. They should use the chart as a review. **LEP**

Reform Group	Goals	Accomplishments

Auditory Learners

Organize auditory learners into small groups. Ask each group to select one of the following topics to research: *Texas outlaws and law enforcement during the late 1800s, the life of a farm family during the late 1800s, the life of a reform leader mentioned in the chapter, the Galveston hurricane of 1900, the Greer County Dispute.* Have students in each group use their research to write a short skit. Each group member should play a role in the skit. Have the groups present their skits to the class. See other activities labeled **A.**

Visual Learners

Direct visual learners to conduct research to find political cartoons dealing with one of the reform groups mentioned in the chapter. Have them study the cartoons and then create one or more additional cartoons. Ask them to display and discuss their cartoons. See other activities labeled **V.**

Tactile/Kinesthetic Learners

Have students work individually or in pairs or small groups to create a poster, collage, or other graphic to illustrate the main ideas of Chapter 23. Display their finished work in the classroom. See other activities labeled **TK.**

Gifted Students

Have students work together to complete the following activity. Point out to students that during the late 1800s, there was a debate on the acceptable level of government involvement in the economy. This same debate continues today. Have students research these current issues and present a debate for the class. See other activities labeled **G.**

VOCABULARY

In addition to the boldfaced terms in each section, some students might benefit from discussing the meanings of these terms.

Section 1: *conservative* (p. 468); *shrewd* (p. 469); *pensions* (p. 469); *cornerstone* (p. 470).

Section 2: *maximum* (p. 474); *uniform* (p. 474).

Section 3: *attorney general* (p. 478); *brought suit* (p. 478); *pardons* (p. 479).

Section 4: *natural disaster* (p. 480); *commission* (p. 481); *minimum wage* (p. 482).

CHRONOLOGY

Ask students to study the Chapter 23 Time Line and identify the relationships among the events.

GRAPHIC ORGANIZER

Have students skim the chapter and complete the Chapter 23 Graphic Organizer. *(You might wish to use this activity to review rather than to introduce the chapter.)*

ENRICHMENT

Have students complete the Chapter 23 Enrichment Worksheet.

Past Learning (I) Review with students the results of Reconstruction in Texas. Ask: What political party was in power *(the Democratic party)*? What was the status of black Texans? *(Though Reconstruction brought emancipation, blacks were resented and discriminated against by many whites.)* Who was governor *(Coke)*?

Vocabulary (I) You may wish to preteach the following boldfaced terms: *reforms* (p. 468); *segregation* (p. 470); *Jim Crow laws* (p. 470). **LEP**

CHAPTER 23 OVERVIEW

In the years following Reconstruction, the West Texas frontier disappeared as railroads crisscrossed the state and new industries emerged. The Democratic party was in control of state government. Aid was given to railroads, and other businesses were free to direct their own affairs. These economic changes soon began to affect Texas politics. Various political groups surfaced, seeking reforms.

Essential Elements
3A, 3C, 3E, 3F, 4A, 4E, 4F, 7G, 8A, 8B, 8C, 8D

CHAPTER

23

TEXAS IN THE AGE OF REFORM

The Story Continues...

Many changes occurred in Texas between 1874 and 1900. The cattle kingdom expanded, railroads were built throughout the state, new industries developed, and the frontier of West Texas disappeared. The natural environment of Texas was permanently transformed. After Reconstruction, the government was cautious in its actions. Limiting spending and fighting crime were major concerns.

With the growth in economy came new demands on the government. Some Texans demanded **reforms**, or changes to improve government or society. Many people wanted the government to regulate the affairs of the railroads and other businesses. Some people worked for equal rights, for the improvement of working conditions, and for better city governments. Other Texans worked to conserve the natural beauty of their state. This chapter looks at Texas government and Texas politics, and their relationship to economics during the late 1800s and early 1900s—the Age of Reform.

As you read the chapter, look for the answers to these questions:

1. Who controlled the government in Texas after Reconstruction, and what was that government like?
2. Who called for reform and why?
3. How did James S. Hogg bring reform to Texas?
4. What changes did Progressives work for in Texas?

Photo Courtesy of The Bayou Bend Collection/Archives, The Museum of Fine Arts, Houston

Progressive governor James S. Hogg is sketched here with his family in 1891. His daughter Ima (left) spent many years working to preserve the cultural heritage of Texas.

1 Politics After Reconstruction

Richard Coke followed Edmund J. Davis as governor in 1874. Reconstruction in Texas was over. For the next fifteen years, conservative Democrats dominated politics in the state. They controlled the governor's office and the state legislature. These Democrats had several goals. They promoted the building of railroads through generous land

Synthesis (I) Write the following headings on the chalk-board: *Democrats, Republicans.* Ask students to copy the headings on a sheet of paper. Have them write in note form under the appropriate heading statements that could be used to characterize each party after Reconstruction.

Example:

Democrats
1. Dominated politics in Texas

Republicans
1. Supported by most black voters

Have students share their lists as you create a master list on the chalkboard. **A, V, TK, LEP**

grants. They tried to limit government spending to reduce or eliminate the state's debt. They worked to bring to justice outlaws who threatened peace and security in West Texas. The Democrats also passed laws to restrict the civil rights of black Texans, however.

The Conservative Era. Law enforcement was a constant challenge as the Texas population expanded westward. It seemed there were never enough law officers along the frontier. Outlaws took advantage of this situation to steal cattle and horses, to rob trains, and to take part in other illegal activities.

On September 19, 1877, the famous Texas outlaw Sam Bass and his gang held up a train at Big Spring, Nebraska. With some $60,000 in gold pieces, they escaped southward to Texas. In the months that followed, Bass and the gang robbed trains in the state.

To deal with outlaws like Bass, John Wesley Hardin, and Wild Bill Longley, the Texas legislature had created the Frontier Battalion of Texas Rangers in 1874. Major John B. Jones, a dedicated and shrewd officer, was made the leader of the group. It was Jones who directed the effort to bring Sam Bass to justice.

Jones and the Texas Rangers learned that Bass meant to hold up a bank in Round Rock. They set an ambush to catch Bass and the outlaw gang. On July 19, 1878, the day of the attempted holdup, Bass was shot but managed to escape. The Rangers caught him the next day but he died of his wounds. Similar actions by the Rangers soon ended much of the lawlessness in Texas.

Under Governor Coke and Governor Richard Hubbard both, the debt of the state increased. Law officers had to be paid to fight crime. Money was also spent to provide pensions for war veterans. New buildings were constructed for Texas Agricultural and Mechanical College, which had been established in 1871. When Governor Hubbard left office in January 1879, the state debt had risen to approximately $5.5 million, despite attempts to limit spending.

The new governor, Oran M. Roberts, immediately took steps to reduce the state debt. He reduced the pensions for veterans, cut support for public schools, reduced the number of Texas Rangers, and cut spending for the state prison. Many citizens were unhappy with the cutbacks, but the financial condition of state government improved.

Western History Collections, University of Oklahoma Library

John B. Jones fought for Terry's Texas Rangers during the Civil War. After the war, the Texas Rangers gained much fame under Jones' command. He was present when Sam Bass was shot in Round Rock.

Culver Pictures

Sam Bass led a gang that held up several stagecoaches and trains in Texas before he died of a gunshot wound received while attempting to rob a bank in Round Rock.

Biography
Oran Milo Roberts, born in South Carolina in 1815, moved to Texas in 1841. He became associate justice of the Texas Supreme Court in 1857.

After the Civil War, Roberts was elected to the United States Senate. Having been a strong secessionist, he was refused the seat by Radical Republicans. After his two terms as governor of Texas, Roberts lived in Austin. He became a professor of law at the University of Texas and wrote a number of history books, including *A Description of Texas, Its Advantages and Resources* (1881), *The Elements of Texas Pleading* (1890), and *Our Federal Relations, from a Southern View of Them* (1890).

Economics (I) Have students review the discussion of the free enterprise system in the subsection "Government and Business" on page 471. Draw on the chalkboard the following continuum:

Agree ————————— Disagree

Ask students to position on the continuum their level of agreement or disagreement with each of the following statements. Each statement reflects a basic premise of free enterprise.

1. Individuals should have the right to purchase any legal product for which they have the money *(economic freedom)*.
2. Government should involve itself in the economy as little as possible *(limited government)*.
3. Anyone with the necessary resources should be able to open a legal business and offer a product or service for sale to consumers *(competition)*.
4. Individuals should have the right to acquire and dispose of property *(private property)*.
5. Profits, bonuses, and salary increases are appropriate

Texas A&M Public Relations Department

Texas Agricultural and Mechanical College was established in 1871 at College Station near Bryan. Texas A&M was the first state-supported college founded in Texas.

Archives Division, Texas State Library

O.M. Roberts was elected governor in 1878. His administration was marked by cutbacks in various public services. He later became a professor of law at the University of Texas.

Historical Sidelight

African Americans made up a majority of the population in fourteen counties along the Gulf Coast and in East Texas. In thirteen other counties blacks made up at least one half of the population. In the late 1800s, white Democrats began organizing to eliminate these areas of black control of government, often by operating outside the law.

Although state spending was cut, some important advances were made in the field of education during Roberts' two terms. In 1881, Galveston was chosen as the site for the University of Texas Medical School. The cornerstone was laid for the Main Building of the University of Texas at Austin in November 1882. A school to train black teachers, Prairie View State Normal School, was opened in Prairie View, and Sam Houston Normal Institute began operation in Huntsville.

One-Party Rule. In the years after 1874, the Democrats succeeded in removing the Republican party as a major force in Texas. The large majority of white voters supported the Democrats. The Democratic party won nearly all state and local offices. The Republican party did not cease to function, but it had very little power.

Most black voters supported the Republicans, and they, too, had little power in the years after 1874. Political rights of blacks were restricted during the late 1800s. A large percentage of black Texans were tenant farmers. They were sometimes denied loans or other needed services if they tried to vote. Groups such as the Ku Klux Klan used violence to keep blacks from taking part in politics. The Democratic party had a rule prohibiting black Texans from voting in primary elections. This method of political discrimination was known as a "white primary."

During these years, the Republican party in Texas was led by an African American, Norris Wright Cuney. Cuney was a delegate to the Republican national conventions from 1872 to 1896. He also served as an alderman, or city legislator, for Galveston from 1883 to 1887. Blacks other than Cuney were politically active throughout the late nineteenth century. In counties with large black populations, local offices were sometimes won by black Texans. At least one African American served in every legislature except one before 1897.

Many Anglos throughout the South resisted black political participation, however. They also avoided social contact with blacks as equals. For years after the Civil War, this separation was customary and informal. Then it was written into the law. Under the Democrats, more and more laws were passed to enforce **segregation**, or separating and keeping apart, of the races. These **Jim Crow laws** were named for a black character in nineteenth-century song-ways to motivate workers and stimulate economic growth *(economic incentives)*.

After students complete the activity, tell them to be alert for discussions in the chapter that pertain to these issues. **A, V, TK**

EXTENSION

Community Involvement (II) Ask interested students to contact the local office of the National Association for the Advancement of Colored People to find out about the work the organization is currently doing to promote equal rights. Have students present their findings to the class. **A, G**

Independent Practice (II) Have students work in pairs to compose a brief dialogue between a white Democrat and an African American Republican in the late 1800s, discussing how the two parties differ. Invite students to present their dialogues to the class. **A**

RETEACHING

Have students copy each of the three subheadings from Section 1 on a sheet of paper. Then ask them to write under each heading a one-sentence summary of the material found in each subsection. Invite several students to read their summaries aloud. **LEP, A**

Austin History Center, Austin Public Library

The University of Texas opened for classes in 1883 at Austin. The main campus was on 40 acres of land. The Main Building, shown in this painting, was completed in 1899.

Institute of Texan Cultures

Norris Wright Cuney was the leader of the Republican party in Texas for many years during the late 1800s.

Dallas Public Library

Jim Crow laws extended even to death and burial.

and-dance acts. They extended separation of the races to all places, not only where it had become informal custom. It became illegal for black Texans and, in some cases, Hispanic Texans to eat in the same restaurants, stay in the same hotels, attend the same schools, or even be treated in the same hospitals as Anglo Texans.

The Jim Crow laws did far more than just keep the races separate. They denied equal rights and equal opportunities to minority citizens. Black and Hispanic Texans were discriminated against in the areas of employment, housing, and education, and they were not given equal protection under the law. These unfair laws led to decades of racial discrimination and misunderstanding.

Government and Business. The conservative Democrats, and most other Texans as well, held similar views about the relationship between government and business. The economic system of the United States operates under a set of ideas called free enterprise. Under this system, individuals are free to own and operate businesses for profit. In the late 1800s, most people accepted the idea that government should do little to interfere with business.

In the 1800s, the free enterprise system was changing. Very large companies were developing. These companies

Chapter 23 **471**

Ask students: Do you think that a role of the government should be to regulate businesses? Why or why not? Allow time for several students to voice varying opinions.

ASSESSMENT

Have students complete the Section 1 Review on page 472.

FOCUS

Student Experiences (I) Ask students if any of them have parents, grandparents, or other relatives who are or were farmers. Ask if they are aware of concerns facing farmers today. Point out that many farmers in recent years have experienced hard times because of falling land and crop prices coupled with rising production costs. Many farmers have been unable to repay loans and have lost their land.

Answers to Section 1 Review

Define: *reforms*—changes to improve government or society; *segregation*—the separation of people by race; *Jim Crow laws*—laws passed to enforce segregation

Identify: Sam Bass—Texas outlaw killed by Texas Rangers in 1878; John B. Jones—leader of the Texas Rangers who killed Sam Bass; Oran M. Roberts—governor of Texas who worked to reduce state debt; Norris Wright Cuney—African American Texan who headed the state Republican party after Reconstruction

1. He reduced pensions for veterans, cut support for public schools, reduced the number of Texas Rangers, and cut spending for the state prison.

(Continued on page 473)

Essential Elements
3A, 3B, 3D, 3F, 4A, 4B, 4F, 7A, 7E, 8B, 8C, 8D

Mural by Charles Campbell, Kenedy Post Office

Raw cotton was taken to the cotton gin, where the seeds were separated from the fiber. Farmers produced more crops, but the prices of farm products fell.

SECTION REVIEW

Define: reforms, segregation, Jim Crow laws
Identify: Sam Bass, John B. Jones, Oran M. Roberts, Norris Wright Cuney

1. What actions did Governor Roberts take to cut the state debt?
2. In what ways did Jim Crow laws keep groups apart?
3. In what two ways were businesses becoming too powerful, according to the views of some Texans?

Using Historical Imagination: If you had been a veteran of the Civil War, how do you think you would have reacted when Governor Roberts cut the pensions for veterans? Why?

Writing Persuasively: Imagine that you are Norris Wright Cuney. Write a letter to Governor Roberts, in an effort to persuade him that Jim Crow laws are unfair to African Americans.

controlled millions of dollars and employed hundreds of workers. Some people began to worry that large companies were becoming too powerful. They accused big businesses of using their wealth and power to influence lawmakers to pass laws favorable to them. Others said big businesses used their wealth and power to limit competition. For example, one wealthy railroad line might buy the other lines in its area. Once this happened, shippers had only one choice for transporting their goods. The railroad company might raise its rates. Either the shippers paid the rates or their goods were not transported.

In the 1870s and 1880s, some Texans began to voice the opinion that limits had to be placed on businesses. These people felt that the government needed to make more rules for regulating business than it had in the past. ○

2 Demands for Reform

Texans in increasing numbers demanded reform in the 1870s and 1880s. Various groups with common goals joined together to achieve political changes. From 1890 to 1915, these groups played an important role in state government.

The Farmers Protest. Many farmers in Texas and throughout the United States faced serious problems in the late 1800s. They were producing more crops than ever, but prices of farm products continued to fall. As a result, many farmers were earning less money each year.

During the study of Section 2, have students use this discussion to compare problems facing farmers in the late 1800s with those facing farmers today.

INSTRUCTION

Vocabulary (I) You may wish to preteach the following boldfaced terms: *interstate* (p. 475); *platform* (p. 475); *labor unions* (p. 477); *strike* (p. 477); *prohibition* (p. 478). **LEP**

Cooperative Learning (I) Organize students into four groups with each group representing one of the following: the Grange, the Farmers' Alliance, the Populist party, the Knights of Labor. Have students in each group work together to complete the information below.

Our members include:
Our purpose is to:
Our goals include:
Our accomplishments include:

Have a spokesperson from each group present the group's responses to the class. **A, LEP**

Barker Texas History Center

Even as they earned less, farmers had to pay more for many goods and services. Farmers claimed that railroad rates were too high. The price of manufactured goods, including farm equipment, household goods, and clothing, also rose. Taxes on land either remained the same or rose, as did interest rates on loans.

Farmers became especially upset with railroad companies. High railroad rates for shipping were but one source of anger. Farmers in Texas also complained that railroad companies were not paying taxes on the full value of their property. Less money was being collected in taxes from the railroads than was possible. Further, many farmers who bought land from the railroads complained that the prices were too high.

The Grange. An early farmer organization was the Patrons of Husbandry, known as the Grange. It was established after the Civil War to promote social activities among farmers. It also worked to encourage the sharing of information about crops and livestock.

The Grange turned its attention in the 1870s to farm problems. One idea of Grange members was to combine efforts at buying goods. By purchasing in large amounts, they expected suppliers to sell to them at lower prices than if they bought individually. The Grange established 150 stores across Texas to pass on lower-priced goods to members.

Separate public schools were created for black students in the late 1800s.

Mural by Jerry Bywaters, Farmersville Post Office

Texas farmers faced more and more problems during the late nineteenth century. Many joined farm organizations such as the Grange.

2. The laws made it illegal for black Texans and, in some cases, Hispanic Texans to eat in the same restaurants, stay in the same hotels, attend the same schools, or be treated in the same hospitals as Anglo Texans.

3. They used their wealth and power to influence lawmakers and to limit competition.

Using Historical Imagination: Answers will vary, but students should recognize that most veterans would feel that they earned their pensions.

Writing Persuasively: Letters will vary but should demonstrate understanding of the unfairness of Jim Crow laws.

The National Grange

The Grange promoted farmers and farm life. These scenes are from a Grange organization poster of the late nineteenth century.

The Grange also applied pressure on the legislature to deal with railroad rates. One of their targets was the policy of railroads to charge more for short hauls than for longer ones. For example, it cost more to ship cotton from Austin to Waco than from Austin to New Orleans. Railroads commonly charged more for hauls where they had little or no competition. On longer hauls where a shipper could choose from among two or three competing railroad lines, rates were lower. Each company lowered its rates in order to encourage shippers to use its line. Railroad companies also claimed that longer hauls were more profitable. Therefore, they set their rates in such a way as to encourage more long-haul business.

Because of pressure from the Grange, the legislature passed an act in 1879 setting maximum freight charges. A law in 1882 reduced fares for passengers using railroads in Texas. Still another law in 1883 set uniform rates for the same kind of service and declared practices favoring one shipper over another to be illegal. It also said that railroads had to post rate changes at least five days in advance. All of these laws proved difficult to enforce because Texas had no government agency to check on the railroad companies.

The Farmers' Alliance. Around 1875, Grange members and other farmers in Texas formed a new organization called the Farmers' Alliance. The purpose of the Alliance was to take political action to help farmers. Eventually the Farmers' Alliance spread to other states. By 1887, it claimed about 3 million members. One of the more important leaders of the Alliance in Texas was Charles W. Macune.

The Alliance took some ideas from the Grange. It called for a policy of cooperative buying of goods. The Alliance also encouraged members to market their farm products together. To do this, members were to haul cotton to one central location. Then the cotton could be sold in large lots by auction. Buyers would have to compete with one another for the lots. In this way, it was hoped that farmers would get higher prices for the cotton than if they continued to sell it individually.

Like the Grange, the Farmers' Alliance wanted action against the railroad companies. Its program called for evaluating lands owned by the railroads at their full value for purposes of taxation. The Alliance wanted the state to sell public lands in small lots to settlers only. They were worried that too much land was being given to railroad companies. Farmers charged that the railroad companies were reselling the land to settlers at unusually high rates.

The Farmers' Alliance also wanted an interstate commerce act. The purpose of such an act would be to regulate railroad companies that operated **interstate**, or between at least two different states. The United States Supreme Court had ruled that a state legislature could not pass laws regulating railroad companies that operated across state lines. Therefore, it was left to the federal government to do so.

The Populists. Some members of the Alliance supported the Democrats. Others, however, helped to form a new political party. It was called the People's party, and its members were known as Populists.

Much of the Populist **platform**, or statement of political goals, was taken from the Farmers' Alliance. But the

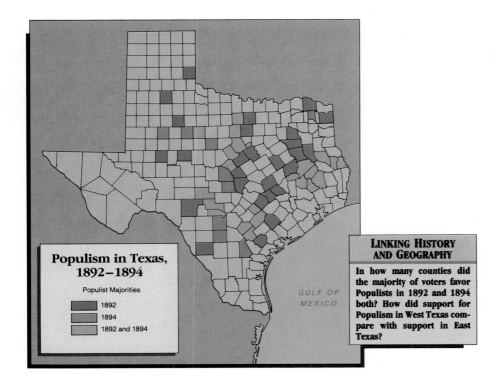

Populism in Texas, 1892–1894

Populist Majorities

- 1892
- 1894
- 1892 and 1894

GULF OF MEXICO

LINKING HISTORY AND GEOGRAPHY

In how many counties did the majority of voters favor Populists in 1892 and 1894 both? How did support for Populism in West Texas compare with support in East Texas?

party added other goals as well. The platform called for government ownership of railroads, telegraph lines, and telephones. It also called for the establishment of national warehouses. Farmers would be allowed to store their produce in these warehouses until prices rose. In the meantime, the government would loan money to the farmers who deposited crops in the warehouses. The Populists believed that railroads should return unneeded land to the government. A number of proposals called for more direct involvement of the people in making government policies and electing officials. These were meant to stop control of government by big business.

Some factory workers and other laborers joined the Populists. The Populists also tried to enlist the support of black farmers. John Rayner was the most important black Populist in Texas. Rayner traveled around East Texas, eventually gaining the support of about 25,000 blacks for the People's party.

Caption Response
Populists

This mural shows various laborers. Many farmers, as well as other laborers, joined the People's party. What were members of this political party called?

Mural by Maxwell B. Starr, Rockdale Post Office

In the 1890s, the Populists ran candidates for national and state office. The party succeeded in having 22 people elected to the Texas House of Representatives in 1894. Thomas L. Nugent ran unsuccessfully for governor as a Populist in 1892 and 1894.

In 1896, the Populists nominated William Jennings Bryan of Nebraska for president. The Democrats chose Bryan as well. Many programs of the Populists were taken over by the Democrats. Bryan ran, and lost, as the Democratic candidate. The People's party began to decline shortly afterward. Although some of the Populist policies were adopted, farm troubles continued. None of the reforms solved the basic problem of low farm prices.

Other Reform Groups. Farmers were only one group demanding reforms in the late 1800s. Workers in industry formed **labor unions** to work for higher wages and better working conditions. Unions often supported Populists.

Some 30,000 Texans joined a national union called the Knights of Labor. It included factory workers, laborers, miners, and railroad workers. For a time, the Knights enjoyed success. A prime weapon of the union was the **strike**, or work stoppage. In 1886, Texas railroad workers belonging to the Knights staged a strike against the Texas and Pacific and the Southern Pacific railroad companies. They said wages were too low and work hours were too long. They also said that the companies failed to provide promised medical services that workers had paid for. Attempts to settle the issues by discussion failed. Violence broke out in some cities when strikers attempted to stop trains from operating. The companies tried to keep the trains moving. They hired people to take the place of those on strike and armed guards to fire at the strikers.

Many Texans were opposed to labor unions and especially strikes. These people believed that workers had no right to force a company into stopping its services. Texans were very upset over violence during the strike. Many workers were arrested. The union declined rapidly as a result of its failure to win the strike.

Other labor unions were formed during the late 1800s and early 1900s. Some Texans joined the United Mine Workers, and others joined the American Federation of Labor. Both organizations have members across the nation and continue to work for their interests today.

Blagg-Huey Library, Texas Woman's University

Don't Fail
TO HEAR
Mrs. Nannie Webb Curtis
SUNDAY, JUNE 18th (1911)
First Baptist Church
At 4 P. M.
Columbus St. Baptist
At 8:15 P. M.

Mrs. Curtis is without doubt one of the most powerful Prohibition Speakers on the American Platform.

No Vituperation! She captivates her auditors with her irresistible logic, pathetic appeals and affability of manner. Wit and humor flash vividly through her addresses. She never fails to please even those who do not agree with her on the great question.

DON'T MISS THIS OPPORTUNITY
REMEMBER THE TIME AND PLACE

This poster announces a prohibitionist meeting featuring speaker Nannie Webb Curtis.

Blagg-Huey Library, Texas Woman's University

Helen Stoddard was an important leader of the Women's Christian Temperance Union in Texas.

Historical Sidelight
The Knights of Labor included members of all races and creeds, as well as of both sexes.

ASSESSMENT

Have students complete the Section 2 Review on page 478.

SECTION 3

FOCUS

Past Learning (I) Review with students the definition of *free enterprise*. Ask: How was the free enterprise system changing during the late 1800s? What were some concerns regarding big businesses?

Answers to Section 2 Review

Define: *interstate*—between at least two different states; *platform*—a statement of political goals; *labor unions*—organizations formed to work for higher wages and better working conditions for workers; *strike*—work stoppage; *prohibition*—a ban on the making and selling of alcoholic drinks

Identify: Charles W. Macune—important leader of the Farmers' Alliance in Texas; John Rayner—most important black Populist in Texas; William Jennings Bryan—1896 unsuccessful Democratic candidate for president; Helen Stoddard—a leader of Women's Christian Temperance Union in Texas

1. Possible answers include: farmers were earning less money but paying more for goods and services, railroad rates were too high, railroad companies were not paying enough taxes, and railroads charged too much for land they sold to farmers.
2. There was no competition on short hauls.
3. It wanted the railroad companies that operated between states to be regulated.

(Continued on page 479)

Essential Elements

3A, 3D, 3F, 4G, 7E, 7F, 7G, 8A, 8B, 8D, 9B, 9D

SECTION 2 REVIEW

Define: interstate, platform, labor unions, strike, prohibition

Identify: Charles W. Macune, John Rayner, William Jennings Bryan, Helen Stoddard

1. What were two reasons that farmers were upset about their conditions in the late 1800s?
2. Why did railroads charge more for short hauls than for long hauls?
3. Why did the Farmers' Alliance want an interstate commerce act?
4. What were two goals of the Populists?
5. Why did railroad workers go on strike in 1886?

Exploring Economics: What part did economics play in the various reform movements?

Comparing Perspectives: Choose a labor union from the section, and write a short speech in defense of it. Then write a short speech against that labor union.

In 1882, a part of the Women's Christian Temperance Union was formed in Texas, led by Helen Stoddard and Nannie Webb Curtis. The WCTU supported **prohibition**, or a ban on the making and selling of alcoholic drinks. Prohibition became a major issue in Texas politics. Under the Constitution of 1876, some counties had voted to become "dry," meaning they did not allow liquor sales. The issue of stopping sales statewide continued for years. ⊙

🔳 The Triumph of Reform

Many issues of reform had been taken over by the Democratic party in the late 1880s. Not all Democrats supported reform, but one who did was James Stephen Hogg. He became the most famous reform leader in Texas and was regarded by many Texans as the champion of the common people against the giant corporations.

Hogg as Attorney General. James Stephen Hogg stood six feet, three inches in height and weighed 250 pounds. He could talk to crowds for hours about politics, and people tended to listen. In 1886, he was elected attorney general of Texas.

After being elected, Hogg directed his first efforts against insurance companies in Texas. He thought that these companies were not following Texas laws. Hogg disliked the fact that most of them had headquarters in other states. The money being paid by Texans to these companies was therefore being taken out of Texas. Other companies lacked the funds to back the claims of people who bought insurance. Hogg brought suit against many insurance companies, forcing a number of them to quit operating in Texas. Others moved their offices into the state. It was claimed that Hogg saved more than $1 million for Texans who had purchased insurance policies.

Hogg next attacked the railroad organization known as the Texas Traffic Association. The attorney general accused the association of illegal practices. The railroads worked together in a **pool**. This is an arrangement whereby companies in the same industry divide up the business. Each takes a share of the market and agrees not to compete for any more. They also agree to set prices. Attorney General Hogg and most Texans regarded such practices as a violation of the spirit of free enterprise.

INSTRUCTION

Vocabulary (I) You may wish to preteach the following boldfaced terms: *pool* (p. 478); *trust* (p. 479); *monopoly* (p. 479). **LEP**

Cooperative Learning (I) Organize students into small groups. Assign each group to imagine that it is a farmer, small shipper, or other small business owner who has been financially hurt by a trust. Have each group prepare a statement to the attorney general telling how it has been hurt and why the government should regulate business. Have a

spokesperson from each group read the group's statement aloud. **A, LEP**

RETEACHING

Write the following headings on the chalkboard: *Hogg as Attorney General, Hogg as Governor.* Have students copy the headings on a sheet of paper and then list the accomplishments of James Hogg under the appropriate heading. Have students share their responses as you record them on the chalkboard. **A, LEP**

During Hogg's first term in office, the federal government passed an important law to regulate railroads. One of the authors of the new law was Senator John H. Reagan of Texas. The law was the Interstate Commerce Act, passed in 1887. It made pooling illegal and forbade railroads to charge more for short hauls than for long ones over the same line. Provision was made for regulating companies that operated in more than one state. Enforcing this law proved difficult. Still, it was a major step in bringing government control over railroad operations.

In 1888, James Hogg was elected to a second term as attorney general. He helped the state pass an antitrust law in 1889. A **trust** is a combination of companies in the same business that operate under the same leadership. Such combinations could establish a **monopoly**, or a large enough share of a business or industry to control prices. Without competition, a trust can set high prices for its goods or services. Texas was the second state in the nation to pass a law against trusts. In 1890, the United States government also passed such a law for the nation as a whole.

Hogg as Governor. James Hogg was elected governor of Texas in 1890. He enjoyed the support of members of the Farmers' Alliance and a majority of all Texas voters. His administration acted to pass a number of laws regulating business. These laws were called the "Hogg Laws."

Perhaps the most notable accomplishment of Governor Hogg was the establishment of the Texas Railroad Commission. The commission was set up to oversee the operation of railroads throughout the state. Hogg appointed John H. Reagan head of the commission. Most Texans saw this as a wise move, and citizens and railroad company officials alike came to regard Reagan as fair.

Under Governor Hogg more money was provided for the public school system. The school term was increased from four months to six. More money was provided for the University of Texas and colleges in the state. The governor also sought to reform the prison system. He believed that a governor had to handle so many requests for pardons that he or she could not be fair. Therefore, a Board of Pardon Advisers was established. The board reviewed requests and made recommendations to the governor. In this way, the governor did not have to review the hundreds of requests personally.

Institute of Texan Cultures, from Original in Texas State Capitol

Former attorney general James Stephen Hogg was the first native Texan to become governor of Texas. He was born near Rusk. He was a popular governor, and his administration passed a great number of important and progressive reforms.

Archives Division, Texas State Library

John H. Reagan, the former postmaster of the Confederacy, was appointed head of the newly formed Railroad Commission in 1891.

4. Possible answers: government ownership of railroads, telegraph lines, and telephones; the establishment of national warehouses; and the return of unneeded railroad land to the government.
5. They struck for higher pay, shorter hours, and medical services they had paid for.

Exploring Economics: Most reform movements were based on economics. Farmers called for reforms because they were earning less money but paying more for taxes and railroad services. Many of the Populists' goals were designed to help the economic condition of farmers. Labor unions sought higher wages and better working conditions for workers.

Comparing Perspectives: Speeches should be based on information presented in Section 2 and should demonstrate sound reasoning.

Biography
James Stephen Hogg was the son of a Confederate officer killed in the Civil War. During Reconstruction, the family was forced to sell off its plantation piece by piece. After his term as governor, Hogg set about rebuilding the family fortune while remaining politically active.

CLOSURE

Ask students: In your opinion, what was James Hogg's most significant accomplishment as attorney general? as governor? Allow time for students to express varying opinions.

ASSESSMENT

Have students complete the Section 3 Review on page 480.

FOCUS

Student Experiences (I) Write the term *progressive* on the chalkboard. Challenge students to provide a definition. Call on volunteers to use the term in a complete sentence. Tell students that they will learn how the term relates to early twentieth-century politics in Section 4.

Answers to Section 3 Review

Define: *pool*—arrangement whereby companies in the same industry divide up business; *trust*—combination of companies in the same business operating under the same leadership; *monopoly*—a large enough share of a business or industry to control prices

Identify: James Stephen Hogg—popular reform governor of Texas; Texas Traffic Association—railroad organization accused by James Hogg of illegal practices; John H. Reagan—head of the Texas Railroad Commission, helped write the Interstate Commerce Act; Charles Culberson—became governor of Texas in 1895

1. He believed that insurance companies did not obey Texas laws, and that because they were headquartered in other states, the money they earned from Texans did not stay in Texas. He brought suit against many insurance companies, forcing some to quit operating in Texas and others to move their offices into Texas.

(Continued on page 481)

Essential Elements
3A, 3F, 4F, 7E, 7F, 9A, 9B, 9E, 9G

480 *Unit 9*

SECTION 3 REVIEW

Define: pool, trust, monopoly
Identify: James Stephen Hogg, Texas Traffic Association, John H. Reagan, Charles Culberson

1. Why did Hogg dislike insurance companies? How did he change them?
2. What was the job of the Texas Railroad Commission?
3. What was the Greer County Dispute, and how was it settled?

Sequencing Events: List these reform actions by James S. Hogg in chronological order: "Hogg Laws," establishing Texas Railroad Commission, establishing Board of Pardon Advisers, Interstate Commerce Act, lawsuit against insurance companies

Exploring Economics: In what way was pooling considered to be a violation of the spirit of free enterprise?

Charles Culberson became governor when Hogg's second term was over in 1895. Culberson had been attorney general during Governor Hogg's administration and supported many of his views. The idea that government could set policies to protect the interests of the public was firmly established. In the following years, however, Texans would continue to debate how much regulation was necessary.

The Greer County Dispute. Shortly after Charles Culberson became governor, a long dispute between Texas and Oklahoma was settled. The dispute was over control of an area of land along the Red River. Texans thought the land belonged to Texas and had organized Greer County there. Oklahomans claimed the land as part of their territory. Charles Culberson, while attorney general, argued for Texas before the United States Supreme Court. The Court ruled, however, that the land belonged to Oklahoma. The boundary in that area of the Red River was set as it is today. ✪

◾ The Progressive Era

Some of the reforms begun in the late 1800s carried over into the new century. They became part of a political movement called the Progressive movement. **Progressive** means forward-looking or relating to progress. Unlike the reformers of the late 1880s, the Progressives were most active in cities. Their concerns were more those of industry than of agriculture. For this reason, the Progressives were less important in Texas than in the large urban areas of the northeastern United States.

The Galveston Disaster. Early in September 1900, there were signs that a major storm was heading for Galveston. Life went on as usual. Such storms were nothing new.

On September 8, a huge hurricane swept over Galveston. The storm packed winds of 120 miles per hour. Huge waves battered the city, destroying buildings and drowning people. In the following days, as the thick layers of mud were cleared away, it became clear that a major disaster had occurred. Six thousand people had lost their lives in the worst natural disaster in the history of the United States.

Many people in Galveston felt that the old city government could not cope with the disaster. Under the old

INSTRUCTION

Vocabulary (I) You may wish to preteach the following boldfaced terms: *progressive* (p. 480); *suffrage* (p. 482). **LEP**

TEXAS VOICES

Analysis (II) Direct students to the third paragraph of the special feature "Texas Voices." Invite a student to read the first sentence aloud. Ask another student to explain the quotation in his or her own words. *(Possible answer: De-*

mocracy depends on informed citizens.) Ask: Do you agree or disagree with this view? Why or why not? Allow time for students to express varying opinions. **A, G**

Cooperative Learning (I) Organize students into groups of four or five. Tell students that they are part of a present-day Progressive movement. Have each group create a list of reforms that it is seeking in society today. Groups should also provide suggested methods for achieving their goals. Have a spokesperson from each group present the group's list. **A**

TEXAS VOICES

*T*exas' first native-born governor, James Stephen Hogg, was the most visible leader of the reform movement in Texas during the late 1800s. Serving two terms as attorney general and two terms as governor, Hogg was at the center of the political movement that aimed to change Texas government and society. One of Governor Hogg's contributions was to help create a public school system in Texas. The following excerpt is from a speech in which he discussed the importance of a public education system in preparing Texas citizens for the responsibilities of democracy:

One of the causes which moved the patriot fathers to the separation from Mexico was that said [the Mexican] government failed to establish any public system of education. By the first Constitution, the people made it the duty of Texas to provide such a system.

The school term, for a number of years past, outside of cities and towns, has not greatly exceeded four-and-a-half months each year. Only 402,000 of the 565,672 children reported to be within the age [school age] attended the schools the past year. To meet the constitutional demands for six months' schools becomes a responsible duty. . . . If the people ever expect to have an efficient system of public free schools, they must prepare to pay for it.

No greater principle was ever uttered than when our fathers said, "Unless the people are educated and enlightened, it is idle to expect the continuance of civil liberty or the capacity for self-government." Herein lies the best reason for informing people by undisguised [taxation] methods that after all they must pay the expenses of maintaining public schools and everything else connected with city, county, state, and federal government. When they are educated to fully understand [this responsibility, then] they may claim the capacity of self-government.

2. Its job was to oversee the operation of the railroads.
3. The dispute was between Texas and Oklahoma over control of an area of land along the Red River. The Supreme Court ruled that the land belonged to Oklahoma.

Sequencing Events: Lawsuit against insurance companies, Interstate Commerce Act, "Hogg Laws," establishing Texas Railroad Commission, establishing Board of Pardon Advisers

Exploring Economics: Pooling restricted competition, which is an essential element of free enterprise.

Essential Elements
2B, 2C, 3F, 4D, 7E, 7F, 9A

system, there was an elected mayor and a city council. To rebuild the city, a new type of local government was established. Under the new system, voters elected a city commission with five members. Each member, besides helping with decisions affecting the whole city, was in charge of a different department such as water services. Better organization resulted, and services became more efficient.

The new government of Galveston proved a success. Commission plans were later adopted by hundreds of cities in other parts of the United States. In choosing commissioners, more emphasis was placed on knowledge of city services and less on politics. Cities hired more people with college degrees in specialized fields. The commission plan represented a major reform of the Progressive movement, which sought better, more honest city government.

Barker Texas History Center

Elected president of the Texas Equal Suffrage Association in 1911, Minnie Fisher Cunningham led the crusade that won the vote for women in Texas.

SECTION ★ 4 ★ REVIEW

Define: progressive, suffrage
Identify: Texas Equal Rights Association, Rebecca Hays, Minnie Fisher Cunningham, Edward M. House

1. Why was the Galveston disaster important nationally? in Texas?
2. What were two changes sought by the Progressives?
3. Which political party remained in control of Texas during the period of reform?

Seeing Cause and Effect: How did the Galveston disaster lead to a new kind of city government?

Using Historical Imagination: If you were a Texas woman in the 1890s, would you have campaigned for the right to vote? Why or why not?

Other Progressive Programs. Progressives in Texas and elsewhere sought other changes. They wanted to limit child labor. They supported the rights of labor unions to organize. Many Progressives wanted laws to guarantee a minimum wage for workers. They also wanted to place a limit on the number of hours people had to work in industry. With the support of Progressives, laws were passed providing for the inspection of food to make sure it was safe. Drugs had to be inspected and carefully labeled before they could be sold.

Progressives also became involved in the struggle for women's **suffrage**, or right to vote. They worked with organizations such as the Texas Equal Rights Association. The association was organized in 1893 "to advance education and equal rights of women and to secure suffrage to them by appropriate national and state legislation." An early leader in the movement was Rebecca Hays of Galveston. Leaders such as Minnie Fisher Cunningham worked for voting rights, too. It would be some years before the goal of suffrage groups was reached.

Politics and the Progressive Era. During the period of reform, the Democratic party remained in control of Texas politics. The party took over some programs of the Progressives as it had taken some from the Populists. In many cases, the Democrats supported certain reforms to prevent even more radical changes.

Perhaps the most important Democratic leader in the late 1800s and early 1900s was Edward M. House. From 1898 to 1912, House directed the party. He was so skillful in getting others to work together that he could practically choose the party's candidate for governor. And the Democratic candidate was always elected.

House had supported the elections of James Hogg and Charles Culberson. Under his direction, Joseph Sayers, S.W.T. Lanham, and Thomas M. Campbell were elected governors. Some of these governors supported various Progressive programs, but others did not. House himself was not a Progressive, but he worked to bring peace and stability to the Democratic party. Because he worked behind the scenes, few Texans knew much about his importance. House became better known to Texans, as well as to other Americans, as the chief adviser to President Woodrow Wilson. ●

Pose the following questions for class discussion: Which of the Progressive reforms mentioned in Section 4 was the most significant? Why do you think so?

ASSESSMENT

Have students complete the Section 4 Review on page 482.

CITIES OF TEXAS

Geography (I) Have students read the special feature and then make a statement explaining how the geographic theme of *movement* might relate to the founding of Brownsville and McAllen. Then have students study the chart and make a statement linking geography and economics. **A, LEP**

CITIES OF TEXAS

Brownsville and McAllen

Population:
Brownsville—98,962;
McAllen—84,021

Metro area population:
Brownsville—260,120;
McAllen—383,545

Size: Brownsville—28.8 square miles; McAllen—29.7 square miles

Relative location: Far southern tip of Texas in the lower Rio Grande valley

Region: Southern edge of the South Texas Plains

County: Brownsville is the county seat of Cameron County; McAllen is in Hidalgo County.

Special features: Both cities have "twin" cities in Mexico, directly across the Rio Grande. Matamoros is across from Brownsville. Reynosa is across the river from McAllen.

Origin of name: Brownsville took its name from Fort Brown, originally established in 1846 by General Zachary Taylor. McAllen is named for John McAllen, a rancher who helped bring the railroad to the area.

Landmarks: Citrus groves and vegetable fields in the Rio Grande valley, of which Brownsville and McAllen are the two most populous cities

Economy: Agriculture is the mainstay of the Rio Grande valley's economy. Citrus fruits and vegetables are the major products. There are also oil refineries,

chemical plants, and food-processing operations. In recent years, tourism has increased, becoming an important part of the area's economy.

History: Brownsville was the site of an army post established in 1846. By 1849, settlers arrived and made Brownsville the first settlement in the lower Rio Grande valley. With the development of railroad lines and a ship channel to the Gulf of Mexico, it grew and remains one of the largest cities in the region.

McAllen was established as a townsite on the St. Louis, Brownsville, and Mexico Railroad in 1904. Building of McAllen began in 1905.

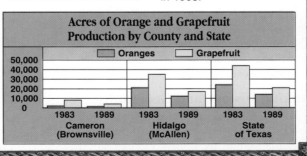

Acres of Orange and Grapefruit Production by County and State

Seeing Cause and Effect: Many people in Galveston felt that the old city government could not cope with the disaster. To rebuild the city, a new type of local government was established. The new local government focused on people who were experts instead of politicians.

Using Historical Imagination: Answers will vary. Students should give reasons for their answers.

Essential Elements
3D, 5B, 5C, 9A

CHAPTER 23 REVIEW

Understanding Main Ideas

1. What were the goals of the conservative Democrats in Texas following Reconstruction?
2. How was segregation enforced in Texas?
3. What reforms were called for in Texas, and who called for them?
4. List three complaints that Texas farmers had against railroad companies.
5. What reforms did James S. Hogg bring to Texas?
6. What were the goals of the Progressive movement?

Thinking Critically

1. **Exploring Economics:** Suppose that there are five companies in your area that provide telegraph services. Explain how one of them might limit competition from the others.
2. **Synthesizing Information:** How do you think owners of railroad companies reacted to demands for regulation? Explain your answer.
3. **Classifying Information:** Create a chart with the headings *Government*, *Economics*, and *Civil Rights* at the top. List the reforms described in the chapter under these headings.

Linking History and Geography

1. Why were reforms that benefited farmers more important in Texas than reforms benefiting industry and people in cities?

2. Where in Texas do you think most members of the Grange and the Farmers' Alliance came from? Why?

TAAS Practice
Using Primary Sources

In 1890, N.B. Ashby, a member of the Farmers' Alliance, wrote a book about the farmers' problems. In the following selection, he says railroads should be owned by the government:

> Rome had her great highways built at public expense. These roads were the arteries for her commerce, and the nerves which kept up communication between Rome . . . and the provinces. Those highways were public; they belonged to the State. What the great "ways," as they were called, were to Rome and the Romans, the railways are to the United States and its citizens. . . . Our railways have been built at public expense as public highways. But our highways, the railroads, have been surrendered to private corporations.
>
> We have our great "ways," but they are controlled by . . . private greed; our Roman "ways" are not of the public, but of the corporation. Whoever controlled the great "ways" of Rome was master of Rome and the Romans. Such must be our fate as well. The railways are our veins and arteries of commerce. Whoever controls the commerce of a country as the railways control ours, will be the masters of the country.

1. Ashby compares the railroads and the Roman roads to
   A nerves and arteries
   B commerce
   C a heart
   D road traffic

leges, and established a Board of Pardon Advisers.

6. Progressive goals included: a change in city government, a limit on child labor, the rights of labor unions to organize, a guaranteed minimum wage, a limit on working hours in industry, food and drug inspection, and women's suffrage.

Thinking Critically

1. **Exploring Economics:** Answers will vary. One company might buy the other four.
2. **Synthesizing Information:** Answers will vary but should suggest that railroads opposed regulation because it would restrict their methods of operating and lessen their profits.

3. **Classifying Information:** *Government*—change in city government, Texas Railroad Commission, Board of Pardon Advisers; *Economics*—minimum wage, limited working hours, Interstate Commerce Act, Antitrust Act; *Civil Rights*—women's suffrage

Linking History and Geography

1. Farmers were in the majority in Texas.
2. Most members probably came from eastern, southern, and central Texas. These were the state's farming regions.

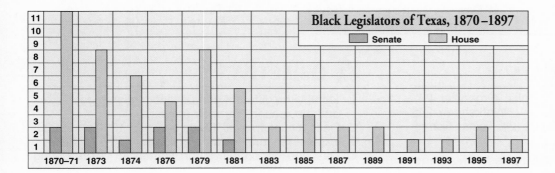

Black Legislators of Texas, 1870–1897
■ Senate   ■ House

2. Ashby thinks that whoever controls the railroads also controls
   A   the wealth
   B   the country
   C   the Romans
   D   the corporation

TAAS *Practice*
Writing Persuasively

Imagine that you are a Texas railroad worker on strike in 1886. Write a letter to a fellow worker, persuading him or her to support your position. Remind your fellow worker of the difficulties that most railroad workers have faced, and explain clearly your reasons for striking.

Practicing Skills

1. **Analyzing Information:** How did education benefit from the reform movement in Texas? Give examples.
2. **Interpreting Graphs:** Study the bar graph above. In what years did the Texas government have the most black legislators? In what year did the number of representatives in the House increase the most from the previous

session? What was the trend of black legislators in the Senate from 1870 to 1897?

Enriching Your Study of History

1. **Individual Project:** Imagine that you are a member of one of the organizations described in the chapter. Write a letter to a newspaper editor, describing a reform you think will benefit Texas. Explain why you think this reform is necessary.
2. **Cooperative Project:** Your teacher will assign to you and a partner one of these topics to research: Texas Rangers, Jim Crow laws, the Grange, Farmers' Alliance, Populists, Knights of Labor, United Mine Workers, American Federation of Labor, Women's Christian Temperance Union, Texas Traffic Association, Progressives. You and your partner will cooperate to research your topic. Then you will prepare a brief written and oral report to share with the class. Each of you should plan ahead of time to be responsible for giving one-half of your oral report to the class.

TAAS *Practice*
Using Primary Sources
1. A
2. B

TAAS *Practice*
Writing Persuasively

Letters will vary but should demonstrate knowledge of the issues facing railroad workers in 1886.

Practicing Skills

1. **Analyzing Information:** More schools were built, more money was set aside for education, and the school year was lengthened from four months to six.
2. **Interpreting Graphs:** 1870–1871; 1879. The trend was a decrease in the number of black legislators in the Senate.

Enriching Your Study of History

1. **Individual Project:** Letters should demonstrate knowledge of the goals of the organizations discussed and should be supported with sound reasoning.
2. **Cooperative Project:** Reports should demonstrate thorough research of the topic selected.

FROM FARM TO CITY

⬛ TEACHER MATERIALS

Core: Chapter 24 Time Line; Graphic Organizer 24; Enrichment Worksheet 24; Review Worksheet 24; Reteaching Worksheet 24; Chapter 24 Tests, Forms A & B

Additional: Geography and Graph Skills 24, Map and Chart Transparencies 23, Informal Evaluation Forms, Test Generator

OBJECTIVES

1. Identify the different groups that immigrated to Texas and the reasons for their moves.
2. Describe life in rural Texas between 1900 and 1920.
3. Explain reasons for urban growth.
4. Describe opportunities for women in Texas during the early 1900s.
5. Discuss Texans' leisure time and entertainment activities.
6. Identify economic resources that led to urban development in Texas.
7. Discuss Progressive reforms in the state.
8. Identify and discuss major political issues in Texas between 1900 and 1920.
9. Explain Texas' role in world affairs.

RESOURCES

BOOKS FOR TEACHERS

Berry, Wendell. *The Gift of Good Land: Further Essays, Cultural and Agricultural*. San Francisco: North Point Press, 1981. Farmer-poet Wendell Berry discusses farming in America.

The Czech Texans. San Antonio: University of Texas Institute of Texas Cultures at San Antonio, 1972. Includes information on Alois Polanski, important Fayetteville settler.

Dos Passos, John. *U.S.A.* New York: Modern Library, 1937. Political changes in the United States in the early part of the century.

Gammond, Peter. *Scott Joplin and the Ragtime Era*. New York: St. Martin's Press, 1975. Musical history of the ragtime period.

Gould, Lewis L. *Progressives and Prohibitionists*. Austin: University of Texas Press, 1973. Story of the Democrats during the Wilson years.

McCallum, Jane Y. *A Texas Suffragist*. Austin: E.C. Temple, 1988. Writings from the diaries of Jane Y. McCallum.

Rogers, Mary Beth, Sherry A. Smith, and Janelle D. Scott. *We Can Fly*. Dallas: E-Heart Press, 1983. Stories about Katherine Stinson and other Texas women.

Snyder, Gary. *The Practice of the Wild*. San Francisco: North Point Press, 1990. Examination of the changes in American land and culture.

MULTIMEDIA MATERIALS

Conversations with Great Americans. The Industrial Era and Modern Times (software) Focus Media, Inc., 839 Stewart Avenue, P.O. Box 865, Garden City, New York, 11530. Students interact with figures of modern times.

The Farmer in Changing America. (video, 27 min.) Encyclopaedia Britannica Educational Corporation, 310 South Michigan Avenue, Chicago, Illinois, 60604. The change from agriculture to agribusiness.

The Rise of Big Business. (video, 27 min.) Encyclopaedia Britannica Educational Corporation, 310 South Michigan Avenue, Chicago, Illinois, 60604. The effects of such men as Carnegie, Rockefeller, and Morgan on American life.

The Rise of Labor. (video, 30 min.) Encyclopaedia Britannica Educational Corporation, 310 South Michigan Avenue, Chicago, Illinois, 60604. The history of labor in America.

Two Farms: Hungary and Wisconsin. (video, 22 min.) Learning Corporation of America, distributed by Simon and Schuster Communications, 108 Wilmot Road, Deerfield, Illinois, 60015. Parallels are drawn between farms in Hungary and America. Includes some common themes of farming everywhere.

World War I: A Documentary on the Role of the USA. (video, 28 min.) Encyclopaedia Britannica Educational Corporation, 310 South Michigan Avenue, Chicago, Illinois, 60604. The importance of the United States in World War I.

 # GENERAL STRATEGIES

STUDENTS WITH SPECIAL NEEDS

Limited English Proficient Students (LEP)

Provide students with a time line of important dates mentioned in the chapter (do not include the events). Have the students skim the chapter and write on the time line the corresponding events. See other activities labeled **LEP.**

Students Having Difficulty with the Chapter

Help students outline the information in Chapter 24 to use as a review. Before beginning the study of a section, have students write the section title and section subheadings on a sheet of paper in outline form. As they read the section, have them write under each subheading three to five facts from each subsection. **LEP**

Auditory Learners

Ask auditory learners to gather information and report on the colleges and universities in their area. The report should include the date the institutions were established, the purpose for which they were founded, their source of funding, and other noteworthy facts. See other activities labeled **A.**

Visual Learners

Direct visual learners to the murals that are featured throughout Chapters 23 and 24. Point out the credit lines of the illustrations (most are from post offices or other government buildings). Ask students to contact the library as well as a local or state historical society to investigate the origin of these murals. See other activities labeled **V.**

Tactile/Kinesthetic Learners

Have tactile/kinesthetic learners work together to create a large, illustrated time line based on the information from Chapter 24. Display the time line in the classroom. See other activities labeled **TK.**

Gifted Students

Have students conduct research at a local public library or historical society to find copies of newspaper articles from the early 1900s written about events mentioned in Chapter 24. Have them present an oral report on their findings. See other activities labeled **G.**

VOCABULARY

In addition to the boldfaced terms in each section, some students might benefit from discussing the meanings of these terms.

Section 1: *descent* (p. 487); *threshers* (p. 488); *mortgages* (p. 489); *statistics* (p. 491).

Section 2: *controversial* (p. 497); *barred* (p. 499).

Section 3: *casualties* (p. 503).

CHRONOLOGY

Have students study the Chapter 24 Time Line and identify relationships among the events.

GRAPHIC ORGANIZER

Have students skim the chapter and complete the Chapter 24 Graphic Organizer. *(You might wish to use this activity to review rather than to introduce the chapter.)*

ENRICHMENT

Have students complete the Chapter 24 Enrichment Worksheet.

FOCUS

Student Experiences (I) Write the following headings on the chalkboard: *Students Born in Texas, Students Born in Other States, Students Born in Other Countries.* On a world map, have each student point out the location of his or her birth. Tally each response under the appropriate heading.

Tell students that in 1900 more than one of every four Texans was born outside the state. Compare the class statistics with those of 1900.

CHAPTER 24 OVERVIEW

Although most Texans still lived in rural areas in the early 1900s, a shift in population was underway. As more Texans moved to the state's growing cities, different ways of life developed. New professions, more forms of entertainment, and wider opportunities for education emerged. Great changes were taking place in the state's economy. New industries developed and old ones expanded. These changes affected politics in Texas as new laws and institutions were created to meet the needs of a rapidly changing society.

Essential Elements
4A, 4B, 4D, 4E, 4F, 4H, 4I, 5B, 5C, 7E, 9A, 9B

CHAPTER 24

FROM FARM TO CITY

The Story Continues...

In 1900, the population of Texas was more than 3 million—the sixth largest in the nation. Just 40 years earlier, Texas had been ranked twenty-sixth. This growing population began responding to changes in the economy. Many Texans were moving into cities to find careers in industry, entertainment, and education. Agriculture grew, and new industries grew because of it.

The changing economy affected politics in Texas as well. People demanded reforms to meet the challenges of their changing society. This chapter looks at the many changes that occurred between 1900 and 1920. It compares and contrasts farm life and city life. It also describes the effects of city life on Texans. Finally, the chapter looks at the role of Texas in world affairs.

As you read the chapter, look for the answers to these questions:

1. How was life in the cities different from life on the farms in the early 1900s?
2. What important events in politics occurred between 1900 and 1920?
3. What was the role of Texas in the Spanish-American War, in the Mexican Revolution, and in World War I?

Barker Texas History Center

Mexican Texans made up about ten percent of the population of Texas around 1900. This family lived in South Texas.

■ The Growth of Urban Texas

More than 80 percent of Texans lived on farms or in small towns in 1900. Nearly six of every ten Texans made a living in agriculture. But the commercial revolution had spread into every region of the state. Small trading centers were blooming into large towns and major cities. New technology and new work habits were affecting life on the farm. People from other countries continued to move to Texas, adding to the rich mix of cultures.

INSTRUCTION

Vocabulary (I) You may wish to preteach the following boldfaced terms: *aviation* (p. 492); *ragtime* (p. 493); *welfare* (p. 496). **LEP**

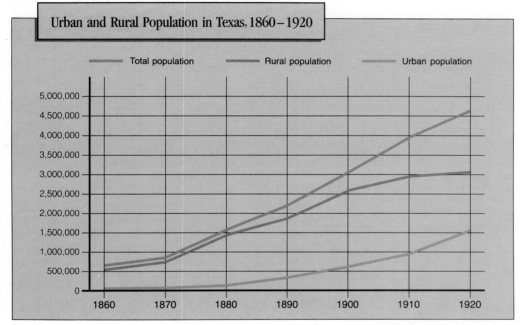

Urban and Rural Population in Texas, 1860–1920

— Total population   — Rural population   — Urban population

Which population category grew the least between 1910 and 1920? Which grew the most?

Transparency 23
An overhead transparency of this graph can be found in the Teacher's Resource Binder.

Caption Response
Rural grew the least; urban grew the most.

The Mix of Cultures. More than one in every four Texans in 1900 had been born in another state. Most of those born outside Texas were from the southern United States. Texans born in other countries numbered around 200,000. Many came to farm or ranch, but others found jobs in oil fields, refineries, and elsewhere in industry.

In 1900, African American Texans made up approximately twenty percent of the population. Most blacks lived on farms in the eastern part of the state.

Mexican Texans made up about ten percent of the population. The number of Texans of Mexican descent was increasing in the early 1900s. Most were living in southern and southwestern areas of the state. But like African American Texans, they were beginning to move to other regions in search of jobs.

Another large ethnic group was made up of German Texans. Almost 50,000 Texans in 1900 had been born in Germany. German communities existed in several Central Texas counties. Large German communities thrived in San Antonio and Houston.

This photograph of immigrants at Galveston Harbor was taken around 1910. European immigrants entered Texas through ports on the Gulf coast.

From 1900 to 1920, more immigrants came to the United States than at any other time in history. The majority came from eastern and southern Europe. Many chose Texas as a place to live. As a result, increased numbers of people arrived in Texas from Poland, Czechoslovakia, Yugoslavia, and Italy. Immigrants also came from Holland, Sweden, Norway, and Russia. Not all came from Europe. Small numbers of new arrivals were from the Middle East, China, and Japan. In 1900 there were 836 Chinese Texans. Most of them had arrived as railroad workers and stayed to open businesses in the growing cities.

Life in Rural Texas. In many ways, life on the farm in the early 1900s was much like it had been during the nineteenth century. Everyone in the family had to work. Men and women were busy from sunup to sundown. Some children did not attend school. Others went part-time. They were needed to help pick cotton, clean the house, and take care of the farm animals.

While work remained demanding, it was changing in some ways. A growing number of farmers were using machinery. Steam-powered tractors were used, and by 1915, there were tractors that ran on gasoline. New plows, binders, and threshers were coming into use. Gasoline engines were applied to cotton gins and cottonseed-processing equipment. Some farmers used these engines to power pumps for irrigation.

Modern conveniences made life more comfortable for those who could afford them. Telephones were installed in some rural areas in the early 1900s. Fewer farms received electric service for lights than for telephones.

New machinery on the farm, such as steam-powered tractors, allowed farmers to increase greatly their crop production.

488 Unit 9

The increased use of machinery allowed farmers to grow more crops on the same amount of land. But in many ways, modern technology did not make life much easier. Many Texas farmers had debts to pay. They owed on mortgages and loans for farm equipment. By 1900, more than half of the Texas farmers were tenant farmers, renting their land. Farm families had to work hard just to keep up with their debts, or they could become tied to the land by them.

The Growth of Cities. The majority of Texans lived in the eastern one-third of the state, where most towns and cities were located. Towns were growing in West Texas as well, however.

In 1900, San Antonio was the largest city in Texas, with a population of 53,321. Houston ranked second, with 44,633 persons. Dallas was the third largest city, with a population of 42,638. These cities were followed in size by Galveston and Fort Worth.

Texas cities were smaller and more peaceful than the crowded, bustling cities of the northeastern United States. There was more space for growth, and the countryside was close by. Nevertheless, Texas cities were challenged to provide necessary services to their growing populations.

A major complaint against the cities was the lack of paved streets. Electric streetcars, automobiles, freight wagons, buggies, and people on foot competed for space on city streets. Cities began paving their main streets by 1900. Some cities used brick and stone, while others even tried wooden blocks. Houston soon had 26 miles of paved streets.

Barker Texas History Center

Electric streetcars competed for space with horses and buggies on Dallas streets around the turn of the century.

LONE STAR LEGACY

The Automobile Rolls into Texas

During the early 1900s, Texas transportation changed from the horse to the
horseless carriage. The automobile arrived. Its coming affected the state's
economy and improved the lives
of urban and rural Texans alike.
Education, medicine, farming,
and industry were altered. Suddenly, people could drive to a
nearby town and back in a single afternoon.

The first automobile to be
driven across Texas soil is
thought to have come to Houston.
According to the March 16, 1897 edition of *The Houston Daily Post*:

> Yesterday an electric horseless carriage
> was seen on the streets. J. Frank Picker-
> ing, a traveling agent for Montgomery
> Ward, accompanied by a *Post* reporter,
> drove over the city streets. The horseless
> carriage was built especially for the
> above company at a cost of $3,000 as an
> advertising novelty. It is run by a set of
> storage batteries [with] 28 cells. . . . The
> tires are solid rubber. The carriage
> weighs about 2,000 pounds.

At first, rural Texans resented the automobile. City dwellers sometimes used country roads to test the speed of their cars. Early
efforts at speed records often resulted in
dead chickens and frightened horses. But
farmers began to profit from their losses by
setting up toll gates on roads and car ferries
on rivers. The first rural car mechanics
charged far more to repair a car than a buggy.

Soon, however, farmers began to see the
advantages of owning an automobile. Manufacturers began to tailor them to fit the
farmers' needs. Removable back
seats allowed for hauling produce
to market and tools to the fields.
Back wheels were replaced with
tractor wheels. The car and its
engine were used to cut fodder,
unload hay, generate electricity, pump water, saw wood, and
run grain mills.

Almost overnight, education
and medicine became more available to rural Texans. The car made
it possible to have traveling libraries, and
doctors could drive from farm to farm to make
house calls to their patients.

Using Historical Imagination

Imagine that you are a Texas farmer in 1913.
In your diary, explain how your new automobile has changed your life.

Inset: **Early auto**   Right: **"Horseless carriage"**   Inset: *Smith County Historical Society Archives.*   Right: *The Granger Collection*

Mural by Julius Woeltz, Amarillo Federal Building

The growing oil industry provided jobs for thousands of Texans in the early twentieth century.

City governments strained to provide other services as well. Clean water was of primary importance. Sewage systems had to be built. Public health received more attention with larger numbers of people living crowded together.

New Opportunities. People on the farms pointed to the cities' fast pace of life and unhealthy conditions as reasons not to move there. Probably most Texans considered country life more healthful. Food was fresh, water was clean, and there was plenty of open space.

Statistics support the view that it was healthier to live in rural areas than urban ones in the early 1900s. But people moved to the cities in large numbers anyway. If health conditions were worse, there were more doctors and hospitals in the city to treat illnesses.

Most people moved to the cities in search of jobs or to establish businesses. A whole range of new occupations could be found in the early 1900s. There were jobs in the oil industry, including the refineries. Hundreds of people worked for railroad companies. They drove trains, loaded freight, and repaired tracks, locomotives, and cars. Hospitals needed doctors and nurses. Telephone and electric companies were expanding.

Multicultural Perspective
The lack of trained physicians caused many Texans to turn to other methods of treatment. Many Mexican American families depended on the *curandero*, who used herbs and folk medicine to treat illnesses. *Curanderos* were highly respected in their communities.

Historical Sidelight
In 1900, Texas claimed 136 African American physicians—more than in any other state.

From the collections of Dallas Historical Society

This photograph of a Dallas telephone office was taken in the early 1920s. Operators often worked long shifts, seven days a week. A wide variety of job choices was not usually available to women at this time.

Humanities Research Center, The University of Texas at Austin

Katherine Stinson's younger sister Marjorie is shown taking the oath of an airmail pilot. Marjorie and Katherine Stinson were pioneers in the field of aviation.

New opportunities were created in cities for women. Many people thought it was improper for married women to work outside the home. Yet single women in increasing numbers were finding jobs. Most telephone operators were women, as were most nurses. By the early 1900s, a majority of teachers in the public schools were women. Better opportunities for education were available for urban Texans than for those in the country. Public schools were built in nearly all towns and cities at a time when many rural areas were without them. The new colleges and universities were located in urban areas.

Single and married women alike created their own opportunities. In 1910, airplanes were attracting attention in Texas and across the United States. Katherine Stinson and her mother opened a flying school in 1913. Stinson and her sister both became pilots. Katherine Stinson was the first skywriter and stunt flyer in the history of **aviation**, or human flight. Through her efforts, advances were made in aviation, and people saw that a woman could fly as well as a man. Stinson said of her flying: "My mother never warned me not to do this or that for fear of being hurt. Of course I got hurt, but I was never afraid."

In Dallas, Carrie Marcus Neiman, along with her husband and brother, opened a department store. She helped to bring the latest fashions to Texas women. Neiman-Marcus stores are world-famous today.

Leisure Time and Entertainment. Texans had more leisure time and a wider variety of entertainments after 1900. Most new forms of entertainment centered in the cities. Railroads and automobiles allowed rural people to travel to towns and cities to take part in these activities.

Horse racing continued to be a popular sport in Texas in the early 1900s. Professional boxing, or prizefighting, was followed by many Texans as well. The sport was outlawed in Texas in 1895, however, just as a championship fight was about to be held in Dallas. A black Texan, Jack Johnson, became the heavyweight champion of the world in 1908. Johnson, a dock worker from Galveston, won the title in Australia and held it until 1915.

Team sports were gaining a large following in many Texas towns and cities in the early 1900s. The Texas League of Professional Baseball Clubs was organized in 1887. Many players got their start in Texas before going on to fame in the major leagues. Tris Speaker, later a member of the Baseball Hall of Fame, began his career in Cleburne before playing for the Boston Red Sox and Cleveland Indians. Another member of the Hall of Fame was Rogers Hornsby, who compiled the second highest batting average in baseball history.

In 1893, the University of Texas began playing a popular new game called football. Soon Texas A&M, Texas Christian, and other colleges organized teams. The Southwest Athletic Conference was begun in 1914.

Baseball, football, and other sports were started in the high schools of Texas. Carroll Monroe played on the Greenville teams coached by Clyde Littlefield. Littlefield later became a famous coach at the University of Texas. Monroe recalled a football game, billed as the state championship, played between Greenville and Port Arthur in the autumn of 1919:

> It was quite a ball game and was played on an abandoned rice field. After scoring three touchdowns, all of which were called back by the officials for offside or clipping the wrong player, Greenville finally scored two safeties and we won 4–0. The score was not announced by the officials until after we were on the train out of the city, for our own protection. That was the year we defeated Forest Avenue of Dallas, in a pouring rain, 13–0. After scoring two touchdowns and one goal after the first quarter, we kicked the ball on first down the remainder of the game on Littlefield's orders.

The first statewide football championships were played with all schools, large and small, in the same class. Soon, the first girls' teams were organized in sports such as basketball.

While sports were gaining in popularity, traditional forms of entertainment were still popular. A special treat for Texas towns in the late 1800s and early 1900s was the circus. One of the best known to travel around the state was that of Mollie Bailey. Her show toured Texas for about 30 years. In 1906, the first railroad cars were developed to haul circus animals and equipment.

Nearly every Texas town had a theater or concert hall. Operas, plays, and concerts were regular events on Friday and Saturday nights. Scott Joplin, a black Texan, established **ragtime**, one of the most popular forms of music during this period. Joplin was a talented pianist and composer. [See "Spirit of Texas" feature on page 494.]

William F. English, Institute of Texan Cultures

Jack Johnson became the heavyweight boxing champion of the world in 1908. He was born in Galveston.

Neiman-Marcus, Dallas

Carrie Neiman brought stylish fashion to Texas. Along with her husband and brother, Carrie Neiman opened Neiman-Marcus in Dallas in 1907.

Historical Sidelight
The first local football teams were not officially sanctioned by high schools and included players up to 22 or 23 years of age. The University Interscholastic League gradually established uniform rules of eligibility.

Music and History (I) Locate and play for students some of the music of Scott Joplin and other ragtime composers.
A, LEP

Essential Elements
4D, 4I, 9A

Scott Joplin: King of Ragtime

About 100 years ago, young Scott Joplin, son of a freed slave, learned to play his mother's banjo and his father's fiddle. Although his family in Texarkana was poor, they valued music so much that they managed to purchase a piano. Scott quickly began to pick out tunes on that piano, and the rest became music history.

In 1917 Joplin, who is known worldwide today as "The King of Ragtime," died in poverty, thinking himself a failure. He was frustrated because his music, a forerunner of today's popular styles, was not taken seriously by the public. It would be more than 50 years before the ragtime style he created would become fully appreciated as serious music. Some critics, however, say that ragtime never died. They insist that it was instead absorbed by jazz and other forms of popular music.

Four years before his death, Joplin wrote a letter to the music editor of a magazine that had criticized ragtime. Scott Joplin's concern was to preserve the music's quality:

I have often sat in theatres and listened to beautiful ragtime melodies set to almost vulgar words as a song, and I have wondered why some composers will continue to make the public hate ragtime melodies because the melodies are set to such bad words.

I have often heard people say after they had heard a ragtime song, "I like the music, but I don't like the words." And most people who say that they don't like ragtime have reference to the words and not the music.

If someone were to put vulgar words to a strain of Beethoven's beautiful symphonies, people would begin saying: "I don't like Beethoven's symphonies." So it is with the unwholesome words and not the ragtime melodies that many people hate.

Ragtime rhythm is a syncopation original with the [black] people. ... But the other races throughout the world today are learning to write and make use of ragtime melodies. It is the rage in England today. When composers put decent words to ragtime melodies there will be very little kicking from the public about ragtime.

More than half a century later, Scott Joplin finally became famous for his ragtime music. In 1973, Joplin's tune "The Entertainer" became the theme song for the Oscar-winning movie *The Sting*. Books were written about his life. In 1976, Joplin was posthumously (after his death) awarded a Pulitzer Prize for his contributions to American music. Today, the ragtime pieces and operas of this turn-of-the-century musical genius are known throughout the world.

Scott Joplin wrote more than 500 pieces of music, including a ballet and two operas. Among his best-loved works are "Maple Leaf Rag," "The Easy Winners," "The Cascades," and the opera *Treemonisha*.

Inset: **Scott Joplin**

The Granger Collection

Cities and Industry. The growth of cities was linked to the development of industry and transportation. Industries grew through the development and use of Texas' natural resources. Because these resources vary from region to region, different resources were important to each city.

Several resources contributed to the growth of Houston. It became a major market for rice and cotton raised on farms in Southeast Texas. The forests of East Texas provided timber. Industries were established to make paper and other products from wood. When oil was discovered at Spindletop and other nearby fields, Houston, Beaumont, and Port Arthur became centers of the oil industry. Businesses were started to sell drilling equipment. Refineries were established. Railroads linked Houston to cities, farms, and forests. During the late 1800s and early 1900s, city leaders worked for the development of a wider channel to link Houston by water to Galveston Bay. The channel gave the city a direct outlet to the Gulf of Mexico.

Cotton aided the growth of Dallas as well as Houston. In the early 1900s, the North Texas city was the largest inland cotton market in the world. Thousands of bales were shipped to Dallas from the farms of the Blackland Prairie region. To serve the farmers, businesspeople began building cotton gins. Soon, Dallas was a world leader in the manufacture of cotton gins and other kinds of farm equipment. Oil and natural-gas fields nearby contributed to the economy.

In San Antonio, the federal government was important to the economy. Military bases were established there in

Historical Sidelight
The railroad accounted for the growth of the lumber industry in Texas. By the 1880s, one wage earner in six worked in a saw-mill. The lumber industry in Texas depended on African American workers for a large proportion of its work force.

The lumber industry of East Texas has continued to be important to the state's economy throughout the twentieth century.

Mural by Alexander Levin, Jasper Post Office

RETEACHING

Organize the class into two groups. Ask each group to make up twenty questions based on information from Section 1. Encourage students to vary the format and difficulty of the questions. Have students from each group exchange papers and answer the questions. Then have partners work together to discuss and correct answers. **LEP, A**

CLOSURE

Ask students to list the accomplishments of urban Progressives as you copy their responses on the chalkboard. Then ask students to comment on the incongruity of the "Progressives" working to strengthen segregation. Allow time for several students' comments.

ASSESSMENT

Have students complete the Section 1 Review on page 497.

Answers to
Section 1 Review

Define: *aviation*—human flight; *ragtime*—form of music established by Scott Joplin; *welfare*—care and well-being

(Continued on page 497)

Historical Sidelight
The purpose of normal schools was to train teachers. The schools typically offered two years of courses. Later, normal schools became state teacher's colleges.

Information Services, Rice University

Rice University opened for instruction at Houston in 1912. The university is renowned for its academic excellence.

Publication Services, Southern Methodist University

Southern Methodist University at Dallas opened in 1915 with an enrollment of 706. The campus consisted of two buildings. It has grown into a large complex of academic structures and offers a wide range of educational degrees.

the early 1900s. People were hired to work on the bases. Soldiers spent their money in San Antonio's stores. Because of the many nearby cattle ranches, businesses in San Antonio made a wide variety of leather goods, including boots. Flour mills and breweries were also built. The city became an important source for building stone and cement.

Progressivism in the City. New laws and new institutions were created to meet the demands of city life. Galveston led the way by creating a new type of city government. A commission was established to run the city after the terrible hurricane in 1900. Other cities soon took steps to make their local government more efficient.

Steps were taken by government and private groups to provide for the **welfare**, or care and well-being, of all. Texans on the farm generally lived in large families. People with special needs were cared for by the family. Neighbors could be counted on too. But in the cities, large numbers of strangers were thrown together. Many single people as well as small families lived in the cities. Institutions were needed to care for people in time of need.

Churches and private groups established charities to provide needy people with food, clothing, and shelter. If the head of a household was injured or lost a job, someone was there to help. During the late 1800s and early 1900s, attitudes were changing about care for people who were disabled. New schools were built for the handicapped. Homes were established for orphans. Patients with mental illnesses received better treatment.

Texans in the cities worked to establish better public schools. They also sought education for more people. After 1900, elementary schools were found in nearly every town and city. Most urban areas soon had junior and senior high schools. New normal schools were opened to train teachers. Other new colleges were established as well, both public and private. Two private colleges, Rice University in Houston and Southern Methodist University in Dallas, were opened in 1912 and 1915, respectively. The University of Texas received new funds, especially after 1923, when oil was discovered on land set aside for the school in West Texas. Millions of dollars of income from oil leases have gone to that university and to Texas A&M.

Women were especially active in bringing about improvements in education. Various women's organizations

SECTION 2

FOCUS

Past Learning (I) Review with students the definitions of the terms *prohibition* and *suffrage*. Have students imagine that it is 1900. Ask them to select the issue of prohibition or women's suffrage and write a sentence attacking or defending it. Call on volunteers to read their sentences aloud.

INSTRUCTION

Vocabulary (I) You may wish to preteach the following boldfaced terms: *faculty* (p. 499); *impeached* (p. 499). **LEP**

put pressure on the legislature to pass a law in 1915 making school attendance compulsory. Olga Kohlberg established Texas' first public kindergarten in El Paso in 1893. Jovita Idar established a free kindergarten in San Antonio in 1917. Women's clubs in Dallas and other cities raised money to set up nurseries to care for children whose mothers worked outside the home. Approximately 80 percent of the public libraries in Texas were established by women's clubs in the early 1900s.

Urban Progressives were not, however, concerned with reforming the system of segregation or insuring the voting rights of minority Texans. At the same time that the reform movement to give women the right to vote was gaining support, steps were taken to deny suffrage to black Texans. Democratic party officials restricted voting in local primary elections to whites. And in 1902, Texas began to require a poll tax, a tax on voters. As a result, by the early 1920s, only about ten percent of eligible black voters went to the polls.

The Progressive era also strengthened segregation in Texas. The state legislature and city governments passed more Jim Crow laws. In 1916, for example, Dallas imposed segregated housing, which meant that blacks had little choice in where they could live. Public facilities, restaurants, and hotels—even drinking fountains—were segregated. Black Texans also faced increased racial violence. Between 1900 and 1910, Texas ranked third in the number of lynchings. Race riots often occurred. ✪

2 Politics in an Urban Age

Prohibition and women's suffrage were two major issues of Texas politics between 1900 and 1920. Both issues were subjects of heated debate. One of the most controversial governors in the history of the state added to the excitement of the era.

The Prohibition Debate. Support for prohibition, or the elimination of alcoholic beverages, became stronger in the early 1900s. More leaders ran for election on the issue of prohibition. Organizations such as the Women's Christian Temperance Union and the Texas Anti-Saloon League worked for prohibition. It was a major political issue in every election from 1908 to 1918.

El Paso Public Library

Olga Kohlberg brought new ideas about early childhood education to Texas from her native Germany.

SECTION ★ REVIEW

Define: aviation, ragtime, welfare

Identify: Katherine Stinson, Carrie Marcus Neiman, Jack Johnson, Olga Kohlberg

1. What percent of the Texas population in 1900 was African American and Mexican American?
2. What jobs did children have on farms?
3. How were Texas cities different from cities of the Northeast?
4. What new opportunities were there for women?
5. Who established most libraries in Texas?

Analyzing Information: How would a poll tax keep black voters from voting?

Exploring Economics: Imagine that you are eighteen and living on your parents' farm in 1925. What economic opportunities does the city offer you? What kind of job might you get?

Identify: Katherine Stinson—pioneer in aviation; Carrie Marcus Neiman—helped open the famous Neiman-Marcus department store; Jack Johnson—African American Texan who became the heavyweight boxing champion of the world in 1908; Olga Kohlberg—opened Texas' first public kindergarten

1. African American: about twenty percent; Mexican American: about ten percent
2. Children picked cotton, cleaned house, and cared for farm animals.
3. Texas cities were smaller, less crowded, and more peaceful.
4. There were many new jobs open to women, including telephone operator, nurse, and teacher; and there were more educational opportunities.
5. Most libraries were established by women's clubs.

Analyzing Information: Because many blacks were poor, paying a poll tax was a burden.

Exploring Economics: There are many more jobs and a wider variety of jobs available in the city. Starting a business there would be easier. Possible jobs include: factory work; delivery work; railroad jobs such as repair work, driving trains, or loading freight; and teaching.

Essential Elements
4B, 4E, 4G, 4I, 7B, 7D, 7E, 7F, 7G, 9A

Analysis (II) Ask students: What was Governor Ferguson's view of prohibition? *(He thought that too much attention was being paid to prohibition.)* Where did the bulk of Ferguson's campaign money come from *(Texas brewers who opposed prohibition)*? Ask students to use their responses to these questions to draw a conclusion regarding Governor Ferguson's guilt or innocence. **A, G**

Cooperative Learning (I) Organize students into three groups. Ask one group to research the history of the women's suffrage movement in Texas. Have students in the second group imagine that they are members of the Texas Equal Suffrage Association. Have students in the third group imagine that they are opposed to granting women the right to vote. Ask the second and third groups to stage a debate on giving women the right to vote. After the debate, have the first group report on the history of the women's suffrage movement in Texas. **A**

Constitutional Heritage

Section 1 of the Eighteenth Amendment to the Constitution reads:

After one year from the ratification of this article the manufacture, sale, or transportation of intoxicating liquors within, the importation thereof into, or the exportation thereof from the United States and all territory subject to the jurisdiction thereof for beverage purposes is hereby prohibited.

The amendment was repealed in 1933 by the Twenty-first Amendment.

Archives Division, Texas State Library

James E. Ferguson was elected to the governorship in 1914 and again in 1916. Several important measures were passed during his first administration. Controversy marked his second term, however, and he was removed from office in 1917.

Blagg-Huey Library, Texas Woman's University

Christia Adair worked for women's suffrage and other civil rights issues. She continued to fight discrimination against women and minorities for many decades.

The Democratic party split between those against and those for prohibition. City people tended to oppose prohibition. Gradually, those favoring prohibition were able to have laws passed in their favor. In 1917, Texas adopted a law forbidding the sale of alcoholic drinks within ten miles of an army post. A law in 1918 closed all saloons in the state. The United States Congress passed an amendment to the Constitution supporting prohibition. In 1919, Texas ratified the amendment. The making and selling of alcoholic drinks was forbidden across the country.

Farmer Jim. James E. Ferguson was one of the Democrats who thought too much attention was being paid to prohibition. Running for governor in 1914, Ferguson said the issue kept Texans from dealing with more important matters. He told the people that attention should be turned to helping the many tenant farmers in the state. His appeal to farmers earned Ferguson the nickname "Farmer Jim."

Ferguson was outspoken and colorful. His supporters said he was the champion of the farmers and the poor. Those opposed to Ferguson said he did not tell the truth and that he aroused people for his own benefit. Most Texas voters seemed to like Ferguson, and he was elected governor in 1914 and 1916.

Several important reforms were made during Ferguson's first term. An act was passed to aid tenant farmers. The law set a limit on the amount of rent a landowner could charge a tenant. In 1915, Ferguson supported the law making school attendance compulsory. Further, he supported an act providing for better schools in rural areas. The state would provide funds to rural communities that approved local taxes for schools.

Other important laws were passed during Ferguson's second term. Many Texans wanted better roads. A law was passed establishing a highway commission. One task of the commission was to oversee the spending of money provided by the federal government for roads. The legislature also provided approximately $1 million in aid to Texas public schools.

Throughout his term, Ferguson developed strong enemies. Some accused him of misusing state funds. He soon ran into serious trouble over money for the University of Texas. The legislature passed a bill that included $1.6 million for the school. Ferguson vetoed that part of the act

Guided Practice (I) Direct the class to play a "Who Am I?" game, using the names of persons mentioned in this section. Have a student stand and provide a clue to the class. *(Example: "I became president of the Texas Woman Suffrage Association in 1913. Who am I?")* Other students should then guess the person's name *(Eleanor Brackenridge)*. Continue the activity until all of the names have been correctly identified. **A, LEP**

EXTENSION

Community Involvement (I) Encourage students to invite to class a representative of the local chapter of Students

Against Drunk Driving (SADD) or Mothers Against Drunk Driving (MADD) to talk about the organization's efforts to curb alcohol abuse. **A, LEP**

Independent Practice (II) Ask students to write a paragraph in response to the following questions: From what you have read in Section 2, do you think Governor Ferguson should have been removed from office? Why or why not? Invite two volunteers with differing opinions to read their paragraphs aloud. **A**

providing money for the university. The governor was upset that the university had not removed certain **faculty**, or teachers and staff members. Former students and other supporters of the University of Texas from around the state were angry at Ferguson. They wanted the governor to be **impeached**, or charged with crimes while in office.

Under the constitution of the state, the House of Representatives made 21 charges against the governor. It was the duty of the Senate to act as a court to try the charges. The Senate decided that ten of the charges were true. The governor was found guilty of using state funds for personal benefit. It was also determined that he had acquired more than $150,000 during his campaign for governor. The money came from Texas brewers (beer manufacturers) who opposed prohibition.

James Ferguson was removed from office. Lieutenant Governor William Hobby became the new governor. Ferguson was barred from serving again in public office, but Texans had not heard the last of him. In the following years, he and his wife, Miriam, worked to regain control of the governor's office.

The Women's Movement Grows. Women became more active in politics as new opportunities were opening for them. Women helped establish libraries, museums, health clinics, and schools. Through their efforts, Texas State College for Women was established at Denton in 1903. Women led the effort to pass laws limiting child labor in industry and making school attendance compulsory. At the same time, they worked to gain the rights to vote and to hold public office. Their goal was to be able to participate in making the laws.

The struggle for women's suffrage received a boost in 1913, when Eleanor Brackenridge became president of the Texas Woman Suffrage Association. The name was changed to the Texas Equal Suffrage Association in 1916. Minnie Fisher Cunningham, Annie Webb Blanton, and Jane McCallum were other important suffrage leaders. Campaigns were held across the state to gain voting rights for women.

Women throughout the United States were working for voting rights at the same time. In 1919, a special session of the Texas legislature ratified the Nineteenth Amendment to the Constitution. This law gave women across the country the right to vote when it went into effect in 1920.

Humanities Research Center, The University of Texas at Austin

Dr. Annie Webb Blanton was an important suffrage leader in Texas. In 1918, she became the first woman in Texas to win election to a statewide office, the superintendent of public instruction.

Blagg-Huey Library, Texas Woman's University

Jovita Idar, a newspaper journalist, established a free kindergarten in San Antonio in 1917. She also organized groups to fight discrimination against Mexican Texans in South Texas and supported educational opportunities for women.

Constitutional Heritage
Section 1 of the Nineteenth Amendment to the Constitution reads:
The right of citizens of the United States to vote shall not be denied or abridged by the United States or by any State on account of sex.

500 *Unit 9*

TEXAS VOICES

*J*ane McCallum and Minnie Fisher Cunningham were leaders of the women's suffrage movement in Texas. For years they worked to promote universal suffrage. McCallum and Cunningham were backed by thousands of Texas women who aided the suffragist cause. Yet by 1919, both leaders had sought cooperation from men as well. They saw the necessity of support from male voters and male legislators in order to secure women's voting rights. The following excerpts are from letters by Cunningham and McCallum, respectively, encouraging the cooperation of men in the struggle for women's suffrage:

> In the name of Democracy, America raised a standard [flag] and went across the seas to do battle for this ideal. We called our boys and young men to that standard, and they came by the millions; for the sake of it, they died by thousands and tens of thousands. Democracy is a government by the people. Women are people. What we found worth sending them to die for, shall we not find worth living and working for?

> It is almost impossible to realize that this is the deciding day, the ONLY day, in fact, in the whole history of the world that Texas men can go on record as making Texas mothers and wives inexpressibly proud by giving us the ballot.... Never for a minute do we doubt the verdict of our men . . . but our task is to awaken them, and get them to the polls! We must and we will.

SECTION 2 REVIEW

Define: faculty, impeached
Identify: Annie Webb Blanton, Nineteenth Amendment, Christia Adair, Jovita Idar

1. What were the purpose and the result of the prohibition amendment?
2. Why was Governor Ferguson called "Farmer Jim"?
3. Why did women want the right to vote and hold office?

Evaluating Information: Were people in cities right or wrong to oppose prohibition? Why?

Using Historical Imagination: How do you think women reacted when the Nineteenth Amendment was passed? Why?

It also paved the way for women to participate fully in the democratic political process. Since 1920, Texas women in increasing numbers have been elected to local and state offices.

Annie Webb Blanton was the first woman to win election to a Texas state office. She became the superintendent of public instruction in 1918. Blanton had been the first president of the Texas State Teachers Association. Jane McCallum later became secretary of state of Texas.

The Texas Equal Suffrage Association had no black members. In spite of this, Christia Adair, a black Texan, worked for women's suffrage. She continued efforts for many years to gain equal rights for all black Texans.

In South Texas, Jovita Idar organized people to support women's suffrage as well as rights for Mexican Texans. Idar helped establish schools and campaigned for justice for Mexican Texans accused of breaking the law. ✪

500 *Unit 9*

ASSESSMENT
Have students complete the Section 2 Review on page 500.

SECTION 3

FOCUS

Past Learning (I) Invite a volunteer to point out Cuba on a wall map. Reinforce the geographic theme of *location*. Remind students that events occurring in faraway places can have a significant impact on their lives. Tell them to keep this in mind as they study Section 3.

INSTRUCTION

Multicultural Perspective (II) Divide the class into two groups. Have students in one group write a newspaper editorial about the border troubles with Mexico from the perspective of a Mexican Texan. Have students in the other group write an editorial from the perspective of an Anglo Texan. Use completed editorials to create an "editorial page" display for the bulletin board. V

3 Texans and World Affairs

The United States emerged as a major world power in the late 1800s. A number of conflicts with other countries arose. Texans played important roles in world affairs.

The Spanish-American War. The Cuban people revolted against Spain in the late 1890s. Many people in the United States were upset over Spanish treatment of the Cubans. Many American businesspeople owned property in Cuba. They hoped the United States would help make Cuba independent and protect their interests. When the United States battleship *Maine* exploded in the harbor of Havana, Cuba, many people blamed the Spaniards. The United States soon declared war on Spain.

Texas was chosen as a major site to train soldiers. Approximately 10,000 Texans joined the army. One of the most famous units in the war, the Rough Riders, was organized in San Antonio. Many Texans served in this unit under Theodore Roosevelt, who later would become president of the United States.

United States forces invaded Cuba as well as the Philippines in the Pacific. Spanish forces were quickly defeated. The United States acquired new territory from Spain after the Spanish-American War.

Border Troubles. Texas has a generally warm climate and plenty of land. These were two reasons that the United States military chose Texas as a major training ground. A number of bases were established in the state, especially in the San Antonio area.

Texas was the staging area for American troops sent to the Rio Grande during the Mexican Revolution of 1910. The president of Mexico, Porfirio Díaz, was overthrown. Forces led by Venustiano Carranza and Francisco "Pancho" Villa were soon fighting each other.

Pancho Villa became upset when Carranza's government was recognized by the United States. Villa began attacking Americans. His soldiers shot sixteen United States citizens in Mexico. They then raided across the border into New Mexico and Texas.

President Woodrow Wilson sent troops to the border area. Governor Colquitt sent Texas Rangers as well. In the spring of 1916, the United States invaded northern Mexico to chase Pancho Villa. They failed and soon withdrew.

The Granger Collection

Theodore Roosevelt became the twenty-sixth president of the United States in 1901. He led the Rough Riders during the Spanish-American War.

Essential Elements
4C, 4E, 4I, 5B, 9A, 9B, 9E

Historical Sidelight
The fairgrounds in San Antonio served as the headquarters for the Rough Riders. Roosevelt recruited practically anyone who could ride and shoot, including cowboys and ex-Texas Rangers. Instead of the typical army uniform, the volunteers wore boots, leggings, brown pants, flannel shirts, slouch hats, and bandanas.

Guided Practice (I) Locate and bring to class examples of recruiting and other types of posters that were used to promote the war effort during World War I. Have students work in pairs or small groups to create either a recruiting poster or one for the campaign to conserve food. Posters should be directed at Texans and should include a drawing and a slogan. Display completed posters in the classroom. **V, TK**

EXTENSION

Research (II) Have students select one of the conflicts mentioned in this section and conduct additional research. Encourage them to supplement their reports with maps. **A, V; TK, G**

Independent Practice (II) Have students use the information in Section 3 to create a chart detailing Texas' role in world affairs during the late 1800s and early 1900s. Allow students to develop their own column headings. Invite volunteers to discuss their charts with the class. **A, V, TK**

Answers to Section 3 Review

Identify: Rough Riders—army unit organized in San Antonio for service in the Spanish-American War; Pancho Villa—Mexican leader who raided the United States; the Allies—nations that fought together in World War I, including Britain, France, Russia, and the United States

(Continued on page 503)

502 *Unit 9*

Brown Brothers

Pancho Villa was a revolutionary hero to many Mexicans. He wanted to be president of Mexico. Angered by the United States government, Villa and his soldiers raided border areas and killed sixteen United States citizens. Villa was pursued by United States troops but was never caught.

The invasion caused bad feelings between Mexico and the United States for many years.

Many Texans dismissed these conflicts in the Valley as a problem with "Mexican bandits," but the reality was more complicated. It was also a struggle between Mexican Texans and Anglo Texans over land and civil rights. The Valley was changing from a ranching society to a farming society, and many Mexican families who had lived in the area for generations were being forced to sell their land. Thousands of Mexican Texans joined a revolutionary movement called the Plan de San Diego. The plan (first signed in San Diego, Texas) proclaimed independence and meant to establish an independent republic along the Texas border. Supporters of the plan raided trains, irrigation pumping stations, and ranches, killing scores of people. These raids brought about a violent response from Anglo authorities and the Texas Rangers. Hundreds of Mexican Texans were killed. Thousands more were driven out of Texas or forced to sell their land to Anglos. As historian David Montejano notes, "The conflict turned the Valley into a virtual war zone during 1915–1917."

World War I. In 1914, a major war broke out in Europe. It was later called World War I. Soon Britain, France, Italy, and Russia were fighting against Germany, Austria-Hungary, and Turkey. President Wilson asked the people of the United States to remain neutral, not take sides. Thousands of people had come to the United States from the countries on both sides fighting the war.

Eventually, many Americans turned against the Germans in support of the British. In 1915, the German navy sank a passenger ship, the *Lusitania*. More than 1,000 people drowned, including 128 Americans. In 1917, the United States declared war on Germany.

Texans and the War. About 200,000 Texans served in the armed forces during World War I. Five hundred were female nurses. Besides serving in the military, Texans played important roles in the federal government. Edward M. House was the closest adviser to President Wilson. Thomas Watt Gregory served as attorney general. Albert Sidney Burleson was postmaster general. David F. Houston served as secretary of agriculture.

Four major military camps were set up in Texas. Soldiers trained at Camp Bowie in Fort Worth, Camp Travis

RETEACHING

Have students write a cause-and-effect statement for each of the subsections of Section 3. Call on volunteers to read their statements aloud. **A, LEP**

CLOSURE

Call on students to summarize the role of Texans in one of the world events mentioned in Section 3.

ASSESSMENT

Have students complete the Section 3 Review on page 503.

Library of Congress

President Woodrow Wilson (center) appointed a number of Texans to important federal posts. Included in this photo are Thomas Gregory (rear, second from right), David F. Houston (front, third from left) and Albert S. Burleson (far right).

in San Antonio, Camp Logan in Houston, and Camp MacArthur in Waco. Pilots were trained at Kelly Field in San Antonio as well as other airfields in the state. Marjorie Stinson trained pilots at her Stinson Flying School.

The United States Army arrived in France in 1917 to help the Allies, as Britain, France, and Russia were known. Most United States troops were in the fighting only a short time before the war ended, but they helped bring victory to the Allies. The Thirty-sixth Division had many Texans in its ranks. It suffered 2,601 casualties in one stretch of fighting lasting only 23 days. Approximately 5,000 Texans gave their lives during the war.

Wartime at Home. Texans at home supported the war effort in a number of ways. They raised money by buying Liberty Bonds. They worked for the Red Cross and other organizations to aid soldiers and sailors. More women took jobs in factories when men left to join the military.

The war caused shortages of food and other goods. People were asked to eat less flour, sugar, and meat. Signs appeared in stores asking people to "go wheatless," or eat fewer wheat products.

Celebrations were held when the terrible war ended in 1918. People looked forward to a more normal life again. Many thought that the war would bring a lasting peace. ✪

SECTION  REVIEW

Identify: Rough Riders, Pancho Villa, the Allies

1. What event caused the United States to declare war on Spain?
2. What was the Plan de San Diego?
3. Why did the United States enter World War I?
4. Which four Texans served in President Wilson's government?
5. List three ways that Texans at home supported the war effort during World War I.

Evaluating Information: Should the United States have remained neutral, rather than joining World War I? Explain.

Exploring Multicultural Perspectives: Imagine that you are a Mexican Texan living in the Valley. Why might you support the Plan de San Diego?

1. The United States blamed Spain for the explosion of the United States battleship *Maine* in the harbor of Havana, Cuba.
2. It was a revolutionary movement that wanted to establish an independent republic along the Texas border.
3. The United States entered the war after Germany sank the *Lusitania,* a passenger ship.
4. Thomas Watt Gregory, Albert Sidney Burleson, David F. Houston, and Edward M. House
5. Possible answers include: raising money by buying Liberty Bonds, working for the Red Cross and other organizations, working in factories, and eating less of certain foods because of shortages.

Evaluating Information: Answers will vary but should be supported by sound reasoning.

Exploring Multicultural Perspectives: Answers will vary, but students should recognize that the conflict involved many Mexican families who had lived in the area for generations and were being forced to sell their land.

CHAPTER REVIEW RESOURCES

1. Chapter Review Worksheet 24
2. Chapter 24 Test, Form A
3. Reteaching Worksheet 24
4. Chapter 24 Test, Form B
5. **Informal Evaluation Forms:** Portfolio Assessment
6. *Texas, Our Texas* **Test Generator**

Essential Elements
4A, 4B, 4E, 4H, 4I, 5C, 9A, 9B, 9G

in the war, and many soldiers trained in Texas; Mexican border troubles—the Texas Rangers fought, Texas served as the staging area for the United States' effort against Mexico, many Mexican Texans were killed and many more were driven out of Texas or forced to sell their land to Anglos; World War I—many Texans fought in the war, many Texans played important roles in the federal govern-

CHAPTER 24 REVIEW ANSWERS

Understanding Main Ideas

1. African Americans—lived mainly in the eastern part of Texas; Mexican Texans—lived mainly in southern and southwestern areas of Texas; German Texans—were concentrated in Central Texas, San Antonio, and Houston
2. All of the family members worked, farmers used more machinery, and some families had modern conveniences such as electric lights and the telephone.
3. Urban population increased, industry grew, many businesses started, streets were paved and other services were provided, new forms of entertainment were offered, many cities reformed their governments, and charities were begun to help people.
4. Texans enjoyed team sports, such as football and baseball; the circus; and theater and music events.
5. The prohibition amendment and the Nineteenth Amendment were passed, women became more active in politics, and Governor James Ferguson was removed from office.
6. The Spanish-American War—many Texans fought

CHAPTER 24 REVIEW

Understanding Main Ideas

1. What were the major ethnic groups in Texas in 1900? In what parts of the state did each group live?
2. What was life like on Texas farms in the early 1900s?
3. How did city life change during the early 1900s?
4. Describe the three forms of entertainment enjoyed by Texans in the early 1900s.
5. What changes in politics occurred between 1900 and 1920?
6. Texans were involved in three different conflicts between the United States and foreign countries between 1898 and 1918. What were they? What role did Texans play in these conflicts?

Thinking Critically

1. **Synthesizing Information:** How did women affect the development of city life? How was the development of cities important to women?
2. **Making Decisions:** Would you have preferred to live in rural or urban Texas in the early 1900s? Consider the advantages and disadvantages of city and country life, and explain your choice.
3. **Exploring Multicultural Perspectives:** Imagine that you are a black seventh-grader in the 1920s. Write a diary entry that shows what your daily life is like under Jim Crow laws. If you prefer, you may write more than one entry in your diary.

Linking History and Geography

1. How did geography affect the selection of Texas as a site for army bases?
2. List the major resources important to the economies of Houston, Dallas, and San Antonio. How did these resources affect the economic development of these cities?

TAAS Practice
Using Primary Sources

In the late 1800s, music was very popular. Few people were shy about singing or playing musical instruments. Many people had a piano in the parlor. People often sang songs while working and as entertainment in the evenings. The following song was popular during this time:

Come, boys, I have something to tell you,
Come near, I would whisper it low;
You are thinking of leaving the homestead.
Don't be in a hurry to go.
The city has many attractions,
But think of the vices and sins,
When once in the vortex of fashion,
How soon the course downward begins.

(Chorus:)
Stay on the farm, stay on the farm,
Though profits come in rather slow.
Stay on the farm, stay on the farm;
Don't be in a hurry to go.

1. This song warns that although the city has many attractions, it is
   A boring
   B full of temptation
   C lively and exciting
   D educational

ment, four major military camps were set up in the state, and pilots were trained in Texas.

Thinking Critically

1. **Synthesizing Information:** Answers will vary but should reflect the increased opportunities for women in cities and the important roles played by women in improving education and other aspects of urban life.

2. **Making Decisions:** Answers will vary. Explanations should be based on information provided in the chapter.
3. **Exploring Multicultural Perspectives:** Diary entries will vary but should demonstrate knowledge of the Jim Crow laws and their impact on the lives of African Americans.

Linking History and Geography

1. Texas had a warm climate and plenty of available land.
2. Houston—rice, cotton, timber, oil; Dallas—cotton, oil, natural gas; San Antonio—cattle, building stone, cement. Industries grew through the development of these resources. For example, Dallas became the largest inland cotton market in the world, which led to the city becoming a world leader in the manufacture of cotton gins.

TAAS Practice
Using Primary Sources
1. B   2. C

TAAS Practice
Writing Descriptively
Letters will vary but should incorporate details regarding urban and rural life.

Practicing Skills
1. **Interpreting Graphs:** Between 1900 and 1920, the population grew more than 1,500,000. The greatest growth in urban population occurred between 1910 and 1920. The greatest growth in rural population occurred between 1870 and 1880.
2. **Interpreting Charts:** Loose hay was the cheapest crop to produce by hand as well as by machine. It took 70 hours longer. It cost $7.09 more.

Enriching Your Study of History
1. **Individual Project:** Posters should be persuasive and creative.
2. **Cooperative Project:** Maps should be based on the information presented on pages 495–96 of the textbook.
3. **Cooperative Project:** Reports should demonstrate thorough research.

Time and Labor Costs for Selected Crops				
Crop	Time Worked		Labor Cost	
	Hours by Hand	Hours by Machine	Hand	Machine
Corn	38	15	$ 3.62	$ 1.51
Oats	66	7	3.72	1.07
Hay: loose	21	3	1.75	.42
Hay: baled	35	11	3.06	1.28
Potatoes	108	38	10.89	3.80
Cotton	167	78	7.87	7.87
Rice: rough	62	17	5.64	1.00
Sugarcane	351	191	31.94	11.31

2. The line "I would whisper it low" tells us that the author
   A has a low voice
   B doesn't like to sing
   C knows that he or she has something unpopular to say
   D knows that he or she has something popular to say

TAAS Practice
Writing Descriptively
Imagine that you are a Texan who has recently moved from the farm to the city. Write a letter to a cousin in New York, explaining why you decided to move to the city. Describe your new life and compare it to your old life.

Practicing Skills
1. **Interpreting Graphs:** Study the graph on page 487. Approximately how much did the total population grow between 1900 and 1920? When did the greatest growth in the urban population occur? When did the greatest growth in the rural population occur?
2. **Interpreting Charts:** Study the chart above. Which crop was the cheapest to produce by hand? by machine? How much longer did it take to produce potatoes by hand than by machine? How much more did it cost?

Enriching Your Study of History
1. **Individual Project:** Create a poster urging Texans to vote for the Nineteenth Amendment.
2. **Cooperative Project:** Working with a partner, create a resource map of Texas in the early 1900s. Use the information on pages 495 and 496 as your guide. Your teacher will display the maps in your classroom.
3. **Cooperative Project:** Your teacher will organize your class into ten teams and assign each team to research and report orally on one of the following topics pertaining to the early 1900s: immigration to the United States, inventions, automobiles, trains, aviators or airplanes, boxing, Texas baseball players or teams, Texas college football, popular music, the oil industry in Texas. Your team should select one member to present your team's report aloud to the class.

UNIT REVIEW RESOURCES

1. Unit Review Worksheet 24
2. Unit 9 Test, Form A
3. Reteaching Worksheet 9
4. Unit 9 Test, Form B
5. **Informal Evaluation Forms:** Portfolio Assessment
6. *Texas, Our Texas* **Test Generator**

Essential Elements
3D, 4A, 4C, 7E, 9A, 9B, 9D

worked outside the home. By 1920 women had earned the right to vote, more women were involved in politics, and more women were employed outside the home.

UNIT 9 REVIEW ANSWERS

Connecting Main Ideas

1. Possible answers include: the Grange—reduce railroad rates; the Farmers' Alliance—regulate railroads; Populists—government ownership of railroads, telegraph lines, and telephones, and other goals aimed at helping farmers; Knights of Labor—higher wages and better working conditions; Women's Christian Temperance Union and Texas Anti-Saloon League—prohibition; Texas Equal Rights Association and Texas Equal Suffrage Association—voting rights for women
2. They addressed the problems of farmers at a time when most Texans made their living in agriculture.
3. Cities grew because of the growth of industry, improvements in transportation, and the large number of people moving to the cities seeking new opportunities.
4. More schools were built, the school year was lengthened, kindergartens were opened, schools for Mexican Texans and African Americans were opened, and more government money was set aside for education.
5. In 1880 women had few rights, and very few women

UNIT 9

REVIEW

Connecting Main Ideas

1. Select three reform groups discussed in Unit 9, and identify their major goal or goals.
2. Why did the Populists have a greater impact in Texas than the Progressives?
3. What were the main reasons for the growth of cities in Texas during the early 1900s?
4. What changes occurred in Texas education during the Age of Reform?
5. Compare and contrast the role of women in Texas in 1880 to the role of women in Texas in 1920.

Practicing Critical Thinking Skills

1. **Exploring Economics:** What efforts were made to limit the power of railroads in Texas? Why were farmers particularly interested in limiting the power of Texas railroads?
2. **Evaluating Information:** Which of these international events do you think was most important to Texans: the Spanish-American War, the Texas-Mexico border dispute, World War I? Explain your answer.
3. **Analyzing Information:** Women were most involved in calling for which reforms? Why do you think this was the case?

TAAS *Practice*
Writing Informatively

Imagine that you are a railroad worker in 1886. Write a letter to your employer, explaining why you are going on strike.

Exploring Local History

1. Are there any farm organizations in your county? Refer to the map on page 475. Did the Populists gain control of your county during the 1890s?
2. Ask a parent, a guardian, or an adult friend: Do you or any of your relatives belong to a union? If so, why? If not, why not?

Using Historical Imagination

1. **Individual Project:** Imagine that you are Governor James S. Hogg. Write a speech in which you tell how you would like to be remembered by Texans. Give specific examples of your accomplishments.
2. **Cooperative Project:** Your teacher will divide your class into groups, each representing a reform group in Texas. Your group will prepare a presentation for the class, describing your group and its goals, and explaining why it is important to Texas that you achieve those goals.

For Extending Your Knowledge

Erdman, Loula Grace. *The Edge of Time.* New York: Dodd, Mead, 1950. A novel about a year in the life of a Texas homesteader and his bride.

Humphrey, William. *The Ordways.* New York: Knopf, 1965. A poignant story of a family who settled in northeast Texas after the Civil War.

O'Donnell, Mary King. *Quincie Bolliver.* Boston: Houghton Mifflin, 1941. The story of a muleskinner's daughter who grows up during the oil-boom days.

Practicing Critical Thinking Skills

1. **Exploring Economics:** The Grange and the Farmers' Alliance worked to lower railroad rates, to force railroad companies to pay more taxes, and to force railroads to sell their land at lower prices. Governor Hogg established the Texas Railroad Commission to oversee the operation of the railroads and helped pass the Interstate Commerce Act. Farmers wanted to limit the power of Texas railroads because farmers relied on the railroads to transport goods to market.

2. **Evaluating Information:** Answers will vary but should be based on sound reasoning and should be supported by information presented in the textbook.

3. **Analyzing Information:** Women called for reforms in schools, in civil rights, in community service, and in child labor. Answers to the second part of the question will vary. These are issues that affected families and children—areas of traditional concern to women.

TAAS **Practice**
Writing Informatively:
Letters will vary but should demonstrate knowledge of issues facing railroad workers and the purpose of labor strikes.

Exploring Local History

1. Students should conduct research to locate any farm organizations in their county. To answer the second part of the question, students should locate their county on the map on page 475.
2. Answers will vary but should indicate that students performed the activity.

Using Historical Imagination

1. **Individual Project:** Speeches will vary but should highlight the reforms carried out by Hogg.
2. **Cooperative Project:** Presentations should be based on information presented in the unit.

Skill Lesson
Practicing the Skill

1. Visual detail—informs readers by helping them visualize the subject; chronological narrative—informs readers by describing a sequence of events; comparison and contrast—informs readers by comparing one thing with another and pointing out similarities and differences
2. Paragraphs will vary but should demonstrate one method of informative writing.

SKILL LESSON

Writing Informatively

Often when you write, you want to pass along facts or news to your readers. You want to inform them.

There are three methods of writing informatively: using visual details, using chronological narrative, and using comparison and contrast.

1. **Visual Detail.** The purpose of using visual details is to inform readers by making them "see," or visualize in their minds, the subject you are describing. Read the following selection from *The Path to Power,* Robert Caro's biography of Lyndon Johnson. The selection describes the time in 1907 that Johnson's mother traveled to her new home near Johnson City.

> As they rode away from comfortable, bustling Fredericksburg and its neat green fields, the land faded to brown, and then gray. It became more and more rocky, more and more barren. The farmhouses were farther and farther apart. Dotting the hills were hulks of deserted farmhouses, crumbling rectangles of logs out of which reared tall stone fireplaces which stood in the hills like tombstones—monuments to . . . other couples who had tried to earn a living there.

Notice that Caro uses visual details to describe the change in the landscape. This type of informative writing depends on interesting details to make what you are describing come to life.

2. **Chronological Narrative.** Chronological narrative informs the reader by describing a sequence of events in time.

Read the following selection from the same book, and notice how Caro uses time to inform the reader. He employs time words such as *one year* and *the next year* to describe a particular order of events.

> The early settlers in the Hill Country couldn't believe how fast the brush spread. . . . One year they would be riding untrammeled [freely] across open meadows; the next year, in the same meadows, their horses had to step cautiously through scrub a foot or two high; the next year, the scrub was up to a rider's shins as he sat on his horse.

3. **Comparison and Contrast.** Comparing and contrasting informs the reader by comparing one thing with another and pointing out the similarities and differences. Read the following selection, also by Caro, and notice how he compares and contrasts two places.

> If the 1870s and '80s and '90s were a desperate time for farmers, nowhere were times more desperate than in the Hill Country. In other areas, farmers might believe that railroads were fleecing [robbing] them; the Hill Country didn't have railroads—because laying tracks through hills was too expensive in a sparsely populated district—and the cost of getting crops to market by wagon (crops that often spoiled because of the length of the trip) ate up farmers' profits. . . . In other areas, farmers felt the price for their crops was too low; in the Hill Country, the problem was trying to get crops to grow at all.

Practicing the Skill

1. What are the three methods of informative writing? How are they different?
2. Choose one method of informative writing, and write a paragraph on a subject related to your school.

INTRODUCING THE UNIT

Connecting with Past Learning

As you draw on the chalkboard the following diagrams, have students recall previous discussions on supply and demand.

   a. Supply ↑   **Demand** ↓   **Price** ___

   b. Supply ↓   **Demand** ↑   **Price** ___

Complete the diagrams to indicate low or falling prices in (a) and high or rising prices in (b). Ask students for examples of products today that might fit each diagram *(oil, expensive*

sports cars). Have students keep the diagrams in mind as they study Chapter 25.

MOTIVATOR

The 1929 stock market crash is introduced in this unit. An interesting way to involve students in the content is by having them follow stocks through the business pages of their local newspaper. Organize the class into three groups, and have each group suggest five companies they wish to follow. Provide stock market listings to each group, and have group members circle their stocks, using a colored marker.

UNIT 10 OVERVIEW

Unit 10 examines Texas history from 1920 through World War II. Chapter 25 explores the mood of intolerance that swept the nation after World War I, including the rise of the new Ku Klux Klan. The prosperity of the 1920s, which saw the expansion of the oil industry and the impact of the automobile, is discussed. The chapter examines advances in education, the development of the state's highway system, and the organized efforts to achieve civil rights by African Americans and Mexican Americans. It concludes with events leading up to the Great Depression.

   Chapter 26 describes the Great Depression and its impact on the people of Texas. Proposals and attempts to deal with the economic crisis are examined. The chapter concludes with a discussion of the roles of Texas and Texans in World War II.

Materials Available at the Unit Level:
Unit 10 Making Global Connections
Oral History Handbook
Informal Evaluation Forms

UNIT 10
CHANGE AND CHALLENGE

After reading their stock quotations, each group should then choose three stocks to follow throughout the study of Unit 10. Teach students how to read the stock quotations by making a transparency or chart of the following:

	Price per Share			Change
	High	Low	Close	
[Stock Name]	28	27	28	+1

Point out that a change of +1 point indicates a gain of $1.00.

Each group should record its stocks' daily quotations on a poster board. At the end of the unit, award a prize to the group that earned the most from its investments in the stock market. *(Students should note the differences between the closing quotes on the first and last days of their charts.)*

TEXAS AND THE WORLD

Organize students into small groups and direct them to the time line on this page. Ask each group to select one world event from the time line and brainstorm about how that event might relate to events in Texas. Have a spokesperson from each group share the group's conclusions. Continue the activity for other key events on the time line.

Texans faced a severe economic depression in the 1930s. This Great Depression affected people all over the United States and in many other parts of the world. Added to the misery caused by the depressed economy was a long drought in the Great Plains region. Winds blowing over the drought area carried away the soil in thick, dark clouds. Crops were ruined and livestock were killed. Alexandre Hogue painted *Dust Bowl, 1933,* on the opposite page, to show the stark landscape in the affected area, which included the Texas Panhandle.

The Great Depression of the 1930s followed a period of prosperity during the 1920s. In the 1920s, business was good, and industries expanded. The period was a hard one for farmers, however. They experienced hard times even as others enjoyed prosperity.

The challenge of the Depression was followed by a second world war. As they had during World War I, Texans responded to the call to support the war effort. Texans helped bring victory for the United States through their efforts at home and on the battlefield.

Unit 10 discusses the changes faced by Texans in the 1920s and the tremendous challenges of the 1930s and 1940s. Chapter 25 focuses on the economic and political changes of the 1920s. Chapter 26 tells the story of the challenges of the Great Depression and World War II and the role of Texans in meeting those challenges.

UNIT 10 OBJECTIVES

1. Describe the mood of intolerance in the aftermath of World War I and its impact on immigrants and minorities in the state.
2. Discuss Texas' industrial growth during the 1920s, including the expansion of the oil industry.
3. Analyze the impact of the automobile on the lives of Texans.
4. List major political issues and achievements in Texas in the 1920s.
5. Discuss events leading to the Great Depression.
6. Describe the effects of the Great Depression on Texans.
7. Identify New Deal relief programs in Texas and discuss Texas politics during the New Deal years.
8. Summarize the role of Texas and Texans in World War II.

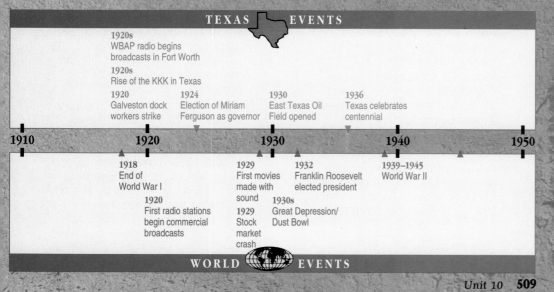

TEXAS EVENTS

1920s
WBAP radio begins broadcasts in Fort Worth

1920s
Rise of the KKK in Texas

1920
Galveston dock workers strike

1924
Election of Miriam Ferguson as governor

1930
East Texas Oil Field opened

1936
Texas celebrates centennial

1910 — 1920 — 1930 — 1940 — 1950

1918
End of World War I

1920
First radio stations begin commercial broadcasts

1929
First movies made with sound

1929
Stock market crash

1932
Franklin Roosevelt elected president

1930s
Great Depression/ Dust Bowl

1939–1945
World War II

WORLD EVENTS

CHAPTER 25

BOOM AND BUST

TEACHER'S TIME LINE				
Section 1 Pp. 510–14 1 Day	**Section 2** Pp. 514–18 1 Day	**Section 3** Pp. 518–21 1 Day	**Section 4** Pp. 521–22 1 Day	**Review and Assessment** 1 Day

⬥ TEACHER MATERIALS

Core: Chapter 25 Time Line; Graphic Organizer 25; Enrichment Worksheet 25; Review Worksheet 25; Reteaching Worksheet 25; Chapter 25 Tests, Forms A & B

Additional: Geography and Graph Skills 25, Informal Evaluation Forms, Test Generator

⬥ OBJECTIVES

1. Describe the mood of Texans following World War I and its impact on various groups.
2. Discuss the organization and operation of the Ku Klux Klan.
3. Outline the growth of the Texas oil industry in the 1920s.
4. Describe the impact of the automobile on Texas.
5. Compare economic conditions in agriculture to conditions in business and industry.
6. List important developments in education and politics in Texas.
7. Identify causes of the Great Depression.

⬥ RESOURCES

BOOKS FOR TEACHERS

Barr, Alwyn. *Black Texans*. Austin: Jenkins, 1973. A history of black Texans from 1528–1971.

Brown, Norman. *Hood, Bonnet, and Little Brown Jug*. College Station: Texas A & M Press, 1983. Study of Texas politics during the years 1921–1928.

Faulk, John Henry. *Papers*. Austin: Barker Center Manuscripts, 1881–1991. Includes work on Leadbelly and other important black artists.

Federal Writers' Project. *Texas: A Guide to the Lone Star State*. New York: Hastings, 1940.

American Guide Series, compiled by Texas Writers' Project, Work Projects Administration.

Lay, Shawn. *War, Revolution, and the Ku Klux Klan*. El Paso: Texas Western Press, 1985. Study of intolerance in El Paso.

Reed, S.G. *A History of Texas Railroads*. New York: Arno, 1981. Comprehensive story of Texas railroads.

MULTIMEDIA MATERIALS

America in the Thirties: Depression and Optimism. (video, 30 min.) Southwest Media Services Inc., P.O. Box 140, Wimberley,

Texas, 78676. Examination of the relationship between government and personal liberty during the Depression.

Franklin D. Roosevelt. (video, 53 min.) Coronet Film & Video, 108 Wilmot Road, Deerfield, Illinois, 60015. Life and career of this president.

United States in the 20th Century Series: 1920 To 1932, (video, 18 min.) and *1932 To 1940*. (video, 21 min.) Coronet Film & Video, 108 Wilmot Road, Deerfield, Illinois, 60015. Examination of events leading up to and following the Depression.

🔷 GENERAL STRATEGIES

STUDENTS WITH SPECIAL NEEDS

Limited English Proficient Students (LEP)

Pair LEP students with English proficient students. Have the students skim the chapter and examine the illustrations. The LEP student should describe each illustration and then read the caption aloud. The partner should then help clarify any unfamiliar terms or ideas. See other activities labeled **LEP.**

Students Having Difficulty with the Chapter

Pair students and ask them to skim the chapter to find the bold-faced vocabulary terms. Have them write the terms on a series of index cards. They should write the term on one side of the card and the definition on the other side. Have them use the cards as flashcards until both students in each pair have mastered the vocabulary. If time permits, have them continue the activity, using the names of important people in the chapter and identifying clues. **LEP**

Auditory Learners

Have students work in groups to prepare a five-minute radio broadcast for the 1920s. The program should include an important news feature, a business story, an en-tertainment announcement, and a sports report. Have groups present their programs to the class. *(If possible, allow students to tape their broadcasts.)* See other activities labeled **A.**

Visual Learners

Have visual learners work together to research how the automobile changed American life. Ask them to use their findings to prepare a classroom bulletin board display. See other activities labeled **V.**

Tactile/Kinesthetic Learners

Have students complete a chart on the governors of Texas during the 1920s. The chart should include the following headings: *Governor, Term of Office, Events of Office.* After students have completed the chart, ask them to rank the governors according to their accomplishments. See other activities labeled **TK.**

Gifted Students

Instruct students to work in small groups to classify the information presented in Chapter 25. Ask them to complete a chart describing the following topics: *Social Developments, Political Developments, Economic Developments.* Under each heading, students should list three or more developments discussed in the chapter. Encourage them to conduct additional research. Then ask them to select one of the three topics and present an oral report. See other activities labeled **G.**

VOCABULARY

In addition to the boldfaced terms in each section, some students might benefit from discussing the meanings of these terms.

Section 1: *prosperity* (p. 510); *aftermath* (p. 510).

Section 2: *amassed* (p. 515); *registered* (p. 517); *fads* (p. 518).

Section 3: *launched* (p. 519); *lagged* (p. 519); *offensive* (p. 520); *accommodations* (p. 521).

Section 4: *plight* (p. 521); *laid off* (p. 522).

CHRONOLOGY

Have students study the Chapter 25 Time Line and identify relationships among the events.

GRAPHIC ORGANIZER

Have students skim the chapter and complete the Chapter 25 Graphic Organizer. *(You might wish to use this activity to review rather than to introduce the chapter.)*

ENRICHMENT

Have students complete the Chapter 25 Enrichment Worksheet.

SECTION 1

FOCUS

Student Experiences (I) With the class, create on the chalkboard a word web using the phrase *the 1920s.* Include various terms for the time period, such as *Jazz Age.* Have students assess their overall impression of the decade as positive or negative. Ask them to summarize their ideas by completing the following sentence: "I would (would not) like to have lived during the 1920s because. . . ." Have students save the statements for use in Section 4.

INSTRUCTION

Vocabulary (I) You may wish to preteach the following boldfaced term: *intolerance* (p. 511). **LEP**

CHAPTER 25 OVERVIEW

World War I left Americans with many emotional wounds to heal. A distrust of foreigners, labor unrest, and a resurgence of the Ku Klux Klan created new tensions. After a brief economic slowdown, a period of prosperity ushered in the Jazz Age, a time of escape and rapid change. By the end of the decade, however, the period of prosperity came to an end. The problems of farmers mounted and businesses across the country failed.

Essential Elements
4C, 4E, 4G, 6B, 7A, 7B, 7E, 7F, 7G, 8A, 8B, 8C

CHAPTER 25

BOOM AND BUST

The Story Continues...

When World War I ended in 1918, Texans faced new problems and challenges that demanded attention. The economy slowed for a short time, then recovered. With the recovery came a period of prosperity. Business and industry expanded in Texas and the rest of the United States. People continued to move to cities to take jobs in industry. New inventions such as the radio brought entertainment and information to millions. New roads and highways were built as more Texans bought automobiles.

Many farmers faced hard times, however. Agriculture changed and expanded, even though prices for many products were low. Debts mounted for an increasing number of farmers. By the end of the 1920s, many Americans found themselves in the middle of a severe economic crisis.

As you read the chapter, look for the answers to these questions:

1. What was the mood of Texans after World War I, and how was that mood reflected in race relations, business, and politics?
2. How did the economic boom of the 1920s affect Texas?
3. What important events and changes occurred in Texas politics in the 1920s?
4. What caused the economy to go into a depression, and how were Texans affected by it?

■ The Aftermath of World War I

Parades and celebrations greeted the soldiers returning from World War I. The fighting was over, but feelings and emotions about the war did not end. They affected how people thought and acted in the war's aftermath.

The Mood of Intolerance. In order to win the war, citizens needed to work together. Government leaders at all levels put great emphasis on loyalty and patriotism.

National Archives

This American poster from World War I reflects the mood of intolerance that affected people after the war.

Daughters of the Republic of Texas Library

▲ A triumphal arch was erected in San Antonio to welcome the soldiers returning from World War I. What famous Texas structure can you see in this photograph?

Laws were passed to punish anyone who spoke against, or committed acts against, the war effort.

As one result of the government's efforts to support the war, a mood of **intolerance** developed. Intolerance means an unwillingness to accept different ideas, people, or opinions. A large number of people thought that loyalty and patriotism meant that everyone had to act and think alike.

During and after the war, the mood of intolerance affected attitudes toward German Americans. The United States fought Germany in the war. As a result, many people disliked Germany and Germans, including people of German ancestry in the United States. The study of the German language in schools was often omitted during the war. Governor Hobby vetoed a bill to provide money for the German department at the University of Texas. Many libraries removed books from their shelves about German history or language. German Texans in New Braunfels, Fredericksburg, and other places were sometimes threatened or attacked. People even stopped using words of German origin such as *sauerkraut*. Instead, many began calling that dish "liberty cabbage."

Archives Division, Texas State Library

Lieutenant Governor William Hobby became governor of Texas when James Ferguson was removed from office in 1917. He won a full term in the election of 1918. Hobby's administration faced problems created by World War I.

Literature (II) Organize students into pairs to research the literature of the 1920s. Suggestions might include the works of F. Scott Fitzgerald, Edna St. Vincent Millay, Eugene O'Neill, and Sinclair Lewis. Encourage students to research to find Texas writers of the period as well. Have one student in each pair present an oral book report. The other student should create an illustrated book jacket or prepare a series of drawings to accompany the book report. **A, V, TK, G**

Guided Practice (I) Ask students to select one of the three subsections of Section 1 and create an illustration to accompany the text. Call on volunteers to display and discuss their illustrations. **A, V, TK, LEP**

Barker Texas History Center

Black veterans of World War I returned from battle to face the same discrimination they had experienced before the war. This photograph shows black delegates to the American Legion National Convention in San Antonio. These delegates were veterans of World War I.

A general fear developed about anyone thought to be different from the majority. Recent immigrants were suspected of not being loyal to the United States. Roman Catholics and Jews were also targets of suspicion.

Tension between blacks and whites increased during and after the war. Of the 200,000 Texans who served in the armed forces during the war, 30,000 were blacks. Black soldiers felt that unfair treatment should end because they had served their country in the war. Many whites were angry when blacks demanded equal rights. This tension erupted into violence at times. A riot in Houston between black soldiers and whites resulted in seventeen deaths. On questionable evidence, thirteen black soldiers were hanged for their part in the conflict.

Labor Unrest. During World War I, there was a shortage of workers in industry. To help increase production, the government encouraged owners of businesses to provide better wages and working conditions for workers. After the war, the economy slowed during the change from making war materials to making products for everyday use. For a time there were fewer jobs. Some businesses sought to cut back on the number of their workers or to reduce wages.

The changes after the war helped create unrest and conflict. In some cities, there was conflict between black

TEXAS VOICES

Historical Imagination (I) Ask students to imagine that they were African American students in Lula Byars' classroom. Have them write their recollections of the all-black rural school. Invite volunteers to read their writings aloud. **A**

Independent Practice (I) Have students choose one of the subsections of Section 1 and write a series of statements or create a diagram showing cause and effect. Call on volunteers to copy their statements or diagrams on the chalkboard. **V, TK, LEP**

RETEACHING

Ask students to write a paragraph establishing a connection between the following topics discussed in Section 1: *World War I, German Texans, Houston race riot, labor unrest, the Ku Klux Klan.* Call on volunteers to read their paragraphs aloud. **A, LEP**

workers and white workers competing for jobs in industry. In other places, workers went on strike for higher wages or better working conditions.

In 1920, dock workers in Galveston went on strike. Ship companies hired people to take the place of those on strike, and violence followed between the strikers and the companies. Governor Hobby placed Galveston under martial law. Troops were stationed there to enforce the laws. Martial law was also declared in Denison and several other towns, following a strike by railroad workers in 1922.

The Rise of the KKK. A new Ku Klux Klan was organized during World War I and soon appeared in Texas. The first such group had operated during Reconstruction, and the new Klan in the 1920s used similar methods against people it opposed. The Klan was a secret organization. Its members wore long white robes. They covered their faces with hoods and used secret handshakes when greeting one another. They threatened, attacked, and sometimes murdered people they disliked.

TEXAS VOICES

*H*ow did segregation and the Jim Crow laws affect the lives of black Texans, particularly students? The following recollection of African American school-teacher Lula Byars gives us an idea. Byars describes her first school, the all-black rural school of the Lytton Springs Common School District, during the 1920s:

The building, it was just one big room, and it was very, very poorly equipped. Sometimes the windowpanes were out. I remember once or twice nailing a piece of cardboard over the window to keep the cold wind out. The floors were not covered, and there were splinters, big splinters, in the floors. And there was no paint—it was unpainted. The walls were naked and bare. It was a horrible-looking sight, I'll be honest.

And there was no equipment. The only thing in there that you could use to work with was a blackboard and a couple of erasers, and maybe a little crayon. But everything else, you just had to devise your own equipment. And there was no water there. We had to carry water from across some of the neighbors' places. They had a few textbooks they had brought us from the other [all-Anglo] school. They would give the other school the new books and give us the old, raggedy, nasty, dirty tore-up books! And snakes were terrible out there. There were holes and cracks in the building; I guess they came in through those. Several times we killed snakes in the building.

Essential Elements
4D, 4I, 9A

CLOSURE
Point out to students that following a dramatic upheaval, such as a world war, people's attitudes are greatly affected because their lives have been unalterably changed.

ASSESSMENT
Have students complete the Section 1 Review on page 514.

SECTION 2

FOCUS
Student Experiences (I) Ask students to name activities they enjoy. *(Most students will probably mention listening to music, playing sports or attending sports events, going to movies, and shopping.)* Then ask students to consider how often these activities require the use of an automobile. Tell students to keep this discussion in mind as they study Section 2.

Answers to Section 1 Review
Define: *intolerance*—an unwillingness to accept different ideas, people, or opinions

1. Possible answers include: the study of the German language in schools was forbidden, Governor Hobby vetoed a bill to provide money for the German department at the University of Texas, many libraries removed books about German history or language, German Texans were sometimes threatened or attacked, people stopped using words of German origin.
2. They reduced wages or cut back on the number of their workers.
3. The Ku Klux Klan gained enough support to help elect mayors, sheriffs, members of the legislature, and a United States senator.

Evaluating Information: Answers will vary but should be supported by sound reasoning.

Analyzing Information: By claiming that it wanted to ensure loyalty to the United States, the Klan appealed to the fears of many Texans following World War I.

Essential Elements
4A, 4B, 4F, 4H, 4I, 5B, 5C, 6A, 6B, 8A, 8C, 9A

SECTION ★1★ REVIEW

Define: intolerance

1. List three ways in which the mood of intolerance during and after World War I affected German Texans.
2. How did businesses react to the slowing of the economy after World War I?
3. What success did the Ku Klux Klan have in politics during the 1920s?

Evaluating Information: Why do you think patriotism and national loyalty become important during a war?

Analyzing Information: How did the Ku Klux Klan use patriotism and national loyalty to influence Texans?

The Klan appealed to the fears of many Texans following World War I. There was concern over crime and labor unrest. Some people worried about the loss of traditional values because of the growth of cities and new styles of life. Others were uneasy over new roles for women in business and government.

The leaders of the Ku Klux Klan claimed they wanted to ensure loyalty to the United States and to fight crime. They also claimed to support honest government and traditional family life. Yet the organization was against Roman Catholics, Jews, and blacks, often using violence to restrict their rights. A number of blacks were lynched, or hanged without a trial, by the Ku Klux Klan.

The Klan became a powerful force in Texas politics in the 1920s. It gained enough support to decide the outcome of many elections. It helped elect mayors, sheriffs, members of the legislature, and a United States senator. The Ku Klux Klan was a major issue in the election for governor in 1924. Miriam Ferguson led those opposed to the Klan and won the governor's race. Following its defeat in the election, the Klan began to decline. Many Texans came to realize that the organization was causing much of the crime and violence that it had pledged to end. ○

② The Boom of the Twenties

By 1920, a business boom was underway in the United States, including Texas. Texas also enjoyed one of the highest population growth rates in the nation. By 1930, the number of Texans topped 5.8 million.

Industrial Growth. Following the war, American businesses switched from making tanks, guns, and ammunition to making **consumer goods**. These are products for personal use, including automobiles, refrigerators, and radios. Large department stores opened in cities such as Dallas and Houston to sell goods to Texans.

Meat-packing and other industries that process farm and ranch products continued to be important to Texas, as did the oil industry. In the 1920s, the oil industry in Texas entered a new period of expansion. New fields were discovered during and just after World War I at Ranger and Burkburnett. In the 1920s, other fields opened at Mexia, Borger, and Big Spring.

INSTRUCTION

Vocabulary (I) You may wish to preteach the following boldfaced terms: *consumer goods* (p. 514); *wildcatter* (p. 515). **LEP**

Map Work (I) Have students work individually or in pairs to create a map illustrating the growth of the Texas oil industry in the 1920s. Ask students to include on their maps a map legend and direction indicator. Select several maps to display in the classroom. **V, TK, LEP**

Minnesota Historical Society

This young woman seems to be enjoying the prosperity of the 1920s as she poses beside her 1924 Lincoln.

In 1930, the biggest oil discovery in Texas history was made near Henderson. C. M. "Dad" Joiner was a **wildcatter**, one of the oil operators who work on their own in search of new fields. Joiner had struck oil in Oklahoma. Always willing to take a risk, he lost most of his money when later holes proved dry. He thought there was oil near Henderson and leased land owned by Daisy Bradford. In September 1930, the Bradford Number 3 well "blew in," opening one of the greatest fields in the world. The great East Texas Oil Field extended from Henderson and Kilgore north to Longview and Gladewater.

Oil discoveries brought fortunes for a number of Texans. Clint Murchison, Sid Richardson, and H. L. Hunt amassed millions of dollars. Howard Hughes of Houston made a fortune from the development of a new type of drill bit. The bit made it possible to drill through very hard rock to reach oil deep underground. Howard Hughes, Jr., used the family wealth to become one of the most powerful business leaders of the twentieth century.

Oil and other industries aided the growth of urban Texas. Following the war, thousands of people left rural

Hughes Tool Company

Howard Hughes, Jr., of Houston was a powerful business leader and one of the wealthiest men of his generation.

Geography
Using a map of Texas, have students determine the location of the East Texas Oil Field, which extended from Henderson and Kilgore north to Longview and Gladewater.

CITIES OF TEXAS

Geography (I) Organize students into four groups. Provide each group one of the following: a globe, a world map, a map of the United States, a map of Texas. Each group should use its assigned reference to describe in various ways the relative location of the five cities listed in the chart in the special feature. **A, V, LEP**

Brainstorming (I) Challenge students to expand on the discussion "Texas and the Automobile" on page 517. Ask the class to speculate further on how the automobile transformed Texas society in the 1920s. *(Ideas might include: changes in living places, jobs created by automobile manufacturing, businesses that grew as a result of the automobile, and the effects of the automobile on social behavior.)* Then pose the following question for class discussion: How might Texas society change today if suddenly there were no more automobiles? **A**

Guided Practice (I) You may wish to obtain silent movies of the 1920s from your local library. Show the movies accompanied by a record or tape of 1920s music. Then have students compare films of the silent era with those of today. **A, V, LEP**

CITIES OF TEXAS

Dallas

Population: 1,006,877

Metro area population: 2,553,362

Size: 378 square miles

Relative location: On the Trinity River in northeast Texas, about 60 miles south of the Red River

Region: On the western edge of the Gulf Coastal Plains, within the Blackland Prairie

County: County seat of Dallas County

Special feature: One of the nation's largest inland cities, Dallas is the financial, trade, insurance, and fashion center of the Southwest.

Origin of name: In 1841, John Neely Bryan named the small settlement after a friend called Dallas.

Landmarks: The Dallas skyline, featuring Reunion Tower

Economy: Banking, fashion, and industry combine to make Dallas a commercial center of Texas and the Southwest. Many national corporations headquarter in

Dallas, ranging from insurance to petroleum to electronics to clothing.

History: John Neely Bryan and his wife, Margaret, settled the present site of Dallas in 1841. For many years, the location had been a trading and meeting place for Indians and Anglo traders. Slowly, the settlement grew around Bryan's log cabin on the Trinity River. By the 1870s, the railroad's arrival helped make Dallas a thriving market and business center.

Recreation facilities: Nearby lakes and parks offer numerous recreation opportunities in the Dallas area. Professional sports attract fans from around the state. The Texas State Fair, the Dallas Zoo, and the Dallas Arboretum and Botanical Garden are favorite family outing destinations.

Cultural activities: Dallas has a symphony orchestra, a ballet company, a civic opera, and numerous theatrical productions. Museums and art galleries serve a variety of cultural tastes.

Selected U.S. Cities	Dallas	New York	Chicago	Omaha	Los Angeles
Unemployment Rate	4.5%	7.0%	6.1%	3.3%	5.9%
Average Personal Income	$18,580	$20,396	$19,060	$15,873	$18,790
Average January Temperature	44.0°	31.8°	21.0°	20.2°	56.0°
Average July Temperature	86.3°	76.4°	73.0°	77.7°	69.0°
Average Annual Snowfall	3.1 inches	26.1 inches	40.3 inches	31.1 inches	— (trace)

EXTENSION

Creating (I) Organize students into groups. Assign each group either a major appliance or a modern invention that became available to Texas consumers in the 1920s (for example, refrigerator, vacuum cleaner, washing machine, portable camera). Have each group prepare a classroom display showing how the invention changed American life. Displays should include drawings, photographs, and copies of clippings from old newspapers and magazines. **A, V, TK**

Independent Practice (I) Provide students with the following scenario: You are a teenager in Houston in 1929. Your cousin from the Northeast is coming for a weekend visit. Write a letter to your cousin telling about the forms of entertainment you have planned. Call on volunteers to read their letters aloud. **A, LEP**

RETEACHING

List on the chalkboard the following topics: *Industrial Growth, The Automobile, The Jazz Age.* Ask students to write a brief paragraph explaining how each topic reflects "the boom of the Twenties." Invite volunteers to read their paragraphs aloud. **LEP, A**

areas to find jobs in the city. The population of rural Texas grew only nine percent during the 1920s, while the urban population jumped 58 percent. By 1930, about 41 percent of all Texans lived in urban areas, and fifteen cities had populations of 25,000 or more. Both Dallas and San Antonio had populations of more than 200,000 each. Houston had nearly 300,000 residents.

Texas and the Automobile. The demand for oil products was spurred by the tremendous growth of the automobile industry. Texas had 14,286 registered autos in 1910. The number of registered vehicles passed the million mark by 1926.

The love affair with automobiles required new roads and highways. Prior to 1920, many counties failed to provide for good paved roads. Under Governor Neff, the Texas Highway Commission was strengthened. Several thousand miles of roads were put completely under state control. Thereafter, a system of state highways was built to connect the major cities of Texas.

Buses and trucks came into use along with automobiles. Companies established truck lines to haul freight both within and between cities. Trucks soon presented a challenge to railroads for freight business. Bus lines began competing with the railroads for passengers.

Autos, trucks, and buses brought many economic benefits to Texans. Farmers could more easily haul products to towns or to the nearest railroad center. They could haul supplies and equipment back to farms. People in rural areas could more easily travel to towns and cities for entertainment and shopping.

At the same time, new problems arose because of automobiles. Small towns not on a major highway lost importance to larger towns and cities nearby. People found it easier to shop at a large department store in the city than at several small local stores. Many local businesses found it hard to compete. Some people complained that the auto destroyed traditional styles of life. Young people were more likely to drive around in the family auto than to spend time with parents and other family members.

The Jazz Age. Jazz was a new form of music in the 1920s, and the period is sometimes referred to by historians as the Jazz Age. The name implies a time of glitter and excitement. Other people call the era the Roaring Twenties.

The Granger Collection

The Roaring Twenties revolutionized the social habits of Americans. The era was marked by jazz music, fads, crazes, and new standards of appropriate behavior.

Austin History Center, Austin Public Library

The automobile changed the face of the nation, including Texas. This photograph from the 1920s reflects the spirit of the Jazz Age.

Economics

Remind students that the concept of competition is important to the free enterprise system. Refer students to the special feature on free enterprise on page 331. Discuss with students how motorized vehicles competed with the railroads for freight business as well as passenger business.

CLOSURE

Write on the chalkboard the title of Section 2: "The Boom of the Twenties." Call on volunteers to explain in their own words what the title means.

ASSESSMENT

Have students complete the Section 2 Review on page 518.

SECTION 3

FOCUS

Past Learning (I) Ask students to recall the discussion in Chapter 24 of the administration of Governor James Ferguson. Remind students that Ferguson was impeached and removed from office but that "Texans had not heard the last of him." Point out that students will meet up with the Fergusons again in this section.

Answers to Section 2 Review

Define: *consumer goods*—products for personal use; *wildcatter*—an oil operator who works independently in search of new fields

Identify: C.M. Joiner—wildcatter who opened the East Texas Oil Field; Daisy Bradford—owner of the land on which Joiner's well was located; Sid Richardson—Texan who became wealthy from oil discoveries; Howard Hughes—Texan who became wealthy from the development of a new type of drill bit

1. One of the greatest oil fields was the East Texas Oil Field, which extended from Henderson and Kilgore north to Longview and Gladewater.
2. The small towns lost importance as residents traveled to bigger towns to shop.
3. The Jazz Age got its name from jazz music, which became popular in the 1920s.

Using Historical Imagination: Answers will vary but should reflect Joiner's long search for a gusher and that the Bradford Number 3 opened one of the greatest fields in the world.

Evaluating Information: Answers will vary but should be supported with sound reasoning.

Essential Elements
4B, 4D, 4E, 4F, 4G, 4I, 5B, 8C, 9A, 9B, 9D

Motion pictures were the rage of the 1920s, and lavish theaters were built to screen the latest films. This photograph is of the interior of the Majestic Theatre in Houston.

Harris County Heritage Society, courtesy Texas Historical Foundation

SECTION 2 REVIEW

Define: consumer goods, wildcatter

Identify: C.M. Joiner, Daisy Bradford, Sid Richardson, Howard Hughes

1. What and where was one of the greatest oil fields in the world in 1930?
2. How were small towns affected by the coming of the automobile?
3. How did the Jazz Age get its name?

Using Historical Imagination: How do you think C.M. Joiner reacted when the Bradford Number 3 "blew in"?

Evaluating Information: Do you agree with those people who say that the automobile destroyed traditional values? Why or why not?

There were new fashions and new forms of entertainment, and business was booming. Jazz had black origins, and the 1920s were a time in which black culture and lifestyles enjoyed nation-wide interest and popularity.

Actually, life for the average Texan did not fit the image of the Jazz Age. Most Texans did not take part in fads or dress in crazy new styles. But many did embrace new forms of entertainment. Texans danced the Charleston at clubs in Houston, San Antonio, Dallas, and Galveston. Automobile trips were popular. People attended football games on Saturdays or went shopping in the new stores.

Motion pictures became one of the most popular forms of entertainment. By the middle of the 1920s, nearly every town had a movie house. The films were in black and white and had no sound. Usually a phonograph was played to accompany the movie, or someone played the piano. By 1929, the first "talkies," or movies with sound, were being made. Much to the delight of Texans, cowboy adventures were popular subjects for movies. Radio was another invention introduced in the 1920s. The first commercial station to air in Texas was WBAP in Fort Worth. Southern folk music and country music were played. Stations also broadcast news, sports, and advertisements. ✪

3 Politics and People

Unlike the Progressive era, there was little demand for reform in the 1920s. In fact, some leaders reacted against the reforms made during World War I and earlier. Nevertheless, population and economic growth created the need for

INSTRUCTION

Synthesis (I) Ask students to use the information in Section 3 to create a chart using the following labels: *Political Issue, Progress Made.* **V, TK, LEP**

Cooperative Learning (I) Divide the class into two groups. Explain to students in the first group that it is 1926 and they are working on the campaign to reelect Governor Miriam Ferguson. Explain to students in the second group that they are working on the campaign to elect Dan Moody. Each

group should create a series of campaign posters and write a speech that its candidate will present to voters. Each group should then select a person to play the role of the candidate. Allow students to stage an election day during which the campaign posters are displayed and each candidate presents the campaign speech. **A, V, TK, LEP**

Guided Practice (I) Provide the class with copies of a road atlas map of Texas. Ask students to highlight the interstate highways. **V, TK, LEP**

some changes. African Americans and Mexican Americans launched the fight for civil rights.

Political Issues. Among the major issues of the 1920s was education. Despite progress made in the late 1800s and early 1900s, Texas lagged behind many other states in funding public schools.

During World War I, the state began providing transportation at public expense for students who lived far from schools. The legislature also authorized certain school districts to combine, or consolidate. Because many districts in rural areas were very small, there were too few people to provide money through taxation to run the schools. Therefore, these districts began combining. Over 1,500 schools had consolidated by 1930. The state also began providing free textbooks for public school students.

Governor Pat M. Neff worked for better schools. During his terms, more money was provided for rural schools. In response to requests for a college in West Texas, the legislature authorized the creation of Texas Technological College (now Texas Tech University) in Lubbock. It was established in 1923 and opened in 1925, as did South Texas State Teachers College in Kingsville.

The State Board of Education was created in 1929. Margie Neal, the first woman elected to the Texas Senate, introduced the bill that created the board.

Highway construction was another major issue of the 1920s. Governor Neff was among those who supported the expansion of the system of state highways. He also used his influence to begin a system of state parks.

Return of the Fergusons. In January 1925, Austin was alive with excitement. Opera star May Peterson Thompson sang "Put On Your Old Gray Bonnet." She rode a horse up the steps of the capitol. The occasion was the inaugural of Miriam A. Ferguson as governor of Texas. Ferguson was the first female governor of the state and only the second female governor of any state in the country.

The election of Miriam Ferguson closed a long and colorful campaign. The campaign was organized by Miriam's husband, James E. Ferguson, the former governor who had been impeached and could not legally be elected again. Reporters referred to Miriam Ferguson as "Ma" and called James Ferguson "Pa." People who had supported James were asked to show their support for him by voting

Texas Tech University

Texas Tech University at Lubbock was established in 1923, a response to 32 years of West Texas requests for a major university.

Archives Division, Texas State Library

Pat Neff was elected governor in 1920 and reelected in 1922. After leaving the governor's office, Neff served as president of Baylor University.

Historical Sidelight
To encourage economic development in the late 1800s, political leaders decided to sell most of Texas' public lands. By 1900, 266,807 square miles of territory were privately owned. When the State Parks Board was created in 1923, there was little state-owned land to set aside for recreational use. At first, the board had to rely on donations of land for parks.

EXTENSION

Research (II) Have students research and write a biographical sketch of one of the governors of Texas in the 1920s. Invite volunteers to read their biographies aloud. **A**

Independent Practice (II) Ask students to review the subsection "The Fight for Civil Rights" on pages 520–21. Then have them create a poster, collage, banner, or other visual that might be used to illustrate the discussion. Encourage students to be creative. Allow time for students to display and discuss their illustrations. **A, V, TK**

RETEACHING

Have students use the information in Section 3 to create a time line of significant events. After students have completed their time lines, call on volunteers to select and summarize one of the events. **A, V, TK, LEP**

CLOSURE

Point out to students that the NAACP and LULAC remain active in Texas in supporting the civil rights of African Americans and Mexican Americans.

Historical Sidelight

One of Governor Moody's main concerns was the problem of Texas prisons and prison management. The prison system was faced with rising costs and a growing prison population. In 1930, Moody appointed Lee Simmons, a businessman from Sherman, to manage the prison system. After Simmons took over, the system improved greatly.

Answers to Section 3 Review

Identify: Margie Neal—first woman elected to the Texas Senate; Dan Moody—youngest governor ever elected in Texas; C.F. Richardson—African American publisher and editor of the *Houston Informer;* Lawrence A. Nixon—African American physician who filed suit against Texas' restrictive voting laws

1. There were too few people in rural areas to provide enough money through taxation to run the schools.

2. She was criticized for awarding highway department contracts to friends of James Ferguson and for her overuse of the power to pardon prisoners.

(Continued on page 521)

Archives Division, Texas State Library

Miriam A. Ferguson was the first woman to serve as governor of Texas. She was elected to office in 1924. Governor Ferguson openly fought the Ku Klux Klan, cut taxes, and issued many pardons and paroles to Texas prisoners. She won a second term in the election of 1932.

Archives Division, Texas State Library

Dan Moody was elected governor in 1926. He was 33 years old. He won a second term in 1928. The growing problems of the Great Depression dominated his second term.

for Miriam. One slogan was "Me for Ma—and I ain't got a dern thing against Pa!" Miriam Ferguson took a strong stand against the Ku Klux Klan, claiming it stood for violence and hatred. The Klan backed Judge Felix D. Robertson for governor, but Ferguson won.

The administration of Miriam Ferguson was marked by controversy. While she was governor, some people were upset over the system for awarding contracts to build highways. James Ferguson sat at the meetings of the highway commission. It was claimed that contracts to build roads were not being awarded to the lowest bidder or to the company that would do the best job. Instead, they were being given to friends of James Ferguson. Attorney General Dan Moody brought suit against two companies that had been awarded contracts in the past. One company refunded money to the state. An investigation of the highway department found that the lack of bidding had cost Texas a great deal of money.

Governor Ferguson was criticized not only about the highway department but also about her use of the power to pardon prisoners. During her term, Ferguson pardoned many more people than had other governors.

Among those who criticized the governor was Dan Moody. In 1926, Moody ran for election against Miriam Ferguson and won. He was the youngest governor ever elected in Texas. As governor, Moody reorganized the highway department to bring about cheaper and more efficient operation. He also helped reorganize the prison system and cut back on the number of pardons granted. Jane McCallum, who had worked for a number of reforms in education, child care, and women's rights, was appointed secretary of state.

The defeat of Miriam Ferguson in the 1926 election did not end her political career. She was again elected governor of Texas in 1932.

The Fight for Civil Rights. During the 1920s, blacks made their first organized efforts to fight discrimination and segregation in Texas. They established a local chapter of the National Association for the Advancement of Colored People (NAACP) in Houston in 1912. By 1930 there were 30 NAACP chapters active in the state. African American newspapers also took the offensive against prejudice. C.F. Richardson, publisher and editor of the *Houston Informer,*

ASSESSMENT
Have students complete the Section 3 Review on page 521.

SECTION 4

FOCUS

Student Experiences (I) Ask students to consider what happens when a person's income declines but his or her expenses remain the same or rise. *(The person cannot buy*

as many goods and services.) Allow time for several students to respond. Point out that this is what happened to Texas farmers during the 1920s.

INSTRUCTION

Vocabulary (I) You may wish to preteach the following boldfaced terms: *stocks* (p. 522); *depression* (p. 522). **LEP**

was especially outspoken. His editorials attacking discrimination, segregation, and racial violence led to threats on his life by the Ku Klux Klan. Yet Richardson refused to let racial threats silence him.

Black political activity in the 1920s centered on a campaign to regain the right to vote. In 1923, the Texas legislature passed a law to keep blacks from voting in the Democratic primary. Lawrence A. Nixon, a black physician, filed suit against the state's restrictive voting laws. Although Nixon won a victory in the United States Supreme Court in 1927, the struggle to regain the vote would continue into the 1940s.

Mexican Americans also launched their fight for equal rights in the 1920s. The Mexican population of Texas soared, as thousands fled the turmoil that surrounded the Mexican Revolution of 1910. By 1930, an estimated 695,000 Mexican Americans resided in the state. Mexican Texans faced prejudice almost as severe as that which faced blacks. Throughout South Texas, Mexican Americans were discriminated against in education and public accommodations. In some counties they were not allowed to vote in the Democratic primary. To fight for their rights, Mexican Americans organized the League of United Latin American Citizens (LULAC) in 1929. It became the best-known Mexican American civil rights organization. ✪

4 The Economy in Crisis

The period of the 1920s was prosperous for Texas in general. Agriculture, however, was a weak link in the economy. In Texas and the rest of the United States, thousands of farmers faced hard times. An economic crisis began in 1929 that soon brought hard times to millions.

The Plight of the Farmers. The growth and expansion of Texas agriculture continued in the 1920s. Much of the ranchland of the Panhandle was sold to farmers. The production of cotton and wheat spread to many counties in the region. The flatness of the land made it ideal for the use of large farm machines, so large farms developed that used machinery to plow the land and harvest the crops. Wells supplied underground water to irrigate the soil. The amount of land in West Texas planted in cotton grew from 45,000 acres in 1909 to more than 2 million acres in 1924.

SECTION 3 REVIEW

Identify: Margie Neal, Dan Moody, C.F. Richardson, Lawrence A. Nixon

1. Why were some school districts consolidated?
2. For what actions was Governor Miriam Ferguson criticized during her first term?
3. What two major civil rights organizations were founded in the early 1900s?

Exploring Multicultural Perspectives: Imagine that you are a black civil rights worker in the 1920s. Write a letter to the members of LULAC, pointing out what they have in common with African Americans.

Evaluating Information: How do you think people who supported James E. Ferguson's impeachment reacted when Miriam Ferguson became governor? Explain.

Barker Texas History Center

Jane McCallum was appointed secretary of state by Governor Moody in 1927. Her "Petticoat Lobby," as the press called it, helped enact reforms for women and children in Texas.

3. The National Association for the Advancement of Colored People (NAACP) and the League of United Latin American Citizens (LULAC)

Exploring Multicultural Perspectives: Letters will vary but should mention the common struggle of African Americans and Mexican Americans to combat discrimination and to gain civil rights.

Evaluating Information: Answers will vary, but students should recognize that people who supported James Ferguson's impeachment probably would not support Miriam Ferguson.

Essential Elements
4A, 5A, 8A, 8C, 9A, 9B, 9E

Economics (II) Have students work in pairs to develop and write a 1920s newspaper editorial titled "The Economy in Crisis." Editorials should explain the economic crisis gripping the nation and offer possible solutions. Encourage students to supplement their editorial with an editorial cartoon or other illustration. Display the editorials on the bulletin board. **V, TK, G**

Guided Practice (I) Ask students to draw a cause-and-effect diagram of the events leading to the Great Depression. Call on volunteers to copy their diagrams on the chalkboard. **V, TK, LEP**

RETEACHING
With the class, outline on the chalkboard the information presented in Section 4. Allow time for students to ask questions to clarify ideas and interpretations. **LEP, A, V**

CLOSURE
Refer students to the statements that they developed for the Section 1 Focus activity. Ask them if the information presented in the chapter has altered their overall impression of the 1920s.

The Granger Collection

The Wall Street crash of 1929 was a significant event at the time, though few people realized how bleak the coming depression would be.

Answers to Section 4 Review

Define: *stocks*—shares of ownership in companies; *depression*—severe slowdown in the economy

Identify: Wall Street—site of the New York Stock Exchange

1. It shifted to the Gulf Coast.
2. A large number of people rushed to sell their stocks, resulting in a drastic loss in stock value.

Exploring Economics: Farmers grew more crops to make up for the low prices they received; however, demand for farm products did not keep up with the supply. An oversupply of farm products resulted, pushing thousands of farmers into debt.

Predicting Consequences: Students should recognize that because people had less money to spend, demand for farm products probably declined even further.

SECTION 4 REVIEW

Define: stocks, depression
Identify: Wall Street

1. To what region of Texas did the cattle industry shift in the 1920s?
2. What started the stock market crash?

Exploring Economics: Why did farmers decide to grow more crops? Why was growing more crops not a good idea?

Predicting Consequences: From what you have learned in this chapter, how do you think the Great Depression affected farmers in the 1930s? Explain.

The Panhandle remained an important area for raising cattle, but less so than in the 1800s. The center of the cattle industry shifted to the Gulf Coast. The Panhandle was still well suited for raising cattle, but farmers there thought they would be more prosperous by raising cash crops.

Even as Texas farmers produced more, prices for many farm products dropped. In order to keep their income at the same level, farmers produced even more. Demand for farm products did not keep up with the supply. Thus there was an oversupply of many farm products. Costs for machinery, taxes, and loans remained at the same level or rose. Thousands of farmers fell into debt. Farm families suffered, and so did businesses that sold goods to farmers.

The Wall Street Crash. Shares of ownership in companies are called **stocks**. Many stocks are bought and sold at the New York Stock Exchange on Wall Street in New York City. Companies sell shares of stock to raise money for uses such as buying new equipment or buildings. During the 1920s, the price of many stocks rose steeply. Thousands of Americans bought stock in order to sell it later for what they hoped would be a large profit. Banks made loans to people for this purpose.

In October 1929, a panic began when a large number of people rushed to sell their stocks. As a result of the panic, the stock market "crashed," meaning thousands of shares of stock lost their value, some becoming almost worthless.

The effects of the crash were soon felt in the economy. Many banks were forced to close because they had made too many loans to people who could not repay them. People who had savings in the banks sometimes lost all their money.

A **depression**, or severe slowdown in the economy, soon took place. The stock market crash did not cause the depression, but it was part of the problem. Many businesses had expanded too quickly. They had borrowed vast sums to do so. At the same time, workers were not earning enough to buy all of the goods being produced.

In the early 1930s, signs of the Great Depression were clear in Texas. Factories shut their doors or laid off the workers they could no longer afford to pay. Banks and stores closed or cut back on business. By 1933, one out of every four American workers was out of work. ✪

CHAPTER REVIEW RESOURCES

1. Chapter Review Worksheet 25
2. Chapter 25 Test, Form A
3. Reteaching Worksheet 25
4. Chapter 25 Test, Form B
5. **Informal Evaluation Forms:** Portfolio Assessment
6. *Texas, Our Texas* **Test Generator**

CHAPTER 25 REVIEW

Understanding Main Ideas

1. Why was there a mood of intolerance after World War I? How was that intolerance shown?
2. What methods did the Ku Klux Klan use to achieve its aims?
3. List three changes in Texas during the boom of the early 1920s.
4. What changes were made in Texas politics during the 1920s?
5. Why were farmers in a crisis in the late 1920s?
6. How did the stock market crash of 1929 affect Texans?

Thinking Critically

1. **Analyzing Information:** How did motor vehicles and the expansion of the highway system make school consolidation possible?
2. **Exploring Economics:** Explain how the loss of jobs or income by one group affects other businesses in an economy.
3. **Evaluating Information:** How did the Ku Klux Klan's claims about its purpose differ from its actions?

Linking History and Geography

1. Why did ranching decline in the Panhandle during the 1920s? What region then became the center of the Texas cattle industry?
2. Why is the Panhandle well suited to the use of large machinery on large farms? In what part of Texas would this use not be suitable?

TAAS Practice
Using Primary Sources

Beginning in 1977, Annie Mae Hunt, a black Texan born in 1909, told her life story to Ruthe Winegarten. In the following excerpt from her oral history, Hunt tells about the work that she did during hard times:

> When I was raising [my] first three kids in Dallas during the Depression . . . I had jobs. Like mama, like daughter. I'd wash and iron. Like on Monday morning, I'd get up, I'd go out to Mrs. X's house, wash for her, hang her clothes up. Then I'd go on down to wash for another woman. I've done four washes in one day. I'd come on back, and these things I had just hung out for Mrs. X, they'd be ready. I'd take them down, and I'd sprinkle them and put them in a basket. And then she had other things for me to do. I could iron a shirt or a child's dress so a fly couldn't stand on the collar. A fly, he would slip off!
>
> And then I'd go on down to this other woman where I just got through settin' the washing, and I'd wash it out. Then if I had time to, I would go wash in another place, and stay there and take the clothes in. A lot of times, I'd have to look for places to wash. . . . And I cooked. I was a very good cook. Everybody liked my cooking. I didn't have to worry about no jobs, because I always had a job as long as I was cleanin' house and cookin'. And I did that for a long time.

1. Hunt earned money during tough times by doing laundry for
   A her daughter
   B her mother
   C one other person
   D several other people

CHAPTER 25 REVIEW ANSWERS

Understanding Main Ideas

1. During the war, leaders emphasized loyalty and patriotism. Many people thought that loyalty meant that everyone had to act and think alike. Because America had fought Germany in the war, German Americans were disliked. Recent immigrants, Roman Catholics, and Jews were all targets of suspicion, and tension between blacks and whites increased.
2. Klan members threatened, attacked, and sometimes murdered people they did not like, and the Klan influenced elections.
3. Possible answers include: the oil industry grew, more people moved to the cities, the automobile became popular, buses and trucks came into use, and new forms of entertainment developed.
4. Achievements were made in funding and improving education, the system of state highways was expanded, a system of state parks was begun, Miriam Ferguson was elected governor, African Americans and Mexican Americans organized to fight for civil rights.

5. As farmers increased production, demand did not keep up with supply. As a result, thousands of farmers fell into debt.

6. Many workers were laid off, banks and businesses closed or cut back on business, and people had less money to spend.

Thinking Critically

1. Analyzing Information: Students could be transported from rural areas.

2. Exploring Economics: Answers will vary, but students should explain that when workers do not have the money to buy goods, factories must lower or end production, which can lead to other workers losing their jobs or having their wages reduced, which in turn allows the cycle to continue.

3. Evaluating Information: The Klan claimed to want to fight crime and to promote honest government. Yet, the organization committed crimes and used its power to influence elections.

Linking History and Geography

1. Ranching declined as more people turned to raising cash crops. The Gulf Coast became the center of the cattle industry.

2. The Panhandle is flat and nearly treeless. Large machinery on large farms would not be suitable in East Texas, which is forested, or in far West Texas, which is mountainous.

TAAS *Practice*
Using Primary Sources

1. D   2. B

TAAS *Practice*
Writing Persuasively

Letters will vary but should demonstrate sound reasoning.

Practicing Skills

1. Interpreting Pictures: Answers will vary, but students should point out the American flags and the large crowd that has gathered.

2. Interpreting Maps: Amarillo, Wichita Falls, San Angelo, Beaumont, Port Arthur, Corpus Christi, Laredo; in eastern Texas

Enriching Your Study of History

1. Individual Project: Reports should demonstrate thorough research.

2. Cooperative Project: Posters should call for the right of African Americans to vote in Texas.

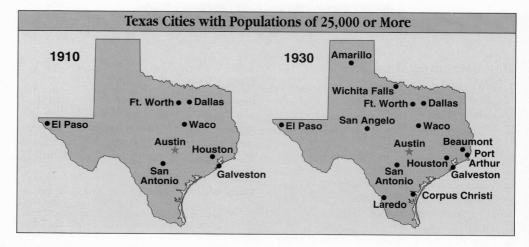

Texas Cities with Populations of 25,000 or More

1910

Ft. Worth • Dallas
• El Paso   • Waco
Austin   Houston
San   Galveston
Antonio

1930

Amarillo
Wichita Falls
Ft. Worth • Dallas
San Angelo
• El Paso   • Waco
Austin   Beaumont
Houston   Port Arthur
San   Galveston
Antonio   Corpus Christi
Laredo

2. Hunt did not worry about being out of work during the Depression because
A she was a skilled hairdresser
B she was a skilled housekeeper
C she was not a skilled cook
D she was not skilled at ironing

TAAS *Practice*
Writing Persuasively

Imagine that you are C.F. Richardson. Write a letter to the Ku Klux Klan, explaining why its members cannot keep you from working for African Americans' civil rights.

Practicing Skills

1. Interpreting Pictures: Look carefully at the top photograph on page 511. In your opinion, how does it show the spirit of national loyalty and patriotism during World War I? Use specific examples to illustrate your answer.

2. Interpreting Maps: Study the two maps above. Which cities grew to a population of 25,000 or more between 1910 and 1930? In what part of the state was most of the population growth during this time?

Enriching Your Study of History

1. Individual Project: Choose one of the new forms of entertainment during the 1920s (jazz, movies, radio). Prepare a brief report of interesting facts about the entertainment form you have chosen, and share these facts with your classmates.

2. Cooperative Project: Work with a partner to create a poster that might have been designed in the 1920s. It should call for the right of African Americans to vote in Texas. Your teacher will display the poster in your classroom.

HARD TIMES

TEACHER'S TIME LINE			
Section 1 Pp. 525–31 1 Day	**Section 2** Pp. 532–35 1 Day	**Section 3** Pp. 535–39 1 Day	**Review and Assessment** 1 Day

 ## TEACHER MATERIALS

Core: Chapter 26 Time Line; Graphic Organizer 26; Enrichment Worksheet 26; Review Worksheet 26; Reteaching Worksheet 26; Chapter 26 Tests, Forms A & B

Additional: Geography and Graph Skills 26, Informal Evaluation Forms, Test Generator

OBJECTIVES

1. Discuss the impact of the Great Depression on the people of Texas and the rest of the United States.
2. Identify problems created by the Dust Bowl years.
3. Explain the state government's actions to help remedy the crisis in Texas created by the Depression.
4. List and describe the New Deal programs.
5. Identify Texans who played important roles in Roosevelt's New Deal government.
6. Discuss major events during the administrations of Texas governors in the 1930s and early 1940s.
7. List ways in which Texans contributed to the World War II effort at home and abroad.

 ## RESOURCES

BOOKS FOR TEACHERS

Dilena, James G., et al. *Pearl Harbor and Hiroshima.* Tokyo: Takeyama Associates, 1989. Personal narratives of the two events.

Gard, Wayne. *Texas Kingfish.* New York: Editorial Publications, 1941. Life and times of W. Lee O'Daniel.

Guthrie, Woody. *Bound for Glory.* New York: New American Library, 1983. Autobiography of Woody Guthrie.

Markusen, Ann, et al. *The Rise of the Gunbelt.* New York: Oxford University Press, 1991. The effect of militarism on American industry.

Salmond, John A. *The Civilian Conservation Corps, 1933–1942.* Durham: Duke University Press, 1967. A case study of this New Deal program.

Smith, Douglas L. *The New Deal in the Urban South.* Baton Rouge: Louisiana State University Press, 1988. A look at New Deal programs in cities in the South.

Steinbeck, John. *The Grapes of Wrath.* New York: The Viking Press, 1967. The classic novel of the Dust Bowl.

Timmons, Bascom Nolly. *Garner of Texas: A Personal History.* New York: Harper, 1948. Life and times of this politician.

MULTIMEDIA MATERIALS

Black Olympians 1904–1984: Athletics and Social Change in America. (video, 28 min.) Churchill Films, 12210 Nebraska Avenue, Los Angeles, California, 90025. Includes coverage of Jesse Owens during the German games preceding World War II.

Growing up in the Great Depression. (video, 28 min.) Coronet Film & Video, 108 Wilmot Road, Deerfield, Illinois, 60015. A look at life during the Great Depression.

Hiroshima and Nagasaki: The Harvest of Nuclear War. (video, 46 min.) University of California

Extension Media Center, 2176 Shattuck Avenue, Berkeley, California, 94704. Powerful documentary about the dropping of the atomic bombs.

Praise the Lord and Pass the Ammunition. (video, 30 min.) PBS Video, 1320 Braddock Place, Alexandria, Virginia, 22314. Pre-World War II migration from small towns and farms to the war plants.

While the Storm Clouds Gather. (video, 30 min.) PBS Video, 1320 Braddock Place, Alexandria, Virginia, 22314. Context of American family life leading up to World War II.

World War Two. (video, 30 min.) Southwest Media Services, Inc., P.O. Box 140, Wimberley, Texas, 78676. Comprehensive examination of World War II.

GENERAL STRATEGIES

STUDENTS WITH SPECIAL NEEDS

Limited English Proficient Students (LEP)
Have students use the boldfaced vocabulary terms to review the chapter. Instruct them to look up each term in the textbook to find the definition. They should then write sentences, using the terms in context. Call on volunteers to read their sentences aloud. Allow time to clarify and discuss definitions. See other activities labeled **LEP.**

Students Having Difficulty with the Chapter
Have students work in pairs to practice placing events in correct chronological order. Write on separate index cards ten to fifteen significant events from the chapter. Provide each pair with a set of the cards. Have students place the cards in the correct order and then number them. Allow them to use the textbook to check and correct their results. **LEP**

Auditory Learners
Assign students to locate family members or people in the community who lived in Texas during the years of the Great Depression and/or World War II. Each student should prepare ten questions for an interview. Discuss the questions as a class, and develop a standard list of ten questions to be used by all students participating. After conducting interviews, the students should meet as a group in front of the rest of the class to discuss similarities and differences in their findings. See other activities labeled **A.**

Visual Learners
Locate and read to students descriptions or stories about the Dust Bowl years in Texas. Have students create a visual interpretation of the selections you have read. Encourage students to be creative. See other activities labeled **V.**

Tactile/Kinesthetic Learners
Direct tactile/kinesthetic learners to Monroe Brannon's account of the Depression years on page 527. Challenge students to make an item of clothing from a feed or fertilizer sack. See other activities labeled **TK.**

Gifted Students
Direct students to work together to locate national unemployment statistics for the years 1929–1939. Ask them to plot the statistics on a graph for classroom display. Have a spokesperson from the group use the graph to explain to the rest of the class how unemployment rose and fell during this period. Group members should be prepared to answer questions from the class. See other activities labeled **G.**

VOCABULARY
In addition to the boldfaced terms in each section, some students might benefit from discussing the meanings of these terms.

Section 2: *vigor* (p. 532); *minimum wage* (p. 533); *furrows* (p. 533); *exposition* (p. 534).

Section 3: *dictators* (p. 535); *ration* (p. 537); *war bonds* (p. 537); *atomic bombs* (p. 538); *nuclear weapons* (p. 538).

CHRONOLOGY
Have students study the Chapter 26 Time Line and identify relationships among the events.

GRAPHIC ORGANIZER
Have students skim the chapter and complete the Chapter 26 Graphic Organizer. *(You might wish to use this activity to review rather than to introduce the chapter.)*

ENRICHMENT
Have students complete the Chapter 26 Enrichment Worksheet.

SECTION **1**

FOCUS

Predicting (I) Write on the chalkboard the following statements from Section 1:

"By 1933, one in every four American workers was unemployed."

"Cotton fell from eighteen cents per pound in 1928 to just five cents per pound in 1932."

Use these statements as the basis for a class discussion about the impact of the Great Depression on the people of Texas. Have students study the photographs and captions on pages 525–27.

HARD TIMES

CHAPTER

26

The Story Continues...

After the stock market crash of 1929, the whole world fell into an economic depression. Banks closed, people lost their life savings, businesses suffered, and millions of people found themselves without work.

While Texans and all Americans struggled to overcome this Great Depression, trouble was brewing overseas. Japan, Germany, and Italy built large armies and navies and attacked neighboring countries. Then in 1939, World War II began. The United States became involved two years later. The attention of Texas and the United States turned from the Depression to the war. This chapter looks at the Depression and the war—hard times demanding the best efforts of all Texans.

As you read the chapter, look for the answers to these questions:

1. What effects did the Great Depression have upon Texas?
2. How did the New Deal help Texans, and what happened in Texas politics during the Depression?
3. What were the major events of World War II, and how did that war affect Texas and the rest of the United States?

1 The Great Depression

The slowdown in the economy during the 1930s was so severe that historians call it the Great Depression. Its effects were felt throughout the world. People were afraid and uncertain of the future.

Rising Unemployment. As business and industry cut back on production, thousands of American workers became **unemployed**, or without work. Because they were unemployed, these workers could not buy as much food, clothing, and other goods as they once had. Thus, demand

Library of Congress

This photograph, taken at Weslaco in 1939, shows a migrant worker with her family. Thousands of Texans lost everything during the Depression and took whatever work they could find.

CHAPTER 26 OVERVIEW

The Great Depression lasted throughout the 1930s. Its effects were felt worldwide as businesses shut their doors. It took a second world war to bring the Depression to an end.

Essential Elements
4A, 4F, 4I, 5A, 5B, 5D, 6B, 7C, 8A, 8B, 9E, 9F

INSTRUCTION

Vocabulary (I) You may wish to preteach the following boldfaced terms: *unemployed* (p. 525); *relief* (p. 526); *proration* (p. 531); *scrip* (p. 531). **LEP**

Problem Solving (I) Use the Section 1 subsection "Rising Unemployment" to prompt a discussion on homelessness. Point out to students that homelessness is a problem that affects many people today. Then discuss what students have seen on television and in newspapers about the homeless. *(Be sensitive to the possibility that one or more of your students may be homeless, and structure the activity accordingly.)* Organize the class into four or five groups, and have each group design a program to aid the homeless. Read some of the best plans aloud. **A**

Historical Sidelight

The 1930s was also a time when women in the garment, cigar, and pecan-shelling industries were organizing to fight wage cuts and long hours. Mexican American women in particular went on strike and sometimes went to jail in the protest against poor wages and working conditions. Women pecan shellers received four to six cents an hour for a 54-hour week, for example.

Geography

On a map of the United States, have students determine how many miles it is from a Texas city such as El Paso or Dallas to the Central Valley in California. Then ask students to estimate how long they think it would have taken to make the trip in a 1920s automobile.

The San Antonio Light Collection, Institute of Texan Cultures

Hundreds line up in hopes of landing a job at the Texas Furniture Company at San Antonio. Many businesses were forced to close down as the Depression became worse during the early 1930s.

for these products fell. When demand fell, business and industry were hurt even further.

By 1933, one in every four American workers was unemployed. Most of these workers supported families. Thus, when a worker lost a job, it affected many other people as well. By late 1933, ten percent of all families in the United States were on **relief**, or received aid to survive.

Churches, the Salvation Army, and other private organizations tried to help as many people as possible. They gave out food and clothing and sometimes provided a place for people to sleep. Still, these organizations could not help everyone who needed aid. Some families moved in with relatives. A number of people living in the cities moved back to the farm so that they could at least have enough to eat.

During the Depression years, thousands of people were left homeless. Some begged on the streets. Others wandered about the country in search of jobs or relief aid. Thousands hitched rides on freight trains. Railroad company police in cities such as El Paso and Corpus Christi spent much of their time clearing the freight cars of riders.

The Depression in Texas. Some Texans made the long trip to California, hoping to find work picking fruit or vegetables on the farms there. So many people traveled to California from Texas and other states that the California

526 Unit 10

526 Unit 10

Painting by Otis Dozier, Dallas Museum of Art

This painting, *The Annual Move*, shows members of a farm family packing up their belongings as they are forced off their land. Many banks were forced to take over the property of Texas farmers.

state police began stopping travelers at the border and making them turn back.

Prices for food and other products dipped sharply during the Depression. Bread cost as little as four cents a loaf. Hamburgers were only five cents. But even at those prices, many people could not afford to buy food.

Throughout Texas, when money was not available, people found ways to make do with what they had. Monroe Brannon of Panola County remembered:

> People around here just didn't have much money for anything, including clothes. During that time, people used cloth feed sacks to make garments to wear. People that had those sacks on hand washed them out and made clothes for their children. All of our children's underwear was made out of the sacks.

Compared to many other areas of the United States, the Depression was less severe in Texas. Only seven percent of families in Texas were on relief in 1933.

There were two major reasons that Texas fared better than some other states. First, many Texans lived on farms. Even though farmers faced hard times, many continued to

Library of Congress

These migrant cotton pickers near Robstown are taking a lunch break. This photograph was taken in 1936.

LONE STAR LEGACY
Using Historical Imagination:
Answers will vary but should be
constructive and creative.

LONE STAR LEGACY

Recycling: A Texas Tradition

Recycling, or the reuse of materials, may seem like a new idea, part of our recent concern about environmental issues. Yet Texans have always recycled in some ways. Previous generations may have recycled for different reasons, but the reuse of material goods is an old Texas tradition.

The farms and ranches of frontier Texas were commonly poor in material goods, and money was in short supply. Things that were "worn out" for their original use were still thought of as too valuable to throw away. Texans were very clever then at recycling. A worn-out saw blade might be used to form the arch of a mud or stone fireplace. A used-up file might be transformed into a kitchen knife or forged into a new cutting edge for an axe.

During World War I and World War II, Texans recycled to help the war effort. Metals, tires, and other materials were in short supply overseas, and Texas adults and children searched junk yards and vacant lots to recover these items. The government then recycled them for American troops.

Early and late in Texas history, most Texans had to recycle during hard economic times to make ends meet. During the Great Depression of the 1930s, manufactured products were scarce or very expensive. Many people went back to the old ways of the frontier. People had to be creative and make the best use of what they had. When one child outgrew clothes, for example, they would be passed on to a younger brother or sister. Women made dresses and shirts from old coat linings and cloth bags in which products such as feed and flour had been packaged. Many Texans made their own soap from cooking grease and lye, as early settlers had done. Women and girls made hair curlers from cloth rags or cardboard, and students constructed lunchpails from empty lard cans or syrup cans.

Today, recycling is an important way to show our concern for the environment. Recycling prevents pollution and saves natural resources, energy, and money.

Using Historical Imagination
Imagine that you are living in the days of the Great Depression. What can you do to help your family make the best use of what you have?

Texans recycle to show their concern for the environment.

Inset: Park Street   Right: David Brownell / The Image Bank

Guided Practice (I) Organize students into pairs. Have one student in each pair assume the role of a Texas oil-field worker during the Depression and the other the role of a West Texas farmer. Ask students to write dialogue for a conversation that might have taken place between the two, focusing on how the Depression has affected them. Allow time for several pairs of students to present their conversations aloud. **A**

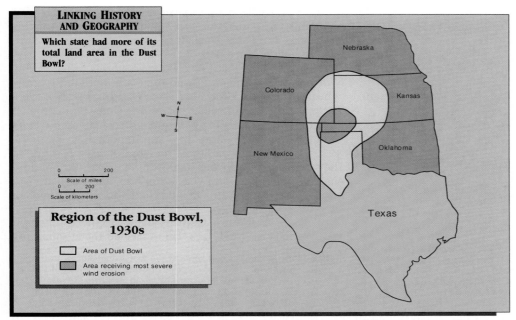

LINKING HISTORY AND GEOGRAPHY

Which state had more of its total land area in the Dust Bowl?

Region of the Dust Bowl, 1930s

☐ Area of Dust Bowl

☐ Area receiving most severe wind erosion

grow crops. They could at least feed their families, which was often impossible to do in urban areas.

Second, the Texas oil industry continued to provide thousands of jobs during the Depression. The great East Texas Oil Field opened in 1930, and fields in other parts of the state were being worked as well. Demand for oil was less than it might have been during good economic times. Still, Texas helped to supply an important portion of the world's oil, and workers were needed to drill wells and to refine and ship oil and its products.

The Dust Bowl and the Farmers. If farmers thought conditions could not be worse than they had been in the 1920s, they were mistaken. Crop prices dropped even lower during the 1930s. Cotton fell from eighteen cents per pound in 1928 to just five cents per pound in 1932. Prices for other farm products also fell. Many farmers could grow food to survive, but few were able to make money to pay their debts. There were reports that some farmers burned cotton and corn as fuel during winter months instead of trying to sell the crops. Milk producers poured milk into sewers in Houston and Galveston when they could not sell it for a profit.

Library of Congress, courtesy
Texas Historical Foundation

This photograph shows a dust storm rolling through Amarillo in 1936.

EXTENSION

Music and History (I) Ask students to locate and bring to class records or tapes of songs from the Great Depression. Point out that Woody Guthrie's Dust Bowl ballads are readily available. You might suggest that students who possess musical talent perform one or more of the songs. **A, LEP**

Independent Practice (II) Ask students to write an essay addressing the following questions: What caused the Dust Bowl? What can we learn from the Dust Bowl years? What environmental issues are of major concern today? Allow time for several students to read their essays aloud. Use the essays to prompt a discussion on environmental issues that affect your community. **A, G**

Environmental Awareness
The dangers of soil erosion were known to a few Texas farmers as early as the 1880s. One farmer in East Texas built a farm terrace to prevent soil erosion. In 1910, the Farmers Cooperative Demonstration Work began educating farmers on the problems associated with soil erosion.

Biography
Woody Guthrie was born in Oklahoma in 1912. When he was sixteen years old, he began traveling around the United States. As he traveled, he wrote songs about the people he met—mostly migrant workers and ordinary people who were affected by the Great Depression and the Dust Bowl. Of the more than 1,000 songs written by Guthrie, perhaps the most famous is "This Land Is Your Land."

The Granger Collection

YEARS OF DUST

RESETTLEMENT ADMINISTRATION
Rescues Victims
Restores Land to Proper Use

The gloom of hard times is shown in this poster by Ben Shahn. The Dust Bowl in the Panhandle only added to the problems that Texas farmers had been facing for years.

Archives Division, Texas State Library

Ross Sterling was elected governor in 1930. The problems of the Depression worsened during his administration, and he was defeated in the 1932 election by former governor Miriam Ferguson.

Farmers in West Texas faced a terrible problem during the 1930s. Giant dust storms swept the Great Plains, earning the region the name Dust Bowl. Many Texas counties in the Panhandle were part of the Dust Bowl.

The problems that led to the dust storms began during World War I. Farmers plowed huge areas of land to grow wheat for the war effort, and acres of natural grasses were destroyed. A long drought struck the Great Plains region in the 1930s. Much of the Panhandle receives no more than twenty inches of precipitation in normal years. In the 1930s, it received even less. The winds started blowing in the spring as they always had. But the wheat did not hold the soil like the natural vegetation had, and there are few trees in the Great Plains to stop the wind. Huge clouds of dust were stirred up.

Folksinger Woody Guthrie lived in the Panhandle during the Dust Bowl days. He described the storms:

> If you want to find some of the worst dust storms in the history of the whole world, I guess, where they get the blackest and the thickest, just go to Amarillo, Texas.
> I remember the particular evening of April 14, 1935. . . . It got so black when that thing hit, we all run into the house. . . . We sat there in a little old room, and it got so dark you couldn't see your hand before your face.

Pauline Robertson of Amarillo was thirteen years old when the first great dust storm struck her city. She and some friends were outside playing when they saw a huge dark cloud approaching:

> We were running away from it and toward home when the wind hit, pelting our bare legs with gravel. We choked and gasped and ran as the air thickened with brown dust. . . . Just as we reached my front porch everything went completely black. The porchlight was consumed by the blackness. We couldn't see each other's faces. We couldn't see our own hands. I remember gasping, "I can't breathe!"

The drought and the dust ruined crops. Thousands of cattle died or had to be killed for lack of food. People in the Panhandle made jokes about the terrible conditions even as they struggled for survival. One tale was about a man who fainted after being struck in the face by a drop of water. His wife had to throw three buckets of sand on him before he woke up.

Crisis in Government. Governor Ross Sterling took office in January 1931. His administration faced one

RETEACHING
Ask students to list on a sheet of paper five effects of the Great Depression on Texas. Call on volunteers to read their lists aloud as you create a master list on the chalkboard.
A, LEP

CLOSURE
Point out to students that while the United States had experienced depressions before, none lasted so long or affected so many.

ASSESSMENT
Have students complete the Section 1 Review on page 531.

emergency after another as the Depression worsened. Even as the state took in less money, demand for services rose because so many people needed help.

The governor faced one of his most serious crises over oil production in East Texas. When the East Texas Oil Field opened in 1930, producers scrambled to drill new wells. By 1935, there were more than 17,000 wells in the East Texas field. There were more than 700 within the city of Kilgore alone. So much oil was being pumped that there was soon an oversupply. The price of oil dropped sharply from a dollar per barrel to less than 20¢ per barrel.

Governor Sterling and others were worried that the oil industry might be ruined. He tried to get producers to agree to cut back production so that the price of oil would rise again. The producers could not agree among themselves, however. Each one wanted to produce as much as possible in order to earn more money.

In August 1931, Governor Sterling declared martial law in East Texas. The National Guard was sent into the region to enforce **proration**. This is a plan whereby each well is limited to producing a certain amount each day. Many producers fought against proration in the courts. They argued that the government had no right to tell them how to use their property. Eventually, new laws were passed that gave the Texas Railroad Commission and the federal government more authority to regulate the oil industry.

During the Depression, local governments were facing emergencies also. Funds had to be cut in nearly every public school district. Schools bought fewer supplies and textbooks. Teachers were sometimes paid in **scrip**, or paper notes. These notes were like a promise of payment at a later date. Corpus Christi schools were forced to close for a time when the bank holding their money failed. Many libraries were closed, or their services were reduced. Houston turned off half of its streetlights at night to save money. Fort Worth shut down its zoo.

Average citizens as well as leaders in business and government were unsure about how to deal with the problems of the Depression. Many Texans had long believed that government should not interfere too much in the economy. But hope began to fade that the Depression would end soon. Because the Depression affected the entire United States, people began to look to the federal government for help in the crisis. ✪

SECTION ★1★ REVIEW

Define: unemployed, relief, proration, scrip

Identify: Dust Bowl, Woody Guthrie, Pauline Robertson, Ross Sterling

1. In 1933, how many American workers were unemployed?
2. What were the two reasons that Texans were better off than other Americans during the Depression?
3. What were two causes of the 1930s dust storms?
4. How did the Depression affect local school districts?

Exploring Economics: Use the terms *supply* and *demand* to explain the oil crisis in 1931.

Solving Problems: Do you think the Depression could be ended only if the government stepped in? Why or why not?

Answers to Section 1 Review

Define: *unemployed*—without work; *relief*—aid to survive; *proration*—plan whereby each well is limited to producing a certain amount each day; *scrip*—paper notes given as promise of payment

Identify: Dust Bowl—name given to Great Plains region during dust storms and drought of the 1930s; Woody Guthrie—folksinger who lived in the Panhandle during the Dust Bowl days; Pauline Robertson—lived in Amarillo during the Dust Bowl days; Ross Sterling—governor of Texas during the Depression

1. One in every four American workers was unemployed.
2. Many Texans lived on farms on which they could grow their own food, and the oil industry provided many jobs.
3. During World War I, all of the natural grasses that held the soil were destroyed to make room for wheat, and in the 1930s, there was a severe drought.
4. Funds were cut, schools bought fewer supplies, and teachers were sometimes paid in scrip.

Exploring Economics: Possible answer: The oil crisis began when the supply of oil was greater than the demand for oil.

Solving Problems: Answers will vary but should be based on sound reasoning.

SECTION 2

FOCUS

Past Learning (I) Write on the chalkboard the following names: *Herbert Hoover, Franklin Roosevelt.* Ask students to provide associations for each person. Point out to students that many people blamed President Hoover for the Depression and that Roosevelt was elected in 1932 by a landslide.

INSTRUCTION

Vocabulary (I) You may wish to preteach the following boldfaced terms: *social security* (p. 532); *repealed* (p. 534); *centennial* (p. 534). **LEP**

Essential Elements
4A, 4F, 4I, 8B, 8D, 9A, 9B

The Granger Collection

Franklin Delano Roosevelt was first elected president of the United States in 1932. His New Deal platform and his personal vigor gave hope to millions during the dark days of the Great Depression.

The San Antonio Light Collection, Institute of Texan Cultures

Several federal agencies operated work camps during the Depression. This photograph of Mr. and Mrs. Theron's wedding was taken at the Civil Works Administration Camp at San Antonio.

❷ President Roosevelt and the New Deal

Many people throughout the United States blamed President Herbert Hoover for the Depression. Groups of shacks and cardboard houses that sprang up in the cities were called "Hoovervilles." Sometimes people had nothing to eat but jackrabbits or armadillos, which they called "Hoover hogs."

President Hoover and many other Americans were against direct government aid to individuals. Instead, Hoover supported limited aid to businesses to help them recover from the Depression. He believed that once they recovered, businesses would be able to provide jobs and wealth once again. Because the Depression did not end, however, most Texans and other Americans supported greater government action. In 1932, Franklin D. Roosevelt was elected president, promising "a new deal for the American people." This platform, along with his personal vigor, inspired hope in millions of people.

The New Deal. President Roosevelt and his advisers asked Congress for a wide variety of laws to fight the Depression. The president's program was called the New Deal. The program did not end the Depression, but it gave hope to millions of Americans. One law gave aid to banks to enable them to reopen and remain strong. Another act provided payments to farmers not to grow crops on part of their land. In this way, it was hoped that farm prices could be raised. Still another New Deal act gave federal money to states so that they could provide food and other aid to the poor.

One of the most important New Deal programs was established to provide jobs for the unemployed. Several agencies were set up with money to pay workers for a number of tasks. Workers built dams, repaired and built roads, constructed parks, and planted trees. The idea behind creating jobs was to give workers money to spend. Then they would be able to buy more goods, thus increasing business and helping the whole economy.

One purpose of the New Deal was to provide Americans with security for the future. In 1935, the **social security** system was established. It provided for pensions, or regular payments, to retired citizens. It also provided payments to unemployed workers while they sought other jobs. The

Comparison (II) Through class discussion, have students compare President Hoover's response to the Depression with Roosevelt's. Conclude by asking students to work in pairs to draw political cartoons that illustrate President Hoover's policies. **A, V, TK**

Analysis (I) Ask students to recall the programs they developed to help the homeless in Section 1. Ask them to comment on any similarities between their proposals and New Deal programs. Ask: In your opinion, which New Deal program helped Texans the most? **A**

Guided Practice (I) Organize students into small groups. Assign each group a New Deal program, which group members are to research in the library. Have each group describe to the rest of the class its program's purpose and success. Suggest to students that they illustrate their presentations with posters, drawings, or photographs. **V, TK, LEP**

system was paid for partly by workers and partly by their employers. A minimum wage was set in 1938.

The New Deal in Texas. Agencies set up under the New Deal provided money for relief in Texas. One of these agencies was the Federal Emergency Relief Administration. In 1933 and 1934, this and other federal agencies poured $50 million into Texas.

Several federal agencies operated in Texas to provide jobs for the unemployed. From 1933 to 1938, the Civilian Conservation Corps employed more than 100,000 Texans. Most CCC workers were young people or veterans of World War I. They built or repaired bridges, dams, and roads. Crews in the Panhandle planted trees to prevent future dust bowls. In Central Texas, crews built roadside parks.

The National Youth Administration was created in 1935 to provide jobs to people of high school and college age. It was directed in Texas by Lyndon B. Johnson, who would later become president of the United States.

Other agencies providing jobs for Texans were the Public Works Administration and the Works Progress Administration. Projects built by workers under the PWA and the WPA can still be seen throughout the state. The PWA aided construction of dams along the Colorado River. The dams control flooding and generate electricity. During the 1930s, such projects helped bring electric power to rural areas throughout Texas.

The federal government worked with farmers in the Panhandle to prevent further dust storms. Farmers were told to plow with the natural shape of the land. Ridges and furrows would prevent erosion by water or wind. The CCC helped plant trees and grasses to break the force of the wind. Reservoirs were built to store water for irrigation.

Texans in the New Deal. A number of Texans served under President Roosevelt during the New Deal years. John Nance Garner of Uvalde was vice president of the United States during Roosevelt's first two terms in office. He had previously served as speaker of the United States House of Representatives.

Jesse Jones of Houston had been appointed by President Hoover to be head of the agency that loaned money to businesses. Jones continued to work for President Roosevelt, who appointed him head of all government lending agencies. Jones later became secretary of commerce.

Garner Museum, Uvalde

Texan John Nance Garner was Franklin Roosevelt's vice president from 1933 to 1941. Garner, sometimes known as "Cactus Jack," had also served as speaker of the House of Representatives.

Sam Rayburn Library, Bonham

Samuel T. Rayburn, a former school teacher, was elected to the United States Congress in 1912. That date marked the beginning of more than 48 years of national service in public offices by Rayburn.

Relating Past to Present
Have a volunteer find out what the minimum wage was in 1938 and what it is today.

Historical Sidelight
Garner State Park, in Uvalde County, was deeded to the state by private owners in 1934. Named after Vice President John Nance Garner, the park comprises 1,420 acres.

534 *Unit 10*

Archives Division, Texas State Library

James V. Allred served two terms as governor during the Depression.

From the collection of Dallas Historical Society

TEXAS

CENTENNIAL·CELEBRATIONS

This 1936 poster celebrates 100 years of Texas independence.

Archives Division, Texas State Library

W. Lee O'Daniel was elected governor over many opponents in 1938.

Members of Congress from Texas generally supported New Deal programs. Among the best-known Texans in the Congress was Sam Rayburn of Bonham. Rayburn was a member of Congress for more than 40 years, serving for a long period as speaker of the House of Representatives.

Texas Politics. Miriam Ferguson was governor of Texas when the New Deal began. Her second term was quieter and less controversial than her first term. Ferguson supported New Deal policies for relief and employment. In 1933, the legislature approved bonds in the amount of $20 million for relief aid to Texans. During Ferguson's term, prohibition was ended at the national level. The Eighteenth Amendment, which established prohibition, was **repealed**, or removed as a law. Voters approved the repeal of prohibition in Texas in 1935.

James V. Allred of Wichita Falls was elected governor in 1934 and reelected in 1936. The Texas Employment Commission was established in 1936. It works to match people with available jobs around the state. The commission also administers payments to unemployed workers. In 1936, Texas approved plans for unemployment payments under the social security system. Governor Allred supported these efforts and others, including a plan to provide payments to public school teachers upon retirement.

During Governor Allred's first term, Texas celebrated its **centennial**, or 100th birthday since independence. The main celebration took place at an exposition in Dallas. In other areas of Texas, historic buildings were restored, historic markers were placed, and statues were erected. As part of the celebration, the San Jacinto Monument near Houston was built on the site of the Texans' victory over General Santa Anna in 1836.

During the Great Depression, there was little difference among the plans of candidates for office. Issues related to the Depression were important throughout the 1930s. In 1938, however, a candidate ran for governor with a style that was unlike that of anyone else.

W. Lee O'Daniel was sales manager of a flour-milling company in Fort Worth. In the late 1920s, he organized a radio show that featured country music by a group called the Lightcrust Doughboys. The show opened with the words "Please pass the biscuits, Pappy!" Soon the show's host was known as "Pappy" Lee O'Daniel. O'Daniel also

Point out to students that not everyone supported Roosevelt's New Deal. Leaders of big business, the wealthy, and people who believed that government was becoming too powerful opposed it.

ASSESSMENT

Have students complete the Section 2 Review on page 535.

Past Learning (I) Ask students to recall the general mood of Americans following World War I *(one of intolerance)*. Point out that Americans did not want to become involved in another world war. By 1941, however, events in Europe and Asia would soon draw Americans, including Texans, into World War II.

---

became president of his own flour company. In 1938, he announced that he was a candidate for governor.

O'Daniel had no experience in politics or government. He admitted that he had never voted. Yet he proved to be a very effective and popular speaker, especially over the radio. O'Daniel's campaign drew huge crowds around the state. He told his audiences, "Go ahead and try me for two years. You can't be any worse off than you have been." O'Daniel was elected by a wide margin in 1938 and 1940. He gave up the governor's office in 1941 to take a seat in the United States Senate. ✪

⓷ Texas in World War II

The Depression of the 1930s affected nations in many areas of the world. In Germany, Italy, and Japan, dictators took control of government. They promised easy solutions to the Depression. Each country built a strong army and attacked its neighbors. In 1939, World War II began when Britain and France went to war with Germany and Italy. Soon Germany, Italy, and Japan signed an agreement to work together as the Axis powers. The Soviet Union joined the war on the side of Britain and France. Throughout most of 1941, the United States stayed out of the war.

The United States Enters the War. On December 7, 1941, Japanese warplanes attacked the United States Navy fleet at Pearl Harbor, Hawaii. A black Texan from Waco, Doris Miller, was aboard the ship USS *West Virginia* when bombs began falling from the Japanese planes. Miller raced to the deck and dragged the wounded captain of the ship to safety. He manned a machine gun and began firing at the Japanese attack planes, downing four. For his actions, Miller was awarded the Navy Cross. As a result of the attack, the United States declared war on Japan. The United States joined the Allies—Britain, France, and the Soviet Union—to fight the Axis nations.

Texans Join the War Effort. As it had in World War I, Texas served as a major site for military training. During the war, there were fifteen army camps and about 40 airfields in Texas. San Antonio became the largest aviation training center in the world. Kelly, Randolph, Brooks, and Lackland air bases were all located there. The navy operated training centers at Corpus Christi, Kingsville, Beeville, and

---

SECTION ★2★ REVIEW

Define: social security, repealed, centennial

Identify: Herbert Hoover, Franklin D. Roosevelt, John Nance Garner, Sam Rayburn

1. What kinds of jobs were created by the New Deal?
2. What efforts were made to prevent the creation of more dust bowls?
3. What Texan was vice president during the first terms of Roosevelt's presidency?
4. How did Texas celebrate the centennial in 1936?

Exploring Economics: Why did President Roosevelt think that the economy would improve if the government could provide more people with jobs?

Evaluating Information: Why do you think Texans elected W. Lee O'Daniel to two terms as governor although he had never even voted or been in politics?

Dwight D. Eisenhower Library

General Dwight D. Eisenhower served as commander of all Allied forces in Europe during the war. In this photograph, he discusses plans for the invasion of France on D Day, June 6, 1944. Eisenhower was elected president as a Republican in 1952 and was reelected in 1956.

Sam Rayburn—well-known Texan who served Congress for more than 40 years, for a long period as speaker of the House of Representatives

1. Building dams, repairing and building roads, constructing parks, planting trees
2. Farmers plowed with the natural shape of the land, and they plowed ridges and furrows to prevent erosion. The CCC helped plant trees and grasses to break the force of winds, and reservoirs were built to store water for irrigation.
3. John Nance Garner
4. An exposition was held in Dallas. In other areas of Texas, historic buildings were restored, historic markers were placed, and statues were erected. In Houston, the San Jacinto Monument was built.

Exploring Economics: Roosevelt believed that more jobs would provide people with money to buy more goods, which would increase business and help the whole economy.

Evaluating Information: Answers will vary. Students might suggest that the Depression left Texans feeling desperate for change.

Essential Elements
4A, 4C, 4I, 5B, 6B, 9A, 9B, 9D, 9E

INSTRUCTION

Vocabulary (I) You may wish to preteach the following boldfaced term: *synthetic* (p. 538). **LEP**

Map Work (I) Provide each student with a blank outline map of Texas. Ask students to label on the map the Texas place names mentioned in Section 3. They should write next to each place name the significance of the site as it relates to Texas in World War II. Encourage students to use map symbols and a map legend as well. **V, TK, LEP**

TEXAS VOICES

Analysis (I) Ask students to provide adjectives other than *heroic* that might be used to describe Audie Murphy. Ask students if they know anyone personally who has served in combat. Ask: Could these same terms be used to describe that person? **A, LEP**

Illustrating (I) Have students draw posters calling for Texans to support the war effort. Suggestions might include posters urging men and women to volunteer for service or posters designed to boost the morale of those on the home front. Display the posters in the classroom. **V, TK, LEP**

Essential Elements
4C, 4I, 9A

TEXAS VOICES

Audie Murphy was born in Hunt County, Texas, on a small farm near Greenville. In 1942, just before his eighteenth birthday, he joined the army and was sent to Europe during World War II. During his tour of duty, Audie Murphy became the nation's most decorated soldier of the war. For his gallantry in action he received many military honors. The Congressional Medal of Honor was his twenty-fourth medal. He returned home to a hero's welcome and was hounded by newspapers and magazines. Murphy refused to discuss his battlefield actions in detail. He did, however, describe the fear that gripped soldiers just before going into battle:

> When you are moving into combat, why try fooling yourself. Fear is right there beside you. It strikes first in the stomach. . . . Sometimes it takes more courage to get up and run [under enemy gunfire] than to stay [in a sheltered spot]. You either just do it or you don't. I got so scared the first day in combat I just decided to go along with it.

As one of the greatest heroes of the war, Murphy was sought after to make speeches to American audiences. He was very modest. Typically, he chose to focus on the role of people at home in supporting the war, as in this speech:

> I would like to take this opportunity to pay a tribute to the mothers and fathers who are here. For it is they who perhaps suffer most in time of war. Too, I would like to express my gratitude for the swell job you have done on the home front. You have given us everything we asked for in the way of tools for modern warfare. . . . Though I need not remind you that the war is but half won, there is now no doubt in anyone's mind what the final outcome will be. I would like today to say to each of you here at home, congratulations on a job well done.

Doris Miller YMCA, Waco, Institute of Texan Cultures

Doris Miller was a hero at Pearl Harbor. He later fought in the South Pacific and was lost at sea when the warship he was serving on, *Liscome Bay*, was sunk in the Gilbert Islands in 1943. A Navy destroyer ship, the USS *Miller*, was named in his honor in 1972.

Grand Prairie. Texas A&M University trained about 20,000 soldiers, including 14,000 officers. More than 1,250,000 troops were trained in Texas during the war years.

Approximately 750,000 Texans served in the armed forces in World War II. Thirty-six Texans received the nation's highest military award, the Congressional Medal of Honor. The most decorated of all soldiers was Audie Murphy of Farmersville. He received every combat award given by the United States Army. Commander Samuel Dealey of Dallas was the most decorated member of the United States Navy.

More than 8,000 Texas women served in the Women's Army Corps, or WAC, commanded by Oveta Culp Hobby

536 *Unit 10*

Guided Practice (I) Have students use the information in this and previous sections to draw a time line spanning the years 1929–45. Ask them to choose two events from the time line and write a sentence showing their relationship. **TK, LEP**

EXTENSION

Research (II) Have interested students conduct research to find more information on activities on the home front in Texas during World War II. Encourage students to illustrate their reports. Some students might focus their reports on a comparison between activities in Texas in World War I and World War II. **A, V, TK, G**

Independent Practice (II) Have students use their historical imagination to write a biography of one of the following: a Texan who fought in World War II or a person who worked on the home front in Texas. Biographies should be based on the information in Section 3. Collect the biographies and compile them into a booklet titled "Texas in World War II." Display the booklet in the classroom for students to read. **V, TK**

of Houston. Another 4,000 Texas women served in Women Accepted for Volunteer Emergency Services, or WAVES, a branch of the navy. Avenger Field in Sweetwater served as the location for training Women's Air Force Service Pilots, or WASP. Around 1,000 female pilots trained there. During the war, they performed every type of aviation task except flying in combat.

More than 150 generals and a dozen admirals in World War II were from Texas. General Dwight D. Eisenhower was born in Denison and served as commander of all Allied forces in Europe. Admiral Chester W. Nimitz of Fredericksburg was commander of the United States fleet in the Pacific.

On the Home Front. The war called for sacrifices at home. Meats, gasoline, sugar, rubber products, and other items were put on the ration list. People were given ration stamps in order to purchase items that were in short supply. Texans collected scrap iron and old tires for the war effort. Many grew vegetables in backyard "victory gardens." Texans bought war bonds and helped the Red Cross and other service organizations.

The programs of the New Deal did not end the Depression, but the war did. The beginning of the war gave a

The Texas Collection, Baylor University

By 1945, at the age of twenty, Texan Audie Murphy was the nation's most decorated soldier of World War II. After the war, he starred in several Hollywood films.

Admiral Nimitz State Historical Park, Fredericksburg

Admiral Chester W. Nimitz of Fredericksburg was commander of the Pacific Fleet during World War II.

This photograph of Women's Air Force Service Pilots was taken in December 1944 at Waco Army Air Field.

Multicultural Perspective
Students should be made aware that by the end of 1942, more than 110,000 Japanese Americans had been relocated from their homes on the West Coast to internment camps scattered from California to Arkansas. Their only "crime" was being of Japanese ancestry. Many people feared that Japanese Americans were spies and that the Japanese attack on Pearl Harbor was preliminary to an attack on the West Coast.

Randolph Air Force Base

RETEACHING
Have students create on the chalkboard a chart listing three negative and three positive effects of World War II on Texas society and economy. **V, TK, LEP**

CLOSURE
List on the chalkboard the subsection headings from Section 3. Have the class work together to outline the section.

ASSESSMENT
Have students complete the Section 3 Review on page 538.

Answers to Section 3 Review

Define: *synthetic*—human-made
Identify: Audie Murphy—Texan who was the most decorated soldier of World War II; Oveta Culp Hobby—Texan who commanded the Women's Army Corps during World War II; Dwight D. Eisenhower—Texan who served as commander of the Allied forces in Europe; Chester W. Nimitz—Texan who commanded the U.S. fleet in the Pacific

1. Japan attacked the United States Navy.
2. Women's Army Corps (WAC), Women Accepted for Volunteer Emergency Services (WAVES), Women's Air Force Service Pilots (WASP)
3. The war ended the Depression.
4. By dropping two atomic bombs on Japan

Evaluating Information: Answers will vary. Students might suggest that by gardening at home, people were supporting the war effort and promoting an Allied victory.

Seeing Cause and Effect: Japanese attacked Pearl Harbor—the U.S. entered the war; many goods came to be in short supply—goods were rationed; factories opened to make war supplies—the economy improved; the United States dropped atomic bombs on Japan—Japan surrendered

Lieutenant Governor Coke Stevenson of Junction became governor when "Pappy" O'Daniel resigned in 1941 to enter the United States Senate. Stevenson was elected to a full term in 1942 and reelected in 1944.

SECTION ⭐3⭐ REVIEW

Define: synthetic
Identify: Audie Murphy, Oveta Culp Hobby, Dwight D. Eisenhower, Chester W. Nimitz

1. What happened at Pearl Harbor on December 7, 1941?
2. In which three military branches did women serve during the war?
3. What effect did the war have on the Depression?
4. How did President Truman force the Japanese to surrender?

Evaluating Information: Why do you think backyard gardens during the war were called "victory gardens"? Were they helpful to the war effort? Why or why not?

Seeing Cause and Effect: Write the effect that resulted from each of these causes: Japanese attacked Pearl Harbor; many goods came to be in short supply; factories opened to make war supplies; the United States dropped atomic bombs on Japan.

great boost to the economy of Texas. New factories were opened to make war supplies, and thousands of new jobs were created. Aircraft factories were built at Fort Worth, Garland, and Grand Prairie. Shipyards operated in Houston, Galveston, Port Arthur, Orange, Beaumont, Brownsville, and Rockport. Steel mills operated in Houston and Daingerfield. The chemical industry in Texas started during World War II. **Synthetic**, or human-made, rubber was produced near the oil fields in Beaumont, Houston, and Borger.

Immigration from Mexico increased as people moved to Texas during the war to find jobs. Women took a number of different jobs in industry when thousands of men left their jobs to join the military forces. Large numbers of black Texans moved to the cities to work in wartime industries as well. Old prejudices against African Americans remained, however. Tensions between blacks and whites erupted into a riot in Beaumont in 1943. Two blacks were killed, and a number of homes were destroyed.

The Allies Achieve Victory. During 1942 and 1943, American and Allied forces attacked in the Pacific and in North Africa. They invaded Italy in 1943. In June 1944, the Allies invaded France and took control of that country from the Germans.

The price of the war in human lives was terrible. Millions of people were killed in Europe and Asia. As Allied forces moved into Germany, they discovered death camps where the Germans had murdered an estimated 12 million people, including at least 6 million Jews.

In 1945, a new age in human history opened when the United States dropped atomic bombs on two Japanese cities, Hiroshima and Nagasaki. This was the first and only use of nuclear weapons. Both cities were destroyed, killing thousands of people. By dropping the bombs, President Harry Truman hoped to force Japan to surrender. He was sure that an invasion of Japan would cost even more lives than the bombings.

The use of atomic bombs forced Japan to surrender to the Allies in August 1945. Germany and Italy had surrendered in May. World War II was over. Approximately 23,000 Texans did not come home. They were among the 400,000 or more Americans who died during the war, of whom around 290,000 were killed in combat. ⊙

Illustrating (I) Ask students to select and illustrate five of the topics presented in the special feature. For example, students might illustrate "Relative location" by drawing a Texas map showing the location of Midland and Odessa in relation to the location of El Paso and Fort Worth. Encourage students to be creative. **V, TK**

Reading a Graph (I) Direct students to study the line graph in the special feature. Ask students: In what county is Odessa located (*Ector*)? Have students study the line graph and point to the line corresponding to Ector County. Call on students to tell you how many oil rigs were operating in Ector County on specific dates. Have students make comparison statements about the number of rigs operating in other counties on the same dates. **A, V, LEP**

CITIES OF TEXAS

Midland and Odessa

Population:
Midland—89,443
Odessa—89,699

Metro area population:
Midland—106,611
Odessa—118,934

Size: Midland—53.3 square miles; Odessa—29.3 square miles

Relative location: In the Permian Basin of West Texas, halfway between El Paso and Fort Worth

Region: At the southern edge of the High Plains where the Edwards Plateau meets the Mountains and Basins region

County: Midland—county seat of Midland County; Odessa—county seat of Ector County

Special feature: The oil-rich Permian Basin makes the area one of the nation's major producers of petroleum products.

Origin of name: Midland is named for its location on the Chihuahua Trail, midway between El Paso and Fort Worth. Odessa was named for its resemblance

to the Odessa region of Ukraine in Eastern Europe.

Landmarks: Many oil wells

Economy: The major income of both cities comes from the petroleum and gas industry, but farming and ranching also are strong. The area is a central trade and banking center for the vast West Texas region.

History: Odessa was established in 1881 as a stop on the Texas and Pacific Railroad. Midland was established in 1885 by farming families. Both grew slowly until the oil boom of the 1920s.

Recreation facilities: Golf courses, parks, and the Midland Angels baseball team are among the recreation choices.

Cultural facilities: Odessa offers a symphony orchestra, Civic Music Association, the Art Institute of the Permian Basin, and the Globe of the Southwest Shakespearean Theatre. Midland offers a number of museums, including the Permian Basin Petroleum Museum.

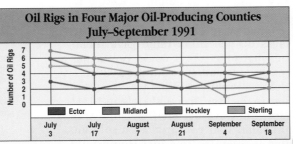

Oil Rigs in Four Major Oil-Producing Counties
July–September 1991

Number of Oil Rigs

Ector   Midland   Hockley   Sterling

| July 3 | July 17 | August 7 | August 21 | September 4 | September 18 |

Essential Elements
4B, 5B, 5C, 9B

CHAPTER REVIEW RESOURCES

1. Chapter Review Worksheet 26
2. Chapter 26 Test, Form A
3. Reteaching Worksheet 26
4. Chapter 26 Test, Form B
5. **Informal Evaluation Forms:** Portfolio Assessment
6. *Texas, Our Texas* **Test Generator**

Essential Elements
4A, 4C, 8A, 9A, 9B, 9E, 9F

CHAPTER 26 REVIEW ANSWERS

Understanding Main Ideas

1. Texans suffered less than people in the rest of the country because Texans were better able to grow their own food and because the oil industry provided thousands of jobs.
2. The Dust Bowl problems came about because the natural grasses of the Great Plains had been destroyed, leaving nothing to hold down the soil, and a severe drought turned the soil to dust. Farmers learned to plow with the shape of the land and to create furrows and ridges that prevented erosion. Trees and grasses were planted to block the wind, and reservoirs were built to hold water for irrigation.
3. Programs were created to provide jobs, the social security system was established to provide pensions for retired people and payments to unemployed workers, and a minimum wage was set.
4. Possible answers: Governor Sterling declared martial law in East Texas to save the oil industry, and the Prohibition amendment was repealed.

CHAPTER 26 REVIEW

Understanding Main Ideas

1. How did the Great Depression affect Texas in comparison to the United States as a whole?
2. What caused the Dust Bowl problems? What was done to correct the problems?
3. What were three actions taken by the federal government to fight the effects of the Depression?
4. Describe two major events that took place in Texas politics during the Depression.
5. What was the role of women in World War II? How did they contribute to the war effort?
6. What are three ways in which Texas contributed to the war effort of the Allied Forces?

Thinking Critically

1. **Exploring Economics:** How did low prices during the Depression hurt farmers and business owners? Why were low food prices of little benefit to American consumers?
2. **Evaluating Information:** Franklin D. Roosevelt and W. Lee O'Daniel both made great use of radio. What advantages do you think radio gave them? In what other ways could politicians reach large audiences in the 1930s?
3. **Solving Problems:** What was the problem in the East Texas Oil Field in 1931? How did Governor Sterling handle the problem? Can you propose a solution that is different from his? How would

you have persuaded the oil producers to accept your plan?

Linking History and Geography

1. Why did many Texans move to California during the Depression? What did California have to offer people that Texas did not?
2. Why could the Dust Bowl not have happened in East Texas?

TAAS Practice
Using Primary Sources

In August 1945, Ted Dealey, president of *The Dallas Morning News*, traveled to Japan to witness the official end of World War II. He sent back articles to his readers in Texas. The following selection comes from the article Dealey wrote after observing the Japanese surrender aboard the battleship *Missouri* on September 2, 1945:

A pile driver [jackhammer] banging away under a full head of steam could not have slammed and packed as much stark drama into a bare twenty minutes of time as Gen. Douglas MacArthur and his fighting companions of the United Nations did on the decks of the United States battlewagon *Missouri* this dull and leaden Sunday morning. . . .

Standing erect and grim, youthful-looking in spite of his years, handsome as an eagle, . . . MacArthur made you proud you were an American and proud, too, that such an American as he was here to speak for the mothers and fathers back home whose hero sons will never come back to welcome arms. . . . [At this point, the Japanese and Americans sign the official papers of surrender.]

All of a sudden at this significant

5. Women served in the Women's Army Corps, Women Accepted for Volunteer Emergency Services, and Women's Air Force Service Pilots. Women at home took jobs in industry.
6. Texas served as a major military training site, Texas factories produced war goods, and approximately 750,000 Texans served in the armed forces.

Thinking Critically

1. **Exploring Economics:** Low prices meant that farmers and business owners received less income. Low food prices were of little benefit to consumers because most people could not afford to buy much, regardless of the price.
2. **Evaluating Information:** Answers will vary but should suggest that radio al-

lowed them to reach large audiences. Politicians also could travel around the country by automobile or train.
3. **Solving Problems:** Overproduction caused low prices. Governor Sterling declared martial law to enforce proration. Solutions will vary but should be logical, and students should be persuasive in their arguments to the oil producers.

Linking History and Geography

1. Unemployed Texans moved to California to find jobs. California had fruit and vegetable farms.
2. East Texas is not as flat and has many trees that protect the soil from the wind.

TAAS **Practice**
Using Primary Sources
1. C
2. C

TAAS **Practice**
Writing Descriptively
Letters will vary but should reflect the effects of the Depression on workers and the promise of New Deal programs.

Practicing Skills
1. **Exploring Primary Sources:** Answers will vary but should reflect the information presented in the two accounts.
2. **Interpreting Tables:** 1937; April; 1934

Enriching Your Study of History
1. **Individual Project:** Speeches should be persuasive and should demonstrate knowledge of the effects of the Depression on Texans.
2. **Cooperative Project:** Songs should demonstrate careful research and practice.
3. **Cooperative Project:** Projects should demonstrate a cooperative effort.

---

moment—almost marvelous to relate—the sun broke through the clouds and bathed the decks of the *Missouri* for a few moments, and a few moments only, in bright sunshine. It was as if an omen from above.

1. According to the selection, Dealey considered General MacArthur to be
   A a kind and considerate person
   B a soft-spoken person
   C a great American leader
   D a person of many talents
2. To Dealey, the sudden breakthrough of sunshine was a symbol of
   A a beautiful day
   B friendship
   C peace
   D a long trip home

TAAS **Practice**
Writing Descriptively
Imagine that you are an unemployed worker in Texas during the Depression. You have just obtained a job through a New Deal program. Write a letter to Governor O'Daniel, describing how your life has been recently and how it will improve now that you have work.

Practicing Skills
1. **Exploring Primary Sources:** Reread the two accounts of the Dust Bowl days on page 530. What do you think would be the worst thing about being caught in the middle of a dust storm? Explain your answer.
2. **Interpreting Tables:** Study the table on this page. In which year were there the most dust storms? In which month during the five years were there the most dust storms? In which year were there the fewest dust storms?

Dust Storms, 1933–1937					
Month	1933	1934	1935	1936	1937
January	4	2	2	0	9
February	4	0	7	9	14
March	14	6	11	18	18
April	17	6	20	16	21
May	12	2	6	14	23
June	7	2	1	1	17
July	3	0	1	2	15
August	3	1	1	1	10
September	3	0	0	0	7
October	0	1	2	1	–
November	2	2	1	7	–
December	1	0	1	4	–
Total	70	22	53	73	134

Enriching Your Study of History

1. **Individual Project:** Imagine that you are a candidate for the Texas legislature during the Depression. Write a brief radio speech in which you will attempt to persuade listeners to vote for you.
2. **Cooperative Project:** Working with a partner, conduct research to find a song that was popular during the Depression or World War II. Learn the song and teach it to your class.
3. **Cooperative Project:** Your teacher will organize your class into groups of four or five. Your group may choose to write and perform a play about a Texas family living during the Great Depression. Or your group may choose instead to research posters of World War II. Create your own 1940s-style poster, encouraging people to buy war bonds, to start a victory garden, or to donate metal or rubber goods for recycling.

UNIT REVIEW RESOURCES

1. Unit Review Worksheet 10
2. Unit 10 Test, Form A
3. Reteaching Worksheet 10
4. Unit 10 Test, Form B
5. **Informal Evaluation Forms:** Portfolio Assessment
6. *Texas, Our Texas* **Test Generator**

Essential Elements
4A, 4C, 4F, 5D, 7C, 9A, 9B, 9C, 9G

UNIT 10

UNIT 10 REVIEW ANSWERS

Connecting Main Ideas

1. After the war, there was a mood of intolerance. Immigrants and minorities were mistreated, labor unrest occurred, and the Ku Klux Klan resurfaced, using violent tactics and gaining power by influencing elections.
2. Farmers were able to haul their goods to market and transport supplies to their farms. Bus and truck lines developed and competed with the railroads.
3. During the 1920s, farm product prices remained low and many farmers fell into debt. Crop prices dropped even lower during the 1930s, and in the Great Plains, drought and dust storms ruined crops.
4. Employment fell slightly after World War I, but then picked up as the nation entered a period of prosperity. Unemployment was high during the Depression, but by the end of World War II, there were many new industries and government programs providing jobs.
5. During the 1920s, new oil fields opened and the industry boomed. During the Depression, the demand for oil dropped along with the price of oil. In an attempt to save

REVIEW

Connecting Main Ideas

1. After World War I, what was the mood of Texans in general? How was that mood reflected in race relations, in business, and in politics?
2. What economic benefits in Texas resulted from improvements in transportation during the 1920s?
3. Explain why farmers in general did not participate in the prosperity of the 1920s and 1930s.
4. How did employment in Texas change between the end of World War I and the end of World War II?
5. Describe the most important changes in the oil industry from the 1920s to World War II.
6. In what ways was the radio important in the 1920s, 1930s, and 1940s?

Practicing Critical Thinking Skills

1. **Exploring Economics:** How did the prosperity of the early 1920s lead to the Depression of the 1930s? Give examples to illustrate.
2. **Evaluating Information:** How do you think the lives of farmers in the Dust Bowl might have been different if they could have used the methods learned during the New Deal to avoid the damages of drought? Explain.
3. **Making Decisions:** If you had been a farmer in the Panhandle during the Dust Bowl days, would you have stayed, or would you have left your farm for California or a large city? Why?

TAAS *Practice*
Writing Informatively

Imagine that you have a brother or sister in military service during World War II, and that you work in a weapons factory. Write a letter to your brother or sister, telling him or her how you are helping in the war effort.

Exploring Local History

1. What projects in your community or county were carried out during the New Deal? Were they carried out by the PWA, the WPA, or the CCC?
2. Ask a parent, a guardian, or an adult friend what they remember, or what stories they were told, about the Depression or the Dust Bowl days in Texas. Share what you have learned with the class.

For Extending Your Knowledge

Davis, Clare Ogden. *The Woman of It.* New York: J.H. Sears, 1929. A novel about the political struggle between women voters and the Ku Klux Klan.

Graham, Don. *No Name on the Bullet: A Biography of Audie Murphy.* New York: Penguin Books, 1990. The illustrated story of the life of World War II's most decorated American soldier.

Owens, William A. *This Stubborn Soil.* Austin: University of Texas Press, 1983. An autobiography about farm life in the Depression.

Wilson, John W. *High John the Conqueror.* New York: Macmillan, 1948. A novel about black life in a white world, the Brazos Bottoms.

the oil industry, the governor declared martial law in East Texas to enforce proration. Eventually, the Texas Railroad Commission gained more authority to regulate the oil industry.

6. The radio provided a new form of entertainment, became an important campaign tool for political candidates, and provided a source for national and world news.

Practicing Critical Thinking Skills

1. **Exploring Economics:** During the prosperity of the early 1920s, people invested in the stock market. In 1929 a panic occurred when a large number of people rushed to sell their stock. As a result, the stock market crashed. The value of stocks dropped drastically. Many banks were forced to close because people could not afford to repay loans. Businesses failed and people lost jobs. The Depression followed.

2. **Evaluating Information:** Answers will vary but should mention that the drought would not have been as damaging had the farmers been using methods to preserve the soil.

3. **Making Decisions:** Answers will vary but should demonstrate sound reasoning.

TAAS *Practice*
Writing Informatively:
Letters will vary but should reflect knowledge of the war effort at home.

Exploring Local History
1. Answers should demonstrate thorough research of local history.
2. Responses will vary but should indicate that students performed the activity.

Skill Lesson
Practicing the Skill
1. Students should select and list in the appropriate columns five facts and five opinions.
2. The writer supports night games, arguing that many more people attend the night games, which brings in more money.
3. Students should demonstrate the ability to distinguish fact from opinion.
4. Paragraphs should demonstrate the ability to write from an objective and a subjective point of view.

SKILL LESSON

Distinguishing Fact From Opinion

We consider television news stories to be based upon fact. They are about something generally assumed to be true. Likewise, front-page stories in the newspaper are usually factual. Such accounts are intended to present the facts *objectively*, or without taking sides. When you read objective stories, it is difficult to tell anything about the person who wrote them. That person tries to keep his or her personality and opinions out of the story.

Facts can be proven. That is, you can check the facts in one account by comparing them against facts in other accounts of the same event.

An account based upon opinion, however, presents facts *subjectively*. This means that facts are told or written from a personal point of view. In reading the account, we can usually tell the viewpoint of the person who wrote it.

In some cases, a piece of writing can contain both fact and opinion. In persuasive writing, for example, the author uses facts and opinions to persuade the reader to accept his or her point of view. Similarly, in descriptive writing we may find a mixture of fact and opinion. A descriptive passage often reveals the author's point of view.

The selection that follows is from a newspaper editorial in the *Hereford Brand* of October 31, 1935. As you read it, ask yourself which statements are facts and which are opinions.

Hereford football fans are more determined than ever to have lights for night play here after watching the display under the arcs at Friona last week. They not only liked the night game, but also approved the crowd of between 1,000 and 1,500 fans who packed the stadium. Its share in the gate receipts was more than $90, which should prove rather conclusively that night football does pay. It was the largest crowd ever to see a game at Friona, we believe, and although the importance and interest attached to the game had something to do with it, the fact that it was a night game accounted for a large portion of that crowd. Judging from the string of cars on the highway following the tilt [game] as people returned to Hereford, more local fans attended the game than had witnessed any ... home contest this season. Tomorrow the Whitefaces [Hereford team] play Tulia in the most important game within the section—much more important and probably a much closer tilt than the Friona melee [struggle]. It will give us a chance to form a more accurate opinion of the night game. In comparison, there should be fully 2,000 people at the Tulia game. Estimate the crowd tomorrow and then decide what floodlights would be worth to Hereford from a purely financial standpoint.

Practicing the Skill

1. Make two columns, one titled *Facts* and one titled *Opinions*. List at least five facts and at least five opinions that can be found in the selection.

2. What is the writer's opinion of night football? How can you tell?

3. Choose an editorial from a recent newspaper. Underline every fact and circle every opinion.

4. Select a topic about which you know a great deal. Then, write two paragraphs about your topic. One paragraph should be completely objective. The other should be completely subjective.

INTRODUCING THE UNIT

Connecting with Past Learning

Ask students to imagine that they have been invited to contribute a time capsule for a space shuttle mission to the moon. The capsule should include items that represent the past and the future of Texas. Have each student list five items to include in the capsule. Create on the chalkboard a class list. Conclude the activity by having the class rank the items in order of importance.

MOTIVATOR

Organize the class into three groups, and assign one of the chapters in the unit to each group. Have students skim their assigned chapter and list on a sheet of paper the names of people and places they find. Then ask them to close their textbooks and write a sentence identifying as many of the places or names on their lists as possible. Upon completion of the unit, allow students to make corrections to their lists.

UNIT 11 OVERVIEW

Unit 11 examines Texas in the years after World War II. Chapter 27 discusses political and social changes occurring after 1945 and presents major developments in transportation and communications. The chapter also introduces the civil rights movement and its impact on Texas.

Chapter 28 focuses on Texas in the 1970s and 1980s, with emphasis on population growth, politics, and economics. It concludes with a discussion of the challenges facing future Texans.

Chapter 29 begins with a discussion of how Texas' cultural heritage has been expressed. The chapter then introduces the many men and women who have contributed to the preservation of Texas culture.

UNIT 11 MODERN TIMES

Materials Available at the Unit Level:
Unit 11   Making Global Connections
Oral History Handbook
Informal Evaluation Forms

TEXAS AND THE WORLD

Organize students into small groups, and ask the groups to study the time line on this page. Have students select one of the world events and brainstorm about how that event is related to events in Texas. Ask volunteers to share their group's response. Continue the activity for other key events on the time line.

World War II had a major impact on Texas. Industries sprang up to aid the war effort. Military bases were expanded around the state to train soldiers, sailors, and pilots. The war boosted the state's economy, and thousands of people moved to cities and nearby towns to take jobs. By war's end, a majority of Texans were living in urban areas for the first time in the history of the state.

Since World War II, Texas has become a major economic force in the United States and the world. Population growth has been explosive as thousands of people from other states and other countries enter the state each year. Growth has brought new opportunities for Texans of all backgrounds even as it has challenged Texas to provide services for its citizens.

Unit 11 describes trends in Texas from the end of World War II in 1945 to the present. Chapter 27 examines economic, social, and political developments in the 1950s and 1960s, while Chapter 28 looks at events from the 1970s to the present. Chapter 29 concludes the unit with a study of Texas' rich culture.

UNIT 11 OBJECTIVES

1. Identify postwar developments in transportation and communication and their impact on life in Texas.
2. Discuss the civil rights movement in Texas, identifying significant organizations, political leaders, and legislation.
3. Identify and discuss postwar political issues in Texas, and identify key figures.
4. Discuss the effects of rapid population growth on the cities of Texas.
5. Describe Texas' modern economy, and identify contributing factors.
6. Identify challenges facing Texans in the future.
7. Discuss Texas' cultural heritage, and identify important Texas artists and writers of the past and present.

TEXAS EVENTS

1929
LULAC established

1940s
First Texas TV stations

1948
American GI Forum established

1960s
Major professional sports teams organized

1960
Supreme Court rules for Texas in Tidelands controversy

1963
President Kennedy assassinated, Lyndon Johnson becomes president

1986
Texas celebrates sesquicentennial

1990
Ann Richards elected governor

1930 — 1940 — 1950 — 1960 — 1970 — 1980 — 1990

1939–1945
World War II

1944
GI Bill passed

1949
Tidelands controversy

1950s
Interstate highway system begun

1954
Brown v. Board of Education case

1964
Civil Rights Act passed

1965
Voting Rights Act passed

1965–1973
U.S. in Vietnam War

1970s
Oil shortage

1980s
Oil prices drop sharply

1988
George Bush elected president

WORLD EVENTS

CHAPTER 27

POSTWAR TEXAS

TEACHER'S TIME LINE

Section 1
Pp. 546–50
1 Day

Section 2
Pp. 550–54
1 Day

Section 3
Pp. 554–58
1 Day

Review and Assessment
1 Day

★ TEACHER MATERIALS

Core: Chapter 27 Time Line; Graphic Organizer 27; Enrichment Worksheet 27; Review Worksheet 27; Reteaching Worksheet 27; Chapter 27 Tests, Forms A & B

Additional: Geography and Graph Skills 27, Informal Evaluation Forms, Test Generator

★ OBJECTIVES

1. Describe the ways in which education, employment, population, transportation, and communication in Texas changed after World War II.
2. List and describe three federal laws designed to end discrimination.
3. Identify three provisions of the Gilmer-Aiken Law.
4. Recognize the contributions to Texas of significant individuals discussed in the chapter.
5. Discuss the significance of the Supreme Court's decision in *Brown v. Board of Education of Topeka*.
6. Discuss the Tidelands controversy.
7. Identify Lyndon B. Johnson and his Great Society program.

★ RESOURCES

BOOKS FOR TEACHERS

Berry, Margaret Catherine. *The University of Texas*. Austin: University of Texas Press, 1980. Pictorial study of the university.

Farmer, James. *Lay Bare the Heart*. New York: Arbor House, 1985. Autobiography of Farmer, including his work in the civil rights movement.

García, Clotilde P. *Clotilde García Papers*. Austin: Benson Latin American Collection. Documents of the García family, including Dr. Hector P. García.

Garrow, David J. *We Shall Overcome*. Brooklyn: Carlson Pub.,

1989. Story of the civil rights movement in the South in the 1950s and 1960s.

Hardeman, D.B. *Rayburn: A Biography*. Austin: Texas Monthly Press, 1987. Life and times of this great speaker of the House.

Kellogg, Charles Flint. *NAACP*. Baltimore: Johns Hopkins Press, 1967. History of the National Association for the Advancement of Colored People.

Loevy, Robert D. *To End All Segregation*. Lanham: University Press of America, 1990. The politics of the Civil Rights Act of 1964.

Moore, Charles. *Powerful Days*. New York: Stewart, Tabori & Chang, 1991. Photographs of the civil rights movement by Charles Moore.

MULTIMEDIA MATERIALS

Committee on Un-American Activities. (video, 45 min.) University of California Extension Media Center, 2176 Shattuck Avenue, Berkeley, California, 94704. History of the Un-American Activities Committee, whose efforts affected all Americans.

The Fateful Decade: From Little Rock to the Civil Rights Bill.

(video, 27 min.) Southwest Media Services, Inc., P.O. Box 140, Wimberley, Texas, 78676. History of the civil rights movement leading up to Johnson's Civil Rights Act of 1964.

Free At Last. (video, 30 min.) University of California Extension Media Center, 2176 Shattuck Avenue, Berkeley, California, 94704. History of the African-American struggle for civil rights.

Martin Luther King, Jr. (video, 24 min.) Encyclopaedia Britannica Educational Corporation, 310 South Michigan Avenue, Chicago, Illinois, 60604. A look at the great leader of the civil rights movement.

Yo Soy Chicano. (video, 59 min.) University of California Extension Media Center, 2176 Shattuck Avenue, Berkeley, California, 94704. The Mexican American experience.

GENERAL STRATEGIES

STUDENTS WITH SPECIAL NEEDS

Limited English Proficient Students (LEP)
Create on the chalkboard word webs around the dates *1950s* and *1960s.* Ask students to complete the word webs by naming people, events, or terms that they associate with these years. Then have students skim the chapter to complete the word webs. Allow time for discussion of terms that are unfamiliar to students. See other activities labeled **LEP.**

Students Having Difficulty with the Chapter
Organize students into small groups that include students who are performing well and those who are having difficulty. Instruct each group to skim the chapter to find important events of postwar Texas and then to construct a time line. Students may choose to illustrate their time lines with drawings of the events. **LEP**

Auditory Learners
Select and write on the chalkboard the names of ten significant persons mentioned in Chapter 27. Have students review the discussion about each person and list three to five facts about each. Then organize a "What's My Line?" game. Select four panelists and one mystery guest. The mystery guest will draw from a "hat" the person he or she represents. The object is for the mystery guest to answer correctly panel members' yes/no questions. If the identity of the mystery guest remains unsolved after five questions, the guest "wins." The panel members win if they identify the guest before five questions are answered *no.* The rest of the class should monitor the guests' responses and correct incorrect answers. Offer all students an opportunity to participate in the activity. See other activities labeled **A.**

Visual Learners
Have students work in pairs or small groups to create a television commercial that might have appeared in the 1950s. You might wish to videotape the commercials. See other activities labeled **V.**

Tactile/Kinesthetic Learners
Have tactile/kinesthetic students work in pairs or small groups to create a classroom bulletin board display titled "Postwar Texas." Displays should incorporate the main ideas presented in each of the chapter's three sections. See other activities labeled **TK.**

Gifted Students
Have gifted students investigate and report on the current activities and goals of one of the following organizations: LULAC, NAACP, CORE, NOW. Encourage students to contact the organization directly. See other activities labeled **G.**

VOCABULARY
In addition to the boldfaced terms in each section, some students might benefit from discussing the meanings of these terms.

Section 1: *momentum* (p. 546); *freeways* (p. 548); *postwar* (p. 548); *tuition* (p. 549).

Section 2: *forerunner* (p. 553); *unconstitutional* (p. 553); *assassinated* (p. 553).

Section 3: *uniform* (p. 554); *consecutive* (p. 555); *margins* (p. 558); *communist* (p. 558).

CHRONOLOGY
Have students study the Chapter 27 Time Line and identify relationships among the events.

GRAPHIC ORGANIZER
Have students skim the chapter and complete the Chapter 27 Graphic Organizer. *(You might wish to use this activity to review rather than to introduce the chapter.)*

ENRICHMENT
Have students complete the Chapter 27 Enrichment Worksheet.

SECTION 1

FOCUS

Student Experiences (I) Ask students if they live in a rural area, an urban area, or a suburban area. Invite a volunteer to provide definitions to distinguish among the three terms.

INSTRUCTION

Vocabulary (I) You may wish to preteach the following boldfaced terms: *urbanization* (p. 547); *suburbs* (p. 547); *commute* (p. 549). **LEP**

CHAPTER 27 OVERVIEW

In the years after World War II, the growth of business and industry attracted more people than ever to towns and cities. Soon, more Texans lived in urban areas than in rural areas for the first time in history. Jobs were plentiful, and Texans in general enjoyed more wealth than ever before. At the same time, great political and social changes were taking place. In the 1960s, the civil rights movement demanded equal rights for all Americans in voting, education, housing, and employment.

Essential Elements
4A, 4B, 4D, 4E, 4H, 5B, 8A, 8C, 9A, 9B, 9E

CHAPTER 27

POSTWAR TEXAS

The Story Continues...

After World War II, veterans returned to Texas to find that the economy was improving. Many industries began making consumer goods once again, while others continued to provide weapons systems. The ongoing need for weapons and for military bases was a result of the Cold War, a war of words and ideas between the United States and the Soviet Union. As the economy improved, important political and social changes occurred. Many of the women who had worked during the war stayed home to raise families during the 1950s, but some continued to work. Beginning in the 1960s, Texas women joined a growing national movement calling for equal rights for women. The Mexican American and African American movements for equal rights also gained momentum in the 1960s. This chapter looks at these and other changes that took place after World War II.

As you read the chapter, look for the answers to these questions:

1. In what ways did education, employment, entertainment, and lifestyles in Texas change after World War II?
2. What changes took place in civil rights, and how were they brought about?
3. What changes occurred in government in Texas and the United States during the 1960s?

Texas/Dallas History and Archives Division, Dallas Public Library

Texas became a truly urban state during the post-World War II years. This photograph of downtown Dallas was taken during the late 1940s.

1 The Urbanization of Texas

New industries developed during World War II that attracted thousands of Texans to urban areas. Many of these persons remained in the cities at the war's end. Tensions between the United States and the Soviet Union soon resulted in a military standoff known as the Cold War. Military spending for bases and weapons systems contributed

Reading Graphs (I) Ask students to study the graphs on this page. Ask: What was Texas' rural population in 1930 *(nearly 3.5 million)*? How much had the state's urban population grown by 1950 *(by about 2.6 million)*? With the class, discuss reasons for the population shift. **A, V**

Guided Practice (I) Provide each student with a copy of a Texas highway map. Have students use the map to plan a trip by car between two Texas cities. Explain that their trip must include a farm-to-market road, a state highway, and an interstate highway. Students should use a colored marker to designate which roads they will travel. Call on volunteers to share their maps with the class. **A, V, TK, LEP**

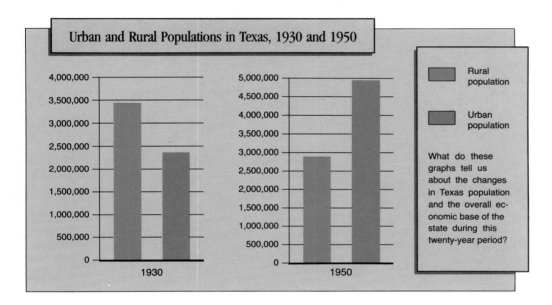

Urban and Rural Populations in Texas, 1930 and 1950

Rural population

Urban population

What do these graphs tell us about the changes in Texas population and the overall economic base of the state during this twenty-year period?

Caption Response
Between 1930 and 1950, the Texas population shifted from rural to urban. The economic base shifted from agriculture to industry.

greatly to Texas' continued prosperity. Opportunities for education, entertainment, and jobs all contributed to the growth and spread of cities, or **urbanization**.

Population Changes. Urbanization in Texas took place later than in the United States as a whole. In 1940, a little more than 45 percent of Texans lived in urban areas. But by 1950, almost 60 percent lived in towns and cities with populations greater than 2,500. During this same period, the rural population of Texas dropped by 400,000.

Houston was the largest city in the state in 1950, with a population of 596,163. Dallas was the second largest city, with a population of 434,462, and San Antonio was the third largest city, with a little more than 400,000 people. Next in order came Fort Worth, Austin, El Paso, Corpus Christi, Beaumont, Waco, and Amarillo.

Suburbs, or towns and cities on the edge of larger cities, were also growing in Texas. Many suburbs were springing up around Houston. Others were appearing between Dallas and Fort Worth. Thousands of Texans moved to suburbs to live but drove to the larger cities to shop and work.

Transportation and Communication. The growth of urban areas was aided by the widespread use of motor

Research (II) Have students research and create a chart showing the estimated travel time for a trip from Dallas to Houston using the following means of transportation: covered wagon, railroad, automobile, airplane. Ask students to display and discuss their findings. **A, V, TK, G**

Geography
The longest highway in Texas is Interstate 10, which extends 878.7 miles from Orange to Houston to San Antonio to Junction to El Paso. Have students identify Interstate 10 on a Texas highway map. The shortest highway is Loop 168 in downtown Tenaha in Shelby County. The road is less than three-quarters of a mile long—about 391 feet. Challenge students to locate the road on a Texas highway map.

Barker Texas History Center

The G.I. Bill of Rights enabled thousands of World War II veterans to attend college. This photograph shows veterans at the University of Texas.

vehicles after World War II. In 1950, there were more than 3 million registered motor vehicles in Texas. Most families found it possible to buy an automobile, and many were buying two cars. (They were much less expensive at this time.) The automobile was no longer a luxury but a necessity.

Thousands of miles of new highways and roads were built in the 1950s. Texas soon had more miles of roads than any other state. The state government contracted for 6,860 miles of new roads in 1950 alone. New funds were also provided to expand the system of farm-to-market roads. The interstate highway system was planned by the federal government in the 1950s. Nonstop freeways of four or more lanes were soon under construction to link major cities.

Air travel became more common for thousands of Texans in the postwar era. Passenger service had begun in the 1920s. In 1928, Dallas, Fort Worth, Houston, Galveston, and San Antonio had air service. There were eleven regularly scheduled airlines operating in Texas by 1950 and nearly 500 airports around the state. Most of these airports were small, private fields, but it was possible by 1950 to fly to nearly any town or city in Texas. Love Field in Dallas became one of the busiest airports in the United States.

A major new form of communication and entertainment came to Texas in the late 1940s: television. The first station was established in Fort Worth as WBAP-TV. In 1950, there were six stations around the state. There were three stations in the Dallas–Fort Worth area, two in San Antonio, and one in Houston.

Few Texas families in 1950 owned a television set. People in cities gathered on the street to look at the new sets in store windows. Soon, however, the television became a common feature in nearly every Texas home. Most people began receiving much of their news and entertainment from television programs.

New Educational Opportunities. Before World War II ended, government leaders made plans to help soldiers and sailors adjust to life after the war. In 1944, the United States Congress passed the Servicemen's Readjustment Act. It was better known as the G.I. Bill of Rights.

Under the new law, veterans of the war received unemployment payments for up to one year. This was done to enable them to look for jobs. Veterans were also provided loans at low rates of interest to buy homes or farms or to

Independent Practice (II) Provide each student with a blank outline map of Texas. Ask students to locate and label on the map the following cities: Houston, Dallas, San Antonio, Fort Worth, Austin, El Paso, Corpus Christi, Beaumont, Waco, Amarillo. Then ask them to use an appropriate reference to find the population of each city in 1950 and today. They should write the population figures next to the city. Then ask them to rank the cities according to population in 1950 and today. Call on volunteers to share their findings and identify possible reasons for population changes. **A, V, TK**

RETEACHING
Have students work in pairs to develop a series of cause-and-effect statements based on the information in Section 1. Call on volunteers to read their statements aloud. **A, LEP**

establish businesses. Thousands of Texas veterans settled in cities and bought homes or started businesses.

The G.I. Bill had a major impact on education. Under the bill, the federal government provided money so that veterans could attend college. The government paid tuition or entrance fees as well as the cost of books and housing.

The number of people attending college in Texas jumped as a result of the G.I. Bill. During the 1944–1945 school year, there were about 22,000 students in Texas' public colleges. By 1946–1947, the number of students increased to more than 54,000.

During the 1950s, it became much more common for Texans to attend college after high school. New colleges and universities were established in the state's cities. More junior colleges were also established to provide the first two years of college courses. Colleges and universities began offering more courses for part-time students so that people could hold jobs while continuing their education.

Urban Styles of Life. New styles of life developed in Texas as urbanization increased. It became more common for people to **commute** to work, meaning they lived in one area but drove elsewhere to their job or place of business. Automobiles and new highways made commuting possible. Many teenagers also drove cars to school.

Shopping habits in cities changed. Shopping centers sprang up in the suburbs and along major city highways. Theaters and restaurants were built in the shopping centers. Downtown business centers in some cities declined as more people chose to go to the new shopping centers, where parking was easy.

During the 1950s, pay increased for Texans even as their hours of work declined. Thus they had more leisure time. Watching television became a popular pastime. Concerts, movies, and theater productions continued to be popular. Large amusement parks were built, offering food, rides, and shows for people of all ages.

Sports became more popular than ever during the 1950s and 1960s. Millions of Texans played golf and tennis or went swimming. Towns and cities formed teams for children and adults in softball, baseball, football, and basketball. Fans turned out to support high school and college teams across Texas. The first major professional sports teams were organized in Texas in the postwar years. Dallas had the first

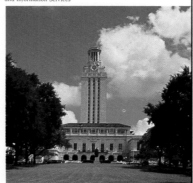

The University of Texas News and Information Services

The Main Building at the University of Texas at Austin, with its famous tower, is a local landmark. It was completed in 1937.

Ralph Barrera / Austin American-Statesman

During the 1970s and 1980s, girls' junior high and high school basketball greatly increased in popularity.

Historical Sidelight
The initials *G.I.* are thought to derive from the phrase *government issue.* Soldiers were issued uniforms and equipment stamped "government issue."

List on the chalkboard the following topics: *education, employment, entertainment, styles of life.* Call on volunteers to select one of the topics and summarize the changes that occurred in Texas after World War II.

ASSESSMENT

Have students complete the Section 1 Review on page 550.

FOCUS

Student Experiences (I) Challenge students to identify present-day African American and Mexican American leaders at the local, state, or national level. If students are unable to do so, assign them to study a local newspaper or national news magazine and report back to the class.

Answers to Section 1 Review

Define: *urbanization*—the growth and spread of cities; *suburbs*—towns and cities on the edge of larger cities; *commute*—to live in one area but drive elsewhere to a job or place of business

Identify: G.I. Bill of Rights—act passed in 1944 that provided unemployment payments, low-interest loans, and money for education to veterans

1. Most people from the suburbs commuted to larger cities to shop and work.
2. They watched them in store windows.
3. College enrollments in Texas increased.
4. Downtown centers declined as more people chose to go to the new shopping centers in the suburbs, where parking was easy.

Evaluating Information: Answers will vary but should be supported with sound reasoning.

Synthesizing Information: Workers had more leisure time to spend on entertainment such as sports and television.

Essential Elements
4C, 4D, 4E, 4F, 4G, 4I, 6A, 6B, 7D, 7E, 7F, 9A

SECTION 1 REVIEW

Define: urbanization, suburbs, commute
Identify: G.I. Bill of Rights

1. Where did people who lived in suburbs shop and work?
2. When televisions first became available, how did most people watch them?
3. What effect did the G.I. Bill have on college enrollments in Texas?
4. Why did shopping in Texas' downtown centers decline in the 1950s?

Evaluating Information: What do you think are the advantages of television over radio? of radio over television? Explain.

Synthesizing Information: How did higher pay and fewer working hours affect workers?

Institute of Texan Cultures

Dr. Hector P. García founded the American GI Forum to help veterans receive health and education benefits.

---

professional football team, which lasted only one season in 1952. The Dallas Cowboys and Houston Oilers began playing football in 1960. Major-league baseball came to Texas in 1962 with the Houston Colt .45's. After moving into the new Astrodome arena in 1965, they were called the Astros. Professional baseball came to North Texas when the Texas Rangers team arrived in Arlington in 1972. ☯

2 The Civil Rights Movement

Life for millions of Americans improved after World War II. Yet not everyone shared in the prosperity. This was especially true for ethnic **minority groups**, or small groups within a population. Blacks and Mexican Americans generally earned less than other Americans. They had fewer opportunities for education or well-paying jobs. Laws and customs denied minorities voting rights and other opportunities.

Fighting Discrimination. People of all backgrounds had fought and died for the United States during World War II. Among the war veterans were thousands of African Americans and Mexican Americans. Members of these minority groups had also supported the war effort at home, working on farms and in factories. When the war ended, they expected to be treated as equals.

Veterans of World War II fought to end **discrimination**, or unfair treatment of people on the basis of their ancestry. One such veteran in Texas was Hector García, a medical doctor. In 1948, Dr. García founded an organization called the American GI Forum. Its purpose was to help veterans obtain an education and health care.

García soon turned his attention to rights for Mexican Texans. He became involved after the director of a funeral home would not let a Mexican Texan family use the chapel to hold services for their son, a war veteran. Soon García was traveling about Texas and other states to organize people to fight for their rights. War veterans demanded that restaurants and hotels serve Mexican Texans on an equal basis. They encouraged people to register to vote. Then they could help elect new leaders who would support passing laws to end discrimination.

The struggle for equal rights was not a new one. The League of United Latin American Citizens, or LULAC, had

INSTRUCTION

Vocabulary (I) You may wish to preteach the following boldfaced terms: *minority groups* (p. 550); *discrimination* (p. 550); *integrate* (p. 553); *civil rights* (p. 553). **LEP**

CITIES OF TEXAS

Illustrating (I) Ask students to read the special feature and then create a travel poster or collage incorporating the information presented. Invite volunteers to display and discuss their posters. Challenge students to incorporate into their posters information from the line graph. **A, V, TK, LEP**

Cooperative Learning (I) Organize students into groups of four or five. Ask members of each group to imagine that they are one of the founders of LULAC, the NAACP, CORE, or NOW. Have them write a list of goals for the organization. Then ask them to write a list of challenges they will face in achieving their goals. Have a spokesperson from each group share the group's lists with the class. **A, LEP**

Fort Worth

Population: 447,619

Metro area population: 1,332,053

Size: 289.4 square miles

Relative location: In north central Texas, 35 miles west of Dallas

Region: Grand Prairie subregion of the Central Plains region

County: County seat of Tarrant County

Special feature: Long known as "Cowtown" because of its stockyards and its historic ties to cattle trails and the cowboy culture

Origin of name: Originally a fort named for General William Jenkins Worth, who served in the Mexican War

Landmarks: Stockyards of the Old West alongside a modern downtown skyline

Economy: Fort Worth has a diverse economy that includes meatpacking, petroleum products, and various manufacturing plants. It is a major center of aviation and electronics manufacturing companies.

History: Fort Worth was established in 1849 as a military outpost, originally known as Camp Worth. Located on the historic Chisholm Trail, Fort Worth grew to be a major center of trade and commerce after a stagecoach line passed through, followed in 1876 by the railroad.

Recreation facilities: Numerous events revolve around Fort Worth's annual Southwestern Exposition and Livestock Show. Parks, lakes, and sporting events dominate outdoor recreation. The city also features the Colonial National Golf Tournament. Six Flags Over Texas theme park is also nearby in Arlington.

Cultural facilities: A symphony, opera, ballet, and art galleries make Fort Worth a major cultural center. The Amon Carter Museum holds one of the country's finest collections of western art, while the Kimbell Art Museum has gained worldwide recognition. The city is home to the Van Cliburn International Piano Competition, which draws the world's best pianists.

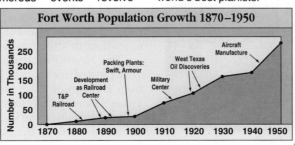

Fort Worth Population Growth 1870–1950

TEXAS VOICES

Analysis (I) Direct students to number a sheet of paper from one to four, allowing space for writing. Then have students explain in their own words each of the four paragraphs from James Farmer's autobiography. For each of the four paragraphs, call on a volunteer to read his or her explanation aloud. **A, LEP**

Guided Practice (I) Have students list on a sheet of paper the following names: Hector P. García, Heman Marion Sweatt, James Farmer, Martin Luther King, Jr., Lyndon B. Johnson. Ask students to write a brief summary of each person's role in the civil rights movement. After students have completed their summaries, ask: In your opinion, which of these people has had the greatest impact on civil rights and why? Allow time for students to express varying opinions. **A**

Essential Elements
4E, 4I, 9A

TEXAS VOICES

James Farmer, a native of Marshall, was a major leader of the civil rights movement from the 1940s through the 1960s. He was one of the founders of the Congress of Racial Equality (CORE). As CORE's national chairman, Farmer worked with prominent African Americans to fight racial discrimination. Farmer dedicated his life's work to improving the lives of all Americans. He was intent upon making the United States a fair and true democracy.

In his autobiography, *Lay Bare the Heart,* James Farmer wrote the following words about his two daughters and about the other Americans whom he considers as his "children":

 A great comfort . . . has been the fact that my daughters—thanks to Lula [his wife], not to me—have turned out well. Both are sensitive and compassionate persons, and that is a joy to behold. Both understand and celebrate the fact that I have other children, millions of others. . . . Most have never seen my face and do not know my name. From the early days . . . to the present, like all who have fought to cleanse this nation, I have helped to pave the roads on which America's black children walk toward new vistas that I shared in shaping.

Vast numbers of these black progeny [children] of the [civil rights] movement know little of the past; they only know the present. Yet in some vague way, they know that the unknown past has made the greater hope of the present possible. They can accomplish much now and aspire to anything in this country. If I am one of their fathers, I am also one of the children of the many fathers and mothers who went before them.

Those who are not black are my children, too. The movement is as much a part of the American experience as is any other odyssey [eventful journey] crowding the pages of the nation's past. . . .

Living was tenuous [difficult] in movement days, but the grasping at liberty, and the reaching toward happiness ennobled life for this nation.

Institute of Texan Cultures

James Farmer helped create CORE, an organization to advance equality for African Americans.

been formed in Corpus Christi in 1929 to support rights for Spanish-speaking people. James Farmer of Marshall became the head of an organization called CORE—the Congress of Racial Equality. The National Association for the Advancement of Colored People—the NAACP—had been formed in the early 1900s to work toward equal rights for black Americans. These and other such organizations were given new strength after World War II.

The NAACP's struggle to regain full voting rights in Texas ended in victory in 1944. Lonnie Smith, a black dentist from Houston, filed a lawsuit to gain the right to vote in Texas' Democratic primary. Because black Texans were not allowed to vote in the Democratic party elections, they had almost no voice in the political system. The United States Supreme Court struck down the white primary in the decision *Smith v. Allwright.* School segregation was another

EXTENSION

Research (III) Challenge students to research and report on specific examples of prejudice and discrimination that existed in Texas in the 1950s. **A, G**

Independent Practice (I) Have students prepare a pictorial essay of the civil rights movement. They may include drawings or pictures cut from magazines. Invite volunteers to display and discuss their projects. **A, V, TK, LEP**

RETEACHING

Use the persons mentioned in Section 2 and identifying clues to create a matching review for students. Have students exchange completed papers with a partner, using their textbooks to check and correct answers. **LEP**

NAACP target in the struggle to end segregation. Another Houston black, Heman Marion Sweatt, filed a suit against the University of Texas in order to enroll in the whites-only University of Texas Law School. In *Sweatt v. Painter* (1950), the Supreme Court ordered the end of segregated professional schools.

Sweatt v. Painter was a forerunner of the much more far-reaching court decision in 1954, *Brown v. Board of Education of Topeka*. The Supreme Court ruled that maintaining separate school systems for black students and white students was unconstitutional. The Court also directed states to begin to **integrate** their public school systems, or allow students of all backgrounds to attend the same schools. Under pressure from the federal government, integration began in school districts in Texas and throughout the South.

Other forms of discrimination and segregation were attacked also. Blacks held demonstrations and marches to demand the right to vote. They also sought the right to eat at the same restaurants and stay in the same hotels as whites.

The movement for **civil rights**, or rights of citizenship, gained national attention through the efforts of a Baptist minister from Georgia, Dr. Martin Luther King, Jr. King led demonstrations against discrimination and segregation throughout the South. He gained the support of millions of Americans of all backgrounds. With this support, he put pressure on leaders in the federal government to pass laws supporting equal rights for all Americans.

New Laws. King gained the support of President John F. Kennedy. When Kennedy was assassinated, President Lyndon B. Johnson continued the cause of civil rights. Under President Johnson, the Civil Rights Act of 1964 was passed. This law made it illegal to discriminate against people on the basis of their ancestry in restaurants, hotels, hospitals, and other public places.

Congress passed the Voting Rights Act in 1965. This law ensured the right of blacks and all others to vote. Federal officials were given the power to register voters in districts where local officials were not allowing blacks to register. A federal law was also passed to make it illegal to discriminate against people in renting or selling houses. As federal laws were passed, old state laws that discriminated were struck down by the courts. Women's groups were among those encouraged by the new laws against discrimination. In

The Granger Collection

Dr. Martin Luther King, Jr., challenged the nation to examine the discrimination and segregation existing in the United States. King led many nonviolent demonstrations in support of civil rights, and the movement gained wide support, partly because of King's excellent speaking ability. He was assassinated in Memphis, Tennessee, in 1968.

Lyndon Baines Johnson Library

Dr. Ralph Abernathy and Dr. Martin Luther King, Jr., were present when President Johnson signed the Voting Rights Act on August 6, 1965.

Constitutional Heritage
Remind students that the United States Constitution is the highest law in the land. The *Brown* case affected only citizens of Kansas, but the Supreme Court ruling—that segregation in schools was unconstitutional—affected people in every state.

ASSESSMENT

Have students complete the Section 2 Review on page 554.

Essential Elements (For Section 3)
4A, 4C, 4D, 4E, 4G, 4I, 5C, 7D, 7E, 9A

SECTION 3

FOCUS

Student Experiences (I) Ask students if any of them have visited Lyndon Johnson's boyhood home in Johnson City, Texas. Invite them to share recollections of their visit. Ask students if any of them have visited other presidents' homes or birthplaces.

Answers to Section 2 Review

Define: *minority groups*—small groups within a population; *discrimination*—unfair treatment of people on the basis of ancestry; *integrate*—to allow students of all backgrounds to attend the same schools; *civil rights*— rights of citizenship

Identify: Dr. Hector P. García—Texas veteran of World War II who established the American GI Forum and worked to gain rights for Mexican Texans; Dr. Martin Luther King, Jr.—Baptist minister and civil rights leader; Henry B. González—in 1956, became first Mexican Texan elected to the Texas Senate in more than 100 years and, in 1961, the first Mexican Texan to be elected to the United States House of Representatives; Barbara Jordan—black Texan elected to the Texas Senate in 1966 after serving in the state House of Representatives, later elected to the United States House of Representatives

1. The Supreme Court ruled that maintaining separate school systems for black students and white students was unconstitutional. The Court also directed states to begin integrating their public school systems.

(Continued on page 555)

SECTION ⭐ 2 REVIEW

Define: minority groups, discrimination, integrate, civil rights

Identify: Dr. Hector P. García, Dr. Martin Luther King, Jr., Henry B. González, Barbara Jordan

1. What was the ruling of the Supreme Court in the case of *Brown v. Board of Education of Topeka?*
2. What was the Civil Rights Act of 1964?
3. How did the large number of minority voters affect government in Texas?

Evaluating Information: Which do you think was more important, the Civil Rights Act of 1964 or the Voting Rights Act of 1965? Why?

Analyzing Information: Why was it important for African Americans and Mexican Americans to have leaders in local, state, and federal government?

20th Congressional District, courtesy Henry B. González

Henry B. González served as a council member for the city of San Antonio and as a state senator. He was elected to a seat in the United States Congress in 1961.

1966, author Betty Friedan founded the National Organization for Women (NOW). Its goal was to end legal restrictions on women and to see that they got equal employment in all fields. NOW chapters sprang up across Texas.

New Leaders. Because of the new laws and the work of civil rights organizations, blacks and Mexican Americans in large numbers registered to vote. They elected new leaders at the local, state, and national levels. In 1956, Henry B. González became the first Mexican Texan elected to the Texas Senate in more than 100 years. In 1961, González was elected to the United States House of Representatives, the first Mexican Texan to hold that office. Other Mexican Texans were elected to city, county, and state offices.

Black leaders were elected in the 1960s for the first time since Reconstruction. One of the best-known new leaders was Barbara Jordan of Houston. She was elected to the Texas Senate in 1966 after serving in the state House of Representatives. Prior to Jordan's election, no black Texan had served in the state Senate in a century. Jordan was later elected to the United States House of Representatives. ⊙

3 Postwar Politics

National as well as state issues of major importance faced Texas leaders in the years after World War II. One of the most important issues involved a dispute between Texas and the federal government over land. Texas gained national attention when Lyndon B. Johnson became president of the United States during the 1960s, one of the nation's most important periods.

The State Scene. Beauford Jester was elected governor of Texas in 1946 and 1948. It was during these two terms that one of the most important programs for education in the state's history was adopted. The program was contained in the Gilmer-Aiken Law.

Under the law, the Texas Education Agency was established. Its task was to set and review standards for schools and for teachers. It was also given the task of providing uniform textbooks for students throughout the state. Funds were provided so that each child in the state could attend school for a minimum of nine months each year. A college degree and training certificate were required of all teachers. A minimum salary was established for all teachers as well.

INSTRUCTION

Vocabulary (I) You may wish to preteach the following boldfaced terms: *tidelands* (p. 555); *sales tax* (p. 555). **LEP**

Analysis (I) Pose the following question for class discussion: How is Lyndon Johnson's Great Society program similar to Franklin Roosevelt's New Deal program? *(You may wish to have students review the discussion of Roosevelt's New Deal on pages 532–34.)* **A**

Governor Jester died in July 1949 while still in office. Allan Shivers became the new governor. Shivers was later elected to three terms of his own, becoming the first Texas governor to serve three consecutive terms.

In 1949, the most important issue to Texans was the Tidelands controversy. This was a dispute between the states and the federal government over control and ownership of **tidelands**, or underwater lands bordering the coast. Most states along the oceans or the Gulf of Mexico claimed land under the water out to a limit of three miles. The federal government argued that the states had given up control of this public land when they joined the United States.

In 1953, Congress passed a law recognizing the states' ownership of tidelands. Still, a suit was filed by the federal government against Texas, which claimed tidelands to a limit of 10.36 miles. Huge deposits of oil lay under the tidelands, and Texas received millions of dollars in income from this oil each year. The federal government wanted to limit the Texas claim to the customary three miles. Texas argued that its 10.36-mile boundary had been established when it became independent from Mexico. The United States recognized that boundary when it annexed Texas. Texas also pointed out that because it was an independent country at the time of annexation, it had not given up control of its public lands to the United States. In 1960, the Supreme Court ruled in favor of Texas.

A key figure in Texas' victory was Price Daniel, who served Texas as attorney general and United States senator. Daniel became governor of Texas in 1957 and served three consecutive terms. The state's first **sales tax** was adopted while Daniel was governor. A sales tax is a tax paid by consumers when they buy certain goods.

A Texan in the White House. John B. Connally became the governor of Texas in January 1963. In November, President John F. Kennedy came to Texas to talk to Connally and other leaders. Kennedy was gathering support for the elections in 1964.

On November 22, 1963, President Kennedy and Governor Connally rode in an open car escorted through downtown Dallas. Large crowds had gathered to see the president. Jacqueline Kennedy, wife of the president, and Nellie Connally, wife of the governor, also rode in the car. At approximately 12:30 p.m., shots rang out. One bullet struck the

Photo by Nancy Schiff, courtesy of Professor Barbara Jordan's Office

Barbara Jordan of Houston served in the United States House of Representatives. She was the first black congresswoman from the South. Jordan became nationally known during the 1974 Watergate hearings, which investigated the election campaign of President Richard Nixon.

2. The Civil Rights Act of 1964 made it illegal to discriminate on the basis of ancestry in restaurants, hotels, hospitals, and other public places.
3. Minority voters elected leaders who would represent them.

Evaluating Information: Answers will vary but should demonstrate sound reasoning based on information presented in the textbook.

Analyzing Information: African American and Mexican American leaders would ensure that the needs and concerns of these minority groups would be addressed.

Historical Sidelight
The Tidelands controversy was a large issue in the presidential election of 1952. President Truman angered many Texans when he vetoed two congressional bills that would have given the states title to the tidelands. Democratic candidate Adlai Stevenson did not side with the states' tidelands claims either. Republican candidate Dwight D. Eisenhower declared in favor of state ownership of the tidelands.

Led by Governor Shivers, Texas Democrats broke from the national Democratic party, and Dwight Eisenhower carried the state of Texas. More Texans voted in that presidential election than had ever voted in a presidential election before.

Guided Practice (I) Ask students to write a paragraph summarizing President Johnson's accomplishments. Call on volunteers to read their paragraphs aloud. **A, LEP**

EXTENSION

Research (III) Ask interested students to conduct library research and present to the class a summary of the various theories surrounding the assassination of President Kennedy. Allow time for the class to ask questions. **A, G**

Walt Sisco, courtesy of Jim Bishop

In this photograph, President John F. Kennedy is shown smiling at onlookers only minutes before he was assassinated. Jacqueline Bouvier Kennedy is seated next to her husband. Governor Connally is seated directly in front of President Kennedy.

Lyndon Baines Johnson Library

After serving in the United States House of Representatives and Senate, Lyndon Johnson was elected vice president in 1960 and became president when John Kennedy was slain in 1963. Johnson was elected to a full term as president in 1964. He chose not to seek reelection in 1968 and returned to his ranch near Johnson City. He died on January 22, 1973.

Historical Sidelight
The hardworking Senator Johnson was quoted as saying, "I seldom think of politics more than eighteen hours a day."

president and another hit Governor Connally. President Kennedy was then struck by a second bullet. Amid the shouting and confusion that followed, the car carrying the president sped away.

The president died of his wounds a short time later at a Dallas hospital. Governor Connally recovered to serve Texas for three terms. Later that day, Vice President Lyndon Baines Johnson was sworn in as the new president. Lee Harvey Oswald was arrested for the murder but was shot and killed by Jack Ruby, owner of a Dallas nightclub.

Lyndon Johnson was born near Stonewall, Texas, in 1908. He grew up in nearby Johnson City. Johnson attended Southwest Texas State Teachers College in San Marcos and taught school upon graduation. Ambitious and hard working, Johnson became involved in politics during the 1930s. He was a strong supporter of the New Deal and President Franklin Roosevelt. Under the New Deal, Johnson became director in Texas of the National Youth Administration.

In 1937, Lyndon Johnson was elected to the United States House of Representatives. He was elected to the United States Senate in 1948. Johnson became known as one of the most skilled politicians in the national government. He was expert at getting bills passed that he supported. When someone opposed him, he liked to take the person aside to talk privately. Few members of Congress were able to resist Johnson, who nearly always persuaded others to support his plans. As a Democrat, he became majority leader in the Senate in 1955. This is a position held by a member of the party with a majority of seats. Texas benefited in a number of ways from having one of its citizens in this powerful position. Through Johnson's efforts, the Manned Spacecraft Center was established in Houston. Today, this headquarters of the National Aeronautics and Space Administration is called the Lyndon B. Johnson Space Center.

The Great Society and Vietnam. President Kennedy had supported civil rights and had challenged Americans to build a better society for all. When Johnson became president, he took up Kennedy's plans and greatly expanded them. In his first address to Congress, Johnson urged passage of a civil rights law:

> We have talked long enough in this country about equal rights. We have talked for one hundred years or more. It is time now to write the next chapter, and to write it in the books of law. I urge you again as I did in 1957 and 1960, to

Analysis (II) Invite a volunteer to read aloud the final paragraph of Sam Rayburn's words of advice. Pose the following questions for class discussion: Think of the politicians you have read about or seen on television. Do you think that they always tell the truth? Are they knowledgeable about our country's history? Are they always honest, fair, and just? Do they talk too much? Encourage students to provide examples to support their responses. **A**

Independent Practice (I) Ask students to list on a sheet of paper the governors of Texas mentioned in this section. Have them write next to each name one significant event that occurred during that governor's term. Finally, ask them to select one of the events and write a brief summary. Call on volunteers to read their summaries aloud. **A, LEP**

SPIRIT OF TEXAS

"Mr. Sam" Rayburn: A Life in Public Service

Samuel Taliaferro Rayburn grew up on a farm in North Texas and attended a one-room schoolhouse in Flag Springs. He decided around age 21 that he wished to go into politics. He said that one day he hoped to become Speaker of the House of Representatives. He studied law at the University of Texas and practiced law in Bonham after being admitted to the bar in 1908.

Rayburn spent his entire adult life as a public servant. As one of the nation's most famous politicians, he was known especially for his honesty. "There are no degrees in honorableness," he once said. "You are or you aren't."

Rayburn's political career began in 1906, when he was elected as a Democrat to the Texas House of Representatives. He became Speaker of the House in 1911, during his third term. In 1912, Rayburn was elected to the United States House of Representatives. There, he represented his district of North Texas. His "down-home" manner and outstanding ability advanced him in the House.

Known to friends and fellow politicians as "Mr. Sam," Rayburn served 48 years and eight months as a congressman, a record. He was reelected to the House 24 times. The last 21 of his years in Congress, he served as Speaker of the House of Representatives of the United States. During his long term of office, Rayburn participated in the passage of much of the important legislation of the twentieth century. He held office during World War I and World War II, and he was active in supporting legislation that put the New Deal into effect during the Great Depression. He called himself a Democrat "without prefix, without suffix, and without apology."

Sam Rayburn once recalled his childhood, offering the following words of advice to young people who would like a career in public service:

When I was a boy, perhaps eight or nine years old, I made up my mind that I was going to make politics and public affairs my life's work. I have never regretted that decision for a moment. For most of my adult life I have been studying and working on our public problems as a lawmaker, and it has been interesting and rewarding and satisfying all the way. It can be for others, too. Although there's no substitute for hard work, determination, and common sense, here are suggestions I have for young people entering politics.

Study the history of our country. Study everything you can about political science. . . . Be honest and candid. Always tell the truth. Be calm and deliberate in your judgments. Be fair, be just. Learn to listen. Don't talk too much.

Painting of Sam Rayburn by Victor Lallier, Dallas

The Sam Rayburn Library

Essential Elements
4I, 6A, 6B, 7D, 7F, 7G

NASA

Mission Control at the Johnson Space Center directed astronauts to the moon and now guides United States space exploration.

SECTION ⭐3 REVIEW

Define: tidelands, sales tax
Identify: Beauford Jester, John F. Kennedy, Lyndon B. Johnson, Economic Opportunity Act

1. What was the Tidelands controversy?
2. How did Lyndon Johnson first become president?
3. What was the Great Society?

Using Historical Imagination: Imagine that it is 1963 and you just heard over the radio that President Kennedy and Governor Connally have been shot. How would you react? Explain.

Synthesizing Information: Why did President Johnson believe that the Great Society could be created in the United States?

enact a civil rights law so that we can move forward to eliminate from this Nation every trace of discrimination and oppression that is based upon race or color.

Johnson believed that the United States had enough power and wealth to provide equal rights, education, jobs, and decent housing for all citizens. Using his knowledge and influence with Congress, Johnson supported passage of the Civil Rights Act of 1964. Congress also passed the Economic Opportunity Act. The purpose of this act was to enable poor people to become better prepared for holding jobs and earning money. One part of the act provided funds for preschool programs. Another part set up the Job Corps to train people who had dropped out of school.

President Johnson won the election in 1964 by one of the largest margins in United States history. Using this support, he launched a program that he called the Great Society. Under the program, Congress passed a law establishing health insurance for Americans over the age of 65. Millions of dollars of federal aid were provided for public schools. An act was passed to provide money to help poor people pay their rent. The Voting Rights Act of 1965 was also passed.

Not everyone supported President Johnson. Some argued that the federal government was spending too much on social programs. Others thought that the federal government had too much power over the states. The most serious opposition grew because of the involvement of the United States in a war in Vietnam in Southeast Asia.

Presidents Eisenhower and Kennedy had supported sending Americans to South Vietnam to help train that country's military forces. The government of South Vietnam was fighting against Communist forces backed by North Vietnam. In 1965, President Johnson ordered American troops to South Vietnam to take a direct part in the fighting. American casualties mounted, as did the cost of the war.

Gradually, many people in the United States turned against the war. They wanted President Johnson to bring American troops home. Students demonstrated on college campuses around the country. As a result of the deep division in the country over the war, President Johnson announced that he would not run for reelection. He spent his remaining time in the White House trying to bring about peace in Vietnam. After retiring from public office in 1969, Lyndon Johnson returned home to Texas. He died in 1973 and was buried in his beloved Texas Hill Country. ⭘

CHAPTER 27 REVIEW

Understanding Main Ideas

1. Describe three changes in Texans' lifestyles that occurred after World War II.
2. What effect did the development of shopping centers have on many downtown business centers?
3. What effect did World War II have on demands for equal rights by women and minority groups?
4. Describe three laws passed by the federal government in an effort to end discrimination or to ensure equal rights for all Americans.
5. List three important provisions of the Gilmer-Aiken Law.
6. How did President Johnson involve the United States in the Vietnam War, and how did that involvement affect his political career?

Thinking Critically

1. **Evaluating Information:** What do you think are the best and worst things about urbanization? Why?
2. **Analyzing Information:** Why do you think war veterans in particular were concerned with equal rights?
3. **Exploring Economics:** In your opinion, why did President Johnson think that the United States as a whole would benefit from the Great Society?

Linking History and Geography

1. What were the major cities of Texas in 1950? In which part of Texas were the cities located, east or west?

2. What valuable resource was Texas seeking to control in the Tidelands controversy?

TAAS Practice
Using Primary Sources

When Barbara Jordan was campaigning for the office of United States representative from Texas, Lyndon Johnson urged people to vote for her. In the following selection, Johnson introduced Jordan to a crowd of people at a campaign party in Austin, Texas:

> Barbara Jordan proved to us that black is beautiful before we knew what that meant. She is a woman of keen intellect and unusual legislative ability, a symbol proving that We Can Overcome. Wherever she goes she is going to be at the top. Wherever she goes all of us are going to be behind her. Those with hurting consciences because they have discriminated against blacks and women can vote for Barbara Jordan and feel good.

1. Johnson believed that Jordan would get to the top because
   A she was black
   B she was creative
   C she was smart and talented
   D she was beautiful and tough
2. Johnson said that people could feel good about voting for Jordan because
   A it would make up for any times they had discriminated against someone
   B he knew she would win
   C she would have all of the people behind her
   D she would prove that We Can Overcome

CHAPTER 27 REVIEW ANSWERS

Understanding Main Ideas

1. Possible answers include: As urbanization increased, more people commuted to work; shopping centers sprung up in the suburbs and along highways; people had more leisure time.
2. The development of shopping centers diverted shoppers away from downtown and led to the decline of many downtown business centers.
3. Women and minority groups had participated in the war effort. When the war ended, they expected to be treated as equals. These groups did not share in the postwar prosperity, however. This inequality led to greater demands for equal rights by women and minority groups.
4. The Civil Rights Act of 1964 made it illegal to discriminate in public places against people on the basis of ancestry. The Voting Rights Act of 1965 ensured the right of blacks and all others to vote. Another federal law was passed to make it illegal to discriminate against people when renting or selling houses.
5. Under the law, the Texas Education Agency was established. Its tasks were to set and review standards for schools and teachers and to provide uniform textbooks for students throughout the state. Funds were provided so that each child in the state could attend school for a minimum of nine months per year, a college degree and training certificate were required of all teachers, and a minimum salary for teachers was set.

6. In 1965, Johnson ordered American combat troops to South Vietnam. As costs and American casualties mounted, Americans became more divided over the war. Because of this deep division, Johnson chose not to seek reelection, thereby ending his political career.

Thinking Critically

1. **Evaluating Information:** Answers will vary but should be supported by sound reasoning and should be based on information presented in the textbook.
2. **Analyzing Information:** Answers may vary but should suggest that veterans had risked their lives for the war effort and expected to be treated fairly.
3. **Exploring Economics:** Opinions will vary but should reflect the idea that the Great Society programs would provide people with the education and jobs necessary for them to become productive members of society.

Linking History and Geography

1. Major cities were Houston, Dallas, and San Antonio. They were located in the eastern part of the state.
2. Oil

TAAS Practice
Using Primary Sources

1. C
2. A

TAAS Practice
Writing Persuasively

Letters will vary but should demonstrate sound reasoning.

Practicing Skills

1. **Sequencing Historical Data:** Time lines should include the major events of Johnson's life.

2. Interpreting Pictures: The 1990 photograph shows high-rise buildings, office towers, and a paved street and sidewalks that came about as a result of the automobile and urbanization.

Enriching Your Study of History

1. **Individual Project:** Songs should demonstrate careful research.

2. Cooperative Project: Brochures should be based on the information presented in the chapter and should demonstrate a cooperative effort.
3. Cooperative Project: Television shows should be based on actual programs of the 1950s and 1960s and should demonstrate a cooperative effort.

Archives Division. Texas State Library

Military Square in San Antonio, 1880

Patrick Dunn

A twentieth-century skyline and modern paving give a new look to the City of the Alamo.

TAAS *Practice*
Writing Persuasively

Imagine that you are a civil rights leader in 1965. Write a letter to your senator, urging him or her to support the Voting Rights Act and explaining why he or she should support the act.

Practicing Skills

1. **Sequencing Historical Data:** Use the information in the chapter and information from an encyclopedia to create a time line of the life of Lyndon Baines Johnson.
2. **Interpreting Pictures:** Compare the photograph of San Antonio in 1880 (above, left) with the photograph of San Antonio in 1990 (above, right). Judging from these two pictures, what effects did the automobile and urbanization have on the San Antonio landscape? Explain how you arrived at this conclusion.

Enriching Your Study of History

1. **Individual Project:** Conduct research to find a song that was sung by people supporting the civil rights movement or by people protesting the war in Vietnam. Share the lyrics of that song with your class, and explain the song's message.
2. **Cooperative Project:** Imagine that you and your partner work for the chamber of commerce of a new suburb in the 1960s. You and your partner will create an advertising brochure. Imagine that you would send this brochure to various businesspeople to convince them to move to your suburb.
3. **Cooperative Project:** Your group will create and perform in a television show, based upon real programs of the 1950s or 1960s. Your parents or guardians and adult friends may help you understand what these programs were like.

CHALLENGES OF A MODERN STATE

TEACHER'S TIME LINE

Section 1	**Section 2**	**Section 3**	**Review and**
Pp. 561–69	Pp. 569–72	Pp. 572–74	**Assessment**
1 Day	1 Day	1 Day	1 Day

⭐ TEACHER MATERIALS

Core: Chapter 28 Time Line; Graphic Organizer 28; Enrichment Worksheet 28; Review Worksheet 28; Reteaching Worksheet 28, Chapter 28 Tests, Forms A & B

Additional: Geography and Graph Skills 28, Informal Evaluation Forms, Test Generator

⭐ OBJECTIVES

1. Discuss reasons for population growth in Texas in the 1970s and 1980s.
2. Describe Texas' modern economy, and discuss the impact of changes in agriculture and the oil industry.
3. Identify major political issues and people in Texas politics from the 1970s to the present.
4. Discuss the challenges facing Texans in the future.

⭐ RESOURCES

BOOKS FOR TEACHERS

Ashman, Charles R. *Connally: The Adventures of Big Bad John*. New York: Morrow, 1974. Life and times of the former Texas governor.

Carson, Rachel. *Silent Spring*. Boston: Houghton Mifflin, 1962. Seminal work on the problems of the environment in our times.

Daniels, A. Pat. *Texas Avenue at Main Street*. Houston: Allen Press, 1964. Detailed and focused story of the development of Houston, Texas.

Diehl, Kemper. *Cisneros*. San Antonio: Corona Pub. Co., 1985. Portrait of the former San Antonio mayor.

Governor Mark White: A Retrospective. Austin: State of Texas, 1987. Examination of the work of the former governor.

Hardeman, D. B. *Shivers of Texas*. New York: Harper & Brothers, 1956. Story of some of the tragic aspects of the former governor.

Pester, John Edward. *Defense Spending and Uneven Interregional Urban Development*. Austin: University of Texas Press, 1986. Study of defense spending in the Sunbelt states, including Texas.

Tower, John. *Consequences*. Boston: Little Brown, 1991. Memoirs of the former senator from Texas.

MULTIMEDIA MATERIALS

Black Women Writers. (video, 28 min.) Southwest Media Services Inc., P.O. Box 140, Wimberley, Texas, 78676. Black women writers (including a Texan) discuss important issues of the times.

Why Vietnam? Churchill Films, 12210 Nebraska Avenue, Los Angeles, California, 90025.

—*Part I: The Roots of U.S. Involvement*. (video, 55 min.) Tracks events leading up to the war.

—*Part II: The Vets; The Vietnamese; Lessons from the War*. (video, 46 min.) Lessons of the war.

STUDENTS WITH SPECIAL NEEDS

Limited English Proficient Students (LEP)

Ask each student to create a fill-in-the-blank review using the names, places, events, and terms discussed in the chapter. Have students exchange and complete the reviews. Allow partners to work together to discuss and correct their answers. See other activities labeled **LEP.**

Students Having Difficulty with the Chapter

Organize the class into three groups, and assign each group one of the sections in Chapter 28. Have the more proficient students in each group help the others skim the headings and main ideas in their assigned section. Then have each group prepare a series of drawings illustrating the main ideas. **LEP**

Auditory Learners

Have auditory learners develop an oral history project by asking family and community members to describe their reactions to events in Texas during the periods discussed in the chapter. Topics might include the state's economic boom of the late 1970s and early 1980s, the impact of the drop in oil prices in the mid 1980s, the Sharpstown Affair, various state elections, Governor White's education reforms, and so on. Have students compile the responses in written form or on tape. See other activities labeled **A.**

Visual Learners

Have visual learners work in small groups to develop brochures to attract businesses from other parts of the country to their area of Texas. Encourage students to examine carefully the information in the chapter before creating their brochures. See other activities labeled **V.**

Tactile/Kinesthetic Learners

Direct students to work in pairs to collect newspaper and magazine articles related to political and economic issues facing Texas. Ask them to sort the articles according to major topics and issues. Then have students create a poster titled "Texas Political and Economic Issues of the 1990s." See other activities labeled **TK.**

Gifted Students

Have gifted students work independently or in pairs throughout the study of Chapter 28 to collect current news articles that reflect the challenges facing Texas in the future. Ask them to compile the articles into book form and make them available to other members of the class to review. See other activities labeled **G.**

VOCABULARY

In addition to the boldfaced terms in each section, some students might benefit from discussing the meanings of these terms.

Section 1: *depressed economy* (p. 563); *trends* (p. 564); *strains* (p. 565); *diversify* (p. 566).

Section 2: *bribes* (p. 569); *exert* (p. 570); *revenue* (p. 571); *lottery* (p. 571).

Section 3: *mobile* (p. 572); *carpooling* (p. 572); *landfill* (p. 573); *extracurricular* (p. 574); *populace* (p. 574); *satellite* (p. 574).

CHRONOLOGY

Have students study the Chapter 28 Time Line and identify relationships among the events.

GRAPHIC ORGANIZER

Have students skim the chapter and complete the Chapter 28 Graphic Organizer. *(You might wish to use this activity to review rather than to introduce the chapter.)*

ENRICHMENT

Have students complete the Chapter 28 Enrichment Worksheet.

Student Experiences (I) With students, discuss changes related to population and the economy that they have observed in their city, town, or community. Ask students to identify challenges that their community faces.

Vocabulary (I) You may wish to preteach the following boldfaced terms: *Sunbelt* (p. 562); *metropolitan areas* (p. 564); *demographers* (p. 564); *economic downturn* (p. 566). **LEP**

CHALLENGES OF A MODERN STATE

CHAPTER

28

The Story Continues...

The Texas population growth and shift to urban areas that began in the 1930s and 1940s continues today. As more and more people have moved to cities, the major industries have changed. Many people now hold service jobs and jobs in advanced technology industries. The government, too, has changed, partly to meet the new demands that have resulted, and partly to meet the changing attitudes of voters.

As Texans move into the twenty-first century, they face many challenges. The growing population means more people to educate, more pollution and waste to contend with, and a greater need for communications and transportation. Texans are already meeting these needs.

As you read the chapter, look for the answers to these questions:

1. What changes are occurring in Texas, and how are Texans meeting these changes?
2. What changes occurred in Texas politics from the 1970s to the present?
3. What challenges face Texans in the future?

1 Texas in Transition

Texas has always been a land of opportunity. It has continued to be that in the 1970s and 1980s on into the 1990s. Yet many changes are occurring in the United States and in the world today. These changes will present new challenges as Texans of the 1990s look to the future.

The Sunbelt and Migration. A majority of Americans lived in the Northeast and Midwest until the 1960s. Then a major shift in population began in the United States. More and more people moved, or migrated, to the South and West. This southern and western rim of the country

Scott Newton

Ann Richards, the second woman to be elected governor of Texas, took office in 1991.

CHAPTER 28 OVERVIEW

Today, Texas faces the challenge of meeting the needs of a rapidly growing population. Developments in communications and transportation must keep pace, the environment must be maintained, and education must be made available to all Texans.

Essential Elements
4A, 4B, 4D, 4E, 4F, 4I, 5B, 5D, 7C, 8A, 8C, 9A

Writing (II) Ask students to imagine that they are speech-writers for Henry Cisneros or some other present-day Texas leader or politician. Have them write a speech, outlining their own view of Texas' role in the future. Invite several volunteers to present their speeches to the class. **A**

Essential Elements
4E, 4I, 9A

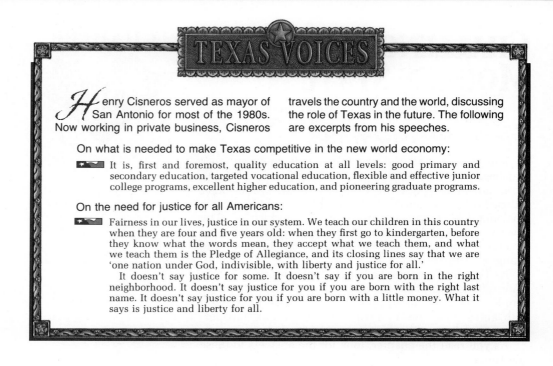

TEXAS VOICES

*H*enry Cisneros served as mayor of San Antonio for most of the 1980s. Now working in private business, Cisneros travels the country and the world, discussing the role of Texas in the future. The following are excerpts from his speeches.

On what is needed to make Texas competitive in the new world economy:

It is, first and foremost, quality education at all levels: good primary and secondary education, targeted vocational education, flexible and effective junior college programs, excellent higher education, and pioneering graduate programs.

On the need for justice for all Americans:

Fairness in our lives, justice in our system. We teach our children in this country when they are four and five years old: when they first go to kindergarten, before they know what the words mean, they accept what we teach them, and what we teach them is the Pledge of Allegiance, and its closing lines say that we are 'one nation under God, indivisible, with liberty and justice for all.'

It doesn't say justice for some. It doesn't say if you are born in the right neighborhood. It doesn't say justice for you if you are born with the right last name. It doesn't say justice for you if you are born with a little money. What it says is justice and liberty for all.

is often called the **Sunbelt** because of its mild and sunny climate. By the 1980s, a majority of the population lived in the South and West.

During the 1970s and early 1980s, thousands of people entered Texas from other regions of the United States and from other countries. The Texas economy prospered in those years, while tough economic times struck major industries in the North and Northeast. Many workers lost their jobs in heavy industries such as steel and automobile manufacturing.

As Texas boomed, people moved here by the thousands, attracted by Texas' healthy economy. Many large corporations moved their headquarters to Texas. Retired people moved to Texas because of its mild climate and its many recreational facilities.

Population Growth. In 1970, Texas ranked fourth in population in the nation, with 11,196,730 people. By 1980, that number had jumped to 14,228,383—third among the

Michael Murphy, Texas Tourist Development Agency

Corpus Christi, often called the "Sparkling City by the Sea," is a favorite resort area. The city is also a major deep-water port. A variety of industries add to the city's economy.

states. The 1990 census showed Texas still in third place with 16,986,510 people. At the present rate of growth, however, Texas will probably pass New York in population during the 1990s and be second in population only to California.

Not all of the population growth in Texas came from northern migration. Many of the people moving to Texas came from southern states. Immigration to Texas from Mexico also expanded the population. Mexico experienced a depressed economy in the 1970s and 1980s. As a result, more than a million Mexican citizens entered the United States in search of employment. In these same decades, thousands of Asian Americans also moved to Texas. Many settled along the Gulf Coast.

Urban Texas. By 1988, more than 80 percent of all Texans lived in urban areas. This is a greater percentage than for the United States as a whole. In fact, Texas is one of the most urbanized states in the nation.

The largest cities in Texas are Houston, Dallas, and San Antonio. Houston is the largest, with a population of more

Robert M. Simmons

During 1986, a train of wagons traveled throughout the state to celebrate the 150th birthday of Texas and remind Texans of their heritage.

Sullivan / TexaStock

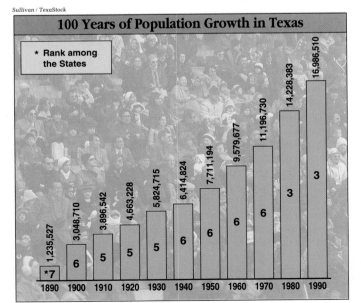

100 Years of Population Growth in Texas

* Rank among the States

1890	1900	1910	1920	1930	1940	1950	1960	1970	1980	1990
1,235,527	3,048,710	3,896,542	4,663,228	5,824,715	6,414,824	7,711,194	9,579,677	11,196,730	14,228,383	16,986,510
*7	6	5	5	5	6	6	6	6	3	3

Between which two years did Texas show the greatest growth in national rank? Between which two years did Texas show the greatest growth in population?

Caption Response
1970 and 1980; 1970 and 1980

Kevin Vandivier

Houston is the largest city in Texas and the fourth-largest city in the United States.

Public Relations Department.
Stephen F. Austin State University

Stephen F. Austin State University was established in Nacogdoches in 1923. A public university, Stephen F. Austin State offers diverse educational programs, ranging from forestry to the fine arts.

than 1.6 million. It is the nation's fourth-largest city. Dallas, the second-largest city in Texas, is home to a little more than 1 million people. Third is San Antonio, with a population of 935,933. El Paso, Austin, and Fort Worth all have populations of more than 450,000.

Suburbs and clusters of smaller cities and towns surround the major Texas cities. Cities combined with the areas of heavy population around them are called **metropolitan areas**. Houston has more than 3 million people within its metropolitan area, and so does the Dallas-Fort Worth Metroplex. According to the 1990 census, Texas had the largest number of metropolitan areas in the nation, 28.

Scholars called **demographers** study population changes and trends. Demographers have made projections, or estimates of future trends, for the population of Texas cities. These estimates predict rapid growth for urban areas and suburbs in the years ahead. Demographers have listed the 50 areas of the United States that they estimate will grow the fastest in the next two decades, and five of them are in Texas. They are Houston, Dallas, San Antonio,

564 *Unit 11*

Austin, and Fort Worth. Austin is one of only four cities in the United States expected to double its population by the year 2005.

Demographers also forecast changes in the ethnic make-up of the Texas population. Minority groups continue to increase in number, and they will play a greater role in the future political changes facing Texas. Already in the early 1990s, African Americans, Mexican Americans, Asian Americans, Native Americans, and other ethnic groups account for more than 50 percent of the Texas population.

The Modern Economy. The Texas economy of the 1990s is a diverse one. Texans earn their living in fields such as the oil industry, farming and ranching, manufacturing, electronics, computer technology, and retail trade. This variety of economic activity enables Texans to enjoy a high standard of living. It also allows Texas to compete successfully with other regions of the United States and with other countries throughout the world.

Until early in this century, most Texans worked on farms and ranches. Today, only about one percent of Texas workers are directly engaged in agriculture. Yet Texas is still a giant among agriculture-producing states. It is a leader in the production of cattle, sheep, cotton, and grain sorghum. Texas is also a major supplier of wheat, vegetables, and fruit.

Many changes have taken place on Texas farms in recent years. The size of the average farm has increased, while the number of people who live and work on farms has decreased. Modern farm machinery, fertilizers, and new strains of crops enable Texas farmers to grow more on the same amount of land.

Since the early 1900s, oil has been the major industry in Texas. Texas workers and the state government became increasingly dependent on income from the oil industry. Many of Texas' boom years occurred when the world faced oil shortages and oil prices rose as a result. For example, the mid 1970s and early 1980s both were periods when the price of oil skyrocketed on international markets. As a result, the oil industry prospered in Texas, and that benefited the entire Texas economy.

The economy suffered, however, when oil prices dropped. A surplus of oil in the world in 1982 caused the price of a barrel of oil to drop from $34 to less than $20.

Texas Christian University

Texas Christian University was established at Fort Worth in 1910. The university was first established as Add-Ran College at Throp Spring in 1873. TCU has gained an excellent academic reputation among Texas universities.

Taylor Johnson / Austin American-Statesman

Austin experienced rapid growth during the 1970s and 1980s. Many important companies opened offices in Austin, and the city became a major center for high technology.

EXTENSION

Illustrating (III) Ask interested students to conduct research to find statistical information regarding oil prices per barrel for the years 1979 to the present. Have them create a bar or line graph to display their findings. Ask students to provide a summary statement about the relationship of oil prices to the Texas economy. **V, TK, G**

University of Texas Medical Center

M. D. Anderson Hospital and Cancer Center, part of the Texas Medical Center in Houston, is world renowned as a health research and treatment facility.

Economics

In the early 1980s, two of the first high-technology companies to announce their headquartering in Austin were Microelectronics and Computer Technology Corporation, better known as MCC, and Advanced Micro Devices. The announcements created a furor of building and speculating.

The announcements by these companies were not the cure-alls that they seemed, however. Economic problems—the oil slump, a worldwide recession, foreign competition—continued to plague Texas. Despite moves to Austin by other high-technology companies, by the early 1990s, many of the office buildings erected in Austin during the early 1980s still had vacancies.

HRW photo by Eric Beggs

Retail businesses, such as this clothing store, employ many Texans.

When oil company profits dipped in the mid 1980s, the Texas economy was hard hit. Workers were laid off or had their pay cut. Available money for investment in economic growth was gone. The amount of tax dollars taken in by state government fell sharply. Many businesses, not just the oil industry, were affected by the **economic downturn**, or decline in business activity. A number of banks and S&Ls—savings and loan companies—went broke.

Recognizing the heavy dependence of the Texas economy on oil, business and government leaders in recent years have encouraged the growth of new and diverse industries. As a result, Texas is rapidly becoming a leader in the fields of electronics and computer technology. The Dallas-Fort Worth area is home to many national and local companies that are moving the Texas economy into a new age of advanced technology. Austin is another high-technology center, with numerous research facilities owned by the government and by private industry. Houston is a leader in high-technology medical research and the development of computer-driven machinery.

As high technology replaces more traditional manufacturing jobs, new jobs are being created in the service industries. At least twenty percent of Texans are employed at jobs in the service industry. These jobs include health care, auto services, food services, and a wide array of business services.

The largest number of Texans today are employed in wholesale trade and retail trade. This is the exchange of goods and services to stores and consumers. Construction is another major field of employment. More than two percent of Texas workers are employed in the building of homes and offices, which are needed for our expanding population.

Economic Challenges. The need to diversify the Texas economy has created new challenges as Texans look to the twenty-first century. Jobs lost in manufacturing because of increased use of computers have been replaced by new jobs in the computer field itself. Farmers who make less money from their crops because of dwindling water supplies and increased foreign competition are forced to diversify. Today, Texas farmers are switching to new crops such as soybeans, sunflowers, and higher-yielding strains of corn and wheat. Some farmland or ranchland that once

Illustrating (I) Ask students to create two drawings: one illustrating Houston today and another illustrating Houston as capital of the Republic of Texas. Invite students to display their drawings in the classroom. **V, TK, LEP**

Writing (I) Have students read the special feature and study the pie graph. Then ask them to write a paragraph telling in what occupation they would like to work if they lived in Houston and why. Call on volunteers to read their paragraphs aloud. **A, V**

CITIES OF TEXAS

Houston

Essential Elements
4B, 4H, 5B, 9B

Population: 1,630,553

Metro area population: 3,301,937

Size: 579.5 square miles

Relative location: The southeast corner of Texas, between the Trinity and Brazos rivers, approximately 50 miles from the Gulf of Mexico

Region: Gulf Coastal Plains

County: County seat of Harris County

Special feature: The largest city in Texas and the South

Origin of name: Named for Sam Houston, commander-in-chief of the Texas forces during the Texas Revolution and the first president of the Republic of Texas

Landmarks: The Houston skyline, the Astrodome, the San Jacinto Monument

Economy: The third-largest port in the nation, Houston is a center of trade and commerce for Texas, the South, and the Gulf of Mexico. The city is located at the heart of major oil

production facilities, including oil refining and petrochemical plants.

History: A small riverboat landing was established on Buffalo Bayou in 1836 by two brothers, Augustus and John Allen. For two years, the town served as capital of the Republic of Texas. Throughout the 1800s, Houston grew steadily as

a center of the southeast Texas cotton and timber industry. The oil industry helped Houston become the fourth-largest city in the United States today.

Recreation facilities: Near the Gulf of Mexico, Houston offers tourists a wide variety of outdoor and sporting activities.

Cultural activities: Symphony, opera, and ballet productions are prominent in Houston's cultural life. There are numerous museums, including the Museum of Fine Arts. Additional attractions are the Hermann Park Zoo and Zoological Gardens, the Planetarium, and the Lyndon B. Johnson Space Center.

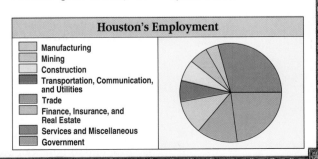

Houston's Employment

- Manufacturing
- Mining
- Construction
- Transportation, Communication, and Utilities
- Trade
- Finance, Insurance, and Real Estate
- Services and Miscellaneous
- Government

Independent Practice (II) Present the following situation to students: It is 1981 and you have just been laid off from your steel industry job in the Northeast. You have decided to relocate to Texas. Write a letter to an employer in a specific Texas city, explaining why you have chosen to relocate and the kind of job you are seeking. Ask students to base their letters on the information presented in Section 1. Call on volunteers to read their letters aloud. **A**

RETEACHING
With the class, outline on the chalkboard the information in Section 1. Use the section subheadings as subtopics.
LEP, A, V

The Image Bank

In recent years, the film industry has been attracted to Texas, where there is a wide variety of scenery and talent.

was used to produce grazing cattle today is being used to grow grapes for the profitable Texas wine industry. Businesses and communities that once depended on oil revenue have begun to offer new products and retrain workers in new skills. And in support of the Texas Film Commission, Governor Richards and others have sought to attract more of the movie industry from California to Texas.

Changes outside the state also present new opportunities in the Texas economic future. The United States government has enacted new trade laws with Mexico, which will open up trade between the two countries. Texans should benefit greatly from this new relationship, as Texas and its neighbor Mexico become stronger economically and more dependent on each other.

CLOSURE

Ask students: Do you think the economic outlook for Texas is positive or negative? Encourage students to give reasons for their answers.

ASSESSMENT

Have students complete the Section 1 Review on page 569.

SECTION 2

FOCUS

Past Learning (I) Challenge students to name Texas' current governor and the governor's political party. Point out to students that the Democratic party has been the majority party in Texas since the days of the Republic.

Political changes in other parts of the world will affect Texas in the future. Western European countries began unifying their economy in 1992 and could rival Japan and the United States as the world's most dominant economic power. Texas businesspeople are trying to improve our state's economic ties, both to Japan and to the new European economy. The state government has an office dedicated to helping Texans sell products in Europe. New opportunities are also opening up in the former Soviet Union as it moves toward a free-market economy. Soon, it may be common to see Texans selling cattle and cotton in Moscow, demonstrating oilfield products in Siberia, and singing the Texas blues in St. Petersburg. ✪

② Politics and Parties

Texas government has grown and changed along with its population and economy. As tax resources have tightened, the amount of money needed for government services has grown. Since the successes of the civil rights movement of the 1960s, Texans of all backgrounds have become involved in deciding the direction of state government. Another major change since the 1960s has been the growth of the Republican party. Texas today is a two-party state.

Modern Politics. By the 1960s, Democrats had won every election for governor in Texas for about 100 years. Preston Smith was elected governor in 1968 and again in 1970. The three previous governors—Democrats Allan Shivers, Price Daniel, and John Connally—had each been elected to three consecutive terms. This three-term pattern was broken when Dolph Briscoe defeated Smith in the 1972 Democratic primary. (Connally later switched parties.)

Briscoe was swept into office amid demands for reform in state government. A scandal involving a number of state officials had been uncovered in 1971. The scandal was known as the Sharpstown Affair. Several state government officials were accused of accepting bribes from Frank Sharp, a Houston banker. Sharp wanted members of the state government to pass laws that favored his business interests. The speaker of the House and another state representative were convicted of hatching a secret plan to pass legislation that was favorable to Sharp.

Several reforms were enacted by the Texas legislature as a result of the Sharpstown Affair. Meetings and records

SECTION ★ REVIEW

Define: Sunbelt, metropolitan areas, demographers, economic downturn

1. Why did many people from other parts of the country move to Texas during the 1970s and early 1980s?
2. What was Texas' rank in population size in 1990?
3. What two new industries are rapidly growing in Texas?
4. Why are Texas farmers having to diversify?

Analyzing Information: List three reasons that the population of Austin may double in the next two decades.

Synthesizing Information: What factors are leading to a change in the relationship between Mexico and Texas?

Archives Division, Texas State Library

Dolph Briscoe of Uvalde was elected governor in 1972. The increasing cost of government was a major concern during his terms in office.

Answers to Section 1 Review

Define: *Sunbelt*—the southern and western rim of the nation that is known for its mild, sunny climate; *metropolitan areas*—cities combined with the areas of heavy population around them; *demographers*—scholars who study population changes and trends; *economic downturn*—decline in business activity

1. Texas' booming economy drew people to the state.
2. Third
3. Electronics and computer technology
4. Farmers are having to diversify because of dwindling water supplies and increased foreign competition.

Analyzing Information: Possible answers include: Austin is the state capital, it is a high-technology center, more businesses from other parts of the country will move to Austin, businesses will start up to meet the needs of a growing population.

Synthesizing Information: The United States government has enacted new trade laws with Mexico, and immigration from Mexico is growing.

Essential Elements
4A, 4B, 4D, 4E, 4F, 4G, 4I, 9A, 7C, 9E, 9F, 9G

Photo by Greg Vimont, courtesy of the Office of the Governor

Mark White was elected governor in 1982. His administration placed great emphasis on education.

Larry Kolvoord

John Tower was the first Republican elected to the United States Senate from Texas since Reconstruction. Tower won election in 1961 and served in the Senate for more than twenty years.

were made open to the public. Elected officials had to report how they acquired and spent donations to their election campaigns.

The length of the governor's term of office was changed in 1972, when Texas voters approved lengthening the term from two to four years. In 1974, an attempt was made to rewrite the Texas Constitution, originally written in 1876 and now cluttered with hundreds of confusing amendments. Delegates to the 1974 constitutional convention never agreed on a finished document to submit to Texas voters for approval, however.

A small number of legislators had helped to expose the Sharpstown scandal. Among them was Frances "Sissy" Farenthold. She ran unsuccessfully for governor in 1972 and was nominated as candidate for vice president of the United States in the same year. Farenthold was one of a growing number of women taking part in politics since the 1960s, when the women's rights movement encouraged their participation. Several women have served in the Texas legislature. In the late 1980s, Texas' three largest cities each elected a woman as mayor: Kathy Whitmire of Houston, Annette Strauss of Dallas, and Lila Cockrell of San Antonio. In 1983, Ann Richards became state treasurer, and in 1990 she was elected governor of Texas.

The civil rights movement of the 1960s helped remove barriers from the political system for all Texans. African Americans and Mexican Americans are today represented in the Texas legislature, in offices of state government, and in local government positions throughout Texas.

Texas is also gaining power in the national government as its population grows. It has the third-greatest number of representatives in Congress, trailing only California and New York. Texans hold powerful positions in the federal government and exert influence worldwide. Following two terms as vice president in the 1980s, George Bush was elected president of the United States in 1988. Bush had worked in Midland's oil industry in the 1950s and 1960s. He served as a congressman from Houston in the late 1960s. President Bush's secretary of state, James Baker, is another Texan.

A Two-Party State. Dolph Briscoe ran for reelection as governor in 1978 but lost the nomination of the Democratic party to Attorney General John Hill. Many political experts

Independent Practice (II) Write on the chalkboard the following statement from the text: "Texas today is a two-party state." Ask students to write a brief paragraph explaining the statement and to list examples from the textbook that support the statement. Call on volunteers to read aloud their paragraphs and lists. **A**

RETEACHING
Use the names mentioned in Section 2 to create a "Who Am I?" game for students. One student should provide a clue from the textbook, while the rest of the class guesses the identity. Continue the activity until all of the students have participated. **A, LEP**

thought that Hill could not lose to a Republican candidate. They were wrong. Dallas businessman William Clements became the first Republican governor of Texas since Reconstruction days.

Republicans had begun to gain some support in Texas in the 1950s. A majority of Texans supported Dwight Eisenhower, the Republican candidate for president and winner in the elections of 1952 and 1956. Texas voters also gave a majority of their support to Republicans Richard Nixon in 1972 and Ronald Reagan in 1980 and 1984. George Bush won the Texas vote in 1988. In 1961, John Tower became the first Republican senator from Texas since Reconstruction. In 1984, Phil Gramm became the second Republican elected to the United States Senate from Texas. Today, Gramm has become a powerful force in the Senate, where he serves with Democratic senator Lloyd Bentsen.

Despite the gains made by Republicans, Democrats won the governor's office again in 1982. Mark White became governor after defeating William Clements, but Clements challenged White in the election of 1986 and won. Even though the Democrats continued to win the majority in the Texas legislature and in local elections statewide, it was clear by the mid 1980s that Texas had become a true two-party state for the first time in its history.

In the 1990 election for governor, Midland oilman and rancher Clayton Williams was the Republican candidate. The Democrats ran State Treasurer Ann Richards. Richards won, becoming the second female governor in Texas history, Miriam Ferguson being the first.

Political Issues in the Future. Many complex and controversial issues face Texans and their government in the 1990s. Funding for state and local services is a major problem facing lawmakers. The federal government began reducing money to the states in the 1980s. This action has forced many states to raise taxes and to find new sources of revenue. For example, Texas legalized horse-race betting in 1987 and in 1991 approved a state lottery to raise funds. Some people have proposed a state income tax as well.

In recent years, the state has had to raise money for environmental protection programs. The crucial need to protect our fragile resources—air, land, and water—will increase the burden on state taxpayers. The ability to raise

Archives Division, Texas State Library

William Clements became the first Republican governor of Texas since Reconstruction when he was elected to office in 1978.

James Newberry

The slogan "Don't mess with Texas" has been part of one of the nation's most successful campaigns against littering.

SECTION 3

FOCUS

Predicting (I) Ask students to raise their hands if they have ever visited Dallas-Fort Worth, Houston, San Antonio, or Austin. *(If your students live in or near one of these cities, delete its name.)* Ask: What common challenge do you think these cities face? *(Lead students to conclude that Texas' large urban areas must deal with problems created by rapid population growth.)*

SECTION 2 REVIEW

Identify: Frances "Sissy" Farenthold, Ann Richards, William Clements, Phil Gramm

1. What reforms were enacted in response to the Sharpstown Affair?
2. How did the majority of Texans vote in presidential elections during the 1970s and 1980s?
3. What are two programs that will require state funding?

Making Decisions: If you were a state senator, would you vote in favor of a state lottery? Why or why not?

Seeing Cause and Effect: Match each cause to its effect. *Causes:* Frank Sharp wanted laws that favored his business; the legislature wished to prevent anything like the Sharpstown Affair from recurring; Republicans were elected to state office in the 1970s and 1980s; the federal government began reducing money to the states. *Effects:* Texas legalized horse-race betting; Texas was once again a two-party state; leaders planned to accept bribes from Sharp; legislative reforms were enacted.

Texas Department of Transportation

Lakes and reservoirs give Texans a source of water and recreation.

needed revenues and keep taxes relatively low will be the political challenge of the future. State government finds itself trying to address old problems as well as new ones. Funding for education, highways, and the crowded prison system are issues that arise during every session of the Texas legislature. ✪

3 Challenges Ahead

A changing economy and a steadily growing population present major challenges for Texas in the years ahead. An expanding and mobile population will demand farsighted approaches to dealing with problems in our cities. Environmental issues will increasingly dominate our political debates. Education will be the key to facing the challenges of the future, for each citizen holds a responsibility to participate in the decision-making as Texas becomes a more important part of the world community.

The Challenge of Growth. Rapid population growth has created problems in many areas of Texas, even as it has brought new opportunities. If present trends continue, the main area of growth in Texas will be within a triangle in the heartland of the state—from Dallas-Fort Worth down to the Houston area and over to San Antonio and Austin.

These high-growth areas face tremendous challenges to provide basic city services. These services include roads, sewer lines, water lines, and solid waste disposal. State and local governments must also pay a large part of educational costs. They are challenged to provide balanced programs to create jobs, protect local environments, and provide more recreational facilities for their citizens.

Traffic congestion has become an unpleasant fact of life in a number of Texas cities. Because the number of private vehicles using Texas roads and highways continues to grow, state and local governments both are trying to encourage other means of transportation. Some cities have expanded bus service. Large urban areas continue to expand their huge system of freeways, in some cases creating special express lanes for carpooling Texans. In some Texas cities, streetcars are making a comeback. A plan is underway to connect Texas' major cities by a high-speed rail line.

Another increasing problem in Texas is the growth of crime. Drug abuse, lack of educational and economic

Brainstorming (I) Organize students into three groups, and assign each group one of the issues discussed in the subsection "The Challenge of Growth" *(providing basic city services, traffic congestion, growth of crime)*. Ask each group to brainstorm to develop a local government plan to deal with its assigned issue. Have a spokesperson from each group present the group's plan to the class. **A**

Guided Practice (I) Ask each student to list three things that he or she is doing to fulfill his or her responsibility to maintain the environment. Have students share their lists as you create a class list on the chalkboard. **A, TK, LEP**

EXTENSION

Research (II) Ask interested students to work together to research and prepare oral reports on Texas' underground aquifer system. Students should detail the aquifers' origins and use, using diagrams and drawings. **A, V, TK, G**

---

opportunities, and a breakdown of the family unit are often cited as causes for the state's soaring crime rate. In the 1990s, the state has struggled to meet its drug and crime problems by increasing emphasis on drug education, law enforcement, and prison reform.

The Challenge of the Environment. Texans of today depend on the land no less than did Texans of 150 years ago. We now realize that all our abundant natural resources are precious and must be protected. We must exercise care in the use of resources such as timber and soil. The Dust Bowl of the 1930s serves as a reminder of what can happen when steps toward conservation are not taken. Today, soil conservation districts operate throughout Texas. The purpose of these districts is to help farmers save the soil from erosion.

Stopping pollution of the air and water is another environmental priority. In 1970, Congress created the Environmental Protection Agency to direct efforts to control air and water pollution. To direct the effort at the state level, Texas has the Air Control Board and the Texas Water Commission. Nearly all Texas cities have agencies to control pollution as well.

Management of our existing water supply is another environmental challenge. The growth of Texas has put a serious strain on reservoirs and aquifers. The aquifers in Texas are lowering every year from the demands of cities and of farmers who use them to irrigate their crops. Politicians from various regions of the state often find themselves at odds over water management. As water supplies become more critical, a statewide water plan that benefits all Texans must be devised.

More people and more industry in Texas means more garbage and waste materials. Disposal of solid waste is an important issue in the 1990s as landfill space becomes scarcer. Every citizen can do his or her part by recycling materials rather than throwing them away without thinking.

Cooperation between government and industry is necessary in the fight to maintain our environment. But every citizen has a responsibility as well. By not littering, by recycling whenever possible, and by avoiding needless destruction of plant and animal life, Texans can help keep Texas clean, healthful, and beautiful.

Texas Department of Agriculture

The underground aquifer system provides much-needed water for many agricultural areas of the state. Water problems are likely to become increasingly important as the water level of the aquifer system drops. What steps do you think should be taken to help solve our water problems?

Texas Department of Agriculture

Soil conservation districts work with Texas farmers and ranchers in developing practices to save the land.

Making Decisions: Answers will vary but should demonstrate sound reasoning.

Seeing Cause and Effect: Frank Sharp wanted laws that favored his business—leaders planned to accept bribes from Sharp; the legislature wished to prevent anything like the Sharpstown Affair from recurring—legislative reforms were enacted; Republicans were elected to state office in the 1970s and 1980s—Texas was once again a two-party state; the federal government began reducing money to the states—Texas legalized horse-race betting.

Caption Response
Answers will vary but should demonstrate sound reasoning.

Environmental Awareness
An Austin-based organization, Children's Alliance for the Protection of the Environment, provides answers to environmental questions from children all over the world. Your students can write to the organization at:

CAPE
P.O. Box 307
Austin, TX 78767

Public Relations Department. Texas Instruments

The computer industry has grown rapidly in recent years, and many major computer companies are now located in Texas.

SECTION 3 REVIEW

Identify: Environmental Protection Agency, Mark White

1. List two ways in which Texas cities are meeting traffic problems.
2. What can Texas citizens do to help protect their environment?
3. What were two results of Governor White's education committee?

Evaluating Information: What do you think is the most serious problem facing Texas today? Explain your answer.

Writing Persuasively: Write a letter to your state representatives, urging them to take action on some challenge facing Texas today. Give reasons that they should act on this issue.

The Challenge of Education. There is a growing competition among major countries in the world. New technology has replaced older methods in business and industry. For these reasons, the education needs of Texans have changed and will continue to change in the years ahead. Texas must be prepared to meet the competition by having informed citizens, new ideas and skills, and new products.

In 1984, Governor Mark White appointed a committee to study the needs and problems of education in Texas. As a result of the committee's findings, the state legislature enacted a major reform program to strengthen the public school system. Requirements for passing courses were raised for all students. General examinations of basic skills were required at several different levels of schooling. Higher standards were required of students who wished to participate in extracurricular activities. Higher standards for teachers were encouraged as well.

Governor Clements and Governor Richards have since carried forward Governor White's demand for higher quality in Texas education. Better-educated Texans will help the state compete in the growing fields of technology and computer science. They will help Texas create more and better-paying jobs. We know that new businesses flourish in, and companies move to, locations with a highly educated populace. Our economic future is no longer tied only to oil or cattle, but rather to information and ideas.

Besides being important to the economy, well-educated people are necessary to a democratic society. Citizens must be aware of their rights and responsibilities. In the past, Texans have been able to meet change and challenge. They have long been admired for their independent spirit and willingness to take a chance. Sound education will enable Texans to meet the future with the same hope and courage.

Texas and the Future. Modern technology is rapidly revolutionizing the world. Satellite communications, computer technology, and cable television have shrunk the world to what one scholar called "the global village." No one is isolated from the rest of the world anymore. As a result, many changes await Texans of the future, and change always presents problems. Yet the opportunities for Texans in this global village are tremendous. Our history has been an exciting one, but the future of Texas on the world stage promises even greater adventures to come. ○

CHAPTER 28 REVIEW

Understanding Main Ideas

1. How has the Texas population changed in the past twenty years, and how is it expected to change in the future?
2. Describe two future challenges to the Texas economy.
3. What important change has occurred in Texas politics in the last twenty years?
4. What important issues face state government today?
5. Describe two challenges to Texas and how they are currently being met.
6. Why is protection of the environment important?

Thinking Critically

1. **Exploring Economics:** How are population growth and economic growth related?
2. **Synthesizing Information:** How will Texas depend on other nations even more in the future?
3. **Analyzing Information:** As more Texans move to cities, and as Texas depends more on service and technology industries, what do you think may happen to farmers and ranchers?

Linking History and Geography

1. Why is protection of reservoirs and aquifers an important issue for state government leaders?
2. What reasons can you give for having a landfill in your community? What reasons can you give against it?

TAAS *Practice*
Using Primary Sources

In October 1990, Bob Bullock, then Texas Comptroller of Public Accounts, wrote an article for a state business journal, *Texas Town & City.* The following selection is from Bullock's article:

Texas is a popular location for film and video projects that have a multi-million-dollar impact on state and local economies. Some 184 film and television projects with budgets totaling nearly $628 million have been filmed entirely or primarily in Texas since 1983. With typical productions spending up to 50 percent of their budgets in the location area, it's not surprising that film crews have become welcome visitors in many Texas communities.

Texas offers filmmakers dramatic and varied scenery, relatively low production costs, and a large community of Texas-based film professionals, including writers, actors, and technicians of every kind.

And the movie and video industry offers Texas something in return: literally millions in local spending, for everything from hotels and catering to construction materials to employment for the state's growing body of home-grown film talent.

The rise of location filming has ended the days when most films were made on Hollywood back lots, regardless of the story's setting. The portability and reliability of modern film equipment makes it possible for today's filmmakers to move their productions wherever the script or the "look" dictate; the sunset Indiana Jones rode into in the final scene of his latest movie was shot near Amarillo. . . .

Filmmakers and industry analysts have estimated that the cost of making a movie in Texas can be as much as 30 percent lower than equivalent costs for a Hollywood production.

CHAPTER 28 REVIEW ANSWERS

Understanding Main Ideas

1. The population has grown, and Texas now ranks third in population in the nation. Much of the growth has resulted from northern migration and immigration from Mexico. During the 1990s, Texas is expected to pass New York and be second in population only to California.
2. Possible answers include: diversifying the economy, strengthening economic ties to other countries, and providing jobs.
3. Texas has become a two-party state.
4. Possible answers include: funding government programs, dealing with rapid population growth, providing educational and economic opportunities, and protecting the environment.
5. Possible answers include: meeting the needs of a growing population—cities are finding alternate means of transportation; drug and crime problems—increased emphasis on drug education, law enforcement, and prison reform; protection of the environment—the operation of soil conservation districts, the Air Control Board and the Texas Water Commission; education—the carrying forward of Governor

White's demand for higher quality in Texas education.

6. Because most resources are difficult, if not impossible, to replace, it is important to protect them. Protection of the environment will keep Texas a clean, healthful, and beautiful state.

Thinking Critically

1. **Exploring Economics:** Businesses and jobs are created to meet the needs of a growing population.
2. **Synthesizing Information:** Neighboring Texas and Mexico will become more dependent upon each other as the United States' new trade agreement opens up trade with Mexico. Texas businesspeople are working to improve economic ties to Japan and to the new unified economy of Europe. As the former Soviet Union moves toward a free-market economy, new trade opportunities are opening up.
3. **Analyzing Information:** Answers will vary, but students should recognize that the number of farmers and ranchers may continue to decline. As the population grows, however, the demand for the goods produced by farmers and ranchers may rise.

Linking History and Geography

1. Texas' population growth has strained the state's reservoirs and aquifers. It is up to the state's leaders to deal with water management.
2. Answers will vary but should demonstrate sound reasoning.

TAAS *Practice*
Using Primary Sources

1. A
2. C

TAAS *Practice*
Writing Persuasively

Speeches should be clear and persuasive.

Practicing Skills

1. **Writing Persuasively:** Letters should be persuasive and supported by sound reasoning.

---

2. **Comparing Pie Graphs:** El Paso; services, miscellaneous; El Paso

Enriching Your Study of History

1. **Individual Project:** Reports should demonstrate thorough research.
2. **Cooperative Project:** Brochures should demonstrate knowledge of the factors that might entice businesses to relocate to Texas.

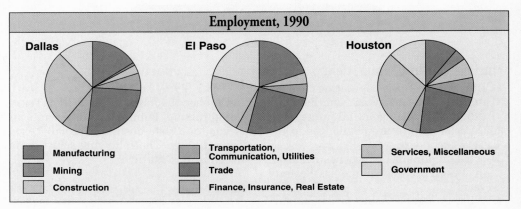

Employment, 1990

Dallas El Paso Houston

Manufacturing

Mining

Construction

Transportation, Communication, Utilities

Trade

Finance, Insurance, Real Estate

Services, Miscellaneous

Government

1. One reason **not** given for the film industry's move to Texas is
   A viewers prefer Western movies
   B it costs less to make movies in Texas than in Hollywood
   C Texas offers a variety of scenery
   D there are many Texans who are able to work in the movie industry
2. Bullock says the move of the film industry to Texas is good because
   A many people like movies made in Texas
   B some Texas actors will become famous
   C it will help the Texas economy
   D the movie industry will grow

TAAS *Practice*
Writing Persuasively

Imagine that you are the mayor of your town or city. Write a short speech urging your fellow citizens to do what they can to protect the environment. Give clear, concrete examples of things that your fellow citizens can do to help.

Practicing Skills

1. **Writing Persuasively:** Write a letter to the editor of your newspaper, taking a stand on the issue of lengthening the school year to improve education.
2. **Comparing Pie Graphs:** Study the pie graphs on this page. Which city has no employees in the mining industry? Which industry employs the most people? Which city has the most employees in government?

Enriching Your Study of History

1. **Individual Project:** Use your library to find out more about one of the following: the high-speed rail line, the savings-and-loan crisis, Mark White's education programs, the film industry in Texas, changes in Texas' relationship with Mexico. Present your findings to the class.
2. **Cooperative Project:** Working with a partner, create a brochure to send to prospective businesses, urging them to move to Texas.

TEXANS AND THEIR CULTURE

TEACHER'S TIME LINE

Section 1	Section 2	Section 3	Review and Assessment
Pp. 577–79	Pp. 579–83	Pp. 583–88	
1 Day	1 Day	1 Day	1 Day

TEACHER MATERIALS

Core: Chapter 29 Time Line; Graphic Organizer 29; Enrichment Worksheet 29; Review Worksheet 29; Reteaching Worksheet 29; Chapter 29 Tests, Forms A & B

Additional: Geography and Graph Skills 29, Informal Evaluation Forms, Test Generator

OBJECTIVES

1. Cite influences of various groups on Texas culture.
2. Discuss the musical tradition of Texas, and identify significant Texas musicians.
3. Explain the images of Texas in popular culture.
4. Cite Texans who have played roles in or have contributed to popular entertainment.
5. Discuss the art and literature of Texas, and identify important artists, writers, and historians of Texas.

RESOURCES

BOOKS FOR TEACHERS

Dobie, J. Frank. *A Guide to Life and Literature of the Southwest*. Dallas: Southern Methodist University Press, 1942. Dobie's guide to culture in the Southwest.

Dobkins, Betty Eakle. *The Spanish Element in Texas Water Law*. Austin: University of Texas Press, 1959. Influence of Spanish law and traditions on Texas water laws.

Dugger, Ronnie, ed. *Three Men in Texas*. Austin: University of Texas Press, 1967. Life and times of Bedichek, Webb, and Dobie.

Eby, Frederick. *The Development of Education in Texas*. New York: Macmillan, 1925. History of education in Texas.

MacCorkle, Stuart A. *Cities from Scratch*. San Antonio: Naylor, 1974. Early city planning of new towns in Texas.

The Melting Pot. San Antonio: Institute of Texan Cultures, 1977. Study of cuisine of different ethnic groups in Texas.

Paredes, Américo. *A Texas-Mexican Cancionero*. Chicago: University of Illinois Press, 1976. Study of the folksongs along the lower Texas-Mexico border.

Texas Historian. Austin: Texas State Historical Association, published five times per year. Student writings on local history as a way to preserve Texas' cultural heritage.

MULTIMEDIA MATERIALS

Art and Architecture Series. (filmstrips/cassettes) Institute of Texan Cultures, P.O. Box 1226, San Antonio, TX 78294. Presents the lives and works of Texas architects and artists.

—*Festivals and Ethnic Gatherings*. A look at ethnic celebrations across the state.

—*Health, Medicine, and Healing Series*. Two-part series on Mexican-American folk healing.

Singin' Texas. (cassette) E-Heart Press, 3700 Mockingbird Ln., Dallas, TX 75205. Cassette of song reproductions, with songbook selected by folklorist F.E. Abernethy.

◈ GENERAL STRATEGIES

STUDENTS WITH SPECIAL NEEDS

Limited English Proficient Students (LEP)
Have students skim the chapter and create two lists: one of the names, terms, or titles that are familiar to them, and another of those that are unfamiliar. As students study the chapter, have them write next to the items on both lists significant facts to remember. Have them use their lists to review the chapter. See other activities labeled **LEP.**

Students Having Difficulty with the Chapter
Invite students to bring in and share with the rest of the class samples of music, art, or literature that they enjoy. Use their interests as a motivating tool to encourage further study of the topics discussed in the chapter. **LEP**

Auditory Learners
Ask students to select one of the Texas musicians, writers, or artists mentioned in the chapter. Have them research the person's life and prepare an oral report. Reports should focus on how living in Texas influenced the person's life and work. If the person the student selects is still living, suggest that the student write a letter to the person, explaining this activity and asking for information. See other activities labeled **A.**

Visual Learners
Have visual learners select an aspect of current Texas culture that interests them. Ask them to prepare a collage or other visual to illustrate their topic. Have them write a brief summary explaining the topic's importance to Texas culture. See other activities labeled **V.**

Tactile/Kinesthetic Learners
Ask students to create a sketch, painting, or sculpture that reflects an aspect of Texas life that they would like to see preserved. For example, students might focus on the heritage of a particular ethnic group or on some aspect of the environment. See other activities labeled **TK.**

Gifted Students
Ask gifted students to write a song, poem, play, short story, or television script that reflects some aspect of life in Texas. Encourage students to share their work with the rest of the class. See other activities labeled **G.**

VOCABULARY
In addition to the boldfaced terms in each section, some students might benefit from discussing the meanings of these terms.

Section 1: *pictographs* (p. 578); *folklore* (p. 579); *rhythm* (p. 579).

Section 2: *folk music* (p. 579); *gospel music* (p. 579); *classical music* (p. 579); *symphony* (p. 579); *innovators* (p. 580); *boogie-woogie* (p. 580); *miniseries* (p. 582).

Section 3: *stylized* (p. 583); *vibrant* (p. 583); *contemporary* (p. 584); *corridos* (p. 586).

CHRONOLOGY
Have students study the Chapter 29 Time Line and identify relationships among the events.

GRAPHIC ORGANIZER
Have students skim the chapter and complete the Chapter 29 Graphic Organizer. *(You might wish to use this activity to review rather than to introduce the chapter.)*

ENRICHMENT
Have students complete the Chapter 29 Enrichment Worksheet.

SECTION 1

FOCUS

Student Experiences (I) On the chalkboard, write the following: *Texas Culture.* Ask the class to brainstorm about ideas that come to mind when they think about this topic. List their responses on the board. Ask students to keep the list in mind as they study this and other sections of the chapter.

INSTRUCTION

Multicultural Perspective (I) Organize students into four groups, and assign each group one of the following peoples: *Native Americans, European Immigrants, Mexican Americans, African Americans.* Have each group plan a presentation honoring its assigned group's contributions to Texas culture. Students might bring in samples of food and music, present a play, create a three-dimensional display, and so on. Encourage students to be creative. **A, V, TK, LEP**

TEXANS AND THEIR CULTURE

CHAPTER 29

The Story Continues...

The culture of Texas has been shaped by the rich variety of peoples who have lived here. Native Americans, Spaniards and other Europeans, Mexican Americans, Anglo Americans, African Americans, and Asian Americans all have contributed much to the culture of the Lone Star State. Musicians, artists, performers, and writers carry on many of the traditions that their ancestors brought to Texas. In this chapter, you will read about the contributions of the various cultures that have influenced the Texas culture of today. You will read about Texas musicians, artists, performers, and writers of the twentieth century and how they have influenced the culture of Texas and the nation.

As you read the chapter, look for the answers to these questions:

1. What are the various cultures that have influenced the culture of Texas?
2. How have Texans played a part in the nation's popular culture?
3. Who are important Texas artists and writers of the twentieth century, and how have they portrayed their state?

1 A Land of Many Cultures

Since colonization of Texas began, our state has been a land of many cultures. The culture of a people includes its customs, traditions, values, ideas, art, music, and literature. Texas culture is rich and varied because of the diversity of the peoples who have called Texas their home over many centuries.

Smiley / TexaStock

Dancers such as these preserve and communicate their cultural heritage by performing traditional Mexican dances for a variety of audiences.

CHAPTER 29 OVERVIEW

The cultural heritage of Texas continues to be reflected in the literature, art, and music produced by Texans of diverse backgrounds.

Essential Elements
1A, 1B, 4B, 4E, 4F, 4H, 9A, 9B

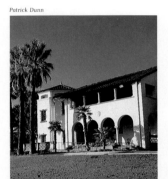

Patrick Dunn

The Marion Koogler McNay Institute in San Antonio is a splendid example of Spanish architecture. It was originally the McNay home, built in 1927, but today it is an art museum.

Roberto Valladares / The Image Bank

Mariachis continue the soulful popular music traditions of Mexico.

The Native Americans. Our knowledge of the cultures and lifestyles of the prehistoric Texans is limited because they had no written histories. The evidence we have of the way they lived comes from pictographs and artifacts. Through their artwork on cliffsides and rock walls, we are able to glimpse their methods of hunting and farming. There is also evidence of the importance of religion in the lives of the first Texans.

The various Indian groups who emerged later in Texas took part in complex cultural activities. From their stories and songs, as well as from their oral traditions passed on to following generations, we learn about Indian cultures. Many of the Indian cultural activities revolved around family, community, and religion. Their ceremonies of dance and song reflected their respect for nature and their elders, as well as for future generations.

The Europeans. The first European culture in Texas was Spanish. Spaniards brought the Roman Catholic faith, with its traditions, literature, and music. Spanish influence is still evident today in Texas. It is present in Texans' architecture, language, food, and music. The first historical accounts of Texas were written by Spaniards.

Other European immigrants left their cultural mark on life in Texas as well. By the 1830s, Anglos became the majority, and they dominated much of Texas cultural life. English became the most common language. Texas' laws, economic system, religion, and education system all reflected English traditions.

Eventually, Texas was populated by Europeans from many countries and cultures. The German Texans retained their native language, clothing, food, and celebrations. Texans still participate in saengerfests, or German singing concerts. French, Scottish, Irish, and Swedish settlers, among others, also contributed to Texas culture. Their special customs, foods, clothing styles, dances, and music add to the cultural diversity that is Texas.

The Mexican Americans. Although Mexican influences are evident throughout the entire southwestern United States, they are particularly strong in the Texas cities of San Antonio and El Paso, and throughout South Texas. Language, place names, food, and traditions of the Roman Catholic church are vivid examples of the influence of Mexican culture.

Ask students: In your opinion, which group mentioned in Section 1 has had the strongest influence on Texas culture? Allow time for students to express varying opinions.

ASSESSMENT

Have students complete the Section 1 Review on page 579.

Student Experiences (I) Challenge students to name well-known musicians from Texas. Allow students to call out their responses as you copy them on the chalkboard. Have students skim Section 2 to find if the musicians they have named are included in the discussion.

Today, these influences have become part of the lives of most Texans, not just those of Hispanic ancestry. Mexican influences are also important to the development of Texas folk music. And of course, the cowboy, the popular image of the Texan to the rest of the world, has historic origins in the Mexican vaquero.

The African Americans. Since African Americans came to Texas with the Spaniards, their impact on the cultural life of Texas has been enormous. African American folklore included stories and tales from the southern United States during the years of slavery. Texas blacks also brought with them a rich African heritage that has influenced clothing styles, games, oral expressions, and religious practice.

The African musical style, with its strong emphasis on rhythm, became the heart of the American popular music known today as rock and roll, or simply rock. American jazz also stems from African American roots. Much of the art of the black community reflects the struggles and achievements of this rich African heritage. ✪

2 Music and Popular Culture

One cultural value common to all the ethnic groups in Texas today is a love of music. Music has provided pleasure and entertainment to every generation of Texans. The music of Texas, and other forms of popular entertainment such as films, stage plays, and television, together have a strong impact on life throughout the United States.

Texas Music and Musicians. People of all backgrounds have contributed to the rich musical tradition of Texas. Texans have played, written, and enjoyed listening to folk music, gospel music, classical music, and popular music. Many Texas musicians have helped create the styles and trends that have made music a reflection of the way Americans live and think.

Classical music concerts have been held in Texas since the days of the Republic. Today, most major Texas cities have their own symphony orchestras, and many Texas colleges and universities train young musicians in classical styles. In the 1950s, Van Cliburn of Kilgore became known as one of the best classical pianists in the world when

SECTION REVIEW

1. What are two ways in which we have learned about Indian cultures?
2. What evidence of Spanish influence still exists today in Texas?
3. In what part of the state is the Mexican influence strongest?
4. Name two styles of music that come from the African American tradition.

Classifying Information: Make a chart showing the cultural influences in Texas. Columns should be titled *Native Americans, Europeans, Mexican Americans,* and *African Americans.*

Writing Descriptively: Write a paragraph describing the influences in your life of the various cultures of Texas.

Sullivan / TexaStock

Gospel music and spirituals reflect the strong religious and musical heritage of African American culture.

Answers to Section 1 Review

1. We have learned about Indian cultures from pictographs and artifacts.
2. Architecture, language, food, and music all show evidence of Spanish influence in Texas.
3. Mexican influence is strongest in San Antonio, El Paso, and throughout South Texas.
4. Jazz and rock both come from the African American tradition.

Classifying Information: Native Americans—song and dance ceremonies, respect for family and nature; Europeans—Roman Catholic faith, architecture, language, food, music, laws, economic system, education system, clothing styles; Mexican Americans—language, place names, food, traditions of the Roman Catholic church; African Americans—clothing styles, games, oral expressions, religious practice, music

Writing Descriptively: Paragraphs will vary but should be based on information discussed in the textbook and should relate to students' lives.

Essential Elements
4E, 4H, 4I, 9A, 9B

INSTRUCTION

Music and History (I) Locate and play for students a sampling of each kind of music discussed in the section. Challenge students to identify the type of music being played.
A, LEP

Guided Practice (I) If possible, assign students to watch a performance of public television's "Austin City Limits." Have students assume the role of a music critic and write a review of the performance. Invite volunteers to read their reviews aloud. **A, V, LEP**

Barker Texas History Center

The folk music of Huddie "Leadbelly" Ledbetter gained national acclaim in the 1930s and 1940s. One of his most famous songs was "Goodnight, Irene."

Scott Newton / Austin City Limits

Flaco Jiménez, son of master accordionist Santiago Jiménez, carries on his father's Mexican music tradition while adding his own unique flavor.

Historical Sidelight
Bob Wills was once a member of W. Lee "Pappy" O'Daniel's Lightcrust Doughboys.

he won the Tchaikovsky International Competition in Moscow.

Although millions of Texans enjoy classical music, most Texans enjoy listening to popular music. Popular music is the common, informal music that people hear every day on their radios, stereos, and televisions. Texans have had their greatest musical influence nationally in the field of popular music.

The first Texan to have a major impact on American popular music was Scott Joplin. He helped develop the style known as ragtime, a musical sound that swept the country at the turn of the twentieth century. Joplin's music also experienced a revival in the early 1970s, when his song "The Entertainer" was used as the theme music for *The Sting*, the hit movie of 1973.

By the 1920s, other black Texans were contributing to new forms of popular music. Blind Lemon Jefferson from Wortham was one of the first to record blues music. Texan Huddie "Leadbelly" Ledbetter became known nationally for writing and singing African American folk songs.

Two black musicians from Dallas made their mark on the music world from the 1930s to the 1950s. Charlie Christian and Aaron "T-Bone" Walker were innovators in the development of the electric guitar. Walker's boogie-woogie sound was a forerunner of rock music.

Another early Texas composer of popular songs was David Guion, an Anglo from Ballinger. Guion wrote songs in the 1920s and 1930s about cowboys, Indians, and life on the Texas frontier. In the 1930s and 1940s, Texas cowboy songs were especially popular across the United States. "Singing cowboys" Gene Autry and Tex Ritter recorded dozens of Western songs and starred in many Hollywood movies about cowboys. Many of the cowboy songs, such as Autry's "My Adobe Hacienda," were influenced by the music of Mexican vaqueros and were accompanied by a Spanish guitar.

In the 1930s, a new style of western music called western swing appeared. It was developed by Bob Wills of Turkey, Texas. Wills borrowed from the various ethnic sounds that he had heard growing up in Texas: Mexican ballads, the blues of black Texans, and the sounds of rural southern music. Blending these diverse elements and using instruments such as fiddles, Wills created a unique sound of his own.

EXTENSION
Music and History (I) Invite students who are musically skilled to perform for the class a style of music discussed in the section. **A, LEP, G, TK**

Independent Practice (II) Ask students to write an essay titled "The Image of Texas in Popular Culture." Allow students to include in their essays information that may not be included in the textbook. Invite volunteers to read their essays aloud. **A, G**

Since the 1930s, a style of Texas music known as *conjunto* has been popular in the American Southwest and northern Mexico. One of its innovators was Narciso Martínez from South Texas. He combined German polkas, Mexican waltzes, and Czech mazurkas to create his special style. Other stars in the Mexican American community have included accordion master Santiago Jiménez and singer Lydia Mendoza. Today, Flaco Jiménez, son of Santiago, carries on this Mexican music tradition.

Recent Texas Popular Music. Millions of Texans, as well as people in the rest of the country, have enjoyed rock music since the 1950s. One of rock's early stars was Buddy Holly from Lubbock. With his band called the Crickets, he recorded many best-selling records. Holly was a brilliant innovator in rock and roll until a plane crash ended his life at the age of 22. A legendary Texas rock star of the 1960s was blues-rock singer Janis Joplin from Port Arthur. She was lead singer of a group called Big Brother and the Holding Company. Before his death in 1988, Roy Orbison of Wink had a successful career that spanned three decades. Leading today's Texas-style rock is ZZ Top, a three-man group from Houston that has had best-selling hits for twenty years.

Texans have always been outstanding in the country music field. One of the best-known performers in America today is Willie Nelson, whose music bridges country, blues, and rock styles. Nelson has frequently teamed with singer-songwriter Waylon Jennings of Littlefield and singer-songwriter Kris Kristofferson of Brownsville. Nelson has appeared in several films with Kristofferson, and he has performed and recorded with Jennings and Kristofferson both. Individually and together, these three added a new dimension to country-western music. For years, it had been dominated by traditional country musicians and singers such as Texan George Jones. Current stars George Strait and Clint Black carry on that tradition.

In recent years, Texas music has received worldwide acclaim for what has been called the Austin Sound. Austin musicians have experimented with various styles, often combining blues, country, and rock. Public television's popular music program "Austin City Limits" has showcased Austin musicians to a national audience since the mid 1970s. Notable leaders of the Austin Sound include

Buddy Holly Memorial Society

Buddy Holly of Lubbock was one of the pioneers of rock and roll music. He was only 22 years old when he died in a plane crash in 1959, but he left a number of hit songs and a style of music that remains popular.

Scott Newton / Austin City Limits

Singer and songwriter Willie Nelson is one of the best-known Texas performers in the United States. His music bridges various popular styles and thus appeals to a wide variety of people.

Biography
Buddy Holly's musical influence spread across the ocean. The first song that the Beatles recorded was Holly's "That'll Be the Day." The Beatles' name may have been a take-off on Holly's group, the Crickets.

Cultural Sidelight
For several years, the annual Fiesta in San Antonio has paid a tribute to the blues tradition by featuring talented African American female blues artists. The June 1991 Fiesta included performances by Ernie Mae Miller of Austin, Pearl Johnson of Fort Worth, Lavelle White of Houston, and Barbara Lynn of Beaumont.

RETEACHING
Create for students or have students work in pairs to create a crossword puzzle with identifying clues, based on the people mentioned in Section 2. Have students exchange the puzzles to complete. **V, TK, LEP**

CLOSURE
Encourage students to name their favorite movies, books, or television shows about Texas, as well as musicians, actors, and other performers from Texas.

Scott Newton / Austin City Limits

Grammy-award winner Lyle Lovett has expanded the boundaries of country music and given the nation a taste of Texas-style humor in the process.

Kimberleh Jones / Shooting Star

Lonesome Dove **was a hit movie made for television. Based on Larry McMurtry's prize-winning novel of the same name, the film starred Robert Duvall, Diane Lane, Texan Tommy Lee Jones, and Rick Schroder (above).**

Biography
More recent works of Horton Foote include the films *Convicts* and *The Habitation of Dragons*, and the television movie *Edna Harris,* about the struggles of a heroic farm woman. Foote still lives in the same Wharton home that his family moved into when he was one year old.

blues guitarist Stevie Ray Vaughan (who died in a helicopter crash in 1990), Jerry Jeff Walker, Marcia Ball, Lyle Lovett, and Joe Ely.

Texas in Popular Culture. Popular culture is the image of people and society as portrayed in television shows, stage plays, and films. Texas has been the subject of numerous dramatic works in the past 50 years, and Texans have played important roles in producing, writing, and performing these works.

The most visible image of Texas and Texans in early motion pictures and television was the cowboy. Because of the many films and TV programs about the West, people in other parts of the world mistakenly thought that all Texans rode horses and worked on ranches! More recent views of Texas in popular entertainment reflect more accurately the diversity of the state's people and lifestyles.

A movie classic about Texas is *Giant,* released in 1956. This film depicted the changes that Texans faced as oil and cattle became less dominant in Texas life. In 1963, *Hud* looked at ranch life in rural Texas and how it affected those who yearned for city life. *The Last Picture Show,* released in 1971, showed the conflicts, hopes, and dreams of Texans living and working in a small town. More recent films set in Texas include *Tender Mercies* (1983) and *The Trip to Bountiful* (1986), both with screenplays by Horton Foote from Wharton. *Terms of Endearment* (1983), based on a novel by Texas writer Larry McMurtry, won the Academy Award for Best Picture.

Television also has used Texas as a setting for many of its dramatic programs. The long-running series "Dallas" created a glamorous image of life in Texas of the 1980s for audiences around the world. The star of "Dallas" was Texan Larry Hagman, who played one of TV's favorite villains, wheeler-dealer oilman J.R. Ewing. One of television's most critically acclaimed miniseries about Texas was *Lonesome Dove,* based on Larry McMurtry's prize-winning novel about the trail-drive era.

Texans have contributed greatly to the Broadway stage in New York, as well as to films and television. Mary Martin of Weatherford was a stage star for many years and is best loved for her performance in the title role of *Peter Pan.* Texas writers such as Horton Foote have had their works produced on the New York stage as well as on the

582 *Unit 11*

ASSESSMENT

Have students complete the Section 2 Review on page 583.

SECTION 3

FOCUS

Student Experiences (I) Challenge students to name as many Texas writers and artists as they can. Point out that, like Texas musicians, Texas' writers and artists have contributed greatly to the state's cultural heritage.

movie screen. One of Broadway's most successful stars today is dancer-choreographer Tommy Tune of Houston. Tune has won several Tony Awards for his directing, choreography (creating dance numbers), and performing in Broadway musicals such as *The Will Rogers Follies*.

Other Texans who have played leading roles in recent decades on stage, on television, and/or in movies include sisters Debbie Allen and Phylicia Allen Rashad of Houston, Gary Busey of Goose Creek, Carol Burnett of San Antonio, Dabney Coleman of Austin, Shelley Duvall of Houston, Morgan Fairchild of Dallas, Farrah Fawcett of Corpus Christi, Lukas Haas of Austin, Tommy Lee Jones of San Saba, brothers Dennis and Randy Quaid of Houston, Debbie Reynolds of El Paso, Sissy Spacek of Quitman, Patrick Swayze of Houston, and Rip Torn of Temple. Two outstanding television journalists today are Texans Bill Moyers of Marshall and Dan Rather of Wharton. ✪

3 Texans in Art and Literature

Texas writers and artists have produced many notable works in this century. These works reflect the creative spirit of Texans throughout their history. Some of their art and literature reflects life in Texas, but much of it deals with themes that are common to all people.

Texas Artists. Artists can be like historians, preserving the history of a place at a given time. Early Texas artists captured views of a frontier state, with its wide-open spaces and pleasing landscapes.

Some modern painters and sculptors have concentrated on the ethnic diversity in Texas. John Biggers, long-time head of the art department at Texas Southern University, has produced works of art that portray African American views and experiences. San Antonian Porfirio Salinas received national acclaim for his Texas landscapes. Austinite Amado Peña, Jr., who paints stylized Indians in scenes of the Southwest, is fondly regarded for encouraging and teaching young students to be artists. Noted Texas sculptors include El Paso-born Luís Jiménez, Jr.,—also known for his vibrant drawings—Octavio Medellin, James Surls, Bonnie MacCleary, and Charles Umlauf.

Clearly the most important modern artist from Texas is Robert Rauschenberg of Port Arthur. One of the most

---

SECTION ★2★ REVIEW

Identify: Huddie "Leadbelly" Ledbetter, Narciso Martínez, Janis Joplin, *Giant*

1. What caused ragtime music to become popular again in the early 1970s?
2. How has the TV program "Austin City Limits" affected Texas musicians?
3. Until recently, what image did many people outside Texas have of Texans?

Analyzing Information: What effect can popular culture have on how others view a group of people? Give examples.

Evaluating Information: Which form of popular culture do you think has the greatest influence on the way people view themselves: movies, television, or stage plays? Explain.

Earlie Hudnall,
courtesy Dr. John Biggers

Dr. John Biggers has painted numerous works of famous black Texans.

Geography (I) Ask students to consider and provide examples of how the geography of a place can influence the work of an artist or writer. Allow time for class discussion. Then have students imagine that they are going to paint a picture, create a sculpture, or write a book, poem, or play. Ask them to write a brief paragraph identifying what geographic factors (physical as well as cultural) might be reflected in their work. Allow time for students to discuss their paragraphs. **A, LEP**

Book Report (II) Assign interested students to read and prepare a book report on *Lonesome Dove.* Select one or two students to present their reports aloud. **A, G**

Essential Elements
4B, 4H, 4I, 9A

TEXAS VOICES

*L*arry McMurtry is Texas' best-known writer of the last 30 years. His early novels took place in small Texas towns. They told the stories of the changes that affected the people there. Later, he wrote of urban Texas and the lives of Texas city dwellers. In 1985, McMurtry set his story in nineteenth-century Texas. That novel, *Lonesome Dove,* focused on the lives of two men who drove cattle from Lonesome Dove, Texas, to Montana. For his best-selling work about the Texas frontier, Larry McMurtry won the Pulitzer Prize. Following are the opening passages of the novel:

When Augustus came out on the porch the blue pigs were eating a rattlesnake—not a very big one. It had probably just been crawling around looking for shade when it ran into the pigs. They were having a fine tug-of-war with it, and its rattling days were over. The sow [female] had it by the neck, and the shoat [male] had the tail.

"You pigs git," Augustus said, kicking the shoat. "Head on down to the creek if you want to eat that snake." It was the porch he begrudged them, not the snake. Pigs on the porch just made things hotter, and things were already hot enough. He stepped down into the dusty yard and walked around to the springhouse to get his jug. The sun was still high, sulled in the sky like a mule, but Augustus had a keen eye for sun, and to his eye the long light from the west had taken on an encouraging slant.

Evening took a long time getting to Lonesome Dove, but when it came it was a comfort. For most of the hours of the day—and most of the months of the year—the sun had the town trapped deep in dust, far out in the chaparral flats, a heaven for snakes and horned toads, roadrunners and stinging lizards, but a hell for pigs and Tennesseans. There was not even a respectable shade tree within twenty or thirty miles; in fact, the actual location of the nearest decent shade was a matter of vigorous debate.

Barker Texas History Center

Walter Prescott Webb was one of the most important historians of his generation.

respected contemporary artists in the world, Rauschenberg has been in the forefront of the art scene since the 1950s. His work covers a broad range of art styles and movements, but he may be best known for his "combine" paintings. These works introduced three-dimensional objects to the traditionally flat surface of the canvas.

Texas Historians. No Texas historian has had greater impact on historical writing than Walter Prescott Webb. After growing up in West Texas, Webb became an influential professor of history at the University of Texas. Among his well-respected books are *The Texas Rangers* and the award-winning *The Great Plains.*

Other modern Texan historians of note include Eugene C. Barker, author of *The Life of Stephen F. Austin* and

Guided Practice (I) Ask each student to list five people from Section 3 who they believe have made the most significant contributions to Texas culture. From the students' lists, compile on the chalkboard a class list. Have the class vote to decide on the five people to be included in a "Texas Hall of Fame." Invite students to prepare an acceptance speech for each person selected. **A, LEP**

EXTENSION

Role Playing (II) Invite interested students to select one of the authors mentioned in Section 3. Ask them to present a "reading" to the class of a portion of the author's work. **A, G**

Independent Practice (II) Have students imagine that they are Texas artists who wish to reflect life in Texas in their work. Ask them to create a drawing or series of drawings. Invite volunteers to display and discuss their drawings. **A, V, TK**

respected professor of history at the University of Texas for 38 years. In 1950, the University of Texas named in his honor the Eugene C. Barker Texas History Center. Historian and librarian Carlos Eduardo Castañeda also had a long and distinguished association with the university. He wrote a seven-volume history titled *Our Catholic Heritage in Texas, 1519–1936.* T.R. Fehrenbach gained renown for his *Lone Star: A History of Texas and the Texans,* among other works. Another notable historian is Félix D. Almaráz, Jr., author of *Tragic Cavalier: Governor Manuel Salcedo of Texas, 1808–1813.*

Today, a new generation of Texas historians is taking a long look at Texas history, exploding old myths and uncovering long-ignored facts.These writers are exploring minority viewpoints of Texas' past. Among the Hispanic Texas historians are Arnoldo De Léon, author of *The Tejano Community, 1836–1900,* and David Montejano, author of *Anglos and Mexicans in the Making of Texas, 1836–1986.* Among contemporary historians reexamining the role of African Americans in Texas history is Cary D. Wintz, author of *Reconstruction in Texas.*

The Literature of Texas. In the mid twentieth century, the most distinguished writer of fiction from Texas was Katherine Anne Porter, born in Indian Creek. Although as an adult Porter lived in New York and Washington, D.C., she wrote several stories set in Texas. Her stories are often included in literature textbooks, and her novel *Ship of Fools* is an American classic.

No discussion of Texas writers would be complete without mention of J. Frank Dobie, a major figure in Texas literature. Growing up on a ranch in Live Oak County, Dobie was acquainted with black, Anglo, and Hispanic cowboys. He developed an appreciation of the legends, the myths, and the many cultures of Texas. His writing reflected that appreciation.

Among Dobie's best-known books are *The Longhorns, The Mustangs,* and *A Vaquero of the Brush Country.* Through his stories of Southwestern and Texas folklore, Dobie helped readers develop an appreciation of Texas' Indian, Spanish, African American, and Mexican heritage. He also was a major influence on Texas writers of the future, encouraging those who came after him to write about the Texas that they knew. In 1936, Dobie helped

Barker Texas History Center

Historian Carlos E. Castañeda wrote much about the period of Spanish rule in Texas. Castañeda had a long and distinguished academic career.

Walter Bennett, Time Magazine

Katherine Anne Porter is perhaps the best-known and most acclaimed Texas author of the twentieth century.

Historical Sidelight
The "Big Three" of Texas' literary tradition—folklorist J. Frank Dobie, historian Walter Prescott Webb, and naturalist Roy Bedichek—were great friends. They supported, critiqued, and motivated each other. In the late 1960s, a young Larry McMurtry criticized them for focusing on nature and ignoring urban people and issues. McMurtry later succumbed to the Texas tradition with *Lonesome Dove,* his book honoring the days of cattle drives.

Provide students with two lists: one of the artists, historians, and writers mentioned in Section 3, and another of their works (in random order). Have students match each name to the appropriate title. Allow students to work with a partner to check and correct their answers. **LEP**

CLOSURE
Ask students: What lies ahead for Texas culture? *(It will become even more diverse as immigration from various countries increases.)*

ASSESSMENT
Have students complete the Section 3 Review on page 586.

Answers to Section 3 Review

Identify: Robert Rauschenberg—most important modern artist from Texas, best known for his "combine" paintings; Carlos Eduardo Castañeda—Texas historian and librarian; Katherine Anne Porter—distinguished fiction writer from Texas; Larry McMurtry—Texas' best-known writer today

1. Texas artists' works have shown views of Texas as a frontier state, with its wide-open spaces and beautiful landscapes. Some Texas artists have focused on Texas' ethnic diversity.
2. They have attempted to point out the falsehoods in the traditional myths and to point out facts that have been ignored. A new generation of writers is exploring minority viewpoints.
3. The organization was formed to promote Texas literature and encourage Texas writers. J. Frank Dobie helped found it.
4. It will change as people from other cultures come to Texas and add their contributions to the existing culture.

(Continued on page 587)

586 *Unit 11*

Humanities Research Center, The University of Texas at Austin

J. Frank Dobie's writings reflected an appreciation of Texas' multicultural heritage.

SECTION ★3★ REVIEW

Identify: Robert Rauschenberg, Carlos Eduardo Castañeda, Katherine Anne Porter, Larry McMurtry

1. What have modern painters and sculptors shown about Texas?
2. How have modern historians reacted to the traditional myths about Texas?
3. What is the purpose of the Texas Institute of Letters? Who helped found the Institute?
4. Why will Texas culture change in the future?

Exploring Multicultural Perspectives: Imagine that you are a Mexican American artist. You are hired to paint a mural about the Mexican War (1846–1848). How will you depict this time in history? Why?

Synthesizing Information: In what ways are artists and historians reinterpreting the past?

586 *Unit 11*

---

organize the Texas Institute of Letters to promote Texas literature and encourage Texas writers.

Partly because of Dobie's influence, the list of notable Texas writers has greatly expanded in recent times. J. Mason Brewer has written about the experiences and folklore of black Texans. Américo Paredes has written about the folklore of Mexican Texans and is distinguished for his studies of corridos in works such as *A Texas-Mexican Cancionero: Folksongs of the Lower Border*. William Owens was another respected writer on Texas folk music and the close relationship Texans have with the land.

A.C. Greene and John Graves are two well-known and respected writers who have observed the relationship between the land of Texas and its impact on people's lives. Greene once called Graves' book *Goodbye to a River* "the best book ever written about Texas." Another successful writer is Shelby Hearon. She has achieved wide recognition for her books *Armadillo in the Grass, Hannah's House,* and *A Small Town*. Poets Rosemary Catacalos, Pat Mora, and Sandra Cisneros have become well known early in their writing careers. They write of their experiences as women and about their ethnic heritage.

Texas' best-known writer today is Larry McMurtry. His novels have had great critical and commercial success, and several of them have become movie hits. They include *Horseman Pass By, The Last Picture Show, Terms of Endearment, Lonesome Dove,* and *Texasville*. McMurtry's stories examine the effects of change as Texas has grown from a rural to an urban state.

The Future of Texas Culture. The culture of Texas continues to become more complex, to become a more accurate expression of the diverse heritage of all Texas people. As we look to the future of Texas culture, one thing is certain. It will continue to be diverse, as it has been in the past. The economic and political changes of the future will insure that Texans will have roots in every part of the world. Immigration to Texas is increasing from Central and South America, from Asia, and from all regions of the United States. All these people will bring to Texas their own special lifestyles and customs. The Texas of the future will be a more interesting and exciting place, as the cultures of the world interact and contribute their own distinctive qualities to the culture of the Lone Star State. ✪

Geography (I) Ask students to explain briefly how the geographic theme *relationships within places* relates to botanist Lance Rosier and his work in the Big Thicket. Ask: What was Lance Rosier's contribution to Texas? **A**

SPIRIT OF TEXAS

Lance Rosier: East Texas Naturalist

Lance Rosier was a hunter who never killed an animal. He was a plant hunter, a self-taught master botanist of the Big Thicket. He knew where to find each of the 20 species of wild orchids that grew there. He knew the many species of ferns, mosses, and mushrooms—and a hundred other plants of the Big Thicket.

Born near the community of Saratoga, Texas, Rosier became interested in plants when he was a boy. He was never happier than when he was tramping about some part of the Big Thicket's 400,000 acres looking for wildflowers. He came to know the Thicket as no other person on earth could.

During the 1930s, Rosier worked as a guide for biologists who were busy surveying the Big Thicket. Gradually over the years, although he had only a sixth-grade education, Rosier learned the common and scientific names (in Latin) for thousands of different plant species. Many professional botanists with PhD's were friends of his, and they freely admitted that no one knew the plants of the Big Thicket, "the biological crossroads of North America," like the little man from Saratoga.

By the 1950s, conservationists were fighting to preserve representative areas of the Big Thicket as a national park. Rosier played a key part in this effort. Tirelessly, day after day and year after year, he took small groups of interested naturalists, reporters, and writers on tours of the Thicket. He was a wonderful guide. He knew the land, the plants, and the animals. His patience was endless, and he gave freely of his time to anyone who showed up at the door of his small home in Saratoga.

Lance Rosier's abilities as a woodsman and guide were frequently amazing. Naturalist Campbell Loughmiller, in his book *Big Thicket Legacy*, remembered:

> Once on an overcast day we walked two miles straight through the woods with Lance to photograph a small orchid he said would be blooming. We didn't waste ten steps. He stopped at a point that had no distinguishing feature, no landmark, and when we did not find it readily I was a little discouraged but not surprised. "It should be here," Lance said, "I saw it two years ago. Oh, here it is!"

Lance Rosier worked for 30 years to save the Big Thicket. Unfortunately, however, he did not live long enough to see his dream come true. He died in 1970. Still, the preservation of the Thicket was his legacy to later generations. Today, 84,550 acres of wilderness are protected within the Big Thicket National Preserve. One section of the preserve lies just southeast of Saratoga. It is named the Lance Rosier Unit and is a fitting memorial.

Inset: **Lance Rosier**

Peter Koch

Exploring Multicultural Perspectives: Answers will vary, but students should display sensitivity to the emotions of Mexican Americans regarding this period of history.

Synthesizing Information: They are examining the past and attempting to weed out the myths as well as pointing out facts that have been ignored.

Essential Elements
4I, 7C, 9A

Essential Elements
4I, 5D, 7C

LONE STAR LEGACY

Using Historical Imagination:
Students' fund-raising speeches should be persuasive. Students should explain that wildflowers help preserve plant and animal life, reduce soil erosion, and protect against pollution from chemical fertilizers.

LONESTAR LEGACY

Texas Wildflowers: Preserving Our Resources

When people drive the highways of Texas in spring, they see endless fields of colorful wildflowers. These native plants owe their abundance, in part, to the National Wildflower Research Center. Located just east of Austin, the Wildflower Center has studied the uses and benefits of wildflowers since 1982. The Center also has promoted the growing of wildflowers that are native to each region of the state.

Texans who take great pride in our fields of wildflowers have Claudia Taylor "Lady Bird" Johnson to thank. Widow of former president Lyndon Johnson, she is the key supporter of the study and promotion of wildflowers.

Lady Bird Johnson began her wildflower campaign in the 1960s, when she was First Lady. She was the head of the White House Committee on Beautification. Through her efforts, cities all over the United States began tree-planting programs, anti-litter campaigns, billboard and junkyard removals, and local beautification projects.

The National Wildflower Research Center has helped people throughout the country find simple and effective ways to protect our environment. Wildflowers help preserve natural resources in a number of ways. They reduce soil erosion, they protect against pollution from chemical fertilizers, and they save water. They help preserve plant and animal life in their native region. They also help maintain the diversity of nature and preserve its delicate balance.

Aside from the environmental benefits, the use of wildflowers is quite economical. In the home landscape or along the Texas highways, wildflowers save us all money. They require little labor to maintain, little water, and no fertilizer.

When Lady Bird Johnson donated the land near Austin for the Wildflower Center in 1982, she explained that the Center was, "for me, a dream come true." She dedicated it on her seventieth birthday. The Wildflower Center was her gift to future generations of Texans.

Using Historical Imagination
Imagine that you are Lady Bird Johnson in 1968. Write a speech to the United States Senate, asking for funding for your wildflower program. Explain how wildflowers help, as well as beautify, the environment.

Inset: **Lady Bird Johnson**   Right: **Texas wildflowers**   Inset: Painting by Aaron Shikler. photo by H.K. Barnett   Right: Paul Montgomery

588   *Unit 11*

1. Chapter Review Worksheet 29
2. Chapter 29 Test, Form A
3. Reteaching Worksheet 29
4. Chapter 29 Test, Form B
5. **Informal Evaluation Forms:** Portfolio Assessment
6. *Texas, Our Texas* **Test Generator**

Essential Elements
4H, 4I, 5B, 6A, 9A, 9B

CHAPTER 29 REVIEW

Understanding Main Ideas

1. Name the various cultural groups who have influenced Texas culture, and give one example of the influence of each on Texas today.
2. List five well-known Texas musicians and the type of music each performs.
3. What are two styles of music that originated in Texas?
4. What are three films, plays, or TV programs that have portrayed Texas?
5. Name two Texas artists and describe their work.
6. Who are three well-known Texas writers? Name one book by each.

Thinking Critically

1. **Synthesizing Information:** In what ways have musicians, artists, and writers portrayed the diversity of Texas culture?
2. **Comparing Perspectives:** How might art by a Mexican Texan differ from art by an African American Texan?
3. **Classifying Information:** Create a "Texas Culture Chart." Use the headings *Music, Art, Popular Culture,* and *Literature.* Under each heading, list at least three Texans, and give a brief description of their contributions. You may include people not mentioned in your textbook.

Linking History and Geography

1. Where would you be most likely to hear *conjunto* music? Why?

2. How might the work of landscape painters in the Panhandle differ from that of painters along the Rio Grande valley?

TAAS Practice
Using Primary Sources

Mike Kelley has written a humor column for the *Austin American-Statesman* since 1977. The following excerpt is from his column of August 13, 1978, titled "I'm Just Not Gonna Take 'Ite' Anymore":

Look, I'm tired of being an ite.

For most of my life, I was a Commerceite, that being a resident of the hub of the universe: Commerce, Texas.

Now, for eight years, on and off, I've been an Austinite. And proud of it, thank you very much.

But this ite thing, this suffix, I never have and do not care for. Say it out loud. "Ite." It has an abrasive quality. . . . It is annoying.
. . .

How much more mellifluous and euphonious [pleasant sounding] are the alternatives.

Consider the ian, for example. People in Corpus Christi are not Corpus Christites. They are Corpus Christians. . . . How trippingly off the tongue rolls the appellation [name] "Abilenian. . . ."

But the ite. It sounds like something you'd bump into in a cave. "Yeah, I jumped over the stalagmites and ducked under the stalactites but then I was impaled on an outcropping of Austinites. . . . "

How do other places do this? Are people who live in Cowtown Fort Worthies? Are the residents of that border city Eagle Passions? . . . If you live in the Dickens County town of McAdoo, are you a McAdoodle? . . .

As for Austin, what are we to do? Let us not lay on generations yet unborn the burden

Understanding Main Ideas

1. Students should give one example for each of the following cultural groups: Native Americans—oral tradition, songs and dances, respect for nature; Europeans—architecture, language, food, music, religion, clothing, celebrations, dances; Mexican Americans—language, place names, food, traditions of the Roman Catholic church; African Americans—music, folklore, clothing, games, religion, oral expressions.
2. Students should list five of the following: Van Cliburn—classical; Scott Joplin—ragtime; Blind Lemon Jefferson—blues; Huddie "Leadbelly" Ledbetter—folk; Charlie Christian and Aaron "T-Bone" Walker—electric guitar; David Guion—songs about life on the frontier; Bob Wills—western swing; Santiago and Flaco Jiménez—*conjunto;* Buddy Holly, Janis Joplin—rock and roll; ZZ Top—Texas-style rock; Willie Nelson, Waylon Jennings, Kris Kristofferson, George Jones, George Strait, Clint Black—country; Stevie Ray Vaughan, Jerry Jeff Walker, Marcia Ball, Lyle Lovett, Joe Ely—Austin Sound.
3. Ragtime and western swing
4. Possible answers include: *Giant,* "Dallas," "Lonesome Dove."
5. Students should list two of the following: John Biggers—works that portray the African American experience; Porfirio Salinas—Texas landscapes; Amado Peña, Jr.—stylized Indians in scenes of the Southwest; Luís Jiménez, Jr.—sculptures and drawings; Robert Rauschenberg—"combine" paintings.

6. Students should name three of the following: Larry McMurtry—*Lonesome Dove;* Katherine Anne Porter—*Ship of Fools;* J. Frank Dobie—*The Longhorns;* Américo Paredes—*A Texas-Mexican Cancionero;* John Graves—*Goodbye to a River;* Shelby Hearon—*Armadillo in the Grass.*

Thinking Critically

1. Synthesizing Information: They have incorporated their own backgrounds, experiences, and cultures into their work.

2. Comparing Perspectives: Answers will vary but should suggest that the art of a Mexican Texan might reflect the Mexican culture, while that of an African American Texan might reflect the African American experience.

3. Classifying Information: Lists and descriptions will vary and may include Texans not mentioned in the chapter.

Linking History and Geography

1. You would most likely hear *conjunto* music throughout the American Southwest and northern Mexico. One of its innovators was from South Texas, and it features Mexican influences.

2. Painters would most likely paint the landscapes with which they are familiar. Landscape painters from the Panhandle might feature flat, grassy plains, windmills, or buffalo, whereas painters along the Rio Grande valley might feature lush vegetation, palm trees, and the Gulf of Mexico.

TAAS Practice
Using Primary Sources

1. C
2. B

TAAS Practice
Writing Persuasively

Letters will vary but should be persuasive and demonstrate knowledge of the diversity of Texas music.

Practicing Skills

1. Creating Maps: Maps should include the persons mentioned in the chapter, along with their hometowns and a map legend.

of sounding like a geologic formation or some new kind of car wax. . . .

Austinian might be okay, but it's a little heavy. . . . What we need is something with flair. . . . How about we start calling the men here Austineros, the women Austinitas, and all be known collectively as Austinos?

1. Kelley says he does not like the sound of the word *Austinite* because
  A it is euphonious
  B it is melodious
  C it is abrasive and annoying
  D it is too much like *Commerceite*
2. Kelley proposes to change the name of his town's citizens to
  A a name that sounds like a car wax
  B a name that shows some flair
  C a name that is more geological
  D a name that is more like *Austinian*

TAAS Practice
Writing Persuasively

Imagine that you are hosting a festival of Texas music. Write a letter to the governor of Texas, urging her to attend your festival. Give reasons that she should attend.

Practicing Skills

1. Creating Maps: Make a map of Texas and include the hometowns of several musicians, performers, artists, and writers mentioned in this chapter. Create a map legend that shows who came from which location on the map.
2. Interpreting Pictures: Look carefully at the sculpture pictured above. Titled *Vaquero*, it is by Texas artist Luís Jiménez, Jr. of El Paso. How do you think this work reflects the artist's cultural heritage? Explain.

---

2. Interpreting Pictures: Answers will vary, but students may suggest that the sculpture is a tribute to the Hispanic tradition behind the western cowboy.

Enriching Your Study of History

1. Individual Project: Reviews should indicate that students have viewed a film mentioned in the chapter.

Courtesy Lisa Sette Gallery

Enriching Your Study of History

1. Individual Project: View one of the films mentioned in this chapter. Then write a review of the movie as if you were a film critic on television, and read your review to your class.
2. Individual Project: Choose one of the Texas artists, writers, or historians mentioned in this chapter, and conduct research to find more biographical information on that person. Prepare a written report for your teacher, and deliver the report orally to the class. You also may wish to draw a portrait of the person you have chosen.
3. Cooperative Project: Your teacher will organize your class into four groups. With your group, choose one of the styles of music described in this chapter. Prepare a presentation for your class which explores the history of that style and gives brief biographies of its well-known Texas musicians. Play some of that music for your class.

2. **Individual Project:** Reports and drawings should be based on outside research.
3. **Cooperative Project:** Presentations should be based on thorough research and should demonstrate a cooperative effort.

UNIT REVIEW RESOURCES
1. Unit Review Worksheet 11
2. Unit 11 Test, Form A
3. Reteaching Worksheet 11
4. Unit 11 Test, Form B
5. **Informal Evaluation Forms:** Portfolio Assessment
6. *Texas, Our Texas* **Test Generator**

Essential Elements
4A, 4B, 4E, 4F, 9A, 9F

UNIT 11

REVIEW

Connecting Main Ideas

1. How did the number of Texans living in urban areas in 1940 compare to the number in 1988?
2. How did the growth of television affect Texas culture?
3. How did the civil rights legislation of the 1960s change government in Texas?
4. How has the Texas government met the changes that have come about with the growing number of automobile drivers?
5. What challenges will the Texas government face in the next ten years?

Practicing Critical Thinking Skills

1. **Synthesizing Information:** How do you think the growing diversity among Texans will help Texas as it becomes more dependent economically on other parts of the world?
2. **Evaluating Information:** Predict three ways that government in Texas will change in the next decade. Give reasons for your predictions.
3. **Exploring Multicultural Perspectives:** Imagine that you are an African American leader in Texas government. Write a paragraph describing how times have changed for you as a black person since you were a teenager in the 1950s.

TAAS Practice
Writing Descriptively

Imagine that you are governor of Texas in the year 2010. Write a speech telling how Texas has changed in the past 20 years.

Exploring Local History

1. How is the population of your community today different from what it was in 1960? How have the changes in population affected your community?
2. Ask parents or guardians and adult friends to write down their favorite ethnic recipes. As a class, compile all the recipes into book form, then sell the book in your community. Vote on a local charity to which you will donate the proceeds of your book sales.

Using Historical Imagination

1. **Individual Project:** Write the words to a song to be sung in one of the music styles described in Chapter 29. Your song could be about your community and how it is changing. Then share your song with the class.
2. **Cooperative Project:** With a partner, choose a business or organization that has been in your community for ten years or more. Interview managers or owners about how their business or organization has changed to meet the needs of a changing Texas. Share your findings with your classmates.

For Extending Your Knowledge

Porter, Katherine Anne. *The Collected Stories of Katherine Anne Porter.* New York: Harcourt, Brace, and World, 1965. A collection of Porter's best stories, many of them set in Texas.

Willoughby, Larry. *Texas Rhythm, Texas Rhyme.* Austin: Tonkawa Free Press, 1990. A pictorial history of Texas music by the author of *Texas, Our Texas.*

UNIT 11 REVIEW ANSWERS

Connecting Main Ideas

1. Just over 45 percent of Texans lived in urban areas in 1940 compared to about 80 percent in 1988.
2. When television first became available, people began getting their news and entertainment from it. Then television began portraying Texas in shows such as the miniseries "Lonesome Dove." The music known as the Austin Sound can be seen around the country on Austin City Limits. Television has spread Texas culture across the country and even the world.
3. More minorities became active in government, political candidates began trying to reach minority voters, and more legislation was passed to meet the needs and concerns of minority groups.
4. To counter traffic congestion and pollution, the government has had to build more highways, provide alternate means of transportation, and promote carpooling.
5. The government will face challenges such as funding services for a growing population, developing land- and water-use policies, fighting crime and drug abuse, and providing education services.

Practicing Critical Thinking Skills

1. **Synthesizing Information:** Answers will vary but should suggest that the growing diversity among Texans will enable the state to deal more effectively with other cultures.

2. **Evaluating Information:** Answers will vary but might include: more women and minorities in government, more legislation for environmental and education issues, alternate methods of funding.

3. **Exploring Multicultural Perspectives:** Paragraphs should focus on civil rights achievements and the increased opportunities for African Americans since the 1950s.

TAAS *Practice*
Writing Descriptively:
Speeches will vary but should be based on information presented in the textbook.

Exploring Local History

1. Answers should be based on research of local history.
2. Books should illustrate ethnic diversity and should be based on a cooperative class effort.

Using Historical Imagination

1. **Individual Project:** Songs should demonstrate one of the music styles described in Chapter 29.
2. **Cooperative Project:** Reports should be based on personal interviews with persons in the community.

Skill Lesson
Practicing the Skill
In writing their drafts, students should follow the four problem-solving stages outlined in the textbook.

SKILL LESSON

Solving Problems

As Texas cities grow, so do the challenges facing city planners. Some of these challenges are: how best to determine zoning (designating how an area may be used), how to fight crime, and how to control air and water pollution.

Complicated problems such as these are best approached through the following steps:

1. *Come to a clear understanding of the problem that must be solved.* No solution is possible until you clearly understand all the parts of the problem.
2. *Devise possible solutions to the problem.* Try to think of as many ways as possible to solve the problem.
3. *Evaluate the costs and benefits of each possible solution.* Analyze each alternative to see how well it would work and what it would cost.
4. *Choose the best solution to the problem.* Make your decision.

Practicing the Skill

Devising a Watershed Ordinance to Protect Austin's Town Lake
Town Lake is a long, narrow, scenic lake that passes through the heart of Texas' capital city. Zilker Park lies along both of its banks. High cliffs, rich in wildlife, border Town Lake to the south and west. Many springs, among them the famous Barton Springs, flow into the lake, as do several major creeks. Everyone agrees that Town Lake is of major importance to the city of Austin. It is a recreational center, a tourist attraction, and a major source of the city's drinking water.

Unfortunately, Town Lake is becoming increasingly polluted. Fish from the lake are no longer safe to eat. But why? The source of Town Lake's pollution is urban runoff.

Urban runoff takes several forms. We have all seen floating cans, bottles, and plastic containers that people have carelessly tossed away. These become part of the runoff. There are also pesticides from thousands of lawns and gardens. Chemicals such as car motor oil wash into drains from streets and parking lots. As in any urban area, large areas of Austin are covered with buildings, paved streets and sidewalks, shopping malls, and paved parking areas. During periods of heavy rainfall, runoff from these hard surfaces is rapid and whatever debris is present quickly ends up in Town Lake. As the city grows, urban runoff becomes worse.

The problem facing Austin's city planners is how best to save Town Lake while still allowing development and economic growth. To help solve such problems, city planners can draft a watershed ordinance—a law to control pollution from runoff.

Imagine that you are one of these city planners. Following the problem-solving stages listed on this page, think of a set of possible solutions to the problem, and decide on your best solution. Then write the first draft of a watershed ordinance to save Town Lake.

HANDBOOK OVERVIEW

The final two chapters of *Texas, Our Texas* make up the "Handbook of Texas Government and Citizenship." Chapter 30 presents an overview of state and local government in Texas, detailing the functions of the three branches of government. The chapter concludes with a discussion of the role of government in public education.

Chapter 31 describes the role of citizens in a democratic government, emphasizing the right to vote. The chapter also examines political parties and interest groups, and it introduces students to methods of citizen participation in the legislative and judicial processes.

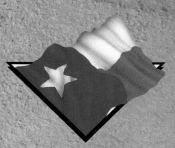

HANDBOOK OF TEXAS GOVERNMENT AND CITIZENSHIP

Janice C. May, PhD
Associate Professor of Government
University of Texas at Austin

HANDBOOK OBJECTIVES

1. Identify the Texas Constitution as the state's fundamental law.
2. Describe the basic principles of the Texas Constitution.
3. List the three branches of government, and discuss the role and functions of each in Texas government.
4. Discuss the role of local government in Texas, and describe the three forms of municipal government.
5. Identify the responsibilities of local, state, and national government in providing public education.
6. Discuss the privileges of citizens in a democratic government.
7. Identify opportunities for citizen participation in Texas government and politics.

TEXAS GOVERNMENT

TEACHER'S TIME LINE

Section 1	Section 2	Section 3	Section 4	Section 5	Section 6	Review and Assessment
Pp. 594–96	Pp. 596–98	Pp. 598–600	Pp. 600–02	Pp. 602–04	Pp. 604–05	
1 Day	1 Day	1 Day	1 Day	1 Day	1 Day	1 Day

⬥ TEACHER MATERIALS

Core: Graphic Organizer 30; Enrichment Worksheet 30; Review Worksheet 30; Reteaching Worksheet 30; Chapter 30 Tests, Forms A & B

Additional: Geography and Graph Skills 30, Map and Chart Transparencies 24, Oral History Handbook, Informal Evaluation Forms, Test Generator

⬥ OBJECTIVES

1. Explain the basic principles underlying the Texas Constitution.
2. Identify the basic rights guaranteed in the Texas Bill of Rights.
3. List the three branches of state government, and describe their functions.
4. Explain how Texans are represented in the bicameral legislature.
5. Explain the basic organization of the state court system.
6. Describe the basic units of local government and their functions.
7. Describe the basic organization of school districts.
8. Explain the role of state, local, and national governments in public education.

⬥ RESOURCES

BOOKS FOR TEACHERS

Buchanan, Bruce. *Electing a President*. Austin: University of Texas Press, 1991. Examination of the Bush campaign for president.

Law in the Lone Star State. Law in a Changing Society Program. Austin: State Bar of Texas, 1976. A look at the relationship between law and society.

May, Janice, Stuart A. MacCorkle, and Dick Smith. *Texas Government*. New York: McGraw-Hill, 1980. Examination of the government in Texas.

Richards, Ann. *Straight from the Heart: My Life in Politics and Other Places*. New York: Simon and Schuster, 1989. An autobiography by Ann Richards.

Texas Legislative Handbook. Austin: Texas State Directory, biennial. The official handbook of the legislature of Texas.

Ullman, John. *Lloyd M. Bentsen, Jr.: Democratic Senator from Texas*. Washington: Grossman Publishers, 1972. Life and times of Bentsen.

MULTIMEDIA MATERIALS

Great Cities of Texas. (filmstrips/cassettes) Texas Instructional Media, P.O. Box 33581, San Antonio, TX 78233. Eight-part series looks at the history of cities in Texas.

Inside the Texas Legislature. (film, 33 min.) University of Texas at Austin Film Library, Education Annex Building, University of Texas at Austin, Austin, TX 78712. Scenes of Texas legislature in session.

STUDENTS WITH SPECIAL NEEDS

Limited English Proficient Students (LEP)

Pair LEP students with language proficient students. Have the language proficient students act as "tutors" throughout the study of Chapter 30. If possible, allow time at the end of each class session for partners to work together to clarify the discussion. See other activities labeled **LEP**.

Students Having Difficulty with the Chapter

Assign students to work in pairs or small groups to outline the chapter, using the following headings:

I. The Texas Constitution
II. The Texas Legislature
III. The Texas Executive
IV. The Texas Judiciary
V. Local Government

Have the students use their outlines to review the chapter. **LEP**

Auditory Learners

Organize students into pairs to play "checkers." You will need checkerboards and checkers for each pair of students. Each time players make a move, they must answer a question about Texas government. (You will need to prepare duplicate sets of questions so that each pair of players has a set.) A player who answers a question incorrectly loses a turn. Allow approximately twenty minutes for the game. The player with the most checkers on the board when the time is up wins. See other activities labeled **A.**

Visual Learners

Have visual learners work in pairs or small groups to prepare visuals illustrating state government. Topics might include:

Three Branches of Government and Their Functions
Changing the Texas Constitution
Texas Senate and Texas House: Qualifications, Selection, Terms of Office, Districts, Salary, Leadership
Powers of the Legislature
Texas Governor: Qualifications, Selection, Term of Office, Salary, Powers
Texas Judiciary: Qualifications, Selection, Terms of Office, Case Types, Jurisdictions, Court Structure
Local Government: City, County, Special Districts

See other activities labeled **V.**

Tactile/Kinesthetic Learners

Have tactile/kinesthetic learners work together to prepare a directory of city, county, school district, and state officials for the current year. The government pages of the local telephone directory and *The Texas Almanac* are useful sources. Students might wish to reproduce and distribute the directories to promote civic awareness. See other activities labeled **TK.**

Gifted Students

Assign gifted students a state government official to interview in person, by phone, or in writing. Have students prepare in advance of the interview questions designed to find out the official's role and specific duties in the government. Ask students to share their information with the class. See other activities labeled **G.**

VOCABULARY

In addition to the boldfaced terms in each section, some students might benefit from discussing the meanings of these terms.

Section 1: *inferior* (p. 594); *principles* (p. 594); *inherent* (p. 595); *interpretation* (p. 596).

Section 2: *will* (p. 596); *presiding* (p. 597); *bills* (p. 597); *human services* (p. 598); *suspended* (p. 598).

Section 3: *comptroller* (p. 598); *consent* (p. 599).

Section 4: *vacancy* (p. 600); *presides* (p. 602).

Section 5: *charters* (p. 602); *trustees* (p. 604).

Section 6: *certification* (p. 605); *vocational* (p. 605).

GRAPHIC ORGANIZER

Have students skim the chapter and complete the Chapter 30 Graphic Organizer. *(You might wish to use this activity to review rather than to introduce the chapter.)*

ENRICHMENT

Have students complete the Chapter 30 Enrichment Worksheet.

SECTION 1

FOCUS

Past Learning (I) Begin a class discussion by asking the students to name some of the responsibilities of state governments. Ask them if they think that the role of state government is important. Point out that it is important for state governments to share governing responsibilities with the federal government.

INSTRUCTION

Vocabulary (I) You may wish to preteach the following boldfaced terms: *popular sovereignty* (p. 594); *limited government* (p. 595). **LEP**

Guided Practice (I) Organize students into pairs or small groups, and provide each group with a copy of the Texas Constitution and of the United States Constitution. Ask students to compare the two documents. Allow time for each group to express some of its findings. **A, V, LEP**

CHAPTER 30 OVERVIEW

The government of Texas is based on the Texas Constitution of 1876. Like the United States Constitution, the document organizes government into three levels, incorporating the system of checks and balances. Chapter 30 explores the structure and functions of Texas government at the state and local levels.

Essential Elements
3B, 4F, 7B, 7G, 7F, 9A, 9B

Taylor Johnson

The Texas Constitution is the highest state law. It is inferior only to the United States Constitution and valid federal laws.

CHAPTER 30

TEXAS GOVERNMENT

Government Focus

Texas government today is a product of the past. The basic framework of today's state government was set by the Texas Constitution of 1876. Many of the constitution's ideas can be traced to earlier Texas constitutions and to English and Spanish law. Since 1876, however, it has been amended more than 330 times, making it a product of the present as well. Chapter 30 is about the state and local governments of Texas. The chapter examines the structure of state government, the kinds of local governments, and the role of government in public education.

As you read the chapter, look for the answers to these questions:

1. On what basic principles does the Texas Constitution rest, and how can it be changed?
2. What is the role of the Texas legislature, and how does it carry out that role?
3. What is the role of the executive branch, and of what does it consist?
4. What is the role of the judicial branch, and of what does it consist?
5. What types of local governments are in Texas, and what are their functions?
6. What is the role of government in providing for education?

■ The Texas Constitution

The Texas Constitution is the state's fundamental, or basic, law. It is also the highest state law. It is inferior only to the United States Constitution and, provided they are constitutional, other federal laws and rules.

Principles. The Texas Constitution rests on several basic principles. The first is called **popular sovereignty**, which means that all political power comes from the

Independent Practice (II) Ask students to write a brief essay on how the Bill of Rights affects their lives. Encourage them to provide specific examples. Invite volunteers to read their essays aloud. **A, G**

RETEACHING
Have students write a summary sentence of each of the Section 1 subsections. **LEP**

people. It is because of this idea that the Texas Constitution is sometimes said to be the people's document. The Texas Constitution states: "All political power is inherent in the people, and all free governments are founded on their authority and instituted for their benefit."

A second principle is that of **limited government**. The Texas Constitution limits, or restricts, government in what it can do and how it can do it. This is especially true with respect to the people's rights and freedoms.

The third principle concerns the kind of government established by the Texas Constitution. It is a republican form of government, which means that the people elect representatives who are responsible to the citizens of the state.

The Bill of Rights. The first article of the Texas Constitution is the Bill of Rights. The article lists many basic rights such as the freedoms of speech, press, assembly, and religion. It also lists rights of persons accused of crimes, rights of people who are victims of crimes, property rights, and equality of rights. Section 29 of the article makes it clear that the rights are never to be taken away.

Three Branches of Government. Article II of the Texas Constitution requires the separation of three branches of government—the legislative, executive, and judicial. The legislative power to make laws is given to the legislative department. The executive power to carry out the laws is given to the executive department. The judicial power to hear and decide legal disputes is given to the judicial department, or courts.

None of the three departments is allowed to exercise the powers of the others unless the Texas Constitution says

Historical Sidelight
During the 1830s, Texans expressed major grievances against the Mexican government over lack of these rights.

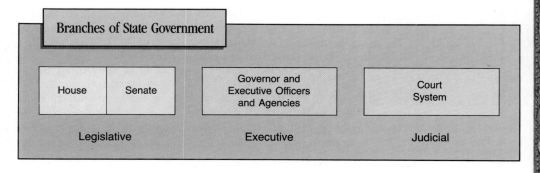

Branches of State Government

House	Senate	Governor and Executive Officers and Agencies	Court System
Legislative		Executive	Judicial

CLOSURE

Ask students: From what you have read in Section 1, do you think that the Texas Constitution is still a workable plan of government?

ASSESSMENT

Have students complete the Section 1 Review on page 596.

SECTION 2

FOCUS

Past Learning (I) Ask students to name the three branches of government. Ask: What is the role of the legislative branch *(to make laws)*?

Answers to Section 1 Review

Define: *popular sovereignty*— basic principle that all political power comes from the people; *limited government*—basic principle that limits government in what it can do and how it can do it

Identify: amendments—additions that change some part of the law

1. It is a government in which people are elected to represent others.
2. Possible answers include: freedom of speech, freedom of press, freedom of assembly, freedom of religion.
3. Executive, legislative, judicial
4. The legislature proposes the amendment, and the voters vote on it.

Analyzing Information: A divided government ensures that no one branch of government gains too much power and that each branch checks the actions of the others.

Interpreting Charts: Governor, executive officers, agencies

Essential Elements
3B, 4F, 7B, 7F, 8D, 9A, 9B

SECTION ① REVIEW

Define: popular sovereignty, limited government
Identify: amendments

1. What is a republican government?
2. What are two rights protected by the Bill of Rights?
3. What are the three branches of the government?
4. What are the two steps involved in amending the constitution?

Analyzing Information: Why is it important for the state government to be divided into three branches?

Interpreting Charts: Study the chart on page 595. Of what does the executive branch consist?

Taylor Johnson

The speaker of the House presides over state representatives, who meet in the House chamber at the capitol every two years and during special sessions.

so. The reason for this restriction is the fear that one department or person might gain too much power and take away rights of the people. Articles III, IV, and V establish the legislative, executive, and judicial branches. The remaining articles of most importance are those on suffrage, finance, education, local government, and the procedures for changing the constitution.

Changing the Texas Constitution. The Texas Constitution has had many amendments, or additions that change some part of the law, since 1876. There is a two-step process for enacting amendments. First, the Texas legislature must propose the amendment. To do so requires a vote of two-thirds of the members of each house. Second, the voters of Texas must decide on the amendment in an election. A majority of the voters must vote "yes" to adopt an amendment.

The Texas Constitution may also be changed by a constitutional convention called by the Texas legislature. The convention consists of delegates elected by the people. All Texas constitutions have been drafted by conventions. The constitution also changes by custom and by interpretation. A change by interpretation occurs when the Texas courts decide a case in which they must rule on what the Texas Constitution means when the meaning is not clear. ✪

② The Texas Legislature

The legislature is the first department described in the Texas Constitution. It is considered to be the strongest of the three branches and the closest to the will of the people.

Structure and Qualifications. The Texas legislature is **bicameral**, or composed of two houses, or chambers. *Bi* means "two" and *camera* means "chamber." Both houses must agree before any bill becomes law. The House of Representatives is the larger body, with 150 members. The Senate has only 31 members.

Representatives and senators must be United States citizens and residents of Texas. Representatives must be at least 21 years of age. Senators must be at least 26 years of age.

Selection, Term of Office, Districts, and Salary. All representatives are elected every two years in a general election. They serve two-year terms. Senators serve four-

INSTRUCTION

Vocabulary (I) You may wish to preteach the following bold-faced terms: *bicameral* (p. 596); *appropriations bill* (p. 597); *balanced budget* (p. 598). **LEP**

Guided Practice (I) Have students work in pairs or small groups to create charts showing for the Texas House and Senate the following information: *Selection, Qualifications, Term of Office, Powers.* **V, TK, LEP**

EXTENSION

Creating (I) Assign students to clip from current newspapers articles that deal with activities of Texas senators and representatives. Have students work together to organize the articles into a bulletin board display. **V, TK, LEP**

RETEACHING

Ask students to use the information in Section 2 to create a diagram illustrating the composition and functions of the Texas legislature. Call on a volunteer to copy the diagram on the chalkboard. **V, TK, LEP**

year terms, but all are not elected at the same time. Every two years, when representatives are elected, only half the senators are elected.

Each legislator is elected from a single-member district. The voters elect only one representative from each House district and one member from each Senate district. Texas is divided into 150 House districts and 31 Senate districts. The boundaries of these districts are drawn by the legislature after every federal census. Each district must contain roughly the same number of people.

The salary of legislators is fixed by the constitution at $7,200 per year. Legislators also receive payment of their expenses up to a certain limit. Because the salary is set by the constitution, voters must approve any changes by an amendment.

Sessions. The Texas legislature meets every two years for no more than 140 days. Regular sessions are in odd-numbered years. Special sessions of no more than 30 days may be called by the governor. Because the legislature does not meet often or for very long, the governor calls special sessions about once a year.

Leadership. At the beginning of every regular session, the members of the House of Representatives elect a speaker as the presiding officer. The presiding officer of the Senate is the lieutenant governor, who is elected by the voters of the state to a four-year term. Under the constitution, the lieutenant governor is the member of the executive branch who becomes governor should something happen to the person in that office. The lieutenant governor is also head of the Senate, with a great deal of power in the legislative branch. Some people consider the lieutenant governor to be more powerful than the governor in Texas.

The two presiding officers in the legislature are given important powers over the members. They appoint members of committees, which study and report on proposed laws. They also regulate the flow of proposed laws through the legislature.

Powers of the Legislature. The Texas legislature passes laws. These laws affect the daily lives of Texans from birth to burial. At a recent session, more than 4,500 bills were introduced and about 950 passed. Thirty-six were vetoed.

The most important of all bills is the **appropriations bill**. The appropriations bill tells in dollars and cents

Taylor Johnson

The lieutenant governor presides over state senators, who meet in the Senate chamber at the capitol during legislative sessions.

Government and Citizenship
Senators are not elected at the same time in order to ensure that there are experienced senators in the legislature at all times.

Remind students that the legislature is considered to be the strongest of the three branches of Texas government. Ask them to provide two reasons from the textbook to support this concept. *(The legislature passes laws that affect all Texans, and it has the power to impeach and remove officials from office.)*

ASSESSMENT

Have students complete the Section 2 Review on page 598.

FOCUS

Student Experiences (I) Ask students to name the current chief executive of the state of Texas. Challenge them to name other executive officers of Texas.

Answers to Section 2 Review

Define: *bicameral*—composed of two houses; *appropriations bill*—bill that tells which state programs will be supported for the next two years; *balanced budget*—a budget in which revenue is equal to expenditures

1. House of Representatives
2. After each census
3. Once a year
4. The lieutenant governor presides over the Senate and is the member of the executive branch who becomes governor should something happen to the person in that office.
5. Through taxation

Synthesizing Information: The lieutenant governor presides over the Senate, which has a great deal of power in the legislative branch.

Evaluating Information: In order to raise money for the budget, the legislature passes tax bills. The tax money comes from voters.

Essential Elements
3B, 4F, 4I, 7B, 7F, 9A, 9B, 9F

SECTION 2 REVIEW

Define: bicameral, appropriations bill, balanced budget

1. Which house of the Texas legislature is the larger?
2. When are the legislative districts determined?
3. About how often do special sessions occur?
4. What is the role of the lieutenant governor?
5. How does the state pay for its budget?

Synthesizing Information: Why would some people consider the lieutenant governor to be more powerful than the governor?

Evaluating Information: Why is it important for legislators to have the support of the voters in their districts when they wish to increase the budget?

Shelley Boyd / TexaStock

Ann Richards was elected governor of Texas in 1990. She is shown here at the swearing-in of Lena Guerrero as chairperson of the Texas Railroad Commission.

---

which state programs will be supported for the next two years. Public education is the number-one budget item. It accounts for about half of the total. The next two major items in order of importance are health and human services, and transportation. To raise money for the budget, the legislature passes tax bills. These must originate in the House of Representatives. The major state tax is the sales tax. Taxes on motor fuels are next in importance. The state also raises money from fees, licenses, the state lottery, and federal aid.

The Texas Constitution places a number of restrictions on spending and borrowing money by state government. The legislature must pass a **balanced budget**. This is a budget in which revenue, or income, is equal to expenditures, or spending. This requirement can be suspended in an emergency, but it has never been done.

The Texas Constitution permits the legislature to exercise some nonlegislative powers. One is the power to impeach and remove officials from office. Very few Texas officers have been removed by impeachment. The best-known case was the removal of Governor James Ferguson in 1917. ✪

3 The Texas Executive

The executive department is the second branch established by the Texas Constitution. In Article IV, the governor is described as the "chief executive." Other executive officers listed are the lieutenant governor, secretary of state, comptroller of public accounts, treasurer, commissioner of the general land office, and the attorney general. All of these except the secretary of state, who is appointed by the governor, are elected officers.

The governor is by far the best-known public officer in Texas government. The governor is the "first citizen" of the state and the official representative of Texas in relations with other governments.

Selection, Term, and Qualifications. The governor is elected by the voters for a four-year term. Elections for governor are held in even-numbered years when there is no election for president of the United States. There is no limit on the number of terms a governor may serve. There are few legal qualifications for the office. The governor

INSTRUCTION

Guided Practice (I) Ask students to use the information in Section 3 to create a chart titled "The Texas Executive." Labels should include: *Selection, Term, Qualifications, Powers.* **V, TK, LEP**

EXTENSION

Illustrating (II) Have students research and create charts identifying Texas' current executive officers. **V, TK, G**

Independent Practice (II) Ask students to imagine that they are the governor of Texas and that they are approaching the close of their term of office. Ask: What will be the focus of your "state of the state" message? What issues will you mention? Allow time for several students to respond. **A**

RETEACHING

Ask students to write a paragraph summarizing the responsibilities of the governor of Texas. Call on volunteers to read their paragraphs aloud. **A, LEP**

must be at least 30 years of age, a United States citizen, and a resident of Texas at least five years. The governor's salary, determined by the legislature, was $93,432 per year in 1991.

Powers of the Governor. Texans have always been fearful of too much power in the executive branch. They especially disliked Edmund J. Davis' strong governorship during Reconstruction. As a result, the Texas governor has less power than governors of most of the other states. Still, a strong leader in the office can guide the people of Texas to reach selected goals.

In relation to the legislature, the governor has the veto power. This power enables the governor to kill a bill passed by the legislature. The legislature can override a veto if two-thirds of the members of each house vote to do so. They rarely do this, however. The governor also has a special "line item" veto. With this veto, the governor can kill items, or parts, of a proposed appropriation bill.

The governor has the power to call special sessions of the legislature. The governor also has the responsibility of giving a "state of the state" message at the beginning of each regular legislative session and at the close of his or her term of office.

As commander-in-chief of the state's military forces, the governor can declare martial law in an emergency and call out the National Guard to keep order. The governor may pardon a person convicted of a crime, but only upon the recommendation of the Board of Pardons and Paroles.

The weakness of the Texas governor shows up in relation to the rest of the executive branch. The governor shares powers with other elected executive officers. The governor appoints many members of state agencies with the advice and consent of the Senate but cannot remove them without the Senate's approval.

Unlike governors with strong powers, the Texas governor lacks control of the budget process. The Texas governor can propose a budget, but the legislature virtually ignores it. Instead, the legislature works through its own Legislative Budget Board. The lieutenant governor chairs this agency. This is one reason that the lieutenant governor is considered to be more powerful than the governor.

Administrative Agencies. In addition to the governor, the executive branch includes about 200 agencies to administer, or carry out, laws passed by the legislature. These

Charles Guerrero / TexaStock

As attorney general of Texas, Dan Morales represents the state in all lawsuits and pleas in the state Supreme Court. His is an elective office.

CLOSURE

Assign students to read a local daily newspaper for one week to gather newspaper articles that illustrate the use of the powers of the governor of Texas. Allow time for students to share and discuss the articles.

ASSESSMENT

Have students complete the Section 3 Review on page 600.

SECTION 4

FOCUS

Student Experiences (I) If possible, in advance of the study of Section 4 organize a field trip to your county courthouse. Or you may wish to invite a municipal or county court judge to speak to the class. Encourage students to ask questions.

Answers to Section 3 Review

Identify: line item veto—veto power that enables the governor to kill parts of a proposed appropriation bill

1. The governor must be at least 30 years old, a United States citizen, and a resident of Texas at least five years.
2. Possible answers include: veto power, the power to call special legislative sessions, the power to declare martial law, the power to pardon a convicted criminal.
3. To carry out the laws passed by the legislative branch

Solving Problems: Answers will vary but might suggest that the governor threaten to use the line item veto or promise to sign some future bill.

Using Historical Imagination: Speeches will vary but should be based on sound reasoning.

Essential Elements
3B, 4F, 7B, 7E, 7F, 7G, 9A, 9B

SECTION ⭐3 REVIEW

Identify: line item veto

1. What are the requirements for being governor of Texas?
2. What are two powers of the governor?
3. What is the function of the executive agencies?

Solving Problems: If you were governor of Texas and you disagreed with the budget proposed by the Legislative Budget Board, how might you convince the board to change its budget?

Using Historical Imagination: Imagine that you were governor of Texas during the Great Depression. Write a brief speech to a crowd of unemployed workers, telling them how you will improve their prospects for jobs.

Thomas P. Murray

Nine justices sit on the bench of the Texas Supreme Court. The supreme court is located in Austin.

agencies have about 190,000 employees and spend about $30 billion each year.

In general, the agencies regulate Texas society and provide services to the people of Texas. Among the most important regulatory agencies is the Texas Railroad Commission. It is known for its power to regulate the oil and natural gas industries in Texas rather than railroads, its original purpose. A major service agency is the Department of Mental Health and Mental Retardation. The largest of state agencies, it provides services to the mentally ill and the retarded. ✪

◢ The Texas Judiciary

The third department of Texas state government is the judiciary, or court system. It is composed of courts and judges who hear and decide cases. The judges interpret and apply Texas law and, to a certain extent, federal law in the interests of justice.

Selection, Terms, and Qualifications. With the exception of some judges at the local level, Texas judges are elected by the voters. Most judges below the level of the state supreme court become judges by appointment to fill a vacancy. Vacancies occur when a judge dies, resigns, or is removed from office. A judge who is appointed to office usually wins at the next election.

Unlike federal judges, Texas judges are not given terms for life. In fact, their terms are rather brief. Judges at higher level courts serve six years, while those at lower levels serve four years. It is common, however, for judges to be reelected many times. Judges must retire at the age of 75. They can be removed for breaking the law or for inability to perform their duties. The legislature may remove judges through the impeachment process. Also, the legislature may tell the governor to remove a judge if two-thirds of the members of each house vote in favor of it. The Texas Supreme Court also may remove judges.

The qualifications for being a judge vary by level of court. Judges must be United States citizens and residents of Texas. With the exception of some judges at the local level, they must be attorneys trained in the law.

Cases and Courts. Texas courts hear millions of cases each year. Most hear civil and criminal cases both. Civil

INSTRUCTION

Vocabulary (I) You may wish to preteach the following boldfaced terms: *jurisdiction* (p. 601); *appellate court* (p. 601). **LEP**

Guided Practice (I) Ask students to select one of the Section 4 subsections and create a chart, diagram, or other visual to illustrate the discussion. Invite students to display and discuss their illustrations. **A, V, TK, LEP**

EXTENSION

Community Involvement (II) Have students research to find a recent court decision (from any level of the Texas judicial system) that provoked controversy. Have them write a paragraph describing the case and their reaction to the decision. **G**

RETEACHING

Provide students with a list of statements based on the information in Section 4. Have them identify the statements as true or false. Then ask them to rewrite the false statements to make them true. **LEP**

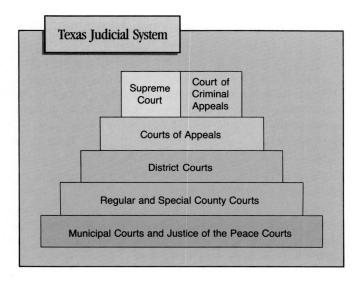

Texas Judicial System

Supreme Court | Court of Criminal Appeals

Courts of Appeals

District Courts

Regular and Special County Courts

Municipal Courts and Justice of the Peace Courts

What are the second-highest courts in the Texas judicial system?

cases are legal disputes between private parties, as between citizens and businesses or other organizations. A criminal case involves a crime against the public or state.

Each court has a **jurisdiction**, or authority to hear certain kinds of cases. The jurisdiction of lower courts is also limited to a geographic area. For example, county courts hear cases only within their county. The Texas Supreme Court, on the other hand, hears certain kinds of cases from the entire state.

Trial courts have original jurisdiction, which means they have the power to hear a case at its place of origin. A person has the right under the Texas Bill of Rights to ask for a jury trial in either a civil or a criminal case. Most trials are conducted without a jury. A judge hands down a decision.

A person who loses a case at a trial court may appeal the case to an **appellate court**. These courts review cases to determine whether errors were made, usually in the interpretation of the law. An appellate court may uphold a lower court decision or reverse it. An appellate court may order a new trial or take other action under the law.

Court Structure. The Texas judiciary is very complex. The 2,567 courts are arranged in five levels, with more than 3,000 judges. The court system is arranged like a

Scott Newton

Judge Morris Overstreet was elected to the Texas Court of Criminal Appeals in 1990 and took office in January 1991. Previously, he served as judge in the County Court-at-Law for Potter County in Amarillo.

Caption Response
Courts of appeals

Government and Citizenship
An example of a civil case is one in which one person sues another over a property dispute. Other civil cases may involve disputes over money or business contracts.

Ask students: In your opinion, should judges be appointed by the governor or elected by the voters? Why do you think so? Allow time for students to express varying viewpoints.

ASSESSMENT

Have students complete the Section 4 Review on page 602.

Student Experiences (I) Challenge students to name their county commissioners. Focus discussion on the importance of citizens becoming involved in local government.

Answers to Section 4 Review

Define: *jurisdiction*—a court's authority to hear certain kinds of cases; *appellate court*—courts that review cases of lower courts to determine whether errors were made

1. With the exception of some at the local level, Texas judges are elected by the voters.
2. The appellate court reviews cases that were decided in a lower court to determine whether errors were made. The appellate court may uphold the lower court's decision or reverse it. The appellate court may order a new trial or take some other legal action.
3. The Texas Supreme Court and the Texas Court of Criminal Appeals

Evaluating Information: Opinions will vary but should demonstrate the knowledge that a person who loses a case may appeal to an appellate court.

Exploring Economics: The state saves money by determining cases without a jury.

Essential Elements
3B, 4D, 4F, 7B, 7D, 7F, 7G, 9A, 9B

SECTION ✪ 4 REVIEW

Define: jurisdiction, appellate court

1. How are judges selected?
2. What is the job of the appellate court?
3. What are the two highest Texas courts?

Evaluating Information: In your opinion, why is it important for the court system to include appellate courts?

Exploring Economics: What is the financial advantage for the state to determine most cases without a jury trial?

Michael Lyon / TexaStock

During the last decade, several Texas cities have elected women to the office of mayor, including Dallas, San Antonio, and Corpus Christi. Above is Mayor Florence Shapiro of Plano.

---

pyramid. The numerous lower courts are at the bottom, and two highest courts are at the top. Both of the two highest courts are appellate courts with some original jurisdiction. One is the Texas Supreme Court, which hears only civil cases. The other is the Texas Court of Criminal Appeals, which hears only criminal cases. Texas is one of only two states with more than one highest court. The two highest courts are each composed of nine justices. The chief justice, who presides over the supreme court, is the official representative of the entire judiciary. ✪

5 Local Government

Texans are governed by local as well as state government. Legally, local governments are "creatures" of the state. The state may create, change, or abolish them. In practice and under the constitution, a great deal of self-government is permitted at the local level.

There are more than 4,400 units of local government in Texas. There are 254 counties and more than 1,100 **municipalities**, or city, town, and village governments. There are another 1,700 special districts and more than 1,000 school districts.

Counties and Municipalities. Texas is divided into 254 counties, the largest number of any state. County governments help carry out state law and also serve as local government. The governing body of the county is the county commissioners court. It is misnamed, because its function is to administer the law rather than to act as a court. An elected county judge presides over the commissioners court, which has four other members. The judge also presides over the county court. Voters elect a host of other county officials. The best known is the sheriff, the chief law enforcement officer.

Eighty percent of Texans live in urban areas under a municipal government. Municipalities with populations of over 5,000 are eligible for home-rule charters. These they draft and adopt within guidelines set by the legislature. The charters enable the people of a town or city to choose their own form of government. They may then make rules, so long as the rules are not in conflict with state law. Most home-rule cities have a council-manager form of government. The elected city council decides on policies.

INSTRUCTION

Vocabulary (I) You may wish to preteach the following boldfaced term: *municipalities* (p. 602). **LEP**

Guided Practice (I) Organize students into pairs, and provide each pair with a scrambled version of the chart on this page. Have students work together to reconstruct the chart. **V, TK, LEP**

EXTENSION

Community Involvement (II) Encourage students to attend and report on a local school board meeting or a city council meeting. **A**

RETEACHING

Have each student create a matching review, using the information in Section 5. Have students exchange and complete the reviews. Allow partners to work together to check and correct their answers. **LEP**

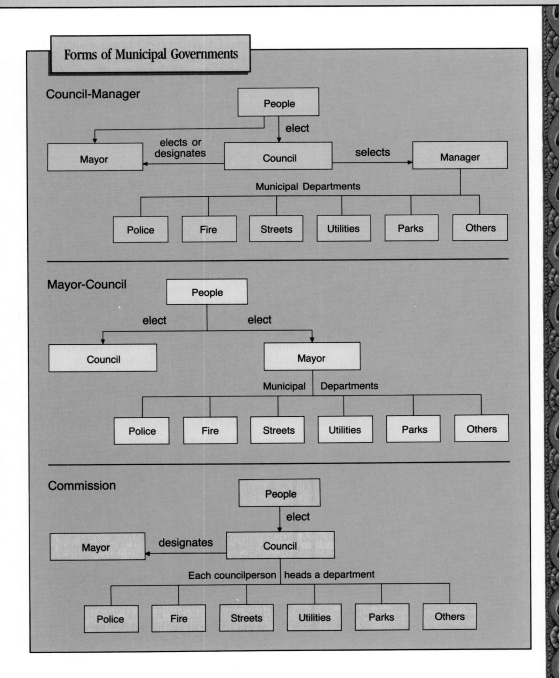

Forms of Municipal Governments

Council-Manager

Mayor-Council

Commission

Transparency 24
An overhead transparency of this chart can be found in the Teacher's Resource Binder.

CLOSURE
Ask students to describe the relationship of local governments to the state.

ASSESSMENT

Have students complete the Section 5 Review on page 604.

SECTION 6

FOCUS

Predicting (I) Ask students: Is your public education free? What is the source of the money that buys your books and pays teachers and administrators? *(Lead students to speculate on the role of federal, state, and local governments in funding public education.)*

**Answers to
Section 5 Review**

Define: *municipalities*—city, town, or village governments

1. To administer the law of the county
2. To handle a specific government service or several related services
3. By an elected board of trustees

Interpreting Charts: Councilpersons in a commission form of government must head a department.

Synthesizing Information: Answers should include three of the following: federal government, state government, county government, local government, special districts, school district.

Essential Elements
3B, 4D, 4F, 7B, 7G, 9A, 9B, 9G

SECTION  REVIEW

Define: municipalities

1. What is the job of the county commissioners court?
2. Why are special districts formed?
3. How are independent school districts governed?

Interpreting Charts: Study the chart of municipal governments on page 603. What job do councilpersons in a commission form of government have that councilpersons in a mayor-council form of government do not?

Synthesizing Information: Describe three forms of government under which you are presently governed.

A trained city manager, who is appointed by the council, carries out the policies of government.

Some Texas cities have a mayor-council form of government. The mayor and the council are elected by the voters. Other cities have a commission form of government, developed in Galveston around 1900.

Special Districts. The most numerous local governments are special districts. They are created to handle one government service or several related ones. Most special districts are related to water resources. The governing body of the district may be elected by the voters or appointed by another unit of government. Districts often include a number of counties or parts of counties under their authority.

School Districts. One kind of special district is the school district. It has the responsibility for public education. Most school districts are concerned with providing elementary and secondary education. There are other kinds, however, including community college districts.

The most common type of school district is the independent school district. It is so named because it is governed by its own elected board of trustees. The number of trustees and their terms of office vary by district. The board appoints a superintendent to be the chief administrator of the schools within the district. ✪

⬛ Government and Public Education

The many units of local government in Texas interact with one another, with the state, and with the national government. The state and the United States also interact. This interaction makes for a very complex system in Texas. One major area in which interaction takes place is in providing public education. The national, state, and local governments all have responsibilities for providing public education for the children of Texas.

The State Role. Of the three levels of government, the state of Texas bears the major burden of providing elementary and secondary education. Article VII of the constitution commands the legislature to establish, support, and maintain "an efficient system of public free schools."

The state legislature is the source of public school laws. The laws cover many subjects. They require children to

INSTRUCTION

Guided Practice (I) Have students work independently or in pairs to create a diagram illustrating the role of local, state, and national government in public education. **V, TK, LEP**

RETEACHING

Call on students to summarize the role of national, state, and local government in providing public education in Texas. **A, LEP**

CLOSURE

Ask students: In your opinion, which level of government—local, state, or national—should bear the major responsibility for providing public education?

ASSESSMENT

Have students complete the Section 6 Review on page 605.

Photo by David E. Kennedy, TexaStock

All students in the Texas public school system are provided with an education by state, federal, and local funding.

attend school, and they list subjects to be taught. The state also provides about 40 percent of the money for schools. One source of money is the permanent school fund, established in 1854. Another source is taxation.

Public education is directed by the state board of education, with members elected from fifteen districts. The governor appoints a commissioner of education, who oversees the operations of the Texas Education Agency. This agency supervises the entire public school system. It administers the foundation school program, the most important state program for funding the public schools. The agency reviews standards for schools and for the certification of teachers. It also reviews textbooks and other learning materials used in Texas public school classrooms.

The Local Role. Texans have long believed in local control of schools. The state has chosen to allow local school districts to exercise many responsibilities. One of the most important is to set the local tax rate on property. The property tax is, by far, the most important local source of money for the schools. Local districts provide about 50 percent of the funds for public education.

The National Role. The national government provides about eight percent of Texas public school funds. The money is used for special programs such as vocational education. The federal courts have also played a major role in public education. Through their rulings, for example, Texas schools were integrated in the 1960s. ✪

SECTION ⑥ REVIEW

1. What level of government bears the major burden for public education?
2. What is the most important local source of money for schools?
3. About what percentage of public school funds are provided by the federal government?

Evaluating Information: Should the federal government be responsible for covering more of the expenses of education? Why or why not?

Making Decisions: What requirements and qualities would you look for in a commissioner of education? Explain your answer.

CHAPTER REVIEW RESOURCES

1. Chapter Review Worksheet 30
2. Chapter 30 Test, Form A
3. Reteaching Worksheet 30
4. Chapter 30 Test, Form B
5. **Informal Evaluation Forms:** Portfolio Assessment
6. *Texas, Our Texas* **Test Generator**

Essential Elements
3B, 8B, 9A, 9B, 9G

CHAPTER 30 REVIEW ANSWERS

Understanding Main Ideas

1. Popular sovereignty, limited government, republican form of government
2. They are the Texas Senate and the House of Representatives. Their job is to make laws.
3. Its job is to carry out the laws. The executive branch is made up of the governor, other executive officers, and executive agencies.
4. It is divided into civil courts and criminal courts. Civil courts hear disputes between private parties. Criminal courts hear cases that involve a crime against the public or the state.
5. Counties, municipalities, special districts
6. Federal, state, and local governments are all responsible for public education. The state government bears the major burden.

Thinking Critically

1. **Analyzing Information:** The governor has the power to appoint officials, veto proposed laws, and call special sessions of the legislature. The lieutenant governor chairs the Legislative Budget Board and is head of the Senate, with power to ap-

CHAPTER 30 REVIEW

Understanding Main Ideas

1. What are the three basic principles underlying the Texas Constitution?
2. What two houses make up the Texas legislature, and what is their job?
3. What is the job of the executive branch, and who makes up that branch?
4. Into what types of courts is the judicial branch divided, and what is the job of each?
5. What are the three levels of local government?
6. What are the three levels of government responsible for public education? Which level bears the major burden of education?

Thinking Critically

1. **Analyzing Information:** Compare the powers of the governor and lieutenant governor.
2. **Exploring Economics:** Why does control of the state budget process give an official much power?
3. **Making Decisions:** List three goals that you, as governor, would support for Texas. Explain why these are important goals.

Linking History and Government

1. To what sources can some provisions of the Texas Constitution be traced?
2. Whose governorship influenced Texas legislators to weaken the power of the executive branch? Why did the legislators respond to the governor thusly?

TAAS *Practice*
Using Primary Sources

In 1988, Ann Richards gave the keynote address at the National Democratic Convention. In the following excerpt from her book *Straight From the Heart*, she describes what she wanted to express:

> Right from the beginning of the speech I wanted to make it clear that "We're about to have some fun." I wanted an overall feeling that made people know that politics does not have to be all gloom and doom and lofty rhetoric [fancy words and ideas], that it is, . . . next to baseball and football, the All-American pastime. . . .
>
> I knew several things that had to be done in the speech. I wanted to say, from the beginning, that I know that my accent is different from yours, and for the majority of you in that television audience I know I don't sound like you. And I wanted to say it in a way that would be funny so that they would accept me and my accent.
>
> I wanted to say, also right away, I realize that I am female, and that not many females get to do what I am doing, but I hope you will listen to me. And I wanted to say something that would make the women feel good about me being there. . . .
>
> I wanted to say, "I am no different [from you]. All you people sitting out there in your living rooms listening to this person speak, I am an American who cares intensely about her country and its politics."

1. Richards thought that because she was female, some of the audience
   A might not listen to her
   B might expect her to be dull
   C might want her to tell stories about her family
   D might think she had an accent

point committee members and control the flow of proposed laws. Because of the lieutenant governor's power in the budget process, many consider the lieutenant governor to be more powerful than the governor.

2. **Exploring Economics:** Answers will vary but should reflect the idea that control of the budget gives an official

great influence over other agencies and areas of government. Agencies and programs have an interest in the budget because appropriations bills determine how much money will be spent on programs.

3. **Making Decisions:** Answers will vary but should demonstrate sound reasoning.

1. To earlier Texas constitutions and to English and Spanish law
2. Legislators weakened the governorship because of Republican governor Edmund J. Davis. During Reconstruction, Davis and his supporters had a majority in the legislature. They passed a series of laws favorable to Republicans, many of which gave more powers to the governor. At first opportunity, angry Democrats decreased the powers of the governor.

TAAS Practice
Using Primary Sources
1. A
2. C

TAAS Practice
Writing Informatively
Letters will vary but should provide detailed explanations.

Practicing Skills
1. **Making a Chart:** Charts should illustrate the three branches of the Texas state government and their functions.
2. **Interpreting Pie Graphs:** Education received the most money. Health, welfare, and rehabilitation agencies gained the most between 1990 and 1991.

Enriching Your Study of History
1. **Individual Project:** Posters should demonstrate thorough research.
2. **Cooperative Project:** Students should report on their observations of a local government session or of a judicial proceeding.

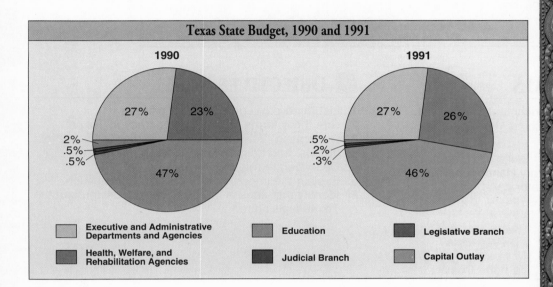

Texas State Budget, 1990 and 1991

1990 — 27%, 23%, 2%, .5%, .5%, 47%

1991 — 27%, 26%, .5%, .2%, .3%, 46%

- Executive and Administrative Departments and Agencies
- Health, Welfare, and Rehabilitation Agencies
- Education
- Judicial Branch
- Legislative Branch
- Capital Outlay

2. Richards wanted to make her listeners understand that
   A she needed a good laugh
   B they could not have a good time in politics
   C she was one of them
   D they deserved a good speech

TAAS Practice
Writing Informatively
Imagine that you are running for the office of mayor of your community. Write the voters a letter explaining why they should vote for you. Be sure to explain your stand on current community issues.

Practicing Skills
1. **Making a Chart:** Create a chart showing the three branches of the Texas state government. Include the function of each branch.

2. **Interpreting Pie Graphs:** Study the two pie graphs above. Which program received the most money in both budgets? Which program gained the most between 1990 and 1991?

Enriching Your Study of Government
1. **Individual Project:** Through research, find out what form of government your community has, and who are the people holding office in that government. Then create a poster chart showing what you have discovered.

2. **Cooperative Project:** With a partner, attend a session of your local community government, or of a judicial proceeding. Watch and listen carefully. Take notes on the proceedings as you observe, in order to prepare a report telling the class what you observed.

CITIZENSHIP IN TEXAS

TEACHER'S TIME LINE

Section 1	Section 2	Section 3	Section 4	Section 5	Review and Assessment
Pp. 608–09	Pp. 609–11	Pp. 612–13	Pp. 613–15	Pp. 615–16	
1 Day	1 Day	1 Day	1 Day	1 Day	1 Day

▥ TEACHER MATERIALS

Core: Graphic Organizer 31; Enrichment Worksheet 31; Review Worksheet 31; Reteaching Worksheet 31; Chapter 31 Tests, Forms A & B

Additional: Geography and Graph Skills 31, Map and Chart Transparencies 25, Oral History Handbook, Informal Evaluation Forms, Test Generator

▥ OBJECTIVES

1. List three privileges of Texas citizens.
2. Cite three forms of direct democracy in Texas.
3. Distinguish between political parties and interest groups, and describe the purpose of each.
4. Describe the role of lobbyists.
5. Explain the importance of political participation.
6. Identify the steps in the passage of a bill through the Texas legislature.

▥ RESOURCES

BOOKS FOR TEACHERS

Faulk, John Henry. *Papers.* Barker Center Manuscripts, 1881–1991. Collection of his works, reflecting his literary, political, and intellectual career.

Geoghegan, Thomas. *Which Side Are You On? Trying to be for Labor When It's Flat on Its Back.* New York: Farrar Straus Giroux, 1991. A look at the current state of the labor movement.

Lipartito, Kenneth J., and Joseph A. Pratt. *Baker & Botts in the Development of Modern Houston.* Austin: University of Texas Press, 1991. Examination of the economic impact of this law firm on Houston, Texas.

Ostrom, Vincent. *The Meaning of American Federalism: Constituting a Self-Governing Society.* San Francisco: Institute for Contemporary Studies, 1991. Collection of essays that defend the concept of federalism and stress the idea that true self-government requires the active participation of citizens.

Thoreau, Henry D. *Walden; and, Civil Disobedience.* New York: Penguin, 1983. Thoreau's philosophy of responsible citizenship.

MULTIMEDIA MATERIALS

A Heritage Restored. (film, 20 min.) Copy in each regional education service center, no charge. Tour of Texas governor's mansion, an example of historical restoration.

Texans Who Built Texas. (video, 30 min.) Texas Education Agency, Resource Center on Publication, 1701 Congress, Austin, TX 78701. Send blank tape for copy, no charge. Trip through Texas State Cemetery as review of Texas history.

Texas: Of All These Wonders. (film, 26 min.) Southwest Media Services, Inc., P.O. Box 140, Wimberley, Texas, 78676. A look at the diversity of the state.

STUDENTS WITH SPECIAL NEEDS

Limited English Proficient Students (LEP)

Bring to class as many used magazines as possible. (Ask students to bring magazines from home, with permission from parents or guardians.) Throughout the study of the chapter, have students cut from the magazines pictures that might be used to illustrate each of the chapter's five sections. Ask the students to assemble their pictures into a collage for classroom display. See other activities labeled **LEP.**

Students Having Difficulty with the Chapter

Have students create an outline of the chapter, using the section and subsection headings as topics and subtopics. They should use their completed outline to review the chapter. **LEP**

Auditory Learners

Invite a member of the Democratic party and the Republican party to class. In advance, have students prepare questions to ask the speakers, focusing on the differences between the two parties. See other activities labeled **A.**

Visual Learners

Have visual learners create a diagram of the three branches of government. Instruct students to draw their diagrams so that they reflect the powers of each of the branches. Ask them to add to their diagrams drawings representing the role of citizens in the democratic process. Invite students to display and discuss their diagrams. See other activities labeled **V.**

Tactile/Kinesthetic Learners

Ask students to work together to create a classroom mural illustrating the role of citizens in Texas government today. Encourage students to be creative. See other activities labeled **TK.**

Gifted Students

Invite students to work in pairs to research a recent election for governor in Texas. Ask one student to assume the role of the Democratic candidate and the other the role of the Republican candidate and then stage a debate for the class. Have the other class members "vote" for the candidate of their choice. See other activities labeled **G.**

VOCABULARY

In addition to the boldfaced terms in each section, some students might benefit from discussing the meanings of these terms.

Section 1: *privileges* (p. 608); *preference* (p. 609).

Section 2: *probation* (p. 610); *incompetent* (p. 610); *odd-numbered* (p. 610); *propositions* (p. 610); *repeal* (p. 611).

Section 3: *primary election* (p. 612); *disclose* (p. 613).

Section 4: *chambers* (p. 613); *testify* (p. 614); *override* (p. 614).

Section 5: *judicial process* (p. 615); *summoned* (p. 615); *jury duty* (p. 615); *verdict* (p. 616); *unanimous* (p. 616); *jurors* (p. 616); *indict* (p. 616).

GRAPHIC ORGANIZER

Have students skim the chapter and complete the Chapter 31 Graphic Organizer. *(You might wish to use this activity to review rather than to introduce the chapter.)*

ENRICHMENT

Have students complete the Chapter 31 Enrichment Worksheet.

SECTION ■1

FOCUS

Predicting (I) Write on the chalkboard the term *dual citizenship*. Ask students to speculate on its meaning. Point out to students that if they were born in Texas or have become a citizen of Texas by legal procedure, they are citizens of Texas as well as of the United States. They are "dual citizens."

INSTRUCTION

Vocabulary (I) You may wish to preteach the following boldfaced term: *naturalized citizen* (p. 608). **LEP**

Guided Practice (I) Ask students to write a paragraph explaining the difference between a right and a privilege in regard to citizenship. Students should provide an example of each. Call on volunteers to read their paragraphs aloud. **A, LEP**

CHAPTER 31 OVERVIEW

The citizens of Texas enjoy certain privileges in return for their allegiance to the state. As citizens of a democratic government, they have the opportunity to participate in democratic processes.

Essential Elements
4E, 7B, 7F, 7G, 9A

Government and Citizenship
The naturalization process consists of three steps. First, an applicant must submit an application form, fingerprint card, and biographical information sheet. Second, the applicant takes an examination that proves qualification in age and residence, character and loyalty, and education. Third, a judge reviews the case. If the judge decides to grant the applicant citizenship, the applicant takes the Oath of Allegiance and becomes a naturalized citizen.

CHAPTER 31

CITIZENSHIP IN TEXAS

Citizenship Focus

As a citizen of a democratic state, a person gives allegiance to that state and in return is protected. Chapter 31 looks at what it means to be a citizen of Texas and at the rights and responsibilities of citizens in a democratic government.

As you read the chapter, look for the answers to these questions:

1. What privileges do citizens enjoy?
2. In what ways do citizens participate in government?
3. What is the role of political parties and interest groups in Texas politics and government?
4. How are laws made, and how can citizens be involved in the lawmaking process?
5. How do citizens participate in the judicial process?

Larry Kolvoord / TexaStock

Most Texans enjoy dual citizenship. They are citizens of the United States and also citizens of Texas.

■1 Texas Citizenship

In Texas, most persons enjoy two citizenships. They are citizens of the United States and of the state of Texas. This "dual citizenship" is defined in the Fourteenth Amendment of the United States Constitution. It reads in part, "All persons born or naturalized in the United States and subject to the jurisdiction thereof, are citizens of the United States and of the State wherein they reside." A **naturalized citizen** is one who is not born a United States citizen but becomes one by a legal procedure.

The original purpose of the Fourteenth Amendment was to ensure that black people—former slaves as well as free blacks—would have citizenship. Before the Civil War, black Americans were denied citizenship. The United States Supreme Court had ruled before the war that African Americans could never become citizens.

Citizen Privileges. As is true in all states, citizens of Texas enjoy certain privileges not extended to noncitizens.

RETEACHING
Have each student use the information in Section 1 to develop a true/false quiz. Ask students to exchange their papers and complete the quiz. Allow partners to work together
to check and correct their answers. **LEP**

CLOSURE
Ask students to summarize and explain the importance of
the Fourteenth Amendment.

ASSESSMENT
Have students complete the Section 1 Review on page 609.

SECTION 2

FOCUS
Student Experiences (I) Distribute to students copies of a
voter registration card. Lead a class discussion of the information contained on the card and the purpose and importance of voter registration.

Only Texas citizens can vote in state elections and run
for office to represent Texans. Texas citizens also enjoy
privileges such as paying lower fees than out-of-state
students to attend state colleges and universities. Texans
receive preference in admission to state colleges and
universities. Texas citizens may hunt and fish in the state
on payment of lower fees and in preference to non-Texans.

Citizenship in a Democracy. Citizens enjoy many freedoms, stated in the Bill of Rights. But perhaps more
important, citizens can use their rights to participate in
decisions that affect their lives. In a democracy, people
have the right to participate in their government, which
makes and enforces laws under which they live. ✪

② Participation in Elections

Citizens of the state have many opportunities to participate in Texas government and politics. One way to take
part is to keep up with the news or to "talk politics" with
friends. More active participation includes writing a letter
to the editor of a newspaper to express your opinion. Other
ways might be to donate money to a campaign, attend a
political meeting, work in a campaign, or run for office.
The primary activity for most citizens is voting.

The Right to Vote. Today it is relatively easy to qualify
for, and to exercise, the right to vote. A voter must be a
United States citizen, a Texas resident, and at least eighteen
years of age. The person must have registered to vote at
least 30 days before the election.

Registration is required so that a person's qualifications
to vote may be checked for accuracy before an election.

Michael D. Sullivan / TexaStock

SECTION ★ 1 ★ REVIEW

Define: naturalized citizen

1. What is one privilege extended to Texas citizens that
noncitizens do not enjoy?
2. Where are a citizen's rights
stated?

Analyzing Information: Why
are noncitizens not given the
same rights as citizens?

**Exploring Multicultural Per-
spectives:** If you were an African
American when the Fourteenth
Amendment was passed, how
would you have reacted? Why?

Eligible voters must register to vote
in elections. Sometimes voter registration drives are held at various
places to sign up citizens qualified to
cast their votes in upcoming elections.
Once registered, a citizen remains
eligible to vote as long as she or he
meets certain qualifications.

Answers to Section 1 Review

Define: *naturalized citizen*—
person who is not born in the
United States but becomes a
citizen by a legal procedure

1. Possible answers include:
voting, running for office,
paying lower college and
university fees, preference in
admission to state colleges
and universities, lower hunting and fishing fees.
2. In the Bill of Rights

Analyzing Information: Answers will vary but might point
out that citizens are protected
by rights in return for their allegiance to their state and country.

**Exploring Multicultural Per-
spectives:** Answers will vary
but should be based on an understanding of the Fourteenth
Amendment and its effect on
African Americans.

Essential Elements
4F, 7A, 7B, 7D, 7E, 7F, 7G, 9A,
9B

INSTRUCTION

Vocabulary (I) You may wish to preteach the following boldfaced terms: *felony* (p. 610); *direct democracy* (p. 610); *initiative* (p. 611); *referendum* (p. 611); *recall* (p. 611). **LEP**

Guided Practice (I) List on the chalkboard the years 1991 through 2000. Have students use the information provided in Section 2 and the years listed on the chalkboard to determine when the following will take place in Texas. *(Note: Provide students with the clue "1992" for (d).)*

(a) General and special elections at the state level *(1992, 1994, 1996, 1998, 2000)*

(b) General elections at the local level *(1991, 1993, 1995, 1997, 1999)*

(c) Special elections at the local level *(These can be called during any year.)*

(d) Presidential elections *(1992, 1996, 2000)*

Copy students' responses on the chalkboard. **A, LEP**

For the citizen, registration is fairly simple. It requires little more than filling out a form. Once registered, the voter's name remains on the registration rolls as long as the voter remains qualified. This is called permanent registration.

A few citizens are disqualified from voting. A person cannot vote if convicted of a **felony**, which is a serious crime such as armed robbery or murder. Felons regain their voting rights two years after their prison term ends or two years after completing probation. If pardoned, they may regain voting rights earlier. Mentally incompetent people, or those judged unable to make their own decisions, are not permitted to vote.

Elections. The Texas voter is kept very busy. Texans vote on many more issues than do voters in some states, and elections are numerous. There are many elective offices and candidates on the Texas ballot. In one Houston election, more than 120 names appeared on the ballot. Proposed amendments to the Texas Constitution add to the length of the ballot in many elections.

Several kinds of elections crowd the voter's calendar. At the state level, there are general and special elections. The number of people voting is highest for general elections, held in even-numbered years. General elections take place on the first Tuesday after the first Monday in November. Every four years, when the names of presidential candidates appear on the ballot, the elections are called presidential elections. Special elections at the state level are held at other times. These elections are called when it is necessary to fill a vacancy in an office or to vote on a proposed amendment to the Texas Constitution.

Local elections also may be general or special. They are held to elect local officials or to vote on local issues. General elections at the local level are typically held in odd-numbered years. Special elections may be called for either year.

Besides the general and special elections, many Texans vote in primary elections. The purpose of primaries is to nominate candidates from each political party to run for office in the general election. Participation in each party's primary election is limited to its members.

Direct Democracy. Texas voters are allowed, within limits, to engage in **direct democracy**. This means they can decide propositions directly, rather than go through their elected representatives.

Michael D. Sullivan / TexaStock

Registered voters of Texas go to the polls on election days to cast their votes on local, state, and federal issues and candidates.

RETEACHING

Ask students to select one of the Section 2 subsections and create a sketch, diagram, chart, or other visual to illustrate the discussion. Invite volunteers to display and discuss their illustrations. **A, V, TK, LEP**

CLOSURE

Ask students: Why is it important for citizens to vote? Allow time for students to express differing opinions.

ASSESSMENT

Have students complete the Section 2 Review on page 611.

The **initiative** empowers voters to propose, or initiate, ballot propositions. A certain number of voters must sign a petition to have a proposition placed on the ballot. The Texas Constitution does not provide for the initiative, but municipalities may allow it. The **referendum** permits voters to approve or reject a proposition proposed by a lawmaking body and even to repeal a law already passed. In Texas, proposed amendments to the constitution must be submitted by the legislature to the voters in a referendum.

The third device of direct democracy is the **recall**. It is authorized only at the municipal level. It allows voters to remove an elected official prior to the end of a regular term of office. A recall election can be called if a certain number of voters sign a petition to demand one.

Voter Participation Levels. The number of Texans voting in elections varies from year to year. The highest voter turnout is during presidential elections. Voter participation in Texas is below average, compared to other states. In the 1988 presidential election, the voter turnout in Texas was 44.2 percent, while the national average was 50.1 percent.

Scholars who study government and politics cite several reasons for low voter participation in Texas prior to the 1960s. Laws kept blacks from voting. People who could not afford to pay the poll tax could not vote. Requirements of early registration and the need to register every year also contributed to low participation. All of these barriers to voting have been removed because they were declared unconstitutional by the federal courts. The United States Constitution was amended to prohibit the poll tax as a requirement for voting in federal elections.

At the present time, all proposed Texas election laws and procedures must be submitted to the United States attorney general. They must be cleared before they can be adopted. This was a requirement of the Voting Rights Act of 1965, which was amended in 1975 to include Texas among the states that must have their laws cleared. The law also requires Texas to print its ballots in Spanish as well as English and to use both languages in materials given to voters.

The voter participation of African Americans and Mexican Americans in Texas has increased in recent years. But neither these groups nor other Texans have completely overcome the legacy of the past. ✪

City of San Antonio

Former San Antonio mayor Henry Cisneros often speaks at Democratic party functions. The Democratic party dominated state politics for a century after Reconstruction and is still the majority party in Texas. The Republican party has gained strength in Texas, however, in recent years.

SECTION 2 REVIEW

Define: felony, direct democracy, initiative, referendum, recall

1. What requirements must a person meet in order to vote in Texas?
2. What is the purpose of a primary election?
3. How can voters remove an elected official at the municipal level?
4. What requirements did the Voting Rights Act of 1965 and its amendment in 1975 make for Texas elections?

Analyzing Information: How might the law requiring ballots to be printed in Spanish have affected Spanish-speaking voters?

Evaluating Information: Do you think the recall should apply to state elected officials? Why or why not?

Answers to Section 2 Review

Define: *felony*—a serious crime such as armed robbery or murder; *direct democracy*—government in which voters can decide propositions directly, rather than through their elected representatives; *initiative*—empowers voters to propose ballot propositions; *referendum*—permits voters to approve or reject a proposition proposed by a lawmaking body and to repeal a law already passed; *recall*—allows voters to remove an elected official prior to the end of a regular term

1. A person must be a United States citizen, a Texas resident, at least eighteen years of age, and must have registered to vote at least 30 days before the election.
2. To nominate candidates from each political party to run for office in the general election
3. Through a recall election
4. The act and its amendment required that all proposed Texas election laws and procedures be submitted to the United States attorney general to be cleared and that ballots and other voting materials be printed in Spanish as well as in English.

Analyzing Information: Citizens who were more proficient in Spanish than in English would have been encouraged to vote.

Evaluating Information: Answers will vary but should demonstrate sound reasoning.

SECTION 3

FOCUS

Past Learning (I) Ask students to name the two major political parties in Texas *(Democratic and Republican)*. Challenge students to name other political parties that they have learned about in their study of Texas and United States history.

INSTRUCTION

Vocabulary (I) You may wish to preteach the following boldfaced term: *interest group* (p. 612). **LEP**

RETEACHING

Ask students to write a paragraph summarizing the roles and functions of political parties and interest groups. **LEP**

CLOSURE

Ask students to name various interest groups that exist in their school. *(Any club or organization might be considered an interest group.)*

Essential Elements
4F, 4G, 7B, 7D, 7F, 7G, 9A

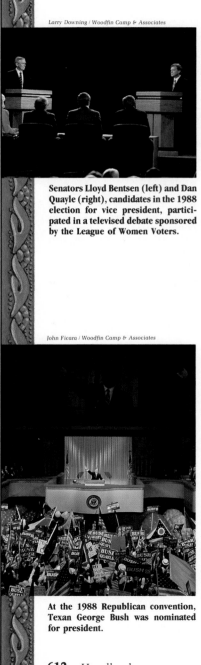

Larry Downing / Woodfin Camp & Associates

Senators Lloyd Bentsen (left) and Dan Quayle (right), candidates in the 1988 election for vice president, participated in a televised debate sponsored by the League of Women Voters.

John Ficara / Woodfin Camp & Associates

At the 1988 Republican convention, Texan George Bush was nominated for president.

3 Political Parties and Interest Groups

To increase their influence and effectiveness in Texas politics and government, Texas citizens join and form groups. The two major kinds of political groups are parties and interest groups.

Political Parties. Political parties are organizations of people with similar views about government. The major parties include people from all walks of life. Parties specialize in winning elections. They hope to control government by electing members to public office. Millions of people vote for, and identify with, parties.

The two major parties in Texas are the Democratic party and the Republican party. For more than 100 years, Texas was dominated by the Democratic party. After the Civil War, the Republican party was seen by a majority of Texans as the party of the North and the Union. Since the 1950s, more Texans have supported the Republican party, but Democrats still hold many state and local offices. Public opinion polls taken in 1991 showed that the number of Texans claiming to be Republicans was only slightly less than the number claiming to be Democrats.

For more citizens, the most common way to participate in party affairs is to vote in a primary election. Another opportunity is presented by party conventions. These are meetings of party delegates for the purpose of deciding party goals and electing party officers. Conventions write the party platform, or statement of goals. In presidential election years, they select presidential candidates. Local and state conventions meet every two years, and national conventions meet every four years.

Interest Groups. An **interest group** is organized to promote and defend the common interests and goals of its members. Interest groups are far more numerous than political parties, but any one group represents a much smaller number of people than does a party. Interest groups concentrate on single issues and interests or related issues and interests. Examples of interest groups in Texas include the League of Women Voters, the Texas Farm Bureau, the Texas State Teachers Association, Mothers Against Drunk Driving, and the AFL-CIO, a labor union.

Texas is known as a strong interest-group state because interest groups are very influential in the Texas legislature.

ASSESSMENT

Have students complete the Section 3 Review on page 613.

SECTION 4

FOCUS

Student Experiences (I) Ask students: When you disagree with a school rule or policy, what can you do to try to change it? Ask students to keep this discussion in mind as they read Section 4.

INSTRUCTION

Vocabulary (I) You may wish to preteach the following boldfaced term: *lobbying* (p. 613). **LEP**

The number of groups is large. Many new groups are being formed to seek representation and influence. One of the newer groups is the Texas Student Lobby, which represents college and university students. Organizations representing minority groups, women, and low-income citizens are also becoming more active. However, most scholars agree that older groups representing business, agriculture, labor unions, and professional workers remain more influential.

Interest groups are interested in more than laws that are passed. They also want to have a say in electing public officials who will be favorable to their goals and ideas. This is why political action committees, or PACs, have been formed. PACs collect money from their members to spend on campaigns. Contributions may go to support a candidate from one of the political parties. They may be used to pay for advertisements on radio, television, or in the newspapers to support or oppose an issue on the election ballot.

Texas election laws regulate PACs, but they do not place any limits on the amount of money PACs can contribute or on the number of PACs. PACs must disclose information about their contributions and how the money is used. ✪

SECTION ③ REVIEW

Define: interest group

1. How has the number of Republicans as compared to Democrats changed in recent years in Texas?
2. What is the purpose of political action committees?

Analyzing Information: Why might minority groups, women, and low-income citizens benefit from forming interest groups?

Evaluating Information: Do you think that a law should be passed to limit the amount of money a PAC can contribute to a candidate? Why or why not?

4 Participation in Making Laws

Citizens have the privilege and the right to participate in the making of laws by the legislature. They may also take part in drawing up rules and regulations for agencies in the executive branch of state government. The most common method of participating in lawmaking is through **lobbying**. Lobbying is defined as communicating with a member of the legislature or the executive branch in order to influence a proposed law.

Legislative Procedures. To be effective in lobbying, it is essential to know something about how laws are made. In general, there are four stages in passing a bill through each of the chambers of the Texas legislature. A bill is first introduced. It is then sent to a committee for consideration. Next, it is debated by the entire chamber. The last stage is final passage of the bill. Because the Texas legislature has two houses, a bill must go through the second house after passing through the first.

The chairperson of the committee to which a bill is referred should be asked to call a public hearing on the

Alon Reininger / Contact Press Images / Woodfin Camp

Senator Phil Gramm of College Station is a strong supporter of the Republican party in Texas.

Guided Practice (I) Refer students to the Section 4 Focus discussion. Then organize the class into small groups, and ask each group to choose a school rule or policy to disagree with. Each group should plan a campaign to have the rule or policy changed. Have a spokesperson from each group present the group's plan to the class. **A**

RETEACHING
Call on several students to describe the sequence of the legislative process. **A, LEP**

Bills into Law

This is a simplified diagram of how a bill becomes a law. The actual procedure is much more complicated than shown here.

Bill is introduced in a house

↓

Sent to committee for study ← Public may attend hearings

↓

Debated by entire chamber ← Public may attend sessions of legislature to show support or to oppose

↓

If passed, sent to other house for consideration →

Other house goes through much the same process. If passed, sent to governor

Governor may veto, sign, or not sign ←

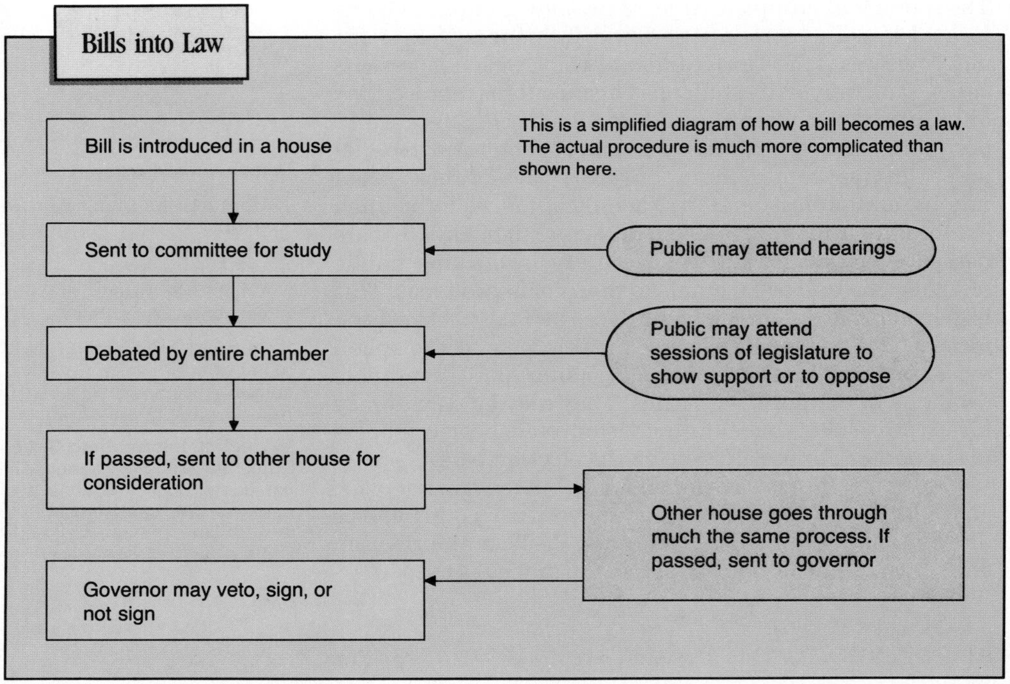

When may the public attend hearings and legislative sessions about a proposed bill?

bill. Members of the public may go to the capitol to testify for the bill or speak against it. If a committee reports favorably on a bill, that bill is likely to be scheduled for debate before the entire chamber. Supporters of the bill may be asked by a legislator to come to the capitol on the day of the debate. Large numbers of people indicate that the bill has support in the state. If the bill is passed by one house, people will have the opportunity to testify and show support when it goes to the other house.

The governor may sign a bill after it passes both houses of the legislature, in which case it becomes a law. The governor may also veto the bill. It will then die unless two-thirds of the members of each house of the legislature vote to override the veto. The governor may decide to do nothing, in which case the bill becomes a law after ten days during a session or twenty days when the session is over.

Influencing the Executive. Citizens have the opportunity to influence the adoption of rules and regulations by

CLOSURE

Ask students to identify three ways that citizens can participate in lawmaking.

ASSESSMENT

Have students complete the Section 4 Review on page 615.

SECTION 5

FOCUS

Student Experiences (I) Ask students if they know anyone
who has ever served on a jury. If so, ask the students to relate to the class what they learned about the case.

Taylor Johnson

The governor's mansion, completed
in 1856 about 300 yards south of the
capitol, is the official residence of the
governor of Texas. The mansion is
open to the public at various times
throughout the year.

the many agencies in the executive branch. These agencies
hold public hearings on proposed changes, and a citizen
may wish to testify at a hearing.

At other times, a citizen may wish to complain about
a problem to a government agency. Many agencies maintain
telephone "hot lines" to provide information and assistance. The office of the attorney general is one of several
that help with complaints by consumers.

Still another way to participate in the executive process
is through appointment by the governor to serve on a board
or commission. Many Texas boards and commissions are
filled with citizens who serve part-time without pay. Many
state boards and commissions exist to regulate a variety of
professions. These boards and commissions usually have
public members. For example, the board of directors of the
State Bar of Texas is the governing authority for the state's
lawyers. It has six members who are not lawyers. They
represent the interests of the public. ○

5 Participation in the Judicial Process

Citizens participate in the Texas judicial process mainly
by serving on a jury. In fact, it is a rare adult who has not
been summoned for jury duty.

SECTION ★ 4 ★ REVIEW

Define: lobbying

1. How many votes are needed
   to override a veto of the
   Texas governor?
2. What is one way in which a
   citizen can affect the executive branch?

Interpreting Charts: Study the
chart on page 614. At what
points can the public become
involved in the passage of a bill
into law?

Analyzing Information: Why is
it important for people to become involved in the legislative
process?

Answers to Section 4 Review

Define: *lobbying*—communicating with a member of the legislature or the executive branch
in order to influence a proposed
law

1. Two-thirds of the members
   of each house
2. Possible answers include:
   by testifying at public hearings, by telephoning hot
   lines, by being appointed by
   the governor to a board or
   commission.

Interpreting Charts: Citizens
can become involved when the
bill is sent to committee and
when the bill is debated by the
entire chamber.

Analyzing Information: Citizens have the privilege and the
right to participate in the making of laws that affect them. It is
important for citizens to see
that government meets their
needs.

Essential Elements
7D, 7F, 7G, 9A, 9B, 9G

INSTRUCTION

Guided Practice (I) Have students work in pairs to prepare a diagram of the information presented in Section 5. Call on volunteers to copy their diagram on the chalkboard. **V, TK, LEP**

RETEACHING

Have each student use the information in Section 5 to create a fill-in-the-blank review. Have students exchange papers and complete the reviews. Allow partners to work together to check and correct their answers. **LEP**

CLOSURE

Ask students: Would you welcome an opportunity to serve as a juror? Why or why not? Allow time for students to express varying viewpoints.

ASSESSMENT

Have students complete the Section 5 Review on page 616.

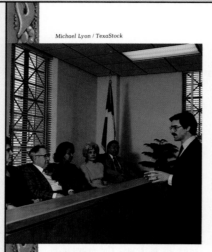

Michael Lyon / TexaStock

Although most trials in Texas courtrooms are conducted without a jury, the Texas Bill of Rights assures that defendants can ask for a jury trial.

Answers to Section 5 Review

1. A juror must be of "sound mind," be able to read and write, be a qualified voter, and not have been convicted of theft or a felony.
2. To investigate crimes and, if necessary, to indict a person of committing a crime

Analyzing Information: It ensures that a person receives a fair trial by a person's peers.

Making Decisions: Answers will vary but might include fairness and free from bias.

SECTION 5 REVIEW

1. What are the requirements for serving on a jury?
2. What is the purpose of a grand jury?

Analyzing Information: Why is a trial by jury an important right of all citizens?

Making Decisions: If you were a lawyer choosing a jury for a trial, what qualities would you look for in a juror?

Jury Duty. The right of trial by jury originated in England. It is protected by the Texas Bill of Rights. Its general purpose is to provide a fair trial by a person's peers, or fellow citizens. Juries may decide criminal and civil cases.

In a criminal case, the trial jury decides whether an accused person is guilty or innocent of the crime as charged. To reach its verdict, a jury considers the facts presented at the trial. It then applies the law as explained by the judge. The Texas jury also decides the punishment or sentence, within limits set by the law. Sentencing occurs separately from the trial on guilt or innocence.

The trial jury in civil cases decides for one side or the other in the suit. It bases its verdict on the facts as presented and the law as explained by the judge. The jury usually decides on the amount of damages awarded to the person bringing the suit, if any.

A trial jury is composed of twelve people in a district court and six in lower courts. A unanimous verdict is required to convict in a criminal case. A decision in a civil case at the district court level requires the agreement of ten of the twelve jurors. The agreement of five of six jurors is necessary for a decision in lower courts.

Most qualified voters are eligible for jury service. There are requirements to ensure that jurors are fair and fit to perform the necessary duties. A juror should be of "sound mind," be able to read and write, and not have been convicted of theft or a felony.

Names for the jury list are drawn at random from those qualified to serve. Those selected are summoned by mail to appear at the courthouse. Failure to do so is a crime. Some people are excused from jury duty by law. Among them are high school and college students. The judge may excuse others. Jurors are paid a small sum while on duty.

Grand Jury. A grand jury is used only in criminal cases or investigations. The purpose of a grand jury is to investigate crimes and, if findings call for it, to indict a person of committing a crime. An indictment is a formal accusation. The Texas Constitution requires a grand jury in felony cases.

The grand jury consists of twelve members. Nine must agree to return an indictment. All proceedings of the jury are secret. Qualifications for grand jurors are similar to those for trial jurors. ✪

Essential Elements
4G, 7D, 7E, 7F, 9A, 9B

CHAPTER 31 REVIEW

Understanding Main Ideas

1. List three privileges given to citizens of Texas that are not given to noncitizens.
2. List three forms of direct democracy used in Texas.
3. What is the purpose of interest groups?
4. What is the purpose of PACs?
5. At what points can citizens become involved in the lawmaking process?
6. What are the requirements for being a juror? What is the juror's job?

Thinking Critically

1. **Synthesizing Information:** Why is the political participation of citizens important to a democracy?
2. **Analyzing Information:** Explain the differences between political parties and interest groups.
3. **Evaluating Information:** What reasons do you think people give for not voting? Should the government require all citizens to vote? Why or why not?

Linking History and Government

1. What are some of the reasons that scholars give for low voter participation in Texas in the past?
2. Why was the Fourteenth Amendment added to the United States Constitution? For what does it provide?

TAAS Practice
Using Primary Sources

The following selection is from an article in the October 12, 1990 issue of *The Texas Observer.* Less than a month before the election for governor, a reporter asked Mesquite resident Ruth Shaver who she would vote for:

Ruth Shaver doesn't have time for electoral politics. She works. . . . Free time is a commodity [product] she lost two years ago when [a corporation] bought out her employer, [a supermarket].

Ann Richards or Clayton Williams? "I don't know," Mrs. Shaver said. "I don't know if it makes a difference and I haven't paid attention because I don't have much time." . . .

Ruth Shaver routinely goes to bed at two in the afternoon, wakes up at 10 p.m., and an hour later drives to Garland where she works at a locally owned grocery store . . . until 7 a.m. Then she leaves and drives the 10 miles to [a drug store where she works]. . . . Then she punches in [at a timeclock] and begins work. By noon, her workday is over.

Ruth Shaver is opposed to crime—her home has been broken into three times in the past two years. . . . More police protection, she said, would be high on her agenda. . . .

But Ruth Shaver is on no one's fundraising list. . . . And no candidate is buying TV ads that are likely to animate her enough to get her to the polls—if she had time to watch the ads and then vote. Like Ruth Shaver, 70 percent of voters sat out the last gubernatorial [governor's] election.

1. One issue that Ruth Shaver might vote to improve is
   A education
   B police protection
   C cutting government salaries
   D trade

CHAPTER 31 REVIEW ANSWERS

Understanding Main Ideas

1. Possible answers include: voting in state elections, running for office, lower college and university fees, preference in admission to state colleges and universities, lower hunting and fishing fees.
2. Initiative, referendum, recall
3. Interest groups inform lawmakers and voters of issues that are important to the members of the interest groups.
4. PACs raise money to elect political candidates who favor an interest group's goals and ideals.
5. Citizens can become involved when a bill is being studied in committee and when it reaches the house floor.
6. A juror must be of "sound mind," be able to read and write, and not have been convicted of theft or a felony. A juror listens to a case and determines guilt or innocence.

Thinking Critically

1. **Synthesizing Information:** A democratic government is based on the participation of citizens.
2. **Analyzing Information:** Interest groups concentrate on single issues and interests or related interests and issues. They might draw their members from more than

one political party. Political parties represent a much larger group of people, whose interests and goals vary widely. Their main goal is to win elections.

3. **Evaluating Information:** Answers will vary but might include lack of interest, inability to get to polling places, and lack of knowledge of issues. Answers to the second part of the question will vary but should be supported with sound reasoning.

Linking History and Government

1. Reasons cited by scholars include: laws that kept blacks from voting, the poll tax, requirements of early registration and registering every year.
2. It was added to ensure citizenship for African Americans. It provides that all persons born or naturalized in the United States are citizens of the United States and of the state in which they live.

TAAS *Practice*
Using Primary Sources
1. B
2. C

TAAS *Practice*
Writing Persuasively
Letters should demonstrate an understanding of the purpose of interest groups and should be based on sound reasoning.

Practicing Skills
1. **Making a Chart:** Charts should be based on the information presented in the chapter.
2. **Interpreting a Bar Graph:** Travis; Hidalgo

Enriching Your Study of Government
1. **Individual Project:** Students should share their findings with the rest of the class.
2. **Cooperative Project:** Reports should be based on thorough research and should demonstrate a cooperative effort.

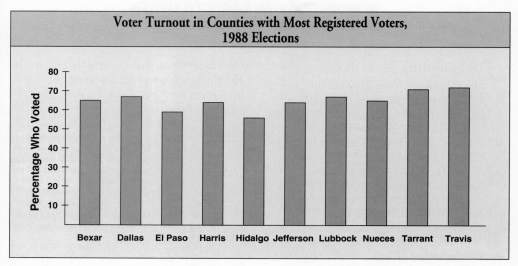

CONTINUED

Voter Turnout in Counties with Most Registered Voters, 1988 Elections

Percentage Who Voted

Bexar Dallas El Paso Harris Hidalgo Jefferson Lubbock Nueces Tarrant Travis

2. The main reason that Shaver does not vote is
   A she works too far from the polls
   B she is not registered to vote
   C she is too busy earning a living
   D she is not on anyone's fundraising list

TAAS *Practice*
Writing Persuasively

Imagine that you are the president of an interest group for bicycle manufacturers. Write a letter to members of Congress, urging them to vote against a proposed law that would make bicycle riding illegal during commuting hours.

Practicing Skills

1. **Making a Chart:** Make a chart showing ways that Texas citizens can participate in government. Use these headings: Politics, Making Laws and Regulations, Participation in the Judicial Process.

2. **Interpreting a Bar Graph:** Study the graph on this page. In which county did the most people vote? In which county did the fewest people vote?

Enriching Your Study of Government

1. **Individual Project:** Ask parents, or guardians, and adult friends if they remember the first time they voted. Find out how often they vote and why they do or do not vote.

2. **Cooperative Project:** With a partner, learn more about a piece of legislation recently passed by the Texas legislature. What was the purpose of the law? Did many legislators vote against the bill? How did the governor vote? Report to the class on your findings.

APPENDIX

SIX FLAGS OVER TEXAS

Through the years, six different national flags have flown over Texas. Early Spanish expeditions into Texas first laid claim to the area for Spain. As a result of explorations by René-Robert Cavelier, Sieur de la Salle, the French flag flew briefly over Texas. Because La Salle's settlement met with ill fate, France soon gave up its claim to the territory. The Spanish flag once again reigned over Texas.

When Mexico gained its independence from Spain, the provinces of Texas and Coahuila were united. The Mexican flag flew over Texas for fifteen years.

The Republic of Texas came into being as a result of the Convention of 1836. The first official flag of the Republic was adopted on December 10.

The flag of the United States then replaced the flag of the Republic when Texas was annexed. Texas became the twenty-eighth state in the United States.

When Texas seceded from the Union in 1861, it joined the Confederate States of America. The United States flag was then replaced by the flag of the Confederate States of America.

On June 19, 1865, the authority of the United States over Texas was proclaimed in the name of President Andrew Johnson. The flag of the United States once again flew over Texas.

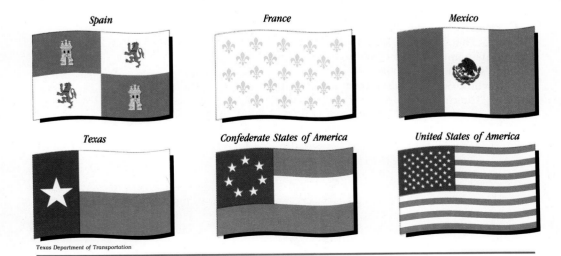

Spain   *France*   *Mexico*

Texas   *Confederate States of America*   *United States of America*

Texas Department of Transportation

STATE SEAL

A white star of five points on an azure-blue field encircled by olive and live oak branches is pictured on the front side of the present seal. The seal bears the inscription "The State of Texas." The reverse side of the seal, adopted in 1961, shows a shield with symbols of the Texas war for independence from Mexico, surrounded by the six flags that have flown over Texas.

Texas Department of Transportation

STATE BIRD

The mockingbird was designated the Texas state bird by the legislature on January 31, 1927. It has the ability to imitate many things it hears. The mockingbird has been characterized as fearless and aggressive in protecting itself and its offspring against enemies.

John Bova / Photo Researchers

STATE FLOWER

The bluebonnet was adopted on March 7, 1901, as the state flower of Texas by the Twenty-seventh Legislature. The flower is said to have received its name from its resemblance to a woman's sunbonnet. It also has been called wolfflower, buffalo clover, and el conejo ("the rabbit").

Reagan Bradshaw

STATE SONG

The Texas state song is "Texas, Our Texas." The music was written by the late William J. Marsh, and the words by Gladys Yoakum Wright and William J. Marsh. It was adopted by the legislature in 1929.

THE PLEDGE TO THE TEXAS FLAG

On April 3, 1965, Governor John Connally signed an act of the Fifty-ninth Legislature, officially designating the following as the pledge to the Texas flag:

Honor the Texas Flag.
I pledge allegiance to thee,
Texas, one and indivisible.

THE UNANIMOUS
DECLARATION OF INDEPENDENCE

made by the
Delegates of the People of Texas
in General Convention
at the Town of Washington
on the 2nd day of March 1836

When a government has ceased to protect the lives, liberty and property of the people, from whom its legitimate powers are derived, and for the advancement of whose happiness it was instituted; and, so far from being a guarantee for the enjoyment of those inestimable and inalienable rights, becomes an instrument in the hands of evil rulers, for their oppression: When the Federal Republican Constitution of their country, which they have sworn to support, no longer has a substantial existence, and the whole nature of their government has been forcibly changed, without their consent, from a restricted federative republic, composed of sovereign states, to a consolidated, central, military despotism in which every interest is disregarded but that of the army and the priesthood — both the eternal enemies of civil liberty, the ever-ready minions of power, and the usual instruments of tyrants: When, long after the spirit of the constitution has departed, moderation is, at length, so far lost, by those in power that even the semblance of freedom is removed, and the forms, themselves, of the constitution discontinued; and so far from their petitions and remonstrances being regarded the agents who bear them are thrown into dungeons; and mercenary armies sent forth to force a new government upon them at the point of the bayonet: When in consequence of such acts of malfeasance and abdication, on the part of the government, anarchy prevails, and civil society is dissolved into its original elements. In such a crisis, the first law of nature, the right of self-preservation — the inherent and inalienable right of the people to appeal to first principles and take their political affairs into their own hands in extreme cases — enjoins it as a right towards themselves and a sacred obligation to their posterity to abolish such government and create another, in its stead, calculated to rescue them from impending dangers, and to secure their future welfare and happiness.

Nations, as well as individuals, are amenable for their acts to the public opinion of mankind. A statement of a part of our grievances is, therefore, submitted to an impartial world, in justification of the hazardous but unavoidable step now taken of severing our political connection with the Mexican people, and assuming an independent attitude among the nations of the earth.

The Mexican government, by its colonization laws, invited and induced the Anglo-American population of Texas to colonize its wilderness under the pledged faith of a written constitution that they should continue to enjoy that constitutional liberty and republican government to which they had been habituated in the land of their birth, the United States of America. In this expectation they have been cruelly disappointed, inasmuch as the Mexican nation has acquiesced in the late changes made in the government by General Antonio Lopez de Santa Anna, who, having overturned the constitution of his country, now offers as the cruel alternative either to abandon our homes, acquired by so many privations, or submit to the most intolerable of all tyranny, the combined despotism of the sword and the priesthood.

It has sacrificed our welfare to the state of Coahuila, by which our interests have been continually depressed through a jealous and partial course of legislation carried on at a far distant seat of government, by a hostile majority, in an unknown tongue; and this too, notwithstanding we have petitioned in the humblest terms, for the establishment of a separate state government, and have, in accordance with the

622 Appendix

provisions of the national constitution, presented to the general Congress a republican constitution which was, without just cause contemptuously rejected.

It incarcerated in a dungeon, for a long time, one of our citizens, for no other cause but a zealous endeavour to procure the acceptance of our constitution and the establishment of a state government.

It has failed and refused to secure on a firm basis, the right of trial by jury; that palladium of civil liberty, and only safe guarantee for the life, liberty, and property of the citizen.

It has failed to establish any public system of education, although possessed of almost boundless resources (the public domain) and, although, it is an axiom, in political science, that unless a people are educated and enlightened it is idle to expect the continuance of civil liberty, or the capacity for self government.

It has suffered the military commandants stationed among us to exercise arbitrary acts of oppression and tyranny; thus trampling upon the most sacred rights of the citizen and rendering the military superior to the civil power.

It has dissolved by force of arms, the State Congress of Coahuila and Texas, and obliged our representatives to fly for their lives from the seat of government; thus depriving us of the fundamental political right of representation.

It has demanded the surrender of a number of our citizens, and ordered military detachments to seize and carry them into the Interior for trial; in contempt of the civil authorities, and in defiance of the laws and the constitution.

It has made piratical attacks upon our commerce, by commissioning foreign desperadoes, and authorizing them to seize our vessels, and convey the property of our citizens to far distant ports for confiscation.

It denies us the right of worshipping the Almighty according to the dictates of our own conscience; by the support of a national religion calculated to promote the temporal interest of its human functionaries rather than the glory of the true and living God.

It had demanded us to deliver up our arms; which are essential to our defence, the rightful property of freemen, and formidable only to tyrannical governments.

It has invaded our country, both by sea and by land, with intent to lay waste our territory and drive us from our homes; and has now a large mercenary army advancing to carry on against us a war of extermination.

It has, through its emissaries, incited the merciless savage, with the tomahawk and scalping knife, to massacre the inhabitants of our defenceless frontiers.

It hath been, during the whole time of our connection with it, the contemptible sport and victim of successive military revolutions; and hath continually exhibited every characteristic of a weak, corrupt, and tyrannical government.

These, and other grievances, were patiently borne by the people of Texas until they reached that point at which forbearance ceases to be a virtue. We then took up arms in defence of the national constitution. We appealed to our Mexican bretheren for assistance. Our appeal has been made in vain. Though months have elapsed, no sympathetic response has yet been heard from the Interior. We are, therefore, forced to the melancholy conclusion that the Mexican people have acquiesced in the destruction of their liberty, and the substitution therfor of a military government — that they are unfit to be free and incapable of self government.

The necessity of self-preservation, therefore, now decrees our eternal political separation.

We, therefore, the delegates, with plenary powers, of the people of Texas, in solemn convention assembled, appealing to a candid world for the necessities of our condition, do hereby resolve and declare that our political connection with the Mexican nation has for-ever ended; and that the people of Texas do now constitute a free sovereign and independent republic, and are fully invested with all the rights and *attributes which properly belong to independent nations; and, conscious of the rectitude of our intentions, we fearlessly and confidently commit the issue to the decision of the Supreme Arbiter of the destinies of nations.*

Richard Ellis President
of the Convention & Delegates
from Red River

Charles B. Stewart
Thos. Barnett
Jas. Collinsworth
Edwin Waller
Asa Brigham
John S. D. Byrom
Franco. Ruiz
J. Antonio Navarro
Jesse B. Badgett
Wm. D. Lacey
William Menefee
Jno. Fisher
Mathew Caldwell
William Mottley
Lorenzo de Zavala
Stephen H. Everitt
Geo. W. Smyth
Elijah Stapp
Claiborne West
Wm. B. Scates

M. B. Menard
A. B. Hardin
J. W. Bunton
Thos. J. Gazley
R. M. Coleman
Sterling C. Robertson
Geo. C. Childress
Bailey Hardeman
Rob. Potter
Thomas Jefferson Rusk
Chas. S. Taylor
John S. Roberts
Robert Hamilton
Collin McKinney
Albert H. Latimer
James Powers
Sam Houston
David Thomas
Edwd. Conrad
Martin Parmer

Edwin O. LeGrand
Stephen W. Blount
Jas. Gaines
Wm. Clark, Jr.
Sydney O. Penington
Wm. Carrol Crawford
Jno. Turner
Benj. Briggs Goodrich
G. W. Barnett
James G. Swisher
Jesse Grimes
S. Rhoads Fisher
John W. Moore
John W. Bower
Saml. A. Maverick from Bejar
Sam P. Carson
A. Briscoe
J. B. Woods
Test. H. S. Kimble Secretary

THE GOVERNORS AND PRESIDENTS OF TEXAS

Spanish Royal Governors of Texas

1523–1526	Francisco de Garay	1722–1727	Fernando Pérez de Almazán
1526–1528	Pánfilo de Narváez	1727–1730	Melchor de Mediavilla y Azcona
1528–1530	Nuno de Guzmán	1730–1734	Juan Antonio Bustillo y Zevallos
1538–1543	Hernando de Soto	1734–1736	Manuel de Sandoval
1691–1692	Domingo Terán de los Ríos	1736–1737	Carlos Benités Franquís de Lugo
1692–1697	Gregorio de Salinas	1737–1741	Prudencio de Orobio Basterra
1698–1702	Francisco Cuerbo y Valdez	1741–1743	Tomás Felipe Wintuisen
1703–1705	Mathias de Aguirre	1743–1744	Justo Boneo y Morales
1705–1708	Martín de Alarcón	1744–1748	Francisco García Larios
1708–1712	Simon Padilla y Cordova	1748–1751	Pedro del Barrio Junco y Espriella
1712–1714	Pedro Fermín de Echevers y Subisa	1751–1759	Jacinto de Barrios y Jáuregui
1714–1716	Juan Valdez	1759–1766	Angel de Martos y Navarrete
1716–1719	Martín de Alarcón	1767–1770	Hugo Oconór
1719–1722	Marqués de San Miguel de Aguayo	1770–1778	Barón de Ripperdá
		1778–1786	Domingo Cabello

1786	Bernardo Bonavía y Zapata	1800–1805	Juan Bautista de Elguezábal
1787–1788	Rafael Martinez Pacheco	1805–1810	Antonio Cordero y Bustamante
1788–1789	The office of governor was ordered suppressed and the province put under a presidial captain.	1811	Juan Bautista de las Casas
		1811–1813	Manuel María de Salcedo
		1814–1817	Ignacio Pérez
		1817	Manuel Pardo
1790–1798	Manuel Muñoz	1817–1822	Antonio Martínez
1798–1800	Josef Irigoyen		

Mexican Governors of Texas

1822–1823	José Felix Trespalacios	1823–1824	Luciano García

Mexican Governors of the Joint State of Coahuila y Texas

1824–1826	Rafael Gonzales	1833–1834	Juan José de Vidauri y Villaseñor
1826–1827	Victor Blanco	1834–1835	Juan José Elguezábal
1827–1830	José María Viesca	1835	José María Cantú
1830–1831	Ramón Eca y Músquiz	1835	Agustín M. Viesca
1831–1832	José María Letona	1835	Marciel Borrego
1832	Ramón Eca y Músquiz	1835	Ramón Eca y Músquiz
1832–1833	Juan Martín de Veramendi		

Provisional Colonial Governors before Independence

Nov. 14, 1835– March 1, 1836	Henry Smith	Jan. 11, 1836– March 1, 1836	James W. Robinson

Presidents of the Republic of Texas

March 16, 1836– Oct. 22, 1836	David G. Burnet	Dec. 13, 1841– Dec. 9, 1844	Sam Houston
Oct. 22, 1836– Dec. 10, 1838	Sam Houston	Dec. 9, 1844– Feb. 19, 1846	Anson Jones
Dec. 10, 1838– Dec. 13, 1841	Mirabeau B. Lamar		

Governors Since Annexation

Feb. 19, 1846– Dec. 21, 1847	J. Pinckney Henderson	Mar. 16, 1861– Nov. 7, 1861	Edward Clark
Dec. 21, 1847– Dec. 21, 1849	George T. Wood	Nov. 7, 1861– Nov. 5, 1863	Francis R. Lubbock
Dec. 21, 1849– Nov. 23, 1853	P. Hansborough Bell	Nov. 5, 1863– June 12, 1865	Pendleton Murrah
Nov. 23, 1853– Dec. 21, 1853	J. W. Henderson	Aug. 2, 1865– Aug. 9, 1866	Andrew J. Hamilton
Dec. 21, 1853– Dec. 21, 1857	Elisha M. Pease	Aug. 9, 1866– Aug. 8, 1867	James W. Throckmorton
Dec. 21, 1857– Dec. 21, 1859	Hardin R. Runnels	Aug. 8, 1867– Sept. 30, 1869	Elisha M. Pease
Dec. 21, 1859– Mar. 16, 1861	Sam Houston	Jan. 8, 1870– Jan. 15, 1874	Edmund J. Davis

Jan. 15, 1874– Dec. 1, 1876	Richard Coke	Jan. 17, 1927– Jan. 20, 1931	Dan Moody
Dec. 1, 1876– Jan. 21, 1879	Richard B. Hubbard	Jan. 20, 1931– Jan. 17, 1933	Ross S. Sterling
Jan. 21, 1879– Jan. 16, 1883	Oran M. Roberts	Jan. 17, 1933– Jan. 15, 1935	Miriam A. Ferguson
Jan. 16, 1883– Jan. 18, 1887	John Ireland	Jan. 15, 1935– Jan. 17, 1939	James V. Allred
Jan. 18, 1887– Jan. 20, 1891	Lawrence Sullivan Ross	Jan. 17, 1939– Aug. 4, 1941	W. Lee O'Daniel
Jan. 20, 1891– Jan. 15, 1895	James S. Hogg	Aug. 4, 1941– Jan. 21, 1947	Coke R. Stevenson
Jan. 15, 1895– Jan. 17, 1899	Charles A. Culberson	Jan. 21, 1947– July 11, 1949	Beauford H. Jester
Jan. 17, 1899– Jan. 20, 1903	Joseph D. Sayers	July 11, 1949– Jan. 15, 1957	Allan Shivers
Jan. 20, 1903– Jan. 15, 1907	S. W. T. Lanham	Jan. 15, 1957– Jan. 15, 1963	Price Daniel
Jan. 15, 1907– Jan. 17, 1911	Thomas M. Campbell	Jan. 15, 1963– Jan. 21, 1969	John Connally
Jan. 17, 1911– Jan. 19, 1915	Oscar Branch Colquitt	Jan. 21, 1969– Jan. 16, 1973	Preston Smith
Jan. 19, 1915– Aug. 25, 1917	James E. Ferguson	Jan. 16, 1973– Jan. 16, 1979	Dolph Briscoe
Aug. 25, 1917– Jan. 18, 1921	William P. Hobby	Jan. 16, 1979– Jan. 18, 1983	William P. Clements
Jan. 18, 1921– Jan. 20, 1925	Pat M. Neff	Jan. 18, 1983– Jan. 20, 1987	Mark White
Jan. 20, 1925– Jan. 17, 1927	Miriam A. Ferguson	Jan. 20, 1987– Jan. 15, 1991	William P. Clements
		Jan. 15, 1991– Present	Ann Richards

POPULATION OF TEXAS' TEN LARGEST CITIES, 1970–1990

	1990	1988	1980	1970
Houston	1,630,553	1,698,090	1,595,138	1,233,535
Dallas	1,006,877	987,360	904,078	844,401
San Antonio	935,933	941,150	786,023	654,153
El Paso	515,342	510,970	425,259	322,261
Austin	465,622	464,690	345,890	253,539
Fort Worth	447,619	426,610	385,164	393,455
Arlington	261,721	257,460	160,123	90,229
Corpus Christi	257,453	260,930	232,134	204,525
Lubbock	186,206	188,090	173,979	149,101
Garland	180,650	180,450	138,857	81,437

COUNTIES IN TEXAS

Name	Named for	County Seat	Organized	Natural Subregion(s)
Anderson	Kenneth L. Anderson	Palestine	1846	Piney Woods, Post Oak Belt
Andrews	Richard Andrews	Andrews	1910	Mountains and Basins, High Plains
Angelina	Angelina River	Lufkin	1846	Piney Woods
Aransas	Río Nuestra Señora de Aranzazu	Rockport	1871	Gulf Coast Plain
Archer	Dr. Branch T. Archer	Archer City	1880	Cross Timbers, Rolling Plains
Armstrong	Armstrong family	Claude	1890	Rolling Plains, High Plains
Atascosa	Spanish word for "boggy"	Jourdanton	1856	South Texas Plains
Austin	Stephen F. Austin	Bellville	1837	Gulf Coast Plain
Bailey	Peter James Bailey	Muleshoe	1917	High Plains
Bandera	Bandera Mountains	Bandera	1856	Edwards Plateau
Bastrop	Baron de Bastrop	Bastrop	1837	Post Oak Belt, Blackland Prairie
Baylor	Henry W. Baylor	Seymour	1879	Rolling Plains
Bee	Gen. Barnard E. Bee	Beeville	1858	Gulf Coast Plain
Bell	Peter Hansborough Bell	Belton	1850	Blackland Prairie, Grand Prairie
Bexar	Duke de Béxar	San Antonio	1837	South Texas Plains, Blackland Prairie, Edwards Plateau
Blanco	Blanco River	Johnson City	1858	Edwards Plateau
Borden	Gail Borden, Jr.	Gail	1891	High Plains, Rolling Plains
Bosque	Bosque River	Meridian	1854	Blackland Prairie
Bowie	James Bowie	Boston	1841	Piney Woods, Post Oak Belt
Brazoria	town of Brazoria	Angleton	1837	Gulf Coast Plain
Brazos	Brazos River	Bryan	1843	Post Oak Belt
Brewster	Henry P. Brewster	Alpine	1887	Mountains and Basins
Briscoe	Andrew Briscoe	Silverton	1892	Rolling Plains, High Plains
Brooks	James A. Brooks	Falfurrias	1912	South Texas Plains
Brown	Henry S. Brown	Brownwood	1857	Cross Timbers
Burleson	Edward Burleson, Jr.	Caldwell	1846	Post Oak Belt
Burnet	David G. Burnet	Burnet	1854	Edwards Plateau, Grand Prairie
Caldwell	Mathew Caldwell	Lockhart	1848	Post Oak Belt, Blackland Prairie
Calhoun	John C. Calhoun	Port Lavaca	1846	Gulf Coast Plain
Callahan	James H. Callahan	Baird	1858	Cross Timbers, Rolling Plains
Cameron	Capt. Ewen Cameron	Brownsville	1848	South Texas Plains
Camp	John L. Camp	Pittsburg	1874	Piney Woods
Carson	Samuel P. Carson	Panhandle	1880	High Plains
Cass	Lewis Cass	Linden	1846	Piney Woods
Castro	Henri Castro	Dimmitt	1891	High Plains
Chambers	Gen. Thomas J. Chambers	Anahuac	1858	Gulf Coast Plain
Cherokee	Indians	Rusk	1846	Piney Woods, Post Oak Belt
Childress	George C. Childress	Childress	1887	Rolling Plains
Clay	Henry Clay	Henrietta	1873	Rolling Plains, Cross Timbers
Cochran	Robert Cochran	Morton	1924	High Plains
Coke	Richard Coke	Robert Lee	1889	Edwards Plateau, Rolling Plains
Coleman	Robert M. Coleman	Coleman	1864	Cross Timbers, Rolling Plains
Collin	Collin McKinney	McKinney	1846	Blackland Prairie
Collingsworth	James Collinsworth	Wellington	1890	High Plains, Rolling Plains

Name	Named for	County Seat	Organized	Natural Subregion(s)
Colorado	Colorado River	Columbus	1837	Gulf Coast Plain
Comal	Comal River	New Braunfels	1846	Edwards Plateau
Comanche	Indians	Comanche	1856	Cross Timbers, Grand Prairie
Concho	Concho River	Paint Rock	1879	Cross Timbers, Edwards Plateau, Rolling Plains
Cooke	Capt. William G. Cooke	Gainesville	1848	Cross Timbers, Post Oak Belt, Grand Prairie
Coryell	James Coryell	Gatesville	1854	Grand Prairie
Cottle	George W. Cottle	Paducah	1892	Rolling Plains
Crane	William C. Crane	Crane	1927	Mountains and Basins, High Plains
Crockett	David Crockett	Crockett	1891	Edwards Plateau, Mountains and Basins
Crosby	Stephen Crosby	Crosbyton	1886	High Plains, Rolling Plains
Culberson	David B. Culberson	Van Horn	1912	Mountains and Basins
Dallam	James W. Dallam	Dalhart	1891	High Plains
Dallas	George M. Dallas	Dallas	1846	Blackland Prairie
Dawson	Nicholas M. Dawson	Lamesa	1905	High Plains, Rolling Plains
Deaf Smith	Erastus "Deaf" Smith	Hereford	1890	High Plains
Delta	Greek letter delta	Cooper	1870	Blackland Prairie, Post Oak Belt
Denton	John B. Denton	Denton	1846	Blackland Prairie, Grand Prairie, Post Oak Belt
DeWitt	Green DeWitt	Cuero	1846	Gulf Coast Plain
Dickens	J. Dickens	Dickens	1891	High Plains, Rolling Plains
Dimmit	Philip Dimmitt	Carrizo Springs	1880	South Texas Plains
Donley	Judge Stockton P. Donley	Clarendon	1882	Rolling Plains, High Plains
Duval	Burr H., John C., and Thomas H. Duval	San Diego	1876	South Texas Plains
Eastland	William M. Eastland	Eastland	1873	Cross Timbers
Ector	Matthew D. Ector	Odessa	1891	High Plains, Mountains and Basins
Edwards	Haden Edwards	Rocksprings	1883	Edwards Plateau
Ellis	Judge Richard Ellis	Waxahachie	1850	Blackland Prairie
El Paso	El Paso del Norte	El Paso	1850	Mountains and Basins
Erath	George B. Erath	Stephenville	1856	Cross Timbers, Grand Prairie
Falls	Brazos River Falls	Marlin	1850	Blackland Prairie, Post Oak Belt
Fannin	James W. Fannin	Bonham	1838	Blackland Prairie, Post Oak Belt
Fayette	Marquis de Lafayette	La Grange	1838	Gulf Coast Plain, Post Oak Belt
Fisher	Samuel R. Fisher	Roby	1886	Rolling Plains
Floyd	Dolphin W. Floyd	Floydada	1890	High Plains
Foard	Maj. Robert L. Foard	Crowell	1891	Rolling Plains
Fort Bend	fort in bend of Brazos River	Richmond	1838	Gulf Coast Plain
Franklin	Judge Benjamin C. Franklin	Mount Vernon	1875	Post Oak Belt
Freestone	freestone rock	Fairfield	1851	Post Oak Belt
Frio	Frio River	Pearsall	1871	South Texas Plains
Gaines	James Gaines	Seminole	1905	High Plains
Galveston	Count Bernardo de Gálvez	Galveston	1839	Gulf Coast Plain
Garza	Garza family	Post	1907	High Plains, Rolling Plains
Gillespie	Capt. Richard A. Gillespie	Fredericksburg	1848	Edwards Plateau
Glasscock	George W. Glasscock, Sr.	Garden City	1887	High Plains, Edwards Plateau
Goliad	town of Goliad	Goliad	1837	Gulf Coast Plain
Gonzales	Rafael Gonzales	Gonzales	1837	Gulf Coast Plain, Post Oak Belt
Gray	Peter W. Gray	Pampa	1902	High Plains

Name	Named for	County Seat	Organized	Natural Subregion(s)
Grayson	Peter W. Grayson	Sherman	1846	Blackland Prairie, Post Oak Belt
Gregg	Gen. John Gregg	Longview	1873	Piney Woods
Grimes	Jesse Grimes	Anderson	1846	Piney Woods, Post Oak Belt, Gulf Coast Plain
Guadalupe	Guadalupe River	Seguin	1846	Post Oak Belt, Blackland Prairie
Hale	Lt. John C. Hale	Plainview	1888	High Plains
Hall	Warren D. C. Hall	Memphis	1890	Rolling Plains
Hamilton	Gen. James Hamilton	Hamilton	1858	Grand Prairie
Hansford	John M. Hansford	Spearman	1889	High Plains
Hardeman	Bailey and Thomas J. Hardeman	Quanah	1884	Rolling Plains
Hardin	Augustine B., Benjamin W., Milton A., Franklin, and William Hardin	Kountze	1858	Piney Woods
Harris	John R. Harris	Houston	1837	Gulf Coast Plain, Piney Woods
Harrison	Jonas Harrison	Marshall	1842	Piney Woods
Hartley	Rufus K. and Oliver C. Hartley	Channing	1891	High Plains
Haskell	Charles R. Haskell	Haskell	1885	Rolling Plains
Hays	John C. "Jack" Hays	San Marcos	1848	Edwards Plateau, Blackland Prairie
Hemphill	John Hemphill	Canadian	1887	High Plains
Henderson	James P. Henderson	Athens	1846	Blackland Prairie, Post Oak Belt
Hidalgo	Miguel Hidalgo y Costilla	Edinburg	1852	South Texas Plains
Hill	George W. Hill	Hillsboro	1853	Blackland Prairie, Grand Prairie, Post Oak Belt
Hockley	Gen. George W. Hockley	Levelland	1921	High Plains
Hood	Gen. John B. Hood	Granbury	1866	Blackland Prairie, Cross Timbers
Hopkins	David Hopkins family	Sulphur Springs	1846	Blackland Prairie, Post Oak Belt
Houston	Sam Houston	Crockett	1837	Piney Woods, Post Oak Belt
Howard	Volney E. Howard	Big Spring	1882	Edwards Plateau, High Plains, Rolling Plains
Hudspeth	Claude B. Hudspeth	Sierra Blanca	1917	Mountains and Basins
Hunt	Memucan Hunt	Greenville	1846	Blackland Prairie
Hutchinson	Anderson Hutchinson	Stinnett	1901	High Plains
Irion	Robert A. Irion	Mertzon	1889	Edwards Plateau
Jack	Patrick C. and William H. Jack	Jacksboro	1857	Cross Timbers
Jackson	Andrew Jackson	Edna	1836	Gulf Coast Plain
Jasper	Sgt. William Jasper	Jasper	1837	Piney Woods
Jeff Davis	Jefferson Davis	Fort Davis	1887	Mountains and Basins
Jefferson	Thomas Jefferson	Beaumont	1837	Gulf Coast Plain, Piney Woods
Jim Hogg	James Stephen Hogg	Hebbronville	1913	South Texas Plains
Jim Wells	Judge James B. Wells	Alice	1912	Gulf Coast Plain, South Texas Plains
Johnson	Col. Middleton T. Johnson	Cleburne	1854	Blackland Prairie, Grand Prairie, Post Oak Belt
Jones	Anson Jones	Anson	1881	Rolling Plains
Karnes	Henry W. Karnes	Karnes City	1854	Gulf Coast Plain, Post Oak Belt
Kaufman	David S. Kaufman	Kaufman	1848	Blackland Prairie, Post Oak Belt
Kendall	George W. Kendall	Boerne	1862	Edwards Plateau
Kenedy	Capt. Mifflin Kenedy	Sarita	1921	South Texas Plains
Kent	Andrew Kent	Jayton	1892	Rolling Plains
Kerr	James Kerr	Kerrville	1856	Edwards Plateau

Name	Named for	County Seat	Organized	Natural Subregion(s)
Kimble	George C. Kimbell	Junction	1876	Edwards Plateau
King	William P. King	Guthrie	1891	Rolling Plains
Kinney	Henry L. Kinney	Brackettville	1874	Edwards Plateau, South Texas Plains
Kleberg	Robert J. Kleberg	Kingsville	1913	Gulf Coast Plain, South Texas Plains
Knox	Gen. Henry Knox	Benjamin	1886	Rolling Plains
Lamar	Mirabeau B. Lamar	Paris	1841	Blackland Prairie, Post Oak Belt
Lamb	Lt. George A. Lamb	Littlefield	1908	High Plains
Lampasas	Lampasas River	Lampasas	1856	Edwards Plateau, Grand Prairie
La Salle	René-Robert Cavelier, Sieur de la Salle	Cotulla	1880	South Texas Plains
Lavaca	Lavaca River	Hallettsville	1846	Gulf Coast Plain, Post Oak Belt
Lee	Gen. Robert E. Lee	Giddings	1874	Post Oak Belt
Leon	Martín de León	Centerville	1846	Post Oak Belt
Liberty	town of Libertad	Liberty	1837	Gulf Coast Plain, Piney Woods
Limestone	limestone rock	Groesbeck	1846	Blackland Prairie, Post Oak Belt
Lipscomb	Abner S. Lipscomb	Lipscomb	1887	High Plains
Live Oak	live oak trees	George West	1856	Gulf Coast Plain, South Texas Plains
Llano	Llano River	Llano	1856	Edwards Plateau
Loving	Oliver Loving	Mentone	1931	Mountains and Basins
Lubbock	Col. Tom S. Lubbock	Lubbock	1891	High Plains
Lynn	W. Lynn	Tahoka	1903	High Plains
Madison	James Madison	Madisonville	1854	Piney Woods, Post Oak Belt
Marion	Gen. Francis Marion	Jefferson	1860	Piney Woods
Martin	Wylie Martin	Stanton	1884	High Plains
Mason	Lt. G. T. Mason	Mason	1858	Edwards Plateau
Matagorda	town of Matagorda, Spanish for "dense cane"	Bay City	1837	Gulf Coast Plain
Maverick	Samuel A. Maverick	Eagle Pass	1871	South Texas Plains
McCulloch	Gen. Ben McCulloch	Brady	1876	Cross Timbers, Edwards Plateau
McLennan	Neil McLennan, Sr.	Waco	1850	Blackland Prairie, Grand Prairie
McMullen	John McMullen	Tilden	1877	South Texas Plains
Medina	Medina River	Hondo	1848	Edwards Plateau, South Texas Plains
Menard	Michel B. Menard	Menard	1871	Edwards Plateau
Midland	location on railroad halfway between Ft. Worth and El Paso	Midland	1885	High Plains, Edwards Plateau
Milam	Benjamin R. Milam	Cameron	1837	Blackland Prairie, Post Oak Belt
Mills	John T. Mills	Goldthwaite	1887	Cross Timbers, Grand Prairie
Mitchell	Eli and Asa Mitchell	Colorado City	1881	High Plains, Rolling Plains
Montague	Daniel Montague	Montague	1858	Cross Timbers, Grand Prairie
Montgomery	Gen. Richard Montgomery	Conroe	1837	Piney Woods
Moore	Commodore Edwin W. Moore	Dumas	1892	High Plains
Morris	William W. Morris	Daingerfield	1875	Piney Woods, Post Oak Belt
Motley	Dr. Junius W. Motley	Matador	1891	High Plains, Rolling Plains
Nacogdoches	Indians	Nacogdoches	1837	Piney Woods
Navarro	José Antonio Navarro	Corsicana	1846	Blackland Prairie, Post Oak Belt
Newton	Corp. John Newton	Newton	1846	Piney Woods
Nolan	Philip Nolan	Sweetwater	1881	Rolling Plains
Nueces	Nueces River	Corpus Christi	1846	Gulf Coast Plain
Ochiltree	William B. Ochiltree	Perryton	1889	High Plains
Oldham	William S. Oldham	Vega	1880	High Plains

630 *Appendix*

Name	Named for	County Seat	Organized	Natural Subregion(s)
Orange	early orange groves	Orange	1852	Gulf Coast Plain, Piney Woods
Palo Pinto	Palo Pinto Creek	Palo Pinto	1857	Cross Timbers
Panola	Indian word for "cotton"	Carthage	1846	Piney Woods
Parker	Isaac Parker	Weatherford	1856	Cross Timbers, Grand Prairie
Parmer	Martin Parmer	Farwell	1907	High Plains
Pecos	Pecos River	Fort Stockton	1872	Mountains and Basins
Polk	James K. Polk	Livingston	1846	Piney Woods
Potter	Robert Potter	Amarillo	1887	High Plains
Presidio	Spanish word for "fort"	Marfa	1875	Mountains and Basins
Rains	Emory Rains	Emory	1870	Blackland Prairie, Post Oak Belt
Randall	Gen. Horace Randall	Canyon	1889	High Plains
Reagan	John H. Reagan	Big Lake	1903	Edwards Plateau, High Plains
Real	Julius Real	Leakey	1913	Edwards Plateau
Red River	Red River	Clarksville	1837	Blackland Prairie, Post Oak Belt
Reeves	George R. Reeves	Pecos	1884	Mountains and Basins
Refugio	Nuestra Señora del Refugio mission	Refugio	1837	Gulf Coast Plain
Roberts	John S. and Oran M. Roberts	Miami	1889	High Plains
Robertson	Sterling C. Robertson	Franklin	1838	Post Oak Belt
Rockwall	wall-like rock formation	Rockwall	1873	Blackland Prairie
Runnels	Hiram G. Runnels	Ballinger	1880	Rolling Plains
Rusk	Thomas J. Rusk	Henderson	1843	Piney Woods
Sabine	Sabine River	Hemphill	1837	Piney Woods
San Augustine	town of San Augustine	San Augustine	1837	Piney Woods
San Jacinto	Battle of San Jacinto	Coldspring	1870	Piney Woods
San Patricio	town of San Patricio	Sinton	1837	Gulf Coast Plain
San Saba	San Saba River	San Saba	1856	Cross Timbers, Edwards Plateau
Schleicher	Gustav Schleicher	Eldorado	1901	Edwards Plateau
Scurry	Gen. William R. Scurry	Snyder	1884	Rolling Plains
Shackelford	Dr. John Shackelford	Albany	1874	Cross Timbers, Rolling Plains
Shelby	Isaac Shelby	Center	1837	Piney Woods
Sherman	Gen. Sidney Sherman	Stratford	1889	High Plains
Smith	Gen. James Smith	Tyler	1846	Piney Woods, Post Oak Belt
Somervell	Gen. Alexander Somervell	Glen Rose	1875	Grand Prairie
Starr	Dr. James H. Starr	Rio Grande City	1848	South Texas Plains
Stephens	Alexander H. Stephens	Breckenridge	1876	Cross Timbers
Sterling	Capt. W. S. Sterling	Sterling City	1891	Edwards Plateau, Rolling Plains
Stonewall	Gen. T. J. "Stonewall" Jackson	Aspermont	1888	Rolling Plains
Sutton	Col. John S. Sutton	Sonora	1890	Edwards Plateau
Swisher	James G. Swisher	Tulia	1890	High Plains
Tarrant	Gen. Edward H. Tarrant	Fort Worth	1850	Grand Prairie, Post Oak Belt
Taylor	Taylor family	Abilene	1878	Rolling Plains
Terrell	Alexander W. Terrell	Sanderson	1905	Edwards Plateau
Terry	Col. Benjamin F. Terry	Brownfield	1904	High Plains
Throckmorton	Dr. William E. Throckmorton	Throckmorton	1879	Cross Timbers, Rolling Plains
Titus	A. J. Titus	Mount Pleasant	1846	Piney Woods, Post Oak Belt
Tom Green	Gen. Tom Green	San Angelo	1875	Edwards Plateau, Rolling Plains
Travis	Col. William B. Travis	Austin	1843	Blackland Prairie, Edwards Plateau, Grand Prairie

Appendix **631**

Name	Named for	County Seat	Organized	Natural Subregion(s)
Trinity	Trinity River	Groveton	1850	Piney Woods
Tyler	John Tyler	Woodville	1846	Piney Woods
Upshur	Abel P. Upshur	Gilmer	1846	Piney Woods
Upton	John C. and William F. Upton	Rankin	1910	High Plains, Mountains and Basins, Edwards Plateau
Uvalde	Juan de Ugalde	Uvalde	1856	Edwards Plateau, South Texas Plains
Val Verde	Battle of Val Verde	Del Rio	1885	Edwards Plateau
Van Zandt	Isaac Van Zandt	Canton	1848	Post Oak Belt
Victoria	Nuestra Señora de Guadalupe de Jesus Victoria mission	Victoria	1837	Gulf Coast Plain
Walker	Samuel H. Walker	Huntsville	1846	Piney Woods
Waller	Edwin Waller	Hempstead	1873	Gulf Coast Plain, Piney Woods
Ward	Thomas W. Ward	Monahans	1892	Mountains and Basins
Washington	George Washington	Brenham	1837	Gulf Coast Plain, Post Oak Belt
Webb	James Webb	Laredo	1848	South Texas Plains
Wharton	William H. and John A. Wharton	Wharton	1846	Gulf Coast Plain
Wheeler	Royal T. Wheeler	Wheeler	1879	High Plains, Rolling Plains
Wichita	Indians	Wichita Falls	1882	Rolling Plains
Wilbarger	Josiah and Mathias Wilbarger	Vernon	1881	Rolling Plains
Willacy	John C. Willacy	Raymondville	1921	South Texas Plains
Williamson	Robert M. Williamson	Georgetown	1848	Blackland Prairie, Grand Prairie
Wilson	James C. Wilson	Floresville	1860	Post Oak Belt, South Texas Plains
Winkler	Judge Clinton M. Winkler	Kermit	1910	Mountains and Basins
Wise	Henry A. Wise	Decatur	1856	Cross Timbers, Grand Prairie
Wood	George T. Wood	Quitman	1850	Piney Woods, Post Oak Belt
Yoakum	Henderson K. Yoakum	Plains	1907	High Plains
Young	Col. William C. Young	Graham	1856	Cross Timbers
Zapata	Antonio Zapata	Zapata	1858	South Texas Plains
Zavala	Lorenzo de Zavala	Crystal City	1884	South Texas Plains

GLOSSARY AND PRONUNCIATION GUIDE

Symbol	Sound	Example	Symbol	Sound	Example	Symbol	Sound	Example
a	ă	lap (LAP)	g	g	go (GOH)	oy	oi	noise (NOYZ)
ah	ä	father (FAH ther)	i	ĭ	hit (HIT)	s	s	salt (SAHLT)
	ŏ	cot (KAHT)	iy	ī	ice (IYS)	sh	sh	ship (SHIP)
	ȯ	straw (STRAH)	j	j	judge (JUHJ)	u	u	foot (FUT)
ay	ā	same (SAYM)	k	k	cat (KAT)	u	ŭ	cup (KUHP)
ch	ch	chin (CHIN)	ny	ñ	canyon (ka nyuhn)		ə	about (uh BOWT)
ee	ē	be (BEE)	oo	ü	rule (ROOL)	y	y	yes (YES)
eh	ĕ	bet (BEHT)	oh	ō	hope (HOHP)		ll	pollo (POH yoh)
er	er	term (TERM)	ow	ou	house (HOWS)	zh	zh	vision (VI zhuhn)

GLOSSARY

The numbers refer to the pages on which the terms first appear.

A

abolitionists (a buh LI shuh nists) people who wanted to abolish slavery, 355

absolute location (ab soh LOOT loh KAY shuhn) the exact location of any place on earth, 23

ad interim (AD IN tehr uhm) temporary, 252

administration (ad mi nis TRAY shuhn) term of office, 267

adobe (uh DOH bee) bricks made by drying clay mud in the sun, 104

alcalde (ahl KAHL deh) A local Spanish official who acted as mayor, sheriff, and judge, 148

allegiance (uh LEE juhnts) loyalty (usually, to a country), 364

allies (A liyz) friends or supporters by treaty, 92

amendment (uh MEHND muhnt) addition that changes a part of a constitution, 390

annexation (a nehk SAY shuhn) the process of a territory or country being added to another country, 263

appellate court (uh PEHL uht KORT) a court that reviews cases tried in lower courts to determine whether errors were made in those courts, 601

appropriations bill (uh proh pree AY shuhnz bil) a proposed law to authorize spending, 597

aquifers (A kwuh ferz) underground formations of natural rock, sand, or gravel in which water is contained, 31

archaeologists (ahr kee AH luh jists) scientists who dig beneath the ground for evidence of past cultures, 76

Archaic Era (ahr KAY ik I ruh) cultural period beginning after 6000 B.C., when the Paleo-Indian culture gradually changed to a different way of life, 83

architects (AHR kuh tehkts) building designers, 333

archives (AHR kiyvz) official records, 283

artifacts (AHR tuh fakts) tools, weapons, and other objects that help show how people lived in the past, 77

assassinated (uh SA suh nay tid) murdered (usually used to mean a sudden and deliberate killing of an important leader), 382

astronomy (uh STRAH nuh mee) the study of the stars and planets, 86

atlatl (AT la tuhl) spear-throwing stick, 81

aviation (ay vee AY shun) human flight, 492

ayuntamiento (ah yoon tah MYEHN toh) Spanish local governing council of landowners, 148

B

balanced budget (BA luhnst BUH jit) budget in which revenue is equal to expenditures, 598

bands (BANDZ) small family groups of nomadic peoples, 91

bayous (BIY yooz) slow-moving, marshy bodies of water, 55

bicameral (biy KA muh ruhl) composed of two houses or chambers, 596

biennial (biy EH nee uhl) occurring once every two years, 297

blizzards (BLI zerdz) winter storms of high winds, snow, and ice, 37

blockade (blah KAYD) to block (usually, by military or naval means), 372

bonds (BAHNDZ) certificates sold with the promise that the issuer will pay back the full amount, plus additional money as interest, after a certain period of time, 447

brand (BRAND) design burned into the hide of cattle as proof of ownership, 427

buckskin (BUHK skin) smooth, tanned deerhide, used to make clothing on the frontier, 200

cabinet (KA buh nit) group of advisers (to the president), 262

capital (KA puh tuhl) city serving as seat of government, 183-184

capitol (KA puh tuhl) building in which a state or national legislature meets, 273

ceded (SEE did) given over, 154

census (SEHN suhs) official population count, 301

centennial (sehn TEH nee uhl) 100th anniversary or its celebration (Texas centennial marks 100 years since independence from Mexico), 534

chapel (CHA puhl) small church, 135

civil rights, (SI vuhl RIYTS) rights of citizenship belonging to all citizens, 553

civil settlements (SI vuhl SEH tuhl muhnts) small villages made up of civilians, people who were neither priests nor soldiers, 133

climate (KLIY muht) patterns of weather over a long period of time, 33

colonists (KAH luh nists) settlers of a new country that is governed by their home country, 135

Comanchería (koh mahn cheh REE ah) land of the Comanches, which stretched from Central Texas northward into Kansas and Colorado, 92

commute (kuh MYOOT) live in one area but drive elsewhere to a job or business, 549

compromise (KAHM pruh miyz) agreement in which each side gives up something it wants in order to reach a settlement, 317

confederacies (kuhn FEH duh ruh seez) groups joined together by agreement, such as the 25 Indian groups who lived in East Texas, 98

conquistadores (kohn KEES tuh dohrz) Spanish soldiers ("conquerors") who led the invasion and exploration of the Americas in the 1500s, 115

conservation (kahn ser VAY shuhn) planned management of resources to prevent their being destroyed, 21

constitution (kahn stuh TOO shuhn) written plan of government, 221

consumer goods (kuhn SOO mer GUDZ) products for personal use, such as automobiles, refrigerators, and radios, 514

continents (KAHN teh nuhnts) the earth's seven major landmasses, 6

corporations (kahr puh RAY shuhnz) groups of people organized into one body to do business, 298

cotton gins (KAH tuhn JINZ) places where cotton fiber is separated from the seeds, 205

countries (KUHN treez) nations of the world, divisions of continents, 6

crop rotation (KRAHP roh TAY shuhn) the practice of not planting the same crop in the same place two years in a row, in order to help keep the soil from wearing out, 99

cultural geography (KUHL cher uhl gee AH gruh fee) study of how the land affects the way people live and how people affect the land, 7

cultures (KUHL cherz) ways of life marked by distinct customs and traditions, 76

customs (KUHS tuhmz) cultural ways of doing things, such as greeting strangers or naming children, 89

customs duties (KUHS tuhmz DOO teez) taxes on goods coming into one country from another country, 218

decree (duh KREE) an official order, handed down by a country's ruler, 218

delegates (DEH luh guhts) representatives to a convention, 224

democracy (duh MAH kruh see) government whose leaders and lawmakers are elected by the people, 213

demographers (duh MAH gruh ferz) scholars who study population developments, 564

depression (duh PREH shuhn) severe slowdown in the economy, 522

diplomats (DIP luh mats) persons who represent a country in foreign affairs, 158

direct democracy (duh REHKT duh MAH kruh see) the ability of voters to decide propositions without going through their elected representatives, 610

direction indicator (duh REHK shuhn IN duh kay ter) map symbol used to tell the map user which way is north, south, east, and west, 12

discrimination (dis kri muh NAY shuhn) unfair treatment of a group of people on the basis of a characteristic they share, such as ancestry, 550

domesticate (duh MEHS tuh kayt) to tame, or control for human use, 84

draft (DRAFT) an act by which people are required by law to serve in the military, 369

drought (DROWT) long period without rain, 38

ecology (i KAHL uh jee) the interrelationships of living things and their environments, 21

economic downturn (EK uh nah mik DOWN tern) a decline in business activity, 566

economy (i KAH nuh mee) system of producing and distributing goods and services, 42

emancipating (i MAN suh pay teeng) freeing, usually of enslaved peoples, 280

empire (EHM piyr) a rule of one country over foreign lands, 114

empresarios (ehm pruh SAH ree ohs) business-people who brought settlers into Texas, 185

environment (ehn VIY ruhn muhnt) natural surroundings, 3

epidemic (eh puh DEH mik) contagious disease affecting large numbers of people at approximately the same time, 139

equator (ee KWAY ter) an imaginary line that circles the earth halfway between the North and South poles, 5

erosion (i ROH zhuhn) slow wearing away (of soil) by wind, water, or ice, 38

escarpments (eh SKAHRP muhnts) long cliffs or steep slopes, 63

ethnic group (ETH nik GROOP) people of the same cultural background, 203

executive branch (eg ZEH kyuh tiv BRANCH) branch of government that carries out the laws and is headed by a president (or governor), 251

exiled (EHG ziyld) forced to flee one's own country for political reasons, 317

expeditions (ehks puh DI shuhnz) journeys of discovery, 114

export (EHK spohrt) send to other areas for sale (usually, to other countries), 205

extermination (ehk ster muh NAY shuhn) complete destruction, 416

extinct (ehk STINKT) no longer existing, disappeared (refers to species of life), 83

F

faction (FAK shuhn) group of people who share a viewpoint on an issue (such as a political faction), 228

faculty (FA kuhl tee) a school's teachers and staff members, 499

fault (FAHLT) uneven break just below the earth's surface, 66

federal government (FEH duh ruhl GUH vern muhnt) government of the United States, 298

felony (FEH luh nee) serious crime such as armed robbery or murder, 610

fiestas (fee EHS tuhz) celebrations, 148

filibusters (FI luh bus terz) from the Spanish word for "freebooters" or "adventurers," persons interested in adventure, in easy wealth, or in overthrowing the Spanish government in Texas, 158

financial panic (fuh NAN chuhl PA nik) situation in which people with money in banks grow fearful and withdraw their savings, resulting in bank failures, 175

foreign relations (FAH ruhn ruh LAY shuhnz) dealings with other countires, 280

Formative Era (FAHR muh tiv IR uh) period of great cultural change after 1000 B.C., in which Indian civilization was forming, 84

freedmen (FREED mehn) freed, or former, enslaved people, 387

free enterprise (FREE EHN ter priyz) economic system in which individuals are free to work for their own profit, 306

friars (FRIY erz) members of a group of Roman Catholic missionaries, or "brothers," 115

frontier (fruhn TEER) edge of settlement, 189

G

garrison (GA ruh suhn) station of troops, 219

globe (GLOHB) a model of the way the earth looks from space, 5

graft (GRAFT) making profit illegally, 412

grist mill (GRIST MIL) machine used for grinding grain into meal or flour, 332

H

historians (his TOH ree uhnz) persons who use the knowledge gained from scientists and scholars to write a history of early people; also those who write the story of the past, 79

hurricanes (HER uh kaynz) huge storms of high winds and heavy rain, 36

I

immigrants (I muh gruhnts) persons who come into a country to settle, 176

impeached (im PEECHT) charged with crimes while in office, 499

inaugural address (uh NAH gyuh ruhl uh DREHS) opening speech when a president (or governor) takes office, 271

industry (IN duhs tree) activity of making products or preparing them for sale, 205

infantry (IN fuhn tree) foot soldiers, 319

initiative (uh NI shuh tiv) procedure enabling voters to propose ballot propositions, 611

insulate (IN suh layt) cover or surround with a material that slows or stops the flow of hot or cold air, 104–105

integrate (IN tuh grayt) allow students of all backgrounds to attend the same schools; mix, 553

interest group (IN trehst GROOP) group of people organized to promote and defend common interests and goals of its members, 612

interstate (IN ter stayt) between at least two different states, 475

intolerance (in TAH luh ruhnts) unwillingness to accept different ideas, people, or opinions, 511

irrigation (i ruh GAY shuhn) supplying water to crops or land by artificial means, 31

J

javelinas (ha vuh LEE nuhz) wild pigs, 104

Jim Crow laws (JIM CROH LAHZ) laws passed after Reconstruction to enforce segregation, 470

judicial branch (joo DI shuhl BRANCH) branch of government that is the court system, 251

junctions (JUHNK shuhnz) meeting places of two or more railroad lines, 450

jurisdiction (ju ris DIK shuhn) authority to hear certain kinds of cases, 601

L

labor unions (LAY ber YOO nyuhnz) organizations of workers formed to work for higher wages and better working conditions, 477

landforms (LAND fohrmz) natural features of the land surface that give the land its shape, 28

land grant (LAND GRANT) form of government aid to encourage construction, as of colleges or railroads (railroad companies received sections of land to encourage the construction of new railway lines), 448

lariat (LA ree uht) long, light rope used by cowboys (from the Spanish words *la reata*), 438

latitude (LAT uh tyood) lines on a globe that run east and west around the earth and measure distances north and south of the equator, 9

legislative branch (LEH jis lay tiv BRANCH) branch of government that makes the laws, 251

legislature (LEH jis lay cher) law-making body, 185

lignite (LIG niyt) a type of soft coal, 58

limited government (LI muh tid GUH vern muhnt) a government whose powers are limited, or restricted, by a constitution, 595

literacy (LI tuh ruh see) the learned ability to read and write, 339

lobbying (LAH bee eeng) communicating with a member of the legislature or the executive branch in an attempt to influence a proposed law, 613

longitude (LOHNJ uh tyood) lines, also called meridians, that circle the earth from North Pole to South Pole and are used to measure distances east and west of the prime meridian, 9

M

maize (MAYZ) a kind of corn cultivated by early American Indians, 84

mammoths (MA muhths) ancient ancestors of the elephant, 80

manufactured products (ma nyoo FAK cherd PRAH duhkts) items made either by hand or by machine in large numbers for sale, 332

map legend (MAP LEJ uhnd) the key to using a map, it tells what a map's symbols mean, 14

maps (MAPS) drawings on a flat surface of all or parts of the earth, 5

martial law (MAHR shuhl LAH) rule by the armed forces (usually, to maintain order) 381

mastodons (MAS tuh dahnz) ancient ancestors of the elephant, 80

matrilineal (mat ruh LIN ee uhl) tracing descent only through people's mother's families, 97

mechanized (MEH kuh niyzd) using machinery to perform tasks, 454

metropolitan areas (meh truh PAH luh tuhn Ar ee uhz) cities combined with areas of heavy population around them, 564

militia (muh LI shuh) group of citizens who serve as an army only when necessary, 182

minority groups (muh NAH ruh tee GROOPS) small groups within a larger population, 550

missions (MI shuhnz) establishments begun by Roman Catholic missionaries, which consisted of a church, houses, and farm buildings, usually built near a presidio, 131

mitotes (muh TOH teez) all-night celebrations held by Indian groups such as the Coahuiltecans, 104

monopoly (muh NAH puh lee) a large enough share of a business or industry to control prices, 479

moral code (MAH ruhl KOHD) set of rules defining right and wrong, 92

municipalities (myoo ni suh PA luh teez) city, town, or village governments, 602

N

naturalized citizen (NA chuh ruh liyzd SI tuh zuhn) one who is not born a United States citizen but who becomes one by a legal procedure, 608

natural resources (NATCH er uhl ree SOHR sez) the vegetation, wildlife, water, minerals, and soil of a place, 20

neutral (NYOO truhl) not belonging to either side in a dispute, 158

nobles (NOH buhlz) persons born of high rank, 115

nomadic (noh MA dik) moving periodically in search of food, or following wild animals from season to season, 79

nominated (NAH muh nay tid) chosen as a candidate for election to office, 293

Northern Hemisphere (NOR thern HEM is feer) the northern half of the planet earth, 4

northers (NAHR therz) air masses or fronts that produce a rapid drop in temperature, 34

O

offensive (uh FEHN siv) forward troop movement (or attack by a military force), 313

order (AHR der) religious group, 115

ordinance (AHR duh nuhnts) an official order, 363

GLOSSARY

P

Paleo-Indians (PAY lee oh IN dee uhnz) first settlers in North America ("ancient Indians"), 79

pardon (PAHR duhn) official forgiveness, 164

parole (puh ROHL) the release of a prisoner under condition of good behavior, 413

pemmican (PEH muh kuhn) food of the Plains Indians, consisting of dried and powdered buffalo meat combined with buffalo fat and juices, and berries, nuts, fruits, or roots, 93

petition (puh TI shuhn) a formal, usually written, request, 175

physical geography (FIZ uh kuhl gee AH gruh fee) the study of the surface and natural features of the earth, 7

platform (PLAT fohrm) statement of political goals, usually of a candidate or party, 475

plaza (PLAH zuh) public square in a city, a town, or a village, 147

political parties (puh LI tuh kuhl PAHR teez) organized groups representing people with similar views about government, 298

poll tax (POHL TAKS) tax that must be paid in order to vote, 267

pool (POOL) arrangement whereby companies in the same industry divide up the business and agree to set prices, 478

popular sovereignty (PAH pyuh ler SAHV ruhn tee) principle that all political power comes from the people, 594–595

prairies (PREH reez) grasslands, 58

precipitation (pruh SI puh TAY shuhn) moisture falling as rain, snow, sleet, hail, or mist, 33

prehistory (pree HIS tuh ree) period of time when no written records of human experiences were kept, 76

presidios (pruh SI dee ohz) small forts in which Spanish soldiers were stationed, 132

prime meridian (PRIYM muh RID ee uhn) line of longitude at 0° that passes through Greenwich, England, 10

progressive (pruh GREH siv) forward-looking or relating to progress, 480

prohibition (proh uh BI shuhn) a legal ban on the making and selling of alcoholic drinks, 478

proration (proh RAY shuhn) plan whereby each oil well is limited to producing a certain amount each day, 531

provisional (pruh VI zhuh nuhl) temporary, 243

R

ragtime (RAG tiym) popular form of music in the late 1800s and early 1900s, originated by Scott Joplin, 493

rancherías (rahn cheh REE ahs) small farming villages, particularly of the Lipan Apaches, 95

ranges (RAYN jehz) groups of mountains, 28

ransom (RAN suhm) pay for the return of, 409

ratify (RA tuh fiy) approve (as a treaty), 269

rebellion (ruh BEHL yuhn) attempt to overthrow an established government, 161

recall (REE kahl) the power of voters to remove an elected official prior to the end of a regular term of office, 611

Reconstruction (ree kuhn STRUHK shuhn) process of bringing the Confederate states back into the United States after the Civil War, 386

referendum (reh fuh RIN duhm) the power of voters to approve or reject a proposition proposed by a law-making body or to repeal a law that has already passed, 611

refinery (ruh FIYN ree) place in which crude oil is processed into various products, 457

reforms (ruh FOHRMZ) changes to improve government or society, 468

regiments (REH juh muhnts) military units of about 1,000 troops, 369

region (REE juhn) geographic area that is somehow different from others near it, 50

reinforcements (ree in FOHRS muhnts) additional troops, 239

relative location (REL uh tiv loh KAY shuhn) where a place is in relation to other places, 22

relief (ruh LEEF) government aid given to people in order to help them survive, 526

remuda (ruh MYOO duh) group of horses on a cattle drive (Spanish for "exchange"), 431

repealed (ruh PEELD) removed as a law, 534

republic (ruh PUH blik) form of government in which voters elect representatives to carry out the wishes of the majority of citizens, 262

reservations (reh zer VAY shuhnz) sections of land set aside, or reserved, for Indian use, 320

revolution (reh vuh LOO shuhn) overthrow of a government, 167

roundup (ROWN duhp) the act of driving or gathering scattered cattle together in one place, 431

rural (RU ruhl) of or relating to the country, 20

S

sales tax (SAYLZ TAKS) tax paid by consumers when they buy certain products, 555

scale indicator (SKAYL IN duh kay ter) a numbered line that tells how much distance on a map represents a certain distance on earth, 13

scrip (SKRIP) paper notes that represent a promise to pay, 531

secede (suh SEED) to withdraw, or separate, from an organization or nation (as Texas separated from the United States), 350

segregation (sehg ruh GAY shuhn) separating or keeping apart groups of people, especially according to race, 470

shaman (SHAH muhn) healer, 119

sharecroppers (SHEHR krah perz) tenant farmers who promise part of their crop to a landowner in return for tools, seeds, or a house, 455

siege (SEEJ) the surrounding of a fortified place in an attempt to force its surrender, 246

socialist (SOH shuh list) society in which all work and rewards are to be shared equally, 306

social security (SOH shuhl suh KYUR uh tee) system that provides pensions to retired citizens and payments to unemployed workers, 532

solar power (SOH ler POW er) energy obtained from sunlight, 44

specie (SPEE shee) gold and silver to back paper money, 267

speculation (speh kyuh LAY shuhn) taking an unusual business risk (such as buying large quantities of land), hoping to make a quick profit, 187

springs (SPREENGZ) natural outpourings of water from underground, 32

squatters (SKWAH terz) persons who settled land on their own without a title, 187

states (STAYTS) major political divisions of a country, or nation, 7

states' rights (STAYTS RIYTS) view that if a state did not agree with a federal law, it could choose not to obey or enforce it, 362

stocks (STAHKS) shares of ownership in a company, 522

strategy (STRA tuh jee) military plans, 239

strike (STRIYK) organized work stoppage, usually by unions, 477

subregions (SUHB ree juhnz) smaller divisions of a region, 52

suburbs (SUH berbz) towns or cities on the edge of a larger city, 547

suffrage (SUHF rehj) the right to vote, 482

Sunbelt (SUHN belt) the southern and western rim of the United States, so called because of its warm climate, 561–562

synthetic (sin THEH tik) human-made (rather than found in nature), 538

T

tallow (TA loh) animal fat used in making soap and candles, 329

tanneries (TA nuh reez) places where animal hides were prepared (made into leather), 332

technology (tehk NAH luh jee) way of using resources, 43

tenant farmers (TEH nuhnt FAHR muhrz) people who rent land on which to grow crops, 455

tepees, (TEE peez) movable homes made from animal skins stretched over long poles, 90

textile (TEK stiyl) cloth, 332

tidelands (TIYD LANDZ) underwater lands bordering the coast, 555

titles (TIY tuhlz) proofs of ownership, 178

tornadoes (tahr NAY dohz) violent circular storms that develop within severe thunderstorms (forming funnel-shaped clouds), 36

tributaries (TRI byuh teh reez) branches of a larger stream or river, 30

trust (TRUHST) group of companies in the same business that operate under the same leadership (to set prices and control competition), 479

U

unanimous (yoo NA nuh muhs) agreed to by all, 250

unemployed (uhn ehm PLOYD) without work, 525

urban (ER buhn) relating to cities or city areas, 20

urbanization (er buhn uh ZAY shuhn) growth and spread of cities, 547

V

vaqueros (vah KEH rohs) the first Texas cowboys, who were Hispanic, 149

venison (VEH nuh suhn) deer meat, 199

veto (VEE toh) cancellation of a proposed law (by a president or governor), 392

viceroy (VIYS roy) Spanish king's representative (in a foreign land), 119

vigilante (vi juh LAN tee) citizen who enforces the law as he or she sees fit, sometimes without following legal procedures, 341

W

water features (WAH ter FEE cherz) rivers, lakes, and streams formed by water draining from the land, 28

welfare (WEL fair) care and well-being, 496

wildcatter (WIYLD ka ter) oil operator who works on her or his own in search of new oil fields, 515

INDEX

c indicates a chart
f indicates a feature
g indicates a graph

m indicates a map
p indicates a photograph or
   illustration

q indicates a quotation

role of lieutenant governor in, 599
Buena Vista, 314
Buffalo, 63, p 74, 83
  described by Spanish explorers, 119, p 119
  destruction of herds, 415–416, p 415, p 416
  and Indian hunting techniques, 81, p 81, 83
  Plains Indian cultures and, 90, 91, 92–93, 94, 95, 97
Buffalo Bayou, 208, 256, 265
Buffalo soldiers, 421–422
Bullock, Bob, q 575
Burleson, Albert Sidney, 502
Burleson, Edward, 240–241, p 241, 277, 280
Burnet, David G., 187, 209, 252, p 252, 255, q 255, 263, 271, q 286, 363, 380
Burnett, Carol, 583
Busey, Gary, 583
Bush, George, 570, 571, p 612
Bustamante, Anastacio, (boos tah MAHN teh, ahn ah STAHS ee yoh), 221–222, p 222
Byars, Lula, f 513, q 513

C

Cabeza de Vaca, Alvar Núñez (kah BEH sah deh VAH kah, AHL vahr NOO nyehs), 117–119, p 118, f 127, q 127, 170
Caddoes, see Native Americans
Caddo Lake, p 21
Camargo, Diego de (kuh MAHR goh, dee EH goh deh), 117
Camino Real (kah MEE noh reh AHL), 143, m 143, 189, 197
Camp Bowie, 502
Camp Logan, 503
Camp MacArthur, 503
Camp Travis, 502–503
Camp Verde, 336
Canadian River, see Rivers
Capitals of Texas, 265, 272–273; see also San Felipe de Austin, Washington-on-the-Brazos
Capitols of Texas (buildings), p front cover, p 265, 273, p 275, 397, p 397, p 565
Cap Rock, see Escarpments
Cárdenas, García López de (KAHR deh nahs, gahr SEE ah LOH pehs deh), 123
Carl of Solms-Braunfels, Prince, see Solms-Braunfels, Prince Carl of

Caro, Robert, q 507
Carpetbaggers, 394
Carranza, Venustiano (kah RAHN zuh, veh noos tee AH noh), 501
Casañas, Francisco (kah SAH nyahs, frahn SEES koh), f 98, q 98
Castañeda, Carlos Eduardo (kahs tah NYEH dah, KAHR lohs ay DWAHR doh), 585, p 585
Castañeda, Lieutenant Francisco (kahs tah NYEH dah, frahn SEES koh), 230
Castro, Henri (KAHS troh, ahn REE), p 305, 306
Catacalos, Rosemary, 586
Cattle, m 15, 425–442, m 429, 468, 551
  branding of, p 427
  in Central Plains, 60, 61, 62
  in Gulf Coastal Plains, 52, 55, 57, 58, 59
  longhorn, p 425, 426–427
  in Panhandle, p 36
  in Rocky Mountains, 68
  in Spanish missions, 146, 149
  on Texas frontier, 329–330, 332
Cattle trails, 428–433
Cavalry, Ninth and Tenth, see Buffalo soldiers
Cazneau, Jane McManus (cahz NOH), 209, 313, 333, f 341, q 341
Centennial celebration, 534
Central America, 85, 86, p 86, 586
Central Texas, p 3, p 22, p 28
  Native Americans of, 94–95, 97
  landforms of, 30
  Rolling Plains of, m 60, 62
Cherokees, see Native Americans
Cheyennes, see Native Americans
"Chicken War," 143–144
Childress, George, C., 250, p 250
Chisholm, Jesse, 430, p 430
Chisholm Trail (CHI zuhm TRAYL), m 429, 430
  Fort Worth and, 551
Chisos Mountains (CHEE sohs), p 25, m 67, 68, 69
Chisum, John, 332, 431
Christian, Charlie, 580
Christianity, see Religion
Chuckwagon, 432, p 432
Churches in Texas, see Religion
Cíbola, Seven Cities of (SEE boh lah), 120–123, 125–127
Cisneros, Henry, (sees NEH rohs), f 562, q 562, p 611
Cisneros, Sandra, 586
Cities; see also individual listings by name

in Blackland Prairie, 59
in Cross Timbers, 61–62
in Edwards Plateau, 66
in Grand Prairie, 61
growth of, 486, 489, 491–492, 572
in Gulf Coast Plain, 55–56
and health, 491
in High Plains, 64–65
and industry, 495–496, 515, 517
in Mountains and Basins, 68
in Piney Woods, 55
in Post Oak Belt, 58
and Progressivism, 496–497
and railroad development, 450–451
in Rolling Plains, 62
in South Texas Plains, 57
since World War II, 546–547
Citizenship, 608–616; see also Voting
  importance of, 608–609
  participation
    in elections, 609–611
    in political parties, 612
    in interest groups, 612–613
    in making laws, 613–615
    in the judicial process, 615–616
    in jury duty, 616
  privileges of, 608–609
City government, 480–481, 491, 602–604, c 603
Civil Rights Act of 1964, 553, 558
Civil rights law, 556, q 556
Civil rights movement, 550, 552–554, 569, 570; see also African Americans, Mexican Americans
Civil War, p 348, 349, 368–383
  battles in Texas, 373–378
  effects on cattle industry, 427–428
  effects on Texas, 382
  events leading to, 360–364, 368
  Texans in, 369–373, 380–381
Civilian Conservation Corps (CCC), 533
Clark, Edward, 364, 380
Clements, William, 571, p 571, 574
Cliburn, Van (KLIY bern, VAN), 579–580
Climate, 33–38, 562
Cloud, Daniel, 250, q 250
Coahuila y Texas, 185, 203, 222, 223
Coahuiltecans, see Native Americans
Coal, 42, 456
Coastal Bend, 51
Coke, Richard, 396–400, p 398, 468, 469
Coleman, Dabney, 583

104–107, f 106, q 106, 133
Karankawas (kuh RAHNG kuh wahz), 101–103, 118, 136, 167, 183
Kickapoos, 322, 415
Kiowas (KIY uh wuhz), 90, m 90, 92–94, p 93, 275, 319, 409–411, p 417, 419
Kiowa-Apaches, 410–411
Lipan Apaches (lee PAHN), 90, m 90, 94–95, p 94, 156, 321, 415
Mayas (MY uhz), 85
Mescalero Apaches (mehs kuh LEH roh), 90, m 90, 95, 421–422
Mound Builders, 85
Plains Indians, 90–97, p 107, 412, 415–416
Pueblos (PWEH blohz), 95, 104
Seminole leader, p 408
Shawnees, 275
and Spaniards, 114–128
Tawakonis (tah wuh KOH neez), 279
Tejas (TAY hahs), 138–139
Tiguas (TEE wuhz), 322
Tonkawas (TAHNG kuh wuhz), 90, m 90, 95, 97, 144, 183, 190, 321
Wacos, 279, 321
Wichitas, m 90, 100–101, p 101, 155, 156, 197
Zuñis (ZOO nyeez), 121–123
Natural gas, 42, 57, 62, 64, 443, 495
Natural regions, 51–52, m 53
Natural resources, 20, 42–45, 456–457, 573; *see also* Agriculture, Economy, Industry, Oil
in Blackland Prairie, 59
in Cross Timbers, 61–62
in Edwards Plateau, 65–66
forests, 43, 57
in Grand Prairie, 60–61
in Gulf Coast Plain, 55–56
in High Plains, 63–65
in Mountains and Basins, 67–68
in Piney Woods, 52, 54–55
in Post Oak Belt, 57–58
in Rolling Plains, 62
in South Texas Plains, 56–57
Navarro, José Antonio (nah VAR roh, hoh SEH ahn TOH nyoh), p 185, 189, 209, 250, 296, 317
Navy, Texas, 279, p 279, 281
Neal, Margie, 519
Neches, Battle of the, 275
Neches River, *see* Rivers
Neff, Pat, 517, 519, p 519

Neill, Colonel James, 244, 245
Neiman, Carrie Marcus, (NEE muhn), 492, p 493
Neiman-Marcus (stores), 492
Nelson, Willie, 581, p 581
Neptune, 375
Neutral Ground, 156, 158, m 158
New Braunfels (BROWN fuhlz), 303, 304
New Bremen, 306
Newcomb, W.W., Jr., f 106, q 106, 110
New Deal, 532–534, 537, 556
New Mexico, 80, 81, 82, 123
New Orleans, Battle of, 164
New Spain, 115, 116, 154, 155, 159
Newspapers, 184, 216, p 330, 339–340, 365
Nimitz, Admiral Chester W., 537, p 537
Nineteenth Amendment, 499
Nixon, Lawrence A., 521
Nocona, Peta, 276, 414
Nolan, Philip, 159–160
Normandy, 306
North American regions, 52, m 53
North Texas, 51, 91
NOW, *see* National Organization for Women
Nueces River, *see* Rivers
Nugent, Thomas L., 477

O'Daniel, W. Lee, 534–535, p 534
Odessa, 64, 452, 460, f 539
O'Donnell, Mary King, 506
Oil, 42, 43–44, 134, 487, 539, c 539, 551, 567; *see also* Industry, Refineries, Spindletop
and automobiles, 515
in Blackland Prairie, 59
in Cross Timbers, 62
East Texas Field, 515, 529
first wells, 457
in Gulf Coast Plain, 55–56
industry, beginning of, 457–460
and jobs, 529
in Post Oak Belt, 58
in Rolling Plains, 62
since 1970s, 566, 568
and urban growth, 495, 515
Old Mill, 240, 241
Old San Antonio Road, 189, 272
Old Stone Fort, 215, p 216
Old Three Hundred, 167, 183, q 184, 209
Olivares, Antonio (oh lee VAH rehs, ahn TOH nyoh), 142
Oliver, Katie, p 408
Olmsted, Frederick Law, 343, q 366

Oñate, Juan de (oh NYAH teh, HWAHN deh), 128
Orange, 3, 538
Orbison, Roy, 581
Ordinance of Secession, 363
Original counties of Texas, 1836, m 268
O'Sullivan, John L., 309, p 309
Oswald, Lee Harvey, 556
Overstreet, Judge Morris, p 601
Owens, William, 542, 586

P

Padilla, Juan Antonio (pah DEE yah, HWAHN ahn TOH nyoh), 189
Padre Island (PAH dray), f 39, p 39
Paleo-Indian cultures, 79–83
Palmito Ranch, Battle of (pahl MEE toh), m 375, 378
Palo Alto, Battle of (PA loh AL toh), 311, p 311, m 312
Palo Duro Canyon (PA loh DOO roh), 65, p 66, f 124, p 124, 125
Battle of, m 418, 419–420
Panhandle, 40, 51, 62
ranches of, 434, 442
Rolling Plains of, 62
Spanish expedition to, 123
vegetation in, 40
Panna Maria, 306
Paredes, Américo (pah REH dehs, ah MEH ree koh), 586
Paris, 58
Parker, Cynthia Ann, 276, f 414, p 414, q 423
Parker, Quanah, 276, p 276, 413–415, p 413, f 414, p 414, 419–420, 422, q 422
Parker's Fort, 275
Parmer, Martin, 250
Paschal, George, 380
Paving (of streets), 489
Pearl Harbor, 535
Pease, Elisha M., 299–300, p 299, 337, 363, 380, p 380, 390, 393–394
Peña, Amado, Jr., 583
Pennybacker, Anna, q 168
People's party, 475–477
Pérez, Antonio (PEH rehs, ahn TOH nyoh), 317
Pérez, Ignacio (PEH rehs, eeg NAH syoh), 165
Permian Basin, m 64, 65
Perry, Henry, 164, 220
Perry, Jim, 437
Petri, Friedrich Richard (PEH tree), p 293, f 303, p 303, p 342, 343, p 409

INDEX